PSYCHOLOGY

The Study of Human Experience

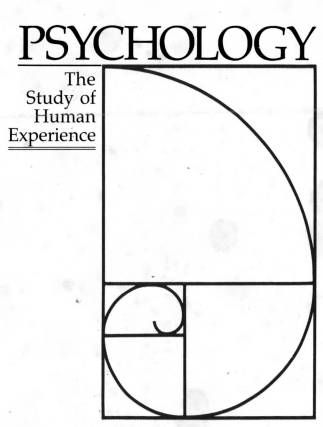

PSYCHOLOGY

The Study of Human Experience

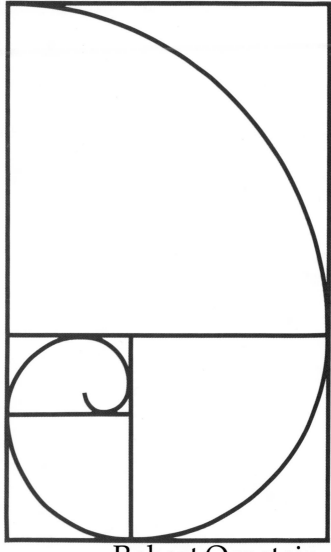

Robert Ornstein

Harcourt Brace Jovanovich, Publishers

San Diego   New York   Chicago   Atlanta   Washington, D.C.

London   Sydney   Toronto

ISBN: 0-15-572670-6

Library of Congress Catalog Card Number: 84-81493
Printed in the United States of America

Cover photos by C. Edelman/© Black Star 1980; © 1984 Peter Read Miller/Focus West; Werner Kalber/PPS; © Jeffrey Jay Foxx 1978.

Text art by Russell Redmond, Paul Slick, Robert Yochum

Copyrights and Acknowledgments and Illustration Credits appear on page 762 and constitute a continuation of the copyright page.

iv

Preface

It can be difficult to say when the writing of a book begins. This one is easy to date. When I sat in my first introductory psychology class 25 years ago, I wanted to study the field in more depth and to understand it enough to write my own book. I thought, smugly, that I would easily write one. But it took, at this reckoning, 25 years.

Why all that time? Well, I did do some other things, but it took some experiences in my own life, some research of my own, reading of the field and meeting the contemporary psychologists who were doing all that famous research . . . and then, 10 years ago, finally I thought I could give it a try.

We are all the stars in our own lives, but we each see our own life and experience from only *one* viewpoint, in one culture, through one set of parents, one sex, one time and place. We can learn much from our own experience, but the experiences of others and of scientists can deepen our understanding of ourself and our life. We may want to know how human life evolved and what makes us unique, one person from another—what makes us think, act, feel, live, love, and learn the way we do. There are pieces to this human puzzle, but they are scattered in studies of the dawn of our ancestors, in genetic analyses of transmission of physical characteristics, in neuroscience and psychophysiology, in studies of the intricate sensory system. There are clues in the analyses of how we think, how we make mistakes in remembering and learning, how we assess others' intelligence, how emotions are expressed by peoples of various cultures, how we face stress and even despair and depression. These experiences can help us understand ourselves, whether it is our misfortune to have them or not. And what of getting older? There are revolutionary findings that will change our ideas of what it means to age and to die.

There was no book, in the field of psychology or out of it, that assembled these pieces into one whole story. There is a real story to tell, I found, and it is the story of our lives. It begins where human life first emerges and continues, in each of us, until we die. In it there are glimpses of the human condition and human possibilities.

This is a book written for the student who wants to know more about why he or she does "stupid" things, what going "crazy" is like, how stress can be reduced, how the brain evolved in different eras, how the dazzling mechanisms of maturation coalesce to produce a three-year-old who can speak sentences never heard before (and why this routine miracle happens in societies throughout the world). This book is written, too, to explore and explain those miracles that seem beyond ordinary understanding: how populations (here, those of our ancestors) can physically grow and change; how *every cell* of the body contains the information necessary to make every other cell of the body; how the senses routinely screen out most of the information that reaches us and how they transform the external world—silent, colorless, odorless—into the rich world of sight, sound, smells, tastes. I hope to show, and clearly, how *extraordinary* the ordinary experience of life really is.

So there is continued analysis of what has to go on "behind the scenes" of our biology, our brain, our senses, our mind, and our society. It is one picture of one animal, struggling to make sense of the world, to love, create, survive, work, reproduce, learn. This animal is us.

This is a book for students, but there are many aspects directed at teaching and teachers. Information is looked at from many viewpoints throughout the book so that students can recall what they have learned in different contexts. This principle, called "multiple encoding," is an important concept, and I have tried to put it to use here. Concepts are developed throughout the book to increase familiarity but also to offer slightly different views so that students can *connect* what they have learned with their own experience.

There is a second principle: everything is learned better if it is related to oneself. The examples are personal, experiences that happened to me and to others. The brain is described as an organ that exists for a purpose that students can follow and relate to themselves. Memory is described as a functioning system, designed to aid the person in operating in the world, not as a wiring diagram of a nonexistent machine. We follow the course of a life, through its stages, as does every reader and student. There is advice as well: how to relax, how children can be encouraged to learn. There are glimpses of others' experiences: creative moments, dreams, being unemployed, getting married. Questions many students ask are addressed: Does everybody dream? What happens to children when there is a divorce?

Can I improve my intelligence? Are whites and blacks different in intelligence? Who stays healthy under stress? Why am I shy? Would I be able to resist harming another?

Although the book was a smug idea 25 years ago, it took 10 years to produce. Two people from Harcourt Brace Jovanovich had major roles in it, one at the beginning and one at the end (I am in the middle). William Jovanovich offered the understanding and encouragement needed to sustain the effort for all this time, as his idea of the book and mine were the same, even 10 years before it appeared! It is quite rare to find that in a publisher. At the end, my acquisitions editor, Marc Boggs, has enabled me to pass the shoals of book production while remaining relatively sane.

Special Acknowledgments

Others have contributed much as well. The book was planned and drafted with the collaboration of Nancy Hechinger, whose enthusiasm and skills repose in the finished book. The beginning of Chapter 12 was written with the collaboration of Dr. Lydia Temoshok. Carolyn Aldwin and Ric Levinson were of great help in working on several of the chapters, as were Thomas Malone and Stephen LaBerge. There are so many research areas, from human evolution to adult development, that one has to keep abreast of, that without these "eyes and ears" . . .

Finally, here it is, and I hope some of you, 25 years from now, will do the same.

Robert Ornstein

Acknowledgments

Christopher M. Aanstoos,
West Georgia College

Harry H. Avis,
Sierra College

Pamela Birrell,
University of Oregon

Frank Costin,
University of Illinois, Champaign-Urbana

Lynette Crane,
City College of San Francisco

Aaron Ettenberg,
University of California, Santa Barbara

Scott Fraser,
University of Southern California

Albert R. Gilgen,
University of Northern Iowa

William J. Gnagey,
Illinois State University

Michael Godsey,
Indian Valley Colleges

Ronald Growney,
University of Connecticut, Storrs

Patrick R. Harrison,
U.S. Naval Academy

Elizabeth S. Henry,
Old Dominion University

Earl Hunt,
University of Washington

John P. Keith,
Clark County Community College

Ross J. Loomis,
Colorado State University

Rick McNeese,
Sam Houston State University

John W. Nichols,
Tulsa Junior College

Patricia Owen,
St. Mary's University

A. Christine Parham,
San Jacinto College Central

Robert Pellegrini,
San Jose State University

James L. Phillips,
Oklahoma State University

Duane Reeder,
Glendale Community College

Gary Schaumburg,
Cerritos College

Thomas R. Scott,
University of Delaware

Michael H. Siegel,
State University of New York, Oneonta

John W. Somervill,
University of Northern Iowa

Tim Stringari,
Canada College

Charles Swencionis,
Yeshiva University

Charles Van Dyne,
Ohio State University

Paul J. Wellman,
Texas A & M University

Barbara Williams,
Palomar College

John W. Wright,
Washington State University

Contents

PART ONE
The Biological World

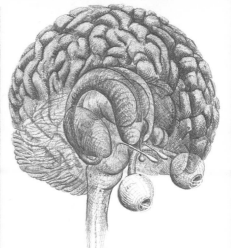

4 The Brain and Nervous System 132

5 Sensory Experience 174

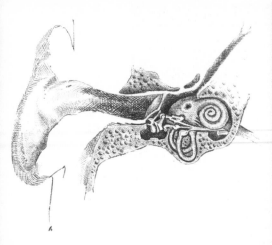
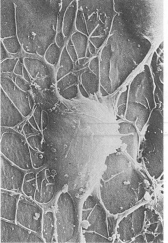

PART TWO
The Mental World

PART THREE
The World of the Individual

PART FOUR
The Social World of the Adult

PSYCHOLOGY

The Study of Human Experience

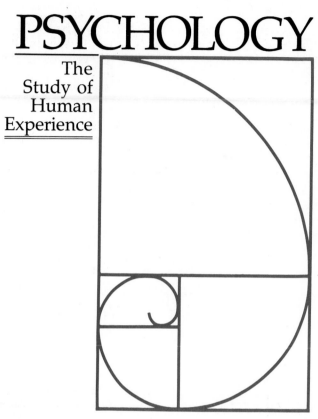

Chapter 1

The Study of Human Experience

AN INTRODUCTORY TALE

There is an ancient tale called "The Elephant in the Dark" about a town where all the inhabitants were blind.

> One day, an elephant appeared in the town square. No one in town had ever heard of or knew of this strange beast. The King of the Blind sent his three wisest men to find out what manner of beast this elephant was. Each sage approached the elephant from a different side. The one whose hand had touched the ear reported back that he had discovered the true nature of the elephant. "It is large and flat, rough—like a rug." The second, who had felt only the trunk, said, "That's not it at all, I know the answer. It is like a trumpet, but capable of dramatic movement." The third touched only the legs, and he disagreed vehemently with the other two, "No, no, no. You've got it all wrong. The elephant is mighty and firm like a pillar." Needless to say, none of the men had discovered the true nature of the elephant. (Adapted from Shah, 1970)

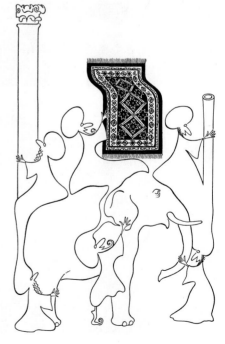

Now, suppose *you* were interested in the experience of a "strange animal," but instead of an elephant it was *you*. How would you approach your study of this person?

You would need to know a lot to understand where you came from, your background, family history, what you are made of, what is inside. How does your brain work? How do you behave, communicate? What is your sex, how are the two sexes similar, how different? What pleases you? How do you act with others of your kind? How do culture groups, family attachments, affect you? How are you like all others of your species?

You would have to ask these questions—and many more. Each question would lead to more questions. You would have to keep probing to achieve your goal. A simple question like, "What is sleep?" might remain unanswered, even after years of searching.

Psychologists are in this situation. They must approach their study from countless directions, study many aspects of a person, ask different questions, use lots of diverse methods. Each aspect of psychology tries to shed some small light on some previously mysterious part of being human: to illuminate the person in the dark. Psychology tries to answer many of the questions we have about ourselves, other people, and the nature of human life: Why do I feel lonely? What is "going crazy" like? What makes someone "creative"? What happens when I take drugs? What is a mystical experience? What makes someone help another?

Psychology, then, can be broadly defined as a complete science of human experience. It involves the study of the brain and nervous system, mental life, our behavior (both alone and in society), our stresses and disorders. However, just what all this means will take us this chapter to begin to define and the rest of the book to flesh out.

PERSPECTIVES ON THE HUMAN EXPERIENCE

In order to study human experience, psychologists observe the "person in the dark" from many different viewpoints. These include the person's biology and development, the mental system, how the person behaves, the influence of society and the environment, and the range of experiences from the difficulties of disordered people to the achievements of exceptional ones. All these different viewpoints combined add to our understanding of the "person in the dark," of what it means to be a human being.

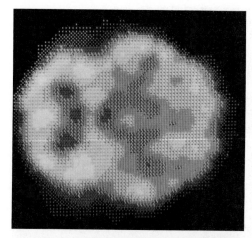

The Biological Approach

We are the product of millions of years of evolution. Each of us comes into the world with an amazing inheritance. We inherit, for instance, a complex brain and nervous system. Studies of the structure and operations of the brain, the **biological approach,** can provide fascinating clues for psychologists. Here is one example:

In 1942, Wilder Penfield, a neurosurgeon, made a startling discovery while performing a preoperative test on a patient with a brain tumor. To see which parts of the brain were active, he stimulated the brain at different locations with electrical current. Penfield probed, no response; again, fingers twitched. Here is the rest of the record:

11–"I heard something, I do not know what it was."
11–(Probe repeated without warning the patient) "Yes, Sir, I think I heard a mother calling her little boy somewhere. It seemed to be something that happened years ago." When asked to explain, she said, "It was somebody in the neighborhood where I live." Then she added that she herself "was somewhere close enough to hear."
12–"Yes, I heard voices down along the river somewhere—a man's voice and a woman's voice calling . . . I think I saw the river."
15–"Just a tiny flash of a feeling of familiarity and a feeling that I knew everything that was going to happen in the near future."
17c– . . . "Oh! I had the same very, very familiar memory, in an office somewhere. I could see the desks. I was there and someone was calling to me, a man leaning on a desk with a pencil in his hand."
I warned her I was going to stimulate, but I did not do so. "Nothing."
18a–(Stimulation without warning) "I had a little memory—a scene in a play—they were talking and I could see it—I was just seeing it in my memory." (Penfield, 1975)

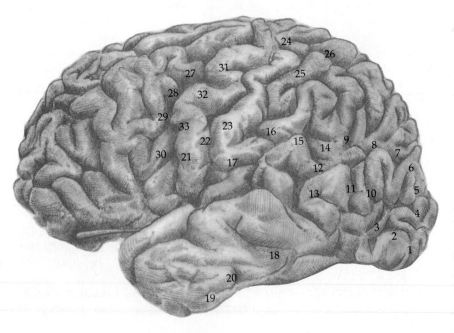

FIGURE 1–1
Electrical Stimulation of the Brain
The numbers indicate the locations at which Penfield stimulated the brain with his electrode. (After Penfield, 1975)

Penfield's electrode seemed to work like this: each time it was inserted into the particular spot, a very similar experience was called up. Penfield writes: "I was more astonished each time my electrode brought forth such a response. How could it be? This had to do with the mind. I called such responses 'experiential' " (Penfield, 1975).

So, disturbances of the *brain's* electrical activity can influence the *mind* dramatically, although you should not conclude that *all* experiences are stored within the brain (Loftus & Loftus, 1975). Injuries to the brain, surgery, drugs that affect the chemistry of the brain, all can have striking effects on the mind. The biological underpinnings of our experience are an increasingly important part of the study of psychology.

The Study of the Mind: The Cognitive Approach

The word cognitive comes from the Latin verb *to know* and the central object of study in **cognitive psychology** is the mind. But the mind is *not* a physical organ like the brain. Rather, it involves many hidden activities, such as thinking, memory, language, consciousness.

Some cognitive psychologists attempt to observe, as directly as possible, the operations of the mind. One question that would interest a cognitive psychologist is: "How many things can a person do at once?" The common wisdom is that "you can't do two things at once." But is that "wisdom" true?

Divided Attention

Ulric Neisser and his colleagues decided to see if it was possible to do two extremely complex activities at once: reading on one subject while writing on another. Two students, Diane and John, were enlisted as subjects. They read short stories while copying down a list of words that was being dictated to them rapidly. At first Diane and John found the task impossible. They read slowly and when they were tested later for story comprehension, they did poorly. But after six weeks of training, they could perform both tasks easily. Later the demonstration was extended. While Diane and John were reading, they took dictation, not simply of words, but of whole sentences. Again, it was difficult at first, but within weeks they were reading one subject, writing on another at the same time, at normal speed and with normal comprehension (Hirst, Neisser, & Spelke, 1978).

Therefore it is possible to learn to increase mental capacity and to divide attention. However, cognitive psychologists also focus on our mental limitations. Here is one example: Suppose you were buying a toaster, and it cost $30 at the store you were at. Then you discovered that it was $20 at a store 20 minutes away. Would you make the trip? Most people, in an experiment similar to this one, said they would. Suppose, again, that you were going to buy a car, which cost $8,320. Again, you discover that another dealer (20 minutes away) is selling the same car for $8,310. Would you go? Most likely not.

But notice what has happened here: the situation is actually the same. In *both* instances you are being asked to drive 20 minutes for a savings of

John B. Watson
(1878–1958)

$10. The savings is the same; the drive is the same. But the $10 *seems* like a lot compared with the $30 for the toaster, and almost nothing compared with the price of the car (Kahneman, Slovic, & Tversky, 1982). This illustrates one important aspect of our mental life: we judge things by *comparing* them with others.

Behaviorism: What People Do

Many psychologists prefer to study behavior because it can be studied "objectively"—a person's behavior can be recorded by external observers.

Behaviorism, as this perspective is called, grew out of a desire to make psychology objective. In the late nineteenth century when the scientific study of psychology began, attention was focused on the mind. The primary method researchers used was **introspection;** that is, they studied how their own minds worked and examined the contents of their own experience. The problem was that the investigators could not agree. John Watson (1914) proposed that introspection was therefore useless if psychology was to become a science, and that the study of observable behavior was a more proper subject for psychology.

There is an important assumption behaviorists make: it is that people do what they do because of the conditions in their environment. A condition is a "prerequisite circumstance for an event." Conditions can be physically present in the environment or they can be experiences learned in the past. Because behavior is dependent on the conditions, behaviorists reason, if the conditions change, behavior can also change. Therefore, fundamental to behaviorism is a strong and optimistic belief in the ability to learn, the possibility of improvement through change in the environment.

> Give me a dozen healthy infants, well-formed, and my own specified world to bring them up in and I'll guarantee to take any one at random and train him to become any type of specialist I might select—doctor, lawyer, artist, merchant-chief, and, yes, even beggar-man and thief, regardless of his talents, penchants, tendencies, abilities, vocations, and race of his ancestors. (Watson, 1925)

The scientific program of behaviorism is "control the conditions and you will see the order" (Skinner, 1972), so behaviorists seek to experimentally alter the conditions in the environment of an animal and observe the changes in behavior that follow. And through behavioral studies of learning, animals have learned to choose between difficult alternatives, to perform complicated tricks. Using a complicated series of learning trials, pigeons can even become quality control inspectors (Figure 1–2).

In a sense, every psychologist has been influenced by behaviorism, and behaviorism has led to important discoveries about how we learn and remember, how we act alone, with other people, and in society at large. Consider this important issue: Why do people act violently?

Some recent investigations concern the effect of television on violent behavior. A child of 10 has seen thousands of acts of violence on televi-

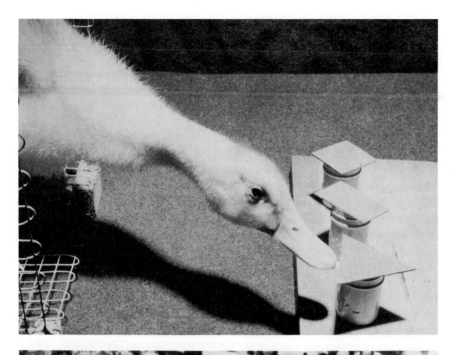

FIGURE 1–2
Conditioned Behavior
The scientific alteration of the conditions in their environment can shape the responses of animals so they learn various new ways of behaving.

sion, acts such as robberies, rapes, murders, and fights. Do these "conditions" affect how aggressive a child will be? A study of the behavior of people in different circumstances is the best way to find out. Some psychologists propose that watching "fictional" violence may be beneficial, because the viewer experiences a *catharsis*; that is, viewing violence allows the violent feelings to be released and the viewer will then be *less* likely to act aggressively. Other psychologists believe that people learn by observation and imitation; they propose that the more violence a child sees the *more* likely he or she is to act violently.

In an important study, children of different ages were shown films of adults (and other children) in such acts of violence as hitting dolls and hitting other people. After the movie the children's behavior was observed. The pictures in Figure 1–3 show the results: children who watched violence subsequently acted more violently (Bandura, 1973).

The Social Environment

Suppose you were sitting in a room and you heard a scream from the room next to you. Would you help? If you were sitting alone the chances are that you would, but if you were with six other people who did not help, the chances are that you would not! (Darley & Latané, 1968). Human beings are quite dependent on each other: as we are social animals, other people *intensify* our actions: runners are faster when they run with others, people act more aggressively in crowds than when alone. The study of how other people and our environment affect us is the **social environmental perspective.**

Some social psychological studies such as the one above are stimulated by life events. In 1964 a young woman named Kitty Genovese was mugged and stabbed to death in New York City. The murder of a woman is, unfortunately, not unusual, but what made this case horribly remarkable was that she screamed repeatedly and was heard by at least 38 people who watched the crime from the safety of their homes. No one tried to help her; no one even called the police. This apathy shocked many people, including psychologists. This murder initiated many studies of why nobody tried to help. The question that many psychologists have since tried to answer is "What makes a person stop to help?"

The Good Samaritan Experiment

A divinity student was told to go to a certain building to tape a sermon. He did not know that on the way he would find a man, slumped and groaning in a doorway (who was actually one of the psychologists, acting the part). Would the divinity student stop to help, and under what conditions?

Sixty divinity students were divided into three groups: one-third were told that they were late and had to hurry, one-third were told to go to the building, but not necessarily to hurry; one-third were told there was a delay in the taping and to take their time. In addition, all the students were assigned a topic for their sermon. Half were to talk on the biblical parable of the Good Samaritan; half were assigned a nonreligious topic.

FIGURE 1–3
Imitating Violent Behavior
Hitting and kicking an inflated doll were among the ways nursery-school children like this little girl responded to seeing a film showing adults and other children acting violently.

**FIGURE 1–4   Experimental Conditions
in the Good Samaritan Experiment**

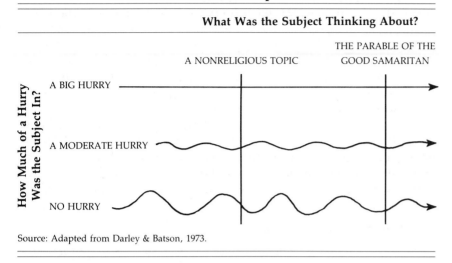

What Was the Subject Thinking About?

Source: Adapted from Darley & Batson, 1973.

The experimenters then were interested to know if either the pressure of time or what you are thinking about will influence "helping behavior." What happened?

Only 40 percent of the divinity students stopped to help; 60 percent did not. Analysis of those who did stop to help showed that the pressure of time seems to have more of an influence on behavior than what is on minds. (See Figure 1–4.) Of the students who were in no hurry 63 percent stopped; only 10 percent of the rushed students did; 53 percent of those thinking about the Good Samaritan stopped to help. The results strongly indicate that if people are in a hurry, they are not likely to stop to help.

The Range of Human Experiences

A complete study of the human experience needs to include all these factors: our biology, our mental life, our behavior, and our environment. In addition to these factors there are two other perspectives that yield much information: studies of people in difficulty, called the clinical approach, and studies of the important positive attributes of people, called the humanistic approach.

The Clinical Approach

The **clinical approach** is based on the idea that observing a person who is unable to perform a function can offer information on how that function usually operates. Here are several examples:

1. *A Biological Malfunction*: A man is interviewed in a hospital. His interviewer asks: "Can you tell me what work you have been doing?" He answers: "If you had said that, poomer, near the fortunate, tamppoo all around the fourth of marz. Oh, I get all confused!" (Gardner, 1978). This

**FIGURE 1–5
What Makes a Person Stop to Help?**
Psychologists study the social environment to discover factors accounting for bystander apathy, bystander intervention, and similar behavior that can affect our lives.

man has a variety of *aphasia*, impairment of language, which is caused by damage to a particular part of the brain. If people with damage in this area of the brain have specific difficulties with language, then we can assume that that part of the brain has an important role in normal language production. The study of people with aphasia has led to insights into the nature of language itself and how the brain produces language.

Nature of Language   See Chapter 4, pp. 145–46 and Chapter 10, pp. 385–92.

2. *Mental Errors*: Mental errors are of great interest to psychologists. Psychologists examine such errors to analyze the workings of normal thought. One class of errors is called *capture errors*. Suppose you have planned to stop at a fish store on your way home, but you find yourself in your driveway at home, having totally forgotten your plan. The route home was such a well-formed habit that it *captured* you. A student gave as an example:

> "I was using a copying machine and I was counting the pages. I found myself counting: 1, 2, 3, 4, 5, 6, 7, 8, 9, 10, Jack, Queen, King." (Norman, 1979, 1982)

3. *A Case of Psychological Paralysis*: Sigmund Freud was an important clinician. One of Freud's cases was a patient whose hand was entirely paralyzed, as if covered by a numbing glove. Freud knew that the anatomy of the hand makes it impossible for a paralysis to stop at the wrist, and so the cause of the paralysis must have been psychological. By hypnotizing the patient and allowing her to talk freely, he revealed the psychological factors in the paralysis. Once these factors were brought to the attention of the patient, the paralysis disappeared and she regained the use of her hand (Breuer & Freud, 1895/1955). From this case and other similar observations, the mental factors in health and disease have begun to be uncovered.

The Humanistic Approach

A natural emphasis on helping people in difficulty has made psychology focus on disorders. But to achieve full understanding of any organism one must also know the extent of its capabilities. One of the first questions you might ask that "person in the dark" would be: "What are you really good at? What is the best you can do?"

In psychology the approach that emphasizes the important positive aspects of human experience is called **humanistic.** Abraham Maslow, the founder and leading theorist of humanistic psychology, thought that humans' natural inclination is toward "growth" and "development"; toward improvement in health, intellectual creativity, achievement, love, and understanding. Maslow theorized that we all have within us certain "potentials" and, given the opportunity, we strive to make those potentials "actual." He consequently called this process **self-actualization.** Maslow studied people who he determined had developed their potential to its fullest, to find out what made it possible for them to become "self-actualized"—scientific geniuses like Einstein, virtuoso musicians like Arthur Rubinstein, or great world leaders like Mahatma Gandhi. Maslow wrote:

> If we want to answer the question how tall can the human species grow, then obviously it is well to pick out the ones who are already tallest and study them. If we want to know how fast a human being can run, then it is no use to average out the speed of a "good sample" of the population: it is far better to collect Olympic gold medal winners and see how well they can do. If we want to know the possibilities for spiritual growth, value growth, or moral development in human beings, then I maintain that we can learn most by studying our most moral, ethical or saintly people.
>
> On the whole I think it fair to say that human history is a record of the ways in which human nature has been sold short. The highest possibilities of human nature have practically always been underrated. Even when "good specimens": the saints and sages and great leaders of history, have been available for study, the temptation too often has been to consider them not human but supernaturally endowed. (Maslow, 1970)

Humanistic psychologists also treat people with difficulties. But their humanistic perspective encourages them to emphasize the positive elements in people, the possibilities for "growth and development."

Martin Luther King, Jr., left, and Albert Einstein and Eleanor Roosevelt, below, are among the rare individuals exemplifying what humanistic psychologist Abraham Maslow termed self-actualization.

A Concluding Note on the Perspectives

Unfortunately, for individuals trying to understand themselves, and even worse for psychologists, we are very complex animals. There are many factors that determine our lives, so it is only through more and more observations from different viewpoints—biological, cognitive, behavioral, social and environmental, clinical, and humanistic—that a complete picture can begin to emerge. But how these observations *themselves* are made is important for psychology as a science, and it is to this we now turn.

HOW SCIENTIFIC PSYCHOLOGY DIFFERS FROM EVERYDAY PSYCHOLOGY

In a sense, we often act like psychologists each day: we consistently try to understand ourselves and others. We ask many questions of ourselves: Why do I make so many mistakes? How intelligent am I? Some of the questions we have are more general: Is a person's personality and character formed in the first years of life? Is an aggressive person always aggressive? The difference between us as "everyday psychologists" and the scientific psychologist is a matter of degree. In ordinary life we often cannot control what happens, and so our guesses are imprecise. In science, many people study the same problem for years, carefully checking their conclusions. Although our individual experiences are unique, other people have fallen in love before, created art before, taken drugs before, even experienced the death of a loved one before. Precise study of others' experience may help you understand your own.

Science Goes beyond Personal Experience

You are the star of your own life: you see things from the point of view of one woman or man, rich or poor, old or young. Our ordinary knowledge is limited by the situations we encounter and by our circumstances in life, where we are born, whom we meet, what our opportunities are. Because scientific psychology attempts to be more objective, it examines human experience from many different viewpoints (such as the perspectives mentioned), and its knowledge is more generally applicable and reliable.

In life we make snap judgments and we need to respond quickly to specific situations. We may like or dislike someone or something on a whim or the flimsiest èvidence. But in scientific psychology, judgments are slow, measured, and tentative. And so the knowledge of psychology changes slowly. The knowledge of science is gathered at a slow pace; it is the most conservative and surest form of human knowledge.

Personal and Scientific Knowledge of Dreams

Sometimes our understanding about ourselves may be wrong. Many people are convinced, based on the best evidence of their own experience, that they do not dream. They are wrong: they do dream. In a pioneering experiment, a group of researchers brought people into the lab and observed them while they slept. They noticed that about every 90 minutes throughout the night every sleeper's eyes moved rapidly. If these people were awakened during these "rapid eye movement" periods, they almost invariably said that they were dreaming. In the morning, the same people often had no recollection of the past night's events—that they had been awakened or that they had reported a dream (Aserinsky & Kleitman, 1953). So in this case scientific knowledge is more accurate about people's personal experience than they are themselves. This experiment has been repeated often over the last 20 years and the relation of rapid eye movement periods of sleep to dreams has been observed in every sleeping person. All of us, no matter what we think, dream every night.

Sleep and Dream Research See Chapter 7, pp. 263–71.

Some Aims and Virtues of Science

People, being human, do science the way they do everything else. They make guesses and mistakes; they argue; they try out ideas to see what works, and discard what does not. Science has a reputation for being difficult to learn and to do, but it is basically quite simple. Scientific methods are extensions and refinements of those we use every day to answer questions about ourselves and about the world we live in. Scientists, as individuals, make the same mistakes everyone else does (Kahneman et al., 1982). But science differs from ordinary inquiry in that it is a systematic and formal process of gathering information—with specific rules for testing ideas, interpreting results, and correcting mistakes. We shall consider some of these methods for gathering information and interpretation later in this chapter.

Apart from the rules governing scientific investigation, there are several important characteristics of science, in theory at least, which differentiate it from other forms of gathering knowledge. In addition to enabling us to go beyond personal experience, science seeks the simplest and most unifying solutions to problems, and science is self-correcting.

FIGURE 1–6
The Scientific Study of Sleep
Sleep is studied in the laboratory by recording the subject's brain waves, eye movements, and heart activity through the night, as in these photographs from the Dartmouth Sleep Laboratory.

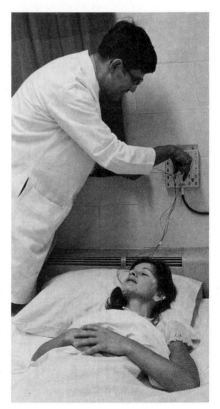

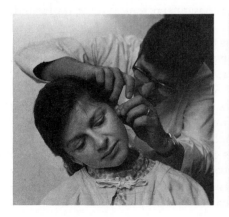

Order, Simplicity, and Unity

The world often seems chaotic: things happen all at once, we have to "make sense" out of it. The first assumption of science is that there is *order* in the world, and the second is that there is *unity* in it. The goal of science is to find the order in things that appear disordered and the unity in the apparent diversity in the most economical way. Albert Einstein (1956) wrote: "The great aim of science is to cover the greatest number of phenomena with the fewest number of ideas."

Scientific Knowledge is Cumulative

Science differs from other forms of study because its discoveries build on one another; one generation's knowledge is superseded by the next. Thus, the first task of the young scientist is to know what has already been discovered. If not, trouble can result. Suppose, while sitting under an apple tree, you realized, in a sudden flash of insight, that the fall of an apple and the movement of the planets were related; you would not be heralded as a genius as was Isaac Newton, for precisely the same insight 300 years ago. You would be criticized for not doing your homework, considered somewhat of a dolt for not boning up on what was already known.

Each generation of scientists can begin where the last left off. A text such as this contains information on the human brain, mental operations, development, social behavior, and therapies unknown to the most learned investigator of the 1930s. Isaac Newton said: "If I have seen farther than others, it is because I have stood on the shoulders of giants."

Corrections and Replication

Scientific knowledge is refined and checked. In communicating results, scientists expose the whole scaffolding that supports their discoveries—what they were trying to do, how they did it, how they interpreted the results. A scientific discovery has to be reliably repeatable, like a recipe. An example: Aserinsky and Kleitman first discovered in 1953 that people dream every night. They published their findings in a scientific journal, and their findings have been repeated, or **replicated,** in many labs around the world.

Because you will read largely of the achievements, psychology may seem to you like a very certain, even boring, step-by-step process, with everything neatly in place. But for every "solution," for every successful experiment and breakthrough, there have been scores of blind alleys, mistakes, and failures. And science, though it strives to be objective and unbiased, is not cool and detached. There exist heated arguments regarding important questions. Right now there is great disagreement on such issues, among others, as the role of race in intelligence, on whether "intelligence" itself can be measured, on how important the early years of childhood are to adult life, on whether or not sex differences are biologically predetermined.

Scientific Ideas and Tests

In both life and science, ideas are tested against experience. In everyday psychology the worth of a guess or hunch is judged against what happens. However, because our ordinary guesses are vague and we do not always have all the information, confirming everyday guesses is haphazard.

Scientific psychology is more specific. The ideas are precisely defined, and tested against experience in specific ways. Among the many ways psychologists test ideas about human experiences, we consider some major ones: observation, demonstration, and experiment. Scientists are trained to be especially precise observers. Of the three methods, the observational is closest to life: occurrences in life are reported and recorded but not interfered with. Demonstrations are the most immediately compelling: a phenomenon is presented to other people so that it can be determined how they personally experience it. The experimental method is the most creative. The experimenter intervenes, arranges a situation, controls all the parts of an experience, and records the results. While observation has the advantage of being most representative of life, experiments have the advantage of being more precise, controllable, and repeatable.

Observation

The raw material for much scientific investigation begins with observations, sometimes tragic ones as in the case of Kitty Genovese. However, observation is sometimes the only way to understand a phenomenon. If you want to discover how city life affects a person's experience, the only valid manner of study is to observe people in crowded cities. In

FIGURE 1–7
The Pace of City Life
The observation that people in cities move at a faster pace helps psychologists understand such phenomena as bystander apathy.

Good Samaritan Experiment
See pp. 10–11.

the Good Samaritan experiment it was discovered that people are less likely to help out others when they are in a hurry. One important associated observation is that people walk faster in cities than in the country. The larger the city, the faster people walk (Freedman, Sears, & Carlsmith, 1978). The faster walk of city dwellers may mean they are in a hurry or that they notice less of what is going on around them, or both. This is one explanation of why people are less likely to stop and help in cities.

Formal observations are made in three ways: (1) *case histories*, (2) *measurements and tests*, (3) *questionnaires* in which feelings and opinions may be reported.

FIGURE 1–8
Art and Autism: A Case History
Nadia's precocious artistic ability (this drawing was done when she was only five and a half years old) showed that she could perceive and conceptualize complex ideas and images her autism prevented her from formulating verbally. (Selfe, 1977)

Case Histories

Some experiences are unique in that the only available evidence will be the psychologist's report of it. This report is called a **case history.** The story of the glove paralysis was one. Here is another.

A Case of Autism.   Autism is a childhood disorder in which children seem completely lost in fantasy. They create and inhabit a world of their own and are usually inaccessible through the normal channels of communication—speech, gestures, etc. For years researchers and therapists could find no way to reach them. In some rare cases children have found a way to break through the barrier and communicate. Nadia is one of these. You see one of her drawings (Figure 1–8). Her drawings give us a glimpse into the world of an autistic child and clues to the operation of an otherwise impenetrable mind. Nadia's drawings have been extremely helpful to psychologists who are discovering ways to reach and help these children (Selfe, 1977).

Measurements

Measurement is as central to psychology as it is to all science; it enables psychologists to make **quantitative** as well as **qualitative** distinctions. A qualitative distinction would be: X is an aggressive person, Y is not. A quantitative distinction would tell us *how much more* aggressive X is than Y, and in which situations.

Some measurements are subtle. When you walk into a room you may hear a clock ticking or a fan whirring, but after a while you do not notice these noises; you seem to tune them out. Psychologists can measure the changing response of the brain to external noises and use these measures to demonstrate that the brain begins to ignore persistent noises and other continuously present stimuli. When we first hear a click, the brain responds one way. A few minutes later the same noise causes a different reaction (Figure 1–9). The brain ceases to respond to the con-

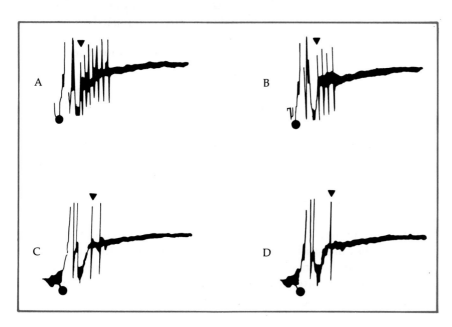

FIGURE 1–9
Measuring Habituation
The brain's ability to "tune out" such stimuli as persistent external noises is called habituation. It can be measured by noting the decreasing firing rate, as shown here, of a neuron under constant stimulation. (Grives & Thompson, 1973)

outlines the plot, and assembles the characters. The difference here is that the scientist does not decide *what* will happen, but can only set events in motion and record what unfolds.

Variables

Life is sometimes chaotic—things change or "vary" all the time. In an experiment we try to hold most conditions constant. The few things that are changed in an experiment are thus called the *variables*. There are two kinds of variables: those the experimenter changes, called **independent variables**—for instance, an experimenter may *vary* the number of hours an animal is deprived of food—and those the experimenter measures, called **dependent variables,** which in this case might be how much the animal eats.

The Sample: Experimental and Control Groups

People are often part of the experiment; they are called **subjects.** (Sometimes animals are the subjects.) Whatever kind of subject is used, it must be selected to *represent accurately* the entire population under study. The group of subjects is called the **sample.** The appropriate *sample sizes* vary depending on what is being studied. The smaller the differences from individual to individual on the specific measure, the smaller the sample size has to be. To study the effect of light on pupil dilation, a few subjects, perhaps fewer than 10, are enough. The purely physical aspects of vision are fundamentally the same for all human beings. Although people's eyes are similar, their opinions are not. To determine something such as the most popular television shows or voter preferences in polls taken before a national election, a sample of about 1,200 people is used. Here individuality, personal preference, prejudices, background, and geography play an important role. The sample has to be large enough to average out the individual differences.

The sample is usually divided into two groups: the **experimental group** and the **control group.** The experimental group is the one you intervene with, the one you study to judge the effect of those elements you change and manipulate. The control group is similar to the experimental group in every respect *except* the independent variable. A control group is necessary because we have to know what would have happened had you not intervened. When the experiment is over, the two outcomes are compared.

An Example: Suppose you want to know if a certain psychotherapy is effective. The findings are that, two years after treatment, 75 percent of the people who had undergone psychotherapy are improved. Could you then say that psychotherapy is effective? Not yet, because you do not know what would have happened to these people if they had not received psychotherapeutic treatment. In this case, the control group would have to be a similar group of people who want to have psychotherapy, but for one reason or another, are unable to obtain it. Suppose that after the same two years, 95 percent of these people are improved. That figure would certainly change your opinion on the benefits of psychotherapy. It would mean that psychotherapy is *less* effective than doing nothing! Or you might find that only 35 percent of the control

FIGURE 1–11
The Control Group and the Experimental Group, Both Drawn from the Sample and Observed during the Experiment

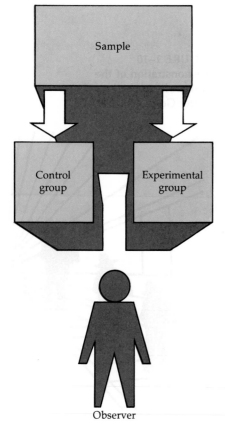

group improved; then you would conclude that psychotherapy is effective, and you would have a good idea just how effective. Please note that in these two examples the *results* of psychotherapy are the same, but our judgment of its effectiveness depends on what would have happened if there were no therapy.

In experiments, the control group represents "what would have happened anyway." The control group is one more way to insure sound and measured judgments; it is the standard from which we can make scientific comparison.

Where Experiments Take Place

Psychological experiments take place in two locations: the laboratory and the field. When place is not the important factor, the lab is the location of choice. The conditions are most easily controlled in the lab and there are the fewest distractions. For instance, when Darley and Batson were conducting the Good Samaritan experiment, the janitor of a nearby building walked out, just as one of the divinity students went by. "Feeling any better today, buddy?" he said to the man lying in the alley. One morning's preparation shot. Most experiments using animals are done in a lab. With human beings, basic psychological processes such as perception, learning, and memory are studied in the lab.

Good Samaritan Experiment
See pp. 10–11.

THINKING LIKE AN EXPERIMENTAL PSYCHOLOGIST

Here we will trace the development of one study, comprised of several experiments. Recall that the experimenter's job is to select a very few variables to alter and to observe, and that the procedures for doing an experiment derive from normal common sense. This particular series of experiments also shows a few other things: part of it takes place in the field, part in the lab, and it shows (in a very small way) the cumulative nature of scientific knowledge.

Suppose you wanted to find out which factors make one person sexually attracted to another? Of course the complete answer is quite complex: it includes the background of the person, expectations, whether the person is "involved." However, to think like an experimental psychologist, you might try to isolate one part of the puzzle. One major factor that you may not have considered may be the circumstances of a meeting. In films or novels it is the daring hero, the one who takes chances, who always gets the girl. Why do many more people fall in love and get married in disasters and wartime than during times of quiescence? Why do people go to horror movies and ride on roller coasters on dates? What all these situations have in common is the element of danger, and danger is arousing. Could a dangerous *location* contribute to sexual arousal?

So, you might try to see what happens when people are put in exciting circumstances. The real experiment we will now follow involves attraction on a wobbly bridge (Dutton & Aron, 1974). A woman interviews two groups of men, each on a different bridge in Vancouver: one bridge is safe, the other very precarious. One is a solid wood structure 10 feet above a stream. This is the "control bridge." The other is the Capilano Suspension Bridge; it is 450 feet long, 5 feet wide, and sways and wobbles over a 230-foot drop to rapids and rocks. This is the "experimental bridge."

What you might do, then, is compare meeting people of the opposite sex in both dangerous and safe circumstances. Men who are crossing one of the bridges were met by an attractive woman interviewer. To each man on both the experimental and control bridges she said she was researching "the effects of scenic attraction on creative expression." She then asked the man to write a brief story based on a picture she showed him of a young woman covering her face with one hand while reaching out with the other. When he finished, she gave the man her name and number and invited him to call her if he wanted more information about the experiment. If you found there were fewer calls from the men who went to the solid control bridge than from those who went to the wobbly experimental bridge, you might conclude that arousing circumstances figure in sexual attraction. The stories were also scored for sexual imagery.

The *independent variables* were the two bridges. The *dependent variables* were the number of phone calls and the men's scores for sexual imagery. The hypothesis was that men on the experimental bridge would be more sexually aroused than men on the control bridge. Therefore, they should (1) telephone the assistant more often than controls, (2) write stories with more sexual imagery.

The results: 12.5 percent of the men who were sent to the secure bridge called the woman for more information. 50 percent of the men who were sent to the wobbly bridge called. Those who met the woman on the wobbly bridge wrote stories with far more sexual imagery than those on the secure bridge.

Therefore we *could* conclude that these results support the hypothesis that dangerous circumstances can lead to arousal and to increased sexual attraction. Now, psychologists are rarely convinced by one study. To think like an experimental psychologist means that you must consider whether the results you have obtained could come about in another way. The results might at first seem definitive, but, as in most studies, there are other possible interpretations of these findings. Let us consider another possible interpretation of the results: it could be that the men who *chose* to cross on the wobbly bridge were more daring than the ones who chose to cross on the secure control bridge. If so, these men might well have been more daring, too, about calling a strange woman up for a date than were the possibly more timid control bridge travelers, and they might also be more sexually daring. Therefore the results might be due to existing differences in the *men* who cross on the bridge, not the *effect* of crossing a dangerous bridge. So, another experiment is necessary.

Experiment II: You would need to rule out differences in the two groups of men. This time the sample was composed *entirely* of men who crossed the wobbly bridge, but they were divided into "aroused" and "nonaroused" groups. The aroused group was interviewed as before—

just as they crossed the bridge. The nonaroused group was interviewed at least 10 minutes later, when the exciting effects of the bridge would have worn off.

The same experiment was done. If the original results were due to *differences* in the men who crossed the bridge, we would expect both groups to this second experiment to be *equally* attracted to the woman. If the original results were due to the arousal of crossing the bridge, then we should expect that the group interviewed *on* the bridge would be *more* attracted to the woman. The results showed the latter to be the case, and this provides further evidence for the idea that general arousal can lead to sexual arousal.

This makes our conclusion clearer. But, again, an experimental psychologist would then wonder whether this result applies to a limited situation or whether it is more general. Is this finding true only under certain conditions (a "damsel in distress" on a wobbly bridge)? Is it just a curiosity or is the relationship between excitement and attraction more basic?

Experiment III: A third experiment was run, this time in the laboratory. A man sat in a room and was told that he was participating in a study to "measure the effect of pain on learning." A woman entered and was introduced as the other subject in the experiment. Actually she was, as

FIGURE 1–12
Does Danger Contribute to Sexual Arousal?
Psychological experiments have been conducted to determine whether or not dangerous situations play a role in sexual arousal.

you will have guessed, in cahoots with the experimenters. The pair was told if they gave an incorrect answer on their test, they would receive an electric shock. One of them would receive a mild shock, the other a severe shock and the experimenter would be measuring which shock level was the more effective learning tool. Now, again thinking like a psychologist, how would you make sure that brave men might choose the severe shock and be likely to call the woman, too?

Before the tests and shocks were to begin, each subject was sent to a different room and asked to fill out a questionnaire "on your present feelings and reactions, since they often influence performance on the learning task." *This was the critical part of the experiment.* There were, actually, no tests or shocks. The first part of the questionnaire measured anxiety. As you might expect, the subjects who expected to receive a strong shock reported much more anxiety than those who anticipated a weak shock. The second part of the questionnaire related directly to arousal and sexual attraction. The men who expected severe shocks and were anxious about them also expressed more attraction for the woman than the calmer men expecting a mild shock.

So what have we found? This series of experiments contributes a little evidence that a man who meets a woman in a dangerous or anxiety-producing circumstance is *more likely* to interpret the feeling of arousal as attraction to the other person. In this experiment we go from an everyday observation—that exciting people and situations are attractive—to a slightly more comprehensive understanding of the general experience. We know a *little* more about the whys of sexual attraction because of our analysis of one of its components and, I hope, a little more about how to think like a psychologist. Of course, this experiment would need to be replicated and many others done before we could conclude that arousal has a general effect on sexual attraction. Then, of course, there would be many other new questions. Some of them will be treated later on in the book.

Some Problems of Experiments: Further Help in Learning to Think Like a Psychologist

Even with all the rules of doing an experiment, there is the possibility that the experimenter may subtly and unconsciously influence or *bias* the results. People so often find what they are looking for that Robert Rosenthal thought that something subtle and unconscious was occurring. He ran a famous experiment that clearly demonstrated the presence of this so-called **experimenter bias:** a group of students were told to run rats through a maze. Half were told that their rats were bred to be especially smart, called (in the trade) *maze bright,* and the other group was told that their rats were *maze dull.* In fact there was no difference: the rats were selected at random; both groups were equal in ability. The independent variable was the expectation of the students. That expectation turned out to be an important difference: the "maze bright" rats learned the maze faster than their supposedly "dull" counterparts (Rosenthal, 1966).

There are two methods psychologists use to minimize the problem of experimenter bias.

1. **Replication.** Every experiment *may* be confirmed in the laboratory of others. The new investigator may have a different bias—perhaps even the desire to disprove the finding.
2. **Double-blind procedure.** The subject of an experiment is usually kept in the dark about the object of an experiment. A double-blind procedure keeps the experimenter in the dark, or blind, as well—unaware of which is the experimental and which is the control group until after the experiment is over and the results have been tabulated.

An Example: Suppose you invent a new sleeping pill, "Snoozie," and you want to test its effect. If the drug works and is a commercial success, you stand to make a lot of money. Suppose further that you give one group Snoozie and the other a sugar pill. Then you interview both groups on the drug's effects. If the people who took the pill knew that the pill was supposed to make them drowsy, they might report feeling that way. Subjects in experiments generally try to be cooperative, and the expectation of the feeling might lead to the feeling.

Similarly, if you *know* who has taken Snoozie and who has taken the sugar pill, you might influence the results by your questions during the interview: "Don't you feel slightly sleepy? Not even a teensy-weensy bit?" But if you do not know who took which pill, you cannot influence the results with questions. In the Dutton and Aron experiment, the attractive female *confederate* (the one who asked the questions) was kept in the dark about the real purpose of the experiment.

What Does It Mean? Statistics

Psychologists use these methods—demonstration, observation, and experiment—to gather data. Once the evidence is in hand, the next step is to *evaluate* and *interpret* it. **Statistics** is the formal set of rules for evaluation of evidence. It enables scientific judgments to be more precise and quantitative than ordinary judgments. If a study shows a difference between the groups, as we saw in the wobbly bridge experiment, we need to know if it is a **significant difference.**

An Example: Suppose you are interested in improving the mathematical skills of third graders. You have two gadgets designed to encourage the learning process, and you want to see which works better. One is a computer that flashes and wiggles when the child gives a correct answer. The other is a set of mathematical instruments that make noise and project the problems on the ceiling.

You have two groups of children, and you give the computer to one group, the mechanical toy to the other. You find that both groups show a 15 percent improvement in learning over their previous work (and over a third control group, which was given no toy to play with). Would you say that both methods are equally effective? At first glance, it seems so, but a statistical analysis shows they are *not*.

The statistical test reveals that the improvement for the first group is *significant*, the second not.

FIGURE 1–13

Group 1 (computer) % improvement for each of the children:
     10, 20, 15, 10, 25, 15, 15, 10, 20, 10
Group 2 (mechanical)
     50, −10, −20, 85, 55, −30, 60, −15, −25, 0

Let us take a closer look at the evidence. In the first group, all the children using the computer made some improvement. The computer's effect on learning, as the statistical test showed, is constant and meaningful. But in the second group, 4 out of the 10 children were helped by the mechanical toy, but 6 out of the 10 children showed no improvement or worsened. Both gadgets were not equally effective as a learning tool, even though the *average* difference is the same. A good psychologist would continue to work, however, to find out *why* the mechanical instrument toy provided such different results for different children.

Mean and Median

There are two major measures scientists use to analyze data: the mean and the median. The **mean** is the arithmetic average. **Median** comes from the Latin word for middle, and that is what the median is. If you rank the results in numerical order, the figure in the middle of the lists is the median.

FIGURE 1–14

Avenue A (in thousands of dollars)
     10, 10, 15, 15, 15, 17.5, 20, 20, 25, 25, 75
Avenue B
     15, 15, 20, 20, 20, 22.5, 24, 25, 27, 29, 30

Which is the more well-to-do street? The *average*, or mean, income is the same for both streets, $22,500. But in this case 10 of the 11 families in Avenue B had higher incomes than their corresponding families in Avenue A. In this case the more accurate measure is the median. For Avenue A, it is $17,500; for B it is $22,500. That figure better reflects the consistent difference in income of the residents of the two streets. The median is used when an extreme value might unduly influence the average, as when a high scorer on a test might affect the average or, as in this case, one family's income might elevate the average of the incomes of the families on Avenue A.

Correlation

Is there any *relationship* between a person's high school SAT score and college grades? Between years of drinking and decline of intelligence? Between a father's intelligence and his son's? We cannot do experiments to find out, but we can measure the relationship. When the relationship of two things is important to measure, psychologists compute a statistic called a **correlation** (the word itself is "co," which means with, and "relation").

The correlation is an important tool, for there are many studies that do not allow experimentation. For instance, suppose you want to determine how much brain damage affects speech. Obviously, you could not produce brain damage in your subjects for this purpose, but you could study people with brain damage to determine the relationship of the amount of damage to speech impairment.

The Natural Experiment

Sometimes things happen in life which cannot be duplicated but which can provide important evidence, and the correlation method can be used to interpret the results. For instance, to find out which is the more important factor in human intelligence, heredity or the environment in which a person grows up, the most obvious thing to do would be to find a pair of identical twins (who are as close genetically as two human beings can possibly be); separate them at birth; let one child grow up in an intellectually enriched environment and the other in a similarly deprived one; then observe what happens. This is unthinkable—no one

FIGURE 1–15
Experiments and
Natural Experiments
This flow chart shows that the principal difference between the two types of experiments is that in a natural experiment—such as the one conducted by Scarr and associates—the creation of the independent variable involves assessment of specified characteristics like occupations, IQs, and interests.

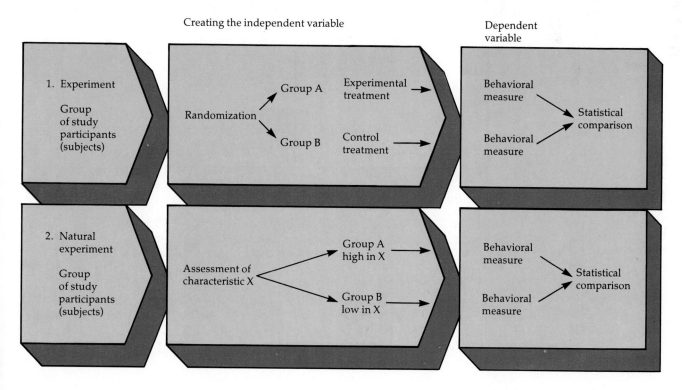

would manipulate people's lives for the sake of psychological knowledge; but, again, a psychologist might use correlation to study existing circumstances where this occurs.

In one study, Sandra Scarr and her associates found groups of adopted children for whom the occupations, IQs, and interests of the natural parents were known and who were raised by couples with children of their own. Scarr et al. then compared the IQs and interests of adopted children reared in families with natural children, using correlations (see Figure 1–15). They found startling evidence that *IQ and even interests seem to be inherited* (Scarr & Weinberg, 1978).

An Example: Is there a relationship between high school and college grades? First we plot one person's high school grades on one axis of a graph and college grades on the other. If the college grades are relatively low and the high school grades are high, the graph will look approximately like Figure 1–16A. If the high school grades are low and the college grades are high, it will look something like Figure 1–16B. If both are high, 1–16C. If both are low, 1–16D. Then we plot the grades of a very large sample of students on the graph.

If everyone who did well in high school got high grades in college, and everyone who did poorly in high school got low grades in college, that would be a perfect correlation. The relationships described in Figures 1–16A–D are high correlations, not perfect ones. A perfect correlation would indicate a perfect relationship: Whenever X happens, Y happens; the more X, the more Y. On the graph a perfect correlation would look like Figure 1–16E. This 100 percent relationship is written in statistics as a correlation of 1.0, either positive or negative. Such a relationship is almost never found.

Heritability of Intelligence
See Chapter 11, pp. 408–14.

FIGURE 1–16
Plotting Data on Scatter Diagrams to Reveal Possible Correlations

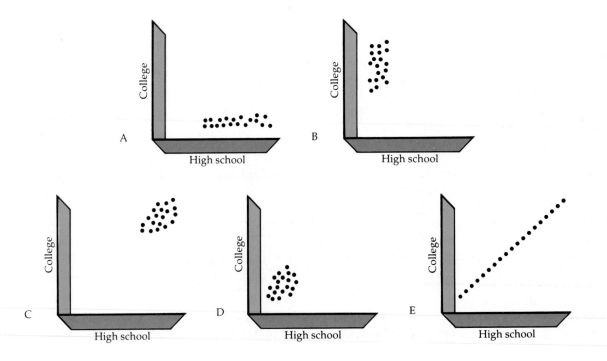

If there is no correlation it means there is no relation between X and Y (e.g., grades in high school and eye color). This lack of relationship is written 0.0. Most correlations fall somewhere between these two figures. There has to be a certain degree of relationship, usually at least 0.2, to be considered important. In addition, the relationship may be positive or negative. A *positive correlation* means the more of X, the more of Y. A *negative correlation* means the more X happens, the less Y happens (e.g., the more food you eat, the less weight you lose). A negative correlation is distinguished from a positive correlation by a minus sign in front of the figure, as in -0.4. A positive correlation would be written simply 0.4.

A CONCLUDING NOTE

So, we have covered a lot of ground, to begin a definition of psychology. It is a science of human experience. This involves specific perspectives, methods of study, and statistical rules of interpretation.

The *perspectives* psychology encompasses are our biological inheritance, studies of the mind, studies of behavior and social environment, and studies of the full range of disorders (the clinical perspective) and of great achievements (the humanistic perspective).

Psychologists use many different methods to go beyond ordinary experience. They include systematic observation, including measurements and tests, demonstrations such as illusions, and experiments, like the study at the wobbly bridge.

All these elements enable us to go beyond our own personal experience, to more fully understand ourselves, what our limits are, and what we are capable of.

How This Book Is Organized

Psychology tells a story, and that story follows the course of our lives—where we come from, how each of us grows from an infant to an adult, how we learn, think, remember, what our consciousness is like, how we argue with and love other people, how groups affect us, how we develop as we get older. We will follow that story, our story, in this book.

Think of it this way: at the beginning is biology (inner circle of Figure 1–17), followed by the normal processes of socialization and development out of which develops the mind (second circle). Then, our life with other individuals: how we communicate, how we express feelings, how we get into trouble (third circle). Finally, there is the "world" of society and of our adult life. Each stage is more complex and filled with more challenges than the last. This book follows "the story" from the biological, through the development of mind, to the study of the individual, and finally to the adult social world.

The first section of this book is The Biological World, and it begins where human beings first developed, in East Africa about 4 million years ago. It continues with the development of a person, from birth to adolescence. The section ends with the study of the most complex thing in the universe, the human brain, and how the senses act to inform the brain.

The second section of this book is The Mental World. It begins with perception, how we organize the world, and continues with the study of how our consciousness changes and how we can change consciousness. The section continues with the basic processes of learning to associate things in the world with things in the mind, and then goes on to the mystery of how we remember. The section ends with a chapter on thinking, how we create and make mistakes, and one on intelligence: can we assess intelligence, and can we increase it?

The third section is The World of the Individual, and it begins with our feelings and our relations with other people. The first chapters are on what "moves" us: our emotions and our motives—*why* we do what we do. Then we deal with a most complex subject: what one's personality is "really" like. If you have ever tried to understand another person (let alone yourself) you will not be surprised to find that the answer is puzzling. The final three chapters of this section deal with our problems: the

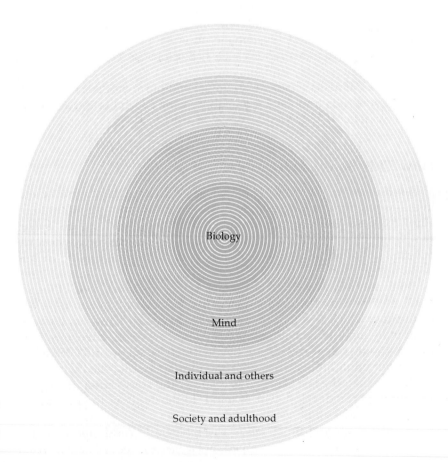

FIGURE 1–17
The Organization of This Book and of Human Experience
Our study of psychology—like the course of our individual lives—starts with The Biological World before moving on to The Mental World, The World of the Individual, and The Social World of the Adult. Each stage augments and amplifies the others.

Biology

Mind

Individual and others

Society and adulthood

first is on the normal problems of living—stress, social changes, and how they affect health (and how to be healthier). The second deals with the abnormal; with such disorders as when sadness becomes debilitating depression, when withdrawal becomes catatonia. The last chapter covers the psychotherapies—the attempts to relieve these difficulties.

The final section, The Social World of the Adult, is still more complex: it deals with our life in current society. The first chapter deals with the effect other people have on us, in small groups, in crowds, and in cities. The final chapter deals with the process of growing up that lies ahead: job, marriage, family, aging, and, finally, death.

So, our story actually begins *before* our birth and ends after our death. In it we can obtain a few glimpses of why we are the way we are, and what we can become. It is our story, and I hope you find something illuminating, here and there, in these chapters.

Summary

1. Psychology is the complete science of the human experience. It involves the study of the brain and nervous system, our mental life, behavior—both alone and in society—stresses, and disorders.

2. In order to study human experience, psychologists must observe human beings from different viewpoints—biological, cognitive, behavioral, social and environmental, clinical, and humanistic. The difference between scientific psychology and everyday psychology is a matter of degree. Scientific psychology, however, goes beyond individual experience and is more comprehensive. It deals with the nature of human experience from many different viewpoints, such as those we have already mentioned. In scientific psychology, judgments are objective.

   Scientists as individuals make the same mistakes everyone else does. But science differs from ordinary inquiry in that it is a *systematic formal process* of gathering information, with specific rules for testing ideas and interpreting the results.

3. Scientific knowledge is *cumulative,* and it involves specific procedures for *correction* and *replication.* Scientific methods include observations, which involve case histories, measurements, tests, and questionnaires; demonstrations; and experiments.

4. Experiments involve developing a *hypothesis,* manipulating independent variables, and measuring dependent variables.

5. An important part of the experiment is obtaining a *sample* of the population. The sample should be selected to *represent* accurately the entire population under study. This sample is usually divided into the experimental and the control group.

6. One series of experiments involved determining the factors promoting sexual attraction. In the study cited by Dutton and Aron, the independent variables were two bridges—one wobbly, one secure. The hypothesis was that the arousal produced by walking on the wobbly bridge would lead to increased sexual attraction. A woman was asked to meet men on each of the bridges,

and the number of phone calls (the dependent variables) she later received was taken as a measure of sexual attraction. The men called *more* often when they met the woman on a wobbly bridge than on the secure bridge.

7. Statistics enable psychologists to go beyond personal experience by giving them a way to *evaluate* and *interpret* the information gained.

   An important statistical test is whether a difference obtained is *significant:* how likely it was that the observed difference would have occurred by chance.

8. *Correlation* is an important statistical procedure that measures the *relationship* between two factors such as a person's high school SAT score and college grades. Zero correlation means that there is *no* relationship between two factors. A positive correlation means that an increase in one factor is associated with an increase in the other. In this case higher SAT scores would mean higher college grades. A negative correlation means an increase in one factor is associated with a decrease in the other, as when, for example, the more you eat, the less weight you lose.

9. Psychology, like this book, can be divided into four sections, each one concerning a perspective on the human condition. The first section is the biological world; the second, the mental world; the third, the world of the individual; and the fourth, the social world of the adult.

Terms and Concepts

behaviorism
biological approach
case history
clinical approach
cognitive psychology
control group
correlation
dependent variable
double-blind procedure
experimental group
experimenter bias
humanistic approach
hypothesis
independent variable
introspection

mean
measurements
median
qualitative
quantitative
questionnaire
replication
sample
self-actualization
significant difference
social environmental perspective
statistics
subjects
tests

Suggestions for Further Reading

Hall, E. (1978). *Why we do what we do: A look at psychology.* Boston: Houghton Mifflin.

   A charming and clearly written introduction to how behavior might be studied and how psychology touches every part of a person's life.

Hilgard, E. R. (Ed.). (1978). *American psychology in historical perspective.* Washington: American Psychological Association.

   Addresses of presidents of the American Psychological Association from William James to Jerome Bruner, giving rich examples of the diversity of psychologists and the development of psychology.

Janis, I. L. (Ed.). (1977). *Current trends in psychology: Readings from American scientists.* Los Altos, CA: William Kaufmann.

A large collection of articles written by eminent psychologists on the different areas of psychology. Important information from firsthand sources.

Miller, G. A., & Buckhout, R. (1973). *Psychology: The science of mental life* (2nd ed.). New York: Harper & Row.

An extremely well-written introduction to psychology, following the "mental" or cognitive approach. It is well organized and follows psychology through the contributions of numerous eminent psychologists.

Shah, I. (1970). *Tales of the dervishes.* New York: E. P. Dutton.

An important collection of stories, many of which, such as "The Elephant in the Dark" used in this chapter, are illustrative of modern psychological phenomena.

*A*t the beginning we are a cell so small that it is invisible to the naked eye.

This joining of father and mother becomes, among other things, a brain of ten billion working cells. If that seems enormous, consider that a machine comparable to your brain would need to be a ten-story building the size of Texas.

If that cell has an extravagant future, it also has an extravagant past. It contains our genetic code developed over millions of years of evolution. That cell grows in a predictable sequence: embryo to fetus, infant to toddler, child to adolescent.

Only recently have we begun to understand these sequences: the evolution of modern humans; the development of every child; and the growth of our brain and senses.

This Part is, then, the beginning of the common human story: where we came from, what is in us at birth, and how we develop.

Part One

The Biological World

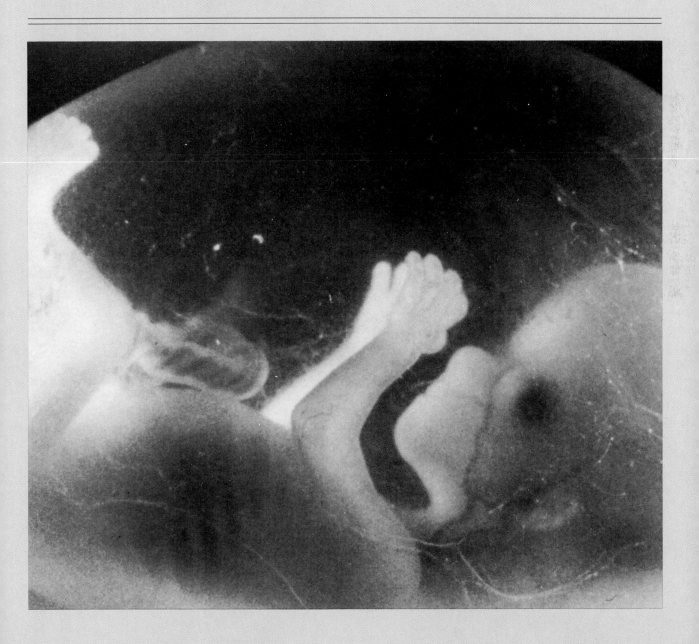

Chapter 2

Where We Come From: Evolution and Genetics

INTRODUCTION

There is a footprint in Africa, impressed in the sand more than three and a half million years ago. That spot records that the ancestors of human beings had begun diverging from the rest of creation. The footprint is of a creature comfortable standing up on two legs instead of four. The step of that creature, however tentative, set into motion a series of changes that made modern humans who we are. The shift from walking on all fours to walking on two increased our ancestors' reliance on vision. The weight of the body that was supported by the front limbs was shifted to the legs and the pelvis. As a result, the front limbs were freed for other activities, such as toolmaking and tool carrying. The pelvis thickened to carry all the weight of the upper body; this changed the entire process of childbirth, making humans a species born "immature." The brain became larger and eventually words were spoken.

We are the result of these changes and we thus have certain distinct physical features. We stand up on two legs and walk erect. We are the most sexual animal; other animals typically mate a few times a year when they are in heat, humans have sexual intercourse regularly at any time of the year. We have the largest brain of any animal in relation to body size, and we have hands capable of very fine movements.

However, these physical features are *not* the only things that make us such an unusual animal. Many animals have distinct physical characteristics. The lion has its mane, the penguin its feathers, the deer its antlers. But most animals are able to survive only in their own original habitat. A lion suddenly transported to New York would not survive the winter, a penguin could not survive New York summer. However, human beings can and do live all over the world, in the bleak heights of the Himalayas, in the deserts of Africa, in the frozen north of Alaska, and in crowded cities all over the world. *We are an animal that lives far outside our original habitat*, and who makes drastic changes in the environment to suit itself. Think of the differences between your life, with television, air and space travel, and the life of a Stone Age tribesman.

Our major concern in this chapter is to discover how we became such

FIGURE 2–1
The footprint of one of our prehuman ancestors, left in the sands of Africa more than three and a half million years ago and discovered by Mary Leakey.

39

a unique animal. To do this we first look at the long sweep of human history, a history of *millions* of years. We will then consider the scientific theory of how our ancestors changed over time, a process known as evolution. Then we will discuss the distinctive features of the human organism and human life, and problems caused by the fact that we live in a world very different from our ancestors' 25,000 years ago. Finally, we consider the mechanisms of inheritance, how physical characteristics are passed on from one generation to the next.

In all this, one moment is especially significant: it is that first time our ancestors stood upright and began to move away from the trees and into a new world, one filled with new circumstances and challenges. In a way, we are still doing that.

Principles and Issues in Human Origins

Most chapters in this book begin with a discussion of major issues and principles of psychology. These issues and principles are important since they provide a general understanding of many of the specialized topics presented in the book.

The Nature/Nurture Question

Are we "naturally" violent? Are men more aggressive than women? Are white people more intelligent than black? These questions reflect one of the oldest issues in psychology. In psychology the controversy has often centered on whether we are *completely determined* by either "nature" or "nurture."

The **nature** view holds that we are governed by our **innate** characteristics. One type of innate characteristic familiar to most people is instinct. Instincts are inborn, fixed patterns of behavior, such as the salmon's

Upright Posture and Locomotion: A Human Inheritance Apes can walk upright better than monkeys can, but the human ability to stand and travel efficiently on two legs is far greater, having resulted from numerous anatomical adaptations over hundreds of generations. (After Leakey & Lewin, 1977)

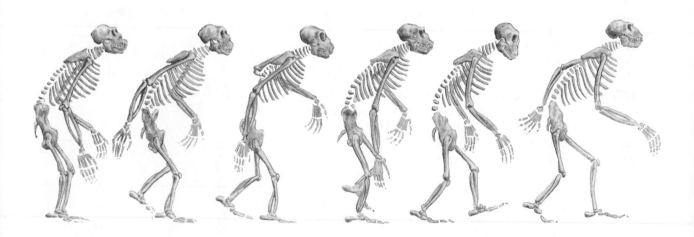

inevitable return to the river of its birth. Some people might think the love or attachment of a mother for her child is a human instinct (Bowlby, 1969). However, because human behavior is more complex than the salmon's, proponents of the nature view have had to assume the existence of hundreds of human instincts, all acting together, to account for our behavior.

The **nurture** view has been prominent in psychology for most of this century. It emphasizes that people are almost completely the product of their environment and that it is only circumstances that make one person into a thief, another into a banker (Skinner, 1972; Watson, 1925).

Both these views are, of course extreme. Neither is sufficient to explain the full range of human behavior. Human beings have certain universal patterns of behavior in common, such as language and tool making. At the same time, an individual's specific experience affects the way in which these universal patterns will be expressed in his own life. For instance, all normal humans are capable of learning language (nature), but the *particular* language they learn depends on their specific experiences (nurture). Most human behavior is the *product of both factors*, as the area of a rectangle is determined by its length *and* width. Some behaviors may be more determined by "nature," some by "nurture," but all are shaped by differing proportions of both.

The Principle of Adaptation

The first order of business in life is to survive. To survive, an individual must be able to function in its environment. **Adaptation** is the process whereby an organism changes—adapts—in order to fit better in its environment.

Any trait (such as color vision or speech) has **adaptive value** if it enables an organism to function better in its environment. Human adap-

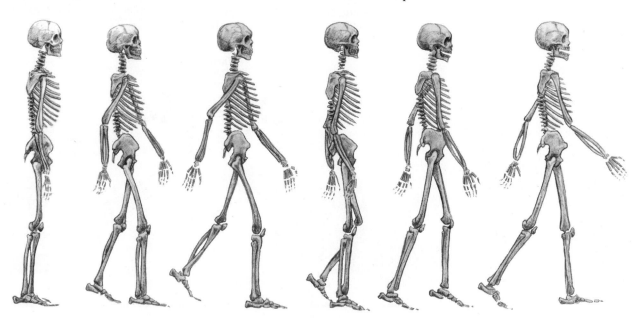

tation takes many different forms because we are always changing to meet new circumstances, and these adaptations involve different mechanisms. For example, when we enter a darkened theater our eyes gradually adapt to the change in illumination, so we continue to see well. This is a variety of **sensory adaptation** called dark adaptation. When we put on a new set of glasses, the world seems curved at first, but we adjust. This is a form of **perceptual adaptation.** Many kinds of adaptations will be treated in detail in subsequent chapters in the book: adapting to different temperatures, adapting to the stress of the modern world, as well as the failure to adapt which results in stress, will be discussed.

Adaptation   See Chapter 5, pp. 179 and 209–10; Chapter 6, pp. 232–33; and Chapter 15, pp. 526, 534.

In this chapter we consider how our ancestors, through a long series of *physical* changes called **evolution,** developed specific characteristics, like walking and talking, which allowed them to adapt to their environment.

Feedback and Systems

It is necessary in science, including psychology, and certainly in textbook writing, to consider individual topics separately. For instance, this book begins with the "biological world," which considers development, the brain, and the senses separately. We then go to the mental, individual, and social worlds. There would be no way to make sense of all the different findings in psychology without presenting different topics separately. But events in the world are not isolated: they constantly affect one another. To help us analyze this interaction, we need to understand what *systems* are and how they are held together by *feedback*.

Systems

A **system** is any group of things that *function together for a common purpose* (Miller, 1978). System is thus another very *general* concept. Sys-

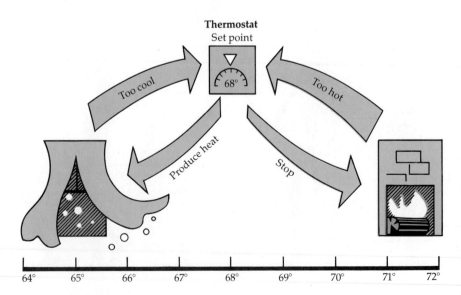

tems exist at all levels and in all areas of life. A system can be widely dispersed and complex as is the "educational system" of the United States. This system includes the actions of individual schools, colleges, teachers, government agencies and even textbook writers. A system can be small and precise, such as the human visual system, in which the eyes, the optic nerve, and parts of the brain function together for the common purpose of sight. Each of us is part of many different systems at once: biological systems, education systems, social systems, legal systems, cultural systems, political systems, ecological systems, and many others.

Feedback

What connects things into a system is feedback. **Feedback** is information about the operation of a system, used within the system to attain its goals. There is a cycle of feedback: information from one part of the system (A) affects other parts of the system (B), which affect the initial part (A). This cyclic action is known as a **feedback loop** (Figure 2–2).

Negative feedback keeps a system in a predetermined condition. Positive feedback allows the system to continually change, sometimes in unexpected directions.

Negative Feedback. An important function of any living organism is the maintenance of the body's internal state. We need to eat, drink, and maintain a certain body temperature to survive. For example, the brain monitors blood temperature in much the same way as a thermostat monitors heat (Figure 2–3). Similarly, the brain monitors blood sugar levels. A low blood sugar level triggers activity aimed at restoring the proper level: hunger pangs occur, and these "tell" us to look for food. *Homeostasis* is an example of a negative feedback loop. The term negative comes from the way the information is "fed back"; in this case the information triggers changes in the opposite (−) direction: *low* blood sugar signals us to *increase* it, high blood sugar would signal the reverse reaction.

FIGURE 2–2
Basic Feedback Loop
Information from one part of the system (A) affects some other part (B), which in response feeds back information that affects the part (A) that initiated the interaction.

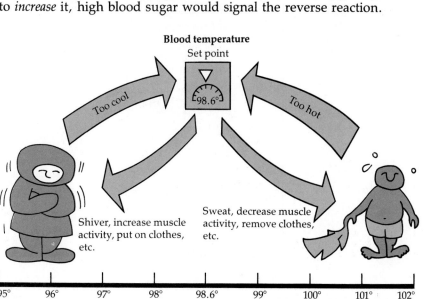

FIGURE 2–3
Negative Feedback Loops
Maintain Predetermined Conditions
A thermostat (far left) is a simple example of a negative feedback loop in action. If it is set at 68°, whenever the room temperature falls below 68°, the heating system will go on; if the room reaches 68°, the heat will go off. In the same way, the body's "thermostat" is set at about 98.6°, and if we get too hot or too cold, our automatic or intentional responses (left) produce negative feedback that keeps our blood at 98.6°.

Positive Feedback. Instead of keeping things constant, a positive feedback loop describes a process by which things may change dramatically: changes in one element of the system change the rest of the system, which then changes the original element, and so on.

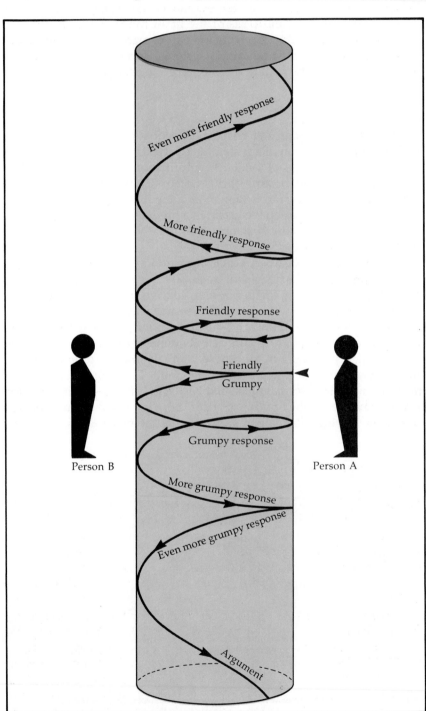

FIGURE 2–4
Positive Feedback: The Mechanism of Adaptation and Change
In positive feedback loops, things change rapidly, dramatically, and in the same direction. Thus, friendliness elicits a friendly response, which prompts an even friendlier response in turn—in an escalating cycle. Situations can also change in the other direction, because just as friendliness begets more friendliness, grumpiness begets increasingly grumpy responses. Human development has involved a long, ongoing process of positive feedback in which innumerable interacting changes and responses have facilitated adaptations to new situations and to the various adaptive changes themselves.

While negative feedback keeps a system at a steady state, *positive feedback is the mechanism of adaptation and change.* In the very simple example in Figure 2–4, one response changes the situation so that the other person can give a friendly response. This makes it possible for the original person to be still more friendly in return. The same loop can also occur with unpleasant feelings: a grumpy statement can evoke a similarly grumpy response, which can lead quickly to an argument. Positive feedback loops explain how things can change rapidly and dramatically. In positive feedback, the change is in the *same* direction (+), friendliness begets more friendliness.

THE ORIGINS AND DEVELOPMENT OF HUMAN BEINGS

This is a story about human origins. It has to be a story because we cannot be completely sure of events that occurred millions of years ago, but it is an important story because it is our common "family history."

We now have a fairly good idea how our ancestors, over millions of years, underwent successive physical changes to better adapt to their new circumstances. Each change, such as standing on two legs, a bigger brain, the uniquely human style of sex, fed into a positive feedback loop. We are the result of this long process of feedback.

The only records we have of these important changes are a few fragments of tools and some skeletons preserved as fossils. But with new evidence being discovered, the full story of human history is emerging. In this section we trace the line of our species from its earliest beginnings four million years ago to the present day. In the following section we will discuss the importance of individual changes that took place and see how the positive feedback loop of human evolution may have worked.

A Note on Evolutionary Time

Before we embark on our journey back through the millennia, it is necessary to reset one's idea of time: In evolutionary time, a few million years, give or take a few thousand, is not very much. Given the time scale of the history of the earth, mankind has developed and multiplied with unprecedented speed. In only a few million years, humans have spread from the African plains to inhabit every part of the planet, and grown from a population of scattered few thousand to well over four billion.

If someone were to chart the entire history of the earth on a single year's calendar, making midnight on December 31 represent today, the first form of life would appear about April 1. Fish appear about November 20. The first recognizable human ancestor would not appear until the *morning of December 31.* The first human being would appear at about 11:45 P.M. All that has happened in recorded history (the subject of history classes) would occur in the final *minute* of the year. (See Figure 2–5.)

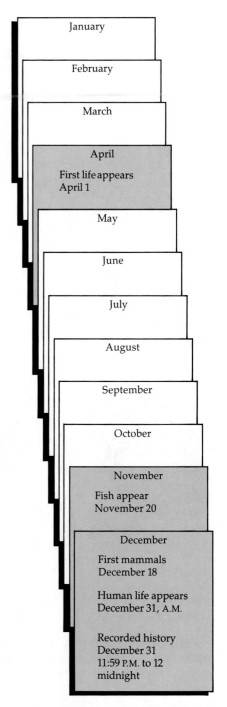

FIGURE 2–5
The History of Earth in a Single Year

Prehumans

Between 25 and 13 million years ago a series of events began that led to the emergence of two primates: humans and chimpanzees. Our prehuman ancestors descended from tree-dwelling animals. Sometime before 13 million years ago, the forest of East Africa began to thin out, forcing many of the tree-dwelling primates out of their homes and inviting others to try living in new ecological niches on the ground. The ones that had no trouble holding on to their tree homes evolved into chimpanzees. Of those who were forced or attracted out, some did not adapt and became extinct (Lancaster, 1978), while others learned to live out of the trees. They took up residence in the surrounding grasslands, prospered and survived, and evolved into prehumans and the first members of the hominid family. **Hominids** include us and all our humanlike ancestors. The change from prehuman to human involved the development of four important hominid characteristics: increasingly upright stance, increased use of tools, increased size of the brain, and the emergence of a cooperative society.

FIGURE 2–6
From Prehuman to Human
The characteristics and abilities that distinguish modern human beings gradually emerged over millions of years of adaptation by our humanlike ancestors.

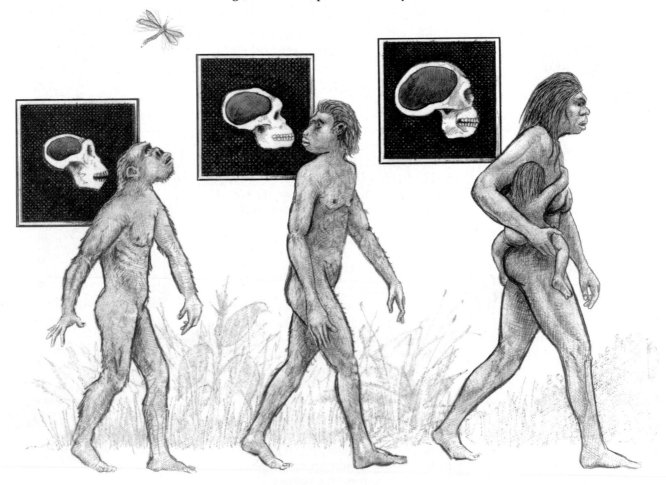

Australopithecus   Homo habilis   Homo erectus

Prehumans had both apelike and humanlike characteristics. Here we will consider only those aspects that are closer to humans. The first humanlike ancestor was *Ramapithecus,* who first appeared sometime between 9 and 13 million years ago. The first hominids we could call our direct ancestors were tiny **Australopithecus,** (3–4 million years ago) and a new species, **Homo habilis,** (1.5 million years ago). Of these species *Homo habilis* (which means handy man) seems to have been predominant, although this is not certain. The superior advantages that might have insured the survival of *Homo habilis* were the ability to use tools and to hunt. In addition to having these social skills, these hominids were physically more nearly human: their brains were larger and they walked more upright. (See Figure 2–6.)

Tool use probably made *Homo habilis* a more efficient worker. Tools would have made it possible to build shelters and construct primitive

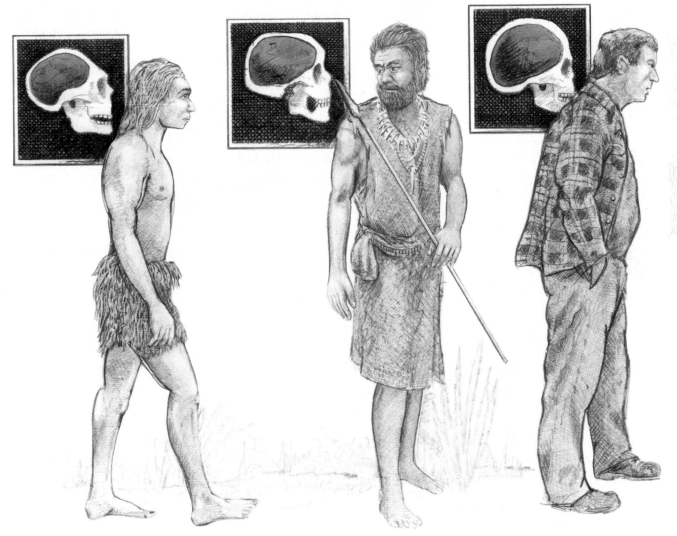

Neanderthal   Cro-Magnon   Modern Homo sapiens

settlements. Perhaps more important, *Homo habilis* hunted in groups. Feeding a family on fruits and berries is a difficult chore; most of every day must be spent foraging for food. But a group of hunters can bring home enough food for several families for days. Food sharing allowed *Homo habilis* to begin to establish a stable home base and a more permanent cooperative society (Lancaster, 1978). Consider what hunting requires: speed and accuracy are obvious, but the ability to plan, communicate, and cooperate are even more important. These abilities are the distinct precursors of superior human intelligence: the ability to think and reason, speak a language, and create a culture.

Humans

Why do we have the abilities we have? How did the grunts and gestures of our ancestors change into the precision and grace of language? And how did the human brain grow to its great size? How did some apparent disadvantages, such as the helplessness of human children, turn into important advantages?

It took 6 to 9 million years for the prehuman brain to grow significantly, for some communal living to develop, for the invention and use of tools (Figure 2–7). But once these things happened, *they affected each other*, and began to work together. As would be expected in a positive feedback loop, this process spurred further and more rapid change. It has been only about one and a half million years since the emergence of the creature who was probably one of the first humans, *Homo erectus*. In this time the brain has doubled in size, primitive tools have developed into complex technology, and civilizations have risen and fallen.

FIGURE 2–7   Comparison of Cranial Capacities

	Range of Cranial Capacity (cc)	Average Cranial Capacity (cc)
Lemur	10–70	—
Chimpanzee	282–500	383
Gorilla	340–752	505
Australopithecus africanus	435–530	450
A. robustus	—	500
A. boisei	506–530	515
Homo habilis	600–752	666
H. erectus	775–1,225	950
Modern adult human	1,000–2,000	1,330

Source: Campbell, 1982.

Physical differences between prehumans and modern humans are obvious (Figure 2–6). Our skull has grown much larger to accommodate a larger brain. The brain of *Australopithecus* was 450 cc; our brains are between 1,000 and 2,000 cc (Campbell, 1982). Humans stand more fully erect and walk and run better than prehumans. As human evolution progressed, society became increasingly stable: home bases were permanent and more central to life. Social organization grew in complexity.

Homo erectus: 1.6 Million to about 500,000 Years Ago

What most distinguished *Homo erectus* from his predecessors was a large brain and the complexity of behavior that it made possible.

Homo erectus, the name means "upright man," stood fully erect and walked as we do. Their appearance was generally modern: they were probably over five feet tall and their skeletons were very similar to ours, at least from the neck down. Like modern humans, *Homo erectus* moved around a great deal. Although the remains of earlier prehumans are confined to East Africa and India, *Homo erectus* migrated from these areas and settled in places as far north as present-day Germany and as far east as China.

In 1965 archaeologists uncovered a well-preserved settlement called **Terra Amata,** which unlocked many of the secrets of the behavior of *Homo erectus* (de Lumley, 1969). Today, in a housing complex built on that same site, people engage in many of the same activities as their ancestors 400,000 years ago. We know from the remains at Terra Amata that the culture of *Homo erectus* was very advanced. Cooking pots, skins, marrow scrapers, and other advanced tools have been unearthed.

Homo erectus built elaborate shelters, invented clothing, and used fire in a controlled manner.

The taming of fire is an important landmark in human history. Along with the inventions of clothing and shelter, it made life in cold climates possible. Even today 75 percent of the earth's population use fire as their primary source of warmth (Eckholm, 1978). Cooked food does not spoil as fast as raw and is more versatile. The use of fire is also a social landmark. People are drawn to fires not only for warmth but also for socializing. Because brain size had increased considerably by this time, and because of the increased social time spent around a fire, it is possible that *Homo erectus* was the first hominid to begin to use speech.

Neanderthal: From before 100,000 to about 40,000 Years Ago

Neanderthals are the cave men of popular folklore. They have been portrayed as brutish and dim witted (possibly because of their physical appearance), but this image now seems to be wrong.

Neanderthals first appeared during the Ice Age. The range they inhabited was similar to that of *Homo erectus:* probably from Germany to China, predominantly in northern regions. They had adapted so specifically to cold weather climates that many scholars think they became extinct when the Ice Age ended.

Figure 2–8 depicts an important event in human history. A cave near what is now Shanidar, Iraq, marks the spot where, on a day 60,000 years

ago, a Neanderthal man was buried. But this was not just a burial, it was a funeral—an organized ceremony. The fossilized remains of several kinds of flowers and grains are distributed in an orderly fashion around the skeleton. The bones of the deceased lie on a woven bed.

Evidence of a deliberate burial this far in the past is impressive. Evidence of an organized ceremony is even more impressive. What is most impressive, however, is that the particular species of flowers found at the burial are still used today in local herbal medicine, which suggests that Neanderthals had an advanced understanding of the medicinal properties of plants (Leakey & Lewin, 1977).

Neanderthal culture was advanced and modern in many ways. There was division of labor, increased inventiveness (as seen by the tools and other found artifacts), and even organized conflict. It is possible that Neanderthals were the first humans to wage wars. In addition, it is now believed that Neanderthals were the first humans to conceive of a spiritual life. There is evidence of worship and ritual: bear skulls and bones are carefully placed in caves.

Neanderthals probably further developed inventions and discoveries of *Homo erectus*. Their shelters were more elaborate. They clothed themselves in skins for warmth and created quite complex tools. The tendency toward cooperation first noticed in *Australopithecus* had probably evolved by this time into the first genuine human society. Thus Neanderthals were not very different from us (their brains were 1,500 cc, the same as ours). The biologists Singer and Hilgard (1978) write: "A Neanderthal man dressed in blue jeans and a sweatshirt would not attract much attention at the checkout line of the local supermarket."

Homo sapiens

Cro-Magnon

In 1868, French railway workers were cutting through a hillside when they came upon four human skeletons. The skeletons looked modern, but the tools and objects lying next to them did not: stone tools, seashells, and animal teeth with holes drilled in them, apparently for stringing as an ornament. These skeletons have proved to be the earliest remains (from sometime about 50,000 years ago) of our own species, *Homo sapiens* ("intelligent man"). They were called **"Cro-Magnon"** after the site of their discovery. There are significant physical differences in the shape of the skull of a Cro-Magnon and a Neanderthal (Figure 2–6). Between their eras the entire shape of the face altered and the physiological apparatus for producing a great range of sounds was different. The brain did not change much in size but actually moved higher in the skull. The palate (inside the mouth) enlarged, which allowed greater precision in speech.

Speech is the most sophisticated "tool" humans have. With the first development of language, the pace of evolution, which had quickened since *Homo erectus*, began to proceed with unprecedented speed. Because of their language skill, Cro-Magnons had a tremendous advantage over Neanderthals: they could plan, organize, and cooperate much more efficiently. The tools Cro-Magnon used in hunting and in daily life were considerably more elaborate than those of Neanderthal. Shelters and settlements, too, were more complex. A major innovation of Cro-Magnon is art. The Cro-Magnon paintings found on the caves of **Lascaux** in France, done 15,000 years ago, are as beautiful as anything ever created (Figure 2–9).

Art and language are both significant milestones in human evolution, because they signify a mind capable of abstraction, symbolism, and invention. Making art is an abstraction of a world not present and often a representation of a world view or a spiritual system. Language, too, is abstract, involving the use of arbitrary sounds to represent real objects in the world. Fifteen thousand years ago, one commentator has it, our ancestors were fully human (Marshak, 1978).

Hunting, Gathering, and the Agricultural Revolution

Hunter-Gatherers

For most of history, humans have lived in hunting-and-gathering societies; many still do. In this kind of society there are two main activities: the search for meat and the gathering of available fruits, vegetables, and grains. Such **hunter-gatherers** lead a nomadic existence, moving as grains become scarce or following the seasonal migration of animals. But their lives are not necessarily impoverished; one anthropologist calls hunter-gatherer societies the "original affluent societies." His study showed (Figure 2–10) that an individual in a contemporary hunter-gatherer tribe spends less time working and has more leisure time than an average Frenchman today (Johnson, 1978). Still, the life of hunter-gatherers does not make for a very *stable* society—their life changes as they migrate.

The Agricultural Revolution

The invention of agriculture liberated humans from the uncertainties of the nomadic life of hunter-gatherers. The first crops, planted about 10,000 years ago, represent the first large-scale attempt to master the environment. A hunter-gatherer is at the mercy of nature; a farmer can control it to some extent. The cultivation of crops transformed human societies from mobile hunting-and-gathering ones to stable groups. Freed from the continual search for food, people now literally "put down roots." Agriculture thus made possible the beginning of civilization as we know it. In what is now Iran and Iraq, our recent ancestors began to grow grains and to domesticate animals and build permanent settlements. These first, tentative, settlements later developed into communi-

FIGURE 2–9
Cro-Magnon Art
The Cro-Magnon paintings (far right) from the caves of Lascaux, France, reveal highly developed artistic ability and sensibility, powers of abstraction, and an appreciation both of the realistic details and of the spiritual essence of life and living things.

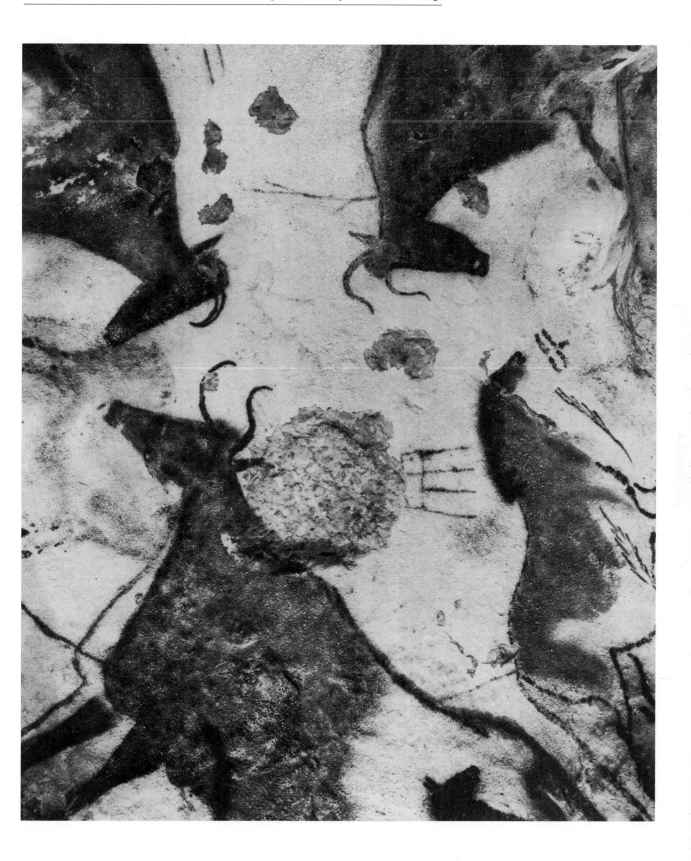

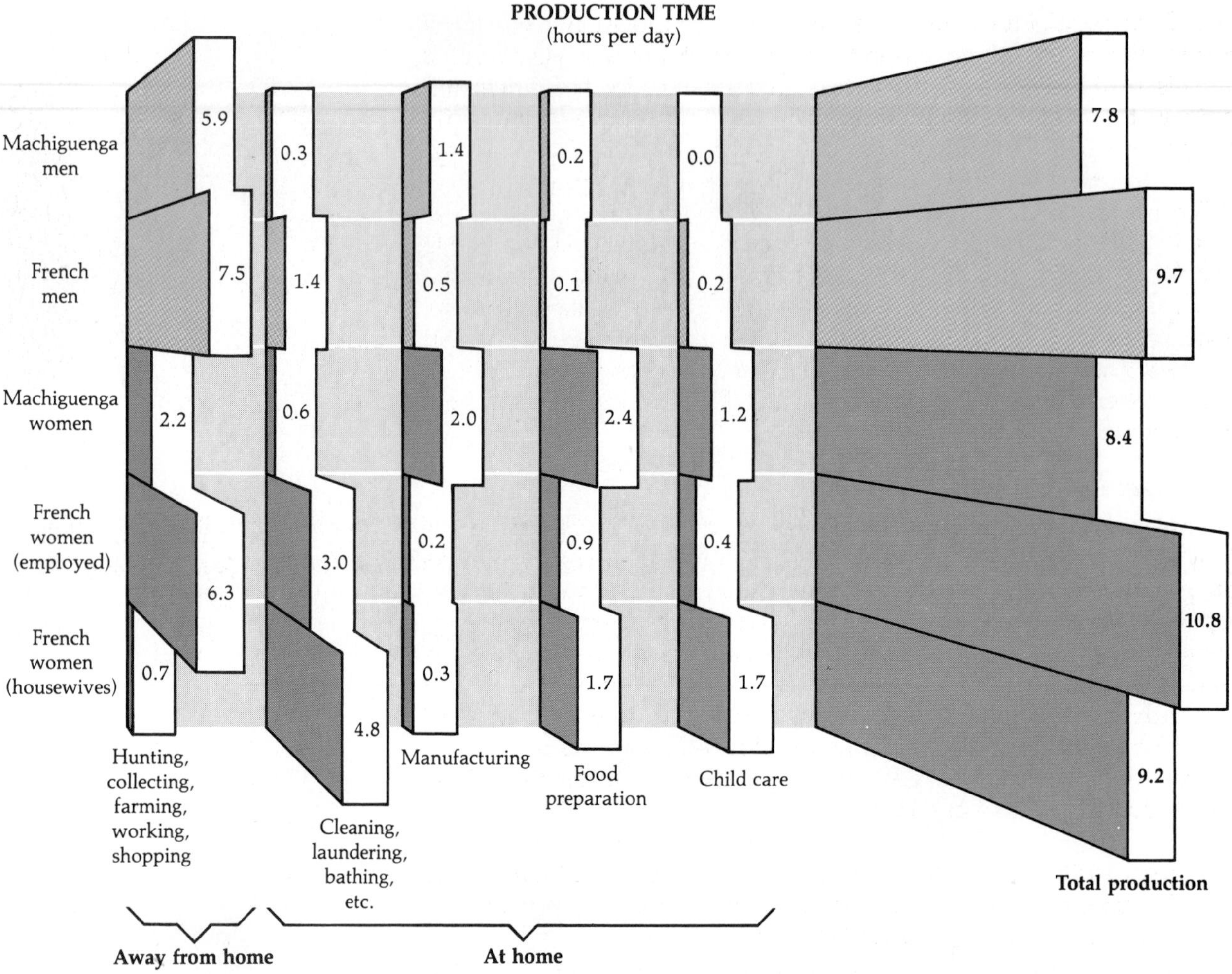

PRODUCTION TIME
(hours per day)

	Hunting, collecting, farming, working, shopping	Cleaning, laundering, bathing, etc.	Manufacturing	Food preparation	Child care	Total production
Machiguenga men	5.9	0.3	1.4	0.2	0.0	7.8
French men	7.5	1.4	0.5	0.1	0.2	9.7
Machiguenga women	2.2	0.6	2.0	2.4	1.2	8.4
French women (employed)	6.3	3.0	0.2	0.9	0.4	10.8
French women (housewives)	0.7	4.8	0.3	1.7	1.7	9.2

Away from home | At home

FIGURE 2–10
The Affluence of Hunting-and-Gathering Societies
Hunter-gatherers, such as the Machiguenga, lack the material wealth of modern French men and women, but—as this chart shows—spend less time working and caring for their homes and possessions; so they are richer in leisure time than the average member of our modern, technological society. (After Johnson, 1978)

ties and, still later, into cities. Then, almost in an instant, the great ancient civilizations emerged in those regions where agriculture was first developed—in China, India, and the Near East. The pace of change quickened again. In a few thousand years, human society changed from nomadic to settled, and the foundations of advanced human culture were cemented.

The Process of Adaptation and Evolution

So far we have described the physical changes our ancestors underwent in adapting to the world. Now we turn our attention to the question of how those changes occurred. *How* did the pelvis change? *How* did the brain become larger?

Before modern science, it was generally believed that all creatures were individually created to suit their special environments. Organisms were thought fixed—humans were created as humans, monkeys were created monkeys, and so on. This view was overthrown by the work of the Swedish botanist Linnaeus in the seventeenth century. He classified animals so that their similarities became apparent. By the nineteenth century, the commonly held scientific view was that all animals did change and had developed from earlier forms of life. But how that change occurred, the specific mechanism, remained a mystery.

The answer finally appeared when the English naturalist, Charles Darwin (1809–1882) proposed his theory of how adaptation occurs. He called the process "descent with modification." In 1859 he published a revolutionary book, *The Origin of Species*, in which he described the mechanism by which organisms adapt to the environment—**natural selection.** Darwin's theory, combined with modern genetics, is the basis of the modern *theory of evolution,* now the accepted explanation of how organisms change over time.

Charles Darwin
(1809–1882)

Natural Selection

How populations change over time is their *evolution;* natural selection is the key element. A "population" is a group of similar organisms who can produce fertile offspring. For a group of animals to survive as a population, each generation must replace itself through sexual reproduction. Any group of organisms produces far more offspring than is needed to replace itself. One salmon lays thousands of eggs, a cat can give birth to several litters of 6 or 7 kittens in her lifetime, a woman can have 10 or more children. But, Darwin observed, populations usually remain at a fairly constant size from one generation to the next. That observation led to two important insights.

1. Some individuals produce more surviving offspring than others. *Therefore, the individuals who do survive must in some way be more fit, better able to live in and adapt to their environment.*
2. Although the offspring are by and large like the parents, they also *differ from them* in many important respects.

Sexual reproduction results in offspring that are *combinations* of two different *individuals,* not an exact copy of one. Differences between the offspring and the parents that enable the offspring to adapt better, to be more successful and reproduce, would be likely to be passed on to the next generation, and that generation would change, or evolve (Darwin, 1859; Gould, 1979).

Let us illustrate this with an example that Darwin used—animal breeding. To breed a small poodle, we would look for the smallest female and the smallest male poodle and then breed them. The dogs in the resulting litter will most probably be smaller on the average than the parents. If we repeat this process with the offspring, each succeeding generation, *on average,* will be smaller than the previous one. In this case we are breeding for a specific characteristic by *artificial* selection. In nature, however, there is no such deliberate manipulation. With natural selection, successful organisms are "chosen" by the environment. People choose their own mates, produce offspring that, because they are combinations of their parents' characteristics, differ slightly from their parents. Traits that are adaptive, therefore, are passed on.

Adaptive Value

Darwin's ideas thus became known as the "survival of the fittest." The popular idea regarding the "survival of the fittest" is that life is a struggle between different *individuals* to survive. But that is incorrect. The struggle for survival referred to in the theory of evolution is the struggle of a *species,* not an individual.

One important insight Darwin had is that the advantage of a new trait is not seen in the individual who inherits the trait, but in *succeeding generations.* The process works like this: individuals born with characteristics that enable them to adapt better to their environment reproduce more successfully and pass on those characteristics to others. Thus when we speak of adaptation, or "survival of the fittest," we refer to *a match between the traits of a population and its environment.* Sunlight stimulates the production of vitamin D, which is a necessary nutrient for humans. Humans can absorb sunlight through the skin. In a tropical environment, where there is an abundance of sunlight, humans run the risk of producing excessive vitamin D. Therefore, those individuals who can in some way block out some of the sun's rays will be better adapted to that environment. A mechanism blocking the sun's rays would thus have *adaptive value.* In a northerly environment, where there is not much sunlight, there would be an adaptive value to those individuals with some mechanism for stimulating production of vitamin D. Many anthropologists use this logic to explain different skin colors in human populations. As people settled farther and farther north, those who best survived had lighter skin color, which allows sunlight to be absorbed through the skin at a higher rate. There is a relationship between skin color and proximity

---

HOW ADAPTATIONS ADD UP

Very slight differences of advantages can effect enormous changes over time. Let us say that in some prehuman population, half the individuals are four feet tall and half are five feet tall. The average height of the entire population is 4.5 feet. Suppose there is some adaptive value in being tall. Tall people see farther, climb faster, run faster, and are more robust. Suppose that on the average the five-footers have 2.9 surviving children, the four-footers have 2.7 surviving children, and those in each group breed only among themselves. This is not a significant difference in one generation, but note what happens to the population over several generations (see Figure 2–11). In about 1,200 years, or 60 generations, the "short" four-footers account for less than two percent of the population. The average height of the entire group is now 4.98 feet. No single individual changed, but the average height of the population has grown over time.

to the equator: the closer to the equator, the darker the skin (Dobzhansky, 1962).

Thus Darwin's insight allowed us to understand how our ancestors became us, how populations could change over time.

To recap, the process by which the environment selects the individuals best adapted to it is *natural selection*. The change in the composition of population that follows natural selection is its *evolution*.

The Impact of Darwin's Theory

Although the principles of evolution are fairly simple and straightforward, they have probably had more impact than any others in the human sciences. The notion of evolution changed forever our conception of ourselves and our place in the universe. It now provides the paradigm for almost all research in the life sciences and has greatly influenced psychology.

Our View of Ourselves

For most of human history the dominant view was that human beings were at the center of the universe. It was believed that the sun and the planets revolved around the earth and that the earth was the center of the universe. Human beings were believed to be specially created to dwell at the center of creation. Two major events dealt stunning blows to

FIGURE 2–11
Adaptation, Reproduction, Success, and Survival
Changes in the average height of this imaginary prehuman population are due to differential reproductive "success." Height happens to be adaptive in this example, so more taller individuals survive to reproduce their kind, which make up a larger and larger percentage of a population with an increasing average height.

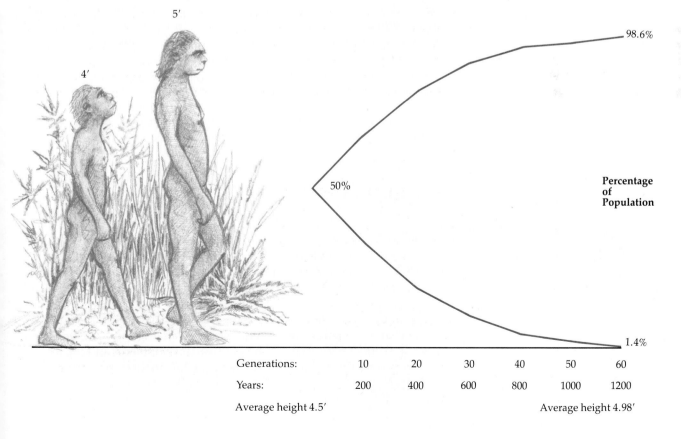

| Generations: | 10 | 20 | 30 | 40 | 50 | 60 |
| Years: | 200 | 400 | 600 | 800 | 1000 | 1200 |

Average height 4.5'   Average height 4.98'

this conception of ourselves. The first came in 1543 when the Polish astronomer, Nicholas Copernicus, demonstrated that the planets did *not* revolve around the earth, that our planet was simply one of many that revolved around the sun. The Catholic Church considered this theory heretical for many years, until the weight of evidence supporting the theory was undeniable and it had to be accepted. Still, the Copernican system did not upset the belief that human beings were unique creatures, created especially to rule the earth.

Then came Darwin, whose theory placed humans under the same rules of life that applied to all animals. All organisms, it was thought, have a common ancestor and, adding insult to injury, we are descended from apes. The Victorian world was appalled at this aspect of Darwin's theory. There is a tremendous difference between thinking of yourself as "created in God's own image" and "descended from the apes." One proper Victorian lady said, on hearing Darwin's theory, "I pray that it is not true, but if it is true, I pray that it does not become widely known" (Leakey & Lewin, 1977).

Darwin himself was the subject of considerable controversy and ridicule. He was immediately lampooned in cartoons and attacked in sermons, debates and editorials. His theory has continued to be controversial to this day. In 1925, an American biology teacher was fired for teaching the principles of evolution in a Tennessee school, in violation of a state law. The controversy ended in court, in the famous "Monkey Trial." Today, in the United States, many fundamentalist Christian groups still object to the teaching of evolution in public schools, at least in the absence of any teaching of "creationism," the idea that God literally created the world as written in the Bible.

Darwin's work, and the later development of evolutionary theory, did more than simply shock the world. It placed human beings as members of the animal kingdom, subject to the same forces that act on all animals, and it opened the modern era of scientific investigations of human nature.

THE HUMAN ADAPTATION

Human beings have many physical, behavioral, and mental characteristics that set us off from other animals. One physical characteristic, standing up, was very important in human evolution: it led, as we shall see, to an increased ability to reproduce. Somewhat later (although it is an oversimplification to completely isolate each characteristic) came tool use, an increasingly large brain, and self-awareness. These physical changes resulted in innumerable behavioral changes, among them the development of a cooperative society. The physical developments and the resulting developments in the human style of life in turn prompted vast changes in human society so that cultures and behavior changed rapidly over a very short time.

Several characteristics set humans apart from other animals. We consider them here in the rough chronological order in which they evolved, but it is better to think of the process of **human adaptation** as the *simultaneous* development of all these characteristics, in a positive feedback loop (Figure 2–12). The effects of the loop have increasingly widened the gap between us and our nearest ancestors.

Characteristics of the Human Adaptation

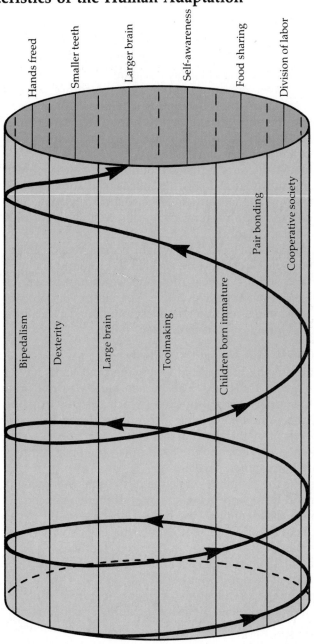

FIGURE 2–12
Human Adaptation:
The Power of Positive Feedback
The characteristics that make the human species unique include the following: (1) We stand on two legs and walk; (2) Children are born comparatively immature and need care for a comparatively long period; (3) Human females are biologically sexually receptive all of the time and usually pair off with one male; (4) Humans have forelimbs capable of fine motor control (dexterity) and use tools; (5) The human brain is larger than that of other animals— relative to body size—is capable of sophisticated communication in language and art, and is specialized to notice changes in the environment and to react quickly to changes; (6) Human life is cooperative, organized around food sharing and division of labor; (7) Like physical characteristics, human society also evolved over time, with human beings demonstrating a capacity to completely change their environment and to live in almost all areas of the earth. These characteristics developed—often simultaneously— over millions of years. Critically important adaptations, such as a large brain, bipedalism, dexterity, toolmaking, and a cooperative society, gradually emerged. Each required and enhanced the others, and related characteristics, in an ever-accelerating spiral of positive feedback.

Bipedalism: Standing up and Walking

Humans are **bipedal,** which means we walk on two feet instead of all four. Chimps and gorillas can stand upright at times, but when they move they usually do so on all fours. A fossil skeleton called Lucy, the first known hominid showing evidence of bipedal locomotion, dates from about 3.75 million years ago, about one million years before the use of tools (Johansen & Edey, 1981).

Walking

Bipedal walking and running are extremely efficient modes of locomotion. People can cover greater distances over time than any other animal. We are the only animals that can climb a tree, swim a mile across a river, and walk 20 miles in a day (Haldane, 1932). Walking enabled our ancestors to travel into new and unexplored territory, which in turn led them into new and often dangerous situations. All other animals live their lives in the environment in which they are born. Humans became immigrants; to survive in new locales they had to invent ways to deal with the unknown and unexpected.

Get down on all fours and look around. The view is more limited than when you stand (Figure 2–13). To four-legged animals smell is important. A standing animal can see farther than it can smell. Since standing animals can spot approaching danger as well as opportunities farther away, a more sophisticated visual system developed along with upright posture. Hands were freed from weight-bearing responsibilities, making tool use possible. Erect posture also led to profound changes in human sexuality and social systems. Although we cannot be completely sure, this complex of factors surrounding bipedalism was probably our first adaptive advantage, resulting, as everything must in evolution, in more surviving offspring (Johansen & Edey, 1981).

Immaturity and Its Consequences

With the freeing of the front limbs, the hind limbs have to bear the entire weight of the body. The human back was not originally "designed" to support upright posture (which partially explains why back pains are a common complaint). To support the additional weight, the human pelvis grew thicker than that of the great apes (Washburn, 1960). The thickened pelvis made the birth canal, the opening through which infants are born, much smaller.

But here is the problem: while the birth canal was becoming smaller, the brain and head were growing larger. If there had been no correction for this new disadvantage, the human species would have eventually died out because of inefficient childbirth. The "solution" was to have human babies born very early in their development. At birth a chimp's brain is about 45 percent of its adult weight, while a human baby's brain is 25 percent of its adult weight (Lovejoy, 1974). Human children have the longest infancy in the animal kingdom (Figure 2–14); they are not as competent and independent as baby chimps or baboons. Within a day, baby baboons can hold onto their mothers by themselves (Campbell, 1982). The human child is completely helpless and will die if not taken care of for years.

FIGURE 2–13
The Value of Bipedalism: Avoiding Danger and Exploiting Opportunities

The Brain.   The major portion of the brain's development occurs outside the womb, exposed to and influenced by many different environments, events, and people. The environment plays a much greater role in the development of the human brain than in any other animal's brain development. And because the environment—the set of experiences one has with the surrounding physical and social world—is different for each person, the specific kinds of abilities each of us develops varies enormously.

The Mother-Father-Infant Relationship.   A helpless infant requires at least one caretaking parent to survive. In other species, because a newborn can fend for itself within a relatively short time, the mother can almost immediately resume her place in the group, providing her young with food and protection for a short time only. But taking care of a human infant is a full-time job. For most of human history, it has been the mother's job. In subsistence societies, like hunter-gatherers, a nursing mother would have a hard time getting enough food for herself while caring for a child (Benshoof & Thornhill, 1979). But parents working together form an efficient team. The father can hunt for meat and bring it home to the mother, who stays close to home gathering fruits and vegetables. *Of all the fathers in the animal kingdom, human fathers take the most active role in the feeding of their young* (Alexander, Hoogland, Howard, Noonan, & Sherman, 1979).

Sexuality

One result of bipedalism is that humans are by far the sexiest mammals. Other mammals are sexually aroused at specific times of the year. All female mammals, except humans, are sexually excitable only when "in heat," which means when *ovulating*. **Ovulation** is the time when the female egg is developed and released from the ovaries, and thus can be fertilized. The period of ovulation is called **estrus.** Female mammals, other than humans, have an *estrus cycle,* which means that they ovulate only a few times a year. In addition, males are generally excited by a female in estrus and a female can only physically receive the male when she is ovulating.

A female in estrus communicates her sexual excitability (or receptivity) by emitting certain odors from the vagina. But without estrus, males cannot tell by smell when females are ovulating. However, in a menstrual cycle with ovulation every month, a woman is always sexually receptive, or—to put it a less potentially offensive way—sex is possible at almost any point. Human beings thus have intercourse frequently throughout the year.

Pair Bonding

Human sexual signals are more visual than other animals. A woman's breasts are always large, even when she is not nursing. In other mammals this is not the case. The man's penis is much larger, relative to body size, than that of any of the great apes. Humans face each other during intercourse; in other mammals the male mounts the female from the rear (Goody, 1976). The frequency of sex, combined with the eye contact during sex and the continual presence of visual sex signals, may, in the

current view, have laid the groundwork for strong emotional bonds based on sexual pleasure. There are also good biological reasons for the pleasure derived from sex: it encourages sexual relations and thus increases the chance of conception. Humans usually like to have sex much more than the demands of conception require. The pleasure each individual derives from the other in sex can lead to strong feelings of attachment or bonds.

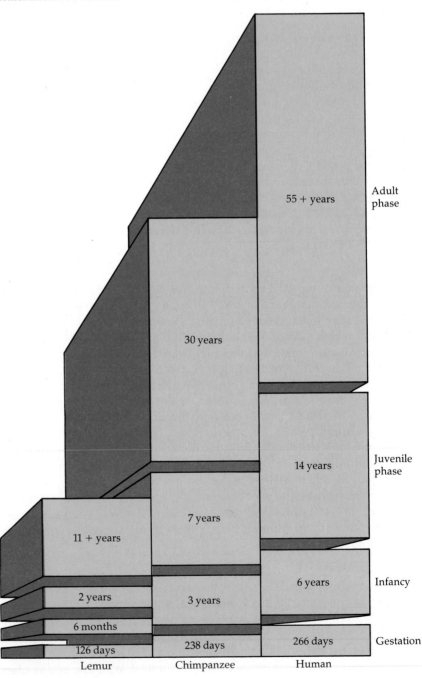

FIGURE 2–14
Help for the Helpless
With the longest infancy of any animal, human young are wholly dependent upon their parents for twice as long as baby chimpanzees. But the long period of protecting the helpless infants gives human family groups greater cohesion and the infants themselves have the time to learn all that is involved in being human.

The human style of sex lays a foundation for a stable society built of family units (Sahlins, 1972). The place sex occupies in human life is unique: we do not have sex merely to replace ourselves in the next generation; we "fall in love" and "make love." The sexual bond, or **pair bonding,** is the basis of the family: fathers stay with, care for, and care about their families. Because both parents participate in child rearing, families can expand faster. The mother can care for several small children at home, if the father brings home most of the food (Benshoof & Thornhill, 1979).

By contrast, consider the female chimpanzee. She lives from 18 to 40 years, but because she bears all the responsibility for her children—nursing, feeding, and protection—it takes her about 16 years to produce and raise two offspring (Gallup, 1977). A human female could theoretically produce and raise a child a year from the onset of menstruation to menopause. Thus one important part of the adaptive value of bipedalism may lie in the human style of sexuality, which creates the family unit and cooperation (Lovejoy, 1981), although this view has been challenged, in that male and female sexual strategies may be different (Symons, 1978, 1980).

SEX DIFFERENCES AND DIVISION OF LABOR

In all of the 800 primitive societies that have been studied, men do the hunting, women do the gathering (Friedl, 1978). The reasons for this may come from the nature of sexual reproduction. A woman carries a child for nine months in her womb, then must carry it around for about a year after birth. In most primitive societies, women nurse their babies for two or three years. It is impossible to be an effective hunter while pregnant, or while nursing or carrying a child (Washburn, 1960). Also, males are physically bigger and stronger than females. Because males do not bear children, the male pelvis is narrower than the female's, with the result that men are usually faster runners.

In every society, human and animal, males do the fighting. This is not only because of their greater physical strength, but is due also to the most basic requirement of a species: survival of the next generation. In a population of 10 males and 10 females, if nine females died in battle, only two or three children could possibly be born to the group the next year, and survival of the population would be in peril. But if nine men died in battle, the 10 surviving females could each produce a child in the next year. So *males are more expendable,* and not as critical to the survival of the species (Leutenegger, 1977).

Even though males are more expendable, in virtually every human society men have held, and continue to hold, the most powerful and respected positions. This male authority is generally referred to as *male dominance.* Why has this occurred?

This question brings up the issue of nature/nurture. Are males "naturally" dominant? Many theorists in the past (all males!) have claimed that males are not only physically stronger but also intellectually superior. But studies in recent years, by both men and women, have not supported this theory.

One new theory suggests that control of a society's most valued resources determines who dominates (Friedl, 1978). Meat is one such valued resource. We need protein to live, and meat is a much more concentrated source of protein than are fruits and vegetables. A large gazelle, caught and brought home by a hunting party, can feed several families for several days. Thus many people can eat well for a long period of time from the labor of a few. As early man developed into modern man—with a larger brain, increased language skills, and increased dexterity—males became more skillful hunters, and consequently meat began to play a more important role in the diet. In hunter-gatherer societies, meat became the most valued resource. Males who procured and distributed it became the dominant members of the community. Today males do not always control protein resources directly. Nevertheless, because men have historically controlled the supply of the most valuable resource, they have acquired a dominant status in nearly every society in human history. As women gain more and more control over currently valuable resources, this "tradition" of male dominance will change (and quickly on an evolutionary time scale).

Cooperation and Human Society

In a mating system governed by estrus, the female is available only at specific times and is available to many males at those times. Mating in most other animal societies is preceded by aggressive competition among males for the females in heat. With the replacement of an estrus cycle by a menstrual cycle and the emergence of pair bonding, this continual sexual competition among males was lessened. Increased cooperation took place, not only within the pair bond but also among members of a society (Johansen & Edey, 1981; Lovejoy, 1981). One characteristic of all human societies studied so far is their cooperation, as defined at least by food sharing and division of labor. The complex and interdependent human society has a biological basis in cooperation.

Every human begins life dependent on the mother. As individuals mature, they recognize increasingly complex networks of interdependence: from family to group to nation to the entire world (Humphrey, 1978). Even organized aggression depends on cooperation. Hunting, which is a primary human adaptation, requires planning, division of labor, signals of a complex order, cooperative carrying home of the kill, and a sharing of the prize with those at home (Lancaster, 1978).

Dexterity and Tool Use

Because most primates are tree-dwelling animals, both the front and hind limbs are needed to grasp branches and vines. Once humans became bipedal and the forelimbs were freed from their weight-bearing function, the limbs developed into hands with great **dexterity,** capable of more precise movements such as those needed for fashioning and **using specialized tools.** Humans began to make tools as early as three million years ago.

Specialized tools for chopping, digging, killing, cooking, washing, and skinning, led to specialized labor by those who used them. Some people took on the tasks of gathering wood or nuts, others digging for roots, still others killing animals (Washburn, 1961). Axes made the hunt more efficient; choppers and scrapers could be used to butcher a large animal at the site of the kill. At home, tools helped scrape the nutritious marrow out of the bones; animal hides could be scraped to make warm clothing.

One way to mark improved dexterity is to look at the change in the tools themselves. Those made by *Homo erectus* about one million years ago took about 35 blows to make. The knives of Cro-Magnon, made about 20,000 years ago, were much more delicately fashioned, requiring at least 250 separate blows (Figure 2–15).

In about 5000 B.C., humans discovered metals and how to make use of them. This advanced technology and created the need for more specialized labor. Specialization led inevitably to greater interdependence among individuals.

The Brain

Central to human adaptation is our large brain. The feedback loop of human evolution caused the brain to evolve faster than any other human organ. It took hundreds of millions of years to create the 400 cc brain of

FIGURE 2–15
The Increasing Complexity of Toolmaking
The growing sophistication of human stone implements, and of their manufacture, is illustrated here. Each wedge symbol represents a blow struck in making the tool and the clusters of symbols stand for the different operations during manufacture. (After Campbell, 1979)

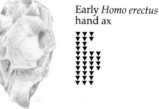

Primitive pebble-chopper

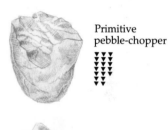

Early *Homo erectus* hand ax

Late *Homo erectus* hand ax

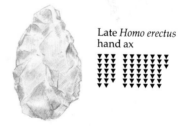

Neanderthal knife

Cro-Magnon knife

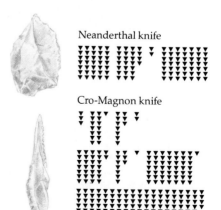

Australopithecus, yet in only a few million years the brain had grown to 1250–1500 cc and had developed the capacity for abstract thought. This kind of thinking hàs been the key to the human adaptation. It has helped us to adapt to every kind of geography and climate. It enables us still today to transcend our biological inheritance.

The brain underlies mental life: the ability to learn, to create, to invent, to think and say things no one has ever thought. The brain increased in size radically from *Ramapithecus* to *Homo sapiens*. Our brain is the largest, relative to body size, of all land mammals, but it is not just the size of the brain that matters. What is especially important is where the brain has increased in size. Although the anatomy of much of our brain is identical with that of other primates, our cerebral cortex, the uppermost part of the brain, is much larger and more intricate than in any other animal. The cortex is the area of the brain devoted to learning, organizing, planning, and other mental activities.

Brain functions will be discussed in detail in Chapter 4, but here is one example of the relation of brain development to human ability. All primates have developed varying degrees of fine motor control. The main mode of locomotion of nonhuman primates is swinging through trees, which requires the ability to grasp tightly onto branches. To do this, an animal must have extremely well-developed motor control in the fine muscles of his limbs. A "kind of grammar" is necessary to know how to get from one place to another, which hand to use, where and how tightly to grasp. Those areas of the brain that control fine motor movements, and which became further developed in toolmaking, are the same ones involved in language (Gallup, 1979). The increasing size of the cerebral cortex thus gave our ancestors great advantages—from control of delicate muscle movements to the development of speech and written language.

Self-awareness

Another result of a larger brain is **self-awareness.** We are conscious of our existence and our mortality—we know who we are, have a sense of personal self. Other animals, cats and dogs, for example, naturally show little evidence of self-awareness, although a version can be experimentally induced even in the pigeon (Skinner, 1981). If you put a cat in front of a mirror, it will approach its own reflection as if the reflection were another animal. A chimpanzee, however, who has a considerably larger brain and a more developed cortex, shows some self-recognition. When Gallup (1979) put chimps in front of a mirror, they acted as though they knew it was a reflection of themselves. In an experiment, Gallup put a red mark on a chimp's forehead, then put him in front of a mirror. The chimp touched the mark on himself—not the mirror. This action indicated that he recognized himself, and knew that something was unusual. All sighted human beings, from the age of 10 months on, can recognize themselves in the mirror.

There is more to self-awareness than simply recognition of a personal self. Awareness of our own existence leads most of us to wonder at some time about the nature of our existence: where do we come from; what will happen when we die? The capacity for self-awareness leads to philosophical questions, to a search for universal principles of human life—morality, spirituality, and religions—and to scholarly pursuits, such as the science of human experience.

The Mind

Although we cannot really separate the mind from the brain, nor describe the mind in a few phrases, it is important to note where and why the human mind evolved. It evolved, first, to aid in the *survival of individuals,* individuals who had to live in circumstances very different from our own. The prehuman's world was smaller than ours, bounded by a few miles rather than continents, comprising small groups of 10 to 100 rather than a planetary population of billions (Washburn, 1961).

Early humans led a nomadic life, moving into new environments with continuously changing circumstances, and thus expanded their recognition of the world. One important aspect of our "mental structure," therefore, is that it seems to have evolved in response to confrontation with a wide variety of situations. To aid this process of adaptation, the mind seems specialized to notice and to react quickly to *changes* in the environment.

In our later discussions we will return to this: the brain and the senses select a small amount of information about changes in the external world and this information becomes part of consciousness. Our thought processes are geared to current information, information that is weighed heavily in making decisions. Although this is speculative, we should note that in human evolution, people who reacted strongly to sudden threats probably survived better than others. Someone who fled at every sign of an approaching animal would be more likely to survive than someone who was calm. The "payoff" of two kinds of mistakes is quite different: there would be less penalty for running from danger, for a "false alarm," than for a lack of concern. In the first instance only time might be wasted; in the second, the organism might be dead.

The human ability to change the environment also aided in the long process of human evolution. Clothing, fire, dwellings, and agriculture all enabled humans to live where none had gone before, in European winters, for instance. However, this inventiveness also creates problems. Once an invention becomes widespread, such as electronics or jet planes, everyone is under pressure to *adapt* to a new situation. *Our ability to judge lags behind our ability to create.*

This kind of mental system may have been helpful in coping with our early environment, but in the complex world of today people are often upset by new situations and changes in their lives (Holmes & Rahe, 1967). This leads to stress-related physical ailments such as ulcers (Selye, 1978). We are thus *always* adapting to our own creations—the airplane, television, nuclear power.

Selection of Information See Chapter 5, pp. 178–79; Chapter 6, p. 217; Chapter 9, pp. 334–37; and Chapter 10, pp. 374–76.

Social-Cultural Evolution

Three and a half million years ago certain primates stood up. One to two million years ago prehumans had begun fashioning tools out of stone. Ten thousand years ago, humans were planting seeds. Since then the rate of human cultural and intellectual development has been dizzying. Although human children born today are biologically about the same as those born 25,000 years ago, they are born into a very different world.

Twenty-five thousand years ago the human population was at most a scattered few million surviving mainly by hunting and gathering. The invention of agriculture 10,000 years ago revolutionized the human experience. Settlements grew up along the fertile flood plains of the Nile, in the Fertile Crescent of the Middle East, and around the Ganges Delta and Huang Ho (Yellow River) in Asia. At the time of the agricultural revolution, the total human population was less than 10 million. Today, almost that many people are born *each month*. In 10,000 years, the population has exploded from 10 million to over 4 billion (Figure 2–16) (Ehrlich, Holdren, & Ehrlich, 1977).

Since surviving offspring are one measure of a species' success, humans must be considered an extremely successful species. The reasons for humankind's spectacular success lie in adaptability. Natural selection favors those who adapt to changing conditions. Physical changes, bipedalism, a larger brain, dexterity, increased visual acuity—combined with the inclination to cooperate and the ability to invent—enable humans to transform their world. The human world has changed more in 10,000 years than in the preceding 4 million. On our calendar of human life, science, civilizations, religions, technology, and architecture all appear in the last few minutes before midnight of December 31. Our ancestors had thousands, sometimes millions of years to adapt to much smaller changes in the environment than those we now face daily in the technological age. What distinguishes modern human development, therefore, is *cultural*, not physical evolution (Campbell, 1982); 25,000 years is too short a time for physical adaptation to the radical changes in the environment (Dubos, 1978).

Calendar of Human Life   See Figure 2–5, p. 45.

FIGURE 2–16
The Human Population
Explosion of Modern Times

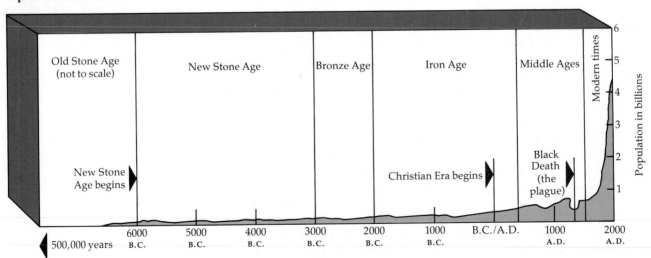

Going beyond Our Inheritance

Although we inherit many essential human characteristics, what most distinguishes us from other animals is our inherited ability *to go beyond our inheritance*. Individual learning can be transmitted quickly between individuals, through language and other symbols. With modern communication networks, new developments can be transmitted to an entire society. Yet the genetic makeup of an educated person does not change in his or her lifetime. Biological evolution cannot match the speed of **cultural evolution,** which is the sum of developments in science, arts, humanities, and technology. Cultural evolution can operate instantaneously, physical evolution only over millions of years. We no longer live entirely in the natural world of our ancestors, but also in a world of our own making.

Thus many of today's serious psychological problems, such as the stress due to crowding, or the overconsumption of food and energy, have their roots in our evolutionary history. They arise in part from our ability to invent our own world. The great technical improvements in health care and agriculture have made it possible for more children to survive infancy, to grow to adulthood, and reproduce. As a result, the world is now overpopulated, the earth's natural resources are being depleted, and overcrowding severely affects human behavior. For most of human history the major problem of all people was getting enough food to eat. Today in America and most Western countries, three-fourths of the people are overweight.

Problems caused by our cultural (psychological) evolution cannot be solved by having physical evolution "catch up"; there is no time to adapt biologically (Dubos, 1978). The solutions, too, must be psychological: new attitudes toward energy, land use, and health, and a better understanding of our mental capabilities. Successful adaptation to a world of our own making will call upon the same capacity that created it: the flexibility and inventiveness of the mind. How that mental structure develops in the individual is a central subject of this book.

GENETICS: THE MECHANISMS OF INHERITANCE

You are your parents' contribution to human evolution. You can probably see a lot of them in your looks and actions. All human beings develop certain characteristics, such as a large brain, erect posture, color vision. But each human being is one of a kind—at once like all other humans and also like no other person who has ever lived. Human uniqueness is the subject of genetics, the science of heredity. Having taken an extremely broad view of evolution, we now take a microscopic view of the physical mechanisms of biological evolution.

We are each dealt a complex genetic "hand" at birth. In every human, there is a set of biological instructions for making a human body and brain. There is an individual component to inheritance: specific physical traits, such as sex and eye color. These traits are set at conception and are unaffected by the environment or your experience. And there is a more subtle inheritance: tendencies to certain physical and mental characteristics. These include a tendency toward tallness, a predisposition to a certain disease—such as diabetes or schizophrenia (a severe form of mental disturbance)—even certain interests and attitudes (Scarr & Weinberg, 1978).

The single cell formed at the moment of conception by the female egg and the male sperm contains all these possibilities. For biological inheritance to take place, a physical substance must be transmitted from each of the parents to the offspring. That substance is the *gene.* The biological program each of us has is called the *genetic code.* **Genetics** is the scientific study of how the characteristics are passed physically from one generation to the next.

The Genetic Code

The **gene** is the basic unit of heredity in all living things. Genes are made of a substance called **DNA** (deoxyribonucleic acid). The DNA molecule consists of two chains twisted into a spiral. The chains consist of four chemical "building blocks": adenine, thymine, guanine, and cytosine. Virtually every living thing is made up of these elements. What differs between living things is only the arrangement of the four elements on the double helix of the DNA molecule. The order in which these substances appear along the double helix is called the **genetic code.** Thus, the essential difference between human beings and turtles, at the

FIGURE 2–17
Chromosomes during the Phases of Mitosis

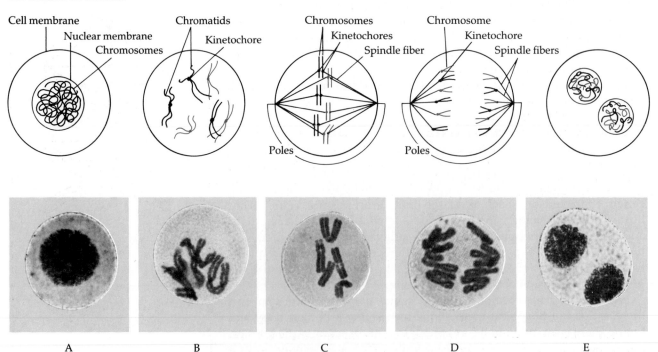

molecular level, is only the arrangement of four chemical substances along the DNA molecule.

Organisms grow by cell division, a process called **mitosis** (Figure 2–17). One cell divides into two, two into four, and so forth. In mitosis, the DNA spirals separate, yet each new cell has exactly the same genetic code as the original cell. That is because each DNA spiral has the ability to "replicate" the instructions of the other spiral. In 1953 two molecular biologists at Cambridge University in England, Watson and Crick, explained how this happens. Each spot on a DNA strand contains specific *pairs* of the four chemicals that make up DNA: guanine and cytosine are always linked; adenine is always paired with thymine. Thus the presence of one, such as adenine, is in itself an instruction: "thymine goes here." Each strand has all the information needed to reproduce a complementary strand and thus create a new double helix.

Chromosomes

Genes are arranged, like beads on a string, on a **chromosome**. Human beings have 46 chromosomes; half the chromosomes come from each parent. These chromosomes carry an individual's entire genetic program. Each human chromosome contains thousands of genes. It is estimated that we have about a million genes. All of them are present in the nucleus of every cell of the body. *Each cell in the body contains all the information necessary to produce all the other cells of the body.*

Dominant and Recessive Genes

Each parent has a set of genes for eye color. At conception, the pair is split apart. The "eye color gene" from the mother pairs up with the "eye color gene" from the father. Now the child has his own set of "eye color genes." But a mother may donate a gene for brown eyes and a father a gene for blue eyes. Which gene will win out? Which gene will be *expressed* in the child's appearance?

All the genes an individual carries are called the **genotype.** But not all genes in an individual are expressed. The portion of our genotype that is expressed is called the **phenotype.**

Gene selection operates on a **dominant/recessive** basis. When *one dominant* gene is present, the trait it governs appears in the person's physical makeup. In this case, the child's eyes will be brown because genes for brown eyes are dominant over those for blue. However, even though only the gene for brown eyes is *expressed,* the gene for blue eye color is still part of the child's genetic makeup. Later, when the child grows up and becomes a parent, his or her own child could have blue eyes, but only if that parent contributes a "blue eye" gene. A *recessive* trait, such as blue eyes, will normally be expressed only if *both* parents contribute the recessive gene.

Sex

An important effect of chromosomes is sex. The chromosomes referred to as pair 23 (Figure 2–19) determine an individual's sex. Chromosomes have two different shapes: one looks like an X, the other like a

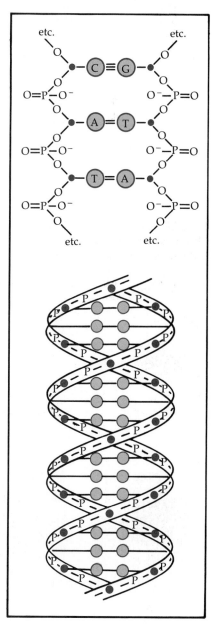

FIGURE 2–18
The Watson-Crick
Model of DNA Structure
The relationship of the four main components of a DNA molecule—adenine (A), guanine (G), cytosine (C), and thymine (T)—is shown below (top). The DNA spiral, or double helix, is depicted in the bottom drawing.

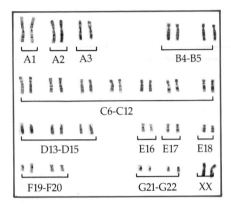

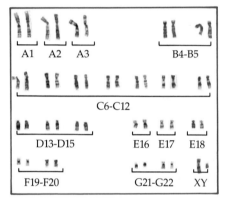

FIGURE 2–19
The 23 Pairs of
Human Chromosomes
The 23rd pair, XX, (top) shows that individual to be a female, while the one below has an XY 23rd pair, indicating those are the chromosomes of a male.

Y. Chromosomes are hence designated X and Y. A female has two X chromosomes in pair 23, a male has one X and one Y chromosome. Thus, because he can contribute either kind of chromosome, the sex of the child is determined by the father: if he donates the X chromosome, the child will be a girl; if he donates the Y chromosome, the child will be a boy.

One might assume, therefore, that the chances of conceiving a male or female are fifty-fifty, but it is not so. For every 100 females conceived, 130 males are conceived. One hypothesis to explain this fact is that sperm carrying Y chromosomes are more mobile than those carrying X chromosomes and reach the egg first.

But, only 106 boys are born for every 100 girls. The XY (male) unit is more fragile than the XX unit in the womb. This fragility continues: more males than females die at every age level in infancy, childhood, and adulthood. Women typically live longer than men, and there are more females in the population than males (Singer & Hilgard, 1978). See Figure 2–20.

Abnormal Chromosomes and Birth Defects

Sometimes a mistake occurs in the process of combining the parents' chromosomes in the fertilized egg. A chromosome can be lost, broken, turned around, or an extra one can be added. If a chromosome is lost at the first cell division (that is, one parent donates only 22, not 23 chromosomes) the fertilized egg almost never develops. Sometimes an extra chromosome can be present. This happens when either the sperm or the egg donates more than one member of one of the 23 pairs. The egg often develops, even with this abnormality, but generally with tragic results. Note in Figure 2–21 that there is an extra chromosome in pair 21. If a child with three chromosomes (a trisome) in pair 21 is born, that individual will have the Down's syndrome: he or she will be very short, have a malformed heart, and be severely mentally retarded. Down's syndrome is quite a common birth defect; it occurs in one out of every 600 live births.

FIGURE 2–20   Approximate Sex Ratio for the Human Species

Conception	120 to 150 males for every 100 females
Birth	105 males for every 100 females
Age 15	100 males for every 100 females
Age 50	90 males for every 100 females
Age 60	70 males for every 100 females
Age 70	60 males for every 100 females
Age 80	50 males for every 100 females
Age 100	20 males for every 100 females

Source: Berger, 1980 as adapted from McMillen, 1979; Nagle, 1979.

In pair 23, the sex chromosomes, another trisome can occur. If, for example, the father donates both X and Y chromosomes, in addition to the mother's X chromosome, a male child with very feminine characteristics (enlarged breasts, more feminine body contours) will be born. In a few recent Olympic contests, the Russians entered males with this abnormal chromosome composition in women's events. Their performances were unusual for females, and so were their genes!

Mutations

Generations can differ in characteristics in two ways: through the sexual recombinations that occur when each parent donates half of the child's chromosomes and through mutations. A **mutation** is a spontaneous change in the structure of one or more genes. Mutations then, are "accidents" in the normal functioning of genetic replication, but differ from abnormal chromosomes. Mutations can occur in a variety of ways: a mistake when the chromosomes from the mother and father are combined at conception, mistakes in DNA replication, and physical damage to DNA molecules, which can be caused by environmental events, such as radiation.

Mutations can affect the life of an individual in different ways: negatively, positively, or not at all. Some mutations have no effect at all. Most mutations are decidedly negative. They result in serious diseases, physical deformity, or mental retardation. Although tragic for the individual, these mutations have little or no effect on the evolution of the species, because the individuals do not usually reproduce successfully. Mutations with a positive effect—that is, those with adaptive value to the individual—probably obey the law of natural selection.

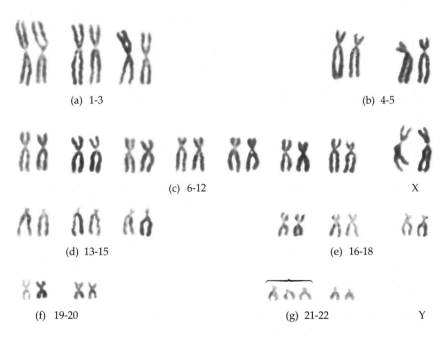

(a) 1-3

(b) 4-5

(c) 6-12

X

(d) 13-15

(e) 16-18

(f) 19-20

(g) 21-22

Y

FIGURE 2–21
**Chromosomal Abnormality
in Down's Syndrome**
The extra chromosome in pair 21, called trisomy 21, is responsible for this relatively common birth defect.

Human Uniqueness

In one mating, the number of genetically different individuals one man and one woman could produce is over 64,000,000,000,000. This astronomical estimate does not even account for the fact that each man and each woman has many possible mates. The possibilities for natural selection and evolution are greater because of this enormous genetic diversity in the human population. The implications of human genetic diversity are profound, both for the science of psychology and for individual self-understanding.

1. In the physical sciences, "one meter" or "one gram" is the same as every other meter or gram. But for the psychologist, "one person" is *never* the same as another person.
2. Every human is biologically unique, a genetic experiment. No one exactly like you will ever happen again.

Twins

The only exception to the rule of genetic uniqueness is identical twins. **Identical twins** are **monozygotic,** developed from the same fertilized egg. (**Fraternal twins** develop when the mother releases two eggs and each is fertilized by different sperms. Fraternal twins are genetically no more alike than any other two siblings.) Because genetic makeup determines much of an individual's behavior and abilities, in addition to physical appearance, genetic similarity is important to psychologists in tracing the role of genetic factors in intelligence, disease, and personality. Because identical twins offer the only possible instance of identical heredity, they are prized as subjects by psychologists interested in tackling the nature/nurture issue. The group next most similar in genetic makeup is siblings, who share many of the same genes from their parents.

There is some degree of genetic similarity between all relatives: parents, aunts, uncles, half-brothers, etc. When we speak of "blood relatives," we are actually speaking about genetic relatives.

DOWN'S SYNDROME

Down's syndrome occurs when three chromosomes instead of the normal two are present in pair 21. Women over 35 are more likely to give birth to children with Down's syndrome. And over 45 the odds can be as bad as 1 in 32. Recently, a simple test has been invented that can inform doctors and parents if the fetus has Down's syndrome. The procedure for this test, **amniocentesis,** is to withdraw a small amount of amniotic fluid (the liquid surrounding the fetus inside the womb) and make a chromosome analysis. If there is an extra chromosome in pair 21, the mother may decide to abort the fetus. Amniocentesis is so successful at detecting this syndrome that the incidence of children born with it has been drastically reduced in women over 35. Evidence now shows that the father can also be responsible for producing a Down's syndrome child. It is now believed that 75 percent of the cases are related to the age of the mother, and the other 25 percent lie with the age of the father (Holmes, 1978).

Genetics, Behavior, and Experience

Some inherited traits may not show up right away, such as myopia (hereditary nearsightedness). Eye color is determined by one gene or at the most a pair of genes, but most human traits are determined by a combination of many. It is possible for a child to have nostrils like the mother's and the bridge of the nose like the father's. Some characteristics are so strong that they come to characterize a family: the Hapsburgs, the ruling family of the Austrian Empire for generations, had a characteristic lip. Some are rather inconsequential: whether you have attached or detached earlobes, whether or not you can roll your tongue, or whether your second toe is longer than your big toe.

Range of Reaction

We are certainly dealt a hand at birth, but how we play the hand is important. Most complex human abilities are determined by an interplay between inheritance and the environment; these are the kinds of abilities governed by what is called the **range of reaction.** The range of reaction is contained in a person's **genetic potential.** The specific genetic endowment may predispose an individual to an ability or a trait. Whether the

The characteristic Hapsburg lip gives most of these relatives a strong family resemblance.

predisposition develops into a reality depends largely on experience. *An Example:* There is probably a genetic component in intelligence, but another influence on the development of intelligence is environment. Height too may be influenced by environment (nutrition). A genetic predisposition for a particular disease may or may not express itself, depending on specific experiences (diet, stress, and culture).

Heredity and Environment

The interaction of the *genotype* (the individual's genetic potential) with the environment determines what part of the genotype will be expressed in the *phenotype.* Every organism, even the simplest bacterium, contains more genetic potential than can be expressed. The expression depends on circumstance and opportunity. *An Example:* Caucasians are generally taller than Orientals because the genetic potential for height in the Caucasian gene pool produces taller people. However, a study of Japanese brought up in North America showed that, with better nutrition, these Japanese grew taller than their countrymen in Japan. Therefore it can be said that Japanese Americans express the upper range of their height potential (Gottesman, 1974).

It is relatively easy to analyze the proportional contributions of heredity and environment in a physical trait, such as height. Mental abilities or disabilities are much more difficult to analyze in this way. **Schizophrenia** is a severe mental disorder, affecting about one percent of the world's

FIGURE 2–22
**Range of Reaction
to the Environment**
One individual may have a genetic potential for greater height than another, but the height each achieves depends on the environment in which each develops. (After Gottesman, 1974)

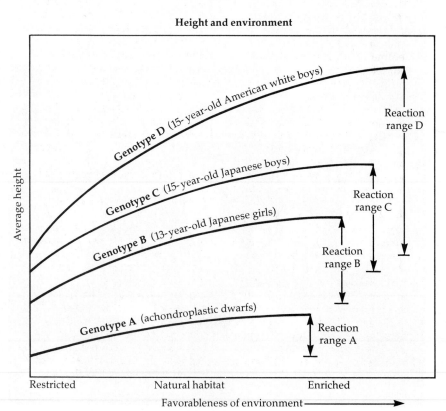

Height and environment

population. Although the causes of schizophrenia are many—early experiences in the home, later life experiences in family and society—there is a genetic component as well.

The genetic contribution was discovered by examining the family histories of schizophrenics and comparing them to those of nonschizophrenics. That comparison revealed a greater number of cases of schizophrenia within the schizophrenics' families than among the families of nonschizophrenics. Moreover, within schizophrenic families, the greater the degree of genetic similarity, the greater the incidence of schizophrenia (Kessler, 1980). (See Figure 2–23.) The identical twin of a schizophrenic is more likely to suffer from the disorder than a fraternal

DO OUR GENES WEAR US?

An understanding of genetic mechanisms has always been central to the study of human adaptation and evolution. Genetic mechanisms explain how characteristics of one individual can be passed to succeeding generations. Indeed, it was only because Darwin's theory of evolution was consistent with the findings of modern genetics in the 1930s and 1940s that evolution became so completely dominant in modern science.

One important question in evolution remains highly controversial: What does natural selection "select"? Darwin's idea was that natural selection is made up of countless individuals, struggling for survival, and these individuals pass on their genes to the succeeding generation. Other investigators have hypothesized that natural selection can work on a *group* of related organisms or on the entire *population* of organisms themselves (the species). Thus, anything that helps a *family unit* to survive will be selected, or anything that helps human beings as a whole will also be selected.

Recently, to these three factors—the individual, the group (such as a tribe) and the population—a fourth has been added: the gene itself. The role of

the gene in evolution is central to a new scientific theory called sociobiology. **Sociobiology** is a new field of study which attempts to account for *social* behavior in *biological* terms. There are, however, many different approaches that attempt to understand the biological basis of social behavior. What is different is that sociobiology concentrates on the *gene* as the determinant of our behavior. According to this view, much of our social behavior is the result of genes trying to insure their *own survival* through their temporary hosts, us. This idea was well stated by Herbert Spencer in the nineteenth century: "A hen is an egg's way of making another egg."

An important example of the sociobiological view is the question of **altruism.** In some extreme situations an individual will give up his or her life for that of others. Why, if the individual is the unit of natural selection, would anyone do this? This behavior could eliminate any chance of that individual passing on his or her characteristics to the next generation. From the point of view of the individual, such behavior would make no sense. But it might make sense from the "point of view" of the *gene:* the

altruistic act insures the survival of those genes that the individual has in common with the others. Thus, the more related any individuals are, the more genes they have in common and the higher the probability of altruism. And in studies of nonhumans this seems to be the case: almost all instances of altruism occur between immediate family members (Hamilton, 1964).

Some writers (Dawkins, 1976) proceed from this analysis to a general theory that most of human behavior is dominated by our "selfish" genes. This is probably too simple. As far as we know, there are no genes for altruism (Maynard Smith, J., 1978). Altruism is a rare occurrence throughout the animal kingdom.

While it is important to note that some of our behavior is dominated by our genes, it seems that natural selection in human beings works mainly in the individual, who exercises conscious choices and passes on a *very large number* of different genes to the offspring (Hamilton, 1964). It is unlikely that *one* individual gene, of the million or so within us, could have a major effect on our behavior.

FIGURE 2–23
Concordance Rates in
Recent Twin Studies
of Schizophrenia (%)

	Identical Twins	Fraternal Twins
Norway	45	15
Denmark	56	26
U.S.A.	43	9
Finland	35	13
U.K.	58	12

Source: Data from Gottesman & Shields, 1972.

twin; a sibling of a schizophrenic has a greater chance of being one than a cousin. The child of a schizophrenic has 12 to 13 times the average chance of being schizophrenic (Kessler, 1980). (See Figure 2–24.) This is a predisposition only; in a favorable and healthy environment the serious disorder of schizophrenia stands less of a chance of being expressed.

At the end of this instant tour of our history, we find that the uniqueness of humanity is the source of our greatest triumphs and problems. Human beings are the only animals who have gone beyond their original "birthplace" to live under almost any conditions on earth—in the desert, on frozen mountains, on the sea, in small settlements, in large cities—and even beyond the boundaries of the earth to live in space, for a while. We inherit a lot of physical characteristics as do other animals, but our most important is this: *the ability to go beyond our inheritance.*

We have created our own environment and thus we are constantly adapting to the change in the world that we, ourselves, have made. This is why we have the pervasive physical and mental "disorders of civilization"—stress, mental disorders, etc. We are always trying to catch up with our own mental leaps, such as electricity, air and space travel, the information explosion, not to mention nuclear power. Our ability to create always leaps ahead of our ability to judge and adapt, and we are continually putting ourselves in unprecedented situations.

We are still immigrants, moving on, in technology and culture if not in territory, and we are constantly adapting to our own creations.

FIGURE 2–24   Estimates of the Risk for Schizophrenia among Relatives of Schizophrenics (%)

	Rosenthal (1970)	Slater & Cowie (1971)
Parents	4.2	4.4
Sibs (neither parent affected)	6.7	8.2
Sibs (one parent affected)	12.5	13.8
All Sibs	7.5	8.5
Children	9.7	12.3
Children (both parents affected)	35.0*	36.6–46.3
Half-Sibs	—	3.2
Aunts and Uncles	1.7	2.0
Nephews and Nieces	2.3	2.3
Grandchildren	2.6	2.8
First Cousins	1.7	2.9

Source: Data from Rosenthal, 1970; Slater & Cowie, 1971.

*Excludes Kallmann's (1938) study.

Summary

1. The perennial question of *"nature/nurture"* concerns whether our biology, thoughts, and behavior are completely determined by either "nature" or "nurture." The nature view holds that we are governed by our innate characteristics such as instincts. Instincts are inborn fixed patterns of behavior such as the salmon's inevitable return to the river of its birth. The nurture view emphasizes that people are almost entirely the product of their environmental circumstances and that these circumstances determine whether one person becomes a beggar and another a banker. More recent thinking in psychology holds that people are a product of *both* factors. Nature sets certain limits and predispositions, and then nurture determines the outcome.

2. *Adaptation* occurs when an organism changes in order to fit better in its environment. There are several varieties of adaptation: sensory adaptation occurs when we walk into a dark room such as in a movie and we can see better after a period of time has passed. When we put on a new set of glasses the world seems curved at first, but we adjust. This is perceptual adaptation. An important form of adaptation took place when our ancestors, through a long series of physical changes called evolution, developed specific characteristics like walking and talking, which allowed them to adapt better to their environment.

3. In science, in psychology, and in this textbook, things are presented separately, as they must be, but in the world things happen as part of larger systems. "System" is any group of things that function together for a common purpose. What connects them together into a system is feedback.

4. *Feedback* is information about the operation of a system, used within the system to attain its goals. There are two different kinds of feedback. One, negative feedback, produces changes in a direction *opposite* an initial change. A thermostat is an example. When the temperature of a room gets too low the thermostat directs the furnace to increase the heat. Positive feedback produces change in the *same* direction as the initial change. An example is how smiling at a person produces a greater smile by that other person, which, in turn, might produce an even greater smile by oneself.

5. The ancestors of human beings emerged over the last 25 million years. The first species that now seems close to being our direct ancestor was tiny *Australopithecus*, who appeared 3 to 4 million years ago. The first recognizably human ancestor was probably *Homo erectus*. They had large brains and fairly complex behavior. They cooked, used skins for covering, had advanced tools, and built elaborate shelters. Neanderthals, the cavemen of popular folklore, appeared during the Ice Age, over 100,000 years ago. They developed much more elaborate rituals and social organization, including ceremonial burial of their dead. Cro-Magnon, somewhere around 75 to 50,000 years ago, is almost indistinguishable from modern human beings. Cro-Magnon had art—as the paintings in the caves of Lascaux are evidence—and developed language.

6. *Hunter-gatherers* lead a nomadic existence, searching for game and for fruits, vegetables, and grains to gather. It is probable that most human cultures, until quite recently, were characterized by such a nomadic existence. The invention of agriculture enabled our ancestors to live in permanent settle-

ments and develop stable social organizations and the beginnings of civilization.

7. How populations change over time is their *evolution*. *Natural selection* is the key element. Organisms in any given situation vary; those organisms with the most "adaptive fitness" to their environment have more surviving and successful offspring, and the population changes. Therefore, the environment "selects" the species best adapted to it by natural selection.

8. Characteristics of *human adaptation* are bipedalism, children born immature, females sexually receptive all the time, forelimbs capable of fine motor control (dexterity), large brain, cooperative life, and an interdependent society.

9. *Bipedalism* (standing on the hind legs) led quite directly to a more delicate set of forelimbs that could become hands and develop tools to use. Bipedalism led also to a thickened pelvic structure, which led to a narrower birth canal and therefore, the need for infants to be born at a comparatively immature stage.

10. Humans are by far the sexiest mammal. All female mammals except humans are sexually excitable only when in *estrus* (when ovulating). With human females there is no time when sex is not possible. Human beings thus have intercourse frequently throughout the entire year. Human sexual signals are more visual than other animals' and are more obvious. The human style of sex lays the foundation for a stable society built of family units.

11. An important aspect of being human is that we seem to *inherit the ability to go beyond our inheritance*. Individual learning can be transmitted quickly between individuals through language and through other communication instruments. This, however, leads to an important and continual human problem: biological evolution cannot match the speed of cultural evolution—the sum of developments in science, arts, humanities, technology, and other means. Thus, many of today's most serious psychological problems—such as stress due to crowding—have their roots in our evolutionary history.

12. The *gene* is the basic unit of heredity. Genes are made of a substance called DNA (deoxyribonucleic acid). The DNA molecule consists of two chains twisted into a spiral made up of four chemical building blocks. The order in which the substances appear along this double spiral, called a "double helix," is the *genetic code*.

13. Organisms grow by cell division in a process called *mitosis*. One cell divides into two, two into four, and so forth. Genes are arranged, like beads on a string, on a *chromosome*. Human beings have 46 chromosomes that carry the individual's entire genetic program. All the genes that an individual carries are called the *genotype*, but not all genes in an individual actually appear in the characteristics of that individual; that portion of a genotype that does appear is called the *phenotype*.

14. Most complex human activities are determined by an interplay between the genetic inheritance and the environment that a person contacts. These are the kinds of abilities governed by the *range of reaction*. A person's genetic inheritance may predispose him to a certain potential, but the environment determines just how much of the potential is developed.

Terms and Concepts

adaptation
adaptive value
altruism
amniocentesis
Australopithecus
bipedalism
chromosome
Cro-Magnon
cultural evolution
dexterity
DNA
dominant gene
Down's syndrome
estrus
evolution
feedback
feedback loop
fraternal twins
gene
genetic code
genetic potential
genetics
genotype
hominids
Homo erectus
Homo habilis
Homo sapiens

human adaptation
hunter-gatherers
identical twins
innate
Lascaux
mitosis
monozygotic
mutation
natural selection
nature/nurture
Neanderthal
negative feedback
ovulation
pair bonding
perceptual adaptation
phenotype
positive feedback
prehumans
range of reaction
recessive gene
schizophrenia
self-awareness
sensory adaptation
sociobiology
system
Terra Amata
tool use

Suggestions for Further Reading

Darwin, C. (1859/1968). *The origin of species*. New York: Penguin Books.
    The classic work on evolution and the development of organisms. Difficult reading but worth looking at this classic book.

Dawkins, R. (1976). *The selfish gene*. New York: Oxford University Press.
    An extremely well-written analysis of human beings as simple carriers for their genes. You will probably never feel the same about yourself after reading this book, although keep in mind its conclusions are controversial.

Evolution. (1979). New York: Scientific American.
    A collection of articles by eminent authorities on evolution and its mechanisms, which forms important background reading for the understanding of this concept.

Gould, S. J. (1977). *Ever since Darwin*. New York: W. W. Norton.
    Essays on evolution and its implications by our current best writer. Useful to explore.

Johansen, D., & Edey, M. A. (1981). *Lucy: The beginnings of human kind*. New York: Simon & Schuster.
    The discovery of what is perhaps our oldest ancestor, written in an engaging "detective story" style.

Symons, D. (1979). *The evolution of human sexuality*. New York: Oxford University Press.

Chapter 3

Early Development (Birth to Adolescence)

INTRODUCTION

The most dazzling biological achievement in the universe begins when one of hundreds of millions of male sperm finds and unites with the female egg. That is the first moment of a new life. That single cell quickly divides, and the new cells divide again and again to form the brain, organs, muscles, skin, and bones. It takes a geometric progression of only about 50 divisions from that original cell to form a baby. No one knows precisely how this happens—why some cells become "brain" and others become "toes" or "tongue."

What we do know is that a speck so small it is hardly visible under a microscope bursts on the scene in about 40 weeks, in the form of a seven pound human baby. Even though that nine-month period of life inside the womb is the period of your most rapid growth, your growth and development have just begun.

From conception to adulthood you change form so drastically and so often that you almost seem to be a series of very different organisms. There are seven periods of human development distinctive enough to bear different names: the ovum, embryo, fetus, newborn, infant, child, and adolescent.

The process of growth and development is one of ever-widening physical and mental competence and abilities. Here we chart the many "stages" of growth from the protected world of the baby to the social world of the adult. By studying human development we can, in effect, watch an adult being "assembled." Starting as a helpless baby, you grow into an adult capable of an extraordinary range of motor abilities, from running to writing. Mentally, you grow from a baby, who can only recognize its mother's odor and face and follow a light, to an adult who can invent and imagine things never before dreamt of. Socially, your world expands—from the moment your umbilical cord is cut—from a singular attachment to your mother to attachment to your family, friends, and, finally, to your community and work.

Although you are helpless and immature at birth, the seeds of your adult abilities are present at the beginning (Figure 3–2). In the study of development, we observe how those seeds begin to bear fruit. As you

FIGURE 3–1
The Moment of Conception

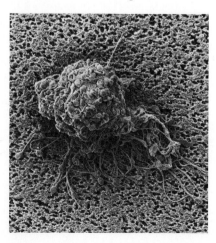

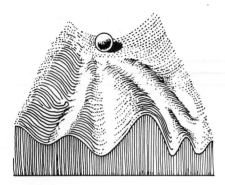

FIGURE 3–2
The Interaction of
Heredity and Environment
In geneticist Conrad Waddington's graphic analogy of the interaction of heredity and environment, the landscape represents possibilities determined by genetic factors, and forces such as wind, gravity, etc. represent environmental influences. The path the ball takes indicates the course of development. There are various paths open, but once development is moving along a particular path—down one of the valleys—it is difficult to change to another course. The analogy helps explain how both heredity and environment play important roles in shaping an individual's personality and abilities. (After Waddington, 1957)

Sequence of Physical Growth
See pp. 90–94.

grow, your life becomes increasingly less determined by your biology and more by your experience—your environment, your family, friends, and the choices you make. This chapter explores the most radical change in our lives by following the development of the human experience from the cell to the self.

Principles and Issues

Nature/Nurture

Human development, at least through childhood, offers an important way to study the nature/nurture issue. By studying a newborn, psychologists can see what we humans know and how we can act without "experience" in the environment. As we age, many of our abilities continue to be governed by an innate sequence of biological development, but increasingly our environment determines how we fare. Nature has its strongest influence early in life. When a child is in the womb, the physical process of growth dominates and his or her specific experience plays a very small but significant part. At 25, individual experiences—language, schooling, profession, culture—tend to have greater influences on our lives than does our biology.

Maturation

Maturation is the emergence of individual characteristics through normal growth processes. *Physical* maturation is controlled by the information contained in the genes and is relatively unaffected by learning or experience. It follows a universal pattern: children all over the world crawl before they walk, have milk teeth before permanent teeth, and mature sexually in puberty. Therefore, in developmental psychology the age of a person is an important factor: behavior appropriate at one age may not be at another. Picture the following scene. You are seated at dinner and the person next to you gets up, walks around the room, asks everyone at the table for food. This individual finally sits down, but interrupts every conversation with deafening yells. If your dinner partner were 25 years old, you might look for the nearest psychotherapist. If your companion were 2 years old, you would no doubt think that child's behavior was "understandable."

Certain experiences can speed up or slow down the rate of physical maturation or affect specific stages, but the sequence of physical growth is the same for all humans. *Psychological* maturation is more complex; it is the development of mental abilities that result from the normal growth of the brain and nervous system. Due to the long period of immaturity in humans, experiences such as language, family, and culture can have profound effects on psychological maturation (Kagan, Kearsley, & Zelazo, 1978).

Adaptation

In the previous chapter we saw how our earliest ancestors, through successive physical adaptations over thousands of years, evolved to meet the demands of a changing world. Although changes occur much more rapidly in an individual's development (years rather than millennia), these changes are quite extreme and require continual adaptation. The worlds of the newborn, infant, child, and adolescent are constantly changing, making constant adaptation necessary.

Egocentrism

The term "egocentric" literally means "self-centered." Although "self-centered" is a term usually used to criticize someone, it is, practically speaking, impossible not to be. The principle of **egocentrism** is one means by which we can differentiate stages in human development.

Jean Piaget (1952) describes a baby as completely egocentric in that it knows no difference between itself and the world. It is not that the baby experiences itself as the center of the world, rather that it *is* the world. As we grow, we discover that there is a world apart from us. At first we think this world revolves around us and our family. We cannot see the world from any viewpoint other than our own. In adolescence, we *know* there are other viewpoints, but believe that ours is the best. In adulthood, we may see ourselves as separate individuals among many. Billie Jean King, the tennis star, said, after entering her 35th Wimbledon tournament: "When you're young, you think you're the center of the universe. When you're older, you realize that you're just a little speck" (*Time*, 1983, July 11). Thus, although we remain egocentric to some degree all our lives, we become progressively less egocentric as we develop.

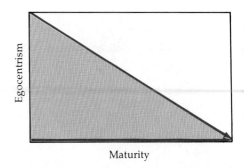

FIGURE 3–3
Egocentrism steadily declines as individuals mature.

THE NEWBORN

Life before Birth

The major influence on development before birth is maturational. The mother and child are the "closest human relationship"; they form a single biological unit for nine months during which the mother and child affect each other in many ways. For the unborn child, physical development is the most rapid and the most vulnerable in the 40 weeks spent inside the mother's womb. The many physical and psychological changes the mother undergoes affect the baby. The mother's emotional state, the drugs she takes, and the food she eats all affect the unborn child. A woman who is exposed to or contracts German measles during the first two months of pregnancy runs a high risk of having a severely retarded or physically deformed child. If she has measles in her ninth month, the child is far less likely to be affected.

There are three distinct periods *in utero* (in the womb): the period of the ovum, of the embryo, and of the fetus. The *period of the ovum* begins at the moment of fertilization and ends about two weeks later when the fertilized egg (ovum) is implanted in the uterus. Once attached to the uterine wall, the ovum becomes an embryo. The **embryonic period** lasts until about the ninth week of pregnancy and is the critical stage of devel-

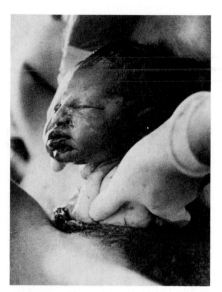

FIGURE 3–4
Passage through the relatively narrow human birth canal compresses the relatively large head of the newborn.

opment for the nervous system. Any serious interference during this period is likely to have tragic effects on the nervous system. In about the ninth week, *the period of the fetus* begins with the baby's first independent reaction to the world. If a physician touches the fetus with a hairlike thread, the fetus responds by flexing its torso and extending its head.

The Birth Process

One of the consequences of the evolution of upright posture in humans is that the pelvis enlarged, thus narrowing the birth canal. Childbirth is therefore more difficult than in other species. Even a normal baby looks mauled at birth—the head is compressed and squeezed during its passage through the birth canal. (Figure 3–4.)

Complications during birth can have a lasting effect on the child's life. Brain injury is possible when the head is compressed during delivery. Children born of difficult labors have a higher than average incidence of mental retardation.

The Newborn: The First Two Weeks

Because newborn babies are so helpless, many psychologists have assumed that babies have almost no mental abilities at birth. But newborns have some important abilities that seem to be the seeds from which adult capacities grow: they identify with other humans almost immediately—they imitate, coo, and smile at the sight of other humans. In this section we discuss what newborns can do, what they know, and what the world of newborns is like.

FOOD, DRUGS, AND THE UNBORN CHILD

How and what the mother eats can have a profound effect on the fetus. Certain quantities of basic nutrients are needed by the fetus in order to develop properly. If the fetus fails to develop properly in important areas, chiefly the nervous system, the result can be fundamental impairment of mental abilities in the child. For example, insufficient protein during pregnancy can lead directly to mental retardation of the child. In a seven-year study in Guatemala, children of mothers who had been given dietary supplements in pregnancy scored higher on intelligence tests (Kagan, 1978).

Because the fetus is especially sensitive at certain periods of development, any drugs the mother takes may affect the child. The baby of a heroin addict may be born addicted to heroin and go through withdrawal at birth. Babies born of alcoholic mothers suffer the **fetal alcohol syndrome:** they are small, have cone-shaped heads, and may be mentally retarded. Even moderate alcohol consumption, such as two drinks per day, can cause malformation of the fetus. Cigarette smoking can also have profound effects on the fetus. Women who smoke are twice as likely to have a miscarriage as nonsmokers. Children of smokers weigh less at birth ("Problems of pregnancy," 1978), and new evidence suggests that children of smoking mothers are more likely to die of crib death than others.

Recent evidence indicates that hormonal substances taken by the mother during pregnancy may have long-term personality effects. Anke Ehrhardt and her colleagues (1981) conducted a follow-up study of children whose mothers had taken *estrogen,* the female sex hormone, as a supplement during pregnancy. They found that even eight years later the boys were judged to be less masculine and the girls more feminine. *Perhaps the best advice pregnant women can be given is to take as few drugs as possible.*

What the Newborn Does: Reflexes

When babies are born they face new experiences such as sounds, heat and cold, movements and pain. Babies are prepared for these changes; for instance, they turn toward interesting noises and away from unpleasant events (MacFarlane, 1978). Newborns know how to signal distress: they cry. A baby's cry gets the attention of the caretaker, usually the mother, who tries to comfort him.

Newborns are capable of certain motor responses immediately after birth. Only two hours after birth, they can follow a slowly moving light in front of their eyes (MacFarlane, 1978). If a nipple or a finger is put into their mouths, they begin to suck on it automatically. If you gently stroke their cheeks or the corner of their mouths, they will turn their heads in that direction. Such unlearned responses of newborns are called **reflexes** and are part of an inborn, unlearned program. Many of these inborn movements are the building blocks of sophisticated motor skills, such as walking and speech. In a series of studies, Trevarthen (1981) recorded the spontaneous lip movements of newborns and found that they were the same as the lip movements required for adult speech. In the first few months of life, an infant makes most of the sounds of every known language (Miller, 1951).

The World of the Newborn

Many psychologists have tried to characterize the newborn's experience. The great psychologist William James (1890) wrote that the newborn's world is a "blooming, buzzing confusion." Jean Piaget characterized it as a transitory world: "There are no permanent objects, only perceptual pictures which appear, dissolve and sometimes reappear" (Piaget, 1952).

These characterizations are in part accurate. The world to the infant probably appears to be more disorganized than to the adult, and seems unstable and meaningless. Because the sensory systems are relatively well developed at birth (Bower, 1977), the newborn's world probably consists of a sequence of sounds, lights, and other sensations, with less stability than adult perception.

Here, let me offer my own characterization of the world of the newborn. The meaningful world of the infant may not be so much confused as it is *simpler,* more *selected,* than the adult world. Newborns are biologically unprepared to function in the adult world, on their own, but they are prepared to function in their *limited* world. For instance, newborns are able to notice objects that are *very close* to them, things that are a part of their very small world. Later on, the newborns' world expands, and so does their awareness. At birth newborns have the ability to focus at a distance of only about 10 inches away, about the distance from the mother's breast to the mother's face. Later on, this range of vision and competence expands. Newborns can distinguish *figures* from ground, can perceive in depth, respond to different smells (Haith, 1980).

Here are a few specific characteristics that researchers now have discovered about the newborn's world:

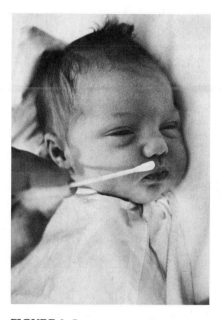

FIGURE 3–5
The newborn's reflexes include the ability to turn away from stimuli such as unpleasant odors.

FIGURE 3–6
Visual Preference of Newborns
In experiments exposing infants to
various visual stimuli, newborns as
young as 10 hours to 5 days old
looked longer at the disc with the
black-and-white face than at simpler
discs showing a bull's eye,
newsprint, or solid colors. (After
Fantz, 1961)

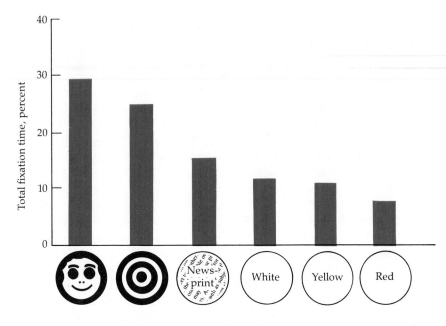

1. *A Preference for Faces.* In one study, Fantz (1961) showed newborns a
set of six discs (Figure 3–6). The babies looked longer at patterned discs
than at single-color discs and *longest* at the faces. Fantz reasoned that this
inborn preference exists because there is an adaptive value in looking at
faces: a baby is totally dependent on adult human beings for survival, so
being attracted to humans is important to survival. At first they look
primarily at the areas of most contour and change, the edges. By six
weeks they look at the mouth, especially when the mother is talking
(Bower, 1978).

2. *A Preference for Small Amounts of Change and Variation.* At two weeks
a baby prefers looking at a disc with a narrow, striped pattern to one
with a solid pattern. Kessen, Haith, and Salapatek (1970) hypothesized

FIGURE 3–7
**Newborns Prefer Moderate
Changes in Visual Stimulation**
The squiggly line patterns show how
various babies scanned the edges of
the triangles. Had they preferred
constant stimulation, they would
have scanned all sides equally. But
the fact that most gave more
attention to the corners indicates
newborns respond primarily to
moderate amounts of visual
variation. (Data from Salapatek &
Kessen, 1966)

that if babies responded primarily to constant stimulation they would scan all sides of a picture of a triangle equally, but if they responded primarily to a moderate amount of change they would look at the corners. Figure 3–7 shows the results: they preferred to look at the corners.

3. *The Rules that Babies Look By.* The baby's visual attention seems to be guided by a set of rules (Haith, 1980): (a) If awake and alert, open your eyes. (b) If you find darkness, search the environment. (c) If you find light, but not edges, begin a broad uncontrolled search of the environment. (d) If you find an edge, look near the edge and try to cross the edge.

We do not yet know if such rules are inborn or learned, but it seems likely that the infant comes into the world with a predisposition to search out new features of the environment.

Differences at Birth

All newborns are not the same. There are very basic differences between newborns (Bee, 1978):

1. *Vigor of response.* Some babies react strongly to a wide range of stimuli; others are slow to respond.
2. *General activity rate.* From birth, some babies move their bodies more than others, turn their heads, etc.
3. *Restlessness during sleep.* Some babies sleep soundly, others move throughout the night.
4. *Irritability.* Babies differ in how much they cry.

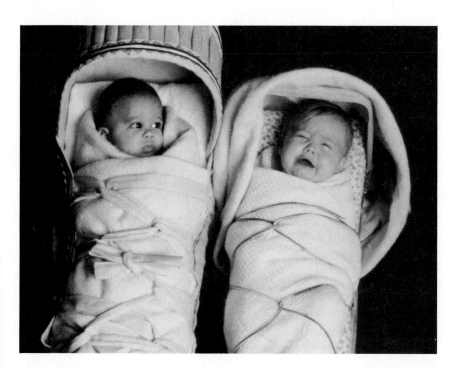

FIGURE 3–8
Differences in
Temperament Appear at Birth
Some babies are more irritable than others. There are variations in responsiveness, levels of activity, restlessness, ability to adapt to change and stress. Some of these differences have been attributed to differences in ethnic background, and all can be increased by differences in child rearing.

FIGURE 3–9
The Achievement of Motor Skills
Not all children achieve these motor skills at exactly these ages. But this sequence is most often observed, as are the milestones of language development described in Figure 3–10. (After Shirley, 1933)

5. *Rate of habituation.* Some babies habituate quickly.
6. *Cuddliness.* Some babies love to be hugged and held more than others.

There is some evidence of significant differences at birth in babies of different ethnic backgrounds. The inborn differences may increase as the baby grows, because different ethnic groups have different styles of child rearing. Daniel Freedman (1979) did some intriguing research in this area. He is married to a Chinese woman, and in the course of their life together they wondered if some of their differences might actually stem from genetic differences. They studied a large sample of Chinese and Caucasian babies of the same age, from the same economic backgrounds, in the same city. They found that Caucasian babies were more irritable. Once they began to cry, they were harder to console than the Chinese babies. The Chinese babies were more adaptable than either Caucasian or black.

THE EARLY YEARS: PHYSICAL GROWTH

As children mature they develop an increasing ability to conceive, plan, and carry out their intentions in more complex circumstances. Small babies are capable of only very gross body movements—they seem to flail about aimlessly. By two years old babies can toddle along on short, chubby legs, manipulate buttons and dials on toys. At six they have still more command over their bodies. They can run, swim, jump, climb trees. They have developed some fine muscle control that allows them to tie their shoelaces, draw, and write. By this time they are either left- or right-handed. They can ride a bike, catch a ball, and dress themselves. Although they still do not have as much motor control or strength as older children, they can actively participate in their play.

Each year between the ages of 5 and 12, children grow 2½ inches and gain 5 pounds. Their muscles strengthen, their heart-lung capacity increases, and their motor coordination develops to the point that they can play, and play well, nearly any game, sport, or musical instrument. The maturation of their brain and nervous systems allows them to develop not only very complex cognitive skills but also the ability to sit still and concentrate for longer periods at home and at school.

The Sequence of Motor Development

Figures 3–9 and 3–10 show when children achieve important motor skills. An infant may skip one or another stage in the sequence (for example, some babies never crawl), but the order in which these skills appear is the same for all children. No one walks before sitting up or standing. Each element in the sequence builds to the next. Although there is some variation in the age at which any one of the particular skills may appear, there are limits: no baby walks at six months or sits up at three weeks.

Physiological Basis of Growth

Underlying the development of motor skills is the maturation of two internal systems: the skeleto-muscular system and the central nervous

FIGURE 3–10 Developmental Milestones in Motor and Language Development

Age	Motor Development	Vocalization and Language
12 weeks	Supports head when in prone position; weight is on elbows; hands mostly open; no grasp reflex.	Markedly less crying than at 8 weeks; when talked to and nodded at, smiles, followed by squealing-gurgling sounds usually called *cooing*, which is vowellike in character and pitch-modulated; sustains cooing for 15–20 seconds.
16 weeks	Plays with a rattle placed in hands (by shaking it and staring at it); head self-supported; tonic neck reflex subsiding.	Responds to human sounds definitely; turns head; eyes seem to search for speaker; occasionally some chuckling sounds.
20 weeks	Sits with props.	The vowellike sounds begin to be interspersed with more consonant sounds; labial fricatives, spirants, and nasals are common; acoustically, all vocalizations are very different from the sounds of the mature language of the environment.
6 months	Sitting: bends forward and uses hands for support; can bear weight when put into standing position, but cannot yet stand holding on; reaching: unilateral grasp: no thumb opposition yet; releases cube when given another.	Cooing changes into babbling resembling one-syllable utterances; neither vowels nor consonants have very fixed recurrences; most common utterances sound somewhat like *ma, mu, da,* or *di.*
8 months	Stands holding on; grasps with thumb opposition; picks up pellet with thumb and fingertips.	Reduplication (or more continuous repetitions) becomes frequent; intonation patterns become distinct; utterances can signal emphasis and emotions.
10 months	Creeps efficiently; takes side steps, holding on; pulls to standing position.	Vocalizations are mixed with sound-play such as gurgling or bubble blowing; appears to wish to imitate sounds, but the imitations are never quite successful; begins to differentiate between words heard by making differential adjustments.

system. At birth the skeleton is mostly cartilage and is very soft. Infants and children need milk because its calcium is used in the manufacture of bone, a process called **ossification.** Ossification occurs as calcium is deposited in the cartilage. The muscles of growing children get stronger and the nerves, which relay instructions between the muscles and brain, develop more precision and control.

As the brain and nervous system mature, the child is able to tackle increasingly complex motor tasks. As a result, attention span increases, enabling the child to make ever more complex plans and carry them out. By about five years of age the brain is 95 percent of adult size. The maturation and growth of the brain and nervous system allow better coordination and motor control, including the fine control needed to draw, color, and write, and the hand-eye coordination needed to catch balls and thread needles.

Age	Motor Development	Vocalization and Language
12 months	Walks when held by one hand; walks on feet and hands—knees in air; mouthing of objects almost stopped; seats self on floor.	Identical sound sequences are replicated with higher relative frequency of occurrence, and words ("mamma" or "dadda") are emerging; definite signs of understanding some words and simple commands ("Show me your eyes").
18 months	Grasp, prehension, and release fully developed; gait stiff, propulsive, and precipitated; sits on child's chair with only fair aim; creeps downstairs backward; has difficulty building tower of three cubes.	Has a definite repertoïre of words—more than 3, but less than 50; still much babbling but now of several syllables with intricate intonation pattern; no attempt at communicating information and no frustration for not being understood; words may include items such as "Thank you" or "Come here," but there is little ability to join any of the lexical items into spontaneous two-item phrases; understanding is progressing rapidly.
24 months	Runs, but falls in sudden turns; can quickly alternate between sitting and standing; climbs stairs up or down.	Vocabulary of more than 50 items (some children seem to be able to name everything in environment); begins spontaneously to join vocabulary items into two word phrases; all phrases appear to be own creations; definite increase in communicative behavior and interest in language.

Source: Lenneberg, 1967.

Adjustments to Growth

The first two years are marked by such rapid growth that the child must continually adapt to a changing body. Children at two are almost twice as tall as they were at birth and are also half their adult height. If as adults we grew at the same rate as we did in our first two years, in two years we would be 11 feet tall. Imagine the number of adaptations you would have to make! An infant's experience may be a gradual version of Alice's experience in Wonderland when she took the drink that suddenly made her tall. She had to adjust constantly her relationship to such familiar objects as tables and chairs. Consider the simple act of lifting a cup to your mouth. You must know not only where the cup is and how to move it toward you, *but you must* also know where *you* are—where your arm is, how long it is, how far to stretch it, and where your mouth is. Growth affects all your sensory systems. For instance, as the head grows, the eyes grow farther apart, which makes it difficult to judge accurately the distance between oneself and an object (Bower, 1981). These constant changes contribute to the instability of the perceptual and mental world of the infant.

Figure 3–11   The Direction of Growth and Development
Children grow physically and develop their motor abilities in two directions at the same time. They experience cephalocaudal growth (from top to bottom) and proximodistal growth (from the center to the periphery). (After Hall et al., 1982)

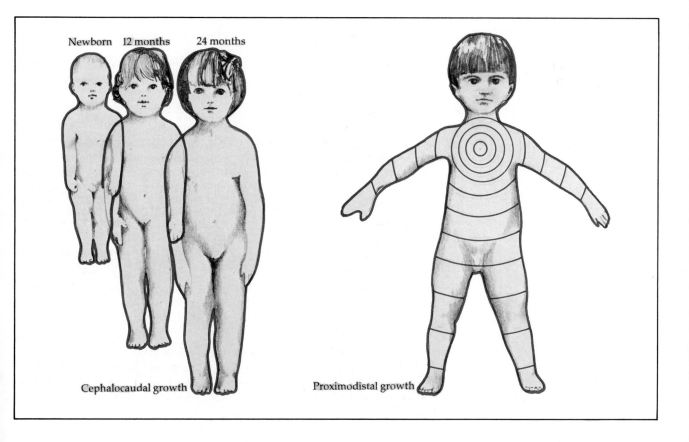

Newborn   12 months   24 months

Cephalocaudal growth

Proximodistal growth

THE EARLY YEARS: COGNITIVE DEVELOPMENT

Imagine the following scene. A father is reading a book to his two-year-old and two-week-old children. The two-year-old laughs, helps turn the pages, points to things and identifies them, asks questions, and asks for the book to be read again. The newborn coos, looks around the room, and dozes off. The infant may be attentive to the world, but is oblivious to the specific activity going on (Flavell, 1977). The two-year-old and the newborn are closer in age than the two-year-old is to the father, yet in terms of cognitive abilities the two-year-old and the father are more nearly alike. They share the same world, one which the newborn has not yet entered. The two-year-old has formed close attachments to people, can organize some activities toward a goal, and is concerned with standards and his or her own competence.

During the early years the child gradually becomes more organized. He is able to focus and direct his attention for longer periods. There are large differences between the way three-year-olds and six-year-olds direct their attention. Children three years and younger focus attention on an exciting event or object, and are easily distracted by the next exciting event that comes along. For that reason they may pay attention to stimuli that are irrelevant to the activity at hand. A six-year-old's attention is more under control, less distractible by outside stimuli (Wright &

ON THE DEVELOPMENT OF CONSCIOUSNESS

The emergence of the consciousness of oneself appears between 18 and 24 months. Indicators that a child has developed this level of consciousness and a sense of self are his competence, planning, and concern with standards (Kagan, 1980, 1981).

1. **Competence.** In one study, Lewis placed two-year-olds on one side of a room and toys on the other; a barrier was placed between them. Children under two lacked the necessary skills to get through the barrier. But two-year-olds planned, manipulated, and persevered well enough to accomplish the goal. Once children achieve a measure of competence, they begin to think of themselves as problem-solvers. Two-year-olds show distress when struggling to do something they know they can do well and smile with satisfaction when they succeed.

2. **Planning.** Two-year-olds' play is more planned and goal-directed than an infant's. By two years children play with complex objects and engage in symbolic play. They can pretend that one object is something else; for example, a block becomes a car by pushing it across the floor and making a "vroom-vroom" noise (Kagan et al., 1980).

3. **Concern with Standards.** If you show a one-year-old a plastic telephone, then replace it with an identical one but with a slight scratch on it, he or she will show no reaction. A two-year-old will examine the telephone, notice the imperfection, and become distressed. When things in the real world do not match his or her "standards," the two-year-old does not like it (Kagan, 1981).

Vlietstra, 1975). By seven years, children have made great cognitive leaps. They know right from left, their memories improve dramatically, and they can distinguish between "p" and "q," "b" and "d." Five-year-olds use simple reasoning, but are not very good at making and carrying out plans. In school they most often work for rewards—praise, attention from peers, gold stars. Seven-year-olds use very complex reasoning, make plans, and are more likely to work for the sake of "getting the right answer" (White, 1966). They can appreciate jokes, puns, and riddles, which means that they understand language well enough to play with the meanings of words.

Piaget's Theory of Cognitive Development

The most influential theory of cognitive development was proposed by a biologist turned psychologist, Jean Piaget (1896–1980). It is impossible to do full justice here to as elaborate and comprehensive a theory as Piaget's. Nevertheless, we will discuss some of the major premises on which Piaget built this theory, some of the developmental factors he considered to be most important, and then follow his outline of the process of cognitive development.

Piaget's theory is rooted in evolutionary theory. Recall that changes in physical structures of a species evolved because they had adaptive value to the species. Piaget believed that our *mental abilities* developed for the same reason, and he felt human psychological adaptation to the environment might be understood by studying how the child's mind develops. Piaget therefore focused his study on how the mind becomes "assembled" during the process of development.

Jean Piaget
(1896–1980)

Piaget's Assumptions and Terms

Piaget makes three basic assumptions:

1. *Knowledge guides action.* Knowledge is built up by the maturation of mental structures and is a tool to be used. The world we experience becomes more complex and detailed as we develop new structures.

2. *Knowledge develops through experience and action.* Babies find out about the world by exploring things with their mouths; young children use their hands and their senses. Gradually we learn to explore abstractly, through books, ideas, etc.

3. *The complexity of mental structures is determined largely by biological age.* A child's knowledge is organized differently at different stages of development. The difference between a child at 10 and at 3 is not merely that the older child has more information, but that the older child has a more complex and capable mind. This growth of mental capacity, or *mental structures*, is what constitutes cognitive development.

Schema

Piaget, like many other psychologists, assumes that the unit of mental life is the **schema** (plural schemata). **Schemata** are the associations formed largely through experience of what goes on in the world. They are our knowledge of how things are organized and relate to each other.

FIGURE 3–12
Innate Form Preferences
By turning their heads to look at the "face" with the features in the right places, rather than at the other "faces," babies less than a day old showed an innate preference that could indicate they were born with a "face" schema. (After Goren, 1970)

FIGURE 3–13
Assimilation and Accommodation in Piaget's Theory of Cognitive Development
Children continually develop their thought processes by assimilating new information about objects and events and accommodating it by changing their existing schemata.

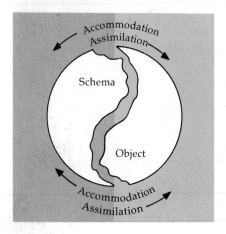

This organization may relate actions to one another, relate different stimuli to one another, or relate outside stimuli to specific actions. For instance, knowing that the general sequence of movements used in picking up a ball is similar to that used in picking up a pencil might be a general schema for "picking things up." A schema may organize parts of an object into a whole—knowing that a nose, eyes, and mouth arranged in a certain way constitute a "face." A "face" schema would explain why babies prefer to look at the elements of a face organized in the usual rather than a disorganized way (Figure 3–12). A schema may also relate perceptions to actions; for example, a baby smiles when she sees another face smile.

Assimilation and Accommodation

The information that a child receives from the environment is interpreted by his or her existing schemata. These schemata *change* and grow during development, according to Piaget, by two processes: assimilation and accommodation.

1. **Assimilation.** When children encounter a new event, they attempt to *assimilate* it into their existing knowledge structure (the schema) in the way that food is assimilated by their system. For example: A young child learns that the family pet is "dog." During a walk the child sees a German shepherd and says "dog"—collies, chihuahuas, poodles are all *assimilated* into this schema. But the child may also say "dog" when seeing a cat or a cow. Then it is clear that the schema was "all animals are dogs."

2. **Accommodation.** When new events cannot be assimilated into existing schemata, a person experiences a sense of *disequilibrium* (imbalance). A change must occur to *accommodate* the new information and restore equilibrium. This usually involves changing or expanding the existing schemata. For instance, in the above example, the child's parent may say, "That's wrong. There are many different kinds of animals. Only some are dogs." Then the schema "all animals are dogs" changes and expands to include the new knowledge.

Each time the child accommodates the schemata to new information, the child's intellectual world expands. Our schemata, which shape our experience, become increasingly more comprehensive and more adaptive as we mature.

Operations

As the child learns about the world, the schemata join together to form repeated mental routines, called **operations.** Operations are rules for transforming and manipulating information. An important characteristic of operations is that they are *reversible.* For example, consider the simple arithmetic operation "if you add 2 of anything to 2 of anything, you will have 4 of anything." The reverse is "if you have 4 of anything and take 2 away, you will have 2." This operation reflects a basic fact about the physical world—that quantities of things change when combined with other quantities—and offers a way to handle any such phenomenon.

Operations grow more complex as cognition develops. Piaget proposed that children gain concepts by *performing operations* on things (recall the assumption that knowledge is attained through action). As simple as $2 + 2 = 4$ is, it is nevertheless an abstract mental concept, the understanding of which requires much repeated experience with counting things. Thus, physical manipulation of the environment leads to knowledge. Piaget developed many experiments to ascertain the level of a child's development in the use of operations, some of which are described in the next section.

Stages of Cognitive Development

Piaget believed that all children, regardless of the culture they live in, go through the same stages of cognitive development in the same sequence. Piaget describes four stages: the sensorimotor, the preoperational, the concrete operational, and the formal operational.

The Sensorimotor Stage (0–2 Years)

In the **sensorimotor stage** children learn primarily through motor and sensory play. Babies are born with certain simple reflexes, innate motor programs, which become organized in the first 18–24 months into complex and controlled movements. During this time practical intelligence of one's effect on the world is developed: the baby may find that crying brings mother, that splashing in the bathtub makes all the bath toys move around. At around 18 months children begin to develop a sense of self and begin to be capable of **representational or symbolic thought.** For example, one important kind of symbol is language. By 2 years the bubbling infants have a vocabulary of about 200 words, which they use effectively in two-word sentences. Another example of representational thought is metaphoric play, such as pretending to stroke a cat or to be an elephant.

One of the most important accomplishments of the early phase of this sensorimotor stage is **object permanence:** babies learn that something continues to exist even when they cannot see it.

FIGURE 3–14
Object Permanence
Because this infant does not yet have the concept of object permanence, it acts as if an object merely hidden from view has ceased to exist.

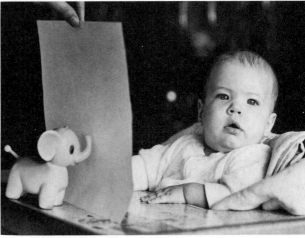

WIT AND WISDOM OF TWO-TO-FIVE-YEAR-OLDS

A look at the way two-year-olds express themselves offers a glimpse of the mental capabilities of the child. Studies of German, French, Russian, Samoan, and many other languages have shown that there is remarkable universality in the kinds of words two-year-olds use and how they use them (Slobin, 1970). The two-year-old can identify objects ("big car"), note their location ("book here"), demand repetition ("more milk"), note what kind of action is taking place ("man sit"), and can ask questions ("where ball?").

K. Chukovsky (1963) has made an extensive study of the language of children between the ages of two and five. He feels that after five, children become less inventive with words as they become more precise and realistic in their use of language. Below are some remarks of toddlers and young children under five. Many of them, you will note, show how important it is for children to have some explanation, *any* explanation, of how the world works.

"Our Granny killed the geese in the wintertime so that they would not catch cold."

"Mommie, I'm so sorry for the baby horses—they cannot pick their noses."

"I sing so much that the room gets big and beautiful."

"What is a knife, the fork's husband?"

"Daddy, please cut this pine tree—it makes the wind. After you cut it down the weather will be nice and Mother will let me go for a walk."

"Mothers give birth to boys too? Then what are fathers for?"

If you hide the object a 5-to-7-month-old infant is reaching for behind a screen or under a cloth, the child will stop reaching. At eight months the baby looks behind the screen or under the cloth. This new ability to search and find is a great advance, an important cognitive step. It is also a source of fun for the child (peek-a-boo, basically a game of object permanence, is a favorite activity). Piaget first discovered this when he showed his seven-month-old daughter his watch on a chain and she reached for it. When he put his watch back in his pocket, she acted as if the watch had disappeared into thin air. At eight months the child began to reach for and search in his pocket. She now knew the watch still existed even though she could not see it.

Preoperational Stage (2–7 Years)

In the **preoperational stage,** children use symbols—they can *represent* objects in drawings and words. Schemata that were just being organized in the sensorimotor stage become more integrated and coordinated in the preoperational stage but are not as yet fully organized, in a logical way. Children at this stage are quite fluent in the use of language, but rely primarily on their senses, on what they see or hear, rather than what they know or imagine. They are unable to use *mental operations*—to reason, to deduce, to wonder about what *might* be.

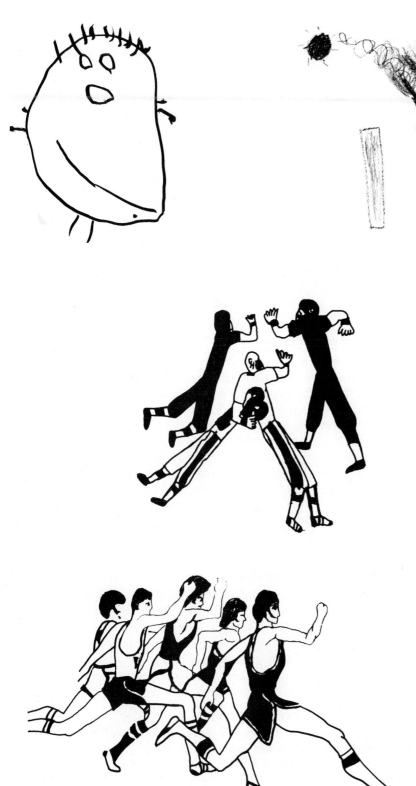

FIGURE 3–15
Cognitive Development
Revealed by Children's Art
Children's cognitive development is apparent in drawings like these. The simple face (top left) drawn by a three-year-old lacks the action and relatively complex composition of the work (top right) by a six-year-old. And although the sports picture (center) by a nine-year-old is exciting and evocative, it is crude compared to the bottom drawing by a twelve-year-old. Artistic skill, like cognitive ability, emerges in stages.

FIGURE 3–16
Conservation
Around age six or seven, children start to understand the concept of conservation. Without it, they do not realize that equal amounts of a liquid in different-shaped containers are still equal, or that equal amounts of clay rolled into different shapes remain equal. Piaget repeatedly demonstrated that lack of this concept characterized preoperational children.

Conservation

One basic operation is conservation. **Conservation** means that an object is understood to be the same even if it looks different. Piaget believed that before age six or seven the child has not yet formed the conservation rule. If you give one three-year-old a sandwich cut into quarters and another three-year-old a sandwich cut in half, the child with the two pieces may complain that he has "less" than the other.

In one of Piaget's most famous conservation experiments, a child holds two balls of clay of equal size and the experimenter asks if there is the same amount of clay in each ball. The child must say "yes" for the experiment to proceed. The experimenter takes one of the balls and flattens it into a pancake right before the child's eyes. Then she again asks the child, "Is there the same amount of clay in each piece of clay?" A preoperational child insists that the pancake has more clay (because it "looks" larger). The older child understands the deeper principle of constancy: "If you roll it up again, it would be the same." Piaget concludes that the younger child is influenced by surface appearances: the information from his senses overrules all other information.

Concrete Operations (7–12 Years)

In the **concrete operational stage** of cognitive development, thinking is no longer dominated by sensory (especially visual) information. Children begin to reason abstractly. Children in the operational stages can carry a task through to completion and understand some of the basic characteristics of things in the world: number, weight, and order.

During the concrete operational stage the child becomes more organized and able to plan, and consequently can focus and direct attention for longer periods. There are large differences between the ways preoperational and concrete operational children direct attention (Wright & Vlietstra, 1975). Younger children direct attention to whatever event or object is most exciting to them and are thus easily distracted. A seven-year-old's attention is more focused, more under control, less distracted by novel stimuli. He or she understands goals and attends more to information relevant to a plan.

Formal Operations (12–Adult)

Higher-order thinking begins in the **formal operational stage.** Adolescents are capable of thinking abstractly, thinking through situations logically and systematically. They can follow a complex scientific experiment from start to finish: they can formulate hypotheses and test them. For the first time, children in the formal operational stage are able to imagine things as they might be instead of how they are. Their new power of abstract thought propels them into the adult world.

Egocentrism and Decentration

Important indicators of cognitive development, according to Piaget, are **egocentrism** and **decentration.** At each stage of development, children become increasingly aware of the world outside themselves and are less focused on themselves. Infants are totally egocentric: they know no differences between themselves and other people or objects in the world. Between 18 and 24 months, children become aware that they are but individuals among many. They "decenter," move away from thinking they are the center of the world and grow increasingly concerned with life outside themselves. The process of decentration continues throughout development, proceeding in stages:

1. The sensorimotor phase of life is totally egocentric: "The world is me." In this phase of life, for example, the children are *thought* to be unable to tell the difference between themselves and any external object.

2. In the preoperational stage children are aware of other people and things but cannot see or imagine the world from any viewpoint but their own: "The world is as I see it." If children see that their mother is sad, they may bring her a toy to cheer her up because that is what cheers *them* up.

3. In the concrete operational stage children recognize that there are ways of looking at things other than their own, but they think their way is the only *valid* one: "I have the right view of the world."

4. In the formal operational stage adolescents characteristically believe that the way they view the world is the *right* way for everyone. "The world *should* be as I view it."

Review and Criticism of Piaget

Piaget has influenced the field of developmental psychology more than any other individual, because he was one of the first to develop a systematic and comprehensive theory of human development. He tested his theory by studying how knowledge matures in the child.

Piaget proposed a quite detailed theory of the acquisition of knowledge through the development of specific mental structures, such as operations, which develop in each child according to specific stages. Like many initial theories in a new area, Piaget's has limitations. Some of the limitations and criticisms are:

1. *Piaget often seems to underestimate the reasoning abilities of children and overestimate their verbal abilities.* For instance, he stated that the preoperational child is incapable of conservation and is unable to see things from another point of view. These assertions, however, seem to depend on Piaget's particular experiments. Consider the conservation experiments. Since young children are easily distracted by stimuli, it is possible that too much information overloads their schemata. Bruner (1978) performed an experiment to test this hypothesis. In Piaget's experiment of conservation of volume, the experimenter shows the child two tumblers, one short and squat, the other tall and thin. He fills the short, squat one with water, and then he pours the water from that tumbler into the other. He asks the child, who has watched this whole procedure, if there is the same amount of water in both tumblers. Because of the difference in shapes, the water is closer to the top of the long, thin tumbler. It appears to be full, unlike the short, squat one. Because of this the young child will usually say "no." Bruner performed this experiment in exactly the same manner, with one difference: before he emptied liquid from one tumbler into the other, he placed a screen between the tumblers and

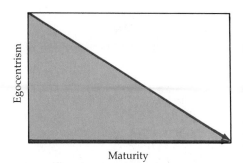

FIGURE 3–17
Decentration
Egocentrism declines as children decenter—stop thinking of themselves as the center of the world. Thus, increasing decentration is a sign of maturation.

the child to block the child's view of the tumblers. When he asked the question, "Is there the same amount of water now?" the four-year-olds, unable to *see* the pouring of water into the tumblers, answered "yes." Thus, it appears that when there is no information overload, constancy can be achieved even at this early stage. Other investigators have changed the experimental situation so that the tasks are more fully explained. In these cases children as young as three years are able to solve conservation problems and to see things from another point of view (Donaldson, 1978a, 1978b).

2. *Stages of cognitive development are not as fixed as Piaget assumed.* Although development does seem to proceed, in general, the way Piaget proposes (for instance, formal operations comes later than sensorimotor, the ability to think more abstractly comes after the ability to perform operations), the idea of discrete "stages of thought" may be too rigid.

According to Piaget, each stage of cognition builds upon an earlier stage, in the way a house is constructed: first the foundation is laid, then the walls, then the roof. Thus, the formal operational child experiences a dramatic transformation of his cognitive abilities, leaving the previous stage behind.

However, children differ from one another and different experiences may hasten or slow the appearance of one or another attribute of a stage (Brainerd, 1978). Not all of a child's cognitive abilities develop at the same time, and *some develop independently of one another* (Gelman, 1978). So there is evidence that development is more continuous and diverse than Piaget allows.

In part, the question of whether development is "continuous" or "discrete" depends upon one's point of view. Consider a child learning to ride a bicycle. From one viewpoint, his or her abilities develop at different rates: leg strength to pedal, eye-hand coordination, balance. However, *when these skills come together, the child is at a different stage:* he or she can now bike to school, to the store, to a friend's house, and do many things that he or she could not do before. Similarly, the development of abstract thought enables the child to entertain fanciful ideas, to explore others' thoughts, which he or she had been unable to do previously.

Many critics feel, though, that the "stages" are useful as generalized *descriptions* of the thinking of an "ideal" child at different points of development, although they are probably not accurate *explanations* of the course of intellectual growth (Brainerd, 1978).

3. *Piaget focuses too much on the cognitive aspects of development.* He sees the child as a miniature scientist and logician, perhaps one in his own mold. This focus has led to a neglect of other important factors in a child's development, such as social relationships, personality, emotions, fantasy, creativity, intuition, and other important aspects of the human experience.

Criticisms are inevitable in a theory and approach as bold and as pioneering as Piaget's. It is only natural that many of his observations would prove too specific, some of his conceptions too rigid, some of his ideas too narrowly based. But it is to his breadth of vision that we owe much research on child development. Piaget's theory remains the most complete and integrated description of intellectual growth from birth to adolescence we have.

Moral Development

Morality is the knowledge of what is right and wrong. Like other aspects of cognition, a child's morals also undergo development, a development dependent on the stage of thought achieved. Piaget (1932) reasoned that moral judgments reflect a child's cognitive abilities at different stages. By observing children's games and recording their reactions to stories about children breaking windows and stealing apples, he described stages of moral development related to cognitive stages.

Kohlberg's Theory of Moral Development

Kohlberg, like Piaget, also assumed that moral reasoning was based on cognitive abilities. However, he thought that moral development was a process that continued throughout adolescence and early adulthood. Kohlberg's focus is on people's *reasons* for doing what they think is right

and how moral reasoning and behavior change as schemata become more complex. Kohlberg suggests that there are three basic levels of moral reasoning, each of which has two stages:

Level I—Premoral:
    Stage 1 Obey rules to avoid punishment (punishment and obedience orientation).
    Stage 2 Conform to obtain rewards, to have favors returned.
Level II—Conventional morality:
    Stage 3 Conform to avoid disapproval, dislike by others ("good-boy" morality, approval by others).
    Stage 4 Conform to avoid "censure" by legitimate authorities and resultant guilt (authorities maintain morality)—obedience to laws.
Level III—Postconventional morality:
    Stage 5 Conform to maintain the respect of the impartial spectator in judging in terms of community welfare (the morality of social contract, of individual rights, and of democratically accepted law).
    Stage 6 Conform to avoid self-condemnation (morality of individual principles of conscience).

These three levels represent a progression of *"sociomoral perspective."* The development of this perspective in an individual is illustrated by one of Kohlberg's long-term subjects, "Joe" (Kohlberg, 1969).

Joe was asked at ages 10, 17, and 24 the same question: "Why shouldn't you steal from a store?" His replies show the changes in his moral reasoning.

1. *At 10.*

> "It is not good to steal from the store. It's against the law. Somebody could see you and call the police."

The reason not to steal is that you might get caught; the law can be enforced by the police. Joe's motivation is to avoid punishment. This level of moral reasoning is **premoral:** Joe considers only his own interests.

2. *At 17.*

> "It is a matter of law. It's one of our rules that we're trying to help protect everyone, protect property, not just to protect a store. It's something that's needed in our society. If we didn't have these laws, people would steal, they wouldn't have to work for a living and our whole society would get out of kilter."

At this stage the concept of law has been extended. It is viewed not so much as rules *against* as rules *for* something. Law is made for the good of society. Joe thinks the law should be maintained. Now his perspective is **conventional.** He has gone beyond individual considerations and takes the view of society as a whole.

3. *At 24.*

> "It is violating another person's rights, in this case to property."
> "Does the law enter in?"
> "Well, the law in most cases is based on what is morally right, so it's not a separate subject, it's a consideration."
> "What does 'morality' or 'morally right' mean to you?"
> "Recognizing the rights of other individuals, first to life, and then to do as he pleases as long as it doesn't interfere with someone else's rights."

Joe's perspective has again widened. Stealing is wrong because it violates the *moral rights* of individuals. Property rights are universal human rights, and the purpose of society is to secure these rights for the individuals who live in it. Joe's moral development has reached the final, **postconventional** level.

Criticism of Kohlberg's Theory

Kohlberg's theory is very complex, and so is his way of assessing an individual's stage of morality. Both of these characteristics have been at the center of a number of controversies, which have resulted in numerous changes by Kohlberg in the theory and assessment.

Some critics point out that Kohlberg's stages are very "western" in their emphasis on democracy and individual judgment. His "stages" might not hold true in a culture in which there is less emphasis on individuals' rights. Others point out that there are methodological flaws; they say Kohlberg's measurements are not very reliable and do not work in the way his theory says (Kurtines & Greif, 1974).

Other criticisms include:

1. The stages of moral development are not fixed and can be greatly modified by experience at both young (Bandura & McDonald, 1963) and older ages (Prentice, 1972). A person at a certain level of moral development may exhibit several different kinds of action (Kohlberg, 1969; Kurtines & Greif, 1974).

2. Does *knowing* what is right and wrong insure moral *behavior?* Some psychologists feel that the correlation between what people say and what they do, between moral principles and moral actions may not always be strong (Mischel, 1981).

There have been numerous studies to ascertain the actual links, if any, between moral judgment and moral behavior. The results have been mixed. However, a recent comprehensive review concludes that the bulk of evidence indicates that individuals at higher levels of development assessed by Kohlberg's scales appear to *behave* more "morally" than those at lower levels. For example, juvenile delinquents are more likely to be at lower stages of moral development than nondelinquents. There is some evidence to suggest that individuals at higher moral stages tend to be more honest and altruistic; at least in their moral judgments. Thus, there seems to be a *general* progression in moral understanding close to the one Kohlberg describes. So moral principles *do* seem to guide action to some extent (Blasi, 1980).

THE EARLY YEARS: PSYCHOSOCIAL DEVELOPMENT

At the age of two, children all over the world can walk and talk and have begun to become part of society. But what children say, how they talk to parents and authorities, what they do, how they play, and what they expect of themselves varies from culture to culture. In psychology, the area of study that focuses on socialization and the development of individual interaction with various groups (family, school, community, nation, etc.) is called **psychosocial development.**

Like other aspects of development, psychosocial development appears to emerge in a predictable sequence. In this section we will touch on one theory of psychosocial development and several major areas of psychosocial development in childhood: attachment, play, sex roles, and divorce.

Stages of Psychosocial Development: Erikson

Erik Erikson divides psychosocial development over the life span into eight stages, which he calls "the eight ages of man" (1950). Each stage has a characteristic "crisis." He believes that the way that crisis is resolved influences the individual's later experience.

1. *First year of life.* The most important influence in the first year of life is the primary caregiver. The crisis that characterizes this year is *basic trust versus mistrust.* Whether the infant develops a sense of basic trust or confidence in the outside world depends on his relationship with his mother or other primary caregiver.

2. *Second year of life.* The important influence at this stage is both parents. The crisis at this stage is *autonomy versus shame and doubt.* A child must learn self-control (toileting, frustration, anger, etc.). If his parents are overly critical, the child may come to doubt his own adequacy (shame). If they allow him to work through difficult problems himself, he develops a sense of self (autonomy).

3. *Third to fifth years of life.* The major influence in life at this stage is the family. The crisis is *initiative versus guilt.* How the family reacts to children's individuality will affect the degree to which they feel free to express themselves. If initiative or innovation is condemned, the child will suffer guilt.

4. *Sixth year to puberty.* The important influences in life at this stage are neighborhood and school. The crisis is *industry versus inferiority.* Children during this stage try to find out how things work. If they succeed, they are likely to become more industrious. If they do not, they may consider themselves inferior.

5. *Adolescence.* Friends are the dominant influences on life in adolescence. The crisis is *identity versus role confusion.* Adolescents are on the brink of adulthood. They have achieved the flexible thinking of the formal operational stage. They can imagine many possibilities for their own life. The choices they make determine who they will become. The danger is role confusion: if adolescents do not succeed in making a choice (dis-

tinguishing among the many possibilities), they may not be able to establish their own sense of identity.

6. *Early Adulthood.* The "job" of early adulthood is to establish intimate bonds of love and friendship. These bonds typically include marriage and children. The crisis is *intimacy versus isolation,* whether one will develop lasting intimate relationships or remain isolated.

7. *Middle adulthood.* At this age, the primary relationships of a person's life are the people he works and lives with. The crisis in this period is *generativity versus self-absorption.* The choice is between concern for others, such as one's family, and a preoccupation with oneself. The danger is becoming too self-absorbed, of becoming concerned primarily with self and not others. .

8. *The aging years.* Here the crisis is *integrity versus despair.* A person can have a sense of satisfaction looking back over his life, a sense of fulfillment, or he can have a sense of despair at lost opportunities and regrettable actions. At this stage the dominant influence is a sense of "mankind is my kind." How one faces the approach of death is largely determined by one's assessment of having lived a worthwhile life or having wasted possibilities.

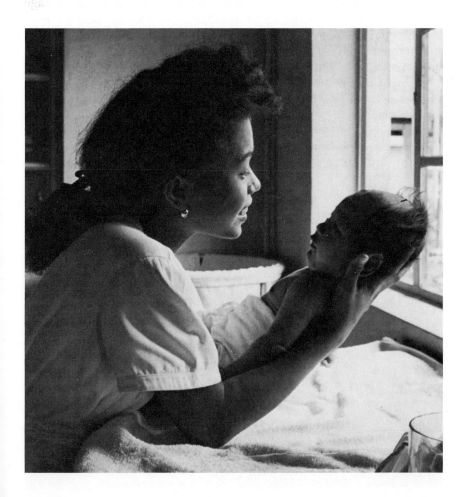

Erikson's theory is considered by most psychologists to be a rather idealized description of development and not an explanation based on research. Erikson's theory has, however, stimulated research in specific areas of social development such as attachment in infancy and search for identity in adolescence, which we will consider in this chapter, and of concerns with adulthood.

Erikson's Theory of Adult Development   See Chapter 19, pp. 666–67.

Attachment

Like physical and mental development, psychosocial development proceeds in stages. As the child matures, his or her social world expands from mother and immediate family to friends, religion, nationality, etc. But, perhaps due to humans' long period of immaturity, the relationships formed in the first few years seem to have a special quality.

Development of Attachment

That special quality is the **attachment** between the infant and the mother or other caregivers. Attachment develops as the infant ages. Even a young infant can tell the difference between the mother and other people: its eyes follow her more than anyone else and it smiles more enthusiastically at her. By eight months, most infants have a strong attachment to their mothers. They smile, coo, and try to stay close to her. When frightened, they go to her and try to cling to her leg or demand to be picked up. As long as she is near, an infant feels freer to explore.

At eight months, the infant often shows extreme distress when the mother leaves. This behavior is called **separation anxiety.** When the mother returns, the child will often cling to her desperately. At this stage, the child cannot be comforted by just anyone—only the mother or primary caregiver brings relief.

Before infants develop separation anxiety, they are also afraid of

FIGURE 3–18
Separation Anxiety
By about eight months of age, most infants become so strongly attached to their mothers that they become extremely distressed when left with anyone else, even a grandparent or other person they know, like, and trust.

strangers. This fear is called **stranger anxiety.** At four or five months infants smile at people almost indiscriminately; they can be comforted by almost anyone, even a stranger. By the last quarter of the first year, however, they are likely to scream and cry if a stranger approaches, especially if they are in a strange place or if their mothers are not around. If they are around the infants will cling tightly to them.

Why Do Infants Develop Attachments to Their Mothers?

The attachment of the baby to the mother is an important event which involves many different factors. It is probably (1) an innate bond which develops due to (2) the necessity for mother love, (3) the gratification of needs, (4) the infant's cognitive development, and (5) the communication between mother (or caregiver) and child.

1. John Bowlby (1969) and Mary Ainsworth (1967) believe that attachment is innate. Bowlby's (1969) hypothesis is that strong attachments have a survival function. Because an infant relies for protection on his primary caregiver, it is safer for the infant to spend most of his time clinging to or close by the mother.

2. Harlow and Harlow (1966) devised a series of ingenious experiments to test the hypothesis that love and care were a necessity. They raised rhesus monkeys with two surrogate mothers made out of wire mesh. One wire mesh "mother" had a feeding bottle attached to its chest; the other was covered with terry cloth. The infant monkeys spent most of their time clinging to the terry cloth mothers. They would go to the wire mother when hungry, but then return to the cloth mother. When frightened, they would run to the cloth mother rather than to the one that fed them (Figure 3–19). This study suggests that food is not the primary basis for attachment.

3. Sigmund Freud believed the basis for attachment lies in the fact that the mother gratifies the baby's needs, especially for food. Similarly, "learning theorists" believe that the pleasure infants feel at having their needs gratified becomes associated with the mother and that such emotional needs are important.

4. Jean Piaget (1932) believed that attachment for the child depends on object permanence. A baby must be able to have a permanent conception of his mother before he can miss her when she is gone. He has to recognize that something is strange or different before he can think it may be something to be afraid of.

5. Babies do not necessarily become attached solely to their primary caregivers (Schaffer & Emerson, 1964). Generally, human infants become more attached to *people who interact with them socially*, whether or not they provide any caregiving functions. Many researchers believe that communication is the primary ingredient in the development of attachment (Maccoby, 1980).

The Strange Situation

Mary Ainsworth and her colleagues have experimented extensively with attachment, separation anxiety, and stranger anxiety, in both the home environment and the laboratory (Ainsworth, Blehar, Waters, & Wall, 1978). She developed an experiment called the **"strange situation,"**

FIGURE 3–19
Love Is Soft
The series of experiments by Harlow and Harlow showed that infant monkeys would go to a wire mesh surrogate mother for food but were more attached to their soft, terry cloth surrogate mother, to whom they clung for warmth, security, and a semblance of affection.

Mary Ainsworth

which has become a classic test of the nature of mother-child attachment. In this experiment a stranger enters a room where a baby and his mother are playing with toys. The mother leaves the room, so that the child is alone with the stranger and the toys. The experimenter observes how the child reacts to his or her mother's departure, how much he or she plays with the toys, how he or she responds to the stranger, and to the mother upon her return (Figure 3–20).

Ainsworth found three basic patterns of attachment:

1. *Unattached infants.* They showed little or no interest in either the mother or the stranger and they exhibited little or no separation or stranger anxiety.

2. *Securely attached infants.* They appeared to be very happy around their mothers, using her as a "security base" for exploration. They appeared to feel freer to play with the toys when she was there; some were friendly to the stranger but were more interested in their mothers. When the mother left the room, they showed varying amounts of distress, but always greeted her happily when she returned.

3. *Insecurely attached infants.* They explored less and stayed close to their mothers, especially when the stranger was there. They either ignored the stranger at first or demanded to be held but then immediately wriggled to get free. They showed great distress when the mother left the room.

Attachment and Competence

Being securely attached may be an advantage in the toddler's early development. Securely attached children are more advanced in cognitive and social skills at 20 months. They play more intensely and enjoyably

FIGURE 3–20
The Infant's Reaction to the Strange Situation
A one-year-old child will cry more and explore its environment less when a stranger enters the room. Presence of a stranger combined with absence of the mother increases these negative effects. Such interactions, over a period of about half an hour, are charted here. (After Ainsworth & Bell, 1970)

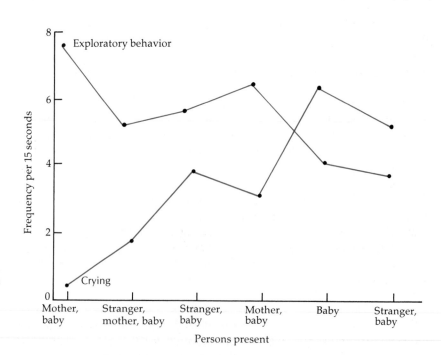

than babies who were judged either unattached or insecurely attached 10 months earlier (Main, 1973). At age two, secure children were more adept at problem solving and approached problems with enthusiasm, interest, and pleasure. They asked adults for help more easily when it was needed. Unattached and insecure children, however, were easily frustrated and gave up on problems. They seldom asked for help; they simply clung to their mothers (Matas, Arend, & Sroufe, 1978). At 3½, children who at 1½ had been judged securely attached, played well with others and tended to be leaders, whereas insecurely attached children tended to be more anxious, withdrawn, and less curious (Waters, Wippman, & Sroufe, 1979). The quality of attachments in the first two years thus appears to be a good indicator of a child's competence and social adjustment for a few years afterward. Of course, this better adjustment may not be due exclusively to attachment behavior in the first year of life, but may be due to a *continuing* good relationship with parents.

Play

For a young child, all the world is a plaything. Children play with their bodies, language, objects, ideas, animals, and other people. *How* they play reflects the degree of their motor, cognitive, and social development. A toddler shrieks with delight at being able to roll a ball back and forth to his mother; a few years later he may hit the winning home run for his Little League team. Play is an important way in which children explore the world and themselves.

Developmental Trends in Play

Children's play reflects four developmental trends (Garvey, 1977):

1. Biological maturation permits increasing motor skill in play.

2. Play becomes more complex and is combined with other aspects of play. Nine-year-olds playing baseball play with more objects, use more skilled motions, interact in an organized way with more people, and use more cognitive skills than a toddler rolling a ball back and forth to his mother.

3. The concrete properties of materials become less important as fantasy and imaginative play become more complex. To a two-year-old a toy is usually the focus of play. For example, the child dials and talks into a toy telephone. An eight-year-old is more likely to use a toy as a prop in a complex situation: the toy telephone may be part of a supermarket he or she has built.

4. As children gain more experience with the outside world, they incorporate new people, situations, and skills into fantasy play. Three-year-olds play house: they pretend to cook, iron, or maybe drive to work. The fantasy play of eight-year-olds is more complicated: they play *Star Wars*, using sticks as laser guns and chairs as spaceships to fly to other planets.

Play with Peers

From a very early age, children are attracted to other children. Infants as young as six months smile in response to other infants and touch each other, but such interactions tend to be relatively infrequent and very brief (Vandell, Wilson, & Buchanan, 1980). One-year-old infants are more likely to engage in solitary than social play, but by two years they are twice as likely to engage in social play. Older toddlers would rather play with their peers than their mothers (Eckerman, Whatley, & Kutz, 1975).

Once infants under one year old have gotten over their initial wariness of unfamiliar children, they play with any responsive child. By 14 months they begin to show preferences in playmates (Bridges, 1933). A toddler's preference for friends is usually related to his mother's friends: the better mothers like each other, the more their children are likely to play with each other (Jacobson, 1977). But even toddlers exercise some independent choice: they are more likely to play with other toddlers whom they perceive to be similar to themselves in age and style. A quiet two-year-old is more likely to enjoy playing with another quiet two-year-old than with a more active toddler or a three-year-old (Rubin, 1980).

Friendships

As children develop and change, their friendships also develop and change. Very young children form friendships on the basis of availability and similarity of physical attributes and activities. Only later do psychological attributes, such as personal needs, interests, or traits, become important. There are four stages in childhood friendships (Selman & Jaquette, 1977):

Stage 0. "Momentary Physical Playmates" (3–5 years). At this age friends are simply the people a child plays with. If you ask a preschooler why he likes someone, you are likely to get a rather circular answer:

ZR: Why is Caleb your friend?
TONY: Because I like him.
ZR: And why do you like him?
TONY: Because he's my friend.
ZR: And why is he your friend?
TONY: (speaking each word distinctly with a tone of mild disgust at the interviewer's obvious denseness): Because . . . I choosed . . . him . . . for . . . my . . . friend. (Rubin, 1980)

Stage 1. "One-Way Assistance" (6–8 years). At this age children begin to have some idea about the psychological aspects of friendships. They are likely to consider a friend as someone who does nice things for them, who tries to please them in some way. But as yet they have little idea of the *reciprocal* nature of friendships. "I like Jamie because he gives me money for popsicles."

Stage 2. "Fairweather Cooperation" (9–12 years). As the child learns to see other people's points of view, he or she understands friendships are reciprocal. But the basis is specific incidents, not a long-term relationship. If you're nice to them, they'll be nice to you. "I'll invite you to my birthday party if you'll invite me to yours."

Stage 3. "Intimate and Mutual Sharing" (11+). By late childhood and

early adolescence, children recognize the unique individuality of others: they know their friends act in certain ways for certain reasons. They form friendships on the basis of shared traits and interests. They share secrets and other intimacies with each other. They express deep feelings about each other and are able to conceptualize relationships. They know that the friendship will exist over time and that they will change. As a 12-year-old put it:

> "You have known your friend so long and loved him so much, and then all of a sudden you are so mad at him, you say, I could just kill you and you still like each other, because you have always been friends and you know in your mind you are going to be friends in a few seconds anyway." (Selman & Jacquette, 1977)

As children grow older, move beyond the family circle, and have more experience with the world, their friendship with peers becomes ever more important.

The Development of Sex Roles

"It's a girl!" "It's a boy!" The first words spoken about a baby are about sex. From the first moments of life on, sex has important influences on an individual's identity, behavior, and personality. One's **gender identity** means that a child knows and identifies with what sex he or she is. A **sex role** is society's expectations of how a male or female should behave. In all cultures some tasks, behaviors, and personality characteristics are defined as "masculine" and others as "feminine."

Biological Factors in Sex Roles

In many different cultures there are consistencies in the roles men and women play; these are based, in part, upon biological predispositions. Men's greater strength allows them to be warriors, hunters, and fishermen. Women's childbearing capacity often ties them more to activities centered around the home: child care, cooking, and gardening. What biological differences there are between men and women can, however, be *almost* completely changed by the culture. For example, among the Guatemalan Indians agriculture is considered a man's work; in Kenya women work the fields. In the United States the majority of physicians are men; in Russia almost all physicians are women.

Social Factors in Sex Roles: The Newborn

A few obvious behavioral differences between boys and girls at birth have been documented. Newborn boys are more active than girls; they are awake more and grimace more. They are more irritable, as well (Moss, 1967). However, these differences are not always found. Some studies have found no differences in activity level, crying, or "soothability" between boy and girl babies.

However, from the first day of life there is an enormous difference in how parents perceive and treat their children. Parents, especially fathers, are more likely to rate their *day*-old daughters as soft, small, delicate and weak, and their boys as strong, firm, and hardy (Rubin, Provenzano, & Luria, 1974), whether they are or not. When asked to interpret their baby's crying, parents generally interpret their son's crying as anger and their daughter's as fear (Condry & Condry, 1976).

Social Factors in Sex Roles: Toddlers and Preschoolers

Parents and other adults also encourage sex-typed behavior in children through the toys and clothes they choose for them, by how they play with them, and by what types of play they encourage. In a hospital nursery girls are often covered in pink blankets, boys in blue. At the age of one there is no difference between boys and girls in the toys they prefer. Boys and girls are equally happy with a doll or a truck. But parents give girls dolls, doll houses, and stuffed animals, while boys are given blocks, trucks, and sports equipment (Rheingold & Cook, 1975). By age three children show a clear preference for sex-typed toys (Maccoby & Jacklin, 1974).

Parents also play with their infant sons and daughters differently. Mothers touch their little girls more and prefer to keep them close by. By age two, girls generally prefer to play closer to their mothers than do boys (Weinraub & Lewis, 1979). Little boys also receive more gross motor stimulation than girls; they are more likely to be tossed, swung, and chased (Maccoby & Jacklin, 1974). And from the age of two on, boys show a higher activity level in their play and are more likely to engage in

FIGURE 3–21
Sex Roles and Sex-typed Behavior
Children of both sexes will happily play with toys and engage in behavior traditionally identified with their own or the other gender. The critical factor is whether and how early adults encourage children in their care to engage in sex-typed behavior.

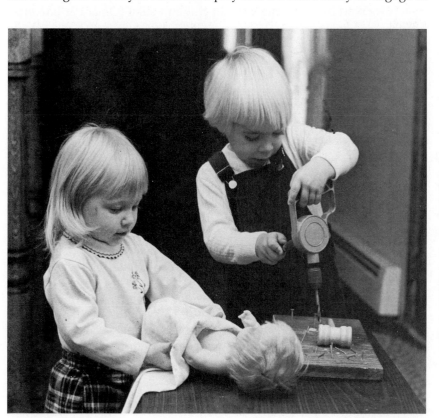

rough and tumble play. In most cultures they are also more likely to be aggressive than girls, to get into more confrontations (Maccoby & Jacklin, 1974). Fathers tend to perpetuate sex roles in their children more than do mothers (Block, 1979). They are more likely to reward their daughters for playing with other girls but punish their sons for playing with girls (Langlois & Downs, 1980).

The Middle Years

Parents place different expectations on their sons and daughters, expectations that are often echoed by the children's teachers. Boys are likely to be encouraged to compete and achieve, to be independent and responsible, and to control their feelings. Fathers, especially, are stricter with their sons than their daughters and punish them more readily. Girls generally get more warmth and physical closeness from their parents; they are more trusted and receive less punishment. They are also encouraged to be nurturant and obedient and are more likely to be closely supervised than boys (Block, 1979).

With all this encouragement, sex roles become much more pronounced in the middle school years. Children play in same-sex groups: girls form small, quiet groups of two and three; boys move in larger, more active groups (Waldrop & Halverson, 1975). Girls and boys differ in the way they play team games. Boys choose teammates on the basis of skill, whereas girls prefer to play with those they like. This pattern has been observed in Swiss and African children alike (Omark & Edelman, 1973).

A Conclusion

In all societies men and women assume different roles. Something this consistent must involve *both* biological and social factors. It is likely that social factors *exaggerate* biological differences. The large behavioral differences between the sexes may be, in part, the result of a positive feedback loop. That is, the slight differences between male and female infants in the early months of life can be amplified by the special way parents treat children of different sexes. For instance, girl babies react more to the human voice; they are more likely to cry in response to another baby's cry and to vocalize in response to their parents' voices. Their response, in turn, encourages the parents, especially the mother, to talk more to their daughters than their sons. By three months, mothers vocalize more to their girl infants than to their boy infants (Lewis & Freedle, 1973). Both mothers and fathers spend more time encouraging infant daughters to smile and vocalize than they do their sons. This may explain why little girls learn to talk earlier than little boys and by two years of age do better on vocabulary tests. Girls and boys may then go down different developmental paths, where further social expectations when they are toddlers and young children continue the process.

Divorce

One important part of the child's social world is whether his parents stay together. Currently, the rate of divorce is at an all-time high. In 1964 there was one divorce for every four marriages, but in 1976 there was one divorce for every two marriages (Wallerstein & Kelly, 1980). Between one-third and one-half of all children growing up in the 1970s experienced the separation or divorce of their parents (Bane, 1976).

Not surprisingly, childless couples are most likely to divorce, and the more children a couple have, the more stable their marriage is. But surprisingly, having sons or daughters seems to be related to how stable the marriage is. Couples who have only daughters are the most likely to divorce, whereas couples who have only sons are the least likely (Glick & Norton, 1977).

The Effects of Divorce on Children

There is surprisingly little known about the effects of divorce on children but, in general, it has been assumed that divorce was better for children than living in a family environment characterized by strife and bitterness. Indeed, parents usually feel that they and their children are better off after the divorce (Albrecht, 1980). However, a new study suggests that the *children themselves* may not feel that way.

Wallerstein and Kelly (1980) studied 131 children and adolescents from white, primarily upper-middle-class divorcing parents. The families were studied during the separation, and again at 18 months and at five years after the first contact. Surprisingly few of the children, especially the youngest, were very aware of parental conflict. At the time of the divorce, only 10 percent approved of it, although 30 percent had witnessed physical violence between the parents. Eighteen months later two-thirds of the children did not see their family as better off than predivorce. More children accepted the divorce with time, especially the adolescents and those who maintained a good relationship with both parents, but five years later, 56 percent still did not find the postdivorce family to be an improvement (Wallerstein & Kelly, 1980).

Initial Reactions to the Divorce

Nearly all children show some degree of distress at the news of parental separation, although it may not be initially apparent. Children feel frightened and more vulnerable; they may feel an enormous sense of loss and may worry about the state of their parents, who will feed them, where they will live. They also worry about their relationship with their parents—if their parents could stop loving each other, why not them too? Will their father prefer his new girl friend to them, or maybe the stepchildren? The children and adolescents may feel angry, rejected, and be torn by conflicting loyalties to both parents. Most of all, the children feel lonely. One parent, generally the father, has left the household, and the mother is less available to them, due to her own grief and often the need to work full time. How children respond to the divorce depends greatly upon their age and how the parents handle the divorce.

Preschool children react with fear, guilt, bewilderment, and regression. Few of these children were prepared for the separation and, in essence, awoke one morning to find a parent gone. This stimulated intense fear of abandonment by both parents and macabre fantasies to explain the loss of one parent.

Children in the middle years (six to eight), on the other hand, respond mostly with grief. They may cry a great deal and express intense yearning for the departed parent. Boys, especially at this age, may express considerable anger at the mother for either causing the divorce or driving the father away.

Nine- to twelve-year-olds are more able to handle grief, but they also express intense anger at their parents. They are also most likely to become involved in the battles between their parents, often taking sides with one against the other, which is particularly detrimental to smooth adjustment to postdivorce life.

Adolescents with a relatively separate identity and strong peer support appear to be able to cope well and more rapidly mature. Others, however, especially those with low self-esteem, tend to regress or "act out" through sexual promiscuity, drugs, or alcohol.

Continued conflict between the parents and the inability to provide consistent care and nurturance can have a devastating impact on the children. The children who do best are those who have easy access to their fathers and maintain a good relation with them, and whose custodial parent (generally the mother) is able to regain her own internal equilibrium and provide a reasonably well-organized and secure household, and also be emotionally available to her children (Wallerstein & Kelly, 1980).

HOW DOES OUR EARLY EXPERIENCE AFFECT US?

Humans are born helpless and have a long period of immaturity. This period, childhood, has been the focus of this chapter. It is a period of great concern to society and to parents, because it is widely believed that the early years completely determine our later experiences. This idea has also been important in psychology. Sigmund Freud, for instance, asserted that most of the major problems of adulthood stem from events in the first few years (Freud, 1920). Recall that Erikson proposes that an individual's basic outlook on the world (trusting or mistrusting) is formed in the first two years. Many investigations have been stimulated by these ideas.

Physical Development

For physical development, the first few years *are* especially important. Improper nutrition, for instance, can cause permanent damage to the brain, resulting in mental retardation and slowed physical growth. McConnell (1978) found that severe protein deficiency in the fetus interferes with the normal development of the brain and can lead to mental retardation. Animals deprived of normal environmental stimuli have smaller brains than those not deprived (Krech, Crutchfield, & Livson, 1974).

Cognitive Development

Although laboratory deprivations are extreme, beyond what may occur in normal life, children deprived of normal stimulation are profoundly affected. Children in radically deprived environments show a much slower growth rate and become mentally retarded as well. There are children who have been prohibited, for some tragic reason, from learning a language in the early years of their life. For these children, the longer they are deprived, the harder it is for them to ever learn to speak.

However, children can *recover* from deprivation to a remarkable extent. In one study, Dennis (1960) observed a group of babies in a Lebanese orphanage. These children were given hardly any stimulation, they lay on their backs all day in bare rooms, in bare cribs. They were touched only when their diapers were changed. At the age of one year,

the children's development was about that of a six-month-old. Some of these babies were later adopted and Dennis was able to follow them and compare their development with that of the children still left in the orphanage. Those in the orphanage remained retarded, but those who were adopted caught up in many aspects of development. This and many other studies show that we are capable of overcoming early deprivations *if later experience compensates*.

Birth Order

Whether our character is *completely* formed by early experience is not clear, but one early experience that has persisting effects is one's rank in the family, called in psychology **birth order.** For millennia the firstborn (male, at least) has been regarded as the heir, the favored one, the one destined to assume family leadership on the death of the father. Recent evidence, somewhat surprisingly, confirms that firstborns are better leaders, but also shows that later birth has its advantages too.

Intellect

Robert Zajonc and his colleagues (1979) propose that a child's intellectual development is related to the intellectual abilities of the people in his immediate environment, namely the family. To determine the intellectual value of that environment Zajonc arbitrarily assigned the parents "intelligence values" of 30 each. Thus the first child is born into an environment of

$$\frac{30 + 30 + 0}{3} = 20.$$

If the next child is born when the first child has an intellectual level of four, the intellectual value of his environment is

$$\frac{30 + 30 + 4 + 0}{4} = 16.$$

The intellectual environment for later children will be lower still. The first child is born into the highest intellectual environment. Each new child is born into a successively lower one. Most older children teach their younger siblings in many ways—games, behavior, language. Zajonc hypothesizes that this informal teaching experience increases the older child's intellectual abilities.

Family size also has an effect on intellectual development. One study examined the scores of almost 800,000 participants in National Merit Scholarship programs in 1962–1965 (Breland, 1977). Average scores declined as family size increased. Firstborns have higher verbal IQs than second-borns, and second-borns scored higher than third-borns. Thus birth order and family size are two aspects of early experience that seem to have a lasting effect—at least on those aspects of intelligence measured by IQ tests. One example of this is that many more eminent scientists are firstborns than would be expected from their number in the population (Zajonc, Markus, & Markus, 1979).

Personality and Psychosocial Development

There are also lasting effects of birth order on personality. Firstborns tend to be more cautious, nervous, and anxious than later-borns. Firstborn and later-born children are treated differently by their parents, and these effects continue into later life. Mothers pay more attention to their firstborns. Mothers are more strict with and protective of firstborns, preventing them from doing things for fear of harm. At just below four years old, firstborns obey their parents more than later-borns (Maccoby, 1980). Later in life, firstborns seem to be more inhibited. They are also more *conformist*, less likely to express antisocial sentiments. Firstborns remain a little more physically fearful as well, preferring a low-contact sport such as baseball to football or skiing. Firstborns are also more nervous. During a power blackout in New York City, people were asked: "How nervous and uneasy were you during the experience?" Firstborns reported more anxiety and distress (Schachter, 1959). Later-borns, being less anxious and inhibited, are more likely to be socially popular, but they are also more likely to harbor doubts about themselves. The reason for this may be that because later-borns do not have as much of their parents' attention as they want, they feel that others do not like them very much.

Although this is a selective review, it should be obvious that early experience is quite important in several respects. There are lasting effects on the brain, on intelligence, and on personality. However, early experience does *not* completely determine our lives. Even an extremely deprived environment can be overcome *if later experience compensates.*

ADOLESCENCE

After late childhood a major developmental change occurs. Increases in the level of sex hormones transform the child's appearance to that of an adult. Sex organs and secondary sex characteristics begin to develop at about the same time. There is a "growth spurt." Although growth in the first few years of life is rapid, young children are not aware enough of themselves or the world to be aware of the physical changes. But teenagers are aware of their growth, and this awareness is often upsetting.

Another source of instability is cognitive: adolescents have just entered the formal operational stage, a more abstract way of thinking and problem solving. These new mental abilities often cause conflicts between themselves and their family and society.

Other factors are personal and social. Adolescents are for the first time preparing to leave home and they enter a world comprised mainly of new friends. And, perhaps most important, for the first time the adolescent is aware of and concerned with sexuality, leading to new desires and explorations. Nevertheless, society and family still regard adolescents as children. Being considered a child allows for more protection (by families and from the law) and also imposes restrictions (curfews, drinking age) which are further causes for conflict.

Physical Growth and Puberty

The beginning of adolescence is marked by a sudden increase in the rate of physical growth, the *growth spurt*, which lasts about three years (see Figure 3–22). Boys at about age 12 and girls at age 10 begin to gain weight. Bones grow thicker and wider, muscle bulk and weight increase (especially, in girls, around the hips). This "pudginess" is a sign that the changes of puberty are fast approaching.

At the peak of their growth spurt, girls may gain 20 pounds and boys as much as 26 pounds in a year. A sharp increase in height follows the weight gain. The stored fat is then redistributed, particularly in boys. Typically, adolescents gain 2–5 inches in height during the growth spurt, fueled by a dramatic increase in caloric intake. Many teenage boys consume up to 6,000 calories a day (about twice what a normal adult eats) (Tanner, 1970).

As in other periods of growth, the body during adolescence does not change uniformly and simultaneously. Hands, head, and feet grow more than the central trunk, which causes many adolescents to feel awkward or "gangly." More upsetting, sometimes one side of the body develops a bit more quickly than the other (one breast, one ear) (Katchadourian, 1977). Almost 50 percent of all adolescents are dissatisfied with their appearance. Boys wish they were taller, girls that they were thinner (Scanlon, 1975).

Puberty

The word puberty comes from the Latin "to be covered with hair," and the appearance of darkened hair on the legs, genitals, and underarms for both sexes, and on the face and chest for boys, is one of the first signs of puberty. In males, the larynx lengthens and the voice deepens

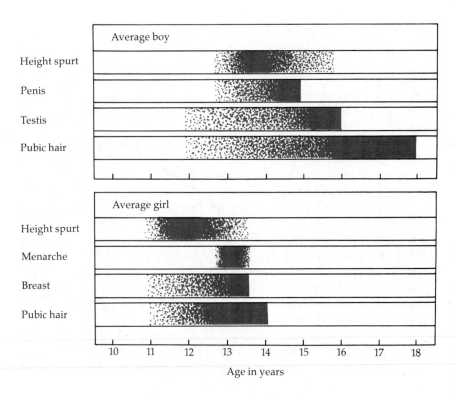

FIGURE 3–22
Physical Development in Puberty
The darkest areas on this chart indicate growth spurts during which adolescent boys and girls grow and change most. Individual patterns of development may vary greatly from these averages. (After Tanner, 1962)

(sometimes "cracking"). Puberty officially begins for boys when they produce live sperm cells. The scrotum, testes, and penis grow and eventually ejaculation is possible. In girls, puberty begins at **menarche,** the onset of menstruation. In girls, breasts and pubic hair develop simultaneously with the growth of the uterus, vagina, clitoris, and labia. Although her menstrual periods may be regular, it may be some time before she produces fertile eggs.

Cognitive Development

At adolescence there is a major shift in thinking—the emergence of *formal operations,* bringing with it the ability to transform the information received. For many adolescents the emergence of the new mental ability causes a radical break in their previous schemata. For the first time they realize that the way they have done things and the way their parents, school, or country operates is not necessarily the only, or "true" way.

Questioning and Idealism

The first exercise of the new level of abstract thought is often an intense period of questioning, searching, and rebellion. The adolescent begins to see that there are many possible choices in life—choices of careers, of life-style, questions of identity: "Who am I? What do I want to do?" On the threshold of adult life, adolescents imagine it to be ideal; experience inevitably tempers some of this idealism. Because teenagers

ADOLESCENT SUICIDE

One of the consequences of the adolescent's new sexual maturity and intellectual idealism can be suicide. It is almost unthinkable for a very young child to contemplate killing himself: a child rarely questions his place in the world, how things *should* be done, what might be possible. But as in adolescence our ability to understand that our situation is not ideal emerges, one tragic "solution" is suicide. One adolescent's suicide note makes the point:

> To my family and friends: I'm sorry it has to be this way. For some reason, I have set unattainable goals for myself. It hurts to live and life is full of so many disappointments and problems . . . Please don't cry

or feel badly. I know what I am doing and why I am doing it. I guess I never really found out what love or responsibility was.
> Bill

I might also add that I had had in recent years no great desire to continue living. Saying goodbye to all of you who I was close to would only make things harder for me. Believe me, I tried to cope with my problems but I couldn't. (Jacobs, 1971)

Adolescence is the first point at which suicide is attempted. First suicide attempts begin with people 15–19 years of age. In most cases of suicide there are long-standing histories of family problems which worsen after puberty (Jacobs, 1971).

cannot reconcile the fact that their parents are less than ideal, adolescence is often a difficult time for both parents and children.

Thus many adolescents become idealistic because for the first time they can imagine what an ideal world and an ideal society might be like. This same ability can also lead the adolescent toward ideologies and to organizations that present an "ideal" life, such as cults led by gurus.

Psychosocial Development

Egocentrism

Although adolescents tend to be idealistic, at the same time they remain emotionally egocentric (Elkind, 1974, 1978). They imagine that their new and thrilling experiences, discoveries, and feelings are unique. A young girl may reproach her mother saying, "But Mother, you don't know how it feels to be in love" (Elkind, 1974, 1978). Adolescents are often so preoccupied with their physical appearance that they assume that everyone else notices minute details about them. They are extremely self-conscious: they may even avoid going to a party when they have a pimple. It may be years before such egocentrism abates, before a young person can acknowledge that others feel as deeply as he does (even those who disagree), and also realizes that no one pays as much attention to him as he pays himself.

Identity and Turbulence

As children move into young adulthood, they begin to realize that their actions may have long-range consequences on their lives. For example, how well you do in high school determines the college you go to, which may be important to your career. Adolescents begin to make their own choices for their lives. Thus adolescence and young adulthood are often marked by a search for one's own identity. "Who am I? What makes me different from other people? Do I want to be like my parents? What am I going to do with my life?"

Not knowing who you are or what you are going to do can be at once an exhilarating and anxiety-provoking situation. College or military service may provide a testing ground for the young person to explore his possibilities. Questioning, searching, and conflicts are characteristic of the teenager's search for identity. This search is made more urgent by the changes in the body and by developments in cognition that occur in adolescence. Adolescence is characteristically a very turbulent time. The rate of juvenile delinquency and heavy drug use attests to that. And in recent years the rate of teenage suicide attempts and successes has increased. Some adolescents, however, never question their predefined roles and travel through adolescence without anxiety, and for these teenagers adolescence is not dramatically turbulent. In a recent study of a sample of teenagers who could be characterized, 35 percent had reported rather smooth sailing through adolescence, indicating that not everyone experiences such crises and storms (Berger, 1980).

Teenage Sexuality

In the last few decades, attitudes toward sex have changed, and all adolescents, girls in particular, have become more sexually active than before. The first major reports on sexual habits of normal people were published in 1948 and 1953 by Kinsey and his colleagues. Their reports were based on interviews with white middle-class people in the 1940s. They found that only 3 percent of women and 40 percent of the men interviewed had sex by the age of 16 (Kinsey, 1953). However, in the mid-seventies a survey of people the same age and background found that 42 percent of 16-year-old boys and 36 percent of the girls had had sex (Haas, 1978).

Boys and girls are more similar now in sexual activity than in previous decades, but their attitudes toward sex differ greatly. Most studies suggest that boys are more interested in sex than girls. Boys approve of casual sex more than girls do. Teenagers were asked when they would like to first have sexual intercourse with someone. Twenty-three percent of the 15- to 16-year-old boys and only 0.5 percent of the girls said, "On a first or second date." Even with the liberalizing of attitudes in the society, losing virginity seems to be a different experience for boys and girls. For boys it is almost a rite of passage into manhood. Their attitudes about it are overwhelmingly positive (Haas, 1978).

Emotional involvement with the sexual partner is more important for young women than it is for young men. In one study, almost half of the young men interviewed said they were not emotionally involved with their first sex partner; over 80 percent of the women said they were in love with their first partner (Simon, Berger, & Gagnon, 1972). This distinction is also reflected in the patterns of male and female sexual activity. Young men typically have more sexual partners than young women, while young women generally have more enduring relationships (Rutter, 1980).

Summary

1. *Maturation* is the emergence of individual characteristics through normal growth processes. *Physical* maturation is controlled by the information in the genes and is relatively unaffected by learning or experience. *Psychological* maturation is more complex; it is the development of mental abilities that result from the normal growth of the brain, the nervous system, and experience in the environment.

2. There are three distinct periods in the womb: the period of the ovum, from fertilization to two weeks; the period of the embryo, from two to nine weeks; and the period of the fetus, from nine weeks until birth.

3. When babies are born they have a large number of innate *reflexes*. Only two hours after birth they can follow a slowly moving light. If a nipple or finger is put into their mouths they will begin to suck automatically.

4. There are several specific characteristics that researchers have discovered about the newborn—a preference for faces, a preference for small amounts of change and variation, and certain rules that guide the baby's vision. Babies open their eyes when awake and alert. They look away from darkness. They look toward the light. They look along edges. There are certain differences in babies at birth: among them are vigor of response, general activity rate, restlessness, irritability, rate of habituation, and cuddliness.

5. The most influential theory of development was proposed by Piaget. Piaget assumes (a) knowledge guides action, (b) knowledge develops through experience and action, and (c) the complexity of mental structures is determined largely by biological age.

6. An important concept is the idea of the *schema* (plural, *schemata*). Schemata are the associations formed largely through the experience of what goes on in the world. They are our knowledge of how things are organized and how they relate to one another. Other important concepts of Piaget's are *assimilation* and *accommodation*. When children encounter a new event, they may attempt to assimilate it into their existing knowledge structure. As long as there is an acceptable fit between the new information and the existing knowledge structure, information can be assimilated. If, however, information cannot be assimilated into existing schemata, children have to *accommodate* this new knowledge by changing their knowledge structure.

7. As children learn about the world, the schemata join together to form repeated mental routines that Piaget calls *operations*—rules for transforming and manipulating information in the world.

8. Piaget's theory posits several *stages of cognitive development*. First is the sensorimotor stage (from 0 to 2 years), in which children learn primarily through motor and sensory play. Second is the preoperational stage (from 2 to 7

years), which finds children less bound by their senses and able to represent objects in drawings and words. Schemata that were just being organized are now able to be used intentionally. The third stage is concrete operations (7 to 12 years), in which thinking abstractly is possible. At this stage children can carry a task through to completion and can understand some of the basic characteristics of things in the world, such as number, weight, and order. The fourth stage, formal operations (from 12 through adulthood), concerns higher-level thinking: thinking abstractly, thinking through situations logically and systematically, and the ability to imagine worlds that do not exist.

9. Important indicators of cognitive development are *egocentrism* and *decentration*. At each stage of development children become increasingly aware of the world outside themselves and less focused only on their own thoughts and points of view.

10. Piaget's theory has been criticized by many, although it is generally accepted as the most useful one. Some of the criticisms are that (a) Piaget underestimates the reasoning abilities of children and overestimates verbal abilities, (b) stages of cognitive development are not exactly fixed, and (c) Piaget focuses more on the cognitive aspects of development than he should and less on social and emotional factors in development.

11. *Morality* is the knowledge of what is right and wrong. Like other aspects of cognition, a child's morals also undergo development. Kohlberg's theory suggests there are three levels of moral reasoning, each with different stages. The first is premoral, in which rules are obeyed to avoid punishment; the second is conventional morality; and the third is postconventional morality.

12. An important theory of *psychosocial development* is that of Erikson. Erikson divides psychosocial development into eight stages, each associated with a characteristic "crisis": In the first year of life the crisis is trust versus mistrust; in the second year, autonomy versus shame and doubt; in the third to fifth years, initiative versus guilt; in the sixth year to puberty, industry versus inferiority; in adolescence, identity versus role confusion; in early adulthood, intimacy versus isolation; in middle adulthood, generativity versus self-absorption; and in the aging years, integrity versus despair.

13. An important part of child development, which has been studied by many, is *attachment*—the quality of the relationship between the infant and the mother or other caregivers. Attachment is probably an innate bond that develops due to the necessity for mother love, the gratification of needs, the infant's cognitive development, and the communication between the mother (or other caregiver) and the child.

14. Attachment is studied in the "strange situation." In this experiment a stranger enters a room where a baby and mother are playing with toys. The mother leaves and the child is alone with the stranger and the toys. Three basic patterns of attachment are observed: (a) unattached infants, (b) securely attached infants, and (c) insecurely attached infants.

15. Children's play reflects four developmental trends: (a) Biological maturation permits increasing skill, (b) play becomes more complex, (c) play becomes more abstract, and (d) children incorporate new people, situations, and skills into their fantasies.

16. Sex roles also develop. *Gender identity* means that a child knows and identifies with what sex he or she is. A *sex role* is society's expectations of how a male or female should behave. From the first day of life there is an enormous difference in how parents perceive and treat their children. Fathers are more likely to rate their one-day-old daughter as soft, small, delicate, and weak, and their boy as strong, firm, and hardy, whether they are or are not. Parents also encourage sex-typed behavior through the toys and clothes they choose, how they play with their children, and what types of play they encourage. It is likely that social factors emphasize and exaggerate the innate biological differences.

17. An important effect on children's lives is *divorce*. A recent study suggests that children have different reactions to divorce, depending on their stage of development. Preschool children may react with fear, guilt, bewilderment, and regression. Children in the middle years (six to eight) respond mostly with grief, while nine- to twelve-year-olds are more able to handle grief but express intense anger. Adolescents, on the other hand, are often able to cope well.

18. The question of how *early experience* affects us is an important area of research in psychology. In physical development, the first few years are especially important. Improper nutrition can cause permanent damage to the brain, resulting in mental retardation and slowed physical growth.

    In cognitive development children deprived of normal stimulation are profoundly affected, but many studies show that they can recover if later experience compensates.

    One important early experience that does have persistent lasting effects is *birth order*. Birth order affects intellectual abilities—the later born the child, the lower the IQ—and has an effect on personality as well. Later in life, firstborns are more inhibited and more conforming than later-borns, less likely to express antisocial sentiments, and remain a little more physically fearful.

19. The last developmental stage in childhood is *adolescence*. During the characteristic growth spurt, girls may gain 20 pounds and boys as much as 26 in a year. At adolescence there is a major shift in thinking—the emergence of formal operations. The first exercise of this new level of abstract thought is often an intense period of questioning, searching, and rebellion. This is what is commonly called the "identity crisis." It is occasioned by the emergence of the ability to imagine a world as the adolescent thinks it *ought to be* rather than the world as it is. Not all adolescents, however, have a turbulent time: 35 percent report rather smooth sailing through the period.

Terms and Concepts

accommodation
assimilation
attachment
birth order
competence
concern with standards
concrete operational stage
conservation
conventional morality

decentration
egocentrism
embryonic period
fetal alcohol syndrome
formal operational stage
gender identity
maturation
menarche
object permanence

operations
ossification
planning
postconventional morality
premoral level
preoperational stage
psychosocial development
reflexes
representational thought

schema
schemata
sensorimotor stage
separation anxiety
sex roles
stranger anxiety
"strange situation"
symbolic thought

Suggestions for Further Reading

Garvey, C. (1977). *Play.* Cambridge: Harvard University Press.
A useful summary of what children go through, how they learn to play, and the stages of play. Written for the general reader.

Phillips, J. L. (1981). *Piaget's theory: A primer.* San Francisco: W. H. Freeman.
Piaget is notably hard to pin down. Phillips provides a useful expansion of the ideas presented in this chapter.

White, S., & White, B. N. (1980). *Childhood pathways of discovery.* New York: Harper & Row.
One of a series of books on "the life cycle," which follows the various stages of a child's growth. Good casual reading, as it is very introductory.

Willemsen, E. (1979). *Understanding infancy.* San Francisco: W. H. Freeman.
An extremely well-done summary of this explosive new area of research and psychology. Highly recommended.

Wolman, B. (Ed.). (1982). *Handbook of developmental psychology.* Englewood Cliffs, NJ: Prentice-Hall.
Developmental psychology has become so large that a standard reference handbook is now needed. This is one to go to for future references.

Chapter 4

The Brain and Nervous System

INTRODUCTION

The most complex and mysterious invention of nature is about the size of a grapefruit. It weighs about as much as this book. It is the one organ you could not have transplanted and still be yourself. It is the brain.

It not only regulates all body functions, but controls our most primitive behavior as well as our most sophisticated activities. It is responsible for the creation of civilization, of music, art, science, and language. Our hopes, thoughts, emotions, and personality are all lodged—somewhere—inside there.

However, those things that make us most human—language, thinking, perception, intelligence, consciousness—represent only *a small fraction of the brain's functions.* What the brain does primarily is to regulate the body. It controls body temperature, blood flow, and digestion; it monitors every sensation, each breath and heartbeat, every movement, every blink and swallow. Much of its work is thus in directing movement: walk this way; take the hand off the stove; lift the arm to catch the ball; smile. Even speech is movement—the tongue, the lungs, the mouth, and the pharynx all must be directed to move to produce speech.

The brain is so complicated that many feel that a perfect understanding of it is beyond our grasp. In a single human brain the number of *potential* interconnections between cells is greater than the number of atoms in the universe.

Although we may never completely unravel the mysteries of the brain, we do know a lot about it. We know something of its evolutionary history. We know how brain cells communicate with one another to direct complex patterns of activity. We have discovered that injuries to certain areas of the brain have specific observable effects on behavior.

Recent discoveries make it clear that the brain is even more flexible than previously thought. It can grow to recover from damage, grow in response to new experience, grow and develop in old age. We know that individuals' brains are different from one another and that there are even differences determined by one's sex. Changes in diet and in the air can

133

have profound effects on brain chemistry, which in turn affect mood and alertness.

The brain sends its commands and receives messages in electrical and chemical languages. The messages are electrical; they are transmitted chemically. The brain produces more chemical substances than any other organ of the body. Some of these chemicals stop pain and aid in healing.

What we do not know is how all of this physics and chemistry finally becomes human experience. The trees that we experience are not present in the brain; there are no birds, no light or sound or thoughts— there is only constant electrical and chemical activity.

WHAT THE BRAIN IS AND WHAT IT DOES

Here is a way to picture the brain's shape and structure. Press your fingers on both sides of your head beneath the earlobes. Between your fingers is the oldest part of the brain, the *brain stem,* largely concerned with arousal and wakefulness. Imagine an area in the center of your head. That is the *limbic system,* which governs emotions and regulates

FIGURE 4–1
The Human Brain: Major Structures and Their Relative Positions

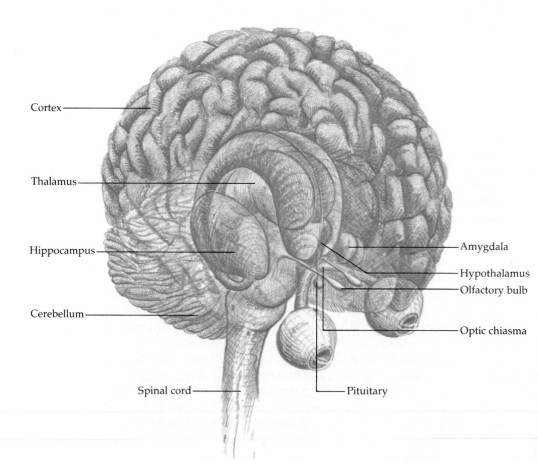

Cortex

Thalamus

Hippocampus

Cerebellum

Amygdala

Hypothalamus

Olfactory bulb

Optic chiasma

Spinal cord

Pituitary

the internal workings of the body. Make two fists and join them at the heels of the hands. This is about the size and shape of the entire brain, divided into two hemispheres, each about the size of a fist. The front of the brain is where your little fingers are; the back, your thumbs. The middle fingers represent the area where the brain controls movement, the index fingers where the brain receives sensory information. Now imagine your hands covered with thick grey gloves. This is the *cortex* (Latin for "bark"). The cortex was the last part of the brain to evolve and the area whose functioning results in the most characteristically human activities, such as language and art.

The cortex is only about one-eighth of an inch thick, and enfolded. If it were spread out, it would be about the size of a newspaper page. Humans have the most enfolded cortex, compared to other animals. Perhaps this is because such a large cortex had to fit into a small head for human babies to survive birth.

What the Brain Does

The brain regulates the action of the other organs of the body and coordinates actions on the external world. Ultimately, everything the brain does is manifested in action, or movements. Roger Sperry, a Nobel Prize–winning neuroscientist who has contributed much to our understanding of the brain, writes:

Roger Sperry

> The brain's primary function is essentially the transforming of sensory patterns into patterns of motor coordination. . . . In man, as in the salamander, the primary business of the brain continues to be the governing, directly or indirectly, of overt behavior. (Sperry, 1952)

There are three main areas of brain function:

1. *Running the body.* The brain directs all voluntary and involuntary movements. It communicates with the body via the glands of the *endocrine system* and three interconnected systems of nerves: *the central nervous system (CNS), the peripheral nervous system (PNS),* and *the autonomic nervous system (ANS)* portion of the PNS. The CNS includes the brain and spinal cord. The brain is the control center of all the neural networks. The spinal cord is the central trunk through which all neural communications pass on the way to the brain. The somatic PNS is a two-way communication system between the brain and muscles for controlling voluntary movements. Involuntary movements, such as heart beat, digestion, blinking, blood flow, swallowing, and heat regulation, are regulated by the autonomic PNS in cooperation with the glands of the endocrine system.

2. *Response to internal and external changes.* The brain responds to changes in the external and internal worlds. Through the senses the brain receives information about occurrences in the outside world. The internal state of the body, for example, blood sugar level and internal pain, is controlled, in part, by the endocrine system. Only the endocrine system will be discussed in this chapter; the sensory systems are the subject of the next chapter.

FIGURE 4–2
The Brain's Response to the Unexpected
The brain responds to an inappropriate word inserted at the end of an otherwise ordinary sentence by registering a marked change in its pattern of electrical activity. (After Hillyard & Kutas, 1980)

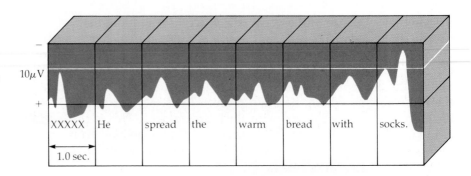

Whether the information is from inside or outside the body, whether an activity is simple or complex, voluntary or involuntary, the brain has *only one way of communicating*. All messages to and from the brain come in the language of neurons, the basic cells of the brain, and that language is firing. The kind of stimulus that gets the brain's attention is one that signals a change from the existing state. The change may be as subtle as a change in air pressure or as jarring as a novel or unexpected statement. For example, if we record the electrical activity of the brain as we read the sentence, "He spread the warm bread with jam," there is little indication of disruption in the electrical activity. However, if we read the sentence, "He spread the warm bread with socks," brain activity changes significantly, an indication of surprise (Kutas & Hillyard, 1980). (See Figure 4–2.) The brain has expectations or models in neural form. Apparently the brain's "model" of possible endings to the sentence "He spread the warm bread with . . ." does not include socks. The brain constantly interprets information it receives, "matching" it against a "model" it develops of the world.

3. *Adaptation.* The brain is the major organ of adaptation. It tells the body what to do based on its information on the changing state of the world. The ability to respond quickly to change and to be flexible in responding are the primary ingredients of adaptability. The more complex the organism, the more adaptable it will be.

A major difference among organisms is flexibility of action. Consider what happens when a frog is confronted by a fallen tree. The frog has such a specialized sensory system and brain that it probably will not notice the tree unless it runs into it. A human can cut it, play seesaw on it, make tables out of it, even make paper for this book. This greater flexibility of action that characterizes the human adaptation is in large part due to a larger brain.

FIGURE 4–3
The Brain's Role in Adaptation
Responding quickly and flexibly to input from the environment and telling the body what to do make the brain the major organ of adaptation to internal and external changes.

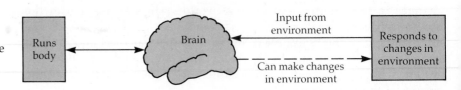

LEVELS OF BRAIN ORGANIZATION

The brain was "built" by the processes of evolution, over a period of hundreds of millions of years. We will take a kind of "archaeological tour" of the brain to discover the four different levels of functions that now exist. The first two are concerned with keeping alive, the second two with doing something new.

Keeping alive:
1. Arousal and wakefulness; the brain stem
2. Emotions and the inner state of the body; the limbic system

Creating anew:
3. Making new associations (learning, memory, perception); the cortex
4. Creating symbols (language, art); the divided hemispheres.

No function is entirely the province of one structure. We do not have four brains, but a highly complex organ with specialized and interdependent units.

Keeping Alive: The Brain Stem

The **brain stem** is the oldest and deepest area of the brain: it evolved over 500 million years ago, before the evolution of mammals (MacLean, 1978). Many scientists refer to this part of the brain as the "reptilian brain," since the human brain stem looks like the entire brain of a reptile, although it has changed in function somewhat. The brain stem sets the general level of alertness and warns the organism of important incoming information; it is concerned with basic life support. Only events that might be of possible use to the organism are monitored and selected by the senses; then they are brought inside and sent to the brain for interpretation and response.

About midway up the brain stem, and winding through it, is the **reticular activating system** (RAS) (Figure 4–4). The RAS arouses the cortex to important incoming stimulation. Like a telephone bell, the RAS seems to alert the cortex in a general way about arriving information (such as "visual stimulus on its way"). This is what happens when a sleeping dog is stimulated by electrodes in the RAS: it awakens immediately and searches the environment (Figure 4–4). The RAS also controls the general level of arousal (wakefulness, sleep, attention, excitement, etc.). Therefore, it controls both the *existence* and the *intensity* of consciousness (Brown, 1977).

For most sensory input, information is first received in portions of the lower brain stem, then the thalamus relays the information to the *appropriate* part of the cortex (Figure 4–5). The **thalamus** makes initial judgments on the nature of the information (is it visual or auditory?). It appears that certain areas of the thalamus are specialized for specific kinds of sensory information: for example, an auditory area of the thalamus alerts the auditory cortex.

Keeping Alive: The Limbic System

A person in a coma cannot respond to or interact with the outside world; but he or she continues to live, because the area of the brain that helps maintain and regulate vital body functions continues to operate. This area of the brain is called the limbic system (Figures 4–5 & 4–6).

The **limbic system** is a group of cellular structures between the brain stem and the cortex; it evolved about 150 million years ago. It is often called the "mammalian brain," because the same structure is found in all mammals. The limbic system is the area of the brain that helps to maintain **homeostasis,** a constant environment, in the body. Homeostatic mechanisms located in the limbic system regulate such functions as the maintenance of body temperature, blood pressure, heartbeat rate, and levels of sugar in the blood.

The limbic system also coordinates many of the brain's operations. It assigns priorities to the messages transmitted to the cortex, sending

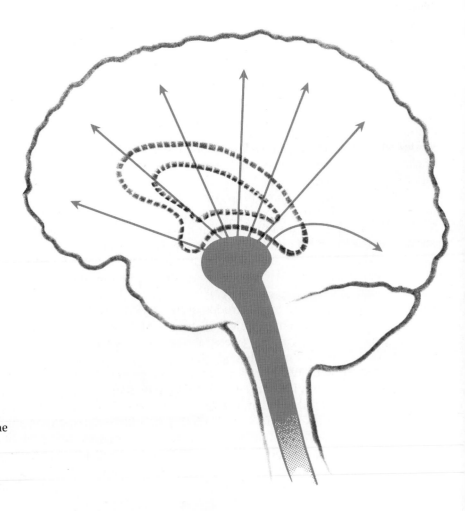

FIGURE 4–4
The Reticular
Activating System (RAS)
The RAS, buried in the brain stem, communicates with wide areas of the cortex, informing it of incoming stimuli and controlling its general level of arousal. (After Thompson, 1975)

some on directly and deferring others. It not only integrates a wide variety of incoming messages but also coordinates and elaborates the complex outgoing messages (or responses) from the brain. Thus, the activity of the limbic system lays the groundwork that makes complex behavior possible.

The limbic system is also strongly involved in the emotional reactions that have to do with survival, such as sexual desire and self-protection through fighting or escaping. One way to remember limbic functions is that they are the "four *f*'s" of survival: feeding, fighting, fleeing, and sexual reproduction.

The limbic system includes five of the most important and mysterious structures of the brain: the hypothalamus, the pituitary gland, the hippocampus, the frontal lobes of the cortex, and the amygdala.

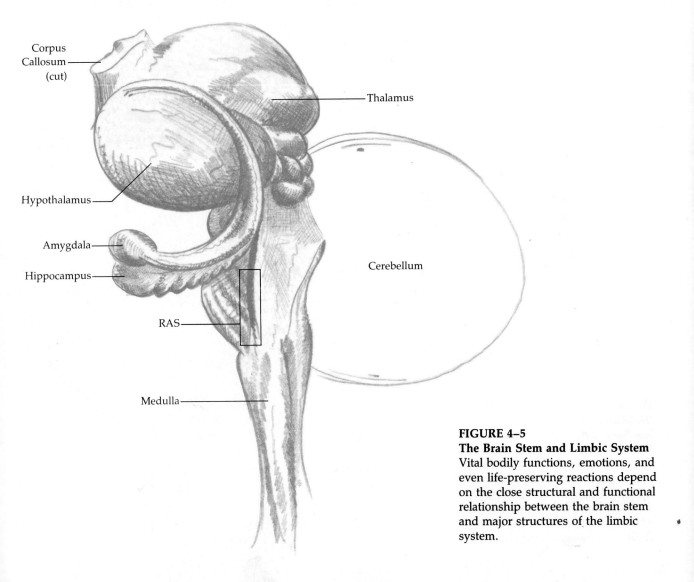

Corpus
Callosum
(cut)

Thalamus

Hypothalamus

Amygdala

Hippocampus

RAS

Cerebellum

Medulla

FIGURE 4–5
The Brain Stem and Limbic System
Vital bodily functions, emotions, and even life-preserving reactions depend on the close structural and functional relationship between the brain stem and major structures of the limbic system.

The Hypothalamus, "The Brain of the Brain" and the Pituitary

The **hypothalamus** is the most amazing part of the brain. It is tiny—about the size of a pea—and weighs about 4 grams. Its major job is to regulate many activities relating to survival: eating, drinking, sleeping, waking, body temperature, balance, heart rate, hormones, sex, emotions. When the hypothalamus is injured, the animal may not eat or drink, no matter how long it has been deprived of food or water. Conversely, stimulation or destruction of certain areas of the hypothalamus cause incessant eating, which can be fatal (Figure 4–7).

Through a combination of electrical and chemical messages, the hypothalamus directs the pituitary gland; the pituitary is the most important part of the neuroendocrine system, a major communication system between brain and body. The neuroendocrine system relies on chemical messengers called hormones. **Hormones** are chemicals manufactured and secreted by special glands, such as the endocrine glands; they are carried through the blood to specific "target cells" in the body. For example, in the male the gonadotropic (literally "toward the gonads") hormone is secreted by the pituitary and is carried to the testes by the bloodstream, where it stimulates the production of testosterone, the primary male hormone involved in both sex and aggressive behavior. The pitu-

Neuroendocrine System   See pp. 164–65.

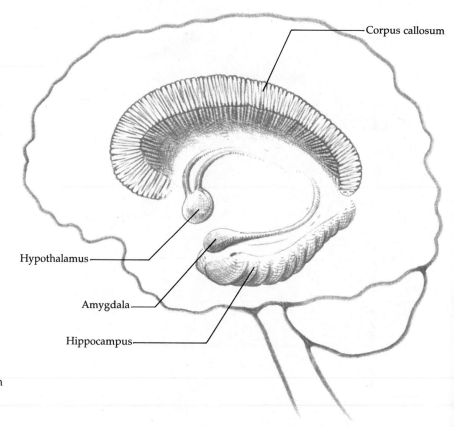

FIGURE 4–6
The Limbic System in Relation to the Cerebral Cortex
Centrally located between the cerebral hemispheres—which are connected by the corpus callosum—and in touch with the frontal lobes and the brain stem, the limbic system is ideally placed for coordinating many of the brain's operations.

itary synthesizes most of the hormones used by the brain to communicate with the major glands of the body (Figure 4–8).

The Hippocampus, Frontal Lobes, and the Amygdala

Information coming to the brain is processed through the hippocampus to determine if it is new or if it matches stored information. The **hippocampus** seems to be involved in three related limbic functions: learning, the recognition of novelty, and the storage of memory. Epileptic seizures often overstimulate and damage parts of the limbic system. When the hippocampus is affected, the result may be a loss or severe impairment of memory for events before and during the seizure.

The **frontal lobes** of the cortex are so intimately linked to limbic functions that many psychobiologists include them as part of the system.

FIGURE 4–7
Eating Itself to Death
When part of its hypothalamus was destroyed, this rat had no way to tell when it was satiated, so it gorged itself to a weight three to four times normal.

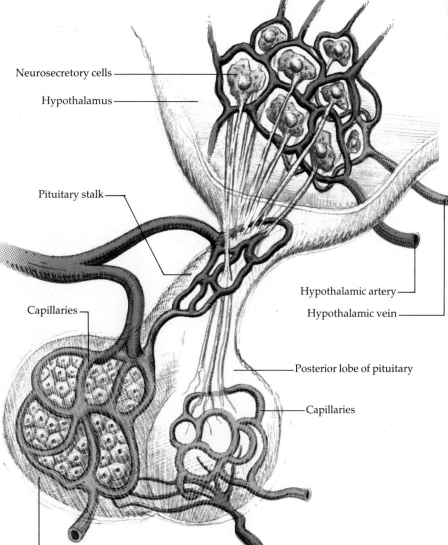

Neurosecretory cells

Hypothalamus

Pituitary stalk

Capillaries

Hypothalamic artery

Hypothalamic vein

Posterior lobe of pituitary

Capillaries

Anterior lobe of pituitary

FIGURE 4–8
The Vital Hypothalamus-Pituitary Link
The hypothalamus is able to integrate functions of the neuroendocrine and nervous systems because it is structurally connected to the cerebral cortex and to the pituitary gland, with which it communicates both by nerve impulses and by chemical messages sent directly or through the general bloodstream. (After Vannini & Pogliani, 1980)

Likewise, limbic functions in humans are under greater cortical control than in other animals. For example, animals, including humans, fight only when they are angry or frightened. What may keep boxers, for instance, from responding to slaps in the face and body as a real threat is the knowledge (stored in the cortex) that a boxing match is a game.

The **amygdala** is a small structure between the hypothalamus and the hippocampus. Its functions are not completely understood, but it appears to have something to do with the maintenance and gratification of internal needs of the body (Cotman & McGaugh, 1980).

CREATING ANEW: THE CEREBRAL CORTEX AND THE DIVIDED HEMISPHERES

The third level of the brain, the *cerebral cortex,* appeared in our ancestors about 50 million years ago. The cortex performs the functions that have greatly increased our adaptability. In the cortex decisions are made; the world is organized; our individual experiences are stored in memory; speech is produced and understood; paintings are seen; music is heard (Figure 4–9).

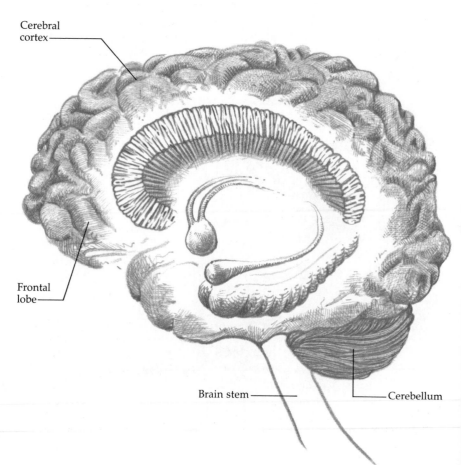

FIGURE 4–9
The Cerebral Cortex
The visible part of the brain is the surface of the cortex, which is thin and enfolded compactly to fit inside the skull. Fifty percent of the cortex is enfolded. The cortex is shown here in relation to the brain stem and cerebellum and to the limbic system, to which it is linked and which it surrounds.

The brains of all primates are divided into two hemispheres. But only in humans are these hemispheres specialized for different functions. This "lateral specialization" is the fourth level of brain organization. It is the most recent development in human evolution, less than four million years old, and perhaps "only" one million years old. The left hemisphere, which controls the right side of the body, also controls language and logical activities, things that happen in a specific order. The right hemisphere, which controls the left side of the body, controls spatial, simultaneous things—which happen all at once—and artistic activities. Each hemisphere is also divided into four different lobes: frontal, temporal, parietal, and occipital (Figure 4–10).

In the next two sections the cerebral cortex and divided hemispheres are discussed in detail. It will seem as though a lot is known about the cerebral cortex. Therefore, I feel compelled to say this: we know very little about *how* the cortex works. We know that certain *activities* are centered in the cortex. We know that memory is a cortical function, but we do not know where memory is stored or how—we do not know how we "retrieve" specific memories. We know that thinking and learning are cortical functions, but we do not know exactly how we "get" a new idea or what happens in the brain when we learn something new. Study of the higher brain functions of the cortex is, and probably always will be, the frontier of research in the neurosciences. Whether we can apply all our marvelous cortical abilities to unraveling the mysteries of the cortex's own operations is a challenging, perhaps impossible task.

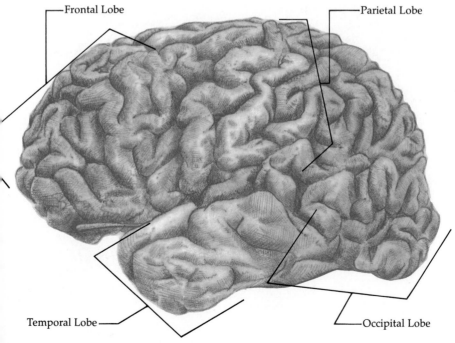

Frontal Lobe

Parietal Lobe

Temporal Lobe

Occipital Lobe

FIGURE 4–10
The Lobes of the Human Brain

The Cerebral Cortex

The **cortex** is the "executive branch" of the brain, responsible for making decisions and judgments on all the information coming into it from the body and the outside world. To do its job it performs three distinct functions: (1) it first receives information from the outside world; (2) it analyzes and compares it with stored information of prior experiences and knowledge, and makes a decision; (3) it then sends its own messages and instructions out to the appropriate muscles and glands.

The Sensory-motor Areas

The **sensory-motor areas** are located at the juncture of the frontal and parietal lobes (Figure 4–11). They are proportionately smaller in humans than in other animals (Figure 4–12). The sensory areas receive information about body position, muscles, touch and pressure from all over the body. The motor areas control the movements of the different parts of the body.

Figure 4–13 shows the body as it is represented in the brain. In the **"homunculus"** different parts of the body are distorted out of proportion to their physical size. The reason for this is that *the more complex the function, the more space the brain devotes to it.* Although the back is larger than the tongue, it makes fewer intricate movements and is less sensitive. Our hands are terribly important to us, giving us information on touch and pressure, and are also capable of extremely complex movements. In a homunculus of a cat's brain, very little space would be devot-

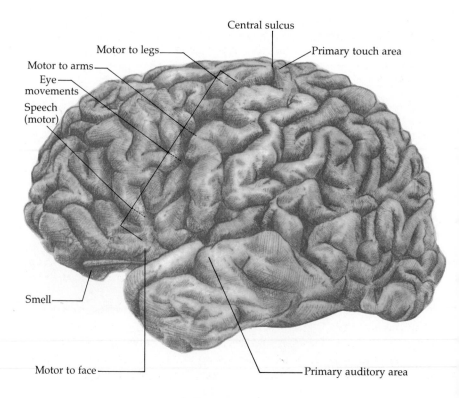

Central sulcus

Motor to legs

Primary touch area

Motor to arms

Eye movements

Speech (motor)

Smell

FIGURE 4–11
Sensory-motor Areas

Motor to face

Primary auditory area

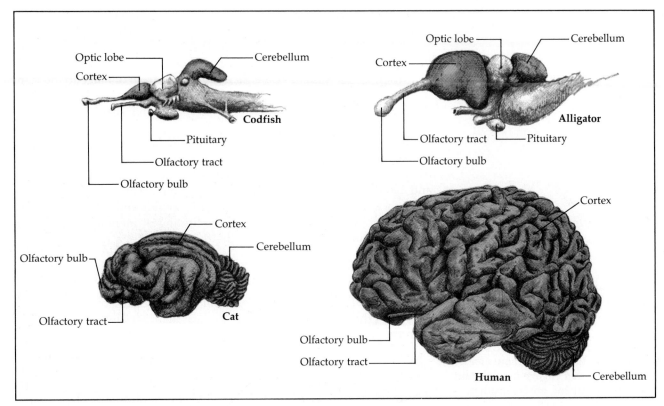

FIGURE 4–12
The Range of Complexity of Animal Brains
Although not drawn to scale, the differences between human and subhuman brains are obvious, particularly the proportionally smaller human sensory-motor areas and the vastly larger human cortex. (After Truex & Carpenter, 1964)

ed to its paws, which provide little sensory information, but a very large area would be devoted to the whiskers, which are far more sensitive (Teyler, 1978). Whiskers are also important to a mouse, as is seen in the fact that its whiskers' arrangement is reflected in the way the corresponding area of the animal's cortex is laid out (see Figure 4–14).

The Occipital Lobes: The Visual Cortex

At the rear of the brain are the **occipital lobes.** Because this area is devoted entirely to vision, it is often called the *visual cortex.* Visual information is sent from the eyes to the visual cortex and is analyzed for orientation, position, and movement. Damage to the occipital lobes can result in blindness even if the rest of the visual system is unaffected.

The Temporal Lobes

The **temporal lobes** (Figure 4–15) have several important functions. A small area in each lobe, about the size of a poker chip, is responsible for hearing; this part is often referred to as the *auditory cortex.* Other temporal lobe functions are involved with perception, memory, and dreaming.

Most of our knowledge of temporal lobe functions comes from people who have suffered some sort of damage to this region. In some cases dramatic hallucinations occur, while in others events occurring after the damage cannot be remembered. Severe damage to certain areas of the left temporal lobe may result in aphasia, language impairment. Here is how a person with temporal lobe damage acts: A man is interviewed in a hospital. His interviewer asks: "Can you tell me what work you have been doing?" He answers: "If you had said that, poomer, near the fortunate, tamppoo all around the fourth of marz. Oh, I get all confused!" (Gardner, 1978). Loss of visual memory results from damage to the right temporal lobe. In one test, people with right temporal lobe damage could not recognize portraits they had studied closely only two minutes before (Kimura, 1963).

When the temporal lobe is electrically stimulated, some people report the feeling of being in two places at once: the memory of an event and the present *coexist* in the person's consciousness. While fully conscious and aware of the operation going on, a person might suddenly feel he is also in a kitchen, 30 or 40 years before: the sounds and smells seem real. Recall that Wilder Penfield's dramatic finding of memory in the brain was made during stimulation of the temporal lobe: a person seems to *relive* specific past experiences.

The Frontal Lobes

The **frontal lobes** are the largest of the four lobes and oversee much of the rest of the brain's activity. This area has an especially rich connection with the limbic system. There is some evidence that an individual's initial appraisal of whether an event is threatening, dangerous or not is carried out in the frontal lobes. They are primarily involved in planning, decision making, and purposeful behavior. If the frontal lobes are destroyed or removed, the individual becomes incapable of planning, carrying out, or comprehending a complex action or idea, and unable to adapt to new situations. Such people are unable to focus attention and are extremely distracted by irrelevant stimuli (Luria, 1973). Although

Physical Stimulation of Memory See Chapter 1, pp. 6–7.

FIGURE 4–13
A Homunculus
of the Sensory-motor Areas
A cross section of the cortex is diagramed to show the relative space devoted to different functions. Parts of the body that engage in important activities involving great sensitivity—such as speech, touch, and dexterity—are shown much larger proportionally than their real relative size in the body. (After Penfield & Rasmussen, 1950)

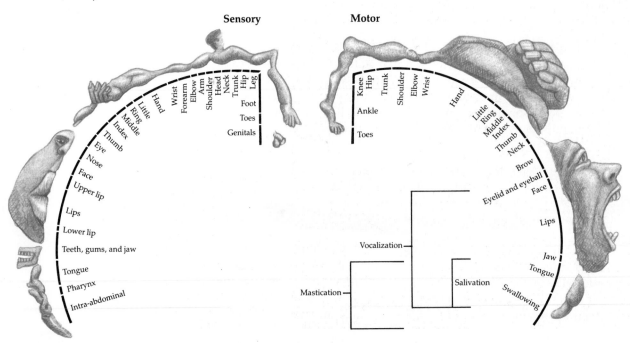

Sensory   Motor

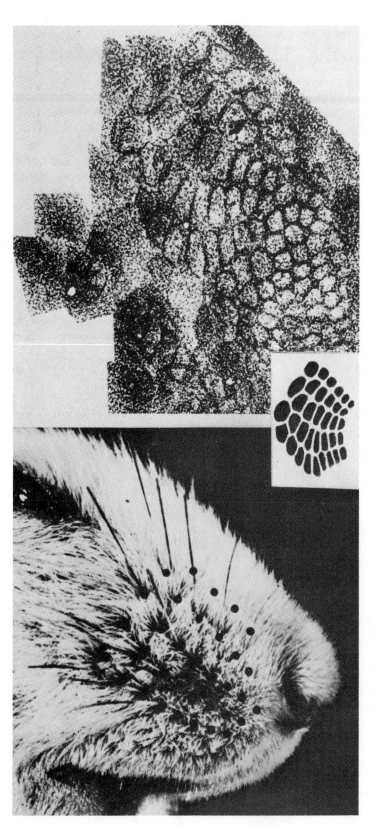

FIGURE 4–14
Brain Function and Structure
Whiskers are so important to a mouse that its brain has a section whose structure almost exactly reflects the external layout of the rat's head. For each row of whiskers in the bottom photograph, there is a row of patches of cells, each corresponding to a whisker, in the rat's cortex (top photograph and diagram inserted between photographs). (After Woolsey & van der Loos, 1950)

many of the most complex functions, such as language and consciousness, seem unimpaired, the loss of the ability to adapt and plan ahead makes all those other abilities useless.

Parietal Lobes

The **parietal lobes** seem to be involved in the *integration* and *analysis* of sensory input. It is probably here that letters come together as words and words are put together into thoughts.

Damage to the parietal lobes can result in a form of *agnosia* (not knowing). The English neurosurgeon Mountcastle (1976) studied a person with parietal lobe damage who was unaware of a whole side of his body, a condition called *amorphosynthesis*. Because his right parietal lobe was damaged, he ignored or did not "know" the left side of his body and of everything else. Drawings done by Mountcastle's patient are shown in Figure 4–16. Notice how all the numbers of the clock are crowded into the right half. Everything on one whole side of the world is either ignored or is crammed into the other side, as in the drawing of the clock. A person with damage to half the parietal lobe may only dress and groom one side of the body (Figure 4–17). Some individuals lose the ability to follow audio or visual cues and cannot recognize familiar objects by touch.

The Two Hemispheres

The cerebral cortex is divided into two hemispheres connected by an enormous structure of 300 million neurons called the **corpus callosum.** Each hemisphere is responsible for the opposite half of the body. The left

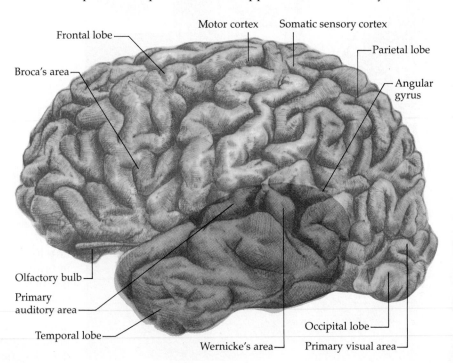

FIGURE 4–15
The Temporal Lobes
The left temporal lobe is here indicated and shown in relation to the rest of the left hemisphere.

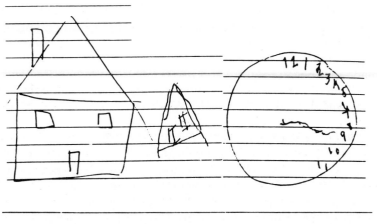

FIGURE 4–16
A One-sided View of the World
A patient with right parietal damage is unaware of the left side of things. The drawings of the watch—the top one made 2 days after the injury and the bottom one 7 days later—in which all the numbers are crowded into the right half of the watch face, show that the patient ignores left-hand external reality. (The far left house drawings are the physician's, which the patient tried to duplicate.) (After Mountcastle, 1976)

FIGURE 4–17
A Shattered Mind
Lovis Corinth, an important turn-of-the-century German artist, did the portrait of his wife (left) in 1910. The portrait on the right was done in 1912, after he had suffered a right-hemisphere stroke that, among other deficits, impaired his ability to render the left side of his subject.

side of the brain controls the right side of the body, the right side of the brain controls the left side of the body. In most right-handers language is the specialty of the left hemisphere, drawing of the right, although left-handers differ. These differences in function appeared at the time humans first began to make and use symbols (both language and art). One commentator has named this level of brain organization the "asymmetric-symbolic" level (Brown, 1977).

Some Facts about Hemispheric Asymmetry

The two hemispheres look about identical, but there are significant anatomical differences. An examination of fetuses and stillborn infants reveals that in 95 percent of the cases the left hemisphere is larger than the right (Geschwind & Levitsky, 1976). The enlarged area is called the *planum temporale* in the temporal lobe. The planum temporale is involved in speech and written language (Figure 4–18).

It has been known for centuries that damage to the temporal lobe of the left hemisphere causes aphasia, the loss of the ability to speak language. Damage to the right hemisphere results in impaired performance of spatial tasks, such as the ability to draw, or to recognize faces.

FIGURE 4–18
Asymmetry of the Cortex
In most people the left hemisphere of the cortex is larger than the right. The boxed drawing shows the temporal lobe in place on the left hemisphere. It is also shown cut loose and turned on end to expose the enlarged section called the planum temporale, which contributes to the brain's asymmetry. This asymmetry is thought to be due to the left hemisphere's linguistic dominance, which is centered in enlarged structures such as Wernicke's area.

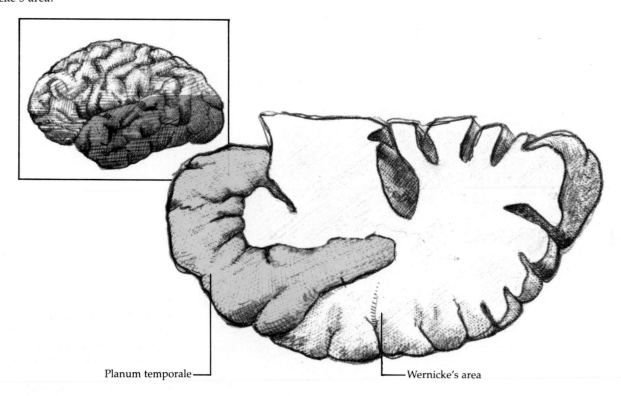

Planum temporale ⎯⏋   ⎣⎯ Wernicke's area

Left hemisphere

Although each hemisphere is specialized to handle different tasks, the division between them is not absolute—they are in constant communication with each other. Rarely is one hemisphere completely idle and the other frantic with activity. The left hemisphere is much more involved and more proficient in language and logic than the right; the right is much more involved in spatial abilities and "gestalt" thinking than the left. But it is oversimplified and misleading, even wrong, to assume that the two hemispheres are *separate* systems, "two brains." An activity as complex as language involves both hemispheres interacting with each other. If either hemisphere is damaged, the remaining "intact" hemisphere can take over, but this becomes less easy as we age. If the left hemisphere is damaged at birth, the right will take over language, although the person may be less adept at language than he or she would have otherwise been (Kohn & Dennis, 1974).

The "Split Brain"

The two cerebral hemispheres communicate through the corpus callosum, which joins the two sides anatomically. Roger Sperry and his colleagues, notably Joseph Bogen, initiated radical treatment for severe epilepsy in humans, in which the callosum was cut, producing a so-called **split brain** (Sperry, 1982).

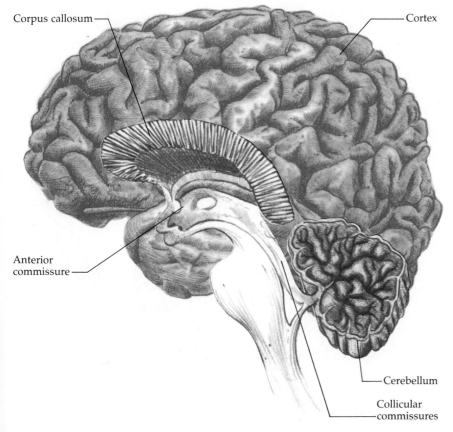

FIGURE 4–19
Splitting the Brain
In split-brain operations, commissures—connective nerve tissue, such as the corpus callosum, through which the two hemispheres communicate—are severed. This procedure has caused radical changes in patients' perception and behavior. (After Sperry, 1964)

After the surgery, if patients held an object, such as a pencil, hidden from sight in the right hand, they could describe it verbally, as would be normal. But if the object was in the left hand they could not describe it at all. Recall that the left hand informs the right hemisphere, which possesses only a limited capability for speech. With the corpus callosum severed, the verbal (left) hemisphere is no longer connected to the right hemisphere, which communicates largely with the left hand; so the *verbal apparatus literally does not know what is in the left hand*. If, however, the patients were offered a set of objects out of sight, such as a key, a book, a pencil, and so on—and were asked to select the previously given object with the left hand—they could choose correctly, although they still could not state verbally just what object they were taking. It was as if you were privately asked to perform an action and I were then expected to discuss it.

Another experiment tested the lateral specialization of the two hemi-

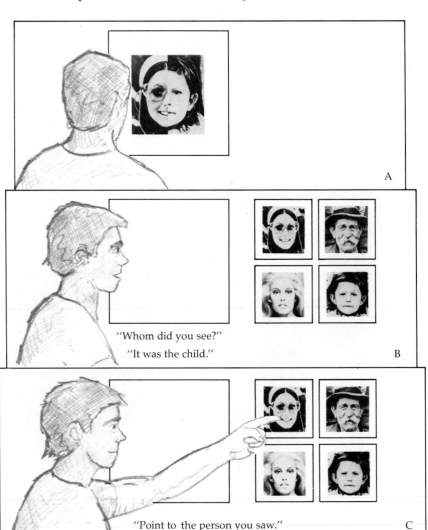

FIGURE 4–20
Hemisphere Specialization and Visual Input
A composite photograph of 2 different faces is flashed before a split-brain subject (A). When shown a group of photographs and asked to pick out the person he saw in the composite, he will *say* it is the face from the right half of the composite (B). But if asked to *point* out which one he originally saw, he will indicate the picture from which the left side of the composite was made (C). Such experiments strongly suggest the two hemispheres are independent to some degree, each performing different functions in different ways. (After Levy, Trevarthen, & Sperry, 1972)

"Whom did you see?"
"It was the child."

"Point to the person you saw."

spheres, using split visual input. The right half of each eye sends its messages to the left hemisphere, the left half to the right hemisphere. In this experiment the word "heart" was flashed before the patients, with the "he" to the left of the eye's fixation point, and the "art" to the right. Normally if any person were asked to report this experience, he or she would report having seen "heart." But the split-brain patients responded differently, depending on which hemisphere was responding.

When asked to point with the left hand to the word seen, the patients pointed to "he." When asked to point with the right hand, they pointed to "art." The simultaneous experience of each hemisphere was unique and independent of each other in these patients. The verbal hemisphere gave one answer, the nonverbal hemisphere another.

Most right-handed people write and draw with the right hand only, but many can also write and draw to some extent with their left. After surgery, Dr. Bogen tested the ability of the split-brain patients to write and draw with either hand. The right hand retained the ability to write, but it could no longer draw very well. (Figure 4–21). In copying the geometrical figures, the left hand certainly conveys the relationship of the parts, even though the line quality may be poor. Note the right hand's performance: the cross contains the correct elements, yet the ability to link the disconnected elements is lacking. No one could consider a cube a set of disconnected corners!

More recent tests of hemisphere functioning confirm that the right hemisphere is superior at part-whole relations, which might indicate that it is responsible for maintaining our internal representation of the world. Robert Nebes (1972) asked split-brain patients to match arcs of circles to completed circles. The right hemisphere was superior in accomplishing this task, which requires the ability to generalize from a segment to the whole.

The Workings of the Normal Brain

As startling as the split-brain studies are, an important question remains: How do the hemispheres operate in *normal* people doing *normal* things? One way we have of finding out what an intact brain is doing is

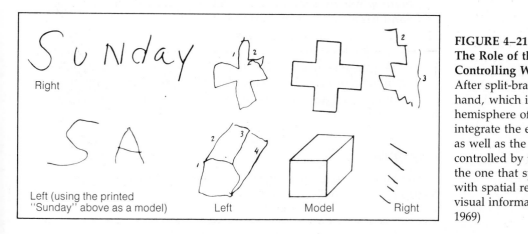

Right

Left (using the printed "Sunday" above as a model)   Left   Model   Right

FIGURE 4–21
The Role of the Hemispheres in Controlling Writing and Drawing
After split-brain surgery, the right hand, which is controlled by the left hemisphere of the cortex, cannot integrate the elements of a drawing as well as the left hand, which is controlled by the right hemisphere, the one that specializes in dealing with spatial relationships and other visual information. (After Bogen, 1969)

measuring electrical activity in the brain through an electroencephalograph (EEG). Brain activity is measured in waves. Alpha wave activity indicates an awake brain on "idle"; beta waves indicate an awake brain actively processing information. In one study (Galin & Ornstein, 1972) the right hemisphere showed more alpha activity than the left while the subject was writing a letter; the left hemisphere showed more beta. While arranging blocks in space, the left hemisphere showed more alpha than the right and the right hemisphere showed beta waves. When people write, they turn off the right side of the brain; while arranging blocks in space they turn off the left hemisphere.

More recent studies show that the primary factor in hemisphere specialization is *not* the type of information (words and pictures versus sounds and shapes) considered, but how the brain processes the information. A recent study compared subjects' brain activity while reading two types of written material: technical passages and two folk tales. There was no change in the level of activity in the left hemisphere, but the right hemisphere was more activated while the subjects were reading the stories than while reading the technical material (Ornstein, Herron, Johnstone, & Swencionis, 1979). This finding might be explained by examining the nature of the material. Technical material is almost exclusively logical. Stories, on the other hand, are simultaneous; many things happen at once; the sense of a story emerges through a combination of style, plot, and evoked images and feelings. Thus, it appears that language *in the form of stories* can stimulate activity of the right hemisphere.

In another experiment brain activity was recorded while subjects mentally rotated objects in space. This operation normally involved the right hemisphere. When asked to do the task analytically, by counting the boxes, subjects by and large "switched over" to their left hemisphere (Ornstein & Swencionis, in press). Thus, in problem solving, people apparently can use their hemispheres differently at will.

THE LANGUAGE OF THE BRAIN

The brain works by sending and receiving information from inside the body and from the outside world in electrical and chemical codes. That "language" of the brain is found in the action of brain cells. Every brain process works through the action of a single type of cell, the neuron. The brain's language is made up of very simple signals sent at varying rates among billions of neurons. Neurons fire an electrical charge. It is in the *pattern of firing* of the neurons of the brain that all experience is to be read—if we can learn to read it.

Neurons

The brain is made up of specialized cells called **neurons** (Figure 4–23). Neurons are the building blocks of the brain and nervous systems. The

FIGURE 4–22
Studying the Workings of the Brain with an Electroencephalograph (EEG)
The electrodes in the skull cap worn by this subject are connected to an electroencephalograph (EEG) that measures the brain's electrical impulses, which are recorded as various kinds of brain waves during different kinds of brain activity.

EDUCATION, SOCIETY, AND THE HEMISPHERES

Some critics have seized on the results of research on hemispheric specialization to justify their rejection of conventional science and educational systems. Like many new discoveries, the nature of the brain's specialization has often been misrepresented. Many concerned people in psychology, education, medicine, and environmental sciences realize that those of us in industrialized societies have not developed our abilities to think in terms of whole systems. When they read about current research in hemispheric specialization, some respond as if all the world's problems would be solved if we simply suppressed our left hemispheres and ran ourselves and society with only the "intuitive" thought of the right hemisphere. Although such conclusions are simplistic, some people have at least realized that our intellectual training overemphasizes analytical skills.

As a result of our preoccupation with isolated facts, it is not surprising that we face so many problems whose solutions depend upon our ability to grasp the relationship of parts to wholes. The problem is not that our technology is "leading us to destruction," but that our technical innovations have outstripped our perspective and judgment. We live in a world that is often difficult for us to understand.

Split- and whole-brain studies have led to a new conception of human knowledge, consciousness, and intelligence. All knowledge cannot be expressed in words, yet our education is based almost exclusively on the written or spoken word. One reason it is difficult to expand our ideas of education and intelligence is that as yet we have no standard way of assessing the nonverbal portion of intelligence.

The two ways of knowing are not competitive but are complementary. Without a holistic perspective our ability to analyze may be as useless to us as it was to the right hand of the split-brain patient. Similarly, an intuitive insight is lost unless we have a way to express it. Many people whom we consider "unintelligent" or "retarded" may in fact possess a different kind of intelligence and may be quite valuable to society. The neurologist Norman Geschwind (1972) has put the dilemma this way:

One must remember that practically all of us have a significant number of special learning disabilities. For example, I am grossly unmusical and cannot carry a tune. We happen to live in a society in which the child who has trouble learning to read is in difficulty. Yet we have all seen some dyslexic children who draw much better than controls, i.e., who have either superior visual-perceptual or visual-motor skills. My suspicion would be that in an illiterate society such a child would be in little difficulty and might, in fact, do better because of his superior visual-perceptual talents, while many of us who function well here might do poorly in a society in which a quite different array of talents was needed to be successful. As demands of society change, will we acquire a new group of the minimally brain-damaged?

nucleus of the neuron is called the *cell body*. It contains the biochemical apparatus for powering the electrical charge and for maintaining the life of the cell. The **axon** extends outward from the cell body. The axon (Figure 4–24) is the "transmitter" end of the neuron; signals sent from the neuron exit through the axon. The **dendrites** (Figure 4–24) which look like the branches of a tree, are the "receiving" end; they receive information from the axons of other neurons. Because of the extensive branching of the dendrites, one neuron is able to communicate with thousands of other neurons (Figure 4–25).

The Neural Impulse: Action Potential

If you could see the brain working, it would be like millions of miniature explosions going on and off each instant as neurons fired their electrical charges. In the pattern and composition of those explosions lie our thought and individuality. An enormous amount of research over the past few years has begun to uncover the secrets of that neural code.

Communication between neurons is carried out by **neurotransmission.** Neurotransmission is accomplished through the release of chemical molecules called *neurotransmitters.* Like a battery, even when a neuron is at rest it possesses an electrical charge. This charge is called the *resting potential.* When the neuron is adequately stimulated by another neuron, it fires. The firing of the neuron releases its stored energy. The neural impulse of a firing neuron is called the **action potential.** The action potential sweeps down the axon. Once it has fired, the neuron is temporarily depleted of energy and does not immediately fire again. This period of time is called the *absolute refractory period.* The neuron then "recharges" a bit and enters the *relative refractory period.* In this period, firing is possible only if there is a greater than normal stimulus. These refractory periods are not long; they are measured in thousandths of a second.

The Myelin Sheath

The axons of many neurons are coated with a fatty substance called the **myelin sheath.** This sheath begins to develop in infancy and contributes to the weight added to the brain after birth. It has three main functions:

1. *Insulation.* By covering the neuron, it prevents loss of electrical potential, just as a cable protects an electrical wire from "leaking" its signals.
2. *Acceleration of transmission.* There are periodic gaps (nodes of Ranvier) in the surface of the sheath. The electrical impulse leaps across the gaps and is transported directly to the next gap. These gaps thus speed up the rate of neural conduction.
3. *Isolation.* For a system to function, the right information must get to the right place. The myelination prevents a neuron from communicating randomly with other neurons.

FIGURE 4–23
The Parts of a Neuron

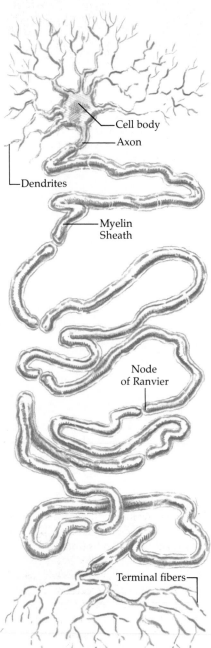

Cell body
Axon
Dendrites
Myelin Sheath
Node of Ranvier
Terminal fibers

Neurotransmission

The action potential inside a neuron is *electrical,* but the transmission of the neural impulse from one neuron to the next is *chemical.* Between the axon of one neuron and the dendrite of the next is a space called the **synapse** (Greek for "connection"). A neuron transmits its signal to the next neuron at the synapse between the two. This is called **neurotransmission.** Neurotransmission across the synapse is achieved by chemicals. The transmitter chemicals are stored in pouches, called *synaptic vesicles,* at the terminal of the axon. When the action potential arrives at the synapse, it initiates a sequence of steps that eventually convey the signal from one neuron to another.

The neuron sending the information is called the *presynaptic* neuron; the neuron receiving information is the *postsynaptic* neuron. In summary, neurotransmission works as follows:

1. Neurotransmitters are stored inside synaptic vesicles in the terminal button of the presynaptic neuron.
2. When the action potential reaches the synapse, it causes some of these neurotransmitters to be released into the synaptic opening, called the *synaptic cleft.*

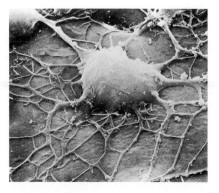

FIGURE 4–24
The Dendrites of a Single Neuron
This highly magnified photograph shows the branching dendrites through which the neuron can receive information from many other neurons.

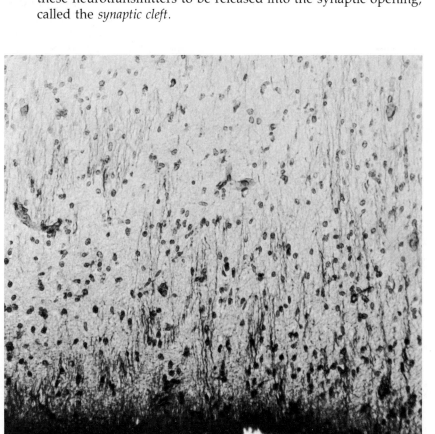

FIGURE 4–25
Neurotransmission: A Living Network of Brain Cells in Continual Communication
Only about one in every hundred neurons can be seen in this picture of a small section of the cerebral cortex, giving you an idea of the intricacy and extent of the network of cells communicating with one another through neurotransmission.

3. The transmitters cross the cleft and either *stimulate* or *inhibit* the firing of the postsynaptic neuron (the neuron receiving the message).
4. After transmission the whole process is deactivated (the refractory period). Some transmitters may break down, some return to the axon of the presynaptic neuron; this process is called *re-uptake*.

The Neurotransmitters

The brain probably has hundreds of different neurotransmitters—new ones are discovered almost monthly. **Acetylcholine** (*ACh*) is one of the major transmitters in the nervous system. ACh is related to the arousal of the organism; it is most concentrated in the brain during sleep. ACh conveys information from the brain to the body. The Amazon Indi-

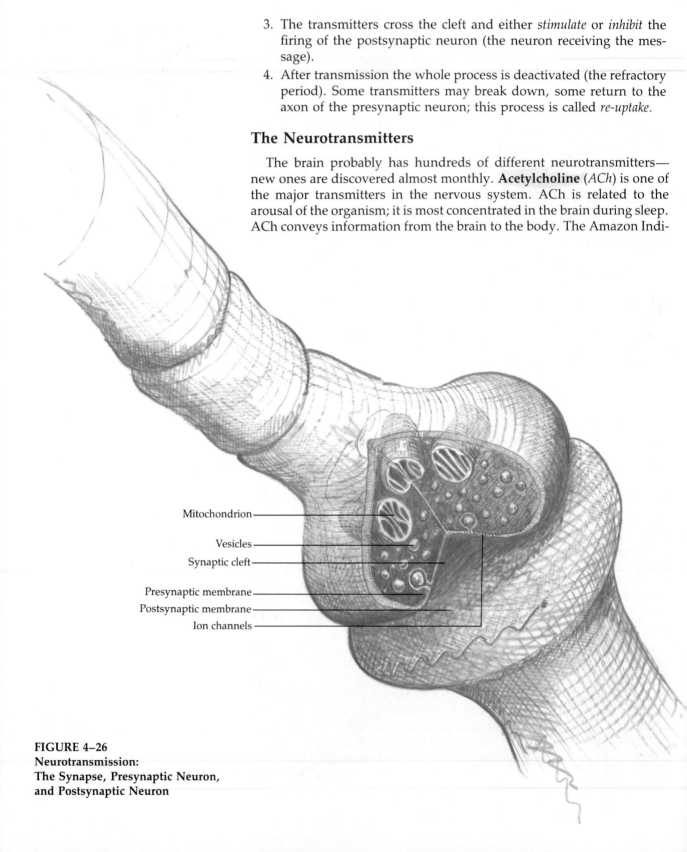

Mitochondrion

Vesicles

Synaptic cleft

Presynaptic membrane

Postsynaptic membrane

Ion channels

FIGURE 4–26
Neurotransmission:
The Synapse, Presynaptic Neuron,
and Postsynaptic Neuron

LOCK AND KEY

Heroin produces exultation; LSD, even in minute quantities, can produce hallucinations. How does this happen? We are born with certain "locks" within us, inside the nervous system. This is why drugs like heroin are so powerful. The drugs are the keys that open these locks.

The nature of this relationship has been discovered only in the past few decades: it is fundamental to our research into how the brain works, how human-made chemicals, like drugs, affect the brain, and how psychological disorders can be aided chemically. The *shape* of the drug or the neurotransmitter molecule is the "key." It "fits" a receptor whose shape matches it, as a key fits into a lock. This lock and key relationship describes how the chemical messages of the body connect with their target cells. The messenger molecules move through the bloodstream or across synapses until they fit the receptors designed for them. Drugs stimulate body processes because they, like neurotransmitters, can open these "locks" within.

Many mental disorders, such as schizophrenia, may be due to alterations in neurotransmission. Many psychoactive drugs, like cocaine, work because they affect the process of neurotransmission. Cocaine may prevent re-uptake, so that the firing of the neurons involved does not cease. This is how cocaine functions as a stimulant.

ans knew the results, though not the mechanism, of neurotransmission when they dipped their arrows in the poison curare. Curare is fatal because it interferes with ACh transmission and paralyzes the victim, who will die quickly without some assistance in breathing.

Various individual neurotransmitters are organized into specific "chemical pathways," transmission networks that connect parts of the brain in complex mosaics unimagined even a few years ago. These pathways are especially noteworthy:

Norepinephrine. The transmitter norepinephrine (formerly called adrenaline) is important in the coding of memory and in the reward system of the brain, a group of structures that are activated in pleasurable moments. The pathway connects the outer brain stem to the cortex. Norepinephrine is found outside the brain in the autonomic nervous system.

Dopamine. The dopamine pathway connects the limbic system to the cortex. It also participates in the brain's reward system and in the control of motor activity. Parkinson's disease, in which the sufferer exhibits severe motor tremors, is caused by a lack of dopamine and can be aided by administration of the drug L-Dopa, which is transformed by the brain into dopamine (Figure 4–27).

Serotonin. The serotonin pathways are widespread in the brain and connect the brain stem and reticular activating system to the cortex and to the limbic system at the hypothalamus and hippocampus. Serotonin controls sleep and many activities associated with sleep. Loss of seroto-

Brain Stem and Limbic System See pp. 137–42.

nin causes insomnia. The drug LSD seems to affect the serotonin system by blocking the firing of serotonin neurons. Because hallucinations are common in LSD trips, many researchers feel that serotonin may be involved in hallucinations and even psychosis. Since serotonin is an inhibitor of neural firing, blocking its transmission speeds up sensory transmission. The great increase in all kinds of neuronal activity leads to a breakup of the normal mode of perception.

Mood and Neurotransmitters

People have long believed that internal substances affect mood, disposition, and even personality. The ancient Greeks believed there were specific body *humors* that determined mood. A characteristically angry person was thought to have an excess of *bile*; a calm one, too much *phlegm*; hence the descriptions "bilious" and "phlegmatic." Although this specific idea now seems wrong, it may be that different concentrations of the various neurotransmitters may affect temperament and mood. Many of the transmitters are involved in excitability, sleep and dreams, and hallucinations.

HOW THE BRAIN CONTROLS THE BODY

The marvelous complexities of the neural and chemical organization of the brain, and of its four different levels of organization, all serve one master: the body. The end point of brain activity is action: plans and ideas as well as walking, turning, dancing, or following something with

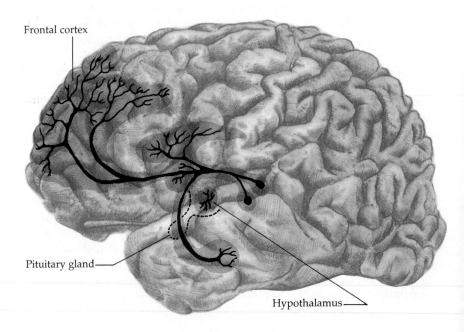

Frontal cortex

Pituitary gland—

Hypothalamus—

FIGURE 4–27
Dopamine Pathways in the Brain

the eyes. The brain, through its neural and chemical connections, monitors activity in every cell in the body. The brain communicates with and controls the body via two kinds of systems: the nervous system and the neuroendocrine system.

The Brain and Nervous Systems

The nervous systems that link the brain to the body are the central nervous system and the peripheral nervous system.

The Central Nervous System

The brain and spinal cord together make up the **central nervous system** (CNS). Just below the brain and physically joined to it is the spinal cord. It is the central trunk of the nervous system. It delivers both the brain's commands to the body and the body's messages to the brain.

Reflexes that protect the body from damage are commanded from the spinal cord. A reflex is an immediate, usually inborn response. Place your hand on a hot stove and you will immediately withdraw it, literally "without thinking." The spinal cord handles such emergencies without involving the brain. These are the only movements that take place without the activity of the brain.

The spinal cord contains all the basic elements of the nervous systems. There are three types of neurons in the spinal cord:

1. **Afferent neurons** bring information to the brain from the sensory system.
2. **Efferent neurons** take messages from the brain and activate muscles and glands.
3. **Interneurons** connect the afferent and efferent neurons.

The spinal cord is encased in the vertebrae and is further protected by the spinal fluid, which acts as a shock absorber. The spinal cord is subject to so many shocks in the course of a day that the average person is a half inch shorter at night than in the morning.

The Peripheral Nervous System

Commands to the muscles move through the **peripheral nervous system** (PNS). Nerves flow from the spinal cord into the muscles and organs of the body. Information is gathered about body states, the position of muscles and limbs, the internal states of organs. If something is awry, action will be taken.

The vast network of nerves in the PNS (Figure 4–29) ultimately reach every organ and muscle of the body. The PNS is divided into two parts: the somatic and autonomic.

1. The **somatic nervous system** (SNS) controls the voluntary movements of the body, as when you reach for a glass or pick up a pencil. These movements originate in the sensory motor area of the brain. Afferent nerves convey information about the skin, sensory organs, muscles, and joints to the brain; efferent nerves bring instructions from the brain to the muscles.

2. **The autonomic nervous system** (ANS) is primarily responsible for running the automatic processes of the body. The heart beats about 70 times per minute without us instructing it to beat; the kidneys purify the blood without our telling them to; the liver and gastrointestinal tract, too, work outside our conscious control. The ANS is largely under the

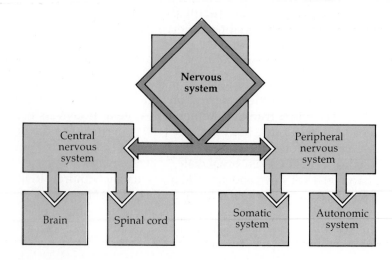

FIGURE 4–28
Subdivisions of the Human Nervous System

direct control of the limbic system (usually without the involvement of the cortex), and this regulates emotional reactions, such as crying, sweating, and stomach pains.

The ANS is divided into two systems:

The **sympathetic system** prepares the internal organs for emergencies, when there are extra demands on the body. It operates "in sympathy" with the emotions, like an accelerator, telling the body to "go." Signs of sympathetic system activation are sweating and other symptoms of arousal. The sympathetic nervous system is usually activated by the unusual: emergencies, ecstasy, excitement.

The **parasympathetic system** is more conservative. It acts like a brake on the sympathetic system and returns the body to normal after an emergency. Typically, when an exciting event has passed, heart rate slows and the dryness of the mouth begins to abate. These changes occur not only because sympathetic activation ceases but because the parasympathetic system actively slows heart rate and deactivates certain internal organs.

The two kinds of signal, "go" and "slow down," are carried by different nerve circuits, and the messages are carried by different neurotransmitters. Norepinephrine carries the sympathetic message, ACh the parasympathetic message. The sympathetic neurons are centralized in the brain, acting on their target from a distance. The parasympathetic system is decentralized; each ganglion (collection of neurons) is located near the organ it serves.

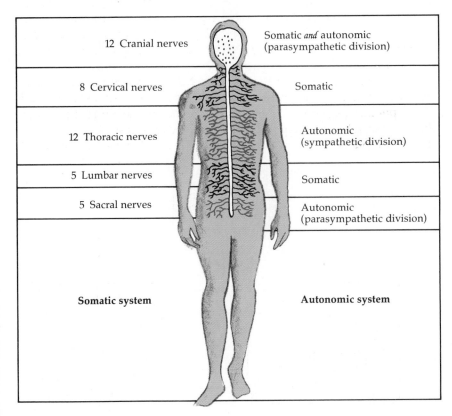

FIGURE 4–29
The Network of Nerves in the Peripheral Nervous System

The Neuroendocrine System

Another way the brain controls the body is via the **neuroendocrine system,** which is made up of the ANS and the endocrine glands. One general way to think of the brain is that each neuron is similar to a little gland, and the brain is a great organ of secretion.

The Brain's Chemical System—
The Neuroendocrine System

The **pituitary** is the control gland of the endocrine system. It lies below the hypothalamus in the limbic system. Many important behaviors, such as sex, are under its direct control. The pituitary also controls many glands, such as the adrenal and thyroid glands. It synthesizes a wide variety of hormones. A **hormone** is a chemical messenger, a molecule secreted by specialized cells called *neurosecretory cells.* Hormones are larger molecules than neurotransmitters and are carried by the bloodstream to specific locations, where they stimulate production of other hormones. Neuroendocrine communication operates on the lock-and-key principle: a hormone secreted into the bloodstream passes many organs until it fits into the intended receptor.

Hormone regulation works through feedback. To stimulate the thyroid gland, the pituitary produces *thyroid releasing hormone* or TRH.

Lock-and-Key Principle   See p. 159.

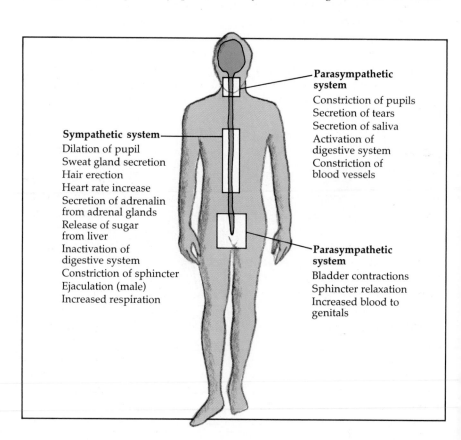

Sympathetic system
Dilation of pupil
Sweat gland secretion
Hair erection
Heart rate increase
Secretion of adrenalin
from adrenal glands
Release of sugar
from liver
Inactivation of
digestive system
Constriction of sphincter
Ejaculation (male)
Increased respiration

**Parasympathetic
system**
Constriction of pupils
Secretion of tears
Secretion of saliva
Activation of
digestive system
Constriction of
blood vessels

**Parasympathetic
system**
Bladder contractions
Sphincter relaxation
Increased blood to
genitals

FIGURE 4–30
**The Functions of the Divisions
of the Autonomic Nervous System**

When the thyroid receives TRH, it produces its own hormone, *thyroxin,* which it releases into the bloodstream. Some thyroxin reaches the pituitary, which then measures the amount of the hormone and either increases or decreases production of TRH. (Figure 4–31). Similar feedback processes operate for other hormones.

Adrenal Glands

The adrenal glands are activated in emergency situations. They have two parts: the outer *adrenal cortex* and the inner *adrenal medulla.* When activated by the ANS, the adrenal medulla secretes epinephrine and norepinephrine. Both of these stimulate the cardiovascular (heart-lung) system. Adrenal gland activity is coordinated with the ANS during emergency situations. If there is injury to the body, adrenal cortisol, an anti-inflammatory agent, travels to the site of the injury.

The Healing Brain: Endorphins and the Intrinsic Pain Relief System

The brain has its own pharmacy; it controls pain and has a significant function in healing. It regulates the conveyance of hormones to wounds, regulates the internal state of organs, and maintains homeostasis. It has recently been discovered that the brain also produces a number of *specific chemicals* related to the direct relief of pain.

For centuries it has been known that opium and its derivatives relieve pain. Drugs like morphine and codeine are routinely used to relieve the pain of injury on the battlefield or after surgery. The brain contains specific receptors for opiates, which fit the receptors by the lock-and-key principle. These receptors are heavily concentrated in the limbic system and in the spinal cord. During pregnancy there are a large number of opiate receptors in the placenta to protect the fetus from pain and shock.

The opiate molecule blocks pain by fitting receptors in areas of the limbic system that seem to be pathways of pain. The discovery of the opiate receptors in the brain led inevitably to the question: what is the brain doing with receptors for a substance (opium) extracted from a poppy? It is unlikely that our evolution was directed toward providing the human brain with receptors for refined products that would be synthesized 150 million years later! Researchers found that the brain *produces its own pain-blocking compounds,* and that the opiates work because they fit the receptors for that built-in system.

These "internal opiates" were identified in the mid 1970s (Snyder, 1980), and are a class of proteins called **endorphins,** meaning "the morphines within." By now, several varieties of endorphins have been identified, among them the *enkephalins* ("in the head"). Enkephalins seem to act as general *modulators* of nervous system activity: they enhance or suppress responsiveness to stimuli. It was initially thought that if endorphins could be extracted in quantity they would provide a safe, nonaddicting pain killer. Unfortunately at least one endorphin, beta-endorphin, is even more addictive than refined opiates such as heroin.

At about the same time endorphins were discovered, another dra-

FIGURE 4–31
Hormone Regulation
This schematic exemplifies the feedback process that regulates hormone production. Here, the level of thyroxin in the blood may trigger the pituitary to produce thyroid releasing hormone (TRH); this signals the thyroid to produce thyroxin, thereby raising the level of that hormone in the blood, which on reaching the pituitary informs it that TRH production can be reduced.

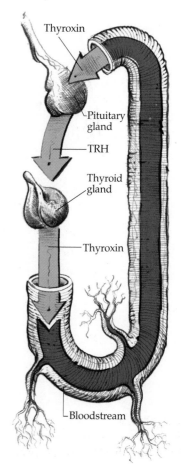

Thyroxin

Pituitary gland

TRH

Thyroid gland

Thyroxin

Bloodstream

matic series of studies was taking place. Electrical stimulation of various specific sites in the brain was shown to enhance or reduce the experience of pain. The most relief from pain comes when areas containing the most endorphin receptors are stimulated. Stimulation in those areas produces marked relief in patients with intractable pain. Repeated stimulation brings increased relief (Beers, 1979). For one patient, the need for stimulation became less and less until minimal and infrequent stimulation was necessary.

The discovery that the brain produces its own painkillers and that it possesses an intrinsic analgesia (pain relief) system has stimulated new research on the many social and psychological factors that directly affect brain chemistry, health, and healing. In one study, young patients with strong postoperative dental pain were given a *placebo,* a nonactive substance whose curative effect lies solely in the taker's belief that it will help. A substantial percentage of patients reported reductions in pain. After the placebo was given, students were given naloxone, a drug that blocks the effect of opiates and endorphins. Naloxone removed the pain-killing effect of the placebo. That means that the patient stimulated his own endorphin production just by believing he had taken a real pain-killing drug (Levine & Fields, 1979).

Naloxone also blocks other effects, such as pain relief from acupuncture (Berger, Watson, Akil, Barchas, & Li, 1980). These findings have led many researchers to wonder whether psychological factors such as emotional state, mood, "will to live," and the doctor-patient relationship may not turn out to be as important as drugs in that they promote the synthesis of endorphins and perhaps other compounds in the brain. It could be that the healing rituals of "primitive" societies and folk medicine have real biological effects by helping to stimulate the brain's own healing system.

THE INDIVIDUAL BRAIN

You may not realize it, but people's brains are as different as their noses. The brain is also responsive to different experiences. The environment determines the specific language or languages that one speaks, and early experience affects brain size as well. There are even temporary reactions caused by changes in local environment, such as nutrition and air quality.

Brain Growth with Experience

Environmental conditions play a greater role in the brain development of humans than in any other animal. Although it is commonly thought that at birth the neurons begin to make connections and that these connections increase as we age and acquire experience, the opposite appears to be the case (Greenough, 1975). There are many *more* connections in the brain of an infant than an elderly adult. Development seems to be a matter of "pruning" the original connections rather than making many new ones. Consider this about infant babbling: in the first weeks, the child utters almost *every sound of every known language* (Miller, 1951) and later on *loses* the ability to make sounds that are not in the language he or she has learned to speak. There is thus a universe of potential sound patterns available to us at birth, but we *learn* only a few of them. Similarly, the brain may be "set up" at birth to do a myriad of different things, but we only get around to doing a few of them.

Severe malnutrition may cause inadequate brain development, a smaller brain than normal, and severe mental retardation (Livingston, Calloway, MacGregor, Fischer, & Hastings, 1975). In controlled experiments rats deprived of normal food show distortions in brain structure and even shrinkage of certain brain structures. The illustration on the top of Figure 4–32 shows a cell from "deprived" ones.

The brain, like a muscle, grows in response to certain experience—the neurons actually become larger. Rats brought up in an enriched environment have a larger cortex than rats brought up in a deprived one. This developmental process goes on as long as the organism lives and is active. Brain growth can be stimulated in *old* rats with stimulation for as little as one week (Connor & Diamond, 1982; Diamond & Connor, 1981). The brain is *modifiable* and it grows with experience and stimulation.

The Brain of the Left-hander

In most right-handed people, language and other sequential abilities are present in the left hemisphere; spatial abilities and simultaneous thinking reside primarily in the right hemisphere. But in left-handed people, brain organization is often different (Herron, 1980).

There are three types of hemispheric organization in left-handers:

1. Those whose cortical organization is similar to right-handers.
2. Those whose organization is reversed.
3. Those who have language and spatial abilities in both hemispheres.

EEG studies of left-handers typically show all three patterns of hemisphere organization in different individuals (Galin, Ornstein, Herron, & Johnstone, 1982).

Left-handers are a distinct minority (about 10 percent of the population is left-handed) and face some difficulty living in a right-handed world. It is quite difficult for them to write any of the "alphabet" languages, which were designed by and for right-handers. Some left-handers write in a "hooked" position, while others write in the same way as right-handers (Figure 4–33). There is controversy about whether being left-handed affects intellectual abilities. Many people argue that because a great percentage of left-handers have "mixed dominance" (language in both sides of the brain) spatial ability is interfered with. However, most investigators who have studied large numbers of subjects show equivocal results (Miller, 1971).

What is less equivocal is the cultural bias against things of the left. The

FIGURE 4–32
Malnutrition and the Brain
A brain cell from an undernourished rat is clearly less developed, with fewer and smaller dendrites. (After McConnell & Berry, 1978)

Undernourished

Normal

word "gauche" (meaning awkward) is the French word for left. The word "sinister" comes from the Latin for left (*sinistra*). Whether brain differences manifest themselves as personality or intellectual traits is unknown, but the existence of strong brain differences is certain.

Sex Differences in the Brain

There are many physical differences between sexes in adulthood. The most notable differences are the reproductive systems, size, body weight, and muscle mass. Males are more active at an early age than are females (Barsley, 1979). Males are characteristically superior to females in gross motor control and spatial abilities (Witelson, 1976).

Behavioral differences between the sexes have physical expression in the brain. Boys show earlier right hemisphere development than girls. Witelson (1976) asked boys and girls 3 to 13 years old to match held objects to visually presented shapes. At 5, boys showed a superiority on the task with objects held in the left hand (compared to their right). Girls did not show a similar superiority until 13. Girls, however, are slightly better than boys on left hemisphere tasks in the grade school years (Buffrey & Gray, 1972). Bryden (1973) presented spoken syllables to boys and girls in kindergarten, second, fourth, sixth, and eighth grades. The girls showed a clear right ear (left hemisphere) advantage by the fourth grade; boys were much later in developing this asymmetry.

In addition to the differences in hemispheric maturation, the hemispheres in males are more specialized than those in females. The representation of analytic and sequential thinking is more clearly present in the left hemisphere of males than in females. For instance, damage to the left hemisphere interfered with verbal abilities more in males than in females (McGlone, 1980).

The Changing Brain

The brain continuously changes in response to a changing environment. Some alterations are in response to temporary, short-term conditions; some to long-range and permanent conditions.

Short-term Changes in the Brain

The relative concentration of the neurotransmitters changes rapidly after a meal. A meal of eggs increases the available levels of ACh in the brain. A meal rich in carbohydrates increases the brain's supply of serotonin (Fernstrom & Wurtman, 1975). Neurotransmitters also seem to respond to changes in the air. Hot, dry winds such as the foehn in central Europe, the scirocco of the Arabian desert, and the Santa Ana of Southern California, are often associated with outbreaks of violence, including suicide (Krueger, 1978). These "ill winds" contain a preponderance of positive ions. An ion is the electrical charge attached to a gaseous molecule. Air full of negatively charged ions has a refreshing and stimulating effect. Negative ions predominate around waterfalls, in clean mountain air, and at beaches, and disappear in polluted urban

FIGURE 4–33
The Trials of Being Left-handed
Whether using the so-called hooked position or the ordinary way of writing, trying to write a language designed for right-handers is but one of the problems of left-handed people in a largely right-handed world.

centers or enclosed spaces. Ionization of the air has a direct effect on the serotonin system of the brain (Krueger, 1978) and the growth of the cortex. Rats raised in a negatively ionized atmosphere have a cortex 9 percent larger than those in nonionized atmosphere (Diamond, 1980).

CONTINUITY BETWEEN ORGANISMS, AND THE STUDY OF BRAIN FUNCTION

A central question in brain research is how brain structures relate to brain functions. But the brain does not give up its secrets easily. Most of our information on the brain comes from the study of lower organisms, people with severe brain damage, and a "listening" technique called EEG.

The principles of neural organization are similar in all animals. Organisms as low on the evolutionary scale as crabs, shrimp, and crayfish are prized by psychobiologists for the light their neural organization sheds on our own. Limbic and cortical functions are studied in rats and monkeys. The advantage of using lower organisms is twofold. Not only are the cells bigger and easier to study, but it is also possible to conduct experiments that would be impossible with humans; for example, removing specific areas of the brain and observing the resulting change in behavior. Because the human brain is so different from that of other organisms, certain functions— language, inventive thought, decision making—can only be studied in humans. As the uniquely human functions are approached, investigation becomes increasingly difficult, since we obviously cannot tamper experimentally with a human brain. People who have suffered strokes and lesions in the brain have provided most of the useful knowledge we have of higher human functions.

A stroke is the cessation of blood to a specific area of the brain; when that occurs the affected brain tissue dies. The investigator then observes which functions of the brain are impaired and can make deductions about the relation of that area of the brain to the particular lost function. If an area is lesioned, or cut, either by accident or surgery, the investigator can similarly observe the change in function. Here is a personal account by a person who had a lesion in the left side of the brain:

I'll look to the right of me and be horrified to discover that half of my body is gone. I'm terrified—sometimes when I'm sitting down I suddenly feel as though my head is the size of a table, every bit as big—while my hands and feet and torso become very small—Another annoying thing that happens is that sometimes when I'm sitting on a chair I suddenly become very tall, but my torso becomes terribly short and my head very very tiny—no bigger than a chicken's head. You can't imagine what this is like even if you tried—it's just got to happen to you. (Luria, 1973)

When the **electroencephalogram** (EEG) was invented in 1929, psychobiologists were able for the first time to listen in on the electrical activity of the brain. Electrodes are attached to the skull at certain locations; these electrodes record electrical impulses and send them via an amplifier to the electroencephalograph, which prints it out. The amount of electricity the brain produces is correlated to different states of arousal and activity of the organism. These states are discussed in terms of waves.

Delta waves (1–3 Hz [cycles per second]) usually occur during sleep.

Theta waves (4–7 Hz) indicate drowsiness and other borderline states of mind.

Alpha waves (8–12 Hz) signal relaxed alertness.

Beta waves (over 12 Hz) indicate brain cells actively processing information—alert and working.

To find out the brain's response to a specific event, researchers record the *evoked potential*. The **evoked potential** is the sum of the electrical activity in the brain associated with a specific event. There is so much "noise" in the brain, the evoked potential is usually an average of the brain's response over many trials to separate the unique response to a particular stimulus from all others. The unique wave found in "he spread warm bread with socks" is an evoked potential. (See Figure 4–2.)

Some newer methods to determine brain function include studies of blood flow to the cortex and **positron emission tomography,** which measures glucose uptake deep within the brain, enabling investigators to "see" into the deeper working of the brain for the first time.

There are also consistent mood changes associated with ionization: an increase in negative ionization seems to elevate mood (Krueger, 1978).

Long-term Alterations

The brain also changes its chemistry, and size, in response to long-term environmental conditions. The brain can often rearrange its organization to compensate for accidents and changes of demands. People with left hemisphere damage can be trained to produce language using the right hemisphere, although this flexibility decreases with age. The right hemisphere takes on language functions in young children who have suffered severe damage to the left hemisphere (Kohn & Dennis 1974). In the deaf, for example, areas of the temporal cortex normally used for the processing of speech sounds are used instead for processing visual information (Neville, 1977).

When a person learns a second language, the brain representation of language changes. Sometimes when the second language is learned, the first language *may migrate from the left hemisphere to the right*. In others, the second language may occupy only the right hemisphere, or it may be represented in both (Albert & Obler, 1978).

The brain is continually changing and developing, responding to influences ranging from the language one hears in infancy to the meal just eaten. The brain has evolved to adapt to conditions in a changing world; our brain still changes continuously to aid us in our adaptation to an unpredictable world.

Summary

1. The brain is primarily concerned with: (a) running the body—controlling body temperature, blood flow, digestion, and heartbeat, among many other bodily processes; (b) response to internal and external changes, through an immense network of sensory systems, and (c) adaptation—the ability to respond in a flexible manner to changes in the world.

2. The brain evolved over millions of years and, in the human, consists of four different levels of organization: the brain stem, the limbic system; the cortex, and the divided hemispheres.

3. The *brain stem* is the area of the brain that evolved earliest and is concerned with basic systems of life support.

4. The *limbic system* is concerned with more advanced systems of life support such as temperature regulation and the maintenance of homeostasis in the body. The limbic system is also involved in emotional reactions.

5. The *cortex* is the "executive branch" of the brain. It is responsible for making decisions and judgments on the information reaching it. It includes these areas of function: (a) the sensory-motor areas, which are largely concerned with the processing of sensory information and the issuance of motor commands; (b) the occipital lobes, concerned largely with the processing and analysis of visual information; (c) the temporal lobes, responsible for hearing

and involved with perception, memory, and dreaming; (d) the frontal lobes, concerned with planning actions, decision making, and purposeful behavior; and (e) the parietal lobes, concerned with integrating and analyzing sensory input. Although the lobes are not fully understood, this is probably where letters come together to make words, words join to make thoughts.

6. The *divided hemispheres* of the brain are not unique to humans, but their division of functions is unique. In the left hemisphere of most right-handed people is the ability to produce spoken and written language, while the right hemisphere seems to contain the ability to produce art. The right hemisphere also is involved in the ability to recognize faces and to move in space.

   Evidence for this hemispheric duality comes from the studies of the "split brains," those in which the connection between the two hemispheres, the *corpus callosum*, is severed. This operation results in two independent hemispheres. The results of testing "split-brain" patients show that each hemisphere is responsible for different functions. Further evidence comes from the study of normal people. The brain's electrical activity, called the "electroencephalogram" or EEG, is recorded, and signs of differences in electrical activity over the hemispheres are analyzed. The results show that the two hemispheres are activated differently in different situations: In speaking, for instance, the left hemisphere is active, the right, relatively idle.

7. The brain operates in electrical and chemical codes. Every brain process works through the action of a single specialized cell called a *neuron*. Neurons fire electrical charges and secrete chemicals across *synapses*,—the gaps between two neurons. There are about 10 billion neurons in the brain and ten times that many supporting cells.

8. Neurons "fire" an electrical potential called the "action potential" within their own cell body and outward through the *axon*. However, the transmission from one neuron to another is chemical,—a process called *neurotransmission*. The transmitter chemicals are stored in synaptic vesicles, tiny "pouches" within the neuron. When the action potential reaches the synapse, it causes some of these neurotransmitter chemicals to be released into the synaptic opening. The transmitters cross this opening and stimulate or inhibit the firing of the "postsynaptic neuron"—the neuron receiving the message. After transmission, the process is deactivated.

9. Of the many neurotransmitters organized into "chemical pathways"—special connections within the brain—these are especially noteworthy:

   1. The *norepinephrine* pathway is important in the coding of memory, and connects the brain stem to the cortex.
   2. The *dopamine* pathway connects the limbic system to the cortex and is involved in the control of motor activity.
   3. The *serotonin* pathways are widely dispersed in the brain. They connect the reticular activating system to the cortex and to the limbic system

10. The brain communicates with the body through the *nervous system* and the *neuroendocrine system*. The nervous system is composed of:

    1. The central nervous system (CNS), which includes the brain and spinal cord. The CNS is involved in reflexes, which are actions that do not involve the cortex.
    2. The peripheral nervous system (PNS), which carries information to and

from the muscles of the body. The PNS is divided into two parts: the somatic nervous system, which controls voluntary movements such as picking up a glass; and the autonomic nervous system, which controls the automatic processes of the body such as heartbeat.

The pituitary is the master gland of the neuroendocrine system. Neuroendocrine regulation of the body is accomplished when the pituitary secretes special chemical messengers called *hormones,* which are released into the bloodstream and stimulate further activity in their target locations. Neuroendocrine communication works on the lock-and-key principle: a hormone secreted into the bloodstream passes many organs until it fits its intended receptor.

11. The brain produces a wide variety of chemicals, most of which are yet to be discovered. One class of chemicals that has been discovered is the *endorphins* (including enkephalins). Endorphins seem to act as general moderators of activity. They have been shown to affect pain relief. They also have profound effects on mood. Their molecular shape is similar to substances that are taken to alter mood, such as opium.

12. Left-handers differ from right-handers in that some have a reversed hemispheric specialization to that described in section six of this summary, above. Some left-handers also have language and spatial abilities dispersed in both hemispheres.

13. There are differences, too, between the male and female brains. Boys show earlier right hemisphere development than girls, who show earlier left hemisphere development than boys. In addition, the two hemispheres of males seem more specialized than those of females.

14. The brain is responsive to short-term changes in its state. Ionization of the air affects the serotonin system and changes mood. Ingested food can change brain chemistry: a meal rich in carbohydrates can also affect serotonin.

15. The brain also can change dramatically over the long term. A stimulating environment, for instance, can stimulate brain growth even in very old organisms. The learning of a new language can also affect the existing organization of function in the brain. We do not know yet how much the brain is capable of change.

Terms and Concepts

acetylcholine	endorphins
action potential	evoked potential
afferent neurons	frontal lobes
amygdala	hippocampus
autonomic nervous system	homeostasis
axon	"homunculus"
brain stem	hormones
central nervous system	hypothalamus
corpus callosum	interneurons
cortex	limbic system
dendrites	myelin sheath
dopamine	neuroendocrine system
efferent neurons	neuron
electroencephalogram	neurotransmission

norepinephrine
occipital lobes
parasympathetic nervous system
parietal lobes
peripheral nervous system
pituitary
positron emission tomography
reticular activating system

sensory-motor areas
serotonin
somatic nervous system
split brain
sympathetic nervous system
synapse
temporal lobes
thalamus

Suggestions for Further Reading

The Behavioral and Brain Sciences.
A quarterly journal, published since 1978, that presents important research areas such as cortical function and intelligence and presents commentary from many scientists. Difficult, but gives a good view of the controversies in the field.

Kolb, B., & Whishaw, I. Q. (1984). *Fundamentals of human neuropsychology.* (2nd ed.). San Francisco: W. H. Freeman.
A good summary of the field.

Ornstein, R., Thompson, R., & Macaulay, D. (1984). *The amazing brain.* Boston: Houghton Mifflin.
Describes in drawings how the brain was "built" and the functional architecture of the cortex. Amplifies material in the text.

Springer, S., & Deutsch, G. (1984). *Left brain, right brain.* (2nd ed.). San Francisco: W. H. Freeman.
Summarizes the enormous work on the functions of the two hemispheres.

174

Chapter 5

Sensory Experience

INTRODUCTION

For years my house had been plagued by squirrels. They nested under the eaves of the roof, held meetings in the recesses of the attic. When they got hungry, they made a nice meal of the side of the house. For years I harbored the most destructive thoughts about them. Then one day I saw an advertisement for a "rodent eliminator." "Rids you once and for all of all pesty rodents!" I was not only delighted, but filled with ideas of how the rodent eliminator would torture the critters that brought me such grief.

The gadget arrived. It was not a giant flame thrower or an electric cage, but a small box with an on-off switch. The instructions advised to set the box near the "rodent infestation" and "watch the rodents disappear forever." I followed the instructions.

When I turned the machine on, nothing happened as far as I could tell. Suddenly, however, there was a great scurrying commotion. The squirrels were running over one another to get out, many more than I had imagined. So many that they had to eat a new hole in the house to get out. Even so, I was delighted.

The rodent eliminator works by emitting a very high frequency wave, one that is beyond the range of human hearing but within the sensitivity of most rodents. Our worlds are different: I heard nothing; the squirrels, in the words of the manual, "will feel that a 747 jet has landed inside their heads." No sound to me and, now, no squirrels either.

Our world appears to us as it does because we are built the way we are. Every organism, then, lives in a somewhat unique world determined by its senses. Consider yourself and a cat, looking at chocolate cake. You see a brown cake and think about tasting sweetness. The cat does not usually see colors or taste sweetness. A cat, however, can see things at night that you cannot, because it has a reflective layer in its eye that doubles the intensity of light.

To function, all organisms need reliable and specific information about the outside world. In this chapter we will examine what kinds of information humans obtain through their senses. Although there is an amazing variety of ways to extract information from the world, humans are limited to sight, hearing, taste, touch, and smell. We also have senses that keep us informed of our internal world: we maintain balance, coordinate and control body movements, and sense internal conditions, like pain and nausea.

The job of the senses is to ''catch'' a small and specific bit of the outside world and ''take it in.'' In later chapters we will see how the mind processes, interprets, and uses this information.

Principles of Sensory Experience

In our discussion of sensory experience, we will need to refer to three important principles of psychology. Since these principles apply to many aspects of human experience, they will prove important elsewhere in the book. They are selectivity, change, and comparison.

Selectivity. The senses are both sensors and censors. Obviously, our senses give us access to and provide information about the outside world. But if we experienced *all* the sensations in the world, our experience would be chaotic. The air in the room you are sitting in now is filled with various forms of energy: radiant electromagnetic, infrared rays, sound waves, radio waves, and more. (See Plate 2.) Yet you are aware of only a small portion of that energy. What we call light is a miniscule portion of the band of radiant **electromagnetic energy.** (See Plate 2.) Selection, then, involves both *inclusion* and *exclusion*. Our senses

The human sensory system simplifies what we experience, selecting important or exceptional stimuli for the brain to respond to. Here, people are responding to an unusual stimulus.

select what is important and *keep the rest of the world out*. And each sense is "designed" to extract a very specific kind of information. You *see* light, you do not hear it. You cannot taste an apricot by squeezing it into your ear!

The abilities of a species evolve because they offer it some adaptive or survival value and suit the natural habitat of the species. Each organism's sensory system simplifies the world to which it needs to attend. The cat has evolved as a basically nocturnal animal and so needs its reflective eye. Insects *see* infrared radiation, which we feel as warmth, a frog sees only things that move.

Change.   The kind of information the senses transmit to the brain concerns *changes* in the external environment; what is important to us are *new events:* the sun coming up, a sudden loud noise, a change in weather. The sensory systems are designed to notice beginnings and endings of events; they cease responding in between. When an air conditioner is turned on in a room, you notice the hum. Soon you become habituated to the noise. When the machine is turned off, you again take note, this time because of the *absence* of the noise. The senses are thus interested in news: loosely speaking, "Let me know when something happens."

Comparison.   How do the senses recognize change? A sensory change is a *difference* in a stimulus from one moment to the next. Because one sensation always follows and precedes another, individual sensations can be compared. One stimulus is louder, softer, brighter, dimmer, warmer, colder, greener, or redder than *something else*.

We compare *relative* differences between stimuli. Put a three-way bulb (50-100-150 W) in a lamp in a dark room. Turn on the lamp: The differ-

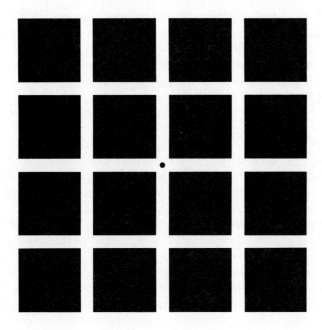

FIGURE 5–1
Stare at the dot at the center of this figure. Those shadowy squares at the intersections of the white lines do not actually exist in the drawing. They are "seen" only because of the way your sensory systems work. (After Verheijen, 1961)

ence between darkness and 50-watt illumination is great. But the next two increases in light, from 50 to 100 and from 100 to 150, do not have the same effect. Although the change in the physical stimulus is exactly the same, you hardly notice the difference.

HOW THE SENSES SIMPLIFY AND ORGANIZE THE WORLD

The senses are the outposts of the brain. All the information about the world comes through the senses. The world is full of different forms of physical energy that have different effects on the body, whether it is the bittersweet taste of chocolate or the sight of a brilliant dawn. While it is the brain that determines these experiences, it is the senses that provide the raw materials of experience.

The senses connect the physical and psychological worlds. In this section we will cover three main areas: (1) applications of the principles of selectivity and adaptation; (2) how the physical and psychological worlds are related; and (3) how physical energy, such as light, is translated into the language of the brain, and how it becomes our experience. This last point is one of the fundamental mysteries of psychology.

Simplification and Selectivity

"Our world" is much simpler than the physical complexity of the entire external world. A primary job of the sensory systems is to discard irrelevant stimuli and to select for transmission to the brain only that small portion of stimuli that is relevant.

The first major basis of selection is the biological nature of the senses themselves. Although there are other ways to obtain information about the world, we have only the methods of sight, hearing, taste, smell, and touch available to us. Second, within each sense only a limited range of stimuli is received in the body. For example, the eye responds to only a minute portion (one-trillionth) of radiant electromagnetic energy. What we see, then, is less than *one-trillionth* of the energy that actually meets the eye. Like other creatures, we are economical; we sense only what is necessary for our survival. The purpose of selectivity is to simplify the world.

Consider an animal that simplifies even more than we do. Jerome Lettvin and his associates (1959) at Massachusetts Institute of Technology devised an experiment in which visual stimulation could be offered to one eye of an immobilized frog. The frog was placed so that its eye was at the center of a hemisphere 7 inches in radius. Small objects were placed in different positions on the inner surface of this hemisphere by means of magnets and could be moved around in the space inside the hemisphere.

The investigators measured "what the frog's eye tells the frog's brain"—the electrical impulses sent to the brain by the eye. There are literally an infinite number of different visual patterns that could be presented to a frog—colors, shapes, movements, and various combinations of all of these. However, when various objects, colors, and patterns were presented to the frog, the investigators noticed a remarkable phenomenon. Out of *all* the different kinds of stimulation present, *only four kinds of "messages" were sent to the brain.*

These four messages contained information relating directly to the two most important aspects of a frog's survival: obtaining food and escaping danger. The first message provided a general outline of the environment. Two of the messages formed a kind of bug-perceiving system: one detected moving edges; the other responded to small dark objects entering the field of vision. Frogs only trap and eat live bugs. A frog surrounded by food that did not move would starve to death, because it has no means for detecting unmoving objects. The fourth message responded to sudden decreases in light, as would happen when a large enemy approaches. The frog's brain is thus "wired" to ignore all but extremely limited types of information. Although higher-level animals, ourselves included, are not as restricted in our sensory experience as the frog, all sensory systems simplify their organism's world by the act of selection.

Sensory Adaptation: Change and Comparison

Adaptation

Once messages from the outside world are selected for transmission to the brain, they are *further simplified.* The senses respond most vigorously to beginnings and endings of events; they respond less to constant stimulation. This decline in response is called *sensory adaptation.* Sensory adaptation reduces the number of irrelevant sensations we experience and therefore the world we experience, allowing us to focus on new events in the environment.

Comparison

Although each sensory system can discriminate millions of different gradients of stimulus, there is not a specific receptor for, say, each shade of color or sound tone. This is an important part of how we are built: we rarely, if ever, experience the same situation twice, so it would be uneconomical to have a system that responded anew to each stimulus. Thus, sensory systems operate primarily by comparison. Our judgments are comparative ones: the color we see at one moment is brighter, redder than the one we just saw; a sound is louder or more complex than an earlier one. (See Plate 3.)

A demonstration of sensory adaptation, change, and comparison: Fill three bowls with water: one hot, one cold, and one tepid. Put one hand in the hot water and the other in the cold water. Wait a few minutes. Now place both hands in the tepid bowl. Notice that the hand that was in the hot water feels cold, while the hand that was in the cold water feels warm. Both hands *adapted* to their relative temperatures. Then, when the hands were in the tepid bowl, they signaled a *change.* Although both hands were in the same bowl of water, each responded differently to it. The particular message of change each hand signaled to the brain is based on a *comparison* of two events.

How the Physical and Psychological Worlds Are Related

The senses relate the external physical world and internal psychological experience. The measurement of this relationship, called *psychophysics*, was the first idea of investigation of scientific psychology in the late nineteenth century. Using the methodology and techniques of physics as their model, the first psychologists tried to determine precisely how changes in the outside world affected the internal world of human experience. They pursued their investigations in a rather straightforward way: they clanged bells, sounded tones of different timbres, and shined lights of varying degrees of brightness at people and then measured how much a stimulus had to change in order for a person to report a change in experience. Here we will discuss first the concept of thresholds and then discuss some of the general psychophysical principles that underlie human sensory experience.

Thresholds

There are some absolute limits to what we can sense, limits set by the range of physical energy to which the senses respond. A light must attain a certain intensity before we notice it; a sound must be loud enough for us to hear it. The least amount of physical energy necessary for us to notice a stimulus is called the **absolute threshold.** The absolute threshold is defined as the minimum strength for a stimulus to be *noticed* by an observer 50 percent of the time.

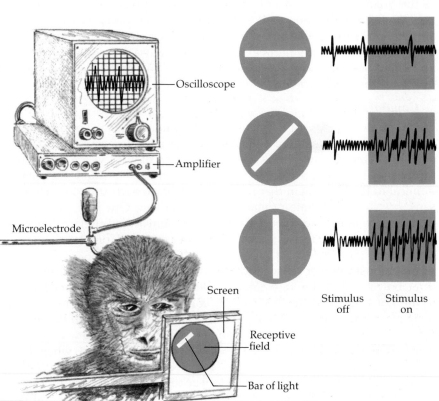

FIGURE 5–2
Measuring Cortical Response to Visual Stimuli
The apparatus on the left monitors how a single neuron in the lightly anesthetized monkey's visual cortex responds to stimuli from a moving bar of light in various orientations. The oscilloscope readings on the right show that the cell makes no response when the stimulus is off or when the monkey is shown a horizontal bar of light, some response to a bar at 45°, and considerable response when a vertical bar of light is the stimulus.

OUR SENSITIVITY

Average absolute thresholds for the five senses have been determined by careful measurement; they are approximately:

Vision: a single flame 30 miles away on a dark, clear night.

Hearing: a watch ticking 20 feet away in a quiet place.

Taste: 1 teaspoon of sugar dissolved in 2 gallons of water.

Smell: 1 drop of perfume in a six-room apartment.

Touch: the wing of a fly alighting on your cheek from a height of one centimeter (Galanter, 1962).

The absolute threshold is not the amount of energy required to *activate* the sensory system, but the amount of energy required for us to *experience* the stimulus. Although the senses have absolute limits, they can be activated with little energy. The eye responds to the smallest quantity of light, the ear to movements in the air only slightly greater than those of the air molecules themselves; although we rarely, if ever, notice these phenomena. But, of course, most sensory experiences are not "absolute." Real experience is composed of things that are brighter, darker, heavier, lighter, or sweeter than other things. An important factor in sensory experience is the *discrimination of differences in stimuli*. This minimum increase in a physical stimulus necessary to notice a difference is called the **difference threshold** or, more commonly, the **just noticeable difference (j.n.d.).** Unlike the absolute threshold, the j.n.d. is not constant. The experience of a stimulus is always relative to its surrounding context. So, for example, if it takes one additional candle to notice a difference in illumination in a room with 10 candles, then in a room with 100 candles you would need 10 additional candles to notice a difference. There would be no noticeable difference if 101 rather than 100 candles were lit (Galanter, 1962).

The Discoverers of General Principles of Sensation: Weber, Fechner, Stevens

Weber's Law.   The first major principle of sensation was discovered by Ernest Weber (1834). He noted that *equal changes in physical intensity do not produce equal changes in experience*. This means that the relationship between the inner world and external world is not a simple one. A single candle flame emits a fixed amount of physical energy, but it is experienced differently depending on the surrounding circumstances. In a darkened room, it provides enormous illumination; in a bright room, it is hardly noticed.

Although the psychological world does not have a one-to-one relationship with the physical world, Weber noted that there is a consistent relationship between them. The amount of added energy in a stimulus required to produce a j.n.d. is always the same proportion of the stimulus. For example, if a 64-watt light is required to notice a change in illumination from 60 watts, then 128 watts would be needed to detect a change from 120 watts. This consistent proportional relationship, known as Weber's Law, is stated mathematically as follows:

$$\frac{\text{CHANGE IN STIMULUS}}{\text{STIMULUS}} = \text{CONSTANT}$$

In our example, $\frac{4}{60} = \frac{1}{15}$ $\frac{8}{120} = \frac{1}{15}$

Fechner.   Gustave Fechner continued Weber's search to discover how the psychological world responds to external reality. Fechner's insight was that it is not the absolute *differences* between lights, sounds, and such that our senses are designed to notice, but the relative intensity of things. Thus, when danger is approaching, the important thing to know is *how fast* it is approaching, not merely how much louder one threatening sound is than another.

A system built to notice relative differences provides great flexibility and makes good sense from an evolutionary point of view. One sensory psychologist writes:

> Our sensory systems are designed to weigh heavily the ratios between stimulus intensities rather than the differences between them. It is not too difficult to understand why such a sensory system is useful. . . . Imagine yourself sitting in front of a fire surrounded by forests, without any effective weapons, listening to the growls of a large and hungry animal. The most important information would be the ratio between the loudness of two successive growls. If the present growl is twice as loud as the last one, you know that the animal has covered half the distance toward you in that time. So you know that it will be arriving in just about that much time! That information is really much more important than estimating the actual loudness of each growl or the actual difference in loudness of two growls. (Ludel, 1978)

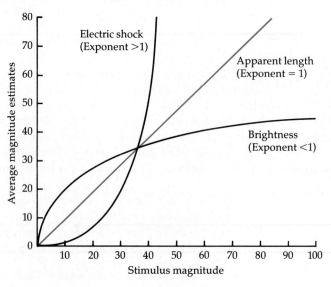

FIGURE 5–3
Power Curves for Different Stimuli
There is great variation in the power curves charting the magnitude of your experience of such stimuli as pain (electric shock), apparent length, and brightness. (After Stevens, 1961)

Stevens.   A third principle, discovered by S. S. Stevens, is that the *different senses transform the information they select differently.* This principle, called the **Power Law,** states that *within each sensory system* equal ratios of stimulus intensity produce equal ratios of change in experience. When these relationships are charted on a graph, they produce characteristic curves. Note in Figure 5–3 that the curves for the experience of length, brightness, and pain are very different (Stevens, 1956).

Scaling sensory experience on a graph reveals a lot about how we are built and the function of our different sensory systems. The flat line that represents the experience of length indicates that the relationship between our experience of length and actual physical length is direct. This makes sense because we do not often have to estimate very long distances visually. On the other hand, we encounter an extremely large range of brightness: we can see a single candle flame on a dark night 30 miles away, and we are able to glance at the sun, which is about 1,000 billion times brighter. Since there is such an enormous range of brightness to judge daily, our sensory system has to attenuate, or turn down, that range because a lot of brightness information has to be assessed in a very small "space." The flattened curve of brightness on the graph indicates that brightness information is indeed compressed. The pain curve is also a good representation of the experience of pain. Because it is important to be aware of potential injury as fast as possible, the experience of pain is amplified, not attenuated. So, a *small amount of pain gets our undivided attention very quickly.* The upward curve on the pain graph shows that we react very strongly to pain. Our amplified response to pain makes it an extremely effective early warning system for possible bodily harm.

Even a small amount of pain gets your attention quickly.

Psychophysics has thus revealed four major related principles. (1) There is a consistent relationship between changes in the physical world and changes in experience. (2) These relationships are proportional. (3) Each sense system has a different internal representation of the outside world. (4) The internal representation of these relationships (shown in Figure 5–3) reveals how closely tied our senses are to our survival.

How Physical Energy Is Changed into Experience: Transduction

Although each sense responds to a different form of physical energy, the brain has only one way of receiving and responding to information. That way is neural firing. Thus, another function of the senses is to transform specific kinds of physical energy, such as waves in the air and mechanical pressure (touch), into the electrical or chemical activation of nerve cells.

The senses routinely perform two miracles. First, each sensory organ transforms a particular kind of physical energy into neural firing. This process is called **transduction.** Each sense has specialized receptors responsible for the transduction of external energy into the language of the brain. The eye transduces light, the ear transduces soundwaves, the nose transduces gaseous molecules. Second, at some point in the sensory and brain system, there is a second transformation: neural firing becomes experience. These two miracles occur every moment of our lives, and are so routine that we are unaware of them. We are on our way to understanding how the first miracle works, but everyone in science remains completely mystified by the second.

VISION

Vision is our dominant sense. Most of our information about the world comes in through our eyes. This is not true for other animals. The sense of smell is much more important for dogs. James Gibson (1966) has classified the basic functions of vision, pointing out that vision is primarily responsible for the control of almost all the basic actions necessary for living in the human world:

Detecting the layout of the surroundings. We can tell the difference between the sky and the earth; we notice large features of the environment and can distinguish objects and other animals.

Detecting change or sequence. We can distinguish between day and night, between fine and gross movements, and between motion and events in the world.

Detecting and controlling movement. We must be able to see what we are doing and where we are going. If we did not have visual feedback our movements would be uncontrolled.

The Eye

Recall that the eye transmits to the brain only a trillionth of the mechanical energy that reaches it. The eyes are like highly sensitive security guards. They let light in but keep out irrelevant stimuli. The most common and difficult question about sight is: "Where is the 'image' we see?" You can see what a camera sees by looking through the lens, but the eye does not work like the camera. The brain does not "see" the image on the retina. Neural impulses, not images, are received by the brain. The visual system works more like television. Your television set does not receive a whole picture, only coded patterns of radiant electromagnetic energy that are translated into colors and shapes.

The eye is the most complex of all the sense organs. In the *retina*, a single layer inside the eye, there are over 120 million receptor cells called *rods*, and 6 million receptor cells called *cones*. The *optic nerve* that connects the eye to the brain contains over a million nerve cells. (Figure 5–4).

Light first enters the eye through the **cornea,** a transparent membrane that covers the front of the eye. It travels inside the eye through the *pupil*, which is an opening in the *iris*, the colored part of the eye. The iris is composed of two kinds of muscles, circular and radial. The circular muscles make the pupil smaller; the radial muscles open it up making the pupil larger. As with the aperture of a camera, the size of the opening of the pupil determines the amount of light that is let in.

Light then passes through the *lens*, which focuses it. The lens is held in place by the interocular (literally, "inside the eye") muscles, which

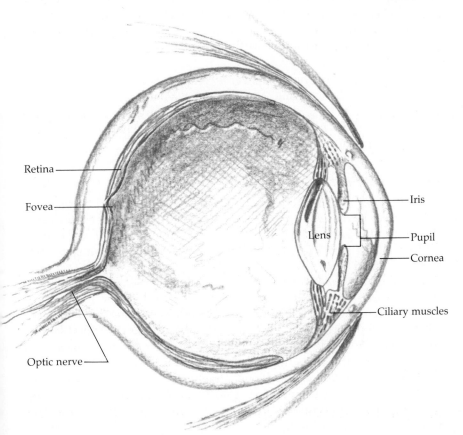

FIGURE 5–4
Major Structures of the Human Eye

pull the lens and change its shape to focus on objects at different distances. If all is working well, the light is put into sharp focus at the retina, at the back of the eye.

The Retina

The **retina** is the center of the process of vision. It begins development as part of the brain, but buds out to become part of the eye in the embryonic period. The retina is comprised of *neural tissue* and is about the thickness of this page. Its job is to transduce waves of light energy (which comes to the eye in the form of electromagnetic stimulation) into neural impulses. The retina has three main layers of nerve cells:

1. **Photoreceptors** ("photo" comes from the Greek word for light). There are two types of photoreceptors: the *rods* and the *cones*. They contain photochemicals that respond to light. (See Figure 5–5 and Plate 4.) (The rods and cones will be discussed in detail in a separate section.)

2. **Intermediate layer.** Three kinds of cells in the intermediate layer all have the job of making connections to the other cells. The *bipolar cells* take information from the rods and cones to the third layer of cells, called *ganglia* (singular: ganglion). The *horizontal cells* transfer information from rods and cones horizontally. The *amacrine cells* transfer information from rods and cones and all cells in the intermediate layer and send it to other intermediate layer cells or to cells in the ganglia (Figure 5–5).

3. **Ganglion cells.** The third layer is composed of ganglion cells. Each ganglion cell has a long *axon*, the part of a neuron that carries information from the cell to other neurons. All the axons from the eye's ganglion cells leave the eye at the same point, where they are bundled together to form the optic nerve.

The Blind Spot

At the point where the ganglion cells leave the eye and become the optic nerve on the way to the brain, there are no photoreceptor cells. Therefore, this part of the eye cannot respond to light and is commonly called the *blind spot*. We are not normally aware of our blind spot. (See Figure 5–6 and Plate 5.)

Although the rods and cones are the first retinal cells to receive light, they face *away* from the light and are at the *innermost* layer of the retina. The reason for this surprising arrangement is the need for oxygen. Although all parts of the eye require oxygen (supplied by blood vessels throughout the eye), the photochemicals of the rods and cones need much more. If the rods and cones were at the *front* of the eye, there would have to be many more blood vessels, which would block so much light that it would be impossible to see. So, the layer of cells right behind the retina has an additional network of blood vessels that supply the rods and cones with the necessary amount of oxygen (Figure 5–5).

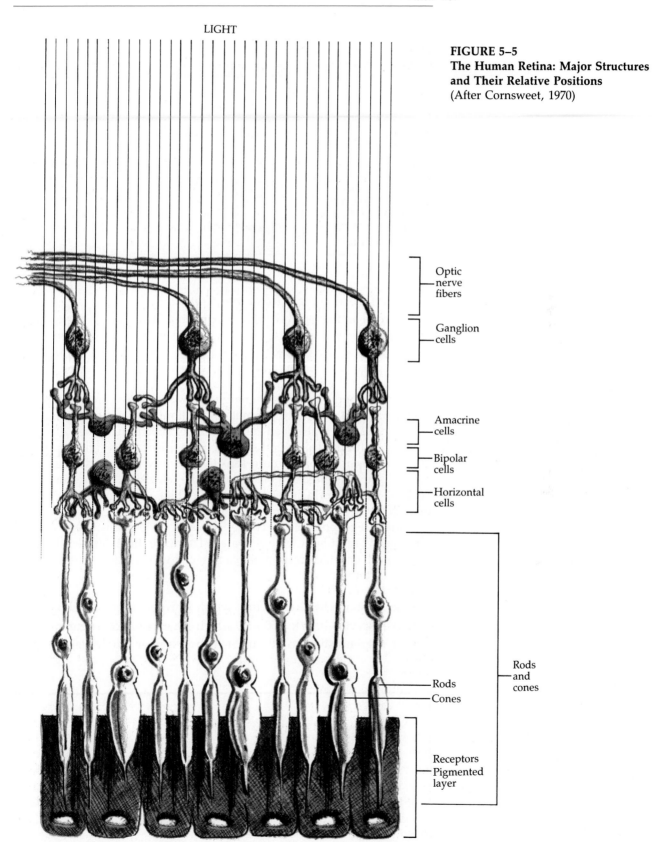

LIGHT

FIGURE 5–5
The Human Retina: Major Structures and Their Relative Positions
(After Cornsweet, 1970)

Optic
nerve
fibers

Ganglion
cells

Amacrine
cells

Bipolar
cells

Horizontal
cells

Rods
and
cones

Rods

Cones

Receptors
Pigmented
layer

LOOKING THROUGH BLOOD VESSELS: A DEMONSTRATION

Blood cells lie between the retina and the outside. Because we are structured to respond to changes, we never see these blood cells, since they are always there. But you can see for yourself that you do look at the world through blood vessels. Get a pen flashlight, a blank piece of paper, and a pencil. Turn on the flashlight and hold it near the outer edge of your eye and jiggle it around. You will see a luminous red spiderweb, which is a reflection of the retinal blood vessels. By looking at the paper immediately, you can trace a map of these vessels.

The Photoreceptors: Rods and Cones

The rods and cones look like their names. And though their shapes are different, their internal structures are similar: they both look like stacks of discs. The photochemicals are inside the discs. The major differences between the rods and cones are the kind of light they respond to and their distribution in the eye.

Rods respond most to light energy at low levels. Rods respond best to wavelengths of 480 nm (nanometers—billionths of a meter) which we experience as the blue-green end of the color spectrum. Some 120 million rods are distributed all over the retina, with the heaviest concentration at the sides: light vision is more sensitive slightly to the side than dead center. The rods are like a black and white television; they sense all the "colors" in the world as relative shades of blue-green grays. They allow us to see when the illumination is low, as at night.

Cones are responsible for color vision and are less sensitive than rods. They need bright light to be activated. There are three different kinds of cones, each of which responds to a range of wavelengths, but responds best to certain ones:

One responds best to 575 nm, which is experienced as red/orange.

One responds best to 550 nm, which we experience as green.

One responds best to 440 nm, which is seen as blue/violet.

FIGURE 5–6
Finding Your Blind Spot
Close your right eye and stare at the circle on the right. Holding the book about a foot from your face, slowly move it back and forth until the square on the left disappears. The square cannot be seen at that point because its image falls on your blind spot.

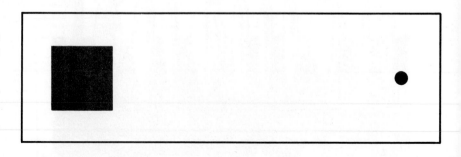

INTERNALLY GENERATED IMAGES

When we dream, we have the impression that we are actually seeing images. In addition, most people can conjure up the image of something or someone in the mind. Hallucinations, too, are visions of things not present. All of these visions are internally generated images, transduced in some way to give the *experience* of sight. The fact is that any stimulus that causes the retinal cells to fire, anything that stimulates the visual cortex (a blow to the head or a probing electrode) will give rise to a visual experience. You can demonstrate this for yourself. Close your eyes and press on your eyelids repeatedly. (If you wear contact lenses, take them off first.) Although no light enters the eye, you should perceive a phosphorescent green light. "Green" is an experience triggered by the firing of certain retinal photoreceptors.

The greatest concentration of cones is in the center of the retina. This area, which has no rods, is called the **fovea.** To examine an object closely, you move your head, body, and eyes until the image of the object falls on your fovea. The fovea is especially well represented in the brain; more brain cells receive input from the fovea than from any other part of the eye. The cones operate like a color television camera, which also has three color sensors: red-yellow, green, blue. These are the three primary colors of light from which all other colors can be made.

Dark Adaptation.   When you enter a darkened movie theater, you can hardly see. Minutes later the outlines of people and seats become visible. Our eyes, through the process of *dark adaptation,* become increasingly sensitive in the dark.

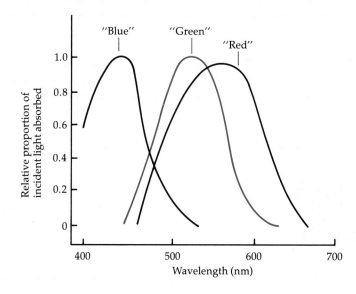

FIGURE 5–7
Relative Wavelength Absorption of Different Kinds of Cones in the Human Eye

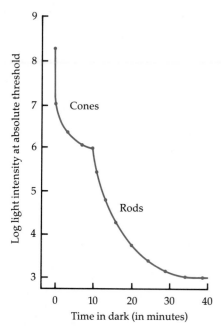

FIGURE 5–8
Testing Dark Adaptation
Subjects whose eyes had become adapted to bright light were then placed in darkness. The curve shows how their retinas adapted to the dark. They became more sensitive to ever fainter flashes of light. The abrupt turn at about 10 minutes is called the *rod-cone break*, indicating where the cones have reached their maximum sensitivity while the rods continue becoming more sensitive over another half hour or so.

The cones quickly adapt to the dark, but within 5 to 10 minutes they stop adapting. The rods continue becoming increasingly sensitive to less light stimulation, reaching their maximum in 30 to 40 minutes. At first you see objects only in black and white, and in shades of blue-green. After about 15 minutes some shading of color becomes visible.

The Basis of Color Vision

An important and distinctive dimension of human visual experience is that we see in color. It is estimated that we can make some eight million distinctions in color! As might be expected, color vision affords us great adaptive value. Seeing in color enables us to make more precise judgments about the outside world. Look at Plate 6. One view shows a scene in black and white. In the color view of the same scene, the ripe fruit immediately stands out.

There is no color in nature. Surfaces vary in the wavelengths of light they reflect. These wavelengths activate one of three different kinds of cones, which in turn send their coded information to the brain. The experience of color is a product of our sensory systems.

Coding of Color

A wiring diagram for the retina has been proposed to explain how it codes color information (Hurvich & Jameson, 1974). (Figure 5–9.) The nature of this coding process determines much of our color experience. We normally experience four colors as primary: red, green, blue, and yellow. These colors are seen as "pure." These colors, like all others, are associated with specific wavelengths of light. What makes these colors "seem" pure is not the color. It is the *way our visual system responds to different wavelengths of light.*

It is thought that three systems of color information are sent from the eye to the brain. Each sends information on two opposite dimensions; therefore, the brain's method for color coding is called an *opponent process.* The first two systems are transmitted only by cone cells and relay information about hue: one transmits the blue-yellow component of color, the other, the red-green. The third system, in which both cones and rods have a part, provides information about the color's brightness (dark-light). Evidence for the opponent process of color coding is drawn from demonstrations of afterimages and color blindness.

Afterimages. Stare at a red square against a white background for a minute. Then take the square away and look at the background. You will see an afterimage of its complementary color, green. Staring at a black square produces white. Blue produces a yellow afterimage. The color of these afterimages results from the brain's opponent process of coding information. (See also Plate 7.)

Color blindness. Color blindness is caused by a defect in one of the three color systems. The most common form is red-green color blindness. In fact, it is quite rare to find impairment of the other two systems. But because of opponent processing, there is no such thing as red-blue color blindness. Many of the tests for color blindness involve discriminating figures composed of color circles against a background composed of other color circles. Color blindness is a genetic defect and occurs predominately in males. Seven out of 100 men have some form of color blindness, while only about one woman in 1,000 suffers from this defect. (See Plate 8.)

WHAT THE EYE TELLS THE BRAIN

Sight does not take place *in* the eyes, but with the *assistance* of the eyes. The first part of visual experience is what the eye tells the brain; the second is what the brain tells the eye.

In each eye there are about 126 million photoreceptor cells whose impulses are channeled into 1 million ganglion cells. Information from the outside world is increasingly simplified and abstracted as the information travels from the outside to the visual cortex of the brain.

Information from the left eye travels via the left optic nerve and information from the right eye goes through the right optic nerve. Notice in Figure 5–10 that a change takes place at an intersection called the *optic chiasma:* some of the axons *cross over.* Those from the left sides of both eyes go off to the left side of the brain while those from the right sides of both eyes go off to the right. Only the arrangement, not the structure, of the axons changes. But the name also changes. After the crossover, the optic nerve is called the *optic tract.*

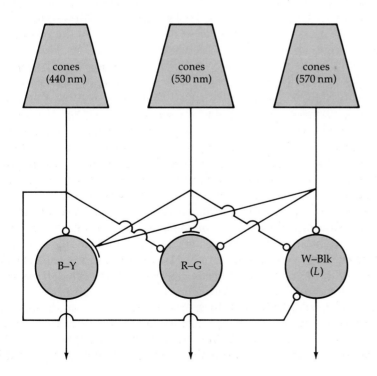

FIGURE 5–9
How the Retina
Codes Color Information
We see primary colors (red, green, blue, yellow) and their variations, as well as experiencing brightness (dark and light, white and black), because of the way our visual system responds to different wavelengths of light. This diagram represents connections in an opponent process that elicits responses from various cone cells. The round and the flat connections may arbitrarily be considered either excitatory or inhibitory and the numbers indicate the wavelength of the cones' maximum sensitivity. (After Hurvich & Jameson, 1974)

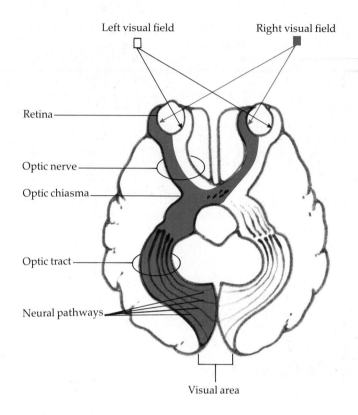

FIGURE 5–10
Visual Pathways in the Brain
The right half of each retina picks up light rays from the left visual field and those from the right visual field fall on the left half of each retina. The optic nerves meet at the optic chiasma, where information from the right sides of both retinas is channeled to the occipital cortex of the right cerebral hemisphere and that from the left sides of both retinas goes to the left hemisphere.

FIGURE 5–11
Feature Analyzers' Responses to Different Receptive Fields
Single cortical cells can be monitored to measure and record their responses to various stimuli. When bars of light (represented on the left, below) are flashed in the subject's eye, the most vigorous neural response is to the vertical bar. This suggests the cell is a feature analyzer intended to detect and react to visual stimuli that have a vertical orientation.

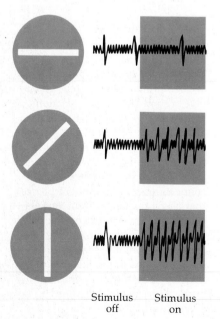

Stimulus off | Stimulus on

Lateral Geniculate Nucleus

The million nerve fibers in each of the two optic tracts reach the brain first at the *lateral geniculate nucleus* (LGN) in the thalamus (*lateral* means "sideways"; a *geniculate* is a bend or joint). Recall that the reticular activating system alerts the cortex to incoming information. The visual cortex is alerted to visual input via the LGN. Because of the similarity between LGN cells and ganglion cells, it appears the LGN is a kind of switching station relaying messages to the visual cortex. While in the LGN, the messages from the two eyes are still separate. The LGN also analyzes color signals. The neural fibers that leave the LGN fan out to inform the visual cortex.

Receptive Fields in the Retina and Visual Cortex

The rate of firing in a single axon can be measured and recorded by a hairlike electrical probe. By flashing a light at an animal's eye and recording the response to individual nerve cells, we can find out which cells respond to the stimulus. The area of stimulation that a cell responds to is called the **receptive field** (Figure 5–11). The function of the cells in the cortex is different from that of cells in the optic tract. When these cortical cells are recorded from individually, they respond best to specific features in the environment and are thus called **feature analyzers.** (However, the cells may actually serve other functions unknown to us.)

There are over 100 million neurons in the human visual cortex, and we do not yet know the extent of their specialization. Isolating and identi-

A million, million spermatozoa,
　　All of them alive
Out of their cataclysm but one poor Noah
　　Dare hope to survive
And among that billion minus one
　　Might have chanced to be
Shakespeare, another Newton, a new Donne
But the One was Me.

Aldous Huxley
"Fifth Philosopher's Song"

PLATE 1A
The Moment of Conception

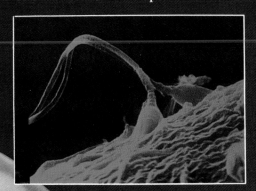

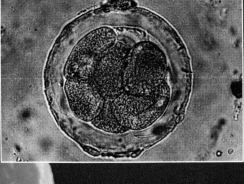

PLATE 1B
The Period of the Ovum
The cells of the fertilized
ovum immediately begin to
divide (above). This period
lasts about 2 weeks, ending
when the ovum is
implanted in the uterine
wall and the embryonic
period begins.

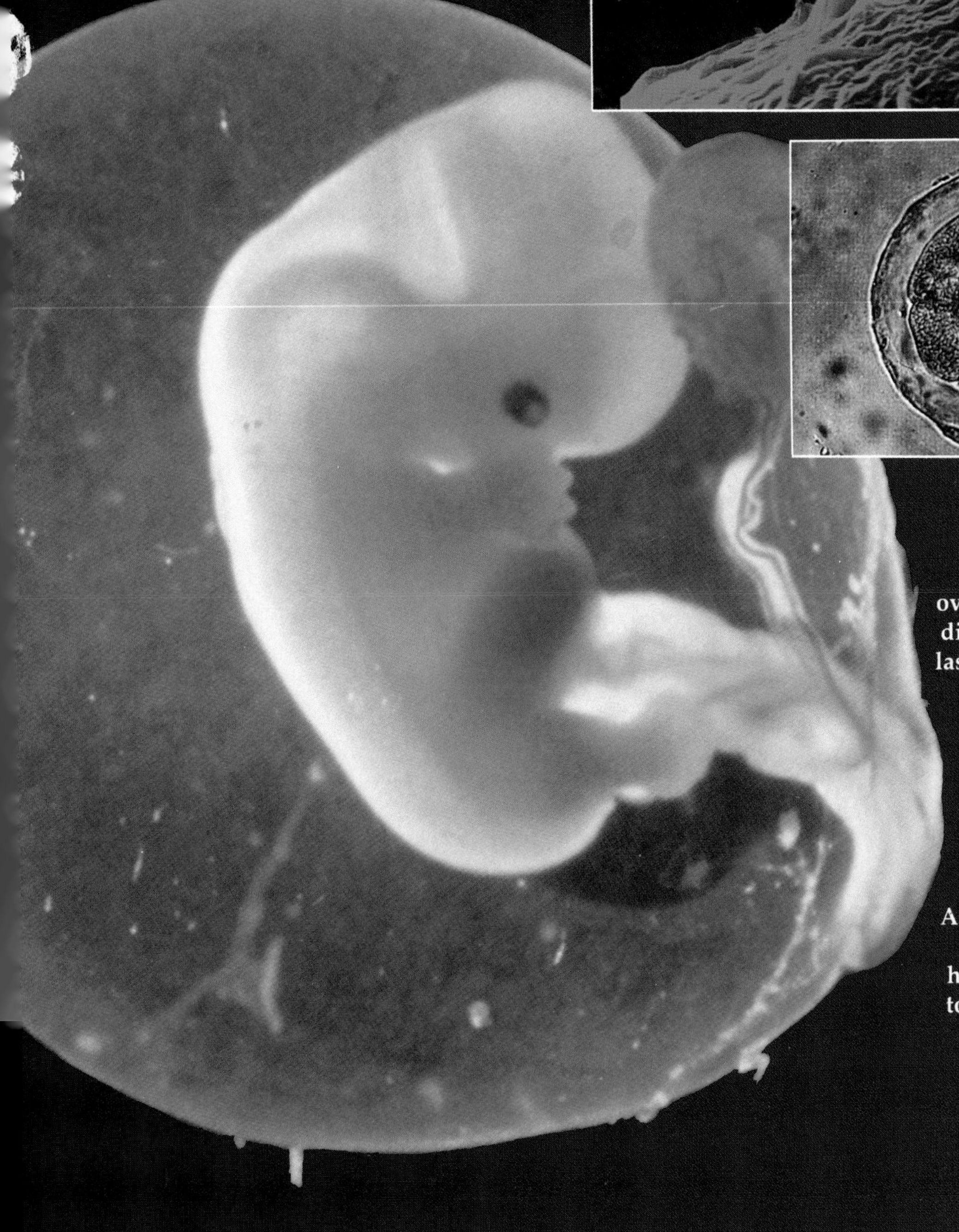

PLATE 1C
The Embryonic Period
At 5 to 6 weeks the embryo
(left) is mostly head and
heart. The heart has begun
to beat; the head and brain
can be discriminated.

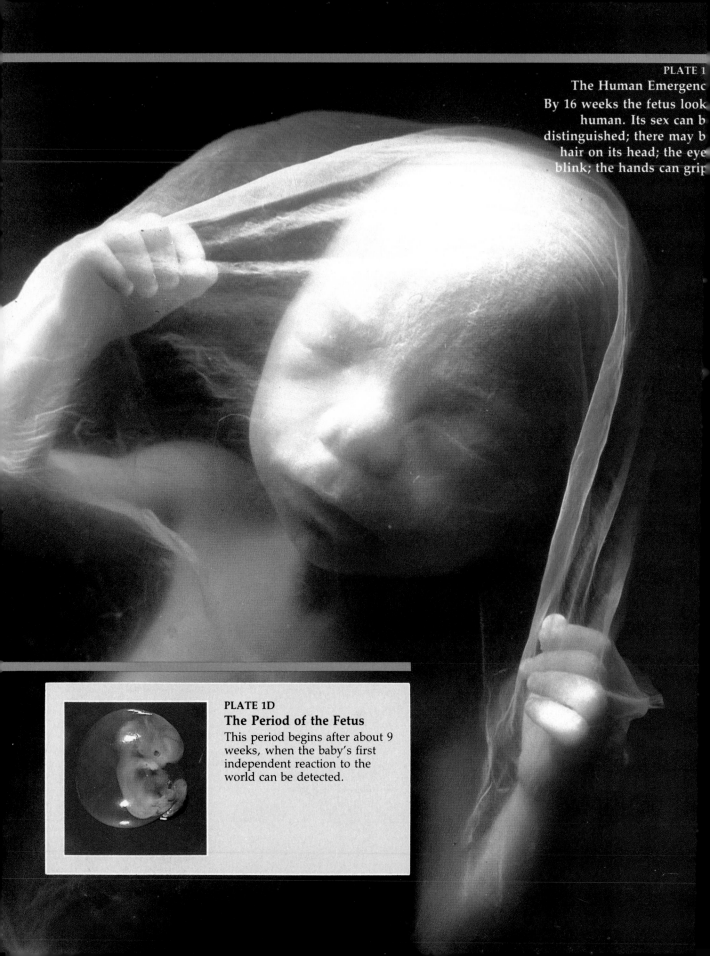

PLATE 1
The Human Emergenc
By 16 weeks the fetus look
human. Its sex can b
distinguished; there may b
hair on its head; the eye
blink; the hands can grip

PLATE 1D
The Period of the Fetus
This period begins after about 9 weeks, when the baby's first independent reaction to the world can be detected.

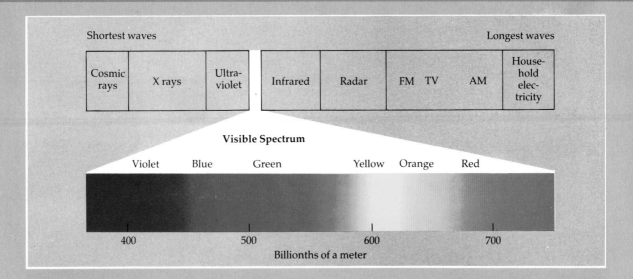

Shortest waves | Longest waves

| Cosmic rays | X rays | Ultra-violet | | Infrared | Radar | FM TV | AM | House-hold electricity |

Visible Spectrum

Violet   Blue   Green   Yellow Orange   Red

400   500   600   700

Billionths of a meter

PLATE 2
The Spectrum of Electromagnetic Energy
The visible spectrum—what our unaided senses
can detect—is a small fraction of the
total range of radiation around us.

PLATE 3
The Spreading Effect
Because we judge sensory
stimuli largely by
comparison, even if the red
in an illustration is actually
all one shade, the so-called
spreading effect of the
adjacent lines can make you
perceive the red as lighter
or darker in different
parts of the drawing.
(After Evans, 1948)

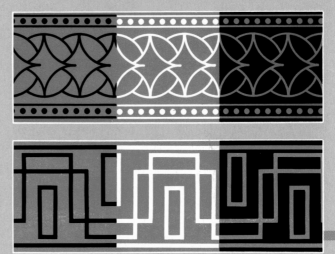

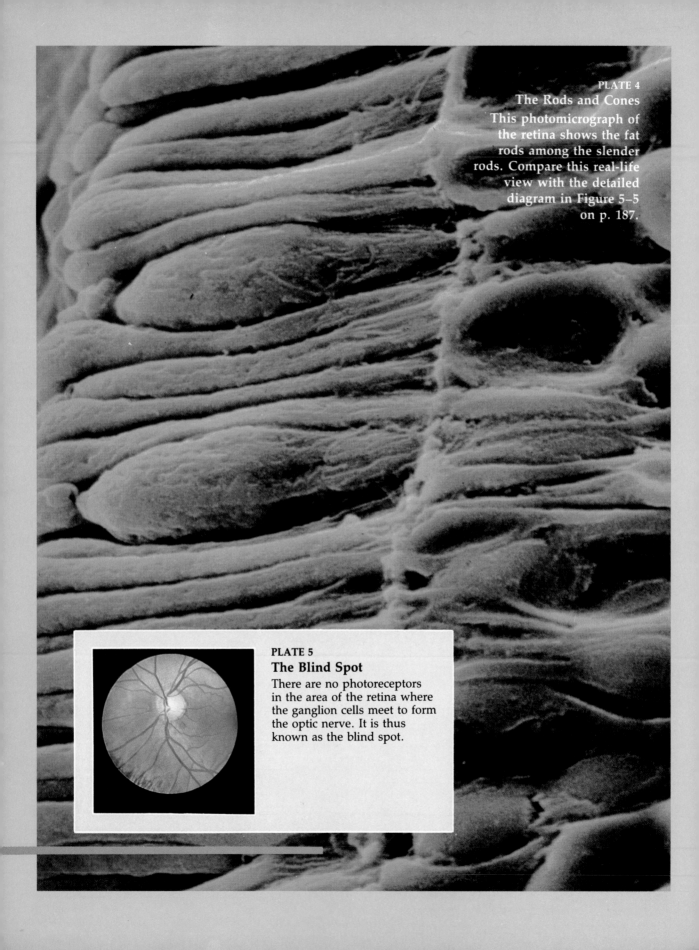

PLATE 4
The Rods and Cones
This photomicrograph of the retina shows the fat rods among the slender rods. Compare this real-life view with the detailed diagram in Figure 5–5 on p. 187.

PLATE 5
The Blind Spot
There are no photoreceptors in the area of the retina where the ganglion cells meet to form the optic nerve. It is thus known as the blind spot.

PLATES 6A AND 6B
The Advantages of Seeing in Color
As these photographs demonstrate, seeing the world in black and white could impair your ability to recognize and quickly exploit opportunities. Seeing in color makes it easier to evaluate what is desirable or dangerous, inviting or inimical.

PLATE 7
Afterimages
Stare at the center of the flag for at least half a minute. Then shift your gaze to the rectangle below the flag and concentrate on the dark spot in its center. What you should see—the red, white, and blue—results from how the brain's opponent process codes information to register complementary colors in an afterimage. (*Flags* was painted by Jasper Johns in 1965 and is from his personal collection)

PLATES 8A AND 8B
The World to a Color-blind Person
The view at the top is what would be seen by a person with red-green color blindness, the most common form of defect in the color-sensing system. The bottom view is what this same scene would look like to a person with normal vision.

PLATE 9
Color Contrast and the Perception of Change
All these gray squares are the same shade. They look different because of their varying degrees of contrast with the color of each background. Such contrasts are among the many kinds of changes our sensory systems are designed to notice and, apparently, to amplify.

PLATE 10
Human Taste Buds
Taste buds, here magnified greatly, are collections of taste cells concentrated in various places on the surface of the tongue to respond to the four basic elements of taste: sour, sweet, bitter, and salty.

PLATES 11A AND 11B
The Relativity of Sensory Experience
Both these pictures are of the same car. But the upper photograph was taken at noon, with white sunlight overhead accentuating the whiteness of the car. The bottom photograph was shot as the sunset bathed the car with its red rays, making it look as red as some red cars would look at noon. And yet it is still perceived as a white car, because it remains relatively whiter than its uniformly redder surroundings. This, like all sensory experience, is a highly relative matter, depending on context, contrast, change, and adaptation.

PLATE 12
Seeing What You Are Prepared to See
See how quickly you can count the number of aces of spades in this illustration; then finish reading this caption. If you are like most people, you may have gotten the wrong total because you have learned spades are black cards, not red. With these anomalous playing cards, Bruner demonstrated how people tend to see what they expect to see, not necessarily what is actually there.

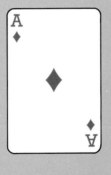

fying receptive fields is one way that investigators can determine the features specific cells are designed to notice. It appears that each species of animal possesses a special set of feature analyzers that pick out the objects and events that are important for it. Recall that in lower animals, such as the frog, selection is extreme. The frog responds to only four specialized aspects of the environment.

The visual system of the cat, which so far is the most thoroughly studied (Hubel, 1979; Hubel & Wiesel, 1962), selects for edges, angles, and objects moving in different directions. In monkeys, some cells seem to respond to specific features of the environment. Gross, Rocha-Miranda, and Bender (1972) experimented with one rhesus monkey. They probed one cell in the cortex and tried to find out what would make it respond. They placed food in front of the monkey, showed it cards, moving objects, and so on. In fact, they tried everything they could think of and found no response. Finally there was a response when they waved their hands "good-bye" to the cell, in front of the monkey's eye. Then Gross et al. showed lots of new stimuli to the cell. The more similar a stimulus was to a monkey's hand, the greater was the response in that cell (Figure 5–12). This example shows that, at least in the monkey, we can identify a single cell that responds strongly to an extremely specific feature.

In the visual cortex of cats, three main categories of cells have been identified, each of which detects specific kinds of patterns (Hubel & Wiesel, 1979).

1. *Simple cells* respond to a bar, line, or edge. Figure 5–13 shows the different kinds of receptive fields of simple cells and the stimulus that will cause them to fire at maximum strength. Because simple cells respond most strongly to particular angles, they are called *orientation detectors*. They are arranged in columns in the visual cortex; each column contains cells that respond to a particular orientation.

2. *Complex cells* respond to orientation and to movement, such as a diagonal line moving from left to right (Figure 5–14).

3. *Hypercomplex cells* respond to bars of light in any orientation. The clumsiness of the term "hypercomplex" reflects the surprising complexity of the cortical selection system. Researchers mapping the cortex of the cat never expected that there would be categories of cells beyond the "complex." It may well be that other cells will be found that respond to even more specialized features of the environment (like the hand-responding cell of the monkey).

Each element of the visual system, including the visual cortex, is designed to select special features of the environment, transmit and analyze that information, and ignore the rest. The cells in the visual cortex are probably the building blocks of more complex visual experiences.

T. N. Wiesel and D. H. Hubel

FIGURE 5–12
The Monkey-Paw Detector
These shapes are arranged in order of their ability to make a single cell in a monkey's brain respond to the sight of them. Some shapes (1) produced no response; some made a neuron react a little (2 and 3). Those shapes somewhat like a monkey's paw (4 and 5) produced a greater response, and the maximum neural response was to the shape most closely resembling a monkey's paw (6). Clearly, there are brain cells intended to detect and react to very complex, highly specific features. (After Gross, 1973)

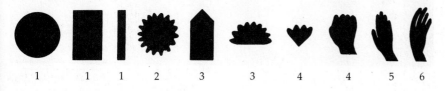

| 1 | 1 | 1 | 2 | 3 | 3 | 4 | 4 | 5 | 6 |

FIGURE 5–13
Receptive Fields of Simple Cells
These cells, from the visual cortex of cats, are arranged in receptive fields whose elongated central regions are oriented for the cells' maximal response to stimuli—dark or light bars, lines, or edges—at particular angles. The + sign shows that a cell gives an on response and a − sign indicates an off response. (After Hubel & Wiesel, 1962)

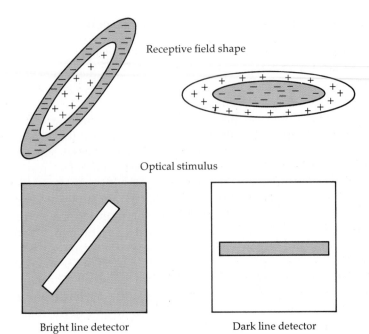

Receptive field shape

Optical stimulus

Bright line detector   Dark line detector

FIGURE 5–14
The Preference of Complex Cells
Like simple cells, these cortical cells respond best to bars and edges at certain angles, but they are especially sensitive to stimuli *moving* within their receptive field. The preference of these cells for extremely specific stimuli is revealed in this drawing, which shows a complex cell responding vigorously to an angled slit of light moving left to right (top), but with less vigor to the same slit of light moving in the opposite direction (bottom). (After Hubel & Wiesel, 1962)

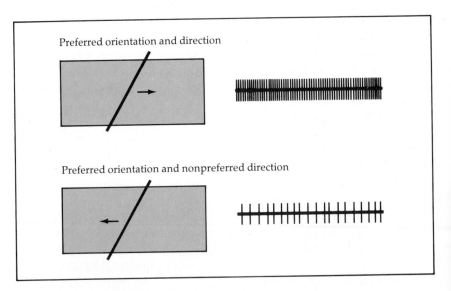

Preferred orientation and direction

Preferred orientation and nonpreferred direction

FIGURE 5–15
How Simultaneous Brightness Contrast Fools Your Eye
All the central squares are the same shade of gray. But how each contrasts with its lighter or darker background triggers the lateral inhibition mechanism of retinal cells and alters your perception so the central squares seem to be of different shades.

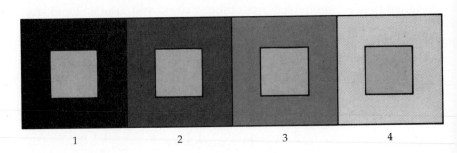

1   2   3   4

Lateral Inhibition

Every sensory experience depends on the previous sensory experience. A lump of coal in bright sunlight reflects more light than this page in the shade. The coal is always experienced as dark and the page as light, because the coal is darker than its surroundings and the page is lighter. In Figure 5–15 all the central squares are exactly the same gray, but the darker the surrounding figure is, the brighter each square appears. An edge or corner or sharp change in color is a clear demarcation between two objects or planes. The demarcation comes from the fact that it is at the point where a significant difference or contrast in brightness is noticed. Things appear brighter at edges and corners than in the middle. At every level, the sensory systems are designed to notice change. (See also Plate 9.)

The physiological mechanism that underlies the experience—which compares the brightness of one object to surrounding brightness—is called **lateral inhibition.** Lateral inhibition describes the way retinal cells fire and affect each other. Most of the evidence on lateral inhibition comes from studies on the horseshoe crab, *Limulus,* whose visual system is both simple and large (Hartline & Ratliff, 1957).

Retinal cells respond to light by firing: the brighter the light, the more they fire. Whenever a cell fires, it inhibits the cells next to it (laterally) from firing. In Figure 5–16 you can see that the brighter the stimulus, the greater the inhibition. Thus, the basic mechanism of lateral inhibition is that the more a retinal cell fires, the more it inhibits neighboring cells from firing. The firing of Cell A inhibits the firing of Cell B.

Lateral inhibition helps us see sharp changes, like corners, in the environment. It may enhance discrimination between two slightly different figures. Because it exaggerates changes in the environment, we can be fooled. Look at the two illustrations in Figure 5–18. If you stare at the center of the left illustration, the light circle disappears. This will not happen if you stare at the center of the right circle.

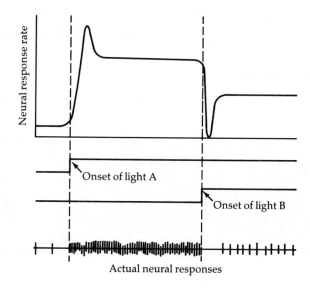

Onset of light A

Onset of light B

Actual neural responses

FIGURE 5–16
A Demonstration
of Lateral Inhibition
The onset of light striking cell A causes neural response; the onset of light striking cell B does not. This is because while a retinal cell is responding to the initial stimulus, neighboring (lateral) cells are inhibited from responding. And the brighter the stimulus, the greater the inhibition. (After Lindsay & Norman, 1977)

FIGURE 5–17
Lateral Inhibition
Accentuates Change
There is a uniform progression of
changes between successive steps in
this photograph. But you do not
perceive the changes as uniform.
Lateral inhibition makes nerve cells
in the retina respond so that changes
are accentuated—the relationship
between the input (light intensity)
and the output (neural activity level)
is not uniform. (After Cornsweet,
1970)

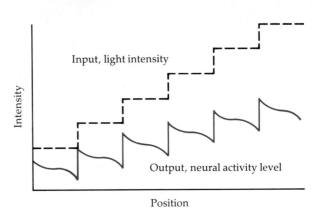

What the Brain Tells the Eye

So far visual experience has been discussed as if it occurred to a stationary observer looking straight ahead. But we are never stationary. We move both the head and the eyes when we see something (Gibson, 1979). The eye is never still. When we look at a painting or photo, our eye seems to trace the outline of the figure (Figure 5–19).

FIGURE 5–18
Sensitivity to the Changes
Presented by Stabilized Images
Your visual system is especially
sensitive to the sharp change
between the light central area and
the darker background shown in the
right-hand illustration. Consequently,
when you stare at it, the distinction
remains sharp because the
photoreceptors continue firing
vigorously, maintaining a stabilized
image. In the left-hand illustration
there is a more gradual change from
the light center to the darker
background. This gives the
photoreceptors little or no change to
trigger their firing, so this
less-stabilized image disappears
when you stare at it.

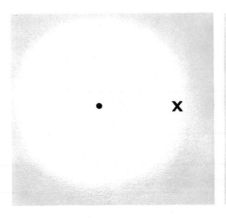

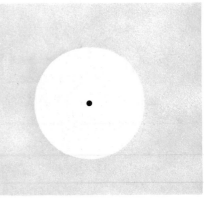

Eye Movements and the Brain

For an organism to see in any practical sense, a systematic relationship between body movements and visual experience must be established. Held and Hein (1963) investigated this relationship using kittens. They raised a group of kittens in total darkness except for an hour each day. During this one hour, one group was allowed to move freely around a patterned cylinder; another sat passively in a gondola pulled by a cat from the active group. Later both groups were exposed to the same visual stimulation. The kittens with an "active" experience with light learned to see normally, but the vision of the other kittens was permanently impaired. Visual information coming in must in some way be correlated, through experience, with the organism's movements.

Our sensory experience is in part determined by our own *movements*. Look straight ahead, then move your eyes sharply to the left. Your *view* of the scene has changed dramatically but the "world" remains stable. Thus, the brain keeps a record of our current movements in order to account for the changes in the *movement-produced stimulation*.

Now, tap your right eye on the right side with your right index finger, so that your eye moves to the left. When it does, the world seems to "jump." The difference between this and the previous movement is that we rarely, if ever, move our eye with our hand, so there is no record of movement signals to account for the change in stimulation.

A second function of eye movements is to stimulate change. Normally our eyes move in sweeps called *saccades*. We hardly ever gaze at any one point too long. Even if you try to fix vision at one point on an object, very small involuntary movements occur. These movements are called *nystagmus*. Portions of the retina are constantly stimulated as a result of both types of eye movements, although at any given moment only some receptor cells are stimulated.

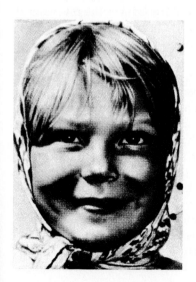

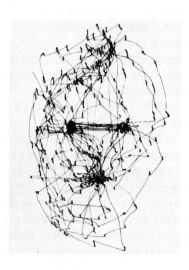

FIGURE 5–19
Your Roving Eye
The pattern of lines trace the eye movements of someone who looked at this picture of the little girl for 3 minutes. The lines not only outline the picture; they indicate points of fixation where the subject's eye paused over areas of visual interest. (After Yarbus, 1967)

Close your eyes, then open them. Whatever you just saw is a result of all the processes discussed here. Light entered, passed through the retina, and information was sent up to the brain. Orientation analyzers have responded, color analyzers have done their job, and many more processes have been activated. Although we can track the sequence from light to the firing of cells on the visual cortex and understand some of the workings of the cells, how all this becomes visual experience somewhere in the brain is still a great mystery.

HEARING

Hearing is our second most important sense. The sensory organ for hearing is the ear. The ear we see (called the *pinna*) has little to do with hearing itself. Its function is to direct sound waves into the auditory channel. The process of hearing begins in the middle and inner ear. The stimuli for hearing are sound waves, which are vibrations of air. Sound waves are invisible, but you can see their effects on the surface of a drum as it is beaten.

The ear, like the other sensory organs, is both highly sensitive and highly selective. The loudest sounds we hear are millions of times louder than the softest. The ear transmits only a fraction of the energy reaching it, but it is precise in what it does transmit. A mosquito buzzing around your ear can keep you up all night, yet the energy in that buzz would have to be 100,000,000,000,000,000 times greater to light a small lamp (Stevens, 1956).

What the Ear Does

The ear picks up vibrations in the air. The auditory system performs the two routine miracles mentioned earlier: it transduces the mechanical energy of sound waves from the outside world into chemical or electrical activity in nerve cells, which in turn becomes the raw material for the experience of sound.

Hearing allows us to locate events by sound. We can discriminate between quite disparate sounds—a birdsong, a car approaching from the left or right, a musical note. When an exciting event occurs in our world, we try to focus on it, visually, by bringing it into the fovea's line of vision. The ear helps guide the eye to that position by sensing differences in loudness. A sound to one side will cause us to turn our heads until the sound is equal in both ears; at that point we will be looking straight at the object. Thus, the ears work in concert with the eyes and other senses.

Hearing gives us feedback on the sounds we make and is especially important for speech. If the auditory feedback from speech is interrupted, distorted, or delayed, speech becomes unclear. A delay of even one second may completely disrupt the ability to speak coherently.

Sound Waves

Sound waves have two major characteristics: amplitude and frequency. *Amplitude* refers to the height of the wave; *frequency* refers to the number of cycles the wave makes each second. Amplitude governs the experience of loudness; the higher the amplitude, the louder the sound. Frequency governs the pitch; a high frequency results in high-pitched tones. The beat in music is the overlapping of the frequencies of two waves. Sound waves must travel through a medium: air, water, or a solid material; so there is no sound in a vacuum.

Sound waves travel through the ear under pressure; sound that is too intense can therefore be painful because of the pressure on sensitive tissue in the ear.

The Ear

The ear is a marvelous physical system of great complexity. It includes a wide-range sound wave analyzer, an amplification system, a two-way communication system, a relay unit, a multichannel transducer that converts mechanical into electrical energy, and a hydraulic balance system. All this is compressed into two cubic centimeters (Stevens & Warshofsky, 1965).

Pressure moves sound waves down the auditory canal to the eardrum, causing it to vibrate. The vibration of the eardrum causes the three bones of the middle ear to vibrate. These bones, named after their shapes, are the hammer, the anvil, and the stirrup. Their vibrations match the original signal in frequency, but are of greater amplitude (25 times greater). The pressure of that magnification forces the waves into the inner ear, where it is transduced into electrical energy in the nerve cells.

The Cochlea

Hearing really begins in the **cochlea** (named for its shape; cochlea is the Latin word for snail). The liquid that fills the cochlea is an ideal medium for transmitting sound waves.

At the base of the cochlea is a structure called the **basilar membrane.** When the stirrup beats on the cochlea at the oval window, the basilar membrane moves just like a whip being cracked again and again. This whipping movement creates a *traveling wave* (Von Békésy, 1949). A short wave produces a high frequency; its bulge is closer to the oval window. On top of the basilar membrane is the *organ of Corti.* The membrane's movements bend the outer hair cells of the organ of Corti and its cells fire. Here the pressure waves are transduced into neural firing, sent up the auditory nerve and then to the brain. The pressure from all this banging is finally released through the round window.

What the Ear Tells the Brain

Although there are far fewer neurons in the auditory nerve than in the optic nerve (28 thousand vs. 1 million), the number of sound discriminations is about equal to the number of visual discriminations. A typical

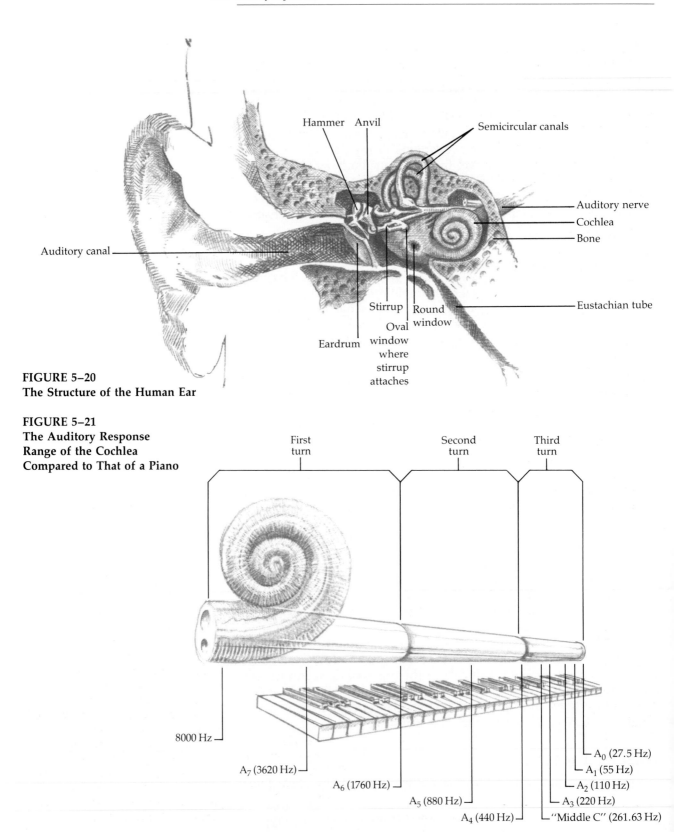

FIGURE 5–20
The Structure of the Human Ear

FIGURE 5–21
The Auditory Response
Range of the Cochlea
Compared to That of a Piano

auditory receptor has a "tuning curve" (Figure 5–22), which represents its ability to respond to tones of different frequencies. The nerve cells in the ear are as sensitive and specific in the kinds of stimuli they respond to as those in the eye. Some cells respond only to complex sounds; others to pure tones, and so on. Each auditory neuron is generally thought to collect information from a specific place in the basilar membrane. The rate of neural firing is therefore related to the membrane's point of movement. As the amplitude of the sound wave increases, the rate of firing of the neurons increases. As the frequency of the wave changes, different neurons begin to fire.

The Auditory Cortex

The first stop after a signal has left the ear on its way to the brain is the *cochlear nucleus*. Many of the fibers of the auditory nerve end here. The axons of the cochlear nucleus of each ear carry the information to the *superior olive* on the opposite side of the brain, where they enter the auditory cortex through the *medial geniculate*. In all these areas the nerve fibers respond similarly in amplitude and frequency to the "tuned" neurons.

Selection and analysis take place in the auditory cortex; 60 percent of the cortical cells there respond to specific tones. These cells behave in much the same way as those in the visual cortex. There are three types; *on cells* respond when a tone starts; *off cells* respond when the tone stops; and *on-off cells* respond when there is any change. The other 40 percent are more specialized. They respond to bursts of specific waves, sharp sounds, or clicks. For example, *frequency sweep detectors* respond to the small changes in frequency produced in normal speech. Some auditory cells with even more specific functions have been found in other animals. For instance, Whitfield (1976) found cells in the auditory system of the squirrel monkey that respond only to the sounds of other squirrel monkeys.

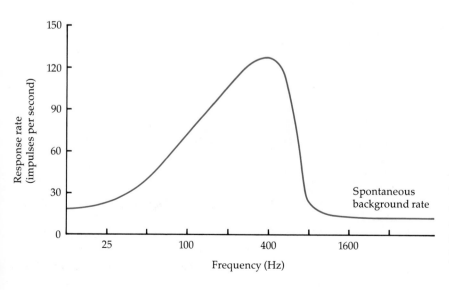

FIGURE 5–22
The Tuning Curve of a Typical Auditory Receptor
When an auditory neuron is presented tones of various frequencies, the pattern of its responses traces a tuning curve such as this one. The point of the receptor's peak response is called the *critical frequency*—in this example, about 400 Hz—which departs most from the neuron's nonresponsive, spontaneous background rate. (After Lindsay & Norman, 1977)

The ear-brain system thus operates on the same basic principles as the eye-brain system. Like the visual system, the auditory system is one of great selectivity and sensitivity. In both systems, physical stimulation of the body by the outside world—the radiation of light or the movement of sound waves—is translated in the body until it somehow becomes the inner world of experience: sight and sound, luminance and tone.

THE CHEMICAL, SKIN, AND INTERNAL SENSES

Our senses of smell, taste, and touch, and the internal senses are much simpler systems than sight and hearing, but they are a substantial part of our sensory experience. Without smell and taste we could not judge if food were fresh or spoiled. People born without a sense of touch feel no pain and must be specially protected from injuring themselves.

The senses we are least aware of are the *internal senses*. These senses keep us standing up, help us maintain balance while moving, inform us of internal feelings, and let us know where each part of the body is in relation to every other part. Without information on our own body position or movements we could not do something as "simple" as walk.

Chemical Senses: Smell and Taste

Smell

Smell helps discriminate tastes and also is useful in judging distance, location, and danger. People usually smell something burning before they see a fire. The nose is the sensory organ for smell and the stimulus it responds to is gaseous molecules carried on currents of air. The receptors for smell, the **olfactory cilia,** are located at the end of the nasal cavity in the outer surface of the **olfactory epithelium** (which means "smell skin") (Figure 5–23). These receptors also analyze the food we eat. It is

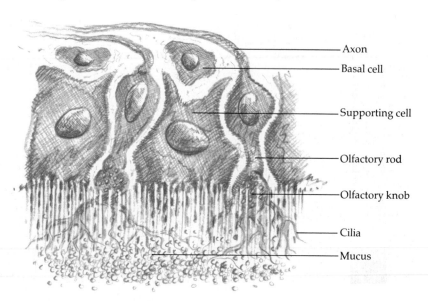

FIGURE 5–23
The Structure of the Olfactory Epithelium
Smells reaching the surface of the olfactory epithelium stimulate the olfactory cilia, which are embedded in mucus secreted by glands situated only in that part of the nasal passage. The cilia protrude from the olfactory knobs, expanded portions of the olfactory rods that extend from the receptors' cell bodies, which are attached by their axons to the brain.

Axon
Basal cell
Supporting cell
Olfactory rod
Olfactory knob
Cilia
Mucus

difficult to taste the difference between an apple, an onion, and a potato if the nose is blocked.

Smell is the most direct sense. The neural information about smell is sent to the brain without any intermediate nerves. Since it is a "straight line" into the brain, smell information is less complex than other sensory information reaching the brain. The direct connection of the nose to the brain may explain certain phenomena. For example, our memory for odors is very good, much better than visual or other kinds of memory. Once a smell has been presented, it is rarely forgotten. The direct connection of the nose to the brain may also make it possible to directly influence brain states by presenting certain odors. In many cultures incense or other strong odors are often used in conjunction with meditation, rhythmic movement, and other spiritual exercises. The goal of these exercises is usually an alteration of the brain state. The strong odors, combined with ritual movements, may aid in the achievement of the desired state. To test this hypothesis, an experiment was conducted in which neural activity in the limbic system of a human subject was recorded while the subject was breathing rhythmically in a room infused with a strong odor. There was a clear indication in the spiking patterns of the EEG that the odor and the rhythmic breathing had stimulated limbic system activity (Galin, Ornstein, & Adams, 1977).

Smell is not the dominant sense in humans as it is in other animals. Recall that one result of the development of erect posture was that as the nose became further elevated from the earth, there was increased reliance on vision. The size of an animal's nose is directly related to the importance of that sense. A dog not only has a much larger snout than we do, but a much larger area of the dog's brain is devoted to smell. Dogs are therefore used to track down a wide variety of things, including specific chemical substances to which human noses are not particularly sensitive. However, there is much speculation about the possible unconscious effect of smell in humans.

Smell and Human Behavior   See box on Pheromones, p. 204.

PHEROMONES

Smell may have a more direct effect on our behavior than was previously thought. Most animals communicate their sexual receptivity through odors. During estrus, the female of a species produces an odor that arouses the male of the species. Such chemical substances used to communicate are called **pheromones.** They have been found in insects and in many mammals. Female mice secrete a substance, *copulin*, which arouses the male.

The evidence in humans is less clear. Although human sexual signals are usually visual and symbolic, some recent evidence indicates that smell plays a role in human sexual behavior. Recent studies also indicate that people can distinguish their own body odor from others. The scent glands in our armpits, which have been generally considered nonfunctional, in any other animal would be considered part of a pheromone system. A difference between the smells of women and men can also be discriminated. People have described the male smell as "musky" and the female as "sweet." Unlike other animals, in humans the male is more odorous than the female. Women are more responsive to the characteristic male odor during ovulation than during menstruation (McClintock, 1971), which would have the adaptive value of increasing the desire for intercourse and the likelihood of conception. There are pronounced ethnic differences in the number of these scent glands: blacks have the most, Caucasians fewer, Orientals the fewest.

Smell may even have an effect on women's menstrual cycles. McClintock (1971) found that women who spend a lot of time together—who are close friends, who live in dormitories or work together—tend to have their menstrual periods at the same time. McClintock and her colleagues found one woman, Geneviève, who had noticed that the menstrual cycle of her roommates changed to conform to her own. In one experiment, Geneviève wore underarm pads to collect secretions of sweat. Sixteen women volunteers were divided into two groups. Each group was asked to smell a particular odor three times a week for four months. The control group was asked to smell alcohol; the experimental group smelled alcohol plus the woman's odor, which they called "eau de Geneviève." At the end of four months, the women in the control group showed no change in their menstrual cycles. But the menstrual cycles of those smelling "eau de Geneviève" shifted from an average discrepancy of 9.3 days to 3.4; some shifted to within a day of Geneviève's cycle.

The research on pheromones in humans is in its infancy. Human sexual life is extremely complex and, obviously, human sexuality is not completely determined by chemical messages. But perhaps our view of scent and its role in our sexual experience will have to be expanded. Musk became a popular male perfume in the late 1970s. In early 1980 an English perfume company began to market a perfume whose base was chemically derived from male sweat. People who say they "feel chemistry" with someone may be right!

Taste

A professional wine taster can often tell the vintage, type of grape, and in some cases the vineyard of a wine from a single sip. Coffee, tea, and liquor manufacturers employ tasters to make decisions on the quality of their products. Our ability to discriminate and remember tastes is remarkably precise. What is especially interesting about human taste is that complex taste sensations are built up on an extremely simple receptor system.

Look at your own tongue in the mirror. The surface of the tongue is covered with small bumps. These bumps are called *papillae,* and each has 200 *taste buds* in and around it. Taste buds are a collection of taste cells. They do not live very long and are replaced every few days. When you burn your tongue on hot food you cannot taste anything in that spot for a few days. This is because the taste buds have been killed and new ones have not yet replaced them.

Many psychologists assume that there are four basic elements in our taste palate: sour, bitter, sweet, and salty. As with our other senses, taste stimuli are "coded" into these basic categories and transmitted to the brain. Each cell has a different threshold for each taste (Figure 5–24). Different parts of the tongue are more sensitive to one taste than another. For example, the tip of the tongue is most sensitive to sweet and salty, while the sides are most sensitive to sour, and the back to bitter (Ludel, 1978). The taste buds also respond to temperature—hot, warm, and cold. (See Figure 5–25 and Plate 10.)

Whereas in all other senses we develop more complexity and sensitivity as we grow older, the opposite occurs in taste. An adult has fewer taste cells than a child. This difference means that children are more sensitive to taste, which helps explain why children are "picky" eaters and why adults add seasoning to food (Ludel, 1978).

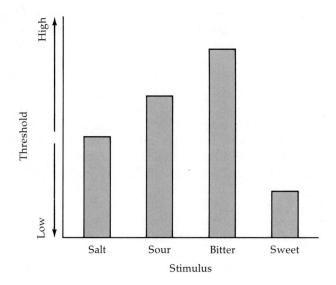

FIGURE 5–24
Taste Buds' Response Thresholds
The single taste bud whose responses are charted here is highly responsive to sweet tastes and fairly sensitive to salt tastes. It is such relatively low thresholds that characterize individual taste buds, not their high thresholds, because taste receptors often have no reaction to certain tastes and therefore have infinitely high thresholds for such stimulation. (After Ludel, 1978)

FIGURE 5–25
Areas of the Human Tongue
and Their Relative Sensitivity
to the Four Basic Tastes
(After Ludel, 1978)

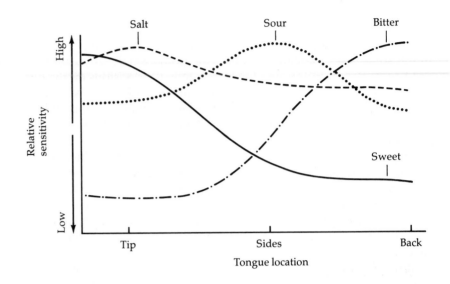

Touching and Feeling

Touching informs and communicates. The skin is the primary sensory organ for touch, and it responds to three dimensions of stimuli: *pressure, pain,* and *temperature*. The skin is the largest sense organ of the body, and one of its most important functions is to define the boundary between ourselves and the outside world. We also obtain information about the surface textures of the outside world through the skin. Touch gives us feedback on our motor movements: whether we are holding a pencil correctly, grasping a screwdriver well, or losing our grip. Touch also communicates; it can express closeness to others. In our culture a good indicator of the closeness of two people is how much they touch each other. Sex is largely an experience of touching, as is the bond between mother and infant.

Different parts of the body are more sensitive to touch than others. The most sensitive regions of the body are the fingers, cheek, nose and lips, genitals, and the soles of the feet. Least sensitive are the arms, back, thighs, and the calf.

The skin has many types of receptors, each of which responds to a different kind of stimulation. One is the *pacinian corpuscle* (Lowenstein, 1960), which looks like an onion (Figure 5–26) and seems to respond directly to *mechanical pressure*, which directly stimulates the nerve. Although there are many different kinds of nerve endings in the skin, they all send their information to the brain via one of two systems, one fast and one slow. The fast one, the *lemniscal system*, is comprised of large nerve fibers that conduct information directly into the cortex. The *spino-thalamic system* is slow and diffuse, is regulated through the reticular activating system, and reaches the brain at the limbic system. These two systems seem to be specialized for the transmission of two types of pain information: the immediate pain of a blow is sent quickly to the brain by the lemniscal system. The slow spinothalamic system conveys chronic pain from long-term injuries and ailments, as well as internal pains such as those resulting from surgery or a toothache (Figure 5–27).

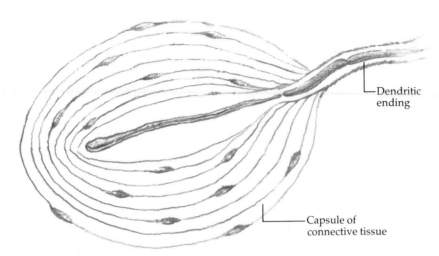

Dendritic ending

Capsule of connective tissue

FIGURE 5–26
The Pacinian Corpuscle
Sensitive to touch, such receptors respond to direct mechanical pressure, adapt to it, and then are ready to respond again soon after the pressure is removed. (After Ludel, 1978)

Internal Senses

While the eyes, ears, nose, and skin inform us primarily of events coming at us, the internal senses relay information on our own movements and bodily functions. We need to be aware of internal processes in order to maintain balance and move. The sense of movement is called *kinesthesis;* the sense of balance is one of the *vestibular senses*. The **somesthetic system** conveys to the brain information concerning sensations in the internal environment, such as deep pain or nausea. We also need to know where each part of the body is in relation to all other parts. The

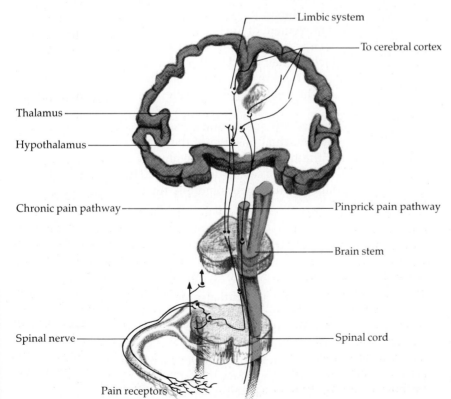

Limbic system

To cerebral cortex

Thalamus

Hypothalamus

Chronic pain pathway

Pinprick pain pathway

Brain stem

Spinal nerve

Spinal cord

Pain receptors

FIGURE 5–27
Pain Pathways
The fast pathway (lemniscal system) carries information on such sudden pain as that from a blow or a pinprick, conducting it directly to the cerebral cortex. Information on chronic pain travels the slow pathway (the spinothalamic system), being routed through the limbic system before coming to the attention of the cortex. (After Snyder, 1977)

sense that performs that function is called **proprioception.** Here we discuss, and briefly, only kinesthesis and the vestibular senses.

Kinesthesis

Close your eyes and consider each movement you must make to walk across the room. The legs must flex, then extend a certain distance, while movements of the arms and back must be coordinated. At every instant you know precisely the position of your body. The sense that makes all this possible is **kinesthesis** (from the Greek word *kine,* meaning movement). Even when we are not moving through space—when we are sitting, lying down, or relaxed—we have kinesthetic feedback. At every moment of life we respond to the unseen force of gravity. You know, without looking at them, where your limbs are, their angle, and what they are doing. Special nerve cells in the muscles, called *joint position receptors,* relay information on movements of the muscles, and nerve endings in the skin and muscles respond to these signals.

As with all other senses, the joint position neurons habituate: if the hand is held in one place, the neurons stop firing. We get no information if we do not move.

The Vestibular Senses

The **vestibular system** consists of organs sensitive to motion, position, and balance. Our organs of balance are in the inner ear next to the cochlea. They are called the *otolith organs* (meaning "ear stone," from their shape) and, as mentioned earlier, are the exception to the rule that sensory systems respond only to differences in stimuli.

The otolith organs contain three semicircular canals that lie in different planes, so that movement of the head in any direction is registered in the canals. The enlarged area at the end of the canals is called the *ampulla,* inside of which are hair cells like those in the organ of Corti. When we tilt our heads, the fluid in the canals stimulates certain hair cells to fire. The firing of the cells signals specific directions of the movements.

The otolith organs are unique among sense organs in that they do not adapt. They signal the actual position of the head. They must respond constantly so that the head and body are always oriented to the only constant force in the world of sensation—gravity. The responses of these organs do not adapt because their stimulus, the force of gravity, never changes.

THE RELATIVITY OF SENSORY EXPERIENCE

Although in this chapter we have analyzed sensory experience separately and noted how each individual process works, sensory experiences do not occur separately. We may see "red" for instance, but we do not see pure "red" alone; it may be on the surface of an automobile, in bright or dim light, or next to a green car. We always see red in comparison to other colors. A photograph of your white car at sunset may be much redder than a tomato at noon. (See Plate 11.)

We are always adapting. Our sensory judgments, and even basic sensory processes, depend on their context. We reset our level of adaptation according to the situation. In winter, a day that is 50° F is experienced as "warm," while the same temperature in summer is "cold." I visited Hawaii one winter when the temperature was 68° F. On the beach were tourists from Minnesota in bikinis; the weather they had left was −20° F. At the end of the beach were Hawaiian workers wearing heavy sheepskin coats. The native workers were experiencing the low end of their temperature range, the tourists the high end (winter). That we constantly maintain a level of adaptation, and interpret experience by comparison to this standard, is a principle to keep well in mind, not only for sensory judgments, but for all kinds of judgments, from wealth to people and politics.

Adaptation-Level Theory

Harry Helson (1964) theorized that, in trying to accommodate to changes in the external world, an organism sets an **adaptation level.** This adaptation level is determined by three factors:

1. *Focal stimuli.* These stimuli are at the center of our attention; they constitute immediate experience.
2. *Background stimuli.* These are the contextual stimuli in which the focal stimulus is embedded, such as the different sequences in brightness contrast and the constant sounds in a room.
3. *Residual stimuli.* These are stimuli that the observer has experienced in the past.

FIGURE 5–28
Adaptation Level
Look at the left-hand photograph. You will quickly form the impression that one man is "tall," that he is probably above average height. Now look at the right-hand photograph. The "tall" man from the other picture is obviously the shorter of the two here. From the initial sensory experience you set an adaptation level, a conviction about what "average" and "tall" are. But the second picture forced you to modify it. We judge people and things against such internal standards, which can be altered by new experience that shows them to be in error.

If you look at a television sportscaster of normal height interviewing a jockey, you are likely to judge the sportscaster as tall. If you see him interviewing a basketball star, he seems small. The height of the sportscaster is the focal stimulus. The heights of the jockey and basketball player are the background stimuli. The residual stimulus is the range of human heights we have experienced. They all combine to create the adaptation level in this situation.

Helson's approach allows us to quantify the relativity of sensory experience. One important finding is **anchoring effects.** An anchoring effect is the effect of preceding stimuli on the judgment of subsequent stimuli. In one experiment people were given either heavy (400–600 g) or light (100–300 g) weights to judge. Then half of each group switched. Those going from the heavy to the light weights experienced the light weights as lighter than those who lifted light weights all along.

Adaptation levels occur in most sensory and judgmental processes. An apple tastes sweet with cheese but sour after ice cream. Sensory judgments of magnitude are also made in comparison to previous experience. As Ernest Weber, the first psychophysicist, pointed out, an inch seems longer compared to a foot than to a yard.

Sensory experience involves a process of *selection, adaptation,* and *comparison.* The senses are at the intersection of the biological world and the world of perception, consciousness, thought, and intelligence. It is to these subjects that we now turn.

Summary

1. The senses use selection, adaptation, and comparison to simplify the incoming information entering the nervous system.

2. The least amount of energy necessary for us to *notice* a stimulus is the absolute threshold. The minimum increase in energy necessary to notice a *difference* in stimuli is the difference threshold or, more commonly, the *just noticeable difference* (j.n.d.).

3. Weber's Law was the first principle of sensation. It states that equal changes in physical intensity do not produce equal changes in experience.

4. Fechner continued Weber's work and discovered that it is the relative intensity of the physical differences that our senses are designed to notice, not the absolute differences.

5. A third principle, discovered by Stevens, is that different senses transform the information they select differently. Pain, for instance, is greatly amplified, while brightness is attenuated.

6. Light strikes the *retina,* the center of the visual system, after passing through the cornea and lens. The retina transduces the light energy into neural impulses.

    Important photoreceptors on the retina are the rods and cones—named after their shape. Rods respond most to light energy at low levels. Cones are primarily responsible for color vision. There are three types of cones: one that responds primarily to red-yellow wave lengths; one to green; and one to blue.

7. In each eye there are about 126 million *photoreceptor cells* whose impulses are channeled to the brain via the *ganglion* cells. On their way to the brain they pass through the *lateral geniculate nucleus* (LGN). Each cell has a *receptive field*—the area of stimulation on the retina to which it is most sensitive.

8. There are specialized cells in the brain *(feature analyzers)*, which respond to various complex features presented on the retina. These features range from bars, lines and edges, to orientation, movement, and other specific features of the environment. One animal study even found that such a cell responded to the shape of the hand.

9. The ear responds to vibrations in the air and, like the visual system, the auditory system transduces what it receives into neural impulses. Pressure waves in the air move down the auditory canal to the eardrum, causing it to vibrate. This causes three bones of the middle ear to vibrate: the hammer, the anvil, and the stirrup. The stirrup beats on the *cochlea* at the oval window and causes the *basilar membrane* to vibrate. These vibrations are transduced into neural signals at the organ of Corti. Although not as well studied as the selection and analysis process of the visual system, that of the auditory system is similar.

10. Other senses, such as smell, taste, and touch, operate on similar principles, although, of course, their receptor apparatus is different.

11. The *vestibular senses* include the sense of balance. The sense of movement is called *kinesthesis*. The somesthetic system conveys to the brain information concerning sensations in the internal environment.

Terms and Concepts

absolute threshold
adaptation level
anchoring effects
basilar membrane
cochlea
cones
cornea
difference threshold
electromagnetic energy
feature analyzers
fovea
ganglion cells
just noticeable difference (j.n.d.)
kinesthesis

lateral inhibition
olfactory cilia
olfactory epithelium
pheromones
photoreceptors
Power Law
proprioception
receptive field
retina
rods
somesthetic system
transduction
vestibular system
Weber's Law

Suggestions for Further Reading

Unfortunately, there are not many books on sensation.

Coren, S., Porac, C., & Ward, L. M. (1979). *Sensation and perception.* New York: Academic Press.
  The best textbook.

Lindsay, P., & Norman, D. (1977). *Human information processing* (2nd ed.). New York: Academic Press.
  A good overview of the senses as they relate to the rest of the mind.

*T*he mind is hard to grasp.

Our biology is tangible: fossils; neurons; pain pathways; receptive fields.

The mind, however, is analyzed in theoretical concepts like those of chemistry before atomic particles were discovered. The "atoms of the mind" are the basic associations: red light "automatically" means "stop." The "elements" are the schemata, joined chains of associations which simplify actions—how to walk, dance, drive. The "compounds" are prototypes and mental routines which "make sense" of all the different information that hits us. You had literally billions of experiences last summer, but how much do you remember?

Ours is a mental system that has only a few components. They combine and recombine to make new creations: new sentences, new ideas, new insights, as particles, once only theoretical, were thought to combine to form new elements, new compounds, and new substances.

Part Two
The Mental World

Chapter 6

Perceiving the World

INTRODUCTION

In the previous chapter we looked at how the senses select information from the world. But in reading about the specifics of neural signals and how they are sent to the brain, you might feel that the functioning of all the senses (visual, auditory, skin, and chemical) somehow does not "add up" to our living experience of our world. Here, for instance, is a simplified and abbreviated example of sensory information as it is transmitted to the brain: "increasing 700 nm waves in the right, accompanied by increasing pressure of sound waves of 60–80 Hz at 40° to the left." Information in this form does not mean much to us. The message "a bear is coming, and fast, on the left" certainly does.

The difference between the two messages is *meaning. Perception is a process that organizes sensory information into the simplest meaningful pattern.*

Usually the translation of sensation into perception is so quick and automatic that we are unaware of the difference. Occasionally, however, you may experience it. I did one morning when I awoke, slowly. I seemed surrounded by bright grayness. I felt a certain heaviness. My back was very warm. I could hear a high pitched sound close by, a lower one farther away. I smelled an odd mixture of aromas. Then these disconnected sensations became organized. I was home in bed, on a cloudy morning, my cat was on my back purring, a lawnmower was working in the distance. Someone in the kitchen was cooking breakfast and had burned the toast.

When I realized the *meaning* of the disconnected sensations, I had shifted between two worlds—I had moved from the world of disconnected "raw" sensations to knowing about the nature of the world. This process goes on all the time: it is the difference between seeing a group of letters printed on a page and recognizing the meaning of the message, like "I love you."

In this chapter we begin our study of how we know and interpret things and events in the world. Perception is an active process. Our perceptions begin with the information our senses receive; they involve not only *reception* and *selection* but also an act of *creation.* In this chapter we examine first how mental processes produce meaning. We then examine the primary achievement of perception: the stable, "constant" experience of the world, even though the world is in constant change. Finally, we consider how we perceive the external world: the world of space, time, other people, and even ourselves.

Principles and Issues

Meaning

Many of the mental processes we consider in Part Two, such as perception, memory, and consciousness, function to discover meaning in the world. In order to interpret the meaning from "raw" sensory information, the perceptual system uses a basic rule of thumb. In effect it asks: What is the simplest *meaningful* thing that the sensory stimuli can be organized into? Thus, we do not experience a "rectangular expanse of red," but a "red book"; when we hear sounds getting louder we know (or assume) an object is approaching; when an object looks smaller and smaller, this *means* it is moving away from us. Two important aspects of perceptual analysis are organization and interpretation.

Organization. Perceptual organization is the connection and coordination of separate sensory stimuli into something meaningful. The disorganized sensations that I felt on awakening were *organized* into one experience: "I'm at home, in bed, on a cloudy morning." This organization "made sense" of all the different sensory information reaching me. Once a number of stimuli are organized into a percept, it becomes difficult to see them once again as separate and disorganized. Look at Figure 6–1 for a few moments. At first it seems to be only a collection of dots

FIGURE 6–1
Organizing Sensory Stimuli
It takes your perception to make a meaningful pattern emerge from what at first seems to be a random collection of spots and dots. And once you have made sense of it, it is hard to recapture your impression of the picture as random or meaningless. (After Carraher & Thurston, 1966)

strewn at random. At some moment you will organize them into a scene of a Dalmation dog near a tree. Once so organized, it is almost impossible to see the picture as a "random" collection of dots again.

Interpretation.   The second step in discovering meaning is interpretation. Consider seeing the bear approaching: first the information from the senses is organized into the perception "bear." But, what is the meaning of "a bear" in your presence? What action do you take? Suppose the "bear" suddenly says "Trick or treat!" Now you remember it is Halloween, and the meaning of "bear" becomes quite different than if you had heard a growl! Determining the meaning of an event thus involves interpretation. Among the different components of interpretation we shall consider later on in this chapter are *inferences* and *assumptions*.

Simplicity

When something is organized it is simplified. The experience of many different "dots" on a page is quite complex: a Dalmation near a tree is organized and simple. Because there is so much information "out there," it is important that we simplify all the information in order to act quickly in the world.

Thus, our experience of the world is far simpler than the external world itself. Our senses select and simplify the physical stimulation to which our bodies are exposed. Perception continues this simplification process. *In any situation we tend to experience the simplest meaningful organization of the stimuli registered.* Look at the two drawings in Figure 6–2: They are both drawings of a cube, but from different angles. The one on the top we see in two dimensions, and we would not normally identify it as a cube. It is simpler to see it as a hexagon than as a cube seen from one of its points. We see the drawing on the bottom as a cube in three dimensions because it is a simpler experience than a group of rectangles. Perceiving the simplest organization enables us to make quick decisions and, therefore, to respond and act quickly.

THE PROCESS OF PERCEPTION

If you do not think about it, nothing seems simpler than perceiving the environment. At this moment I can see ivy and grass, hear kids playing in the street, see the blue sky beyond. Let us consider a simple, typical scene. I walk into a room and see my friend David. I might speak to him, perhaps ask him about a project he is working on. This is a simple, ordinary experience, not worthy of much analysis—or so it would seem.

It takes a lot of work to keep things simple. It might interest you to know that no computer, no matter how large and sophisticated, could accomplish that simple feat. I know hundreds of people, and it is not extraordinary that I know what to talk about with each one. A computer could not even identify David, let alone hold a conversation with him. This simple and ordinary experience is, actually, the result of many difficult and complex operations. We may be aware of *what* we perceive, but we

FIGURE 6–2
Three-dimensionality and Organizational Simplicity
The continuous lines in each drawing make it easier to perceive one as a flat pattern (top) and the other as a three-dimensional cube (bottom). (After Hochberg & McAlister, 1953; Kopfermann, 1930)

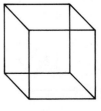

are not normally aware of the mental processes "behind the scenes" that make perception possible. The analysis of these processes is the subject of perception.

Let us go back to David in the room. In order to see David, you first "pick up" information from the environment. Only a few of the millions of stimuli reaching the sense receptors yield any information about David and the room. This "raw" sensory information is first picked up and organized. That expanse of red we see we perceive as the couch, the gray is his shirt, the voice identifies David, not Fred. In addition, your perception of David goes beyond what meets the eyes and ears. Once you have assembled David, you go beyond that immediate information and assume he is the same person he was before, with the same memories, interests, and experiences. Further, perception is continuous. The world changes, David may move around, you may move as well, someone else may enter the room, you may leave.

Perception thus involves "picking up" information about the world, organizing it, and making inferences about the environment in a continuous cycle. Each of these processes will be considered in this section.

Selecting Information Relevant for Survival   See Chapter 5, pp. 178–79.

Picking up Information about the World

Perception, and our analysis of it, begins with the environment to be perceived. To be useful, our perceptions must accurately reflect the world around us. People approaching must be seen if we are to avoid bumping into them. We have to be able to identify food before we can eat it. The senses act as information gatherers and selectors for perception. They select information about color, taste, and sound relevant for survival. What our organism perceives depends on what elements the environment "affords." The characteristics of the environment have been analyzed extensively by specialists called "ecological psychologists." Two characteristics are:

1. *Affordance.* Each object in the environment offers a rich source of information (Doner & Lappin, 1980). This information is called the **affordance** of the environment. A post "affords" information about its right angles; a tomato affords information about its roundness, color,

FIGURE 6–3
The Invariance of Perception
Even though some are close and others farther away, some seen from the front and others from one side or the other at different angles, some blocked from clear view by those in front of them, all the objects in this drawing are clearly perceived as fence posts because they present us unchanging, or invariant, information from all perspectives. (After Gibson, 1950)

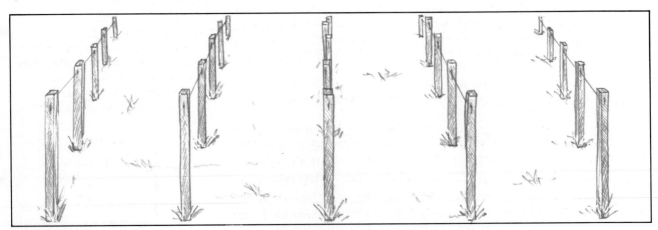

and taste; a tree about its greenness, the color of its fruit, and other attributes.

2. *Invariance.* The external environment contains many different objects. Each offers to the perceiver certain *invariant* features. An **invariant** is a constant pattern of stimulation (Michaels & Carello, 1981). Even a common object such as a post presents unchanging, or invariant, information about itself as we walk around it (Figure 6–3). From every angle, we see that the post has right angles, is perpendicular to the earth, is white. Because perceivers are always in motion, they have the chance to "pick up" many of the invariant features of the environment (Gibson, 1979). There are invariant patterns that are common to all objects: all objects get smaller as their distance from the perceiver increases; lines converge at the horizon; when one object is nearer it blocks out another.

Perception, then, involves an organism "picking up" the information afforded by the environment and using it.

Rules of Organization

The sensory information is most often so complex that it must be simplified and organized. The perceptual system is so specialized for organizing sensory information that it attempts to organize things into a pattern even when there is none. We look up at a cloud and see shapes in it—a whale, a bird.

"Op art," popular in the 1960s, played with this predisposition to organize. Op art is at once intriguing and unsettling because we try continually to organize certain figures that are designed by the artist to have no organization.

Gestalt

The rules of perceptual organization are the basis of the *Gestalt* approach to psychology. **Gestalt** is a German word with no direct English equivalent (which is why it has entered our language in its original form), but it roughly means *to create a form.* A gestalt is the immediate organization of the form of an object. In the Gestalt school of psychology, an object is more than the sum of its parts. For instance, you instantly perceive the lines in Figure 6–5 as a square. You do not see four individual lines, then notice they are all at right angles to one another, then judge that they are of equal length, and then add them up and say, "That's a square." *The figure is immediately perceived as a whole,* not as the sum of its parts.

Principles of Organization

Gestalt psychologists have identified a number of rules governing the organizing principles of perception. Four of the principles of organization are figure-ground, proximity, similarity, and good continuation.

Figure-ground.   What you see in Figure 6–6 depends on which color you decide is the background and which the "figure." These drawings are called "ambiguous figures," because it is not clear which is the figure

FIGURE 6–4
Resistance to Stable Organization
Op art such as this can present many different and changing meaningful patterns of organization. This runs counter to our perceptual preference for stable, invariant patterns of organization. (After Carraher & Thurston, 1968)

FIGURE 6–5
Gestalt:
Perception of the Whole
We tend to organize our perceptions immediately into wholes, rather than seeing them as their constituent parts—which is why you first see this figure as one square, not four lines.

and which is the ground. Depending on what you decide, you see a chalice or two profiles, some stones from an ancient ruin or the word "TIE."

Proximity.   When elements are close together, they tend to be perceived as a unit. That is, they seem to describe a form (Figure 6–7).

Similarity.   Like elements tend to be grouped together (Figure 6–8).

Good Continuation.   It is simpler to see *continuous* patterns and lines. In Figure 6–9, it is more difficult to discern the complicated figure in the middle or bottom drawing than in the top one, which is made up of the same elements, but moved closer together.

Interpretation: Going beyond the Information Given

In spite of the fact that there is a great richness of sensory information reaching us, the information we receive at any one monent is often incomplete. We may catch but a glimpse of our friend David's shirt or hear only a word or two of his voice, yet we recognize him. In order to organize our experience of the world we often need to go beyond the immediate imformation we receive. This fact was often demonstrated in the Middle Ages by jesters. They constructed garments that were white on one side, red on the other; then they walked a straight line between two rows of spectators. The audence was later asked the color of the garments. One group confidently reported that the jesters were dressed

FIGURE 6–6
Seeing Figure and Ground
Because you can perceive either the light or dark portions of these drawings as figures against a background of the opposite shade, the meaning of what you see can vary dramatically.

FIGURE 6–7
Organization by Proximity
Separate elements placed close together tend to be perceived as a unit, seem to describe a form, rather than being seen as distinct and unrelated.

FIGURE 6–8
Organization by Similarity
Our perception tends to recognize similar elements and group them with one another. Thus, you are more likely to see the two halves of the spheres as separate and different, and perceive three groups of the same letters rather than groups of the letters OXT.

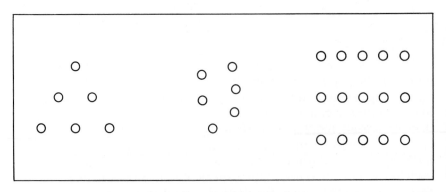

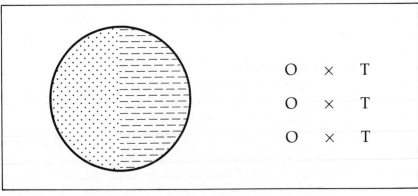

all in white; the other group equally confidently said "red." They nearly came to blows, until the ambiguous garments were shown, so strong is the tendency to fill in the gaps.

In order to act quickly and flexibly in the world, we fill in the gaps of missing information. For example, you probably did not notice the three typographical errors in the previous paragraph (Hochberg, 1978).

One of the most common perceptual operations is one that "cleans up" information and "straightens it out." Look at Figure 6–10. Then cover up the figure and draw the shapes. You probably drew the slanted ellipse as a circle, the "square" with straight sides; you completed and connected the sides of the "triangle," and made the "X" with two straight lines. You cleaned up, corrected, and connected the figures to match your interpretation of them.

Figure 6–11 is composed of three acute angles spaced equidistantly between three squares, each square with a small piece missing at the corners. What you probably saw was three squares and two overlapping triangles. However, the topmost triangle is something you "filled in" by the process of interpretation. We try, in such a perceptual analysis, to experience things in the "best form" available to us.

Unconscious Inferences

We are always unaware of sensory stimuli and usually unaware of the act of perception. We *experience* neither the separate, disconnected stimuli nor the "rules of organization" being applied to them. Rather, we make what is called in psychology **unconscious inferences.** We draw conclusions about reality on the basis of the suggestions and cues brought in by the senses. The nineteenth-century scientist Hermann Helmholtz thus compared the perceiver to an astronomer, forced to fill in the gaps in his information.

> An astronomer, for example, comes to real conscious conclusions of this sort, when he computes the positions of the stars in space, their distances, etc., from the perspective images he has had of them at various times and as they are seen from different parts of the orbit of the earth. His conclusions are based on a conscious knowledge of the laws of

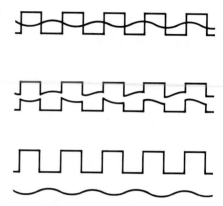

FIGURE 6–9
Organization by Continuity
It is much easier to perceive the whole and the parts of the top figure than to see those identical elements presented in the other two discontinuous drawings.

FIGURE 6–10
Cleaning up Perceptual Information
After looking at these figures for a few seconds, draw what you saw and read in the text on this page what your drawing may indicate about how you interpret what you perceive.

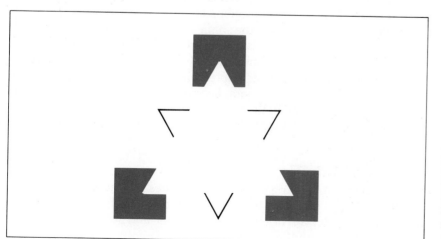

FIGURE 6–11
Filling in Perceptual Information
If you see two triangles in this figure, you are interpreting or subjectively "filling in" the white central one, which does not actually exist. (After Coren, 1972)

optics. In the ordinary acts of vision this knowledge of optics is lacking. Still it may be permissible to speak of the (psychological) acts of ordinary perception as unconscious conclusions, thereby making a distinction of some sort between them and the common so-called conscious conclusions.

Many classic demonstrations in perception show the effect of inferences on our experience. As you look at the cube in Figure 6–12, its structure seems to shift before your eyes. Is the shaded portion a rear or front side? The figure itself does not change, of course. What does change is your *perception* of the cube. The eyes send the brain bits of information about the arrangement of a set of lines. The next step is to *organize* the information and *interpret* what it is. Your perception of the cube shifts because your interpretation changes; indeed the shift in your *experience* is actually a shift in your interpretation. Normally we are not aware that perception involves such inferences, because few figures are ambiguous and it is usually easy to settle on one correct inference.

The Assumptive World

In order to act quickly we must assume a lot about the world we perceive. If I tell you that David is in a room, you immediately assume the room has four walls, a floor, a ceiling, and probably furniture. On entering a room we do not inspect it to determine whether the walls are at right angles, or that the room is still there when we leave it. If we constantly verified everything in our environment there would be no time to do anything. Thus our perceptual experience, such as "David in the room," involves many *assumptions*.

If much of our experience is assumed, then it follows that *if our assumptions change, our perceptions will, too*. This was the hypothesis of Adelbert Ames and his colleagues at Dartmouth in the late 1940s and early 1950s (Ittleson, 1952). They analyzed perception involving a transaction between the organism and the environment. For instance, Hastorf (1950) showed that our judgment of the distance of a thing depends on how big we assume it to be. A Ping-Pong ball seen at one distance might be taken for a tennis ball closer up or could look like a volley ball seen at a greater distance. How we experience the ball and judge our distance from it depends on our assumptions of *what* it is.

Another example involves the shape of rooms. Space is three-dimensional, but the mechanics of vision are two-dimensional. We assume that rooms are rectilinear. But sometimes assumptions are wrong, and the result can be the experience of "impossible" changes in the apparent size of a person who crosses the room, because we do not easily change our learned assumptions about the shape of rooms. (See Figure 6–13.) It is so hard to change this assumption that it makes us see people of grossly different sizes.

Needs and Values

Other determinants of perception are values and needs. Bruner and Goodman (1946) conducted an experiment in which they compared the perceptual experiences of children from poor and well-to-do families.

FIGURE 6–12
Inference and Perceptual Ambiguity
The shaded part of this so-called Necker cube seems to shift from the front to the back as you look at it. But, of course, the figure is not changing, only your perception of it, which changes as your brain organizes and interprets the ambiguous perceptual information it receives. (After Gregory, 1968)

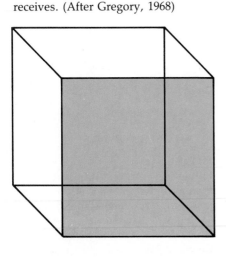

FIGURE 6–13
Perceptual Assumptions
Because we assume rooms are
rectilinear, a "room" like this,
shaped to exploit that assumption,
can distort our perception and fool
us into seeing the boy and the dog as
improbably different sizes.

When shown a certain coin, children from poor homes experienced it as larger than did the richer children. This finding has been repeated in other cultures, such as that of Hong Kong (Dawson, 1975). In another study, students in a class were asked to draw a picture of the teacher. The majority of the honor students drew the teacher slightly smaller than the students in the picture. But the pictures by less-than-average students depict the teacher as much taller than the students (Hochberg, 1978). Albert Hastorf and Hadly Cantril (1954) studied the influence of prejudice on perception at a Princeton-Dartmouth football game. During the game, Princeton's star quarterback was injured. Afterward, Hastorf and Cantril interviewed two groups of fans and recorded their opinions of the game on a questionnaire. The Princeton fans said that Dartmouth had been unduly violent and aggressive toward their quarterback. The Dartmouth fans reported that the game was rough, but fair. Thus, values, needs, and biases also help determine perception.

The Perceptual Cycle

Picking up information, organizing it, and filling in gaps all help explain how we might perceive static objects and events. These processes also help explain how we recognize things we have experienced before. The world is constantly changing, however, and to get along we must be able to discover the meaning of new things and information we encounter. The concept of a *perceptual cycle* helps explain how we handle new information about undiscovered parts of the world.

The **perceptual cycle** is based on the idea that perception is a continuous process directed by schemata (Neisser, 1976). When one person says a glass is "half empty" and another says it is "half full," we have an example of how people search their environment differently. One person is looking at what is gone, the empty space; the other is looking at what is left, the liquid.

Three factors figure in the perceptual cycle: first is our schemata. To review, a unit of mental organization is called a *schema*—plural, schemata. A schema is the framework that ties events together in the mind. Schemata allow us to perceive things as connected and thus act in an organized way. Schemata not only link our past experience with present events, they also direct our discovery of the world. The second factor is our movements and manipulations of the world; the third is sensory information about physical changes in the external world. Figure 6–14 is a diagram of the cycle. The schemata direct exploration: sensory information provided by these exploratory movements modifies the view of the world produced by the brain, which in turn changes the schema. New movements are directed, and exploration begins anew. This continuous cycle produces continually changing experience, and thus different people may "carve out" different perceptual experiences.

Consider the different experiences of a child, an artist, and a botanist as each walks across a park. The child sees everything at the knee level of adults. He or she may notice balls that roll nearby, other children (especially if they have balloons); the bell of the ice cream truck is compelling.

Schemata   See Chapter 3, pp. 97–98.

The artist notices the different colors of green on the grass and trees, the play of light, the shape of the clouds. If in need of a dark-haired woman to model for a painting, every dark-haired woman in view will be examined as a potential model. When the botanist looks at the trees, the scientific name of each one may come to mind and the progress of some spring blossoms seen the week before will be noted. The child may pick up a leaf unconsciously and begin to tear and fold it. The botanist may pick up the same leaf exclaiming, ''My God! This is the first time that the *Fernicus imaginarius* has been seen outside Europe!'' Although the three park strollers are afforded the same sensory stimuli, their experiences are very different. Thus we carve out our individual worlds by *picking out specific information;* the schemata direct the selection of events that follow (Neisser, 1976).

How Perceptual Experience Changes

Our perceptual experience changes in the same two ways that children's schemata change as they get older: assimilation and accommodation. In the perceptual cycle, schemata are constantly updated as the search of the external environment relays information that requires new interpretation.

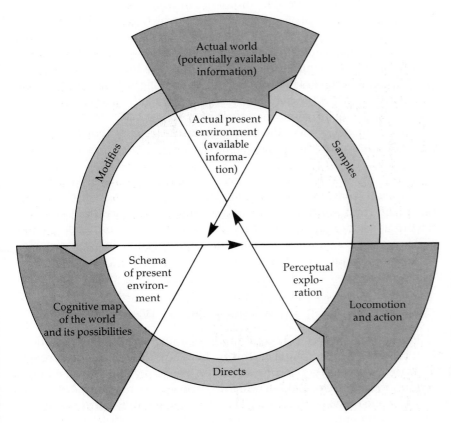

FIGURE 6–14
The Perceptual Cycle
This diagram represents the theory that perception is a continuous process of changing experience directed by schemata, themselves modified by sensory information provided by the selective exploration of the environment. (After Neisser, 1976)

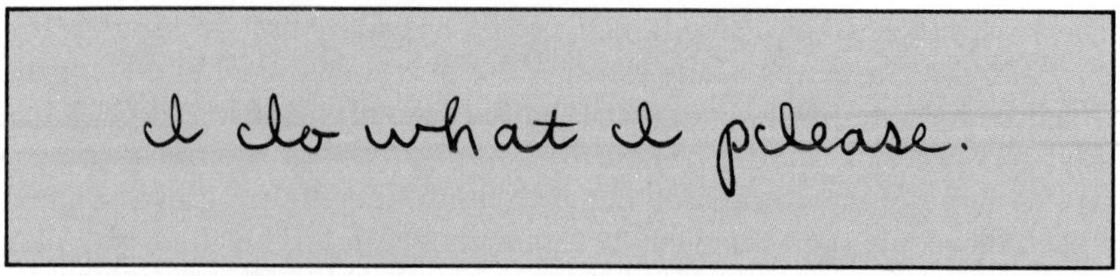

FIGURE 6–15
Assimilation

I do what I please.

Assimilation is the way we interpret incoming information to match our existing schemata. Read the message in Figure 6–15. You probably had no trouble deciphering "I do what I please." But notice that the "l" in "please," the "I," and the "d" in the "do" are identical. That same element is experienced differently, and appropriately, in each case. For instance, we do not perceive the individual letters of words, but rather the words they signify. Thus typographical errors are hard to detect. Similarly, Figure 6–16 is experienced as a rabbit if seen with rabbits, a bird if among birds.

Accommodation is the process by which schemata are changed to fit new information. If the discrepancy between the outside world and our schemata is too great, then the schemata must change to accommodate the new information. Look *quickly* at the playing cards in Plate 12 and then turn away. (Do this before reading any more of this paragraph.) How many aces of spades are there? Now look again, but this time keep in mind that in this illustration an ace of spades may be red or black. Now how many are there? The difference in your two estimates was due to a change in your "playing card schema," which in turn changed your perception of the future, of what you were prepared to see the second time. Our normal "playing card schema" directs us to look for black spades only. When our schemata change, we see things more "as they are." The same process holds in the evaluation of other people and even of scientific theories. Scientific "facts" are actually interpretations of events according to some theory. When events occur that cannot be explained by the theory, the theory is discarded and replaced with a new, more encompassing one.

Perceiving is a very complex act. It begins with the picking up of information from the environment. That information is simplified and organized, and we determine its meaning through assumptions and unconscious inferences. We then search out new information as the cycle of perceptual experience continues and we come to know a stable, continuing, meaningful world.

Two Theories of Perception: Do We Receive or Invent the External World?

Perception involves determining the meaning of outside information, but how do we accomplish this? There are two major theoretical approaches to the process of perception. The *ecological approach* emphasizes the relevance of the external information in perception. A comparison is made between the perceiver and a radio set; they both "tune into" the environment and pick up information they are built to receive (Gib-

FIGURE 6–16
Context and Ambiguity
Depending on its context, this ambiguous figure can be perceived as either a duck or a rabbit.

son, 1979). The *constructivist approach* emphasizes the role of the schemata in perception. This view likens the perceiver to a computer, making judgments and decisions about the external world according to past experience or "programs."

The Ecological Approach

The **ecological approach** emphasizes the richness of the information available to the perceiver. In this view perception is a direct function of stimulation (Gibson, 1979; Michaels & Carello, 1981). For instance, in studying sensation we found that the information for color vision is *directly* present at the receptors, it stimulates the receptors, and we experience color. The proponents of this view say that information about distance, relative size, shape, and perspective are all similarly available to the human perceiver.

This process of human perception is similar to other organisms'. The worm, the fish, the eagle, the tiger, and the human being, to take a few examples, all live in quite different environments. Different organisms have evolved differently in different environments, and each organism has evolved specialized perceptual systems to "pick up" information that is relevant to the organism. This part of the ecological approach is called *evolutionism* (Turvey & Shaw, 1979). This is an important point and deserves emphasis. According to the ecological view, the *environment is different for each organism,* so that the information that is appropriate for each organism is different to a greater or lesser extent. Insofar as perception is successful, it responds directly, as does a radio, to the specific features of the world it is designed to pick up (Gibson, 1979).

If this theory is right, then there should be, waiting to be discovered, cells or networks of cells in the brain that respond to the relative size of two objects, to the convergence at the horizon, and to other features of our natural world, as do the cells in the visual system that respond to color and to corners. If such networks are discovered, we would have a more precise understanding of what is built in and what is built up in the perceptual process.

The Human Visual System See Chapter 5, pp. 190–94.

The Constructivist Approach

The **constructivist approach** has been dominant in psychology for a hundred years. It asserts that because the sensory information reaching the brain is chaotic and disorganized, perception must be a process of constructing a "representation" or model of the world (as an ordinary globe is fashioned to represent the earth). Hence, the information from the senses "sparks off" the creation of an image of what could have caused this sensation. Many of the classic demonstrations described earlier, such as the distorted room and figure-ground illustrations, support the view that perception involves an act of creation as well as "passive" reception of information. We process, infer, and analyze information until we arrive at a reliable solution, the percept. Of course, our percepts must also be correct when checked out in the real world. That is, the percepts we do construct should keep us from bumping into walls, drinking boiling hot fluids, or not recognizing our friends when we see them.

FIGURE 6–17
Shape Constancy
Like most objects we perceive, this cup, though viewed from various angles, is always recognized as a cup. Such changes of orientation may alter the retinal image, but not what is experienced.

Review of the Two Approaches

Each of the views emphasizes different aspects of the perceptual process. The ecological approach deals with the adaptive nature of perception. Like all other organisms, we have evolved in response to a physical environment. It is thus highly likely that we would possess some built-in systems for the reception of external information, things of importance to our survival, like color. However, few cells or neural networks have been found that pick up more organized and complex features of the world. Many psychologists feel that the view that *all* of our perception is "direct" is too extreme, that it cannot account for actual human perception in our complex, invented environment (Hayes-Roth, 1980; Ullman, 1980). The ecological view does not well account for the fact that the same stimulus can mean different things to different people; for example, the meaning of a police siren is not the same to a thief and to the victim. It also ignores the role of assumptions. The ecological approach, then, does not account for the elements of meaning that depend on interpretation.

The constructivist approach assumes that we must invent a stable world anew, each moment, and that this invention is the product of a long period of trial and error. This view, too, seems extreme. It ignores the evolutionary history of humans and other organisms and the specific information in the environment that is important to each organism. Obviously, most organisms evolved to take advantage of their environment, and human beings did, as well.

Perception most likely involves some of both processes. Perhaps some of the basic or "primary" qualities of the environment are "picked up" directly by the perceiver. But even these must be interpreted. What is the *meaning* of the man approaching, of an object disappearing into the distance? We need not restrict ourselves to a one-track view of a complex process like perception; we are probably a little like a radio and a little like a computer.

CONSTANCY: THE STABLE PERCEPTUAL WORLD

The most impressive thing about the perceptual process is how little change we experience even though the sensory information reaching us changes radically. A building may appear as a small dot on the horizon or may completely fill our visual world. Yet we perceive the building to be the same size and shape regardless of our vantage point. The main purpose of all the receiving, organizing, and interpreting that goes on in the perceptual processes is to achieve **constancy,** a stable, constant world.

You can easily demonstrate three kinds of perceptual constancies with your hand. Hold it with the palm facing toward you; then turn the palm away; then turn it so that you see the side of the hand. Even though the sensory impression of the hand is very different in each orientation, you perceive the same shape. That is *shape constancy*. Now hold your hand close to your face; then hold it at arm's length. Even though the image on the retina is very different in each case, the hand seems to be the same size. That is *size constancy.* Now hold your hand under a lamp, then turn the lamp out. What color is your hand? You experience the hand as having the same underlying color and brightness, even though the information is different. That is *brightness and color constancy.*

Shape Constancy

The same object presented in very different aspects is experienced as the same. In Figure 6–17, a cup is seen from several different angles. Even though the actual image is different in each instance, you see the same cup. Changes in the slant of an object cause the retinal image to change, but not your experience of the object.

Size Constancy

The size of the object can be accurately judged whether it is near or far away. As someone walks toward you from the horizon, that person's "image" on your retina can increase by more than 100 times (Figure 6–18), but you do not think the person is actually growing larger and larger before your eyes.

Brightness and Color Constancy

Although the brightness and color of an object vary in different illuminations, they are perceived to be the same. The whiteness of the pages of this book will look about the same to you in sunlight as it does in an unlit room at twilight. In controlled experiments on brightness constancy, people are asked to adjust a light source to match the brightness of a test object. The subjects are shown a test object ("A" in Figure 6–19). The outer circle has a brightness level of 200, the inner circle 100. Then drawing "B" is presented; here the outer circle has a brightness level of 200. The subjects are asked to produce the gray that matches the inner circle of the test object (A). The subjects usually choose accurately—producing a gray with 100 units of brightness. Then they are shown

FIGURE 6–18
Size Constancy
Look at the top photograph. The "small" man on the far right seems normal height, about the same as the man leaning against the lamp post. But in the bottom picture that *identical* figure is ridiculously smaller than the man on the left. What do your responses to these specially prepared photographs tell you about how size constancy works?

FIGURE 6–19
Brightness Constancy
As explained in the accompanying text, it is the relativity of brightness, not absolute values, that remain constant in perception.

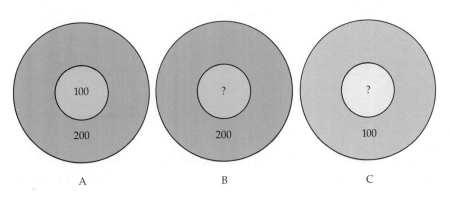

A   B   C

another drawing (C) in which the outer circle has a brightness of 100. Again, they are asked to match the gray of the inner circle to the test object (A). This time they are most likely to produce a gray with brightness level 50. This demonstrates that people do not perceive absolute values of brightness, but instead judge the relative brightness of objects to achieve a sense of constancy.

Likewise with color. A white car at sunset actually reflects the orange-yellow color of the sun (Plate 11). But it appears white to us because it is *relatively whiter* than the surrounding environment.

Illusions

Our perceptual mechanisms work so quickly and so well that we are, for the most part, unaware of all the operations involved in perceiving. Illusions are prized by psychologists not only for their fun, but because they reveal the normal processes of perception. Many illusions elicit a misapplication of the rules that govern constancy. Sometimes we may go from the process of "filling in the gaps" to "jumping to conclusions" as a consequence of the speed necessary to make quick judgments, and we make a mistake.

Here are three illusions:

Comparative Size.   The central circle on the left of Figure 6–20A looks larger than the central circle on the right, although they are the same size. They are perceived incorrectly because the circle surrounded by larger circles is smaller relative to its context than the other central circle. Recall that we ordinarily perceive in a comparative way rather than according to absolute values. This is a basic principle of all cognitive processes, from perception to decision making.

FIGURE 6–20
The Illusion of Comparative Size
The central circle on the left (A) only looks bigger because it is surrounded by smaller circles than the identical central circle next to it. Likewise, the upper horizontal line in the lower part of the right-hand drawing (B) seems longer no matter how you look at it—even turning the book sideways or upside down does not destroy the illusion. Even knowing the lines are the same length cannot overcome the power of the rules of perspective and the principle of comparative values.

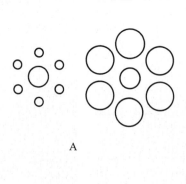

A

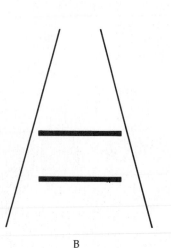

B

The Ponzo Illusion. Look at the two lines at the top of Figure 6–20B. You can see that they are the same length. Now look at the illustration below. Putting two converging lines next to these lines makes the top line seem longer. The rules of perspective that normally help us to judge size and distance accurately have in this case misled us.

Müller-Lyer Illusion. Although both lines in Figure 6–21A are equal in length, the figure with the arrows pointing toward its center looks longer than the figure with the arrows pointing toward its ends. The arrows may be taken as "depth cues" by the brain: the arrows pointing inward probably cause us to judge the line as farther away and thus longer (Gregory, 1973). Figure 6–21B is an example of this illusion in the world. The center vertical line in the picture on the left looks longer and it appears to be farther away. In this illusion, two schemata, "the appearance of things that recede into the background," and "things that approach and open up toward us," have probably been activated and misapplied.

FIGURE 6–21
The Müller-Lyer Illusion
Depth cues can alter our perception of lines of equal length. Because the arrows in the sketch below and the arrowlike intersecting lines at the corners in the photographs make us judge the vertical lines as closer or farther away, we see each line as shorter or longer than the other.

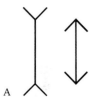

A

B

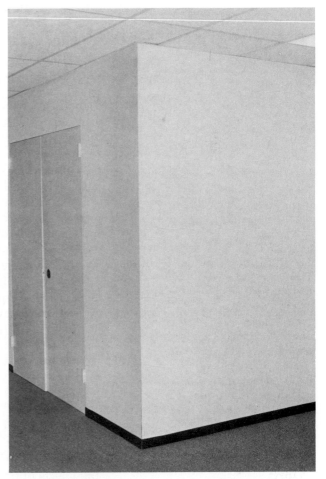

Ivo Köhler

PERCEIVING THE WORLD: SPACE, TIME, PEOPLE, AND PLACE

Controlled laboratory experiments can uncover some of the basic perceptual processes, but our perceptual processes normally operate in a much more complex and changeable environment than that of the laboratory. How these processes work in the real world is the subject of this section.

Adapting to the Environment

Perception is a continuous process by which an organism adapts to the immediate environment. For instance, the optical image on our retina is upside down from what we "see." How is it that we see the world "right side up?" Where is the image reversed? The answer reveals an important principle of perception: the "image" is *never* turned right side up. We do not need such an image; all we need to adapt to the external world is consistent information. The "image" on the retina is, in fact, inverted, consistently obscured by blinks, blind spots, and blood vessels, yet we adapt to all this.

Adaptation to Distortion

In the late nineteenth century the psychologist George Stratton reasoned that if perception is a process of adaptation to the environment, then it ought to be possible to learn to adapt to an entirely different arrangement of visual information, *as long as it was consistent.* To test this hypothesis, Stratton wore a special prism lens over one eye, so that he saw the world turned 180° on its side. The world was topsy-turvy: up/down and left/right were reversed.

Stratton had great difficulty at first in doing even simple things like reaching for or grasping an object. He felt very dizzy when he walked, and he bumped into things. Within days he began to adapt. After only three days of wearing the inverted lens, he wrote: "Walking through the narrow spaces between pieces of furniture required much less art than hitherto. I could watch my hands as they wrote, without hesitating or becoming embarrassed thereby." By the fifth day he could move around the house easily. On the seventh day he enjoyed his evening walk as usual. On the eighth day he removed the lens, and wrote "The reversal of everything from the order to which I had grown accustomed during the last week gave the scene a surprisingly bewildering air which lasted for several hours." Once Stratton had adapted to the new relationship between information and perception, it took some time to unlearn it.

Stratton wrote (1896) of his results:

> The different sense-perceptions, whatever may be the ultimate course of their extension, are organized into one harmonious spatial system. *The harmony is found to consist in having outer experiences meet our expectations.* [Italics added.]

More than 60 years later, Ivo Köhler conducted further experiments in the effects of optical rearrangement on perception. His observers wore various kinds of distorting lenses for weeks. At first they all had great difficulty in seeing the world. But in a few weeks they had adapted. One of Köhler's subjects was able to ski while wearing distorting lenses! People can also adapt to color distortions. In another of Köhler's demonstrations his subjects wore glasses in which one lens was green and one red. In a few hours they sensed no difference in color between the lenses (Köhler, 1962).

Is Perception Innate or Learned?

Suppose a blind man were suddenly able to see after years of blindness. What would he experience? The question of what is innate and what is learned in perception has been studied in many ways, using children, people from other cultures, blind people, and even a person born blind who had an operation to restore sight.

We come into the world with many abilities that enable us to perceive right away. Recall from Chapter 3 that children from birth prefer to look at faces. They are disturbed when the facial elements are rearranged. They seem to be born with, at the very least, the preference to perceive other human beings before other things in the world. The newborn's ability to imitate others, to discriminate between the mother's odor and that of other women, to turn toward sounds—as well as other abilities—all point to the likelihood of innate perceptual abilities.

Visual Cliff

Some perceptual abilities are probably innate but only develop with maturation. Recall that the "world" of the infant or young child is narrow, a very limited physical and social environment. Eleanor Gibson established that depth perception seems to develop only along with a baby's ability to move around. One day, Gibson was having a picnic on the rim of the Grand Canyon when she began to wonder if a baby would perceive the danger of the cliff or blithely ignore it and fall off. To test this question, she constructed an apparatus in her laboratory that she called the "visual cliff" (Figure 6–22). The **visual cliff** is the effect created by two surfaces under glass, both of which have a checkerboard pattern. One is directly underneath the glass, the other is several feet below. A wide board is placed across the glass top, directly over the "break" between the two checkerboard surfaces. If babies, old enough to crawl, are placed on the center board, they will not crawl to their mothers if it means "falling to the 'lower' surface," even though the glass top is solid and perfectly safe. The babies will leave the center board only if they can crawl across what they perceive to be the safe side (Gibson & Walk, 1960).

Recovery from Blindness

One question that has long interested philosophers and psychologists is, "What would be the visual experience of a person who had been born blind but was suddenly able to see?" Richard Gregory had the good fortune to study such a case. At 52 a man called SB, blind from birth, had a successful corneal transplant. When the bandages were removed, he

FIGURE 6–22
Visual Cliff
Babies will not crawl over a "cliff" onto a solid glass surface below which they can see a lower surface to which it appears they could fall. Both crawling infants and young animals seem able to perceive depth and its potential dangers. (After Gibson & Walk, 1960)

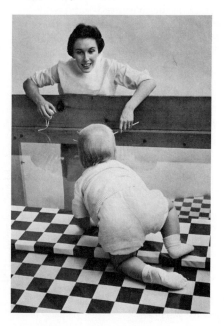

heard the voice of the surgeon, turned to look at him, and saw nothing but a blur. In a few days he could walk around the hospital corridors without touching the walls and could tell time from a wall clock. Even so, he could not see the world as crisply as we do when we open our eyes. He was able almost immediately to recognize objects for which he had already developed an "internal picture" through touch (Gregory, 1973).

He was surprised by the appearance of the moon. He could see and draw objects that he had known previously by touch, but had difficulty with those objects that he had not had the opportunity to touch while blind. For example, his drawings of a London bus even a year after the operation omitted the front of the bus, which he was, of course, unable to touch. Windows and wheels, however, were drawn in pretty fair detail right from the beginning. When Gregory showed SB a lathe, a tool SB was experienced in using, he had no idea what it was. Then SB was asked to touch the lathe; he closed his eyes, examined it thoroughly with his hand, and said, "Now that I have felt it I can see." Although SB had been deprived of sight, he had not been deprived of perception.

Cultural Effects on Perception

Although we appear to have some innate perceptual abilities, a completely prewired, built-in perceptual system seems unlikely. Humans live in all types of environments in the world and have lived in many cultures. It is almost certain that much perceptual experience is learned. Pygmies of the Congo dwell primarily in dense forest and thus rarely see across large distances. As a result they do not develop as strong a concept of size constancy as we do. Colin Turnbull, an anthropologist who studied pygmies, once took his pygmy guide on a trip out of the forest. As they were crossing a wide plain, they saw a herd of buffalo in the distance.

> Kenge looked over the plain and down to a herd of buffalo some miles away. He asked me what kind of insects they were, and I told him buffalo, twice as big as the forest buffalo known to him. He laughed

FIGURE 6–23
Blindness and Perception
Regaining his sight after an operation did not instantly enable the man who drew these pictures to perceive the world as it is. Both the left-hand drawing, done 48 days after the operation, and the other, done a year later, show more detail for parts of the bus the man used—and especially touched—while he was blind. His perceptions from when he was blind still influenced his experience of the world.

loudly and told me not to tell him such stupid stories. . . . We got into the car and drove down to where the animals were grazing. He watched them getting larger and larger, and though he was as courageous as any pygmy, he moved over and sat close to me and muttered that it was witchcraft. . . . When he realized they were real buffalo he was no longer afraid, but what puzzled him was why they had been so small, and whether they had really been small and suddenly grown larger or whether it had been some kind of trickery. (Turnbull, 1961)

I observed the same "mistake" one day while talking to a five-year-old. Seeing his mother from afar, he said, "There's my midget mommy." Children's perceptions tend to be more limited than adults' because they have fewer perceptual schemata. In addition, people from different cultures may not be "fooled" by the same optical tricks, because they do not share the same schemata. For example, illusions like the Müller-Lyer and the Ponzo illusions depend to a certain extent on living in a world in which right angles and straight lines predominate. Our world is a "carpentered world." By contrast, some African tribes, such as the Zulus, live in round huts with round doors and plough their fields in circles; they do not experience the Müller-Lyer illusion as strongly as we do (Segal, Campbell, & Herskovits, 1963).

FIGURE 6–24
Culture and Perception
People who live in round houses do not experience the Müller-Lyer illusion as strongly as we do. (See Figure 6–21, p. 231.)

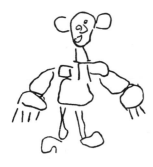

FIGURE 6–25
Drawings by Blind People
The crossed fingers (top), a runner (middle), and a boy (bottom) were drawn by people blind from birth, yet they show awareness of perspective and even of such artistic subtleties as the need to foreshorten one leg of a running person.

SEEING WITHOUT EYES

What do blind people think the world looks like? Are their mental images of people and things very different from ours? Over the past 10 years John Kennedy has conducted experiments that begin to answer these questions. He asked people, blind since birth, to draw pictures. At first you might think that was a ridiculous request; most of the blind people thought it was. A picture is, after all, a two-dimensional representation of a three-dimensional object, and the blind sense their world primarily through touch, a strictly three-dimensional experience. Kennedy gave each subject a plastic sheet that makes a raised line when a ballpoint pen is moved across it (Figure 6–25). He first asked them to draw simple objects—a cup, a hand, a table—and later, more complicated scenes.

To his surprise, Kennedy found that the blind realized almost immediately that some aspects of reality must be sacrificed in a drawing. You cannot draw a cup from all sides at once; a point of view must be selected. The blind artists devised ways to convey their meaning. And their solutions were easily understood by sighted people either at a glance or with brief captions, such as "This is how it would look from the side." What most surprised Kennedy is

that his blind artists understood perspective. (Kennedy, 1974)

There is more to seeing than meets the eye, and more to visual perception than sight. Although we rarely *experience* the difference, sensation and perception are not the same. Perception fills in the gaps left by incomplete sensory information. We recognize a cup even though we see only one side; we are not likely to check for a bottom before pouring coffee. The properties of weight, size, texture, form, function, and color all figure into the final perception of what a thing is. Through touch, a blind person can gain almost all the same information as a sighted person.

In fact, the sense of touch appears to be part of the visual perceptual system. It definitely is so for blind people. Carter Collins and his colleagues on the **Tactile Sensory Replacement** project at the Smith-Kettlewell Institute of Visual Sciences in San Francisco have devised a machine that capitalizes on the blind person's fine-tuned sense of touch. The machine impresses "televised" images onto the skin using electrical stimulation. The felt pattern of the image allows individuals to recognize objects in front of them. In fact, blind people have been able to "see" and work with instruments as precise as an oscilloscope, using

Look at Figure 6–27. Is the hunter closer to the baboon or the rhinoceros? Most of us would say the baboon. However, many Africans who do not share our experience of perspective in drawing do not make the same assumptions we make regarding the pictorial representation of three-dimensionality. Many of these people will answer that the rhinoceros is closer. This seems odd to us. However, if you look at the drawing strictly in two dimensions, the rhinoceros *is* closer to the hunter.

Our conventions for representing three dimensions on a two-dimen-

the TSR device (Figure 6–26).

The reason Collins and his co-workers chose touch instead of another sense is that of all senses touch is the closest to vision: Collins says, "No matter how acute your hearing is, it is a cue for location and distance only— not forms. But the thing about vision and touch is that they are both three-dimensional systems. What you see in front of you is essentially a frame on which patterns of light and shadow are played. You see in three dimensions because you move your neck and eyes and you have binocular vision. When a person wears the TSR vest, the camera moves just as the eyes do in sighted people."

Still I could not understand how such representations might actually "look." I sat blindfolded in the chair, the cones cold against my back. At first I felt only formless waves of sensation. Collins said he was just waving his hand in front of me so that I could get used to the feeling. Suddenly I felt, or saw, I wasn't sure which, a black triangle in the lower left corner of a square. The sensation was hard to get a fix on. I felt vibrations on my back, but the triangle appeared in a square frame in my head. Although there was no color, there were light and dark areas. If you close your eyes and face a strong light or the sun

and pass an object in front of your eyes, a difference appears in the darkness. That difference is approximately what I saw. The TSR image was fuzzy at first, but even within 10 minutes in the chair it became clearer. When Collins confirmed that he was holding a triangle, it became clearer still.

For me, believing that there is a difference between sensation and perception has always required an enormous leap of faith. It is hard to believe that I do not see with my eyes or hear with my ears. Although we are taught that there is a difference between sensation and perception, at the TSR lab I *experienced* the difference for the first time. The sensation was on my back, the perception was in my head. Feeling is believing.
—Nancy Hechinger

We began this book with the story of "The Elephant in the Dark." In a study that echoes this story, Kennedy gave blind children pictures of parts of an elephant (the lines in the pictures were raised, in relief, so they could be felt). In 39 out of 41 cases the children recognized that together the pieces made up a picture of an elephant. These children lacked *sight*, but not perception; the wise men in the story had sight, not perception.

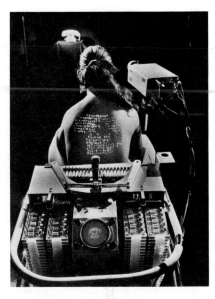

FIGURE 6–26
The Tactile Sensory Replacement device that enables blind people to "see" by television-guided electrical stimulation of their skin.

sional surface can lead to some interesting confusions. Look at the "impossible" object in Figure 6–28, sometimes called the Devil's tuning fork, and try to draw it from memory. The figure itself is obviously not impossible—after all, it's there on the page. But most Western people cannot reproduce the drawing, because we possess a set of schemata that almost automatically interpret the drawing as a fantasy, an object that could not exist in three dimensions. It is our *interpretation,* not the figure itself, that *is* impossible. Here our usual schemata for mentally translating two-dimensional drawings into three-dimensional figures prevent us from seeing the figure as it is. Africans who do not share these conventions have little difficulty in reproducing this figure (Deregowski, 1973).

The Perception of Space

How do we perceive objects and events in space? How do we know when an object is away from us? In 1790 Bishop George Berkeley initiated the modern argument over space perception. He stated that information regarding distance must be inferred, that there is no specific physical stimulus for distance. "We cannot sense distance in and of itself," he wrote. According to this view, distance must be constructed from a set of cues, such as the relative size of an object. Recent research, however, has been able to demonstrate the great amount of distance information directly available to the perceiver.

Internal Cues to Distance

When you focus the lens of a camera you are adjusting the angle at which incoming light is bent and falls on the film. You do this so that the

FIGURE 6–27
**Cultural Assumptions
and Three-dimensionality**
(After Hudson, 1962)

object of interest will be clear in the picture. As a result, things in front of or far behind the object will be less clear. The eye works in a similar way. When we look at objects at different distances, contractions of the ciliary muscles cause the width of our lens to change. This change is called **ocular accommodation.** To demonstrate this for yourself, hold a pen about 10 inches in front of your face. Choose a distant object to look at. When you focus on the far object, the pen becomes blurred. When you focus on the pen, the background becomes blurred. Changes in the width of our lens are monitored by the brain and coupled with other information to develop distance information. This other information includes the convergence of the eyes (the eyes are turned more sharply inward as they look at closer objects) and the different information reaching each eye and ear.

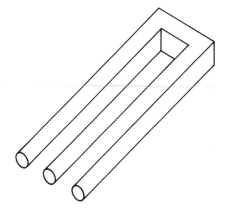

FIGURE 6–28
The Devil's Tuning Fork

Binocular Disparity

Because the eyes are in different locations in the head, each eye receives slightly different information (Figure 6–29). This difference in information—**binocular disparity**—increases the closer we get to something we are looking at. The difference in the left and right images is analyzed by the brain to provide information on distance (Pettigrew, 1972).

Binaural Disparity

Likewise, the difference in location of our two ears also provides us with distance information. A sound directly in front of us strikes both ears at the same time; one to the left strikes the left ear before the right. Also, since sound is composed of physical pressure waves, the wave can strike the two ears at different points in its cycle, producing **binaural disparity.** This information, too, is used to judge distance (Kaufman, 1974).

| What the left eye sees | What both eyes see together | What the right eye sees |

FIGURE 6–29
Binocular Disparity

External Cues to Distance: Stationary Cues

A great amount of information in the external environment contributes to our perception of distance. These "cues" include interposition, perspective, size, texture gradient, and relative brightness.

Interposition

Because most objects are not transparent, an object in front of another will block part of the one behind. This is called **interposition.** In most cases interposition is a simple, reliable, and unambiguous cue to depth, so much so that when the cues are unusual and misleading, the rule of interposition governs our judgment. In Figure 6–30 the circle is perceived as the closest form, with the triangle and the square behind. In looking at Figure 6–31 you probably assumed, like most subjects in laboratory experiments, that the small playing card was in front of the large card.

Perspective

When you look at a long stretch of road or railroad tracks, the parallel lines seem to converge on the horizon. This apparent convergence is

FIGURE 6–30
Interposition

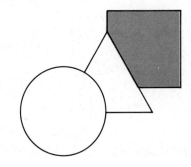

FIGURE 6–31
Interposition Assumed
The normal assumption is that the smaller playing card is in front of the larger one (left) because interposition provides a perceptual cue. But the picture on the right reveals that this assumption can be wrong and our perception confounded by interposition used as a misleading cue.

FIGURES 6–32 and 6–33
The Power of Perspective
We rely on perspective to judge distance and artists rely on it to make their paintings more evocative. Van Gogh's *Hospital Corridor* (left) uses perspective to create a constricting view, capturing his feelings about the place. Escher's *Waterfall* shows the artist's habit of using perspective and other depth cues to fashion scenes in which the laws of nature are playfully violated.

 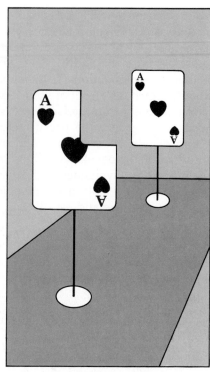

called perspective. Because it is a powerful cue for judging distance, it is crucial in two-dimensional representations of three dimensions. Artists manipulate perspective to create different impressions and evoke different emotions. The exaggerated perspective in Van Gogh's *Hospital Corridor* expresses tension and a closed-in, cramped feeling. In Figure 6–33 M. C. Escher uses perspective and other depth cues to create an "impossible" world in which water runs uphill.

Size

The size of objects on the retina gets smaller as objects recede into the distance. These size differences are valuable depth cues.

Brightness

The closer the object is, the brighter it appears. The amount of light from distant objects that hits the eyes is less because particles in the air diffuse the intensity of light. In the absence of other cues, the brighter of the two objects will be judged to be closer.

FIGURE 6–34
Brightness as a Depth Cue
Because closer objects appear brighter, if no other cues are available, the brighter of two objects will be judged to be closer—sometimes incorrectly.

Texture Gradient

As you look over a uniform surface, like a pebbled beach or grassy field, the *density* of the texture increases with distance (Figure 6–35). A change in density, or **texture gradient,** can also signal a change in the angle of the surface (Figure 6–36). Consequently, information about distance may be quite directly available to the perceiver (Gibson, 1970).

FIGURE 6–35
Texture Gradients as Depth Cues
Because the density of the texture of a uniform surface increases with distance, such texture gradients can help you judge distance.

FIGURE 6–36
Depth Cues in Changes in the Angle of a Surface
Changes in the angle, tilt, or level of an otherwise uniform surface change the density of texture, providing a texture gradient cue to depth.

Movement Cues to Distance

However, as we move around the world, the stimulus information changes. This change of information gives us additional and important information about distance.

Motion Parallax

When you look out of the window of a moving car, objects outside the car appear to move. However, objects at varying distances move in different directions at different speeds. Some objects in the far distance seem to move along with you—the moon may even appear to be following you. Objects quite close, however, move in the opposite direction (Figure 6–37). This difference in movement is called **motion parallax.**

Optical Expansion

As you approach a scene, objects close to you appear to be moving toward you faster than those far away (Figure 6–38). (Gibson, Olum, & Rosenblatt, 1955.) This apparent difference—**optical expansion,** or the "looming effect"—provides information on how fast you are approaching, at what angle, and the relative distances of objects in the scene.

A Note on Space

Although many sources of spatial information are available to us, we probably use only some of them at any given time. It is probably only

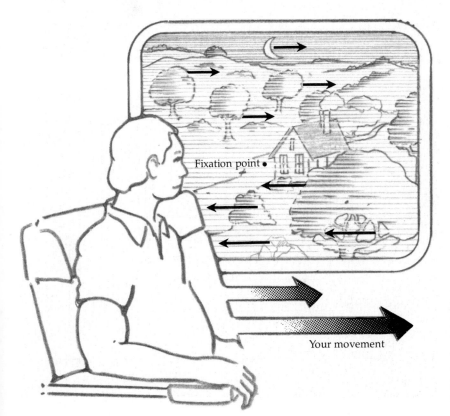

Fixation point ●

Your movement

FIGURE 6–37
Motion Parallax
Relative to a moving observer, various objects seem to move at different speeds and in different directions. This is called motion parallax and it provides movement cues to distance.

when our environment is extremely limited, as in the case of Kenge, the pygmy, that we do not learn all the relevant cues. Berkeley probably underestimated our ability to "pick up" the information in the environment that is available to us (Gibson, 1979).

The Experience of Time

Time is an invisible dimension that underlies our perceptual experience. Our perceptual, intellectual, and emotional events take place in time. We feel these events passing quickly or dragging on. We say we have a "sense" of time, but there is no actual sensory organ (like the eye) for the experience of time. Time is not a physical stimulus in the external world, like the wavelength of light, which can be isolated and measured by scientific analysis.

Kinds of Time

We experience two kinds of time: the time that is *now* and the time that has *passed*.

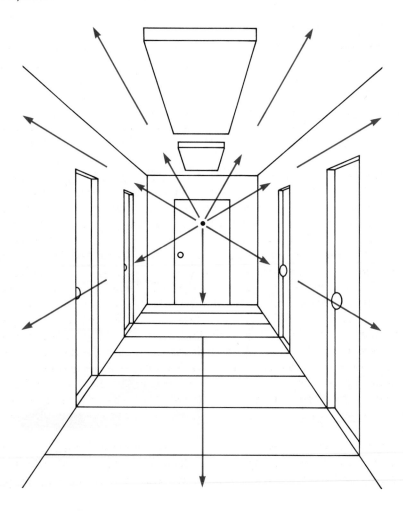

FIGURE 6–38
Optical Expansion
of the Looming Effect
The fact that objects you approach or that are approaching you appear to be moving faster when closer than when farther away gives you cues to speed of approach, angle of approach, and relative distance between objects in the scene affected by optical expansion.

The Time That Is Now—The Present.   The time that is experienced as the present is literally gone the moment you speak of it. As one anonymous poet wrote, "The moment of which I speak is already far away." Generally, however, present time varies, depending on our perspective. "Now" can be this moment, this day, or this year.

The Time That Has Passed—Duration.   The experience of time passing is based primarily on the perception of the duration of events. Albert Einstein once explained his theory of relativity this way: "When you sit with a pretty girl for two hours, it seems like two minutes; when you sit on a hot stove for two minutes, it seems like two hours. That's relativity." Thus duration is perceived according to the nature of the events taking place. Judgment of duration is based on the number of things that occur. The fewer the number of events in a given time, the shorter it will seem (Ornstein, 1969). People who have taken mind-stimulating drugs (like LSD) report that time seems extended under the drug. If you wait an hour with nothing to do, it may seem like an eternity while you are waiting, but that hour will probably disappear from memory and in retrospect seem quite short.

Storage Space and Time

The more that is remembered of a given situation, the longer it seems. A piece of music that contains 40 sounds per minute is experienced as shorter than one with 80 (Ornstein, 1969). In one study, people were given 30 seconds to look at Figure 6–39A. Then they were given 30 seconds to look at Figure 6–39B. Later they were asked which time was the longer. The subjects estimated the time spent looking at the more complicated figure (B) to be 20 percent longer than the time looking at the simple figure (A).

Ultimately, the sense of time is constructed out of memory of experience. Periods of time are judged by how much is remembered about them, how much **storage space** they take up. If you are on an interesting vacation, each day is filled with new experiences, people, and places. At the end of a couple of weeks, it is as if you have been on vacation forever. When you return home, at first your memories and description of the experience are quite complex. "We went to Waikiki Beach, ate mahi-mahi in the famous restaurant, listened to Dorman's orchestra, traveled by sailboat to Maui, stayed in the little cottage . . ." Later your memory may change. It may be simply, "I went to Hawaii for two weeks last year and had a great time." In a study that bears on this, people perceived and remembered an interval containing a successful event as shorter than one with a failure (Harton, 1938). Increased organization and automatization decrease the storage space required and the time needed to recall a memory. Automatic experiences, such as driving an automobile over familiar terrain, seem shorter than the same amount of time in unfamiliar territory.

I conducted an experiment on the effect of organizing memory on the experience of time. Look at Figure 6–40A. Before reading on or turning the page to look at Figure 6–40B, try to describe it. Groups of subjects

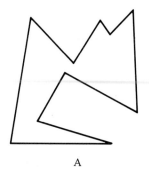

A

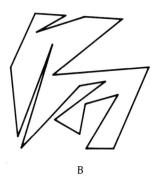

B

FIGURE 6–39
Time Worth Remembering
The same amount of time spent looking at the simpler pattern (A) will be recalled as shorter than the same period spent contemplating the more interesting figure (B). The effect holds true for experiences of all kinds. (After Ornstein, 1969)

FIGURE 6–40A
Try to describe this figure before you read on or turn the page.

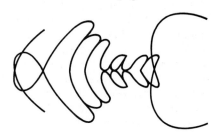

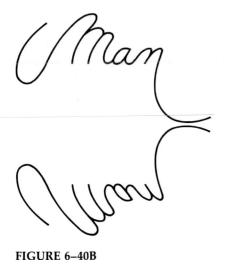

FIGURE 6-40B

were also asked to look at and describe this figure. One group was given no organizing principle, the second and third were given two organizing principles. One group was told the figure was the word *Man* written on top of its mirror image. The other clue was that it was an insect. The more organized the figure was in memory, the easier and faster it could be described. The experience of duration shortened. Our time experience, then, seems to be based on how much we remember and how that memory is organized (Ornstein, 1969).

The Perception of Ourselves and Other People

The perceptual processes described in this chapter allow us to experience a familiar, stable world of objects. Everything from line drawings to facial expressions, from cubes to buildings, is organized and interpreted by perception. However, many other aspects of our lives, from our emotions and personality to our social lives, are strongly influenced by the mechanisms of perception. Many areas, such as our interpretation of our own emotions, will be discussed in later chapters. Here we consider how we experience the world of other people.

Person Perception

In general, we perceive others the same way we perceive everything else: we pick up sensory information, we have selective schemata, we interpret actions and events. As we have seen in the case of the cube, we often experience our interpretations about the nature of external events, and this is more true of our experience of people. We may interpret someone as "overbearing" and from then on are likely to select only those actions that are consistent with our interpretation.

Impressions of People

When we first meet someone, we form a "snap judgment" about his or her basic characteristics. Although we generally have very limited information on meeting someone, nevertheless we tend to form a coherent impression. We "fill in the gaps." Solomon Asch (1946) suggested that this occurs because we assume that people's "traits" form consistent patterns. For example, an "industrious" person is more likely to be considered "intelligent" and "skillful" than "lazy."

However, some traits, like some features of the environment, are more important than others, and they dominate our impression of people. Asch gave two groups of people different lists of traits and asked them to write a paragraph describing the person with those traits. For one group the listed traits were "intelligent-skillful-industrious-warm-determined-practical-cautious." The other group was given a nearly identical list: "intelligent-skillful-industrious-cold-determined-practical-cautious." The two groups reported quite different impressions of the person. The change from "warm" to "cold," with no other change, made people feel much more negative about the person described. This suggests that the "warm-cold dimension" is central to our experience of others.

Prototypes in Person Perception

Not only do we make inferences about traits, but we also tend to relate information about traits and a person's behavior in a simple, organized manner. We tend to judge people around a prototype we have formed of different individuals' behavior. A **prototype** is a typical set of features that exemplify the person or object. For instance, a robin is a prototypical bird, a house calls up the prototype of four walls, a ceiling, paintings on the wall, and so forth. We seem to use these common prototypes in our experience of others. In one study, people were shown a list of traits regarding a person, some of which fit a prototype and some of which did not. For instance, an "extrovert" is a common prototype. Such a person is likely to be outgoing, boisterous, gregarious, loud. Later on, subjects not only recalled more of the traits that fit the prototype (for instance, "loud" in an extrovert), but they also remembered seeing traits that had not been presented, traits that fit the prototype. We are more likely to remember having heard that someone is "excitable" if he is an extrovert than if he is an introvert, even if we have not actually experienced this. We fill in the gaps in experiencing others, just as we do in experiencing objects.

Special Features of Person Perception

However, people are much more complicated than most objects we encounter. They vary greatly in personality, appearance, and circumstances. So, although we use many of the same processes of perception to organize and simplify other people, our perception of others has special aspects (Schneider, Hastorf, & Ellsworth, 1979).

1. *People are causal agents.* We perceive the movement of objects as caused by external forces, but perceive the behavior of people as caused from within.

2. *We see other people as similar to us.* The inner goals and intentions of others are not directly observable, but because we assume that other people are similar to us, we infer something about their inner workings, emotions, goals, and intentions, by reference to our own.

3. *Social interactions are dynamic.* We act upon objects, but generally we do not experience objects as acting on us. However, interactions with other people are dynamic and involve a feedback system. Other people respond to our actions and change their behavior. This changes our own behavior toward another person.

Perception of Ourselves

The processes of perception also influence our experience of ourselves. We make many unconscious inferences about "what is out there." However, we also make such unconscious inferences about our own behavior and feelings. In one experiment, Valins (1966) showed nude photographs from *Playboy* to young men as they listened to the sound of heartbeats. They were told that this sound was their own heartbeat. In many cases, it was not. With some pictures, the experimenters speeded up the rate of the "heartbeat" sounds. Later, the men judged those pictures of women to be the most attractive. This is likely to have occurred because of an unconscious inference: "My heart is beating fast, therefore I'm attracted." We will consider more experiments like this in the chapters on personality and emotion, experiments which show that all of us, women included, show the effects of these unconscious inferences.

Our perception of emotional and social events is determined by the same basic processes of perception we encountered earlier in this chapter. There are specific perceptual processes, such as picking up information, organization, and filling in the gaps by inference that operate in a cycle to make our experiences meaningful. These processes achieve a constant, stable world of objects, other people, and even our own internal feelings. They enable us to make our way through the complex physical and social worlds.

The varied input from the senses is organized and transformed into the rich world of art, music, motion, sunsets, fires, trees, space, time, and people. It seems so simple, but we have seen how much work is necessary "behind the scene." However, our analysis of our experience is still limited. The rules of organization and the processes of perception still do not add up to our conscious experience of the world. In the next chapter we discuss the most flexible aspect of our experience—consciousness.

Summary

1. The distinction between sensation and perception is in meaning: The disconnected and somewhat chaotic sensory impressions are *organized* by the processes of perception into a meaningful whole.

   Two important aspects of perceptual analysis are organization and interpretation. Organization is the connection and coordination of separate sensory stimuli into something meaningful. Interpretation is the judgment of the most likely phenomena that are behind the observed stimuli. *In any situation, we tend to experience the simplest meaningful organization of the stimuli registered.*

2. The process of perception is complex: it requires many separate operations "behind the scenes" in order that the simple "performance" on the stage is experienced. The perceptual process involves *picking up* information about the world, *organizing* it, and making *inferences* about the environment in a *continuous cycle.*

3. An important aspect of perception is that it accurately *"picks up"* information the environment offers. Ecological psychologists have extensively analyzed two characteristics of the environment: (1) *Affordance.* Each object in the environment offers, "affords," a rich source of information available to be perceived. (2) *Invariance.* The external environment contains many different

objects. Each one offers the perceiver certain invariant features. For instance, a post presents unchanging information about itself as we walk around it, including its right angles and the fact that it is perpendicular to the earth.

4. The concept that there are certain rules that *organize* our perceptual experience is the basis of the Gestalt school of psychology. Four principles of organization are figure-ground, proximity, similarity, and good continuation.

5. An important aspect of perception is that we go beyond the information given. We must interpret the sensory information offered to us. This interpretation is performed in *unconscious inferences*. For example, a person may see a little splotch of red in the distance and register that it is a car belonging to a friend. The fact that the car is there at that time could mean that the friend is home from school early, is sick, or is there on an unexpected errand.

   Needs and values are important determinants of inferences. For example, when shown a certain coin, children from poor families experienced it as larger than did children of well-to-do families. In one study, students in a class were asked to draw a picture of their teacher. The honor students drew the teacher as being shorter than themselves, while the poorer students drew themselves as smaller than the teacher. Thus needs and values determine perception in many ways.

6. Perception operates in a cycle—a concept proposed by Neisser. Three factors figure in the *perceptual cycle*. First, because the *schemata* we already possess allow us to perceive things as connected to one another, we can act in an organized way. Schemata not only link our past experience with present events, they also direct our discovery of the world. The second factor in our perceptual experience is our movements and our manipulations of the world. Third is the sensory information about physical changes in the world.

   As we move through the world, the information we receive is changed by our own movements and our own exploration. The process works like this: The schemata direct exploration. The sensory information provided by these exploratory movements modifies the view of the world produced by the brain, which, in turn, changes the schemata. New movements are directed, and exploration begins again. This perceptual cycle is a description of how our experience continually changes and becomes refined.

7. Two important theories of perception concern whether we directly "receive" or "invent" the external world. The *ecological approach* emphasizes that there is an enormous amount of information directly available to the perceiver. For instance, the information for color vision is directly present at the receptors, as is the information for corners, edges, lines, and so on. Similarly, say the proponents of this view, information for distance, relative size, shape, and perspective, is all available to the human perceiver.

   The *constructivist approach* asserts that because sensory information reaching our brain is incomplete and disorganized, perception must be a process of constructing a representation or model of the world. In this view, the information we receive from the sensors "sparks off" the creation of an image of what might have caused this sensation.

   The constructivist view has been dominant in psychology for many decades but is now being challenged by the ecological approach. Perception, most likely, involves several processes of both approaches. Perhaps some of the basic or primary qualities of the environment are directly picked up by the perceiver; however, these still need to be interpreted, probably by the processes described in the constructivist approach.

8. The most important result of all the perceptual processes is how little change we experience, even though the sensory information reaching us changes radically. The main purpose of the receiving, organizing, and interpreting processes is to achieve a stable, *constant* world.

Different forms of constancy have been described by psychologists. In *shape constancy* the same form seen from different angles is still seen as the same shape—a cup seen from different viewpoints seems to have the same shape. In *size constancy* one perceives an object as being the same size no matter what the image on the retina is—a person one hundred feet away seems to be the same size as when two feet away, although appearing to be much bigger. In *brightness and color constancy* the luminance and saturation of an object may vary in different lighting; however, they are perceived to be the same. This page will still appear white whether it is under yellow light, in bright sunlight, or in the gray dusk of an evening. In all those situations, the actual color and brightness being projected to the viewer are very different.

9. Suppose a blind man was suddenly able to see after years of blindness; what would he experience? This question—whether perception is innate or learned—has been studied, using children from other cultures, blind people, and even a person born blind who had an operation to remove his cataracts. The findings show that there are some features, such as the ability to distinguish figure from ground, that seem to be built into the perceptual process at birth, while other, more specific features of the environment seem to be learned.

10. There are very many internal and external cues governing our space perception. Among them are binocular and binaural disparity, interposition, perspective, size, brightness, texture gradient, and the cues provided by our own movement.

We have a very large innate ability to pick up the information in the environment. It is probably when our environment is extremely limited that we do not learn all the relevant cues of the environment.

Terms and Concepts

accommodation
affordance
assimilation
binaural disparity
binocular disparity
constancy
constructivist approach
ecological approach
gestalt
interposition
invariance

motion parallax
ocular accommodation
optical expansion
perceptual cycle
prototypes
storage space
tactile sensory replacement
texture gradient
unconscious inference
visual cliff

Gregory, R. L. (1977). *Eye and brain* (3rd ed.). New York: McGraw-Hill.
  Probably the best single book on many of the immediate phenomena of perception. Well illustrated and especially good on illusions and recovery from blindness.

Hochberg, J. (1978). *Perception* (2nd ed.). Englewood Cliffs, NJ: Prentice-Hall.
  An engaging small book about perception, written mostly from the constructivist viewpoint.

Michaels, C. F., & Carello, C. (1981). *Direct perception.* Englewood Cliffs, NJ: Prentice-Hall.
  The most recent summary of the emerging ecological viewpoint in perception.

**Suggestions for
Further Reading**

Chapter 7

The Varieties of Consciousness

INTRODUCTION

Consciousness is the "front page" of the mind. In this loose analogy, the mind is organized like a newspaper: what is most important that day is on the front page. The most important events are immediate crises, such as a breakdown in transportation or a battle, or new and unexpected situations that require action, such as a flood or a death. Consider the sequence of headlines just before, during, and after the assassination attempt on President Reagan. Notice that one important event moves everything else off the front page. Countless ordinary events each day never make the headlines. We would never see "75 Million Pleasant Dinners Last Night" as a headline, or anything like it. Instead, those who select what goes on the front page ask: Is it unexpected? Is it important? Is it new? Is it a threat?

A similar process goes on in the mind. Countless stimuli reach us at any moment. Many are filtered out by the senses, most are organized and simplified by perception, but we must still select the most important ones remaining at any one moment. Therefore, what is in consciousness at any moment are the items of highest priority to us, those items most needing action. These items may be real emergencies, such as a threat to safety. Some may be immediate concerns, such as: "Watch that car in the left lane, he's weaving all over the road." Some may be chronic concerns, such as solving an intellectual problem; some may simply be new events, such as a person entering the room.

Since our situation and needs for action change, our consciousness changes continually within a day, from sleep and dreaming to "border-line" states on awakening; from tiredness to excitement; from daydreaming to directed thinking. These "daily" alterations in consciousness are much more extreme than we normally realize.

It is also possible to deliberately alter consciousness. Techniques for doing so have been developed in almost every culture. Meditation, for instance, turns down the normally active consciousness and allows a more receptive, inward state to emerge. Under hypnosis, the control of our consciousness is given over to another. A person in hypnosis can

William James
(1842–1910)

withstand normally intolerable levels of pain and uncover memories "lost" from consciousness. Mind-altering drugs, such as LSD and cocaine, affect consciousness by altering the neurotransmitters of the brain.

William James, in a now-classic passage, described the potential varieties of consciousness:

> Our normal waking consciousness, rational consciousness as we call it, is but one special type of consciousness, whilst all about it, parted from it by the filmiest of screens there lie potential forms of consciousness entirely different. We may go through life without suspecting their existence; but apply the requisite stimulus, and at a touch they are there in all their completeness, definite types of mentality which probably somewhere have their field of application and adaptation. No account of the universe in its totality can be final which leaves these other forms of consciousness quite disregarded. How to regard them is the question— for they may determine attitudes though they cannot furnish formulas, and open a region though they fail to give a map. At any rate, they forbid a premature closing of our accounts with reality. (James, 1890)

Principles

Automatization

The reason that only new and important information gets into consciousness is that well-learned actions and patterns of events become automatized. **Automatization** takes place when a series of movements or actions are repeated thousands of times, as in writing a set of letters to make a word. It becomes in essence a set routine. Thus, familiar actions are accomplished "without thinking," without much involvement of consciousness, leaving us free to notice new events.

Watch a baby learning to walk. Notice how he or she concentrates very hard on the sequence of movements required. Eventually, the complex coordination involved in walking will become automatized. Do you remember how it was when you first learned to drive a car? At first, individual actions required to operate the car were painfully uncoordinated. All of your attention was focused on the car. "Let's see. Press the left foot down. Move the gear lever into first. Let the left foot off the clutch. Press on the gas." While learning to operate a car it is very hard to think about anything else—including driving somewhere! However, once the movements become automatized you can carry on a conversation, sing, or admire the scenery without necessarily being conscious of operating the car. The action of shifting gears, even the total activity of driving, becomes automatized.

Mental operations, like physical skills, also become automatized. Sometimes one idea, because of its association, makes one think of a second. When someone says George Washington, such ideas as chopping down a cherry tree, Father of his country, first president, or crossing the Delaware "automatically" come to mind.

Adaptation, Selection, Egocentrism

Adaptation, selectivity, and egocentrism underlie consciousness. Consciousness is adaptive in that it enables us to be flexible enough to initiate the correct action at the correct moment. It is selective in that it focuses on the item with the highest priority for survival at each moment. Consciousness is egocentric because it is geared to what the individual needs most at any one moment.

THE FUNCTIONS OF CONSCIOUSNESS

In animals less complex than humans, needs are met and life is sustained in large part by fixed, innate mechanisms. Recall that the frog sees only a few selected features of the physical world. Human needs and actions are more complex. The unique quality of human consciousness has made it possible for us to survive and thrive in widely different environments, from life on the dry plains of Africa to the frigid mountains in Alaska: no other animal can do that.

There are four main functions of consciousness:

1. *Simplification and selection of information.* Consciousness is a further stage in the process of selecting and simplifying sensory information. Even after sensory and perceptual "editing" there is still far too much potential information for us to know automatically what to act on at any

FIGURE 7–1
Automatization
The division of attention to deal simultaneously with a variety of stimuli requires both conscious processing and automatization, or automatic processing.

moment. Our world is constantly changing and so is our consciousness. William James (1890) described it best:

> We can see that the mind is at every stage a theatre of simultaneous possibilities. Consciousness consists in the comparison of these with each other, the selection of some, and the suppression of others, of the rest by the reinforcing and inhibiting agency of attention. The highest and most celebrated mental products are filtered from the data chosen by the faculty below that, which mass was in turn sifted from a still larger amount of simpler material, and so on. The mind, in short, works on his block of stone. In a sense, the statue stood there from eternity. But there were a thousand different ones beside it. The sculptor alone is to thank for having extracted this one from the rest. . . . Other minds, other worlds, from the same monotonous and inexpressive chaos! My world is but one in a million, alike embedded and alike real to those who may abstract them. How different must be the world in the *consciousness* of ants, cuttle fish, or crab!

2. *Guiding and overseeing actions.* Consciousness connects brain and body states with external occurrences. In order to function in a complex environment, our actions must be guided and planned: we must know when and where to walk, when to speak and what to say, when and how to run, when to eat and drink and sleep. These actions must be coordinated with events in the outside world. At any moment, the *content* of consciousness is what we are prepared to act on in the next moment.

3. *Setting priorities for actions.* It is not enough for our actions to be

FIGURES 7–2 and 7–3
Automatization of Complex Tasks
Activities such as playing a musical instrument, going through the coordinated sequence of movements required to fabricate devices, driving a car, or flying an airplane involve automatization that permits you to accomplish such demanding routine tasks without really thinking or worrying about how you are performing the many separate actions that go into accomplishing these tasks.

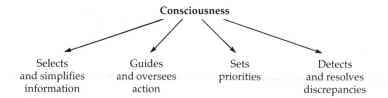

Consciousness

Selects and simplifies information

Guides and oversees action

Sets priorities

Detects and resolves discrepancies

FIGURE 7–4
The Functions of Consciousness

coordinated with events in the outside world; they must also reflect our internal needs. There is thus a *priority system* in consciousness. Certain events enter consciousness more easily than others. Pain can flood consciousness in the same way that a national emergency fills the front page of a newspaper. No matter what you are doing, the sharp pain of a toothache will seize your consciousness and prevent you from giving attention to what you are doing. The priority system of consciousness gives certain events, usually those affecting survival, fast access to consciousness so that immediate action may be taken (Maslow, 1970).

4. *Detecting and resolving discrepancies.* The information selected to enter consciousness is information about changes in the external or internal world that cannot be resolved by the perceptual processes. Generally, when there is a discrepancy between incoming information and our existing schemata, an event is likely to come into consciousness. For instance, a woman in a bikini is hardly noticeable on the beach, as is a man in a business suit on a city street. However, a woman in a bikini on the street or a fully dressed man sunbathing on the beach is unusual, and we become conscious of it.

Survival Needs Take Precedence
See Chapter 13, pp. 468–69.

FIGURE 7–5
Consciousness and Discrepancies
Because consciousness tends to be stimulated by change, contrast, and the unusual, we are sure to become conscious of a perceptual discrepancy like seeing a fully dressed man sunbathing on a beach.

Discrepancies may arise internally. For instance, you are usually not conscious of your breathing. However, when you have a cold your breathing may be quite conscious, and that "tells" you to slow down or to see a doctor. Discrepancies in the external environment are more common. For example, when someone changes the furniture in a room, you become conscious of the new arrangement for a while. The new arrangement of the furniture recedes from consciousness as it becomes familiar. The feeling that you "must" straighten out a crooked painting on the wall is a result of consciousness striving to reduce discrepancies.

THE STRUCTURE OF CONSCIOUSNESS

Continuing the newspaper analogy, the contents of consciousness are those few important events demanding immediate action. But consciousness is only the "front page" of the mind; behind it are many different levels of awareness, containing our plans and expectations, our assumptions, or our basic knowledge of how to operate in the world.

So the mind is divided in the two ways a newspaper is divided: the first is the division between the front page and the rest of the paper, between consciousness and other forms of awareness. The second is the division of the front page (consciousness) itself.

Consciousness and Subconscious Levels of Awareness

Only the most important events that need our attention enter consciousness. But "behind" consciousness, as the later pages of a newspaper follow the front page, are different **levels of awareness** of the outside world.

There is a difference between awareness and consciousness. When something is in awareness *it means that we are keeping track of it*. We are aware of a great deal, much more than we know. For instance, to walk we must be aware of our own movements, the touch of feet on the pavement, whether there is a crack, a curb, or a stone. But we are not *conscious* of these things as we walk, nor are we *conscious* of our breathing, our arm movements, the background noises, or traffic.

Sleep provides a striking example of the difference between awareness and consciousness. During sleep, when our consciousness is shut down, we are nevertheless aware of sounds. If the sounds have a particular significance, our consciousness can be aroused. Sleepers will awaken to their own names or to a word like "fire," although they will not awaken to random words spoken (Oswald, 1962). A mother sleeps through the noise of sirens in the streets, but awakens at the far softer sound of her baby crying. For that to occur, we must have been *aware* of many of the words and sounds of the environment and have selected only the important ones to enter consciousness. Therefore, *when we know we are aware of something, we are conscious of it*.

Awareness

The content of awareness includes our plans, the automatized functions, our expectations and assumptions, all those "things" and more that make up our world, and of which we keep track.

Sometimes we do not notice events in our awareness until they are gone, as when you notice that the clock has stopped ticking. Sometimes we say, "I just heard the clock stop." In order to hear the clock stop, you must have been aware of the ticking at some level of perception. A dramatic illustration of this level of awareness occurred when a train line was torn down some time ago in New York. An elevated railroad once ran along Third Avenue in New York City. At a certain time late each night, a noisy train ran. The train line was torn down some time ago, with some interesting aftereffects. Shortly after the demolition, many people in the neighborhood began to call the police quite late to report "something strange" occurring—unusual noises, suspected thieves or burglars were reported. The police determined that these calls took place at about the same time the late-night train would have passed these peoples' houses had the line not been demolished. What they were "hearing," of course, was the *absence* of the familiar noise of the train.

Preconscious Memories

At a still more basic level of awareness are our **preconscious** *memories.* These consist of the memories that enable us to operate in the world. Preconscious memories are of two kinds, episodic and representational. *Episodic memory* consists of specific memories in our life. *Representational memory* is our stored knowledge of the world, such as our knowledge of language and where Scotland is.

Preconscious memories become conscious as they are needed. That is, preconscious memories can become conscious only when we are in a situation in which they are likely to be activated. For instance, when you speak with a friend whom you have not seen for a long time, you may remember experiences and things about him or her you had not thought of in years.

Nonconscious Processes

Lower still is the **nonconscious** level of awareness. The concerns of this level are primarily the automatic functioning of the body. The pumping of the heart, regulation of blood circulation and pressure, and neurotransmitter production operate without conscious direction. If something goes wrong with one of these processes, however—if, for example, your heart suddenly speeds up—these processes can enter consciousness.

Unconscious

A more controversial level of awareness is called the **unconscious.** The unconscious is the "place," postulated by Sigmund Freud (1900), in which memories and thoughts that are difficult to deal with are hidden. Thus, someone who hates a parent but cannot face the fact will try to prevent the feeling from entering consciousness. This process is called "repression to the unconscious." Freud believed that when thoughts are repressed to the unconscious they may still break into consciousness in uncontrolled ways. Many actions and slips of the tongue thought by Freud and his followers to be examples of this are therefore termed "Freudian slips." For example, a woman who has repressed hatred of

FIGURE 7–6
The Structure of Consciousness

Conscious awareness
Subconscious awareness
Preconscious memories
Nonconscious processes
The unconscious

FIGURE 7–7
Learning to Do Two Things at Once
John and Diane steadily improved their ability to read while writing. After a few weeks their reading speeds were close to their normal rates, as this record of their progress in the experiment shows. (After Hirst et al., 1978)

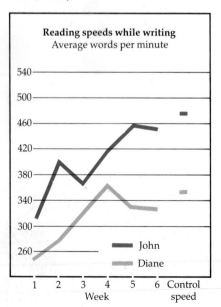

her mother might misplace the invitation to a dinner party to which her mother is also invited; this action may be an expression of that unconscious hatred. Similar is the slip, "I'm so glad you left," on greeting a person one does not wish to see. As interesting as the idea of unconscious wishes and desires is, attempts to validate this theory have not proved very successful. Today many psychologists regard the "unconscious" as a plausible but by no means proven level of consciousness.

Divisions of Consciousness

It is commonly assumed that you cannot perform two complex operations at once. Consciousness, it is believed, has a fixed capacity, so that if two very complex activities are attempted at the same time one will suffer somehow. Normally when we do two things at the same time, at least one is already well learned—we sing an old song while following a new recipe. When this happens, the well-learned task is performed automatically and is below consciousness.

Recently a group of investigators tested these assumptions. They enlisted two students, Diane and John, as subjects to see if people could read and write simultaneously. They read short stories while copying down a list of words that was rapidly being dictated to them. At first Diane and John found the task impossible. They read slowly and did poorly when tested later for comprehension. But after six weeks of training, they could perform both tasks easily and well. The investigators made the experiment more difficult. This time the subjects were required to write down whole sentences rather than a list of words. Again it was difficult at first, but within weeks they could simultaneously write on one subject while reading on another at normal speed and with normal comprehension (Hirst, Spelke, & Neisser, 1978). These studies indicate that division in consciousness can be trained and that the capacity of consciousness may be greater than what we have assumed.

Dissociation

Past experiences are not usually in consciousness, but many are retrievable. Your high school graduation was not in your consciousness a moment ago. Now you are conscious of it and can recall specific experiences associated with it. Some experiences, however, can only be recovered under specific conditions. This division in consciousness is called **dissociation.** Pierre Janet, a nineteenth-century psychiatrist who used hypnosis in his therapy, first introduced the term dissociation in 1899. He suggested to one of his patients under hypnosis that she would write letters to certain people when she came out of her hypnotic state. Later, when she was shown the letters, she had no recollection of having written them and accused Janet of forging her signature. The act of writing had been dissociated, "split off," from normal consciousness.

Probably all of us experience some splits in consciousness at one time or another. Have you never felt "out of it" and just snapped back, with no recollection of the time, as if you had just lost a half hour? When such splits become extreme or a permanent condition, a *multiple personality* may result. A multiple personality is a person in whom two or more distinct consciousnesses coexist. The consciousnesses are so well-developed and distinct that they are more like separate personalities than simply shifting states of consciousness or mood. Such people are usually unaware of the other personalities inside them. Their normal consciousness is dissociated when one of the others emerges.

DAILY VARIATION IN CONSCIOUSNESS

The daily changes in biological rhythms, the borderline states between sleep and dreams, sleep and wakefulness, and daydreams are all variations that occur daily in the structure of consciousness. Our needs for action change during the day so that our consciousness goes through numerous changes each day.

Biological Rhythms

The basic rhythm of human life is **circadian,** which means "about one day." Many factors keep us on a daily rhythm, including the light-dark cycle, the positioning of the sun, work hours, and mealtimes. In studies in which these cues are taken away, the circadian rhythm changes from a 24- to a 25-hour one. After a few weeks in a cueless environment, profound changes in the cycles of sleep-wakefulness and body temperature occur (Czeisler, Weitzman, Moor-Ede, Zimmerman, & Knauer, 1980).

One specific daily rhythm is body temperature: every day there is a peak, a valley, and plateaus. Body temperature is related to mental activity. A person whose temperature peaks in the morning usually is more alert and capable at mental tasks at that time. This is a "morning person." A "night person," on the other hand, feels good-for-nothing in the morning and works best at night. Such a person's body temperature peaks in the evening (Luce, 1970).

Some people experience quite extreme rhythmic variations in consciousness. One salesman found that he suffered a severe thought disturbance every fourth day. On that day he would get ready for work and find that he would remain in his car unable to do anything, tense and frightened. When he became conscious of the regular rhythm of this

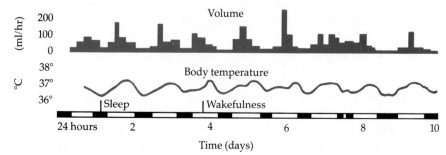

FIGURE 7–8
Circadian Rhythms
Human subjects kept isolated under constant environmental conditions eventually exhibit a circadian day that differs from the normal, 24-hour day by an hour or two. Notice in this chart that biological rhythms do not follow strict 24-hour patterns. (After Ascholl, 1965)

disturbance he arranged his work schedule around it. He never found out what caused the problem, but he did find out how to live with it (Luce, 1970).

Borderline States

Although we are often in an active mode of consciousness during the day, at fairly regular intervals a receptive mode dominates. These periods are called borderline states; they include daydreams and the times just before sleep and just upon waking. When in a borderline state, we experience a decline in active performance but are more imaginative.

Daydreaming

Everyone daydreams almost daily (Singer, 1976). Daydreams usually occur when outside events are boring, automatized, or unchanging (riding in a car or train, listening to a dull lecture); then our consciousness tunes out the outside world and tunes in an inside world.

Recall that we routinely simplify sensory information by tuning out unchanging events in order to direct our attention to novel events. But since consciousness does not turn off when novel events are absent in our environment, *we create our own*. During daydreams we lose consciousness of the external world, and our effectiveness is diminished. Even so, daydreaming may have some important functions. During daydreams our thoughts are more free-flowing and uncensored, making us more receptive to new courses of action and new ideas, even to reflecting "honestly" on our faults and mistakes. Such thoughts are less likely, if ever, to enter consciousness in a normal active state (Singer, 1968).

Singer classifies daydreams into general and specific types. General daydreams are wide-ranging fantasies with a limitless variety of content. Specific daydreams fall into clearer categories (Singer, 1976):

1. *Self-recriminating.* These daydreams are prompted by the question, "What should I have done (or said)?"
2. *Well-controlled and thoughtful.* These daydreams are a form of planning—the day is organized, a party is planned, and so forth.
3. *Autistic.* In these daydreams, material usually associated with night dreams breaks through and disrupts consciousness. Seeing a horse flying through the lecture hall would be one example.
4. *Neurotic or self-conscious.* These daydreams include fantasies: "How I can score the winning point and become revered by all the fans," or "How I can be discovered by a Hollywood director."

Although parents, teachers, and bosses keep telling us not to daydream, everyone does.

Hypnopompic and Hypnogogic States

The state of consciousness we enter just before complete awakening is called **hypnopompic**; the state before sleep is called **hypnogogic** (*hypno* is Greek for "sleep"). The mode of consciousness in both states is receptive. Our images at these times have four qualities: vividness, originality, independence of conscious control, and changeableness (Budzynski, 1977). Many people report that creative insight frequently occurs during these moments (Magoun, 1969).

Sleep and Dreams

Each of us undergoes a radical and dramatic alteration in consciousness—we go to sleep. The outside world is shut off; the content of consciousness is generated entirely from within. During sleep we continue to have conscious experience, called dreams. The nature of sleeping and dreaming has fascinated people for millennia. Why do we sleep? Why do we dream? What do dreams mean? Do dreams mean anything? These and other questions are the subject of this section.

FIGURE 7–9
The Daydream in Art
I and My Village, by Marc Chagall

Sleep and Tiredness

Every animal sleeps, but, surprisingly, no one is sure why. Most people assume sleep is restorative, because we commonly go to sleep tired and awake refreshed. One hypothesis that assumes there is a relationship between sleep and tiredness distinguishes between two kinds of tiredness, each requiring a different kind of sleep (Hartmann, 1973). *Physical tiredness* comes after a day of intense physical effort and is usually experienced as a pleasant feeling because of the relaxed state of the muscles. *Mental tiredness* comes after a day of intense intellectual or emotional activity and is usually experienced as an unpleasant feeling of having been "drained."

Sleep Deprivation and the Functions of Sleeping

There has been little direct evidence to back up the assumption that sleep is restorative. The specific functions of sleep, and therefore of dreaming, remain a mystery. However, some real progress has been made in the last few years on both of these questions. One way to figure out the functions of sleep is to deprive people of it. In 1959 a New York City disc jockey, Peter Tripp, tried to stay awake for 200 hours to benefit charity. For this marathon he was surrounded by psychologists and medical specialists; his physiological and psychological functioning were monitored continuously.

> Almost from the first the overpowering force of sleepiness hit him. Constant company, walks, tests, broadcasts helped, but after about five days he needed a stimulant to keep going. . . . After little more than two days as he changed shoes in the hotel, he pointed out to [a psychiatrist] a very interesting sight. There were cobwebs in his shoes—to the eyes at least. . . . Specks on the table began to look like bugs. . . . He was beginning to have trouble remembering things. By 100 hours . . . he had reached an inexorable turning point. . . . Tests requiring attention or nominal mental agility had become unbearable to him. . . . By 70 hours the tests were torture. By 110 hours there were signs of delirium. Tripp's world had grown grotesque. A doctor walked into the recording booth in a tweed suit that Tripp saw as a suit of furry worms. By about 150 hours he became disoriented, not realizing where he was, and wondering who he was. . . . Sometimes he would back up against a wall and let nobody walk behind him. Yet from 5 to 8 p.m. all his forces were mysteriously summoned, and he efficiently organized his commercials and records and managed a vigorous patter for three hours. . . . On the final morning of the final day [of the 200-hour period] a famous neurologist arrived to examine him. The doctor carried an umbrella although it was a bright day, and had a somewhat archaic mode of dress. . . . [Tripp] came to the morbid conclusion that this man was an undertaker, there for the purpose of burying him. . . . Tripp leapt for the door with several doctors in pursuit. (Luce & Segal, 1966)

With some encouragement, Tripp managed to get through the day, gave his broadcast, and then, following an hour of tests, sank into sleep for 13 hours. When he awakened, the terrors, ghoulish illusions, and mental agony had vanished.

There have been other cases of sleep deprivation, though most have been less extreme than Tripp's. Randy Gardiner, who now holds the record for staying awake, suffered much less. He spent most of his time playing pinball. Except for some mild hallucinations, his performance on the pinball machines was unimpaired. One of the sleep researchers who stayed with Gardiner reported that on the morning of the final day the two played 100 games of pinball and Gardiner won them all (Dement, 1974). A large study of sleep deprivation in 359 servicemen showed that by the third sleepless day 70 percent experienced hallucinations and 7 percent behaved abnormally. However, a good night's sleep restored all to normal. Thus, when people are deprived of sleep there can be a profound disorganization of normal mental processes.

Dreaming and "REM" Sleep

In 1953 Eugene Aserinsky and Nathaniel Kleitman made a chance observation in the course of studying the sleep patterns of infants. They noted that periods of eye movements and bodily activity seemed to alternate regularly with periods of "quiet" sleep. These regular periods of rapid eye movements, called **REM sleep,** were observed precisely by attaching electrodes near the subjects' eyes. During this period, the EEG recording of brain activity indicated light sleep. People of all ages experience some REM sleep every night. Whenever test subjects are awakened just after periods of REM sleep, they almost always give vivid reports of their dreams. In contrast, when awakened after other stages of sleep (collectively called "non-REM" or NREM), they report dreams only a tenth as often (Aserinsky & Kleitman, 1953).

William Dement has been trying to discover the relation of REM sleep to dreaming. As well as finding a highly significant relationship between the length of dream reports and the amount of REM time elapsed before awakening, Dement has produced evidence for a precise correspondence between REM sleep behavior and dream gaze changes (Dement & Kleitman, 1957). One subject who showed many side-to-side eye movements reported dreaming of a tennis match!

The Stages of Sleep

Determining what stages of sleep a person is in is quite involved and requires simultaneous recording of three physiological measures: EEG; the electrooculogram, which records the movements of the eyes (EOG); and chin EMG (electromyogram, a measure of muscle tension). These measures change during the course of a typical night's sleep in roughly the following way: as the subject lies awake in bed before going to sleep, the EEG is likely to exhibit the alpha rhythm illustrated in Figure 7–10A, the EOG reveals blinks and occasional REMs; and the EMG level is relatively high. This state is called "relaxed wakefulness."

As the subject becomes drowsy, the EEG alpha rhythm is gradually replaced by the low-voltage, mixed-frequency activity characteristic of the state shown in Figure 7–10B known as "stage-one sleep." The EOG usually shows slow eye movements (SEM) and the EMG may decrease. Normally, stage-one sleep lasts only a few minutes.

Stage-two sleep is marked by the appearance of 12–14 Hz rhythms on the EEG, called **sleep spindles** (Figure 7–10C). EOG activity is minimal and the EMG usually decreases still further.

Gradually, high-amplitude slow waves begin to appear on the EEG. When 20 to 50 percent of the EEG record is filled with these high-amplitude, slow (delta) waves, stage three is reached (Figure 7–10D). Eventually, delta activity dominates the EEG. When the proportion of delta

FIGURE 7–10

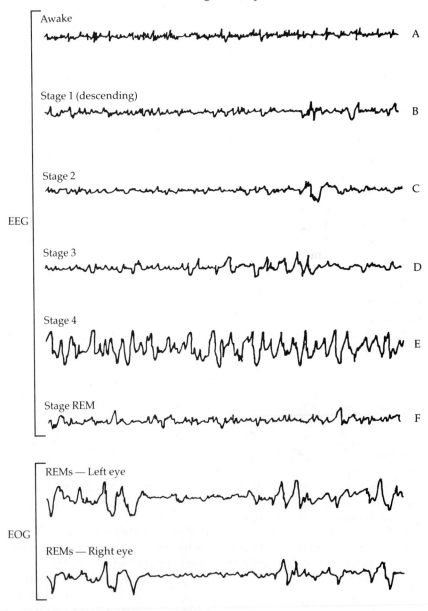

Stages of sleep

EEG

Awake — A

Stage 1 (descending) — B

Stage 2 — C

Stage 3 — D

Stage 4 — E

Stage REM — F

EOG

REMs — Left eye

REMs — Right eye

100μV

2 sec.

activity exceeds 50 percent, the "deepest" stage of sleep, stage four, is reached (Figure 7–10E). During these stages there are no eye movements and EMG is normally low.

After about an hour and a half, the above sequence is reversed. By the time the EEG indicates that stage one has been reached, however, the EMG is at the lowest level of the night and REMs occur in dramatic profusion. This is "stage-one REM," or REM sleep (Figure 7–10F).

REM sleep is extremely curious; many seemingly contradictory phenomena occur at once. The eyes move rapidly, while breathing and heart rate become irregular; there is erection in the male and vaginal engorgement in the female; the vestibular system is stimulated. Although these are all signals of arousal and activation, *all other commands for voluntary movement are blocked* from reaching the muscles at the spinal cord. For instance, you may dream that you are running, but your legs do not move. The brain, breathing, heart rate, and cerebral blood flow are all excited, but the rest of the body is momentarily paralyzed.

Immediately preceding and during REM sleep there is increased activity in the cells of the **pontine reticular formation,** a network of cells located in the pons of the brain. These cells in turn activate eye movement neurons. At the same time, the activity in the pontine reticular formation inhibits a nearby group of cells, the locus cerulus, which in turn affects muscle tone and blocks muscle movements. REM sleep lasts on average 10 minutes.

Generally, the cycle of sleep stages is repeated about three or four times during the night, although the same stage is slightly different at each occurrence. The depth of sleep decreases, there is less and less stage-three and stage-four sleep. Successive REM periods increase in length; 40 minutes is not an unusual length for later REM periods. At the same time, the interval between REM periods decreases from 90 minutes in the early part of a night's sleep to as little as 40 minutes. The typical sequence of sleep stage changes during the night is illustrated in Figure 7–11.

Dreams

Dreams occur in REM sleep, which provides an objective measure of the occurrence of dreaming. With such an external indicator of an internal event, researchers have been able to answer many basic questions about dreams. We all dream every night, whether or not we can recall the content of our dreams. Most people have four or five dream periods a night with about 90-minute intervals, but dream periods become longer throughout the night. Dreams are more frequently recalled if the sleeper is awakened immediately after a REM period.

FIGURE 7–11
The Sequence of Sleep Stages
(After Van de Castle, 1971)

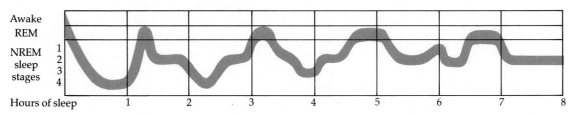

A DIVIDED CONSCIOUSNESS DURING DREAMING?

Sometimes we know we are dreaming while we are dreaming. Some individuals claim to be able to think clearly and act deliberately while sleeping soundly and dreaming vividly. But dreaming and wakefulness are such distinctly different stages of consciousness that communication between the two has been thought to be impossible. If dreamers could signal to an observer that they knew they were dreaming, that would indicate a division within dreaming consciousness that could, perhaps, open a channel of communication between the dreamer and the outside world.

Evidence for such "lucid" dreaming was indicated in an intriguing study. Subjects in this study were able to signal to researchers that they knew they were dreaming. They had been trained to signal dreaming by moving their eyes voluntarily during dreams, producing observable effects on their polygraph records (Laberge, Nagel, Dement, & Zarcone, 1981). The fact that at least some individuals have learned to communicate in this way may make possible a new approach to dream research. Such subjects might be able, for example, to mark the exact time of particular dream events. Perhaps such studies mark the beginning of "on-the-scene" reporting from the dream world (Laberge et al., 1981).

The content of dreams can be influenced by outside stimuli. For instance, many people have dreamt of a loud noise only to awaken to the alarm clock. Dement and Wolpert (1958) sprayed water on subjects' faces during REM periods. When awakened, many subjects reported water imagery in their dreams.

The Functions of Sleep and Dreaming

One theory of dreams by Hans Hartmann associates the two basic kinds of sleep, REM and non-REM sleep, with two kinds of tiredness, physical and mental. He believes that increased physical activity during the day leads to an increase in non-REM sleep (Hartmann, 1973). Minor physical illnesses, such as colds or flu, are also thought to increase non-REM sleep (Brewer & Hartmann, 1973). Some have speculated that non-REM sleep may be a time when physical restoration of the organism occurs, such as in cell repair and protein synthesis (Adam & Oswald, 1977; Takahashe, 1979).

REM sleep is thought to be associated with the kind of tiredness that results from "mental effort." Experimental subjects who wore inverting lenses during the day had more REM sleep at night (Zimmerman, Stoyva, & Metcalf, 1970). This may indicate that part of the process of adapting to the lenses took place during dreams. Similarly, when subjects wore red lenses (Roffwarg, Bowe-Anders, Tauber, & Herman, 1975) or lenses that reduced the visual field (Herman & Roffwarg, 1983), there were dramatic increases in REM periods.

This phenomenon suggests that, to some degree, mental "reprogramming" required by dramatic changes in one's environment may occur in dreaming. For instance, kittens and rats placed in enriched environments showed more REM time than controls in an impoverished environment (McGinty, 1969). Rats show increased REM time after learning something new (Leconte, Hennevin, & Bloch, 1972; Lucero, 1970). Lewin and Gombosh (1973) put human subjects in a "disturbing and perplexing" atmosphere four hours just before sleep. The subjects were asked to perform difficult and annoying tasks with no explanation. During the night their REM time increased. Many studies have shown that REM sleep increases after human subjects have had to learn complex tasks (McGrath & Cohen, 1978). Thus, REM sleep and the dreams it produces might be involved in the reorganization of mental structures (schemata) to accommodate new information. However, there is not enough evidence to say conclusively this is the case. Nevertheless, such a function would help explain why the amount and percentage of REM sleep (see Figure 7–12) typically decrease with age. As less and less new information must be accommodated, there would be less need for REM sleep.

What Do Dreams Mean?

Dreams have been used to predict the future and explain events in both traditional and modern cultures. The belief that the contents of dreams are important is virtually universal. In many cultures a person who can interpret dreams occupies an important place in the community. Many scientists have reported that a breakthrough to the solution of a significant problem came to them in a dream.

The Greeks believed that the gods spoke to them directly in dreams. Hippocrates, the father of medicine, used dreams to diagnose physical ailments. Aristotle believed that dreams were a vehicle for information about body distress that went unnoticed during the day. Two modern theories also assume that something important is released and revealed during dreams: Freud's theory of psychological "energy" and a more recent theory of the biological function of sleep and dreams.

Freud's Dream Theory

The most influential modern theory on the meaning of dreams is Freud's, presented in a brilliant and influential book, *The Interpretation of Dreams* (Freud, 1900). Freud's analysis of the function of dreams is extremely rich and complex, so we can note only two of the main points.

1. *Wish fulfillment.* During dreams the normal conscious controls on the unconscious are released, allowing unconscious wishes to be expressed directly. For Freud, dreams are the "royal road to the unconscious," because dreaming is one of the few times when normally forbidden desires rise to the surface of consciousness. A hungry person might dream of food, the sexually deprived of sex. These "pent up"

FIGURE 7–12
The Need for REM
Sleep Decreases as We Age
Over a lifetime, the average person spends an increasing percentage of each day awake and needs less non-REM and, especially, REM sleep each day. (After Hartmann, 1967)

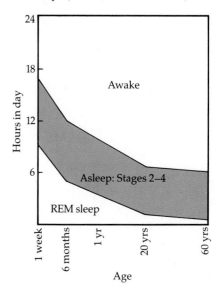

desires are diminished to some extent simply by being expressed in dream consciousness, and they are then less likely to disturb waking consciousness and influence behavior.

2. *Dreams guard sleep.* However, the expression of desires during sleep could pose problems to the sleeper. A dream about killing a rival or sleeping with a friend's spouse might be disturbing even though the dreamer knows it is only a dream. If a dream is upsetting enough, a person may wake up. Since that rarely happens, Freud felt that dreams "guard" sleep by transforming the unconscious desires into disguised symbols. For instance, a snake may stand for the penis, a tunnel for the vagina. It was the aim of Freudian *psychoanalysis* to uncover what these disguised symbols meant to dreamers by encouraging them to free associate to the dream content. In this technique the patients report their dreams and then talk "freely" about what the various parts of each dream make them think of (Hall, 1966).

Psychoanalysis See Chapter 17, pp. 595–97.

Activation Synthesis

A recent theory of dreaming is based on observations of the unique state of the brain and nervous system during REM sleep (Hobson & McCarley, 1977). During REM the pontine reticular formation in the brain stem produces spikes of neuronal activity, the motor input to the muscles is blocked at the level of the brain stem, and the vestibular system is stimulated. Furthermore, during REM sleep the brain may be reprogramming stored information, reshuffling schemata, as it were. The theory is called **activation synthesis** because it assumes that the brain is *activated* in REM sleep and that dreams are a conscious *interpretation* or *synthesis* of the information in consciousness during dreams.

Perception as the Simplification of Sensory Information See Chapter 5, pp. 178–79 and Chapter 6, p. 217.

During wakefulness the processes of perception organize sensory information into the simplest meaningful interpretation. Activation synthesis theory assumes that the *same processes* are at work during dreaming, except that brain systems, such as the vestibular, are activated internally. In dreams, therefore, mental processes attempt to organize this diverse material: falling (from the vestibular activation), the inability to move (from the blocking of motor output), and the specific events of the day needing to be assimilated or accommodated. The "simplest meaningful experience" of all these events becomes, in this theory, the dream.

Many of the experiences commonly reported in dreams (see Figure 7–13) may therefore be our *interpretation* of the brain's state. For example, the commonly reported feeling of being chased and unable to avoid the pursuer, or of being tied up, locked up, or frozen with fright, may well be an interpretation of the blocked motor commands to our muscles during REM. Floating, flying, and falling experiences in dreams may be the interpretation of vestibular activation; the sexual content of dreams may be an interpretation of vaginal engorgement or penile erection.

Dreams are often incoherent, even bizarre. One minute you may be speaking to your boss, the next you may be singing in a cabaret in some exotic city. Such abrupt shifts in imagery may simply be the brain's "making the best of a bad job in producing partially coherent dream

FIGURE 7–13 **The 20 Most Common Dreams**
of 250 College Students and
the Percentage Having Each Type of Dream

Type of Dream	Percentage of Students
Falling	83
Being attacked or pursued	77
Trying repeatedly to do something	71
School, teachers, studying	71
Sexual experiences	66
Arriving too late	64
Eating	62
Being frozen with fright	58
A loved person is dead	57
Being locked up	56
Finding money	56
Swimming	52
Snakes	49
Being dressed inappropriately	46
Being smothered	44
Being nude in public	43
Fire	41
Failing an examination	39
Flying	34
Seeing self as dead	33

Source: R. M. Griffith, O. Miyago, and A. Tago. The universality of typical dreams: Japanese vs. Americans. *American Anthropologist*, 1958. 60, pp. 1173–1179.

imagery from the relatively noisy signals sent up . . . from the brainstem" (Hobson & McCarley, 1977).

Activation synthesis theory has been criticized and is not firmly established. There is no direct evidence as yet that the pontine reticular cells are uniquely associated with REM sleep (Vogel, 1978). However, the theory provides a useful, even if tentative, explanation of the function of dreaming, the common features of dreams (falling, flying, sex), and the lack of strict coherency in dreams (see Figure 7–13). If activation synthesis is correct, then the experience of dreams can be understood as a product of the processes of perception and consciousness at work when the brain is generating its own "raw" information. Of course, dreams still *may* have specific meanings, but these meanings may lie in the *interpretation* of the events.

DELIBERATE ALTERATIONS IN CONSCIOUSNESS

The practices of deliberately changing consciousness are found in almost every human society. These changes may be undertaken simply for amusement, as in recreational drug taking, or as a disciplined way of deepening one's understanding of reality.

Since normal consciousness is geared to action, reducing the requirements for action can offer consciousness a chance to change. In meditation and in many religious practices, the practitioner is removed from normal routines. He or she may simply sit alone in a quiet private area or engage in a highly structured action with no "practical" value (bead stringing). Certain kinds of interventions seem to alter consciousness in a predictable manner. Here we will consider three basic types:

1. Psychological techniques, such as meditation and hypnosis, in which there is a shift in the structure of consciousness from the active to the receptive mode.
2. The attainment of a religious or mystical experience. This alteration is rare, but common to the mystics of all cultures, from the "born again" Christians to Indian monks.
3. The use of drugs that affect brain chemistry and therefore conscious experience.

Meditation Exercises

Concentrative Meditation

Meditation includes a number of techniques whose aim is knowledge of oneself and one's place in the world rather than intellectual knowledge. These techniques aim at shifting consciousness from the active to the receptive. Instead of coming to an intellectual understanding of "different mechanisms of attention," meditation seeks to teach individuals to control their own experiences. Meditation is used by nearly all "traditional psychologies" of the East—among them Sufism, Zen, and Yoga—and in the West by religious orders such as the Franciscans.

The instructions for meditation are strikingly similar in different traditions. In *What the Buddha Taught*, the Buddhist Rahula (1969) gives these instructions:

> You breathe in and out all day and night, but you are never mindful of it, you never for a second concentrate your mind on it. Now you are going to do just this. Breathe in and out as usual, without any effort or strain. Now, bring your mind to concentrate on your breathing-in and breathing-out. Let your mind watch and observe your breathing in and out, let your mind be aware and vigilant of your breathing in and out. . . . Forget all other things, your surroundings, your environment; do not raise your eyes and look at anything. . . .
>
> At the beginning, you will find it extremely difficult to bring your mind to concentrate on your breathing. You will be astonished how your mind runs away. It does not stay. You begin to think of various

things. You hear sounds outside. Your mind is disturbed and distracted. You may be dismayed and disappointed. But if you continue to
practice this exercise twice a day, morning and evening, for about five
or ten minutes at a time, you will gradually, by and by, begin to concentrate your mind on your own breathing. After a certain period you
will experience just that split second when your mind is fully concentrated on your breathing, when you will not hear even sounds nearby,
when no external world exists for you.

In the Christian tradition, meditative exercises are more commonly
called contemplation. Instead of breathing, objects are sometimes used
as the focus of attention, as when a meditator stares at a cross. Many
elements of prayer are derived from the same principles as the *mantra*
(words or sounds often thought to have special meaning) of Eastern
meditation. The Christian Saint John Climacius wrote: "If many words
are used in prayer, all sorts of distracting pictures hover in the mind but
worship is lost. If little is said or only a single word pronounced, the
mind remains concentrated."

That the process of concentrative meditation is similar throughout the
world, at different times and in different places, suggests that there may
be a common experience stimulated by this process. It does not seem to
matter what actual practice is followed, or whether one symbol or another is used; the experience is the same. The important factor seems to
be that *the same information is cycled through the nervous system over and
over.*

The concentrative form of meditation produces the experience of
"one-pointedness" or a "clear" state. Normal experience of the outside
world disappears, to be replaced by what is described in Indian termi-
nology as the "darkness" and the "void." The object of this form of
meditation is, in fact, to divorce oneself from and become nonresponsive
to the outside world. During meditation, muscle tension is lowered and
alpha waves, indicating a state of relaxation, predominate. In a study of
Zen masters in Japan, no disturbance in their EEGs showed up when
external stimuli were presented while they were meditating (Kasamatsu
& Hirai, 1963).

The sensory and perceptual systems are specialized to detect changes
in the environment; concentrative meditation suppresses these systems
by producing unchanging stimulation. Normal conscious experience
ceases and is replaced by a state of receptivity. Concentrative meditation
turns off the outside world. The purpose of "heightening" consciousness in this way is to de-automatize one's response to the world, to
enable a restructuring of schemata and one's approach to the world.

Opening-up Meditation

A second form of meditation is much more closely related to daily
activity. These exercises do not isolate the practitioner, but attempt to
involve everyday events in the training of consciousness. In these exercises, called "just sitting" in Zen, "mindfulness" in Yoga, "self-observation" in Sufism, consciousness is "opened up" to everything that
occurs.

TEACHING STORIES

Another technique for upsetting routine and for deepening consciousness is the narrative containing paradoxes and unusual events. Such a tale is often called a **teaching story** (Shah, 1970, 1971, 1972). One aim of many esoteric traditions is to experience unfamiliar ideas and information. Teaching stories are said to contain certain specially chosen patterns of events that encourage openness to new ideas. Repeated reading of the story allows these patterns to become strengthened in the mind of the person reading them. This use of stories is quite unusual, so we will merely present a few, without explaining them, so that the reader can experience them.

The Man with the Inexplicable Life

There was once a man named Mojud. He lived in a town where he had obtained a post as a small official, and it seemed likely that he would end his days as Inspector of Weights and Measures.

One day when he was walking through the gardens of an ancient building near his home, Khidr, the mysterious Guide of the Sufis, appeared to him, dressed in shimmering green. Khidr said: "Man of bright prospects! Leave your work and meet me at the riverside in three days' time." Then he disappeared.

Mojud went to his superior in trepidation and said that he had to leave. Everyone in the town soon heard of this and they said: "Poor Mojud! He has gone mad." But, as there were many candidates for his job, they soon forgot him.

On the appointed day, Mojud met Khidr, who said to him: "Tear your clothes and throw yourself into the stream. Perhaps someone will save you."

Mojud did so, even though he wondered if he were mad.

Since he could swim, he did not drown, but drifted a long way before a fisherman hauled him into his boat, saying, "Foolish man! The current is strong. What are you trying to do?"

Mojud said: "I do not really know."

"You are mad," said the fisherman, "but I will take you into my reed-hut by the river yonder, and we shall see what can be done for you."

When he discovered that Mojud was well-spoken, he learned from him how to write.

After a few months, Khidr again appeared, this time at the foot of Mojud's bed, and said: "Get up now and leave this fisherman. You will be provided for."

Mojud immediately quit the hut, dressed as a fisherman, and wandered about until he came to a highway. As dawn was breaking, he saw a farmer on a donkey on his way to market. "Do you seek work?" asked the farmer. "Because I need a man to help me to bring back some purchases."

Mojud followed him. He worked for the farmer for nearly two years, by which time he had learned a great deal about agriculture but little else.

One afternoon when he was baling wool, Khidr appeared to him and said: "Leave that work, walk to the city of Mosul, and use your savings to become a skin merchant."

Mojud obeyed.

In Mosul he became known as a skin merchant, never seeing Khidr while he plied his trade for three years. He had saved quite a large sum of money, and was thinking of buying a house, when Khidr appeared and said: "Give me your money, walk out of this

Opening-up exercises emphasize the difference between sensation and perception: the difference between the information that reaches consciousness and the interpretation of that information. This has also been attempted in psychology. The early "introspectionist" psychologists attempted to analyze the elements of their own consciousness. In philosophical and religious traditions the purpose is different: to disassociate one's "models of the world" from the actual world outside; in Zen "to stop conceptualizing while remaining fully awake."

Normal perception involves making quick automatic guesses about

town as far as distant Samarkand, and work for a grocer there." Mojud did so.

Presently he began to show undoubted signs of illumination. He healed the sick, served his fellow men in the shop and during his spare time, and his knowledge of the mysteries became deeper and deeper.

Clerics, philosophers and others visited him and asked: "Under whom did you study?"

"It is difficult to say," said Mojud.

His disciples asked: "How did you start your career?"

He said: "As a small official."

"And you gave it up to devote yourself to self-mortification?"

"No, I just gave it up."

They did not understand him.

People approached him to write the story of his life.

"What have you been in your life?" they asked.

"I jumped into a river, became a fisherman, then walked out of his reed-hut in the middle of one night. After that, I became a farmhand. While I was baling wool, I changed and went to Mosul, where I became a skin

merchant. I saved some money there, but gave it away. Then I walked to Samarkand where I worked for a grocer. And this is where I am now."

"But this inexplicable behaviour throws no light upon your strange gifts and wonderful examples," said the biographers.

"That is so," said Mojud.

So the biographers constructed for Mojud a wonderful and exciting history; because all saints must have their story, and the story must be in accordance with the appetite of the listener, not with the realities of the life.

And nobody is allowed to speak of Khidr directly. That is why this story is not true. It is a representation of a life. This is the real life of one of the greatest Sufis.

The High Cost of Learning

Nasrudin is interested in learning to play the lute. He searches out the lute master and asks, "How much do you charge for lessons?" The lute master replies, "Ten gold pieces for the first month, one gold piece for the succeeding months." "Excellent," says

Nasrudin. "I shall begin with the second month."

See What I Mean?

Nasrudin was walking on the main street of a town, throwing out bread crumbs. His neighbors asked, "What are you doing, Nasrudin?" "Keeping the tigers away." "There have not been tigers in these parts for hundreds of years." "Exactly. Effective, isn't it?"

I Believe You Are Right

During Nasrudin's first case as a magistrate, the plaintiff argues so persuasively that he exclaims, "I believe you are right." The clerk of the court begs him to restrain himself, for the defendant has not yet been heard. Nasrudin is so carried away by the eloquence of the defendant that he cries out as soon as the man has finished his evidence, "I believe you are right." The clerk of the court cannot allow this. "Your honor, they cannot both be right." "I believe you are right," says Nasrudin.

what is outside us. Opening-up meditation attempts to change what consciousness selects. For instance, one exercise might be to listen to all the sounds in and outside of your room: the noises of the buildings and traffic, static on the radio, creaks in the walls. They are ever-present but almost never noticed. Because consciousness evolved as an adaptive advantage for survival, this exercise is extremely hard to do and could be dangerous if it were done all the time. Opening-up meditation exercises also attempt to *de-automatize* perception, to undo some of the selectivity and interpretation that take place in normal perception.

Religious and Mystical Experiences

When combined with other practices of traditional psychologies, meditation is intended to bring about a more "complete" consciousness. The full emergence of this experience is called the "mystical experience."

Upsets to Routine

A major precipitating event for many mystical experiences is a strong upset of normal routine: fasting, extreme physical exertion as in long-distance running. Another way in which the normal processes of consciousness are upset is through specially designed techniques to shock and startle. The Zen *koan* is one such example. A koan is a riddle or paradox, an unsolvable problem: "Show me your face before your father and mother met," or "What is the sound of one hand clapping?" Most people treat these questions logically, at first attempting to find rational answers to these problems. But the koan is first intended to demonstrate to the practitioner that verbal solutions to every question are not possible. There is no textbook in which the "meaning of life" is written down.

De-automatization

One specific aim in both concentrative and opening-up meditation is to dismantle the automatic selectivity of ordinary awareness. One aim of the esoteric traditions is to remove "blindness," to awaken a fresh perception. The word "enlightenment" or "illumination" is often used for progress in these disciplines. The psychological term is *de-automatization*, an undoing of the normal automatization of consciousness (Deikman, 1966).

The Mystical Experience

Many meditation and spiritual exercises result in what are called mystical or religious experiences. They have occurred in many cultures and religious disciplines.

In his classic *The Varieties of Religious Experience*, William James (1917) cites the analysis and description by a Canadian psychiatrist of a mystical experience, which James called "cosmic consciousness."

> "I was walking in a state of quiet, almost passive enjoyment, not actually thinking, but letting ideas, images, and emotions flow of themselves, as it were, through my mind. All at once, without warning of any kind, I found myself wrapped in a flame-colored cloud. For an instant I thought of fire, an immense conflagration somewhere close by in that great city; the next, I knew that the fire was within myself. Directly afterward there came upon me a sense of exultation, an immense joyousness accompanied or immediately followed by an intellectual illumination impossible to describe. Among other things, I did not merely come to believe but I saw that the universe is not composed of dead matter, but is, on the contrary, a living Presence; I became conscious in myself of eternal life. It was not a conviction that I would have eternal life, but a consciousness that I possessed eternal life then; I

saw that all men are immortal; that the cosmic order is such that without any peradventure all things work together for the good of each and all; that the foundation principle of the world, of all the worlds, is what we call love, and that the happiness of each and all is in the long run absolutely certain. The vision lasted a few seconds and was gone; but the memory of it and the sense of the reality of what it taught has remained during the quarter of a century which has since elapsed. I knew that what the vision showed was true. I attained to a point of view from which I saw that it must be true. That view, that conviction, I may say that consciousness, has never, even during periods of the deepest depression, been lost."

James (1890) defines four characteristics of the mystical experience.

1. *Unity or oneness.* Experience becomes comprehensive rather than fragmented; relationships between things normally separate are seen.
2. *A sense of "realness."* The person has the sensation that the relations between things he or she experiences are closer to truth than ordinary experiences.
3. *Ineffability.* The experience is said to be impossible to communicate in ordinary words.
4. *Vividness and richness.* Events take on a glow of freshness and clarity, not present in ordinary consciousness.

Hypnosis

Two hundred years ago Franz Anton Mesmer claimed he had discovered the property of "animal magnetism," a new force of nature through which he could control and influence another person's experience. Miraculous healing cures were claimed. His technique was called mesmerism. It was essentially what we call hypnosis.

Hypnosis is a form of dissociation in which individuals relinquish the normal control of their consciousness to another person. Through a variety of techniques, a hypnotist engages and relaxes the subject's waking consciousness. People under hypnosis have been able to recall events otherwise inaccessible to their waking consciousness; they have also been able to withstand extreme pain.

Although the idea of a "force" transmitted through hypnosis is no longer popular today, there is as yet no accepted scientific explanation of how hypnosis works. The lack of explanation makes many psychologists and physicians uncomfortable with the phenomenon and has stimulated fierce attempts to discredit it. In the nineteenth century, a British surgeon, Esdaile, demonstrated hypnosis to an audience of the Royal College of Physicians. The demonstration was dramatic: a man under hypnosis had his gangrenous leg amputated without anesthetic! The patient showed no evidence of pain and was wheeled away after the successful surgery. Still, Esdaile was ridiculed. In the *Lancet,* a British medical journal, it was asserted that "the patient was an imposter who had been trained not to show pain" (Rosen, 1946).

Hypnotic Suggestibility

Not everyone can be hypnotized. A scale of hypnotic suggestibility has been established that measures how much a given suggestion, such as "your eyes are closing," is actually carried out (Weizenhoffer & Hilgard, 1959). There are several characteristics that suggestible people share. Primary among them is the capacity for imaginative involvement (Hilgard, 1970). Typical forms of such involvement are: reading science fiction or drama; adventurousness in physical activities, like exploration; and adventurousness of a mental nature, like experimentation with drugs.

The Hidden Observer in Hypnosis

In 1960 Kaplan hypnotized a 20-year-old college student. He induced "automatic writing" in which the subject's right hand was able to "write anything it wanted to, not subject to control or restriction of the 'conscious' personality." Then the hypnotist told the subject he would feel no pain in his left hand. He began pricking the left hand with pins, which ordinarily would have been unbearable. The student showed and reported no pain (Kaplan, 1960). This demonstration was one of the first and most important examples of dissociation of consciousness. In dissociation one part of the person is conscious of experiences (and can report them) and another part is not.

Hilgard discovered, however, that even in a dissociated state normal consciousness was not totally cut off or "unconscious" of what was happening. In one study, Hilgard hypnotized a man and gave him the suggestion that he would become completely deaf at the count of three. He then banged two wooden blocks next to the man's ear. The man did not react to the sound. Hilgard said to the man, "Although you are hypnotically deaf, perhaps some part of you is hearing my voice and processing

this information. If there is, I should like the index finger of your right hand to rise as a sign that this is the case." To Hilgard's amazement, the finger rose! Hilgard called this phenomenon the "hidden observer" (Hilgard, 1978).

The **hidden observer** is an important demonstration of the hypothesis that many experiences below consciousness may enter consciousness through hypnosis. For instance, we may be instructed under hypnosis not to feel pain, and indeed report no pain. But because the hidden observer does report pain (Figure 7–14), it may be assumed that the hypnotic state is only one part of awareness (Hilgard, 1978).

The Hypnotic Condition

Although hypnosis is not as radical a change in consciousness as sleep and dreaming, under hypnosis many things can come under conscious control that are otherwise beyond the control of normal consciousness. On command, warts have been removed, migraine headaches relieved, people have stopped smoking, and episodes forgotten. Many people are concerned that hypnosis is dangerous because unethical hypnotists might make subjects do things they would not do in a normal waking state. But that is more the stuff of movies and fiction than reality; a person will not do anything under hypnosis that goes against his or her moral code.

The general characteristics of the hypnotic condition are:

1. Attention can be changed, narrowed, or broadened according to instructions.
2. Distortions of reality can be accepted. For instance, hypnotized persons can imagine and act as if they were young children ("age regression").
3. They will act out roles suggested by the hypnotist.
4. They can be given suggestions about posthypnotic behaviors. (Hilgard, 1966)

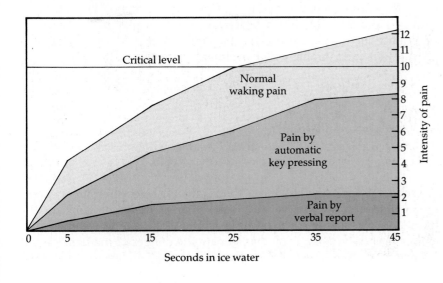

FIGURE 7–14
The Hidden Observer
and Pain under Hypnosis
People who were hypnotized not to feel pain while their hands were in ice water, have signaled pain during the experiment—by automatic key pressing—or reported it later, through the level of awareness called the hidden observer, which seems to be separate from hypnosis. (After Hilgard, 1978)

Later, when acting out the suggestions, they may not realize they are following directions.

Drugs

In nearly every culture, drugs and other biochemical agents have been deliberately used to affect consciousness. These substances range from coffee to the psychedelic drug LSD. Generally, drugs work by stimulating, depressing, or altering neurotransmission.

The effects of drugs are not only pharmacological but social. Taking a drug can be an expression of a desire for social change or a protest against society, an exploration of taboo areas or simply "mental adventurousness." Adolescents often experiment with drugs as part of their general exploration of forbidden activities (Jessor & Jessor, 1977).

The social acceptability of a drug often influences the interpretation of the experience of it. At a conference on drug abuse, concerned professionals discuss the dangers of marijuana, heroin, and amphetamine, while at the same time they smoke cigarettes and drink coffee and alcohol, three drugs that not only alter consciousness but also have very harmful physical effects. Smoking tobacco leads to severe health consequences such as increases in lung cancer and heart attacks, and withdrawal from tobacco can be at least as severe as withdrawal from heroin (Brecher, 1974). Excessive alcohol consumption causes brain damage and other organ degeneration. The physiological effect of coffee is quite similar to that of amphetamine.

The Pattern of Drug Taking

The social acceptance of all drugs that are used to change consciousness often follows a similar pattern. A drug is often introduced into a culture by a minority primarily interested in the drug's effects on consciousness. The drug is then condemned, confiscated, and, finally, taken up by the culture (Brecher, 1974). Coffee provides a good illustration of both this process and the part interpretation can play in the personal experience of a substance. At first coffee was banned throughout Europe. An early Arabic writer comments:

> The sale of coffee has been forbidden. The vessels used for this beverage . . . have been broken to pieces. The dealers in coffee have received the bastinado, and have undergone other ill-treatment without even a plausible excuse. . . . The husks of the plant . . . have been more than once devoted to the flames and in several instances persons making use of it . . . have been severely handled. (Brecher, 1974)

If coffee is offered only under conditions of secrecy and great expectation, its effect will be very different than if the same substance is offered in plastic cups in vending machines. The *interpretation* of drug experiences may make us underestimate the danger of the familiar and overestimate the danger of the unfamiliar.

Classification of Drugs

Drugs that affect consciousness can be divided into five classes:

1. **Analgesics** such as morphine reduce the experience of pain.
2. **Sedatives** induce relaxation and sleep. Barbiturates are a class of sedative.
3. **Stimulants** elevate mood and increase alertness. Amphetamines and cocaine are two well-known stimulants.
4. **Psychoactive drugs** change the overall structure of consciousness. Marijuana, mescaline, and LSD are psychoactive drugs.
5. **Psychiatric drugs** such as antidepressants, antipsychotics, and lithium help to "normalize" consciousness by correcting neurochemical imbalances.

These five classes are not entirely mutually exclusive. For instance, many psychoactive drugs are also stimulants, and some have depressive effects.

Analgesics

The most widespread analgesic is morphine (after Morpheus, the Greek god of dreams). Morphine is the active ingredient in opium, long used in East and Northeast Asia to relieve pain as well as to induce extraordinary dream-like experiences. More recently opiates have become a major recreational drug in the West. Opium is an unrefined extract of the poppy seed pod; morphine is a refined extract of opium and is stronger in its effects. Heroin is derived from morphine and is even more potent in its pure form. ("Street" heroin, however, is usually diluted to below the strength of opium.) The opiate class of drugs kills pain by blocking neurotransmission. They fit into "opiate receptors" in the limbic system and stop pain from reaching the cortex. But the molecular structure of the opiates fits the brain's own opiate receptors imperfectly. It may also fit into other receptors in the limbic system.

The Lock and Key Principle and Pain Control in the Neuroendocrine System   See Chapter 4, pp. 159, 165–66.

Because the limbic system is involved with emotion, the opiates can have a major effect on emotion. Immediately after injection, the opiates produce a pronounced feeling of intoxication and euphoria, called a "rush." The opiates seem to block so many afferent impulses to the cortex (at the limbic system) that the user not only feels no pain but also no signals of normal physiological needs, such as hunger. So while physical pain is relieved, there is also a decrease in anxiety and often in the motivation for food, sex, and work.

But still heroin and other opiates are actually more dangerous psychologically than physiologically. The real physical danger of heroin, for example, is that people who use it often neglect their health by not eating or drinking, or attending to pain. It is not, however, in itself an extremely dangerous substance; alcohol, by contrast, *is* dangerous. Much of the danger of heroin results from two factors: it is addicting and it is illegal. In England people addicted to heroin and other opium derivatives are registered, receive their doses orally, and there are fewer physiological difficulties (Brecher, 1974).

Sedatives

Sedatives depress the activity of the central nervous system, which results first in relaxation, then drowsiness, and finally sleep. In fact, the most common use of sedatives is to induce sleep. Barbiturates are the drugs most commonly prescribed as sleeping pills. They are also sometimes taken, though not prescribed, to produce a state of "sedated inebriation," which some people find pleasant. Quaaludes are also a medically designed sedative commonly abused as a so-called recreational drug. But the most widely used (and abused) sedative is a nonprescription drug—alcohol. Alcohol is the major "drug of choice" in most Western societies. However, it is so dangerous that it is banned in many others, notably in all Moslem societies and by Hindu communities in India.

Alcohol and other sedatives are nonselective depressants of the central nervous system. When taken together, they add to each other's effects (Figure 7–15). In the first stages of drunken behavior, people commonly feel euphoric and uninhibited. Dancing in the streets, wild parties, and other "popular" examples of drunken behavior are expressions of these stages. Later stages are characterized by depression and withdrawal.

Alcohol first acts as a depressant on the brain stem, which explains the loss of inhibitions on behavior—rowdiness, bawdiness, and so on. It later acts on the cortex, which explains loss of muscular control and depressing thoughts. Doses sufficient to depress activity in the brain stem probably do not at first depress cortical activity, thus releasing the cortex from the regulatory controls exerted by the brain stem, such as the excitatory signals from the RAS (Julien, 1978).

Alcohol is used by about 70 percent of people in the United States, and most of them have little trouble with it. There is even evidence that moderate drinking may benefit health. Perhaps because it aids relaxation, moderate drinkers have fewer heart attacks than nondrinkers (Darby, 1978). But alcohol can be addicting. Among the effects of alcohol addiction, or "alcoholism," are liver damage, ulcers, and hypertension.

FIGURE 7–15
The Continuum of the Action of Alcohol and Other Sedatives

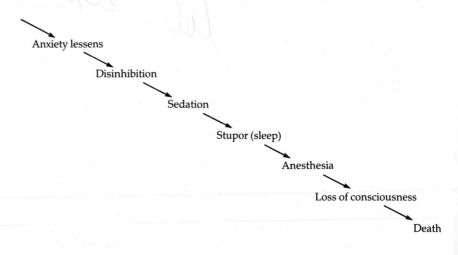

Anxiety lessens

Disinhibition

Sedation

Stupor (sleep)

Anesthesia

Loss of consciousness

Death

An excess of alcohol during pregnancy may result in birth defects. In addition, there are often psychosocial problems: loss of job, family, or status; long-term depression, and even suicide. Withdrawal from alcohol dependence is a difficult and severe experience. The user may suffer delirium tremens (the D.T.'s), frightening visions, auditory hallucinations, and severe trembling. Alcohol withdrawal is a more frightening experience than heroin withdrawal (Brecher, 1974).

Stimulants

Stimulants and drugs like amphetamines elevate mood and increase alertness and reduce fatigue. Since one of their effects is loss of appetite, they are commonly used as diet pills. Amphetamines stimulate neurotransmission at the synapse. Recall that when a neuron fires, the chemical neurotransmitters migrate from one neuron to the next at the synapse. After firing there is a *refractory* period when the neuron is inactive, giving the neurotransmitter time to return to the first neuron. This process is called re-uptake. Amphetamine itself interferes with the re-uptake of the neurotransmitters dopamine and norepinephrine, causing erratic and uncontrolled neural impulses, which can eventually disrupt consciousness. With continued use, the disruptions can become permanent, resulting in a condition known as *amphetamine psychosis.* Chronic use of amphetamines (or, colloquially, "speed") may result in schizophrenia. Among the first signs of an amphetamine breakdown are paranoid delusions, such as, "The CIA is after me." People also often become violent, which may be attributed more to the delusions than the drug

Endorphins: The Brain's Own Painkillers   See Chapter 4, pp. 165–66.

THE CYCLE OF ADDICTION

Any drug that gives pleasure or relief from pain or anxiety is potentially addicting. Pleasure-giving or pain-relieving drugs are especially potentially addicting because their effects on mood are produced by altering brain chemistry. In the short term, mood may be elevated or anxiety reduced, but in the long term the delicate balance of neurochemicals is likely to be upset, leading to more extreme moods and diminished motivation. Another, perhaps larger, dose of the drug will again produce euphoria, but at the cost of a further neurochemical imbalance and consequent mood changes.

Addiction is a cycle, often controlled by the principle of feedback. Consider an example involving taking morphine as a pain killer. Normally, the brain produces its own "opiates," the endorphins, which serve to kill pain. When this supply is inadequate, as in recovery from surgery, additional opiates in the form of morphine may be given. However, since brain chemistry operates on a feedback system, the presence of the morphine is registered in the pituitary and a signal is sent to decrease production of the brain's own painkillers. When the morphine wears off, the pain will therefore be even more excruciating, requiring the administration of more morphine the next time, which leads to a still further reduction in the production of the body's own internal painkillers. Eventually, the primary effect of the drug is no longer to give pleasure but to give *relief from the unpleasant state that develops during abstinence*. Nothing else gives quite the same pleasure either. The addict becomes so conditioned to the intense effect of the drug that lesser stimuli like food and sex are uninteresting.

itself. "An amphetamine party may begin with everyone very elated and talkative, and may end with each person stationed silently at a window, peeking through the curtains for signs of the police" (Snyder, 1980).

Another stimulant that produces euphoric effects, cocaine, is becoming increasingly popular in affluent Western societies. The leaves of the coca plant, from which cocaine is derived, have been chewed by the Indians of Bolivia and Peru for thousands of years to banish fatigue and boredom (Weil, 1979). The drug was introduced to North America and Europe in the late nineteenth century. "Tonics" and patent medicines containing cocaine or other coca extracts were very widely used in the United States until the early twentieth century. One of the most popular of these was Coca-Cola, a drink that contained cocaine for 20 years until it became illegal in the early 1900s.

Sigmund Freud experimented with cocaine and was extremely enthusiastic about it at first. Later, however, he became disillusioned with the drug when he discovered that overuse could lead to severe depression, addiction, and even psychosis. He became an addict, himself. Governments, too, became alarmed at some of the harmful and dangerous aspects of cocaine. By the First World War, cocaine was viewed as a dangerous drug and made illegal. Abuse of cocaine then declined until the early 1970s. Its use has been increasing since then, stimulated at first by the revival of interest in psychoactive drugs. Cocaine, or "coke" as it is commonly called, is usually ingested by sniffing ("snorting") the white powder. This produces a sense of exhilaration and relief from fatigue that lasts approximately a half hour. Most cocaine use is moderated by the high cost of the substance—as much as $100 per half-hour high. Cocaine intoxication, incidentally, shares many of the features of mania. Mania is a psychological disorder characterized by an extremely frantic high mood. Lithium, a drug that can alleviate acute mania, also blocks the euphoric effects of cocaine.

Mania   See Chapter 16, pp. 572, 573–74.

Psychoactive Drugs: Marijuana and LSD

Drugs such as marijuana and LSD are called psychoactive or "psychedelic" because one purpose of their use is to change consciousness. Marijuana and LSD were the primary drugs of the "drug culture" of the 1960s and 1970s, which introduced consciousness-changing drugs to the culture at large.

Marijuana

Although illegal, marijuana is in common use in the United States; it is probably the most common drug used for altering consciousness. More than 60 percent of people under 35 have tried marijuana (Davison & Neale, 1982). The use of marijuana among young people is increasing rapidly. Over one in four people age 18 to 25 now use marijuana regularly, and three out of five have tried it. Women tend to use the drug less often than men.

The leaf of the *Cannabis sativa* plant is the source of marijuana. The leaves are often dried and smoked. When the oil from the plant is collected and dried, this produces hashish, a substance that is more powerful in effect than marijuana. Marijuana or hashish is usually smoked, although some prefer to eat it in cookies and cakes.

Marijuana is an extremely complex substance; it contains more than 400 identified compounds, but it is usually agreed that the primary active agent is THC, one of a variety of "cannabinoids." There may well be other active cannabinoids in marijuana, but this has yet to be demonstrated. The THC content of different preparations of marijuana varies. Prior to 1973, "street" marijuana typically possessed less than one percent THC. Now THC content of 5 percent or more is common. Hashish oil may possess a 20 percent THC content (Lee, Novotny, & Bartle, 1976).

Marijuana is smoked for pleasure, and its users often report that it elevates mood and enhances enjoyment of music and other sensual experiences, including sex. In one survey, Charles Tart interviewed 150 experienced marijuana users in 1968–69. Tart's sample of marijuana smokers distinguished three levels of marijuana intoxication. At low levels, they reported being quiet at parties, "more quiet than if drunk," and interested in subtle musical sounds. At medium levels, they reported they were more noisy and boisterous, experienced new qualities about themselves, and their need for the enjoyment of sex increased. At strong intoxication they became easily distracted, had poorer memory, felt emotions more strongly, and experienced heightened qualities to sexual orgasm (Tart, 1971).

For many, marijuana is primarily a social drug, to be used as an alternative to alcohol at parties. Users often prefer it because they prefer the alteration of consciousness it produces and because they feel that marijuana is not as serious a health hazard as alcohol. In this latter point they are, unfortunately, wrong.

Among the effects of smoking marijuana is impairment of memory. Something learned during marijuana intoxication is difficult to recall when not under the influence. Smoking marijuana seems to interfere with the transfer of information into permanent memory (Tinkelberg & Darley, 1975). Marijuana intoxication is also quite detrimental to driving. It interferes with driving as tested on the road (Klonoff, 1974) and increases the rate of fatal accidents (Sterling-Smith, 1976). Marijuana has some direct effects on health: it interferes with normal lung functioning (Taskin, Calvarese, Simmons, & Shapiro, 1978) and decreases sperm count and motility. Although no definitive studies have been done, it is advisable for pregnant women to avoid the drug altogether.

LSD

LSD is derived from a fungus that grows on rye, called ergot. When ergot-infected rye bread is eaten, a disease known as ergotism results. One symptom of the disease is hallucinations.

LSD is one of the most powerful drugs known. Albert Hoffman first synthesized it in April 1943. In a test, he took what he thought was an infinitesimal dose, about 250 micrograms (250 millionths of a gram).

After 40 minutes, I noted the following symptoms in my laboratory journal: slight giddiness, restlessness, difficulty in concentration, visual

disturbances, laughing . . . [Later:] I lost all count of time, I noticed with dismay that my environment was undergoing progressive changes. My visual field wavered and everything appeared deformed as in a faulty mirror. Space and time became more and more disorganized and I was overcome by a fear that I was going out of my mind. The worst part of it being that I was clearly aware of my condition. My power of observation was unimpaired. . . . Occasionally, I felt as if I were out of my body. I thought I had died. My ego seemed suspended somewhere in space, from where I saw my dead body lying on the sofa. . . . It was particularly striking how acoustic perceptions, such as the noise of water gushing from a tap or the spoken word, were transformed into optical illusions. I then fell asleep and awakened the next morning somewhat tired but otherwise feeling perfectly well. (Hoffman, 1968)

As little as 10 micrograms can produce noticeable effects: mild euphoria, de-automatization (the unravelling of normally associated schemata), a high similar to marijuana. A dose of 250 micrograms causes major effects, which increase up to the usual high dose of 500 mcg. The lethal dose of LSD is unknown. In the only reported case of death due to the drug's direct physiological effects, an autopsy suggested that 320,000 cg (about 1,000 times the normal dose) had been injected intravenously (Grinspoon & Bakalar, 1979).

The drug has a dramatic effect on conscious experience: sensation is enhanced; de-automatization occurs; emotions are greatly amplified; thought processes are transformed. Users may identify themselves with everything from animals to God.

Four main clusters of LSD responses have been identified (Barr, Langs, Holt, Goldberger, & Klein, 1972).

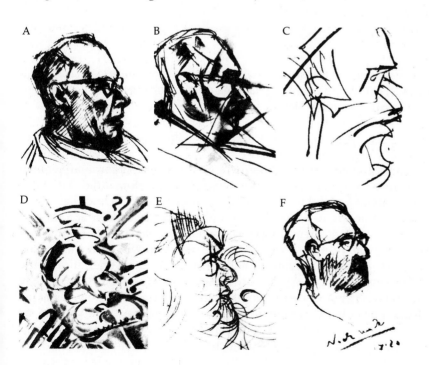

FIGURE 7–16
Drawings Made under the Influence of LSD
The first drawing (A) made 25 minutes after the first dose, shows the drug had not yet taken effect. After a second dose (B) the man had little control of his hand's movements. The man was unhappy with the third drawing (C) and 2 hours and 45 minutes after the first dose the full effect of the LSD was discernible in the highly distorted fourth drawing (D). After 5 hours and 45 minutes the drug's influence was still obvious (E), but the effects were starting to wear off. Eight hours after the first dose the intoxication had worn off, but the quality of the last drawing (F) was not on a par with that of the first.

1. Elation, loss of inhibition, loss of control of attention.
2. Feelings of unreality and of being dissociated, the ability to observe one's self, fear and suspicion, loss of control, regression to infancy.
3. Body-image alterations and physical symptoms.
4. Anxiety and fear of losing control.

The effect of LSD on an individual is influenced by the interpretation: when people take the drug and do not know that they are taking it, the effects can be disastrous. The perceptual distortions that might occasion great interest in those who know they have taken the drug can be terrifying to someone who is ignorant of that fact. Suicides have resulted from failure to interpret the experience of an LSD "trip" properly.

A horrifying example of this failure is an experiment conducted by the U.S. Army. They gave LSD to some subjects without warning them of its effects. One sergeant was so shattered by the experiment that 20 years later he remains a broken man. He cries at the memory of his experience, and still cannot even speak of it. He thought he had "gone crazy." Because no one told him these experiences were to be expected, they had a striking effect. He was unable to work or carry out a normal social life after this episode. Finally, the army awarded him one million dollars in compensation.

We have considered analgesics, sedatives, stimulants, and psychoactive drugs in this section. Psychiatric drugs will be treated later, in Chapter 17, which deals with psychotherapies.

FRONTIERS OF CONSCIOUSNESS RESEARCH

Parapsychology is the study of extraordinary experiences. Parapsychology is an extremely controversial area of research attracting both ardent believers and extreme skeptics.

Parapsychology

In almost everyone's life there are moments of extraordinary coincidence. You "knew" the phone was going to ring before it did. You have a dream about a friend who is in trouble and you wake to find that he has been in an accident. Over the centuries there have been accounts of people who could "read" others' minds, who dreamt of events that occurred in the future, who could move objects at will. These are called *paranormal phenomena;* if they could be demonstrated scientifically the implications would be enormous. If people can foresee events, if they can communicate through thought alone over great distances, if people can influence others' actions or events at a distance, then it would be necessary to completely revise our notions of space, time, and of human consciousness. Since there is so much at stake, it is not surprising that the scientific community sets a high standard of proof regarding these phenomena.

Paranormal abilities (called psi abilities) are classified into two categories: **extrasensory perception** (ESP), the ability to communicate and acquire information about the world by means other than those familiar to us (talking, reading, etc.); and **psychokinesis** (PK), the ability to affect the physical world by mental force alone, such as transporting objects merely by willing.

Experiments in Parapsychology

The first major obstacle to parapsychological research was how to go about studying a phenomenon that might not even exist. Parapsychological research began in the 1930s in the United States in the laboratory of J. B. Rhine at Duke University. In order to rid parapsychology of the "freak show" stigma, Rhine instituted a card-guessing paradigm. Subjects were asked to guess which cards the experimenter was holding. If the subject guessed accurately several times, that would be evidence of ESP. However, in a series of well-controlled experiments over 30 years of extensive research, few positive results were obtained. Few scores were

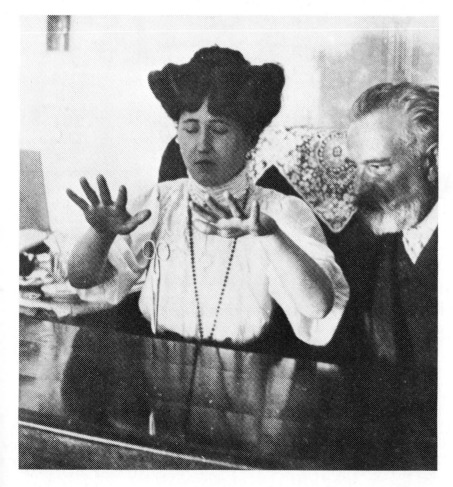

FIGURE 7–17
A "Demonstration" of Paranormal Abilities

above chance; these results could mean that paranormal phenomena do not exist; they could also mean that these kinds of experiments will not discover them.

More recently, researchers in parapsychology have attempted to develop more sophisticated methods than those used by Rhine and to look at more subtle phenomena. Recent attempts fall into several categories (Beloff, 1978):

1. The search for a conducive state of mind. REM sleep and borderline states have been investigated (Honorton, 1974; Ullman, Krippner, & Vaughn, 1973).
2. The search for a method of training psi ability. Such methods include feedback on right and wrong choices (Tart, 1977).
3. The search for people with psi. Often "psychics" and "mediums" with spectacular claims have been studied. The most famous modern psychic is Uri Geller, who claims he can receive telepathic (mental) communication and perform psychokinesis. Most of his "feats," however, have been repeated by professional magicians (Randi, 1975; Targ & Puthoff, 1977).
4. The search for a dependable physiological reaction to extrasensory signals. Perhaps ESP is unavailable to normal consciousness, but can be injected into awareness. Experiments have been conducted in an attempt to influence such processes as heart rate (Tart, Puthoff, & Targ, 1979).

Two major difficulties continually beset parapsychological researchers who report some positive findings: (1) there are no repeatable effects, and (2) when there are mild successes, their effects seem to decline with practice.

Unfortunately, there has not been as yet any reliable demonstration of paranormal abilities. Perhaps you, the current or next generation of researchers, will come up with convincing demonstrations of the existence of paranormal abilities. Until then, whether some individuals have "special gifts" or whether all humans have "hidden" mental abilities remains a fascinating, elusive, unproven area of research.

Self-regulation

For centuries there have been reports from India of extraordinary examples of self-control by Yogis. These adepts were said to be able to control their experience of pain, for example, when lying on a bed of nails or walking across hot coals. Recently, developments in both consciousness research and technology have made it possible to evaluate these claims, which have been confirmed in precise studies (Bagchi & Wenger, 1957).

The Control of Internal Processes

Several internal processes can be consciously controlled. These include the electrical potential of the skin, heart rate, blood pressure, muscle tension, and the electrical activity of the brain (Miller, 1980). Perhaps other controls will be uncovered.

Studies in self-regulation have led to experimental clinical treatments to control seizures without using drugs (Sterman, 1978). Tension headache and anxiety have also been treated experimentally using biofeedback techniques, specifically by reducing tension in the frontalis muscle of the forehead (Budzynski, 1981). (See Figure 7–18.) Migraine headaches have been successfully treated by redirecting blood flow from the head to the hands.

Biofeedback is a method of training people to control internal processes not normally controlled by consciousness. Glandular and muscular activity, brain waves, and blood pressure have all been controlled through the technique of biofeedback (Miller, 1978).

With biofeedback, individuals' physiological responses, such as heart rate, are converted into information and then communicated to them. For instance, their heartbeats may be amplified so they can easily hear the sounds. If they want to slow their heartbeat, they breathe differently, concentrate, try to relax. If they succeed, they will immediately hear a slower heartbeat. When previously unconscious information is vividly brought to consciousness, action can be taken and the internal processes can be altered.

Biofeedback is of interest to researchers because it is a drug-free therapy (therefore free of unwanted side effects) and it is a new way to study consciousness.

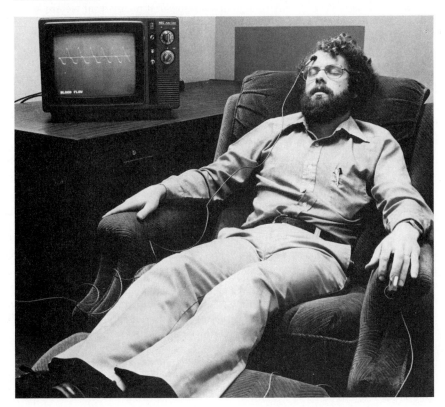

FIGURE 7–18
Biofeedback Being Used for Self-regulation of Internal Processes

Conclusion

The study of consciousness is at once the oldest area of psychological research and one of its most important new areas. Consciousness is so difficult to study objectively that researchers had to wait for the development of new and sophisticated techniques such as biofeedback, the analysis of REM sleep, studies of the physiology of meditation. Investigations so far reveal that human consciousness is much more diverse and variable than most people have thought. Our consciousness changes radically each day because we have many divisions of consciousness, each activated by different circumstances. Finally, we may have more control over internal environment than we have thought.

Summary

1. *Consciousness* has four main functions: (1) selecting information in the inner and outer world; (2) guiding and overseeing actions; (3) setting priorities for actions; and (4) detecting and resolving discrepancies.

2. The structure of the mind can be compared to that of a newspaper. Consciousness is the "front page" of the mind, and below it are many different levels of awareness containing plans, expectations, assumptions, and basic knowledge of how to operate in the world. Below consciousness are the following:

   a. *Awareness.* When something is in awareness, it means that we are keeping track of it. We are aware of a great deal, much more than we are conscious of.

   b. *Preconscious memories.* These enable us to operate in the world; they are of two kinds, episodic and representational. Episodic memory consists of specific memories of our lives. Representational memory is our stored, general knowledge of the world.

   c. *Nonconscious processes.* These are concerned with regulating the automatic functioning of the body.

   d. *Unconscious processes.* The unconscious is the part of the mind, postulated by Sigmund Freud, in which memories and thoughts that are difficult to deal with consciously are hidden.

3. *Dissociation* is a division in consciousness in which an experience can only be recovered under specific conditions. Examples of dissociation include hypnotic trances and multiple personality—thought by many psychologists to be an extreme version of the divisions of consciousness in every person's mind.

4. Consciousness changes throughout each day as our needs for action change. There are *circadian* rhythms that keep us aligned with the daily light-dark cycle, the positioning of the sun, work hours, and mealtimes. One important daily rhythm is body temperature. Every day there is a peak, a valley, and plateaus. Usually, the peak of body temperature corresponds with the time of felt maximum efficiency.

   Consciousness goes through borderline states during the day. Included among these are: *daydreams* in which individuals, unable to receive enough outside stimulation, create their own; *hypnopompic* and *hypnogogic* states, just before waking and just before sleep. In both these times the mode of consciousness is receptive.

5. An important and radical change in consciousness occurs daily when we sleep and dream. In 1953 Aserinsky and Kleitman discovered that during sleep, periods of involuntary, rapid eye movement (REM) and intense bodily activity seemed to alternate regularly with periods of "quiet" sleep. These periods of *REM sleep* were observed precisely by attaching electrodes near the subject's eyes. In many subsequent studies it has been confirmed that we all enter REM periods each night, no matter what we remember, and that REM periods are strongly associated with dreaming.

   Several stages of sleep have been identified. Stage-one sleep is the entrance into sleep and is a relaxed, drowsy period lasting only a few minutes. Stage-two sleep is marked by the appearance of "sleep spindles" on the EEG and a further relaxation in muscle tension, compared with stage-one sleep. Stage-three sleep is reached when 20 to 50 percent of the EEG record is filled with high-amplitude, slow (delta) waves. When delta activity is more than 50 percent, the deepest stage of sleep, stage-four, is reached. These sleep stages follow one another in sequence throughout the night. During these stages there are no eye movements and EMG is normally low.

   During the second alternation of sleep stages, the first REM period appears. The eyes move rapidly; breathing and heart rate become irregular; there is erection in the male and vaginal engorgement in the female; and the vestibular system is activated; but all other commands for voluntary muscle movement are blocked. Dreaming usually occurs in this state, and each REM period lasts, on the average, about ten minutes. The overall cycle of sleep stages is repeated about three or four times each night.

6. The meaning of dreams has been the subject of much philosophical and, more recently, scientific thought. The belief that the contents of dreams are important is virtually universal. Within psychology there have been several influential dream theories, including:

   a. Freud's dream theory. Freud thought that dreams served two functions. The first is wish fulfillment: dreams are one of the few times when normally forbidden desires rise to the surface of consciousness. Thus, these pent up desires are diminished to some extent by being expressed in dream consciousness. Second, dreams guard sleep. The expression of these unconscious desires may become frightening to the sleeper. If the dream is upsetting enough, the person will wake up. Freud felt that dreams guard sleep by *transforming* the unconscious desires into disguised symbols. For instance, a snake might stand for the penis.
   b. Activation synthesis. In this theory many dream phenomena are interpreted as derived from the unique state of the brain and nervous system during sleep. Thus, the experiences of dreams are the result of the perceptual processes' attempt to organize the diverse information in consciousness during dreams and needing to be assimilated or accommodated. For example, the commonly reported feeling of being chased and being unable to avoid the pursuer may well be an interpretation of the blocked motor commands to our muscles during REM sleep. Floating experiences may be the interpretation of vestibular activation. Dreams are often incoherent, and such abrupt shifts in imagery may be the brain's attempt to integrate many diverse signals coming through it during the dream state.

7. Throughout history people have tried to deliberately alter consciousness through several basic methods.

   Meditation includes a number of techniques whose aim is knowledge of oneself and one's place in the world rather than intellectual knowledge. Important in these is *concentrative meditation*, in which a person restricts attention to one unchanging source of stimulation, such as your own breathing, a repeated word, a sound, or an image. This form of meditation seems to produce measurable change in the brain's activity, a shutting off of response to the external world.

   There are many techniques designed to open up and de-automatize consciousness and produce what has been called a religious or mystical experience. Among procedures used to induce these experiences are: upsets to routine, unsolvable problems, and tales of the Sufi tradition, called teaching stories. These stories contain certain specially chosen patterns of events that encourage openness to new ideas. Repeated reading of the stories allows these patterns to become strengthened in the mind. Characteristics of the mystical experience discussed by William James are the feeling of unity, a sense of realness, ineffability, and vividness and richness.

   An important technique to alter consciousness is *hypnosis*, which is a deliberate, voluntary form of dissociation. The individual relinquishes normal control of consciousness to another person, the hypnotist. General characteristics of the hypnotic condition are that attention can be changed—narrowed or broadened—according to instructions. Distortions of reality are accepted; the person can act out roles suggested by the hypnotist and can be given suggestions about posthypnotic behavior.

8. Drugs that affect consciousness can be divided into five classes:
   - *Analgesics* (e.g., morphine) reduce the experience of pain.
   - *Sedatives* (e.g., barbiturates) induce relaxation and sleep.
   - *Stimulants* (e.g., amphetamines) elevate mood and increase alertness.
   - *Psychoactive drugs* (e.g., marijuana and LSD) change the overall structure of consciousness.
   - *Psychiatric drugs* (e.g., lithium) help to normalize consciousness by correcting neurochemical imbalances.

9. The study of parapsychology or of paranormal phenomena is of great interest in psychology. Paranormal abilities (called psi abilities) are classified into two categories: *extrasensory perception* (ESP) and *psychokinesis* (PK). Most studies of parapsychology have failed to convince the scientific community of the validity of the phenomena, at least within the customary scientific framework. Recent attempts to produce repeatable scientific investigations have fallen into several categories: the search for a conducive state of mind, such as REM sleep; the search for a method of training psi ability; the search for special people with psi; and the search for dependable physiological reactions to extrasensory signals. Two major difficulties of parapsychology are that there seem to be no repeatable effects; and, when there are mild successes, these successes seem to decline with practice, which is the opposite of what would normally be expected.

10. It has been recently demonstrated that several internal processes can be consciously controlled: the electrical potential of the skin, heart rate, blood pressure, muscle tension, and the electrical activity of the brain. It is the hope of researchers in these areas that many of the previously "involuntary" processes of the body may be brought under conscious control.

activation synthesis
analgesics
automatization
biofeedback
circadian
dissociation
extrasensory perception
hidden observer
hypnogogic
hypnopompic
hypnosis
levels of awareness
meditation

nonconscious
pontine reticular formation
preconscious
psychiatric drugs
psychoactive drugs
psychokinesis
REM sleep
sedatives
sleep spindles
stimulants
teaching story
unconscious

Suggestions for Further Reading

Brecher, E. M. (1974). *Licit and illicit drugs.* Boston: Little, Brown.

Hilgard, E. R. (1977). *Divided consciousness: Multiple controls in human thought and action.* New York: Wiley-Interscience.
    An intriguing compilation of the varieties of dissociative phenomena and divided consciousness in hypnosis and in other phenomena such as fugue states.

Ornstein, R. E. (Ed.). (1973). *Nature of human consciousness.* San Francisco: W. H. Freeman.

Ornstein, R. E. (1977). *The psychology of consciousness* (2nd ed.). New York: Harcourt Brace Jovanovich.
    Two books that attempt to bring together much of the diverse literature on consciousness for students who wish to take matters in this chapter further.

Shah, I. (1982). *Seeker after truth.* New York: Harper & Row.
    One of many of Idries Shah's books for a person seriously interested in developing a more comprehensive personal understanding. Highly recommended.

Chapter 8

The Basics of Learning

INTRODUCTION

I don't eat Mexican food. My friends always make fun of me because of this. You're so inconsistent, they tell me; you love hot food, like Indian curry; you love tomatoes, onions, garlic, avocadoes. It seems strange to me too; it's not just that I don't care for the food, I simply *can't* bear the thought of eating it, no matter what. Until I did the research for this chapter, I never understood *why* I feel this way about Mexican food.

I certainly do know *when* and *where* I developed my problem. About 20 years ago I was working as a deckhand on a freighter that stopped at the port of Zihuatenejo, on the west coast of Mexico. We arrived one night and I went ashore to enjoy a meal given for the ship's crew. The ship left "Z" early the next morning. It was my time to stand watch on the bow. Before the sun came up a terrific storm arose. The rain poured, the wind blew, and the bow of the ship leaped, time and again, out of the water, crashing into the sea. Again and again the ship heaved. The only way I could stand out there was to tie myself onto the little perch on the bow. So I bounced and heaved (in more than one sense of the word!) along with the ship itself.

When all had calmed down, I returned to my quarters, sick and completely exhausted. I slept for 12 hours. When I awoke I was afraid of returning to the bow of the ship and completely disgusted by the idea of Mexican food. My fear of the bow was, I think, completely understandable, but I got over that fast. I returned to my regular watch two or three days later. However, I have never been able to eat Mexican food again, even though I "knew" the cause of my sickness was the storm, not the dinner, so deep was my association of the dinner with the sickness.

That particular experience is quite unusual, but what we know of our world consists in large part of associating things that occur together: the traffic light flashes red, we hit the brakes without thinking; the light has come to "mean" STOP. When the music begins to swell in a movie, you know that a big clinch is coming, you can almost anticipate the heroine rushing into the hero's arms. When the music becomes low, you know the hero is in trouble. The dinner bell conjures the taste and smell of food: the sound and the smell have become associated. These simple **associations** form the basis of our knowledge of the world: they underlie our ability to know what events occur together, how events are linked to actions, and actions to each other.

Because associations are so basic to the mind, how they are formed has been the subject of more research in psychology than any other topic. We know the specific *conditions* under which simple associations occur (so much so that the process of forming associations is called **conditioning**). We even know that certain kinds of associations, especially those involving food, are probably built in to us. But we will get back to that when we pick up the story of my experiences in Mexico.

Principles and Issues

Association

Association is one of psychology's oldest principles. The study of associations began with the Greek philosophers and was revived by the British empiricists in the seventeenth century. Such philosophers as John Locke, David Hume, and John Stuart Mill felt that the "association of ideas" (an "idea" being what we might now call a sensation or a thought) is the bond that connects all our experience. "Ideas" become associated when they occur close to each other in space or in time. John Locke (1670) wrote:

> A man has suffered pain or sickness in a place; he saw his friend die in such a room, though these have in nature nothing to do with one another, yet when the idea of the place occurs to mind, it brings (the impressions being once made) that of pain and displeasure with it, he confounds them in his mind and can as little bear the one as the other.

The empiricists, who have been quite influential in science's view of the human mind, believed that all knowledge came from experience. They assumed that the mind was, at birth, a blank slate (in Latin, a *tabula rasa*) on which our specific experiences "write." However, we do not have to accept that we are a blank slate at birth to understand the importance of associations. There is, of course, much evidence that some of our abilities and "knowledge" are built in, that infants are prepared to react to their world in a certain way and that different species are *prepared* biologically to learn different things: humans, for instance, learn lan-

FIGURE 8–1
How Ideas Get Associated
This diagram indicates how ideas and sensations may become associated with a place (a room) someone occupied while sick or in pain.

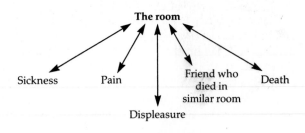

guage easily; other species do not. Associations are learned, but we are biologically "prepared" to learn some things more easily than others.

CLASSICAL OR RESPONDENT CONDITIONING

A student of mine was once watching a television program about how bees make honey from flowers. At one point in the program, the narrator shook a box of flowers to demonstrate how much pollen there is in them. When the yellow stuff appeared on the screen, my student began to sneeze violently. Of course, she was allergic to pollen itself, but not allergic to its *sight* alone. What happened was that, through a long period of experiencing bouts of sneezing after seeing and inhaling pollen, she began to associate sneezing with seeing pollen. Her response had become "conditioned" to the sight of pollen.

We all have similar experiences. One man came to psychotherapy because of a learned fear. He was inside his car, waiting for a red light to change, when his car was struck by another from the rear. His head went into the windshield. Afterward he became extremely fearful not only of driving a car, but even of sitting in one. One woman, who was laughed at once when she spoke in class, was fearful of ever speaking again (Wolpe, 1981).

But *how*, exactly, do these associations develop? What are the rules governing the formation of associations? Once formed, do associations disappear? Some of the earliest scientific experiments designed to answer these questions were by Ivan Pavlov (1849–1936).

FIGURE 8–2
How an Allergic Person Might Become Conditioned to Reacting to the Sight of Pollen

Inhaling pollen from flower . . . causes sneezing.

Repeated pairings (bouts of sneezing after seeing flowers and inhaling pollen) strengthen association of sneezing with sight of flower (pollen).

Just seeing picture of flower . . . causes sneezing.

Ivan Pavlov
(1849–1936)

Pavlov (center) in his laboratory with his assistants, his apparatus, and one of his dogs.

Pavlov's Experiments

Pavlov was a Russian physiologist whose work on digestive processes earned him a Nobel Prize in 1904. But today, he is most remembered for his contribution to the psychology of learning. This work, like many important experiments, began by accident. In order to study the role of salivation in digestion, Pavlov invented a procedure that allowed him to measure saliva precisely. He cut a slit in each laboratory dog's cheek and inserted one end of a tube into the salivary glands, the other end into a measurement device (Figure 8–3). When a piece of meat or meat powder was put in the dog's mouth, the saliva would be caught and measured.

The dogs soon began to ruin Pavlov's experiment. After a few trials with the same dog, the salivation began *before* the food was put in the dog's mouth. The dogs even went so far as to salivate at the sight of the person who usually brought the food or even when they heard the rattling of the food trays: the dogs were learning to anticipate the arrival of food. Pavlov realized that he could study the process of association with this experimental setup. At the time, studying "associations" was the realm of philosophy or psychology—both deemed unscientific by Pavlov. And yet this procedure allowed him to produce an observable, measurable response (salivation) that could objectively be used as an index of

"associative strength," that is, he could *measure* "thinking" and "learning."

Pavlov set out to discover the *conditions* under which a dog would come to associate a previously "neutral" stimulus with food, and hence he gave his research the name **conditioning.** In fact, over 60 percent of the terms we use today in animal learning were first coined by Pavlov (Bower & Hilgard, 1981). First he designed a special environment where he could control all the stimuli. The environment included the apparatus shown in Figure 8–3. The dog is harnessed so he cannot move and must see the experimental stimulus. The laboratory is soundproof; food is delivered by remote control; the experimenter watches from behind a one-way mirror. A light is flashed; the dog notices it, but does not salivate. Food is presented; the dog eats and salivates. Then again: the light is flashed; food is presented. After a number of repetitions or "trials," the dog salivates when the light is flashed, before the food is presented. Later the dog salivates when the light is flashed, even if the food is not presented at all. The change in the response is evidence that the dog has learned to associate the flash of light with the food.

To define terms: When food is in the mouth, salivation always occurs. This salivary reflex is called an **unconditioned response** (UCR). The taste of food is the **unconditioned stimulus** (UCS) that elicits the UCR. The flash of light has an important effect on the dog's behavior, but only under a specific condition: after it has been paired temporally with tasting the food (UCS). The flash of light is called the **conditioned stimulus**

FIGURE 8–3
The kind of apparatus used by Pavlov in his experiments in classical conditioning.

(CS). When the dog salivates at the sight of the light, it is a **conditioned response** (CR). Pavlov used the word "conditional," meaning that the response is conditional upon the presence of the stimulus. The term now used is *conditioned*.

How a previously neutral stimulus (NS) comes to have a significant effect on an organism's behavior is called "classical" or **respondent conditioning.** Here is the process: An unconditioned stimulus (UCS), such as the taste of meat, always elicits the unconditioned response (UCR), such as salivation. After the CS, such as a bell, has been repeatedly paired with the UCS, it elicits a response equivalent to the UCR, which is designated a CR. The UCR and CR are often the same physiological response, as in the salivating dog. In this example, associations in the dog's mind trigger a response that is normally physiologically initiated. However, the conditioned response is not always identical to the unconditioned response. For instance, if a dog is shocked, it will jump and flinch (UCR). If a light is made a CS to the shock, the dog will crouch or freeze (CR) when the light is flashed but no shock is given.

Importance of Basic Conditioning

Pavlov was able to explain how new behaviors can be acquired. This process of building new connections allows an organism more flexibility than if it were limited to the few inborn reflexes with which it is endowed. If we *could not be conditioned we would not be able to survive.* In Pavlov's words:

> The complex conditions of everyday existence require a much more detailed and specialized correlation between the animal and its environment than is afforded by the inborn reflexes alone. This more precise correlation can be established only through the medium of the cerebral hemispheres; and we have found that a great number of all sorts of stimuli always act through the medium of the hemispheres as temporary and interchangeable signals for the comparatively small number of agencies of a general character which determine the inborn reflexes, and that this is the only means by which a most delicate adjustment of the organism to the environment can be established. (Pavlov, 1927)

FIGURE 8–4
The relationship of stimuli to responses before, during, and after classical or respondent conditioning.

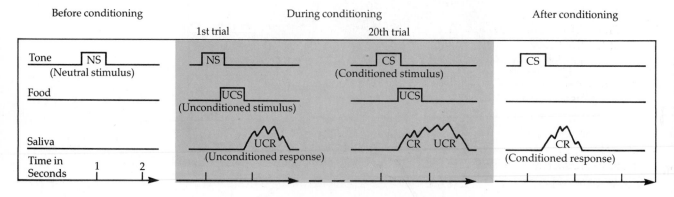

Conditions of Conditioning

Stimulus Significance

If you were sitting in a library reading this sentence and someone dropped a book nearby, you would probably automatically turn and think: "What is it?" Numerous physiological changes would take place preparing you for possible action: you would stop doing what you were doing; your senses would sharpen; and your muscles would tense. This set of responses is called the **orienting reflex** (OR). It occurs in response to any perceived novel or unexpected stimulus.

If a stimulus loses its novelty by repetition, the OR habituates unless the stimulus is made significant by conditioning. Pavlov found that only stimuli that initially elicited an OR could be made conditioned stimuli. This was Pavlov's way of making certain the animals were perceiving the stimuli he used.

There are two classes of stimuli that are significant: those the organism seeks to *approach* and those it tries to *avoid*. There are two corresponding kinds of conditioning, called appetitive and aversive. Food, sex, and water are unconditioned stimuli that an organism might like to approach (when hungry, horny, or thirsty). Shock, pain, and loud noises are stimuli that an organism would usually try to avoid. *Appetitive conditioning* refers to the procedure in which an organism is conditioned to positive, "pleasant" stimuli; *aversive conditioning* refers to conditioning to avoid painful events.

Timing and Frequency of Stimuli

There are bound to be many stimuli in the environment when a UCS is presented; consequently, which stimulus comes to acquire the status of a CS is contingent on when and how often it is paired with the UCS; these contingencies are known as the principles of recency and frequency.

Recency.   There are five different temporal arrangements of CS and UCS.

1. Simultaneous: The CS and the UCS are presented at the same time.
2. Delay: The CS is presented and continues until the UCS is presented.
3. Trace: The CS is presented but is discontinued before presentation of the UCS.
4. Backward: The CS is presented after the UCS.
5. Temporal: The CS in this case is time. The UCS is simply presented at precisely regular intervals.

Delay is the most effective arrangement; backward conditioning is the least. This is probably because stimuli presented just before the UCS can be used to prepare the organism for the UCS; stimuli presented after the UCS are of no such use. Given that the stimulus to be conditioned must occur before the UCS, does it matter how much earlier? If the stimulus precedes the UCS by too much time, say a half hour, it will not effectively predict exactly when the UCS will be presented. On the other hand, if the stimulus precedes the UCS by too little time, say one thousandth of a second, the organism will not be able to react in time to take advantage of the warning. The optimal *interstimulus interval* (ISI) is between these extremes, usually about 0.5 second, for such responses as eyeblink or foot jerks. The optimal ISI for automatic responses like GSR or salivation is much longer—5 to 30 seconds.

Frequency. How often a CS must be presented before it elicits a CR depends on the nature of both the stimulus and the response. Some associations are so easily formed that they require only one trial or a very few. For example, the relationship between food and sickness is so strong that anyone who gets sick is likely to associate the illness with a particular food, even if it happens only once (Revusky & Garcia, 1970). This is something I know well.

Acquisition and Extinction

Other characteristics of the stimulus affect classical conditioning as well. Because of habituation, a constant stimulus such as a shining light is not as effective as an irregular one such as a flashing light. The intensity of competing stimuli is another factor in the acquisition of a CR. Moderate stimuli are most easily conditioned; a weak stimulus may take longer, while an extremely strong stimulus may prevent classical conditioning altogether, by producing disruption. The general principle is: The more often a neutral stimulus (CS) is paired with an unconditioned stimulus (UCS), the faster the conditioned response (CR) will be acquired.

Most conditioned responses are acquired by repeated pairing of UCS and CS. What happens to a CR if it is no longer reinforced? What if the bell sounds, but no food is presented? If after a conditioned response has been acquired, the CS is presented *without* the UCS, the CR gradually decreases. (See Figure 8–5.) The procedure is called **extinction.** The CR has not been completely eliminated, however, if when the CS is presented after some time has elapsed, the CR reappears. This is *spontaneous recovery.*

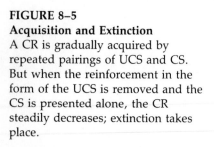

FIGURE 8–5
Acquisition and Extinction
A CR is gradually acquired by repeated pairings of UCS and CS. But when the reinforcement in the form of the UCS is removed and the CS is presented alone, the CR steadily decreases; extinction takes place.

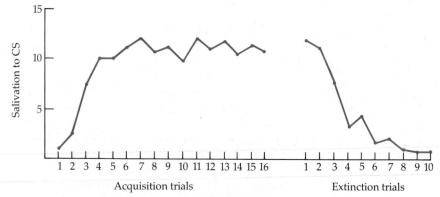

Generalization and Discrimination

Because of the complexities of life, respondent conditioning would have little importance in learning if an organism did not transfer knowledge from one situation to another. We know someone is at the door whether the signal is a bell, a buzzer, a knocker, or chimes. **Generalization** means that once a specific stimulus has become a CS, similar stimuli will elicit the conditioned response. The more similar the stimuli, the stronger the transfer of the conditioned response.

Generalization is common to all forms of learning. Watson & Raynor (1920) gave a one-year-old baby named Albert a white rat to play with. As Albert moved to the rat to pet it, Watson stood behind the baby and banged a steel bar. They repeated the procedure until Albert began to cry (CR) as soon as he saw the rat (CS). Although Albert was only conditioned to fear white rats, this fear *generalized* to a white dog, a rabbit, a fur coat, and even a Santa Claus mask.

Gregory Razran (1939) demonstrated the principle of generalization in an experiment on *semantic conditioning*—the changing of responses to words. Razran conditioned college students to salivate to certain words, by flashing the words "style, urn, freeze" on a screen as they sucked on lollipops. Soon, when those words appeared on the screen the students salivated (CR). New words were then flashed, either homonyms or synonyms of the original list. There was little salivary response to the homonyms "stile, earn, frieze," but the synonyms "fashion, vase, chill" did elicit the CR. Thus the conditioned response can generalize to the *meaning* of words.

Generalization tests the ability to observe similarities. It is also important to note *differences* between stimuli. That ability is called **discrimination.** If a dog is conditioned to salivate to a certain tone, it will, according to the principle of generalization, salivate to a similar tone. If food does not follow the similar tone for several pairings, the dog will no longer respond to that tone, but it will still respond to the original. We say the dog has learned to discriminate between the tones (Pavlov, 1927).

An example of human discrimination can be taken from infants' learning of language (Brown, 1965). Initially, infants are reinforced for saying "da-da" and "ma-ma" in the presence of parents. These words are then generalized and applied to all adults, strangers included. Since infants are not reinforced for these responses, they learn to discriminate and use the words correctly.

What happens if impossible discriminations are demanded? Pavlov and a student in his laboratory found that extremely fine discriminations can cause an animal to become "neurotic." First, they conditioned a dog to salivate (CR) to the sight of a circle (CS) projected on a screen. Then they projected a picture of an elongated ellipse, not followed by food. The dog soon learned to discriminate between the ellipse and the circle. Then Pavlov began presenting the dog with increasingly circular ellipses. The dog was able to make discriminations, but acted strangely.

At the same time, the whole behavior of the animal underwent an abrupt change. The hitherto quiet dog began to squeal in its stand, kept wriggling about, tore off with its feet the apparatus for mechanical stimulation of the skin, and bit through the tubes connecting the animal's room with the observer, a behavior which never happened before. On being taken into the experimental room, the dog now barked violently, which was also contrary to its usual custom; in short, it presented all the symptoms of a condition of acute neurosis (Pavlov, 1927).

Respondent Conditioning in Perspective

Applications

It is possible that Albert, the subject in Watson and Raynor's experiment, is still alive and still afraid of white rats and Santa Claus masks and psychologists in white coats. It is more likely that his fear underwent *extinction* as he encountered many white furry things that were not followed by terrifying sounds. It is also possible that fear can be so intense it generalizes to representations or even thoughts of the CS. Some people are so terrified of flying that they become frightened even thinking about it.

Mary Cover Jones (1924) discovered a method, using extinction and generalization, to help people overcome their fears. The method is called **counterconditioning.** In counterconditioning, an unwanted CR is eliminated by conditioning the subject to another stimulus (CS) that elicits a new conditioned response (CR) that is less disruptive than the unwanted CR. Jones found a child, Peter, who was afraid of rabbits. Peter was put in the high chair and given some candies to eat. While he was enjoying the candy, she brought a rabbit close to the high chair. When Peter screamed, Jones moved the rabbit back until he was appeased. She inched the rabbit closer and closer. After six weeks of trials, the rabbit sat on the high chair with Peter; once the boy even asked for it, when it was not there. What had happened was that the rabbit was no longer a CS associated only with a fearful CR, but became associated with an enjoyable CR, eating candy. Another good "application" comes from taste aversion research; alcoholics given Antabuse will suffer a violent nausea if they drink alcohol. In many cases the taste of alcohol is subsequently avoided because it was paired with sickness!

OPERANT OR INSTRUMENTAL CONDITIONING

Respondent (classical) conditioning describes how we learn to associate different events in the world. Instrumental conditioning describes how we learn to *act* in the world to get what we want. One major principle of instrumental conditioning is familiar enough. *We act in such a way as to seek pleasure and avoid pain.* In psychology this is called the *Law of Effect.*

The Law of Effect

Edward Thorndike (1874–1949) was an early investigator of how an organism learns new behaviors. One of his experiments involved cats trying to escape a locked cage to get food. The cat could escape the cage by unlatching a string that held the door closed. A hungry cat will move around and claw the cage; eventually, it will accidentally loosen the string that releases the door and escape. Each time it is put in the cage, its behavior will become increasingly organized. Instead of random clawing, it will head right for the string and unlatch the door. This is evidence that the cat has learned to open the cage. This work has been called "instrumental" because the cat's action was *instrumental in getting what the cat wanted* (Hilgard & Marquis, 1940).

Thorndike proposed that learning is governed by the Law of Effect: Any action that is followed by a "satisfying state of affairs" is likely to be repeated; similarly, any action that results in an "annoying state of affairs" probably will not be. The Law of Effect is a useful way to predict behavior. If you put your hand into a fire, you get burned and are unlikely to do it again. If, while wandering, you find a beautiful stream, you may go there straight away the next time you are out walking.

B. F. Skinner

Operant Conditioning

In a very important series of studies, B. F. Skinner described two kinds of learning. He gave respondent conditioning its name because it is the *response* of the organism that is conditioned. He renamed instrumental conditioning **operant conditioning** because it is the organism's *operations* or actions that are conditioned in this case. In respondent or classical conditioning the UCS both *precedes* and *reflexively elicits* the response, while in operant conditioning the response *precedes* the UCS (reinforcement) and is *voluntarily emitted*. Operant conditioning involves feedback: the organism's *responses* are part of the system, unlike respondent conditioning. Operant conditioning is based on a principle similar to the Law of Effect. All actions have certain consequences, and those consequences increase or decrease the possibility of reoccurrence of that action. Consequences of actions that increase the probability of the recurrence of those actions are called *reinforcements*. Reinforcements are central to the operant conditioning approach and will be discussed in detail later.

The Skinner Box

Skinner invented a controlled environment commonly known as the "Skinner box." It contains a food tray, a lever, and a water spout. A rat is placed inside the box. Food pellets dropped into the tray by a mechanical device make a clicking sound as the pellets are released. Quickly the rat shows a conditioned response to the click and runs to the tray. At this stage of the experiment, the lever is not connected to the food dispenser, because it is necessary to determine how often the rat presses the bar by chance. The number of times this response is made before conditioning is called the **operant level** of the response. Once the operant level is determined, the lever is hooked up to the food dispensing device. When the rat again presses the bar, it will hear the click of the food dispenser. It takes a few such bar pressings for the rats to begin to change their behav-

forced. Because the UCS is usually something that directly causes a reflexive response, almost any stimulus can become a CS under the right conditions. The critical contingencies in classical conditioning are frequency, recency, and timing (how closely the CS and UCS are paired). Although these contingencies are important in operant conditioning too, the value of the reinforcement to the organism plays an obvious role.

Relativity of Reinforcement. Reinforcements are relative. One hundred dollars is a lot of money to a poor man, less to a rich one. Working for $10,000 a year is perceived one way if it is a first job and another way if one's last salary was $25,000. One man's reinforcement may be another man's punishment. A hungry rat will press a bar for food; a satiated one will not; a job I might be eager to do, a millionaire might turn down.

To change behavior through operant conditioning, an appropriate reinforcement has to be determined. (Psychologists have recently rediscovered what parents have long known: behaviors themselves can be reinforcers. "You can watch TV if you finish your homework first.") Premack (1965) has studied this form of reinforcement. *Premack's principle* states that a more favored behavior can be used to reinforce a less favored behavior. He demonstrated his principle with a group of elementary school children in a room with a pinball machine and chocolate. Some children preferred to play pinball; he called these children "manipulators." The ones who preferred the chocolate he called the "eaters." A few days later the children went back to the room, but this time their play was restricted. Before "manipulators" were allowed to play pinball, they had to eat a piece of chocolate. The result was an increase in their consumption of chocolate. Likewise, the "eaters" had to play pinball first, which caused a parallel increase in manipulating.

Ayllon and Azrin used Premack's principle on psychotic patients in an Illinois State Hospital (1968). Their goal was to teach the patients behaviors and social skills that would make it possible for them to live in the community. Ayllon and Azrin observed the patients carefully and discovered the favorite behaviors of each individual: one liked to sit in a certain chair, another hid things under his mattress, some liked to sit alone, hidden from others. These favored behaviors had to be earned. The price for indulging in them was participating in a new social activity or practicing a new skill: asking questions, following directions, keeping an appointment, keeping clean, and so on. The project was quite successful and has been repeated in a variety of situations in institutions.

Primary and Conditioned Reinforcers. There are two broad categories of reinforcers: primary and conditioned. *Primary reinforcers* include food, water, relief from pain; they need no training, as they are inherently reinforcing.

A *conditioned* (or *secondary*) *reinforcer* is something that is not innately reinforcing but has come to be associated with a primary reinforcer. The most common conditioned reinforcer in human life is money. Although we all work to eat, we do not receive food after work. We work for money, which allows us to obtain the primary reinforcers.

In one study, Wolfe (1936) taught chimps to put a poker chip into a machine to get a grape. Soon, the chimps performed other tasks to earn poker chips. Conditioned reinforcers are especially important when there is a delay between a behavior and a primary reinforcer. Wolfe's chimps were only allowed to use the grape dispensing machine at certain times, but they could earn the chips at all times. When a chimp deposited a chip and had to wait a long time for a grape, the operant strength of the new behavior decreased. As long as the chimp could do something while it waited, like earn chips, the operant strength was maintained. The importance of conditioned reinforcement is enormous: it enables us to wait for payday, to work hard and save for the future.

Physiological Reinforcements.   It appears that electrical stimulation to certain locations of the brain is itself reinforcing. Olds and Milner (1954) implanted electrodes in specific areas in a rat's brain and ran electrical current through them. The rats began to repeat actions that immediately preceded the stimulation. Thus stimulation to a site in the brain was a reinforcer. There are many stimulation sites in the brain that might be reinforcing, especially those areas related to hunger, thirst, and sex. Electrode implantation has also been tried on people suffering from neurological disorders like epilepsy. The patient sits in front of a display of buttons, each of which sends electrical stimulation to a different part of the brain. Heath (1963) found that certain buttons were pressed more than others. The patients reported sensations ranging from intoxication to specific tastes to the intense feeling right before orgasm.

Schedules of Reinforcement

In the last section, we discussed the qualities and characteristics of reinforcers. Now we turn to another important factor affecting reinforcement—timing. In general, the best time for a reinforcer or punishment to be presented is *immediately following the response,* so that no random stimuli become inadvertently associated with the reinforcement. No animals can learn if there is too much of a delay between response and reinforcement or punishment. Grice (1948) had rats run a maze for food. The reinforcement delays for different groups of rats ranged from 0 to 10 seconds. The shorter the delay, the faster the rat learned. The rats who faced a 10-second delay showed no improvement after even hundreds of trials. Likewise, when administering a punishment, it is more effective to do so as soon as the inappropriate response is made: thus, a young child who misbehaves should be punished immediately, not made to wait until daddy comes home.

Continuous and Partial Reinforcement

For conditioning to occur, a reinforcer need not be presented each time a response is made. There are two patterns of reinforcement: continuous (or constant) and partial. **Continuous reinforcement** (CRF) means that each time the animal makes the correct response, it is reinforced. **Partial reinforcement** (PR) means that reinforcement does not always follow the response. Continuous reinforcement, as you might

FIGURE 8–8
Conditioned Reinforcers, Chimpanzees, and People
This chimpanzee earned poker chips (conditioned reinforcers) in a learning experiment and is now using one to get food (primary reinforcer). Most people are rewarded in this way, being paid later for work done now, with money that can be converted into primary reinforcers of their choice.

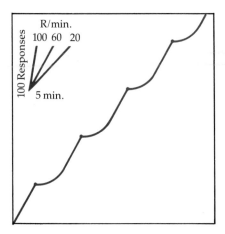

FIGURE 8–9
A Pigeon's Responses
on a Fixed-interval
Schedule of Reinforcement
Note the "scalloping" as the
responses decrease after
reinforcement and increase just
before each scheduled reinforcement.

Superstitious Behavior
See p. 315.

imagine, makes learning very fast; it is almost essential if an animal is to learn a very complex new behavior beyond the bounds of his species' normal behavior. A seal must be reinforced with a fish every time it balances a ball on its nose. Continuous reinforcement is *not* necessary for humans to acquire new skills. In life outside the laboratory or the circus there is not always someone to throw a "fish" for a job well done. Thus, a child who gets an award for reading new words in class may also read alone at home with no decrease in operant strength.

Partial Reinforcement Schedules

There are four kinds of partial reinforcement schedules:

1. **Fixed Interval** (FI). Reinforcement is presented at regular intervals after the correct response. The interval is written as a number. A pigeon who knows how to peck for food may be put on FI-7 (seconds). The pigeon pecks, receives food. Then, no matter how many times it pecks, it will receive no food until 7 seconds have elapsed. As a rule, responding on a FI schedule shows "scalloping," increasing just before reinforcement, and decreasing immediately following it. (See Figure 8–9.) An example of the effect of a FI schedule is an experiment by Mawhinney, Bostow, Laws, Blumenfeld, and Hopkins (1971). The investigators asked their students to use a special room for study. The experimenters observed the actual amount of time the students spent studying in the special room. Once the operant level of studying was determined, manipulation of the conditions began. The teachers gave a test every day; the observers noted that about the same amount of studying went on every day. Later the teachers gave a test once every three weeks (FI-3 weeks). They noted a distinct difference in study habits. Little studying was done immediately after a test, but it increased noticeably later in the three-week interval. Most studying was done in the few days before the test. When the teachers returned to giving a daily test, studying was once again regular.

2. **Variable Interval** (VI). In this schedule, the intervals between reinforcement vary randomly around an average. It is impossible for an animal to adjust its response rate to match the schedule, because it is independent of the number of responses it makes. A VI-5 (minute) schedule means that the intervals could vary from a few seconds to a few minutes, but the average of all the intervals is 5 minutes. When you keep trying to call someone and the line is busy, you are on a VI schedule. Sometimes the call goes through immediately, sometimes the line is busy for hours. The time you dial when the line is free is the only response that is reinforced (by talking to your friend). "Superstitious" behavior often develops in animals (humans included!) on a VI schedule.

3. **Fixed Ratio** (FR). On a fixed ratio schedule, reinforcement is given after a certain number of responses. A rat on a FR-5 schedule is reinforced every fifth time it presses the bar. Some people are paid on a FR schedule. Farm workers may be paid a specified amount for a certain number of bushels; piece workers are paid when they have finished making a certain number of objects. A farm worker who picks seven bushels of lettuce to receive payment is on a FR-7 schedule.

4. **Variable Ratio** (VR). In this schedule, reinforcement occurs after a randomly varying number of responses. A VR-5 schedule means that, on the average, every fifth response will be reinforced. People who gamble on slot machines are on a VR schedule.

The closer a schedule is to continuous reinforcement, the faster learning: a response conditioned on a continuous schedule will undergo extinction the fastest. An animal may be switched from a CRF to a partial reinforcement schedule when adequate operant strength has been reached. The same thing happens to us. If you take tennis lessons, at first your teacher may say "good shot" each time you hit the ball well, but later may only comment occasionally.

An animal's response patterns vary with the kind of schedule it is on. On a FI, the response rate decreases immediately after the reinforcement and gradually increases. On a VI schedule there is not much change in response rate from reinforcement to reinforcement. On both FR and VR schedules, rate of response is rapid, indicating that the animal knows that reinforcement has something to do with the number of responses. In a lab, conditions can be tightly controlled, but in life things are more haphazard. The four schedules of partial reinforcement are analogous to the way things happen in life. As a rule you cannot always be rewarded for every good thing you do. But intermittent rewards for your efforts are enough to keep you trying and they enable you to learn.

The most important effect of partial reinforcement is the increased persistence of the resultant learning. An organism will respond for a longer time without reinforcement when it has received partial rather than continuous reinforcement during learning. VR schedules are particularly resistant to extinction. This helps account for why gamblers

Gamblers are rewarded on a variable ratio schedule, because if they win it is after a randomly varying number of bets—but this also allows them to expect to win at *any* time.

COGNITIVE LEARNING

If you suspect that there is more to learning than classical and operant conditioning, you are right. These two forms of learning are important, but people have additional ways of learning.

Insight

Much learning, from Thorndike's cats escaping their cage to human problem solving, is accomplished by trial and error. There is, however, the experience when the solution to a problem seems to appear in a flash of **insight.** In one experiment, a chimp is placed in a cage with a short stick. A few feet outside the cage is a longer stick, beyond which is some enticing fruit. The chimp immediately tries to reach the fruit, but finds his arms too short. Next he tries the short stick, and fails—it is not long enough either. Then he seems to stop all overt activity for a while. All of a sudden the solution seems to pop into his mind: he uses the short stick to get the long stick, then uses the long stick to get the fruit. What is learned in this case is not a specific association between a stimulus and a response but the organization of objects and events in the environment. The chimp learns to combine familiar objects and behaviors into a new solution to the problem. In a similar experiment, a bunch of bananas was suspended from the ceiling of a room with nothing in it but a few boxes. The chimp jumped in vain, then stopped, pondered, and perused—and then piled the boxes one upon the other, climbed up, and got the bananas (Köhler, 1925).

Köhler points out that the chimp who has learned to use the two sticks has learned a *relationship,* not a response. Thus, this learning will *generalize* to new situations. If there is no stick around, but there is a long wire, the chimp will pick up the wire. Once a new relationship has been learned, it becomes part of the organism's behavioral repertoire.

FIGURE 8–10
Chimpanzee Insight
After apparent contemplation, this chimpanzee used a short stick provided him to pull a longer stick into his cage and used it to reach the fruit.

Latent Learning

Performance is the ultimate test of learning. If an organism shows consistent reductions in errors while performing a task, we say learning has taken place. However, there is evidence that learning can occur without being manifested in performance improvement. Such **latent learning** amounts to a change in ability not yet demonstrated by performance.

The classic demonstration of latent learning was by Tolman and Honzik (1930). Three groups of rats ran a complex maze once a day for two to three weeks. Group A always found food in its goal box; Group B never found food; Group C found no food for the first 10 days. On the 11th, Group C rats found food in their box, and food was presented every day thereafter. Figure 8–11 shows the results. The performance of Group C rats was, for the first 10 days, like that of Group B; but after the 11th day, it was immediately equal to or better than Group A's performance. This demonstrated that Group C had learned during the previous 10 days, though their performance had been low due to the lack of reward.

In Köhler's experiments, the chimps had learned that sticks could be used to reach things, even though chimps usually use sticks for digging food. Tolman believed that learning goes far deeper than what overt behavior expresses, and he conducted an experiment to prove the point.

Two groups of rats were to run a cross-shaped maze, such as the one in Figure 8–12. The maze is open so that the rats can see any objects in the experimental room. There are two start boxes and two goal boxes with food. Half the time the rats begin in start box 1, half the time in 2. Group A rats always find food in goal box 1 no matter which start box

FIGURE 8–11
Latent Learning
The rats in this experiment ran a maze like the one on the left. The graph below charts the different performance curves of the three groups discussed in the accompanying text. (After Tolman & Honzik, 1930)

One-way door

Curtain

Start box

Goal box (food)

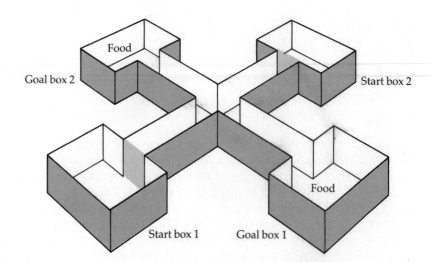

FIGURE 8–12
Learning by Developing Cognitive Maps
The rats who had to run this cross-shaped maze in a natural foraging pattern learned the maze faster than those who always found food by turning one way after leaving their start box. Tolman believed that the more successful foraging group developed wider expectations and
a kind of cognitive map of the relationships in their environment.

they leave from. Sometimes they need to make a right turn to get food, sometimes left. Group B rats find food in goal box 1 when they leave start box 1, and food in goal box 2 when leaving start box 2. Group B rats always turn right to get food.

There was a great difference in the rate at which these two groups learned the maze. One group learned in about eight runs, while some rats in the other group never learned. From a strict conditioning point of view, the prediction would be clear: Group B should learn faster; the learning is simple: "turn right for food"; however, Group A learned faster, not B.

Tolman argued that the way an organism naturally finds food in the environment is through foraging; it comes to know the lay of the land by random exploration. Specifically Tolman noted that organisms learn not only by responding to simple stimuli, but by developing a set of expectations about the relationship of elements in the environment, a sort of *cognitive map.*

Observational Learning

Primates are social animals; remember that an important function of the group is to teach the young how to act in the society. This process is called socialization. Implicit in socialization is the ability to *learn from the experience of others.* One child watches another touch a hot stove and get burned. In the future, they both are less likely to put their hands on the hot stove. The child with the burned finger has learned the lesson by operant conditioning; the other has learned by painless observation.

Albert Bandura, a leading theorist in **observational learning** (also called social learning) writes:

> Learning would be exceedingly laborious, not to mention hazardous, if people had to rely solely on the effects of their own actions to inform them what to do. Fortunately most human behavior is learned observationally through *modeling:* from observing others one forms an idea of

COMPARISON OF THEORIES

The cognitive approach to learning emphasizes that the learner is an active part of the process. Thus the processes of perception, memory, consciousness, and decision making are important intermediary events between a stimulus and response. Human learning depends to a great degree on the ability to recall similarities and relationships among situations, to recombine information, weigh alternative courses of action. This is in accord with much of modern psychology and certainly follows from our analyses of sensation, perception, consciousness. However, the behaviorist approach of Pavlov and Skinner emphasizes the study of observable actions only—measurable responses such as paw presses, and the like.

The differences between the cognitive and behaviorist approaches produced a bitter controversy that lasted more than a generation and centered on one question: Could psychologists study anything other than external, observable responses? With the advent of new technology enabling scientists to make many internal processes observable—such as brain waves and blood pressure—the gates opened. Psychology now studies observable behavior, internal physiological processes, and the unobservable mind all together. After the battle, one psychologist wrote:

Man is a thinking organism possessing capabilities that provide him with some power of self-direction. To the extent that traditional behavioral theories could be faulted it was for providing an incomplete rather than an inaccurate account of human behavior. (Bandura, 1977)

how new behaviors are performed and on later occasions this coded information serves as a guide for action. Because people can learn from example what to do, at least in approximate form, before performing any behavior, they are spared needless errors. (Bandura, 1977)

An Example: Herbert and Harsh (1944) conducted experiments in which one cat had to learn a difficult task, and other cats were allowed to watch—some all the trials, some only part of the trials. In one task the cat had to get some food that was on a revolving turntable. The cat that was learning by "trial and error" took a little over a minute (62 seconds) on the first trial to accomplish the task. Cats that observed half the trials took slightly under a minute (57 seconds), but the cats that had observed all the trials took only 16 seconds to get the food on the first trial.

Modeling

What an organism learns in classical and operant conditioning is clear enough: in the former it is the association between events in the world; in the latter, an association between one's actions and their effect on the environment. One is the result of frequent pairing, the other the result of reinforcements. In observational learning, what the observing organism acquires is an organized set of associations: schemata that direct behavior. These schemata can then direct behavior at appropriate times. Among Peruvian weavers, for example, young girls are taught to weave solely by observing others. For years, the girls simply watch their mothers while they weave the traditional patterns. They do not work on a loom until their teens. Everything from the setting up of the loom to weaving itself, even creating the intricate patterns that set each tribe apart, is learned entirely by observation (Franquemont, 1979).

Observational learning is guided primarily by four processes (Bandura, 1977):

1. *Attention.* The observer attends and perceives the salient features of another's behavior. Many factors are involved in those perceptions: who the observer is, who the person being observed is, what the behaviors are. For example, the prestige of the model is extremely important. In some groups, a scholar is a high-status person; in other groups, a strong fighter would be more respected. Different aspects of behavior would probably be attended to in these two groups.

2. *Retention.* Underlying all learning is memory. Observational learning is the development of schemata that add up to an understanding or a "model" of the world.

3. *Reproduction of the action.* We assume that observational learning has taken place when we observe someone doing something that has been learned by watching. An important process in observational learning is the *conversion of schemata into action.* It is not simple; mistakes are made at first. Trying to learn a new dance when you have only seen someone perform it is a good example. Most people do not get the steps right the first time they try to translate their internal representation into action. But the schemata are usually accurate enough that the discrepancies between the mental model and the action serve as reliable feedback. The dancing improves more rapidly than if observation had not been allowed.

4. *Motivation.* If employees watch another get fired when asking for a raise, they might hesitate to ask for a raise themselves: we can tell they have learned by what they do not do. Behaviors that result in rewarding consequences for others may be adopted; behaviors that have negative consequences will probably not be.

Imitation

The visible behavior resulting from observational learning is called imitation. The ability to imitate is not as simple as it might seem. To imitate, observers must be able to recognize similarities between the model's behavior and their own and must be able to recreate that behavior. The processes of attention, retention, motivation, and reproduction are involved in even the simplest imitation. Imitation may be the earliest form of human complex learning. A four-day-old baby can imitate the mother smiling or sticking out the tongue.

Humans also can imitate behavior when the model is not present. Rosekrans and Hartup (1967) conducted an experiment that shows this kind of imitation, regarding aggression. The question was how the observation of violence on television affects later behavior. Children watched a videotape in which an adult model punched a Bobo doll, shouting, "Wham, bam, I'll knock your head off." Some saw a version in which the model's behavior was punished by another adult's reprimands. Others saw a different version, showing the model being rewarded by the other adult's praise. A control group saw a nonviolent tape.

Modeling of Violent Behavior
See Chapter 1, pp. 8–10.

All the children were later taken to a playroom with lots of normal nursery school toys and a Bobo doll. They were left alone and observed through a one-way mirror. The children's behavior was greatly influenced by their observation of the model. The group that had seen aggression rewarded acted much more aggressively than the group that saw no aggression. Both of these groups were more aggressive than the group that saw aggression punished.

Many psychologists feel that children *learn* to behave aggressively and that many of their lessons in aggression come from television. Their concern is shared by many parents, some of whom have founded Action for Children's Television (ACT). ACT monitors children's television shows and commercials and has been instrumental in banning extremely violent shows.

Imitation is not a rote process, where actions are simply copied. Creativity can be learned by imitation. Zimmerman and Dialessi (1973) developed a technique using imitation to increase the creativity of fifth graders. One test for creativity is the "Uses" Test; the taker is asked to name as many uses as possible for a certain item, a tin can, for example. There are two broad dimensions of creativity measured in the Uses Test: fluency and flexibility. Fluency refers simply to the number of uses in a single category. A tin can may hold coins, flowers, pencils, or nails. Flexibility refers to the number of different categories the object can belong to. A tin can can be a holder of objects, a walkie-talkie, a candle stand; it can be remelted into other objects. Before the test, children watched adult models take the test; a cardboard box was the stimulus item. One group of children watched models who exhibited high or low fluency; the other group watched models with high or low flexibility. The results are that when the models showed high fluency, both the fluency and flexibility for the children increased. Surprisingly, when the model showed high flexibility, both the fluency and flexibility decreased. The children had been influenced in their creativity by the observation of others' performance and had imitated it in some way. The imitation, however, is not a passive or precise process.

Observational learning is a latecomer in the psychology of learning. The exact conditions under which it takes place, the kinds of schedules of reinforcement, have not been firmly established. Generalization and discrimination take place just as in other forms of learning. Observational extinction can be used (watching someone perform an action not punished) to help people overcome fears.

The most important factors in observational learning are the hardest to pin down: the characteristics of the model and the learner, and the interaction between the two. So the process of observational learning certainly is not as well understood as conditioning.

WHAT WE ARE "PREPARED" TO LEARN

Up to this point we have been emphasizing how associations are formed, how they gain strength and decline, how they become organized. But learning is also influenced by the fact that there are basic differences between different organisms at birth. Each organism comes into the world with some abilities "built in": birds learn to fly, we do not. We read and write, birds do not. The set of abilities each organism is born with is its **behavioral repertoire.** This repertoire varies greatly between species. However, there is a more subtle question that psychologists have recently addressed. Are some things easier to learn than others?

The Assumption of Equivalence of Associability

It could also be asked: are all events equally associable? Most students of conditioning, Pavlov, for instance, have assumed that any CS and any UCS could be associated with equal facility. He wrote:

> Any natural phenomenon chosen at will may be converted into a conditional stimulus . . . any visual stimulus, any desired sound, any odor, and the stimulation of any part of the skin. (Pavlov, 1928)

Similarly, Skinner assumed that any response could be conditioned by any reinforcer. It was believed that the laws of learning governing the association of arbitrary events such as we have considered would apply to *all* events. The problem, as we shall see, is that these laws may only apply to arbitrary associations in the lab and not to more normal and biologically adaptive associations in nature.

The Continuum of Preparedness

In an influential paper, Martin Seligman (1970) questioned the assumption of equivalence of associability and suggested that organisms are more predisposed (prepared) to associate some events than others. He proposed that there is a continuum of **preparedness** ranging from prepared to unprepared to contraprepared.

Response Difference

One of the first indications that something was wrong with the classical assumptions about learning came from the Brelands' experiences with the "misbehavior of organisms." They had difficulties in teaching a pig to deposit a coin in a "piggy bank." They termed the phenomenon **instinctive drift:** "learned behavior drifts toward instinctive behavior" (Breland & Breland, 1961).

Many other studies have shown difficulties with getting organisms to learn arbitrary responses. Thorndike's cats had great difficulty learning to escape by scratching or licking themselves. Moreover, when they did learn, the response degenerated to a "mere vestige of a lick or scratch" (Thorndike, 1954). Other experiments showed that dogs found it extremely difficult, if not impossible, to learn to yawn for food. Neither rats nor pigeons are prepared to avoid shock by lever pressing. On the other hand, pigeons easily learned to escape shock by flying, and rats by running. Bolles (1970) has suggested that the easily learned responses in avoidance situations are closely related to innate *species-specific defense reactions* (SSDRs). The idea behind SSDRs is that the organisms do not usually have the opportunity to learn how to escape from predators. A rat cannot afford to try "pressing levers" when it sees a cat. It is counterprepared to do so. It must run if it is to survive. Any avoidance

response inconsistent with an organism's specific defenses will be difficult to condition.

Stimulus Difference

We have just seen that some responses are easier to condition than others. What about stimuli? Again, the assumption of equivalence of associability appears to be mistaken—again, some things are more easily learned than others. For example, dogs are counterprepared to learn to associate different locations of the trainer's voice with "go/no go" responding; yet they easily learn to use voice tone as a discriminative stimulus, as with "go!" "stay!" (Dobrzecka & Konorowski, 1968).

An important series of experiments showing differences in the associability of different stimuli and reinforcers was performed by Garcia and Koelling (1966). They arranged for rats to drink unflavored and saccharin-flavored water while lights flashed and clicking noises were heard. The "bright-noisy" and the "tasty" water were made aversive in three ways: rats were shocked as they drank, or the water was slightly poisoned, or they were given doses of radiation. Afterward the rats were tested with "tasty" water and "bright-noisy" water separately. The rats that had been made ill by poison or radiation avoided the "tasty" water but not the "bright-noisy" water. The rats that had been shocked showed exactly the opposite result, avoiding the "bright-noisy" water but not the "tasty" water.

All of these results can be understood from an evolutionary perspective. To review: successful organisms (the ones that survive) have developed either adaptive fixed action patterns or the ability to quickly learn behaviors relevant to their particular environment or niche.

An example should make this point clear. Think about Garcia and Koelling's experiment. The rats were "prepared" to associate foot shock with external events ("bright-noisy" water) but not with nausea, an internal event. They were also prepared to associate nausea with the taste of water, but not with external events. Doesn't this make sense? How well would a rat survive that decided it was sick because of something it heard or saw? Or a rat that reacted to a sore foot with "it must be something I ate?"

Human Preparedness

You might be thinking that the notion of preparedness applies only or mainly to "animal" learning. But the evolutionary history of *Homo sapiens* has selectively prepared humans for certain kinds of learning. Some of the things we find easy to learn we share with many other species; others appear to be uniquely human.

FIGURE 8–13
The Bright-Noisy Water Experiment
Whether or not a rat avoided the water depended on the water's characteristics and on the consequences that followed drinking it. Avoidance developed if taste and illness were paired or if bright-noisy water was paired with shock—but not if pairings were reversed. The reasons for these associations are discussed in the accompanying text. (After Garcia & Koelling, 1966)

		Consequences	
		Illness	Shock
Cues	Taste	Avoid	—
	Audiovisual	—	Avoid

An example of the first kind of prepared learning is taste aversion—the *"sauce béarnaise"* phenomenon. Seligman describes how the problem of preparedness first became compelling to him. One evening he had gone to the opera with his wife. For dinner, he had one of his favorite dishes—a filet mignon with *béarnaise* sauce. In the middle of the night, Seligman became violently ill. As a result, he developed an aversion to the taste of what was once his favorite sauce. This was in spite of knowing that the cause of his sickness was not food, but flu. Moreover, he had developed no aversion to the opera, his wife, the friend he caught the flu from. The connection between nausea and prior food taste is so strongly prepared that it defies "reason." Similarly, ocean voyagers may acquire aversions to food eaten prior to seasickness, in spite of "knowing" that the cause of their sickness is the ship's motion, not the food (Garcia & Koelling, 1966).

So you now know why I have, for all these years, been unable to eat Mexican food. Of the particular combination of events I experienced, only the meal and the stomach upset—not the storm and the tossing ship—became strongly associated, because the relationship between food and stomach upset is strongly built in to us. I behaved like a subject in one of Garcia's experiments. Even now that I know *why* I can't eat Mexican food, I still can't do anything about it—our "prepared associations" are stronger than I am. Even conscious knowledge of why this happened has made little difference.

This tendency for highly prepared learning to result in superstitious behavior is perhaps demonstrated by phobias as well. A case reported by Seligman and Hager (1972) provides a vivid illustration. A little girl saw a snake while playing in the park. Some hours later she accidentally slammed a car door on her hand. The result? A fear of snakes! Evidently humans are more highly prepared to fear snakes than cars, all logic aside.

As a final—and more positive—example of human preparedness, consider language acquisition. Our species appears to be uniquely prepared to learn language with ease (Lenneberg, 1967). With very informal training, children in all cultures learn the complicated contingencies involved in language use. The conditions under which normal children fail to learn to speak and understand must be impoverished indeed—amounting essentially to complete linguistic isolation. Otherwise, willy-nilly, they learn.

Human Preparedness to Learn Language. See Chapter 10, pp. 385–86.

We have learned a lot about these basic processes of learning. Organisms learn to associate events that occur together, by simple and repeatable procedures in the lab and, sometimes, in life. These simple associations form the groundwork of our knowledge of what goes on in the world; they allow us to understand why particular experiences such as being embarrassed once in class affect us strongly, why we have superstitions, why we behave the way we do—from calling someone on the phone to standing at a slot machine that once hit the jackpot. Some of us even know why we cannot eat certain things, even though there is no "rational" reason why. How we *remember* and organize these learned associations is another story, and it is told in the next chapter.

Summary

1. *Association* is one of psychology's oldest principles. It began with the Greek philosophers and was revived by British empiricists like John Locke, who wrote that the "association of ideas" is the bond that connects all experience. In more recent times the study of association has become more precise. The conditions under which ideas become associated are well studied and evidence shows we are "prepared" biologically to make certain associations.

2. Ivan Pavlov set out to discover the underlying conditions under which an animal could come to associate a previously neutral stimulus with food. He gave his research the name *conditioning*. In Pavlov's experiments with dogs, an innate reflex, such as salivation at the sight of food, (called an unconditioned response or UCR), came to be associated with a new stimulus, such as a bell (conditioned stimulus or CS). The dog, after repeated pairings of the bell and the food, soon tended to associate the bell with the food and to salivate in response to the bell, without the presentation of the food. When the dog salivated at the sound of the bell alone, that was a conditioned response (CR).

3. Pavlov's long series of experiments are the basis of such principles in conditioning as acquisition, extinction, discrimination, generalization, reinforcement, and the timing of conditioned and unconditioned stimuli.

4. *Generalization* is one of the more important principles discovered by Pavlov. It is common to all forms of learning. We know someone is at the door whether the signal is a bell, a buzzer, a knocker, or chimes. Generalization means that once a specific stimulus has become a CS, similar stimuli will elicit the conditioned response.

5. B. F. Skinner extended Pavlov's methods through his study of *operant conditioning*—how we learn to *act* in the world in order to get want we want. One of its primary principles is that we act in such a way as to seek pleasure and avoid pain—the "Law of Effect." Operant conditioning, unlike Pavlov's classical conditioning, involves feedback within a system that includes the organism's responses. In operant conditioning, the consequences of any actions (responses) that increase the probability of the recurrence of those actions are called *reinforcements*.

6. A *reinforcement* is something that strengthens the probability that a certain response will occur. There are two kinds of reinforcement—positive and negative. Something given to the animal after a desired response is a *positive* reinforcement; something unpleasant taken away from the animal after a desired response is a *negative* reinforcement.

   Schedules of reinforcement are central to operant conditioning. Continuous reinforcement means that every time the animal makes the correct response, it is reinforced. Partial reinforcement means that reinforcement does not always follow the response. In partial reinforcement, responses persist long after a reward is terminated. There are four kinds of partial reinforcement schedules: fixed interval, variable interval, fixed ratio, and variable ratio.

7. The laws of associative learning have prepared psychologists for an investigation into more complex forms, such as *cognitive learning*, although for a long period the existence of two different kinds of learning was controversial. However, it has recently been well established that animals as well as people can learn by virtue of *insight*. A chimp who is able to use two sticks to draw a banana into a cage has learned a *relationship*, not a response.

8. Another important form of learning is *observational learning*. Most animals learn from the experience of others through a process known as modeling. Observational learning is guided primarily by attention, retention, reproduction of the action, and motivation. The visible behavior that results from observational learning is called imitation.

9. The assumption of the early investigators was that any response can be equally associated with any stimulus. However, a more subtle question psychologists have recently addressed is: Are all the events equally associable? The concept of *preparedness* suggests that organisms are more predisposed or "prepared" to associate certain events than others. Seligman proposes that there is a continuum of preparedness encompassing responses that an organism is *prepared* to perform, *unprepared* to perform, and even *contraprepared* to perform. Some animals simply *cannot* learn certain arbitrary responses. Thorndike's cats had great difficulty learning to escape from their boxes by scratching or licking themselves. An example of a strongly prepared association is taste aversion—the strong reaction to the taste of a food associated with stomach upset. This kind of association seems to take hold so strongly that even one's knowledge of the conditions under which it occurred (as in the author's own experience) cannot seem to diminish the strength of such a prepared association.

Terms and Concepts

association
behavioral repertoire
conditioned response
conditioned stimulus
conditioning
continuous reinforcement
counterconditioning
discrimination
extinction
fixed interval
fixed ratio
generalization
insight
instinctive drift

latent learning
observational learning
operant (instrumental) conditioning
operant level
operant strength
orienting reflex
partial reinforcement
preparedness
reinforcement
respondent (classical) conditioning
unconditioned response
unconditioned stimulus
variable interval
variable ratio

Suggestions for Further Reading

Chance, P. (1977). *Learning and behavior.* San Francisco: Wadsworth.
   A very good current introduction to more contemporary viewpoints on learning.

Köhler, W. (1925). *The mentality of apes.* New York: Harcourt Brace Jovanovich.
   The classic work on insight studies of learning. Effective counterpoint to the more basic associationist point of view of Pavlov and Skinner.

Pavlov, I. P. (1927). *Conditioned reflexes.* New York: Oxford University Press.

Skinner, B. F. (1938). *The behavior of organisms.* New York: Appleton-Century-Crofts.
   This book and the Pavlov book are the major classics in the discovery of the basic laws of learning. It may be very useful to see how these men wrote and how they related their discoveries to contemporary knowledge.

Chapter 9

Remembering and Forgetting

INTRODUCTION

The other night a friend put on a record that was popular when I was in graduate school. I hadn't listened to the record for 15 years, and as soon as I heard the first note I had a strange experience. I recognized the whole song immediately, but I also *experienced a whole period of my life once again.* I could smell once again the orchard I lived in. I could almost see the faces of friends not seen (or even thought of) in 15 years. There was my old blue '56 Chevy convertible. It had a top that never worked, I remembered. I often drove that car to the beach at night. When I heard that song, I could once again smell the night air, see the night sky, and feel the car slipping around the winding curves of the road out to the beach. As I listened to that song I was transported back in time.

To continue my personal memories for a moment: I once worked in a mental hospital. One day I was taking care of Michael S., a patient who suffered from amnesia, a loss of memory due to a blow to the head. He told me a story I will never forget. "This morning a woman came to see me in my room. I felt attracted to her. She was very pretty, and I liked talking to her. I asked her for her name. 'Ellen,' she said. I asked why she had come to visit me, as I thought she was a hospital volunteer. She slumped and burst into tears. She said, 'Michael, I'm your *wife*. We've been married for twenty years!' I just didn't know what to say. I don't remember her at all."

Our memory is a great mystery. How can a song suddenly bring up memories of an orchard, an automobile, a lost era? How can someone forget a spouse of 20 years? No one really knows, but the answers must lie in the nature of our system of memory. There are different *kinds* of memory, too. Michael lost his memory of Ellen, but not of the English language.

Our memories give meaning to our life, a sense of continuity between the past and present. In order to live, we must be able to remember our friends, our house, how to drive, how to walk, even who we are. We enrich and extend our life through our memories. Thanks to memory, one poet wrote, "we can have roses in December."

Some Principles of Memory

In this chapter we will discuss not so much the *specific* memories of our lives, but the principles and operation of memory itself or our "system of memory." In this, our analysis is like that of perception—not an analysis of what is on stage, but an analysis of the countless operations supporting our experience from behind the scenes. Many of the principles that underlie perception—such as simplicity, organization, and meaning—also hold true for memory.

Three important principles of memory processes are described by William James (1890):

> The more other facts a fact is associated with in the mind, the better possession of it our memory retains. Each of its associates becomes a hook to which it hangs, a means to fish it up when sunk beneath the surface. Together they form a network of attachments by which it is woven into the tissue of our thought. The "secret of a good memory" is the secret of forming diverse and multiple associations with every fact we care to retain. . . . Most men have a good memory for facts connected with their own pursuits. . . . The merchant remembers prices, the politician other politicians' speeches and votes. . . . The great memory for facts which a Darwin and a Spencer reveal in their books is not incompatible with the possession on their part of a brain with only a middling degree of physiological retentiveness. . . . Let a man early in life set himself the task of verifying such a theory as that of evolution, and facts will soon cluster and cling to him like grapes to their stem. Their relations to the theory will hold them fast, and the more of these the mind is able to discern, the greater the erudition will become.

1. *Memory involves associations.* The mind, in the modern analysis, is a network of associations formed from past experiences. The more we associate an event with something we already know, the more our memory of it will "stick" with us. For me, a car, friends, an orchard, the beach, are all associated with a song. When I hear that song, I am reminded of other experiences I had while hearing the song. Listening to that same song, there is no way you could have the same memories; you might never have heard of the song, or it might have been associated with specific events in your life.

2. *Memory selects and simplifies reality.* Because there is simply too much information available to us at any one moment to act on, the senses, the perceptual process, and consciousness all simplify events by selecting only immediately important information, usually information that is relevant to what we are doing. Even after all the filtering out, there are still too many experiences in our past to handle. We remember a few of the many things that happen to us: how many of the billions of momentary experiences you had last summer do you remember? Perhaps one glorious day at the beach, some fine times lazing about, but certainly not *every* bite of food, *every* right turn, *every* conversation, *every* moment of *every* day. *Memories are much simpler than actual experience.*

A PERFECT MEMORY

Just about everybody would like to have a better memory. But an absolutely perfect memory, one permitting us to remember everything that ever happened to us, would paralyze us. The Argentine writer Jorge Luis Borges, in his story "Funes the Memorius," describes what that would be like:

We, at one glance, can perceive three glasses on a table; Funes, all the leaves and tendrils of fruit that make up a grape vine. He knew by heart the forms of the southern clouds at dawn on the 30th of April, 1882, and could compare them in his memory with the mottled streaks on a book in Spanish binding he had only seen once and with the outlines of the foam raised by an oar in the Rio Negro the night before the Quebracho uprising. These memories were not simple ones; each visual image was linked to muscular sensations, thermal sensations, etc. He could reconstruct all his dreams, all his half-dreams. Two or three times he had reconstructed a whole day; he never hesitated, but each reconstruction had required a whole day. He told me: "I alone have more memories than all mankind has probably had since the world has been the world." And again: "My dreams are like you people's waking hours." And again, toward dawn: "My memory, sir, is like a garbage heap." A circle drawn on a blackboard, a right triangle, a lozenge—all these are forms we can fully and intuitively grasp; Ireneo could do the same with the stormy mane of a pony, with the herd of cattle on a hill, with the changing fire and its innumerable ashes, with the many faces of a dead man throughout a long wake. I don't know how many stars he could see in the sky.

Because of Funes's extraordinary memory, it took him the same amount of time to recall events as the events themselves took—an entire day to remember an entire day. As a result, Funes forfeited the future. In ordinary life, we need to act quickly. Memory serves this need by retaining only a *simplified version* of events.

3. *We remember meaningful events.* Perhaps the most important criterion for remembrance is what an event means to us. We remember events of personal importance or aspects of events that at the time appeared important to us. For example, your notes of a lecture transcribe the *meaning* of the lecture, not the shape of the room.

Since we remember meaningful details, we often overlook *familiar* details of everyday life. For instance, which of the drawings in Figure 9–1 is an accurate picture of a penny? Most people cannot readily tell, although we see pennies daily. The reason we cannot tell is that most of the *specific* details of the penny are meaningless to us. We need to remember little more about a penny than that it is a small copper coin with Lincoln on it. Whether Lincoln faces left or right and where the date is are meaningless details to us, and we do not remember them.

FIGURE 9–1
Which drawing of the penny is accurate? It can be very hard to tell, because the few details that identify the real one are not sufficiently meaningful that you would remember them. (After Nickerson & Adams, 1979)

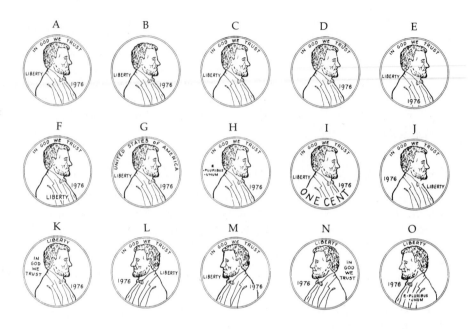

THE FUNCTIONS OF MEMORY

Memory records specific *episodes* in our lives, but it also contains the general rules for operating on the world, called *representational* memory. Memory is continuously *updated* as new events occur, which allows us to respond to continuous changes in the world. Memory allows us to *organize* past experiences and to *make them accessible* when needed.

Episodic Memory

Episodic memory is a record of our individual experiences. They include a movie we saw, a hike in the woods, a certain book, experiences shared with others. These memories are a continuing "autobiographical reference" (Tulving, 1972). Episodic memory can be remarkably precise. Lindsay and Norman (1977) asked students the question: "What were you doing on Monday afternoon in the third week of September two years ago?" Before reading on, try to answer the question yourself (write down your thoughts as you try to recall the event). The following was a typical exchange between a subject (S) and one of the experimenters (E) (Lindsay & Norman, 1977):

s: Come on. How should I know?
E: Just try it anyhow.
s: OK. Let's see: Two years ago . . . I would be in high school in
    Pittsburgh. . . . That would be my senior year. Third week in
    September—that's just after summer—that would be the fall
    term. . . . Let me see. I think I had chemistry lab on Mondays. I
    don't know. I was probably in chemistry lab. Wait a minute—
    that would be the second week of school. I remember he started

off with the atomic table—a big fancy chart. I thought he was crazy trying to make us memorize that thing. You know, I think I can remember sitting. . . .

Episodic memory records quite specific details of particular events. The evidence suggests that specific episodes can endure in memory a long time, sometimes for decades. We will consider some of this evidence later in the chapter.

Representational Memory

Representational memory is a record of our general knowledge of the world, for example, "common sense," and skills. Representational memory thus underlies episodic memory. Episodic memory is specific to one individual. However, people who share the same culture have a generally similar representational memory, such as the rules of language and of inference and logic, general facts of the world such as the effects of gravity, how to cook or ride a bicycle, who is president. This memory underlies our perception, as it allows us to "fill in the gaps" when we get new information, to assume "facts" on the basis of partial information. You know, for example, that the people living in Timbuktu eat and sleep, have children, and work. You know all this even though you may never have visited Timbuktu and witnessed these facts firsthand (Wickelgren, 1977).

Representational memory is of two types: semantic and perceptual-motor memory.

Semantic Memory

Semantic memory includes the knowledge of a specific language, of what words mean and how they are used (Tulving, 1972). This semantic knowledge is vast; the average college student has a vocabulary of 50,000 words in semantic memory. Semantic memory also includes "common

Episodic memory records our individual experiences and is a continuing autobiographical reference.

FIGURE 9–2
Representational Memory
Which map is correct? Most people assume the left one, since Reno is shown east of Los Angeles. But here our representation is intentionally wrong, exploiting the tendency to inaccuracy in common sense representational memory.

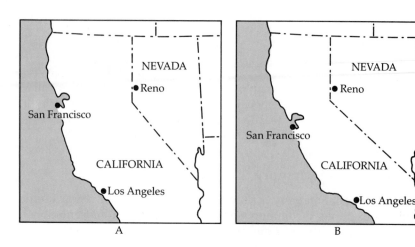

sense" inferences, most so simple that they go unnoticed. Suppose you ask mother where her keys are and she says, "They are either in the bag or on the mantle." You look in the bag and they are not there; you then know without any further information they are on the mantle. Semantic memory also contains the rules for everyday, informal inferences. For instance, if someone says, "I hate country music," you know immediately not to invite that person to the next Willie Nelson concert. The rules for deducing these things are in semantic memory, as are the rules of formal logic and inference.

Perceptual-Motor Memory

Perceptual-motor memory contains the automatized schemata for performing routine actions, whether they are simple, like throwing a ball or getting dressed, or complex, like driving a car or playing baseball. It also guides our movements in space, using the knowledge of perspective and constancy. This kind of memory also underlies much of our ordinary perceptual experience: that we are drinking coffee, not tea, that the milk is sour, or that someone is singing off key.

Updating Our Information about the World

Because our world is always changing, our memory would be useless if its content did not also change; it must be updated. Episodic memory is updated more frequently than representational memory. We must be able to remember where we parked *today,* who is going out with whom *this* week, and countless other temporary episodes (Bjork & Landauer, 1979).

Memory Organizes and Makes Past Experience Accessible

Even though the information stored in memory is a severe reduction of all the experiences that pass in and out of consciousness, an enormous number of events are stored in memory. There would be no point in retaining all these memories if the ones we wanted could not be called up at appropriate times. We would become confused by the irrelevant information. Thus, perhaps the most important function of memory is that it is *organized to make information accessible*. To illustrate how memory is organized, we will use two analogies: the library and the storehouse.

Organization

Memory is organized around relating associated events to each other. When you think about your father, you recall things that relate to your knowledge of him. Memories of other people and other times do not intrude.

If memory were a random collection of bits of information, you would have to rifle through millions of memories simply to recognize a face or the voice of someone calling your name. Suppose you wanted the book *The Theory of the Leisure Class* by Thorstein Veblen. And suppose that the library you go to is a random collection—no book has an assigned place. The only way you would be able to find Veblen's book is to look at one book after another, perhaps tens of thousands, until you found it. Even in a small-town library with a few thousand books, it might take months to find it—a part of your life would be wasted in pursuit of *The Theory of the Leisure Class*.

Perceptual-motor memory permits easy performance of routine actions, both simple and complex.

WHAT DAY IS IT?

Consider this simple question: What day is it? To answer this question a representational knowledge of the days of the week is required. In addition, it is necessary to update—today's answer is not the same as yesterday's or tomorrow's.

If our memory system were simple, like a date counter on a digital watch, we would be able to answer the question just as quickly on one day as on any other. However, if people are asked what day it is on a Wednesday, *it takes twice as long to answer as when they are asked on* *Sunday*. (See Figure 9–3). However, our memory is not only updated; it is updated and stored in simplified schemata. Weekdays take longer to recall than weekends, probably because there are five weekdays and two weekend days. The closer the weekday is to the weekend the faster it is recalled (Shanon, 1979). In the real world, every day is equal, but their *meaning* to us is not. Weekends are perhaps more central to our lives and therefore we may represent our weeks largely with reference to weekends.

In reality, libraries are not just buildings housing books; they are organized systems for locating books. You can find Veblen's book in a number of ways. You can look up the author's name, or, if you have forgotten the author's name, you can look up the title. If you do not remember the author or the title, you can do a quick search through the subject catalog. If the book has been assigned for class, you might even go directly to a special reserved-book section. When you use the library to do research, you learn how rich and extensive the information retrieval system we call a library really is.

Human memory is similarly richly interrelated. If I ask you to tell me what you know about U.S. presidents, a variety of information may come to mind: names of presidents, what the powers of the president are, important policies of past presidents.

If memory becomes disorganized, our efficiency is impaired. Consider the simple question, "What are the months of the year?" You would probably answer by reciting the months in chronological order, begin-

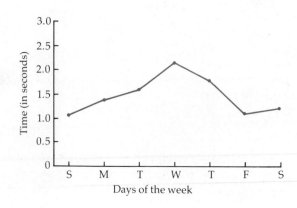

FIGURE 9–3
Timed Responses to the Question "What Day of the Week Is It?"
(After Shanon, 1979)

ning with January. This takes about 5 seconds, because the months are usually organized in memory in that order. Now, try to name the months of the year in reverse order. This usually takes about 12 to 15 seconds. Finally, name the months of the year in alphabetical order. Although you know the months and know how to alphabetize, you probably have rarely had to use these two pieces of knowledge together. There is, in effect, *no* organization to speed the response. It generally takes more than a minute to answer this question and most people make several mistakes.

Accessibility

Only a limited amount of information in memory is accessible at any one time, and this information constantly changes. This helps us adapt to different situations: an old song makes certain memories accessible to me; talking to a good friend brings forward the memory of shared experiences.

The schemata associated with whatever is in consciousness becomes accessible at that time. For instance, during exam week you may have tests in English literature, psychology, and history one right after the other. When you are writing your English exam, the information relevant to English literature is easily accessible. That information recedes when you plunge into your psychology exam.

One analogy for this "dynamic" aspect of memory is the storehouse. In a storehouse, often-ordered items are at the front, where they are easy to get to; items that are rarely called for are tucked away in corners and are less accessible.

In one formal experiment on this phenomenon, subjects were asked to name any fruit that begins with the letter *a*, then asked to name fruits that begin with the letter *p*. The second question was answered faster. The first question summoned up the storehouse of information about fruits, making the names of fruits more readily accessible for the second question (Loftus & Loftus, 1975).

THE PROCESSES OF MEMORY

Although distinguishing between the functions of memory is a relatively straightforward matter, how these functions are performed is a question of much debate. This section describes the overall processes of memory in terms of the memory *cycle* and the memory *system*. The memory cycle describes the process in which we experience something, retain it, and later retrieve it. The memory system includes the different divisions of memory, from momentary visual impressions to the lifelong retention of important moments in our lives.

The Memory Cycle

Recall of a specific event depends on three prior processes. First, of course, is *perception*; the event must be sensed, transduced into neural language, and perceived. The second process is **retention:** the new information must be stored and kept. **Retrieval** is the third process, by which the stored information is brought forward into consciousness at the appropriate time.

Perceptual Encoding

To be remembered, an event must be perceived. This occurs when information brought in by the senses stimulates appropriate receptors, which then relay it by neural firing to the brain. Sensory information is then organized by perceptual processes into the simplest meaningful percepts.

Retention

A remembered event is retained as long as needed. The retention time may be a few seconds, a few years, or forever. Occasionally, we consciously direct retention ("I am going to remember that term"), but usually we select things on the basis of a few rules: something is striking or new, related to other memories, important to our career, and so on.

We cannot, yet, pinpoint the locations in the brain of specific memories or even different kinds of memories. Childhood memories do not seem to be stored in one corner of the brain and memories of songs in another. But the mere fact that we do have memories means that there must be physical changes somewhere in the brain when we remember something.

Retrieval

When a past event is brought into consciousness, we regain, "retrieve," information previously stored. Two types of retrieval are recognition and recall.

Recognition is the ability to correctly identify an object or event. This identification involves a match between present perception and your memory of the information presented to you. The word "recognize" comes from the Latin "to know again." Recognition is the most common experience of memory.

Recall is the ability to summon up stored information in the absence of the actual event or object. An exam question like "Which of Shakespeare's plays is concerned with the emotion of jealousy?" tests *recall*. The same question presented with a choice of answers would test *recognition*: "Jealousy is the central theme of which Shakespeare play? (a) *Merchant of Venice* (b) *Macbeth* (c) *All's Well That Ends Well* (d) *Othello*."

It is easier to recognize something than to recall the same thing, because the stimulus is present and it calls up all the relevant associated schemata. This is why multiple choice tests are easier than tests that require recall. The capacity of recognition memory is enormous. Haber and Standig (1966) showed subjects 2,560 photographs for 10 seconds each. A few days later recognition of the pictures was greater than 90 percent.

The Memory System: Basic Divisions of the Memory Process

Some information, like the name or phone number of someone you have just met, is remembered for only a brief time before it is forgotten altogether. Other information that we use continually, like our own name and address, we do not forget. This difference has led many psychologists to hypothesize that memory has two distinct components: short-term and long-term memory.

Short-term Memory

Information that is retained temporarily, for only a few seconds, is thought to be stored by a process called **short-term memory.** The storage capacity of short-term memory is about seven items, such as a seven-digit number. Short-term memory is regarded like scratch paper; something used quickly for a specific purpose and then discarded. When you look up a phone number, you only have to remember the number long enough to dial it. If you encounter interference—a busy signal or a loud noise next to you—you may have to look the number up again. To avoid this hassle, you may rehearse the number by repeating it. That act can be thought of as constantly replacing the number in short-term memory or nudging it into the more permanent component of memory system: long-term memory.

Long-term Memory

Information retained for more than a few seconds is stored in what is termed **long-term memory.** You do not have to look up your *own* telephone number when you call home, nor do you have to repeat your name over and over to remember it. Both episodic and representational memory are stored in long-term memory. The storage capacity of long-term memory is huge; many psychologists consider it limitless. In the next section, we will consider many aspects of long-term memory—how we remember both in the laboratory and in life, our memory for pictures, faces, and odors.

HOW WE FORGET AND WHAT WE REMEMBER: LONG-TERM MEMORY

The modern scientific study of memory began 100 years ago with controlled experiments to determine the fundamental characteristics of human memory by determining the basic rate of forgetting. More recently, the emphasis has been on research outside the laboratory, on determining how and what we remember and forget of life events. In this section we will examine the empirical evidence on what we forget and how we remember.

The Factors of Forgetting

The first paradigm for controlled research on memory was developed in 1885 by Hermann Ebbinghaus. He devised long lists of **nonsense syllables,** such as "dof," "zam," and "fok." By using such nonsense syllables to test memory, Ebbinghaus hoped to eliminate any effect subjects' personal experience might have on their ability to recall information. In this way, he hoped to obtain a precise measure of learning and memory independent of previous experience. His method was heroic; he used

ALTERNATIVE INTERPRETATIONS
OF THE MEMORY CYCLE AND MEMORY SYSTEM

Although many psychologists accept the twin concepts of a memory cycle and memory system, some recent theorists have challenged both ideas as inadequate descriptions of how memory works.

Memory as a Change with Experience

The concept of a memory cycle is appealing. It describes in a clear manner how an event enters consciousness and is remembered through the stages of encoding, storage, and recall. The findings of many experiments that test the recall of specific kinds of information support this hypothesis. Nevertheless, it is quite unlikely that our memory operates this way all the time. One important cognitive psychologist, William Estes, describes a different view: "Human memory does not, in a literal sense, store anything; it simply changes as a function of experience" (Estes, 1980).

In the viewpoint we considered in the last section, memory is likened to a computer, acquiring information, filing it, bringing it back. The alternative idea, that memory simply produces changes in us, is similar to the ecological approach to perception (described in Chapter 6), which emphasizes that we experience the world directly.

According to this experiential view, changes that take place inside of us in response to experience are analogous to changing the dial on a radio set: when the "tuning" is changed, new stations can be received. The changes that we call "memory" are, to switch the metaphor, more like other changes in the body due to experience. When we exercise, our muscles change their shape and change their performance, but they do not "remember" the plow or the pen.

As in our discussion of two competing theories of perception (Chapter 6), both views of memory probably describe some part of our experience. Both interpretations agree that our experiences change us and that the resultant changes are reflected in memory. They differ on the question of how those changes are reflected in memory. A part of our memory is probably a little like a computer, storing words and phrases and specific events that can later be described. But for much of our life we are not storing information simply because we *might* need it in the future. Rather, our general concern is adaptation: being able to change behavior as a result of experience. For example, we may wish to avoid someone who once caused us pain. Our previous experience produces changes in us. We then begin to pick up information about other people who may cause us pain, by noticing similarities between them and a person who has hurt us before. But in these cases we do not "retrieve" specific information as a computer does. We become "tuned" differently, we perceive and act differently. Probably no single machine analogy is sufficient to explain the complexity of the human mind, even a machine as complex as a computer.

Memory as a Continuous Process

Many psychologists do not believe that *separate* processes for short-term and long-term memory are plausible. Instead, they think of the memory system as a single and *continuous* process. In this view, each repetition of an event causes an increase in the strength of the association of that event and increases the probability that it will be remembered later on.

The single-process hypothesis has advantages (Wickelgren, 1977). There is no sharp distinction between not remembering and fully remembering. You may forget a phone number the first time you dial it, then remember a few of the numbers, and remember more each time you dial.

The single-process hypothesis regards short-term and long-term memory stores, not as separate mechanisms, but as the extreme ends of a single process. More technically, each exposure to a situation increases the probability of its being remembered. In this view, all memories are generated by the same system. Because the continuous memory approach postulates only a single process for all normal memory experience, it has the advantage of being simpler and more inclusive. The majority viewpoint now seems to be shifting toward the single-process hypothesis. No matter how much controversy surrounds the question of how to conceptualize the processes of memory, our observable experience is unmistakable: new information fades quickly in our memory while at the same time we have a relatively stable and permanent knowledge of the world.

himself as a subject over long hours of investigations. He learned a list of syllables by heart, well enough to recite it twice in a row. He then tested his recall of the list over several days. His measure of forgetting was the time needed to relearn the list until he recalled it perfectly. This method yields a precise measurement of the rate of forgetting (Figure 9–4). He discovered that the rate of forgetting is described by a predictable curve; most forgetting occurs immediately and tapers off as time goes on. Ebbinghaus's curve is a general description of the rate at which material with no previous associations is forgotten.

The Decay of Memory

In films, scenes of the distant past are commonly shot in dulled, faded colors. Although the image of memory literally fading with time is appealing, it is simply that—an image. Our memory is more complex than that. For instance, a senile person may not be able to recall the day's events, but may remember clearly events from youth. Motor skills, like riding a bicycle, do not seem to "fade away" over time, even without practice.

In one important test of the "fading" notion, Jenkins and Dallenbach (1924) asked two groups to learn lists of nonsense syllables in the same way Ebbinghaus did. Immediately after the memorization task, one group was allowed to go to sleep, while the second was required to stay awake. If memory fades with time alone, there should be no difference in recall between the two groups if both groups are tested for recall at the same time. However, the results showed that those who slept retained far more than those who had stayed awake (Figure 9–5). The most likely explanation for this result is that the "awake" group had experiences that interfered with retention. The decay of memory is not just "a matter of time"; the particular *events* that occur "in time" are also a factor.

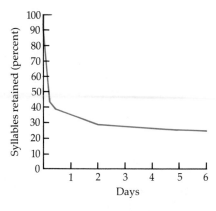

FIGURE 9–4
Ebbinghaus's Curve of Forgetting

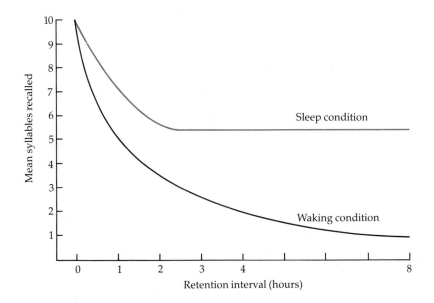

FIGURE 9–5
Sleep and Memory
After memorizing nonsense syllables, subjects who slept had better recall than those who did not. (After Jenkins & Dallenbach, 1924)

Interference

Some kinds of events interfere with memory more than others. Two kinds of interference have been studied in the laboratory. **Proactive interference** occurs when previous knowledge interferes with present memory. The term proactive is a combination of "pro," meaning forward, and "active." Together they mean that the interference *moves forward* from previous to present knowledge. Proactive interference is easily demonstrated in the following test. Two groups learn the same list (B). However, the first group has learned another list (A) before. Both groups are tested for their ability to recall list B.

	Learn	Learn	Test
Group 1	A	B	B
2	—	B	B

On testing, Group 2 can remember more of list B than Group 1 can.

Retroactive interference occurs when new information interferes with memory of old. It can be demonstrated as follows. Two groups learn list C. The first group then learns list D, the other does not. Both groups are tested for their memory of list C.

	Learn	Learn	Test
Group 1	C	D	C
2	C	—	C

On testing, Group 1 will remember less of list C than will Group 2. Similarly, suppose you are making a list of people to invite to a party. You are about to write down John's name, but before you do, someone says, "Hey, don't forget we have to invite June and Sally." You write their names down but then find that you cannot remember the name of the person you first thought of.

Two general factors in interference are:

1. The *longer* the interval between the first and second event, the *less* interference.

2. The more *similar* the items, the *more* interference. A real-life example can occur when you are trying to remember the phone numbers of two people. If the first number is 524-5318 and the second is 883-2299, there will be less interference than if the second is 524-5218.

ON PHONE NUMBERS

Telephone numbers have proved useful in some simple experiments on memory. Although it is not clear exactly what phone number memory tells us about real-world memory, it is clear that memory research has provided some important information to telephone companies. Phone numbers have seven numbers, but the first three are a prefix that designates the exchange in a certain area of town. These prefixes are remembered as a single unit, or chunk, not as three separate numbers. Shepard and Sheenan (1963) thought, therefore, that it would be easier for people to remember phone numbers if the last four digits were dialed first, when the memory of the numbers is freshest. This method reduced the time needed for dialing by 20 percent, and errors made in dialing were cut in half. However, the telephone companies cannot take advantage of this research, since the cost of switching their equipment over to such a method is prohibitive. It does point out, however, the need for people who design machines and equipment to be aware of relevant psychological research.

Primacy and Recency

We seem to be structured, even at the most rudimentary physiological level, to notice and retain elements at transition points. Recall that the senses respond most vigorously at the beginnings and endings of stimuli; in between they habituate, or stop responding.

Habituation   See Chapter 5, p. 177.

We remember the beginnings and endings of events better than middles. A word at the beginning of a list is recalled 70 percent of the time, words in the middle less than 20 percent, and words at the end almost 100 percent (Loftus & Loftus, 1975). Our enhanced recall of beginnings is an example of the effect of **primacy.** Our enhanced recall of endings is an example of the effect of **recency.** The principles of primacy and recency in memory have been extensively demonstrated experimentally using lists of nonsense syllables. They also hold as general principles in many areas of life, from the basic characteristics of the sensory systems to political campaigns, love affairs, and theater performances. In 1980, presidential candidate Ronald Reagan illustrated these principles. He said: "Politics is just like show business. You need a big opening. Then you coast for a while. Then you need a big finish."

Nonsense Syllables   See pp. 339–41.

The Memory for Life Experiences

Although studies in the laboratory make clear some of the basic operations of the memory system, they shed little light on our memories; lists of syllables and numbers are not important parts of our lives. The most memorable events of your life would be impossible to duplicate in the lab. When I was six I almost drowned trying to learn to swim. I remember, as if it just happened, the blue water turning to black as I lost consciousness, the blinding light when my father pulled me out. I will never forget it. If you ask people of your parents' generation where they were when President Kennedy was shot, they often remember every detail. But in pursuit of scientific knowledge we cannot deliberately create such powerful events and then check in on people 20 years later to see what they remember about them.

Psychologists are now trying to develop methods to study what kinds of things people recall in the course of their lives. Some psychologists use themselves as subjects, sometimes they use a common experience as a focus. Some of the studies we will discuss below involve considerable amounts of time—sometimes decades—between the event and the recall test; some involve memory for visual scenes, faces, and odors. One question recently investigated is the nature of differences between one individual's memory and another's.

Memory for Real-world Events: After Six Years

The forgetting curve of Ebbinghaus shows that the greater part of relatively meaningless information, such as nonsense syllables, is quickly forgotten. But how long do you remember a tennis victory, a movie, a passionate kiss? Marigold Linton studied her memory of her life events over a period of six years (Neisser, 1982). During this time she recorded 5,500 events and tested some of them for recall every two months. Her record includes items like: "narrowly beat HEO at tennis today," and "received a call from Maureen, Strassberger's secretary, indicating that she will make the travel arrangements to Washington." She expected that her rate of forgetting would follow the Ebbinghaus curve. Surprisingly, it was much less rapid; the shape of the curve was very different (Figure 9–6). Where Ebbinghaus found that forgetting was rapid at first, Linton's loss of memory for the details of her own life proceeded at a slower, more constant rate. Although there are many differences in the two test situations, the key difference may be that because events in your life have personal meaning they are not quickly forgotten. Many laboratory tasks are designed to have no meaning, so there is no reason to remember them when the experiment is over.

Memory for Very Old Events

To investigate memory for events long past, Bahrick, Bahrick, and Wittlinger (1975) tested the ability of high-school graduates to recognize the names and faces of their former classmates. They chose nine groups from different graduating classes (the youngest had graduated 3.3 months before, the oldest, 47 years before). Each group had about 50 people. All groups were shown photographs and asked to identify any pictures they recognized. The data were quite surprising (Figure 9–7). Recognition of the faces of old classmates remained at over 90 percent for intervals up to 34 years! However, name recognition was not as durable; it dropped after 15 years (still a considerably long interval). This finding suggests that memory for names might be organized differently from memory for faces.

In another test of what is often called "very long-term" memory, Rubin (1977) tested elementary and college students on their recall of

FIGURE 9–6
Linton's Six-year Study of Her Memory of Her Life Events

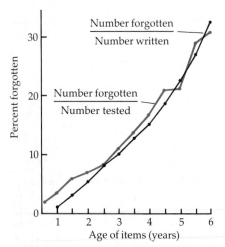

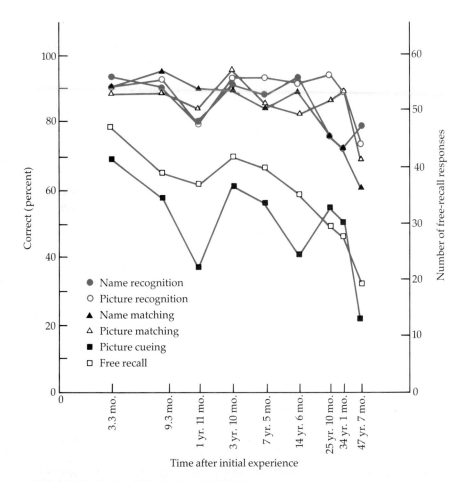

FIGURE 9–7
**Remembering Faces
and Names out of the Past**
When high school graduates were
tested on their ability to recall the
faces of former classmates, even very
old subjects showed remarkable
memory. The retention in various
categories is shown here and the test
itself is discussed in the
accompanying text. (After Bahrick,
Bahrick, & Wittlinger, 1975)

passages most of us learn in school: Hamlet's soliloquy, the Preamble to the Constitution, and the Twenty-third Psalm. There seem to be certain words and phrases that are remembered of each passage, although individuals differ in how many of them they remember. Figure 9–8 shows how many words 50 people remembered of Hamlet's soliloquy "To be, or not to be."

Recognition of Pictures and Odors

Our ability to remember our high-school classmates for so long is impressive. We have an enormous capacity in recognition memory for pictures. In one study, Shepard (1967) selected 612 familiar pictures and allowed subjects to review the pictures (on slides) at their own pace. A recognition test was given immediately afterward; recognition was 96.7 percent. After 120 days more than 50 percent of the pictures were recognized (Figure 9–9).

Are other kinds of information remembered as vividly as pictures? One important component of real-world memories is odor. Marcel Proust, in the famous passage from *Swann's Way*, describes how the smell of madeleine cookies summoned up details of his childhood. Cities have characteristic odors. The London underground has an unpleasant but distinctive odor. I always feel I am *really* in London when I smell it in or near the underground.

Brown University has a collection of more than 100 different odors, ranging from skunk to whiskey. In one experiment, subjects sniffed 48 cotton balls, each saturated with a different odor. Afterward, a second group of odors was presented, including many from the first group. Sixty-nine percent of the odors were recognized (Engen & Ross, 1973). While this is very high, it is not as high as picture recognition. However, there seems to be no decline in odor recognition; recognition was at 70 percent one week later and at 68 percent one month later.

Individual Differences in Memory

We all know people who seem to have a good memory for faces but not numbers; some people can remember stories well but not directions; "absentminded professors" may remember specific details of the Peloponnesian War but cannot remember to pick up their laundry. That individuals differ in memory is a universal observation, and is an observation that is attracting new interest among researchers. In a very early study, Francis Galton (1874) surveyed an eminent group of subjects, British men of science. He found that some relied primarily on vision, others on words. In a more recent (though still exploratory) study, Herrmann and Neisser have developed a questionnaire called the Inventory of Memory Experiences (IME), which asks respondents how often they remember and forget different kinds of things (1978). Their analysis reveals eight characteristics that distinguish individual memories:

1. *Rote memory:* forgetting things like numbers and addresses and having to check them.
2. *Absentmindedness:* forgetting what one has just done or intended to do.

FIGURE 9–8
Very Long-term Memory
Fifty subjects tested on how much of Hamlet's soliloquy they remembered showed the results charted here: each vertical line represents recall by one subject. How much would you recall of such material learned when you were in high school? (After Rubin, 1977)

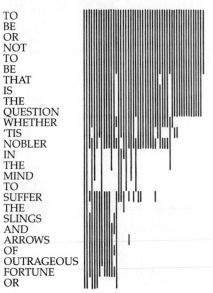

TO
BE
OR
NOT
TO
BE
THAT
IS
THE
QUESTION
WHETHER
'TIS
NOBLER
IN
THE
MIND
TO
SUFFER
THE
SLINGS
AND
ARROWS
OF
OUTRAGEOUS
FORTUNE
OR

3. *Names:* the ability or inability to recall people's names.
4. *People:* recognizing individuals by their appearance.
5. *Conversation:* remembering jokes, stories, and conversations.
6. *Errands:* remembering "things to do."
7. *Retrieval:* inability to recall why something seems familiar.
8. *Place:* where things are.

Although these findings are very tentative, they suggest that an individual's memory may be "assembled" out of these components. One person may have a great memory for jokes and names but forget "things to do." Another may easily remember where things are but have difficulty in remembering why someone's face is familiar. Further research may reveal which of these components of memory are associated with each other.

MEANINGFULNESS AND ORGANIZATION IN MEMORY

The most basic principle of memory is that we remember meaningful events. Of all the information we receive, of all the experiences we have, the things we remember are those that are *most* meaningful to us. The word *mnemosyne* would be extremely difficult to remember if it had no meaning. "It's Greek to me," we say (in fact, Mnemosyne is the Greek goddess of memory). The word *memory* is easier to remember because we know what it *means.* For the same reason, a sentence like "The for time now come good party all men the their to aid to is of" is harder to remember than "Now is the time for all good men to come to the aid of their party."

Meaning differs from individual to individual. Recall how a child, a botanist, and an artist have different perceptual experiences during a "walk in the park." They see only those things that interest them as

Differences in Perceptual Experiences   See Chapter 6, pp. 224–25.

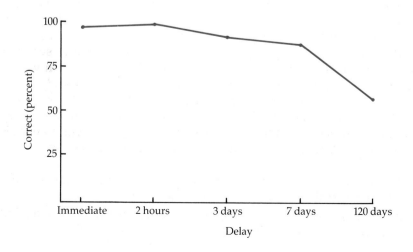

FIGURE 9–9
Recognition of Pictures
The results of Shepard's test of picture recognition and recall are charted on this graph. (After Shepard, 1967)

individuals. The botanist is likely to perceive and remember a plant in detail, because it is of particular professional interest. Meaningful events and nonmeaningful events are distinguished by the strength of association with other items in memory (Winograd, 1980).

The Importance of Context

Read the following story (Dooling & Lachman, 1971) and then, before reading on, jot down what you remember of it.

> With hocked gems financing him, our hero bravely defied all scornful laughter that tried to prevent his scheme. "Your eyes deceive," he had said. "An egg, not a table, correctly typifies this unexplored planet." Now three sturdy sisters sought proof. Forging along, sometimes through calm vastness, yet more often very turbulent peaks and valleys, days become weeks as many doubters spread fearful rumors about the edge. At last from nowhere welcome winged creatures appeared, signifying momentous success.

You probably remembered next to nothing of this passage. Now read the story again, and again jot down your recollections, but this time consider the context: the story is about Columbus's voyage to America. Dooling and Lachman found that people who had been given this context remembered much more than those who had not (1971). The main function of context is to provide a way of organizing information *beforehand*, therefore making it more memorable. A title usually announces an overall context and makes parts of what is read more accessible, as mentioning fruits aided recall of other fruits.

The context of a story can affect what is remembered. Because of context, some events are better remembered, some less well. Although it is difficult to study how different people organize information into a meaningful memory, here is a demonstration of how context, when deliberately altered, can affect memory. Read the following story (Bransford & Johnson, 1974) *once* and do not reread any part of it. Then write down or recite what you remember of it.

> *Watching a Peace March from the 40th Floor*
>
> The view was breathtaking. From the window one could see the crowd below. Everything looked extremely small from such a distance but the colorful costumes could still be seen. Everyone seemed to be moving in one direction in an orderly fashion, and there seemed to be little children as well as adults. The landing was gentle, and luckily the atmosphere was such that no special suits had to be worn. At first there was a great deal of activity. Later, when the speeches started, the crowd quieted down. The man with the television camera took many shots of the setting and the crowds. Everyone was very friendly and seemed glad when the music started.

Did you write down anything about the sentence "The landing was gentle and luckily the atmosphere was such that no special suits had to be worn"? In one experiment, only 18 percent of the subjects recalled something about that sentence. However, with a different context, recollection is improved. Reread the story, but this time under the title, "A Space Trip to an Uninhabited Planet." Now the sentence "The landing was gentle . . . " makes sense. Of the subjects who read the story with this title, 53 percent recalled the sentence. You might try this out on a couple of friends, giving both of them the story, but each a different title. Then compare their recollections.

The word context comes from the Latin word meaning "to weave together." When information is presented in a context that is meaningful to an individual, it is remembered more easily. Information is "weaved" into an already meaningful background. All the schemata associated with the new information are activated.

How Information Is Organized into Meaningful Units

In this section we will examine three processes of organization:

1. How existing schemata influence and often change what we remember.
2. How incoming information is organized into meaningful units or "chunks."
3. How some memory can be reconstructed on the basis of the above two processes.

The Effect of Schemata on Memory

In 1932 F. C. Bartlett published an important book, *Remembering*, in which he demonstrated the important effects of a person's existing knowledge structure on memory. The method he used in his experiments was similar to the child's game "telephone." A subject is given an "original stimulus," either a drawing or a story, and asked to reproduce it. That person then passes on his or her reproduction to the next person, who reproduces it, and so on. Bartlett called this method "serial reproduction." The stimuli Bartlett chose were deliberately exotic, unfamiliar to residents of Cambridge, England, where he did his research.

One example of serial reproduction is a series of drawings that begin with an African drawing, *Portrait d'Homme* (Figure 9–10). In these drawings, the subjects transformed figures to correspond with what was already in memory. According to Bartlett, unfamiliar features *"invariably suffer transformation in the direction of the familiar."* That is, people have a tendency to transform "odd" or unfamiliar figures into conventional or familiar ones. In the reproductions of the African drawing, all the original unconventional characteristics are gone. The final figure is an ordinary, even schematic representation of a face. The one clue to the exotic qualities of the original is the transformation of the name *Portrait d'Homme* (portrait of a man) to *L'Homme Egyptien* (Egyptian man). Bartlett also presented an unusual story to his students, an Indian tale called "The War of the Ghosts." Again, each subject was asked to reproduce what he or she remembered from the previous subject's version of the story. The original story is recounted below:

Original drawing

PORTRAIT D'HOMME

Reproduction 1

PORTRAIT D'HOMME

Reproduction 2

PORTRAIT D'UN HOMME

Reproduction 3

Portrait d'un homme.

Reproduction 4

Portrait d'un homme.

Reproduction 5

Portrait d'un homme!

Reproduction 6

Portrait d'un homme

Reproduction 7

Un homme Egyptien.

Reproduction 8

L'Homme Egyptien.

FIGURE 9–10
Portrait d'Homme
Transforming the unfamiliar in the
direction of the familiar.

The War of the Ghosts

One night two young men from Egulac went down to the river to hunt seals, and while they were there it became foggy and calm. Then they heard war-cries, and they thought: "Maybe this is a war-party." They escaped to the shore, and hid behind a log. Now canoes came up, and they heard the noise of the paddle, and saw one canoe coming up to them. There were five men in the canoe, and they said:

"What do you think? We wish to take you along. We are going up the river to make war on the people."

One of the young men said: "I have no arrows."

"Arrows are in the canoe," they said.

"I will not go along. I might be killed. My relatives do not know where I have gone. But you," he said, turning to the other, "may go with them."

So one of the young men went, but the other returned home.

And the warriors went on up the river to a town on the other side of Kalama. The people came down to the water, and they began to fight, and many were killed. But presently the young man heard one of the warriors say: "Quick, let us go home: that Indian has been hit." Now he thought: "Oh, they are ghosts." He did not feel sick, but they said he had been shot.

So the canoes went back to Egulac, and the young man went ashore to his house, and made a fire. And he told everybody and said: "Behold I accompanied the ghosts, and we went to fight. Many of our fellows were killed, and many of those who attacked us were killed. They said I was hit, and I did not feel sick."

He told it all, and then he became quiet. When the sun rose he fell down. Something black came out of his mouth. His face became contorted. The people jumped up and cried.

He was dead.

Here is one of the final reproductions of the story:

Two Indians from Momapan were fishing for seals when a boat came along containing five warriors. "Come with us," they said to the Indians, "and help us fight the warriors further on." The first Indian replied: "I have a mother at home, and she would grieve greatly if I were not to return." The other Indian said, "I have no weapons." "We have some in the boat," said the warriors. The Indian stepped into the boat.

In the course of the fight further on, the Indian was mortally wounded, and his spirit fled. "Take me to my home," he said, "at Momapan, for I am going to die." "No, you will not die," said a warrior. In spite of this, however, he died, and before he could be carried back to the boat, his spirit had left this world.

Again the effects of the English student's organization are clear: the story has been transformed into a more conventional one. The original distinctive names are gone, though Momapan is added. Bartlett says: "The story has become more coherent, as well as much shorter. No trace of an odd or supernatural element is left: we have a perfectly straightforward story of a fight and a death." Things that do not match the common schemata of an Englishman are omitted or transformed into the familiar: canoes are changed into boats, references to ghosts are omitted. What occurred here is similar to what happened in your recollection of "Watching a Peace March from the 40th Floor." You tended to omit elements that did not "fit in."

Chunking and Coding

A unit of memory is called a chunk. In perceiving and remembering bits of information, **chunking** is the process by which we organize the individual items into chunks by using a code. G E A I M N N is a "list" of seven bits that you might be able to retain briefly. M E A N I N G is a list of the same seven bits, but you have a code, English, that organizes them into a chunk (a single word, "MEANING"). The ability to chunk information greatly expands the storage capacity of memory, because small chunks can be combined into larger chunks that you are also able to remember.

Knowing a code increases the capacity of memory and the ability to remember. Read the following list of numbers quickly: 41236108324972. Now write down what you remember. Most likely you remembered only about seven. But here is a code: begin with 4, multiply it by 3, then repeat the process four times by multiplying each successive total by 3. With that instruction, you need not *memorize* any of the numbers. The code tells you where to begin, what to do, and where to stop. Read the following lists quickly and see if you can devise a code to help you remember.

IB MF BI TW AJ FK
816 449 362 516 941

If you had to reproduce the two lists above, the simple way would be to notice that the top line includes four well-known acronyms (such as IBM) and the bottom row includes the squares of all single-digit numbers in descending order from 9. We could easily reproduce the lists as

IBM FBI TWA JFK
81 64 49 36 25 16 9 4 1

The Reconstructive Nature of Remembering

Various kinds of information can color or change our memory of the past. In one study, researchers showed people a reddish orange disc. One group was told it was a tomato; the other group was told it was an orange. Later the two groups were shown colors and were asked to select the color that most closely matched the color they saw. The groups that had been told the disc was an orange selected a color closer to orange; the groups that had been told the disc was a tomato selected a

FIGURE 9–11
Chunking
It is easier to count the dots on the right (B), because they are arranged in groups, or chunks.

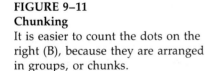

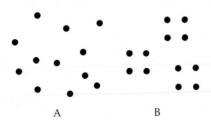

A   B

color closer to red (Loftus, 1978). In another demonstration two groups of subjects were presented with ambiguous doodles (Figure 9–12). Each drawing was labeled with a word. Although both groups saw the same drawings, they were given different labels. For example, the same doodle was presented with the word "eyeglasses" or "dumbbell." Immediately after each presentation, the subjects were asked to reproduce, as accurately as possible, the figure they had seen. The subjects' drawings were influenced by the label they had been given. The drawings reflected an obvious effort to draw pictures according to the verbal labels: for example, an attempt to reproduce eyeglasses or dumbbells, rather than the figure as it was presented (Carmichael et al., 1932).

Eyewitness Testimony

The reconstructive nature of memory is efficient in everyday life. We do not need to know things in complete detail, nor are we capable of recalling literally *every* detail of an experience, even what a penny looks like. And when details are important, perhaps even a matter of life and death, the reconstructive nature of memory can become a problem.

No courtroom testimony is more effective than a witness who stands, points a finger at someone, and says, "It's him. I saw him do it with my own eyes." We have such confidence in our memory that the power of an eyewitness's testimony is not easily overcome, even if it is success-

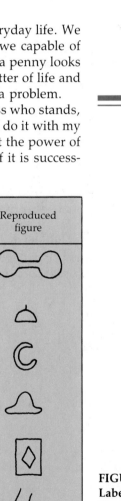

Elizabeth Loftus

Reproduced figure	Word list	Stimulus figure	Word list	Reproduced figure
⊙⊙	Eyeglasses	⊙–⊙	Dumbell	O—O
	Bottle		Stirrup	
	Crescent moon	☽	Letter "C"	C
	Beehive		Hat	
	Curtains in a window		Diamond in a rectangle	
7	Seven	7	Four	4
	Ship's wheel		Sun	
	Hourglass		Table	

FIGURE 9–12
Labeling and Remembering
The name something is given influences our memory of it, as this chart demonstrates. People recalled and reproduced an ambiguous doodle as more like the label given it than did others given another label for the same figure. (After Carmichael, Hogan, & Walters, 1932)

fully challenged by other testimony. But an understanding of the malleability of memory should make us more wary. Many innocent people have been accused and sentenced to prison on the basis of the testimony of an eyewitness.

Memory is influenced not only by previous knowledge but also by events that happen between the time an event is perceived and the time it is recalled. *An Example:* People were shown a film of a traffic accident and later asked questions about what they had seen. The key question in the first part of the test was "How fast were the cars going when they *smashed* into each other?" For some groups the word *smashed* was replaced by less aggressive verbs, such as hit, bumped, or collided. A week later the groups were asked, "Did you see any broken glass?" More of those who had been given the question with the word *smashed* answered "Yes," even though no broken glass was shown in the film (Loftus, Miller, & Burns, 1978).

Levels of Processing

No one theory has yet been able to tie together all the complex phenomena of memory. One recent attempt at such a theory is called **levels of processing.** This theory states that all information presented to us is "processed" at different "depths" or "levels."

For instance, the visual image of a word is received as sensory stimuli, transduced into neural signals, and then transformed by perception into something meaningful. This stage would be a first, shallow level of processing. At a deeper "level," the word and the sentence it is a part of are identified and understood. The meaning of the sentence may trigger associations (images, stories, similar events) on the basis of the subject's past experience. This is the "deepest" level of processing (Craik & Lock-

FIGURE 9–13
Eyewitness Testimony
Memory can be influenced by what is experienced between perceiving an event and when you try to recall it. Thus, being told two cars "smashed" into each other will move your recollection in different directions than hearing the cars collided, scraped, or bumped. (After Loftus & Loftus, 1975)

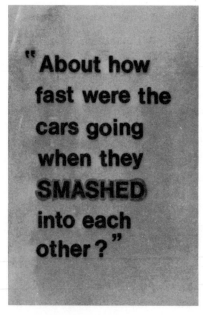

hart, 1972). In one study, Craik and Tulving (1975) hypothesized that the more deeply processed a word was the more likely it would be recalled. Their method was to ask questions about the "semantic qualities" of the word. These qualities were revealed by the following questions:

Structural: Is the word in capital letters?

Phonemic: Does the word rhyme with WEIGHT?

Semantic: Would the word fit into the sentence: "He met a _____ in the street"?

Each type of question was intended to evoke a deeper level of processing, the deepest being the "semantic," which concerned the *meaning* of the word.

Craik and Tulving found that it takes longer to process a word deeply, but recognition and recall of the word increase according to the "depth" at which it was processed. The semantic processing produced a higher amount of recall than the phonemic, the phonemic higher than the structural.

The levels-of-processing theory helps to explain that we may remember the same item differently depending upon how we process it. For instance, reading a page of text in order to type requires only shallow processing, while reading for understanding requires deeper processing: less information is remembered when reading to type than to understand.

Relating Information to Yourself

An important way to "deepen" processing is to try to relate the information to yourself. To the list of questions in Craik and Tulving's experiment Rogers and his colleagues (1977) added the question, "Describes you?" They found that people best remembered words they could relate to themselves (Figure 9–14). Asking yourself questions like "What would have made me do that?" and considering whether "That happened to me once" both increase the likelihood of recall. The reason for this increase in remembering may be that the richest set of associations in memory relate to ourselves. When information can be referred to an event in your own life, it is remembered longer (Bower, Gilligan, & Monteiro, 1981).

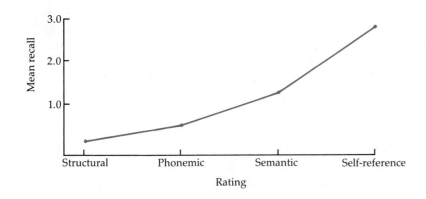

FIGURE 9–14
Memory and Self-reference
You can deepen the processing of what you perceive and want to recall if you relate that information to yourself, to an event in your life. (After Rogers, Kulper, & Kirker, 1977)

Why *Are Meaningful Events Better Remembered?*

Although the idea of levels of processing offers a useful *framework* for understanding memory, it has been criticized as a circular *explanation*: "Deep processing leads to better memory because we remember something that is deeply processed." It is possible that a simpler, and therefore preferable, explanation is that successfully remembering an event depends, primarily, on the number of associations that a particular event calls up. One dominant view in psychology, beginning with the British empiricists like Locke and Hume, and continuing with James and many current researchers, is that the mind is best described as a network of associations. When something arises in consciousness, all the associated schemata arise with it. Associations may be semantic, visual, or emotional.

Something is meaningful to us because it evokes many associations. Because the most meaningful information has the most associations, it is remembered better. They cluster, as James wrote, "like grapes to a stem." Each time an event occurs, the number of associations increases, and memory is improved. Thus, relating information to yourself serves to increase the number of associations, because we have the most items associated with ourselves. Generally, then, the more meaningful something is, the more associations it has, and thus it is more memorable.

IMPROVING MEMORY

More than any other group, students probably have the greatest self-interest in improving memory. A "successful" student is usually one who can retrieve "correct" information easily at exam time. Several of the principles discussed in this chapter may help you remember things better.

Improving Memory by Changing Encoding

For students, it is not useful to have learned something "by heart" if the information cannot be *retrieved* when needed. Exams test your ability to retrieve information, either by recognition or recall. Have you ever heard someone say after an exam, "I knew the answer, but not the way the question was asked"? Concerning this problem, one psychologist writes:

> The critical thing for most of the material you learn in school is to *understand* it, which means encoding it in a way that makes it distinctive from unrelated material and related to all the things it ought to be related to in order for you to use it. . . . The time you spend thinking about material you are reading and relating it to previously stored material is about the most useful thing you can do in learning any new subject matters. (Wickelgren, 1977)

Instead of simply memorizing "by heart," ask "What does this mean?" Talking to a friend or roommate about what you have read is a good way to make sure you have grasped the central meaning.

Relating Information to Yourself

The self is the most efficient "context" for remembering. Try to relate material to your own past experience and knowledge. Psychology is almost tailor-made for efficient studying, since its subject is you. The demonstrations and examples in this book were selected to help you relate concepts to your own experience. So far, every chapter concerns information that bears on your life in some way. As we progress into the more individual aspects of psychology, you may have to associate information to a less familiar context. For example, most people do not suffer from severe psychological abnormalities. However, noticing how you *differ* from someone who is seriously disturbed will help you retain the information.

Techniques for Improving Memory

Techniques for improving memory try to change the way information is organized in memory so that it becomes more accessible. It is always easier to remember something according to a rule than by rote. For example, it is simpler to remember the spelling rule "*i* before *e* except after *c*" and the few exceptions than to learn to spell every word containing *ie* or *ei*.

The SQ3R Method

Learning progresses with active use. The more ways information is encoded, the better it will be retained and, simultaneously, the more access routes to its retrieval. One successful study method that attempts to improve encoding is called **SQ3R,** which stands for "Survey, Question, Read, Recite, Review."

1. *Survey* a chapter before reading it. Look at the outline, the general headings, and the chapter summary; this way you will get an idea of what will be covered. In addition, the length of a section should indicate how important the topic is in relation to other topics covered. Notice the organization of the book you are studying. In this book, the introduction to a chapter provides an overall context for reading the chapter—important concepts are highlighted and topics covered in the chapter are previewed. The chapter summary should provide preliminary schemata for understanding.

2. *Question* the material *before* you read. Ask questions like "I wonder what X means?" "Is X related to Y in an earlier chapter?" Such questioning ignites curiosity and demands an answer. Your active questioning will lead to an active search for an answer.

3. *Read* the material only after a framework for encoding is in place.

4. *Recite* what you have learned from reading. Try to answer the questions you asked before reading. Make sure you understand important concepts and facts featured in the summary or introduction.

5. *Review* the material after you have retained the important information. Implicit in the SQ3R method are *rehearsal* and *relearning*. The greater the familiarity or number of associations, the greater the retention and retrieval. The more time you spend attending to and concentrating on the material, the better your retention will be.

Improving Memory for Meaningless Material

The best way to remember material with no apparent meaning is to *impose a context* that will serve as an aid to memory or will convert the material into something meaningful. Here are two methods for improving memory of "meaningless" events.

Mnemonics

Mnemonics (the first *m* is silent) is basically a technique for aiding memory. There is nothing about the names of the months of the year that gives clues to the number of days they have. The rhyme "Thirty days hath September . . ." is a mnemonic to help you retrieve that information when you need it. To remember which way to change your clocks for Daylight Savings Time, a useful mnemonic is "Spring forward,

A student who crams for an exam in his car may need to improve his study habits and develop recall techniques with a method like SQ3R.

fall back." People often use mnemonics to remember names. To remember someone named Scott McDonald, you may remember that his last name is the same as the fast food restaurant. (A word to the wise: choose your mnemonic carefully. A friend of mine, Betty Cone, said she knew exactly how the principal of the school tried to remember her name, because he always called her Betty Pine.) Mnemonic devices are useful in learning a foreign language. The word for horse in Spanish is *caballo*, pronounced COB-EYE-O. The second syllable sounds like the English word "eye" (Figure 9–15), so a mnemonic might be to visualize a horse kicking an enormous eye. Although this may sound silly, students who use tricks like this have doubled their recall of foreign vocabulary words (Bower, 1978).

One way to remember a list in a certain order is to associate each item with a previously learned, organized set of "peg words." One example is:

One is a bun
Two is a shoe
Three is a tree
Four is a door
Five is a hive
Six is sticks
Seven is heaven
Eight is a gate
Nine is wine
Ten is a hen

Let us say you want to buy the following: lettuce, soup, paper towels, eggs, tomatoes, and chicken. Try to visualize these items with the above peg words. The more striking (often unlikely) the association, the more likely it will be remembered. For example, imagine lettuce on a bun,

FIGURE 9–15
Mnemonic Devices
An image like this could be an effective mnemonic for the Spanish word *caballo*.

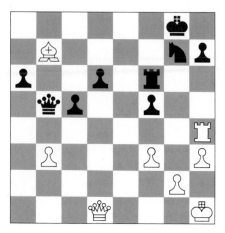

FIGURE 9–16
Look briefly at the positions of the chess pieces and try to reproduce them without looking back at the page.

FIGURE 9–17

| 563908972 |
| 878992111 |
| 389763009 |

soup spilling out of a shoe, a tree with paper towels for leaves, eggs splattered all over the door, a hive-full of tomatoes, a chicken picking up sticks.

Method of Loci

Visualizing items to be recalled is a powerful aid to memory (Bower, 1973). Visualization is especially useful in the **method of loci,** a memory trick devised by the Greeks. The trick here is to create new and different associations to improve recall. Select a group of places that have some relationship with each other. For example, every day you awaken in your bedroom, wash up in the bathroom, have breakfast in the kitchen or dining room, walk or drive along a certain route. Associate the items in order with the different places, such as your bed, the sink, the dining room wall, a tree that you pass. For the shopping list used in the previous section, you could imagine that the sheets on your bed are lettuce, you are eating soup out of the sink, paper towels are on the dining room table, and so on. The method of loci is effective because human memory is associative, and "putting things in their place" increases the number of associations.

Great Feats of Memory

A knowledge of how memory operates will help you improve your memory. But, as with every human ability, there are some people who have extraordinary memories. Some people can play as many as 60 games of chess blindfolded. Some people can multiply long numbers in their heads as fast as a calculator (e.g., 789054.78 × 657483.86). One man could look at 70 unrelated words and recall them perfectly a day later, and sometimes even a year later. These feats are possible using the principles of memory described and mnemonics and the method of loci.

Chunking in Chess

The chess masters who can play several games at once, blindfolded, are not necessarily possessed of supernatural memory, but are simply able to combine or "chunk" larger units of a chess game than ordinary chess players. Figure 9–16 shows a fairly common chess position. Look at it briefly and try, if you have a board, to reproduce it quickly without referring back to the book. In one study, chess masters were able very quickly to reproduce most common chess positions; beginners could not (Chase & Simon, 1973). All positions on the board form one meaningful chunk of information to the masters. When Chase and Simon placed the chess pieces on a board at random, masters and beginners were equally inept at reproducing the positions.

The Great Russian Mnemonist

The most famous case of memorization is "S," studied by the Russian psychologist Luria (1968). To gain a sense of the immensity of his feats, look at the table of numbers in Figure 9–17 for three minutes. Then try to reproduce it without looking. S was able to do it in 40 seconds. Even more impressively, he could repeat it several months later. Luria writes:

"The only difference in the two performances was that for the later one he needed time to revive the entire situation in which the experiment had been carried out; to 'see' the room in which he had been sitting; to 'hear' my voice; to 'reproduce' an image of himself looking at the board." S thus encoded information with as *many meaningful associations as possible* to aid retrieval. He was especially adept at associating information with specific visual imagery. When trying to recall a particular list, he once said: "Yes . . . yes, that was a series you gave me once when you were sitting in your apartment. You were sitting at the table and I was in the rocking chair. . . . You were wearing a gray suit and you looked at me like this" (Luria, 1968).

S also used the method of loci in remembering, and this sometimes led to interesting mistakes. Trying to recall a particular list of words, he imagined a "mental walk" but missed the words "pencil" and "egg."

> I put the image of the pencil near a fence . . . , the one down the street, you know. But what happened was that the image fused with that of the fence and I walked right on past without noticing it. The same thing happened with the word "egg." I had put it up against a white wall and it blended in with the background. How could I possibly spot a white egg up against a white wall?

S had an extraordinary ability to visualize, but even so his methods are merely extensions of the principles discussed in this chapter: *making the associations between information meaningful, by making those associations rich and complex.* Thus, as in the quotation from James at the beginning of the chapter, facts will cluster together in the mind.

Summary

1. Memory involves associations, selection and simplification of reality, and is organized around meaningful events.

2. Memory records specific episodes in our lives, but it also contains rules for operating on the world; the latter is called *representational memory.* Memory is continuously updated as new events occur, which allows us to respond to continuous changes in the world. Memory allows us to organize past experiences and to make them accessible as needed.

3. New information must be stored and kept. The *retention* time may be a few seconds, a few years, or forever. In *retrieval*, a past event is brought into consciousness. We regain, "retrieve," information previously stored. Two types of retrieval are recognition and recall.

4. An important division of the memory process is the distinction between short- and long-term memory. Information retained temporarily, like a telephone number for a few seconds, is thought to be stored by a specific process called *short-term memory.* The storage capacity of short-term memory is about seven items, such as a seven-digit number. Short-term memory is regarded

as something like scratch paper on which immediate information is "written" and continuously erased as new information comes into consciousness.

Information that is retained for more than a few seconds is stored in what is termed *long-term memory*. You do not need to look up your own telephone number when you call home, and you certainly do not need to continuously remember your own name. These memories are relatively permanent. Both episodic and representational forms of memory are stored in long-term memory.

5. Although many psychologists accept the concepts of short- and long-term memory as a specific system, recent theorists have challenged these ideas. William Estes does not feel, for instance, that memory actually stores or retrieves anything, but rather it is more like other changes in the body due to experience.

6. Many psychologists do not believe that separate processes for short- and long-term memory are plausible. Instead, they think of the memory system as a single and continuous process. In this view, each repetition of an event simply causes an increase in the associative strength of that event, thereby increasing the probability that it will be remembered.

7. Some kinds of events *interfere* with memory more than others. Two kinds of interference have been studied in the laboratory. *Proactive interference* occurs when previous knowledge interferes with present memory. *Retroactive interference* occurs when new information interferes with memory of old.

Two general factors in interference are: (1) the longer the interval between the first and second event, the less interference, (2) the more similar the items, the more interference.

8. More recent studies of memory have tended to focus on how real-life events are remembered. Linton found that the loss of memory for details of one's own life proceeds at a very slow, constant rate, unlike the quick decay of memory for intentionally meaningless events learned in laboratory tests. Bahrick and his colleagues found that memory for names might well be organized differently from memory for faces, and other studies have found that odor memory may also differ from any other forms of memory. In an important study, Herrmann and Neisser developed a list of eight characteristics that distinguish individual memories: rote memory, absentmindedness, names, people, conversation, errands, retrieval, and place.

Although these findings are very tentative, they do suggest that an individual's memory may be assembled in some way out of these different components.

9. The most basic principle of memory is that we remember the most meaningful of events. Meaning *differs* from individual to individual. Important determinants of memory are: how existing schemata influence and often change what we remember; how information is organized into meaningful units or "chunks"; and how memories can be reconstructed on the basis of these two processes.

In 1932, Bartlett published an important book, *Remembering*, in which he demonstrated the important effects of a person's existing knowledge structure on memory. He used the method of serial production, in which a drawing or a story was given to successive people in the manner of the children's game, "telephone." According to Bartlett, unfamiliar features "invariably suffer transformation in the direction of the familiar."

10. A unit of memory is called a chunk. In perceiving and remembering bits of information we organize individual items into chunks by using a code. Knowing a code (such as a language) increases the capacity of memory and the ability to remember.

11. One theory that attempts to tie together the complex phenomena of memory is called *levels of processing*. This states that all information that is presented to us is processed at different depths or levels, such as the structural, the phonemic, and the semantic. This view holds that the deeper the level of processing, the more likely it is the event will be remembered. And it helps explain why you can deepen processing by trying to relate information to the rich associations in your memory of personal experiences.

12. One important way to improve memory is called the *SQ3R* method. The more ways information is encoded, the better it will be retained and, simultaneously, the more access routes to its retrieval. SQ3R is a method that emphasizes (1) surveying information before reading it, (2) questioning the material before reading it, (3) reading the material only after a framework for encoding is in place, (4) reciting what has been learned from reading, and (5) reviewing the material after having retained the important information. Implicit in the SQ3R method are rehearsal and relearning. The greater the familiarity (number of associations), the greater the retention and the retrieval. This is a useful lesson to learn in studying this and other chapters.

Terms and Concepts

chunking
episodic memory
levels of processing
long-term memory
method of loci
mnemonics
nonsense syllables
perceptual-motor memory
primacy
proactive interference

recall
recency
recognition
representational memory
retention
retrieval
retroactive interference
semantic memory
short-term memory
SQ3R

Suggestions for Further Reading

Bartlett, F. C. (1932). *Remembering: A study in experimental and social psychology.* Cambridge: Cambridge University Press.
  The classic study of "transformations" in memory and how memory is altered.

Neisser, U. (1982). *Memory observed: Remembering in natural context.* San Francisco: W. H. Freeman.
  A compendium of the different aspects of memory—aspects that have too often been forgotten by psychologists. Includes articles on testifying, forgetting, performing, getting things done, and people who have special memories. Very highly recommended for those who wish to absorb some of the phenomena of memory as opposed to some of the theories.

Norman, D. A. (1982). *Learning and memory.* San Francisco: W. H. Freeman.
  A useful anecdotal and up-to-date viewpoint on the current status of knowledge about learning and memory.

Chapter 10

Thinking and Language

INTRODUCTION

One of the most puzzling questions about the nature of the human mind concerns the value of our thought. On the one hand, we are certainly the most creative species that has ever lived. We have invented everything from agriculture to cities to space travel. On the other hand, we seem almost like idiots at times. We make the same dumb mistakes over and over again.

However, I do not think we should enter an argument about whether we are complete geniuses or complete fools. Instead, let us quickly face ourselves at the outset: We are at the same time *both* miraculously inventive and continually stupid. We are so *because of the nature of our mental processes, including thought.*

Like other aspects of the mind, thinking involves a great deal of simplification. As there are fixed ways the senses act to deal with external information, and rather fixed rules of organization in perception and memory, so we develop set strategies for solving problems and making decisions. Thus, we again select a limited amount of information on which to base our judgments, and we develop rather fixed strategies for considering that information. This makes us prone to our "cardinal sin": we continually overgeneralize from the little information we possess. When the news reports a murder in a distant city, we tend to think of the world as a more murderous place. When someone famous comes down with breast cancer, it becomes a national concern. Yet in each case only a *single instance* has been brought to our attention. It happens all the time, to the dismay of psychologists.

When we come to the study of thinking, our analysis of the mind shifts somewhat. Mental processes, as we have seen, are simplifying processes. But in thought, something different also happens; the information we have is sifted, combined, and changed, so that new ideas and combinations result: new books, new buildings. These creative acts seem to be as characteristic of us as simplification and generalization. The processes we will examine in this chapter share a common theme: we select a few simplified elements, which can be combined and recombined to create new and diverse possibilities.

A similar process underlies our use of language. We have, in English, only a few elements to use—26 letters, 10 numbers. But those few elements can be combined to form an almost infinite number of different sentences. Language is the method most often used for the communication of thoughts, but every sentence we utter is a new creation.

Principles and Issues

Generalization and Overgeneralization

Central to the current analysis of thinking is that we tend to overgeneralize from the information at hand. The ability to generalize saves us a lot of effort. We need not waste time discriminating one car horn from another to get out of the way; different-sounding dinner bells all mean the same thing. Also, we are conscious of only a few things at once. What happens, then, is this: *whatever enters our consciousness is overemphasized.* It does not matter how the information enters, whether it is a television program, a newspaper story, a friend mentioning something, a strong emotional reaction, something easy to remember—all get overemphasized. We ignore other, more compelling evidence, to overemphasize and overgeneralize from the information at hand. Consider this:

> Let us suppose that you wish to buy a new car and have decided [on] either a Volvo or Saab. . . . CONSUMER REPORTS informs you that the consensus of their experts is that the Volvo is mechanically superior, and the consensus of their readership is that the Volvo has the better repair record. Armed with this information, you decide to go and strike a bargain with the Volvo dealer before the week is over. In the interim, however, you go to a cocktail party where you announce this intention to an acquaintance. He reacts with disbelief and alarm: "A Volvo! You've got to be kidding. My brother-in-law had a Volvo. First, that fancy fuel injection computer thing went out. $250. Next he started having trouble with the rear end. Had to replace it. Then the transmission and the clutch. Finally he sold it in three years for junk." (Nisbett & Ross, 1981)

How do you feel about the cars now? Most likely you will strongly reconsider buying the Volvo. But think about it. The information you have received is that *one more* person out of thousands does not like the Volvo. The brother-in-law is not an expert, but you are strongly influenced by a single case.

However, all is not lost with overgeneralization. It probably reflects a tendency to emphasize the most recent information, even at the cost of ignoring past knowledge. Consider this: in 1980 a DC-10 crashed in Chicago. On the day it crashed, what do you think you would have done if you had been scheduled to fly on a DC-10? Probably you would have canceled. Here our tendency to overgeneralize is clearly adaptive: it helps to protect against dangers associated with *changing circumstances.*

This kind of mechanism, with the tendency to trip the emergency reaction, may have gotten our ancestors out of a lot of trouble. So, our tendency to overgeneralize is an important part of our system of thought, with advantages and disadvantages; it simplifies, it allows us to adapt quickly to changes in the world, and it makes mistakes in a stable situation. Overgeneralization figures strongly in the current analysis of thinking.

SOME CHARACTERISTICS OF THOUGHT

Helping us to cut our way through the complex world are the simplifying mental structures that underlie thought. Psychologists have recently studied two different structures: how we classify things into *categories* and how we develop simplifying strategies called *heuristics.*

Categories

We seem to love to classify. Putting something in place may be as concrete as deciding something is an antique, or mulling over whether a person is dishonest or trustworthy.

Classification is a major simplifying factor in mental life. Without it we would have to identify and decide on *each* shading of color, *each* idea, and *each* feeling each time it was encountered. For instance, the range of colors we encounter is huge; the human visual system can discriminate 7,500,000 colors; however, only *eight* color names are commonly used (Brown & Lenneberg, 1954). We consider a sunset "red," an apple "red," and tomatoes "red." Here we use a single category (red) to classify a large number of different objects. A *category,* then, is a number of objects that can be considered equivalent in an important dimension (Rosch, 1978).

The Function of Categories

The first function of categories is *simplicity*—to give the most information with the least effort. It is simpler to call a tomato, a sunset, and an apple "red" than to identify them by "orangey red," and "luminescent red-orange with streaks of blue and black," and "pure red speckled with green." We *can* do all this, but it is unnecessary and wasteful unless we are writing poetry. The word "red" is enough.

Second, categories are not random and arbitrary, but reflect the structure of the world. Most objects in the world are characterized by a combination of predictable features (Garner, 1974). For instance, wings are more likely to have feathers on them than fur; legs are found on animals, not trees. Rooms do not move on their own; people breathe, buildings do not. Certain aspects of the world seem to "go together," and our categories reflect this: we consider dogs more similar to cats than to airplanes.

Thus categories aid us in interacting with the world; they simplify experience and reflect the actual structure of the world. Any system of

A NONEXISTENT CATEGORY SYSTEM

Here is a classification of the animal kingdom attributed to an ancient Chinese encyclopedia, the *Celestial Emporium of Benevolent Knowledge:*

On these remote pages it is written that animals are divided into a. Those that belong to the emperor, b. Embalmed ones, c. Those that are trained, d. Suckling pigs, e. Mermaids, f. Fabulous ones, g. Stray dogs, h. Those that are included in this classification, i. Those that tremble as if they were mad, j. Innumerable ones, k. Those drawn with a very fine camel's hair brush, l. Others, m. Those that have broken a flower vase, n. Those that resemble flies from a distance. (Borges, 1966).

It is clear that this is an impossible, nonexistent category system (in fact, it is an excerpt from a story by the Argentine writer Jorge Luis Borges). The reason this type of categorization system is not found in any culture is that it does not reflect the world.

classification (or **taxonomy**) organizes things by similarities and differences. By doing so, relationships become explicit. Categories help us make relationships and associations among many disparate objects and events.

Natural and Artificial Categories

The categories we have are useful. Some categories are universal, probably due to universals in the world. Color is a good example of a universal and probably innate response to the external environment. Our receptive apparatus for color is reflected in the categories most languages use for colors. Recall that the human visual system codes information in two ways: in black-white, and in color combinations of red, yellow, green, and blue. In a study of almost 100 languages, Berlin and Kay (1969) determined that color terms "always" appear in the following sequence:

			white					purple
black	[then]	red	[then]	yellow	[then]	brown	[then]	pink
			blue					orange
								gray

If a language has only two color terms, they will be black and white; if it has three, they will be black, white, and red; if there is a fourth, it will be either green, yellow, or blue. The fifth and sixth will be the remaining two of green, yellow, and blue. The later terms fill the gaps between the other, more general terms. In addition to these relatively basic **natural categories,** there are other **artificial categories** that refer to the attributes of constructed objects like chairs or buildings. In the case of natural categories, people have no trouble judging a best example of the category. There is more disagreement and difficulty in artificial categories; people find it easier to judge whether something is "more red" than another than whether something is "more of a chair" than another.

Categories not only reflect the structure of the physical world but many of our categories are peculiar to our culture, which are the standards we use for judgments. For example, an American traveling in Italy would probably have to convert 15,000 lira into dollars to find out if that was a good price for a pair of shoes. In the United States the most commonly used measures are inches, feet, yards, miles, fahrenheit, and so forth. If the weather report says it will be 28 degrees Celsius, most of us have to "translate" that figure to know if it will be hot or cold.

Characteristics of Categories

Basic Level

Categories are arranged hierarchically from extremely broad to quite detailed. An example of a broad category is furniture. Furniture is relatively abstract: there are a few specific features common to all items of furniture, but furniture may be many different things: chairs, beds, cabinets, tables. Each of these is also a category. "Tables" have clear perceptual distinctions: they have legs, a flat top, and other features in common, which differentiate them from chairs, for instance. Kitchen, or dining room, or modern, or wood tables are subcategories of table. The category *table,* however, seems to be the level at which we most naturally divide the world. It is called a **basic level category.** *Table* and other basic level categories, like apple, are the categories first learned by children (Rosch, Mervis, Gray, Johnson, & Boyes-Braem, 1976).

Typicality and Prototypes

Categories are arranged around a core of *best examples* or *prototypes.* A **prototype** is the example that most typifies the category (Rosch & Mer-

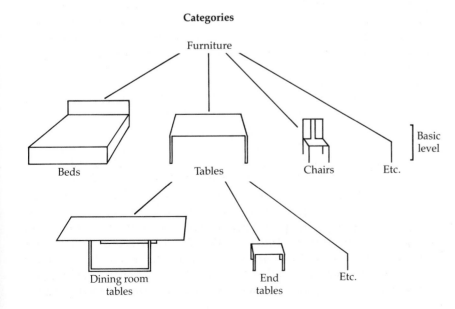

Categories

Furniture

Beds   Tables   Chairs   Etc.   ] Basic level

Dining room tables   End tables   Etc.

FIGURE 10–1
Categories
This diagram shows how the category "furniture" might be divided into a basic level and subcategories.

vis, 1975). **Typical** examples of a category are closest to the prototype, as when a strong, quiet, athletic man is considered a "typical athlete," or an attitude like love of wine is considered "typically French." However, a typical example may not always be the one we meet most frequently. Consider this: which bird do you think is mentioned most often in written English? Most people think it is the robin. A robin flies, has feathers, tugs at worms, makes a nest, sings, announces the arrival of spring; this fits our prototype of a "bird." However, the bird that is most often mentioned is not the robin. It is the chicken. Chicken is not an unfamiliar term or animal, but it does not *typify* our concept of bird. We are more likely to put chicken in the category "food" than "bird."

A robin is thus a more prototypical bird than a chicken. One way to study how people categorize things is to see how quickly they can make a judgment. One study found that the sentence "A robin is a bird" is recognized *more quickly* than the sentence "A chicken is a bird." In another study, Rosch (1975) asked people to fill in the blanks in this sentence, "_____ is virtually _____" with the numbers 100 and 103. There was a clear preference for "103 is virtually 100" over the reverse, "100 is virtually 103." One hundred is a more prototypical number than 103. Our preference for "round numbers" and multiples of 10 is an example of our use of prototypes and categories.

Similarity

Members of a category are by definition similar in some ways to other members of the category. They share a number of attributes. The more shared attributes, the more similar the objects are judged to be. However, similarity is not that simple. Nearly everything in the external world has its varying attributes: some of these may be similar to other objects and some different. Two things can thus be both similar *and* different at the same time.

Consider these statements: Jamaica is like Cuba. Cuba is like Russia. Jamaica is like Russia. These three statements form a loose kind of syllogism. The first two make sense. Jamaica and Cuba are both Caribbean countries. Cuba and Russia have Communist governments. But the third proposition, that Jamaica is like Russia, is odd because they have almost *no* attributes in common. The two other similar relationships led to a confusion.

Another characteristic of similarity is that it is not always symmetrical: "A is like B" is not necessarily the same as "B is like A." In the first instance, A is the subject, B is the *reference;* when these roles are reversed, the meaning is often changed. Consider the sentence: "A rattlesnake is like lightning," which indicates that rattlesnakes are fast and may strike quickly. "Lightning is like a rattlesnake" conveys that lightning is dangerous, perhaps deadly. In both cases the attributes of the reference are attributed to the subject (Glass, Holyoak, & Santa, 1980).

Judgments of similarities are quite complex (Tversky, 1977). Figure 10-2 shows the relationship between two entities. Similarity is where the circles overlap; the nonoverlapping areas represent the distinctive fea-

FIGURE 10–2
Similarity
The area where two circles overlap represents similarity. The nonoverlapping areas represent dissimilar, distinctive features of each entity.

Similarity

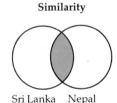

Sri Lanka   Nepal

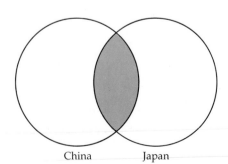

China   Japan

tures of the two. Our judgments of similarity are based on shared attributes; differences, on distinctive attributes. The more familiar with something we are, the more we know about it, which means that two things *can* be both more similar and more different than are another pair. In these diagrams we can represent this with larger circles.

An Example: How similar is China to Japan? How different is it? How similar is Sri Lanka to Nepal? How different is it? Tversky and Gati (1978) found that because people tend to know more about the prominent countries they also judge them to be *both* more similar and more different than are the pair of less prominent countries.

Heuristics

Heuristics are simplifying strategies that we use to make judgments and solve problems. There is a trade-off in the use of heuristics: we may sacrifice accuracy for speed. In life, we must usually rely on incomplete information to make judgments, reason, and solve problems. Heuristics are the rules of thumb that guide our decisions. Three heuristics we often use in thinking are representativeness, availability, and comparison.

Representativeness

Representativeness is the judgment that an object is *typical* of its category. This heuristic involves matching prototypes: a robin, for instance, is quickly judged to be a bird; it is *representative* of birds. A chicken is less so. However, using representativeness as a heuristic can lead to mistakes of overgeneralization. For instance, we often tend to judge *concrete* or *vivid* examples of a category as representative when they are not. Something that we see or hear firsthand overpowers other evidence. When there was a nearly catastrophic accident at the Three Mile Island nuclear reactor in 1979, the effect in influencing people to protest against the use of nuclear power was dramatic. The accident was judged to be representative of nuclear power plants, and it overwhelmed entirely the generally good safety records of these plants.

A single case has a striking influence; statistics can be easily ignored. At the beginning of a movie or novel, a disclaimer may appear that warns against the overuse of representativeness: "Any resemblance to persons living or dead is purely coincidental." More examples of representativeness appear in the next section on decision making.

Availability

Another heuristic we use to make judgments is **availability**—the ease with which relevant instances come to mind (Tversky & Kahneman, 1973). Recall from the chapter on memory that events that occur more frequently to us are more easily retrieved from memory, since they are more accessible for use. The availability heuristic is used when we are asked to guess the frequency or the probability of events. In general it is useful: things that occur more frequently are more available. However, the use of availability can lead to error. A man from Indiana may remark, "Haven't you noticed how many famous Hoosiers there are?" People out of work may overestimate the rate of unemployment (Nisbett & Ross, 1981). In one experiment this question is asked: are there more words in English that start with K or in which K is the third letter? Two-thirds of the people asked this question feel that it is more likely that K begins the word than is third; however, they are wrong. Why are most of us wrong? Probably because of the way we index and categorize words; it is much easier to remember those that *begin* with K. Our judgments most often are based on the "available" evidence (Kahneman & Tversky, 1973).

Comparison

The comedian Henny Youngman was asked: "How do you like your wife?" "Compared to what?" he responded. Youngman's answer points out two psychological processes: We judge by comparison, and our standard of comparison constantly shifts. Most judgments, from the simplest to the most complex, depend upon comparison. Something is judged heavier, lighter, warmer, colder, more or less expensive than *something else.* An outside air temperature of 50 degrees is judged as "warm" in winter but as "cold" in summer; a salary of $300 a week is enormous to a college student and might be an insult to an executive. A 200-gram weight in a series of weights ranging from 100 to 200 grams is experienced as heavy, while in a series of weights of 200 to 500 grams it is experienced as light. We often judge our own state of mind and mood by comparison. *An Example:* it would seem that a person who had the great luck of winning a lottery would be happier over a long period than those who have not. However, lottery winners were no happier one year after winning than before they won and found considerably less pleasure in mundane events than did those who had not won. Why? The lottery winners may have habituated to their new fortune (Brickman, 1975).

One common effect of comparisons is **anchoring:** once a standard has been used in trying to solve a problem, a person is less likely to change or adjust, even if compelling new data are present, or even if common sense would dictate a change. A person is "anchored" in his or her strategy.

The tendency to anchor is taken advantage of by salespeople and advertisers. Suppose a couple goes to buy a car. They are considering two: one costs $6,000 and one $7,000. The $1,000 difference is important to them; they examine the differences between the cars carefully. The salesperson then shows them a $20,000 car, pointing out the features that are similar to those in the $7,000 car. When the couple gets back to deciding between the two cars they are considering buying, the $7,000 car begins to seem like a better deal, even cheap, in comparison. In the ad in Figure 10–3, a fairly expensive item seems less so when displayed with something very costly.

Changing Standards of Comparison

We may apply different standards of comparison to different situations at different times. What is enough money at one time is not enough at another. Kahneman and Tversky conceptualize these changing standards as *psychological accounting*—we shift items into different accounts. For example, suppose you are going to a play and lose $10 on the way. Would you still pay $10 for a ticket? Most people say they would. Now suppose you have bought your $10 ticket and lose it on the way. Would you still pay $10 for another ticket? Most people say no. *The loss in both of these situations is exactly the same:* $10. But they are not the same in "psychological accounting" terms. In the first case the loss is not "applied" to our "ticket account"; in the second, the account has been used up (Tversky & Kahneman, 1981).

A second question: would you drive 20 minutes to save $5? Whether you would or not depends upon comparison. If you are going to buy a toaster and a store close to you has it for $25 and another store 20 minutes away has it on sale for $20, would you drive? Most people say that they would. Suppose you are going to buy a jacket at a nearby store for $165 and a store 20 minutes away has the same one for $160. Most people say that they would not drive the extra miles. *They are less likely to drive when the savings represent a smaller amount of the total.* The savings are equal, but how they are compared is not (Tversky & Kahneman, 1981).

FIGURE 10–3
Standards of Comparison
An advertisement like this, which juxtaposes a fairly costly item (the car) with something extremely expensive (the yacht), makes the car look more accessible, especially to people who would never have thought of buying a yacht in the first place.

COMPARISONS AND CATEGORIES

Categories can affect comparisons. We seem to hold cutoff points for categories. Retailers are aware of this when they price goods at $99.98 rather than $100.00. They know people may be looking for something "under $100.00." The shifting nature of our comparisons is shown in the effect the rise in the cost of gasoline had on American drivers. There was little decline in gasoline consumption as gas rose from 38 cents to 60 cents to 90 cents and even 95 cents; but once gasoline was more than $1.00 a gallon, there was a marked decrease in usage. Later on, as prices remained above $1.00 a gallon, consumption rose again.

DECISION MAKING AND JUDGMENT

What will you major in? Which car should you buy? Which job offer should you accept? What will you have for lunch? Life is one decision after another. Although in a sense every decision is a problem and every problem requires decision making, psychologists distinguish between the two. Problems require finding a series of steps that allow you to reach a goal. Decisions require making a choice among several options. In this section we will consider decision making; in the next, problem solving. There are four basic elements in every decision:

1. A set of *alternatives* to choose from
2. A set of possible *outcomes*
3. The decision maker's *preferences* among the different outcomes
4. The decision maker's judgments of the *probabilities* that a particular choice will lead to a particular outcome

Suppose you have to decide whether or not to buy collision insurance for your car at $300 a year. Your *alternatives* are to buy or not buy the insurance. The *outcomes* are that you do or do not have a collision. Your *preference* is the outcome that will cost the least, but you are not sure which choice will lead to that outcome. This uncertainty can be represented as *probabilities*.

Let us assume that you think you have a 10 percent chance of having a collision in a year and that if you had a collision the cost would be about $2,000. You can quantify the various factors to be dealt with in this problem. Since the numbers are specified, you can compute the expected value of each choice by multiplying the probabilities by the values of the outcomes. According to these numbers, you should choose not to buy the insurance since it costs $300 a year and your expected loss without it would be only $200 a year. Obviously this example is oversimplified. The decision would not be this simple in reality—there are other insurance policies, there may be more factors involved in your preferences than the amount of money (for instance, the "peace of mind" of having insurance), and you may be very unsure about your probability of having a collision.

Even though most decisions are more complex than this example, the four basic elements—alternatives, outcomes, preferences, and probabilities—are present in decision making in one way or another. Often just thinking about decisions in this way can help clarify decision making. For example, you are having trouble getting along with your roommate; you might make a list of alternative things you could do and the possible outcomes of each choice. Then you could consider which outcomes seem most likely from each choice, and which outcomes you would prefer most. This way of thinking about decisions is called **decision analysis.**

Heuristics and Biases in Decision Making

We use heuristics to make decisions. These "shortcuts" probably result in more efficient decision making overall, but they also lead to systematic **biases** preventing impartiality in certain kinds of judgments that people make (Einhorn & Hogarth, 1981). Knowing about these common biases may help you avoid them in your own judgments and decision making.

Availability

When people are asked to judge the relative frequency of different causes of death, they overestimate the frequency of well-publicized causes like homicide, tornadoes, and cancer, and they underestimate the frequency of less remarkable causes like diabetes, asthma, and emphysema. Tversky and Kahneman (1973) read subjects lists of names of well-known people of both sexes. In each list the people of one sex were more famous than those of the other sex. When the subjects were asked to estimate the proportion of men and woman on the lists, they overestimated the proportion for the sex with more famous people on the list. If the list contained very famous women (such as Elizabeth Taylor) and only moderately well-known men (such as Alan Ladd), then subjects overestimated the proportion of women on the list. In both these cases, people's judgments were biased by *how easily they could recall specific examples.*

Representativeness

People often overestimate the probability that something belongs in a particular category. Kahneman and Tversky (1973) told subjects to read the following passage. "This description of Tom W. was written by a psychologist when Tom was in his senior year of high school":

> Tom W. is of high intelligence, although lacking in true creativity. He has a need for order and clarity, and for neat and tidy systems in which every detail finds its appropriate place. His writing is rather dull and mechanical, occasionally enlivened by somewhat corny puns and by

flashes of imagination of the sci-fi type. He has a strong drive for competence. He seems to have little feel and little sympathy for other people and does not enjoy interacting with others. Self-centered, he nonetheless has a deep moral sense.

Imagine that Tom W. is now a graduate student. Rank the following categories in order of the likelihood that they are Tom's area of graduate specialization:

business administration
computer science
engineering
humanities and education
law
library science
medicine
physical and life sciences
social science and social work

If you are like the people Kahneman and Tversky studied, you probably chose computer science or engineering as Tom's most likely area of specialization, and thought that humanities, education, social science, and social work were least likely. The character description probably fits your *prototype* of what "typical" computer science or engineering students are like. The representativeness heuristic leads you to think these are likely categories for his field of study. But there are many more graduate students in humanities, education, social science, and social work than there are in computer science or engineering. Even people who know these *base rates* of students in different fields and who have very little faith in the predictive value of the character sketch disregard the base rates in making their predictions.

Vivid Information

One particularly important consequence of availability and representativeness is that concrete or vivid information is very influential in judgment.

The tendency to disregard statistical information and to overemphasize vivid examples extends even to some of society's most important decision makers. Nisbett and Ross (1981) describe an acquaintance of theirs

who often testifies at congressional committees on behalf of the Environmental Protection Agency. . . . She reported that the bane of her professional existence is the frequency with which she reports test data such as EPA mileage estimates based on samples of ten or more cars, only to be contradicted by a congressman who retorts with information about a single case: "What do you mean, the Blatzmobile gets twenty miles per gallon on the road?" he says. "My neighbor has one, and he only gets fifteen." His fellow legislators then usually respond as if matters were at a stand-off—one EPA estimate versus one colleague's estimate obtained from his neighbor.

PROBLEM SOLVING

People are continuously involved in problem solving. Some of the problems we deal with may be simple and unstructured, such as "What should I make for dinner?"; some may be chronic, such as "How can I get along with my boss better?"; and some may be formal, such as a solution to a problem in chess or logic. Different problems demand different kinds of solutions and approaches. Many everyday problems are fairly simple and may be dealt with by simple trial and error; some life problems involve hypothesis testing. More formal problems may draw on these two methods but also may involve structured analyses and strategies. Some of the strategies involve heuristics. Earlier we emphasized how heuristics interfere with judgment; here we will see how they help in solutions. We will also examine how people go beyond problem solving to the creative invention of new ways to deal with unexpected situations.

Simple Problems and Strategies

We are faced with problems so constantly that we often do not notice that they are problems until they are solved. Trivial ones, such as how to open a tightly closed jar, or how to get the sofa through the door, are usually solved by trial and error. Some problems are more substantial (although not formal) such as "How do I get a checkmate?" or "How does my car work?" We may use hypothesis testing for the solution to these problems.

Trial and Error

You arrive in your hotel room in Tibet. There are three faucets in the shower with strange markings on them. How do you turn the hot water on? The only way to find out is to turn the faucets and see what happens. This is trial and error (Wason & Johnson-Laird, 1972).

Trial and error is the most basic problem-solving strategy. When we are stuck in a situation and do not know anything about it, we try anything to get unstuck. Trial and error usually involves a more or less random series of different actions when there is no logical way to solve the problem. What do you do to stop a car going downhill if the brakes fail?

Hypothesis Testing

Suppose one night you come home and find all the lights out. You check all the switches, turn them on and off—no light. You call the electric company to find out if there has been a power failure. You check the fuse box; nothing. Then the main switch to the house—it is off. You switch it on and the lights brighten your house. What you do, even in this simple situation, is to entertain a series of hypotheses about the problem, in a systematic and structured way. Using **hypothesis testing,** you eliminate each hypothesis until the solution is found. To do this you must have a *set of possible hypotheses* stored, each of which could account for the situation; for example, it could be something wrong in the fuse box or the power line. You must also be able to take appropriate *actions* to test and *eliminate* certain hypotheses (e.g., turning on switches in different rooms eliminates the hypothesis that the lights are out in one room, or on one switch).

Even animals use hypotheses. David Krechevsky (1932) had rats run a maze with four choice points. At each one the rats could turn left or right. Behind each choice point there was a door that could be opened or closed and that either blocked the rats or allowed them to continue. The rats did not treat the situation in a trial-and-error way but seemed to test hypotheses. They would try a series of all right turns or all left ones until they had arrived at a satisfactory solution.

Strategies in Problem Solving

Even situations that allow for hypothesis testing are not that common, because most human actions and interactions are more complex than mazes or home electric problems. In chess, for instance, there are literally millions of possible moves. Players would be stymied unless they used some simplifying strategies and procedures (heuristics).

There are too many kinds of problems to produce a neat classification. They are as varied as which stock to buy, which career to choose, which move to make in tic-tac-toe. However, it is useful to think of problems as having these elements:

1. The *initial state* or starting point of the problem
2. A set of *operations,* or actions, that the problem solver can use to change the state of the problem
3. A *goal* or a description of the states that would be solutions to the problem

Tic-tac-toe is a good example. The initial state is a set of nine empty squares. The operations are marking an X or O in the squares and all the possible ways the squares can be marked. The goal is to get three of your marks in a row before your opponent does. Tic-tac-toe is a completely specified problem. Most puzzles and mathematical problems are similarly well defined; however, many problems in life are not so well defined. For example, if your problem is to write a paper for an English class, you might say that the initial state of the problem is a blank page and all your knowledge about the entire world, or at least about the subject of the paper. The operations are writing words on the page. The goal is a completed paper. However, all of these, especially the goal, are quite difficult to specify precisely. In this and other problems it would be hard to specify all the possible states and operations. But even though many real-world problems are not completely well defined, it is useful to conceive of them as having these elements, since different parts of the problem-solving process can be distinguished.

The Sequence of Problem Solving

Once a problem is identified and its solution begun, there are four basic steps (Polya, 1957):

1. Understanding the problem
2. Planning a solution
3. Carrying out the plan
4. Checking the results

Thus, you must first understand the starting point, the operations, and the goal. Then you plan a sequence of operations to change the initial state into a goal. Finally, you carry out the operations and judge whether the solution is correct. Of course, you may have to repeat the cycle many times before you reach a solution. At each step there are a number of choices to be made. Two of the most important parts of solving problems are how you *represent* the problem and what *strategy* you use to solve it.

Problem Representation

Problem representation, the way you think about or *represent* a problem, may make it harder or easier to solve. Although logical reasoning often helps solve problems, sometimes it makes solution more difficult. Consider the following problem:

> One morning, exactly at sunrise, a Buddhist monk began to climb a tall mountain. A narrow path, no more than a foot or two wide, spiraled around the mountain to a glittering temple at the summit. The monk ascended at varying rates of speed, stopping many times along the way to rest and eat dried fruit he carried with him. He reached the temple shortly before sunset. After several days of fasting and meditation, he began his journey back along the same path, starting [at] sunrise and again walking at variable speeds with many pauses along the way. His average speed descending was, of course, greater than his average climbing speed. Show that there is a spot along the path that the monk will occupy on both trips at exactly the same time of day.

Try to think about this problem verbally and mathematically. Most people find the solution difficult: how can we be sure the monk would find himself at the same spot at the same time on two different days, when we do not know how fast he walked? The way to *represent* this problem is visually. One woman describes her experience: "When you graph the position of the monk on the mountain for the two different days, there must be a point at which they cross, and this is the solution to the problem" (Glass et al., 1980).

However, visual solutions do not always work. Here is another problem. Suppose you take a piece of paper 0.01 inch think and fold it on itself 50 times. How high is it? Most people, visually estimating the solution, may say "five inches" or "two feet" or even "ten feet." They all underestimate the height greatly. Attack the problem mathematically: we find that 50 folds increase the height by two multiplied by two 50 times, or 2^{50} times 0.01 inch. When the problem is solved mathematically the answer is surprising—the "paper" would reach from the Earth to beyond the end of the Universe! Successful problem-solving strategy may involve visual, verbal, mathematical, and other kinds of representation.

Problem-solving Strategies

After you have a representation for your problem, there are several different strategies you can use to solve it. Some strategies will guarantee that you will find the solution if you keep working long enough. These strategies are called **algorithms.** If you follow the procedure exactly, you will reach a correct answer to the problem. One algorithm is a strategy for playing tic-tac-toe, in which you consider all the possible moves you could make and then all the possible replies your opponent could make to that move and then all the possible next moves you could make, and so on. Then you select a move that cannot lead to a win for your opponent. This strategy is called *generate-and-test*, because at each point, you *generate* a set of alternative moves and *test* each one to see if it works. Looking at many alternative actions in this way is called "searching the test (or problem) space." This algorithm works well for tic-tac-toe, but in more complex and interesting problems there are far too many alternatives to consider each one. For example, imagine trying to play chess by listing all moves you could make and all the possible replies by your opponent and all the possible next moves, and so on. Even though this algorithm guarantees in principle that you could solve the problem, there will never be enough time to use it.

Heuristics

People use heuristics in complex situations. They do not guarantee a solution in all cases, but are often very useful in reaching a solution. Some examples of chess-playing heuristics might be "Capture any piece you can" and "Never expose your king." This drastically reduces the amount of information that needs to be considered to solve a problem.

One heuristic that is often useful is called "hill climbing." The goal is to reach the top of a hill; a good strategy is always to walk uphill from where you are. Using this heuristic you would always apply operations that would bring the state of the problem more in line with the goal state. As a simplifying strategy in complex problems, a heuristic may be of some help: for example, someone with a poor sense of direction would remember that in California you always drive west to reach the ocean. This strategy can sometimes get you into trouble if used blindly. In checkers the goal is to capture all the opponent's pieces. Using the hill-climbing strategy, you would try to capture any piece you could, as this would bring you closer to the goal. But to do so indiscriminately could lead you into a trap in which more of your own pieces were captured.

Another heuristic that is often very useful is to break a larger problem into **subgoals.** For example, consider the algebraic problem $2x + y = 8$, $x - y = 1$. You might first set the subgoal of finding x and look for a way to reach it. The two equations added gives $3x = 9$ or $x = 3$. Then y can be easily derived. Breaking problems apart makes the larger one easier to solve (Wickelgren, 1977).

Means-End Analysis

A particularly useful way of breaking a problem into subgoals is called **means-end analysis.** With this heuristic, you work backward from your goal through the things you need to achieve it. For example, if your goal is to cook spaghetti, you need a kitchen to cook in and all the ingredients for spaghetti. Suppose you have enough money, but you have no transportation to the store. Your new subgoal is to get to the store. You might ask to borrow your roommate's bicycle. If you get permission to use it, then your next subgoal is to find the bicycle. If permission is denied, then you may have to "search through the problem space" some more by considering other means of transportation.

Insight

Not all problems are necessarily soluble using only systematic, step-by-step ways like those treated so far. Often a crucial **insight** is needed to solve a problem, a vision of how all the parts fit together or of how to represent the problem differently. Deciding to visually represent the Buddhist monk problem is one example of an insight. "Aha, that's it!" is the feeling of insight when all the different elements of a problem suddenly come together. This experience can come at the end of a directed process of hypothesis testing or seemingly all at once. The mathematician Poincaré (1921) described his insight into a mathematical formula. He had worked constantly on the problem for 15 days and then went on a trip:

> Just at this time I left Caen, where I was living, to go on a geologic excursion under the auspices of the School of Mines. The changes of travel made me forget my mathematical world. Having reached Coutances, we entered an omnibus to go some place or other. At the moment when I put my foot on the step, the idea came to me, without anything in my former thoughts seeming to have paved the way for it. . . . I did not verify the idea . . . as upon taking my seat in the omnibus I went on with a conversation already commenced, but I felt a perfect certainty. On my return to Caen, for conscience's sake, I verified the result at my leisure.

The insight is often visual and seems to consist of a simultaneous vision of the total problem. Some of the earliest experimental work on insight was done by Wolfgang Köhler. Köhler demonstrated that insight can occur even in animals. Recall from the chapter on learning that Köhler hung a bunch of bananas from the ceiling just out of reach of the chimpanzees (Figure 10–4). He also randomly arranged a set of boxes in the cage. After exhausting various approaches in a trial-and-error manner, the chimp suddenly stopped, perused the situation, and then appeared to see the solution: he stacked the boxes one on top of another, stood on the boxes, and reached the bananas. This is insight: the sudden arrangement of a set of elements in a new way.

Studying Problem Solving

How do psychologists study problem solving? One of the most obvious ways is by asking people to introspect (literally "look within") and talk about how they solve problems. It is usually best to have people do this while they are actually solving the problem. If they wait until they

FIGURE 10–4
One of Köhler's Problem-solving Chimpanzees

Herbert Simon

are finished, their memory may distort what they actually did to solve the problem.

The use of this "thinking aloud" technique is called **protocol analysis.** Newell and Simon (1972), for example, used this technique to study how people solved puzzles where each letter stands for a digit and the goal is to figure out which digit each letter stands for. Newell and Simon analyzed such protocols by means of a *problem behavior graph* that shows the path the person followed in solving the problem, including all the false starts and backtracking.

The Problems of "Set" in Problem Solving

One important problem in problem solving (and thinking in general) is that people tend to repeat actions that have been successful in other circumstances. Sometimes this can lead to inefficiency and difficulty in solving new problems. The classical demonstration of this problem involving "set" is in a series of experiments by Luchins (1942). Luchins tested more than 9,000 people on this "water jar" problem: You have three jars; jar A holds 21 quarts, B holds 127 quarts, and C holds 3 quarts. How can you measure out 100 quarts? Most likely you would fill the

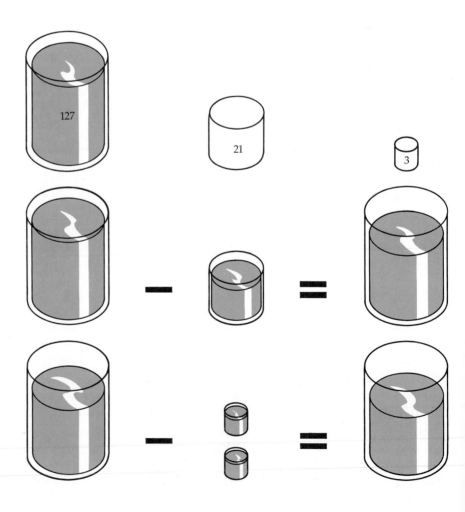

FIGURE 10–5
The Luchins Water Jar Problem

127-quart jar, then pour 21 quarts into jar B, then 3 quarts into jar C twice. Now solve the five problems in Figure 10–5.

This solution can be written as a formula (B − A − 2C). You find you can solve them using the formula. However, look again at the fifth problem. A much simpler solution is A − C. People who see this problem first usually use this simpler solution. But those who work through the other problems first tend to use the more complicated formula and in repeating it with the fifth problem they may fail to see the simpler solution at all. Thus, success and efficiency with one approach and one kind of problem can be responsible for difficulty and inefficiency in solving some new problems.

Creativity

Life is more than solving problems. People go beyond problem solving to inventing solutions. One characteristic of creativity is that it may involve things as simple as cooking a new dish or as grand as a new scientific theory. The need for humans to create is quite basic. We have been inventing ways to deal with unexpected situations for at least a million years.

Generation and Evaluation

Campbell (1960) proposes that creativity works this way: ideas are generated at random; some are retained (selected) because they are useful or have adaptive value. Creativity is thus considered a process similar to natural selection, in which there are random variations, some of which prove useful and are "selected" by the environment. Here the idea is that people generate many ideas, almost at random, and a few of them are appropriate, and become selected. Chance plays a great role in both the generation and the evaluation of ideas.

Generation of ideas is the primary stage. People who have a lot of ideas are more likely to have creative ones. A useful creative idea is rare. Campbell (1960) emphasizes:

> [The tremendous amount of nonproductive thought] must not be underestimated. Think of what a small proportion of thought becomes conscious, and of conscious thought what a small proportion gets uttered, what a still smaller fragment get published, and what a small portion of what is published is used by the next intellectual generation. There is a tremendous wastefulness, slowness and rarity of achievement.

Thousands of small and wrong ideas help prepare the way for an occasional useful one. Thomas Edison was supposed to have evaluated his progress on an invention by saying that he now knew a hundred ways that wouldn't work.

So creativity involves hard work and the relentless generation of ideas and thoughts, to produce a few that pass evaluation. *Evaluation* is the assessment of the worth of an idea. In an important passage, the psy-

FIGURE 10–6   Water Jar Problems

Problem	Jar A	Jar B	Jar C	Goal
		(IN QUARTS)		
1.	2	40	4	30
2.	1	27	6	14
3.	2	16	3	8
4.	7	59	12	28
5.	23	49	3	20

Source: Adapted from Luchins & Luchins, 1959.

chologist Wickelgren (1979) writes that ''it is perhaps more important to *recognize* a good idea than it is to possess one.''

As Pasteur said, ''Chance favors the prepared mind.'' That is, when something unexpected happens, it takes training to recognize whether it is significant.

The Process of Creation

There have been many analyses of creativity and most have come to generally similar conclusions. Creativity involves four processes: preparation, generation, evaluation, and implementation (Johnson, 1972). *Preparation* involves immersion in the subject, and often an especially intense period just before the solution. Poincaré, in the example above of

Edison at work on one of his many inventions.

THE CREATIVE PERSON

People are not totally "creative" or "noncreative." However, there are certain characteristics that may make it easier to express ideas creatively. Some of the characteristics would, however, indicate that people who think unusual thoughts often lead different lives from the rest of us.

Isaac Newton, for instance, spent almost 16 hours a day locked up in his rooms at Cambridge working on his ideas. If you spend too much time being like everybody else, you *decrease* your chances of coming up with something different.

insight, began his discussion by saying that the problem had occupied him constantly for 15 days. Generation and evaluation have already been discussed. *Implementation* involves actually carrying out the idea, after the assessment of its worth. Only a few of the useful ideas get implemented, because only rarely is there anyone to put up with the further work of carrying them out. Thomas Edison said that genius is 1 percent inspiration and 99 percent perspiration.

LANGUAGE

The primary way we express our thoughts, share our ideas, and reveal our solutions and decisions is through speech. Language is probably the greatest human achievement. Talking makes it possible for a group to plan and carry out a very complex activity together; it makes it possible to teach, to transmit to a new generation what happened in the past. In our society and most civilized countries, history and culture are passed down in books. But even among illiterate primitive people the primary vehicle for the transmission of culture is words. Every human culture has a language; every normal human being has the ability to speak.

It is important to note that all language is creation; every sentence we utter is an on-the-spot invention. Unless you are giving a prepared speech, everything you say is instantly put together in response to a new situation. *All children as they grow up can recognize millions of sentences and exclamations that they have never heard before!*

Education increases our store of knowledge, and most of that knowledge is stored in words. Every profession has its own vocabulary. The particular vocabulary, or jargon, speeds up communication among colleagues. Words like "schema," "cognitive," "neurotransmitter pathways" ought to contain meaning for you now. (I hope!)

Even a child of three, with little complex language ability, can communicate basic needs, ideas, and questions. A single word like "hungry" will serve as important communication. "Where's Daddy?" communicates a different, more complex thought. Sentences can be extraordinarily complex in structure, but "I wonder where father might possibly have gone today?" is not a much more complex thought than "Where's Daddy?"

Elements of Language

Speech Acts

The different forms of language are termed speech acts (Austin, 1962). Three important speech acts are associated with different kinds of sentences. A **declarative sentence** conveys specific information, such as "Jamaica is a country in the Caribbean." A *question* demands information, as in "Do you have any quarters?" or "Will you give me a kiss?" An *imperative* conveys a command: "Please give me the salad."

Phonemes

The sounds of a language are called **phonemes.** A particular sound is considered a phoneme only if it is used in language. The sound of *d* is used in words and is a phoneme; the grumbling sound we make when we clear our throat is not. A way to isolate a phoneme is to say a word and systematically change one of the sounds until the word changes into a different word. If a change in a single sound transforms one word into another, this will identify phonemes. There are three phonemes in the word *bat* (b/a/t). A change in the first phoneme can give pat, or vat; a change in the second phoneme can give bit, bet; a change in the third can give ban. The phonemes in standard American English are listed in Figure 10–7. Note that phonemes within words differ between different dialects. Merry, marry and Mary are pronounced identically in parts of the Midwest.

Morphemes

Phonemes are as meaningless as individual letters. The phoneme *b* in *bet, bat,* and *bit* has no common meaning. Phonemes combine to make units of meaning, called **morphemes.** A morpheme can be a word, such as car, but, or teach. Morphemes can be fragments; prefixes and suffixes are themselves morphemes: plurals are indicated by the suffix *s*. Other morpheme prefixes and suffixes include *pre, dis, un, ing, es, est*.

Words such as "dis+em+body" are made up of three morphemes; the high-school spelling bee favorite, antidisestablishmentarianism, is made up of seven morphemes (anti+dis+establish+ment+ari+an+ism). English has only 26 letters, but they combine to make over 90,000 morphemes, which in turn combine to make about 600,000 words, which can be made into an almost infinite number of sentences.

Syntax

A word is the normal unit of meaning. Words form sentences, and spoken sentences form conversations. We speak without being conscious of the elements. Children learning to talk often do not actually know they are speaking words (Donaldson, 1978); however, written language is by nature more formal and self-conscious. The thought contained in a sentence is meaningful only if it follows the specific rules of

---

FIGURE 10–7 Phonemes in General American English

Vowels

ee as in heat	ʌ as in ton
ɪ as in hit	*uh* as in the
ɛ as in head	*er* as in bird
ae as in had	*oi* as in toil
ah as in father	*au* as in shout
aw as in call	*ei* as in take
U as in put	*ou* as in tone
oo as in cool	*ai* as in might

Consonants

t as in tee	*s* as in see
p as in pea	*sh* as in shell
k as in key	*h* as in he
b as in bee	*v* as in view
d as in dawn	*th* as in then
g as in go	*z* as in zoo
m as in me	*zh* as in garage
n as in no	*l* as in law
ng as in sing	*r* as in red
f as in fee	*y* as in you
θ as in thin	*w* as in we

Source: Denes & Pinson, 1963.

language. **Grammar** is the study of those rules of language; how words are arranged to convey meaning is called **syntax.** Although syntax and grammar are the bane of most students in school, we speak fairly grammatically all the time.

There are specific rules in language, both written and spoken. *An Example:* "The boy the ball the road hit on" is meaningless; it is not a sentence. "The boy hit the ball on the road" conveys a thought. When children begin to speak they utter *essentially* grammatical sentences, and though children's sentences are simple and not in perfect syntax, almost every sentence is original, not an imitation of other sentences they have heard.

Surface and Deep Structure

When children begin to speak they are naturally adept and make relatively few grammatical errors. Therefore many scientists characterize the grammar of language as being innate. The leading proponent of this view, called **transformational grammar,** is Noam Chomsky (1966). He believes that an important distinction in syntax is between "surface" and "deep" structure. *Deep structure* is the underlying network of thought conveyed in a sentence. The *surface structure* is the actual sentence that carries the deep structure. A *transformation* occurs that changes the deep structure (or meaning) into the surface structure (the expression in words). Because there are many ways to say the same thing, a single deep structure has many possible variations in surface structure. *An Example:* "The large elephant saw the small mouse" and "The small mouse was seen by the large elephant" have the same deep structure, but have a different surface structure.

Sometimes the surface structure can be confusing and could derive from two different deep structures. In this case, knowing the deep structure is the only way to understand the sentence. In other words, you must have an idea of what the person is talking about. The following sentence is ambiguous: "They are visiting firemen." Figure 10–8 shows a transformational grammar analysis of the two sentences that show the different deep structures. A similar analysis of the two sentences above, about the large elephant and the small mouse, reveals that they share one deep structure.

Meaning

Our discussions of mental activities have emphasized the search for order and meaning and the ability to go beyond the information given, to fill in the gaps. This tendency is called *active processing.* When we listen and when we read, we attend selectively and "fill in" an enormous amount of information. The meaning of something causes us to complete the gaps in the elements of language—words or letters. As we read text, we are able to make good predictions the words we expect to see. These predictions are usually good enough to allow us to fill in the missing "about" in the preceding sentence.

Context determines what we hear. "I went to the new display last night" can get a shocked reaction from someone who heard "I went to the nudist play," because the sounds are the same. A friend of mine reported wondering, as a child, why she never saw pictures of "Gladly the cross-eyed bear" in church, although he was mentioned in prayers and hymns! Active processing is the way we analyze specific sounds and language patterns and how we search for meaning. When the sounds are ambiguous or difficult to hear, we fill in the gaps. Warren and Warren (1970) did an interesting study on this process. People heard the following:

"It was found that the __eel was on the _____." There were four different words that ended the sentence:

axle

orange

shoe

table

They were asked to repeat what they had heard.

Those who had heard "axle" recalled the sentence as: "It was found that the *'wheel'* was on the axle." Those who had heard orange also heard *"peel,"* those who had heard "shoe" inserted *"heel,"* and those who had heard "table" inserted *"meal."* The subjects did not *think* that they were *guessing* the word, but that they had *actually heard* the sentence. They "filled in" the sentence with the most likely element.

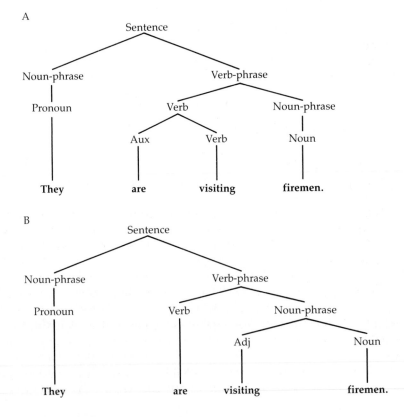

FIGURE 10–8
Transformational Grammar Analysis
Analysis A indicates some people are paying a visit to firemen. Analysis B identifies "they" as firemen who are visiting (or, actually, any important visitors—termed "visiting firemen"). (After Chomsky, 1966)

How We Understand Each Other: Conversational Maxims

We have looked at the structure of language and analyzed some of its elements, such as phonemes, and the ways in which words and thoughts are organized, as into surface and deep structures. But it is hard to go from these elements to an understanding of how we actually communicate. Take the following exchange:

SARAH: I think I have a headache.
JANE: Well, there's a store open around the corner (Miller, 1981).

Now, what are these people doing? What is the relationship between the first and second statements? The relationship between two speakers follows what is called the **cooperativeness principle:** each speaker tries to understand *why* the other said what he or she did. In this case, the implication is that the store sells something that might relieve the headache. Otherwise the exchange makes no sense.

Following the cooperativeness principle, there are four **conversational maxims** that speakers usually obey when they speak (Grice, 1967):

1. Quantity. Make your contribution as informative as required, but not more so. If someone asks "Where do you live?" the answer will depend on where you are. If you live in San Francisco, California, and you are in your neighborhood, you may say "Green Street." If you are in London, you may say "The U.S.A." or "California." It would be idiotic to tell someone in London that you live on "Green Street." If you are in San Francisco, you would never say "I live in the U.S.A." It violates the maxim of quantity. However, sometimes this maxim is deliberately violated.

BILL: How did you like your date last night?
BOB: Well, she had nice shoes.

Here Bob is not being as informative as is usually required and therefore implies something about his date: he says nothing about her personality and most likely means that he did not like her much.

2. Quality. Try to be truthful in conversation. This maxim is often violated in the use of metaphor and in indirect speech. "I hated the movie." "Yes, I thought it was swell too." The second speaker signals agreement by violating the principle.

3. Relation. Contributions should be relevant to the conversation. Suppose the boss says "It's hot in here." You realize that you should turn on the air conditioning or open the windows. Why? Because the statement "It's hot in here" is *not* simply a statement of fact. Since we use the maxim of relation, the statement implies a specific idea about the situation.

4. Manner. Be clear and orderly. When this is violated, the underlying intention usually is still clear. Take the statement in a review: "Ms. Mal-

The sounds of a language are called *phonemes*. A particular sound is considered a phoneme only if it is used in language. Phonemes are meaningless as individual letters but combine to make units of meanings called *morphemes*. A morpheme can be a word, such as car, but, or teach, or can be a fragment, such as a prefix or suffix. A word is the normal unit of meaning. Words form sentences, and spoken sentences form conversations. *Grammar* is the study of specific rules of language; how words are arranged to convey meaning is called *syntax*.

An influential theory of language by Chomsky, called *transformational grammar*, proposes that the grammar of language is innate. In this view there is an important distinction in syntax between surface and deep structure. Deep structure is the underlying network of thought conveyed in a sentence. The surface structure is the actual sentence that carries the deep structure. A transformation occurs that changes the deep structure (meaning) into the surface structure (the expression in words).

An important aspect of determining meaning in a sentence is the ability to go beyond the information given. This tendency is called *active processing*. When we listen and when we read, we attend selectively and fill in an enormous amount of information.

Terms and Concepts	algorithms means-end analysis

Terms and Concepts

algorithms
anchoring
artificial category
availability
basic level category
biases
conversational maxims
cooperativeness principle
decision analysis
declarative sentence
grammar
heuristics
hypothesis testing
insight

means-end analysis
morpheme
natural category
phoneme
problem representation
protocol analysis
prototypes
representativeness
subgoals
syntax
taxonomy
transformational grammar
typicality

Suggestions for Further Reading

Johnson-Laird, T. N., & Wason, P. C. (Eds.). (1977). *Thinking: Readings in cognitive science.* Cambridge: Cambridge University Press.
A useful sourcebook on the general varieties of thinking.

Kahneman, D., Slovic, P., & Tversky, A. (Eds.). (1982). *Judgment under uncertainty.* New York: Cambridge University Press.
A compilation of much of the classic work on how we use "heuristics" in judgment, how we make mistakes, and the nature of the mental system that underlies these processes. Technical, but interesting and worthwhile.

Miller, G. A. (1981). *Language and speech.* San Francisco: W. H. Freeman.
An elegant, entertaining, and witty introduction to the question and the problem of understanding language.

Smith, E. E., & Medin, D. L. (1981). *Categories and concepts.* Cambridge: Harvard University Press.
One controversial theory about how categories are organized and combined to form concepts.

Chapter 11

The Concept and the Controversy of Intelligence

INTRODUCTION

It seems so simple, to understand what is intelligence and who is intelligent. To be intelligent is to use the mind well. We think someone is smart for working out an elegant proof in mathematics, but also for something as mundane as maneuvering a sofa through a small door. We call a move in chess, or a football play, brilliant. The common element is that someone acts with excellence and originality. Yet the concept of intelligence—what it is, who has it, how it can be measured—is perhaps the most controversial topic in psychology.

Many people think that intelligence is a fixed quantity. It is not. It is, rather, a *varied array* of abilities and talents. Although intelligence is not an inherited trait like hair color, there is almost certainly a genetic component to intelligence which describes the range of an individual's potential for intellectual development. Educational institutions are built on the premise that achievement skills can be developed.

The intelligence test is psychology's most visible contribution to society. It directly affects people's lives. Individuals who attain low scores on intelligence tests may be classified as "minimally educable" or "educable mentally retarded," and placed in a special school or classroom designed to meet their special needs. If a test is mistaken, children may mistakenly be placed in a program that will restrict their intellectual growth and affect. It is a serious question whether or not intelligence tests are biased in that they favor verbal, white, middle-class students and are, therefore, unfair in measuring people of different ethnic groups with different cultural standards and even different styles of learning.

But this test bias issue is only one of the controversies in the psychology of intelligence. Others are: What is intelligence? Is there one kind, or many? Do intelligence tests actually test intelligence? Do different races have different intelligence? Why are some people more intelligent than others? How much of intelligence is inherited, and how much is the result of experience and opportunity? These are very serious issues, and we will consider them carefully.

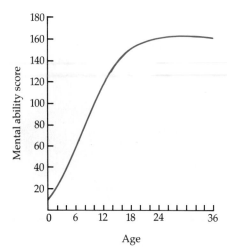

FIGURE 11–1
Increased Mental
Abilities in Childhood
The theory that children's
intelligence increases as they get
older is illustrated by this growth
curve. Clearly, there is a rapid
increase in childhood and a leveling
off in early adulthood. (After Bayley,
1970)

2. Binet realized that to meet society's demands he would have to make intelligence testing applicable to large numbers of people. The questions he posed would help sort children into "bright," "average," and "below average" ranks. To accomplish his goal, he first tested children who *already* were performing at these levels in schools. He scored the differences in their performance on tests of reasoning, judgment, memory, and comprehension. The tests developed with these children were then used to test other children whose scholastic abilities were unknown. The similarity of their performance to the children in the original group could be used as an indicator to predict future success in school.

3. Binet noted that *as children age, their intellectual abilities increase*. The brightest three-year-old is hardly a match for an average nine-year-old. Therefore, age is a critical factor in test performance and must be taken into account in the analysis of the test results and the test itself. Binet used the term "mental level" to refer to the intellectual achievement reached by the student. This concept was later modified into a **mental age** score (Terman & Merrill, 1937).

Cognitive development was measured by Binet's tests and converted into a score that would identify which children were exceptionally smart, normal, or retarded. In addition, Binet reasoned, mental and chronological age are related. A bright child may be defined as one whose mental age is greater than his or her chronological age; a slow child as one whose mental age is less than his or her chronological age. French schools of the time used the results of these tests to design curricula and to assign children to classes. Children whose test scores showed they were below average would either be given special training or else excused from the attendance requirement entirely.

The early Binet tests were given by one examiner to one student and took several hours to administer and to score. Then, once again, a change in society directly affected the field of intelligence testing: World War I broke out. It was a war vastly different from any waged before. It was the first war in which so many millions of men from the general population were required to fight, and the army needed to know the capability of its unknown, untrained, and untried soldiers. Psychologists were called upon to develop intelligence tests that could be administered simultaneously to large groups and which could be easily scored. The specific scores became more important than they had been in Binet's original tests, because they were the primary factor in the determination of assignments of soldiers. Group administration of tests and reliance on the score as the primary measure remained the norm even after the war ended.

Current Intelligence Tests

Many current intelligence tests follow Binet's idea that items testing problem solving, reasoning, and judgment abilities are better measures of intelligence than is sensory acuity. Because in our society a lot rides on an individual's test scores (a person may be put in special classes, denied

The pri
intention:
taught in
school. Tl
different f
with IQs
itations, tl
to do well
sole meas
discussion
of intellige

Tests of

The Se

One of t
eral faculty
investigatic
called *g*, re
gave peopl
tor" *g* cou
nique callee
test scores.
mance can
correspond
each indivi
not closely
represents

The notic
as complex
gent" for tl
mental abili
ity to learn.
ered a mosa
ally" intellig
tasks, while
write well. 1
ment for a t

Even if ea
independc
different
described
pendent
probably
(Thurstor

Thurstone
on mental al
primary fact
ther doubt or

---

admission to schools or professions), it is essential then that the tests be *reliable* and *valid*. **Reliability** means that test scores are reproducible and consistent. For example, if a test is supposed to measure general intelligence or aptitude, then test scores should be the same no matter when or where the test is taken, or by whom it is scored. There should be no unclear or ambiguous questions that could be interpreted differently by different people. Second, a test must have **validity,** which means that it must measure what it is intended to measure. We can measure something like hair color or height *reliably*, but neither of these is a *valid* measure of intelligence. Intelligence tests, modeled after Binet's and still in use today, appear to be a quite strong predictor of a child's success in the existing school system and a predictor of success in society. Whether they are valid measures of "intelligence" is another question to which we will return. Now we will examine the most popular standardized tests of intelligence.

Stanford-Binet

The original Binet test was adapted by Lewis Terman of Stanford University and standardized on American students in 1916 and is known as the Stanford-Binet Intelligence Scale. A new test is *standardized* by giving the test to a representative sample of the test population. An average score is derived and used as the standard against which successive generations of test takers are compared. The Stanford-Binet was restandardized in 1937, 1960, and 1972. The current test departs little in concept from the original Binet test: items are administered by an examiner, and the individual is scored in relation to the standard for his or her age group. Sample items from a Stanford-Binet test appear in Figure 11–2.

The **IQ** originally was a number that related a person's mental age (MA) to his or her chronological age (CA). It is derived by first dividing the mental by the chronological age (MA/CA = IQ), and then multiplying by 100 to remove decimal points. Thus a child who tests at a mental age of 10 when 8 years old has an IQ of 125 ($10/8 = 1.25 \times 100$).

In Binet's day each test item was assigned a score relating to mental age. In the Stanford-Binet, a more efficient and more precise statistical measure was introduced. It was called the **deviation IQ.** Individuals were scored according to their relation to their age group's average score on the test. The current test is further refined: it is standardized with a norm of 100 (that is, the group's average score on the whole test is arbitrarily assigned the value of 100) with a standard deviation of 16. Thus, an individual who scores one standard deviation above the norm is assigned an IQ of 116, two standard deviations above is an IQ of 132. The Stanford-Binet has been continually modified to assess individuals at the upper and lower ends of its range more accurately.

Wechsler Tests

David Wechsler devised the popular Wechsler Adult Intelligence Scale (WAIS-R) and the Wechsler Intelligence Scale for Children (WISC-R). The advantage of WAIS-R and WISC-R over the Binet test is that they test two major areas of intelligence: *verbal* and *performance* (which deals in

tests of mental ability, some excel on some measures, others on different ones (Stevenson, Friedrichs, & Simpson, 1970). These and other findings have led psychologists to consider that there are many *different kinds* of abilities that make up intelligence.

Fluid and Crystallized Intellectual Abilities

Many recent analyses have tried to determine how many and what kinds of intellectual abilities there are. Raymond Cattell (1971) divides intelligence into two major *kinds* of abilities:

Fluid abilities are involved in the perception and registration of the world and are thought to be genetically based and more or less independent of cultural learning. Understanding perceptual relationships and memory span are examples of fluid abilities. **Crystallized abilities** derive from *specific* cultural experiences and are represented by the store of gradually accumulating knowledge. They can be tested by vocabulary measures, mathematics, and social reasoning. The evidence for the difference in the two stems from the fact that fluid abilities seem to reach their peak at the age of 25 and then decline, while crystallized abilities continue improving as long as the individual is active in the culture (Willerman, 1979).

"The Structure of Intellect" Model

The most complex and ambitious attempt to analyze the components of intelligence is Guilford's model of the **structure of intellect** (1967, 1971). Guilford conceives of intelligence as a large set of abilities, each different and distinct from the other. In Guilford's model these abilities are arranged in a cube. Each side of the cube represents a different function of the mind: Contents, Operations, and Products (Figure 11–7).

Contents describe the information in the mind, which is divided into four categories:

1. Figural (pictures and images)
2. Symbolic (letters and numbers)
3. Semantic (the knowledge of language and how it is used)
4. Behavioral (the knowledge needed to deal with other people)

Operations are the working rules of the mind. They involve evaluation, convergent thinking (being able to give the correct answer to a problem), divergent thinking (inventing new ideas), memory, and cognition (discovery).

The *Products* dimension is more abstract, but has to do with how things relate to one another in the mind. Products are: units (which are similar to categories); relations (the similarities between things); systems (organizations of independent parts, like plans or programs); transformations (changes, redefinitions, and modifications of information); and implications (expectations and models of what will happen).

Guilford has devised a number of specific tests to measure specific kinds of mental abilities. In this way each pattern of intelligence of a specific individual might be studied.

FIGURE 11
Occupation
The vertical
bars indicat
men in each
the average
such jobs as
and teacher
of the occup
that some n
have IQs hi;
score in any

Guilford's model may well be wrong in detail and even in its overall shape. It is hardly reasonable that intellect will look like a perfect cube; additionally, Guilford's work has been criticized on the grounds that the factors are neither exhaustive nor are they independent of one another, and some seem arbitrary (Cattell, 1971). Guilford's specific methodology has also been severely criticized (Horn & Knapp, 1973). But I include this model because it is important in its general conception. I agree that each person's intelligence is best considered a *mosaic of specific intellectual abilities and talents which form an individual portrait of intelligence.* For instance, one person may be good at art and bad at math, another the reverse, a third good or bad at both. As we have seen, we consider one person "smart" who picks the right stock, another "smart" who proposes a new theory. Intelligence, then, is probably made up of many *separate* abilities and is different from individual to individual. People are much more individual in their assortment of specific characteristics than we normally give them credit for; although, of course, *some* people are more generally intelligent than *some* others.

An important question remains. Given that we each differ in the abilities in which we are strong, how much effort should an individual devote to strengthening weak areas? In some cases the time and effort would be more efficiently spent strengthening our strong suits. The amount of time it would take for me to become even a passable playwright is disproportionately enormous compared to the time it would take for me to become an expert psychologist. Because life is short, I may do well to choose psychology over the theater. This means that people should not always try to improve their worst aspects, but sometimes develop their best. The idea of a well-rounded, all-around smart person, as appealing as it is, is probably just a concept of ours; it simplifies our personal and professional assessment of people, but does not do justice to our own complexity and that of others.

FIGURE 11–7
Guilford's Model of
the Structure of Intellect
Guilford considered the factors constituting intelligence to be the 120 distinct abilities (blocks in the cube) used to perform each of the mental *operations* on the different *contents* to obtain the various *products*. (After Guilford, 1967)

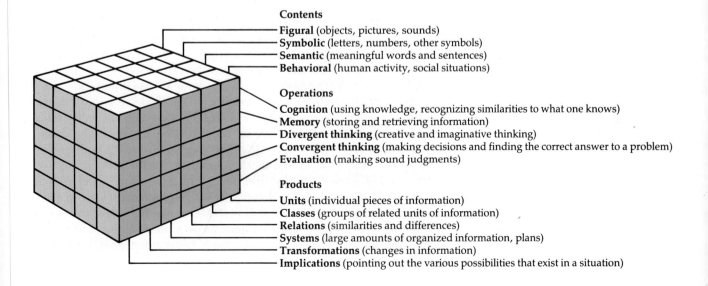

Contents
Figural (objects, pictures, sounds)
Symbolic (letters, numbers, other symbols)
Semantic (meaningful words and sentences)
Behavioral (human activity, social situations)

Operations
Cognition (using knowledge, recognizing similarities to what one knows)
Memory (storing and retrieving information)
Divergent thinking (creative and imaginative thinking)
Convergent thinking (making decisions and finding the correct answer to a problem)
Evaluation (making sound judgments)

Products
Units (individual pieces of information)
Classes (groups of related units of information)
Relations (similarities and differences)
Systems (large amounts of organized information, plans)
Transformations (changes in information)
Implications (pointing out the various possibilities that exist in a situation)

Problems with Studies of Heritability and IQ

There is, it would seem, some relationship between genes and IQ. However, most of these studies have been criticized on several grounds, and the precise estimate of the heritability of intelligence is still in great dispute.

The studies of selective breeding by Tryon and others do not show a strong effect on *intelligence* per se. Searle (1949) showed that the maze-bright animals were superior only in the particular maze that Tryon used. The maze-dull animals were equal in performance to maze-bright rats in several other mazes. This indicates that something other than "intelligence" was inherited. For instance, when the illumination of the mazes was changed, the maze-bright animals performed less well, which suggests that sensitivity to a particular level of illumination may have been inherited, but not "intelligence."

In adoptive studies and in the studies of twins raised apart, the precise estimate of heritability is confounded greatly by the fact that the adoptions are very often not random. In many cases, the environments of two separated twins are quite similar. Some were raised by relatives, often close relatives. In some cases the twins knew each other, and knew that they were twins (Kamin, 1976). The problem with adoptive studies is that adoption agencies go to great lengths to place children in homes that are not only fairly stable and middle class, but also "compatible" with those of their biological parents. For example, in many cases a black child is adopted by a black family, an Oriental by an Oriental one, and so on. Although this matching of children and family is laudable from the

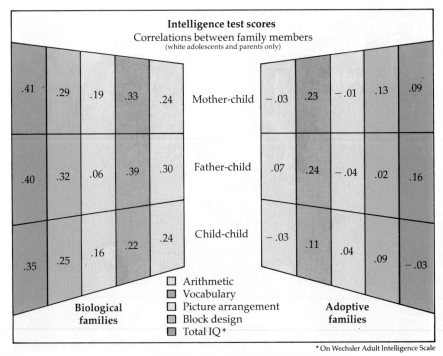

FIGURE 11–10

IQ in Natural and Adoptive Families The IQ scores of children and their natural parents and siblings show a considerably higher correlation than the scores of children and their adoptive families. This suggests there is at least some genetic element in intelligence. (After Scarr & Weinberg, 1978)

Intelligence test scores
Correlations between family members
(white adolescents and parents only)

Biological families:

	Arithmetic	Vocabulary	Picture arrangement	Block design	Total IQ*
Mother-child	.41	.29	.19	.33	.24
Father-child	.40	.32	.06	.39	.30
Child-child	.35	.25	.16	.22	.24

Adoptive families:

	Arithmetic	Vocabulary	Picture arrangement	Block design	Total IQ*
Mother-child	−.03	.23	−.01	.13	.09
Father-child	.07	.24	−.04	.02	.16
Child-child	−.03	.11	.04	.09	−.03

Legend:
☐ Arithmetic
◩ Vocabulary
☐ Picture arrangement
◩ Block design
◼ Total IQ*

*On Wechsler Adult Intelligence Scale

point of view of the child and the family, it makes precise measures of the heritability of IQ more difficult! Because the adoptive family is often quite similar to the biological family, the influence of the often-similar environment may make the observed relationship between the IQ of the biological parents and the child appear greater than it actually is.

The difficulties in these studies make it very difficult to estimate precisely the exact relationship between heritability and the IQ. One of the leading proponents of the genetic argument in the IQ controversy believes that 81 percent of IQ is inherited (Jensen, 1969, 1980). One of the clearest studies that correlated the *unwed* mother's IQ with the child (brought up by another family) gives a much lower estimate of 25 percent (Scarr, 1982). And Kamin points out that the inaccuracies and lack of direct evidence in many of the studies makes it *essentially impossible* to estimate the heritability of the IQ accurately. However, most investigators agree that there is *some heritability* of IQ, although whether it is .1 or .5 is quite difficult to assess. Indeed, it would be surprising if there were no genetic component to IQ. The information encoded in the genes could fill approximately 1,700 thousand pages the size of the one you are reading. Some of that information might be related to the reasoning and problem-solving skills and talents, which have been important in human evolution, and also happen to be tested by the IQ.

Racial Differences in Intelligence

No issue in psychology is more controversial than the question of inherited differences in intelligence among the different races. The evidence is straightforward but it has been subject to different interpretations. The average IQ for black Americans is 85 to 90, for whites it is 100.

In a celebrated article in 1969, Arthur Jensen argued that compensatory education programs that attempt to improve the intelligence of black children fail because the difference in IQ is innate. Another psychologist, Richard Herrnstein, who believes that IQ is inherited, thinks that the United States will eventually develop into a "meritocracy" based on heredity.

> As the wealth and complexity of human society grow, there will be precipitated out of the mass of humanity a low capacity (group of people) that . . . cannot compete for success and achievement and are more likely to be born to parents who have similarly failed. . . . The tendency to be unemployed may run in the genes of the family about as certainly as bad teeth do now. (Herrnstein, 1973)

However, every ethnic group that has migrated to the United States has been the subject of arguments such as the above. For instance, when the descendants of the people who participated in the Italian Renaissance first came to the U.S., they too were considered to be of inferior intelligence (Willerman, 1979).

The question of racial differences in intelligence has enormous ramifications. Let us try to examine and clarify some of the basic concepts underlying this important issue: the concept of intelligence and how it relates to IQ and to the environment in which intelligence is defined and tested.

The Interpretation of Racial Differences in Intelligence

The claim that blacks are *genetically* inferior in intelligence rests on several assumptions: that the IQ is synonymous with intelligence; the IQ is a measure of a fixed trait like eye color; that race is an important biological distinction; that heredity is more important than environment.

1. The IQ score is intelligence:

The IQ is a *test score* developed by Terman from Binet's test designed to discriminate groups of children who could and who could not profit from normal schooling. It is remarkably successful in its purpose. However, there are few psychologists now who would agree that there is any *single* measure of intelligence. The idea that intelligence can be accounted for by a simple factor has been given up in favor of the idea that intellect is a *composite* of different abilities. There is no single number which can adequately indicate a complex human intelligence.

2. The IQ represents a fixed capacity:

Change in the environment strongly affects IQ. A severely impoverished early experience stunts intellectual growth. However, when children in an impoverished environment are provided more stimulation, their IQ increases (Skeels & Dye, 1939). Other enrichment programs, which we will summarize later on in the chapter, produce an increase. The IQ is talked about in everyday language as a measure of a fixed aptitude, but it is actually only a measure of *current achievement* on certain tasks. The quality of education, coaching on test taking, improvements in motivation, more positive attitude to schools, improvements in facility with language, and other factors can increase the test score. There is no disagreement over the fact that less-well-educated people score less well on IQ tests. A very low score on the IQ probably means that the individual needs some compensatory education, as Binet intended, or has some brain damage.

3. "Racial" differences exist, and are important:

The division of the human species into races was first formally classified by Linneaus (1707–1778), who believed that the distinction was important and that races differed (not only in color but also in personality characteristics). However, Linneaus's "racial" classifications are essentially arbitrary. People evolved different skin colors to adapt to different climates. There are any number of ways to categorize and classify human beings into "races": by height, hair color, eye color, nose size, and others. *A person's skin color tells you nothing more about intelligence than hair color.*

The major characteristic differences between races are skin deep: they consist of superficial adaptations such as skin color, eye folds, sweat glands. There is no evidence of differences in brain size, shape, organization, or structure, or in any other mentally relevant classification between races.

In a recent study that investigated 178 different populations divided into 16 different racial subgroups, the genetic differences between different racial groups were almost nonexistent. This means that even if you know the *exact pattern* of someone's genes it is difficult to say what race he or she comes from.

4. The difference between groups of blacks and whites is due to heredity.

Because individual intellectual abilities can be inherited does not mean that group characteristics are inherited. *People get their genes from their parents, not from a group.* There is no way to extrapolate from individual differences to group differences (Ehrlich & Feldman, 1977). There are far more differences between individuals within a racial group than between groups.

However, even if race were a more profound distinction, the evidence is against there being any differences between "black" and "white" genes on intelligence. In a study of heredity and IQ, the ancestry of a group of blacks was compared with the obtained IQ scores. If whites were innately more intelligent than blacks, then blacks with more "white" genes should have scored higher on IQ. But that was not the case: more white genes do not increase IQ (Scarr, 1981).

Another way to compare the possible effects of heredity and environment on IQ is to compare the results of interracial marriages, where the genes for intelligence should be equal. But IQ results are not equal. Children of a black father and a white mother tend to have higher IQs than children of a white father and a black mother (Scarr, 1981). Such a difference can be explained by the fact that white, middle-class women talk to their children more than black mothers do (Willerman, 1979). But it also points out that the environment, especially the mother-child relations, may have an important relationship to IQ, something we will return to when we consider how intelligence might be improved.

In addition, many other factors can influence IQ performance. Educators in Israel were confronted with very large cultural differences in IQ between Jews of European ancestry and Jews from the Arabic countries. European Jews scored higher. These differences were larger than the black-white differences in the United States. However, when children of both cultures are reared communally on the kibbutzim, exposed to the same opportunities and education, the IQ differences disappear and the children average above 100 (Smilansky, 1974).

There are many other factors in the United States that influence IQ scores. Blacks in general have a poorer environment than whites. Early experiences and nutrition have long-lasting effects on intelligence. Environmental deprivations, if continuous, can be devastating to the child. Blacks in the U.S. have more nutritional deficiencies than whites. The larger the size of the family, the more IQ decreases (Zajonc & Markus, 1974). Blacks have larger families than whites. Even when blacks attain the same socioeconomic levels as whites, they often cannot live where they choose, or go to the schools they choose.

414 The Concept and the Controversy of Intelligence

A Conclusion

There are, therefore, many reasons to doubt that there are *important* genetic differences in "intelligence" among racial and ethnic groups. It is important to remember that intelligence is not measured by a single IQ score; that intelligence is still not adequately defined, and that it cannot be reduced to a single quantity or process. Further, the biological differences between the races are superficial, but the environmental differences are profound, in the United States at least.

Based on the observed differences in IQ scores, it is probably not profitable to conclude that blacks are *genetically* inferior to whites. It is probably more profitable to focus attention and effort on enriching the environment of children who score lower on intelligence tests, and to develop other measures of "intelligence" than the IQ alone. Some psychologists have suggested that the concept of intelligence be enlarged to include athletic skills and tests of adaptation to new situations (Gardner, 1984).

In addition to the development of new assessment programs, perhaps we should return to Binet's earliest notion and use the IQ solely to aid in helping children whose environment has been deficient, and to identify those with organic deficits. In the past several years many programs and studies have strengthened the notion that intelligence, or at least some aspects of intelligent behavior, can be taught. It is to this evidence and these new attempts that we now turn.

CAN INTELLIGENCE BE TAUGHT?

Most of the factors that seem to affect the IQ differences between whites and blacks in the United States are experiences in the environment. The environment can be changed: improved nutrition and more stimulating environments have systematically increased IQ test scores. Preschools and Head Start programs in the U.S. and an ambitious program in Israel are currently attempting to increase IQ. These attempts largely concern the remediation of disadvantaged children, those whose IQs are far below normal. Can these children be brought up to the normal range?

Biological Factors in Intelligence: Nutrition

During gestation and in the first year of life, the brain is the fastest-growing organ. It consumes nutrients at twice the rate of the adult brain and is thus heavily dependent upon dietary intake. If there is a severe deficiency in the very first months of pregnancy, there can be lasting and irremediable damage to the brain and therefore to intelligence. Severe childhood malnutrition can produce many effects lasting seven or eight years (Kagan, 1978). However, some effects of early deprivation *can* be overcome by later improvements in nutrition.

One study investigated the effects on children born to Dutch mothers pregnant during a six-month famine during the Nazi occupation. Nutrition was adequate after the famine and there were no deficits in IQ scores found at 19 years of age (Stein et al., 1972). In a study of 11-year-olds, who were malnourished as infants, but given adequate nutrition later on in life, performance on IQ tests was normal (Winnick et al., 1975).

A specific program of nutritional supplements can increase IQ. In one study, iron and B complex were given to one group of pregnant black southern women, another group was given a placebo. At four years of age, the mean IQ of those whose mothers had received supplements was 102, while those whose diets were unsupplemented was 94 (Harrell et al., 1956). Where there is a specific dietary deficiency, food supplements are found to increase IQ. In one study, a group of students deficient in ascorbic acid were regularly given some orange juice. In six months the IQs of those who had been low on ascorbic acid increased an average of 3.5 points. There was no change in IQ for a control group who had no ascorbic acid deficiency.

Nutrition has a profound effect on the brain both in its development and its day-to-day operation. Many recent studies show that the action of neurotransmitters is affected by food intake within hours. Therefore, it should not be surprising that improvements in nutrition could have a great effect on intelligence. It is even conceivable, though unstudied, that differences between what two individuals have eaten within hours of taking a test could explain differences in IQ scores.

Neurotransmitters   See Chapter 4, pp. 157–60.   Neurotransmitters and Food   See Chapter 4, p. 161.

Stimulation in Early Experience

Recall that most of the brain's growth (75 percent of its weight) occurs outside the womb. Therefore, certain early experiences can have a strong effect on brain development and, consequently, intelligence. Studies of rats reared in "enriched" and "deprived" environments show that the "enriched" rats have larger brain size, as measured by the depth of the cortex (Diamond, 1980). Changes in experience cause the rat brain to grow throughout life. Cortical growth continues into very old age if the environment remains stimulating. The brain is quite responsive to changes in the outside environment (Diamond & Connors, 1981). Thus changes in early experience can affect the brain, and perhaps intelligence.

For instance, rural Guatemalan children are reared in windowless huts, have no toys, are rarely spoken to for the first year of life, and show extreme retardation at the end of the year (Kagan & Klein, 1973). When the environment is changed and they are allowed to explore, communicate, and eat better, their development begins to proceed more normally, although it takes many years for them to catch up to children whose first year of life was more normal. There is much less difference between them and normal children at 10 than at 1 (Kagan, 1978).

The human brain is remarkably resilient. Early traumas and deprivations can be overcome if later experience is more benign. The effects of poor nutrition on intelligence can be overturned by improved diet. Intelligence, which suffers in a deprived environment, improves in a normal environment.

Orphanage Studies

Orphanages can have a negative effect on a child's mind, because they are often bleak places that offer little human contact and minimal external stimulation. In Dennis's study in a Lebanese orphanage, the average IQ of the orphans was 63; in a well-baby clinic, 101 (Dennis & Najarian, 1957). When these orphans were simply propped up in their cribs for an hour a day so that they could see what was going on, they showed dramatic improvement.

Howard Skeels (1966) observed the effects of institutionalization on the development of baby girls in an orphanage. At 15 and 18 months, they were sick and retarded. After they were transferred to a more suitable institution, their health was restored and their intelligence scores were higher. Skeels decided to test the hypothesis that stimulation and attention (tender, loving care) is important in the development of intelligence. He placed 13 orphanage children with an average IQ of 64 (range 35–85) in an institution for retarded adults. Each orphan was "adopted" by an older woman. All the adoptees became "favorites" of and were doted on by the patients and staff. A control group was selected, comprising children between 1.5 and 6 years old, who remained in the same or in a similar orphanage. The control group's IQ *dropped* an average of 20 IQ points. The "adopted" orphans *gained* an average of 28 points. This

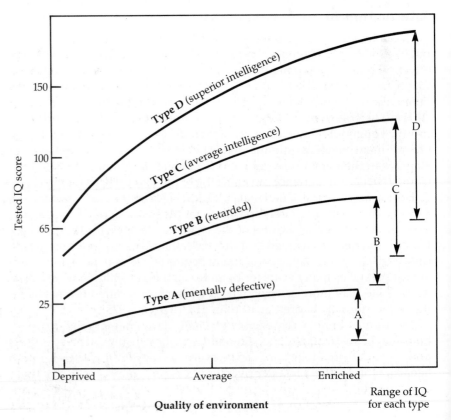

FIGURE 11–11
IQ and the Range of Reaction to the Quality of the Environment
An individual's measured IQ will vary, depending on the quality of the environment in which that person is raised. So even someone with a potential for superior intelligence (Type D) might test fairly low in IQ if raised in a deprived environment. Note that the range of reaction is wider for individuals with a greater genetic potential for higher intelligence. (See also Figure 2–22, p. 76.) (After Gottesman, 1963)

The environmental deprivations experienced by children raised in poverty or in institutions can produce extreme retardation. But if the quality of their environment is improved (including improvements in their diet) such children begin to show more normal development and, eventually, they can catch up to children who enjoyed the benefits of good diet and a stimulating environment from the first year of life.

study has been criticized for some methodological flaws: there were large sex differences in the sample; the differences between the "adopted" and control groups were large at the start (Willerman, 1979). However, the improvements in IQ are so large that they are encouraging to those who seek to aid intellectual development by enriching the environment. The effects were long lasting. As adults, *all* of the orphans in the adopted group were self-supporting, while only 6 of the 11 surviving members of the control group were self-supporting. Eleven of the 13 adopted were high-school graduates and 5 had gone to college. Their IQs were, on the average, 104 (Skeels, 1966).

Programs to Develop IQ: General Enrichment Programs

The results of Skeels and others encouraged development of various enrichment programs aimed at increasing IQ. For example, many parents now send their children to preschools, in the hope that such early training will enhance intellectual development. Children in preschools typically show an initial increase in IQ during the preschool years and a decline to the norm at around the second grade. The programs that emphasize academic skills *alone* are most likely to show a later decline, while those preschools that emphasize *curiosity* and *self-motivation,* such as the Montessori schools, show the greatest long-term gains (Miller & Dyer, 1975).

Head Start

In 1965, a large-scale experimental program of preschool enrichment in underprivileged areas in the United States was initiated. The program was called **Head Start.** All over the country many preschools began trying to enrich the environment of 4-year-olds. There were many different curricula at each Head Start center. This insured that programs might more closely fit a community's needs, and research could be conducted to find out which programs were the most successful. The results followed a pattern similar to the study of more traditional preschools. There is an initial increase in intellectual functioning (Berger, 1980), followed by a decline almost to the level of the norm.

A major setback to the Head Start program came in 1969 when the Westinghouse Report claimed that Head Start did not work, because children in the program showed no improvement in IQ over non–Head Start children. That report led a lot of people to question the concept of enrichment and it prompted Arthur Jensen to conclude that blacks cannot benefit from an improved environment. Jensen proposed that the reason Head Start did not work is that blacks are simply intellectually inferior to whites and that it is a waste of time and money trying to develop compensatory education programs. However, while Jensen's view has gained wide currency, it is extreme and shared by very few people in psychology or education. The evidence of the Westinghouse Report must be examined quite carefully and matched against the original goals of the Head Start program.

Even though the programs are different in different areas and of uneven quality, children in Head Start programs, on the average, get better grades at school and score higher on achievement tests. In addition, the evaluation of the program had, probably, unrealistic expectations. The Head Start enrichment program was evaluated after only a few years of operation, and in a very experimental phase. They were still trying to find out which programs worked and which did not. That extremes of cultural differences and deprivations were not completely overcome by a few hours a day of enrichment over the course of one summer is not surprising. Besides, two major goals of Head Start—preliminary to increases in IQ scores—were improvements in health and nutrition and encouraging parental involvement in their children's education.

Children in the Head Start preschool enrichment program tend, on the average, to get better grades in school and higher scores on achievement tests. Although there is some controversy over whether or not Head Start children show improvement in IQ, they do show improved health and nutrition, and they benefit from their parents' increased involvement in their education.

The "Toy Demonstrators" Program

The most successful interventions to improve IQ, at least in the United States, are those that attempt to *change the pattern of mother-child interaction*. The most successful of these was devised by Phyllis Levenstein (1970). In this program, a "toy demonstrator" visits mother and children *at home*. Usually this is done twice a week for two years, beginning when the child is between 24 and 28 months old. The visitor brings a toy or a book as a gift and demonstrates to the mother how to play games with the child, especially those involving language.

The IQ of the children involved in this program increased during the two years of the program, but, more important, the effect lasted for a long time. Three years after the program ended, the "toy demonstrator" children had IQs 13 points higher than a comparable group who had not been visited. Further, it was found that nonprofessionals were equally successful as demonstrators as the original ones who had been professionals. Some of the mothers who had first been visited later joined the project as toy demonstrators.

The success of this program is probably due to the fact that so many of our intellectual and other skills important in schooling depend on language for expression, and language skills develop within the family. The mother spends much more time with her child than do teachers and has been the primary "teacher" of language (at least in the pretelevision age) as well as other skills (Bruner, 1978). *Changing the mother-child interaction seems to be an important intervention in increasing intelligence.*

Mother-Child Interaction in the Toy Demonstrators Program
Increasing meaningful interaction between mothers and children—especially in games involving the development of language skills—seems to contribute to increasing the children's intelligence.

Instrumental Enrichment

The programs we have discussed so far are **general enrichment** programs; they seek to *generally* raise the amount of stimulation in the environment or of interaction with a child. Many new programs designed to improve intelligence have been designed or are in the works. We focus

here on one promising attempt, instrumental enrichment. **Instrumental enrichment,** which attempts to develop *specific* techniques and assessments for increasing intelligence, is a recent experimental approach in Israel.

Although there is not yet a fully worked out program for a new intelligence assessment, Reuven Feuerstein, the developer of I.E., makes several important distinctions that may well improve the effort to improve intelligence (Feuerstein, 1979):

1. *There is a difference between* **cultural deprivation** *and* **cultural differences.** Individuals who are culturally *deprived* are lacking something in their own culture, while those who are culturally *different* may belong to a culture that is different from the one they are living in. Cultural *differences* can lead to a deficiency or an improvement in the *content* of intelligence, while cultural deprivation in this analysis can lead to a deficiency in the *structure* of the mind. These two distinctions are often confused in testing. A wrong answer on a test by the culturally *different* might simply be due to not knowing the language, whereas a culturally *deprived* person may lack the reasoning and thinking skills necessary to answer. These two kinds of mistakes are very different and indicate very different needs of the person taking the test.

2. *Intelligence has to do with making adaptive responses in new situations.* The Binet-type tests are tests of current *achievement* rather than tests of an underlying mental structure. Therefore, a new kind of intelligence test, to Feuerstein, ought to be one in which the testee *learns* something during the test rather than recalls information. I.E. thus attempts to measure the learning ability of the individual directly.

Cognitive Modifiability

The ability to *change* one's mental structure and contents is called **cognitive modifiability.** Learning, for instance, involves a change in contents: thinking involves a change in the structure of information in consciousness. Since the function of all the mental processes is adaptation to the environment, it should also be the focus of testing.

> The neglect of cognitive process has conspired to produce a widespread belief that intelligence is something that one either has or does not have and that attempts to change the structure and course of intellectual development are futile, if not impossible. (Feuerstein, 1980)

Mediated Learning Experience

People provide us, and especially provide the child, with a mediated learning experience. **Mediated learning experience** means that information about the world, events, and experiences is *interpreted* by others, usually a parent or sibling. Thus the *meaning* of events is often given to us by other people. Consider a child who sees a growling dog and approaches it, but the mother says "watch out!" The child learns to avoid growling animals through its mother's *mediation*. "The mediator selects the stimuli that are most appropriate and then frames, filters and schedules them; he determines the appearance or disappearance of certain stimuli and ignores others" (Feuerstein, 1979). Feuerstein feels that the roots of intelligence may be found in the adequacy of the mediated learning experience. Mediated learning experience can be insufficient even in the presence of a living parent or other dedicated caregiver. One example is the difference in the phrasing of the same basic request, "Please buy three bottles of milk," versus, "Please buy three bottles of milk so that we have enough left for tomorrow when the shops are closed." The second request provides a much greater opportunity for learning on the part of the child than the first, although the same action is required in both cases (Feuerstein, 1979).

There are many possible causes of poor mediated learning experience: obvious ones are schizophrenic parents, parental indifference, or extreme difficulty with a child, as in autism. However, more common interpersonal barriers for excellent mediated learning experience are cultural differences.

Learning Potential Assessment Device (LPAD)

The main target group for instrumental enrichment programs is people who are below the norm on standard tests of intellectual skills like IQ. The aim is remediation of retarded individuals. When testing retarded people, the aim is to identify their specific deficits and point to possible remediation. This is the subject of the **learning potential assessment device** (LPAD). The LPAD differs from other tests in the way it is used and scored, but is similar in the tasks employed. The premise of LPAD design is that if a test is to measure human intelligence, it must be representative of real life. In life we are rarely called upon to recall one paragraph or select a number that fits into a progression, but we are often called upon, in collaboration with other people, to learn. The "tester" in the LPAD is involved in teaching the retarded performer new tasks: the measure of success is how well, under these conditions, the person learns and modifies his or her abilities—that is, demonstrates "cognitive modifiability." This is done in a "test-train-retest" paradigm (how the testee improves or gets worse between the first test and the retest). The tasks are varieties of "content free" intelligence tests. The training consists of exercise sheets designed to guide the testee into learning successful strategies for solving the problem. The tester in the LPAD situation is not an examiner but a "committed teacher." When the student makes a new response or tries a different approach to a problem, the teacher tries to make it happen again.

The Instrumental Enrichment Program

While general enrichment programs improve overall performance on intelligence tests among people who are substandard, the instrumental enrichment program attempts to pinpoint the process of enrichment. The program is designed to provide remedial mediated learning experiences so that retarded children can learn how, in the future, to learn from their own experience. The specific program consists of a wide variety of tasks to be completed under the guidance of a specially trained instructor. The tasks range from the inference of geometric figures in dot patterns to spatial orientations to syllogisms.

Initial Assessment of Instrumental Enrichment

How well does it work? The appropriate comparison for instrumental enrichment is a program of general enrichment. With a sample of Israeli children, the I.E. program shows significant, though not immense, improvement over controls in a general enrichment program, using as assessments the LPAD and other measures such as the Stanford-Binet, the WAIS, Thurstone's Primary Mental Abilities Test, and more. An

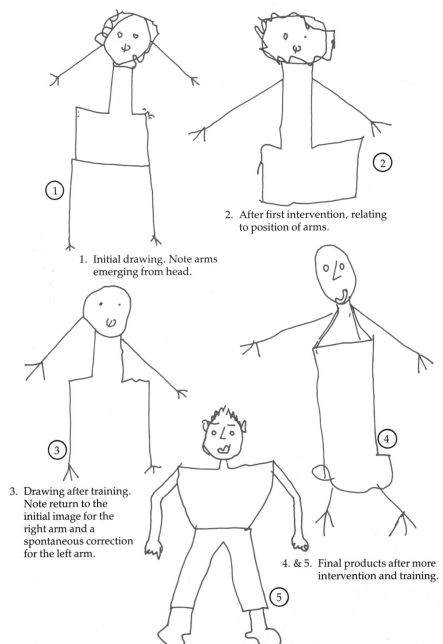

1. Initial drawing. Note arms emerging from head.

2. After first intervention, relating to position of arms.

3. Drawing after training. Note return to the initial image for the right arm and a spontaneous correction for the left arm.

4. & 5. Final products after more intervention and training.

Instrumental Enrichment (I.E.) Using the Learning Potential Assessment Device (LPAD)
LPAD procedures helped an intellectually retarded, culturally deprived ten-year-old show progressive improvement in drawing a human figure. (After Feuerstein, 1979)

assessment of I.E. programs by the Israeli military reveals impressive gains. The results show that, after I.E., formerly retarded service-age youths are equal to controls from the general population. It must be emphasized, however, that the assessments are quite tentative, since few people not involved in the training group have had a chance to make their own independent assessment (Feuerstein & Rand, 1977).

An Evaluation of Instrumental Enrichment

Instrumental enrichment, along with other recent approaches to intelligence, is too experimental for a final evaluation. The strength of the approach is that it attempts to develop a more complete view of intelligence and to remediate specific deficiencies. Yet, I.E. still has certain difficulties to overcome. The tester's role raises questions:

1. Is a good score the reflection of a good interaction between tester and testee rather than the performance of the testee? Feuerstein (1979) acknowledges the possibility but points out that the fact that learning takes place *at all* in a "retarded" person is surprising, significant, and important.

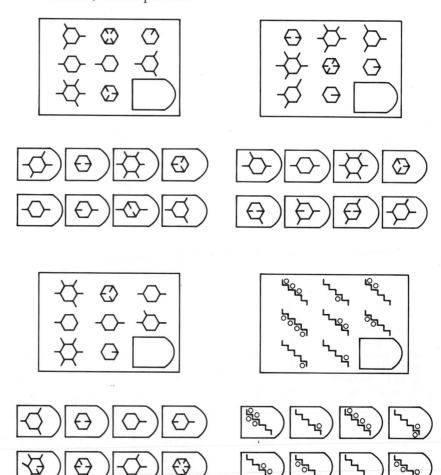

FIGURE 11–12
Examples from an LPAD
Content Free Intelligence Test
(After Feuerstein, 1979)

2. The administration of the test is very complex and is difficult to systematize, which leads to the problem of how to interpret scores, especially low ones. It is difficult to know whether a failure to improve reflects the tester or the testee.

The use of the LPAD raises another question: children showing high modifiability before I.E. are considered good candidates for the program. In no case, in exhaustively documented studies, does Feuerstein describe a child who has shown initially low modifiability and has had that score increased through I.E.

Name: Grade:

Date: School:

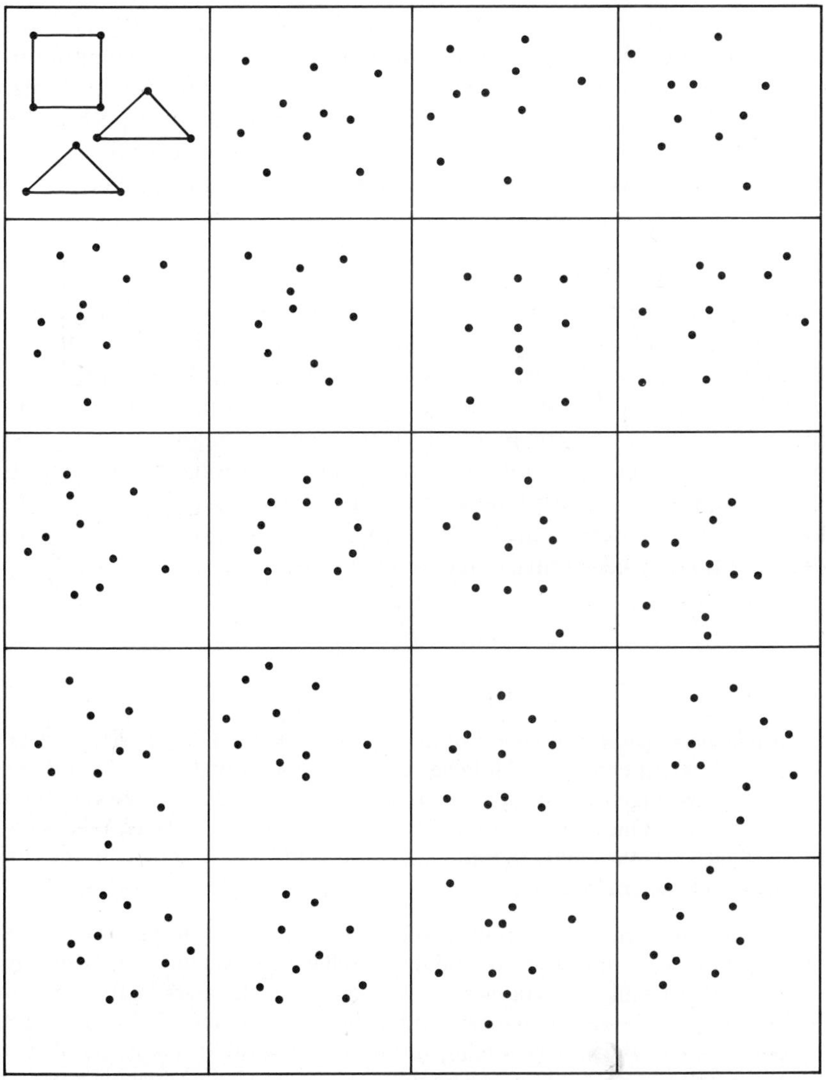

Test

FIGURE 11–13
An Organization of
Dots Test Used in an
Instrumental Enrichment Program
(After Rey & Dupont, 1953)

There is also no agreed-upon "index of modifiability"; the term is not yet fully defined. The scoring of this measure of the important concept "cognitive modifiability" is undeveloped and may be difficult to define, which will continue to make claims of improvement hard to verify and validate. Still, I.E. may provide the basis for both a new assessment of intelligence and a way to improve it. Already elementary school teachers in countries such as Venezuela are required to learn the method.

CONCLUSION

Now we return to one of the most common problems in intelligence research. If intelligence is conceived of as a specific and fixed quantity, it is easy to test, score, standardize and categorize students, but that assessment may be inadequate and sometimes destructive. Defining intelligence by taking into account modern cognitive and developmental psychology is an extremely complex and difficult process. A thorny problem. We are able to measure fairly precisely what most people generally agree is an extremely limited, and therefore not useful, vision of human intelligence. When we try to tackle the subject in all its complexities, intricacies, and forms, our measures do not yield such neat, tidy and efficient scores.

Both general enrichment programs and instrumental enrichment are encouraging. We may develop a new way to analyze intelligence, assess intelligence, and perhaps even improve intelligence. It does seem clear that intellectual skills measured by IQ and other standardized tests can be improved in a beneficial environment and learning situation. Thus the responsibility and the focus of future research might well be placed on the role of teachers and the quality of educational environments. Although not all of the programs may survive, they may make it possible to define more carefully and more completely how and when someone uses the mind well—that is, acts intelligently.

Summary

1. Intelligence has always been a difficult problem to define. Different societies have different concepts of intelligence; different individuals have different ideas of intelligence. Psychology has also had a very difficult time of defining intelligence. One definition that is most useful is from David Wechsler— intelligence is the ability to understand the world and to cope with the challenges of the environment.

2. Around the turn of the century, Alfred Binet and his colleagues laid out an important new approach to studying intelligence. Among Binet's insights were: (1) Directly test actions that are regarded as the mark of an intelligent student, such as comprehension and the ability to reason. (2) In accord with society's demands, make intelligence testing applicable to large numbers of people by sorting children into bright, average, and below average ranks. (3)

As children age, their intellectual abilities increase; the brightest three-year-old is hardly a match for an average nine-year-old. Therefore, age must be considered as a critical factor in testing intelligence, and norms must be developed for each age.

The original Binet test was adapted by Lewis Terman of Stanford University and standardized on American students in 1916. It is known as the Stanford-Binet test.

In the Stanford-Binet a more efficient and precise statistical measure of a student's score is used, called the *deviation IQ*. Individuals are scored according to their relationship to their age group's average score on the test. The current test is now standardized with a norm of 100 (the group's average score on the whole test is arbitrarily assigned the value of 100), and the standard deviation is 16. An individual who scores one standard deviation above the norm is therefore assigned an IQ of 116.

The primary usefulness of IQ tests seems to be close to Binet's original intention: to sort children on skills our culture values, identifying those who are likely to profit from schools. The IQ does appear to discriminate better at the low rather than the high end of the scale. A child with an IQ of 60 is undoubtedly very different from the child with an IQ of 100, but the difference between people with IQs of 130 and 170 is not nearly as great. Although many people have criticized the IQ test as being too heavily relied upon as the sole measure of intelligence, it remains the *single* best instrument for measuring ability to do well in school.

3. One of the first questions in analyzing intelligence is whether intelligence is a general faculty, a trait characteristic of an individual. Charles Spearman, in 1916, employed a statistical technique called *factor analysis* to determine if general intelligence, which he called g, represented an entity related to "cerebral energy." Such notions of a single general intelligence are probably too limited to characterize the diversities of human beings.

A more important distinction seems to be that of Cattell, which divides intelligence into two major *kinds* of abilities. (1) *Fluid abilities* are involved in the perception and registration of the world and are thought to be genetically based and more or less independent of cultural learning. (2) *Crystalized abilities* are derived from specific cultural experiences and are represented by the store of gradually accumulating knowledge.

Another important attempt to analyze the components of intelligence is Guilford's *structure of intellect* model. In it, intelligence is characterized as a cube with different functions of the mind represented on each side: contents, operations, and products.

4. There is much current concern with the question of how much intelligence is genetically based. Studies that seem to measure the heritability of intelligence generally disagree. It is important, however, to note that even if there is a genetic basis for intelligence or specific intelligence skills, this, in itself, does not necessarily mean that one race or another is superior or inferior on these traits. People get their genes from their parents, not from a group. In the United States, for instance, there can be such great differences between the races in early nutrition, early environment, and culture that it would seem unwise to conclude on the basis of current evidence that there are any significant differences in intelligence between racial and ethnic groups.

5. Because of extreme differences in the early environment of different groups, psychologists are turning more attention to the ways in which environment

can be changed and, thereby, intellectual abilities can be increased. Among areas now being investigated are nutrition and more stimulating early environments. Preschools and Head Start programs in the United States and recent programs in Israel and Venezuela are currently attempting to increase IQ.

The effects of severe malnutrition in childhood can produce effects lasting seven or eight years; however, some effects of early deprivation can be overcome by later improvements in nutrition. In one study, a group of students deficient in ascorbic acid were regularly given orange juice and in six months their IQs increased an average of 3.5 points.

Lack of stimulation in early experience has a profound effect on intelligence, but again this can be overcome. Rural Guatemalan children who are reared with little stimulation show extreme retardation at the end of the first year of life. When the environment is changed and they are allowed to explore, communicate, and eat better, their development begins to proceed more normally, although it takes many years for them to catch up to children whose first year of life was more normal. There is much less difference between them and normal children at 10.

6. One of the more successful programs to improve intelligence attempts to change the pattern of mother-child interaction. In this program a "toy demonstrator" visits mothers and children at home. Usually this is done for two years twice a week, beginning when the child is between 24 and 28 months of age. The visitor brings a toy or a book as a gift and demonstrates to the mother how to play games with the child, especially those involving language. The IQs of children involved in this program increased during the two years of the program, but, more important, the effect lasted for a long time.

7. One new and innovative attempt to increase intelligence is *instrumental enrichment*, which makes the following distinctions: (1) There is a difference between *cultural deprivation* and *cultural differences*. Individuals who are culturally deprived are lacking something in their own culture, while those who are culturally different may belong to a culture that is different from the one they are living in. These distinctions are often confused in testing intelligence. (2) Intelligence has to do with making *adaptive* responses in *new* situations. The Binet-type tests are tests of current achievement rather than tests of an underlying mental structure. Therefore, a new kind of intelligence test ought to be one in which the testee learns something during the test rather than recalls information.

An important concept in instrumental enrichment is *cognitive modifiability*— the ability to change one's mental structure and contents. Other people provide the child with a *mediated learning experience*. This means that information about the world, events, and experience is *interpreted* by others. The *learning potential assessment device* (LPAD) involves a testee learning something new in the presence of a tester, who tries to measure how well the person learns. The premise of the LPAD is that in life, we are rarely called upon to recall a paragraph or select a number that fits into a progression, but we are often called upon to learn in collaboration with other people.

The instrumental enrichment program consists of a set of mediated learning experiences so that retarded children, especially, can learn how, in the future, to learn from their own experience. While early results are encouraging, it is too early to tell for certain whether this ambitious and innovative program, or others like it, can be used to develop that most precious of human abilities—intelligence.

Terms and Concepts

cognitive modifiability	instrumental enrichment
crystallized abilities	IQ
cultural deprivation	learning potential assessment device
cultural differences	mediated learning experience
deviation IQ	mental age
factor analysis	reliability
fluid abilities	sensory acuity
general enrichment	structure of intellect
Head Start	validity

Suggestions for Further Reading

Feuerstein, R. (1980). *Instrumental enrichment*. Baltimore: University Park Press.

An important early statement about the possibility of improving intelligence.

Gardner, H. (1984). *Frames of mind*. New York: Basic Books.

A good and complete introduction to the theory of "multiple intelligence."

Glaser, R., & Bond, L. (Eds.). (1981). Testing: Concepts, policy, practice, and research [Special issue]. *American Psychologist, 36* (10).

A good introduction to many of the different aspects of testing.

Scarr, S. (1982). *Race, social class, and individual differences in IQ*. Hillsdale, NJ: Lawrence Erlbaum.

A good overview and presentation of the genetic evidence for the inheritance of some individual differences.

*W*e are a puzzle to our- selves and to others.

Some people seem like different people at different times. One is rude when you thought her nice, another surprises you with his generosity. You may have this same experience about yourself: you are different to your lover than to your boss.

Is someone "emotional," or "money motivated," "generous," or "cynical," we may ask. We discuss it with others and try and come up with a single simple description.

It is the same kind of puzzle as understanding intelligence. But people just cannot be reduced to a single number or phrase. We are a mosaic of abilities, predispositions, moods, and quirks. We are not the same person at all times.

We are a number of people.

Part Three

The World of the Individual

Chapter 12

Emotions and Feelings

INTRODUCTION

One summer evening I was stuck in traffic while driving home from the beach. The man in the car ahead of me got out of his car and walked over to the car next to him, which was driven by a young woman in a bathing suit. As he approached the car she said nothing, but first frowned, then snarled and almost hissed at him. Although there was no verbal communication or intellectual content, the man "got the message." He returned quickly to his car. The woman smiled in relief.

There is something quite important we have not yet considered in our analysis: it is the role emotions play in human experience. Our emotions are vivid experiences, and they communicate our own feelings to other people quite immediately. They also, in a real sense, "tell" us what to do. The woman, as she hissed, was tensed to defend herself, although she might have been unaware of this.

There is an *automatic* and *involuntary* quality to emotions which sets them apart from thinking and reasoning. When frightened we are almost automatically "primed" to run or to defend ourselves. You may decide to be "cool" when someone embarrasses you, but your blush may give you away. To borrow from e e cummings: "feeling is first." Emotions—like fear, anger, joy, surprise—are basic and immediate. We hear a strange noise and feel afraid first; then we determine if there is something to be afraid of.

We will consider, in this chapter, what makes emotions so central to our experiences and so special; which emotions are basic, which have to be interpreted, how we "read" other people, and how we "read" ourselves, too. At the end of the chapter we will continue a part of the story begun in Chapter 2, of how certain emotional experiences, such as love and sex, are unique and important parts of human experience.

WHAT EMOTIONS ARE, WHAT THEY DO, HOW THEY ARE EXPRESSED

We get angry and embarrassed often when we do not want to, or "fall" in love almost by accident. Emotions are similar among all peoples of the world, and even between humans and other animals. The emotions comprise relatively automatic patterns of responding to different situations. They are *involuntary* and seem beyond our conscious control (Averill, 1978). They simplify an organism's experience by preparing it for action. They almost certainly evolved before language and other forms of human knowledge.

The Function of Emotions

The word emotion has roots in the Latin word for movement, so emotions both guide and goad our actions. Although basic emotions and their expressions may be similar in many species of animal life, the role they play in human experience is unique. Human emotional experience is far more complex and intricate than that of any other animal. We are the only animal that laughs when happy, almost the only one that cries when sad (the bear is the other). Before we explore in detail the rich network of human emotional experience, let us first discuss why we have emotions—their function. Emotions *arouse* us, help *organize* experience, *direct* and *sustain* actions, and *communicate* actions.

Arousal

Emotions move us into action; they are a signal that something important is happening. An animal who becomes fearful and excited about an approaching attacker is more ready to respond and to defend itself. It would, therefore, be more likely to survive. A human who experiences sexual love is more likely to reproduce than one who does not. Emotions give action its intensity. Emotions, whether positive or negative, are arousing. We will see later why it is emotions that may be experienced as opposites (elation and anger, fear and lust) that often arouse the emergency system of the body into action.

Organization

Emotions help organize experience. Our emotional state tends to "color" perception of ourselves and others. This is a common experience; for instance, if your professor is in a grumpy mood, you know it is not the time to ask if you can hand your paper in late. The professor's "grumpy mood" may have been initiated by a family argument the night before or perhaps a traffic tie-up on the way to work. But the emotions have "spread" and have come to organize the professor's response to other events. The process is the same as the way finding a dollar causes us to reorganize our memory: we become happier about *everything*.

Emotions, then, can serve as schemata that aid in organizing consciousness (Bower, 1981). In a good mood, everything seems right with the world: we see it through "rose-colored glasses." In a bad mood, everything—from foreign policy to friendships—is seen in a more negative light. Recall that when an event enters consciousness, *all associated schemata* are brought forward as well. So it is with feelings. The presence of a feeling in consciousness influences perception. When you are angry, for instance, you tend to see others as angry as well, even if they are not (Bower, 1981). In an experiment on this, people who were hypnotically induced to feel a certain emotion and then taught something, remembered what they had learned better when they were again in that emotional state than in another one (Bower & Gilligan, 1980).

Directing and Sustaining Actions

An enraged organism is prepared to attack; a fearful one is prepared to flee; a joyous one is willing and eager. Emotions are simplifying guides to behavior, and they have adaptive value. Consider the happiness we derive from sweets. The pleasure derived from sweet-tasting foods encourages us to search for and find more sweet things to eat. Our sweet tooth had adaptive value in our evolutionary history because sweet fruits were more nutritious and unlikely to be poisonous. We avoid situations that cause us fear or other negative reactions. In a colorful passage, the psychologist Silvan Tompkins wrote, "If, instead of pain, we had an orgasm to injury we would be biologically destined to bleed to death" (1979).

Emotions not only initiate and direct action but *sustain* and engage action: when you are afraid you will probably run longer and faster than if you are bored. This is a reaction that is certainly useful in avoiding danger. Coaches recognize this by giving pregame "pep" talks, making the team "emotionally involved." The description athletes use is "pumped up," one case where slang is quite accurate.

Communication

Most animals have evolved display signals, such as odors, postures, facial expressions, and gestures, that communicate information about probable behavior to other animals. These signals and gestures are called "social releasers." A dog cannot say "please go away," and so it snarls. The message gets across. (See Figure 12–1.) Although humans can com-

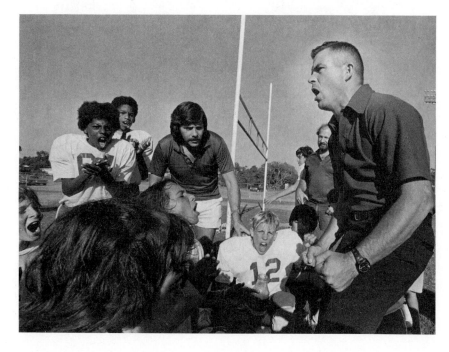

A football coach gets his players "pumped up" emotionally by giving them a pregame pep talk to initiate, direct, and sustain their actions on the field.

municate in language, words are usually accompanied by nonverbal signals with emotional content: facial expression, tone of voice, and body posture often convey meaning or what is "between the lines." A person may express interest in what you are saying, but the blank stare, yawns, and passivity signify boredom.

The Basic Emotions

We rarely experience a "pure emotion," just as we rarely see primary colors. Emotions combine, are shaded and muted. Some psychologists hypothesize that there are several basic or "pure" emotions, similar to the primary colors. These emotions then combine in different mixtures to make complex emotional experiences. But unlike visual or other sensory experience, no one has yet discovered specific structures in the brain or body that correspond to specific emotions (as the specific receptivity of rods and cones corresponds to visual experiences). There are many theories on the origin of emotional experience, which are in general agreement over basic emotions (Izard, 1977; Plutchik, 1984; Tomkins, 1984). We present one current and intriguing theory below (Plutchik, 1980).

Robert Plutchik's theory of emotions compares emotions to color experience. Recall that primary colors—red, green, yellow, and blue—are determined by the receptive characteristics of the eyes. All other

FIGURE 12–1
Some of the Many Facial Expressions Chimpanzees Use to Communicate Emotions
These diagrammatic drawings, done from photographs and descriptions, illustrate "glare," anger (A); "scream calls," fear-anger (B); infant's "cry face," frustration-sadness (C); "hoot face," excitement-affection (D); and "play face," playfulness (E). (After Ekman, 1973)

A

B

C

D

E

PSYCHOLOGICAL TERMS USED TO DESCRIBE VARIOUS ASPECTS OF EMOTIONAL LIFE

Affect is a term used by psychologists to refer to the feeling dimension of life. It may be used to characterize the general outward emotional expression. Someone with a *flat affect* displays little or no emotion.

Emotions are relatively specific and automatic patterns of short-lived responses, physiological and mental, which arouse, communicate, direct, and sustain behavior.

Feelings are the subjective experience of emotions; they can be complex experiences. Jealousy is not, then, an emotion but a feeling comprised of many different emotions, including envy and anger.

Moods are relatively long-lasting states of feeling. A mood sets the emotional backdrop of experience. People who are in a good mood are more likely to help others than someone in a bad mood. Moods color experience. In fact, color words are often used to describe moods: blue mood, a black mood, rosy or sunny mood.

Temperament is the most permanent and characteristic aspect of emotional life. Temperament is a predisposition to specific emotional reactions in certain situations. One person will become angry at social injustice, another will be sad, a third indifferent. One person has a sunny disposition, generally sees the bright side of things; another is a sourpuss and sees misfortune in the same things. (From Ekman, 1984)

---

colors are made up of combinations of these primary colors. Based on evidence from extensive scaling of subjective responses, Plutchik postulates that there are eight "primary emotions" that combine in different ways to make up the simple and complex feelings we experience. These **primary emotions** are *joy, acceptance, fear, surprise, sadness, disgust, anger,* and *anticipation.* These basic emotions produce new combinations in the way they vary on three dimensions.

1. They may vary in *intensity.* Surprise intensified is amazement; intense anger is rage, intense disgust is loathing. Less intense fear is apprehension, less intense disgust is boredom.

2. They may vary in *similarity.* Disgust is more similar to sadness than it is to joy.

3. Emotions also vary on the dimension of **polarity.** Love is the opposite of hate; sadness is the opposite of joy.

The "Emotion Wheel" and the "Emotion Solid"

These considerations have led to a model of emotions that begins with the **emotion wheel** modeled after the color wheel and shown in Figure 12–2. Here the eight primary emotions are arranged in a circle of opposites. More complex emotions are formed from combinations of the simple ones. For example: The combination of the adjacent pair of joy and acceptance yields love; awe is a combination of fear and surprise. The combination of emotions once removed, such as fear and sadness, results in despair; anger and joy make pride. The intensity dimension is described by the **emotion solid,** which conveys that emotions are most distinct from one another at the highest levels of intensity (at the top of the model) and least distinguishable at the lowest end of the model. Loathing is very different from grief; disgust is different, but less so, than sadness; and boredom and pensiveness are quite close.

Are Emotions Universal?

Does everyone have the same emotion? Different things make different people happy, obviously, but is the *experience* of happiness the same to everyone? You have probably noticed individual differences in the role one emotion or another plays in different people's lives. One person is easily angered, another apprehensive. Some people give their emotions more weight in actions and decision making than others; we may even describe someone who does this as "emotional."

But these are all differences in *degree,* not in kind. Research initiated by Charles Darwin in 1872 and continued today confirms that there are universal emotions found in all cultures.

Studies on Universality of Emotion

The evidence for the universality of emotion rests on several different observations: the similarity in emotional expressions among different

FIGURE 12–2
Plutchik's Emotion Wheel
This model has the eight primary emotions arranged in a circle of opposites. More complex emotions (dyads) resulting from combinations of adjacent primaries are shown just outside the wheel. Additional combinations, of primary emotions once removed on the wheel, produce such emotions as despair (from fear and sadness) and pride (from anger and joy). And a similar emotion solid describes the various emotions in terms of their relative intensity. (After Plutchik, 1980)

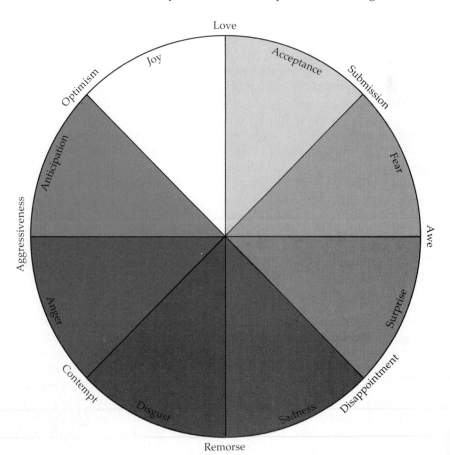

species; the similarity in emotional expression among widely different human groups that have had no contact with each other; the similarity of emotional expression among blind infants, normal infants, and adults.

Charles Darwin (1872) observed that all peoples of the world, from an Oxford Don to an aborigine, express grief by contracting the facial muscles in the same way (Figure 12–3). This is true of the other emotions as well. In a rage, the lips are retracted and teeth clenched. There are similarities in the snarl and in disgust (Figure 12–4). All over the world, flirting is signaled by a lowering of the eyelids or the head, followed by direct eye contact (see Figure 12–5) (Eibl-Eibesfeldt, 1971). Embarrassed people all over the world close their eyes, turn their heads away or cover their faces. And anger is recognizable in all cultures (Figure 12–6).

**FIGURES 12–3, 12–4, 12–5, and 12–6
The Universality of
Emotional Expression**
People in different cultures all over the world express emotion in quite similar ways. This suggests there is an innate component to emotion. You can notice this yourself: you immediately know what these people are feeling. The women in Figure 12–3 (left) are obviously expressing grief. The facial expression of the man in Figure 12–4 (below, left), although he is not part of our culture, is completely recognizable as disgust. One look at the girl in Figure 12–5 (below, center) reveals she is flirting. And people from any culture would instantly realize that the man below (Figure 12–6) is angry.

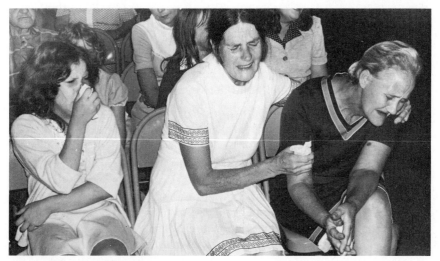

Emotional Expression in Infants

Emotional expression seems to be in large measure maturational—it develops naturally in a predictable sequence. Like motor skills, it begins as undifferentiated and disorganized and gradually becomes more refined and precise.

Bridges (1932) observed the progressive differentiation of emotions in a study of 62 Canadian foundlings over 3 to 4 months. At first, infants show "general excitement" to all stimuli, increased muscle tension, quickness of breath, increased movements. This general arousal gradually becomes differentiated into expressions of distress (at 3 weeks), anger (3 months), disgust (3–6 months), fear of strangers (7–8 months), jealousy and envy (15–18 months). The predictable, reliable sequence of these changes indicates an innate maturational component to emotions.

Crying occurs earlier than smiling, perhaps because crying is more related to immediate survival needs. In addition, *attachment*, the substratum on which feelings of love and belonging develop, seems to be an inborn biological-emotional bond between the mother and the child.

Attachment See Chapter 3, pp. 110–13.

Emotional Responses in Infants Born Blind

Eibl-Eibesfeldt (1970, 1980) filmed children born deaf and blind and found that basic facial expressions—smiling, laughing, pouting, crying, surprise, anger—occurred in appropriate situations. Blind children show the same pattern of development of smiling as sighted children, with the difference that social smiling becomes increasingly responsive to the mother's voice and touch instead of to her face (Fraiberg, 1971).

In humans, emotional expression is primarily expressed in the face (Ekman, 1984; Tomkins, 1984). The facial musculature of animals below

The universality of emotional expression extends to infants (even infants born blind). Although their ability to express various emotions only emerges over time, the forms of emotional expression they gradually develop are similar to those seen in adults.

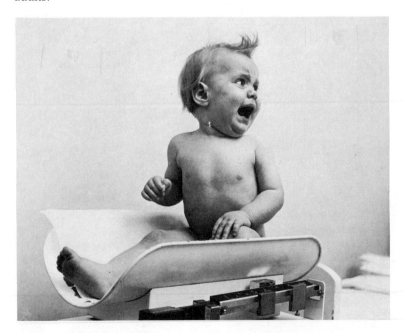

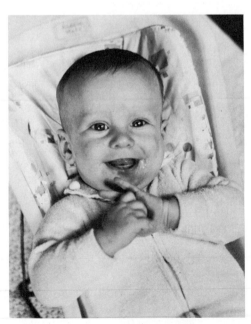

the level of mammals does not permit much more than the opening and closing of the mouth and eyes. Mammals, especially primates and humans, have more complicated patterns of muscles that allow a variety of facial expressions. In addition, because gorillas, chimpanzees, and humans have a more upright posture, their faces are much more conspicuous to others than in lower animals. There is also increasing frontal orientation of the eyes and, in humans, stereoscopic vision, which leads to sharper focus on other animals' faces. Facial hair is relatively lacking in humans and is further accentuated by the framing of head hair. The face is the primary organ of human social communication, followed by bodily gestures (Ekman, 1984), although other body movements, such as hands and feet, are being investigated (Frey, 1982).

HOW WE EXPERIENCE EMOTIONS

Although emotions may be judged by facial expressions, the emotional reactions themselves involve the autonomic nervous system. Interestingly, the actual bodily response pattern in emotions matches quite closely the colloquial expressions: "my heart leapt when I saw her," "I've got butterflies in my stomach." The cardiovascular and gastrointestinal systems are involved in most emotional reactions and signify emergency arousal in the sympathetic nervous system. However, it is important to note that generally similar activation patterns are common to all emotions. That we differentiate emotions, and experience one as fear, one as lust, means that we must interpret our physical reactions. Just as our perceptual processes can be tricked with ambiguous figures and illusions, emotions can sometimes be mislabeled and misunderstood.

It happened to me once. A few years ago, I flew from San Francisco to Los Angeles to give a lecture. I enjoy lecturing and was looking forward to the meeting. I was listening to the speaker who preceded me, waiting for my turn, when a most bizarre thing happened. I began to feel shaky, worried, uneasy. When I noticed this, I began to berate myself, silently: "I should have prepared more . . . I should have written out my speech. . . . Why didn't I fly in last night and get a good night's sleep before the talk?" And there were more worries and ideas on what I should have done.

What was most surprising was that I had never felt like this before in my life. I lecture often on subjects I know well; I was prepared. But was I nervous!

Then it began to dawn on me, slowly. I truly felt "shaky." My arms were shaking, so was my hand. But then I looked around. The *table* was shaking, the glasses on it almost spilled their water. The podium was shaking. I turned around, and there it was. The old air conditioner was rumbling, vibrating everything around it, including me. As soon as I saw the air conditioner, I wasn't nervous.

What happened to me was almost a classic experiment in emotion. It is also similar to what happened to you when you looked at the cube in the perception chapter. There, your hypothesis about the cube became

HOW TO READ FACES

The face of emotion is complex. The brain's control of the facial muscles is exquisite: there is more area devoted to the control of the face than any other surface of the body. This exquisite control is for a purpose: to express feelings. What a person's feeling looks like can be ''read'' as patterns of muscle movements on the face.

We continually send emotional messages to others by our facial expression, a raise of the eyebrows here, downward turn of the mouth there. Our facial expression is a large part of the impression we communicate to others, and sometimes we are unaware of the messages we are sending to others and of the messages others send to us. However, since many expressions of emotions are universal, it is possible to learn how to read the specific messages on the face. The

material in this section, adapted in large part from work of Ekman and Friesen (1983), explains in detail how to identify the emotions in various facial expressions.

The face provides three general types of signals: static (such as skin color), slow (such as wrinkles), and rapid (such as a smile). Emotions are communicated by the rapid movements of the facial muscles, which continually alter the appearance of the face. These changes flash over the face in a matter of seconds. It is rare for a facial expression of emotion to last more than 5 or 10 seconds, and some are much faster. The accompanying pictures illustrate several facial expressions of emotions and the specific characteristics of the emotional expression.

Surprise

Surprise is a sudden experience (Figures 12–7 and 12–7A):
- The brows are raised and are curved and high.
- Horizontal wrinkles mark the forehead.
- The eyelids are opened, the white of the eye is more prominent, particularly above the iris.
- The jaw drops open, but there is no tension in the mouth.

However, each one of these clues may express part of the feeling. And since our perception fills in the gaps, the rest of the face may seem to convey the emotion as well. For example, someone's entire face may seem to be expressing ''mild surprise'' when, in fact, it is only the raised brows that give that impression, as in Figure 12–7B.

FIGURE 12–7

FIGURE 12–7A

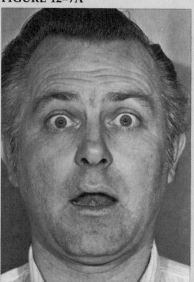

FIGURE 12–7B

Fear

- The brows are raised and drawn together.
- The forehead wrinkles in the center, not sides.
- Both the upper and lower eyelids are raised.
- The mouth is opened and the lips are tensed slightly. (Figures 12–8 and 12–8A.)

  Fear may occur with other emotions as well, as in a "blend" of fear and surprise, where someone looks afraid, but not as afraid as in outright fear.

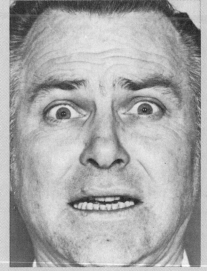

FIGURE 12–8

FIGURE 12–8A

Disgust

Disgust usually involves a response of getting away or getting rid of something offensive. Disgust is shown largely in the lower face and eyelid (Figures 12–9 and 12–9A):

- The upper lip is raised, as is the lower lip.
- The nose is wrinkled.
- The cheeks are raised.

- The brow is lowered.

  If we mix disgust and surprise we get a new expression. This seems to be disbelief or skepticism (Figure 12–9B).

FIGURE 12–9

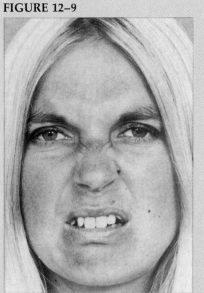

FIGURE 12–9A

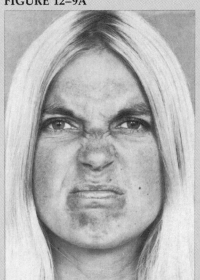

FIGURE 12–9B

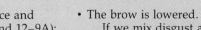

HOW TO READ FACES (continued)

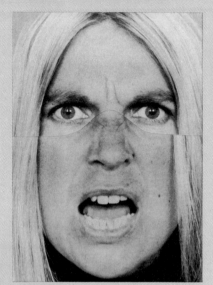

FIGURE 12-10

FIGURE 12-11

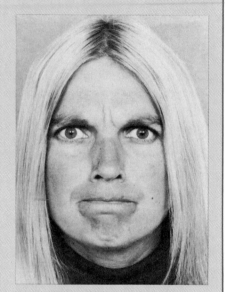

FIGURE 12-10A

Anger

The expression of anger is strong and direct, and the emotion conveys strong displeasure and can be read easily. There is much redundancy in the anger message, making it clear to all.

- The brows are lowered and drawn together, causing vertical lines to appear.
- The eyes may have a hard stare and may bulge out.
- The lips may be either pressed together or open in a squarish shape as in shouting.

Anger often blends with disgust. Here the wrinkled nose blends with the angry eyes and brows. The expression is "How dare you do this to me?" (Figures 12-10 and 12-10A)

Happiness

Happiness is welcome after all these difficult emotions. It is shown in the lower face and eyelids.

- The corners of the lips are drawn back and up.
- The mouth is upturned in a smile, either open or not.
- The cheeks are raised, causing a wrinkle from the outer edges of the mouth to the nose.
- "Laugh lines" or crow's feet wrinkle outward from the outer corners of the eye (Figure 12-11).

Anger can blend with happiness into a gleeful "gotcha" expression.

your experience. My thinking could be explained in this way. "I can feel myself shaking. Why? I'm delivering an important lecture, that must be it. Why didn't I . . ." And you know the rest. The hypothesis about why I was shaking *became* my experience: I'm nervous. The hypothesis that "The whole room is shaking" is very unlikely. But when I saw it was true in this case, my experience changed. I had appraised myself wrongly.

Bodily Changes in Emotions: Activation of Emergency Reaction

The major physiological effect of emotion is **activation.** Emotions turn on (activate) the body's **emergency reaction,** allowing us to prepare for immediate action. Most of the "reactions" involved in emotions involve the activating mechanisms of the sympathetic nervous system. Underlying most strong feelings—anger, fear, joy—are the following: an increase in the secretion of norepinephrine in the bloodstream by the adrenals activates the internal organs; heart rate, blood pressure and blood volume increase, allowing more blood to flow to the muscles and the face. We are "flushed with excitement." Skin resistance decreases; respiration, sweating, salivation, and gastric motility all increase; pupil size increases. There seems nothing in the physical arousal *alone* that differentiates what the emotion is.

FIGURE 12–12
Activation of the Emergency (Fight-or-Flight) Reaction
This drawing illustrates the various ways in which the body responds to activation of its emergency reaction.

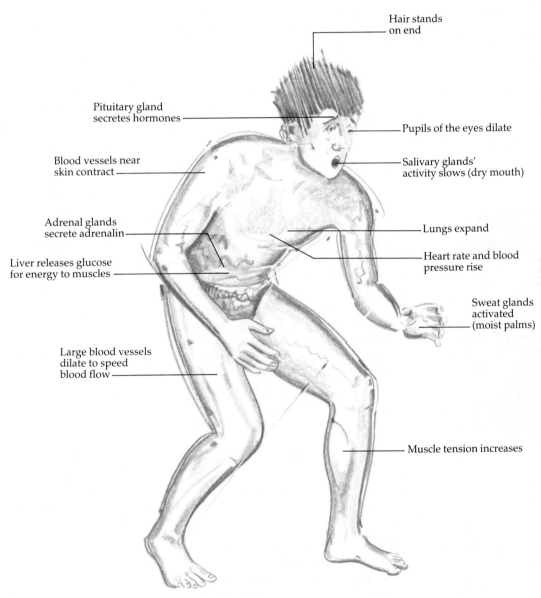

Emergency (fight-or-flight) reaction

Are There Specific Body Patterns to Emotions?

But fear and happiness do feel different, and so do anger and joy. It seems only logical that different emotions would cause quite different bodily reactions. One recent study asked people to assume different emotional expressions. When they did, they *felt* different emotions, such as anger and happiness. Consistently different patterns of autonomic nervous system activity characterized different emotions (Ekman, 1984). However, this has not often been found. What has been found more often is this: Different people seem to show *different* characteristic "emotional" responses to situations. One person may become flushed with anger as well as joy, another may sweat, a third may have stomach reactions (Lacey & Lacey, 1958). In studies of people who experience the same emotion, the pattern of activation is different. In one study of students' anxiety regarding an examination, some sweated, others increased heartbeat (Lacey, Bateman, & Van Lehn, 1953). However, all the individual differences involve specific components of the emergency reaction of the sympathetic division of the autonomic nervous system (ANS). The only specific body pattern that consistently relates to various people's emotional expressions is facial expression.

Emotions and the Brain

Two major brain divisions seem to act differently with respect to the emotions. The limbic system is largely responsible for many emotional reactions. The pleasure center is located in the hypothalamus, and stimulation there gives rise to intense sensations of pleasure. Other areas of the limbic system, when stimulated, can produce rage and attack reactions (Delgado, 1969). These findings have led many psychologists (Papez, 1937) to assume that the relatively automatic aspects of emotion are controlled by the limbic system. Yet in many emotional situations there is conscious control from the cortex. For instance, the "emergency reaction" causes a release of hormones into the blood stream under the regulation of the limbic system. The emergency reaction also often occurs involuntarily, as when trembling with fright before a job interview. Some writers have speculated that the conflict between our "old" emotional brain and the "new" thinking brain is at the root of many of these conflicts between rational thought and our "gut" feelings (Koestler, 1974).

However, most recent analysis about the brain and emotion regards the two cerebral hemispheres. As the two hemispheres are specialized for different kinds of thought, they also seem specialized for emotions: the left hemisphere responds to the verbal content of emotional expression and the right to the tone and gesture (Kolb & Milner, 1980; Safer & Leventhal, 1977).

Since the right hemisphere controls the left side of the body and the left hemisphere the right side, are there differences in the expression of emotions on both sides of the body? Look at Leonardo da Vinci's *Mona Lisa*. She has a smile described as enigmatic, puzzling, ambiguous. Why? Look carefully at each side of her face. Only the left side is smiling, the side controlled by the right hemisphere! Perhaps this is why the expression is so ambiguous.

The celebrated ambiguity of the smile of Leonardo da Vinci's *Mona Lisa* might be attributable to the fact that she is smiling only on the left side, the side controlled by the right hemisphere of the brain. To aid you in considering whether or not this could be the source of the enigma, look at the related picture on p. 448.

Look, too, at the three faces in Figure 12–13. Which of the faces seems to express the emotions most strongly? These three photographs are specially constructed. On the left is a photograph of a man expressing disgust. The middle photograph is a double image, a composite of two right sides of the man's face. On the right is a double image of the left side of the face. Most people feel that the right photograph, which expresses the right cerebral hemisphere, shows the emotion strongest. Similar results have been found with eye movements (Schwartz, Davidson, & Maer 1975) and with interpreting a facial expression. We seem to express emotion on the left side of the face more than the right and interpret it better on the left than the right (Campbell, 1978).

Moscovitch and Olds (1980) unobtrusively recorded the difference in the laterality of facial expression of people seated in restaurants and found the same result. The right hemisphere controls the left side of the face, which is seen better by the viewer's right hemisphere. In a social situation there may be two kinds of messages sent: from left hemisphere to left, through words, and right to right through facial and other expressions. In an intriguing series of recent studies, Davidson (1984) has shown that the left hemisphere may involve different emotions than the right. The left seems to be involved in "positive" emotions, like happiness, the right in "negative" ones, like anger.

Knowing What We Feel

A basic emotional reaction such as fear is probably innate, a shortcut to action. In the long course of evolution emotions probably evolved to match well the needs of most organisms—fear of snakes, for instance, probably saved many lives. However, the situation in human beings is different: the dangers of the modern world are unprecedented in our

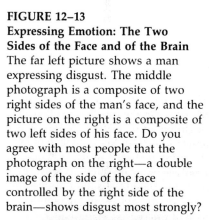

FIGURE 12–13
Expressing Emotion: The Two Sides of the Face and of the Brain
The far left picture shows a man expressing disgust. The middle photograph is a composite of two right sides of the man's face, and the picture on the right is a composite of two left sides of his face. Do you agree with most people that the photograph on the right—a double image of the side of the face controlled by the right side of the brain—shows disgust most strongly?

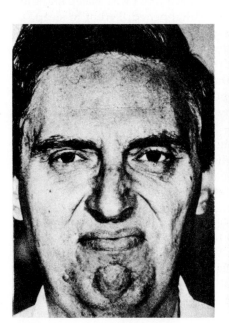
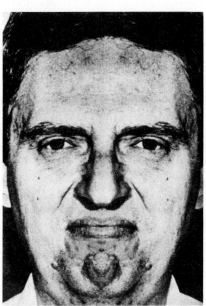
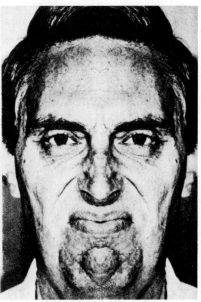

evolutionary history. The fear of nuclear war, for instance, is not as palpable as fear of snakes: there is no identifiable stimulus, no obvious and immediate course of action. The *meaning* of a situation and its appraisal are major factors in human emotional life.

Evaluation, Potency, Activity

There are three basic dimensions to the appraisal process. The first is *evaluation*: is the situation good or bad, benign or threatening? The second is **potency:** is it alive/dead, strong/weak, fast/slow? The third is *activity*: active/passive? Osgood and colleagues (1971) who proposed these dimensions of emotions, describe their value:

> What is important to us now, as it was way back in the age of Neanderthal Man, about the sign of a thing is: First, does it refer to something *good* or *bad* for me (is it an antelope or a saber-toothed tiger)? Second, does it refer to something that is *strong* or *weak* with respect to me (saber-toothed tiger, or a mosquito)? And third, for behavioral purposes, does it refer to something which is *active* or *passive* (is it a saber-toothed tiger or merely a pool of quicksand, which I can simply walk around)?

Meaning: Appraisal and Reappraisal

Emotions, like the rest of human experience, are not a succession of isolated, unrelated feelings and reactions to situations. Perception, consciousness, and memory operate in a cycle. Emotions do too. The cycle involves a primary appraisal of the situation, feedback of that information, and continuous reappraisals, and feedback. Feelings change as new information comes in. One night I awakened to the sound of a strange noise upstairs in my house. I was aroused—fearful. What could the sound be? Did I lock the door? Was the roof falling? With each thought I was prepared to act differently. Then I remembered that a friend of mine had asked to stay over. He must have noticed that I was asleep and then let himself in. Once I realized what had happened, I went to sleep.

The first reaction was the primary appraisal: "Something's happening." I awoke, aroused. *Primary appraisal* arouses the organism. *Reappraisal* considers whether an event is *benign* or *threatening* and what actions to take. When I decided that the noise was only my friend's footsteps, all my plans to call the police or run like mad from the roof caving in vanished. The result of my reappraisal was that I went back to sleep.

Any situation is complex enough that it requires continuous appraisal. When a man sees that his wife prepared his favorite dish, his primary appraisal is benign. When the dish is in front of him, he sees that the dish is burned. This new information causes a sadness or disappointment—which may lead to an action such as visiting a restaurant, resulting in a second feeling (Lazarus, 1968).

Illusions and Emotions

Because inner states in emotions are similar, situations need to be appraised and a conscious interpretation of their meaning must be made. Most times these appraisals are accurate and serve us well. Some-

Look at the smile on this reversed *Mona Lisa.* Is her smile as enigmatic, as ambiguous? Here, because she is smiling only on the right side of her face, the impact is different. Your response may be different because the smile is on the side controlled by the left hemisphere of the brain.

EMOTIONS AND HEALTH

Should You Hold in Your Feelings?

In everyday language we assume an association between the expression of emotions and health. We may urge someone to "let out" anger, or to have a "good cry" and "get it off your chest." The assumption seems to be that the release of "bottled-up" feelings is beneficial. The expression of positive feelings is also believed to be healthy. For years the *Reader's Digest* has carried a column on "Laughter— The Best Medicine." Recently, Norman Cousins, the longtime editor of the *Saturday Review,* described treatment of an incurable illness he contracted in Russia, an undetermined blood disease. After his doctors had given up, Cousins moved from the hospital to a hotel room and "prescribed" humor for himself, notably films providing a dose of the Marx Brothers and round-the-clock administration of Laurel and Hardy. He got better. While there is some anecdotal evidence for laughter, single cases do not provide adequate scientific evidence.

However, there is one area of research—on cancer—where the link between emotional expression and health is supported by many studies. In a long series of studies, Kissen (1962, 1963, 1966a, 1966b) have found that a characteristic of lung cancer patients is that they suppress their emotions. Cancer patients also seem to ignore their negative feelings, such as hostility, depression, and guilt (Bahnson & Bahnson, 1964, 1969).

In a recent study that compared long-term survivors of breast cancer with those who do not survive, Derogatis and

colleagues (1979) found the same pattern. The long-term survivors express much higher levels of anxiety, hostility, alienation, and other negative emotions than short-term survivors. They have more negative moods and express more negative attitudes toward their illness.

That there is a link between "getting it off your chest" and reduced cancer is fairly well established. Why this might be so is not. One link may be hormonal. Hormones can influence the growth of cancerous tumors, and since emotion involves sympathetic activation, it may alter hormonal levels in the body. However, any firm link is yet to be discovered. While "venting" emotions may still cause difficulty in social situations (Tavris, 1982), keeping feelings to yourself may be injurious to your health.

The Benefits of Crying

It may seem strange to think of crying as beneficial. Yet, many people say that "a good cry" makes us feel better. The belief that crying has positive effects is of ancient origin. More than 2,000 years ago, Aristotle theorized that crying at a drama "cleanses the mind" of suppressed emotions by a process called catharsis. **Catharsis** is the reduction of emotional distress by releasing the emotion in controlled circumstances. Crying in response to a sad movie is a textbook case. Many people attend movies and plays that they know beforehand are, shall we say, "elicitors of psychogenic lacrimation,"— "tearjerkers." Such people may cry freely in movies and not regret

the experience at all. The experience that stimulates crying is sought out and, if the resultant crying is the behavioral release of suppressed grief, it is but a short step to a view of crying as therapeutic.

There are some studies of the effects of crying. Borquist (1906) obtained reports of the effects of crying, including the observation of 54 of 57 respondents that crying had positive results. Weiner (1977) found from reports that asthma attacks—long thought to be largely psychosomatic—cease as a result of crying. Grinker (1953) noted that depressed persons do not cry and that recovery is associated with the development of the ability to cry.

While the research on the benefits of crying is intriguing but hardly decisive, other strands of evidence are becoming available. Tears produced by emotional crying—such as those elicited by those "tearjerker" movies—differ in chemical content from those caused by irritants such as onion juice (Frey, 1982). Emotional tears contain more protein than tears induced by irritants. Frey contends that emotional crying is an eliminative process in which tears *actually remove toxic substances from the body.* Crying may "cleanse the mind" in a much more literal sense than even the catharsis theorists imagine. Other researchers are now examining the contents of emotional tears for substances such as endorphins, ACTH, prolactin, and growth hormone, all of which are released by stress. While the research on psychoactive substances in tears is just beginning, there is reason to think that emotional tears may perform a very important function in the maintenance of physical health and emotional balance.

one may insult us, we get angry. Another person snuggles up to us, we become activated in a blizzard of lustful joy.

The *cognitive appraisal theory of emotion* (Schachter & Singer 1962) states that the interpretation of the physiological state leads to different emotional experiences. In this view, our interpretation is made in the same way as most perceptual interpretations: what is the simplest meaningful explanation for my excitement? But, as in most perception, the interpretation can be difficult when the circumstance is ambiguous. One factor that may lead to some ambiguity in life is that arousal is common to quite different emotions. When the situation is ambiguous we may misinterpret our own emotional states. Although this happens infrequently in life, it can be created in the lab.

My experience shaking before a lecture is an example from life. I *interpreted* my shaking as nervousness. Once I understood the situation, I was no longer nervous. But my interpretation had real consequences: I *felt* worried.

The conscious interpretation can affect the internal state itself. In one study, students saw a very arousing film and ANS arousal was measured continuously during the viewing (Speisman, Lazarus, Davison, & Mordkoff, 1964). The measure of arousal of the autonomic nervous system was the skin resistance, the galvanic skin response (GSR). The film was of a ceremony an aboriginal tribe used to mark manhood. The rituals included the subincision of the penis with a knife. Most people find these scenes quite negatively arousing.

One group was shown the film silently. A second group heard a narration that emphasized the cruelty of the ritual. Two other groups heard narrations that minimized the cruelty by denying or intellectualizing it. GSR measures of arousal increased in the narration that emphasized the cruelty, while arousal decreased in the narrations that minimized it (Figure 12–14).

In a well-known study on the effect of interpretation on emotion, Schachter and Singer (1962) injected epinephrine, an activating drug, into students who were told it was a vitamin. Half of the students were placed in a situation with a euphoric person (a confederate of the experimenters) who tossed paper airplanes, used the wastebasket to shoot baskets with wads of paper. These students later reported feeling euphoric. Half of the students were confronted by an insulting and irritated person. They later reported being angry. Schachter and Singer concluded that these results confirmed the theory that emotional experiences depend upon the interpretation of arousal.

There have been many studies that support these general findings, and Schachter's hypothesis, but there have been problems with his experiments. Many people have tried, with little success, to replicate the result of this experiment (Marshall & Zimbardo, 1979). It is no longer permissible to conduct experiments with epinephrine injections—so no further replication attempts can be made. However, many other studies indicate that the interpretation of inner states can have profound effects on emotional experience.

One way to test the theory is to offer *false feedback* on the internal state

itself. If emotional experiences depend in some way on the interpretation of the inner state, then false information should also have an effect on experience. In one study men were shown photographs of nude women, while listening to their own heartbeat. What each actually heard, however, was not his own heart beating, but a recording. One group heard a recording in which the heartbeat increased when 5 of the 10 slides were shown. A second group heard "their" heartbeat decrease at these 5 slides. Later, when asked to rate the attractiveness of the nudes, the group whose heartbeat increased rated the women in the five slides as more attractive; the ones whose heartbeat decreased found the other five more appealing (Valins, 1966).

The false feedback effect is not restricted to men looking at nudes. In another experiment, women were shown slides of people who had experienced violent death. Those who "heard" their heart rates increase in reaction to the slides rated them as significantly more unpleasant and discomforting than those who had not been misinformed.

The study we discussed in Chapter 1, "Sexual Attraction on the Wob-

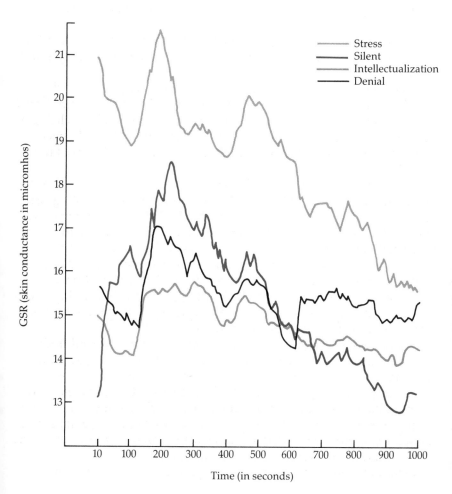

FIGURE 12–14
Cognitive Influences on Emotional Reactions
In the experiment charted in this graph, different groups of people watched a stress-provoking movie. Those who heard a narration that denied or intellectualized the distressing parts of the film, or who saw the film without any narration, had less stressful emotional reactions than people in the group that heard a narration intended to increase stress. (After Speisman, Lazarus, Davison, & Mordkoff, 1964)

bly Bridge," is one instance of this phenomenon. Here the arousal caused by crossing a somewhat dangerous bridge is misinterpreted as excitement on seeing a woman. Other studies have shown similar results, and similar phenomena have been studied in life. For instance, many people find that exercise with a partner of the opposite sex is very sexy. Why? In one study (Cantor, Zillman, & Bryant, 1974), people were asked to exercise for a period of time. The activation resulting from exercise diminished with time; soon after exercise one no longer *feels* activated; however, measures of autonomic activation, such as blood pressure, are still elevated. If people are shown erotic stimuli during this phase, they report *more sexual arousal* than when they have fully recovered from the exercise. The unexplained activation is interpreted, again, as sexual excitement. So activation, especially in contrived or ambiguous situations, is subject to interpretation (Mandler, 1980). However, most situations are *not* ambiguous and our emotions are usually a quite accurate and immediate guide for us.

LOVE AND SEX

Of all our feelings, those involving love and sex have probably inspired the most comment. It is easy to see why: being in love is among the best and most treasured experiences of life; being without love is often dismal. The experience of love is complex; it involves intense feelings of ecstasy, despair, and uncertainty. We do not know when love will strike or why it goes away. As for sex, it is universally regarded as a central human experience—sought, enjoyed, prohibited, denied, encouraged, frustrated. But because sex and love are such complicated, private, intense, and intimate feelings, they are devilishly hard to study. They are complex and are thus very difficult to analyze scientifically. Sex and love are prized experiences and many people do not want any of the secrets of love subjected to the "cold eye" of science. In 1975, Senator William Proxmire of Wisconsin denounced the federal government for funding research on love:

> I believe that 200 million other Americans want to leave some things in life a mystery, and right at the top of things we don't want to know is why a man falls in love with a woman, and vice versa. . . . So National Science Foundation—get out of the love racket. Leave that to Elizabeth Barrett Browning and Irving Berlin. Here, if anywhere, Alexander Pope was right when he observed, "If ignorance is bliss, 'tis folly to be wise."

However, the senator is wrong, on many accounts. Love relationships are central in people's lives—and disruption of them is a major cause of personal distress. The most common precipitating factor in severe depression and suicides is disruption of a love relationship. People are hungry for information: Why do we fall in love with a certain person, why does love turn to hate? Do opposites attract? Love stories are best-

FEELING AND THINKING

How do feelings relate to thinking and decision making? Many psychologists consider that the mental functions such as perception, consciousness, memory, and thinking come before emotions: in this view we first analyze and appraise information, then evaluate it, and experience it emotionally. Recently, however, Robert Zajonc has proposed that feelings come first, or to use his phrase, preferences need no inferences (Zajonc, 1980). Zajonc argues that mental functions are most often in the service of emotions, not the reverse: that we evaluate first and think of the reasons secondly. He offers many examples for his theory. Here is a representative one. Consider the example of a woman trying to decide rationally whom to marry. "Let's see, Jack has more money, one point for him; he wants to live where I do, another point; he's handsomer than Bill . . . wait a minute, this isn't coming out right, I want to marry Bill. Let's see . . ." In a contest between emotion and reason, emotion is more likely to win, in this view.

It may be that the question "Which comes first, emotions or cognitions?" is like asking about the chicken and egg. It is perhaps more profitable to view emotions and thoughts as part of a feedback system in which each influences the other and appraisals are followed by reappraisals. Sometimes emotional evaluation may come first: "I like wine," is an evaluation. But sometimes the evaluation may well come after a long analysis: "I don't like this white wine after all; it's too sweet." Emotions probably influence every mental process: they may cause us to seek out different information, remember differently, think and evaluate differently.

selling books; songs exalt or lament over love. Newspaper columnists and advisors to the lovelorn prosper by the thousands. A scientific analysis, flawed as it might be, would begin to expose some of the essential components of love.

In addition, one might want to study love out of sheer curiosity about the hows and whys of one of the most prized human emotions. It is no less interesting or important than how and why memory works. In a world troubled by wars and discord in national and private affairs, learning how love works is an important task.

Sex is even more difficult to study than love, since sex is the most intimate experience. Cultural and personal taboos have, until the last few decades, made it impossible to study this important aspect of life. For example, many questions about women's orgasms were only settled in the mid-1960s when mores had relaxed enough to permit laboratory investigation.

The study of love and sex is just beginning. So far the data collected allow us to make some generalizations on such questions as: what are the general characteristics of people in love; how may the experience of love be interpreted; why do people fall in love, and who does it; what are the kinds of love? In the discussion of sex we will review the important place sex occupies in human evolution and development, the basic sexual response cycle, differences in sexual behavior between the sexes, and how sexual mores are changing.

The Evolution of Love

Before we turn to contemporary research on love and loving, we should briefly review love's history in our species. Love is unique to human beings. The love "bond" between people is important to the human adaptation and to the survival of humans as a race. Because of our upright posture, the birth canal is small, and this leads to human infants being born, if not "early," at least immature and helpless. The love and attachment between the father and the mother has a key biological role: it ensures that the father remains with the mother and helps care for the offspring. Human fathers are the only males among primates who take a significant role in the care of their own offspring. The father-mother-child unit is "bonded" by love into a family unit, one typical of our species. Any analysis of the nature of our love, far from being trivial, is of the utmost importance to our understanding of ourselves. The analysis of love and its evolutionary history is, of course, rather new (Mellen, 1981) and the current studies of love and loving are also in their infancy; so the findings, as yet, are quite meager.

Characteristics of People in Love

Something dramatic happens to us when we are in love. When you love someone, that person is suddenly unique, the central person in your world, and you may act differently around your lover than around anyone else. The language we use to describe love uses images of movement and distance. We "fall" in love, lovers are "inclined" toward one another, lovers are "close," "as one." The physical and verbal expressions of closeness are related. It is quite easy, on observing people, to tell who are the lovers and who are not (Figure 12–15). There are three characteristics that have been observed as indicators of interest: inclination, closeness, and eye contact. We will treat each of these briefly.

The "Inclination" toward Another. Francis Galton, in 1884, first proposed that the ordinary metaphors of speech are useful for the scientific student of love. He wrote: "When two persons have an "inclination" to one another they visibly incline or slope together when sitting side by side. . . ." Galton never got around to testing this idea, empirically, but recently it has been done. When the posture of people is measured in situations in which they confront people they like and dislike, they are found to lean toward those they like and away from those they dislike.

Closeness. When we are in love, we feel "close" to the other person. Couples walking with distance between them seem less in love than those entwined arm in arm. In one study, men and women students were introduced and sent off on a 30-minute "blind date" for a coke. When they returned they were asked to rate their date's attractiveness. Unknown to the students, the psychologists also rated how closely the couples stood when they returned. There was a high relationship: the more the couple reported liking one another, the closer they stood to each other (Walster & Walster, 1980).

Gaze. When two people are close to one another, each looks more often in the other's eyes. People who like one another more look more in each other's eyes than those who do not (Argyle, 1978).

The Excitement of Sexual Love

One component of emotional experiences is activation or excitement. Love is a grand stirring up of feeling and probably depends upon activation more than most emotional experiences. From most analyses and studies (as well as common observations), it seems that arousal is a strong component of loving. In one study, Walster and her colleagues (1966) sent a group of men on blind dates and then asked them to come in to the lab to fill out a questionnaire. While they were waiting, half were given fairly boring reading material, half were given *Playboy* and other "girlie" magazines. They were then asked to rate their date's attractiveness. It was thought that the *Playboy*-type of magazine would be more arousing and lead to a higher rating of attractiveness of the "blind date." The hypothesis was confirmed. Many of the studies we cited earlier seem to confirm the importance of arousal in sexual attraction. The men on the wobbly bridge in the Dutton and Aron experiment interpreted their arousal as attraction; those given false feedback on their heart rates, and those aroused by exercise, all show increased attraction. The arousal component of love can help make sense of a common problem that occurs when love ends. Many people report that they strongly hate someone they once loved. At first glance that seems odd, but perhaps it is due to the arousal component of sexual love. When the affair

FIGURE 12–15
Each of these couples has the look of people in love.

ends, the positive feelings are replaced by negative feelings, feelings which may be *amplified* by the arousal.

Obstacles to love, such as separation, the exciting effects of dangerous exploits, all heighten love. Women who are hard to get are often thought to be the most desirable. One man, after kidnapping his former lover, said, "The fact that she rejected me only made me want to love her more." The philosopher Bertrand Russell (quoted in Tennov, 1979) wrote: "The belief in the immense value of the lady is a psychological effect of the difficulty of obtaining her, and I think it may be laid down that when a man has no difficulty in obtaining a woman, his feeling toward her does not take the form of romantic love."

Passionate and Companionate Love

The strong form of "being in love" is **passionate love.** It is a state of intense absorption in another, arousal, and longing. This experience seems to have some similar aspects among many people: it is involuntary and there are times when many people wish they were not in love. The French writer Stendhal once commented that if he were murdered while he was in the throes of an unrequited passion he would thank the murderer before he died. The experience often includes:

1. The object of desire is thought about almost all the time and intrudes into thinking. Attention is narrowed to the person involved. One so involved wrote: "Love is a human religion in which another person is believed in."
2. Longing for reciprocation.
3. Dependency of mood on the other's reactions.
4. Inability to react in the same way to more than one person at a time.
5. Fear of rejection.
6. Intensification through adversity.
7. Emphasis and focus on positive qualities of the person, ignoring all negative ones. (Tennov, 1979)

In time, however, most passionate relationships fade somewhat. Arousal is dependent on novelty, so it is probably impossible to maintain such intense feeling for long. When the initial passion fades, there are two possibilities. Either the relationship is burned out and over, or it develops into the more sober kind of "everyday" love, **companionate love.** There is less arousal and excitement, but more friendly affection and deep attachment. Companionate love, to be sure, has its moments of passion, but they are woven into the fabric of life. They do not usurp all other concerns.

Falling in Love

What causes us to fall in love, and what are the characteristics of the "fall"? Each love experience is different, yet there are some similarities of love experiences.

It is commonly thought that women are the romantics; their lives are said to be organized more around love, while men are more concerned with work, money, and other activities. But here the data contradict that common assumption. Hobart (1958) asked hundreds of men and women questions about romance and found that men are much more likely to be romantics than women are. Men fall in love faster and have a more romantic view of love relationships than women do. In another study of the course of love in dating, 20 percent of men fell in love before the fourth date while 15 percent of women did. It is usually the woman who ends the affair, too, and the men who suffer more (Walster & Walster, & Traupmann, 1978).

Attractiveness and Loving

We want someone to love us for ourselves—not for externals like a pretty face. However, physical attractiveness is very important in the initial tumble into love. In one study (Walster, Aronson, Abrahams, & Rottmann, 1966), a panel of college students rated the physical attractiveness of 752 college freshmen; then other information regarding their intelligence, personality, and attitudes was also assembled. Then the experimenters staged a dance at which the freshmen were randomly assigned a date. The freshmen were later asked how satisfied they were with their date, how eager they were for another date, and whether they would ask the person out. *The only determinant of interest was physical attractiveness.* In another study, Berschied found that physical attractiveness was more related to a woman's popularity than to a man's. There was a strong correlation between a woman's physical attractiveness and the number of dates, but the relationship was slight for men (Walster & Walster, 1980).

It may well be that physical attractiveness is most important at the beginning of a love relationship and that with time other "more real" factors come into play, but the evidence so far is not flattering to those who believe that "love" does not depend upon "mere physical" attributes.

Human Sexuality

The Evolution of Human Sexuality

People are, simply, very sexy animals. We have sex more than any other primates do. Our love of sex is one of the reasons for the success of our species. In evolutionary terms, the "survival of the fittest"—who has the most surviving offspring—determines how a population grows, changes, and develops. Survival is more keyed to sex than aggression. Because we made love, not war, we have been successful.

Sex is different for humans than other animals in that the signals for sex are often mental, not biological. It is for this reason that the role of emotions and interpretation of love experiences are so closely related to sexual feelings. There are also biological differences in our sexuality and that of other primates. Recall that other female animals are sexually receptive to the male only for brief periods, during the estrus cycle.

When receptive, a female mates often with many different males, who do not remain to care for the children. Female humans can have sex at any time. Animals have sex only to have offspring; humans like to have sex much more often than the strict demands of reproduction require. This style of continual sexual activity forms the basis of human society.

The human anatomy is "designed" to call attention to the sexual characteristics. Upright posture has transferred emphasis from odor to visual signs of sexuality. There is no reason for a women's breasts to be large except when nursing—except that they are visually appealing and arousing to the male. The male penis is much larger, relative to body size, than that of the great apes. In addition, genitalia are accented with pubic hair. Publications like *Playboy* magazine have not *created* a need for men to look at women sexually, but have merely taken advantage of a natural inclination.

Finally, because how we feel depends on our interpretation of physical arousal, sexual attraction has mental components that include love and attachment.

The Sexual Response Cycle

There are regular physiological changes involved in sexual intercourse and sexual activity (Masters & Johnson, 1966). The four major phases of **the sexual response cycle** (Figure 12–16) are excitement, plateau, orgasm, and resolution.

1. In the *excitement phase,* the physical manifestations of arousal are a general arousal reaction similar to all emotional arousal, combined with an increase of blood flow (**vasocongestion**) to the genitals and increasing muscular tension in the genital area. The penis becomes erect, the vagina is lubricated through vaginal sweat glands.

2. In the *plateau phase,* vasocongestion and muscle tension level off but sexual and general excitement remain high. This is the phase when intercourse occurs. The plateau may be long or short depending on the sexual

FIGURE 12–16
Human Sexual Response Cycles
These graphs show how males and females differ in their patterns of physiological response during sexual activity. (After Masters & Johnson, 1966)

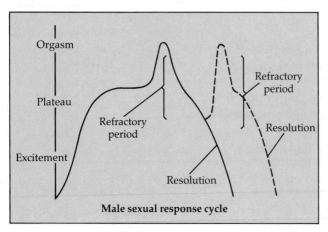

Male sexual response cycle

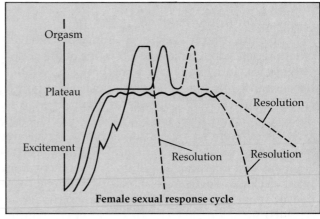

Female sexual response cycle

So we ha
it warns us
wonder tha
So it is with
motives,—i

---

1. Emotions a
lished that
between hu
and involu
counts for v
our respon
functions.
actions, an
display sigr
communica
more primi
mals.

2. Some psych
One viewp
sadness, di:
the way the
In resear
out the wo:
emotions a:
tions are vie
and preliter

3. *Activation* of
as anger, fe
emotions ca
and Friesen
vous systen
seem to sho
sponses to s

4. Recent analy
that the two
The left hen
and the righ
sion, it has b
right hemisp
addition, we
emotion. In
that the left
right. The le:
right in nega

5. There are thr
is *evaluation:*

act, the stimuli, and the training and control of the individual. One person may reach orgasm quickly, another may wish to delay orgasm.

3. The third phase is **orgasm,** which is the briefest and most intense phase. Arousal, muscle tension, heart rate and respiration increase rapidly to a kind of peak. Then there is a sudden reduction of tension accompanied by orgasm. While sexual excitement can be initiated by purely mental means, such as fantasies, orgasm usually results from the stimulation of the genitals. Almost every male has orgasm. During orgasm men ejaculate semen, which contains sperm. From 10 to 30 percent of women never have orgasms, while about 14 percent report that they always have one or more climaxes during intercourse.

The pattern of orgasm differs between the sexes. Men have more times when they have orgasms. Women can have multiple orgasms (that is, several at one encounter).

4. In the *resolution phase,* the participant rests; arousal has subsided. There is mental and physical relaxation and a feeling of well-being. During resolution a man cannot have an erection. After resolution, the cycle can begin again. There is, however, a physical limit to the number of times a day a man could have sexual intercourse. This number decreases as he gets older. Theoretically, there is no limit to the number of times a woman could have sex.

Sex Differences in Sexuality

Dorothy Parker wrote, in her "General review of the sex situation," the following:

> Woman wants monogamy;
> Man delights in novelty
> Love is woman's moon and sun;
> Man has other forms of fun.
> Woman lives but in her lord;
> Count to ten and man is bored.
> With this gist and sum of it;
> What earthly good can come of it?

While some of this poem written in 1926 may be a bit outmoded, especially the part about "woman living for her lord," it contains some basic truth about sex differences in sexual expression and desire. There are real and basic differences in the sexual expression of males and females in all societies, and in most animals.

In Figure 12–17, charting the frequency of orgasms of men and women, note that at all ages men have more sex per week than females. One consistent difference in sexuality is this: In all cultures studied, men desire more sex and more variety in sex than women do. In his monumental survey of human sexual activity, Kinsey (1953) wrote:

> Among all peoples, everywhere in the world, it is understood that the male is more likely than the female to desire sexual relations with a variety of partners.

potency: is it alive or dead, strong or weak? The third is *activity:* is it active or passive? Emotions, like perception, consciousness, and memory operate in a continuous cycle of appraisal, feedback, and reappraisal. Primary appraisal arouses the organism. Reappraisal considers whether an event is benign or threatening and directs which action to take.

In several studies, it has been found that emotional expression seems to be associated with a decrease in certain illnesses, such as cancer. One characteristic of lung cancer patients is that they suppress their emotions. They also seem to ignore their negative feelings, such as hostility, depression, and guilt. A recent study showed that long-term survivors of breast cancer express much higher levels of anxiety, hostility, alienation, and other negative emotions than short-term survivors. They have more negative moods and express more negative attitudes toward their illness. It is not yet clear why there is a fairly well-established link between "getting it off your chest" and reduced cancer, but one link may be hormonal as hormones can influence the growth of cancerous tumors. However, any firm link is yet to be discovered.

Several studies of the effects of illusion or false feedback on emotions demonstrate how conscious interpretation can affect the internal state. In one study, students saw an arousing film featuring a stressful aboriginal manhood ceremony. ANS arousal was measured during the viewing. Some saw the film with a narration designed to increase their stress; others heard stress-reducing narrations, and one group saw the film silently. Measures of arousal increased in the viewers who saw the version with the stressful narration.

In one important study of the effect of interpretation on emotion, Schachter and Singer injected epinephrine, an activating drug, into students who were told it was a vitamin. Half the students were placed with euphoric people; the other half were placed with an insulting and irritated person. The first half reported feeling euphoric, while those confronted by the insulting and irritated person reported being angry. It has been concluded by many that these results show that an emotional experience depends upon the interpretation of arousal. However, there are many problems with these experiments, including many failures.

Although many studies do show that interpretation and false feedback can affect emotional states, in most cases the activation requiring interpretation appears to be characteristic of only quite contrived situations. However, most real-life situations are hardly ambiguous and our emotions usually provide accurate and immediate guidance. This innate network for organizing our experiences probably does not depend upon interpretation.

6. There are several characteristics of people in love that have been described, albeit not thoroughly, in research. They are: inclination toward one another, closeness, and eye contact. An important component of emotional experience is activation or excitement, and this also seems to be quite common in love experiences. People's feelings toward each other seem to be greatly *amplified* by love. A person's faults seem much less strong when one is in love with that person and seem much stronger when that love ends. This strong form of love is *passionate love* and includes the following: (1) thinking about the object of desire almost all the time; (2) longing for reciprocation; (3) dependency of mood on the other's reactions; (4) inability to react in the same way to more than one person at a time; (5) fear of rejection; (6) intensification through adversity; and (7) emphasis and focus on positive qualities of the person. A more sober, less distressing form of love is *companionate love.*

An important but often denied fact in the experience of love is that the main determinant of initial interest is physical attractiveness.

FIGURE 12-
Frequency c
At all ages r
sexually tha
age. But me
activity is ac
twenties, wl
reaching the
in their thirt
Pomeroy, G

7. Sex is very different for humans than for other organisms. Sex signals for human sexuality are often mental rather than biological. However, there is a regular pattern of physiological changes involved in sexual intercourse and sexual activity. The four major phases of the *sexual response cycle* are: (1) excitement in which the physical manifestations of arousal are similar to all emotional arousal—combined with vasocongestion and muscular tension in the genitals; (2) the plateau phase, in which vasocongestion and muscle tension level off, but sexual and general excitement remain high; (3) orgasm, the briefest and most intense phase, during which arousal, muscle tension, heart rate, and respiration increase rapidly to a peak. There is a sudden reduction in tension accompanying orgasm. Almost every male has orgasm, but 10 to 30 percent of women never have orgasms, while about 14 percent report that they always have one or more climaxes during intercourse; and (4) in the resolution phase, the participant's arousal has subsided and there is a general lessening of arousal to external stimuli.

All over the world there are large-scale sex differences in sexuality. At all ages, men have more sex and are interested more often in sex than females. Men desire more sex and more variety in sex than women do. Men seek vicarious, visual, and other sexual stimulation far more than women. With changes in society, such as the acceptability of female sexual expression and contraceptives that allow women to have sex without worrying about pregnancy, these differences will probably continue to decrease in the future, but it seems unlikely that they will disappear entirely.

Terms and Concepts

activation
affect
catharsis
companionate love
emergency reaction
emotions
emotion solid
emotion wheel
feelings
moods
orgasm
passionate love
polarity
potency
primary (basic) emotions
sexual response cycle
temperament
vasocongestion

Suggestions for Further Reading

Ekman, P., & Friesen, W. (1983). *Unmasking the face.* Palo Alto, CA: Consulting Psychologists Press.
Back in print, the complete text of facial expression of emotions.

Mellen, S. L. W. (1981). *The evolution of love.* San Francisco: W. H. Freeman.
An attempt to analyze the place and development of human love.

Scherer, K., & Ekman, P. (Eds.). (1984). *Approaches to emotion.* New York: Lawrence Erlbaum.
An important review of the major studies of emotion. The article by Ekman on expression and emotions is particularly useful.

Symons, D. (1978). *The evolution of human sexuality.* New York: Oxford University Press.
An important attempt to raise the currently taboo question of how innate the differences in sexuality are.

Chapter 13

Needs and Goals

INTRODUCTION

A woman refuses to go anywhere at night, studies late, works extra hours at a waitress job, and saves all her money. Why? She has decided to go to medical school. You might find that you want to do well in this course because you seek knowledge or need a good grade for some reason. You might find that this course does not "mean" much to you, because you are not curious or because you do not need the grade. In all these cases your goals determine your actions.

Motives are much more variable and individual than any other process we have considered so far, and they determine the course of your life. A person motivated by love may forgo the possibility of making a scientific contribution; one motivated by achievement may have little time for a family.

Not only do different people have different motives, but each person has different *levels* of motivation within. Motives range from the universal and incessant, such as hunger and thirst, to the unusual and evanescent, such as the desire for self-actualization. Motives build upon one another. They vary from the simple to the complex in a progression.

As far as we know, we are the only animals aware of our own existence; that awareness, perhaps coupled with the awareness of death, seems to lead to wondering about the purposes of life. In a very real sense, we create our life in the pursuit of our goals. The desire to achieve goals—be they financial, intellectual, family, or others—becomes the moving, motivating force in adult life. Here we will consider many of the different things that stir us to action: those motives common to all animals, such as basic hunger and thirst, as well as those distinct motives, such as creativity and accomplishment, that carve out the beginnings of our individuality.

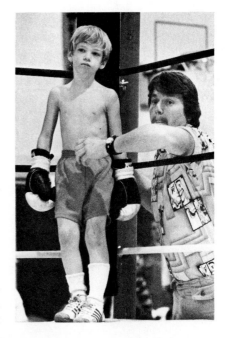

NEEDS AND GOALS

We share with other animals motives called needs, basic to the survival of the individual and the species. Thirst, hunger, temperature regulation are examples. These derive from purely biological needs. But we do not live by bread and wine alone. We *need* to be safe and warm, to care and be cared for. People also look for *meaning* and strive for specific *goals* in life. To be "driven by ambition" is to be moved by a goal, be it the construction of a building or a symphony.

At every moment of life we face an almost infinite number of choices: we can play, loaf, eat, spend, save, study. We can do things enthusiastically, halfheartedly, persistently, or lackadaisically. People who are "well motivated" do better on intelligence tests than others, less motivated, do. People will give up their lives for their country, work all night tending the wounded, or eat nothing but bread and cheese to save for something special. People act in very different ways depending on what motivates them and how well their needs are satisfied.

Specific Needs and Goals

Needs

In our discussion of the variety of human motives, we will divide them into two different categories: needs and goals. **Needs** *are specific deficits that any animal must satisfy, such as hunger and thirst.* We have needs for food, for water, for rest, for safety, and protection, among many. Needs give rise to *drives:* the need itself is a deficiency that drives the organism into action to satisfy it.

Drives

Drives are physiologically based goads to behavior: they literally move us to action. A hungry person is "driven" to find food. A drive is often experienced as a specific feeling such as thirst, hunger, or sex. At one time psychologists hypothesized that all behavior resulted from the reduction of a drive (Hull, 1943). For instance, the hunger drive is increased when the organism has not fed. After eating, that drive is reduced, and the motivation to seek food is lessened. Much of animal and human action is certainly "driven" this way. However, the concept of drive reduction only accounts for behaviors associated with very basic needs, such as hunger and thirst, and does not account for much that is characteristically human, such as curiosity, exploration, and even some behaviors that would seem to *increase* drives, such as watching pornographic movies or going on roller coaster rides, not to mention jumping out of airplanes for "fun."

Instincts

Early on in the development of the understanding of motivation, it was felt that all behaviors, animal and human, could be understood by innate patterns of behavior called **instincts,** which were "programmed" to satisfy needs. In order to be classified as an instinct, the behavior must be typical of every member of the species and must appear without learning on the first occasion the appropriate situation occurs.

Today, there is much less strict emphasis on instincts. It is generally accepted, however, that certain *predispositions* are inherited as part of the human genetic program. Some are specific, such as the patterns of mother-infant attachment; some are general, such as learning a language. It is

FIGURE 13–1
Drive Reduction

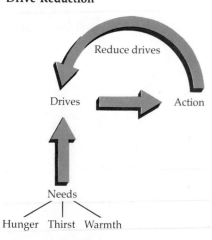

now well recognized that behavior is a mixture of innate and environmental factors. An example is that most humans learn a language; the specific language they learn is determined by their culture.

Goals

What is most unique about human motivation is the creation of goals. *A* **goal** *is a desired outcome that has not yet occurred.* Humans do not merely adjust to the demands of our environment, we adapt the environment to suit ourselves. If the satisfaction of needs is homeostatic adaptation, then the satisfaction of goals is "creative adaptation": changing the environment to meet the goals of the organism (Dubos, 1978). Examples of this are everywhere in human life, though usually unnoticed: the construction of cities, human culture and art, science and technology, novels, businesses. In short, everything that makes human beings unique is related to the ability to create new goals and to make something happen that has never happened before—the ability to go beyond our inheritance.

Abraham Maslow
(1908–1970)

Maslow's Pyramid of Motivation

A significant concept of motivation describes the complexity of human motives as a "pyramid" of different needs and goals. The range of human motives can be described as a hierarchy that can be visualized as a **pyramid of motivation** (Maslow, 1970a). At the bottom are the most basic needs; as one progresses to the top, the needs and then goals become more complex (Figure 13–2).

Prepotence

What distinguishes the different levels of Maslow's hierarchy is the concept of **prepotence:** the *relative strength* of the different needs. In this view, the "stronger" needs are lower on the hierarchy. For instance, given the lack of both friendship and water, the need for water is stronger, "prepotent." The need for water will preempt consciousness until it is satisfied, as you will know if you have ever been deprived of water. The general rule, then, is *once the lower needs are satisfied, the higher ones can be.* This description of motives is similar to our earlier description of the "priority system" of our consciousness.

The prepotence of hunger was dramatically illustrated in a study of 32 conscientious objectors during World War II. Their calorie intake was reduced from a normal 3,500 calories per day to 1,600 per day for a period of six months, during which time they lost an average of 24 percent of their body weight. The thought of food completely "preempted" their consciousness. They talked, dreamed, and read about it more than anything else. They were extremely disturbed by the slightest waste of available food and even licked their plates clean. The motivation for activities not associated with food vanished (Keys, Brozek, Henschel, Mickelson, & Taylor, 1950).

Maslow's pyramid of motivation is a general, and somewhat idealistic, scheme. While thirst is certainly more basic than self-actualization, people may often satisfy many different kinds of needs at one time, and

Priority System of Consciousness See Chapter 7, pp. 253, 256–57, 258–60.

Maslow's Pyramid of Motivation
Efforts must be made to satisfy needs lower in the hierarchy before needs and goals at higher levels can be expected to motivate action. (After Maslow, 1970)

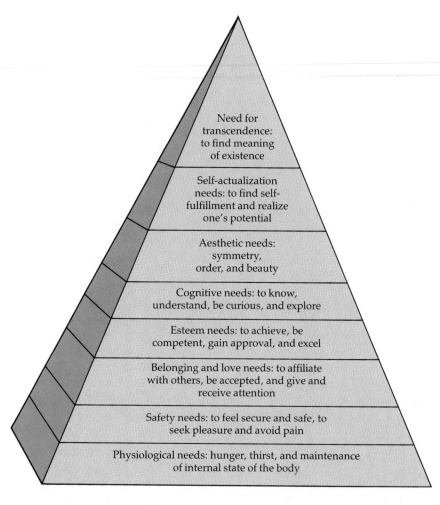

the prepotence of the different levels may vary from individual to individual. The need for transcendence, for instance, may be so strong in one person that friendship and esteem are passed over, and even survival needs are sometimes forgotten. Religious figures such as Moses, the Buddha, and Christ are examples. Still, the hierarchy is a useful way to organize, at least tentatively, the enormous range of human motives. We will follow its general outlines in this chapter, beginning with relatively basic and well-understood motives such as temperature regulation, thirst, and hunger, and continuing through our needs for other people, through curiosity, knowledge, achievement, and religious motives—all less well understood.

PHYSIOLOGICAL AND SAFETY NEEDS

The primary motivation for all organisms is survival. Sufficient oxygen must be inspired, sufficient food of good quality eaten, sufficient liquid must be drunk for animals to stay alive and healthy. All animals, too, try to avoid pain and injury and seek shelter and safety. All these needs operate on the principle of **homeostasis:** *a deficiency in any of them leads to actions designed to correct the deficiency* and to return to the original state.

Because these needs are so vitally important, they have been the subject of the most research, and there is a great understanding of the complex and precise regulation of these processes. Again, many of our experiences seem quite simple: we are thirsty and we drink; we are hungry, we eat. But, again, there is a lot of work "behind the scenes." We will discuss two of the most basic needs, thirst and hunger, and the malfunction of hunger—obesity—and the amazingly sophisticated and (to us) infuriating system that controls weight gain and loss.

We begin with temperature regulation, since the body's own thermostat seems to work on the same feedback principles as an ordinary thermostat, and this process is similar to the feedback control of thirst and hunger. After thirst and hunger, we will consider the basic safety needs of the organism. There is much more precise understanding of these basic needs than the more complex human goals we will examine in the final section of this chapter.

Homeostasis—The Constancy of the Body

As our mental function evolved to maintain constancy in the perceived world, so too our physical structure developed to maintain constancy in the internal world. **Homeostasis,** you will recall, is the tendency to keep the organism in a constant (stasis) state. In general, the regulatory systems of the body seek to maintain constant internal processes—constant temperature, constant water content and food supply. This constancy must be maintained during extremes of temperature, a long period without drink, too much or too little food.

Homeostasis   See Chapter 2, p. 43 and Chapter 4, p. 138.

To review, homeostasis operates by the process of feedback. If the set point of a thermostat is 68°, then external temperatures higher than that will cause the cooling systems to come on, whereas temperatures below 68° will result in heat production. Here 68° is the desired state, and any deviation from that state is minimized by the thermostatic control of heat and cooling.

Homeostatic principles underlie many bodily processes. We eat when we are hungry; we are hungry when our body needs more fuel. When we are cold we shiver, which warms us up. Sweat cools us off when we are hot.

Temperature Regulation

One of the body's most basic homeostats is the mechanism of temperature regulation. In human beings the "set point" temperature, usually 98.6°F (37°C), is maintained by a system of *thermometer neurons* located in the hypothalamus of the brain. The **thermometer neurons** measure blood temperature: if there is a discrepancy of about 1°C from the set point, they alter their firing rate, which triggers actions either to warm or cool the blood. Warming is accomplished by increased muscle tone, shivering, and constriction of the peripheral blood vessels, which decreases heat loss; cooling is achieved by sweating and vasodilation in the arms, legs, and head.

A fever occurs when the hypothalamic set point itself is raised. There is some evidence that the development of a fever itself may be beneficial: the increased body temperature during fever may kill viruses that cause common febrile diseases such as influenza (Dinarello & Wolfe, 1979).

Thirst

Every cell of the body is bathed in fluid; it accounts for 75 percent of body weight. The maintenance of proper fluid intake and regulation is an extremely important and intricate job, since a small loss of fluid can kill us.

How Do We Know We Are Thirsty?

When your mouth feels dry, you take a drink. Like much in our experience, it seems so simple. However, there is an amazingly complicated system to regulate body fluids. Your mouth is dry because there is a drop in the water content of the blood; this dries out the salivary glands. Usually the glands dry out gradually, but occasionally it may occur suddenly, as in the case of exercise on a hot day.

However, thirst can be quenched in several ways, only one of which is wetting down the salivary glands. For instance, water placed directly into the stomach through a tube reduces thirst. Clearly there is a more central mechanism for fluid control than the glands in the mouth. When the water content outside the cells (primarily in the blood) drops, the concentration of salt (which is usually 0.9%) in bodily fluids increases. That causes fluid from the cells to be released into the bloodstream, increasing blood volume and, hence blood pressure. **Pressure receptors** in the veins also detect even the smallest reduction in the water content of the blood. This leads, by means of messages transmitted from the veins by the sympathetic nervous system, to the release of *renin,* an enzyme produced by the kidney. Renin changes blood protein, *angiotensin,* into **angiotensin II,** the "thirst substance," which acts on receptors in the hypothalamus and other parts of the limbic system, which, in turn, activate the sensation of thirst. The hypothalamic receptors can also be activated by salt water and by the neurotransmitter acetylcholine (ACh). So there is a complex system just to indicate that fluid is needed.

How Do We Know When to Stop Drinking?

When the correct amount of fluid is ingested, we stop drinking. However, how we know when to stop drinking is less clear than why we start, because *we stop before the fluid has time to enter the cells of the body.* One factor is that there are *venous pressure receptors* that detect entering fluid. These receptors reduce renin production, which diminishes the conversion of angiotensin to angiotensin II, and so the activity in the area of the hypothalamus concerned with thirst is reduced. However, this cannot be the whole story, because much of the liquid is still unabsorbed when

FIGURE 13–3
Thirst and the
Regulation of Body Fluids
A drop in the water content of your blood, which dries out your salivary glands and makes your mouth dry, is only part of what is involved in thirst. The extremely complex system for regulating body fluids is explained in the accompanying text and Figure 13–4.

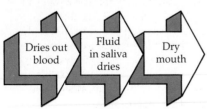

we cease drinking. Perhaps increased stomach volume is used as a feedback signal, but the specific mechanism is not yet understood.

If there is no fluid intake, as occurs in sleep, and the cell fluids are too

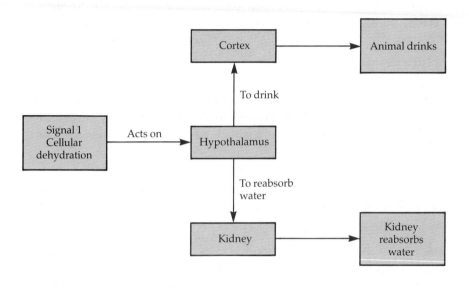

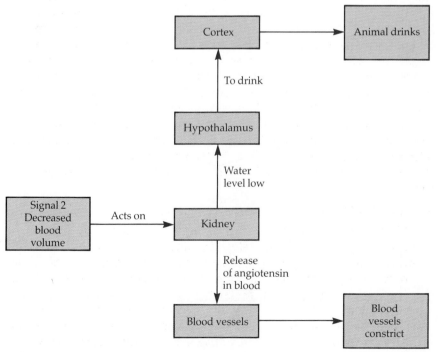

FIGURE 13–4
Regulation of Water Intake
In the upper flow chart cellular dehydration signals the hypothalamus to tell the kidney to reabsorb water and the cerebral cortex to have the animal drink. In the lower flow chart decreased blood volume prompts the kidney to trigger constriction of the blood vessels and to signal the hypothalamus of the need for water intake.

low, a hormonal feedback system is activated. The anterior hypothalamus produces antidiuretic hormone (ADH), which signals the kidneys to divert some of the water in the urine to the bloodstream. The absence of ADH, which may result from damage to the hypothalamus, as in *diabetes insipidus*, leads to an increase of 10 to 15 times the normal amount of urine and almost constant thirst and drinking (Bellows, 1939).

Hunger

Thirst regulation is more complex than temperature regulation, and the processes regulating hunger are even more complex than those regulating thirst. One consequence of this complexity is that while disorders of temperature regulation and thirst are unusual, hunger disorders such as obesity are common.

How Do We Know We Are Hungry?

It seems obvious that we know when we are hungry, but as with thirst there is a complex system underlying our experience. *Gastric* and *metabolic* factors are at work, telling us when to eat and when to stop.

Gastric Factors in Hunger

Walter Cannon, who pioneered much research on the wisdom of the body, emphasized the gastric (stomach) component of hunger. In one experiment, he cajoled his research assistant into swallowing a balloon attached to a graph that recorded the changes in size of the balloon. When the stomach expanded, so did the balloon; when it contracted, the balloon did too. Cannon's assistant's reports of hunger pangs coincided

FIGURE 13–5A
The Lateral Hypothalamus and the Control of Eating
When their lateral hypothalamus is destroyed, rats will not eat or drink. If tube fed, such animals usually resume eating and drinking on their own in time. But those that were starved before the operation increase their eating and those freely fed prior to the operation eat less. Eventually, the two groups' weight and eating and drinking patterns will stabilize at about the same relatively normal level. (After Powley & Kessey, 1970)

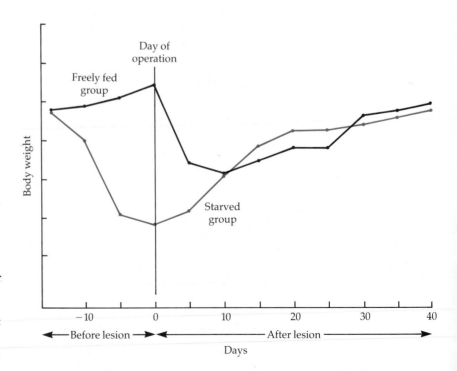

with contractions of the balloon (Cannon, 1929). Thus, Cannon proposed that stomach contractions were the primary signal of hunger.

Metabolic Factors

However, it soon became obvious that there is more to hunger than stomach contractions and more to stomach contractions than simple stomach emptiness. For instance, stomach contractions stop when sugar is injected directly into the bloodstream, even though the stomach is still empty.

The area of most intense research in hunger has been on metabolic factors. These factors relate hunger to the maintenance of energy and body weight. They are registered in the brain in terms of level of blood sugar and the amount of fat deposited in the body.

We get hungry when our blood sugar (glucose) is low (Mayer, 1953). However, we do not stop eating only because blood sugar is restored to the proper level (Thompson, 1975). Although the control of eating is rather complex, it is in some way mediated by fibers in several brain structures, especially the hypothalamus. How this works is seen by what happens when the lateral hypothalamus (LH) of a rat is destroyed. The rat will stop eating, will actually starve to death without tube feeding (Anand & Brobeck, 1951). However, if these rats are tube fed, their normal eating and drinking patterns are gradually restored, which indicates that the LH is not the "eating and drinking center." Destruction of some areas of the hypothalamus leads to very specific deficits; there may be an inability to regulate blood sugar level, but other food regulation capacities, such as response to food deprivation, are left untouched (Blass & Kety, 1974). It is clear that the hypothalamus is intimately involved in feeding, but in a complex way. But other studies indicate that disruption of eating and drinking is associated with lesions in a number of areas outside the hypothalamus (Grossman, 1979).

How Do We Know When to Stop Eating?

The destruction of one region of the hypothalamus, the ventromedial nuclei (VMN), resulted in **hyperphagia** or extreme overeating. This lesion produced some extremely fat rats, who were unable to stop eating (Hetherington & Ranson, 1942). Teitelbaum (1957) discovered that these

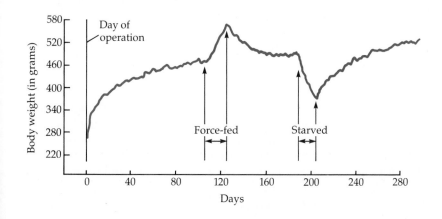

FIGURE 13–5B
The Ventromedial Nuclei and Hyperphagia
Destruction of the ventromedial nuclei of a rat's hypothalamus causes hyperphagia—extreme overeating. The weight of such rats eventually stabilizes at a new, obese level that is only temporarily influenced by either force feeding or starvation. (See also Figure 4–7, p. 141.) (After Hoebel & Teitelbaum, 1966)

rats were picky eaters. They consumed an enormous amount, but were more sensitive to the taste of the food than normal rats. They only ate a lot of what they liked. The same with obese humans. Obese humans and rats with VMN lesions have lost internal mechanisms that control eating, and they seem to eat more because of external cues (Schachter, 1971; Schachter & Rodin, 1974). An internal cue would be stomach contractions or low blood sugar. An external cue would be the lunch whistle or the appearance of food. Thus, there are cognitive factors in the control of eating. Although this "external" versus "internal" distinction does not hold absolutely (Rodin, 1978), there seems to be a difference in how people use external cues for food.

Rats with VMN lesions do not go on eating until they explode, but simply maintain a new, higher body weight (Brooks & Lambert, 1946; King & Gaston, 1977). When the VMN is damaged, growth hormone, which modulates the effect of insulin (Frohman & Bernardi, 1968), decreases; circulating insulin then increases, which in turn decreases the burning of fatty acids, resulting in increased deposits of fat. Normally, circulating insulin increases as soon as the organism begins to eat (Struble & Steffens, 1975). When the VMN is damaged, this normal process may be exaggerated (Steffens, 1970; Steffens, Mogenson, & Stevenson, 1972).

Although we have some idea of what happens when the VMN is damaged, we are less clear about how it works when it is working well. It might be a direct sensory process—food passing through several stages of digestion may be signaled to the VMN—or perhaps the production of insulin is the cue.

Obesity

The search for the edible and the delicious is constant in history, and continues now with new cuisines, new restaurants, new food crazes. Farb and Armelagos (1980) write:

> Humans will swallow almost anything that does not swallow them first. The animals they relish range in size from termites to whales; the Chinese of Hunan Province eat shrimp that are still wiggling, while North Americans and Europeans eat live oysters; some Asians prefer food so putrified that the stench carries for dozens of yards. At various times and places, strong preferences have been shown for the fetuses of rodents, the tongues of larks, the eyes of sheep, the spawn of eels, the stomach contents of whales, and the windpipes of pigs.

Many other pleasures are associated with certain foods: some are thought to be aphrodisiacs; an image of daily love and togetherness might be a family gathered around a holiday table; the cliché has it that the way to a man's heart is through his stomach; Jewish mothers are well known to cure everything with chicken soup.

Our love of and preoccupation with food has had, until recently, great adaptive value. In times when the food supply was not reliable, people who gorged themselves when food was plentiful had more chance of survival when it was not. In addition, when most work required the expenditure of enormous amounts of energy, huge meals were needed as fuel for the manual labor. Until recently, unheated homes made it necessary for people to produce the heat *within* themselves, from what went into their stomachs, not into a furnace. Thus, although we may be biologically programmed to eat greatly, this predisposition may no longer have adaptive value.

Temperature and Food Intake Regulation

However, the body operates like a furnace: metabolism is a process in which fuel (food) is burned to make heat to keep the body warm and to provide energy. When there is more fuel than can be metabolized, it is stored as fat to be used when needed. The regulation is damnably accurate. Each of us eats, over a lifetime, more than 45 tons of food, and weight is quite precisely regulated. Consider this: if you were to eat 200 calories a day more than you burn (one small chocolate bar), without increasing other activities, or if there was no adaptation in the body, you would gain about 20 pounds in a year! Today, with a drastic increase in the availability of food, a decrease in strenuous activities, easier modes of transportation, and central heating, the end product is often fat. In some contemporary Western European countries, like Germany, more than 75 percent of the population is overweight.

The "Set Point"

Weight is gained when there are more calories taken in than are expended. A calorie is a measure of heat production, defined as the amount of energy required to increase the temperature of one gram of water by 1° C. However, losing and gaining weight is *not* simply a matter of decreasing calorie intake, because the homeostatic mechanisms of the body regulate weight around a set point. The **set point** is the body

FIGURE 13–6
Humans are truly omnivorous, able and willing to eat large quantities of any and all kinds of food. In most times and places this has been of great adaptive value to our species.

weight around which the brain, probably involving the hypothalamus, attempts to maintain homeostasis (Cabanac, 1971). The hypothalamus can control eating and drinking and metabolic level to raise or lower caloric expenditure; these activities can be increased or decreased. The set point, not primarily our conscious decisions, keeps weight around a predetermined level. In fact, it is almost impossible to consciously regulate food intake to a few hundred calories a day. Even a nutritionist could not estimate caloric intake that precisely (Bennett, 1983).

That weight is homeostatically regulated around a set point (which may be different from the body weight "we" want) means that it is *more difficult both to gain and to lose weight* than we would predict by merely counting calories.

The brain's regulation of body weight helps us understand why it is easier to lose weight at the beginning of a diet and harder at the end. At the beginning of a diet we may be far away from our set point; the farther away from the set point we are, the easier weight is to lose.

There are common excuses for being overweight:

1. "I've lost hundreds of pounds in my life" (the implication being that it is always gained back).
2. "It doesn't matter how much I eat—I am just naturally fat."
3. "I can gain weight *just looking* at food."

Recent evidence suggests that these clichés are true.

Innate Factors in Obesity

Here is a sad fact: some people *are* born to be fat. It seems that the set point for weight is simply higher in these people. This, as is well known, makes losing weight to a desired ideal difficult if not impossible. Fatness is related to the number and size of the body's fat cells, called **adipocites.** Obese people have three times the number of these fat cells as do people of normal weight (Björntorp, 1972). Fat cells are established in the first two years of life. Overfeeding in those years results in an increased number of fat cells (Knittle, 1971). No amount of weight loss after that age lessens the number of fat cells; they remain, waiting to be bloated. Some researchers think there are other critical periods of fat cell production: from the ages 6 to 10 and during adolescence (Nisbett, 1972).

A person with too many fat cells has a high set point for food consumption and will continue to be hungry even when his or her weight is at the supposed "norm." The problem for the "constitutionally obese" is that their own body norm (another way to describe set point) is higher than the cultural norm. The "naturally obese," or, more properly, the naturally heavy, then face two bleak alternatives: either constant hunger or being thought of as overweight. So these people lose and gain weight constantly; their diets do not work. They are up against a powerful biological barrier.

A Remarkable Finding on Obesity and Health

There is one consolation, however, for people who seem doomed to never match the skinny ideal of the models in jeans ads. For years it has been assumed that thin people are healthier (most actuarial tables of insurance companies reflect this; obese people pay higher rates for life insurance).

It has recently been found (Andres, in press) that, on the contrary, people who are *slightly fat are the healthiest* (see Figure 13–7). Extremely thin and extremely fat people have the highest mortality rate. The ideal weight, defined as the best for health, is higher than we have thought and: (1) men's and women's ideal weights, at each height, are the same; (2) the *ideal* weight increases with age, thus a person 5'11" at 45 should weigh 15 pounds more than at 20. Most of the advice we are given in terms of health is more likely cultural advice (look thin = look young) than based on medical data. Our lower brain centers, evolved over millions of years to adjust weight for health, in this case may well be wiser than our current cultural ideal; so being "overweight" may not be such a losing battle, after all.

Cognitive Factors in Obesity

Obese people seem to have a slightly different cognitive orientation than those of normal weight. They are more responsive to external situations than people of normal weight. When an attractive bowl of cashews is well lit, an obese person will eat more than when the bowl is not well lit. Normals eat the same amount irrespective of light conditions (Ross, 1974). If overweight people have listened to a description of food, they will eat more than normals when it is offered; they eat more when they are bored than when engrossed in a situation (Rodin, 1978).

When people, especially fat people, say "Just looking at food makes me fat!" they are more correct than they expect. In one study, obese people were asked to look at a sizzling steak, with the promise that they would soon be eating it. Just looking at the steak increased the produc-

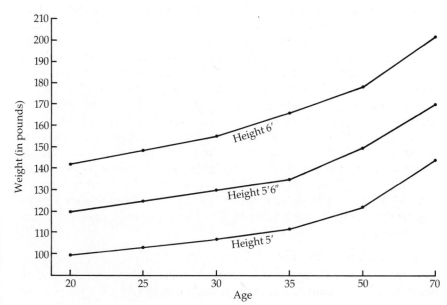

FIGURE 13–7
"Natural Weight"
The most recent research indicates that "natural weight" depends only on your height and age. This table graphs the natural weight for persons 5', 5'6", and 6' at different ages in their lives. Weight within 15 pounds of each of these points should not interfere with health. Thus, a 25-year-old woman or man who is 5'6" can weigh between 110 and 140 with probably little health effect. (After Andres, in press)

tion of insulin, which accelerates the entry of sugar into the existing fat cells, enlarging them, and making the person fatter (Rodin, 1978).

Resetting the Set Point

Overeating and Weight Gain

It is a common observation that we do not gain as much weight on a binge as when we overeat steadily. This observation is confirmed by a number of studies. In one, rats who ingested 80 percent more calories at one feeding than normal gained only 27 percent more weight than rats on the normal diet (Bennett, 1983). Their activity was exactly the same as the rats on the normal diet. How were the extra calories burned up? There is a specialized kind of fat cell whose purpose seems to be the production of heat when there is a sudden caloric oversupply. It is called "brown adipose tissue," often referred to as "brown fat." The function of brown fat has been more firmly established in animals other than adult humans, but brown fat seems to burn up calories at a great rate. Brown fat is activated by either excessive calories or by homeostatic adaptation to cold, so people with brown fat may often be warm in the cold.

Obese rats do not have as many brown fat cells. In a comparison of normal and obese rats fed an identical diet, normal rats lose weight faster, because they produce more heat. Heat production, then, may be as important as food intake in the regulation of weight (Rothwell & Stock, 1979).

Undereating and Weight Loss

When we begin to eat less, the homeostatic mechanisms of the body begin immediately to compensate for the fuel shortage by conserving its

FIGURE 13–8
Obesity and Beauty
People who are fat can be considered healthy, admirable, even beautiful in their own culture. But in other times and places thinness may be equated with health and beauty while obesity is viewed as unattractive, unhealthy, even unnatural.

resources. This is a huge advantage for adaptation if the food supply continues to be short, but it is a great annoyance when we try to lose weight: *we lose less than a simple calorie intake analysis would predict.* This is how it works: a reduction in calorie intake reduces the resting metabolic rate (RMR), so less heat is produced and body resources are conserved. We slow down and we do not expend as much energy. At the beginning of a diet, when weight may be well above the set point, weight loss occurs fairly quickly. As the weight is lowered, the body strives to maintain its set point, RMR is reduced, and weight is lost *less quickly* or not at all.

Starvation

On the other side of the coin, the body's built-in protection against famine lowers the "set point" drastically when the food supply is low. Then, weight loss may be extremely difficult. The body continues to slow down, always conserving resources.

The limits to which the body can conserve were determined in a series of studies, carried out in secret by Jewish doctors in World War II, during the Nazi occupation of Poland. The caloric intake of the residents of the Warsaw ghetto was decreased by the Nazis from about 2,400 per day to about 300; protein intake was cut to about 10 percent of normal. The record these doctors made of the human body was of an organism struggling heroically to adapt. These changes were observed: body temperature dropped, blood pressure decreased, blood circulated at a slower rate, and the body burned fuel in the most efficient way possible. Eventually, some of the stored protein in muscles, including the heart, was burned. If a starvation diet is continued, it can, of course, lead to death (Winick, 1979). However, the changes in metabolism to conserve resources undoubtedly saved many lives in the ghetto and concentration

FIGURE 13-9 Expenditure of Calories

Food	Minutes of Activity					
	CALORIES	WALKING	BICYCLING	SWIMMING	RUNNING	RECLINING
Apple, large	101	19	12	9	5	78
Bacon, 2 strips	96	18	12	9	5	74
Banana, small	88	17	11	8	4	68
Beans, green, 1 cup	27	5	3	2	1	21
Beer, 1 glass	114	22	14	10	6	88
Bread and butter	78	15	10	7	4	60
Cake, 2 layer, 1/12	356	68	43	32	18	274
Carbonated beverage, 1 glass	106	20	13	9	5	82
Carrot, raw	42	8	5	4	2	32
Cereal, dry, 1/2 cup with milk, sugar	200	38	24	18	10	154
Cheese, cottage, 1 tbs.	27	5	3	2	1	21
Cheese, cheddar, 1 oz.	111	21	14	10	6	85
Chicken, fried, 1/2 breast	232	45	28	21	12	178
Chicken, TV dinner	542	104	66	48	28	417
Cookie, plain	15	3	2	1	1	12
Cookie, chocolate chip	51	10	6	5	3	39
Doughnut	151	29	18	13	8	116
Egg, fried	110	21	13	10	6	85
Egg, boiled	77	15	9	7	4	59
French dressing, 1 tbs.	59	11	7	5	3	45
Halibut steak, 1/4 lb.	205	39	25	18	11	158
Ham, 2 slices	167	32	20	15	9	128

Source: Adapted from Konishi, F. (1965). Food energy equivalents of various activities, *Journal of the American Dietetic Association, 46*, 186.

camps, as they probably did when our ancestors were confronted with famine.

Losing Weight

In this culture, obesity may be a cause of stress (e.g., feeling "fat and ugly") or it may be partially a result, as when people cope with frustrations and anxiety by eating more (Polivy & Herman, 1983). Obesity can also compound stress from other causes, making people more susceptible to hypertension, heart disease, diabetes, and other ailments.

Each year there are new wonder diets galore: all fruit, no fruit, all

Food	Minutes of Activity					
	CALORIES	WALKING	BICYCLING	SWIMMING	RUNNING	RECLINING
Hamburger sandwich	350	67	43	31	18	269
Ice cream, ⅙ qt.	193	37	24	17	10	148
Ice cream soda	255	49	31	23	13	196
Ice milk, ⅙ qt.	144	28	18	13	7	111
Mayonnaise, 1 tbs.	92	18	11	8	5	71
Milk, 1 glass	166	32	20	15	9	128
Milk, skim, 1 glass	81	16	10	7	4	62
Milk shake	421	81	51	38	22	324
Orange, medium	68	13	8	6	4	52
Orange juice, 1 glass	120	23	15	11	6	92
Pancake with syrup	124	24	15	11	6	95
Peach, medium	46	9	6	4	2	35
Peas, green, ½ cup	56	11	7	5	3	43
Pie, apple, ⅙	377	73	46	34	19	290
Pizza, cheese, ⅛	180	35	22	16	9	138
Pork chop, loin	314	60	38	28	16	242
Potato chips, 1 serving	108	21	13	10	6	83
Sherbet, ⅙ qt.	177	34	22	16	9	136
Shrimp, French fried	180	35	22	16	9	138
Spaghetti, 1 serving	396	76	48	35	20	305
Steak, T-bone	235	45	29	21	12	181
Strawberry shortcake	400	77	49	36	21	308
Tuna-salad sandwich	278	53	34	25	14	214

meat, no meat, specific schemes of "chemical combinations," tricks like staples in the ear, and almost everything else. Diets come and go in continual fads, indicating that no specific diet can produce an immediate and lasting weight reduction for all people. *There are no miracles in weight loss.*

The homeostatic mechanisms of the body also serve to discourage weight loss: at the beginning, when one may be high above the real set point, weight loss is easier; as one approaches the set point, however, weight loss is more difficult. This causes many people to go off their diet and return to the original weight. Also, people try to establish a new, lower set point; when this cannot be reached, they abandon all discipline. This is known in technical terms as the "what the hell" effect (Polivy & Hermann, 1983). The wonder diet has not been invented, nor has the wonder physical exercise program. There are several principles, however, that should be taken into account in planning weight loss:

1. Some people will always be fatter than others, due to the fat cells determined both genetically and early in life.
2. Because of the homeostatic regulation of the body, both weight gain and weight loss are more difficult than one might think.
3. Some people are more responsive to external cues associated with food, so reducing the variety and attractiveness of food may help.
4. Ultimately, the loss of weight depends simply on burning more calories than you take in, and *this is the only principle that matters.*

Eating less is one means of adjusting weight, but to maintain weight loss, *food intake must be continually decreased as the diet goes along,* since our caloric needs decrease at lower weight. Therefore, a diet low enough in calories to lower weight early in the diet may cause no weight loss or even a weight gain later on.

An alternative is to increase exercise. There have been several serious misunderstandings of the effects of exercise on obesity. It has falsely been believed that exercise requires relatively little calorie expenditure and therefore results in little weight loss and that any increase in calorie expenditure results in appetite increase, which will offset any positive effect. In most studies, however, it has been found that an increase in activity actually decreases the appetite rather than increasing it. The first error is made because people forget that any weight burned in exercise is cumulative, hour to hour, and day to day. Thus, a 170-pound person walking one level mile in 20 minutes will burn about 100 calories. If calorie intake is kept constant and if the increased activity of walking that one mile each day is continued regularly, although the decrease in one day is less than half an ounce, in one year this would cause a reduction of 10 pounds.

Exercise has several effects:

1. It increases the caloric consumption (heat production) during the exercise.
2. Exercise also increases heat production *after* a meal, and there is increased heat production between meals (Gleeson et al., 1979). This means that the increase in calories burned during exercise *continues through the day.* Running a mile burns an average of 100 calories during the run, but more calories are consumed throughout the day. This increases the weight-losing effect of exercise.
3. Exercise reduces appetite.
4. Exercise converts fat to muscle. This does not usually result in weight loss, but in loss of inches of girth, which is what most people usually want (Bennett & Gurin, 1982).

The only sure kind of diet is one that takes your own individuality into account, including eating and exercise habits and metabolism. The simplest way to lose weight is to set up your own feedback system and monitor it consistently. The feedback device can be a scale or a tape measure. You should be able to chart your calorie intake from one of the indexes of caloric contents of foods and the impact of your exercise from the exercise tables. At any initial level of activity and eating you should be able to either increase your exercise or decrease your consumption so that weight is lost. You should be able to find a level of exercise and eating that may aid in losing at least some weight. However, the last few pounds will be the most difficult, so either do not lose them or do not get discouraged. One cheering fact to remember if you do fail is that low weight may not be as healthy as average weight.

Food Intake and Calorie Expenditure   See Figure 13–9, pp. 480–81.

BELONGING AND SAFETY

When the most basic and immediate physiological needs are met, others then need to be satisfied. Safety must be maintained, pain avoided, pleasures sought. There are specifically human needs to belong to groups and social networks, to give and receive attention. Pain and pleasure, belonging, and maternal care will be discussed briefly here.

Pain and Pleasure

Avoiding pain and seeking pleasure guide the behavior of most animals. There exist well-defined pain and pleasure systems in the nervous system. These serve as a feedback system about actions that may be injurious or helpful to the organism's survival or reproductive success. An organism's feelings are, then, one strong guide to action, and it is here that emotions and motives are most closely related.

To review from Chapter 5, there is an innate network for sending pain information to the brain. The lemniscal system quickly transmits sudden pain, as from a blow or a sharp instrument. Sudden pain preempts consciousness, as when you put your hand on something hot. The spino-thalamic system transmits slow pain information, like that of an old injury or a back problem. There is a "pleasure system" in the brain's limbic system, which is probably the final common pathway of the feeling of pleasure. Animals with electrodes in the "pleasure center" will perform almost any action to keep that center stimulated, even forgoing food and drink under certain conditions (Routenberg, 1976).

Belonging

One element that runs through our evolutionary history is cooperation. At first glance you might be surprised to find "belonging" as a human need. After all, we have defined a need as something that, if not satisfied, results in harm to the organism, such as starvation from lack of food. Why, then, is "belonging," or the attention of others, a need, like

Cooperation and Human Society See Chapter 2, p. 65.

food? There is much recent evidence that when people are deprived of belonging to a group, they may suffer health consequences. Human beings are social animals.

In one Australian aboriginal tribe, a person may become the victim of "bone pointing" when a powerful witch casts a spell condemning the unfortunate person to death. The people in the tribe then treat such individuals as if they were actually dead. They do not speak to them or acknowledge their presence, and act as if they cannot see them. Unless the "spell" is lifted, the condemned often do die.

FIGURES 13–10 and 13–11
People Need to Belong
Being part of a group (as at right, top) having even one friend and engaging in social interaction (as at right, bottom) or merely caring for a pet or a house plant provides a sense of belonging that can improve individuals' health and outlook on life.

Is this extreme example just superstition? One study in our society partially repeated these extreme conditions. Experimenters at a military base instructed a group of soldiers to ignore one man completely, and to act as if he literally were not there. The man lost his appetite, became apathetic, and withdrew. He began to develop a "thousand-mile stare" (looking far into the distance, noticed in prisoners of war). Needless to say, the effect was so surprising and devastating that the experiment was soon called off.

In cases when people are deprived of normal social interaction, there are significant negative effects on intelligence and on health. Recall that children in a Lebanese orphanage who were neglected showed much lower intelligence (Dennis & Dennis, 1948). When some children in an orphanage were "adopted" by caring people, their intelligence increased (Skeels & Dye, 1939).

So *people need people, and need the attention of others.* In an extensive study of the effect of social networks on health, Syme and others found that healthy people have a more extensive network of friends than those less healthy. Professor Syme often begins his lectures saying, "When I was young and felt bad, my grandmother used to tell me, 'Go out and play with your friends'; now I find there is good evidence for this" (Syme, 1984).

When people who lack friends or a group are encouraged to join one, their health improves. A large project is under way in San Francisco's "Tenderloin" area seeking to improve the health of the impoverished elderly residents by forming neighborhood associations. The results, although preliminary, show significant health improvements when people belong to a group (Minkler, 1984). Almost any improvement in "belonging" seems to help, whether there is a person involved or not. Patients in a nursing home who were given a plant to care for showed improvements in health (Rodin & Langer, 1978). To belong and perhaps to be needed, by a family, a group, or a club, is an important human need, more of a basic need than we might expect.

Maternal Care

Maternal care in female rats seems largely to be under hormonal control. If the hormones in the blood from a mother rat are transferred to another rat, the latter will begin to exhibit the characteristic maternal behavior pattern of rats, which includes nesting, licking, retrieving, and nursing the young rats (Terkel & Rosenblatt, 1972). In humans, hormonal regulation probably does not completely determine maternal behavior, although hormones under the control of the pituitary do play a specific role in lactation and nursing. Male rats never care for their offspring. Human males may come to take an active role in child care, and some women abandon their children. It may be that the hormones associated with lactation predispose the mother toward loving and caring for the child (Newton & Modahl, 1978), although it is more likely that it is the closeness involved in the activity of nursing itself and other caretaking functions that cement the love bond.

GOALS

Many of the needs we have just discussed are common to all animals: food, drink, avoiding pain, safety. Belonging needs and needs for attention are common to social animals like humans and chimpanzees. But what is uniquely human is not our needs but our goals. Human beings are not only motivated by biological *deficits* but by the invention of *possibilities* (Dubos, 1978). Homeostatic adaptation is important to all organisms and it is to us as well. However, our most important inheritance is the ability to go beyond our inheritance.

The motives we will consider as goals all serve the function of creative adaptation: the ability to create a new world to suit ourselves. These motives are more "mental" than biological; they are highly individual and are capable of being expressed differently by different people. If we had no goals, we would have no civilization: such as the built world of cities and the world of universities and psychology.

What makes us unique also makes us so hard to study: why someone creates or is "driven" to form a new company is not as anatomically clear as the thirst drive. Thus, some of the most meaningful human experiences are not as well understood as some of the most basic. We will consider here several kinds of human goals: competence and excellence, achievement (which has been extensively and imaginatively studied), knowledge and understanding, and self-actualization and transcendence.

Competence and Excellence: Esteem

Competence is how well we can carry out an intended action. It earns us the esteem of others and builds our self-respect. In the early years, competence may involve quite simple tasks, such as getting food into the mouth or lifting a cup. At around two, a child smiles when able to perform a task successfully. Competence is a part of the emerging human consciousness.

Later on there are other challenges to competence: learning new tasks—like riding a bike or reading, making friends, and being liked. Challenges to one's competence appear throughout life, especially to people of high aspiration. The desired *level* of competence increases with age, from the toddler to the student to the worker to the executive.

Achievement

Competence produces its own reward: achievement. The sense of achievement is so reinforcing that it is itself a motivating force in human existence. David McClelland, a major investigator of human motivation, defines the drive for achievement as "competition with a standard of excellence" (McClelland, 1984). In a long series of studies, McClelland and his associates have concentrated their study on what they call the achievement motive, or need for achievement. **Achievement motivation** is what enables us to carry through and complete the goals we set for ourselves. Many human goals are long-term and not immediately attain-

Going Beyond Our Inheritance
See Chapter 2, p. 69.

Competence and the Emergence of Consciousness   See Chapter 3, p. 96.

able. You can quench thirst right away, but it takes years to become a great pianist. The need to achieve keeps you on the path toward a distant goal.

Achievement motivation is different at different times. The value placed on achievement itself and the kinds of achievements that are valued vary within cultures and across time. In nineteenth-century America, the folklore was dominated by stories of remarkable achievements: inventions, mastery over the wild environment, people making huge fortunes. "Success stories" are not as popular today. This ideal of achievement has never been central in such cultures as those of the Egyptians and the American Indians. The rise and fall of a civilization can sometimes be correlated with the achievement level in literature: "striving" is a major theme in early Greek literature, but by the time of the peak of the civilization it had declined (McClelland, 1961). Revolutions bring forth changes in achievement. There was a higher level of achievement in children's books in Russia and China after their communist revolutions than before, and high achievers were the heroes in stories in the early years following the American Revolution.

Characteristics of Achievers

The achievement motive is a *need* for achievement and is a relatively consistent and characteristic component of a person's personality (McClelland et al., 1953). McClelland's study of achievement motivation has revealed striking differences between the personality profiles of people in whom the need for achievement is high and those in whom it is low.

People with a high level of *n-Ach* (a measure of the strength of the achievement motive) set *moderately* high, *realizable* goals. High achievers are more likely to actively pursue success, rather than simply avoid failure. This activity includes a willingness to take some risks. They are more internally motivated than low achievers; a sense of their own competence and excellence is more motivating and rewarding than external rewards, like money. They make decisions and judgments on their own, independently of the opinion of others. They are more likely to associate with others on the basis of their competence than friendship. Their fantasies often concern unique accomplishments (McClelland & Winter, 1971). They like concrete feedback and criticism, and they prefer to direct activities with definable goals and clear-cut results. McClelland suggests that this tendency may be why high achievers are more attracted to business careers than academic ones. A business usually has a definable outcome: "the bottom line"—does it make money? An academic contribution is often more difficult to evaluate.

The need for achievement is probably determined by environmental factors. But achievement does seem to breed achievement. The standards parents set for their children and the parents' accomplishments themselves are critical in the development of n-Ach. Parental training and expectations are the most important factors, specifically reliance in their children from an early age, "getting the child to do things well [and] on his own" (Rosen, 1959).

Socioeconomic class, at least in some older studies, has also been

Nobel Prizewinning Geneticist Barbara McClintock

Jonas Salk

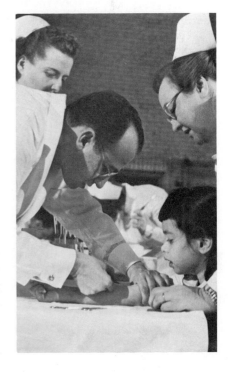

shown to affect n-Ach. Upper- and middle-income homes produce twice as many high achievers as lower-income homes (Rosen, 1956), which probably results from the fact that middle- and upper-class parents are high achievers and set higher standards for their children. For example, over the past few decades, when opportunities for advancement have been more accessible to blacks in the United States, there has been an increase, not only in their income, but also in n-Ach (Banks, McQuarter, & Hubbard, 1977; Rokeach, 1973; Rosen, 1959).

Achievement motivation can be easily and quickly learned, even in adulthood. In one study, businessmen in India took an achievement motivation course. Later it was found that they made more investments, employed more people, and made more money than before they took the course (McClelland, 1971).

Knowledge: Organization, Curiosity, and Exploration

A most important human motive is the search for knowledge and understanding of the world. Systems of education and philosophical, scientific, and fictional works all serve to further our understanding. This is all quite evident to anyone. What might not be so evident is that the search for how the world is organized is so basic to us that our health suffers when our understanding of the world is in disarray (Antonovsky, 1979).

Organization

To review once again: our nervous system is designed to organize the world. It selects only a few meaningful elements from all the stimuli that reach us, organizes them into the most likely occurrences, and remembers only a small organized sample of what has occurred. At each step the world becomes more organized and simplified in the mind. A network of schemata is developed to represent the world so that the external world, so chaotic and changing, becomes stable, simplified, and seemingly coherent in the mind. Instead of thousands of reflecting bits of glass, gray stone, scores of doors opening and closing, several high ceilings, we perceive *one* building. The parts fit together.

There is a sense of organization, or of coherence, to things. When this sense of coherence regarding a person's world is disrupted, he or she is more likely to become ill (Antonovsky, 1979). If the world is disorganized, it is not clear what appropriate action to take in any situation, and it is not clear that we can control our lives to any extent. We will treat these issues more extensively in our discussion of the problems of daily life (Chapter 15), but here it is enough to note that the motive to organize and to understand the world is so basic to us that it affects our health when it is in disorder.

Curiosity and Exploration

The other side of our voracious organizational ability is that we become restless when things get too organized: we get bored, we need to change, we need to create something new. It was, in some part, curiosity and exploration that led our ancestors out of the trees and away from the savannah to every corner of the earth. We explore our environment as

FIGURE 13–12
Curious Monkeys
Experiments have shown that monkeys and other animals are motivated by curiosity and prefer stimulating, complex environments.

much to find what it is like as to find something in particular. Other organisms are also curious. Monkeys will work for the reward of the sight of another monkey. Indeed, even rats are motivated by curiosity: they will choose a more complex environment over a less complex one (Dember, Earl, & Paradise, 1957); they quickly learn to press a bar that makes a new compartment accessible to exploration (Myers & Viller, 1957).

> The inveterate curiosity of the white rat is well known to comparative psychologists, and even better known to the animal caretaker and trainer. One of the best of many stories about the affectionately remembered Fred Brown, for many years animal caretaker at Brown University, is the following: One of the graduate students appeared one day with a group of rats in a large iron pail which was being used for a carrying cage. The rats were milling about the bottom of the pail in an agitated way, which made the student think they had "whirling disease" and would have to be destroyed. But Fred took one look and said, "Now, them rats ain't got the whirling disease. The rats just want to see out." And, sure enough, cutting windows in the sides of the pail cured them. (Hilgard & Marquis, 1961)

Curiosity increases mental activity by conveying more stimulation from the outside environment (Berlyne, 1960). If you had to eat your favorite meal every day, you would soon wince at the sight of it. Too much of a good thing is a bore. A friend of mine is a confirmed chocoholic. When she was in college, the job she was most excited about taking was in a candy store selling chocolates. She could eat all the chocolate she wanted, and for the first few days she was in paradise. After two weeks, however, she never wanted to see chocolate again! We are restless, "stimulus-hungry" creatures, even at the most basic physiological level of our nervous system.

Optimal Level of Arousal

Curiosity keeps us stimulated, but when arousal level is too low—just before sleep, in a boring situation—the level of performance suffers. Likewise, overarousal—being highly excited at bedtime, or restless when you are trying to study—hurts performance. Each of us has an optimum level of arousal. Many psychologists use an n-shaped curve (sometimes called an "inverted-U") to describe this (Figure 13–13). As you can see by the curve, the optimum level is in the middle of an organism's response range. Here pleasure is greatest, reinforcement is most efficient, and the processing of information is most efficient. Recall that the effect of deprivation on learning also is described by an n-shaped curve (Broadbent, 1961).

Many of our behaviors are motivated by the need to achieve our optimum level. Some people cannot study without loud music on; they need to increase their activation level. Others cannot be in a room with any distractions; they need to decrease their level. It is probable that individual differences in optimum level of arousal are relatively stable characteristics in individuals. Many actions in a day—working hard, exercising, resting, having a beer or cup of coffee, turning music off or playing it

FIGURE 13–13
Arousal and Performance
As this n-shaped curve shows, arousal helps performance, but overarousal can lower efficiency of performance. (After Hebb, 1972)

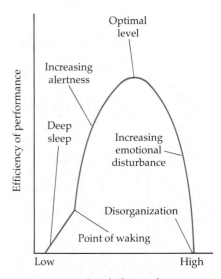

loud—are all attempts to increase or decrease arousal to the optimum level. The maintenance of the optimum level is another feedback process in human motivation; more complex, to be sure, but similar in principle to the homeostatic mechanisms in the body.

But many people also seek to upset homeostasis: to temporarily elevate their arousal level to the high range of the curve, even if it is unpleasant, presumably for the pleasure that occurs when that stimulation is reduced. Thus people do strange, "sensation-seeking" things like riding roller coasters, driving quickly, eating very spicy food, jumping out of airplanes, going to horror movies, watching erotic films, and more (Zuckerman, 1979).

Self-actualization and Transcendence

Humans do not live for bread alone, or even to be safe or to be loved or for their work. Some psychologists have postulated a drive, of sorts, to develop oneself, called self-actualization, and in some a drive to go beyond the normal range of knowledge, to "transcendence" (Maslow, 1970).

Self-actualization

Abraham Maslow was concerned that psychologists typically restricted their study to problems and breakdowns in human functioning because these issues are more easily studied. It is easier and more fun to study mistakes in thinking than errorless thinking; easier to study a need such as hunger than a goal that makes people strive for years to achieve a particular kind of excellence.

Maslow coined the term **self-actualization** to refer to the growth motivation of the healthy individual. He believed this motive to be natural, that every person, unless obstructed, tends toward growth and health. He thought that once the lower motives are fulfilled, people begin to feel the need to expand their inner lives. He studied people whom he determined represented self-actualized, successful individuals—people such as Eleanor Roosevelt, Einstein, and Ghandi—in order to isolate those common characteristics that might be the defining characteristics of the self-actualized individual. Maslow identified the following as the distinguishing features of self-actualized individuals:

Sensation seeking is a commonly observed human activity.

1. Creativity and inventiveness.
2. Problem centering rather than ego centering. Capacity for concern about larger problems of society and humankind.
3. They feel that their life has purpose.
4. Objectivity and detachment; acceptance of self and others.
5. High tolerance of the unknown and of ambiguity.
6. Mystical or peak experiences: peak experiences are events that are of a special quality in that they serve to organize and give direction to one's life.
7. Freedom from prejudice and cultural conventions; an unconventional morality about what is right and wrong. (Maslow, 1970)

Others have followed Maslow's work and have attempted to analyze more carefully the personality characteristics of self-actualized persons. Although there has not been exhaustive research, self-actualized persons have been found to be more sexually permissive (Paxton & Turner, 1978) and to regard their own experiences and morality on their own terms, free from the opinions or influence of other people (Rizzo & Vinacke, 1975).

Although Maslow has been criticized for his lack of systematic observation and lack of precision in his definition of terms, this vagueness is not enough of a reason to discard a model of motivation that may be useful in understanding part of the "farther reaches of human nature."

Transcendence

We seek meaning in all situations, from the meaning of sensory stimulation to the remembrance of actions that mean the most to us. At the most complex level, the search for meaning involves the search for the order of the world and the meaning of life. This is generally termed the "spiritual" aspect of life and is most often represented by the organized religions such as Christianity, Judaism, and Islam, or by spiritual groupings, such as Sufism (Shah, 1982).

Transcendence, then, means to go beyond the ordinary understanding of life. It is the search for knowledge at the highest level. Some of the questions that lead to this kind of search are "What is the meaning of life?" or "What is God?" Although there has been little attention given to this search within psychology since William James's *The Varieties of Religious Experience* was published in 1900, it is a major organizing principle in the lives of many throughout the world. More than 2.5 billion people belong to the major religious groupings of the world, an orientation that determines morality, life-style, what one eats, whom one can marry, and many of the "lower" motives we have considered.

Although many aspects of religions serve social functions, the primary purpose of religious and spiritual activity is to attain a direct knowledge of how the world is organized. This knowledge may take the form of a "born again" experience in contemporary Christianity or a mystical experience, either deliberately stimulated or accidental, or it may take the form of a continuously deepening understanding of the nature of human life. In any case, it is a powerful motivator: for millennia people have fasted, prayed, meditated, given up their possessions, even gone to war, in the service of religious knowledge.

The Motives Combined

At any moment we are doing many things: the brain is monitoring body temperature, food, and water, but we may also be angling to join a club, trying to study, trying to understand a new concept. Sometimes needs combine: a person may combine the basic need for food with that of exploration and become a chef; another combines achievement with understanding and becomes a rich inventor.

Some people *may* move up the hierarchy of motives during their lives, in the idealized way Maslow describes: first satisfying basic physiological and safety needs, belonging and gaining esteem, then developing competence and understanding, and becoming self-actualized. However, probably few people follow this strict sequence. The art collector, Hirschorn, described his motive for collecting: "After the first million, money doesn't make much difference. I tried eating four meals a day and I got sick. I can't change my suits more than three times a day. So I collect art." Sometimes an individual may become dominated by one motive or another. This is true when the lower needs are not satisfied and all thoughts turn to food or to drink or the maintenance of other body processes.

Functional Autonomy

Some motives seem to persist even after they are satisfied. Students may work hard to obtain the esteem of their peers, and may find it so rewarding that they continue to seek esteem for the rest of their lives, neglecting achievement and understanding. Politicians may find that they love to run for office and win, while giving little attention to the process of governing later on, as they continually run for office.

An important determinant of the motives an individual expresses is functional autonomy. **Functional autonomy** is the tendency for any action repeated often enough to become a motive in its own right (Allport, 1961). Functional autonomy may lead an individual to stay at one level of motivation or may lead upward on the hierarchy. The motive to earn money may be prepotent when one is poor, but it may continue on for life, even when the person has enough money, or is even very rich. Habits persist. Sometimes functional autonomy leads to a different outcome. A child may learn to play a musical instrument to gain approval, but might later on develop a love for music.

However, some may skip stages on the way up; some may stay at one level. Some people may operate in a way contrary to Maslow's scheme: relatively basic needs such as esteem and belonging may be forgotten in the search for achievement or for transcendence.

It is in the particular motives that a person expresses that we find roots of individual personality.

Summary

1. *Needs* are specific deficits that any animal must satisfy, such as hunger and thirst. We have needs for food, water, rest, safety, and protection, among many others. Needs give rise to *drives,* which are physiologically based goads to behavior. They move us, literally, to action. *Goals* are desired outcomes that have not yet occurred. It is characteristic of human motivation that we seek to create new situations and cause them to come into existence. Dubos calls this aspect of human motivation "creative adaptation."

2. Instincts are patterns of behaviors classified as follows: they are *typical* of every member of a species, and they must appear without learning the first time the appropriate situation occurs. Examples of animal instincts are the specific songs of birds and the homing instincts of the salmon. In the human genetic program it is generally accepted that certain *predispositions* are inherited, not specific instincts. An example would be the attachment between mother and infant.

3. An important concept in motivation is the hierarchy proposed by Abraham Maslow. At the bottom of this *pyramid of motivation* are physiological needs, then safety, then love and belonging. Higher up are esteem, cognitive needs, aesthetic needs, self-actualization, and transcendence.

   What distinguishes the different levels on this hierarchy is the concept of *prepotence*—once the lower (stronger) needs are satisfied, the higher ones can be. For instance, a starving organism, human or otherwise, will not be able to do anything about its higher needs without satisfying the strong lower need for food.

4. *Homeostasis* is the tendency of an organism to try to maintain a constant (stasis) state. The regulatory systems of the body seek to maintain constant internal processes such as temperature, food supply, and water content. Homeostasis operates by the process of feedback.

   Temperature regulation is maintained by a system of *thermometer neurons* located in the hypothalamus of the brain. Thirst can be quenched in many ways, only one of which is wetting down the salivary glands. For instance, water placed directly into the stomach through a tube reduces thirst. Thirst operates like this: when the fluid content outside the cells (primarily in the blood) drops, *pressure receptors* in the veins eventually detect the consequent reduction in the water content of the blood; then *renin,* an enzyme produced by the kidney, is released and changes blood protein, *angiotensin,* into *angiotensin II,* the "thirst substance," which acts on receptors in the hypothalamus and other parts of the limbic system, which, in turn, activate the sensation of thirst.

   Why we stop drinking is slightly more complicated, because we stop drinking before the fluid has time to enter the cells of the body. One factor is the existence of *venous pressure receptors* that detect entering fluid. These receptors reduce renin production, and, eventually, the activity in the area of the hypothalamus concerned with thirst is reduced.

5. Hunger is more complex than thirst or temperature regulation. One consequence of this complexity is that hunger disorders are quite common. Two major ways we know when to eat and when to stop are the gastric and metabolic components of hunger. Although the control of eating is rather complex, it is in some way mediated by fibers in several brain structures, especially the hypothalamus. When the lateral hypothalamus (LH) of a rat is destroyed, the rat will stop eating and will actually starve to death without

tube feeding. However, if these rats are tube fed, their normal eating and drinking patterns are gradually restored. Destruction of another area of the hypothalamus, the ventromedial nuclei (VMN), results in *hyperphagia* or extreme overeating. Disruption of eating and drinking are also associated with lesions in a number of areas throughout the brain, not only the hypothalamus.

6. One important disorder of food regulation is obesity. The body operates like a furnace, and when there is more fuel than can be metabolized, it is stored as fat and used when needed. Although the regulation is quite accurate, in some Western European countries, such as Germany, more than 75 percent of the population is overweight.

   Set point assumes that there is a specific body weight around which the brain attempts to maintain homeostasis. It is more difficult both to gain and to lose weight by merely counting calories than people think. Important factors in obesity seem to be the number of *adipocites* (fat cells) that people are born with—obese people have three times the number of fat cells as do people of normal weight—and the hypothalamic regulation of the set point. It has, however, recently been found that a moderate amount of "overweight" is actually the healthiest weight for most people; so fighting against a "set point" that is higher than you would normally like may not be worth doing.

   It means that some people will always be unhappy with their weight, but this is more a social than a physiological concern. It is both difficult to starve and to gain a lot of weight as the body adjusts metabolism, absorption, and so on, to maintain a constant weight. Exercise and calorie intake seem to be the only relevant factors affecting set point.

   Exercise seems to increase metabolism during and *after* exercise, burning more calories. It also reduces appetite and converts fat to muscle, producing a thinner appearance, if not actually lowering weight. The complexity of hunger and food regulation is one of the reasons why annual wonder diets come and go, and it can be said with some assurance that they rarely work.

7. When the most basic and immediate physiological needs, such as hunger and thirst, are met, other "higher" ones need to be satisfied: Safety must be maintained, pain avoided and pleasure sought; and social needs, like belonging, met. Belonging is perhaps the most surprising of human needs. When people are deprived of belonging to a group, they may suffer specific health consequences. To belong and be part of something, such as a family, group or club, is an important human need—more of a basic need than we might expect.

   An important aspect of social needs is maternal care. In rats it has been discovered that maternal care seems to be under hormonal control. If the hormones in the blood from a mother rat are transferred to another rat, the latter will begin to exhibit characteristic maternal behavior patterns. In humans it is undoubtedly true that this hormonal regulation is less strict. For example, human males may come to take an active role in child care, and some women abandon their children.

8. *Achievement motivation* has been studied quite extensively by McClelland and his associates. They have correlated different levels of achievement imagery in a culture with the subsequent success of that culture. For example, in nineteenth-century America the folklore was dominated by stories of remarkable achievements.

The achievement *motive* is a *need* for achievement and is a relatively consistent and characteristic component of personality. There are striking differences between the personality profiles of people in whom the need for achievement is high and those in whom it is low. High achievers set moderately high, realizable goals. They more actively *pursue success* rather than simply *avoid failure* and are more willing to take some risks. Low achievers are much less internally motivated. Achievement motivation can be easily and quickly learned even in adulthood.

At a higher level are "cognitive" needs for *knowledge*, for *organizing* the world, for *curiosity*, and *exploration*. Curiosity keeps us stimulated, but when our arousal level is too low the level of performance suffers. The highest level of performance is in the *middle* of an organism's response range. Many behaviors may be motivated by the need to achieve a personal optimum level of arousal. For instance, some people need loud levels of music to study by; others cannot be in a room with any distraction.

9. The highest levels of motivation described by Maslow are self-actualization and transcendence. Distinguishing features of self-actualized individuals are: creativity and inventiveness; problem centering rather than ego centering; feeling of purpose in life; objectivity and detachment; high tolerance of the unknown; peak experiences; and freedom from prejudice and cultural convention. Transcendence means to go beyond the ordinary understanding of life and to develop a search for knowledge at the highest level. Included in this are religious, mystical, and other endeavors, endeavors that are not often studied in contemporary psychology but, nevertheless, claim the allegiance of billions of people throughout the world.

10. Maslow's view is one, idealized view. Some people may move up the hierarchy of motives during their lives, but it is more likely that people do not follow a strict sequence. Some motives are described more by the process of *functional autonomy*—the tendency for any action repeated often enough to become a motive in its own right.

Terms and Concepts

achievement motivation
adipocites
angiotensin II
drives
functional autonomy
goals
homeostasis
hyperphagia
instincts

needs
prepotence
pressure receptors
pyramid of motivation
self-actualization
set point
thermometer neurons
transcendence

Suggestions for Further Reading

Bennett, W., & Gurin, J. (1982). *The dieter's dilemma*. New York: Basic Books.
A good read and synopsis of the "set point" approach to weight regulation.

Maslow, A. (1970). *Motivation and personality* (rev. ed.). New York: Harper & Row.
Maslow's views on motivation and a presentation of the pyramid of motivation.

Chapter 14

The Puzzle of Personality

INTRODUCTION

We have studied different components of ourselves in previous chapters—learning, thinking, intelligence, emotions. But to determine what a *whole* person is like, it is like putting pieces of an enormous puzzle together, something both ordinary people and psychologists do continuously. A divorce lawyer once said to me, "I've seen hundreds of divorces in my career. I can understand why people get divorced, but what I don't understand is when someone, after 5, 10, or even 20 years of marriage says 'I never really knew him.' How is it that someone can live with someone else every day and *never know them?"* This problem occurs to the rest of us, too; we wonder "How could he do that? I always thought he was so conscientious," or "She's not *herself* today."

It would be nice to be able to promise a clear answer to the puzzling question of why other people are so difficult to know. But it is this difficulty that has also made the scientific study of personality so complex and puzzling. It is an area of psychology that, like intelligence, involves characterizing and assessing people. Both intelligence and personality are areas of great controversy in psychology.

Part of the problem lies in the nature of other people and part of the problem lies in our own tendency to simplify. People are certainly the most complex "objects" we ever perceive; they have different genetic predispositions, different histories, and they seem different depending on our individual personality and perception. Two women may discuss the same man. One says, "He's so domineering"; the other, "He's so sweet." People seem to have a lot of different identities within, and they change with different situations. Remember Indiana Jones in *Raiders of the Lost Ark*, who was both a swashbuckling adventurer and a meek professor. None of us are as simple as we might seem.

However, the way we understand the world involves a great deal of simplifying. This simplifying costs us more in the perception of other people than it does in the perception of the outside world. We try so hard to make other people be perfectly coherent—like our perception of

The photographs on this page and the next suggest some of the many social selves each of us may have. The woman pictured shows different sides of herself to different people in her life: she is a wife and lover to her spouse; a mother and homemaker to her child; a professional to people with whom she does business; an athlete to those who see her jogging.

a rock. We categorize or "type" individuals as, for instance, a "hot-tempered redhead" or a "meek professor" or "the strong, silent type," and we are often surprised when people do not behave as they "should."

Here we consider some of the many pieces of the puzzle of personality: how we in ordinary life experience ourselves and others; the formal psychological theories of personality; whether or not we are "really" consistent; and if certain dimensions of personality help to explain our nature—are boys more aggressive than girls, do some people try to control everything, and others act helplessly?

I think it is useful to keep in mind a scene from Lawrence Durrell's *The Alexandria Quartet*. This set of novels is about a group of people living in Alexandria, Egypt, and how they came to know one another. The novels focus on a woman named Justine and how others see her. To one man, Justine is a selfish lover; to another, she is a committed revolutionary. We wonder, all through the books, who is she *"really"*? But the author has anticipated some of the lessons in psychology. Near the end, he portrays a scene of Justine dressing, before a mirror like those in clothing stores. It is a mirror with several panels, in which one can see oneself reflected differently from all angles. We show, he seems to say, different "sides" of ourselves, depending upon the point of view of the onlooker and the situation.

OUR "SELF" AND OTHER PEOPLE

There is a surprising experience that many people have the first time they hear their voice on tape. The voice on tape sounds high-pitched and squeakier than one's own. "That's not *me*, I hope," is a common statement. On tape our voice is heard as we hear others. *There are great differences in how we experience ourselves and how we experience others.* The *self* may be very different from *personality*—how we present ourselves to others and how they experience us. However, the self and the personality are related.

The Self

> A man has as many social selves as there are individuals who recognize him and carry an image of him in their mind . . . he has as many different social selves as there are distinct groups of persons about whose opinions he cares. He generally shows a different side of himself to each of these different groups. . . . We do not show ourselves to our children as to our club companions, to our masters and employers as to our intimate friends. (James, 1890)

Many centuries ago, Socrates proclaimed "Know thyself," but how do we do this? It is unlikely that we are born with a "real" self that we later

"discover"; rather, we construct a self-concept. Through interaction with others we learn to label our feelings and our behaviors. For example, if a child leaves food on his plate, his parents may say, "Charlie doesn't like spinach," and he learns to label that particular feeling as dislike. Similarly, we learn not only the consequences of our behaviors, but also that they are kind or naughty, rude or polite. These labels may be incorporated into our self-concept; for example, "I am a fussy eater" (Kleinke, 1978).

Self-schemata and Observation

Self-schemata are the "cognitive generalizations" that guide the processing of information and interpretation about the self (Markus, 1977). For instance, one man may regard himself as the "strong, silent type," another as "oriented to achievement." Obviously, there are limits to these kinds of interpretation. In a dangerous situation, trying to label one's feelings as "pleasant tingling" may be fruitless if not actually harmful.

We also develop and learn about the self through observation of our internal states and behavior. Most of the time we know how we feel about something. We know we like or dislike a particular person, are excited about or dreading an upcoming event, and so on. But often there is ambiguity—we have mixed feelings or are unaware of some part of them. In this case there may often be a discrepancy between how we expect to feel and how we may actually feel, how we want to behave and what we actually do.

Interpreting Inner Feelings

Perception of the World See Chapter 6, pp. 215–17, 226–28.

In our everyday life, we are generally unaware of interpreting our inner feelings, as we are unaware of the organization and interpretation that guide our perception of the outside world. A parachutist who is about to jump out of a plane does not think "My heart is beating rapidly, therefore I am afraid"; he or she simply feels "afraid." However, in experiments it is fairly easy to demonstrate that this sort of interpretation can occur. If you speed up a person's heart rate, for instance, it can make a person feel more aroused sexually, or more afraid in a threatening situation.

Self-monitoring

People seem to differ in the kind of information they select for their self-concept. A dimension recently explored in psychology is high and low **self-monitoring** (Snyder, 1979). *High self-monitoring* individuals are particularly concerned about how they appear to *others* and how appropriately they behave. They are particularly sensitive to the wishes of others and use others' behavior as a guideline.

By contrast, *low self-monitoring* individuals are not so concerned about others and look to their own standards as a guide. If you are a high self-monitor and go to a meeting where everyone is serious and staid, you will try to act appropriately sedate. If you are a low self-monitor, and are feeling good, you may say to yourself, "I'm really giddy tonight, I'd better go to a party."

Perceiving Other People

We do not perceive behavior as random; rather, we perceive it as coherent and meaningful. We try to "make sense" of others' actions and determine the reasons for their behavior. One important way we judge others is by **attribution,** how we explain what causes their actions. We often try to determine whether something in the situation is causing their behavior (this is called *situational attribution*) or if their behavior reflects something enduring about the person (called a *dispositional attribution*). Since we will consider this extensively in our discussion of social psychology, we will only briefly discuss it here by giving an example of how this process works.

Suppose that during a conversation your psychology professor smiles at you. Is it because the professor likes you (which would be a dispositional cause) or because you related a particularly funny joke (situational cause)?

Social Psychology See Chapter 18.

Fundamental Attribution Error

That people tend to overgeneralize from a small sample of another person's behavior to form a judgment of that person's disposition is the **fundamental attribution error.** What little information is available (Kahneman & Tversky, 1973) is overused: the more you know about someone, the less likely you are to do this. People also tend to attribute *their own* behavior to the situation, and others' to dispositions. If someone cuts ahead of you in line, he is rude. If *you* do it, it is because you are in a hurry. People are more likely to attribute their success to internal dispositions (i.e., intelligence, skill) and their failures to situational factors (i.e., bad luck or task difficulty). When Jimmy Carter won the presidency, he attributed it to his own brilliance in organization, his skill in campaigning, and his motivation. When he lost, he attributed it to the problems of the economy, energy, and the international situation.

Overgeneralization in Perception and Thought See Chapter 5, pp. 178–84; Chapter 6, pp. 220–24; and Chapter 10, pp. 366–67, 371–76.

Egocentric Bias

There is also an **egocentric bias** in judgment: we tend to overestimate our own contributions. In academia two researchers who work on a paper may both believe that it is "theirs," and each thinks up strategies to get his or her name first. It has often seemed to me that alphabetical orders for publication are often suggested by people who have last names beginning with a letter early in the alphabet!

Person Perception

When we first meet a person, we rapidly form an impression of his or her basic characteristics. This impression, or *snap judgment,* is based not only on the person's verbal and nonverbal behavior, but on our past experience. Past experience and the current context direct what we notice about the person. For example, a man in a singles bar may be more likely to notice blonde women if he usually dates blondes, and he is more likely to notice whether the woman is wearing a wedding ring if he meets her in a bar rather than in one of his classes.

In general, we use the same processes in perceiving people that we do in perceiving things. There are differences, however: we think of the behaviors of others as *intentional*, of people being *similar to us*, and of social interactions as *dynamic* (Schneider, Hastorf, & Ellsworth, 1979).

People, unlike objects, are capable of generating their own behavior. The *inner goals* and *intentions* of others are not directly observable, but assuming that others are similar to us, we infer something about their inner workings. Other people do precisely the same thing with our behavior—how we respond to them influences how they respond to us, and vice versa. Our perceptions of other people are different from our perceptions of objects, even though they may both be governed in part by similar processes.

Organizing Information about Other People

Generally we have only partial information about other people, yet somehow we form a coherent impression of them. Solomon Asch (1946) suggested that this is so because people's characteristics, called "traits," form consistent patterns of impressions. For example, we are more likely to associate being "industrious" with being intelligent and skillful than with being "frivolous."

Remember, some traits are more "central" than others; they dominate the impression, and organize it very differently. Asch (1946) gave subjects lists of traits and asked them to write a paragraph describing the characteristics of that person. Group A heard the person described as intelligent-skillful-industrious-*warm*-determined-practical-cautious. Group B heard the person described in nearly identical terms: intelligent-skillful-industrious-*cold*-determined-practical-cautious. The two groups formed quite different impressions of the person, which suggests that *warm* and *cold* are central, organizing traits. Thus, if we think a person is *warm*, we are likely to infer specifically different characteristics than if we think he or she is *cold*. Somehow certain traits seem to go better with other characteristics. How traits are grouped forms a naive, *implicit personality theory* that guides impression formation, or the characteristics we infer about others (Bruner & Tagiuri, 1954).

People appear to use basically the same sorts of processes to understand themselves that they use to understand others. This understanding is based on the schemata by which we perceive the world and on the inferences and judgments we normally make. We all use *implicit personality theories* to organize the people in our world.

FORMAL THEORIES OF PERSONALITY

The extremely diverse formal theories of personality are often derived from radically different assumptions about human nature. Sigmund Freud thought that primitive, unconscious conflicts were the driving force behind personality and that much of civilization arose primarily to check these sexual and aggressive urges. Maslow and Rogers, on the other hand, felt that people have a natural tendency toward self-actualization and that the individual's personality results from conscious choices. Social learning theorists prefer to examine the effect of the social environment on behavior, and they are more likely to see both aggressive and cooperative impulses as deriving from the examples of models. Some psychologists think we have enduring traits, others feel that traits are merely products of the human tendency to characterize and simplify. Whether our actions are chosen or determined, malleable or unchanging, consistent or inconsistent, is perhaps one of the most important subjects for psychology.

Psychoanalysis

Sigmund Freud
(1856–1939)

Sigmund Freud (1856–1939) is one of the most influential figures in modern psychology and many consider him to be the most influential in twentieth-century thought as a whole. His theory of personality, **psychoanalysis,** is the most complete and detailed theory of what motivates people and of the development and structure of personality. It is a theory of another era, when it seemed possible to simply synthesize the evolutionary, biological, developmental, and social factors as they come together in one person. Part of the appeal of Freud is his breathtaking ambition and his startling insights.

Freud studied medicine in the nineteenth century and began his research career in neurology, but later switched to clinical practice. It was through this clinical work that he became interested in the relationship between biology, psychological processes, and civilization, and it was not until his forties that he began formulating his theories of psychoanalysis. There is no single and definitive statement of Freudian psychology; Freud's ideas developed and changed over the course of his long career. His early work has an emphasis on the determining factors of the inherited biological instincts. His later work shows an interest in the *higher mental functions*—in short, conscious processes.

General Characteristics of Psychoanalysis

Determinism

Freud sought to uncover the natural laws that determine behavior. Specifically, Freud followed two principles of determinism current in the biology and physics of the late nineteenth century.

Reductionistic determinism: complex events can be *reduced* to a few simple laws that cause that event.

Historical determinism: events in the past cause present ones. If you bend a branch of a sapling, you determine the future shape that branch will take.

Freud sought to discover the *underlying* psychological structure that determines behavior and to understand how events in the past determine present behavior. Freud's deterministic viewpoint was based upon his conviction that personality is rooted in biology—and that human personality is largely governed by *inherited instincts.*

the superego are: (1) to restrain the aggressive and sexual impulses of the id; (2) to pressure the ego to substitute moralistic goals for realistic ones; and (3) to strive for perfection. While the ego is rational, both the id and the superego are irrational.

The Development of Personality

Freud states that the sexual instincts in large part determine personality and are present at birth—a premise that shocked Victorian-era morality. How this instinct is transformed through a series of stages underlies how the personality is developed.

Very young infants are in the *oral stage*, and derive most of their pleasure from the lips and oral cavity. A little later, oral activity includes biting, a form of aggressiveness.

The oral stage is followed by the *anal stage*, during which the libido is centered around the eliminative functions. In the *phallic stage*, libido becomes concentrated on the genitals. Children become interested in masturbation, which sets the stage for the *Oedipus complex*. (Oedipus was a character in a Greek myth who unknowingly killed his father and married his mother.) Because the mother satisfies its needs, the infant forms a strong attachment, or cathexis, to her. This is similar to other concepts of attachment, except that for Freud the attachment is primarily sexual.

Although infant boys and girls have the same cathexis, the girl is thought to be traumatically disappointed at the discovery that she does not have a penis, and she holds her mother responsible for this lack. Through *penis envy*, she transfers her love to her father. These differences between boys and girls in the Oedipus complex are thought to underlie the sex differences in adult personality.

Following resolution of this conflict, the child enters the *latency period*, in which sexual desires are not prominent. During adolescence, the child enters the last, or *genital stage*. The cathexes of the pregenital period are basically *narcissistic* in character—centered on personal pleasure. In this last stage, however, this self-love becomes appropriately channeled to other "objects"; in other words, the person begins to love others.

Fixation and Regression

Not everyone reaches the genital stage. Some individuals may become **fixated** at earlier stages, and their personalities reflect the characteristics of those stages. For example, a person who is overly dependent and derives a great deal of satisfaction from oral activities such as smoking or eating is said to be fixated at the oral stage. Someone who is overly concerned with controlling things, or is compulsive, may be fixated at the anal stage. Under stress, a person may **regress** to earlier stages. Thus, according to Freud, the *foundations of personality are laid down by the time a person is five years old*, and there is very little that one can do to change afterward.

Neuroses and Civilization

For Freud, the central problem in human life is the conflict between our biological inheritance and the demands of human society—an analysis much influenced by Darwin's ideas on evolution. Other animals can

Darwin's Ideas   See Chapter 2, pp. 54–58.

freely give expression to their instincts for sex and aggression. However, for humans to coexist in civilization, these instincts must be restrained. Our personality develops as a function of that need for restraint—people cannot have sex with anyone they choose any time they want, or kill their rivals.

For Freud, almost all that is generally thought noble in our culture—religion, justice, the family—exists primarily to *control* our animal instincts. Freud believed that this conflict puts a tremendous strain on the individual, which may result in neuroses. **Neuroses** are unconscious conflicts between the desires of the id and the demands of the superego, and they often occur as a result of *traumatic experiences* in early childhood. Normally the ego can control these conflicts. But when it cannot, too much tension or anxiety may result, which threatens to destroy the ego.

Neurosis and Specific Defense Mechanisms

Defense mechanisms are unconscious processes used by the ego to distort the image of reality in order to ward off anxiety. The ego may simply *deny*, or refuse to believe that an anxiety-provoking desire exists or that a traumatic event occurred. It may *repress* the memory or desire into the unconscious; it may *displace* it onto another object; or it may *project* onto another person. In *reaction formation*, the ego may not only deny that it has a particular desire, but construct elaborate positions or arguments against it. For example, people who crusade against something may actually have an irrational desire to participate in the very thing they believe they are against. The rabid anti-homosexual may have latent homosexual tendencies; the censor, after all, has to watch pornographic films in order to censor them. More positively, the ego can transform or *sublimate* an illicit desire into an acceptable one—a person with murderous tendencies may create a stirring thriller movie instead.

Evaluation of Freud's Theory of Personality

Freud was a genius, and his genius lay in his ability to synthesize a great many ideas current in biology, medicine, philosophy, and psychology at the turn of the century. Some of his radical ideas stemmed from the evolutionary ideas of his time: we are animals and share most of our characteristics with other animals. He was able, in a plausible way, to connect these ideas to the psychological problems of his patients. It remains a brilliant synthesis.

One of Freud's major and lasting contributions is that he focused psychology's attention on many of the most fundamental questions about personality and human nature. Are we the prisoners of our animal instincts? How much of our personality is inherited, how much is determined by early childhood experiences? Do we know what motivates us? Why and how do personality and civilization develop? Why are people often unhappy and wracked by guilt and anxiety? How much conscious control can a person have over his or her life?

However, Freud's specific concepts are difficult to test experimentally. When this has been possible, they do not seem to hold up well. For example, Freud thought the Oedipus conflict is universal, but it is not. It depends on how the culture organizes the family structure (Malinowski, 1928). In addition, there is little evidence that specific disorders, such as impotence, can be traced to specific difficulties in early childhood experience. Most important, it does not seem to be true that our psychological problems are so deeply rooted that removing one symptom (such as fear of snakes) may lead to "symptom substitution." If you remove a symptom it does not always reappear in a new form (Mischel, 1976). Further, the idea that all our personality stems from sexual "energy" is too simple an analysis. There are many determinants of personality.

Freud's work *was* an astonishing synthesis and has set the agenda for almost all psychologists who followed him, especially those involved in personality. In some ways our situation is worse than Freud imagined, in some ways better. It is not only sex that controls our lives but many other forces beyond our control—the food we eat, the structure of our nervous system, the weather, and the electrical charge in the air.

From the perspective of current scientific knowledge, it is most clear that Freud *underestimated people's ability to continue to develop and change throughout their lives.* Aggressive and sexual "instincts" can be modified more than Freud thought (Bandura, 1977). Personality is certainly not fixed by age five but continues to develop throughout the life span. Therefore, the "rider" (our conscious capacity for development and change) has been found to have much more control than Freud thought.

Neo-Freudians

A major problem with Freud's theory is that much of our behavior does not seem to be linked to unconscious forces of sex and aggression or to conflict between the id and the superego. *Many behaviors, then, have little to do with unconscious drives or conflicts.* For example, infants playing with their hands seem to be motivated by curiosity and the search for new knowledge more than the release of "tension." Exploration is only one of many behaviors that do not seem to serve tension reduction needs, but rather serve "higher" mental needs, like achievement. Furthermore, Freud neglected some major social influences on behavior. Later psychologists (called "Neo-Freudians") sought to modify Freud's theories by de-emphasizing the reductionistic determinism, emphasizing the higher mental functions, and including social influences as important determinants of personality.

Ego Psychology

One group of neo-Freudians was called *ego psychologists.* They emphasized that the ego, the conscious part of the personality, played a large role in personality. The ego is thought to be responsible for such behaviors as exploration and mastery.

Other neo-Freudians, such as Adler and Sullivan, minimized the importance of instincts in favor of social interactions and processes. Adler assumed that humans are motivated primarily by *social urges,* such as participation and cooperation, and Sullivan defined personality in terms of interpersonal interactions. Personality results from the observation of social interactions with others and is defined as "the relatively enduring pattern of recurrent interpersonal situations which characterize a human life" (Adler, 1929).

Erik Erikson

While Erik Erikson is generally considered an ego psychologist because of his emphasis on the development of the ego throughout a person's life, he was also interested in the formative effect on personality of social interaction. His theory of psychosocial stages demonstrates the shift to ego processes and social influences in psychoanalytical thought.

Erikson's theory differs from Freud's in two basic ways. First, he suggested that the ultimate goal of people is *not* to reduce tension, but, rather, to *become integrated human beings.* Secondly, although early childhood experiences are important, Erikson emphasized that *development continues throughout the life span* as people encounter a widening range of human relationships. Thus, Erikson described psycho*social* rather than psycho*sexual* stages. Personality develops through the resolution of the crises associated with each stage.

Carl Jung
(1875–1962)

Jung's Analytical Psychology

Carl Jung was an early disciple of Freud's who was also interested in the role that instincts and the transformation of energy play in the development of personality. Like Freud, he was a creative and original thinker whose complex theories synthesized and reflected a number of important historical trends in scientific and philosophic thought. However, Jung disagreed with Freud on a number of important points. First, Jung rejected Freud's strong emphasis on sexuality as the *primary* motivator. Secondly, Jung also rejected Freud's extreme determinism, that all behavior is determined by unconscious forces from the past. He emphasized that humans also strive toward goals and thus are motivated by future events.

Jung formed his own school, called **analytical psychology,** which studied *individuation,* development of the self through the process by which the unconscious and the conscious unite. Jung divided personality into the *ego,* the *personal unconscious,* and the *collective unconscious.*

The Ego

The ego is the conscious mind and is composed of thoughts, feelings, perceptions, and memories. It is the center of consciousness and forms the basis for our sense of identity and continuity.

The Personal Unconscious

The personal unconscious consists of memories that have been forgotten, suppressed, or were too weak to enter consciousness in the first place. Within the personal unconscious are **complexes**—organized groups or constellations of memories, thoughts, feelings, and perceptions. For example, someone for whom experiences with mother figures are particularly strong, perhaps because of a domineering mother, is said to have a mother complex. That person's thoughts, feelings, and actions will be guided by his or her conception of the mother. If the complex becomes strong enough, it may function like an autonomous personality and may even take control of the person's personality and utilize the psyche for its own ends. For example, Napoleon was dominated by the lust for power.

The Collective Unconscious

The **collective unconscious** is the most innovative and significant of Jung's contributions. It is the inherited foundation of personality, the racial (in the sense of the human race) experience common to all people. It consists of *archetypes*, which are not racial memories *per se*, but are the inherited predispositions to have certain experiences or to react to the world in a certain way.

Archetypes are such universal images as God, birth, rebirth, the hero, the child, the wise man, and the earth mother. These archetypes are often found all over the world in legends and literature, and they may contribute to the formation of complexes in the personal unconscious. The archetypes provide the sources of psychic energy for the personality and provide a fund of wisdom and creativity that the ego can draw on.

Jung agreed with Freud about the importance of dreams, but he felt that dreams are the way in which both the personal and collective unconscious seek to provide information to the conscious. Jung's viewpoint has been important, as it has built a bridge between the western, psychoanalytic viewpoint on the "depth" of consciousness and the tradi-

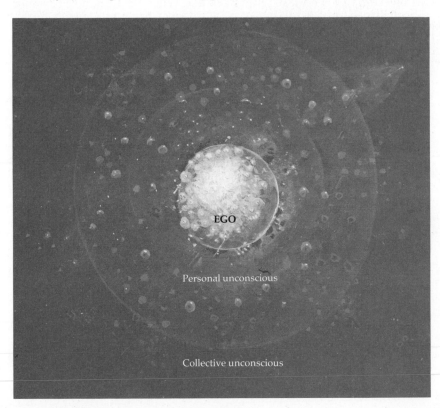

FIGURE 14–2

A Visual Interpretation of the Relationships among Jung's Concepts of the Ego, the Personal Unconscious, and the Collective Unconscious

tional, "esoteric," eastern viewpoints on the great range of influences on personality.

Humanistic Psychology

A common criticism of psychoanalytic and other clinically oriented theories is that they are based on the study of emotionally disordered people and thus result in pessimistic, negative, and limited conceptions of humans. The proponents of **humanistic psychology** argue that psychology should study the healthy, growth-oriented side of human nature.

Abraham Maslow

Maslow, as we have seen, proposed a hierarchical theory of motivation, which includes not only the basic needs of hunger and security and the psychosocial needs of belonging and esteem, but also the higher needs of self-actualization and transcendence (similar to Jung's individuation and development of the self). While the lower needs, if unfulfilled, may preempt the higher ones, they are all biologically based, which means that all people have a need for self-actualization. This hierarchy of motives extends the psychoanalytic and ego psychology to one that includes basic social curiosity and achievement as determinants of personality.

Maslow's Hierarchy of Motivation   See Chapter 13, pp. 467–68.

Rogers's Self-theory

Carl Rogers exemplifies the humanistic view that each person has the possibility for healthy, creative growth. His theory rejects Freud's historical determinism to emphasize *immediacy* of a person's experience at the moment.

Rogers divides personality into the *organism*, the locus of all experience, and the *self*, which is part of the organism that becomes differentiated and consists of the perceptions of the "I" or "me" and its relationships to others and to the environment, as well as the values attached to these relationships. In addition to the self, there is an *ideal self*, which is what the person would like to be.

In this view, the primary motivational force is self-actualization. But people also have two needs: the need for positive regard from others and the need for self-regard. However, these two needs are sometimes at odds, because others evaluate a person's behavior both positively and negatively, which sets up conditions for self-regard. Both the organism and the self have related, but separate, self-actualizing tendencies. If the self is relatively congruent with the total experience of the organism, then the actualizing tendency is unified. But if they are incongruent, the self and the organism may work at cross purposes, resulting in maladjustment—the person may be unhappy and dissatisfied. Incongruence results in part from differences between the self as perceived and the self as experienced (organism). Rogers (1959) writes:

> If an individual should experience only unconditional positive regard, then no conditions of worth would develop, self-regard would be unconditional, the need for positive regard and self-regard would never

be at variance with organismic evaluation, and the individual would continue to be psychologically adjusted, and would be fully functioning.

In contrast to Freud's emphasis on unconscious determinants of behavior, Rogers emphasizes that personality develops through people making deliberate and conscious choices based on their understanding of their self. When people cannot make adequate choices, because their self-perceptions are no longer congruent with external reality, they are thought to be maladjusted.

Like the other personality theorists we have discussed, Rogers is primarily a clinician and therefore bases his theory on his experience with his patients, although he made a major effort to test his theory. However, experimental psychologists have also made their contribution to the study of personality, as we will discuss in the next section.

Social Learning Theory

Social learning theory emphasizes that most behavior is learned rather than instinctually determined. Its advocates generally reject the idea of an unconscious in favor of an analysis of immediate, situational influences on behavior. Social learning theorists currently emphasize cognitive influences on behavior, such as:

1. Competencies: both cognitive and social
2. Encoding strategies and personal constructs
3. Expectancies: anticipated outcomes in particular situations
4. Subjective values: likes and dislikes
5. Self-regulatory systems and plans: rules for the performance and the organization and evaluation of complex behavior sequences (after Mischel, 1981)

Social Learning See Chapter 8, pp. 318–21.

Social learning is more an approach to personality than a theory of it. It puts the emphasis on the social situations that make us what we are: we are more likely to be aggressive if we see another person acting aggressively (Bandura, 1977); we can be made to torture another by a seemingly bland set of circumstances (Milgram, 1974); people put in an imitation prisonlike environment immediately take on their designated social roles and the "guards" become brutal, the "prisoners" oppressed (Zimbardo, 1972). The piece that social learning theory fits into the personality puzzle is the role of the outside world, not our inherited predispositions or our possibilities. It is an important and valuable addition (Bandura, 1977; Mischel, 1981).

Types, Traits, and the Measurement of Personality

Some personality psychologists are less interested in identifying the general rules that govern the motivational and developmental aspects of personality than they are in devising ways to accurately describe personality characteristics and *individual differences*.

Instead of grand conceptions about the structure of personality, some psychologists have tried to determine how people's personalities differ. The research parallels that of intelligence—from a general approach to more and more detailed analyses. There is a movement in psychology away from simple descriptions of personality toward an understanding of the different abilities that constitute a person. The search has gone through general personality *types*, to specific traits, to abilities.

Types

A "type of person" is one with many consistent characteristics; for example, a person is either male *or* female. One of the best known personality typologies is introversion-extroversion (Jung, 1921). Introverted people are oriented toward the inner, subjective world, while extroverted ones are oriented toward the external, outer world. An introverted person, especially under stress, prefers to be alone, tends to avoid others, and is shy. The extrovert, on the other hand, is sociable and outgoing and, under stress, seeks the company of others. We all use "type" descriptions when describing others, the "strong, silent type," for example.

Traits

People are not so consistent, however; they may be friendly and outgoing on one occasion, shy and withdrawn on others. Thus, most psychologists prefer to describe personalities in terms of *traits*. Traits are discrete characteristics assumed to be relatively stable, like "resourceful," or "conscientious."

Allport (1937) divided traits into:

1. **Cardinal traits,** which are highly generalized dispositions that organize the whole personality. For example, John McEnroe's cardinal trait could be said to be competitiveness.
2. **Secondary traits,** which occur in only a few specific situations. For example, a person may be generally calm, but become anxious on airplanes; so anxiety is a secondary trait.

Some traits appear to be more closely related to others; central traits organize other traits. One way to test this idea is to construct a *correlational matrix*, which shows the strength of relationships on a scale from −1 (completely opposite) to 0 (no relationship) to +1 (identity). For example, Wishner (1960) found that there was a high (.48) correlation between warmth and imaginativeness, but no correlation between strength and warmth.

But if a researcher wishes to consider many traits (and there are 18,000 adjectives in the English language to describe people [Allport & Odbert, 1936]), a correlational matrix can become too complicated and essentially uninterpretable. In these circumstances, a *factor analysis*, which reduces a correlation matrix to a few basic dimensions, is useful.

FIGURE 14-3   Cattell's Basic Trait Dimensions

	1		5		10	
Reserved						Outgoing
Less intelligent						More intelligent
Affected by feelings						Emotionally stable
Submissive						Dominant
Serious						Happy-go-lucky
Expedient						Conscientious
Timid						Venturesome
Tough-minded						Sensitive
Trusting						Suspicious
Practical						Imaginative
Forthright						Shrewd
Self-assured						Apprehensive
Conservative						Experimenting
Group-dependent						Self-sufficient
Uncontrolled						Controlled
Relaxed						Tense

Source: Adapted from Cattell, 1973.

Measures

Raymond Cattell, who also analyzed intelligence, gathered personality traits from many different sources, including lists of adjectives, personality tests, and observations of behavior in real-life situations, and through a series of complex factor analyses developed sixteen *factors* that he believes are the basic trait dimensions. Each factor is represented by two expressions (see Figure 14–3), one indicating a high score, the other a low score. From this he developed the Sixteen Personality Factor Questionnaire, or 16 P-F, which is a list of 100 yes or no questions. By plotting a person's test score on a graph, a psychologist can discover that individual's *personality profile*.

There are literally hundreds of personality tests, most based on various trait assumptions. The *Minnesota Multiphasic Personality Inventory* (MMPI), a personality "atlas" consisting of more than 500 items, was originally devised to distinguish between normals and people with psychiatric difficulties such as paranoia, anxiety, and depression. It also reveals personality profiles and is probably the most extensively used test in personality psychology.

The description and measurement of traits and their behavior correlates play a central role in understanding personality. However, some psychologists question the usefulness of even a trait approach, pointing out that people's behavior is very flexible and can be modified to fit various situations.

People learn their social behavior mostly from direct reinforcement by others. However, learning can also be observational (vicarious), or reinforcement may be self-administered (Bandura, 1977). Thus, a person's actions in a given situation depend upon situational characteristics, the appraisal of the situation, and past reinforcement or observation of others' behavior in similar situations. Behavior will be consistent only to the extent to which a person *generalizes* across situations. But more often, people *discriminate* between situations and adjust their behavior accordingly. For example, some students may be intellectually aggressive around their peers but very meek with their professors.

To recap a bit, the tradition of theories of personality begins with Sigmund Freud, and many of the later theories are reactions to and developments of Freud. Freud's theory about human personality was startling, especially in the context of the nineteenth century. He saw us doomed to live within society, the prisoners of our outmoded instincts of sex and aggression. Later theorists reacted to this bleak description and put more pieces back into the puzzle of our personality.

Some felt that the ego was stronger than did Freud, and some thought we have access to a deeper, collective unconscious than Freud thought. Some believed that our personality develops socially with other people and continues to develop through the life span. Each theorist, like the protagonists in the story of the Elephant in the Dark, seems to have a piece of the puzzle—our biological inheritance, conscious processes, social environment, our capacity for growth. No one has yet been able to fit these pieces together; we may just be too complex for that. Another approach is more research-oriented than these theories, and it is to this we now turn to find yet new pieces of the puzzle.

DIMENSIONS OF PERSONALITY

So personality remains a puzzle, both in our everyday lives and in formal theories in psychology. We all have our own implicit theories of personality, and we use them not only to type other people (she is a brave person, he is honest), but also to understand and predict (i.e., Jane is nicer than Mary, so I will ask her for a favor).

Different Dimensions of Personality

We assume that people are consistent and that their behavior is understandable, that boys are more aggressive than girls, that some people are more in control of their lives than others. Most personality theorists have the same assumptions and use the concepts of personality structures, motivation, past experience, conflicts, and so on, to explain behavior. Furthermore, most people's self-descriptions are remarkably stable across time, even over a number of years or decades (Block & Block, 1980; Costa, McRae, & Arenberg, 1980).

Sex Differences in Personality and Behavior

There are clear-cut differences in the behavior and personality of men and women. While obviously this does not hold true for all men and all women, there are a number of dimensions along which they differ. These differences may partly be based in biology, but it is clear that differences in socialization, both in early childhood and throughout the life span, contribute heavily to these differences.

Recently, Jean Block (1981), in an extensive review of the literature, has identified seven dimensions along which men and women differ.

Aggression.   Male animals, including humans, are consistently more aggressive than females. Males engage in more rough-and-tumble play, use more physical aggression, try to dominate peers more, are more likely to engage in antisocial behavior, and human males prefer television programs with more aggressive content.

Activity Level.   Males are more active than females, are more curious, engage in more exploratory behaviors, and have more accidents requiring emergency medical treatment than females do. They also perceive themselves as more daring and adventurous.

Impulsivity.   Impulsivity is the inability to delay gratification and to control impulses. Males are more impulsive; they tend to be more mischievous than females, and they are more likely to have temper tantrums, engage in disruptive behaviors, and overreact to frustration. Men operate machinery such as automobiles more impatiently and impulsively than women do.

Susceptibility to Anxiety.   However, females are more likely to be fearful, anxious, and less self-confident than males. They have a less favorable attitude toward their own competence, score higher on measures of social desirability, and are more compliant. In group situations characterized by uncertainty, they are more influenced by peer pressure than males are.

Achievement.   Sex differences with regard to achievement behavior are a little more complex. Women feel less confident in problem-solving situations and tend to underestimate their level of performance; however, they are no less likely to be persistent or motivated in achievement-related situations. Instead, they may be differently motivated than males. Challenging, ego-involving situations may stimulate male achievement, but do not affect or may even impair the performance of females. Social approval may enhance female achievement motivation, a finding made more poignant by the fact that females are less likely to be encouraged in their achievement by their parents, teachers, and college professors.

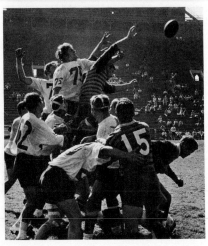

Potency of Self-concept.   Men have greater feelings of personal efficacy than women. They are more interested in feelings of control and describe themselves as more powerful, ambitious, and energetic than females. Women, however, are more likely to describe themselves socially; they see themselves as more generous, sensitive, nurturing, and considerate than males.

Social Orientation.   Women are more empathic than men, and they are more accurate in discerning emotions from nonverbal cues than males are. They are more involved in constructivist, pro-social activities, whereas men engage more in political-social dissent and protest. Friendship patterns also differ. Women are more affiliative and develop more intensive social relations than men, who have more "extensive" relationships—more numerous and less involved. In all cultures, women express more interest in babies and engage in more nurturing activities.

Personal Control

People have a basic tendency to attribute either situational or dispositional causality to behavior. However, people differ in their tendency to perceive their own behavior as internally or externally controlled. Julian Rotter (1966) allowed systematic investigation into this perceived *locus of control* by devising the Internal-External (I-E) scale. This questionnaire examines a person's sense of control over personal achievement, social and political events. The subject must choose between two items such as:

> Becoming a success is a matter of hard work; luck has little or nothing to do with it, **or**
>
> Getting a good job depends mainly on being in the right place at the right time.
>
> *and*
>
> No matter how hard you try, some people just don't like you, **or**
>
> People who can't get others to like them don't understand how to get along with others.

People who perceive events as situationally caused or due to luck are called *externals; internals* believe that events are under personal control. An *internal* would most likely pick "Becoming a success is a matter of hard work . . ." and "People who can't . . ."

There are some very interesting differences between externals and internals. Externals are (1) less likely to delay gratification, (2) are more susceptible to experimenter manipulation, and (3) are less likely to spontaneously notice details about their environment (Lefcourt, 1976). Demographically, men are generally more internal than women, internality increases with age, and minorities and lower socioeconomic groups are generally more external than higher socioeconomic groups. To take two extremes: if you are an older, white, wealthy male, you are quite likely to believe that you have personal control over your achievements and social behavior and that political events are amenable to control. However, if you are a young, poor black woman, you are less likely to perceive personal control over your life than to believe that what happens to you is a matter of luck or external forces. And you are likely to be correct!

Consistency in Behavior

We assume that a child whom we perceive as honest, for example, does not lie to his or her parents and friends, does not cheat at school or on the playground, and does not steal from the corner store. But what would happen if you actually followed the child around for several days and kept a record of whether or not his or her actions were honest?

Hartshorne and his colleagues (Hartshorne & May, 1928, 1929) did

that. They studied over 8,000 children and assessed their "moral character" by their behavior in a number of diverse circumstances—cheating in the classroom and on exams, stealing money, lying, and cheating during games—and found that there was very little **consistency** of behavior across situations, that behavior is *situation specific*. Hartshorne and May concluded that being honest in one situation does not mean that a person will be honest in a different situation. This finding has been demonstrated repeatedly (Bem & Allen, 1974).

Errors in Perception

Perhaps people really are not so consistent and consistency lies only in how we perceive ourselves and others. Bem and Allen (1974) describe four reasons to believe our experiences are in error on this matter:

1. We hold implicit personality theories which lead us to generalize beyond our observations and fill in the missing data with consistent data of our own manufacture.

2. We overestimate the degree to which behavior can be attributed to internal dispositions, and underestimate the influence of the situation, which also leads to over-generalization.

3. Our sample of behavior is unrepresentative; how we act tends to shape how others respond to us. For example, you may think that your psychology professor is a very nice man, because you're usually nice to him and he responds in kind.

4. We tend to overgeneralize from the few behaviors which are consistent, due to the similarities in situations. For example, you may think Anne is a competent person because you only see her in class and in the laboratory but she may be completely incompetent in the kitchen.

Just as Allport suggested that some traits may go well together in personalities, Walter Mischel and his associates suggest that there might be a tendency to perceive some traits as linked, using "prototypes" (Cantor & Mischel, 1977). To the extent that people shape their behavior, or presentation of personality, to conform to the roles they assume, and to the extent that we perceive others in terms of those roles, we are likely to see their behavior as consistent. But if we see them in other roles, the behavior may well change. Contrast, for example, how the police captain and his attorney girl friend (and later wife) in the television show *Hill Street Blues* act toward each other at work, where their roles often force them into conflict, and off the job, where they are very close and loving. Granted that these processes do exist, and that we do tend to overgeneralize about others, still our intuition *feels* correct. We see that our psychology professor is friendly to others as well, makes special efforts to help people with problems, and really seems to be *generally* a nice person.

Differences in Consistency in Different Individuals and in Different Traits

Some people are more consistent than others (Snyder, 1979). Epstein (1979) found that some people are almost completely consistent, with average correlation coefficients in the .90s, whereas others were inconsistent.

Furthermore, people are quite accurate in predicting how consistently they demonstrate certain traits across situations. Bem and Allen (1974) studied consistent and inconsistent people. They then measured their behavior across situations in three ways:

1. The subjects filled out another questionnaire about friendly behavior in specific situations.
2. Their parents and friends rated their friendliness.
3. The subjects' behavior was observed while in the waiting room and in a group discussion.

All three measures showed the same results: individuals who said they were consistently friendly were more likely to be friendly in specific situations, judged friendly by their parents and peers, and demonstrate friendly behavior in the waiting room and in the group discussion. However, these findings were much weaker for the trait "conscientious.' Thus "being friendly" means about the same thing to most people, but people have very different conceptions about what being conscientious entails. However, even Bem and Allen's "highly consistent" individuals responded *differently* in different situations, even though they gave the overall impression of being consistent. How is that possible?

Time, Meaning, and Situations

That most people's self-descriptions are remarkably stable across time, even over a number of years or decades (i.e., Block & Block, 1980; Costa, McRae, & Arenberg, 1980), gives us a possible solution to this dilemma. Perhaps being consistent *across situations* is not as important as being consistent *across time*. Lutsky and colleagues (1978) measured consistency in conscientiousness both across time and situations. People were found to be very consistent over time in the same situations, but not consistent in different situations.

The Eye of the Beholder

An important key comes from the recent work of Walter Mischel and his colleagues (Mischel, 1983). We probably judge other people in much the same way we judge other objects. We try to *make* them more stable than they are. We may quickly judge someone, for instance, as a prototypical "kindly old man" and then try to fit his actions into the "correct" category. Or more likely, we *select* a few "key features" that go along with being, in this example, kindly, and restrict our observation to them, largely *in the same situation*, over time. Because behavior *is* consistent in the same situation over time, we can maintain our coherent perception ("He is honest," "she is conscientious") and simply ignore many other situations and behaviors of that person (Mischel & Peake, 1982). Thus, we may be able to impose a kind of simplifying consistency on other people through our perceptual processes. Some consistency, of course, must actually be there, but some is contributed by ourselves. This is why people *are actually less consistent than they seem to us.* Consistency perhaps, in addition to beauty, may lie in the eye of the beholder.

A NOTE ON PERSONALITY

We have gone through many of the approaches to the study of the most complex subject in psychology, what our personalities are like. Each approach has something to contribute. I do not want to review them now, but to make another point, one more personally relevant. The assumption that other people can be simply and easily understood, and that they are consistent whether good or bad, is an assumption that causes much trouble. *And if there is one lesson to be learned from the study of personality, it is that human personality is quite complex and that we are very hard to categorize simply.* So the next time someone you think well of does something that you do not like, consider that you do not have to change your assessment so quickly. If you say, "I thought he was kind" and find that the person does something that you do not consider kind, there may be many reasons for it. You may not have enough information. *He* may not consider the action unkind. He may be inconsistent; there may be other parts of his personality operating. People do act very differently to other people, at different times and in different situations. This very complexity, however, is probably what keeps most of us interested in each other and, of course, most puzzled, as we try to piece each other together.

Summary

1. Personality is a puzzle, both to individuals and to psychologists. People (including ourselves) are the most "complex" objects that we will study. There are great differences, for instance, between how we experience ourselves and other people. The self may be very different from personality, which is how we present ourselves to others and how they experience us. Important to self-observation are *self-schemata*—the cognitive generalizations that guide the processing of information and interpretation about the self. We also develop and learn about the self through observation of our own internal states and behavior. People seem to differ in the kind of information they select for their self-concept. One dimension is *self-monitoring*. High self-monitoring individuals are particularly concerned with others' opinions, while low self-monitoring individuals are not so concerned about others and look to their own standards for a guide.

2. We do not perceive other people's behavior as random; rather, we try to judge other people's actions and *attribute* them to a simplifying prototype. People tend to overgeneralize from a small sample of a person's behavior to a judgment of a person's disposition; this is called the *fundamental attribution error*. Available information is overused: the more you know about someone, the less likely you are to do this. A related phenomenon is *egocentric bias* in judgment: we tend to overestimate our own contributions, obviously because they are more available to us.

3. In perceiving other people, we use the same processes that we do in perceiving things. However, there are differences: we think of the behavior of others as *intentional*, of people being *similar to us*, and of social interactions as *dynamic*. People's inner goals and intentions are not directly observable, but we infer their workings. Somehow we group certain traits with others to

form a naive, *implicit personality theory* that guides our impression formation of other people.

4. The most important theory of personality in psychology's history has been that of Sigmund Freud. His theory of personality, called *psychoanalysis*, is the most complete and detailed theory about what motivates people, how the personality develops, and how it is structured. Its general characteristics include: (1) determinism and (2) the postulation of the unconscious, a pool of information below consciousness, which cannot be observed directly either by the person or other people, but determines personality. Freud compared personality to a horse with the rider atop to describe how the unconscious and conscious parts function.

Freud felt that animal instincts, which he likened to the horse, provided the energy which fuels action. The primary source of this energy, called *libido*, is the sexual instinct. There are many sexual instincts, which are linked, he felt, to erogenous zones. In developing his theory, Freud developed the more general conception of many different life instincts subsumed under one category. *Eros* comprises the positive, pleasurable, growth-oriented instincts. Eros is balanced by *Thanatos*, the death instinct. The structure of personality for Freud is divided into the id, ego, and superego. The *id* is the initial, infant personality, unconcerned with the demands of the world. The *ego* mediates between the demands of the id and the reality of external constraints and is guided by the *reality principle*. The *superego*, the last part of the personality to develop, is the internal representation of society's values and morals.

For Freud, infants develop in specific stages, each attributable to different kinds of sexual urges. They go through the oral, anal, and phallic stages—which set the stage for the Oedipus complex—and during adolescence enter the last, or genital stage.

Another important point of Freud's theory was that *defense mechanisms* are unconscious processes used by the ego to distort the image of reality in order to ward off anxiety. Among defense mechanisms are denial, repression, displacement, projection, reaction formation, and sublimation.

5. Freud was a genius and considered to be the most influential psychologist—certainly of the late nineteenth and early twentieth century. His ideas, however, have been less influential in scientific psychology because they are very difficult to test experimentally. He was able, in a plausible way, to connect the ideas of evolution and our continuity with other animals to current psychological problems and current mental life. He raised many of the most fundamental questions that everyone interested in personality and human nature must answer: Are we the prisoners of our animal instincts? How much of our personality is inherited? Will we ever be able to know what motivates us? It is most clear that Freud underestimated people's ability to continue to develop and change throughout life.

6. The neo-Freudians developed a personality theory that emphasizes those aspects of the person that have little to do with unconscious drives or conflicts. One group was called ego psychologists, who emphasized that the ego, the conscious part of the personality, played a large role in personality. Erik Erikson was interested in the formative effect of social interaction on personality. He suggested that the ultimate goal of people is not to reduce tension in the way that Freud described but, rather, to become integrated human beings. Secondly, Erikson emphasized that development continues throughout the life span and described psycho*social* rather than psycho*sexual* stages.

7. Jung was an early disciple of Freud's who emphasized that the determinants of personality are more extensive than Freud believed and formed his own school, called *analytical psychology*, which studied individuation, the process by which the unconscious and the conscious unite. Jung divided personality into the ego, the personal unconscious, and the collective unconscious. The *collective unconscious* is the most innovative and significant of Jung's contributions. it is the inherited foundation of personality, the racial (human) experience common to all people. It consists of archetypes, which are inherited predispositions to have certain specific experiences or to react to the world in a certain way. Archetypes include such universal images as God, birth, rebirth, the hero, the child, the wise man, and the earth mother. These archetypes are often found all over the world in legends and literature, and they may contribute to the formation of complexes in the personal unconscious.

8. *Humanistic psychology* emphasizes the study of positive aspects of human nature, not the more pessimistic and negative viewpoint that is associated with Freudian psychology. Rogers's self-theory exemplifies the humanistic view that each person has the possibility for healthy, creative growth. His theory rejects Freud's historical determinism to emphasize the immediacy of a person's experience at the moment. Rogers divides personality into three structures: the organism, the self, and the ideal self. In this view, the primary force for motivation is self-actualization. Rogers emphasizes that personality develops through people making deliberate and conscious choices based on their understanding of their self.

9. Social learning theorists emphasize that most behavior is learned rather than instinctually determined. They include: (1) competencies, (2) encoding strategies and personal constructs, (3) expectancies, (4) subjective values, and (5) self-regulatory systems and plans. Social learning is more an approach to personality than a theory of it. It is a way of studying personality emphasizing the social situations and the contingencies of a person's life.

10. A *type* of person is one with many consistent characteristics—a person being either male or female, extrovert or introvert. However, people are not so consistent; they may be friendly and outgoing on one occasion, shy and withdrawn on others. Thus, most psychologists prefer to describe personality in terms of *traits*, which are characteristics that seem to be relatively stable, like "resourceful." Allport divided traits into: (1) *cardinal traits*, which are highly generalized dispositions and (2) *secondary traits*, which occur in only a few instances, like specific anxieties. Some traits seem to be more closely related to others; central traits seem to organize other traits.

   Some research on personality emphasizes different dimensions of personality. One important dimension is sex differences in personality and behavior. Jean Block, in an extensive review of the literature, has identified seven dimensions along which men and women differ: aggression, activity level, impulsivity, susceptibility to anxiety, achievement, potency of self-concept, and social orientation. Another important dimension in personality is how much personal control people have over their lives. People who perceive events as situationally caused or due to luck are called externals; internals believe that events are under personal control.

11. How consistent is our personality and behavior? We are much less consistent than we would like to believe: our behavior is situation specific. However, it has recently been found that some people are more consistent than others. A

resolution of the question of whether we are consistent or not is offered by Mischel and his associates, in which he emphasizes that we probably judge other people in much the same way that we judge other objects. We try to *make* them more stable than they are, or, more likely, we select a few key features that go along with being representative of the prototype that we have selected. For instance, if we judge someone as kindly, we restrict our observations to those instances in which a person *is* kind, largely in the same situation over time. Behavior *is* consistent in the same situation over time but is inconsistent in different situations at the same time. Because of this we can maintain our consistent perception by simply ignoring different contingencies. This is why people are actually less consistent than they seem to us. *Consistency*, in addition to beauty, may lie in the eye of the beholder.

Terms and Concepts

analytical psychology
attribution
cardinal traits
cathexis
collective unconscious
complexes
consistency
defense mechanisms
ego
egocentric bias
Eros
fixation
fundamental attribution error
humanistic psychology

id
libido
neuroses
pleasure principle
psychoanalysis
reality principle
regression
secondary traits
self-monitoring
self-schemata
social learning theory
superego
Thanatos
unconscious

Suggestions for Further Reading

Erikson, E. H. (1958). *Young man Luther*. New York: Norton.
An example of how a theory of personality may be used in analyzing a life.

Freud, S. (1962). *New introductory lectures on psychoanalysis*. London: Hogarth Press.
Perhaps the best statement of Freud's ideas. However, Freud changed his theory throughout his career, and there is no single definitive work.

Mischel, W. (1981). *Personality and assessment* (3rd ed.). New York: Wiley.
A classic text on personality by one of the leaders in research on consistency.

Singer, J. L. (1984). *The human personality*. San Diego: Harcourt Brace Jovanovich.
A recent, but somewhat idiosyncratic view of personality. Well written.

Chapter 15

The Problems of Everyday Life

INTRODUCTION

Human life is different, as far as we know, from the lives of other animals. This difference is not due to our *physically* distinct characteristics: after all, a bird has its wings, a deer has its antlers, a fish has its gills. There is a more fundamental distinction between human life and other animals' lives. This difference is the wellspring of our creativity, as well as the source of many of our current problems.

All species are evolved to suit their original habitat. In other species the adaptation has already taken place and is set in fixed physical behaviors like flying and hibernation, as well as in behavior patterns like the homing instinct of the salmon. Human beings, however, have gone outside our original home in subtropical East Africa, live all over the earth, and have built a new environment—in crowded cities, in skyscrapers. We can live for brief periods even outside earth itself.

In concluding our discussion of evolution we said that our ancestors first stood up and walked into new environments. They had to adapt to many unexpected situations and we are still doing that. We are now changing our environment faster and faster. This is one reason why many of the problems we now face are of our own making. We now need, constantly, to adapt to changes in the world we *ourselves* make, like air and space travel, computers, even nuclear power and nuclear weapons. Our ability to create, obviously, always leaps ahead of our ability to adapt, and we are forever trying to adapt to new and changed situations. In the words of the comic strip character, Pogo: "We have met the enemy and it is us."

If there are too many changes in our lives, such as the death of a spouse, a new job, or a move to a new city, our ability to adapt may be taxed to the limit and we can become ill. The common word for the deleterious effects of change is stress. Some situations, like crowding or divorce, are commonly stressful. Everybody hates going back to work on Mondays, so much that 75 percent of deaths that occur at work occur on Mondays. However, stress is not a specific bodily reaction, the way flu is a reaction to a specific virus. What can occur to different people under stress are different bodily reactions such as ulcers, high blood pressure, diabetes, and premature heart attacks.

However, these biological reactions do not occur to *everyone* in the same circumstances. An unexpected change, such as pregnancy, may be depressing to one person or exhilarating to another, depending upon how that person interprets the event. Some people are "hardy" and can deal effectively with changes; some are not. How a person copes with a situation is very important. Some people love the excitement of a political campaign, others cannot stand the uncertainty.

Because the changes are occurring so fast in modern society, many people find that their ordinary coping strategies do not always work. Psychologists have recently begun to address this problem and are developing ways to deal with the problems of everyday life, ways to relax, to assert oneself, to overcome shyness, to modify behavior toward healthiness. The "problems of daily life" are created by the society we have created. We can begin to develop some of the solutions.

STRESSFUL SITUATIONS

Stress is the failure of adaptability. It occurs when the environmental or internal demands exceed the adaptive resources of an organism (Lazarus & Launier, 1978). These situations can include *catastrophes* like earthquakes, wars, and fires; *major life events* such as the death of a spouse; *chronic life strains* like poor working conditions; or *minor "hassles"* like waiting in long lines or having a check bounce.

Catastrophes and Wars

Combat

The study of stressful situations began with the realization that men in combat suffer extreme psychological distress, which may severely impair their functioning and even lead to psychosis (e.g., Grinker & Spiegel, 1945). This was called "shell shock" in World War I, "combat fatigue" in World War II, and "acute combat reaction" in Vietnam. Combat is one of the most difficult life circumstances, because it involves so many different types of stress. Under combat conditions, a soldier may have to make extreme demands on his body, going without sleep, food, or shelter. He may be called upon to commit extreme acts like killing. Finally, he may see his buddies become injured, disfigured, or die, and may fear for his own life. Four decades later, there is a high incidence of psychiatric and neuropsychological difficulties in World War II veterans who had been exposed to high combat stress for prolonged periods (Klonoff, McDougall, Clark, Kramer, & Horgan, 1976). Even though soldiers may appear fine while on active duty, many experience delayed reactions that may not show up for months or even years after their discharge (Shatan, 1978).

Natural Disasters

Natural disasters, such as fires and floods, earthquakes, and tornadoes, put people in grave physical danger and often result in widespread destruction; these are extremely stressful situations. People are more likely to panic if the danger is *unexpected* and *imminent*, with no clear means of escape (Janis & Mann, 1977). If the danger is anticipated, difficulties may be lessened.

In addition to physical disruption, catastrophes may adversely affect persons for a long time, because they shatter people's stable organization of the world (e.g. not knowing when another earthquake may strike) (Seligman, 1975).

Stressful Life Events

Fortunately such extreme situations in which many people's lives are threatened are very rare so we will study more common sources of stress to understand the impact of stress on health and well-being. For several decades, researchers noticed a connection between stressful life events and illness (Dohrenwend & Dohrenwend, 1974). This is a very important finding and deserves emphasis: *People are more likely to become ill after experiencing major changes in their lives.* We will trace the history of this finding.

Life Change Units

In the 1960s, Thomas Holmes, Richard Rahe, and colleagues devised two questionnaires, the *Schedule of Recent Events* (SRE) and the *Social Readjustment Rating Scale* (SRRS), which assess the "major life changes" a person has experienced in the recent past. These life events include:

1. Positive events such as marriage, vacations, and outstanding personal achievements
2. Negative events such as marital separation, death of a close friend, and jail terms

FIGURE 15–1 Social Readjustment Rating Scale

Rank	Life Event	Life Change Units
1	Death of spouse	100
2	Divorce	73
3	Marital separation	65
4	Jail term	63
5	Death of close family member	63
6	Personal injury or illness	53
7	Marriage	50
8	Fired at work	47
9	Marital reconciliation	45
10	Retirement	45
11	Change in health of family member	44
12	Pregnancy	40
13	Sex difficulties	39
14	Gain of new family member	39
15	Business readjustment	39
16	Change in financial state	38
17	Death of close friend	37
18	Change to different line of work	36
19	Change in number of arguments with spouse	35
20	Mortgage over $10,000	31
21	Foreclosure of mortgage or loan	30
22	Change in responsibilities at work	29
23	Son or daughter leaving home	29
24	Trouble with in-laws	29
25	Outstanding personal achievement	28
26	Wife begin or stop work	26
27	Begin or end school	26
28	Change in living conditions	25
29	Revision of personal habits	24
30	Trouble with boss	23
31	Change in work hours or conditions	20
32	Change in residence	20
33	Change in schools	20
34	Change in recreation	19
35	Change in church activities	19
36	Change in social activities	18
37	Mortgage or loan less than $10,000	17
38	Change in sleeping habits	16
39	Change in number of family get-togethers	15
40	Change in eating habits	15
41	Vacation	13
42	Christmas	12
43	Minor violations of the law	11

Source: Holmes & Rahe, 1967.

3. Neutral events, such as changes in work hours, recreation, or number of family get-togethers

Not all changes are equally stressful, so Holmes and Rahe (1967) asked people to rate the relative extent of adjustment required, setting marriage at an arbitrary value of 50 **life change units** (LCU). The relative rankings are given in Figure 15–1. The amount of stress a person experiences within a year or so is considered to be mild if his or her LCU score is 150–199, moderate if it is 200–299, and high if it is over 300 LCU.

People who score high on this measure are more likely to have such problems as diabetes, leukemia, rheumatoid arthritis, cardiovascular disease, schizophrenia, psychosomatic symptoms, depression, and difficulties in pregnancy. Increases in life change are also related to behavioral problems like increased risk of traffic accidents and children ingesting poisons (Rahe & Arthur, 1978).

Although these early findings were startling, some researchers began questioning some of the assumptions of the scale and the way it was used. (1) *Negative* life events are more *strongly* related to illness, positive events are only *weakly* related, and not everyone who experiences major life changes gets sick. (2) The *nonoccurrence* of a desired event may also be stressful, as when a person would like to marry someone but does not. (3) Life events are not necessarily *discrete* episodes that occur at once, but are often events that take place over a span of time, with far-reaching consequences for many areas of a person's life (Lazarus, 1976).

Chronic Life Strains

Thus, *chronic conditions* such as an unhappy marriage or poor working conditions are not really "events" per se, but may be very stressful (Pearlin, 1980). **Chronic life strains** can be produced by the way in which a society is organized and by a person's position in that society. For example, a society that accepts some unemployment (for the greater economic good) assures that some of its members will be under the great stress of unemployment.

Consequently, how a society is structured and what sorts of demands are placed upon its members may increase stress.

FIGURE 15–2
Dealing with Stressful Life Events
Illness is not the inevitable reaction to life changes and stress. Each of us has various ways of deflecting, defusing, or interpreting stressful events to permit coping and possibly to prevent physiological reactions and illness. How such physiological defenses can filter upsets and upheavals is shown diagrammatically below. (After Rahe, 1974)

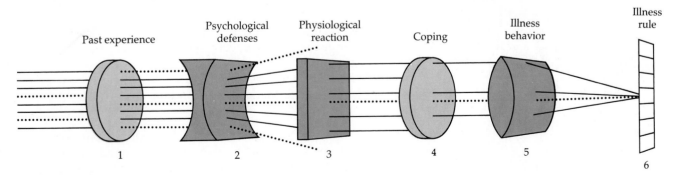

Social Roles

Leonard Pearlin and his associates surveyed 2,300 adults in the urban Chicago area to find out what types of things they found stressful and how they generally coped with them. They identified problems associated with four different roles in life: marriage, parenthood, household economics, and work.

Employment Stresses

Work is a central part of an individual's life. Through employment, we earn enough to feed, clothe, and shelter ourselves and our families, gain friends and social contacts, and may derive pleasure from our work and enhance our sense of mastery and self-esteem. However, the work environment may also involve dangers and stresses that outstrip our capacity to adapt to them (Dubos, 1979).

Setting aside physical dangers, such as carcinogens, there is a growing body of evidence to suggest that **organizational stress** can effect major physical and mental disease and even mortality (Kahn, Hein, House, McLean, & Kasl, 1980). Workers in jobs with high levels of stress have more of a variety of diseases, including cardiovascular disease, diabetes, and emotional disorders such as depression (Cobb & Rose, 1973; Kahn et al., 1980; McLean, 1979).

People in certain occupations show a higher than expected incidence of stress-related disorders. They are:

general and construction laborers
secretaries
inspectors
clinical laboratory technicians
office managers
managers
administrators
foremen
waiters and waitresses
machine operators
farm workers
painters (Smith, Colligan, Horning, & Hurrel, 1978)

Why these particular jobs may be more stressful is unclear. We currently have no index by which to compare the relative stressfulness of different occupations.

However, there are some general factors which may be related to stress at work (Cooper & Marshall, 1976; Kahn et al., 1980; McLean, 1979).

Work Load.   Having too much work to do is an obvious source of stress. One study of 100 young coronary patients found that fully 70 percent of them were either working two jobs or working 60 hours a week (Russek & Zohman, 1958). Having to do a great deal of work in a

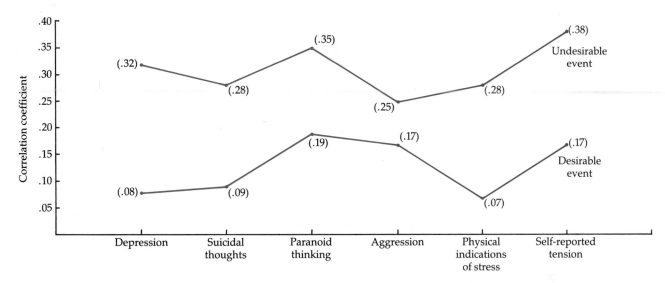

FIGURE 15–3
**Psychological Distress
in Response to Life Events**
This graph charts the findings of a
study using a modified version of the
Holmes and Rahe scale (see Figure
15–1) to rate life events against six
variables. Undesirable (negative)
events are much more highly
correlated with distress than
desirable (positive) events are. (After
Vinokur & Selzer, 1975)

short space of time with the pace set by a machine, as in the lumber
industry and on many assembly lines, is another type of work overload.
One worker described the experience:

> God I hated that assembly line. I hated it. I used to fall asleep on the job
> standing up and still keep doing my work. There's nothing more boring
> and more repetitious in the world. On top of it, you don't feel human.
> The machine's running you, you're not running it. (Rubin, 1976)

Relationships. Relationships with one's co-workers and supervisors
at work can be both a source of stress—in the form of conflict, competition, and depersonalization—or a "buffer" (a protective factor) against
other types of stresses on the job (French & Caplan, 1970; McLean, 1979).
Although there is a great deal of anecdotal evidence about stress deriving from relationships at work, and everyone has undoubtedly experienced this at some point, there has been little systematic research in this
area (McLean, 1979). One yacht broker said,

> Sometimes you feel like you're appreciated and needed. Other times
> they make you feel like you're a parasite. . . . The frustration, the humil-
> iation—but that's in any business, isn't it? Some of the people you trust
> the most want to chisel you the most. (Terkel, 1976)

Unemployment. However, being out of work may be even more
stressful than having work one doesn't like. When unemployment
increases, there are higher incidences of mental hospital admissions and
even deaths in subsequent years (Brenner, 1973, 1976). The cost of
unemployment, in the form of increased use of physical and mental
health services, is far more than anyone thought, and perhaps more than
needed to keep people employed. Workers laid off due to factory clos-
ings suffered from more emotional disorders and physical disease than

FIGURE 15–4
Ten Most Frequent Hassles

College Sample (N=34)	% of Times Checked
1. Troubling thoughts about future	76.6
2. Not getting enough sleep	72.5
3. Wasting time	71.1
4. Inconsiderate smokers	70.7
5. Physical appearance	69.9
6. Too many things to do	69.2
7. Misplacing or losing things	67.0
8. Not enough time to do the things you need to do	66.3
9. Concerns about meeting high standards	64.0
10. Being lonely	60.8

Middle-aged Sample (N=100)	% of Times Checked
1. Concerns about weight	52.4
2. Health of a family member	48.1
3. Rising prices of common goods	43.7
4. Home maintenance	42.8
5. Too many things to do	38.6
6. Misplacing or losing things	38.1
7. Yard work or outside home maintenance	38.1
8. Property, investment or taxes	37.6
9. Crime	37.1
10. Physical appearance	35.9

Source: Kanner, Coyne, Schaefer, & Lazarus

did employed workers in similar plants, especially if there was a greater than average time to reemployment or if the worker had lower than average social support from friends (Cobb & Kasl, 1977).

Hassles and Uplifts

Hassles

For all our concern with disasters, unemployment, even divorce, these life events are uncommon. Psychologists have also been investigating the effects of daily annoyances, like traffic jams, foul-ups at work, and arguments; our **hassles.** For example, getting a divorce may be stressful not only because of the emotional loss and conflict, but also because there is an increase in the number of hassles a person experiences: fixing the car, cooking meals, arranging child care, and so on. In one sample of middle-aged people, hassles were better predictors of both psychosomatic symptoms (Kanner, Coyne, Schaefer, & Lazarus, 1971) and physical symptoms (Delongis, Coyne, Dakof, Folkman, & Lazarus, 1982) than life events. This may have been due in part to the particularly low incidence of life events in that age and socioeconomic group, but it is clear that the quality of an individual's life needs to be taken into consideration in understanding health problems.

Uplifts

Stress alone may not be enough to predict illness; perhaps *positive* events, **uplifts,** can balance out negative ones. For example, a person

Olympian Phil Mahre (below, right) shows justifiable elation at the combined uplifts of winning a gold medal in the slalom in the 1984 winter games and hearing that his wife had given birth to a baby son that same day. Such uplifts are in marked contrast to common hassles (like the one at left).

with a very active life may have a lot of hassles, but he or she may also be doing something that gives a great deal of pleasure. An athlete preparing for the Olympics is a good example. Trying to balance school and work-outs, having enough time for dates or outings, watching the weight, scrounging up money to pay coaches and go to competitions, may be a lot of hassle. But, for an athlete, the sheer joy of mastering new skills, winning matches, and maybe being the best in the world more than compensates for the hassles.

Lazarus and his colleagues devised an "Uplifts Scale" to assess the positive things a person experiences. Not unexpectedly, people of different ages and occupations have different patterns of hassles and uplifts (see Figure 15–4). Kanner and colleagues (1971) found that college students were "struggling with the academic and social problems typically associated with attending college (wasting time, concerns about meeting high standards, being lonely.)" And while the middle-aged sample found pleasure and satisfaction primarily in their family and in good health, the students preferred hedonic ("fun") activities such as laughing, entertainment, music, and the like.

REACTIONS TO STRESS

Imagine that you are a nurse who works in the evening. To get home you must walk a couple of blocks to your car through a dangerous area. It's dark, and there are few people around. You begin to hear footsteps behind you, but when you turn around, there doesn't seem to be anyone there. You start walking faster, but the footsteps keep pace. You remember that a nurse was mugged last week not too far from here and begin to feel afraid—your heart starts to pound, your mouth gets dry, your stomach may churn, and your hands get clammy. The footsteps get closer, and you can't decide if you should run for it or turn and face the mugger. Suddenly you whirl around and the person in the shadows seems to be huge and menacing. He steps into the light and it's just the security guard, who offers to escort you to your car. Although you feel relieved, you worry about the next night and wonder if you shouldn't switch to the day shift.

This is an example of the immediate, situational reaction to stress. It includes *physiological* changes in heart rate and respiration, in skin conductance, as well as more subtle, hormonal changes, and *psychological* reactions, such as fear, anger, guilt, and anxiety.

General Physiological Reactions

The basic reaction to stress is the *emergency reaction*, which can take various forms: the fight-or-flight reaction, the general adaptation syndrome, and the stress associated with both positive and negative events.

The Fight-or-Flight Emergency Reaction

If our prehistoric ancestors were confronted by a charging animal, it would be adaptive if they were instantly aroused, ready for action—to

FIGURE 15–4A
Ten Most Frequent Uplifts

College Sample (N=34)	% of Times Checked
1. Completing a task	83.7
2. Relating well with friends	81.6
3. Giving a present	81.3
4. Having fun	81.3
5. Getting love	81.3
6. Giving love	80.0
7. Being visited, phoned, or sent a letter	79.0
8. Laughing	79.0
9. Entertainment	78.4
10. Music	78.0

Middle-aged Sample (N=100)	% of Times Checked
1. Relating well with your spouse or lover	76.3
2. Relating well with friends	74.4
3. Completing a task	73.3
4. Feeling healthy	72.7
5. Getting enough sleep	69.7
6. Eating out	68.4
7. Meeting your responsibilities	68.1
8. Visiting, phoning, or writing someone	67.7
9. Spending time with family	66.7
10. Home (inside) pleasing to you	65.5

Source: Kanner, Coyne, Schaefer, & Lazarus

Hans Selye

fight or to flee (Cannon, 1929). This **fight-or-flight emergency reaction** is mediated by the sympathetic nervous system and includes these changes:

1. The rate and strength of the heartbeat increase, allowing oxygen to be pumped more rapidly.
2. The spleen contracts, releasing stored red blood cells to carry this oxygen.
3. The liver releases stored sugar for the use of the muscles.
4. The blood supply is redistributed from the skin and viscera to the muscles and brain.
5. Respiration deepens.
6. The pupils dilate.
7. The blood's ability to seal wounds in increased (Gray, 1973).

When you take an exam or ask for a date, your heart pounds, your hands sweat, your stomach churns, and you feel more alert. These reactions may be more appropriate to prehistoric than modern times.

The General Adaptation Syndrome

Hans Selye defined stress as the general reaction of the body to change. As a medical student in the 1920s, he noticed something that eluded his professors. No matter the type of illness a patient had, one thing was common to all—they all *looked* sick. Selye set out to study the "syndrome of just being sick," the physiological reactions to extreme change. This response, called the **general adaptation syndrome,** occurs in three stages.

Alarm Reaction.   The first stage is similar to the fight-or-flight reaction. No organism can remain in this state for long.

Resistance.   Many of the physiological changes associated with the alarm reaction are reversed and the organism has *increased* resistance to the stressor. For example, in one study Selye (1956) subjected rats to prolonged cold. After five weeks of cold, these animals—having developed resistance—could withstand even colder temperatures than rats that had been kept at room temperature.

Exhaustion.   In exhaustion, the body's "adaptation energy" has run out. After several months of cold, the rats lost their resistance and became less tolerant of the cold than ordinary rats. The rats at this point were very prone to sickness and death.

Eustress and Distress: Positive and Negative Events

It is important to remember that not everyone who is stressed becomes ill. In the early studies of the effects of life events, about 30 percent of the people with a high number of life change units did not develop illness (Rahe & Arthur, 1978). In part to account for findings such as these, Selye divided stress into two types: **distress** (from the

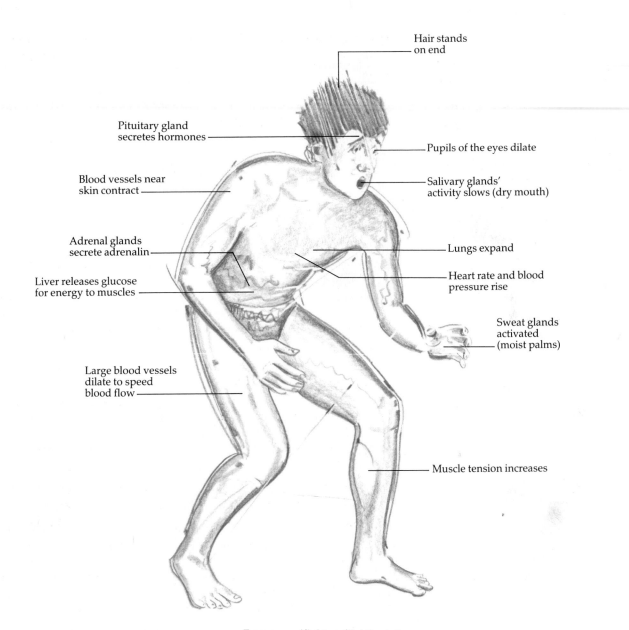

Hair stands on end

Pituitary gland secretes hormones

Pupils of the eyes dilate

Blood vessels near skin contract

Salivary glands' activity slows (dry mouth)

Adrenal glands secrete adrenalin

Lungs expand

Liver releases glucose for energy to muscles

Heart rate and blood pressure rise

Sweat glands activated (moist palms)

Large blood vessels dilate to speed blood flow

Muscle tension increases

Emergency (fight-or-flight) reaction

FIGURE 15–5
Changes that occur when the fight-or-flight emergency reaction is activated.

Latin, dis = bad), and **eustress** (from the Greek, eu = good). Both kinds have the same physiological effect—as clearly as we can determine now—but in general, eustress is less harmful than distress. Why? Euphoria is short-lived, distress lasts a long time. The stress of falling in love, for example, does not last long, though the less intense pleasure of being in love may. The distress of taking on a job one may not be up to, or of living with a dying spouse, may continue for years.

Specific Physiological Reactions

While there may be general arousal states in reaction to stress, different kinds of people may have specific physiological responses to stress. Two important areas of research are ulcers and heart attacks.

Ulcers and "Executive" Responsibility

In a classic laboratory study, Joseph Brady (1958) studied the development of ulcers in monkeys who could react actively or passively to shock. He linked two monkeys to a machine that gave them a shock every 20 seconds, unless one of the monkeys (the "executive") pressed a lever that turned off the next shock.

The executive monkey had to respond and developed deep bleeding ulcers, while the "passive" monkey, who had no control over the shocks, did not, even though he was shocked as much as the "executive." Brady concluded that active decision making was more stressful than passive.

In laboratory studies, however, what may seem to be minor procedures may profoundly affect the results. Brady did not randomly assign the monkeys to the executive or passive conditions; instead, whichever monkey reacted first and pressed the bar became the executive monkey. However, the more emotionally responsive a monkey is, the sooner it reacts.

J. M. Weiss (1968) later repeated this experiment, using rats assigned to the executive or passive positions, and found that the executive rats got fewer and less severe ulcers than the passive ones, who lost more weight, defecated more, and drank less than the executives. He concluded that a "sense of control" mitigated the effects of stress.

An ingenious experiment resolved the discrepancy between the two experiments. If the executive animal had already learned how to turn off the shock, being in control was associated with fewer stress responses. However, if the executive animal was just learning how to control the shock, the situation was more stressful for the executive animal than for the passive one. In other words, being in control may be less stressful than not having any control; but trying to learn how to control something in the midst of a stressful situation may be even more stressful than not having any control.

A sense of control is also important for humans. People who thought they could control an aversive noise were less bothered by it and made fewer errors on a task—even though they did not turn off the noise—than people who were not given that option (Glass, Singer, & Friedman, 1969). Somehow, a sense of control allowed the people to feel less stressed and to perform their work better, which is also seen in the work setting. However, the relationship of perceived control to stress probably is not that simple. For instance, the inability to surrender control in situations about which we can do very little—like surgery—may contribute to stress.

Heart Attacks

Stress can cause heart diseases. The striking rise (see Figure 15–6) of heart disease in this century is not entirely due to changes in diet, exercise, cholesterol, and smoking. These factors account for only half the occurrences of heart diseases. Sir William Osler, a physician at the turn of the century, noted that his typical patient with coronary heart disease was "not the delicate, neurotic person . . . but the robust, the vigorous in mind and body, the keen and ambitious man . . . whose engine is always at full speed ahead" (Rosenman, 1978).

People who have heart attacks often appear healthy but have a specific reaction to the stresses of their lives. This has been called **Type A behavior.** The Type A, coronary-prone individuals described by Friedman and Rosenman (1980) are aggressive, hostile, competitive, and time-urgent. They are also fast-paced, impatient and irritable, are deeply involved in their work, and deny failure, fatigue, and illness. They try to get more and more done in less and less time, do not care very much about relationships with their co-workers, but are very anxious about the opinions of their supervisors.

Type A's are twice as likely to develop heart disease as Type B's, who may be as occupationally successful as Type A's, but who tend to be calmer, not as time-urgent, more concerned with quality rather than quantity of work, more organized, and less prone to frustration.

The difference is not that "Type A's" do more directly damaging things like smoking, eating too much, or not exercising. If these factors are statistically controlled, this specific reaction contributes as much to the development of heart disease as any other risk factor (Brand, Rosenman, Sholtz, & Friedman, 1976).

The specific physiological reaction that may damage the heart is the Type A's extreme responsiveness to situations. Type A's show a greater emergency reaction to challenge than do Type B's. They shift more often and more extremely into the "emergency reaction" of high heart rate and blood pressure (as well as the other associated changes) and back again; the constantly increasing and decreasing blood volume can directly weaken the arterial walls. The high amounts of epinephrine and norepinephrine in the blood during the emergency reaction cause the blood to clot faster, increasing the rate of atherosclerosis, the formation of deposits on the walls of the arteries. This prevents blood from reaching the heart muscle and is the disease process behind heart attack. In addition to this underlying disease, ephinephrine and norepinephrine may precipitate a heart attack, because they also make the heart beat irregularly (cardiac arrhythmia) (Rosenman, 1978).

However, people who respond in this manner can learn to change their responses. When Type A's are taught to modify their behavior and

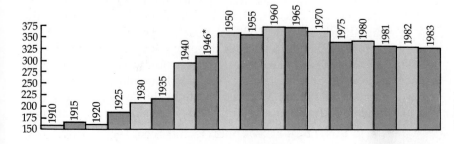

FIGURE 15–6
Deaths Due to Heart Disease (per 100,000) 1910–1983

to react less to challenging situations, their heart attacks decrease (Rosenman, in press).

The Immune System

The immune system is the body's defense against disease and toxins. It is a highly complex system involving many components. Many researchers believe that the state of the immune system is more important in the development of diseases than exposure to disease entities (viral or bacterial) or toxins. For example, some viruses, like herpes simplex, are always present in the body, but they only become active when something goes wrong with the immune system. Many researchers believe that cells that could become cancerous constantly circulate in the body, but in healthy persons they are routinely eliminated by the immune system. These "mutant" cells can only take root when some factor, either genetic or environmental, has suppressed the functioning of the immune system. Thus, the immune system may hold the key to curing or preventing cancer and a wide variety of other illnesses, perhaps including schizophrenia (Solomon & Amkraut, 1981).

Some of the most exciting research today involves the effect of psychological processes, especially stress, on immune system functioning. Both life events and some personality and coping characteristics affect susceptibility to and recovery from disease. Greer (1981) has even found that how women cope with breast cancer has a greater impact on recovery than the size of the tumor or the type of treatment. New techniques have allowed researchers to directly measure indicators of immune system functioning, and they are beginning to link emotions with some changes in immune system reactions. For example, ten weeks after the death of a spouse, the bereaved spouses had a tenfold decrease in one kind of immune system responsivity (Bartrop, Lazarus, Luckhurst, Kiloh, & Penny, 1977).

How Does Stress Cause Disease?

We know a fair amount about the mechanisms of the general physiological reactions of stress, but are just beginning to understand the more specific ones. The emergency reaction is mediated by the sympathetic nervous system. Its synapses directly stimulate the heart to beat faster and peripheral blood vessels to clamp down. The principal neurotransmitters at these synapses are epinephrine and norepinephrine. At the same time, the sympathetic nervous system stimulates the adrenal medulla to secrete a great deal of epinephrine and some norepinephrine, which are thus doubly assured of reaching the target organs.

If the emergency reaction is extreme or long enough to bring on the general adaptation syndrome, the hypothalamus stimulates the pituitary gland to release ACTH (adrenocorticotrophic hormone) into the blood. ACTH stimulates the adrenal cortex to release other hormones, the mineralocorticoids and glucocorticoids. If mainly mineralocorticoids are released, the body has made a decision to fight the stressor. These hormones stimulate the immune system to attack the stressor and stimulate the liver to fight the stressor. If mainly glucocorticoids are produced, the body has made the decision to peacefully coexist with the stressor.

The interplay of glucocorticoids and mineralocorticoids is complex, and we are just beginning to understand how psychology affects the immune system. There are many parts to the immune system, and each may bear its own relation to psychological processes.

COGNITIVE RESPONSES TO STRESS

Cognitive factors may alter the physiological responses to external stressful stimuli. Here we will consider frustration, anxiety, "learned helplessness" and depression. Because people differ in the ways they handle the problems of everyday life, we will discuss what stress means to individuals and how they cope with it.

Frustration and Conflict

Frustration is a normal reaction to stress. It results when a desired outcome is thwarted or delayed (Lazarus, 1976). A person may also feel threatened if he or she anticipates harm or frustration.

Conflicts

There are three types of conflicts that may result in threat or frustration: (1) when needs or motives are in opposition, (2) when external demands are incompatible, (3) when an internal need or motive opposes an external demand (Lazarus, 1976). Obviously, if the motivation or demands are weak, little threat or frustration may be felt. However, when they are strong, the conflict may be severe.

An example of *internal conflicting demands* is found in combat stress (Grinker & Spiegel, 1945). A soldier has a very strong need to survive, but he may also need to be respected by others, which requires that he live up to their expectations—that is, go into combat. Usually, the soldier overcomes or at least puts aside his fear of death and completes his combat tour of duty. But sometimes the conflict is so severe that it results in neurotic symptoms, and the soldier would be removed from combat for a reasonably honorable reason.

A person may also be subject to two external *conflicting demands,* as when one parent insists a child become an athlete and the other demands excellence in music to the exclusion of athletics. The frustration and threat of failure may be so great that the child ends up doing neither.

Finally, most people experience *internal demands* or desires that *conflict with external ones*. A child may want to eat nothing but junk food, but the parents will forbid it and insist vegetables also be eaten.

The Consequences of Frustration

At one time psychologists thought that *all* frustrations increase the probability of *aggressive* behavior, and that *all* aggression was due to

frustration. This was called the "frustration-aggression hypothesis," proposed by Dollard and associates (1939). Aggression *is* a common response to frustration. However, aggression may occur in the absence of frustration (Bandura, 1965). Frustration may lead to many things besides aggression (Mischel, 1976). A frustrated person may become depressed, or feel guilty, disappointed, apathetic, anxious, or fearful—to mention only a few.

Stress Emotions: Fear and Anxiety

One of the most important of the "stress emotions" is anxiety, which is often seen to be at the root of a variety of psychological disorders. Fear and anxiety are closely related, but there are differences.

Fear is an immediate and specific emotional reaction to a specific threatening stimulus. For example, young birds show fear if the shadow of a hawk—even a wooden one—passes over them. However, as we go up the phylogenetic scale, fear may become highly symbolic and/or more future oriented than immediate, and psychologists may term this feeling anxiety, rather than fear.

Anxiety is a more general reaction and may develop in response to the anticipation that something harmful *may* occur in the future. This harm may be not just physical but also psychological, as in a threat to a person's self-esteem. The stimulus for fear is usually clear and immediate, but when a situation is ambiguous and the person is not sure what is going to occur, he or she may feel a vague sense of apprehension and become anxious (Lazarus, 1976).

The stress emotions, while unpleasant, usually alert a person to the fact that something is (potentially) wrong and that action is necessary. For example, a student who is slightly anxious about an upcoming test is more likely to study harder than one who does not particularly care about it and is not anxious. Healthy fear may keep someone from walking alone at night in dangerous sections of town. However, when emotional reactions become too great, they disrupt. The student may be too anxious to study for the test, or a person may become too afraid to leave the house even during the daytime.

Antianxiety Drugs

Antianxiety drugs (alcohol, barbiturates, Valium, etc.) may be useful in helping a person to function. However, these drugs lessen anxiety at a cost—they seem to interfere with complex learning (Gray, 1978) and inhibit REM sleep, or dreaming (Greenberg & Pearlman, 1974). Antianxiety drugs may reduce the fear of the consequences of action without lessening a person's aggression; in some situations this may be useful, but in others it may be harmful. For example, giving Valium to an anxious parent with a tendency toward child abuse may actually increase the parent's aggression toward the child (Gray, 1978). Thus, such drugs should be used sparingly and with full consideration of the consequences of using them.

Learned Helplessness

Anxiety at its extreme can lead to hopelessness and helplessness. Hopelessness and helplessness can affect development, can contribute to depression and even to death.

When a person or animal discovers that it has no control over events that affect it, the result can be a decrease in motivation, a decrease in the ability to learn new responses, and an increase in emotional disturbance. This has been termed **learned helplessness,** learning that one's actions do not lead to one's goals (Seligman, 1975). The basic experiment to investigate learned helplessness uses three groups of subjects. Those in one group learn that their actions can lead to a desired outcome—generally, avoiding an aversive stimulus. A second group experiences exactly the same stress as their counterparts in the first group, but their actions do not affect it. A third group receives no previous learning experiences. Later, all three groups are tested on a new task.

In one study, a group of dogs in a restraining hammock were trained to turn off shock by pressing a panel with their noses. The second group received shocks identical to their partners in the first group, only without any control. A third group received no shock in the hammock. Twenty-four hours later, all three groups received escape-avoidance training in a shuttle box. The first group and the third group performed well and learned to jump over a barrier to avoid shock. The second group was slower to respond and six of the eight dogs in this group failed to escape. It was not the shock itself, but *inability to control the shock* which caused the "helpless" failure to escape. Similar responses have been found in cats, fish, rats, and people (Seligman, 1975).

Seligman describes how learned helplessness can lead to depression:

> When a traumatic event first occurs, it causes a heightened state of emotionality that can loosely be called fear. This state continues until one of two things happens: if the subject learns that he can control the trauma, fear is reduced and may disappear altogether; or if the subject finally learns he cannot control the trauma, fear will decrease and be replaced with depression. (Seligman, 1975)

If depression, or at least depression developed mainly in reaction to external events, really is learned helplessness, this theory has important implications for treating and preventing depression. Considering Seligman's dogs who failed to escape shock in the shuttle box, it would seem that forced experiences of successful shock escape would teach them that they were not helpless. So, Seligman put long leashes on these dogs and dragged them over the barrier, forcing them to escape. After 25 to 200 draggings, each dog began to initiate its own response and thereafter *never failed to escape.* The experience of control can reverse the learning of helplessness.

Perhaps more important, the experience of control before the helplessness experience can prevent the animal or person from learning helplessness. Seligman tested this by giving one group of dogs ten escape trials in the shuttle box before they received inescapable shocks in the hammock. These dogs were able to escape normally when placed in the shuttle box 24 hours later (Seligman, 1975). However, not all depressed individuals feel helpless. One group recently studied felt that they had as much control as normal, nondepressed people, but were found to have inadequate coping strategies (Coyne, Aldwin, & Lazarus, 1981).

Appraisal of Meaning and Coping

There are individual differences in response to stress, in part due to the fact that human beings are not passive responders to their environment—we actively interact with situations and the people in them, we anticipate and control some events.

Appraisal: The Meaning of an Event

A specific event, such as divorce, may be associated with stress and disease *on the average*, but the same event may have different meanings to different people. The ending of a marriage, for instance, may result in a decrease in stress for one partner, who was unhappy, and an increase for the other, who was content and now must cope with a new and difficult situation.

Thus, an important factor in the study of stress is **appraisal**—what the event means. Obviously there are a number of dimensions along which a person can evaluate an event, but for the study of stress the main dimensions are whether there is *harm* or *loss*, whether the situation is a *threat*, a *challenge*, or *benign* (Lazarus & Launier, 1978). A *harm/loss* situation is one in which the damage has been done and the person must cope with it; a *threat* situation is one in which a person tries to ward off a possible or impending harm; or a person may feel *challenged* by an event, that is, perceive possible benefits in a stressful situation. Situations judged as *benign* are not stressful.

Coping

In stressful situations, people actively try to solve the problem as well as deal with their emotions. **Coping** is thought or behavior that is directed at managing the problem or the emotions (Folkman & Lazarus, 1980).

There are two kinds of coping: *problem-focused coping* includes such strategies as making and executing plans, asking people for advice, or getting information. *Emotion-focused coping* includes such diverse processes as trying not to think about a problem, expressing your feelings to

FIGURE 15–7
Whether events are stressful or not often depends on what they mean to us, which is determined by our appraisal of their various possible meanings.

someone, drinking to forget about problems, or looking on the bright side. Emotion-focused coping may serve to keep the person from being overwhelmed, making it possible to engage in problem-focused activities, and problem-focused coping can help to calm the emotions. In almost all situations, people use both problem- and emotion-focused coping, although the types of problems a person faces and how he or she appraises them influence what strategies a person will use to cope, whether they increase or reduce stress (Folkman & Lazarus, 1980).

Stress, Control, and Social Support

We have already seen that "belonging" seems to be a basic human need. Thus, one important way of coping is to seek **social support,** the company and attention of others. Stanley Rachman (1978) examined possible reasons why some soldiers in World War II showed signs of severe stress and others did not, despite almost identical situations. Those soldiers who tried to be "as good as they could" in their jobs seemed to be protected against the effects of stress, as did those who were in tightly knit fighting groups. These findings agree with other studies. Social cohesion reduces stress (Antonovsky, 1979), and commitment to vocation, seeking challenge, and feeling a sense of control over one's life protect people with equal amounts of life stress from illness (Kobasa, 1984). Thus, working hard and maintaining strong social networks may be good ways to stay healthy under considerable stress.

An Israeli psychologist, Anton Antonovsky, predicted terrible effects on the health of Israelis following the stress of the 1967 Six Day War, but he was stunned to find none. If anything, people might have been healthier afterward. It seemed that Israelis pulled together during the war. In a more precise analysis, Antonovsky found that the social and personality dimension most protective against stress is *flexibility,* or the ability to perceive and try alternatives rather than beating one's head against the wall, and he measured it as flexibility of perception of social roles, flexibility of values, and flexibility of personal behavior—*ties to others* and *community ties.*

The Need to Belong   See Chapter 13, pp. 483–85.

Social support, "belonging," improves individuals' ability to cope with stress.

LEARNED HEALTHINESS

The 1979 Surgeon General's Report on Health Promotion and Disease Prevention found the major causes of death for people ages 25 to 64 years in the United States to be heart disease, cancer, stroke, cirrhosis of the liver, all other accidents, motor vehicle accidents, and homicide. Many of these diseases can be modified by individual actions. For example, cirrhosis of the liver is primarily attributable to alcoholism; accidents and homicide are obviously behavioral; and we can modify risk factors associated with the development of heart disease and cancer, such as smoking. Hypertension is a powerful risk factor in heart disease and can be controlled through diet, exercise, and medication. Type A behavior can be modified; changes in this behavior can reduce heart disease.

If helplessness can be learned, why not healthiness?

General Factors in Health

Stress Inoculation

Many psychologists are beginning to develop generalized ways of teaching people coping skills. One popular technique for stress management is through "verbal self-instruction" (Meichenbaum, 1977). *Anticipation* can reduce stress, through considering some possible causes of and alternatives to action. The self-statements in this technique serve to assess the reality of the stressful situation, control negative, anxiety-arousing thoughts or images; acknowledge anxiety and perhaps relabel it; in other words, people can "psych themselves up" to perform well. In addition, the clients practice coping with possible intense fear and then reinforce themselves for having coped.

Relaxation

One factor in stress reactions is the extreme responsiveness to situations, which contributes to a chronic emergency reaction. However, people can learn to relax through a variety of techniques, including biofeedback, self-hypnosis, and deep muscle relaxation. The goal of learning relaxation is not to be relaxed *all* the time, but to be able to relax in times of stress and not to react so extremely when stressed. To do this, relaxation must be practiced the way you would practice tennis or any other physical activity to train your responses. It is a form of physical education.

Deep Muscle Relaxation Drill:

1. Find a comfortable chair in a dimly lit room. Your neck should be supported, but you should not lie down. Remove or loosen tight clothing, shoes, glasses, or watches, and remove contact lenses.

2. Right-handed people should begin by tensing the right hand for a while, making a fist, then letting it go. Notice the feeling as it relaxes, the contrast with the tension, and feel this relaxation deepen. Suggest that it be heavy and warm, but don't insist. It's important to adopt a passive attitude toward your response, because getting upset over "failure" to respond properly will defeat the purpose of relaxation. Just notice what feelings you do have as you relax. Continue with the rest of the right side of the body, moving to forearm, upper arm, shoulder, foot, lower leg, and upper leg. Then follow the same procedure with the left side of the body. If you are left-handed, begin with the left side. Your body should feel like a heavy, warm mass. After some practice, you will not need to tense the muscles before relaxing them.

3. Now relax the muscles of the hips and let a wave of relaxation pass from your abdomen to your chest. Don't tense these muscles, tell them to be heavy and warm. You should start breathing from the diaphragm, more slowly than before. When this happens, continue.

4. Let the wave of relaxation continue into the shoulders, neck, jaw, and face muscles. Pay special attention to your throat, mouth,

SELF-STATEMENTS

Preparing for a Stressor

What is it you have to do?

You can develop a plan to deal with it.

Just think about what you can do about it. That's better than getting anxious.

No negative self-statements: just think rationally.

Don't worry: worry won't help anything.

Maybe what you think is anxiety is eagerness to confront the stressor.

Confronting and Handling a Stressor

Just "psych" yourself up—you can meet this challenge.

You can convince yourself to do it. You can reason your fear away.

One step at a time: you can handle the situation.

Don't think about fear; just think about what you have to do. Stay relevant.

This anxiety is what the doctor said you would feel. It's a reminder to use your coping exercises.

This tenseness can be an ally; a cue to cope.

Relax; you're in control. Take a slow deep breath. Ah, good.

Coping with the Feeling of Being Overwhelmed

When fear comes, just pause.

Keep the focus on the present; what is it you have to do?

Label your fear from 0 to 10 and watch it change.

You should expect your fear to rise.

Don't try to eliminate fear totally; just keep it manageable.

Reinforcing Self-statements

It worked; you did it.

Wait until you tell your therapist (or group) about this.

It wasn't as bad as you expected.

You made more out of your fear than it was worth.

Your damn ideas—that's the problem. When you control them, you control your fear. It's getting better each time you use the procedures.

You can be pleased with the progress you're making.

You did it! (Meichenbaum, 1977)

---

eyes, and forehead. Finish the exercise by telling your forehead to feel cool.

Practice this twice a day, 15 to 20 minutes if possible, but even a few minutes is better than missing completely. Don't practice within an hour after meals. You may want to practice before an expected stressful experience, but don't practice more than four times a day.

With practice you will be able to reach a state of deep relaxation in a few minutes, or some relaxation in just seconds. When you are able to achieve deep muscle relaxation, repeat to yourself some pleasant phrase, such as, "I am deeply relaxed," or "I feel heavy and warm." Use this each time you are relaxed and it will become a conditioned stimulus, a cue phrase, so that you can repeat it at any time and achieve at least some relaxation.

Instant Relaxation:

1. Sit in a comfortable position, but not necessarily in a completely supported chair, as at the beginning. You have reached the stage now where you have enough skill that you should be able to accomplish some relaxation anywhere, even standing up.

2. Take a deep breath, hold it for a slow count of five (about five seconds), and while exhaling slowly, tell all your muscles to relax. Repeat this two or three times. Use your cue phrase.

3. If possible, imagine a pleasant scene.

Whenever you notice yourself feeling stressed (tense muscles, dry mouth, excessive perspiring, or other signs) or when you expect what is normally a stressful situation to occur, use instant relaxation for 30 to 60 seconds. You can do this even when you are in a stressful situation, arguing with someone, just after a minor accident, or waiting in line. Even one deep, slowly exhaled breath, combined with your cue phrase, will give you some relaxation. Use this relaxed state to ask yourself, "How else could I approach this situation to get what I want without it being so stressful? Is this problem worth getting this upset about? If so, what options are open to me which I'm not considering?"

Exercise

Some of the problems of contemporary life are directly related to our having evolved to meet very different conditions from those we now face. The primitive hunter, nomad, and farmer humans evolved as dependent on strength, speed, and agility. This vigorous life has been replaced in the last few hundred years with a more sedentary existence for many people, but no evolutionary change has occurred to allow our cardiovascular system, lungs, skeletal muscles, skeleton, and nervous system to function optimally without exercise. Chronic degenerative diseases such as obesity, atherosclerosis (hardening of the arteries), and diabetes are linked, in part, to lack of exercise (Haskell, 1979).

Exercises that best enhance cardiovascular and metabolic capacity involve continuous effort for extended periods of time. These are considered endurance or "aerobic" (with oxygen) conditioning exercises, and they include hiking, jogging, brisk walking, running, swimming, cycling, certain calisthenics, and active sports and games. These exercises need to be performed long and hard enough to impose an overload demand on the body. Without this overload there is no adaptation and no benefit.

Most beneficial changes produced by exercise occur when the system is extended beyond 50 percent of its capacity. These changes usually increase muscle endurance, strength, and power, as well as the capacity and efficiency of the heart and vascular system to transport blood to muscles. People who exercise moderately on a regular basis are less likely to develop heart disease, and if they do, are more likely to recover than people who do not exercise. They are less likely to develop diabetes. In general, active people have fewer heart attacks, have them at older ages, and have less severe ones than people who are not active, either on or off the job. This relationship holds up even when smoking, body weight, education, and ethnic and religious background (all of which are related to risk of heart disease) are considered.

Although exercise will not provide any protection against the development of chronic pulmonary diseases, such as asthma, emphysema, or bronchitis, or reverse tissue damage once it has occurred, exercise causes an improvement in breathing efficiency, resulting in an effective increase in respiratory working capacity.

Psychological benefits from exercise may be particularly attributable to a reduction in blood levels of epinephrine and norepinephrine, and also to expectation. Reported benefits include: self-esteem and self-confidence (often related to improved physical appearance); elevation in mood; increased capacity for general coping; and improvement in job functioning. Exercise may also lift a person's depression.

Specific Techniques

Relaxation, exercise, and stress inoculation are general techniques that can be applied to many different situations. However, many people suffer from the stress associated with such problems as lack of assertiveness, shyness, and obesity. These "problems of daily life" can, to some extent, be overcome with some specific psychological techniques.

Shyness

More than 80 percent of Americans (based on some 5,000 questioned) have been shy at some point in their lives. Forty percent consider themselves shy now—84 million Americans (Zimbardo, 1977). These include many successful people who have struggled with and overcome shyness, such as Carol Burnett, Barbara Walters, Lawrence Welk, Melvin Belli, Nancy Walker, and Johnny Carson.

Shy people generally have low self-esteem and lack specific social skills. Zimbardo (1977) suggests ways to build self-esteem, and develop specific and successful social skills. Some specific techniques include: make a contract with yourself about your shyness goals and how you

will work toward them. Start talking in nonthreatening situations and gradually work up to more difficult ones. Pay attention to dressing and grooming. Give and accept truthful compliments. Learn techniques for starting a conversation, keeping it going, and knowing when it should end. Follow generally accepted but unstated rules about how to make a date.

If important social skills are lacking, they can be taught by rehearsal in a role-playing situation. Self-evaluations can be changed by rehearsing different kinds of self-talk, for example,

1. *Situation.* Let's suppose you've been fixed up on a blind date. You've taken her to a movie and then for some coffee afterwards. Now she begins to talk about a political candidate, some man you've never heard of; she says, "What do you think of him?" You say to yourself:

2. *Self-talk.* An example of self-talk might be: "She's got me now. I'd better bullshit her or she'll put me down. I hate politics anyway so this chick is obviously not my type . . . Boy, that's really jumping to conclusions. This is only one area and it really doesn't show what type of person she is. Anyway, what's the point of making up stuff about somebody I never heard of? She'll see right through me if I lie. It's not such a big deal to admit I don't know something. There are probably lots of things I know that she doesn't."

3. *Self-talk reinforcement.* "Yeah, that's a better way to think about it. She's just human, trying to discuss something intelligently, I don't have to get scared or put off by her." (Meichenbaum, 1977)

Self-assertion

Assertiveness is another technique useful in reducing frustration. Although a person who is always assertive can be unpleasant, the person who *cannot* be assertive when *necessary* can contribute to increasing stress and frustration.

Bower and Bower (1976) have devised a technique for asserting yourself in most situations, from dealing with the auto repairman who is "ripping you off" to the spouse who criticized you in front of other people. The technique is called "DESC Scripts," an acronym for Describe, Express, Specify, and Consequences.

DESCRIBE—Begin your script by describing as specifically and objectively as possible the behavior that is bothersome to you:

"You said these car repairs would cost $35 and now you're charging $110."

"The last three times we have been with other people you have criticized me in front of them."

EXPRESS—Say what you feel and think about this behavior:

'This makes me angry because I feel I'm being ripped off." (to the car repairman)

"This makes me feel humiliated and hurt." (to the husband)

SPECIFY—Ask for a different, specific behavior:

"I would like you to adjust my bill back to the original estimate unless you can clearly justify these extra charges."

"I would like you to quit criticizing me and I will signal you every time that you start to do it."

CONSEQUENCES—Spell out concretely and simply what your reward will be for changing the behavior. Sometimes you have to specify the negative consequences of not following the changes:
"If you do this, I will tell all of my friends that I have gotten good service at Bob's repair shop."
"If you quit criticizing me I'll feel a lot better and bake you your favorite apple pie."

The best way to make such a script work is to write it out ahead of time and rehearse it in front of a mirror. After several repetitions, you will be able to adapt it as necessary on the spot and deliver it effectively.

CONCLUSION

We all experience stress, no matter how lucky, wealthy, happy, or intelligent we are, or how supportive our friends and family are. Stressful situations may range from catastrophes to major changes such as divorce, from chronic problems to minor hassles such as bouncing a check. Stress may result in profound and often damaging physiological changes and may contribute to many prevalent diseases.

But even in the most stressful circumstances, people differ in how they experience stress—how severe they think it is, what meaning they give to it, what they do to cope with it. Situations that some view as a challenge, others may view as simply annoying, and yet others as terribly frightening. How we appraise situations depends upon the type of situation, our previous experiences and values, and what resources we have to deal with the situation. Important resources are friends and relatives who are willing to help—our social support system—and the coping strategies we can use to manage the problem and our emotions. Coping strategies may help us or they may make the situation worse—as when an obese person feels so bad about being fat that he or she goes on an eating binge. Psychologists are devising new ways to help people cope with stress by teaching people to relax and by teaching them specific coping skills to deal with the problems of everyday life.

Summary

1. *Stress* is the failure of adaptability. There are numerous situations that cause the environmental or internal demands to exceed the adaptive resources of an organism. These include catastrophes, major life events, chronic life strains, or minor hassles.

2. Stressful life events have been studied extensively in their relationship to health. People are more likely to become ill after experiencing major changes in their lives. Holmes, Rahe, and colleagues devised two questionnaires, the Schedule of Recent Events and the Social Readjustment Rating Scale, which assess major life changes a person has experienced in the recent past. These include:

1. positive events, such as marriage, vacations, and achievements
2. negative events, such as marital separation, death of a close friend, and jail terms
3. neutral events, such as changes in work hours, recreation, and family get-togethers

A number of studies have shown that the more life changes a person experiences, the more likely he or she is to get ill. Other important stressors include those of employment: workload, relationships, and unemployment. However it has also recently been found that the number of daily *hassles* also seems to strongly affect health.

3. The emergency reaction is the basic reaction to stress. It includes the *fight-or-flight emergency reaction*, the *general adaptation syndrome*, and the stress associated with both positive and negative events. The emergency reaction includes an increase in the rate and strength of the heartbeat, contraction of the spleen, the liver releasing stored sugar for the use of the muscles, a redistribution of the blood supply, a deepening of respiration, dilation of the pupils, and an increase in the blood's ability to seal wounds.

   The general adaptation syndrome occurs in three stages: (1) an alarm reaction similar to the fight-or-flight reaction; (2) resistance, the organism has increased resistance to the stressor; and (3) exhaustion in which the body's adaptation energy seems to run out.

   An important effect of stress is on heart disease. People who have heart attacks often appear healthy but have a specific reaction to the stresses of their lives. This has been called *Type A behavior*. The Type A, coronary-prone individuals are described as being aggressive, hostile, competitive, time-urgent, fast-paced, impatient, and irritable. They are twice as likely to develop heart disease as Type B people, who may be as occupationally successful as Type A's, but are calmer and less time-urgent. The specific psychological reaction that may damage the heart is the Type A's extreme response to situations. Type A's show a greater emergency reaction to challenge than do Type B's. The constantly increasing and decreasing blood volume can directly weaken the arterial walls. However, people who respond in this manner can learn to change these responses and react less to challenging situations.

4. *Frustration* is a normal reaction to stress. It results when a desired outcome is thwarted or delayed. There are three types of conflicts that may result in threat or frustration: (1) when needs or motives are in opposition, (2) when external demands are incompatible, and (3) when an internal need or motive opposes an external demand.

   The consequences of frustration or threat include the stress emotions, fear and anxiety, which can be modified by the taking of antianxiety drugs, such as alcohol, barbiturates, and the like. However, these drugs lessen anxiety at a cost—they seem to interfere with complex learning and inhibit REM sleep, or dreaming.

   Anxiety at its extreme can lead to hopelessness and helplessness. When a person or animal discovers that it has no control over events that affect it, the result can be a decrease in motivation, a decrease in the ability to learn new responses, and an increase in emotional disturbance. This has been termed *learned helplessness*, which can lead eventually to depression.

5. In stressful situations, people actively try to solve the problem as well as deal with their emotions. *Coping* is thought or behavior that is directed at managing the problem or the emotions. There are two kinds of coping: *problem-focused* coping includes such strategies as making and executing plans, ask-

ing for advice, or getting information; *emotion-focused* coping includes trying not to think about a problem, expressing your feelings to someone or trying to look on the bright side.

6. An important new area of psychological research is learning to improve one's health. Many diseases can be modified by individual actions. Hypertension can be modified through diet, exercise, and medication. Type A behavior can be modified. We can modify risk factors associated with the development of heart disease or cancer. Among the generalized ways of trying to teach people coping skills are stress inoculation, which involves anticipation of the problems and self-statements designed to help coping. Other general approaches include relaxation, which may lessen the extremity of the reaction to stress. Included in relaxation are deep muscle relaxation drills and instant relaxation exercises.

Exercise itself may also have direct effects on health, including the enhancement of cardiovascular and metabolic capacity, and the prevention of degenerative diseases that affect the cardiovascular system, lungs, skeletal muscles, skeleton, and nervous system. Improvements in these functions lessen the deleterious effects of stressors. Most beneficial effects of exercise occur when the system is extended beyond 50 percent of its capacity. Reported psychological benefits include increases in self-esteem and self-confidence, elevation in mood, increased capacity for general coping, and improvement in job functioning.

7. An important problem that many Americans face is shyness. Forty percent consider themselves shy. Shy people generally have low self-esteem and lack specific social skills. Some specific techniques designed to overcome shyness are rehearsal of important social skills through role playing, including imagining new situations that cause shyness, developing self-talk to improve social relations, and self-talk reinforcement.

Terms and Concepts

anxiety
appraisal
chronic life strains
coping
distress
eustress
fear
fight-or-flight emergency reaction
frustration

general adaptation syndrome
hassles
learned helplessness
life change units
organizational stress
social support
stress
Type A behavior
uplifts

Suggestions for Further Reading

Dohrenwend, B. S. (1974). *Stressful life events*. New York: Wiley.
A useful review of the effects of different life events on stress.

Levine, S., & Ursin, H. (1980). *Coping and health*. New York: Plenum.
A text on coping: how different people try to deal with stress.

Seligman, M. (1974). *Helplessness*. San Francisco: W. H. Freeman.
A very important and readable book on the persistent problem of how feeling helpless leads to major disorder.

Selye, H. (1956). *The stress of life*. New York: McGraw-Hill.
The classic book by the developer of the concept of stress.

Chapter 16

Psychological Disorders

INTRODUCTION

For some people, the problems of living get to be too much and their adaptability is stretched beyond their capacity—they snap. When this happens, all or almost all of such individuals' efforts are devoted toward their problems, their fears, their distorted thoughts; there remains little in life undisturbed. Then a "disorder" results. These psychological disorders are *exaggerations* or *extremes* of the normal patterns of thought, action, emotions, personality, and coping that we have studied. Part of the difference is this: everybody does crazy things, sometimes, but normally the order in life returns. When it is impossible to return to the control of daily life, a person may need to seek help.

If there is a "line" between a normal reaction to difficulties and a disordered one it is somewhat like the difference between a brief bout with the flu and a chronic illness. It is one thing to cry when a love affair ends, or to feel sadness when a parent dies; it is another to be so disturbed that for three years you cannot go out to a party. It is one thing to be anxious about going to a party and another to be so afraid of meeting people that you cannot go outside your house at all.

In this chapter we will look, closely, at the breakdown of human adaptation: sadness becomes depression, happiness becomes mania, fear becomes phobia, concern becomes paranoia. Some disorders are mild: they may interfere with work, mood, or relationships. Some disorders are more extreme: the person seems to lose all contact with the world as it is normally experienced. Some people can be incapacitated by their condition, some are even dangerous to others or to themselves, some are just different.

Psychological disorders do not afflict only an unlucky few. One clinical psychologist wrote: "They are, rather, the state of being of all of us at *some time* [italics added] in our lives" (McNeil, 1967). These disorders take an enormous toll on society. Scores of millions are so depressed that they cannot function adequately. Hundreds of thousands are paralyzed because of fear of crowds, snakes, or elevators. Ten million people in the United States are alcoholics who cannot live without drink. More than a

million are schizophrenic, closest to our ordinary idea of someone "crazy."

Every year a million college students leave school because of emotional problems. A decade ago one out of every five Americans said that at one time or another they felt they were going to have a nervous breakdown (*Roche Report*, 1971). More recently, in 1978 the President's Commission on Mental Health predicted that, given current trends, one out of every seven people in the United States will need professional help for psychological problems.

We will first describe the classification system now used for disorders, and then consider what people who experience these disorders are like and how they feel. We must also address two very serious questions regarding psychological disorders. The first concerns labeling, and it is an issue similar to the controversy on classification of people by intelligence test scores. Being diagnosed as disordered has serious consequences, often as serious as being sentenced for a crime. Often a person's civil rights are withdrawn; employment is hard to find; friends withdraw. The effect of categorizing someone as disordered may be worse than their problems.

The second question concerns the interpretation of the disorders: are they "illnesses" or problems of living. There are many theories proposed to explain why things go so wrong with people. The theories have serious implications and consequences because they determine how the disorders are treated. The various psychological approaches to the cause of disorder will be discussed in the next chapter on psychotherapy.

THE NATURE OF PSYCHOLOGICAL DISORDERS

To review, the mental processes work to maintain order in a chaotic world. We select a small amount of information, interpret and organize it simply into categories, and remember a small, meaningful bit of what happens. Disorders can occur when there is a malfunction, breakdown, or misapplication of one or more of these processes.

Suppose you have failing hearing and do not know it. You may think that others are whispering in your presence. Normal perceptual processes interpret the sensory input in the simplest meaningful way: people are whispering because they do not want you to hear them. The reason for that may be they do not like you or may be conspiring against you or plan to exclude you from some activity. A condition know as *sensory paranoia* may result from this kind of interpretation of faulty information. Order and disorder are two sides to the same coin (Maher, 1964).

Disorders may differ from person to person, but here are some fundamental qualities that characterize the experience of disorder.

Loss of Control.   The feeling that one's feelings and thoughts are beyond one's competence. Life is meaningless: there is no organization to life, one's actions do not matter. Helplessness is one aspect of this. In more severe cases it is easy to see why, in earlier ages, the idea that people were "possessed" by the devil or a spirit was popular. When one is possessed one has no control.

Unhappiness or Distress. Although there is a romantic notion that mad people are happy to be different from others, or have made a breakthrough, the experience is more of a break*down*. They are almost always unhappy about it. People considered disordered often make other people unhappy as well: they may be dangerous, or so unable to function that others' lives are disturbed, in families or in jobs.

Isolation from Others. The individuals may physically separate themselves from others or feel themselves withdraw while in company.

The Causation of Disorder

There is no single cause for psychological disorders, as there is for polio. Psychologists analyze disorders as arising from biological, mental, and situational factors.

Biological. A person's genetic inheritance may predispose him or her to certain disorders, such as depression or antisocial actions. Other biological disorders, such as inadequate sensory input, may predispose a person to a disorder, as in the example of sensory paranoia above.

Mental. Each person is influenced by the particular experiences of his or her life. A person may grow up under extreme or unusual circumstances: being beaten by the father or never receiving affection from either parent. He or she may have a strange series of accidents that create an unusual view of the world: suppose everyone in the family was murdered or had terrible luck in business. The person may take this unusual experience as representative, overgeneralize from it, and think and act very differently from the rest of us.

Situational. In everyone's life there are times of extreme stress, times when one is more vulnerable and less able to cope with the problems of living. Violence and riots occur more during heat waves; there are more admissions to mental hospitals during times of economic hardship and recessions.

We cannot predict with assurance an *individual's* disorder. However, psychologists have succeeded in producing an acceptable classification of the *patterns* of disorder.

Classification of Disorders

Psychological disorders are difficult to classify, for they are complex and more subject to the interpretation of the person, the family, and the observer than are medical diseases. For instance, homosexuality was considered a disorder until the early 1970s, and is no longer.

The most widely used classification system is in the American Psychiatric Association's *Diagnostic and Statistical Manual of Mental Disorders* (*DSM*). The *DSM* was first published in 1952, and there have been two major revisions, in 1968 and in 1980.

FIGURE 16–1 *DSM-III* Diagnostic Categories

Disorders usually first evident in infancy, childhood, or adolescence
Organic mental disorders
Substance use disorders
Schizophrenic disorders
Paranoid disorders
Psychotic disorders not elsewhere classified
Affective disorders
Anxiety disorders
Somatoform disorders
Dissociative disorders (hysterical neuroses, dissociative type)
Psychosexual disorders
Factitious disorders
Disorders of impulse control not elsewhere classified
Adjustment disorder
Psychological factors affecting physical condition
Personality disorders

Source: American Psychiatric Association, 1980.

Although the *DSM* classification has been criticized for being modeled too strongly along medical lines, we follow the general guidelines of *DSM-III* here, because it provides an acceptable way of categorizing disorders, both the mild and the severe. However, because of space limitations, we have had to eliminate whole categories of disorders. We begin with the group of mild disorders previously called "neuroses," such as obsessions and phobias, then consider disorders of personality, and examine drug use and abuse (called "substance use disorders" in *DSM-III*). We then focus on depression, the major affective disorder, and schizophrenia, the major thought disorder. Our descriptions of disorders are based largely on material in *DSM-III*. (See Figure 16–1.)

The use of the term "disorder" is intended to be a neutral one. The problems described are not diseases, nor are they simply alternate lifestyles. Something is definitely wrong with many of the people described herein, and they often need help.

MILD DISORDERS: ANXIETY AND SOMATOFORM

The distinguishing feature of this group of disorders is that the individual recognizes and is disturbed by the symptoms he or she is experiencing. There is generally no disturbance of thought processes, his or her behavior is not way out of line with normal social conventions.

These disorders are fairly consistent: that is, they become part of the "background noise" of the individual's life and are not normally precipitated by a specific stressful life event. Finally, there is no evidence that any genetic or organic factors contribute to the development of these disorders. Here is a fairly typical case:

A 25-year-old married insurance salesman is admitted to the medical service of a hospital by his internist when he arrives at the emergency room, for the fourth time in a month, insisting that he is having a heart attack. The cardiologist's workup is completely negative.

The patient states that his "heart problem" started six months ago when he had a sudden episode of terror, chest pain, palpitations, sweating, and shortness of breath while driving across a bridge on his way to visit a prospective client. His father and uncle had both had heart problems, and the patient was sure he was developing a similar illness. Not wanting to alarm his wife and family, he initially said nothing; but when the attacks began to recur several times a month, he consulted his internist. The internist found nothing wrong and told him he should try to relax, take more time off from work, and develop some leisure interests. In spite of his attempts to follow this advice the attacks recurred with increasing intensity and frequency.

The patient claims that he believes the doctors who say there is nothing wrong with his heart, but during an attack he still becomes concerned that he is having a heart attack and will die. (Spitzer, Skodol, Gibbon, & Williams, 1981b)

Before the *DSM-III*, such disorders were classified together as "Neurotic Disorders." The term neurosis (from "inflamed nerves") was used by Freud to describe a symptom, or group of symptoms, that, while painful, did not interfere with the person's perception of reality. He also meant to imply by the term that the cause of the maladaptive symptoms was anxiety-arousing unconscious conflicts. However, although the word neurotic is used in everday speech, clinicians and psychologists have had a hard time agreeing on a useful definition. In *DSM-III* the disorders formerly called *neurotic* fall into five categories: *affective, anxiety, somatoform, dissociative,* and *psychosexual*. In this section we will discuss anxiety and somatoform. Mild affective disorder will be considered briefly in our discussion of depression. Dissociative disorders were touched on in the chapters on personality and consciousness.

Causes of Mild Disorders

The causes of mild disorders seem to be entirely psychosocial: maladaptive coping strategies, learning of inappropriate contingencies, difficulty in interpersonal relationships, especially familial ones.

Both anxiety and somatoform disorders are largely found in contemporary Western civilization. There is no recorded example of these disorders in undeveloped countries or among primitive tribes, such as the aborigines of Australia (Kidson & Jones, 1952). In our own culture anxiety disorders are more often experienced by middle- and upper-class people who express general dissatisfaction with life, complain of being unhappy, and are often called "the worried well." Their dissatisfaction is experienced in the rather abstract, pervasive feeling of anxiety. People in lower economic classes or with little education who experience mild disorders are more likely to experience somatoform disorders. (The prefix *soma* refers to the body.) The major symptoms are physical complaints

that have no physical cause. Mild disorders may be an extremely maladaptive reaction to stress.

Anxiety Disorders

Generalized Anxiety Disorder

People suffering from **generalized anxiety** live in constant tension and worry. They seem uneasy when they are around people and are unusually sensitive to comments and criticisms by other people. Often they are so terrified of making a mistake that they cannot concentrate or make decisions. Their posture is often strained and rigid, resulting in sore muscles (especially in the neck and shoulders). They may have chronic insomnia and gastrointestinal problems (such as diarrhea), perspire heavily, and experience high blood pressure, heart palpitations, and breathlessness. It does not matter how well they are actually doing in life, people with a generalized anxiety disorder are worried that something will go wrong, that they have made the wrong decisions.

OBSESSIVE-COMPULSIVE DISORDERS

Obsessive-compulsive disorders are the least common of all the mild disorders but are quite interesting because they are clear-cut exaggerations of feelings we all have at one time or another. In an obsession the mind is flooded with a specific thought. In a compulsive disorder the person feels compelled to repeat a certain action over and over. Scientists or artists may be "obsessed" with their work and allow few intrusions. You may check during the day to see that you have brought the tickets to a concert you are going to that evening. But an obsessive-compulsive's life is interfered with, rather than enhanced, by this problem. Davison and Neale (1982) report a client who washed her hands more than 500 times a day to prevent contamination from germs. Below are two excerpts from a case history of Georgia M., who was obsessively neat. The first excerpt is an account by Georgia M., the second is by her husband.

"I can't get to sleep unless I am sure everything in the house is in its proper place so that when I get up in the morning the house is organized. I work like mad to set everything straight before I go to bed, but, when I get up in the morning, I can think of a thousand things that I ought to do. I know some of the things are ridiculous, but I feel better if I get them done, and I can't stand to know something needs doing and I haven't done it. I never told anybody but once I found just one dirty shirt and washed, dried, and ironed it that day. I felt stupid running a whole wash for one shirt but I couldn't bear to leave it undone. It would have bothered me all day just thinking about that one dirty shirt in the laundry basket.

"What really bothers me is this whole business of sex. My husband acts like he wants it all the time and he always brings it up at a time when it's impossible because I have so

A 27-year-old, married electrician complains of dizziness, sweating palms, heart palpitations, and ringing of the ears of more than eighteen months' duration. He has also experienced dry throat, periods of uncontrollable shaking, and a constant "edgy" and watchful feeling that often interfered with his ability to concentrate. These feelings have been present most of the time over the previous two years; they have not been limited to discrete periods.

Because of these symptoms he had seen a family practitioner, a neurologist, a neurosurgeon, a chiropractor, and an ENT specialist. He had been placed on a hypoglycemic diet, received physiotherapy for a pinched nerve, and told he might have "an inner ear problem."

For the past two years he has had few social contacts because of his nervous symptoms. Although he has sometimes had to leave work when the symptoms became intolerable, he continues to work for the same company for which he has worked since his apprenticeship following high-school graduation. He tends to hide his symptoms from his wife and children, to whom he wants to appear "perfect," and reports few problems with them as a result of his nervousness. (Spitzer et al., 1981)

much to do. By nighttime I am tired and we live on different sleep schedules. I always have a million things to do and he's ready to go to bed. I like to make preparations, too. I think we both ought to take a shower and the bed should have clean sheets on it. But, he gets mad and says "the hell with it" and sulks. He's just like a big overgrown kid. In the last month he hasn't said anything about sex and I am beginning to think he is fooling around with some other woman. I got so suspicious that I thought about following him once or twice, but, with the kids and the house to take care of, I couldn't get free."

"You remember that old joke about getting up in the middle of the night to go to the john and coming back to the bedroom to find your wife has made the bed? It's no joke. Sometimes I think she never sleeps. I got up one night at 4 a.m. and there she was doing the laundry downstairs. . . . If I forget to leave my dirty shoes outside the back door she gives me a look like I had just crapped in the middle of an operating room. I stay out of the house a lot and I'm about half-stoned when I do have to be home. She even made us get rid of the dog because she said he was always filthy. When we used to have people over for supper she would jitterbug around everybody till they couldn't digest their food. I hated to call them up and ask them over because I could always hear them hem and haw and make up excuses not to come over. Even the kids are walking down the street nervous about getting dirt on them. I'm going out of my mind but you can't talk to her. She just blows up and spends twice as much time cleaning things. We have guys in to wash the walls so often I think the house is going to fall down from being scrubbed all the time." (McNeil, 1967)

Causes.　There are several possible causes of generalized anxiety. It may be an extreme reaction to an early trauma. For example, whenever she heard a siren or accident reports, a young housewife experienced severe anxiety that someone in her family was hurt. Often the feelings of anxiety are caused by the person's fears that he or she will not be able to control dangerous impulses. For example, a young man had persistent fantasies about strangling his girl friend. "When we are alone in the car, I can't get my mind off her nice white throat and what it would be like to choke her to death" (Coleman et al., 1980). Learning is also important: overanxious parents tend to have overanxious children (Jenkins, 1966, 1969).

Phobic Disorders: The Fears

Phobia is Greek for fear. In psychology the term refers to an extreme or unfounded fear of an object or place. In general, fear is an adaptive emotion, an efficient warning system that gets us out of dangerous situations. Fear of snakes is one of the most common of all fears. And it is justified, since many snakes are poisonous, and it is wise to avoid one you see while hiking. However, if your fear of snakes is so great that you cannot leave your apartment on the thirty-fourth floor in New York City, then it is a disordered fear, or a phobia. The most common phobias are *zoophobia* (fear of animals), *claustrophobia* (fear of closed spaces), *acrophobia* (fear of heights). **Agoraphobia,** fear of being alone in public places that might be difficult to escape, is classified separately in *DSM-III.*

People with a phobic disorder experience anxiety whenever they try to confront their fear. Barbara Gordon was a successful television producer who suffered from agoraphobia. She was so afraid that she could not leave her office for lunch or go out without some definite destination in mind. She wrote of the experience in her book, *I'm Dancing as Fast as I Can:*

You don't dash, I said to myself, you flee, as if moving quickly will somehow help you beat the terror. There it was, the old fear, back again, whenever I had to go someplace. And I was at this point, afraid of the fear. My anxiety attacks had become so intense that I was often immobilized, paralyzed. So I hadn't dashed very far when the terror, greater than yesterday's, less than tomorrow's, swallowed me up like a vacuum cleaner. I walked along holding on to the walls of the corridor, praying I wouldn't bump into anyone I knew.

Age is a critical factor in the determination of phobias. Most children are extremely "phobic": afraid of the dark or of a certain kind of animal. Many parents of preschoolers have to check their children's closets for gorillas and monsters. These fears are not considered pathological in early childhood. However, one childhood phobia may require some professional help: *schoolphobia*, in which a child experiences stomachaches whenever he or she has to go to school. In general, phobias begin in late teens or early adulthood. Women are more likely to suffer from a phobia than men. Agoraphobia is found in about 0.5 percent of the population. Simple phobias (phobias directed toward a specific object) are thought to be quite common, but are usually not intrusive enough on someone's life to impel the individual to seek treatment.

Causes. Most investigators agree that there are three primary factors that contribute to the development of a phobia.

1. *Faulty learning.* Recall the case of Little Albert, who became afraid of white furry things because they were associated with a frightening, loud noise. In that instance the child generalized incorrectly from a specific trauma. A fear is also likely to be maintained if it is acceded to by a child's parents.

The Case of Little Albert See Chapter 8, pp. 305, 306.

2. *Displacement of anxiety.* Freudian analysis holds that anxiety is the result of guilt, transference, or repression. The phobia may relieve individuals of anxiety and responsibilities and gain them increased attention from those they live with. A child who has schoolphobia may actually fear separation from his or her mother. By refusing to go to school, the child gets to stay home with her.

3. *A defense mechanism to counteract dangerous impulses.* A man avoids speaking in public because he is afraid he will expose his genitals. A woman avoids skyscrapers because she is afraid she will jump off.

Somatoform Disorders

Somatoform disorders are those in which the individual complains of a physical ailment or pain for which there is no organic or physiological explanation. *DSM-III* classifies several kinds of somatoform disorders: somatization, conversion, psychogenic pain, hypochondriasis, atypical. Here we discuss hypochondriasis, because it is probably the most common.

Hypochondriasis

Hypochondriasis is characterized by an individual's misinterpretation of body functions. This often leads to the fear of disease or to the belief that he or she is already suffering from one. The belief that he or she already has a disease continues even in the face of medical evidence that there is none. The feigned "illness" may cause serious restrictions in social activities, at work and at home. Certain bodily functions, such as heartbeat or perspiration or even minor coughing or irregular bowel movements, can be interpreted as symptoms of a serious disease. Sometimes the person believes that he or she has a specific disease.

Hypochondriacs are famous for "doctor shopping." They go to doctor after doctor with their list of symptoms and medical knowledge picked up from popular journals and previous physicians. They search for the doctor who can find the serious disease they know they have. Below is a letter (Menninger, 1945) written by such a woman:

Dear Mother and Husband:

I have suffered terribly today with drawing in throat. My nerves are terrible. My head feels queer. But my stomach hasn't cramped quite so hard. I've been on the verge of a nervous chill all day, but I have been fighting it hard. It's night and bedtime, but, Oh, how I hate to go to bed. Nobody knows or realizes how badly I feel because I fight to stay up outdoors if possible . . .

These long afternoons and nights are awful. There are plenty of patients well enough to visit with but I'm in too much pain. The nurses ignore any complaining. They just laugh or scold. With supper so early, and evening so long, I am so nervous I can't sleep until so late. I haven't slept well since I've been here. My heart pains as much as when I was at home. More so at night. I put hot water bottle on it. I don't know if I should or not. I've been wanting to ask some Dr.

I had headache so badly in the back of my head last night and put hot water bottle there. My nurse said not to.

They don't give much medicine here. Mostly Christian Science it seems! Well, I must close or I never will get to sleep. My nurse gets off at 8:15 so she makes me go to bed by then.

My eyes are bothering me more.

Come up as soon as you can. My nose runs terrible every time I eat.

The trains and ducks and water pipes are noisy at night.

Annie

Causes. There are three broad areas that seem to be predisposing factors in the development of hypochondriasis.

1. *Early childhood learning.* Overanxious parents, who comment on their children's every sneeze and pamper them unduly when they are sick, may be unwittingly teaching hypochondriacs how to gain love and attention.

2. *Dissatisfaction with life.* People who become hypochondriacs later in life (men in their thirties, women in their forties) generally do so in reaction to a sense that they have not made much of their lives: they have not achieved what they wanted professionally or marriage may not have turned out satisfactorily. Hypochondriasis then is the maladaptive behavior they "choose" over what they perceive to be a life full of wrong choices.

3. *Reinforcement of the behavior.* Because people with hypochondriacal disorders gain attention from families, friends and doctors, they are rein-

forced and more or less encouraged to persist in them. In addition, these individuals will not have to worry about disappointing people as they present themselves as "sick," not healthy enough to live up to the expectations of others.

PERSONALITY DISORDERS

People with personality disorders perceive, relate to, and think about themselves and their environment in maladaptive ways. One distinguishing feature of personality disorders is that the symptoms tend to be "acted out" in the world, rather than simply in the mind of the person. The entire personality seems to be typified by the disorder.

People with personality disorders do not usually seek treatment. They do not feel anything is wrong, and often it is the people who live with them who do. The following is a list of the major personality disorders and brief definitions from *DSM-III*.

Paranoid: "pervasive and unwarranted suspiciousness and mistrust of people, hypersensitivity"

Schizoid: "a defect in the capacity to form social relationships, evidenced by the absence of warm, tender feeling for others, indifference to praise, criticism, and the feeling of others"

Histrionic: "overly dramatic, reactive, and intensely expressed behavior and characteristic disturbances in interpersonal relationships"

Narcissistic: "a grandiose sense of self-importance or uniqueness"

Borderline: "instability in a variety of areas, including interpersonal behavior, mood, and self image. No single feature is invariably present"

Avoidant: "hypersensitivity to potential rejection, humiliation, or shame; an unwillingness to enter into relationships unless given unusually strong guarantees of uncritical acceptance"

Dependent: "the individual passively allows others to assume responsibility for major areas of his or her life, because of a lack of self-confidence and an inability to function independently"

Compulsive: "restricted ability to express warm and tender emotions . . . excessive devotion to work and productivity to the exclusion of pleasure; and indecisiveness (bye, bye, I think)"

Passive-Aggressive: "resistance to demands for adequate performance in both occupational and social functioning; the resistance is expressed indirectly rather than directly [the result is] pervasive and persistent social or occupational ineffectiveness"

Antisocial: "a history of continuous and chronic antisocial behavior in which the rights of others are violated." We will discuss the antisocial personality disorder in detail below.

Causes.   Except in the case of the antisocial personality (ASP) there is little evidence of any biological factors leading to the development of personality disorders. For the most part there is little information about why people develop personality disorders or why they develop the specific ones that they do. In addition, because individuals with such a disorder have little desire to change, treatment of these individuals is rarely successful.

Antisocial Behavior: Sociopathic Personality

Suppose you saw this advertisement:

> Are you adventurous? Psychologists studying adventurous carefree people who've led exciting impulsive lives. If you're the kind of person who'd do almost anything for a dare and want to participate in a paid experiment, send name, address, phone number and short biography proving how interesting you are.

This ad was written by a psychologist and appeared in several underground newspapers in Boston, and it attracted a number of people who psychological tests revealed fit the clinical picture of an *antisocial personality* (also called *psychopath* or *sociopath*) (Wisdom, 1977). Most antisocial personalities seen and studied by psychologists are institutionalized, usually in prisons or reformatories. Wisdom wanted to see if ASPs were similar to those institutionalized. They are. (One respondent, however, determined the true purpose of the ad: He wrote: "Are you looking for hookers or are you trying to make a listing of all the sociopaths in Boston?")

The repetitive pattern of antisocial behavior usually begins before the age of 15 and is mainly characterized by the individual's inability to feel either positive emotions or guilt. The following behaviors characterize an **antisocial personality** (Cleckley, 1954):

1. Superficial charm, average or above average intelligence.
2. Absence of irrationality characteristic of severe disorders, absence of anxiety characteristic of milder ones; at ease in situations that would unsettle an average person.
3. No sense of responsibility about anything, big or small.
4. No sense of shame.
5. Tells lies or doesn't care if he is caught.
6. No guilt or regret about any of his antisocial actions.
7. Poor judgment—doesn't learn from experience.
8. Lack of genuine insight.
9. Callousness, insincerity, incapacity for love and close attachments.
10. Little response to special consideration and the kindness of others.
11. No history of suicide attempts.
12. Unrestrained and unconventional sex life.
13. No life plans or goals, no order except for a "persistent pattern of self-defeat."

A Case of Antisocial Personality

The psychologist Elton McNeil described one such person whom he knew, not as a patient, but as a friend. One day McNeil and Dan F. were at a restaurant. When the order arrived Dan F. yelled at the waitress, telling her that it was not fit to eat, and demanded that she taste the food. He asked for the manager. When a second plate of food was brought, he shoved it aside, saying that it could not be fit to eat, either. McNeil asked about the scene:

"Dan," I said, "I have a sneaking suspicion that this whole scene came about just because you really weren't hungry."

Dan laughed loudly in agreement and said, "What the hell, they'll be on their toes next time."

"Was that the only reason for this display?" I asked.

"No," he replied, "I wanted to show you how gutless the rest of the world is. If you shove a little they all jump. Next time I come in, they'll be all over me to make sure everything is exactly as I want it. That's the only way they can tell the difference between class and plain ordinary. When I travel I go first class."

"Yes," I responded, "but how do they feel about you as a person—as a fellow human being?"

"Who cares?" he laughed. "If they were on top they would do the same to me. The more you walk on them, the more they like it. It's like royalty in the old days. It makes them nervous if everyone is equal to everyone else. Watch. When we leave I'll put my arm around that waitress and ask her if she still loves me, pat her on the fanny, and she'll be ready to roll over any time I wiggle my little finger."

He was convincing. I believed him. That's exactly what he did on the way out and there was no mistaking the look in her eye. She was ready any time he was, and she thought he was a lot of man . . .

One night, a colleague of Dan's committed suicide. My phone started ringing early the next morning with the inevitable question "Why?" The executives at the station called but Dan F. never did. When I did talk to him, he did not mention the suicide. Later, when I brought it to his attention, all he could say was that it was "the way the ball bounces." At the station, however, he was the one who collected money for the deceased and presented it personally to the new widow. As Dan observed, she was really built and had possibilities.

Dan F. had been married twice before, a fact he had failed to communicate to his present wife, and as he described it, was still married only part time. He had established a reasonable basis for frequent nights out since his variety show required that he keep in touch with entertainers in town. He was currently involved sexually with girls ranging from the station manager's secretary (calculated) to the weather girl (incidental, based on a shared interest in Chinese food). The females of the "show biz" species seemed to dote on the high-handed treatment he accorded them. They regularly refused to believe he was "as bad as he pretended to be," and he was always surrounded by intense and glamorous women who needed to own him to feel complete as human beings.

Dan F. had charm plus. He always seemed to know when to say the right thing with exactly the proper degree of concern, seriousness, and understanding for the benighted victim of a harsh world. *But, he was dead inside* [italics added]. People amused him and he watched them with the kind of interest most of us show when examining a tank of guppies. Once, on a whim, he called each of the burlesque theaters in town and left word with the burlesque queens that he was holding a party beginning at midnight with each of them as an honored guest. He indeed held the party, charging it to the station as a talent search, and spent the evening pouring liquor into the girls. By about 3 a.m. the hotel suite was a shambles, but he thought it was hilarious. He had invited the camera and floor crew from the television station and had carefully constructed a fictional identity for each: one was an independent film producer, another a casting director, a third an influential writer, and still another a talent agent. This giant hoax was easy to get away with since Dan had read correctly and with painful accuracy the not so secret dreams, ambitions, drives, and personal needs of these entertainers. What was staggering was the elaborateness of the cruel joke. He worked incessantly adding a touch here and a touch there to make it perfect. (McNeil, 1967)

Causes of Antisocial Personality: Psychosocial

It is estimated that 3 percent of American men and less than 1 percent of American woman have ASP disorder. The psychosocial factors thought to be important are:

1. Extreme poverty and poor education.
2. Poor family background: if the father suffers from the disorder, the child is removed from the home and gets little discipline.

Biological Factors in Antisocial Personality

Dan F. describes his situation:

I can remember the first time in my life when I began to suspect I was a little different from most people. When I was in high school my best friend got leukemia and died and I went to his funeral. Everybody else was crying and feeling sorry for themselves and as they were praying to get him into heaven I suddenly realized that I wasn't feeling anything at all. He was a nice guy but what the hell. That night I thought about it some more and found out that I wouldn't miss my mother and father if they died and that I wasn't too nuts about my brothers and sisters, for that matter. I figured there wasn't anybody I really cared for but, then, I didn't need any of them anyway so I rolled over and went to sleep. (McNeil, 1967)

The antisocial personality seems to be associated with *decreased emotional response*, especially to unpleasant stimuli. In studies measuring autonomic system reactions, ASPs had less activation to shock (Hare & Craigen, 1974; Lykken, 1957). When one is punished or slapped as a child for doing the wrong thing, the activated feeling of hurt and guilt makes it less likely that the action would be repeated. People with "flat" emotions would not feel the hurt and would be less likely to learn law-abiding behavior (Mednick, 1977).

Thus, one characteristic of these people is extreme calm, perhaps due to the underarousal. There is a constant search in these people for exciting situations; they attack others verbally, set up wild scenes like the burlesque queen party. This may be due to a characteristic underarousal and the need for extreme stimulation (Quay, 1965).

Genetic Factors

There is evidence for genetic factors in this disorder. The children of criminal fathers have less reactive ANS responses than the children of noncriminals. In a very large study, Wadsworth compared the pulse rate of boys just before a mild stress, at age 11, to later records of delinquency. Those with low increases in pulse rate were much more likely to become delinquent (Mednick, 1977). There is a higher rate of criminality and antisocial behavior in the biological relatives of adopted criminals than in the general population (Hutchings & Mednick, 1975). In studies of the antisocial personality, the same relationship holds: the transmission is significant from the biological father (Schulsinger, 1972). What might be inherited, then, is an ANS less responsive to stimulation. In the appropriate situation this could lead to some deficiencies in learning law-abiding behavior, to less responsiveness to others' feelings, and to the need to create excitement—all characteristic of the antisocial personality.

SUBSTANCE USE DISORDERS

The use of mood- or consciousness-altering drugs is common in every culture. Alcohol is the most common recreational drug in our society; the use of illegal drugs such as marijuana and heroin is widespread in certain subcultures of American society. "Substance use" is not considered a disorder unless there is a *consistent pattern of excessive use resulting in impairment of social or occupational functioning.* Disordered individuals may be dependent on the drug (substance), may not be able to get through the day without it, or cannot stop or restrict their use even if they know that they should.

Some disorders may be minor, such as caffeine intoxication:

> A 35-year-old secretary sought consultation for "anxiety attacks." A thorough history revealed that the attacks occurred in the mid-to-late afternoon, when she became restless, nervous, and easily excited and sometimes was noted to be flushed, sweating, and, according to co-workers, "talking a mile a minute." In response to careful questioning, she acknowledged drinking five or six cups of coffee each day before the usual time the attacks occurred. (Spitzer et al., 1981)

The *DSM-III* criterion for a disorder requires the disturbance in behavior caused by the drug to be of at least one month's duration. There are two forms of **substance use disorders:** abuse and dependence. Dependence is more severe: the drug-dependent person begins to show increased *tolerance;* he or she requires greater amounts of the drug. In addition, the person experiences specific physiological symptoms if the drug is withdrawn.

There are five categories of substances that may invite abuse or dependence: *alcohol*; barbiturates or other *sedatives*; *analgesics*, painkillers or narcotics, which include heroin; *stimulants* like amphetamines; and *psychoactive drugs* such as marijuana and LSD.

Incidence

The prevalence of substance use disorders varies with the particular substance. Sixteen percent of Americans over three recent years reported alcohol-related problems. Because many of the other drugs are illegal or prescribed, there are no accurate figures of the incidence of their abuse. It is more common for men than women to have a substance use disorder. Abuse and dependence do not usually appear until adulthood: alcoholic disorder in the twenties, thirties, and forties; problems with marijuana, cocaine, or heroin and other narcotics start earlier, in late teens and early twenties. Substance abuse and dependence may lead to physical problems such as malnutrition or hepatitis. A major complication of alcohol abuse is traffic accidents. Half of all highway deaths in America involve either a pedestrian or driver who has been drinking. Twenty-five percent of all suicides and more than one-half of all murderers *and* their victims are thought to be drunk at the time of the murder.

Alcohol   Stimulants

Causes

The use of a drug may begin for recreational purposes and also to alleviate fear and anxiety in social settings. The effect of the drug in alleviating anxiety is the reinforcer that maintains, and creates, the abuse or dependence. The factors that contribute to the abuse of the different drugs vary. Although alcohol abuse tends to run in families, and there is some evidence for genetic involvement in alcoholism, the important factors seem to be psychosocial. These psychosocial factors may include stress, marital problems and the desire for tension reduction. Sociocultural influences also play a part: rapid changes in socioeconomic status (especially downward) may lead to alcoholism.

In narcotic addiction there is some evidence of neurological causes. Recall that the brain produces its own painkillers and mood modulators: endorphins. Specific endorphins fit as a key does to a lock, to specific receptors in the brain, especially in the limbic system. Morphine (of which heroin is a derivative) fits these locks as well. Some researchers hypothesize that morphine addiction may occur in people whose brain produces too few endorphins (Coleman et al., 1980).

But in narcotic addiction too, sociocultural factors are more important. In the United States, heroin addiction is more common in the lower economic groups. During the Vietnam War heroin addiction was a seri-

Analgesics   Sedatives   Psychoactive Drugs

FIGURE 16–2   Substances Inviting Abuse and Dependence

Alcohol

Whiskey	Liqueur
Vodka	Wine
Gin	Beer
Brandy	

Sedatives

Barbiturates	Chloral hydrate
Amytal	Miltown, Equanil
Nembutal	(meprobamate)
Seconal	Methaqualone (Quaalude,
Phenobarbital	Sopor)
Tuinal	Valium
Doriden (glutethimide)	

Analgesics (painkillers, opiates, narcotics)

Opium	Percodan
Heroin	Demerol
Dilaudid	Methadone
Morphine	Cough syrup (Cheracol,
Codeine	Hycodan, Robitussin AC, etc.)

Stimulants

Amphetamines	Cocaine
Benzedrine	Preludin
Methedrine	Caffeine
Dexedrine	Coffee, tea, Coca-Cola
Desoxyn	No-Doz, APC
Biphetamine	Nicotine (and coal tar)

Psychoactive drugs

Marijuana, hashish (cannabis)	Mescaline (peyote)
THC (tetrahydrocannabinol)	PCP (phencyclidine)
LSD	DMT (dimethyltryptamine)
Psilocybin	Glue

Source: Adapted from Fort, 1970.

ous problem. However, the great majority of heroin addicts gave up their addiction when they returned to the States. All substance use disorders involve an extremely high mortality rate. Heroin addiction, however, is often short-lived, which is not true of alcohol or the other narcotics. Although the death rate among heroin users is high, due in large part to impurities and continual injections without proper hygiene, if a person survives, dependence rarely lasts more than nine years.

SEVERE MENTAL DISORDERS: DEPRESSION

Depression is known as the "common cold of psychological disorders" (Seligman, 1973). The word "depressed" is widely used in our everyday vocabulary. People say they are depressed when they are sad or upset or in a bad mood: "I'm depressed . . . the store is out of chocolate chip cookies and I was thinking about them all day." However, a **depression** serious enough to be considered a severe mental disorder *consists of an overwhelming sadness that immobilizes and arrests the entire course of a person's life.* Below are two examples of people suffering from depression: the first is by British writer John Custance, and the second is the story of a college student:

> I was utterly miserable and wanted to die, but my fears, troubles and words were of normal human mischances which might happen to anybody. I feared poverty, failure in life, inability to educate my children, making my wife miserable, losing her, ending up in the gutter as the most revolting type of beggar and so on. My fears had in fact become so overpowering as to appear to me like certainties, but they were only earthly fears. (1951)

> Nancy entered the university with a superb high-school record. She had been president and salutatorian of her class, and a popular and pretty cheerleader. Everything she wanted had always fallen into her lap; good grades came easily and boys fell over themselves competing for her attentions. She was an only child, and her parents doted on her, rushing to fulfill her every whim; her successes were their triumphs, her failures their agony. Her friends nicknamed her Golden Girl.
>
> When I met her in her sophomore year, she was no longer a Golden Girl. She said that she felt empty, that nothing touched her any more; her classes were boring and the whole academic system seemed an oppressive conspiracy to stifle her creativity. The previous semester she had received two F's. She had "made it" with a succession of young men, and was currently living with a dropout. She felt exploited and worthless after each sexual adventure; her current relationship was on the rocks, and she felt little but contempt for him and for herself. She had used soft drugs extensively and had once enjoyed being carried away on them. But now even drugs had little appeal.
>
> She was majoring in philosophy, and had a marked emotional attraction to Existentialism: like the existentialists, she believed that life is absurd and that people must create their own meaning. This belief filled her with despair. Her despair increased when she perceived her own attempts to create meaning—participation in the movements for women's liberation and against the war in Vietnam—as fruitless. When I reminded her that she had been a talented student and was still an attractive and valuable human being, she burst into tears: "I fooled you, too." (Seligman, 1975)

Classification of Depression

Depression is classified in *DSM-III* in the category of **affective disorders:** a disturbance of *mood* is the distinguishing feature. There are two major categories of serious depressive disorders. In *major depressive disorder* (sometimes called *unipolar depression*) an individual suffers only from depression. In the other, *bipolar depression*, a person suffers from depression, but also experiences the "polar" opposite: mania. **Mania** is excessive elation. An individual in a manic episode is caught up in a frenzy of overexcitability and activity: a happiness that is as out of control as is the sadness. Both forms of the illness vary from mild to extremely severe. A person who is severely depressed or manic may be hospitalized. All of the affective disorders involve either mania or depression or both. Here we will describe the essential features of both, and in the following sections begin to examine the causes of the disorder.

Clinical Criteria for Depression

Although we use the word "depressed" loosely, before a clinician would diagnose a person as depressed, at least four of the following symptoms have to be present *every day* for two weeks:

1. *Loss of interest and pleasure.* This is an almost universal symptom. The individual is indifferent to the activities that usually provide interest and pleasure. This loss of interest extends to friends and family. The depressed person often withdraws from people and activities.

2. *Appetite disturbance.* The most common appetite disturbance is loss, although some people experience an increase in appetite, causing a significant change in the person's normal weight. A fairly accurate description of a depressed person is that he or she is "wasting away." One sign that a person is pulling out of a depressive episode is weight gain.

3. *Sleep disturbance.* The most common sleep disturbance is insomnia, although sometimes there is the opposite, hypersomnia.

4. *Psychomotor disturbance.* The depressed individuals exhibit either psychomotor agitation or retardation. In agitation, they cannot sit still, pull their hair, pace up and down the floor, wring their hands, occasionally burst into shouting and complaining. In retardation, speech is slowed and monotonous. They move slowly as if carrying a heavy weight.

5. *Decrease in energy level.* This is another practically universal trait. People feel tired consistently whether or not they have slept or done anything physically taxing. The prospect of having to do even the smallest task is overwhelming.

6. *Sense of worthlessness.* Nearly every person suffering from depression experiences a sense of worthlessness. The degree varies from general feelings of inadequacy and negative self-evaluations to feelings of delusional proportion.

7. *Difficulty in concentrating.* Thinking seems to be slowed; the depressed person has trouble making decisions, often complains of memory disturbances, and is easily distracted.

8. *Thoughts about death.* A depressed person often seems preoccupied with death: may be afraid of it, wish for it, and plan or attempt suicide.

9. *Miscellaneous associated symptoms.* Other features that might be experienced by the depressed persons are anxiety, phobias, over-concern with health, tearfulness, irritability.

Manic Episodes

You look like a couple of bright, alert, hard working, clean-cut, energetic, go-getters and I could use you in my organization! I need guys that are loyal and enthusiastic about the great opportunities life offers on this planet! It's yours for the taking! Too many people pass opportunity by without hearing it knock because they don't know how to grasp the moment and strike while the iron is hot! You've got to grab it when it comes up for air, pick up the ball and run! You've got to be decisive! decisive! decisive! No shilly-shallying! Sweat! Yeah, sweat with a goal! Push, push, push, and you can push over a mountain! Two mountains, maybe. It's not luck! Hell, if it wasn't for bad luck I wouldn't have any luck at all! Be there firstest with the mostest! my guts and your blood! That's the system! I know, you know, he, she, or it knows it's the only way to travel! Get'em off balance, baby, and the rest is leverage! Use your head and save your heels! What's this deal? Who are these guys? Have you got a telephone and a secretary I can have instanter if not sooner? What I need is office space and the old LDO [long-distance operator]. (McNeil, 1967)

The features of mania are the mirror image of depression. *DSM-III* characterizes the mood as predominantly elevated, expansive, or irritable. The experience of elevated moods is commonly felt as pure euphoria, and those who know the disturbed people well recognize that the euphoria is a bit excessive: their friends are "not themselves." The happiness has no specific cause and is not under the person's control. The quality of expansion is seen in the manic person's unbounded enthusiasm for everyone and everything. The two qualities of euphoria and expansiveness when not too extreme are infectious, which is what enables some manics to be very effective manipulators. Their enthusiasm often can get people to do whatever they want.

Sometimes irritability is the dominant mood of a manic episode instead of euphoria. This irritability usually shows itself whenever someone stands in the way of something the manic wants.

Incidence

Affective disorders afflict 5 to 8 percent of all people at some time in their lives. Of these people 6 percent of the women and 3 percent of the men have an episode serious enough to require hospitalization.

Bipolar disorder (depression with both depressive and manic periods) is experienced by 0.4 to 1.2 percent of the population. Although women are more likely than men to suffer from *unipolar* (only depression) *disorder*, there is no sex difference in the bipolar form. A major depression can occur at any age. A person with the bipolar form of the disorder generally experiences his or her manic episode before the age of 30. The average age of onset for bipolar is 28, for unipolar, 36.

Causes of Major Depressive Disorder

The causal factors contributing to either unipolar or bipolar disorder are divided into factors *within* (*en*dogenous) and *without* (*ex*ogenous). Endogenous factors include genetic predisposition and biochemical components. Exogenous factors include undue stress, a precipitating event, psychosocial factors including helplessness, personality predispositions, and sociocultural factors. It is unlikely that endogenous factors alone can account for a severe disorder; although it is possible that depression may be caused by exogenous factors alone. First, we will discuss endogenous factors and then exogenous ones.

Endogenous Factors in Depressive Disorders

One way to separate genetic and learned factors is to compare two kinds of twins. Fraternal twins (called dizygotic, DZ) are the product of two eggs and are no more alike, genetically, than any brother and sister.

Identical twins (MZ for monozygotic, or one egg) have an identical genetic makeup. A "concordance rate" indicates the degree to which when one twin has the disorder so does the other. There is an extremely high concordance rate in both unipolar and bipolar forms of the disorder in MZ twins. In bipolar disorder the concordance rate in MZ twins is 72 percent, in DZ twins, 14 percent; for unipolar disorder, the rate is 40 percent for MZ, 11 percent for DZ (Price, 1968; Slater & Cowie, 1971; Zerbing & Rudin, 1967). This finding is particularly interesting because the bipolar form of the disorder is rarer than the unipolar.

There is probably more of a predisposing genetic factor in bipolar depression. Studies of families of bipolar depressives reveal that 11 percent of close relatives also had experienced bipolar depression, 0.5 percent had had the unipolar form. Seven percent of close relatives of people with unipolar depression also had experienced a major depression, 0.4 percent had experienced the bipolar form (Winokur, Clayton, & Reich, 1969). Other severe psychological disorders and suicide are more prevalent in families of people with bipolar disorder. Winokur was able to locate and interview the close relatives of 61 bipolar patients. He found that there was a risk of an affective disorder in 56 percent of the mothers and 13 percent of the fathers, and he found a much lower incidence in a similar study of unipolar patients. The evidence so far points to a probable genetic component in bipolar disorder, but it is not so clear in unipolar.

Some studies (Cadoret, Winokur, & Clayton, 1971) suggest that a predisposition to bipolar depression may be transmitted as a dominant gene on the X chromosome. Specific X chromosome traits, such as red-green color blindness, have been traced through several generations of families, as has a predisposition to bipolar depression. This finding has not always been reproduced and is controversial. Even if it is proved conclusively, it would indicate only inherited vulnerability to, not a certainty of, depression.

Exogenous Causes of Depression

Stress and other precipitating causes are important factors in the onset of depression. Depressed patients report two to three times as many disruptive events as normal in the period just before a depression. The kinds of events reported are threatening: marital separation, children leaving home. Marital separation increases the probability of depression by five to six times (Deykin, Klerman, & Armor, 1966). Still, fewer than 10 percent who separate from their spouse become clinically depressed. Women who develop depression often do so after menopause.

There also seem to be personality characteristics that predispose one to depression. Cohen et al. (1954) found depressives to be, by and large, conventional, well behaved, often successful, hard working, and conscientious to the point of obsessiveness. They also found that the typical family background of bipolar depressed individuals included parents who used their children to gain social acceptance for themselves. The children were told that they had to behave better and do better than other kids. Consequently, the children felt that they had to earn their parents' love by superior effort. As adults these people tended to be dependent on others and worked hard to make other people like them. They still believed that they could not be loved without extra effort.

An Interesting Finding about Realism

Most people—psychologists among them—believe that a depressed person has an overly negative perception of how others feel about him or her. However, one study shows that depressed people are generally *more* realistic in their self-perception than nondepressed people. Normal people overestimate how much others like them; depressives are fairly accurate in this regard. One sign that depression is abating is that the realism *decreases* and depressives begin to think people view them more favorably than they do (Lewinshohn, Mischel, & Barton, 1980).

Suicide

The most serious and tragic outcome of depression is suicide. Three-quarters of suicides are depressed at time of death (Leonard, 1971). Suicide is among the ten leading causes of death in Western countries. Over 200,000 attempt suicide each year in the United States. This means that 5 million living Americans have tried to kill themselves. Each year about 15 percent of those who attempt it succeed. Three times as many women as men attempt to kill themselves; but three times as many men as

women are successful. This fact may have something to do with the way they choose to commit suicide. Women are more likely to try to overdose on drugs, especially barbiturates; men are likely to use firearms.

Most commonly a person who commits suicide is in the 24 to 44 age group. However, in recent years there has been an enormous increase in the number of young adults 15 to 24 who have tried. In the next year it is estimated that 80,000 of this group will attempt suicide and about 4,000 will succeed. One characteristic of this group of suicides is that they generally come from privileged backgrounds. The rate is higher at larger, more prestigious colleges and universities (Peck & Schrut, 1971). College students are apt to commit suicide at the beginnings and ends of quarters and semesters. In college students there is no sex difference in either attempts or successes. Groups at high risk to commit suicide are the elderly (white), alcoholics, separated and divorced men and women, migrants, and members of some native American tribes. Among the professions, physicians have the highest rate, followed by dentists, lawyers, and psychologists. The most common factors that trigger the suicide attempt are relationship problems and marital discord.

SCHIZOPHRENIA: THE UNIQUELY HUMAN DISORDER

Schizophrenia is the name for a group of disorders that involve *severe deterioration of mental abilities.* For example:

> A twenty-one-year-old student (found that) "As I think, my thoughts leave my head on a type of mental ticker-tape. Everyone around has only to pass the tape through their mind and they know my thoughts."

This fundamental disorganization causes disturbances in every area of life: social functioning, feeling, and behavior. The nature of these disturbances is listed below, although no single feature is *always* present in schizophrenia.

1. *Content of thought delusions* are the most common disturbances of thought. Common delusions are the belief that someone is spying on the individual, or spreading rumors. Often inappropriate, unusual, or impossible significance is given to events. For example, one man was convinced the singer Cher was parodying him on one of her television broadcasts. Other common delusions, which do not appear in other severe psychological disorders, are:

- *Thought broadcast*, the belief that one's thoughts can be heard by others.
- *Thought insertion*, that others are inserting thoughts into one's mind.
- *Thought withdrawal*, the sensation that one's thoughts are being stolen from one's mind.
- *Delusions of being controlled*, the belief that one's actions and thoughts are being controlled.

Artist Louis Wain (1860–1939) was noted for his pictures of cats in human situations (below, top). Although he was institutionalized, he continued to paint, but his paintings (below, bottom) reflected perceptual distortions and mental deterioration associated with schizophrenia.

2. *Form of thought.* This disturbance involves unusual patterns of formal thought. Typically, this involves loosening of associations, ideas shift from one topic to another with no apparent connections. The speaker typically is unaware of the bizarreness of this thought process. Often the associations are so loose as to render speech incoherent and incomprehensible. Also, although a lot is spoken, little seems to be said: there is little content.

3. *Perception hallucinations* are the most characteristic perceptual disturbance. Auditory hallucinations ("voices") are the most common, although visual and smell (olfactory) ones occur. Many investigators believe that a breakdown in perceptual filtering is also characteristic of people with schizophrenic disorder.

4. *Affect.* Affect often appears blunt, flat, or inappropriate. A blunt affect means that there is little intensity in feeling; flat affect means that there are virtually no signs of emotions; inappropriate affect, that the emotion expressed does not fit the situation (for example, giggling at a funeral).

5. *Sense of self.* There is severe disturbance in the sense of self, as indicated by the delusions of being controlled or of one's most private thoughts being public. Laing writes that the schizophrenic "may say that he is made of glass, of such transparency and fragility that a look directed at him splinters him to bits and penetrates straight through him" (1959).

6. *Volition.* There is often an impairment in goal-directed activity due either to lack of interest, inability to complete something, or lack of initiative.

7. *Relationship to the external world.* The tendency of individuals with schizophrenia is to withdraw from the world. Often their strange behavior may cause people to withdraw from them. At any rate, in the withdrawn state they become totally immersed in their own fantasies, delusions, and illogical conclusions.

8. *Psychomotor behavior.* There are several different patterns of psychomotor disturbance. In extreme cases, a person may maintain a rigid posture for hours, in others he or she may assume bizarre postures or make strange gestures. Often there is a "waxy flexibility" to body and muscle movements.

9. *Associated features.* Almost any other symptom of any psychological disorder may be present in the schizophrenic. For example, *anhedonia*— a defect in the capacity for pleasure—depression, anxiety, memory impairment.

Before we begin our discussion of schizophrenia, here is an extraordinary case history that highlights practically every known cause of the development of the disorder. The case is the story of Mr. and Mrs. Henry Genain who in the 1930s gave birth to quadruplet girls, all of whom developed a different form of schizophrenia. The family came to the attention of researchers at NIMH (National Institute of Mental Health) who have made an extensive study of the case. The name is fictitious; it is derived from the Greek words meaning "dire gene"; the town the family lived in was called *Envira*, to signify the environment, and the girls were given the names *Nora*, *Iris*, *Myra*, and *Hester*, the first letter of each spelling out NIMH (Rosenthal, 1963):

Mr. and Mrs. Genain were married because Mr. Genain said he would kill Mrs. if they did not. The quads were born prematurely; had a low birthweight, but except for Hester, were all healthy. Hester had an abdominal problem that required her to wear a truss for several years. Because quads are so rare, a lot of publicity and fame surrounded their early life. Their parents charged admission for people to come see them. Because of the fame, the girls tended to stick together and had few friends in the outside world. The isolation was encouraged by the parents, who were afraid of the dangers in the outside world, particularly men. The parents treated the girls differently. Nora and Myra were favored. Iris and Hester were picked on, and considered oversexed by their parents because they were caught masturbating. Eventually, Mr. and Mrs. Genain had these two girls circumcised.

Mr. Genain was a minor politician in Envira; he drank too much, was domineering at home, and fearful of the world. The family's life was organized around his fears. He prowled around the house with a shotgun worried that his girls would be raped. He never let them leave the house alone. He was promiscuous and had sexually molested at least two of the quads. They often had to dress and undress, even change their sanitary napkins, in front of him.

Mrs. Genain was terrified of sex and of Mr. Genain. When told by her daughters of his sexual advances, she said that he was just testing them to see if their virtue was intact.

By the age of 18, Hester could no longer be managed at home. She tore her clothing, broke furniture, had severe stomach pains. She was hospitalized and developed catatonia and finally the hebephrenic form of schizophrenia. She was hospitalized most of her life.

Nora began to show signs of the disorder at 20. She stood on her knees and elbows until they bled; she walked and talked in her sleep. She was hospitalized at 22. Although she was primarily catatonic, she showed some hebephrenic signs.

Iris had a spastic colon. She began to hear voices shortly after Nora was hospitalized. She drooled at meals and couldn't swallow anything. She had persistent delusions that people were paying undue attention to her. She was hospitalized.

Myra made it until her 24th year, when she began vomiting violently, suffered panic and insomnia. She withdrew from all contact with people and was hospitalized. Myra is the only one of the quads who was able to live outside of the hospital and she is on drugs for schizophrenics.

[Rosenthal writes] Thus the quads manifested the full range of possible outcomes associated with schizophrenic breakdown . . . we have four genetically identical young women, all of whom experienced schizophrenic disorders. The disorders, however, were very different in severity, chronicity and eventual outcome. Quite obviously these differences must be [due] to differences in the environment the [quads] experienced.

Incidence

It is estimated that 1 percent of all populations suffer from a form of schizophrenic disorder. It is more likely in urban than rural areas. As mentioned before, Farris and Dunham (1965) and others have found a greater instance of people hospitalized for schizophrenia in the lower socioeconomic sections of the city. There is no sex difference in schizophrenic disorder.

Kinds of Schizophrenic Disorders

Schizophrenia was first classified as a separate disorder by Bleuer, who chose the term to indicate "the splitting of the different psychic functions" was the most important characteristic (*schiz* means splitting, *phren* refers to the mind). Although the term schizophrenia is used, it is really a group of disorders. Most psychologists divide them into the following categories:

Hebephrenic. This is the most severely disorganized form of schizophrenia, characterized by extreme disturbance of affect. Most often the hebephrenic appears silly. There is more disintegration of personality in hebephrenia than any other form of schizophrenia, and it has the worst prognosis for recovery. It often begins in childhood.

Paranoid. This type is dominated by delusions of being persecuted and is marked by extreme suspiciousness. Speech is generally coherent. Sirhan Sirhan, who assassinated Bobby Kennedy, was diagnosed as a paranoid schizophrenic.

Catatonic. This type is characterized by unusual motor activity: either excitement or stupor. In catatonia with stupor a person might maintain a posture for days that a normal person would find difficult to maintain for more than a few minutes. One woman explained that the reason she held her arm outstretched in front of her, palm outstretched, was that the forces of good and evil were warring on the palm of her hand and she did not want to upset the balance in favor of evil.

Undifferentiated. This type is a rapidly changing mix of all or most of

A catatonic person sometimes assumes awkward and uncomfortable postures and maintains them for extended periods.

the primary symptoms of schizophrenia. Many people exhibit signs of undifferentiated type in the beginning stages of the disorder.

Causes of Schizophrenia

Genetic Factors

Genes are a necessary but not sufficient cause in the development of schizophrenic disorder. Kringlen (1967) in a study in Norway found a 38 percent concordance rate in MZ twins and only 10 percent in DZ twins. In America studies also have shown high concordance rates. Cohen, Allen, and Pollen found a 23.5 percent rate in MZ twins, 5.3 percent in DZ twins; Gottesman and Shields found 42 percent concordance for MZ, 9 percent for DZ. thus, although the concordance rate is high, it is not perfect. It indicates a predisposition, not a certainty.

Heston (1966) found that 16.6 percent of children reared apart from their schizophrenic parents developed schizophrenic disorder. Children of schizophrenics are often retarded, neurotic, or psychopathic (Heston, 1966), have unusual peer relations, are suspicious, and exhibit strange mental activity and group behavior.

The risk of developing schizophrenia is 5 to 15 times higher in siblings of schizophrenics than in the general population. The risk for developing schizophrenia is 1 percent in the general population, less than 5 percent in parents of schizophrenics, averages 10 percent in siblings, 11 percent in the children. If both parents are schizophrenic, a child runs a 35 to 45 percent or more chance of developing the disorder. In studies of twins reared apart, MZ twins showed a concordance rate of 50 to 60 percent, DZ twins 10 to 15 percent (Rosenthal et al., 1971). Thus although the evidence for genetic factors is impressive, the biochemist Solomon Snyder offers a caution: "Schizophrenia runs in families, but so does attendance at Harvard." In addition, the great majority of people who become schizophrenic do *not* have a schizophrenic relative.

Biochemical and Neurophysiological Causes

In the 1950s it was established that the presence of certain chemical agents, such as LSD and mescaline, in the bloodstream could evoke schizophrenic symptoms. Researchers were excited by the possibility of discovering a substance produced in the body that might be the dominant causal factor. So far there have been no breakthroughs, but one promising theory is called the **dopamine hypothesis:** Schizophrenia is caused by a surplus of dopamine, a neurotransmitter of the catecholamine group, at important synapses. Alternatively, it may be that there is a surplus of dopamine receptor sites. Support for the dopamine hypothesis comes from the fact that the very effective antipsychotic drugs given to patients to control their schizophrenic symptoms work by blocking dopamine at synapse receptor sites (Snyder, 1979).

There is also evidence of neurophysiological abnormalities that might be causal factors. One hypothesis is that the disturbance might be due to imbalances in the exciting and inhibiting processes, leading to inappropriate arousal. Disturbances of these processes would interfere with the normal attentional process (Wynne, Cromwell, & Mattysse, 1978). A woman who had suffered a schizophrenic episode, and later became a psychiatric nurse, writes: "I had very little ability to sort the relevant from the irrelevant. The filter had broken down. Completely unrelated events became intricately connected in my mind". These attentional deficiencies generally occur before the onset of the episode.

Another predisposing factor is the adequacy of sensory information. For instance, paranoids have been tested and found to have poorer hearing than normals. In an ingenious experiment based upon these findings, Zimbardo and colleagues (1981) studied the relationship between paranoia and deafness. They gave subjects under hypnosis the suggestion that they would experience partial deafness and would be unaware of the suggestion. When subjects awoke, they began to develop paranoid tendencies because they could not hear the conversations going on around them. Presumably the paranoia "explained" why the people they were talking to were excluding them by talking so low that they could not hear the conversation.

Psychosocial Factors

Most of the psychosocial factors that may contribute to the development of schizophrenia seem to include the common element of an environment filled with "double messages," such as "I want you to do this/ Don't do this"; "I love you/I hate you."

Gregory Bateson (1959) stressed the importance of these conflicting and confusing communications in the families of schizophrenics and proposed a **double-bind theory.** A double bind is a situation in which a person is called on to respond to a message that contains two meanings.

> A young man who had fairly well recovered from an acute schizo-phrenic episode was visited in the hospital by his mother. He was glad to see her and impulsively put his arm around her shoulders, where-upon she stiffened. He withdrew his arm and she asked, "Don't you love me anymore?" He blushed and she said, "Dear, you must not be so easily embarrassed and afraid of your feelings." The patient was able to stay with her only a few minutes more and following her departure he assaulted an aide . . .

> The impossible dilemma thus becomes: "If I am to keep my tie to my mother, I must not show her that I love her, but if I do not show her that I love her, then I will lose her." (Bateson, 1959)

The double-bind theory is, however, controversial. With all the evidence we have so far, there is still no way we can predict who will suffer from this most tragic of all psychological disorders or how it can be prevented or cured.

Why Does Schizophrenia Persist in Populations?

The consistency of schizophrenia leads one to ask how such maladaptive behavior persists. Remember, in natural selection maladaptive qualities "die out." Jarvick and Deckard (1977) propose an interesting explanation. The personality of many nonpsychotic relatives of schizophrenics might represent "a selective advantage." Their outlook of general suspiciousness and distrust of peers might make them better candidates for survival in difficult circumstances where there is a scarcity of resources, war and strife. Their improved chances of survival mean that they are more likely to contribute to the gene pool of the species. "They, rather than their trusting peers are the ones more likely to survive long enough to ensure the survival of their progeny." Other evidence suggests that the genes that predispose schizophrenia may be double-edged. Some correlation has been found of giftedness and social prominence among relatives of schizophrenics. They often show schizoid (schizlike) tendencies causing them to be slightly detached in relationships. This detachment allows them to pursue with greater intensity their chosen vocations. Such people often achieve great success in science, art, or the pursuit of power.

THE IMPORTANCE OF BEING NORMAL

It is possible to classify someone as "disordered," but does this do justice to the person? McNeil (1967) writes:

Each of us is neurotic in one sense or another. Each of us carries through life a set of unsolved problems, prejudices, and biases in response to our fellow human beings. Since neurosis so often disguises itself as normality and so often is indistinguishable from it, a major problem of adjustment is focused on the correct or incorrect diagnosis each of us makes of the other. The disorder of a single life usually has repercussions in the lives of others, and that is the issue. Normality, then, becomes a very relative term and its limits are more elastic than most of us suspect. We are all, simultaneously, normal and abnormal.

Normality

A society comprises a group of people who share common standards of permissible thought and behavior. A person who deviates too far from these standards is often considered abnormal. These standards are called **norms.** There are two different kinds of norms. One is *statistical;* it refers to the most common or average incidence of a particular quality. The second is *ethical*. It refers to qualities considered by the majority to be desirable or valuable. Allport (1937) wrote, "No system of ethics in the civilized world holds up as a model for its children the ideal of becoming a merely average man. It is not the actualities, but rather the potentialities of human nature that somehow provide us with a standard for a sound and healthy personality." Thus, Isaac Stern is not a normal violin player; Eric Heiden is not a normal skater. Great artists, athletes, scientists, inventors, politicians, entrepreneurs, are all "abnormal" in that they deviate from the ordinary. But these kinds of abnormalities are not worrisome. When we characterize someone as abnormal, we are referring to patterns of thought and behavior that are maladaptive—they interfere with or interrupt a desirable, useful, or healthy conduct of life.

The "dividing line" between normal and abnormal is not often easy to determine. It is often a subjective determination, and abnormality is often in the eye of the observer. Let us examine some of the components.

1. *Time*. It is quite normal to be depressed when someone you love dies or stops loving you. It is abnormal when the depression persists and becomes the pervasive life experience over an extremely long period of time.

2. *Exaggeration of normal behavior*. It is not abnormal to be neat and clean. But if you could not begin work unless you had showered and washed your hair several times, had everything in your room sterilized and neatly stacked in piles of three, it would be abnormal.

3. *Age*. Behavior perfectly fitting for a two-year-old would be highly inappropriate for a twenty- or forty-year-old.

4. *Sociocultural factors*. Normality is a changing value, a reflection of society and culture at a particular time. A century ago it would have been abnormal for a woman to have premarital sex, now it is not. Homosexuality used to be classified as a disease, now it is not. Society relaxes or restricts the boundaries of what behaviors it will accept and tolerate.

Dangers of Labels

If you were told that someone was "schizophrenic" or "depressive," you might evaluate their behavior differently than you would without the label. In an important experiment, David Rosenhan and seven normal people posed as *pseudopatients* and gained admission to mental hospitals, complaining of hearing voices that said their life was "empty" and "hollow." These symptoms were chosen because they were the determining feature of "existential psychosis," a disorder that has been theorized in literature, but has never been seen in clinical practice. They showed no other symptoms and were admitted to the mental hospitals with the diagnosis of schizophrenia.

Once they were in the hospital, they behaved normally. Even though they acted normally, *not one of the pseudopatients was ever discovered by the staff.* In fact, all of their behavior was categorized in terms of their diagnosis of schizophrenia. For instance, one patient who was writing notes about his experience in full view of doctors and nurses found the following notation on his record: "engages in writing behavior." When they were finally released, they were classified as "schizophrenics in remission."

In a second experiment, Rosenhan told the staff at a mental hospital that over the next three months one or more new pseudopatients would try to gain admission to the hospital. The hospital admitted 193 patients in that period. Forty-one of these patients were judged by at least one of the staff members to be pseudopatients. Nineteen of these were identified by at least two staff members. As you may have guessed, *no pseudopatient was actually sent to the hospital;* thus, the line between "normal" and abnormal is certainly blurred.

The labeling of schizophrenia depends on background. American and British doctors differ consistently on the diagnosis of schizophrenia. Americans are more likely to diagnose patients as schizophrenic (Cooper, Kendell, Gurland, Sharpe, Copeland, & Simon, 1972).

To be labeled schizophrenic or "insane" often has permanent consequences. Individuals who have been diagnosed schizophrenic will be considered "in remission" for five years before a diagnosis of "no mental disorder" is made. Aside from the debilitating effect this may have on these people psychologically, it may also interfere with their ability to find work and with their personal relationships. For instance, friends and family may treat them as "disturbed." Often this is a self-fulfilling judgment.

Langer and Abelson (1974) wanted to test the effect of labeling on a clinician's judgment. The subjects were three groups of clinicians with clear-cut theoretical points of view: one was behaviorist, the other two were traditionally psychoanalytic. Half of each group was told that they were going to see a videotape interview of a "job applicant." The other half were told that the person on the tape was a "patient." At the end of the tape all clinicians answered a questionnaire. All groups found the "job applicant" to be fairly well adjusted. The behaviorists did not change their judgment when the person was labeled a "patient." The traditional analysts, however, found the "patient" to be significantly more disturbed than the "job applicant."

Thus, being considered disordered, or "insane," has consequences for a person's life, as does being considered "mentally retarded." One of the consequences, of course, is how disorders are treated, and it is to this we now turn.

Summary

1. Psychological disorders are not restricted to a few people. They are the state of being of all of us at some time in our lives. In the United States, hundreds of thousands are paralyzed because of fear of crowds, snakes, or elevators. Ten million people in the U.S. are alcoholics; more than one million are schizophrenics.

2. Disorders differ from person to person. There are several qualities that characterize the experience of disorder: (1) loss of control, (2) unhappiness or distress, and (3) isolation from others.

   There is no single cause for psychological disorders. Psychologists analyze disorders as arising from biological, mental, and situational factors.

3. The most widely used classification system is in the *Diagnostic and Statistical Manual of Mental Disorders* (*DSM*) of the American Psychiatric Association. Its most recent revision was in 1980. The *DSM-III* characterizes both mild and severe disorders.

4. Mild disorders include anxiety and somatoform disorders. The cause of mild disorders seems to be entirely psychological: maladaptive coping strategies, learning of inappropriate contingencies, and difficulty in family or personal relationships.

   People suffering from *generalized anxiety* live in constant tension and worry. They seem uneasy when they are around people and are unusually sensitive to comments and criticism from others.

   Phobia is the Greek word for fear. In psychology, *phobic* disorder means an extreme or unfounded fear of an object or a place. There is a wide variety of phobias, such as zoophobia (fear of animals), claustrophobia (fear of closed spaces), and acrophobia (fear of height).

   There are three primary factors which contribute to the development of phobias: faulty learning, displacement of anxiety, and the development of a defense mechanism to counteract dangerous impulses.

   Somatoform disorders are those in which an individual complains of a physical ailment or pain for which there is no organic or physiological explanation. There are several kinds of somatoform disorders: somatization, conversion, psychogenic pain, hypochondriasis, and atypical. *Hypochondriasis* is characterized by an individual's misinterpretation of body functions, usually leading to the belief that one has a disease. Three predisposing factors to hypochondriasis are early childhood learning, dissatisfaction with life, and reinforcement of the behavior.

5. Personality disorders are quite common, and people with personality disorders perceive, relate to, and think about themselves and their environment in maladaptive ways. Personality disorders tend to have symptoms that are "acted out" in the world rather than simply in the mind of the person. Some of the major personality disorders are:

- *Paranoid:* pervasive and unwarranted suspiciousness and mistrust of people
- *Schizoid:* defect in the capacity to form social relationships
- *Avoidant:* hypersensitivity to potential rejection
- *Compulsive:* restricted ability to express warm and tender emotions
- *Antisocial:* history of chronic and continuous antisocial behavior in which the rights of others are violated.

The *antisocial personality* (also called psychopath or sociopath) is very well studied and, typically, is developed in an individual with an inability to feel either positive emotions or guilt, with an insensitivity to the needs of other people. They seem to have an autonomic nervous system that is less likely to react to punishment. Therefore, they do not seem to develop the normal social conscience. This decreased emotional response, especially to unpleasant stimuli, seems to be an important characteristic of these people. Wild scenes such as loud parties, extreme manipulation of others, and a consistent disregard for other people's feelings are examples of the antisocial personality. There is evidence for genetic factors in this disorder.

6. Substance use disorders are those disturbances in behavior that are caused by a drug and exist for at least one month. There are five categories of substances that may invite abuse or dependence: alcohol, barbiturates or other sedatives; analgesics, painkillers or narcotics, which include heroin; stimulants like amphetamines; and psychoactive drugs such as marijuana and LSD. It is more common for men than women to have a substance use disorder. Abuse and dependence do not usually appear until adulthood: alcoholic disorder in the twenties, thirties, and forties; problems with heroin, marijuana, and cocaine start earlier, in late teens and early twenties. The causes of disorders may be genetic, or the important causal factors can be psychosocial and sociocultural.

7. A severe mental disorder of great importance to Americans is *depression.* Serious depression consists of an overwhelming sadness that immobilizes and arrests the entire course of a person's life. There are two kinds of depression: *unipolar depression,* in which the person is simply depressed; the second is *bipolar depression,* in which the person also suffers the "polar" opposite, *mania.* In order to diagnose a person as depressed, at least four of the following symptoms have to be present every day for two weeks:

1. Loss of interest and pleasure
2. Appetite disturbance
3. Sleep disturbance
4. Psychomotor disturbance
5. Decrease in energy level
6. Sense of worthlessness
7. Difficulty in concentrating
8. Thoughts about death
9. Miscellaneous associated symptoms

The features of mania are the mirror-image of depression. The mood is characterized as predominantly elevated, expansive, or irritable. There are large swings between euphoria and extreme annoyance.

There are certain endogenous factors in depression. Studies of families of bipolar depressives reveal that eleven percent of close relatives also had experienced bipolar depression. The concordance rate is extremely high in both unipolar and bipolar forms of the disorder in monozygotic (identical) twins. Exogenous causes of depression generally include stress and other precipitating events. Depressives are, by and large, conventional, well behaved, often successful, hard working, and conscientious. The most serious and tragic outcome of depression is suicide. Three-quarters of suicides are depressed at the time of death, and suicide is in the top ten causes of death in Western countries. Over two hundred thousand people attempt suicide in the United States each year, most commonly a person in the 24 to 44 age group, although there has been a sharp rise in the number of those attempting suicide in the 15 to 24 year group.

8. *Schizophrenia* is a uniquely human disorder. It is the name for a group of disorders that involve severe deterioration of mental abilities. This fundamental thought disorganization causes disturbances in every area of life: social functioning, feeling, and behavior. The schizophrenic may be disturbed in any of the following ways:

   1. Content of thought delusions
   2. Form of thought
   3. Perception hallucinations
   4. Affect
   5. Sense of self
   6. Volition
   7. Relationship to the external world
   8. Psychomotor behavior
   9. Associated features

   The following are categories of schizophrenic disorders:

   1. Hebephrenic—the most severely disorganized form of schizophrenia, characterized by extreme disturbance of affect.
   2. Paranoid—dominated by delusions of being persecuted
   3. Catatonic—unusual motor activity, either excitement or stupor
   4. Undifferentiated—rapidly changing mix of all or most of the primary symptoms of schizophrenia

   There is a strong genetic component of schizophrenics. One study showed a 38 percent concordance rate in monozygotic twins. The risk of developing schizophrenia is 5 to 15 times higher in siblings of schizophrenics than in the general population. Its incidence is about 1 percent in the general population. The causes of schizophrenia may also include biochemical and neurophysiological factors. There are many psychosocial factors in schizophrenia. One controversial factor is described by the double-bind theory in which the families of schizophrenics offer the patient messages containing two meanings, such as I want you to do this/don't do this, or I love you/I hate you.

9. And now a word about being normal. It is possible to classify someone as disordered, but does this do justice to the person? It is important to realize, as Elton McNeill points out, that only a small segment of the disturbed person's total behavior actually deviates very grossly from normal behavior. Over a 24-hour period, mentally disturbed individuals are overtly disturbed no more than one percent of the time and their acculturation may be indistinguishable from the normal. The dividing line between normal and abnormal is not often easy to determine, but it involves several components:

   1. Time. It is quite normal to be depressed when someone you love dies, but it is abnormal when that feeling becomes the pervasive experience over an extremely long period of time.

2. Exaggeration of normal behavior. Neatness is not abnormal, but having to wash every room every time you enter it would be.
3. Age. Behavior that is fitting for an infant is not for a thirty-year-old.
4. Sociocultural factors. Normality is a reflection of society and culture at a particular time. Homosexuality, for instance, used to be classified a disease, now it is not.

Terms and Concepts

affective disorders
agoraphobia
antisocial personality
depression
dopamine hypothesis
double-bind theory
generalized anxiety
hypochondriasis

mania
norms
obsessive-compulsive disorders
phobia
schizophrenia
somatoform disorders
substance use disorders

Suggestions for Further Reading

Good reviews of the literature are to be found in:

Altrocchi, J. (1980). *Abnormal behavior*. New York: Harcourt Brace Jovanovich.
An encyclopedic overview of disorder. Useful for reference.

Brecher, E. M. (1974). *Licit and illicit drugs*. Boston: Little, Brown.
An important and readable book. Traces the history of drug dependence over many cultures and throughout history.

Snyder, S. (1980). *Biological aspects of mental disorder*. New York: Oxford University Press.
A good analysis of the biological underpinnings of such disorders as schizophrenia.

Winokur, G. (1981). *Depression: The facts*. New York: Oxford University Press.
One of the few balanced treatments of depression.

Chapter 17

Psychotherapies

INTRODUCTION

For as long as people have suffered psychologically, there have been attempts to relieve that suffering. Psychotherapy is an attempt to restore adaptive functioning. Throughout history there have been many forms of psychotherapy, most of which reflect differing beliefs about the factors contributing to mental disorder.

How a psychological disorder is characterized leads to specific kinds of treatment, and it is in their differing characterizations that the various approaches to psychology affect what is done. If you believe that psychological disorder is caused by demons that invade a person's body and take possession of his or her faculties, it would follow that the treatment be geared at getting the demons out of the body. If you think that psychological disorder has its origins in events and issues of early childhood, treatment may attempt to root out these events. If you believe that disordered behavior results from learning inappropriate responses, such as inordinate fear of social interactions, you may try to teach a new, more adaptive set of responses. If you believe that the problem is essentially biological, you may administer biological treatment, for example drugs or surgery. If you conceive of the problem as a person's difficulty in cognitive patterns, you may try to help the person restructure his or her ways of thinking. If you believe that a psychological problem is the result of some blockage in the normal development of self, then you would seek to find out where the block is, what caused it, and then unblock it.

Here we examine the psychotherapies that developed out of the major theoretical approaches of psychology: psychoanalytic, behavioristic, cognitive, humanistic, and psychobiological. These approaches differ enormously in their fundamental views of human nature. For example, psychoanalytic theory holds a distinctly pessimistic view; humanistic theory is explicitly positive.

Although all psychotherapies have as their goal the restoration of normal functioning, they vary widely in method, approach, and assumptions. An important question to ask when considering these various forms of psychotherapy is: do they work? This question is a sticky and difficult one. In the last section of this chapter we will review the evidence on the effectiveness, or the lack of it, of psychotherapy.

EARLY APPROACHES AND METHODS OF TREATMENT

Conceptions of Disorder: Medieval Approaches

One widespread prescientific belief was that mental disorder is caused by demons who enter and possess the victim. One treatment that followed from that idea was called **trephining.** Holes were drilled into a person's head to let the demons out. Other treatments following from the concept of demon possession included floggings, burnings, and other forms of torture. These treatments were not *intended* to be cruel to the victim—but to the devil.

Industrial Revolution

During the Industrial Revolution it was commonly thought that mental disorders were a moral problem. Disorder was considered to be a result of idleness or bad character. Mad people were lumped together with criminals and vagrants, chained and thrown into dungeons. The "insane" were considered dangerous nuisances to society and were also used as warnings. They were often put on view so that young people would see the consequences of deviant behavior. In this period, there was only confinement, not treatment.

Trephining
In this medieval treatment, holes were cut into a mentally disturbed person's head in the hope that the demons would pass out through them.

Before reformers like Pinel (shown above, right, unchaining the inmates of a Paris asylum) and Dix began having an impact, people with mental disorders continued to be "treated" with such devices as the "circulating swing" (above, left), which seemed to involve as much torture as treatment.

The Nineteenth Century

A series of reforms were begun by Philippe Pinel (1745–1826) in France during the Revolution and later by Dorothea Dix (1802–87) and others in America. Finally, research and advances in biology, medicine, and neurology encouraged development of the "biomedical paradigm." Insanity began to be viewed as a disease. This paradigm led to more humane treatment; the onus of blame was off the victim. Under this paradigm a disease was treated by a doctor, usually with a certain amount of compassion.

A great advance in the late nineteenth century was the discovery of the cause of one type of disorder, general paresis. **General paresis** is a slow, degenerative disease that eventually erodes mental faculties. Paresis was discovered to be caused by syphilis. Understanding the cause of the disease led to an effective treatment. The elimination of paresis is one of the few decisive victories in the war against mental disorder. That victory led to the hope that a specific biological cause could be found for every pathology. That hope spurred important research: mental disorders received more attention from medical and scientific researchers.

A Short History of the Classification of Disorders

As more and more serious investigators set to work to unravel the mysteries of the malfunctioning of the human mind, classification became more precise. One of the major contributors to the biomedical point of view was Emil Kraepelin (1856–1926). He noted that mental disorder was not a monolithic entity, but several *distinct* disorders with their own particular patterns of symptoms. He devised the first classification system of mental disorders. His system is the basis for the *DSM* classification system used today by clinicians. It was Kraepelin's firm belief that a specific brain pathology is responsible for each mental disturbance. Many have joined him in that belief and hope, but there has been no recent success as spectacular as the victory over general paresis.

The Current Controversy over Disorders

Although the advantages of the biomedical over the "demonological" and "societal menace" paradigms are great, many feel that it too has limitations. Thomas Szasz is a current and outspoken critic. In a controversial and influential article entitled "The Myth of Mental Illness," he writes,

> I submit that the idea of mental illness is now being put to work to obscure certain difficulties which at present may be inherent—not that they need to be modifiable—in the social intercourse of persons. If this is true, the concept functions as a disguise: for instead of calling attention to conflicting human needs, aspirations, and values, the notions of mental illness provide an amoral and impersonal "thing" (an "illness") as an explanation for *problems in living*. . . . We may recall in this connection that not so long ago it was devils and witches who were held responsible for men's problems in social living. The belief in mental illness as something other than man's trouble in getting along with his fellow men, is the proper heir to the belief in demonology and witchcraft. Mental illness exists or is "real" in exactly the same sense in which witches existed or were real. . . . Sustained adherence to the myth of mental illness allows people to avoid facing [the] problem [of what to do with themselves], believing that mental health, conceived as the absence of mental illness, automatically insures the making of right and safe choices in one's conduct of life. But the facts are all the other way; it is the making of good choices in life that others regard retrospectively as good mental health. (Szasz, 1961)

Psychotherapists

Currently much treatment involves psychotherapists. There are many different kinds of psychotherapists. A **psychiatrist** is a medical doctor whose specialty is the treatment of psychological problems. He or she is licensed to dispense drugs, if they are indicated in treatment. A **psychoanalyst** is a psychotherapist trained in the psychoanalytic techniques first formulated by Sigmund Freud; almost all psychoanalysts are physicians, but some are not. A **clinical psychologist** holds a Ph.D. in psychology and may specialize in a particular form of psychotherapy, such as behavior modification, sex therapy, and so on. Some clinical psychologists are also involved in testing and research, but many concentrate solely on therapy and guidance counseling in schools or industry. A **psychiatric social worker** usually holds an advanced degree (M.S. or Ph.D.) and usually concentrates on social or community-based problems.

PSYCHOANALYSIS

One of the most influential perspectives on the causes of mental disorder is Freud's psychoanalytic theory. As we have seen in Chapter 15, psychoanalysis is a "psychology of conflict": the conflict between the biological and social, or civilized, selves. Freud believed that inherited basic "instincts" underlie the state and functioning of the mind.

In Freud's terms, psychological distress arises from fundamental unresolved conflicts of the id and the ego. Thus, unconscious wishes and desires cause anxiety and fear and are repressed, or pushed out of consciousness. Ego-defense mechanisms are set up which result in abnormal or maladaptive behavior. Freud believed that the roots of disorder could be found in early childhood, often in the troublesome resolution of the Oedipus complex.

One of Freud's cases concerned "Little Hans." Little Hans was a five-year-old boy who was so afraid of horses that he would not leave his house. (Freud's analysis was, by the way, based on letters from Hans's father; he only met the boy once.) Before Hans became so afraid of horses, he was a perfectly normal boy in every respect, although he showed an "uncommon" interest in his penis. Once his mother caught him playing with it and told him she would cut it off if she ever caught him at it again. At four he tried to "seduce" his mother. About six months later he was out walking with his nurse when a horse and carriage rolled over in front of them. He began crying and said that he wanted to go home to hug his mother.

From that day on, he was terrified of horses and would not leave the house. Freud's analysis was that Hans's real fear was that he had so desired his mother that he subconsciously wanted his father out of the way. Since he really feared his impulses, he transferred his fear to horses to relieve himself of guilt. Freud hypothesized that even though his mother had actually threatened to castrate him, it was his father who represented that threat. By avoiding horses, he avoided castration, and by staying home he got to stay close to his mother.

The Psychoanalytic Method of Treatment

Because Freud believed that disorder is caused by conflicts between unconscious and conscious desires, he believed that therapy should bring those unconscious desires into consciousness where they may be acknowledged and analyzed. However, the unconscious does not give up its secret desires easily or without struggle: the ego "edits" and represses those desires. The maladaptive behavior that brings the person to the therapist is the external symptom of underlying unconscious conflicts.

In his therapy, Freud used hypnosis to bring the unconscious to the surface. Later he developed the technique of **free association:** in it, the patient is asked to say anything that comes into his or her mind, without criticism or editing—no matter how obscene, unimportant, or silly it

Sigmund Freud's Office

Characteristics of Psychoanalysis
See Chapter 14, pp. 503–8.

may seem. Free association is quite difficult to do, because we are used to speaking in context; we are careful of the connections we make in speech; we exercise control and usually are modest about personal subjects.

The patient, as characterized in psychoanalysis, may often lie on a couch facing away from the analyst. Removing normal eye-to-eye contact helps remove some restraints. Although the analyst usually listens passively, occasionally he or she interrupts the patient's free flow of ideas to highlight or suggest connections between things that the patient is saying and things that have been said. A psychoanalyst often asks the patient to recall dreams and use the contents of dreams as starting points for free association. Thus, the interpretation of dreams is a cornerstone of Freudian analysis.

The psychoanalytic situation is very formalized and controlled. As a rule, the analyst adopts a posture of noninterference in the flow of the patient's ideas. The reason for this is that Freud believed that psychological problems come from within, and the cure also must come from within. Therefore, as much as possible, *the thoughts, images, and connections in therapy must come from within the patient,* because the thoughts and associations that emerge are not haphazard but come to the surface because of the internal pressure of the repressed desires and feelings.

The patients who seek psychoanalysis commit themselves to a very long process of self-evaluation, criticism, and examination. Psychoanalysis usually requires four to five 50-minute sessions a week for anywhere from one to several years.

These conditions, then, exclude a great number of people from treatment: most psychotics, people with personality disorders who are not highly motivated to change, nonverbal people, and poor people.

Phases of Treatment

There are four phases in psychoanalysis: the opening phase, transference, "working through," and resolution of the transference.

1. The *opening* phase of treatment usually lasts from three to six months. In this time, the analyst begins to learn the patient's history and the general nature of his or her unconscious conflicts. One of the greatest signals of an unconscious conflict in the opening phase is *resistance*.

Resistance is the characteristic way that the patient unconsciously works *against* revealing his or her feelings or thoughts. *For example*, every time a patient starts to talk about his or her mother, he or she might change the subject, tell a joke, say that the thought is too silly, and so forth. Another sign of resistance to therapy is when the patient "forgets" an appointment or is late. Resistance serves to reduce the anxiety of the patient by not allowing anxiety-producing thoughts to surface.

2. *Transference.* One of the most important concepts in psychoanalytic therapy is how the patient perceives the analyst. At a certain point in treatment, **transference** takes place as the patient "transfers" onto the *analyst* attitudes toward people about whom he or she has conflicting feelings. For example, a man who has difficulty getting along with people in authority may have had a domineering father who demanded perfection of his son and strict obedience to all his rules. At a certain point in therapy, the patient may begin to show anger at the analyst for requiring the patient to follow the rules of analysis. The analyst comes to play a role in the patient's life whose significance is all out of proportion with reality.

Freud believed that transference is extremely important and is the patient's way of recreating and reenacting forgotten or repressed memories from earliest childhood. Instead of recalling events, the patient repeats them.

3. *Working through.* The therapist then proceeds to an analysis of the transference. This is a most critical stage, because patients begin to see, in a very concrete way, the nature of their misconceptions, maladaptive responses, and misinterpretations, since they have "transferred" them to the analyst. Once they begin to understand these things, they can begin to evaluate more realistically and begin to change their actions and responses and those of others.

The analysis of the transference should offer patients some insight into the nature of the unconscious conflicts that have been troubling and disrupting their lives. Usually during this phase the patients recall some extremely important event, desire, or fantasy of their youth. The recollection and their ability to express it produces in them a catharsis. A **catharsis** is the release of stored up or held back feelings; it is an intensely emotional experience. The immediate result of a catharsis is pleasurable—relief.

4. *Resolution of the transference.* This is the last phase of the treatment, in which the patients and therapist agree that the goals they set out to achieve have been accomplished. This means that the patients ought to be behaving in different ways and no longer experiencing anxiety in situations that used to make them very anxious.

BEHAVIOR THERAPY

The Case of Little Albert   See Chapter 8, pp. 305, 306.

The behavioristic point of view holds that psychological disorders are the result of "faulty learning." Psychotherapy then is a process of learning. A behaviorist would view Freud's analysis of Little Hans as unnecessarily complex. Little Hans's fear could be better explained by respondent conditioning. Recall "Little Albert." A loud noise presented at the same time as a white rat caused Albert to be afraid of rats, rabbits, and Santa Claus. In Little Hans's case, it is conceivable that the commotion associated with the tipping over of a horse and carriage would have been frightening. Because his parents reinforced the fear by letting him stay home, the fear was maintained.

Behavior therapy proceeds from the assumption that the behavior that is causing the person distress *is* the problem, unlike psychoanalysis, which assumes that it is only the symptom of an underlying neurosis. As a prominent behavior therapist, Hans Eysenck, wrote, "There is no neurosis underlying the symptom, but merely the symptom itself. Get rid of the symptom . . . and you have eliminated the neurosis." While this is probably an overstatement—most behaviorists would agree that there are many cognitive components feeding into fears and anxiety—it is probably also true that by changing a person's overt behavior, the underlying problems may also be realigned.

Two varieties of therapy are related to the two primary modes of learning: the form generally called behavior therapy is based on respondent conditioning; the other, called behavior modification, is based on the theory of operant conditioning.

Behavior therapy aims to reduce the anxiety that the person experiences in response to certain key external stimuli (Wolpe, 1958). Anxiety is the underlying cause of the "neurotic" behavior. Behavior therapy techniques are based on respondent conditioning, and they decondition those anxiety-producing autonomic responses.

Behavior modification is based on operant conditioning and attempts to change behaviors by changing the stimuli and conditions. For example, someone who feels helpless or trapped may feel depressed; a person who is punished may become fearful; a person who cannot fight back or is frustrated because someone else is trying to control him or her may feel anger. Behavior modification may employ reinforcement or extinction to alter such situations and people's responses to them.

Behavior therapy has a wide range of applications and methods. The person is considered a "client," not a patient. Therapy may be individual, group, a family, or even a community. Therapy may last for a single session or forever (as, for example, in the cases of autistic children). Problems that have been treated with behavior therapy of one form or another include test anxiety, sexual dysfunctions, phobias, addictions, interpersonal and personality problems.

Methods of Behavior Therapy

A first, crucial step in a successful therapeutic program is the establishment of a good relationship between therapist and client. The therapist helps create this good working situation by showing the client that he or she does not judge, but rather accepts and understands. In addition, although having the expertise to help achieve the client's goals, the therapist does not "do" therapy on the client—they work together to accomplish agreed-upon outcomes. In this phase of treatment, the therapist often asks the client to give an account of the history of the problem and of his or her own personal development.

The therapist's focus on past history is fundamentally different from the psychoanalyst's. It is not believed that solving the problems of early childhood will solve the problems of adult life. Instead, the aim is to *discover where and how the inappropriate conditioning* was acquired. The therapist also tries to obtain detailed accounts of current situations in which the problem arises. To get the account, the therapist may not rely solely on the client's own verbal report. The person may be asked to keep detailed diaries of events and feelings during the week; the therapist may interview members of the client's family or engage the client in role playing. In **role playing** the therapist creates a hypothetical situation that is likely to cause the client anxiety and they act it out together. *An example:* a woman thinks she deserves a raise but cannot bring herself to ask her boss for one. She says that if her boss thought she deserved a raise he would give her one. The therapist might then adopt the role of the boss and she would act out asking for more money. A possible interchange might be:

c: Mr. Big Shot, I'd like to talk—when you have some time.

t: That's not a very effective opening. You are giving me an out right away.

c: Okay. Mr. Big Shot, I'd like to make an appointment to talk to you about a matter of great importance to me.

t: (That's better.) Well, I have some time now, what is it?

c: Well, I was wondering if, uh, well I know that there are budget problems and that I am still in a sort of training period in the firm, but I . . .

t: (You're giving me reasons to say no. It might be better to give me reasons to say yes.)

c: Mr. Big Shot, I have been with the company for a year now, and I believe that you will agree with me that my work has been . . . (I can't say this about myself!)

t: (Then who will?)

c: My work has been very good. Sales in my division have increased 35 percent under my direction. But my salary has not increased. I think I deserve a raise.

t: (That's pretty good.)

c: What if he says no?

t: (All right. Let's tackle that.) Yes, your work has been very good. However, budgets for this year are very fixed, and there are many fine people in your department. I don't think it would be possible at this time. Let's talk about it in a few months.

c: Now what? Should I say I will quit if I don't get a raise?

> What if he says go ahead. I knew this would happen.
>
> T: Think about what he said and try to find a way to pin him down.
>
> C: I could say that I wanted a definite time or . . .

Reconditioning Techniques in Behavior Therapy

Once an understanding of the problem is achieved, reconditioning proceeds. There are several behavior therapy techniques that have been developed to do this. Here we will mention systematic desensitization, flooding, and assertiveness training.

1. **Systematic Desensitization** is based on the phenomenon of *counterconditioning*. The idea is to *eliminate* an unwanted conditioned response by conditioning the client to another stimulus that elicits a response (usually relaxation) incompatible with the original response.

Systematic desensitization is very effective in helping people overcome phobias. Generally, the therapist asks the client to imagine or role play an anxiety-provoking situation. When the client begins to be anxious, the therapist instructs him or her in relaxation techniques. When the client is able to relax, the therapist presents a situation *more* likely to produce anxiety. The client again learns to relax. Thus, the therapist arranges the situations in a hierarchical order, and the client reduces fear step by step. *An example:* a person who is afraid of elevators might first be asked to imagine an elevator, then to imagine being alone in the elevator. Later he or she may go and stand beside the elevator, then may stand inside it. Finally, the client will ride it.

2. **Flooding** is similar to systematic desensitization in that the therapist deliberately presents the client with fear- or anxiety-provoking stimuli (either in imagination or in real life). The difference is that flooding is more intensive and does not rely on relaxation. It is most effective in severe phobias.

In this technique, the therapist literally "floods" the client's mind with a continuing narrative (or presentation) of situations that evoke fear and anxiety. When the person begins to experience anxiety, the therapist, now aware of being on the right track, elaborates on the story in order to make the person more and more anxious. For example, a woman with agoraphobia is afraid to leave the house. The therapist might begin by asking her to close her eyes and to imagine going out of the house, then imagine meeting someone in the street, imagine a group of children running down the sidewalk bumping into her, imagine getting on a public bus at rush hour. The therapist might go with the client into a crowd or a store. Eventually, the client will notice that her anxiety diminishes even if she does not run away. Then she may be assigned to try to imagine going places on her own and, finally, actually going to specific places on her own. Flooding is extremely intense; there is no letup until the client begins to feel the fear and anxiety dissipate. But it is an extremely effective and fast form of therapy for phobias.

3. **Assertiveness Training** is used when the problem entails difficulties in interpersonal relationships. Assertiveness training teaches people that they have a right to their feelings and opinions, to be themselves as long as they do not hurt others. The therapist may use role playing or

assign clients tasks to force them to confront and overcome their inability to assert themselves. In the example above of the woman who is afraid to ask for a raise, she may find it difficult to ask people for something directly. She may think that people will think she is pushy or demanding or fear that they will not do what she wants. A therapist may give her assignments such as going into a department store and asking a sales-clerk to show her a number of things, and then not buy anything; or calling her sister and asking her to drive her to an appointment.

Behavior Modification

Behavior modification techniques have been used in the treatment of a wide range of problems—from compulsive gambling to obesity to anti-social behavior in reform schools—to break maladaptive habits. The popular Smokenders programs is based on behavior modification. People who sign up come to a group meeting. They are allowed to smoke, but they agree on a date six weeks in advance as the day when they will quit smoking. Each person is given a little card and a pencil that fits into a pack of cigarettes. They are then free to smoke as much as they want for the first week, but they must note every cigarette. In later weeks they are asked to cut back on their smoking and to take notice of the kinds of situations in which they really want to smoke. A great amount of group support emerges and becomes an important reinforcer. By the time of their "quit date" they have cut back substantially on their smoking; they see that they can live without cigarettes in many situations where they thought it was impossible. Each person's family is brought into the rein-forcing circle by being encouraged to be demonstrative in their sup-port.

COGNITIVE THERAPIES OR COGNITIVE-BEHAVIORAL THERAPIES

Cognitive or cognitive-behavioral psychology combines many of the techniques of behaviorism with cognitive psychology. The main empha-sis is on the effects of thought on behavior. We will discuss three forms of cognitive therapy: rational-emotive, cognitive restructuring, and stress inoculation. These therapies differ in method and emphasis, but they share two major assumptions: (1) cognitive processes influence behavior and (2) behavior can be changed by a restructuring of the indi-vidual's cognitive system. This is achieved by bringing the individual's own thought processes into consciousness and holding them up to real-ity. The process of cognitive therapy is one of hypothesis testing. As in the behavior therapies, the client and therapist work together and the therapist takes an active role.

Rational-emotive Therapy

Rational-emotive therapy (RET) was developed by Albert Ellis (1970), who bases his therapy on the assumption that a person's perceptual interpretation becomes his or her "world." In this view, a well-adapted person is one in whom there is a good match between behaviors, self-perception, and reality. Maladaptive behavior can result from unrealistic beliefs or expectations. A person might believe that he or she must be loved by everyone, must always show perfect control, must be good at everything he or she does. Because these are unrealistic goals, they are self-defeating. A person may feel a failure and thus no good. This feeling is a consequence of the *interpretation*, not of any external event.

Ellis devised a list of what he calls "core irrational beliefs," which are the source of maladaptive behavior. Not all of these are present in any one case (Ellis, 1970):

1. One should be loved by everyone for everything one does.
2. Certain acts are awful or wicked and people who perform them should be punished.
3. It is horrible when things are not the way we would like them to be.
4. Human misery is produced by external causes or outside persons or events rather than by the view that one takes of these conditions.
5. If something may be dangerous or fearsome, one should be terribly upset about it.
6. It is better to avoid life problems if possible than to face them.
7. One needs something stronger or more powerful than oneself to rely on.
8. One should be thoroughly competent, intelligent, and achieving in all respects.
9. Because something once affected one's life, it will indefinitely affect it.
10. One must have certain and perfect self-control.
11. Happiness can be achieved by inertia and inaction.
12. We have virtually no control over our emotions and cannot help having certain feelings.

In **Rational-emotive therapy** the therapist determines what the underlying belief system of the individual is. In contrast to psychoanalysis and behavior therapy, the therapist confronts the client with his or her belief system and *directly* forces him or her to examine it against reality. For example, a woman's lover breaks a date with her. She interprets this to mean that he does not love her and is trying to avoid her. A RET therapist might point out that her lover might have had a good reason (a customer came in from out of town, a paper was due).

In RET the awareness of the client is *constantly directed* to the *inconsistencies* between his or her beliefs and external reality. At first the therapist is quite active in disputing the beliefs. There has been some criticism of RET on this point. A person might hold very strict religious beliefs, which may be at the core of the problem. If the religion says that sex is bad, the client may feel sinful every time he or she has and enjoys sex. The therapist may attack the religious belief.

RET holds a generally humanistic view of human nature. It is founded on belief in the worth and value of human beings and their potential for growth and self-understanding and self-acceptance.

Cognitive Restructuring Therapy

Cognitive restructuring therapy was developed by Aaron Beck (1976). Becks' assumption is that disorders result from individuals' negative beliefs about events in the world and about themselves. Because people tend to set unrealistic goals for themselves, their efforts are usually self-defeating, and thus their negative beliefs are reinforced. Beck proposed that there are four major areas where a person's thought processes make the beliefs self-fulfilling.

1. He tends to be *absolute* in his thinking; things are black or white, all or nothing. *Example,* you must approve of everything I do, or you don't like anything about me.

2. He tends to *generalize* a few negative events to every aspect of life. *Example,* I didn't get into the college of my choice, so I am a hopeless failure and not really college material and not smart enough to have friends who go to college.

3. He tends to *magnify* the importance of negative events. *Example,* because X broke up with me, I will never love again because I am not worth loving anyway.

4. He tends to be *selective* in his perceptions, noticing only those events which confirm his negative beliefs about himself. *Example,* a man becomes depressed and worried about losing his job because his boss made two or three critical comments on a report he prepared. He does not pay attention to the fact that the boss liked the report in general and is using it at an important meeting.

The therapist in **cognitive restructuring therapy** does not dispute clients' beliefs directly (as does the RET therapist). Rather, he or she encourages clients to engage in experiments that will help them to confirm or disconfirm their beliefs. The client and therapist may develop a hypothesis, and then the client has the assignment of gathering information to support or demolish it. For example, a depressed man may decide to wallpaper his living room. His wife papers one side, and he does the other. He predicts that he will not be as good as his wife at the job. His work will be sloppier. When he finishes the papering, he may point out all the places on his side where the pattern does not exactly match or the seams are slightly off kilter. He will point to the excellent job on his wife's side of the room. His wife, or the therapist, may counter that no one can notice the small mistakes if they are not pointed out and, in addition, indicate mistakes on the wife's side of the room that the man had chosen not to notice. Below is an excerpt from a case of a severely depressed man:

Therapist and patient set an initial goal of his becoming physically active (i.e., doing more things no matter how small or trivial). The patient and his wife kept a separate list of his activities. The list included raking leaves, having dinner, and assisting his wife in apartment sales, etc. His cognitive distortions were identified by comparing his assessment of each activity with that of his wife. Alternative ways of interpreting his experiences were then considered.

In comparing his wife's resume of his past experiences, he became aware that he had:

1. Undervalued his past by failing to mention any previous accomplishments.
2. Regarded himself as far more responsible for his "failures" than she did.
3. Concluded that he was worthless since he had not succeeded in attaining goals in the past.

When the two accounts were contrasted, he could discern many of his cognitive distortions. In subsequent sessions, his wife continued to serve as an "objectifier."

In mid-therapy, the patient compiled a list of new attitudes that he had acquired since initiating therapy. These included:

1. I am starting at a lower level of functioning at my job, but it will improve if I persist.
2. I know that once I get going in the morning, everything will run all right for the rest of the day.
3. I can't achieve everything at once.
4. I have my periods of ups and downs, but in the long run I feel better.
5. My expectations from my job and life should be scaled down to a realistic level.
6. Giving in to avoidance never helps and only leads to further avoidance.

He was instructed to re-read this list daily for several weeks, even though he already knew the content. (Rush, Khatami, & Beck, 1975)

Symptoms of Depression See Chapter 16, pp. 571–73.

If you recall the major characteristics of a person suffering from depression, you will see that the above list of attitudes is in direct opposition to the thought patterns of a depressed person. They are a form of conceptual antidotes. An important part of cognitive restructuring therapy, especially in the treatment of depression, is the assignment or scheduling of tasks that interfere with the "conduct" of the disorder. For example, a depressed person might find no pleasure in doing things that once gave pleasure. The therapist may ask him or her to list those things: going to a movie, listening to records, going for walks, cooking meals. The "assignment," then, may be to engage in a certain number of these activities before the next session. The client may be prevented from giving in to the inclination to do nothing but think about how worthless he or she is. The client will feel he or she has accomplished something by completing such assignments—which is in itself rewarding. And he or she may even begin to discover the pleasure once felt in participating in these activities. As part of the therapy, the client is called upon to monitor his or her thoughts and to question constantly whether they are realistic.

Stress Inoculation Therapy

Stress inoculation therapy is based on Meichenbaum's theory of stress inoculation. Meichenbaum proposes that by altering the way people talk to themselves, the way they approach stressful problems will be changed. The training takes place in three phases. *First,* the therapist and client *examine the situations* causing stress and try to uncover the beliefs and attitudes being carried into these situations. The therapist focuses attention on how what the clients say to themselves in these situations affects their behavior. For example, a graduate student experiences great stress every time he has to give a lecture. Often the effects of the stress are so overpowering that he begins to stutter; his mind has gone blank on occasion. In the first phase of training, he may reveal that before he enters the classroom he says to himself, "I know I am going to do a lousy job. I am not well enough prepared. What if a student asks a question I cannot answer? I wonder if the professor will be in class today to judge my performance." When the client realizes how damaging his self-statements are, he and the therapist can work up a new set of statements that will be more constructive.

Causes of Stress   See Chapter 15, pp. 526–33.

The *second* phase is called *acquisition* and *rehearsal.* The client rehearses and learns the new set of statements. Meichenbaum (1974) suggests the following list of self-statements for a person who, like the hypothetical student above, feels overwhelmed by the task he or she must do:

> When the fear comes, just pause.
> Keep the focus on the present; what is it you have to do?
> Label your fear from 0–10 and watch it change.
> You should expect your fear to rise.
> Don't try to eliminate fear totally; just keep it manageable.
> You can convince youself to do it. You can reason fear away.
> It will be over shortly.
> It's not the worst thing that can happen.
> Just think about something else.
> Do something that will prevent you from thinking about fear.
> Describe what is around you. That way you won't think about worrying.

Application and *practice* are the *third* phase of the training. The client begins to use the new set of statements in real situations. Usually he or she begins with situations that are only slightly stressful and gradually works up to increasingly stressing situations. Stress inoculation training is most helpful in cases where the situations that cause distress are clearly defined: for example, fear of speaking in front of crowds. Some believe that stress inoculation training may prove to be an effective preventive treatment. Maladaptive behaviors may be prevented from developing if a person has the stress inoculation coping strategy in his or her behavioral repertoire (Mahoney & Arnkoff, 1978).

HUMANISTIC THERAPIES

Humanistic therapies are founded on the primary positive assumption that human beings, if unobstructed, will tend toward growth, health, and the realization of their potentials.

Person-centered Psychotherapy

Carl Rogers

In this view (Rogers, 1959), psychological disorders arise from a blocking of a person's natural inclination toward self-actualization. These blocks arise because of unrealistic demands people make on themselves. For example, individuals might believe that it is wrong to feel anger or hostility toward others. Rather than admit to feeling these "wrong" emotions, they deny and suppress them. In denying the feelings, people may actually numb themselves emotionally or lose touch with these feelings. When individuals lose touch with their real experience, the self is necessarily fragmented, less integrated. This state makes relationships and a whole variety of behaviors difficult and maladjusted.

The purpose of this form of psychotherapy is to release "an already existing capacity in a potentially competent individual" (Rogers, 1959). In the right situation with the proper conditions, clients can learn to unblock themselves and allow their "self-actualizing capacity" to emerge. In **person-centered** (formerly called "client-centered") **therapy,** perhaps the most important element is the relationship between the therapist and client, particularly the client's perception of the therapist. The necessary condition for successful therapy is that the client perceive in the therapist three qualities: genuineness, empathy, and unconditional positive regard. Rogers (1974) writes:

> In the first place the therapist must achieve a strong, accurate empathy. But such deep sensitivity to moment-to-moment "being" of another person requires that the therapist first accept, and to some degree prize, the other person. That is to say, a sufficiently strong empathy can scarcely exist without a considerable degree of unconditional positive regard. However, since neither of these conditions can possibly be meaningful in the relationship unless they are real, the therapist must be, both in these respects and in others, integrated and genuine within the therapeutic encounter. Therefore, it seems to me that genuineness or congruence is the most basic of the three conditions.

Person-centered therapy is also called *nondirective.* The therapist gains the trust of clients by showing that his or her concern for them (what they are experiencing and what happens to them) is based on his or her ability to accept the clients unjudgmentally. The therapist respects the clients' feelings, privacy, and reluctance. Whereas a psychoanalyst directs and interferes, and to some extent shapes patients' revelations and the connections they make, a person-centered therapist does not probe; unless it is necessary he or she does not express either approval or disapproval, does not interpret what clients say. More often, he or she repeats or paraphrases what clients have said. These restatements should help clients further clarify their feelings and demonstrate that the therapist understands the clients because he or she is experiencing what they are experiencing.

T: Just kind of fell, sunk way down deep in these lousy, lousy feelings, hum? Is that something like it?

C: No.

T: No? (Silence of 20 seconds)

C: No. I just ain't no good to nobody, never was, and never will be.

T: Feeling that now, hum? That you're just no good to yourself, no good to anybody. Never will be any good to anybody. Just that you're completely worthless, huh? Those really are lousy feelings. Just that you're no good at *all*, hm?

C: Yeah. (Muttering in a low, discouraged voice.) That's what this guy I went to town with just the other day told me.

T: This guy that you went to town with really told you that you were no good? Is that what you're saying? Did I get that right?

C: M-hm.

T: I guess the meaning of that if I get it right is that here's somebody that meant something to you and what does he think of you? Why, he's told you that he thinks you're no good at all. And that just really knocks the props out from under you. (C. weeps quietly.) It just brings the tears. (Silence of 20 seconds.)

C: I don't care though. (Rather defiantly.)

T: You tell yourself you don't care at all, but somehow I guess some part of you cares because some part of you weeps over it. (Rogers, 1970)

Rogers found that therapy usually progresses in three stages. In the first stage, the clients express predominantly negative feelings toward themselves, the world, and the future. In the second stage they begin to feel and express a few glimmers of hope. They show a few tenuous signs that they are beginning to accept themselves. Finally, positive feelings emerge which allow them to care about others, to have more self-confidence, and to make plans for the future. At this point therapy is concluded because the person has allowed his or her "self-actualizing capacity" out.

One of Rogers's major contributions was his interest in evaluating objectively the outcomes of psychotherapy. This is in contrast to psychoanalysts, who from the beginning of psychoanalysis have resisted developing empirical research to support its methods.

BIOLOGICAL THERAPIES

The evidence on possible biological factors in disorders comes from two sources. First, many disorders are first felt and experienced as somatic complaints. Modern psychotherapy began with Freud's discovery of the power the mind held over the body. His first patients were primarily *hysterics,* people who complained of a physical problem (usually paralysis or loss of some other sensory modality) that had no underlying physical cause.

Second, brain and body states influence mood and thought: even nutrition and the weather produce noticeable changes. Stress can cause physical disease, but it is also possible for *physical disease* to cause *psychological distress.* A study of 100 patients about to be committed to a state mental hospital found that 46 percent had undiagnosed medical illnesses that "specifically related to their psychiatric symptoms or exacerbated them significantly." When these people were treated for their medical ailments, 61 percent had reduced psychiatric symptoms. The most common illnesses were Addison's disease, Wilson's disease, low levels of arsenic poisoning, and dietary deficiencies (Hall, Gardner, Stickney, LeCann, & Popkin, 1980). Certain diseases and medical treatments can have mood-altering side effects: depression is a side effect of the degenerative blood disease lupus and of the strong chemotherapy used in the treatment of cancer. In this section, we will examine the two main kinds of biological therapy: electroconvulsive shock and drugs.

Electroconvulsive Therapy

Shock treatments began as a result of an observation, which later proved to be wrong, that epileptics do not suffer schizophrenia. It was thought that the intense electrical activity that causes epileptic convulsions was incompatible with schizophrenia. In 1938 two Italian psychiatrists, Cerletti and Bini, developed a method whereby an electrical current of about 160 volts was passed through the head from one hemisphere to the other. The patient first loses consciousness and then undergoes convulsive seizures. When the patient wakes up, he or she has amnesia for the period immediately preceding the administration of the shocks and may be disoriented and experience loss of memory for a period lasting up to a few months.

A patient undergoing **electroconvulsive therapy** (ECT) may receive a series of several (usually fewer than 12) shocks. When the treatment is completed there is often a complete cessation of disordered symptoms. In the early days of ECT, the convulsions were often so severe that bones were fractured. However, people are now premedicated with a muscle relaxant, which has obliterated that side effect. A new method of ECT, called unilateral ECT, passes the electrical current through only one side of the brain (usually the right hemisphere), which results in fewer of the disorienting side effects, at least verbal ones, of bilateral ECT (Squire, 1977; Squire & Slater, 1978).

Sometimes the cure seems miraculously effective; in other cases the effects are short-lived. Since the development of antipsychotic drugs, the use of ECT has been in decline, because it is an extremely violent and drastic intervention. The over-administration of ECT may cause significant brain damage (Allen, 1951; Alpers & Hughes, 1942). No one really knows why shock works. Recently it has been hypothesized that the mechanism may simply be the increased amount of electrical firing it induces in the brain, which may facilitate and stimulate the release of greater amounts of neurotransmitters. It is believed that the inhibition of certain neurotransmitters might underlie severe disorders such as depression and schizophrenia. Today, only in the most severe cases of depression or schizophrenia is ECT used. And it is the *most effective treatment* (Snyder, 1980).

In recent years antipsychotic drugs have made it possible for mental institutions to try becoming more open therapeutic communities (below, bottom) instead of human warehouses in which long-term patients spent years in locked wards (below, top).

Pharmacotherapy: The Administration of Drugs

A major change in the treatment of mental disorders came in the 1950s with the development of drugs that relieved the major symptoms of several different psychological disorders. **Pharmacotherapy** involves administering drugs from four main categories: antipsychotics, antidepressants, antianxiety drugs, and lithium compound (used exclusively to resolve manic episodes and to control mood swings in bipolar disorder).

Antipsychotic Drugs

Antipsychotic drugs are used in the treatment of severe disorders, such as schizophrenia. They serve to calm the patient (they are often called the major tranquilizers) and they also reduce the experience of some of the major symptoms of the disorder, namely hallucinations and delusions. It is important to realize what a tremendous impact the use of these drugs has had in mental hospitals. Here is the experience of one psychologist regarding the change that drugs make:

> [I] worked several months in the maximum security ward of (a mental) hospital immediately prior to the introduction of this type of medication in 1955. The ward patients fulfilled the oft-heard stereotypes of individuals "gone mad." Bizarreness, nudity, wild screaming, and the ever present threat of violence pervaded the atmosphere. Fearfulness and a near-total preoccupation with the maintenance of control characterized the attitudes of staff. Such staff attitudes were not unrealistic in terms of the frequency of occurrence of serious physical assaults by patients, but they were hardly conducive to the development of maintenance of an effective therapeutic program.
>
> Then, quite suddenly—within a period of perhaps a month—all of this dramatically changed. The patients were receiving antipsychotic medication. The ward became a place in which one could seriously get to know one's patients on a personal level and perhaps even initiate programs of "milieu therapy," and the like, promising reports of which had begun to appear in the professional literature. A new era in hospital treatment had arrived, aided enormously and in many instances actually made possible by the development of these extraordinary drugs. (Coleman et al., 1980)

The first antipsychotic drug used in the United States was *reserpine*. It had been shown to have a calming effect on patients and helped to reduce manic and schizophrenic symptoms. However, it has severe side effects such as producing low blood pressure and sometimes depression; it may also be carcinogenic. Reserpine is no longer in widespread use because of the introduction of new antipsychotic drugs. One such drug is *chlorpromazine* (trade name, Thorazine). Because it has fewer side effects than reserpine, it became the most widely prescribed drug in the treatment of schizophrenia. Different drug companies manufacture several other compounds of the phenothiazine group, which are all basically variants on chlorpromazine. In 1970 it was estimated that more than 85 percent of patients in all mental hospitals were taking an antipsychotic drug (Davison & Neale, 1974).

An important result of the use of antipsychotic drugs has been a drastic reduction in the number of people in mental hospitals. Many people who might have been kept in institutions for the rest of their lives are able now to live fairly normal lives. After the development of antipsychotic drugs, the number of people in state and county mental hospitals decreased each year. In 1955 there were almost 560,000; in 1980 there were only 132,000 (Coleman et al., 1980). An unfortunate consequence of reducing the number of people hospitalized has been a dramatic increase in the number of released mental patients without homes or jobs who are living as street people in our major cities.

Chlorpromazine and the other antipsychotics are not free from side effects such as jaundice, stiffness in the muscles, and dryness of the mouth. The most serious side effects are those that affect the motor control areas of the brain: facial muscles may become so rigid as to make eating difficult, tremors resembling Parkinson's disease may result. With

Antipsychotic drugs have made it possible for large numbers of mental patients to be released from institutions. Unfortunately, many of them have become homeless street people as hopeless as when they were locked in the back wards of mental hospitals.

extended use these drugs may also cause infertility and cessation of menstruation.

The antipsychotic drugs treat schizophrenia but do not cure it. Although a schizophrenic taking an antipsychotic drug no longer shows overt signs of abnormal behavior, the evidence suggests that the symptoms are merely "suppressed" or masked by the drug. It may be that the way they work is analogous to the way insulin controls diabetes. As long as diabetics receive doses of insulin, their disease is under control. If they stop taking insulin, it will reappear. However, the analogy is not perfect, because it is not yet clear exactly how the antipsychotics work. We do not know if they work on the basic mechanism of schizophrenia, perhaps supplementing a short supply of some chemical agent in the brain. They may only reduce the intensity of the internal experience or inhibit the overt symptoms.

The dopamine hypothesis described in the last chapter presumes that the drugs work by inhibiting the production of dopamine at the synapse receptor sites. In one study, half of a group of schizophrenics were given a placebo and the other half were maintained on their antipsychotic drug. At the end of the six months, the placebo group showed a relapse rate of 60 percent compared to 30 percent of the group on the drugs (Hogarty & Goldberg, 1973; Leff & Wind, 1971). It is still too early to know what the long-term side effects of prolonged treatment with these drugs might be.

Dopamine Hypothesis on Causes of Schizophrenia   See Chapter 16, p. 582.

Antidepressants

The main evidence that biochemical abnormalities play an important role in depression is the effectiveness of drugs used to treat depressive symptoms and the action of these drugs on the neurotransmitters (Snyder, 1980). Serotonin and norepinephrine are two important transmitters

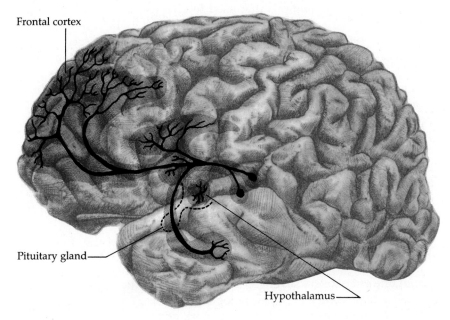

Frontal cortex

Pituitary gland

Hypothalamus

FIGURE 17–1
Dopamine Pathways in the Brain

Alcohol remains the most widely used antianxiety drug—usually self-prescribed.

FIGURE 17–2
Antianxiety Drugs and Electrical Activity in the Brain
Antianxiety drugs like Librium (chlordiazepoxide) alter the rhythm of theta brain waves, and this rhythm can be artificially "driven" to test how such drugs work. The graph below shows that the drug raises the minimum threshold needed to drive the theta rhythm. (After Gray, 1978)

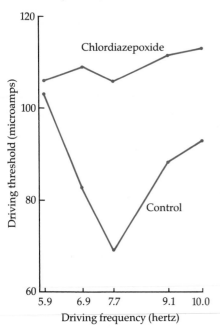

that operate, among other places, along limbic system pathways. Recall that the limbic system of the brain governs emotions. It is believed that depletion of serotonin and norepinephrine may be related to depressive symptoms.

To see how this belief was arrived at we will examine how the major antidepressant drugs work. The first class of drugs are *monoamine oxidase* (MAO) *inhibitors*. They work by blocking the work of an enzyme, monoamine oxidase, which destroys both neurotransmitters. Thus MAO inhibitors allow serotonin and norepinephrine concentrations to build up.

Tricyclics are a class of drugs that work by *preventing the inactivation* of serotonin and norepinephrine in the synapse. Recall that neurotransmitters are normally inactivated during the absolute refractory period following transmission across the synapse. During this time, the re-uptake mechanism brings the chemicals back into the presynaptic neuron. *Tricyclics block the re-uptake mechanism*, allowing the released serotonin and norepinephrine to go to work. Tricyclics have side effects; they are sedatives, cause dryness in the mouth, blurry vision, and difficulty in urinating.

Antianxiety Drugs

People suffering from any one of the mild disorders have in common the experience of anxiety. Although there are a variety of ways to relieve anxiety, the most common method of treatment is with drugs. The oldest and most widely used antianxiety drug is alcohol, and it is usually self-prescribed.

Before the 1950s, the tranquilizers most often prescribed by doctors were sedatives. Today two drugs of the benzodiazepine group are the most popular: Librium and Valium. These drugs work very effectively to reduce the experience of anxiety; people are able to return to work, to sleep, to confront situations that used to give rise to anxiety reactions.

Antianxiety drugs are the most prescribed drugs in America (Coleman et al., 1980). There is a growing concern over the overuse of these drugs; first, because they are addicting: second, because their indiscriminate use may prevent people from developing coping strategies from within to handle their fears (Gray, 1978b). How the antianxiety drugs work is not fully known. One promising approach is Jeffrey Gray's. Gray proposes that anxiety is represented in the brain by increased electrical activity in the parts of the brain that contain the neurotransmitters norepinephrine and serotonin. This increased activity may stimulate increased firing of the neurons and hence the flow of the neurotransmitters. Antianxiety drugs may work by blocking the synthesis of norepinephrine and serotonin at the neuron receptor sites (Gray, 1978a, 1978b).

THE EFFECTIVENESS OF PSYCHOTHERAPY

About one out of every seven (30 million) people in the United States will consult a professional for a psychological problem. What will be the outcome? Do therapies work? Does one work better than another? If they work, do we know why? What does "work" in this context mean, anyway? The question of the effectiveness of psychotherapy is very difficult to answer. Circumstantial evidence would say that it should—why else would 30 million people spend a lot of money and time seeking it out?

Empirical evidence is hard to come by; we still do not know what causes psychological *dis*order; it is equally difficult to assess why we become "ordered" again. There are many variables to consider: the cause and nature of the disorder, the particular experience and personality of the individual seeking therapy, the therapist and the nature of the interaction.

It is also quite difficult to obtain an objective measure of effectiveness. For example, it can be assumed that when individuals enter therapy, they are troubled and therapy may be declared finished when they feel better. Would we then judge that the therapy was effective? Suppose they sought additional therapy six months later? What if they went to another psychotherapist?

Early "Outcome" Studies

There was virtually no objective data on the effectiveness of psychotherapy until the mid-1940s. Freud and most followers of the psychoanalytic school generally maintained that psychoanalysis is too complex to be studied. Carl Rogers was the first pioneer in the gathering of psychotherapy outcome data. With the development of behavioral therapies, data collection became customary.

The recent research on the question of psychotherapy's effectiveness was initiated by an influential paper presented by Hans Eysenck in 1952, "The Effects of Psychotherapy: An Evaluation." Eysenck divided those seeking psychotherapy in two groups. The members of one group were put on a waiting list; the others received psychotherapy. At the end of the study, he found that "roughly two-thirds of a group of neurotic patients will recover or improve to a marked extent within about two years of the onset of their illness." This improvement or recovery was the case whether the person had received therapy or not. He called this two-out-of-three figure the rate of **spontaneous remission,** meaning that the patient perceived his or her neurosis had subsided without medical or psychiatric interference. This two-thirds figure then would be a baseline figure to consider when judging the effectiveness of any therapy. Although Eysenck claimed that at the time he wrote his report there was no evidence of the usefulness of psychotherapies, about 80 percent of the studies since then have shown positive results (Smith, Glass, & Miller, 1980). The questions then remain—which ones work better and why?

Psychoanalysis

Psychoanalysis is the most difficult to evaluate. First, few psychoanalysts undertake research on outcomes. Second, psychoanalysis is available to a very few individuals and suitable for a few disorders. Freud felt that psychoanalysis was effective in the treatment of mild or "neurotic" disorders only, so more serious disorders—schizophrenia, personality disorders, depressions—are not usually treated by psychoanalysis. Because of the time and expense, psychoanalysis is a route open to a very few. A study conducted by the Menninger Foundation found, however, that psychoanalysis is effective for individuals who scored high on scales of ego strength at the beginning of therapy (Smith et al., 1980).

Behavior Therapy

The advent of behavior therapy had several important advantages for the study of outcomes; primarily, the methods are precise and so easily measured, and secondly, the desired outcome is explicit at the beginning—the modification of a certain behavior. How close one is to that predetermined goal at the end is a good measure of success. The outcome of studies show behavior therapy is most useful when someone has a specific behavior to change: specific phobias, breaking of habits like smoking, controlling eating, addictions, sexual dysfunctions. Like psychoanalysis and most other therapies, behavior therapy is not usually successful with severe disorders.

Cognitive-behavioral therapies are so new that the results are naturally more tentative. But the first results are promising enough that this area of psychotherapy is growing rapidly (Coleman et al., 1980).

Although outcome research was initiated by Rogers of the humanistic school, evidence on the humanistic therapies is extremely difficult to quantify; the goals of the therapy are often hard to evaluate.

Recent Comparative Outcome Studies: Controversies

A recent major study compared the results of all the major outcome studies in order to assess which therapy was best. The only therapies that showed a consistent significant advantage over any of the others were the drug therapies (Luborsky, Singer, & Luborsky, 1975). A wide range of disorders can be treated with drugs, particularly the severe ones: depression and schizophrenia. In one important study, Hogarty and Goldberg (1973) divided 374 recently released schizophrenics into four groups (1) those who received chlorpromazine alone, (2) those who received a placebo alone, (3) those who received chlorpromazine and psychotherapy, and (4) those who received a placebo and psychotherapy. At the end of one year, the rehospitalization rate was as follows: for the first group, 33 percent; for the second, 72.5 percent; for the third, 26 percent; for the fourth, 63 percent. Thus, drug therapy with psychotherapy was only slightly more effective than drug therapy alone; and both were substantially more effective than psychotherapy or minimal (counting placebo treatment as minimal). The Luborsky study also revealed no significant difference in results in individual versus group therapy or between therapies with a time limit (e.g., ten sessions) and ones where time was unrestricted.

The results of Luborsky's study make it clear that if there is a successful outcome it is not because one or the other school has the right answer. The approach and treatment hardly seem to matter. *The most important factor in therapeutic success is the therapist-client relationship.* Each therapy recognizes the importance of the therapist's establishing a good trusting relationship at the start of therapy.

Factors Affecting Therapy

Therapists

What makes a good therapist? One area of research compares the effects of experienced and nonexperienced therapists. There have been many studies where an experienced therapist is matched against: (a) undergraduates, (b) housewives, (c) graduate students, and (d) inexperienced but trained therapists. In general, inexperienced or nonprofessional people are far more directive and less interpretive, and they act the way most nonprofessionals imagine therapy. A panel of judges can pick out experienced from inexperienced therapists. However, professional therapists are not always more effective than amateurs. In fact, in a comparison of twelve outcome studies using inexperienced versus experienced therapists, only *five* showed that patients of experienced therapists achieved better outcomes (Smith et al., 1980).

Attention

We saw in Chapter 13 that the need to belong is quite basic to us. It follows then that some people seeking therapy might be helped by the "attention" they receive from the therapist. In one study, Paul divided a sample of college students seeking therapy for "performance anxiety" into two groups. One group became involved with an insight-oriented therapy (e.g., psychoanalysis, person-centered); the other group received "attention-placebo" treatment. Attention-placebo means that a person was merely convinced that a therapist was interested in him or her but received no actual treatment. At the end of two years, both groups showed the same rate of improvement (Paul, 1965).

A Recent Study on the Outcome of Psychotherapy

The controversy over whether or not psychotherapy works has stimulated some recent, comprehensive studies to help answer the question. In an extremely large review of all published studies on the effects of psychotherapy, Smith and colleagues (1980) find these effects:

1. The *average* effect of psychotherapy is *positive* in almost all kinds of therapies.
2. The amount of effect is fairly large, enough to move a person who is at the mean (50th percentile) of a population up to the 80th percentile rank.
3. Cognitive therapies seem the most effective of all therapies, but all are effective.
4. There is a significant positive effect of "attention-placebo," but it is not as strong as psychotherapy.
5. Drug therapy is as effective as psychotherapy, and the effects of drug therapy and psychotherapy add to one another. Thus drug + psychotherapy is the most effective treatment, on the average.

Thus, after three decades of research and almost a century of treatment, we have evidence that most therapies are largely effective; some may be due simply to attention, some to the specific technique, some due to drugs; but the main point in the end is that psychotherapy, on the average, can help people, if the correct factors are applied to the right people.

Summary

1. In the late eighteenth century, a series of humane reforms began to treat disordered people as victims of disease rather than as if something had "possessed" them. A great advance in the late nineteenth century was the discovery of the cause of one type of disorder, *general paresis*—a slow degenerative disease that eventually erodes mental faculties. It was discovered to be caused by syphilis, and the elimination of syphilis by medical means is one of the few decisive victories in the war against mental disorder. That victory led to the hope that a specific biological cause could be found for every pathology.

2. One of the most important innovations in the history of mental disease was the development of classifications of mental disorders. Kraepelin noted that mental disorder was not a monolithic entity, but several distinct disorders, each with its own particular pattern of symptoms. His system remains the foundation of the modern general classification of disorders.

   Currently, much treatment of mental disease is administered by psychotherapists. A *psychiatrist* is a medical doctor whose specialty is the treatment of psychological problems. A *psychoanalyst* is a psychotherapist trained in psychoanalytic techniques first formulated by Freud. A *clinical psychologist* holds a Ph.D. in psychology and may specialize in a particular form of psychotherapy. A *psychiatric social worker* usually holds an advanced degree and concentrates on social or community-based problems.

3. The psychoanalytic method of treatment is based on the theories of Freud, who believed that disorders are caused by conflicts between conscious and unconscious desires. Therapy, in this system, is designed to bring these desires into consciousness where they may be acknowledged and analyzed. Among the important techniques Freud developed was *free association*, in which a patient is asked to say anything that comes to mind, without criticism or editing. The idea is that the thoughts, images, and connections in therapy must come from within the patient.

   Psychoanalysis is usually very expensive, requiring four or five 50-minute sessions per week, for anywhere from one to several years.

4. There are four phases of treatment in psychoanalysis: (1) the opening phase usually lasts from three to six months, in which there is usually the emergence of resistance in the patient. *Resistance* is the way the patient unconsciously works against revealing feelings or thoughts; (2) *transference*—one of the most important concepts in psychoanalytic therapy is how patients perceive the analyst. At a certain point in treatment, patients transfer their feelings toward people in their lives onto the analyst and, therefore, these feelings can come to the surface; (3) working through—the therapist then proceeds to an analysis of this transference. Patients begin to see, in a concrete way, the nature of their misconceptions, having transferred them to the analyst; and (4) resolution of the transference—this is the last phase of the

treatment, in which patients and the therapist agree that the goals they set out to achieve have been accomplished.

5. In behavior therapy, the approach is to work directly on problems, which are considered to be the result of "faulty learning." Psychotherapy, then, is the process of relearning. Two varieties of behavior therapy are related to the two primary modes of learning: the form generally called behavior therapy is based upon respondent conditioning; behavior modification is based on operant conditioning. *Behavior therapy* aims to reduce the anxiety that a person experiences in response to certain key external stimuli. Anxiety is the underlying cause of neurotic behavior. Behavior therapy aims to decondition those anxiety-producing autonomic responses. *Behavior modification*, based on operant conditioning, attempts to change behaviors by changing the stimuli and conditions. Behavior therapy has a wide variety of applications and methods. Therapy may involve an individual, group, family, or community. This form of therapy has been useful in treating test anxiety, sexual dysfunctions, phobias, addictions, and interpersonal and personality problems.

6. Important reconditioning techniques in behavior therapy include: (1) *systematic desensitization*—this technique eliminates an unwanted, conditioned response by conditioning the client to another stimulus that elicits a response (usually relaxation) incompatible with the original one. For example, a person who is afraid of elevators might first be asked to imagine an elevator and then to imagine being alone in an elevator. Later the client may go stand beside an elevator and then finally stand inside and ride it. (2) *Flooding* is similar to systematic desensitization in that the therapist deliberately presents the client with fear or anxiety-provoking stimuli. Flooding, however, is more intensive and does not rely on relaxation. It is most effective in severe phobias. (3) Assertiveness training is used when a person's problem involves difficulties in interpersonal relationships. This training teaches people that they have a right to their own feelings and to be themselves as long as they do not hurt others.

7. In *rational-emotive therapy* (RET), the therapist determines what the underlying belief system of the individual is. In this therapy, the person is confronted directly with this belief system and is forced to examine it against reality. For example, if a woman's lover breaks a date with her, an RET therapist might point out that her lover might have had good reason for doing so and that it does not necessarily mean that the lover has abandoned her. In RET, the client is continually directed to the inconsistencies between beliefs and external reality, with the therapist quite active in the disputing of these beliefs.

8. *Cognitive restructuring therapy* is similar to RET in that it works on beliefs. This therapy contends that there are four major areas where people's thought processes make their beliefs self-fulfilling: (1) they are absolute in their thinking—things are black or white, all or nothing; (2) they generalize a few negative events to every aspect of their lives; (3) they tend to magnify the importance of negative events; and (4) they tend to be selective in perception, noticing only those events which confirm negative beliefs about themselves.

9. In person-centered psychotherapies, psychological disorders are thought to arise from a blocking of a person's natural inclination toward self-actualization. The purpose of this form of psychotherapy is to release an already

existing capacity in a potentially competent individual. This therapy is also called nondirective. It usually progresses in three stages. In the first stage, the client expresses predominantly negative feelings both inwardly and toward the world and the future. In the second stage, the client begins to feel hope. In the third stage, impromptu feelings emerge that allow the client to care about others, to have more self-confidence, and to make plans for the future.

10. A different approach to therapy is through biological factors. Much recent research has shown that the areas of the "mental" and "physical" are not as unrelated as previously thought. Brain states affect mental states; body states affect brain states. Therefore, the relationship between the body and biology and therapy is potentially quite important.

One important form of therapy is *electroconvulsive therapy* (ECT). A patient undergoing ECT may receive a series of several shock treatments, usually fewer than a dozen. When the treatment is completed, there is often a complete cessation of disordered symptoms, especially those of depression. Sometimes the cure seems extremely effective, but, in other cases, the effects are short-lived. Since the invention of antipsychotic drugs, the use of ECT has been in decline because it is an extremely violent and drastic intervention. Today, only in the most severe cases of depression or schizophrenia is ECT used; but still, it is the most effective treatment of such severely disordered cases.

Pharmacotherapy has perhaps been the most revolutionary change in the treatment of mental disorder. Drugs were developed that relieved the major symptoms of several different psychological disorders. Antipsychotic drugs are used in the treatment of severe disorders, such as schizophrenia. They serve to calm the patient and reduce the experience of delusions and hallucinations. Examples of antipsychotic drugs are reserpine and chlorpromazine.

Antidepressants are an effective class of drugs used to treat depressive symptoms. These drugs seem to act on the neurotransmitters, especially serotonin and norepinephrine. Tricyclics are a class of antidepressants that work by preventing the inactivation of serotonin and norepinephrine. They thus block the "re-uptake" portion of neurotransmission and allow the serotonin and norepinephrine to go to work.

Antianxiety drugs are widely used in our culture. Among the most popular are librium and valium. These drugs work very effectively to reduce the experience of anxiety; people are able to return to work, to sleep, and to confront situations that used to cause them difficulties. These drugs are the most prescribed drugs in the United States, and there is growing concern because they are addicting and their indiscriminate use may prevent people from developing coping strategies from within to handle their fears.

11. It is quite controversial how effective psychotherapy is. Early outcome studies, especially those by Hans Eysenck, showed patients improved as much without therapy as with it. Among therapies psychoanalysis is the most difficult to evaluate, because there is little emphasis on successful outcome, and it is available only to very few people. Behavior therapy is much easier to evaluate, because its procedures are quite specific, and the criteria for successful outcome are also quite specific. Behavior therapy has also been shown in a number of cases to be quite effective with specific phobias and habits. Cognitive-behavioral therapies have also been shown to be successful in certain well-defined situations.

A recent, major review of the effects of therapy has helped to integrate many of the findings: it has shown that, on the average, people in therapy are statistically better off after therapy than people in matched situations who do not enter therapy. It is still quite clear that not everyone is helped by every form of psychotherapy to the maximum extent. It must be emphasized that psychotherapy is still a discipline in its infancy, and much research still needs to be done on the diagnosis, understanding, and treatment of psychological disorders.

Terms and Concepts

assertiveness training
behavior modification
behavior therapy
catharsis
clinical psychologist
cognitive restructuring therapy
electroconvulsive therapy
flooding
free association
general paresis
person-centered therapy
pharmacotherapy

psychiatric social worker
psychiatrist
psychoanalyst
rational-emotive therapy
resistance
role playing
spontaneous remission
stress inoculation therapy
systematic desensitization
transference
trephining

Suggestions for Further Reading

Many of the major therapies are summarized by their innovators:

Freud, S. (1900). *The interpretation of dreams.* London: Hogarth Press.
    The classic statement of psychoanalysis.

Meichenbaum, D. (1977). *Cognitive behavior modification.* New York: Plenum.
    A very readable account of this therapeutic approach.

Rogers, C. (1970). *On becoming a person: A therapist's view of psychotherapy.* Boston: Houghton Mifflin.
    A warm, humane account of being a therapist.

Smith, M. L.; Glass, G. V.; and Miller, T. I. (1980). *The benefits of psychotherapy.* Baltimore: Johns Hopkins University Press.
    A technical account of how the different methods of therapy are evaluated and analyzed. Useful to look at.

Also see Brecher and Snyder in Chapter 16 Suggestions for Further Reading.

*I*f our earliest development is primarily biological, our later development is social. Other people often determine how and where we work, what we like to eat, how we think. We conform, obey, accept. We may make extreme decisions, such as whether or not to kill, while in a group.

The experiences of adulthood—marriage, becoming a grandparent, work—make many people aware that they are part of something larger than their individual selves. We are workers, citizens, members of a political party. Some people become "citizens of the world," concerned with life on the planet as a whole.

So, we expand **away** from our biology during our adulthood.

Until the end, when our biology reclaims us once again.

Part Four

The Social World of the Adult

Chapter 18

Social Psychology

INTRODUCTION

Imagine that you are sitting alone in a room and you hear someone cry for help from the next room. Would you help? Probably. Now, imagine that you are sitting with a few other people when you hear a cry for help. Would you go to help? Yes again? In fact, you are three times *less* likely to help if there are six people in the room than if you are alone. The group we are in has a profound effect on us, on our behavior, attitudes, and experience. We obey the authority of groups; we compare our attitudes with those of the group; we make decisions we never would have made if we were alone. We change ourselves and so *conform* to the groups we belong to.

It is often said that we are "social animals"; what this means is that the presence of other people *intensifies* and *directs* an individual's behavior, a phenomenon known since the early days of psychology as the **coaction effect.** Bicyclists ride faster racing against other people than alone against the clock; children reel in their fishing lines faster in groups than alone (Triplett, 1897).

How we develop as adults depends not only on the groups we belong to, but also where we fit into those groups. How do you know where you belong? As in all matters of perception and judgment, by comparison. In your family or school, you are old or young compared to someone else, smarter or funnier than someone else.

We make many social judgments by comparing ourselves to a standard, called the *reference group.* This standard may shift our comparisons. Am I a fast runner? Yes, in comparison to other middle-aged joggers whom I pass on the track each morning. No, in comparison to a member of the U.S. Olympic team.

We are all changed by the groups in which we live, and we will examine these varied effects in this chapter. Social psychology is the study of the general effect of other people on our experience. They may be individual friends, and they may form groups to which we belong; they may not even be present but affect our judgment. First we focus on the individual within the group: how we conform, why we obey orders, then

Social life is characterized by various interactions involving cooperation or competition by members of groups large and small.

how we make judgments about others. Later we consider the function of the groups we live in, how they inhibit or enhance actions, bring out the best and the worst in us. Then we consider an important social problem: aggression. Finally we examine the effect of living in society, the larger groups in which we live, such as crowds, cities, and the built environment.

SOCIAL INFLUENCE

We constantly interact with other people who belong to a variety of groups: large ones such as business, professional, political, or social groups; small groups such as family, friends, club, or team. A fundamental part of our lives is determining how we stand compared to the rest of the group and how we fit into the group.

Social Comparison

How we stand is sometimes based upon an objective comparison. You can easily determine if you are taller or heavier by a simple measurement. But most of the time there is no objective "yardstick" with which to compare ourselves with others. Most social situations are very complex. There is no objective scale to tell you whether your attitudes or behavior are normal for a particular group.

Leon Festinger, one of the leading social psychologists, proposed an important theory of **social comparison** (1954). It states: if there is no objective measure of comparison, we seek out other people and compare our attitudes or behaviors to theirs. However, not just anyone will do for comparison. We compare ourselves to those we admire or whom we believe are like us: most of us would not compare our political beliefs to a group of drunks, unless we aspire to inebriation. For example, assume that you are opposed to draft registration and want to find out if your opposition is "normal." You probably would not compare your opinion to that of the Army Chief of Staff. Instead, you would compare yourself to someone who is like you in many ways, such as another college student. If you find out that most college students share your antidraft attitude, you would believe your attitude is normal.

Reference Groups

The group we choose to compare ourselves to is the **reference group.** When attitudes and behavior agree with the reference group, we consider ourselves part of it. When we do not fit in, there is often a heavy price to pay: we might be disliked, rejected, or treated badly. When there are differences between our attitudes and the group's, there may be "pressure" to change attitudes, to *conform.* The pressure that forces us to try to be like everyone else is **social pressure** or **conformity pressure.**

We conform when we comply with a request to do something we would not ordinarily do. You may be against the draft, but would probably join the Army if drafted. Even at the height of antiwar protests, most young men complied with their draft orders. *However, most people are sure they would not carry out an order they consider wrong.* But are they right?

Obedience to authority has been extensively studied by Stanley Milgram (1964). He demonstrated that under the right circumstances ordinary people will comply with the commands of an authority figure even when the request is extreme and uncalled for, and even when there is no threat of punishment. This is a classic and controversial study in psychology.

In Milgram's original (1960–63) study, men responded to a newspaper advertisement for "participants in a psychology experiment" at Yale University, which would take about one hour and for which they would be paid $4.50. When each subject arrived for the experiment, he was introduced to the experimenter and another subject (actually a confederate of the experimenter). The subjects were told that the experiment was "an investigation of the effects of punishment on learning." The subject and confederate drew lots to see who would be the "teacher" and who would be the "learner." The drawing was rigged, however, so that the confederate was always the learner and the real subject was always the teacher. The experimenter said that the teacher's job was to administer an electric shock every time the learner made a mistake. Then the experimenter took the teacher and learner to an adjoining room and strapped the learner into a chair and attached electrodes to his wrist. The learner expressed concern about receiving shocks, stating that he had a heart condition. The experimenter assured him and the teacher that there were no physical risks in the experiment. The teacher and the experimenter then returned to the original room.

The teacher was asked first to read a series of word pairs to the learner, then to read the first word of each pair along with four choice words. For each pair, the learner was to recall which word had been the second in the original pair. When the learner answered correctly, the teacher was to press a switch that lit a light in the learner's room. When the learner was wrong, the teacher was supposed to read the correct

Pictures of some of the events in the Milgram experiment on obedience to authority, the details of which are provided in the accompanying text.

FIGURE 18–1
Obedience to Authority
In the Milgram experiment, all subjects followed instructions and administered what they thought were painful shocks of up to 300 volts. Only above 300 volts did some subjects refuse to go on administering shocks to the protesting "learner." (After Milgram, 1963)

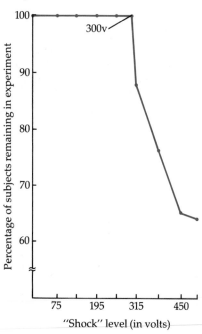

answer aloud and punish the learner by pressing a switch that delivered an electric shock to the learner. There were 30 switches, which ranged from 15 volts (labeled Slight Shock) to 420 volts (labeled Danger: Severe Shock). The two final switches, for 435 and 450 volts, were simply labeled **XXX.** Each time the learner made a mistake, the teacher was to administer a shock one level higher (15 more volts) than the last shock.

Unbeknown to the subject (teacher) the learner had been instructed to make frequent mistakes and never actually received any shocks. Following a prearranged script, the learner began to complain about the shocks, express concern over his heart condition, and beg to be released. After the teacher administered 300 volts, the learner began to pound the walls; after that he no longer answered.

Whenever the teacher showed hesitation about giving a shock, the experimenter instructed, but did not threaten or force the "teacher" to follow the directions. Now, consider this carefully: *how much shock would you have given?* Almost no one says they will give the maximum shock (Aronson, 1984). The results are, well, shocking! Although the "teachers" knew that the learner had a heart condition and heard him beg to be released, *62.5 percent* of the teachers in the experiment complied *completely* with the experimenter's request and gave the *maximum* shock of 450 volts. Even more startling, only 22.5 percent gave less than 300 volts and in one variation of the experiment **no one** *gave less than 300 volts.*

This experiment, extreme though it is, shows how strong social influence can be. The subjects gave the maximum shock because they were in a situation in which the pressure to comply with the requests of the experimenter (an authority figure) outweighed their own judgment. But, think how abstract and subtle the pressure is. The subjects had agreed to be in an experiment; they had accepted money for their participation; they felt an obligation to the experimenter; the experimenter assured them there was no danger. They may have felt the scientists, dressed in doctorlike white coats, would not ask them to do anything really dangerous. Perhaps they felt that whatever happened was the researcher's responsibility. This experiment by no means proves that people are weak willed and always obedient. It does point out, however, that it is hard not to comply, obey, or conform when there is social "pressure" urging us on.

Conformity to a Group

A single individual can sometimes pressure us to change our behavior, but more often our judgments, attitudes, and actions are influenced by groups. The more desirable and important we find the group, the more difficult it is to resist its pressure.

Opinions and Social Influence

It is difficult to resist such conformity pressure even when the group is merely a random collection of strangers and there is no explicit request to comply. Solomon Asch conducted an important study of the social influences on conformity. Volunteers were solicited for a psychology experiment on visual perception. One real subject and six other subjects, who were actually confederates of the experimenters, were seated around a circular table and shown a board with a vertical line on it. A second board was shown with three vertical lines, one of which was the same length as the first line and two of which were obviously different in length. (See Figure 18–2.) The subjects were asked simply to identify which line on the second board was the same length as the one on the first. The subjects answered in turn; the real subject responded last. Although all of the confederates picked the same obviously incorrect line, although there was no overt demand for group unanimity of response, although common sense tells you it would be very easy to resist this pressure, 32 percent of the real subjects conformed to the group pressure; they gave the incorrect answer. The pressure of even a group formed of a random collection of people that you have never met before can be considerable.

Conforming in College

So far we have seen that social pressure *can* change people's *behavior*, but there is no evidence that there was any change in what they actually *believed*. An important question, then, is, do people change their beliefs to match their group? The foremost study of this question was a study begun in 1935 at Bennington College, then a small college for women in Vermont. Today this college is well known for its liberal political atmosphere, and most of the entering students come from liberal backgrounds (it is also coed). At the time of this study, however, Bennington College had just graduated its first senior class, and it had not yet gained

FIGURE 18–2
Social Influence
In the Asch study, subjects viewed display A and then were asked to choose the line in display B that matched it. (After Asch, 1958)

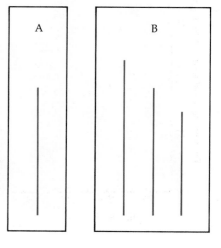

a wide reputation. The professors *were* largely extremely liberal; however, the bulk of the new students came from very conservative families, families that could afford to send their daughters to an expensive school even during the Great Depression. Thus, there was a wide difference in beliefs between the conservative attitudes of the new students and the prevailing liberal attitudes of their new reference group, the college community. The stage was set for a real-life study of conformity pressure on beliefs. Theodore Newcomb and his colleagues (1943) charted its effects on these students for over a quarter of a century.

Over the four years in college the once-conservative students increasingly adopted the liberal attitudes of their new reference group: 62 percent of the freshman class were Republican, 43 percent of the sophomore class, but only 15 percent of the juniors/seniors.

How did these changes come about? First, many of the students reported that they made a deliberate shift in their choice of reference group. They threw over the attitudes of their conservative parents in favor of those of the liberal students and faculty that they wanted to be like. Second, the liberal faculty and students tended to reject conservative students, labeling them immature, and "not intellectual." Third, there was an intellectual influence: the liberal environment provided students with new information on issues and events. Twenty-five years later, most of the students were still politically liberal; the change that had been initiated by the college reference group persisted (Newcomb, Koenig, Flacks, & Warwick, 1967).

Newcomb explained this persistence by noting that after college they actively sought out other liberals and joined liberal groups. These new groups became the new reference groups and provided a continuing source of liberal information and identification. College can, then, act as an important reference group in a person's life. Many of the reference group changes we make in college become our reference groups for life.

Factors in Conformity

The rules that people in different groups conform to differ: Indians dress like Indians, Americans like Americans . . . when in Rome, you do as the Romans do. When you change your reference group you change many things about yourself. A recent law school graduate who takes a job in a prestigious New York law firm may find he or she needs an entire new wardrobe, a different one than a lawyer in a small town in the Sierras. Several factors determine to what extent we conform.

One factor is *group unanimity.* People are most likely to conform when faced with unanimous group opinion. In the Asch experiment conformity was 32 percent. If, however, there is even *one* other person who does not go along, conformity drops drastically to about 8 percent; it does not even matter if the other dissenter's answer is wrong (Wilder & Allen, 1973).

Another important factor in conformity is *group size.* If you are sitting with someone in a lecture who says that it is boring, you may or may not agree. If 10 other people say it is boring, you may begin to agree with the other people's judgment. In the Asch experiment, there is only 2.8 percent conformity with only one other person in the room, 12.8 percent with two, about 30 percent with four people. Conformity does not increase with groups over four (Asch, 1951). Thus, apparently we take a consensus of opinion from other people to *define* our social reality; once defined, further confirmation is unnecessary, a surplus.

ATTITUDES AND PREJUDICE

There is a subtle effect of all this pressure to change: conformity pressures directed at attitudes can indirectly produce other types of change. One of the major areas of investigation in this field in the 1960s (a time of important new legislation guaranteeing civil rights to blacks) was how to change attitudes and behavior. Many minority groups have followed the leadership of the blacks in demanding a fair and equal share. Social psychologists were approached to help devise ways to counter long-held attitudes of "in" majority groups that resisted the changes.

Attitudes

Attitudes typically consist of several components. An attitude about another person (say, a negative one) consists of a *cognitive* component (e.g., your belief that the person is conceited and domineering), an *emotional* component (e.g., your dislike of that person), and a *behavioral* component (e.g., your tendency to avoid that person at parties).

Consistency of Attitudes

We hold many different attitudes at once and we are motivated to make all of our attitudes simpler and consistent with one another. **Cognitive consistency** theories attempt to define exactly how we achieve consistency between our attitudes.

One cognitive consistency theory is called the *balance theory* (Heider, 1946, 1958). This theory describes the relationship between an attitude about a person (like vs. dislike) and attitudes about other things. The basic formulation of this theory is quite simple: if you like someone, you want to have the same attitudes as that person; if you dislike someone, you want the opposite attitudes. Both of these two states are "balanced" or "consistent."

An example of a state of balanced attitudes from the Bennington College experiment: A student likes a professor (positive attitude about someone); both the student and the professor have liberal political attitudes (shared positive attitude about politics). This state is balanced because the student likes both the professor and his politics. An unbalanced state would be if the student liked the professor but held political attitudes that were the opposite of the professor's. This was exactly the case for many of the Bennington freshmen. They admired and liked the liberal professors, but held conservative attitudes. According to Heider, this unbalanced state is psychologically uncomfortable and motivates the students to create balance by changing their attitude about the professor or about politics. Balance can be achieved in one of two ways. First, a student could change her attitude about the professor and decide she dislikes him. The other way (which seems to have been chosen by most of the Bennington students) is to change political attitudes from conservative to liberal.

Attitudes and Behavior

There is another relationship between attitudes and behavior that seems appealing and obvious: an attitude about a person, object, or event can influence our *behavior* toward that person, object, or event. Everyday experience is full of examples of attitudes affecting behavior: if you like one political candidate more than another, you are more likely to say positive things about that candidate and vote for him or her in the election. If someone you like enjoys Japanese movies, you may find yourself suddenly finding that Japanese film festivals are fascinating!

Given how obvious this relationship between attitudes and behavior seems to be, you might be surprised to find that it has been controversial in social psychology. But this controversy is centered on the definitions and measurements of attitude and behaviors. Research in which *both* attitudes and behaviors relating to a person or event have been properly measured supports the ordinary view that attitudes can and do cause behaviors (Azjen & Fishbein, 1974).

Behaviors and Attitudes

There is a less obvious relationship between attitudes and behavior: *behavior* can influence *attitudes*. The major theory of this relationship concerns cognitive dissonance (Festinger, 1957). Like Heider's balance theory, the *theory of cognitive dissonance* assumes the need for cognitive consistency.

Cognitive dissonance occurs whenever an individual holds two cognitions (e.g., beliefs, attitudes, or knowledge of behaviors) that are *inconsistent* with each other. A dissonance (literally, disharmony) is a discrepancy, and we try constantly to resolve discrepancies.

Consider these two statements: (1) I know cigarette smoking causes cancer; (2) I smoke. A rational person would be uncomfortable trying to live with these two contradictory facts. He or she can solve the discrepancies in several ways: give up smoking, or consider cancer not a bad thing; assume that a cure will be found by the time he or she gets the disease, or, in the extreme, ignore the data (Festinger suggested the person can give up reading!).

Dissonance would also occur if you liked someone but were aware that you had insulted that person in public. Dissonance arises since you would not usually harm or insult someone you like. Like any state of disequilibrium, dissonance is uncomfortable and motivates the person to reduce it. Dissonance can be reduced by changing one of the cognitions so that it no longer is inconsistent with the second cognition, or by attempting to reduce the importance of one of the dissonant cognitions. For example, you can decide you really do not like the person you insulted, or that what you said was a joke, not an insult. Dissonance can also be reduced by *adding* other cognitions that are consistent with one of the beliefs. You could compensate for the insult by doing something especially nice for the person you slighted.

The following experiment was the first, and remains the most famous, demonstration of the theory that behavior can change attitudes (Festinger & Carlsmith, 1959). Sixty undergraduates were randomly assigned to one of three experimental conditions. Each subject was first asked to perform a dull, repetitive task—placing 12 spools in a tray, emptying the tray, placing the spools in the tray, emptying it, and so forth for one hour. Afterward, one third of the subjects were paid $1 and asked to tell a waiting subject (who was in cahoots with the experimenters) that the task was enjoyable and interesting. Another third of the subjects were paid $20 to say the same thing. The final third, control subjects, simply performed the repetitive task and were not asked to tell anyone how they liked the job. Later, the subjects were asked to fill out a questionnaire unrelated to the purpose of the experiment and then to rate how much they had actually enjoyed the task. *All initially thought that the task was extremely dull.*

Before performing the task, all subjects thought it would be boring. Festinger and Carlsmith predicted that subjects in the $1 condition would experience dissonance and change their attitude about the task, and that subjects in the $20 condition would not experience dissonance and would not change their attitude. The $1 subjects' unconscious reasoning would be, "I wouldn't lie about such a silly thing for $1, so I must have really enjoyed it." The $20 subjects would think, "Hell, for $20 it's no skin off my back to lie about such an insignificant thing." The $20 would give them a *valid* reason for the inconsistency. The results confirmed this prediction (Figure 18–3). When asked after the experiment by someone other than the experimenter to rate their "true" attitude toward the task, the $1 subjects evaluated the task as significantly more enjoyable than did the $20 subjects and the control subjects.

This experiment indicates that behavior (the statement to the confederate) produced a change in attitude. The inconsistency between the subjects' behavior and initial attitude produced an uncomfortable state

FIGURE 18–3
Behavior, Incentive, and Attitude Change
Paid to perform what they knew would be a boring task, those paid only $1 had more reason to change their attitude about the work to make it consistent with their behavior than did those paid $20, an amount that gave them sufficient reason to perpetuate the inconsistency. (After Festinger & Carlsmith, 1959)

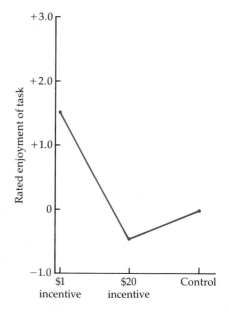

that prompted them to change their *attitude* so that it was now consistent with their *behavior*. The finding has important implications. A teacher whose income is far less than that of a friend who is a banker may decide that making money is "selling out." A starving artist claims that successful artists aren't "pure." It also means that *the fewer inducements you provide someone to do something*, the *more* likely you are to create attitude change. For instance, chronically underpaid workers, such as nurses, teachers, and social workers, often speak of the "psychic income" of their jobs.

Self-perception Theory

Daryl Bem (1972), however, characterized these and similar results somewhat differently in his *theory of self-perception*. Bem argues that our justification in situations like the Festinger and Carlsmith experiment was produced not by a need to reduce dissonance, but by a search for self-understanding.

Bem hypothesizes that in judging our *own* attitude we put ourselves into the role of an outside observer who witnesses his own behavior. In the Festinger and Carlsmith study, the observer sees himself perform a task that appears dull and uninteresting and sees himself tell someone that it is interesting after being paid only $1. The observer then probably infers that this must be his own true attitude. However, if the observer sees the subject being paid $20, he could well think that for $20 he would probably be willing to lie about his enjoyment of the task. Self-perception theory assumes that when a person is asked to describe his *own* attitudes, he bases his judgment on the same evidence as an outside observer would.

Comparing the dissonance and self-perception interpretations, it is clear that both assume that behavior can influence attitudes. People often rely on their behavior and their circumstances to infer what their internal experience, for example, attitude, is (e.g., "I didn't realize I liked X so much until I defended him to my friends" or "I must like chemistry because I got an A on the exam"). The theories differ only in the specific mechanisms postulated to explain how behavior influences attitudes. Dissonance theory assumes that the attitude was produced by the attempt to reduce discrepancy; self-perception theory assumes that the attitude was produced by the subjects' attempt to infer or discover their true beliefs.

Both theories offer interesting and compelling explanations for the link between behavior and attitudes, and many psychologists have assumed that only one explanation can be adequate. But both have advantages. "Dissonance" helps us understand that constancy and consistency are quite important. Self-perception is useful in that it emphasizes that sometimes we must *infer* what is happening to us, as subjects in the Schacter and Singer experiment did. Although this self-perception theory seems appealing, it overlooks an important point: *we usually do know what our attitudes and feelings are*. Perhaps in some ambiguous situations we must *infer* our attitudes, but it is unlikely that we do so very often. A more reasonable position, one that is being advocated by some

Schacter and Singer Experiment on Interpretation of Emotion
See Chapter 12, p. 450.

psychologists, is that both theories have their applications and merely emphasize two different roads that lead to the same destination.

Prejudice

One of the major problems in our society today is prejudice. Some people are denied jobs, housing, and basic civil and human rights because other people hold different attitudes. Yet in a sense we are all prejudiced about many things. *Prejudice* literally means ''to prejudge.'' We come to most situations ready to prejudge, a disposition that is most often useful. We are all prejudiced to seek out order and meaning in situations, to look at the simplest possible explanations of our own and others' behaviors. Our attitudes ''prejudice'' us. We may well be prejudiced against eating steak, for or against capital punishment, for women's rights.

However, the simple aspect of prejudice is not what most people mean by prejudice in current society. **Prejudice** is a *negative judgmental attitude toward an identifiable group of people, based on a simplistic overgeneralization.*

Stereotypes

Prejudice derives from mechanisms similar to those that we use to experience the world and develop our ideas and attitudes. We are able to judge many different objects and people because of our efficient *simplification* processes: we sort the infinite variety of things we encounter into simpler categories, and we assume all members of a category are similar. The problem comes when we overextend our simplifying strategies.

Simplification of Experience
See Chapter 6, p. 217.

Central to categories are prototypes. However, when a prototype is *over*extended it becomes a *stereo*type. A **stereotype** is a generalized assumption attributing identical characteristics to all members of a group, for example, Americans are materialistic, blondes are dumb, the elderly are wise, Irish are drunks.

When we judge someone according to a stereotype we attempt to fit an individual's actions and qualities into a consistent personality. Gordon Allport, in *The Nature of Prejudice* (1954), gives this example:

MR. X: The trouble with Jews is that they only take care of their own group.

MR. Y: But the record of the Community Chest campaign shows that they give more generously, in proportion to their numbers, to the general charities of their community than do non-Jews.

MR. X: That shows they are always trying to buy favor and intrude into Christian affairs. They think of nothing but money, that is why there are so many Jewish bankers.

MR. Y: But a recent study shows that the percentage of Jews in the banking business is negligible, far smaller than the percentage of non-Jews.

MR. X: That's just it: they don't go in for respectable businesses. They are only in the movie business or run night clubs.

If a stereotype is widely accepted it can have lasting effects on the group so stereotyped. One study, done in the days before the recent black pride movement, showed that black children, even as young as three years old, felt that whiteness was superior. For instance, they rejected black dolls in favor of white and classified the white dolls as better than the black (Clark & Clark, 1947).

Jane Elliot did a study on the effects of prejudice. A teacher announced to her class that brown-eyed people were superior to blue-eyed people (more intelligent, better behaved). Brown-eyed children were given many more privileges. Blue-eyed children had to sit in the back of the room, wait at the end of lines. Blue-eyed children began to falter at their lessons and described themselves in negative terms, for example, bad, sad, stupid. The brown-eyed children had become nasty, vicious, discriminating little third graders. The next day, Elliot said she had made a mistake: in fact, blue-eyed people were superior. The moods and actions of the two groups reversed. Friendships that had previously existed between brown- and blue-eyed children vanished and were replaced with hostility. On the third day, she told the students what she had done and reassured them they were all equal (Elliot, 1977).

In our society, there has long been a stereotype that women are intellectually inferior to men. In one study, male college students were asked to judge the accomplishments of highly successful physicians, male and female. Even though the accomplishments were equal, the males rated the females as less competent than the males (Feldman-Summers & Kiesler, 1974). Women also seemed to believe the female stereotype. A number of female students were asked to read several scholarly articles and to evaluate them. The articles were signed by either John T. McKay or Joan T. McKay. The articles were rated more highly when written by John than by Joan (Goldberg, 1968).

Some Causes (and Some Cures, Perhaps) of Prejudice

Although there is certainly a tendency to simplify and oversimplify the world and those in it, prejudice arises more regularly in certain situations and in certain groups.

Conformity.   People want to fit in well with the groups they belong to. One way to fit in well is to adopt and conform to many of the existing attitudes of that group without questioning or examining them. Many of the "attitudes" are prejudices.

Conformity of attitude can also work to reduce prejudice. When prejudiced people join less prejudiced groups, they adopt more tolerant attitudes. Army recruits from the South showed less prejudice to blacks after spending time with less prejudiced recruits from the North (Pettigrew, 1961). Another way to reduce prejudice is to increase contact with the prejudged group. *The more you know about someone, the less likely you are to make sweeping judgments about him or her.* This fact holds true in our judgments about groups of people. Because society has become less segregated in the past thirty years, we should expect less prejudice towards blacks. Indeed, there is less prejudice among people in public housing, where black and white families live together, than among people who live in segregated areas (Jahoda & West, 1951; Works, 1961).

Prejudice seems to be reduced through increased contact with members of the prejudged group, as happens when black firefighters and white firefighters work closely together.

Competition and Conflict within a Group. When there is intense competition for limited resources, prejudice and discrimination are likely to flourish. Greely and Sheatsly (1971) found that the strongest antiblack prejudice was found in people who were one step above blacks on the socioeconomic scale, and it was most severe especially when the two were in close competition for jobs.

One interesting study shows both how prejudice can develop and how it might be changed (Sherif, Harvey, White, Hood, & Sherif, 1961). Twenty-two boys who came to summer camp at Robbers Grave, Oklahoma, were divided into two different groups, the "eagles" and the "rattlers." Each group was encouraged to cooperate and to work together as a team toward goals, such as making improvements to the camp grounds. The first phase of the experiment was then to create strong group affiliation and cohesion of a random grouping of individuals.

Once each group had become a cohesive unit, they were pitted against one another in competitive sports events. Initially, the boys showed good sportsmanship, but gradually there arose resentment, hostility, and discrimination between the teams.

In the second phase of the experiment, the goal was to decrease the ill will between the groups. Simply eliminating competition did not work. The experimenters found that when both groups worked together toward a common goal, hostility decreased, cooperation and fellowship increased. Once a truck broke down and all the campers were needed to tow it up a hill (pulling on a large rope). The cooperative effort probably reduced the feelings of differences between the groups and allowed the two groups to share a sense of accomplishment and to discover similarities in each other.

Cooperative Interdependence

A systematic attempt to use the principle of cooperation is called *cooperative interdependence*. Cook and his colleagues used the principle of cooperative interdependence with groups of young, white, rural southerners and blacks. The principle is that prejudice will fade when two separate groups meet each other in a close relationship, as equals, with shared goals and the need to cooperate to achieve them. (Contact with out-group members is not sufficient, interdependence is necessary. A black janitor in an all-white building would not reduce racial prejudice. Black and white tenants working together to pull off a rent strike would.) They engaged small, mixed groups to work in a management-training game. The situation was "running a railroad." The object was to keep the business running well. Participants had to fill various jobs—communications, shipping, equipment maintenance. In each of the groups a confederate was planted, in some cases white, in some cases black. The idea was to find out how well the confederate was liked or disliked and why. Cook hypothesized that attraction to the confederate might be based on several factors:

1. The success or failure of the group efforts
2. The competence level of the minority person's behavior
3. A subject's participation in decision making

4. The race of the confederate
5. A subject's opportunity to help a minority group member

The most consistent factor in reducing prejudice was the success or failure of the group. The more successful the group, the more the confederate was liked, whether or not the person was black or white (Blanchard, Adelman, & Cook, 1975; Blanchard, Weigel, & Cook, 1975).

Another systematic attempt at reducing prejudice through cooperation is the "jigsaw classroom technique," developed by Eliot Aronson. Classrooms often stress individual competition. Here the stress is on interdependence. Students are divided into groups. Each group is assigned a project and each member of the group is given information about one part of the assignment, one puzzle piece. The only way the assignment can be completed is if each member teaches and shares his or her information with the others. Thus, each person is an important and invaluable resource. In addition, the teacher gives grades based on group cooperation rather than individual effort (Aronson, 1984).

Thus, two major psychological principles can work to reduce prejudice:

1. Stereotypes can be overcome by increasing the availability of information about the groups and especially by increasing direct knowledge of a variety of individuals within the group.
2. Association and cooperation with members of a discriminated group as equals.

ATTRIBUTION

The reasons we give for our own or others' behavior are called **attribution,** as in "To what do you *attribute* your success?" There are, broadly, two kinds of attribution:

Dispositional: We judge that a person does something because of who he or she is.

Situational: A person does something because of his or her situation.

For example, Olympic decathlon winner Bruce Jenner in a television commercial promotes a certain camera. You may wonder what caused him to do this. Does he *really* think the camera is terrific or was he paid a large amount of money to make the commercial? An attribution to the former proposition is *dispositional* and an attribution to the latter is *situational.*

Discounting and Covariance

What do we base attributions on? Harold Kelley (1967), in his *attribution theory,* argues that we use one of two logical rules. The first is the **discounting principle,** used in cases where you are forced to attribute the behavior of a single person in a single situation on a single occasion. For example, in the case of Bruce Jenner's endorsement of a camera: If you explain his behavior using the discounting principle, you discount the importance of any causal factors to the extent that other plausible causes or determinants can be identified. For example, if you find that a situational factor constitutes a "sufficient" explanation for behavior, no dispositional attribution will be made.

Thus, if you discover that Jenner was paid a large sum of money for the commercial, you may conclude that this (situational) factor is reason enough for his behavior. If, on the other hand, his endorsement occurred in spite of situational forces, you would make a dispositional attribution. If, for example, Bruce Jenner did the commercial for free, you may infer that a *disposition,* his delight with the camera, caused his behavior.

A second principle, the **covariation principle,** is used in cases where we have multiple observations rather than a single one. For example, you may have observed Bruce Jenner in a number of commercials talking about a variety of products. In this case, you apply the covariation principle by assessing the degree to which his behavior occurs in the presence of, but fails in the absence of, each possible cause. Accordingly, if you note that he always says positive things when he is paid large sums of money, but never says positive things when he is not paid money, you might infer that money was the cause of his behavior.

Errors in Attribution

One of the most frequent errors in attribution is called the **fundamental attribution error** (Ross, 1977). This is the tendency to underestimate the impact of situational forces and to overestimate the role of dispositional forces in controlling behavior. For instance, Jones and Harris (1967) found that listeners were willing to attribute a subject's pro-Castro statement to that subject's private opinions even when the listeners knew he was being influenced by a situational force (he was reading a prepared speech given him by the experimenter). Another example is people's reaction to the Milgram experiment cited earlier. Most people, perhaps you included, are stunned by the results of this study primarily because they infer that the "teachers" who gave the maximum amount of punishment were dispositionally "evil." What the experiment actually demonstrates, however, is that the behavior was almost totally controlled by situational forces and *pressures.*

Milgram Experiment on Obedience to Authority See pp. 625–27.

A particular type of situational force that individuals commonly overlook when making attributions are how social roles determine behavior. Social roles typically are unequal in situations; the dominant one is usually "in control." This control allows a person to display knowledge or skills while concealing various deficiencies. In these situations, people overgeneralize and make dispositional rather than situational attributions. In an important demonstration of this, Ross, Amabile, and Steinmetz (1977) set up an experiment in which one subject was randomly assigned the role of "questioner" in a "college bowl" quiz and one subject was assigned the role of "answerer." The questioner was asked to compose a set of challenging questions from his or her store of knowledge and to pose these questions to the answerer. Later, both subjects were asked to rate the general knowledge of both the questioner and answerer.

Before looking at the results of this experiment, note that the questioner had an advantage in this situation—being able to *display* his or her own "wealth of knowledge" by composing difficult questions to which he or she knew the answers. (It is always easier to make up difficult questions than to answer them.) The role also guaranteed that the questioner could *conceal* his or her lack of knowledge in many other areas. The answerer, on the other hand, was prevented any such display. Did the subjects make allowance for this "role-based situational cause" of behavior? No. They overlooked it and inferred instead that *the questioner was smarter than the answerer*. They made a *dispositional* rather than a *situational* attribution.

Reasons for the Fundamental Attribution Error

Although one would not expect it, given the formal rules of attribution theory, there is a difference between attributions about one's self and others in at least some situations. One explanation calls on Tversky's principle of availability; it emphasizes the differing *information available* to the individual (actor) performing a behavior and an observer witnessing that behavior. For example, the actor knows what he or she is thinking at that moment and knows extensive details of his or her past history (e.g., how he or she has behaved in the situation in the past). The observer is unaware of this information. This difference in information in turn can produce the differing tendency to commit the fundamental attribution error. In an example of this, Nisbett and Ross (1981) demonstrated that the more well known an actor is to an observer (and presumably the more the observer knows about that actor's thoughts, feelings, and background), the more likely the observer is to attribute the actor's behavior to situational rather than dispositional causes. This implies that the more information we have to base our attributions on, the less likely we are to make the fundamental attribution error.

False Consensus

False consensus is another error. It is the tendency of individuals to *overestimate the commonness of their own responses in a situation and to underestimate the commonness of the responses of others who acted differently* (Ross, Greene, & House, 1977). In one study, subjects were asked to complete a questionnaire containing such questions as "Are you shy?" "Where do you prefer to live?" When asked to estimate the percentage of people who responded as did they on each question, subjects overestimated the percentage of people who agreed.

One explanation of this error emphasizes the biased information available to each person. Much of our knowledge about the behavior of others comes from those we know and associate with. But we tend to know and associate with people who share our interests, background, and attitudes. These people usually do respond as we do in a large number of circumstances. Given this biased sample of information about the

Availability Principle See Chapter 10, pp. 371–72.

behavior of others, it is not surprising that we believe our behavior to be more common and representative than it actually is. Thus, according to Ross,

> the specific behaviors we have chosen, or would choose, are likely to be more readily retrievable from memory and more easily imagined than opposite behavior. In Kahneman and Tversky's . . . terms, the behavior choices we favor may be more cognitively "available," and we are apt to be misled by this ease or difficulty of access in estimating the likelihood of relevant behavioral options. (Ross, 1977)

Why Do We Make Errors in Attribution?

Occasionally the attributions people make are different from those they would make if they used the principles of discounting and covariation. Why? One obvious answer is that using these rules requires more resources and information than the individual usually has. The discounting rule requires that we have extensive knowledge of characteristics of individuals and the impact of specific situational factors such as money, social roles, and so on. We seek simple and quick judgments of everything and this information burden is just too much. It also requires a lot of time to sift through all the alternatives. In an experiment, people are usually given sufficient information and time, but in life we usually have neither. An attribution about Bruce Jenner's behavior, for instance, is a snap judgment about someone you do not know much about. You do not know how much he was paid, what he was thinking, or whether he uses the camera.

The covariation rule has similar limitations: it requires an individual to perform a logical and statistical task. However, in life we do not have all the relevant information. There are many possible causes for each of the many behaviors we witness each day. When judging a celebrity endorsement, we do not know how he has acted in other situations, how he has acted in the same situation on other occasions, or even how other people have acted in that situation. Because of the lack of information and the principle of simplicity, we rely on the available information which may be biased or unrepresentative.

So we follow the *same* principles in making judgments of others as we do everything else. We *select* and *simplify* and use the information *available* to come to the best quick assessment. We use comparison and interpretation. That most of us seem successful in our ordinary judgments for the most part indicates that the simplifying system probably helps us more than it hurts. Psychologists are, of course, interested in the errors and distortions because they allow us to study the process of judgment and attribution.

AGGRESSION AND VIOLENCE

Aggression is intentionally harming another. The injury caused by aggression can be psychological, due to verbal abuse, for example, as well as physical (Bandura, 1979). Aggression is an attribution as well as

an act. Whether one judges an act to be aggressive depends on one's values, and this, in turn, partly depends on one's culture and one's place in it. For instance, some types of harm-causing behavior, such as self-defense, are almost universally considered legitimate and not "aggressive." The harm caused by favored members of society is usually attributed to accident or circumstance; when harm is caused by disfavored members, to personal intent. (Bandura, 1979) A peace march may be considered "nonviolent protest" or "aggressive provocation," depending on the interpretation.

It is possible to distinguish two basic types of aggression. *Hostile aggression* is motivated by anger or hatred and is intended only to make the victim suffer. *Instrumental aggression* is motivated by an incentive, usually economic. The victim may be injured incidentally, as when a purse snatcher causes an old lady to fall, breaking her hip. Undoubtedly, hostile and instrumental aggression are often combined in the same act.

Approaches to Aggression

Freud

Freud held that aggression is an instinct. He called it *Thanatos* or the death instinct: a destructive energy that accumulates until it is discharged either inwardly, as in self-destructive behavior, or outwardly, in the destruction of others. He believed that, as an instinct, aggression could never be eliminated from human beings. "The aim of life," he wrote, "is death." As with other instincts, our innate aggression was more useful in days before settled society, when killing one's enemies was important for survival. Civilization puts curbs on aggression and makes it necessary for us to redirect these instinctual urges.

Ethology

Like Freud, ethologists contend that aggression is instinctive. A complex theory of aggression is proposed by Lorenz (1966) and others. Their analysis, simplified, is as follows: In animals, aggression is most often directed at other species. Animals have evolved innate *inhibitions* against fatal aggression toward members of their *own* species. These inhibitions involve either behavior patterns or physical characteristics, such as coloration, which "turn off" an aggressor before he can do serious damage. *The strength of the inhibition corresponds to the strength of a species' offensive weapons.* Thus, wolves, as predators, are well equipped for violence and also possess strong inhibitions against killing other wolves.

However, the human inheritance has provided us with very weak "natural" instruments of physical aggression. We are weak for our size and we do not have the strength of a tiger, the jaws of a shark. Since we inherit weak weapons, we also *inherit weak inhibitions* on personal aggression. However, human beings, as we have seen, go beyond their inheritance. We have invented weapons that are vastly more destructive than any inherited ones. But we have not evolved corresponding inhibitions. Our lack of inhibition against violence toward members of our own species explains why, under the circumstances, we have become so dangerous to ourselves. A whole city can be destroyed by the push of a button by someone in an underground fortification, for whom a few million people are only a point on a map.

Appeasement behavior in wolves, such as assuming a submissive posture, inhibits fatal aggression within the species. (After Schenkel, 1967)

Social Learning Theory

According to *social learning theory,* there is no aggressive instinct (Bandura, 1979). The biological basis of aggression is the same as that of all learning. Organisms, especially human beings, have the ability to learn vicariously, by observing the behavior of models, especially people who are perceived as important controllers of reward and punishment (Bandura, 1977). Thus, nonaggressive models are useful in reducing aggression in others (Baron & Kepner, 1970) and appear to be more effective than threats of retaliation. Threatened punishment works to subdue aggression, but only if certain conditions are satisfied:

1. The instrumental value of the aggression is low. [There is little to be gained by aggression.]
2. The threatened punishment is severe.
3. The potential aggressor understands that punishment is highly likely.
4. The potential aggressor is not awfully angry (Baron, 1977).

Aggressive behavior is not elicited merely by learning how to do it, but by rewards and punishments, both experienced and anticipated, on the basis of what the learners observe to be the consequences of others' behavior, as well as of theirs (Bandura, 1973).

Factors That Affect Aggressive Response

1. *Arousal.* In addition to incentives and provocation, environmental factors that affect *arousal* also can influence the likelihood of aggressive behavior. Physiological arousal increases the probability of aggression,

but only when aggression has become a dominant response (Zillman, Johnson, & Day, 1974). A high level of sexual arousal increases aggression, and a low level inhibits it, presumably by simply distracting attention from the provocation (Bandura, 1973).

2. *Crowding* is an intensifier of feelings, pleasant or unpleasant. If one is in an aggressive mood, crowding is likely to make one feel more aggressive (Freedman, 1975).

3. *Noise* increases the chance of aggressive behavior when aggression is dominant in the response hierarchy (Bandura, 1973).

4. *High temperatures* also facilitate violence. The long, hot summer has been implicated in the precipitation of urban riots. Riots occur relatively more frequently in very hot weather (Carlsmith & Anderson, 1979).

5. *Alcohol* in small amounts tends to reduce aggression, while larger amounts make aggression more likely (Taylor, Gammon, & Capasso, 1976).

6. *Marijuana* in large amounts inhibits aggression (Taylor, Vardaris, Rawitch, Gammon, Cranston, & Lubetkin, 1976).

7. *Tranquilizers*, surprisingly, do not lessen aggressive behavior. In fact, they may even increase it. Since tranquilizing drugs seem to work by interfering with the transmission of the neurotransmitter norepinephrine, which is associated with general arousal, they provide evidence that aggression is not a function of mere arousal. *Cognitive mediation* of arousal, how we *interpret* our physiological state, is crucial (Bandura, 1977; Schachter & Singer, 1962).

There are also personality differences in aggression. Comparatively low aggression is found among people with a high need for social approval (Taylor, 1970). People who feel that they have some control over what happens to them (internal locus of control) are more likely to use aggression instrumentally—as a means to an end—than are those who feel that they cannot affect what happens to them no matter what they do. Persons with Type A personalities—highly competitive "driven" types—exhibit more aggression when strongly provoked than Type B personalities (Carver & Glass, 1977).

Situations That Affect Aggression

Through observation, we learn a great deal about situations and behaviors without ever having been in them. A "role" is a pattern of behavior that is determined by the situation. Examples are waiter, housewife, boss. When placed in a situation, we know how to play the roles we have learned. Sometimes our roles can be destructive.

A Study of Prisons

In one of psychology's most important studies, Philip Zimbardo sought to investigate the degree to which behavior can be situationally determined. He simulated a "prison" in the basement of the psychology building at Stanford University (Haney, Banks, & Zimbardo, 1973; Zimbardo, 1972). He randomly assigned male students to the roles of prisoner and guard. The local police even cooperated by picking up the prisoners in squad cars, complete with siren. Prisoners were treated realistically. They were fingerprinted, stripped, "skin searched" and given demeaning uniforms. The uniforms were dresses, with no underclothing, intended to "emasculate" the male prisoners. The prisoners also wore a chain locked around one ankle. Guards were also uniformed, and they were given handcuffs, cell and gate keys, and billy clubs, even though physical violence was prohibited. The guards were told to maintain "law and order" and to be stern with the prisoners.

Soon the experiment took an unsettling turn. Some of the guards identified with their roles and began to enjoy their power over the prisoners. The prisoners rebelled at first, but after the rebellion was put down, the guards became more aggressive and the prisoners became more passive. Five prisoners were released early because of their severe anxiety and rage reactions. The experiment had to be terminated after only six days, rather than the two weeks originally scheduled, due to the distress of the prisoners.

The guards, on the other hand, were disappointed with the early termination of the experiment. They quickly grew to enjoy their power roles. Outside the situation the guards were normal, nondestructive people, as measured by standard psychological tests, but the apparently complete power over the prisoners resulted in arrogant, aggressive, and cruel behavior.

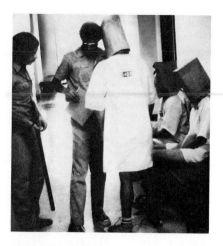

FIGURE 18–4
The Stanford "Prison" Study
Students playing their roles as prisoners and guards in the "prison" in the basement of the psychology building at Stanford University.

This all being an experiment, the "prisoners" could have left. They did not, having assumed the role of a weak and submissive prisoner, accepting punishment.

However, not *all* the guards behaved in a "corrupt" manner. Only one-third were described as "quite inventive in their techniques of breaking the spirit of the prisoners." The rest were described as "tough but fair" or "good guards from the prisoner's point of view since they did small favors and were friendly" (Zimbardo, 1972).

Prisoners in Nazi concentration camps showed an interesting difference from Zimbardo's subjects. Among them, middle-class prisoners without strong beliefs fared worst. They claimed their imprisonment was a mistake. They groveled and were unable to oppose any of the actions of their oppressors. "The SS made fun of them and mistreated them badly" (Bettelheim, 1960). Those who were explicitly political prisoners were much better able to maintain self-respect, because they had *expected* persecution.

Earlier we saw that Milgram also demonstrated the willingness of ordinary people to harm others. How can we learn to avoid doing harm? Two important possibilities are provided by social learning theory and ethology:

1. Through observation we can learn not only such antisocial but also **prosocial behavior.** For instance, the presence of two *disobedient models* eliminated the obedience of most subjects in Milgram's experiment (Milgram, 1974).

2. Ethologists believe that the more closely we observe the suffering of others, the less likely we are to harm them. In the Milgram experiment if the "teachers" heard more of the suffering of the

FIGURE 18–5
Environment and Aggression
A car abandoned in New York City, as part of an experiment in the motives for vandalism, began being stripped within minutes by various people, starting with a "respectable" middle-class family. When a car was similarly abandoned on a street in Palo Alto, California—a much smaller urban area—it went untouched for a week.

"students" the level of the maximum shock they delivered tended to be lower. The closer they were, the less they would shock the "students" (Milgram, 1974).

Another important determinant of violence is city size: large cities are more prone to violence and crime than small cities and rural areas (Fischer, 1976). Does this mean that city violence is due to the large number of violence-prone individuals who dwell in cities?

A member of a large crowd may tend to act with less inhibition than an individual alone. Similarly, residents of large cities seem more likely to indulge in vandalism than those who live in less urban areas. Zimbardo (1973) demonstrated this by abandoning a car in New York City (large urban) and a similar car in Palo Alto, California (small urban). In New York, the car was systematically looted and vandalized, beginning within 10 minutes. Surprisingly, this violence was not started by juvenile delinquents, but by a middle-class family who methodically stripped the car of valuable parts. In Palo Alto, however, the car stood untouched for a week, except for one thoughtful passerby who lowered the hood to prevent the engine from getting wet during a rainstorm. Zimbardo did not conclude that New Yorkers are inherently more violent than Californians, but that large, urban environments disinhibit aggression.

Criminals

For some people, violence is a way of life. There are relatively few such people, but they make their numbers felt by being involved in much of the total violence. Such people are *undercontrolled aggressors* or, simply, violent people (Megargee, 1966).

In an innovative study, Hans Toch (1969) had prisoners and parolees interview other prisoners and parolees who had a history of violence. As a result of this research, Toch was able to separate violence-prone individuals into types defined by the goals or reasons served by violence. Pleasure in hurting others is the motive of only quite a small percentage of the sample of violent men. The pattern most frequently encountered is that of men who engage in violence to compensate for feelings of inferiority—to promote or defend their self-image.

Career Criminals

Career criminals may have come to their "profession" early in life. Criminologist Frank Schmalleger put the formative years of the criminal in these terms:

> Criminality is an attitude toward life that, more often than not, begins in youth, generally in the preteens or early teen years. Many of the inmates I have met have been in trouble nearly all of their lives. When interviewed, they recall that as children they craved excitement. Constantly seeking thrills, they saw most other children as weak, and they now see conforming adults in the same light.

It is quite important to note, contrary to the saying, that crime *does usually pay*. The chances of even the habitual criminal avoiding prison are 300 to 1 for small crimes and 100 to 1 for more serious ones (Schmalleger,

1979). Yet even prison is hardly a deterrent to a criminal. Career criminals expect to be caught eventually. Prison is sometimes thought of as a vacation, or just an "occupational hazard." Many feel that even with the certainty of a prison term, the "costs" are still low enough relative to the benefits to make the criminal occupation worthwhile.

The career criminal often finds the idea of geting a job abhorrent: he has one already. Naturally, there are differences among criminals in skills and status. Those who have a real skill—for example, safecracking—and are exposed to danger are most highly regarded. Schmalleger (1979) goes on to suggest that, since criminality is a world view, the only way to change the criminal into a conformist is by a process similar to religious conversion—a total change induced by forcing the criminal to face the consequences of his or her antisocial behavior pattern.

Television and Violence

Since television is so available to all, any situation it portrays is amplified. There have been many instances of violence, some of it quite brutal, which were imitated from televison. Television is a violent place and the content of programs exaggerates the amount of crime in society. The viewing of so much crime has its effects: the heavy television viewer perceives society as more violent than the light viewer (Gerbner & Gross, 1976).

Adults as well as children appear to learn violent behavior from television. The wide television exposure of the first airplane hijacking in the United States was followed by a large number of hijackings in only a few years (Bandura, 1979). In one case, a child was found putting ground glass in his parents' dinner to see if it would work as well as it did on television (Liebert & Baron, 1972). When Tylenol was laced with cyanide, a series of other tamperings and poisonings followed. Even Halloween candy was doctored.

The airing of the program "The Doomsday Flight," which involved a bomb threat to an airliner, was followed by twelve bomb threats to airlines in a week. This was an 800 percent increase from the previous

Career criminals form tight-knit groups within prison society that are characterized by a camaraderie much like that of fraternal organizations. Criminal attitudes are reinforced within these groups, and many associations formed in prison continue after inmates are released.

month. When the show appeared in Australia, one airliner was threatened with a bomb threat (Liebert, & Baron, 1972).

The exact imitation of aggressive models on television has also been observed in the laboratory. Children who observed an adult beat up a bobo doll imitated the behavior almost exactly when given the opportunity (Bandura, Ross, & Ross, 1961). The photographs in Figure 1–3 (Bandura film) indicate the extent of the imitation. When the aggressive model was on film, or even when the aggression was performed by a cartoon character, the children exhibited the same amount of violence. Comparable results have been obtained from older children and young adults viewing movies of actual violence or television programs. The viewing of violent programs, as indicated in many studies, increases the general aggressiveness of the viewers. (Baron 1977).

The exact imitation of an aggressive model on television is comparatively rare. However, continuous observation of aggressive models as on television can lead to more *generalized* aggressiveness (Bandura, 1979). This is accomplished by such mechanisms as:

1. Increasing arousal, especially among children (Osborn & Endsley, 1971).
2. Lowering restraint, making aggression more likely in conjunction with provocation or an aggressive model.
3. Desensitization: Adults who view a lot of violent television have a lower physiological response to violent scenes than those who watch less violence.

Television *itself* cannot be directly blamed for violent behavior. The *content* of television programs responds to demand: programs with aggression and violence are popular. However, there have been many studies and reports of the effect of television on violence, and the relationship of televised violence to social violence is clear: televised violence does increase the probability of violent behavior among viewers.

LIVING IN SOCIETY

So far we have discussed how others affect our attitudes and behavior. In this section we will examine how groups work and how the society affects our experience.

Many of the factors that affect our lives are outside our personal control. If you were born after the invention of the atom bomb, and after the invention of television, you have only known a world quite different from that of someone in 1900. Margaret Mead called the postwar generations "immigrants in time," because the rapid rate of change today forces us all to face a new world and make up new rules to live by.

The world we have created affects us: the shape of buildings we live in affects us. The size of the city we live in determines how fast we walk and talk. Decisions made by governments affect the ages at which we can vote, drink, drive. Every day we face very large-scale problems we did not, individually, create. We are running out of energy, becoming overcrowded and dehumanized; there is violence in the streets of our cities and the threat of war. The sheer numbers of people are forcing us all to lead very different lives.

Groups

You may be a college student and a member of a film club, a diet group, a political discussion society, and more groups, all at once. Our social reality is altered by the people we meet and the groups we belong to. Indeed, life is enhanced and enriched by the groups we are a part of. Groups usually intensify experience for better and for worse; they can make our opinions more extreme, make it less likely that we will help someone, encourage us to loaf instead of work, and turn a set of individuals into a mob.

Groups and Attitudes

People are *more* likely to take risks in groups than while alone. This phenomenon is called **risky shift** or the *extremity shift*. Suppose you, like the subjects in one study, (Kogan & Wallach, 1967) were given this problem:

> Mr. E. is president of a metals corporation in the United States. The corporation is quite prosperous and Mr. E. has considered the possibility of expansion by building an additional plant in a new location. His choice is between building another plant in the United States, where there would be a moderate return on the initial investment, or building a plant in a foreign country, where lower labor costs and easy access to raw materials would mean a much higher return on the initial investment. However, there is a history of political instability and revolution in the foreign country under consideration. In fact, the leaders of a small minority party are committed to nationalizing, that is, taking over all foreign investments.
>
> Imagine that you are advising Mr. E. Listed below are several probabilities of continued political stability in the foreign country under consideration. Please check the *lowest* probability that you would consider acceptable in order for Mr. E.'s corporation to build in that country.
>
> The chances are 1 in 10 that the foreign country will remain politically stable.
>
> The chances are 3 in 10 that the foreign country will remain politically stable.
>
> The chances are 5 in 10 that the foreign country will remain politically stable.
>
> The chances are 7 in 10 that the foreign country will remain politically stable.
>
> The chances are 9 in 10 that the foreign country will remain politically stable.
>
> Place a check here if you think Mr. E.'s corporation should not build a plant in the foreign country, no matter what the probabilities.

After listening to the problem, everyone made individual decisions, then they were brought together as a group. In one group, two people had chosen 9 in 10, two 7 in 10, and two, 5 in 10. After the discussion the unanimous decision was for 5 in 10. The decision had shifted to the most extreme of the choices, and the most "risky" position.

Group discussions tend to *magnify* initial attitudes, as well. In one study, a group of prejudiced and unprejudiced high school students were tested on their attitudes toward issues such as property rights and open housing. Then the students were put in discussion groups with like-minded people; when questioned again after the discussion, the differences in attitude between the two groups increased (Myers & Lamm, 1975).

One important factor in the change of opinion in groups is social comparison. People want to be thought of positively and will modify their opinions to become liked. In one experiment, subjects were shown "sneak previews" of others' opinions. When the opinions of others were known, the subjects changed their own opinion in the *more extreme direction*. Thus a snowball effect of opinion change is created. Groups can take on a life of their own.

In a series of studies designed to determine the underlying effect of being in a group, (Darley & Latané, 1968), people were asked to enter a booth in which they sat alone and listened to a discussion by college students. Although the subject did not know it, the discussion was on tape. In the first part of the discussion, one of the "discussants" said he was epileptic. During the discussion, the subject heard what clearly sounded like an epileptic seizure.

Darley and Latané changed one variable in the different conditions of the experiment: in some cases the person in the booth thought he was the only one listening to the discussion; in others the person in the booth thought he was part of a group of three, in another, a group of six. The effects (see Figure 18–6) were, unfortunately, startling: 85 percent of those who believed that they were the only other discussant tried to help the epileptic immediately by reporting it to the experimenter; 60 percent of those in a three-person group tried to help. Only 30 percent of those in six-person groups notified the experimenter. It is not the supposed "apathy" of others that stops us from helping, it is a group effect: we believe that someone else must be doing something about the emergency.

As you can see, this laboratory situation was similar to the Kitty Genovese situation. The 38 onlookers must have thought that someone else had called the police, so there was no reason to get involved.

Another way groups prevent us from helping was demonstrated by Latané and Rodin (1969). They hypothesized that the behavior of others helps us define a situation. A subject sitting alone in a waiting room hears noises in the adjoining room—someone climbing on a chair to reach something—then he hears a crash and a woman moaning and groaning in pain. Of the subjects who were alone, 70 percent rushed to the woman's aid. When the same scenario was played out when two subjects were waiting, the figure dropped to 40 percent. Apparently each had waited for the other to define the situation as an emergency. Indeed, it has been found that once a situation is so defined (that is, someone stops to help), others are more likely to stop and offer assistance (Bryan and Test, 1967).

FIGURE 18–6
Groups and Individual Responsibility
When subjects of the experiment charted below thought they were alone, most took action to help a person seeming to have a seizure. Far fewer subjects took action when they believed they were part of a group that had witnessed the victim's plight. (After Darley & Latané, 1968)

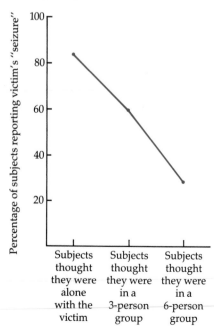

Social Loafing

When people are asked to perform physically exerting tasks like clapping and shouting, they do them much less vigorously in groups than alone. Latané and his colleagues (1980) measured the intensity of the noise produced by people alone and in groups: it decreases when group size increases. The average sound generated per person decreases with group size. In studies of behavior in society, these same effects have been found. Factory workers produce less per person in larger groups than in smaller ones (Campbell, 1963). The proportion of members taking part in church activities is lower in large than in small churches (Wicker, 1969).

Thus, we have a great potential for loafing. Some political ideologies unwittingly seem to maximize this potential. In Russia large numbers work in one field after another, day after day, and have no "sense of responsibility and no direct dependence on the results of their labor" (Smith, 1976). However, each man is also given a one-acre plot of land that he and his family may work on their own. These plots account for less than 1 percent of the total land yet they produce 27 percent of the produce (Smith, 1976).

This productivity problem is not limited to communist countries. People in small companies work harder and feel more personal loyalty and satisfaction than people in large corporations. One lesson to learn from this is to keep work and social groups as small as possible to maximize efficiency. Volvo Corporation in Sweden has begun to change how an automobile is made. Instead of a large assembly line where each person is responsible only for one small task, workers are divided into small groups who work together (as in the jigsaw classroom technique) to complete an engine or other major component. When groups are designed to intensify responsibility rather than alienation or loafing, they become more efficient. (On the other hand, if you want an easy job . . .)

Judith Rodin

Crowding

Your "self" extends beyond your body. Anything that we control we consider part of us (Miller, 1980). For instance, when someone hits our car, we say "he hit *my* rear end" not "the car's rear end." The space around us, somehow, becomes part of us.

The space we live in is also a medium of communication. How close we approach another person may indicate what culture we come from, how much we like the other person, and whether our meeting is casual or for business. Too many people in the same space produces crowding and loss of privacy, but both individuals and cultures differ on what is "too many people."

Personal Space

Edward T. Hall wrote, "We treat space somewhat as we treat sex. It is there but we don't talk about it." Hall developed a method of analysis called **proxemics,** which makes our spatial habits explicit. This analysis begins with the concept of *personal space,* which Hall defines as a "small, protective sphere or bubble that an organism maintains between itself and others." *Individual distance,* by contrast, is the basic minimum distance members of species keep between themselves. The maintenance of a fixed individual distance seems innate in most animals, but is different in different human cultures. Such distance is classified in four basic types (Hall, 1966):

Intimate: from actually touching to 18 inches
Personal: up to four feet
Social: four to twelve feet
Public: more than twelve feet

Distances that may be considered "invasions" depend on one's culture, and this can easily lead to misunderstandings. People from the Middle East and southern Europe interact with each other at close range, touching frequently and gazing intently into each other's eyes. North Americans and the English tend to find this very disconcerting. One person interacting with another whose cultural distance is less than his or her own can be driven across a room trying to avoid this "rude pursuer."

English and Americans also differ in their concept of "proper" space. The English are accustomed to less exclusive space than Americans, so they learn ways to enhance mutual privacy when they are with others. The technique of "reserve" serves this function. English people often speak quietly and diplomatically and interact less with the people in their immediate environment than do Americans (Hall, 1966).

Members of different cultures appear to need widely varying amounts of space. In Hong Kong, the world's most densely populated city, low-cost housing provides only 35 square feet of living space per person. One architect reports:

> When the construction supervisor of one Hong Kong project was asked what the effects of doubling the amount of floor area would be upon the living patterns, he replied, "with 60 square feet per person, the tenants would sublet!" (*American Institute of Planners Newsletter,* 1967)

Privacy

Privacy is the need to be alone when desired. We can enhance privacy by different means: *behavioral,* words and body language (the English we discussed above); *spatial* (a large house on spacious grounds is also favored by some of the English); or by *security measures* (locks and alarms).

Privacy is expressed in different ways, but it has a distinct meaning. Americans create physical barriers while, as we have seen, the English specialize more in psychological barriers. The Japanese developed the movable wall to make space multifunctional while preserving situational privacy (Hall, 1966).

The Experience of Crowding

Crowding is having more people around than one desires. It might seem that the experience of crowding would simply be a function of the number of people in a given amount of space—the population density (a physical measure of the number of people in a given area) (Aiello & Thompson, 1980; Freedman, 1975; Stokols, 1972). Yet this is not always the case. The *experience* of crowding depends on many factors: population density and the individual and social interpretation of that density.

The experience of crowding can be triggered in a number of ways, only some of which are related to density. The effect of density in social pathology has been studied in rats and mice (Calhoun, 1973). In an experimental situation, populations of these animals were allowed to increase without external restraint by predators, disease, or lack of food or water. These colonies grew rapidly at first, then leveled off, and finally declined. The mouse population eventually died out completely. In the process, several curious patterns developed. Dominant males staked out the favorable areas and the females in their territories produced more offspring than others. As population grew, territorial defense broke down, females became more aggressive in order to protect their litters, but maternal behavior and live births declined. A large population of nonreproducing females developed along with nonviolent and asexual males, which Calhoun called the "beautiful ones." They only ate, drank, slept, and groomed. When mice from this environment were transferred to one of low density, most could not establish a society or reproduce (Marsden, 1972).

Yet density was not the principal cause of this deterioration. Rather, as Calhoun notes, *"rate and quality of social interaction* are paramount issues. . . . Despite the thousandfold increase in human numbers since the beginning of culture, some forty to fifty thousand years ago, there has been no change in effective density" (Calhoun, 1973).

Responses to Population Density

When an animal population in the wild becomes too large, it suddenly may decline or "crash." For instance, the victims of a population crash among Sika deer were not sick or undernourished in general, but did have enlarged *adrenal glands*, indicating an extreme stress reaction (Christian, Flyger, & Davis, 1960). This is consistent with the evidence on other animals: the adrenals of lone mice in very small enclosures did not enlarge (Freedman, 1975).

The human response to density is much more flexible. Males and females may differ in response to density. In a laboratory setting, a mock jury deliberation, groups of women often became less aggressive—gave lighter sentences—in small rooms than in large ones, while men tended to do just the reverse (Freedman et al., 1972). Similar effects have been found for competition in all-girl and all-boy groups (Freedman et al., 1972). Although this type of relationship has not always been found, it has occurred often enough to suggest that men and women may respond differently to high-density situations.

In general, crowding *amplifies* what is occurring (as do other parts of our social life), whether this is positive or negative (Freedman, 1975). Parties and football games are crowded environments most of us seek out for pleasure—the excitement of the crowd increases ours. Going to a "crowded bar" after an irritating day at the office may result in a sudden lifting of bad mood. People who are put into situations that violate their distance preferences react physiologically and become less creative—less able to deal with complexity—than under preferred conditions (Aiello & Thompson, 1980).

The Built Environment: Buildings, Cities, and Growth on the Planet

"We shape our buildings, and thereafter our buildings shape us." When he said this, Winston Churchill was referring to the reconstruction of the sixteenth-century House of Commons. Commons was destroyed by bombing in World War II, and many in England wanted to reconstruct the building along more modern lines. Churchill, however, felt that the design of the building had, in some part, determined the course of British politics. The oblong shape of the Commons room encouraged the existence of two opposed parties with a number of leaders rather than just one, and encouraged confrontation rather than cooperation. The building was rebuilt and as it had been, brick by brick.

Although Churchill was speaking of a political institution, his observation that "our buildings shape us" is universally applicable. Our built environment has a profound effect on how well we live and work. Failure to recognize this can lead good intentions into disaster.

Buildings: Effect of Physical Structure on the Social Environment

The Pruitt-Igoe housing project in St. Louis was built in the 1950s as a radical new approach to improving life: it was intended to replace the slums of the black ghetto (Jacobs, 1959). It was assumed that new housing would automatically be better. So a large high-rise project was built

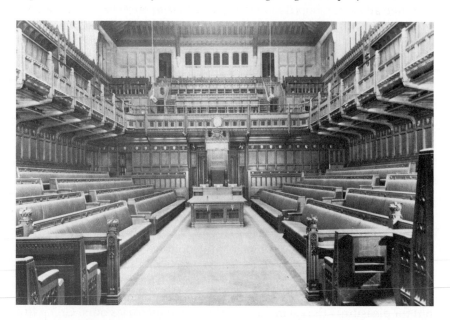

The British House of Commons

The Pruitt-Igoe Housing Project

that effectively, and instantly, "replaced" the slum, but without the benefits of the ghetto. Twenty years later, part of it was torn down because people would not live in it. Why?

Many housing projects contain design flaws that a knowledge of human needs and of the relationship of spatial arrangements to behavior could have prevented. *High rises are usually set off in an open space.* This seems like a good, humane idea at first glance. On closer inspection it is clearly the opposite. In poor neighborhoods, there is frequently a network of affiliation which makes an area a community, even if it is run-down. The streets are made relatively safe by the single fact that so many people are on them, especially if they contain a mix of dwellings and shops, and other people keep an eye on the street from their windows. In high rises with spacious grounds, full surveillance by occupants is not possible and from the fourth or fifth floor up probably would not be very effective anyway. The open spaces therefore become a "no man's land" in which people are justifiably afraid to walk (Jacobs, 1959).

Other problems are related to a *lack of surveillance.* High rises for the poor may have one elevator to serve a thousand people. It is not likely that you would be able to recognize all of your neighbors under these conditions, so criminals are less easily detected. The elevators and stairwells are also "blind" areas where crimes can be committed without much chance of detection and where children play without supervision (Newman, 1979).

However, the effects of the structure of buildings are not all bad. A graduate student housing complex at MIT helped to show that orientation of housing in space can *encourage* or *discourage social interaction.* The housing at MIT is arranged in U-shaped courts with most front doors facing other front doors. At the ends of the U, however, apartment doors opened out onto the street. There was a clear effect of the apartment location on friendship: the people who lived in the center apartments had twice as many friends as those who lived at the ends. The structures we build do shape us (Festinger, Schachter & Back, 1950).

FIGURE 18–7
Modifying the Built Environment
Before the Clason Point housing project in New York City was modified, the crime rate was rising and the buildings were deteriorating. The modification assigned parts of the grounds to the residents to treat as their own front and rear yards. This ended the totally open access from all directions and, along with other modifications and increased community interest that developed, contributed to lowering the crime rate and improving the residents' attitudes about both their built environment and their social environment. (After Newman, 1979)

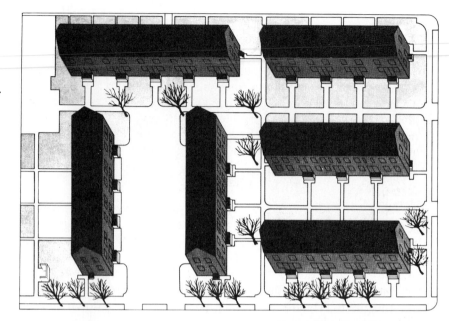

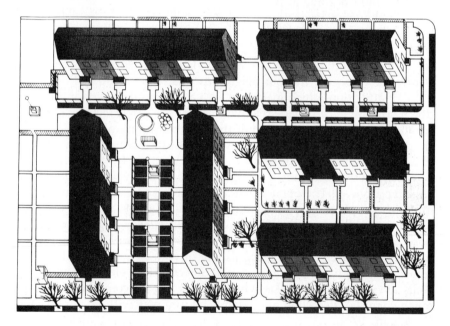

Cities

Increasing population, crowds, and attendant structures come together in a new entity: the city. Until the eighteenth century, even the moderately big city (500,000) was a rarity. Now cities are becoming huge, in area as well as population. Until the twentieth century, there had been only one predominantly urban nation, Great Britain. The United States has become an urban nation. One out of every three Americans lives in a city of over 100,000 people. The world is becoming an urban society.

Density

Why do we flock to the cities? One reason is purely economic. Easy access to services and economies of scale make concentration attractive to business and government; people come to the city for jobs or higher pay. Yet these are not the only attractions of cities. In cities, people create high-density situations intentionally, not only in formal institutions, but on the street, showing a higher preference for congested situations than noncity people. Cities are where most innovation occurs. From art to crime, the city is the center of creativity, diffusing its culture to an often reluctant countryside (Fischer, 1976).

Helping

The murder of Kitty Genovese and the studies of bystander intervention indicate that the greater the group size, the less likelihood of aid (Darley & Bateson, 1973). City people appear to be less willing to help strangers, probably due to fear (Milgram, 1970). City dwellers are less likely to speak to or establish eye contact with strangers than small town people are (Newman & McCauley, 1977).

Bystander Intervention   See p. 648 and Chapter 1, pp. 10–11.

Speed

The pace of cities is faster than that of other human environments. All over the world, city people walk faster than others. Also, density increases the amount of maneuvering necessary to avoid bumping into others, which could increase the pace experienced in cities (Milgram, 1970). People who live on busy streets engage in less social contact and are more dissatisfied with their homes than those who live on quiet streets. They also show more stress and withdrawal.

The Effects of Noise

Noise is unwanted sound (Farr, 1967). It does not have to come from airplanes or freeways. It can originate in the home from luxuries such as dishwashers, vacuum cleaners, and garbage disposals. Annoyance can be produced when sound is unexpected, interfering, inappropriate, intermittent, or reverberating. We are also much more tolerant of our own sounds than those of others (Farr, 1967). Under the high-density conditions of cities, other people's sounds are abundant and, even if they are not loud, can be unpleasant.

Cities are noisy places, especially given the predominance of machines. Noise can be harmful to the concentration and auditory discrimination of those who live near the noise source. In one study, children who lived on various floors of a high-rise built over an expressway were tested for auditory discrimination and reading skill. The children on the lower floors were exposed to a great deal of noise and had impaired hearing and reading (Cohen, Glass, & Singer, 1973).

The harmful effect of noise is not entirely due to its intensity. The unpleasantness of noise and its physiologically arousing effect are both reduced by partial *control* over the noise source. When subjects could turn the noise off, the noise itself did not seem so bad (Corah & Botta, 1970). A person's altered perception of noise is enough to reduce the negative effects even though control is seldom exercised (Glass & Singer,

1972). The effect of noise is reduced by making the noise *predictable*. This is why listening to familiar sounds, such as loud rock music, is not disruptive to the person who puts it on and *is* disruptive and annoying to parents or neighbors.

Institutions

A consequence of living in society is large organizations and institutions. Although the complex experience of our institutions is far beyond the scope of this book, we can concentrate on how a sense of personal control is important in many institutions.

Work

We do not just "produce" on the job. In a way a job produces us. For instance, a bureaucrat is anyone who works in an organization characterized by a *hierarchy of authority*, and bureaucrats are widely despised in our society—even though so much of society is bureaucratic—for being dull, rigid people. In an interesting study by Kohn (1971; 1978), quite the opposite was found to be the case. For the typical bureaucrat there are a number of employees of the organization above and below him or her in the hierarchy. Surprisingly, such people were more tolerant of nonconformity, more intellectually flexible, and more receptive to change than their nonbureaucratic counterparts. Educational differences account for some of this but not all.

Bureaucracies are complex, demanding work environments that require subtle decision making but also provide more job security than most other work places. Kohn (1978) concludes, "Bureaucracies allow their employees much more opportunity to exercise their ingenuity and their skills than is commonly understood."

The Unhappiness of Work

Work can also make people profoundly unhappy:

> Work is . . . about violence—to the spirit as well as to the body. It is about ulcers as well as accidents, about shouting matches as well as fistfights, about nervous breakdowns as well as kicking the dog around. It is, above all . . . about daily humiliations. (Terkel, 1975)

One way workers improve their quality of life is retaining some *control* and owning the factories they work in. Twenty percent of Sears Roebuck is owned by workers who participate in a profit-sharing program. In the worker-owned plywood mills of the Pacific Northwest, worker productivity is 26 to 43 percent higher than in others.

Some firms have endeavored to humanize the work environment. The Volvo plant at Kalmar, Sweden, has no assembly line but is organized in small separate groups with work areas that even have separate entrances. Noise has also been kept to a minimum. In this factory, absenteeism was one-fourth lower than in a Volvo factory of the same capacity that has an assembly line.

At the Ralston Purina pet food plant, jobs were expanded so that workers took part in much more of the production process than they did previously. Generally, work place reform involves:

1. Making the work place more pleasant physically
2. Involving workers in decision making
3. Organizing jobs in more meaningful units
4. Establishing team spirit by having workers organized in small groups
5. Making hours flexible

Summary

1. An important feature of how we judge ourselves in relation to others is *social comparison*. The theory of *social comparison* states that if there is no objective measure of comparison, we seek out other people and compare our attitudes or behaviors to theirs. We compare ourselves to those we admire or whom we believe are like us. The group we choose to compare ourselves to is the *reference group*. The pressure that forces us to try to be like everyone else is termed *social pressure* or *conformity pressure*.

2. An important experiment on conformity was performed by Milgram. In this study men responded to a newspaper advertisement for participants in a psychology experiment. They were eventually chosen to play the role of a "teacher." It was the job of the teacher to administer an electric shock to a learner each time he made a mistake. On this shock machine there were 30 switches that ranged from 15 to 450 volts. (In reality, the learner was a confederate of the experimenters, received no actual shocks, and merely acted out being shocked.) The results were astounding. More than 60 percent of the "teachers" in the experiment complied completely with the experimenter's request and gave the maximum shock; and even more startling, in one variation of the experiment **no one** gave less than 300 volts.

3. Opinions and social influence in a group cause us to conform. In a study by Asch, volunteers were solicited for an experiment on visual perception. When six observers, who were confederates of the experimenter, all denied that one line length was the same as another, their obviously incorrect answer influenced the real subject of the experiment, the new member of the group. Of these real subjects, 32 percent conformed and also gave the wrong answer. The pressure of even a group formed by a random collection of people that you have never met before is considerable. In other studies it has been shown that social pressure can change people's beliefs.

   Important factors in conformity are group unanimity and group size. The more unanimous the other people's opinions and the larger the group, the more likely you are to conform.

4. Attitudes typically consist of several components: cognitive, emotional, and behavioral. *Cognitive consistency* theories attempt to define exactly how we achieve consistency between our attitudes. The *theory of cognitive dissonance* holds that cognitive dissonance occurs whenever an individual holds two

cognitions (e.g., beliefs, attitudes, or knowledge of behaviors) that are inconsistent with one another. In an important experiment, Festinger and Carlsmith asked groups of people to perform an extremely boring task and to tell another waiting person that they liked the task. It was thought that people who were paid one dollar for the experiment would experience dissonance and actually try to believe that the task was more pleasant, but that another group, which was paid twenty dollars for it, would persist in believing the task was dull. The results bore this out. People paid one dollar for the boring task *did* rate the task more pleasurable than people paid twenty dollars for the task. This finding may have very general implications. It may mean that the fewer inducements you provide for someone to do something, the more likely you are to create attitude change.

5. *Prejudice* is a negative judgmental attitude toward an identifiable group of people, based on a simplistic overgeneralization. Prejudice derives from mechanisms similar to those that we use to experience the world and develop our ideas and attitudes. We are able to judge things by means of simplification, by creating prototypes and their simplifying structures. However, when a prototype is overextended it becomes a *stereotype*, and we then attribute identical characteristics to all members of a group; for example, Americans are materialistic, the elderly are wise, and so on. If a stereotype is widely accepted, it can have lasting effects on the group so stereotyped.

   One way to overcome prejudice is to increase contact with the prejudged group. The more you know about someone, the less likely you are to make sweeping judgments about that person and about members of a group.

   A systematic attempt to use the principle of cooperation between groups, known to reduce prejudice, is called cooperative interdependence.

6. An important factor in developing *attributions* is the *discounting principle*, used in cases in which you are forced to attribute the behavior of a single person in a single situation on a single occasion. If you find a celebrity was paid a large amount of money to endorse a camera, you may discount the importance of other information. If, on the other hand, the celebrity's endorsement occurred in spite of situational forces, and the commercial was done for free, you might believe the endorser really did like the camera.

   A second principle, *covariation*, is used in cases where we have multiple observations. If you observe the celebrity in a number of commercials talking about a variety of products, you may note that the endorser always says positive things when paid a sum of money; then, you might easily infer that money was the cause of this behavior.

   The *fundamental attribution error* is the tendency to underestimate the impact of situational forces and to overestimate the role of dispositional forces in controlling behavior. We typically overlook the degree to which social roles determine behavior and overgeneralize from a small bit of evidence. The reason for the fundamental attribution error is that the information available to us is very different between an actor and someone observing a behavior. The more well known an actor is to an observer, the more likely the observer is to attribute the actor's behavior to situational rather than dispositional causes.

   We tend to make attribution errors because avoiding them requires more resources and information than we usually have. It is more likely that, as with everything else we do, in making judgments about other people we select, simplify, and use the available information to come to the best quick assessment. Most of us are ordinarily successful using this method.

7. *Aggression* is intentionally harming another. It is an attribution as well as an act, because what one judges to be aggressive depends on one's culture and one's place in it.

   There are two types of aggression. Hostile aggression is motivated by anger and hatred and instrumental aggression is motivated by an incentive, usually economic. The two often are combined in the same act.

   Freud considered aggression an instinct, calling it *Thanatos* or the death instinct. Because civilization puts curbs on aggression, Freud contended that it becomes necessary for us to redirect our destructive instinctual urges.

   Like Freud, ethologists such as Lorenz see aggression as instinctual. They point out that animals have evolved innate inhibitions against fatal aggression toward members of their own species. The strength of this inhibition corresponds to the strength of a species' offensive weapons. Thus, wolves, as predators, are well equipped for violence and also possess strong inhibitions against killing others of their kind. However, the human inheritance has provided us with very weak natural instruments of physical aggression. We are weak for our size, and we do not have the strength of a tiger or the jaws of a shark. Since we inherit weak weapons, we also inherit weak inhibitions on personal aggression. Human beings have developed weapons and other systems that are vastly more destructive than any inherited ones. However, we have not evolved corresponding inhibitions. This lack of inhibition against violence toward members of our own species explains why, under the circumstances, we have become so dangerous to ourselves. We are able to destroy a whole city by the push of a button.

   Social learning theory holds that there is no necessarily aggressive instinct and a threatened punishment works to subdue aggression, but only if certain conditions are satisfied: (1) there is little to be gained by aggression; (2) the threatened punishment is severe; (3) the potential aggressor understands that punishment is highly likely; and (4) the potential aggressor is not very angry.

   Factors that affect aggressive response are arousal, crowding, noise, high temperatures, and use of alcohol, marijuana, and tranquilizers.

   Psychologists have devoted some study to specific situations that cause people to behave aggressively. In one of psychology's most important studies, Philip Zimbardo sought to investigate the degree to which behavior can be situationally determined. He simulated a "prison" in the basement of Stanford University and found that student subjects soon took on their assigned social roles of prisoners and guards. The "prisoners," for instance, assumed the weak and submissive role of a prisoner, and a number of the "guards" behaved in a corrupt and threatening manner. The experiment caused so much distress that it had to be terminated after only six days.

8. Two important ways that we may learn to avoid aggression and develop *prosocial behavior* are: (1) through observation of other people behaving in a prosocial way and (2) by more closely observing the suffering of others—we are then less likely to harm them. It seems a human being needs feedback from other individuals that harm is being done.

9. The effects of televised aggression can lead to more generalized aggressiveness. This is accomplished by such means as: (1) increasing arousal, especially among children; (2) lowering restraint; and (3) desensitization: adults who view a lot of violent television have a lower physiological response to violent scenes than those who watch less violence.

10. As groups come to intensify behavior, they also come to intensify attitudes. People are more likely to take risks in groups than while alone. This phenomenon is called *risky shift*. In several studies of risky shift, group discussions tended to magnify initial attitudes as well as final decisions. When the opinions of others were known, subjects often changed their own opinion in the more extreme direction. Thus, a snowball effect of opinion change was created and groups took on a life of their own.

11. Crowding can be an important dimension of social life. Crowds serve to *intensify* our social interaction. Different people maintain a different amount of personal space, the small protective sphere that we maintain between ourselves and others. This distance is classified in four basic types: intimate, from actually touching to 18 inches; personal, up to 4 feet; social, 4 to 12 feet; and public, more than 12 feet. Individuals in different cultures have varying ideas about the amount of personal and living space needed. In Hong Kong, for example, low-cost housing provides only 35 square feet per person, an amount that would be completely intolerable to most Americans.

12. Crowding is having more people around than one desires. The effects of crowds on people are the same as those of groups: they intensify behavior. Human response to density is quite flexible. Males and females may differ in response to density. For instance, in a laboratory situation, a mock jury deliberation, groups of women often became less aggressive, gave lighter sentences, in small rooms than in large rooms, while men tended to do just the reverse.

13. Churchill said, "We shape our buildings, and thereafter our buildings shape us." Our built environment, the structure and arrangement of the buildings in which we live and work, can have profound effects—both positive and negative—on our social and individual lives. Our high-rise, high-density cities encourage creativity but create problems and influences such as interference with bystander intervention when someone is in trouble, an increasingly faster way of life, bothersome noise, and feelings of insecurity in the face of crime and crowding.

14. Studies of the work place have also been quite important in social psychology. One way that psychologists have recommended that workers improve their quality of life is to offer some greater degree of *control* to the workers and ownership of the factories in which they work. For instance 20 percent of Sears Roebuck is owned by workers who participate in a profit-sharing program. Generally work place reform means: (1) making the workplace more pleasant physically; (2) involving workers in decision making; (3) organizing jobs in more meaningful units; (4) establishing team spirit by having workers organized in small groups; and (5) making hours flexible.

Terms and Concepts

aggression
attribution
coaction effect
cognitive consistency
cognitive dissonance
conformity pressure
covariation principle
discounting principle
fundamental attribution error

prejudice
prosocial behavior
proxemics
reference group
risky shift
social comparison
social pressure
stereotype

Aronson, E. (1984). *The social animal*. San Francisco: W. H. Freeman.
Probably the most literate and readable introduction to social psychology.

Bem, D. J. (1970). *Beliefs, attitudes and human affairs*. Belmont, CA: Brooks/Cole.
A very nicely done small book on beliefs, which covers some material not covered in this text, such as why certain beliefs seem to go together. Recommended.

Festinger, L. (1957). *A theory of cognitive dissonance*. Stanford, CA: Stanford University Press.
Perhaps the most influential of current theories, in its original edition. It is useful sometimes to read these important theories as they are stated.

Milgram, S. (1974). *Obedience to authority: An experimental view*. New York: Harper & Row.
The famous study, well presented by its author.

**Suggestions for
Further Reading**

Chapter 19

Development in Adulthood

INTRODUCTION

The British writer Orwell said: "At 50 you have the face you deserve." If early development is primarily a series of *stages* of growth, then later development is primarily *self-development*: a series of choices. Early adult life is based on the important choices of work and love, and they set the course for the years to come.

More and more people are discovering that the process of choice and self-development continues as long as we live. People change careers in middle age, leave unhappy marriages and form new ones. The study of adult development is new, yet many of the common stereotypes about the "declines" in aging have already been challenged. People in restrictive situations may experience physical decline, but it can be arrested if they are returned to a normal social life. Barring illness, there is little decline in brain functioning in the aged with normal levels of stimulation. I once watched a friend direct a film that had a part in it for a woman 65 years old. The actress engaged for the part was about 65, and the director told her to act like a 65-year-old woman in the scene. Since she was one, she did so. She smiled, almost leaped around the room, walked with a spring in her step, all things that she usually did. This did not satisfy my friend. The woman was acting too young for him. Finally, for expensive time on the set was adding up, he got the idea. He told her: "Act like you are 110 years old." He got the effect.

More than three-quarters of your life will be spent as an adult, and the majority of successes, joys, and sorrows lie ahead. You will fall in love, probably marry, achieve some important goals and fail at others. There are transitions you may face: becoming a professional, getting married, becoming a parent, perhaps facing divorce. You will also probably face your parents' death, and your own certainly. In this chapter we will follow the developing adult from conceptions of the life span: a new and important area in psychology. Then we look at the "love and work" years of early adulthood, the middle years from about 40 to 65, and late adulthood including death and bereavement.

CONCEPTIONS OF THE LIFE SPAN

Early Development   See
Chapter 3

Until recently, the study of psychological development usually ended at adolescence, partly because the changes in early life are so fascinating and so swift. There is more research now on the continuing development of the adult, and, as in personality, there are many conflicting theories.

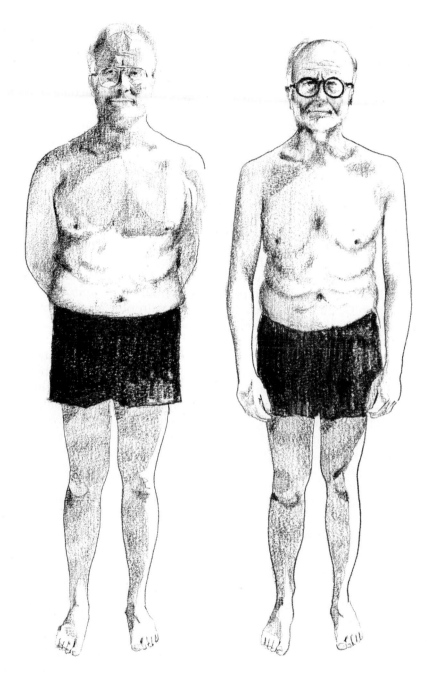

Theories of Adult Development

The "father" of the modern study of adult development is Carl Jung. Jung was a disciple of Freud who later split from him due to many disagreements. One that concerns us here is that Jung felt Freud too strongly emphasized that childhood development almost completely determined adult characteristics: "the child is the father to the man." Jung extended the study of development to the entire life cycle. Jung also felt that the social world of the adult was much more important in adult life than Freud thought.

Erik Erikson is the second great figure in adult development and has stimulated much of the more recent research and theories. Erikson postulates that we develop in a series of eight crises, the outcome of each one determining later directions.

There has been much recent interest in adult development, in part due to the general aging of the population and in part due to the recognition that humans continually grow and change, and some of these changes are predictable. Two recent theories, of Gould and Levinson, attempt to describe the series of development "tasks" or "transitions" that adults experience.

Jung

Jung (1953) thought that we develop in adulthood through dealing with problems and that different developmental stages have different types of problems. In *puberty,* prohibitions and limitations become internalized, and conflict with the self begins. *Youth* runs from puberty to about age 35, during which the self deals with problems of sexuality, widening horizons, and establishing oneself in the world. But around age 35 or 40, subtle changes begin to take place. There may be changes in character: traits and interests long suppressed from childhood may begin to assert themselves. More commonly, men who have buried themselves in their careers may find themselves becoming more interested in their families; however, at the same time, many women may be completing childrearing and be looking forward to starting a career. Conversely, a person may become more rigid in his or her convictions and principles, as if these were somehow endangered and it is all the more necessary to reinforce them.

Jung characterized a person's values in the first half of life as expanding, *outward* directed. In the second half, he felt the values must become more *inner* directed, including self-knowledge, cultural concerns, and preparation for death.

Erikson

Erik Erikson recognized that development processes occur in a social context, hence his term **psychosocial development.** Erikson viewed the life course as a series of eight successive stages. Each stage has a particular *developmental task,* a dialectical conflict that the person must resolve. The adult developmental tasks are: identity versus role confusion, intimacy versus isolation, generativity versus self-absorption, and integrity versus despair. The resolution of each task forms the basis for the next stage; if the task is not resolved, damaging consequences result, which interfere with the successful completion of the next stage. An adolescent who has not successfully negotiated his or her identity crisis, for example, may have difficulty forming intimate bonds with another in early adulthood.

Erikson's writings provide a rich descriptive framework for understanding the life cycle. But unfortunately they are difficult to translate into "objective" measures. Vaillant (1977) simplified the concepts of the

Erik Erikson

Stages of Psychosocial Development   See Chapter 3, pp. 108–10.

stages in order to measure them (for example, a long marriage indicated the achievement of intimacy) and found some evidence for this hierarchical concept. In a large longitudinal study, the men judged to be "Best Outcomes" (in terms of adaptive criteria such as socioeconomic success, length of marriage, status in the community, etc.) had resolved Erikson's developmental tasks, but the "Worst Outcomes" had not. Men who had achieved intimacy were more likely to be involved in tasks that reflected generativity. The "Worst Outcomes" often had childhoods that were rated not conducive to developing basic trust, autonomy, and initiative; as adolescents, they tended to have less integrated and secure identities. They were less likely to achieve intimacy in marriage, and tended to reject responsibility for others in midlife.

False Assumptions and Life Transitions

Both Roger Gould (1972, 1978) and Daniel Levinson (1977, 1978) describe stages that are somewhat similar to those of Erikson and Jung. Gould feels that major life stages are characterized by major **"false assumptions"** about identity and intimacy. Development involves working through these misconceptions.

Levinson's conception of the life cycle involves a series of stable *life structures* that alternate with *transitional periods*. Life structures are patterns of person-environment transactions that involve three elements: the sociocultural world, roles, and aspects of the self. Within each life structure, a person chooses and pursues certain goals, like settling down or furthering a career. But each life structure excludes other possible developments; so every six to eight years a person goes through a transitional period, lasting four to six years, in which the old life structure is terminated and work begins toward the next one. These transitional periods are often times of crisis.

Social Factors in Development

Social psychologists and sociologists view the life span in terms of progression through successive *roles* and *statuses*. For example, a woman may become a school child, an adolescent, a college student, wife, mother, working mother, chemist, grandparent, retiree, and so forth. The process of learning *norms*—behavior appropriate to a given role—is termed *socialization*, a continuous process across the life span. The number and kinds of roles that a person can learn in a lifetime are determined in part by what a culture offers.

Within a culture, there are **timetables,** generally agreed upon times for entering or completing certain roles. Neugarten and her associates (1965) asked a middle-aged, middle-class sample about the appropriate ages for a number of events and found a very high consensus. Furthermore, there are different timetables for different roles—there is a wider range of ages at which it is acceptable to become a father, for example, than to graduate from college—and these timetables may vary by social class, ethnicity, sex, and so on. Generally, the higher the social class, the later the age for various roles (Neugarten & Hagestad, 1976). For example, poor women tend to marry and have children earlier than middle-class women. Cultures may also have different timetables for roles. In

GOULD'S LIST OF FALSE ASSUMPTIONS

Age

16–22   *Major False Assumption to be Challenged:* "I'll always belong to my parents and believe in their world."

Component Assumptions:

1. If I get any more independent, it will be a disaster.
2. I can see the world only through my parents' assumptions.
3. Only my parents can guarantee my safety.
4. My parents must be my only family.
5. I don't own my body.

22–28   *Major False Assumption to be Challenged:* "Doing things my parents' way, with will power and perseverance, will bring results. But if I become too frustrated, confused, or tired, or am simply unable to cope, they will step in and show me the right way."

Component Assumptions:

1. Rewards will come automatically if we do what we are supposed to.
2. There is only one right way to do things.
3. Those in a special relationship with us can do for us what we haven't been able to do for ourselves.

Age

28–34   *Major False Assumption to Be Challenged:* "Life is simple and controllable. There are no significant coexisting contradictory forces within me."

Component Assumptions:

1. What I know intellectually, I know emotionally.
2. I am not like my parents in ways I don't want to be.
3. I can see the reality of those close to me quite clearly.
4. Threats to my security aren't real.

35–45   *Major False Assumption to Be Challenged:* "There is no evil or death in the world. The sinister has been destroyed."

Component Assumptions:

1. The illusion of safety can last forever.
2. Death can't happen to me or my loved ones.
3. It is impossible to live without a protector (women).
4. There is no life beyond this family.
5. I am innocent.

the United States, a fifteen-year-old boy is still in school with few adult responsibilities; in traditional cultures, he may be considered a man and have a family to support.

BIOLOGICAL AND COGNITIVE DEVELOPMENT

While many of the theories concern the development of personality and character, much of the research evidence has been directed toward the predictable biological and cognitive changes in aging, in part because they are easier to study and in part because they are more uniform across a wide range of different people.

Biological Development

When we are young, we cannot imagine not being able to bend over easily or trot across the street. But as we grow older, we experience first subtle changes in our bodies, then increasing physical limitations.

LEVINSON'S THEORY OF ADULT DEVELOPMENT

Age	Stage	Age	Stage
17–22	*Early Adult Transition.* Tasks: Move out of preadult world and make preliminary steps into the adult world by separating from parents and exploring work and intimacy.	40–45	*Midlife Transition.* Tasks: To evaluate how well one has achieved the goals set, and to work on self-individuation by resolving conflicts between four polarities: young/old, creation/destruction (death), masculine/feminine, and attachment/separateness.
22–28	*Entering the Adult World.* Tasks: Explore possibilities for adult living, while creating a stable life structure by developing a career and getting married.	45–50	*Entering Middle Adulthood.* Tasks: To build a new life structure based on the outcome of the midlife transition.
28–33	*Age 30 Transition.* Tasks: Work on flaws in the "novice" life structure by examining and refocusing work and relationships.	50–55	*Age 50 Transition**
33–40	*Settling Down.* Tasks: Establish a niche in society and work at advancement by making choices about work, relationships, and personal interests, and working on long-range goals.	55–60	*Second Middle Adult Structure**
		60–65	*Late Adult Transition**

*The men Levinson studied had not yet reached these stages.

Age- and Disease-related Changes

Age-related changes in bodily functioning are different from disease-related changes. Birren and his associates (1963) studied 47 men aged 67 to 91 who appeared very healthy. They were given lengthy and extensive examinations of medical, physiological, psychological, and social functioning. On the basis of the medical examinations, they were divided into two groups. The men in Group A were optimally healthy on every measure, but the ones in Group B, who appeared healthy, actually had subclinical diseases: the beginnings of diabetes, heart disease, and the like. Many of the decrements generally associated with being old were absent in the healthy men, but were present in the men in Group B, an indication that impairments are often more a function of disease than of age *per se.*

Why Do We Age?

No one really knows why we age. Part of the problem is the need to distinguish between the effects and the causes of aging. For example, it has long been known that waste products accumulate in the cells, but whether this causes or is a symptom of aging is unknown (Curtis, 1966).

Aging results from many different processes, some of which are genetically controlled. In shorter-lived species, genetics is more important than in humans (Medvedev, 1975). Research on the cells is the best evidence for the possibility of genetic programming. Animal cells grown in the laboratory have a limited number of times that they divide (about

---

THE COHORT EFFECT

If we were to take a cross section of people aged 20, 30, 40, 50, 60, 70, 80, and 90, we would find that height decreases with age, and we might be tempted to conclude that people grow shorter after age 20. However, this conclusion does not take into account that in this century successive generations have grown taller. That is, the average height of twenty-year-olds in 1970 is greater than that of twenty-year-olds in 1920. This is known as a **cohort**. A **longitudinal study** attempts to control for this by selecting a group, or panel, of people and studying them over a number of years or decades.

---

30), after which they die, no matter how good their environmental conditions are (Hayflick, 1980). The biologist Hayflick comments:

> Over a period of time the information in the information processing system represented by the transcription and translation of the genetic message in DNA into RNA and into other enzymes might be increasingly subject to error. Such errors would give rise to faulty enzyme molecules and lead to a decline in the functional abilities of the cell. The situation would be analogous to an error in the instructions of an automatic machine tool: the tool would turn out faulty parts that, when they were assembled into the final product, would reduce its efficiency or keep it from working altogether. (Hayflick, 1980)

There are many other biological factors in aging. Background radiation may damage the DNA; the mechanisms that repair the cells may break down; biochemical changes in the cells may contribute to their malfunctioning and result in disease such as cancer, diabetes, hypertension, and others. (Blumenthal & Burns, 1964; Makinodan, 1977; Shock, 1977).

Changes in the Body

There are predictable changes in the body: height generally increases up to about age 45, then slowly decreases; shoulder width increases until about age 35, then decreases; chest diameter increases until about age 54, then decreases slightly; the pelvis *widens* with age; the ear and the nose lengthen, and the nose also broadens (Rossman, 1977).

The relative composition of the body also changes with age. As muscle mass decreases, the percentage of fat increases. Because fat has less water than muscle, the percentage of body water also decreases. Fat tends to become concentrated in the trunk and decreases in the extremities, so the hands, feet, arms, and legs become thinner, while the abdomen, waist, and hips thicken.

Other changes are associated with aging: the skin becomes drier, loses its elasticity, wrinkles, and may develop "age spots," deposits of pigmentation. Hair becomes gray by losing pigmentation. Beginning in the thirties, hair is lost, and later on perhaps teeth as well, either to decay or periodontal (gum) disease. The voice becomes less powerful and more restricted in range, which may result from atrophy of the muscles of the larynx, upper respiratory congestion, or gradual changes that limit the capacity and control of expelled air (Timiras, 1972).

The senses also decline in sensitivity with age (Fozard, Wolf, Bell, Farland, & Podolsky, 1977). Visual acuity, the ability to focus on near objects, and adaptation to darkness all decline in the elderly. Loss of hearing is marked in older persons (Corso, 1977), especially at the higher frequencies (Weiss, 1959). The number of taste buds declines and there is an increase in the threshold for smell. However, other factors, such as disease or smoking, play an important role in this (Engen, 1977). The number of nerve endings in the skin decreases with age (Selmanowitz, Lorer, & Orentreich, 1970), but this does not mean that the elderly are any less susceptible to pain (Kimmel, 1980).

Changes in the Brain

There is *less* change in the aging brain than in the rest of the body. It is commonly thought that the brain loses cells as we age. However, we came into the world with more brain cells than we need. One result of development is the "pruning" (Greenough, 1982) of brain cells, possibly for more efficient functioning. Studies of rats, under controlled conditions, shows that most brain cells are lost in *the first years* of life, and few, if any, are lost afterward (Diamond et al., 1981).

Even brains in older rats can *increase* in size if the rats are placed in an enriched environment—that is, one that has a lot of sensory stimulation and activities that the rats can engage in. So the brain continues to adapt and develop throughout life depending on the environment. Thus, the elderly in bland institutional settings seem disoriented or confused; justices of the Supreme Court are at the height of their mental abilities. As Diamond (1984) reminds us, "Use it or lose it."

How Long Can We Live?

Most people in the United States can expect to live into their seventies, although this varies by sex and race.

Exactly how long a person can live is a matter of some debate. Some villagers in the Caucasus mountains in Russia and Turkey claim to be extremely old: 120, 130, and even 150 and 160 years old (Medvedev, 1974). While many of these elderly do live a very long time and are exceptionally healthy, many question the validity of the claims to extreme old age. The problem is that there is very little valid documentation such as birth certificates or church records to back up these claims. For example, Berdyshev (1966) investigated claims in the Caucasus and Altai areas and stated:

> We met many old persons who produced oral statements . . . where their age was 150 to 180 years old. But detailed analysis of their family backgrounds and other data proved an arbitrary exaggeration of their real age, sometimes by 2 or 3 times. (Quoted in Medvedev, 1974)

Vulnerability to disease can be reduced, so people can live closer to their maximal life span.

Some of the Caucasus villagers who claim to be over 100 years old.

However, not all of aging can be controlled by our environment and behavior. People who live long lives generally had parents and grandparents who also lived a long time, indicating that genes may play a large role. But certain things we do are harmful and can be avoided. Granich and Patterson (1971) studied the healthy elderly men that Birren had examined 11 years previously, and found that not smoking cigarettes and greater organization of daily living, including gratifying pursuits and pastimes, were associated with long life.

Kyucharyants (1974) asked one elderly woman in the Caucasus who claimed to be 138 years old whether a fountain of youth existed in her village. She replied, "Of course, it exists, young man: It is inside each of us. Only not everyone knows how to use it."

Cognition

Along with biological changes, changes in many major mental functions occur with age, although there is less decline in intelligence and memory than is commonly thought.

Intelligence

As we age, what happens to our intellectual capacity? If we measure IQ in a cross-sectional sample, we find that IQ scores decline with age, and we might conclude that people lose their intellectual capacity as they grow older. However, if we control for cohort effects and examine IQ in a longitudinal sample, the results are very different—the older the person, the *higher* the IQ (Botwinick, 1977).

There are problems with both kinds of measures: cross-sectional studies confound cohort variables—the older a person is, the less education he or she is likely to have had and the less familiarity with taking tests. However, longitudinal results are also misleading, because of "selective dropout"—the less intelligent, less healthy, less well-adapted person is more likely to drop out of a longitudinal study, and so an increasingly select and more intelligent sample remains in a longitudinal study, increasing the IQ level.

Taking all of these factors into consideration, verbal abilities seem to remain relatively constant or increase slightly with age, whereas measures of performance decline. However, these declines are not found often before age 50 or 60, and even then they are relatively small (Botwinick, 1977).

Memory and Learning

Are the elderly more forgetful than younger people? Age differences in primary memory are minimal, if the tasks do not require reorganizing the material or dividing attention (Craik, 1977). However, the elderly perform worse than younger groups if the tasks involve long-term memory. Schonfield and Robertson (1966) found that the elderly had more difficulty in recalling information than younger people, but did not find age differences in recognition, and concluded that older people do not retrieve information from storage as well as younger ones. Perhaps this difficulty in retrieval is due to the fact that the elderly do not use as much mnemonics, or verbal mediators and imagery, as younger people (Craik, 1977). If the subjects are taught to use mnemonics, all age groups improve, but older people improve much more (Hulicka & Grossman, 1967).

Many studies based on laboratory research show that the elderly do not learn as well as younger people. Several reasons for this have been found: (1) they may take longer to process and retrieve information; (2) they fail to encode or organize the information as well as younger people; (3) they prefer preestablished habits; and (4) they may be very uncomfortable in laboratory situations (Arenberg & Robertson-Tchabo, 1977).

EARLY ADULTHOOD: WORK AND MARRIAGE

In adolescence, most people begin separating themselves from their parents and their own childhood assumptions. Above all else, adolescence is a time of exploration (Norton, 1976). If individuals do not saddle themselves prematurely with adult responsibilities and commitments, this pattern of exploration continues in early adulthood. College or military service can provide a hiatus of a sort, in which young persons may be physically separate from their parents, while not completely independent, and can build a basis for living in the adult world (Levinson, 1978).

The Dream

It is during this period of life that people may form their "dream," a hazy, unarticulated idea of what they want to do with their lives. During this time, people begin experimenting with different jobs or careers, different styles of interpersonal relationships (Levinson, 1978).

Work and Career

While there is no definite biological event that signals the beginning of early adulthood, for most people there are several hallmarks of this period: beginning a career, getting married, and becoming a parent. People generally assume that in their early twenties they must decide upon an occupation and become "launched in a well-defined line of work." Actually, the process is far more complicated and diffuse than that, and it might be more useful to speak of the process of "forming a career," which may last several years or even decades (Levinson, 1978). Kimmel (1980) identifies six factors that influence occupational "choice": background factors, role models, experience, interests, personality, and research.

Background factors include socioeconomic status, ethnic origin, intelligence, race, sex, and education. These may set "boundaries" on the range of occupational choice. For example, a person who has been placed in the "vocational track" in high school may have a more difficult time in becoming a lawyer than someone who took college preparatory courses, or there may be ethnic preferences for occupations.

A person may also choose an occupation on the basis of identification with a *role model*, that is, a woman may decide to become a diamond cutter like her uncle. Of course, such a person may be more than a model, he or she may also provide entry opportunities. An important figure in this regard is a **mentor,** not precisely a role model or "father figure," but someone who eases the youth into adulthood (Levinson, 1978). A mentor ideally aids a person in developing his or her own autonomy and interests, commitment to an occupation, and understanding of the "dream." The mentor may be a teacher, an older colleague, a family friend.

A person's *experience* is also an important factor. A man may want to become a doctor because of a serious illness as a child; a woman might spend a summer on the rodeo circuit and decide that that is what she really wants to do. And, of course, a person's *interests* and *personality* may be better expressed in or matched to one occupation or another (Bolles, 1972; Holland, 1973). Finally, a person may *research* the job market and decide that the best opportunities exist in computer programming or setting up a mail order business and obtain the specialized training needed in those fields.

Marriage

While many relationships, especially the ones that involve a mentor, are extremely important to a person's development, marriage generally has a profound impact and is considered a major developmental milestone. If you ask a person why he or she marries, the automatic answer will often be, "Because I love so-and-so." However, if one probes a little deeper, the developmental aspects of marriage become more apparent.

Reasons for Marriage

Some people marry to *become adults*, to step out of the role of being a child and into being a wife, mother, father, husband. Others see it as a way of gaining security.

> I was only seventeen when I got married the first time. . . . I guess the biggest thing was that there was no other way if I wanted to get away from that house and to be a person in myself instead of just a kid in that family. All three of us girls married when we were very young, and I guess we did it for the same reason. All three of us got divorced, too, only for my sisters it didn't work out as lucky as for me. (Rubin, 1976)

> I got married because I wanted the security of a marriage and a home. In fact, I needed it very much. . . . I was ready to be married and have somebody take care of me. (Rubin, 1976)

Instrumental gain is often an important reason for marrying. A woman may "marry up" in a quest for social mobility, or a man may "marry the boss's daughter"; a medical student may marry to have someone to help put him or her through medical school.

"Well, marriage," says the doctor who needed a helpmate through medical school, "it was a practicality. People always seem to come back to it as the final answer, just like democracy." (Sheehy, 1976)

For many men, marriage appears to be almost a matter of *chance*, or a feeling that it was somehow an appropriate thing to do at the time.

I don't know exactly why I married her instead of somebody else. I guess everybody always knows they're going to have to get married. I mean, everybody has to some time, don't they? What else is there to do but get married? (Rubin, 1976)

Within six months before or after our graduation from law school, all but one of my friends got married. I don't think it could be that everybody met the right girl by coincidence. There must have been an element of its being the right time. Not to take away from Jeanie. (Sheehy, 1976)

For the "blue collar" people that Rubin studied, the overwhelming reason for marriage was *pregnancy*. Forty-four percent "got caught."

I had gone with this girl for two years, and I suppose we expected to get married, but not yet. She was eighteen and I was nineteen when she got pregnant. Once that happened, there was nothing else to do but get married. My one consolation was that I outlasted everybody else. Everybody I knew then was getting married because the girl got pregnant; nobody got married without that. And most of them were getting caught a lot sooner than I did. (Rubin, 1976).

The Marriage Adjustment

But few people enter marriage with any realistic expectations about what it is like (Bernard, 1972), and even in the best of marriages there are many adjustments to be made:

I found it awfully hard to leave Renn as free as he wanted to be left, for quite a while. Of course, the transition from courtship to marriage is quite something. I think that I expected some of those same attentions to hold over and found it a little difficult when at times they didn't. And I made demands on Renn which he didn't want to have made on him because of that, demands for time and attention. . . . I had sort of a picture of a glorious future when we did everything together, which is really very silly, because I don't think it does anybody that much good. You've got to have independent things so that you bring something new into the relationship all the time. (White, 1952).

Especially when people marry very young, the responsibilities that come with marriage often seem very shocking. Asked if there was some period of adjustment after getting married, young people gave such responses as:

Was there? Wow! Before I got married, I only had to do for myself; after, there was somebody else along all the time. . . . Then, I suddenly found

BECOMING A PARENT

For many years, psychologists studied the effect of the mother on the baby. But more recently, it has been realized that having a baby has a profound effect not only on the mother, but on the whole family. The early studies viewed becoming a parent as a crisis with serious ramifications for the mental health of both parents (Bibring, 1959). Surveys showed that women with very young children are more likely to be depressed, anxious, and unhappy than women without children (Bernard, 1972; Pearlin and Johnson, 1977; Rossi, 1968). But if becoming a parent is so distressing, why would 90 percent of all women want to have a baby (Prosser, 1978)? Social scientists began to examine more closely what effect becoming a parent has on normal, healthy men and women and have found that it is not so much a crisis as a developmental stage—it is disruptive, with the possibility of harm, but also the possibility of growth (Grossman, Eichler, & Winickhoff, 1980).

Becoming a parent for the first time can signal that the person has become an adult, with adult responsibilities for caring and providing for someone else (Hoffman, 1978). A woman may come to identify herself more as a mother, as opposed to other possible identities (artist, comic, sexy, etc.), and often becomes more sympathetic to and understanding of her own mother (Cowan, Cowan, Coie, & Coie, 1978).

Having a very young infant is time-consuming and tiring, and sheer exhaustion may account for low morale. A woman who shifts from full-time employment to full-time motherhood may find this disruptive (Cowan et al., 1978). Furthermore, the loss of her income may produce financial strain at a time when expenses increase, creating additional stress.

But all this may be offset by the sheer exhilaration of becoming a parent. While many have described the joy, awe, and sense of fulfillment a woman feels upon

I had to worry about where we'd live and whether we had enough money, and all those things like that. Before, I could always get a job and make enough money to take care of me and give something to the house. Then, after we got married, I suddenly had all those responsibilities. Before, it didn't make any difference if I didn't feel like going to work sometimes. Then, all of a sudden, it made one hell of a difference because the rent might not get paid, or, if it got paid, there might not be enough food money. (Rubin, 1976)

These hardships are often compounded by the fact that in early adulthood, financial and job security tend to be very low. However, barring such disasters, *the first year of marriage is often remembered as the happiest time* (Brim, 1968; Gould, 1972).

"His" and "Her" Marriages

The experience of marriage may be very different for men and women, so much so that one theorist proposes both "his" and "her" marriages need to be thought of separately. And it does seem that mar-

giving birth, men may experience similar feelings. Asked to describe his reaction during his wife's delivery, one man said:

> It was very powerful. There we were—my wife pushing and I pushing with her—then the baby slipped out. The doctor suctioned her and cut the cord, and the nurse cleaned her up and brought her to me. She was crying, and her color changed from blue to pink. I held her, my bright-eyed little child, and she looked right at me and quieted in my arms. (Fein, 1978)

One woman who had twins said of her husband:

> He's having a love affair with the babies. He holds them and changes them and sings to them and feeds them, things he wouldn't have considered doing if we only had one baby. But with two he felt he had a responsibility to help out. And helping out has freed him to be a more loving man. (Fein, 1978)

Whether motherhood is a positive, rather than negative, experience depends on the mother's characteristics, the child's, and the relationship with the husband. If the marital relationship is poor, or the husband is very anxious, or the mother has a history of anxiety or depression, or if the infant is very difficult—for example, sick, handicapped or very temperamental—the mother's satisfaction is likely to be very poor (Grossman et al., 1980). The woman may feel frustrated, depressed, and resentful, and her relationship with her husband and with the child may deteriorate. But if these three elements are reasonably OK, then becoming a parent is likely to be an enriching, rewarding experience for both parents. The woman may become more self-assured, and the marital relationship become closer (Cowan et al., 1978; Hoffman, 1978).

riage is quite different for "him" and "her."

Statistically speaking, marriage appears to be very beneficial—at least for *men*. Compared to men who are divorced, widowed, or who have never married, married men live much longer, have fewer mental and physical illnesses (Lynch, 1977), and appear happier. Divorced and widowed men also tend to remarry very quickly (Bernard, 1972). However, married *women* have higher rates of depression than married men, perhaps because they are often restricted and may feel that they are "only housewives."

Some psychologists feel that marriage may be actually harmful to women (Bernard, 1972; Gove, 1972). Married women have higher rates of mental illness than married men, while single women have lower rates of mental illness than single men (Gove, 1972). However, these differences are very small.

Marital Satisfaction

There are four factors in satisfying marriages (Rogers, 1972). The first is *commitment to the relationship* and to working together on it as it changes

and evolves over time. The second is *communication,* and the third is *role flexibility.* The fourth is having a *separate identity* and greater acceptance of oneself as a unique person, while accepting the partner's growth and autonomy.

Of these, the nature of the communication between the spouses is the key element in marital satisfaction (Gottman, 1979). There is, for instance, high correlation (.82) between how well couples communicate and their marital satisfaction (Navran, 1967). In a study of happy and unhappy married couples, he found that the former talked to each other more about a wider range of subjects. They showed more sensitivity to each other's feelings and conveyed the sense that they understood what was being said to them. Happily married couples tried to keep open verbal and nonverbal communication. They also were more playful with each other (Betcher, 1981).

In contrast, unhappily married people use less "give and take" in resolving differences (Locke, 1951), tend to distort nonverbal communication (Kahn, 1970), and fail to develop a private communication system (Gottman, 1979). Instead, they tend to "mirror" each other's behavior sequences: complaint is met with complaint, proposals with counterproposals, negative affect with negative affect (Murstein, Cerreto, & MacDonald, 1977).

Divorce

If the marriage becomes unhappy enough, the decision may be made to divorce. The rate of divorce is at an all-time high. Between 1970 and 1979, the divorce rate nearly doubled. Currently, one-third of all marriages can expect to end in divorce (Glick & Norton, 1977).

Some people are more likely to divorce than others. People who were married when they were teenagers and have little education and low incomes are most likely to divorce (Glick & Norton, 1977). Low incomes are likely to put great strains on marriage, and people who marry very young are less likely to have the maturity necessary to cope with the various problems of a marital relationship, household economics, and childrearing.

Obviously, such a widespread phenomenon has attracted a great deal of attention, and there is legitimate concern for what effect divorce has on individuals and society as a whole. How stressful is divorce? Is it harder on men or on women? What are the problems divorced men and women are likely to face? Which is worse, living with a "bad" marriage or divorcing? What are the best strategies for coping with divorce? And perhaps most important of all: what does it do to the children?

Effects of Divorce on Adults

There are four periods of the divorce process: marital distress, the decision to divorce, separation, and postdivorce. There is no doubt that the whole process is very painful: people who are separating are often lonely, anxious, angry, depressed, feel rejected, have low self-esteem, and are likely to have disturbances in their sleeping or eating patterns (Goode, 1956; Weiss, 1976). Separated and divorced individuals are also more likely to be admitted to psychiatric hospitals than any other group, including the widowed, and have higher rates of illness and disability (Bloom, Asher, & White, 1978).

Separation

The separation period is more stressful than either the preceding marital distress (Chiriboga & Cutler, 1977) or the postdivorce period (Bloom et al., 1978). The process of separation is just as painful whether one is leaving a relatively "good" marriage or a relatively "bad" one (Bloom & White, 1981). However, postdivorce, both men and women are likely to state that their situation is better than it was before the divorce (Albrecht, 1980). Nevertheless, it still takes approximately three years after the divorce for adults to regain their sense of equilibrium (Hetherington, Cox, & Cox, 1978).

The Stress of Divorce

The early studies of divorce, such as Goode (1956), assumed that divorce was more stressful for women, and, indeed, women are more likely than men to report divorce as being traumatic and stressful (Albrecht, 1980). However, assessments of emotional distress and psychosomatic symptoms show that divorce is at least as painful a process for men, if not more so (Chiriboga, 1977; Hetherington et al., 1978). Women appear to be more intensely distressed than men at the beginning of the divorce process, whereas men's distress may show up later on in the process (Chiriboga, 1977; Hetherington et al., 1977). Divorce appears to be most disruptive for middle-aged men and women (Chiriboga, Roberts, & Stein, 1978).

Coping with Divorce

Getting divorced, especially when there are children, may bring about a host of problems. These include difficulties involving contacts with the former spouse, interpersonal relations, loneliness, practical problems, financial concerns, and parent-child interactions (Berman & Turk, 1981). Income generally drops precipitiously, although this may be more true for women than for men (Bloom et al., 1978; White and Bloom, 1981). Only about one-third of ex-husbands contribute to the financial support of their children and former wives (Brandwein, Brown, & Fox, 1974). Half of all households headed by single women are at or below the poverty level (U.S. Bureau of the Census, 1975).

There are practical problems of taking over the tasks previously done by the ex-spouse, such as cooking and laundry, household and car maintenance, and child care and discipline. Men with primary custody of children are especially likely to feel disorganized and have problems coping with practical demands (Hetherington et al., 1977).

Social adjustment is also difficult. A person may discover that some friends were actually closer to the other spouse, and social networks become disrupted. Women with children may have an especially hard time dating, although men usually enter into a "flurry" of social activity (Hetherington et al., 1977). Contacts with former spouses are often distressing, and there may be increased problems with parent-child interactions, especially when mothers must discipline male children (Wallerstein & Kelly, 1980).

Sexual Relationships after Divorce

Overall, sexual and social experiences appear to be the best resource for coping with divorce. Men who had an extramarital affair (even if unrelated to the divorce) tend to have an easier time adjusting to divorce (White & Bloom, 1981), and the establishment of a satisfying heterosexual relationship, for both men and women, seems to help the most in recovering from divorce (Berman & Turk, 1981; Chiriboga et al., 1978; Hetherington et al., 1977; White & Bloom, 1981).

MIDDLE ADULTHOOD

For people who have followed the traditional family and career patterns (marry in the early twenties, children, career), the thirties are generally a time of "settling down" (Levinson, 1978). If the marriage has survived the tumultuous beginnings, the husband and wife have largely learned how to accommodate to each other.

With the children a little older, parenthood is a little easier. Jobs have become more stable, and financial security is a little better. A person has generally developed some skills and acquires some seniority at work and is less likely to be fired or laid off. He or she may have had some rewarding promotions and may feel well on the way to becoming established in the field.

But for others, the thirties is a time for some crucial decisions. A woman who has intentionally forgone children for the sake of a career must now make the decision whether or not to become a mother, as the "biological clock" is running out. Past the age of 30 or 35, a woman faces increasing risk of difficulty in pregnancy, and after she is 40 her child has an increased risk of birth defects, especially Down's syndrome.

If a person has not yet settled into a career, or is unhappy with the present one, he or she may feel time pressure to find a career that better suits his or her needs or interests. Women who have been full-time homemakers may start going back to school or working.

Middle Age

Middle age is more of a social stage of life than connected with a specific biological event, although most researchers set its boundaries from about age 40 to about 65. However, since it is socially influenced, the boundaries of middle age differ in different groups. In the upper middle class, the forties are considered the prime of life, and middle age is considered to start at about age 50; but in the lower socioeconomic groups, the thirties are considered the prime of life, and middle age is perceived as starting at age 40 (Neugarten & Petersen, 1957). In this latter group, marriage and parenthood begin earlier in life, thus children leave the home when the parents are younger. In addition, the earnings and prestige of blue collar jobs tend to peak in the thirties, while for the upper middle class, the peak is usually in the forties and sometimes fifties (Kimmel, 1980).

The "Midlife Crisis"

In midlife, adults are generally at the height of their accomplishments and achievements in society, and they are often perceived as stable and reliable, the "stalwart pillars of family and society" (Brim, 1978, 1979). But young people are often surprised to learn that their parents may be undergoing a transition and upheaval not dissimilar to their own. These marker events and the awareness of one's own mortality may trigger a **midlife crisis** (Jacques, 1965) in which people review and assess their early adulthood. They may try to change those facets of their life with which they are dissatisfied and attempt to resolve the psychological issues introduced by entering the final half of life (Levinson, 1978). A midlife crisis occurs when a person discovers that he or she is not happy with life—because goals either have not been attained or do not bring the expected satisfactions. The awareness of one's own mortality—that a whole lifetime no longer lies ahead—may also prompt radical changes.

No one knows how many people experience a midlife crisis. Vaillant (1977) suggests that men whose lives have been primarily determined by their parents and who have not developed their own sense of autonomy and direction may rebel in midlife. Two personality types are particularly prone to depression in midlife (Block, 1971). "Early maturing" men who were socially very gregarious, primarily athletically oriented, and non-intellectual may have a hard time with the passing of their youth. "Lonely, independent" women, on the other hand, who primarily invested in their intellect to the exclusion of social relations, may become depressed as the chance to have a family fades. The woman who remains strongly involved with her children may have difficulty in the "empty nest" stage (Bart, 1971). Finally, contrary to the popular stereotype of the high-flying executive having a midlife crisis, it may be the poorer people who are more likely to become depressed at midlife (Peck & Havighurst, 1960).

Of course, it may not be possible to equate depression with midlife crisis. Midlife is a time of transition for many, and transitions do tend to be stressful (Lowenthal, Fiske, Thurner, & Chiriboga, 1974). However, many of these transitions are eagerly anticipated and provide opportunities for growth as well as crisis. Middle age may be a spicier time of life than youth realizes.

Menopause and the "Empty Nest"

Not all the important events in middle age cause a crisis. Menopause and the "empty nest" are good examples of this. Menopause generally occurs between the ages of 48 and 51 (Talbert, 1977) and may be associated with hot flashes, irritability, crying spells, and depression. However, in a study of over 700 Japanese and American women, 75 percent reported none of the symptoms usually associated with menopause (Goodman, Stewart, & Gilbert, 1977). It is primarily younger women who feel that menopause is a disagreeable event; older women (aged 45–55) were more likely to feel that menopause creates no major changes (Neugarten, Wood, Kraines, & Loomis, 1963). While loss of fertility may have a profound effect on a woman's self-esteem, many others feel that not having to worry about menstruation or getting pregnant is positive.

Similarly, the **empty nest period,** in which the children leave home and become increasingly independent, is often thought to be a time of crisis for the family. The loss of the motherhood role to a woman who lacks other important roles may lead to depression (Bart, 1971). However, not all women become depressed. In an analysis of ethnic differences, Bart found that Jewish mothers had the highest rate of depression, WASPs an intermediate rate, and blacks the lowest. This may reflect differences in family patterns and interpretations among these groups. First, older black women are more likely to retain a maternal role by being involved in child care in an extended family network, and second,

> since black women traditionally work, they are less likely to develop the extreme identification, the vicarious living through their children, that is characteristic of Jewish mothers (Bart, 1971).

For many, however, the empty nest period is a time of great satisfaction—once the adolescent rebellion is over, families may have improved relationships with their children. The husband and wife may take great pride in the accomplishments of their offspring, may be greatly pleased to see their children establishing families of their own, and may enjoy becoming grandparents (Neugarten & Weinstein, 1964). For a woman, the empty nest period may be a time of decreased responsibility, a time when she can finally pursue her own interests (Deutscher, 1964).

But other responsibilities may also keep a woman at home at this stage of her life. With increasing age, the middle-aged person's own parents are likely to become more dependent and may need extensive assistance. This responsibility usually falls to the woman (Gray & Smith, 1960; Robinson & Thurner, 1979; Townsend, 1968) and may entail great sacrifices of time and money. While having an active, healthy parent may be a source of comfort and reassurance in middle age, having to care for parents who show increasing signs of mental deterioration may be a source of great stress (Robinson & Thurner, 1972).

Nevertheless, the middle years are often times of the most satisfaction and happiness. The decrease in family responsibilities may encourage new ventures for both the woman, who may return to school or the work force, and the man, who may decide to take a risk and switch occupations to one he thinks might be more rewarding. The couple may find that they have time again not only for themselves but also for each other, and the increased privacy and leisure time may improve their sexual relationship. Many start saving and planning for their retirement, and look forward to various leisure activities such as traveling.

LATE ADULTHOOD

At the end of life our biology begins to claim us once again. There are certainly some declines in mental and physical functions, but if a person remains active, these are usually minimal. People who are *forced* to retire may begin to decline in functioning. Others, who find retirement a time of pleasure, may flourish.

For most older people, the traditional, "frail old person" stereotype does not apply. Due to better nutrition and medical care, many elderly are active and vigorous well into their seventies. Neugarten (1974) suggested that the elderly should be considered the "young-old" and the "old-old." The young-old, aged 55 to 75, have good health, relative economic security, and leisure time resulting from a decrease in traditional work and family responsibilities. The old-old are more likely to be frail and in ill health. Another myth about old age is that most adult children abandon their parents to nursing or old age homes. But only 4 to 5 percent of the elderly are institutionalized: families go through great sacrifices to maintain their parents at home (Lowenthal, 1964). Most elderly live near their children and have very frequent contact with them (Shanas, 1979).

There are, however, some inescapable facts of life that everyone faces in late adulthood. Bereavement and grief are a part of this phase of life. Just before death, we do decline, although we might cling to life for a while, to reach another birthday or to have an anniversary. Everyone dies, yet until recently, research on death has been as taboo as research on sex. The early evidence is that people go through a series of stages of dying, and it is not that unpleasant.

Retirement

Retirement at the end of life, with its implications of leisure time, is a recent phenomenon. Previously most people had worked until they were too ill to continue. But with better health and more economic security, many people look forward to (or dread) their retirement years.

Attitudes toward Retirement

The people who most look forward to retirement have an adequate income and care little about their work. Retirement is perceived as a chance to have fun and perhaps practice a skill or hobby that work left little time for. Retirement is dreaded most by those with erratic work histories and those who will not have sufficient funds for an adequate income after retirement. Professional people, or those who have a great deal invested in and derive much satisfaction from their work, tend to keep working longer. After retirement they may continue to work part-time or consult.

Most people's lives are structured by the demands of their jobs. Work provides an income and (it is hoped) satisfaction from a sense of having done something well, from practicing a skill or helping others. It also provides opportunities for social interaction and friendships. In retirement, people are more or less removed from their previous patterns of social interaction and sources of satisfaction. Retired spouses tend to see a lot more of each other (which may or may not be a good thing), and incomes are generally halved upon retirement. For most people, old age is associated with loss (roles, jobs, decreased income, death of one's spouse, decreased parental responsibilities, and, perhaps, diminished health and vigor).

The most important things that affect a person's adjustment to retirement are health and an adequate income. Some elderly may feel useless and regret the lack of responsibility. Others may have parents in their eighties and nineties who require a good deal of care or may assume major responsibility for raising their grandchildren, especially if their adult children are single parents. Others may start new careers.

Adjustment to Retirement

One of the most controversial theories in adult development is **disengagement theory.** In 1961, Cummings and Henry proposed that it is normal for the elderly to withdraw, or disengage, from society. They cite decreased energy levels, fewer social interactions, less investment in family relations, and so on, and suggest that disengagement is the most adaptive pattern for the elderly. This provoked a storm of controversy, and other studies found that *the elderly who kept active were the most satisfied with their lives* (Shanas et al., 1968; Havighurst, Neugarten, & Tobin, 1968).

Both sides assume that there is only one adaptive pattern for the elderly: disengagement *or* activity. However, there can be many adaptive styles: whether activity or disengagement is adaptive depends upon the individual. An individual who chooses relative activity or inactivity is likely to be satisfied; one who is forced against his or her wishes to be either active or inactive is likely to be unhappy (Neugarten, Havighurst, & Tobin, 1968).

Aging and Personality

There are very few well-documented changes in personality with age. One of the most consistent findings was noted by Jung in the 1930s. In later life people compensate for those aspects of their personality that were neglected in the first half—men begin to express the more feminine, or nurturant and receptive, tendencies, and women begin to express the more masculine, or aggressive and dominant, aspects (Neugarten, 1964). Lowenthal, Thurner, and Chiriboga (1975) noted:

> The preretired men are mellow—and significantly less dissatisfied and unhappy—compared to men at earlier stages . . . they see themselves as less hostile and more reasonable. They feel less ambitious but also less restless than any of the younger men. Unlike the middle-aged, they do not seem to feel the need to control others or to drive themselves. Rather, they manifest a concern for warm interpersonal relations. . . . In sum, the preretired men seem the group most comfortable, not only with others, but with themselves as well.

After describing the relatively poor self-image of newly wed and middle-aged women, they stated that, on the other hand:

> It is in the preretirement stage that women seem finally to hit their stride. The problems with competence, independence, and interpersonal relations . . . appear resolved. The preretired women see themselves as less dependent and helpless and as more assertive: "I don't have the fears and tragedies that I had when I was younger. I can say what I feel, I am not embarrassed by many things any more, and my personality is better."

It is interesting that women with careers did not experience this shift (Neugarten, 1964), although it is not clear if they became more nurturant.

Also, with increasing age, men and women often become more introspective, more reflective (Neugarten, 1977). Some introspective elderly note how their personality has developed with aging:

> I've become more tolerant of people, tolerant of their faults or objectionable features. I'll admit I have faults of my own and that I've made mistakes. I realize that other people have the same privilege. I don't carry my worries home from the plant any more. I used to worry, wake up in the night, but I don't do that anymore. (Reichard, Livson, & Peterson, 1962)

Integrity versus Despair

Erikson (1953) suggested that the self has a last developmental task: integrity versus despair. In this "crisis," a person evaluates his or her life and what meaning it may have had. Out of this may come integrity and wisdom; alternatively, a person may despair at the realization that there is no time left to start again. Butler (1963) has suggested that life review may facilitate the resolution of this crisis, and there is some evidence to suggest that reminiscence may be related to adaptive functioning in the elderly (Havighurst & Glaser, 1972). The achievement of integrity may allow a person to face his or her own death, and that of friends and family members, with more equanimity.

Bereavement and Widowhood

In the past, people of all ages had very frequent contact with death. The death of infants was more common than not, and longer-lived people could expect to bury two or three spouses. The death of a loved one at any age is a great loss, especially for very young children whose parent dies or for parents who lose a child. But the most traumatic bereavement may be the loss of a spouse.

Most women live longer than men and marry men older than themselves. There are far more widowed women than widowers in old age: if a woman marries a man ten years older than herself, she stands an 80 percent chance of being widowed by age 55 (Metropolitan Life Insurance Company, 1969).

The stressful effect of losing a spouse is reflected in health and mortality statistics. The bereaved person's health generally deteriorates, with loss of weight, sleeplessness, depression, general irritability, and an increased use of tranquilizers, alcohol, and cigarettes commonly reported (Weiner, Gerber, Battin, & Arlon, 1975). Not only do the bereaved visit their physicians more often (Parkes, 1972), they also face an increased risk of death in the first year after bereavement (Rees & Lutkins, 1967). Parkes and his colleagues (1969) found that a large percentage of these deaths were due to heart disease. Indeed, dying of "a broken heart" or grief was a recognized cause of death not so very long ago.

There are many reasons why widowhood is so traumatic. A widow's income generally drops dramatically (Parkes, 1972). As in divorce, the bereaved must now learn many new roles and skills formerly handled by the spouse: cooking, taking care of the car, managing the budget, repairs around the home, doing the laundry, and so forth. The social life changes—in a couple-oriented society, a woman may feel "like a fifth wheel" if she goes out with married friends, and she may gradually lose

contact with them. Many cultures place severe restrictions on widows (Lopata, 1979).

But the loss of the person you have loved and spent many years with is undoubtedly the hardest to bear. A person's identity may become so entwined with that of the spouse that many people feel as if they have lost a part of themselves.

"I feel as if half of myself was missing," said one widow, and another spoke of "a great emptiness." (Parkes, 1972)

Many widowed men and women sense the "presence" of their spouse, and actually feel that they have seen, heard, or spoken to their spouse. Nearly 50 percent of both a British sample (Morris, 1958) and a Welsh one (Rees, 1971) had such experiences, and Yamamoto and his colleagues (1969) found this in 90 percent of their sample of 20 Japanese widows. Such experiences are most likely to occur to people who had happy marriages. Most found the experience helpful (Rees, 1971), although some were very disturbed by "seeing" their spouse (Morris, 1974).

The Grief of Widowhood

Many other aspects of the grief reaction are similar the world over (Glick et al., 1974). The initial reaction is one of shock and disbelief, especially if the death was unexpected. For many, the shock is so great that they feel "numb," which prevents them from being overwhelmed by grief and allows them to carry on, at least briefly. But the numbness lasts only a few hours or days, and gives way to overwhelming grief and despair. Lindemann (1944) describes the "pangs of grief":

The picture showed by persons in acute grief is remarkably uniform. Common to all is the following syndrome: sensations of somatic distress occurring in waves lasting from twenty minutes to an hour at a time, a feeling of tightness in the throat, choking with a shortness of breath, need for sighing, an empty feeling in the abdomen, lack of muscular power, and an intense subjective distress described as tension or mental pain.

While such intense mourning generally lasts only a few weeks, the effects of bereavement last much longer, with exhaustion, loss of appetite, and inability to initiate activity; feelings of emptiness, guilt, apathy, hostility, and that life has no meaning are common. The person may feel unable to surrender the past—brooding over memories or refusing to let go of possessions—and may have feelings of unreality. It should be emphasized that these characteristics are not pathological, but are *normal* reactions to bereavement, which can continue for about a year.

Death and Dying

The death of others close to us reminds us of our own mortality. Everyone goes through specific life stages, from the egg to the embryo to

These pictures of Frank Tugend, from the book *Gramp*, by his grandsons Mark and Dan Jury, are part of the record of this 81-year-old man's final weeks of life and of his death, which took place at home and were witnessed by his family. Gramp's physical and mental decline put great stress on his family, but they maintained that the trying experience taught them a lot about life and themselves.

the fetus, the infant, the adolescent, adulthood. These periods are marked by specific maturational changes. Adulthood is less dominated by biology, as conscious choices determine how our adulthood develops. But we are never free of our physical nature, and as the end of life approaches, the last stage is biological and is common to all.

The Years before Death

Most people believe, somehow, that death is something that happens to others, not to them. But in late age, "cues" remind a person of his or her own death: parents and friends may die, health may deteriorate, and so on. People may begin to think in terms of how many years left to live rather than how many years since birth (Neugarten, 1964).

People who are close to death may experience subtle psychological changes before any obvious physical decline. There can be a marked decrease in intelligence scores *a few months* or *a year* before death, which Riegel and Riegel (1972) termed **terminal drop.** While there is some controversy about the timing and size of the decline, Botwinick, West, and Starandt (1978) found that slower response, slower learning and memory, a depression, lessened sense of control and self-rated health, strongly indicate people who are going to die.

Psychological Intervention in the Years before Death

The effect of psychological and personal processes on health, well-being and mortality in the elderly should not be underestimated. Kastenbaum and his colleagues have done a series of studies on raising the morale on geriatric wards in hospitals (Kastenbaum, 1965). Even beer and wine parties for patients and staff have a remarkable effect both on the morale of the staff and on physiological and psychological well-being in even severely impaired elderly. On one "hopeless" ward, elderly who had gross impairment showed marked gains; for example, incontinence was reduced. Other researchers have given plants to elderly in nursing homes. The aged who were asked to take care of their own plants (as opposed to being instructed that the staff would have that responsibility) were significantly happier, more alert, and spent more time interacting with others. A follow-up study showed that in a given period the responsibility-induced group was not only healthier than the comparison group, but also that less than half as many of them died. (Rodin & Langer, 1977).

There is also some clinical and anecdotal evidence that psychological factors can affect the timing of a person's death, either by the person dying prematurely—"losing the will to live" (Pattison, 1977)—or postponing death until a special occasion. There are fewer deaths than would be expected before a person's birthday, before presidential elections, and before important holidays (Phillips & Feldman, 1973). They concluded that this **anniversary effect** results from the persons postponing death.

The Stages of Death

Although research in this area is just beginning, one recent study describes five stages that a dying person goes through. These should not be thought of as necessarily sequential, but rather reflect common characteristics of the terminally ill (Kübler-Ross, 1969, 1975). The first stage is *denial* and *isolation*, which may function positively to keep the person from being overwhelmed with grief and to maintain hope. The second stage, *anger*, is a natural reaction to disrupted plans and loss of personal control. It is also a way of asserting that the person is still alive. In the third stage, the person may *bargain with fate*, that is, offering to devote the remaining life to God in exchange for a little more time. *Depression*, the fourth stage, is an understandable reaction to increasing debilitation, the tremendous financial burden of hospitalization, fear of losing loved ones. The dying may sometimes be unable to communicate with or may feel rejected by his or her family. Finally, some may *accept* impending death, sometimes aided by religious faith or by the understanding that one has lived a full and meaningful life. Kübler-Ross believes that if one has accepted his or her death, it is easier to die in peace and dignity.

While acknowledging the importance of Kübler-Ross's work, some researchers caution against a too literal interpretation (Kastenbaum, 1977.) They point out that these "stages" are not sequential; a person may go from anger to denial to hope to fear, and so on. There are many questions not addressed: Does age matter? The type of illness and setting? Are there personality, sex, or ethnic differences? It is clear that people do not die in the same manner. Hinton (1967) found that about half of his sample of patients openly acknowledged and accepted their death, though only a quarter showed a high degree of acceptance and composure. Another quarter expressed distress, and the remainder said very little about it.

Paradise, by Hieronymous Bosch

The Experience of Dying

While the *dying process* may be more or less painful or distressing, there have been intriguing clinical reports that the *experience of death* may be quite different. Ring (1980) studied 102 men and women who had "near-death experiences"—who had been very close to death or actually clinically dead and revived—and found highly interesting results. These people reported experiencing *intense feelings of peace* or *joy*, or felt that they *left their body* and *traveled* through a *dark tunnel*. In addition, they reported *seeing a brilliant light* or *beautiful colors*. A few reported *speaking with deceased relatives* or friends or a *"presence"* who convinced the person to return. They may also have felt that they had taken stock of their life by reviewing all or parts of it, sometimes in movie form.

This "core experience" seems to be ordered in five distinct stages: (1) feelings of peace and affective well-being; (2) body separation; (3) entering the darkness; (4) seeing the light; (5) entering the light. People who experienced the first stage reported a cessation of pain and intense feelings of joy, peace, or calm, usually unlike anything they had previously experienced. This has led to some speculation that endorphins are involved (Thomas, 1982). In the second stage, some people reported a sense of being detached from their bodies, and some even felt they were somehow looking down at their bodies. Those who did also reported an unusual brightness of the environment.

The next stage seemed to be one of transition. People would experience moving through a dark space, sometimes described as a tunnel. At the end of the "tunnel," there was often a brilliant light. Although very bright, it did not hurt the eyes, and was described as very comforting and beautiful. Finally, a very few people reported entering the light, which was somehow a different land—a field or valley, always very bright and beautiful, and indescribable.

There were other elements of the core experience, which cut across stages. These were the life review, encounter with "a presence" or deceased loved ones, and making the decision to return. In the life review, a person may experience all or part of his or her life in the form of visual, instantaneous images. This experience is usually positive, although people report a sense of detachment, and sometimes also an ability to "edit"—to move backward or forward or to "skip" certain parts.

Twenty people in Ring's sample experienced a "presence," which was rarely seen, but that somehow communicated directly with the person, offering him or her the opportunity to go back. This presence was sometimes interpreted within a religious framework—that is, as being God or Jesus for Christians and Krishna for Hindus (Osis & Hanalosen, 1977). Alternatively, a person may "be greeted" by the "spirits" of deceased loved ones, usually relatives, who inform the person that it is not time yet, and that he or she must go back.

The frequency and intensity of the core experience tended to be greatest for illness victims, moderate for accident victims, and very low for attempted suicides. Interestingly, the few attempted suicides who had core experiences did not use drugs, which may suppress the experience, but they still had fewer "transcendent" elements, and their experiences tended to differ from the non-suicides. While not everyone in Ring's sample experienced all or any of these phenomena, *not one person had a negative experience.*

The Soul Hovering Over the Body Reluctantly Parting with Life, **by William Blake**

No one is really sure why some people have these experiences, or why some people have them and others do not—or at least do not remember them. (Ring reported one person whose eyewitnesses said he revived speaking of these things, but later on did not remember.) We know little about this and it is quite controversial. There were no demographic differences (age, sex, social class, marital status, religion) in Ring's sample between experiencers and nonexperiencers. While the experiences may be interpreted within a religious framework, religiousness is unrelated to the likelihood or to the depth of the core experiences.

> I believe in the basis of all religions. They're all connected as far as I'm concerned.

> I don't think of religion as a religion any more. God is above all religions. God is the religion, so, therefore, the various religions have no effect whatsoever on me.

Finally, it did not appear to be due to suggestion, because people who had *not* previously heard of this phenomenon were *more* likely to experience it. Regardless of whether or not a person had a core experience, the experience of nearly dying almost always had a positive effect on the person's life.

Everyone who had a brush with death came away a different person. As one young man said,

> [I had an] awareness that something more was going on in life than just the physical part of it. . . . It was just a total awareness of not just the material and how much we can buy. . . . There's more than just consuming life. There's a point where you have to *give* to it and that's real important. And there was an awareness at that point that I had to give more of myself *out* of life. That awareness has come to me.

Ring summarizes:

> The typical near-death survivor emerges from his experience with a heightened sense of appreciation for life, determined to live life to the fullest. He has a purpose in living, even though he cannot articulate just what this purpose is.

This study is, of course, exploratory. However, it indicates that our ideas about death, or at least dying, may need to change, as have our ideas about adulthood. Some psychologists think these experiences are simple hallucinations (Siegel, 1980), but the common elements in the experience indicate that perhaps dying is not a terrible experience after all, hallucination or not.

So, at the end, our biology reclaims us once again, quietly and pleasantly. It completes the story begun before we were born.

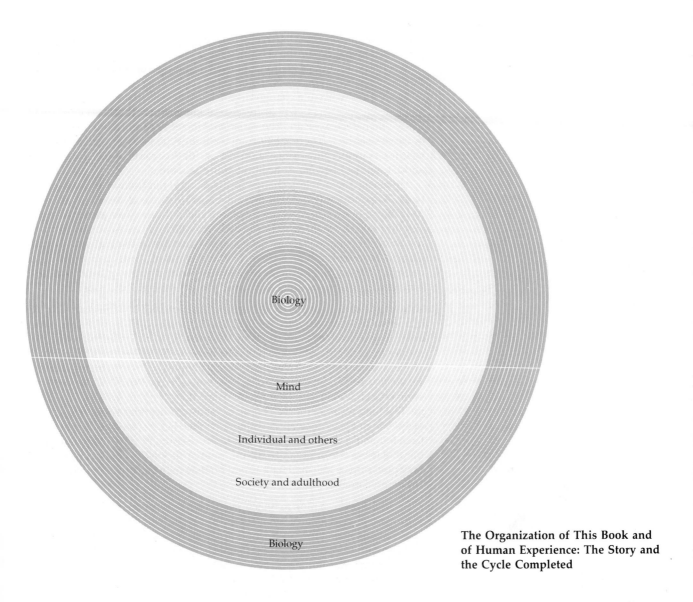

Biology

Mind

Individual and others

Society and adulthood

Biology

The Organization of This Book and of Human Experience: The Story and the Cycle Completed

Summary

1. There has been much recent interest among psychologists in the developmental processes of adulthood. One theory of adult development is that of Levinson. It postulates that at different ages adults go through certain stages of development, including several transitional periods. They are: ages 17 to 22, early adult transition; 22 to 28, entering the adult world; 28 to 33, age 30 transition; 33 to 40, settling down; 40 to 45, midlife transition; 45 to 50, entering middle adulthood; 50 to 55, age 50 transition; 55 to 60, second middle adult structure; and 60 to 65, late adult transition.

2. There are several biological changes that predictably occur in adulthood, but nobody really knows why we age. Aging results from many different processes, some of which are genetically controlled. There are many biological factors in aging, however—background radiation may damage the DNA,

the information in the DNA cells may degrade as replication occurs, the mechanisms that repair the cells may break down, and changes in the cells may contribute to their malfunctioning and may result in diseases such as cancer, diabetes, hypertension, and so forth.

There are predictable changes in the body: height generally increases up to about age 45, then slowly decreases; shoulder width increases until about age 35, then decreases; and chest diameter increases until about age 54, then decreases slightly. The relative composition of the body also changes with age: for example, muscle mass decreases, the percentage of fat increases, and fat tends to become concentrated in the trunk.

However, there is less change in the aging brain than in the rest of the body. It is commonly thought that the brain loses cells as we age, but this is probably not the case. Most brain cells are lost in the first few years of life and very few later if we develop normally. Diamond and her associates recently found that it is possible to actually increase the size of the brain in very old animals by offering them an enriched environment. Instead of thinking of ourselves as people who are destined to inevitably decline, at least in mental functioning in age, we might consider the old saying, "use it or lose it."

3. As we age, what happens to our intellectual capacity? If we measure our IQ in a cross-sectional sample, we find that IQ scores decline with age; however, if we control for *cohort effects* and examine IQ in a *longitudinal sample*, the results are very different—the older the person, the higher the IQ. Taking all of these factors into consideration, verbal abilities seem to remain relatively constant or increase slightly with age, whereas measures of performance seem to decline. The elderly perform worse than younger groups if the tasks involve long-term memory. There are many studies that show that elderly people do not learn as well as younger people. Several reasons for this have been found: (1) they may take longer to process and retrieve information, (2) they fail to encode or organize the information as well as younger people, (3) they prefer preestablished habits, and (4) they may be very uncomfortable in laboratory situations.

4. Early adulthood is a time in which many people form their "dream," a hazy and unarticulated idea of what they want to do with their lives. The hallmarks of this period for most people are beginning a career, getting married, and becoming a parent. Of all these, marriage has the most profound impact on a person's development. Few people enter marriage with any realistic expectations about what it is like, and many commentators regard the needs of males and females as so different that they refer to "his" and "her" marriages. However, barring disaster, *the first year of marriage is often remembered as the happiest time of people's lives.*

Statistically speaking, marriage appears to be very beneficial—at least for men. Compared to men who are divorced, widowed, or who have never married, married men live longer, have fewer mental and physical illnesses, and appear happier. However, married women have higher rates of depression than married men.

There are four factors in satisfying marriages: (1) commitment to the relationship, (2) communication, (3) role flexibility, and (4) having a separate identity and greater acceptance of oneself as a unique person, while accepting the partner's growth and autonomy.

5. The rate of divorce is at an all-time high. One-third of all marriages currently can expect to end in divorce. There are four periods of the divorce process: marital distress, the decision to divorce, separation, and postdivorce. The separation period is the most stressful. It is just as painful whether one is

leaving a relatively "good" or a relatively "bad" marriage. However, in post-divorce both men and women are likely to state that their situation is better than it was before the divorce. The social adjustment after divorce can be quite difficult. People may discover that the friends they thought were "theirs" were actually closer to their spouse, and friendships and other social networks may become disrupted. Women with children may have an especially hard time dating, although men usually enter into a "flurry" of social activity. Overall, sexual and social experiences appear to be the best resource for coping with the stress of divorce.

6. For people who have followed traditional family and career patterns, the thirties—middle adulthood—are generally a time of settling down. Middle age is more of a social stage in life than a specific biological event, although most researchers set it from about age 40 to about 65. No one knows how many people experience a *midlife crisis*. Contrary to the popular stereotype of a high-flying executive having a midlife crisis, it may be poorer people who are likely to become depressed at midlife. The woman who remains strongly involved with her children may have difficulty with the *empty nest period* when children leave home and become increasingly independent.

   Menopause generally occurs between the ages of 48 to 51 and may be associated with hot flashes, irritability, crying spells, and depression. However, one study reported that 75 percent did not have any of these symptoms. It is primarily *younger* women who have not experienced menopause who feel that it is a disagreeable event.

7. In late adulthood our biology begins to claim us once again. Retirement is a recent phenomenon, and a number of studies have found that the elderly who kept active were the most satisfied with their lives—a finding that supports the idea of "use it or lose it."

8. As people age, their friends tend to age, and older people begin to have more contact with death and dying. Most women live longer than men and marry men older than themselves. Therefore, if a woman marries a man ten years older than herself, she stands an 80 percent chance of being widowed by age 55. The stressful effect of losing a spouse is reflected in health and mortality statistics. The bereaved person's health generally deteriorates.

   There are many reasons why widowhood is so traumatic. The widow's income generally drops dramatically, and the bereaved must learn many new roles and skills formerly handled by the spouse.

   The death of others close to us reminds us of our own mortality. In late age, there are many "cues" that remind people of their own death: parents and friends may die, or health may deteriorate. People may shift their thinking: they now consider how many years they have left to live rather than how many years since birth. There can be a marked decrease in intelligence scores very close to death, which is called the *terminal drop*.

   Although research on the stages of death is just beginning, one recent study describes five stages that a dying person goes through. They include: denial and isolation, which may function positively to keep the person from being overwhelmed with grief; anger, a natural reaction to disrupted plans and loss of personal control; trying to bargain with fate; depression; and finally, for some people, acceptance of their impending death. These stages are not sequential, but reflect common characteristics of the terminally ill. There are also quite tentative, but intriguing, reports that while the *dying process* may be more or less painful or distressing, the *experience of death* is quite unique. At the end, it is our biology that reclaims us, quietly and pleasantly, when we return to the biological pool.

Terms and Concepts

anniversary effect

cohort effect

disengagement theory

empty nest period

false assumptions

longitudinal study

mentor

midlife crisis

psychosocial development

terminal drop

timetables

Suggestions for Further Reading

Blythe, R. (1979). *The view in winter: Reflections on old age.* New York: Harcourt Brace Jovanovich.

How people see themselves as they age, in their own words. Wonderful reading.

Dubos, R. (1978, January). Health and creative adaptation. *Human Nature.*

An important summary of how our built environment extends and limits our abilities.

Hall, E. T. (1969). *The hidden dimension.* New York: Anchor Press.

Perhaps the most worthwhile book ever written on our personal space. It is well written and presents an important viewpoint often lacking in social and adult development.

Levinson, D. (1978). *The seasons of a man's life.* New York: Knopf.

One of the first modern developmental studies of adulthood. It is often criticized for focusing on well-educated males, but it remains important.

Ring, K. (1980). *Life at death.* New York: Coward, McCann and Geoghegan.

A study that breaks modern psychology's taboos. It investigates the experiences of people who have clinically died and were revived. It is quite controversial, but it raises some very important questions at the bounds of psychology and, obviously, about the nature of life itself.

Appendix

Statistics: Making Sense of Fallible Data

by Geoffrey Iverson, Northwestern University

INTRODUCTION

Take a long hard look at the world. Try to describe what you see. All of it, as precisely, as completely as you can.

You will soon give up in frustration. There is just too much going on, too much detail, too much change, too much that appears arbitrary. No two peas, no two people, no two pearls are exactly alike. Sometimes dogs chase cats, sometimes they do not.

Fortunately, we spend little time bogged down in this mire of detail. The world, as it actually is, as it really occurs, is something we hardly notice. Individual detail is sacrificed for the sake of clarity; attention is confined to trends, tendencies, regularities that (somehow) manifest themselves despite idiosyncrasy and happenstance.

When sailing, you know the importance of gauging wind direction. For this, a triangular piece of cloth—a flag—is often employed. Despite the fact that the flag never stays put, is never in exactly the same position twice, it serves its purpose as a directional indicator pretty well. There is constancy in its motion, a regularity that is unaffected by irregular, moment-to-moment fluctuations. Such regularity emerges almost automatically, a useful end product of visual processing and short-term memory. No conscious calculation is involved, and none is needed. For we have inherited an amazingly powerful and flexible visual system that, as long as our eyes are open, provides us with the information needed to successfully navigate our way through a world seething with inconsequential detail. "How do we extract stability from the irregular, unpredict-able motion of a flag?" is a question for the psychophysics and physiology of vision. We ask a different, less specific question, one which does not require a detailed discussion of vision: How might we describe things so as to reveal, on a piece of paper, the hidden regularity in "fallible" (i.e., variable) data, be they sensory or otherwise?

Suppose we can measure the direction of the tip of the flag at any designated time. This might be done, for instance, by taking a movie of the flag—a sequence of still shots, each of which yields an instantaneous measurement. Let us record these measurements as compass positions, that is, in degrees with respect to the fixed direction North. (See Figure 1) We have recorded 20 such measurements

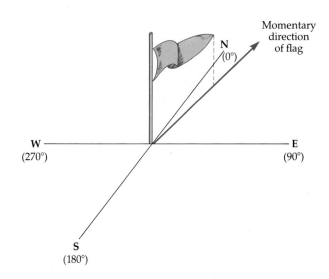

Figure 1　Direction of flag (degrees of compass).

Movie frame	1	2	3	4	5	6	7	8	9	10
Direction of flag (degrees)	10.2	5.8	7.1	3.0	8.9	5.4	4.8	6.2	4.1	7.4
Movie frame	11	12	13	14	15	16	17	18	19	20
Direction of flag (degrees)	3.8	5.3	6.0	6.9	5.1	5.7	8.3	5.2	4.3	4.9

Table 1 Twenty instantaneous measurements of flag direction.

as they occur in our movie, frame by frame. These are given in Table 1. But there is no simple, unitary direction of wind peering up at us from Table 1, just a bunch of rather different numbers. Perhaps we would be better off drawing a graph. In Figure 2 we have plotted the measurements of Table 1 as flag positions versus movie frame numbers. This graph is a history of the flag position over time, exactly as it was recorded in the sequence of movie frames.

Does Figure 2 remind you of anything? If you have any interest in the goings on of the stock mar-

ket, it might occur to you that the graph of Figure 2 is not unlike, say, the Dow-Jones average. To make this analogy clearer, in Figure 3 we have plotted "typical" Dow behavior for a "typical" week. Although the units have changed between Figures 2 and 3 (Figure 2 plots position, while Figure 3 plots the Dow index), the appearance of each figure is essentially the same. If we can come to terms with one figure, may we not come to terms with the other? Note that in Figure 3 each day's trading has been divided into four separate values, taken in succession: an opening figure, a morning figure, an afternoon figure and a closing figure.

Let us try a description of Figure 3 along the lines of Wall Street: The events of the weekend were immediately apparent. In a run that showed only a minor correction after lunch, the Dow dropped 22 points on Monday. A rally early on Tuesday was not sustained, though by Tuesday's close there was a hint of recovery. This promise persisted, somewhat nervously, through Wednesday and Thursday, but on Friday the market began to slide again and by week's end the Dow had dropped 16 points altogether.

Can we profit from this blow-by-blow description of the stock market in gauging direction? I suggest not. There ought to be a better way of visualizing the data of Table 1 than is conveyed by Figure 2. Let us

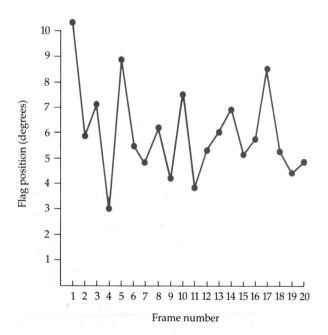

Figure 2 Motion of a flag depicted graphically. (Source: Table 1)

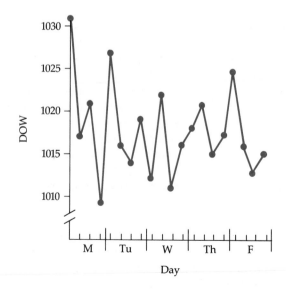

Figure 3 Hypothetical weekly record of Dow–Jones average. (Source: Figure 2)

see what happens if we represent each of the twenty measurements given in Table 1 by a cross (x) on a line:

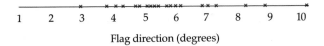

Flag direction (degrees)

Figure 4 (Source: Table 1)

The picture that emerges is reasonably easy to interpret. While the x's are scattered about alright, this scatter is confined to a modest range of roughly 7° (3° to a little over 10°). Moreover, there is a marked concentration of crosses lying between 4° and 6°, and it is not unreasonable to summarize things in the following practical form: The wind direction is approximately 5° east of north.

As a visual representation, the picture above is pretty ugly. We can achieve a more pleasing picture by sacrificing unnecessary precision. We therefore round the measurements of Table 1 to the nearest whole degree. Thus, the first measurement, 10.2° becomes 10°; the next, 5.8°, is rounded to 6°; and so on. In this way we obtain the following list of rounded measurements:

Frame number	1	2	3	4	5	6	7	8	9	10
Direction	10	6	7	3	9	5	5	6	4	7
Frame number	11	12	13	14	15	16	17	18	19	20
Direction	4	5	6	7	5	6	8	5	4	5

Table 2 Data of Table 1 rounded to nearest whole number.

Many of our measurements are now identical. This suggests the following strategy: Count the number of times that each of the rounded measurements occurs in Table 2, recording these counts in a new table—an inventory, if you will—as has been done in Table 3.

Direction	1	2	3	4	5	6	7	8	9	10
Frequency	0	0	1	3	6	4	3	1	1	1

Table 3 Frequency with which each direction occurs in Table 2.

The inventory of Table 3 allows a simple, elegant picture to emerge in the alternative form of a bar graph, or *histogram* (Figure 5). The original twenty individual, distinct measurements of wind direction are reduced to a visual form that reveals their collective regularity at a glance. Curiously, but significantly, this regularity was achieved by throwing away information. (This, by the way, is true of vision and our other senses. If what we see, hear, feel etc. were faithful copies of sensory stimuli, the world would appear to be quite chaotic.)

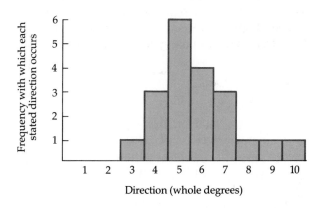

Direction (whole degrees)

Figure 5 Frequency with which each direction occurs in Table 2.

The process we just went through is a rudimentary example of a *statistical analysis*, a process of organizing evidence, typically numerical, so as to reveal tendencies, trends, regularities, and so on that are often present in collections of measurements but that are quite difficult, even impossible to detect in any individual measurement.

A major benefit of a statistical description of data is the simple, clear picture that often emerges: the forest is emphasized at the expense of the individual trees. But you would be right to critically examine this unqualified endorsement of statistical description over individual point-by-point description. For, while we rejected the "Wall Street" description of the motion of a flag in favor of the simplicity manifest in a bar graph, should we not, likewise, regard the Dow in the same way? A full answer is complicated, and we content ourselves with a simple "No." To appreciate the difference between the stock market and a piece of cloth flapping in a steady breeze, we need to free ourselves from the shackles of mechanical habit, of blindly following a recipe. The recipe, "construct a histogram" applied to the data of Figure 2, leads to the highly interpretable picture of Figure 5; applied to the very similar data of Figure 3 it would lead to a very similar picture, but one that most stock market analysts would label as worthless.

There seems to be a paradox here. To resolve it, let us examine in more detail what one preserves in a histogram, and more important, what one throws away.

It is useful to go back to the source of our data, namely, a movie, a sequence of individual photographs, each of which gives rise to an individual measurement. Suppose we ran our movie backward. Would the wind direction change? Of course not. Even more drastically, suppose we arbitrarily shuffled the order of the frames that make up our movie—thereby creating a new one. Would the wind direction change? Again the answer is "no," no matter what the order. While the momentary fluctuations of the flag are different for each of the (roughly) 2.4 billion billion movies created by shuffling the order of 20 individual frames, the histogram and estimate of wind direction accompanying each such movie would remain exactly the same. But this is emphatically not so for the analogous stock market descriptions. Taking into account the precise sequence of events is of obvious importance for deciding when to buy, when to sell; similar considerations of sequential order are (at least over the short haul) quite irrelevant when one is out sailing. To follow the recipe "construct a histogram" is to implicitly assume that the order of measurements is irrelevant to the object or system under study. We do not usually care if a big cloud follows a little one, or vice versa; only that it might rain. But we behave and feel very differently if the prime lending rate is on the increase rather than on the decline.

In psychology, as in any science, we place a premium on "stable," replicable measurements; a great deal of experience, common sense, and ingenuity goes into this endeavor. Is there any reason to distinguish in ability two students who in a one-semester course receive respective homework grades of A, B, B, C, A, B, B, B, C and C, B, B, A, B, B, A, C, B? Each student's performance is characterized by the same histogram; each is a solid "B." This is not to say that people do not learn, do not change their behavior, do not adopt new habits, change their opinions . . . Of course they do. But to understand learning or to measure a change in some behavior requires us to measure knowledge or behavior "before and after" learning or change. Those static "before and after" measurements are crucial, for it is by way of comparison that we are able to detect change or acknowledge that learning has taken place. Just as important as the role statistics plays for the *description* of stable practical measurement is the related role it plays in detecting change.

The question "Has the wind changed?" is one that requires the apparatus of *statistical inference*. Moreover, at least in some circumstances, the issue may not be settled with the mere detection of change. If the wind changes direction by 1°, what do we (usually) care? What we do with the outcome of a statistical analysis, what actions we take, is an issue for *decision theory*. Unfortunately, decision theory remains in its infancy, and we shall not have much to say about it.

To summarize, statistics divides itself into three major areas, *descriptive statistics, statistical inference,* and *decision theory*. These form a sort of hierarchy in that issues which are unresolved at one level become the dominant focus at the next. We devote the rest of our discussion to a sketch of the first two levels of statistical enquiry, description and inference.

DESCRIPTIVE STATISTICS

The major function of description is to *accurately* represent a set of observations of the world in as condensed a form as seems appropriate. Weather reports, the Dow-Jones average, baseball "stats," grade point averages, IQs, Nielsen ratings are all examples of the use of descriptive statistics.

Condensing a large set of measurements or facts without destroying their collective integrity is termed *data reduction*, and it is characterized by a number of useful procedures (which we shall call *algorithms*) of wide applicability. We have already seen in action one of the most widely used algorithms, namely "form a histogram." We have also seen that blind application of this algorithm may lead nowhere, or worse, to potential misrepresentation. Yet a sensitive, informed descriptive analysis can be of great power and beauty. A good description often allows data to "speak for themselves."

A common form of data reduction is provided by a *table*. Baseball statistics are usefully represented in this form. A historically early example presenting tabulated data is given in Table 4.

Tables are very useful devices for collecting information related to some specific issue. The visual format of a sensibly organized table allows the eye to quickly pick out clusters of related information that might otherwise go unnoticed. Indeed, important questions and hypotheses often emerge from a scrutiny of tabulated information. Tables are most commonly used to list categories of some focus of interest; for example, diseases and other causes of death. Typically, numerical information accompanies each category; thus, for instance, we see from Table 4 that in 1632 *62* Londoners died "Suddenly" (of a heart attack?), while but *46* were "Kil'd by several accidents."

The algorithms "form a table" and "form a bar graph" are sometimes equivalent. For example, there is no more, nor less information in Table 3 than is represented by the histogram of Figure 5. However it would not be very natural to represent a grocery list as a bar graph. (If you are not sure why, try it).

2 lb. apples	$1.48
1 qt. milk	.64
3 lb. onions	$1.00
• •	•
• •	•
• •	•

In many applications, categories are artificially formed by grouping measurements (of a single entity) that fall into a narrow range, *bin*, or *interval* of values. Rounding measurements is a typical way of creating categories in this manner (recall the transition from Table 1 to Table 3). When categories of a single quantity, such as wind direction, reaction time, height, weight, are involved, a histogram is often preferred to a table (compare Table 3 with the visual clarity of Figure 5). Our next example, which requires some preamble, is a beautiful illustration of the power of a well-constructed histogram.

As you know, the nervous system is composed of billions of neurons more-or-less grouped into bundles according to "purpose." Information is transmitted by these neurons both electrically and chemically. The easiest, most direct measurements are those of electrical activity and, not surprisingly, recordings of neural events (action potentials, or

The Diseases, and Casualties this year being 1632.

Disease	Count	Disease	Count
Abortive, and Stillborn	445	Grief	11
Affrighted	1	Jaundies	43
Aged	628	Jawfaln	8
Ague	43	Impostume	74
Apoplex, and Meagrom	17	Kil'd by several accidents	46
Bit with a mad dog	1	King's Evil	38
Bleeding	3	Lethargie	2
Bloody flux, scowring, and flux	348	Livergrown	87
Brused, Issues, sores, and ulcers	28	Lunatique	5
Burnt, and Scalded	5	Made away themselves	15
Burst, and Rupture	9	Measles	80
Cancer, and Wolf	10	Murthered	7
Canker	1	Over-laid, and starved at nurse	7
Childbed	171	Palsie	25
Chrisomes, and Infants	2268	Piles	1
Cold, and Cough	55	Plague	8
Colick, Stone, and Strangury	56	Planet	13
Consumption	1797	Pleurisie, and Spleen	36
Convulsion	241	Purples, and spotted Feaver	38
Cut of the Stone	5	Quinsie	7
Dead in the street, and starved	6	Rising of the Lights	98
Dropsie, and Swelling	267	Sciatica	1
Drowned	34	Scurvey, and Itch	9
Executed, and prest to death	18	Suddenly	62
Falling Sickness	7	Surfet	86
Fever	1108	Swine Pox	6
Fistula	13	Teeth	470
Flocks, and small Pox	531	Thrush, and Sore mouth	40
French Pox	12	Tympany	13
Gangrene	5	Tissick	34
Gout	4	Vomiting	1
		Worms	27

| Christened | { Males.... 4994
Females . 4590
In all .... 9584 } | Buried | { Males.... 4932
Females . 4603
In all .... 9535 } | Whereof,
of the
Plague.8 |

Increased in the Burials in the 122 Parishes, and at the Pesthouse this year 993
Decreased of the Plague in the 122 Parishes, and at the Pesthouse this year 266

Table 4 A mortality table for the year 1632, London. (Source: John Graunt, "Natural and Political Observations made upon the Bills of Mortality," 1662)

"spikes") from a single cell are of great importance for neurophysiology. It is possible to record the activity induced in a primary auditory neuron by an externally applied tone of fixed frequency and intensity. Our very ability to hear, particularly to distinguish one sound from another, strongly suggests that the nervous activity induced by physical sound is a sort of "code," a running record of those aspects of a physical stimulus that are crucial for its recognition and eventual meaning. Physiologists spend a good deal of effort attempting to decode neural activity, especially the activity produced in response to simple stimuli such as pure tones. To a physicist however, a tone is an undulating pressure wave, as depicted in Figure 6.

An obvious feature of a tone is its *period*, the time between two consecutive peaks of physical pressure. The question naturally arises: Is periodicity present in the activity of a single auditory neuron? As we shall see below, the answer is "Yes," but it is not at all obvious at first glance. For, a spike train recorded in response to a tone looks something like that depicted in Figure 7. Disappointingly there does not appear to be any semblance of periodic behavior. But it is there alright. The way to see it is to form an *interval histogram*, that is, an inventory of intervals between successive spikes (Presenting a tone over and over again allows the inventory to grow arbitrarily large). An example of such a histogram is displayed in Figure 8. It is apparent that the intervals between neural spikes are clustered at precise multiples of the stimulus period: in other words, each cluster is separated by exactly one stimulus period. The activity of a single auditory neuron

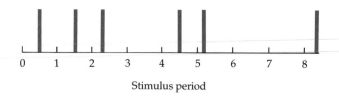

Stimulus period

Figure 7 Neural responses to a pure tone.

is locked in synchrony with the stimulus (at least at moderate to low frequencies), thus preserving ("coding") the periodicity of the stimulus.

I shall leave the interpretation of the following example to you, except for an intellectual challenge: do you see a rough similarity between the periodicity evident in Figure 8 and the data of Figure 9 concerning times at which pregnancies are aborted in women?

It is not uncommon to reduce the information in a histogram or table even further. We did this in our discussion of how to use a flag to measure the direction of a steady breeze. Recall that we reduced twenty individual measurements first to a histogram and then to a single summary statement: "The wind direction is approximately 5° east of north." There are two key issues here, one having to do with the term "approximately," the other being the numerical value "5°." We shall deal with the latter first, taking up the former somewhat later on.

Frequently it is useful to summarize in part a set of data or histogram by a single number, a measure of *location* or *central tendency*. When we look at the histogram of Figure 5, is it not apparent that the data

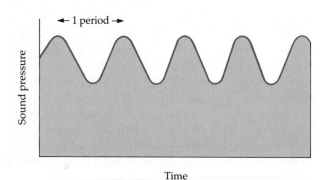

Time

Figure 6 A pure tone as regarded by physics.

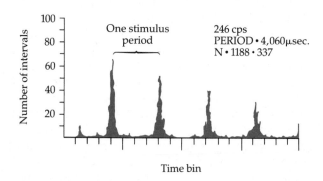

Figure 8 Interval histogram of a single auditory neuron driven by a pure tone of period 4,060 microseconds—roughly middle C. (Source: Rose et al., 1967)

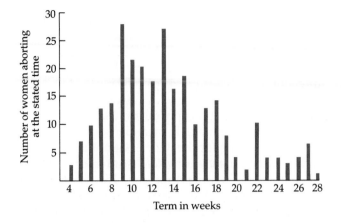

Figure 9   Abortion in women. (Source: data of T.V. Pearce, 1930)

are fairly evenly distributed about a value of 5° or so? We can be even more systematic about this.

There are a number of useful indices of location employed in practice, and of these, three are usually singled out as having the widest application. They are the *mode*, the *mean*, and the *median*. The mode is easy to define: it is the most frequently occurring category (the tallest bar in a histogram). In Figure 5, the category "5°" occurs more often than any other, so the mode of that histogram is 5°. The median of a set of measurements is that value that divides the set in two: half the measurements fall below the median, half above. The median of the set of directions recorded in Table 1 is somewhere between 5.3° and 5.7°, and it is sufficient for our purposes to record the median as 5.5°. Finally, the mean of a set of measurements is just their arithmetic average. If we compute the arithmetic average of the twenty values listed in Table 1, we find that it is 5.9°. These three numerical values, 5°, 5.5°, 5.9° are different, but sufficiently close in magnitude that no one would (usually) care which was selected. This close agreement will occur whenever a histogram is more or less "heaped symmetrically" about its mode, but there are many examples of data that do not distribute themselves in this way. Income provides a notorious example. The average income of people who work in a factory is dramatically influenced by a few large managerial salaries together with many much smaller salaries paid to workers on the production line. The average of one $100,000 salary and ten $10,000 salaries is $18,182, hardly representative of

anyone's income. Both the modal, and median salaries are more reasonable reflections of reality: $10,000.

A histogram may occur as a "mixture" of two or more others. It is not uncommon for such mixtures to be accompanied by two or more distinct modes. Notice, in Figure 10, the bimodal nature of a "living histogram" of men and women arranged according to height. If one were to construct two histograms, one for each sex, they would each be characterized by a single mode.

This example should not be taken as indicating that more than one mode necessarily indicates the presence of more than one underlying structure. It can certainly occur that a single system is naturally characterized by several modes. An example is provided by gambling. Have you not noticed playing poker, say, that you are either "hot," or "cold"? In fact in a simple game between two players, involving the tossing of a fair (unbiased) coin, it is common for one player to be ahead for the entire duration of the game! Despite this, over many such games of the same length, the average winnings will be zero for each player. An appropriately constructed histogram would be diagrammatically U-shaped, showing two pronounced modes (always ahead, and always behind), with a mean of zero in between. Both the modes and the mean are reflections of single underlying mechanism: pure chance.

Figure 10   A bimodal histogram of college students arranged by height.

An additional comment is in order before we proceed further. The calculation of a mean requires the arithmetic operations of addition and multiplication. These operations may be inappropriate, indeed meaningless, if applied without thought. For example, we may jocularly categorize the major interests of teenagers as "sex," "drugs," and "rock 'n' roll." What is the average category of interest? The answer is not to be found in some verbal contrivance such as "averaging" the category labels to get "drolex." There simply is no answer, for the question as posed is meaningless. Likewise, to compute a median requires that a meaningful *order* be established for the category values or labels. Only the mode remains unaffected by such considerations of meaningfulness (or *scale type* in more traditional jargon). One can always sensibly ask: What is the most frequent category? Alas, the answer may be none, many—or worse—may be irrelevant.

A histogram is not often well represented by a mere measure of location, for such measures are essentially blind to the "width" or dispersion of the histogram. It is one thing to know that the modal direction of a breeze is 5° east of north, but quite another to know that it varies over a 7° range. To quote the mean direction of the Mississippi is to quite ignore its incredible meander.

To compensate for the deficiencies of measures in location, measures of *variability* (scatter, spread, dispersion, . . .) are introduced. The *range* of a set of measurements is one such measure: this is simply the difference between the largest and smallest of a set of measurements. The range of the data listed in Table 1 is $10.2° - 3.0° = 7.2°$.

Just as there are several useful indices of location, so too there are a number of measures of variability in use. The most outstanding of these is *variance*, together with its closely related sibling, *standard deviation*. Like the mean, variance is an arithmetic average, not of a set of raw measurements, but of squared *deviations*. A deviation is computed for each raw measurement by subtracting from it the value of the common mean. These deviations are squared so as to eliminate the distinction between positive and negative values, and they are subsequently averaged to produce the variance. In Figure 11 these arithmetic operations are illustrated on the data of Table 1.

The variance of the data of Table 1 is given by the average of the squared deviations listed in the rightmost column of Figure 11. We see that

$$\text{variance} = \frac{60.644}{20} = 3.032.$$

(Note in passing that the average of the middle column, that is, the average of the (unsquared) deviations, is zero. This is no accident—it is a simple algebraic consequence of the definition of a deviation and provides a useful check on intermediate calculations). Standard deviation arises from variance by extracting a square root: thus, for the above data,

$$\text{standard deviation} = \sqrt{3.032} = 1.74$$

Why bother with standard deviation when variance will do? The reason is one of convenience; a standard deviation possesses the same units as the original data, and may be pictured as a "distance" from the mean value. Standard deviation provides a

Original measurement	Deviations	Squared deviations
(Flag directions)	(Measurement– Mean)	
10.2	4.28	18.318
5.8	–0.12	0.014
7.1	1.18	1.392
3.0	–2.92	8.526
8.9	2.98	8.880
5.4	–0.52	0.270
4.8	–1.12	1.254
6.2	0.28	0.078
4.1	–1.82	3.312
7.4	1.48	2.190
3.8	–2.12	4.494
5.3	–0.62	0.384
6.0	0.08	0.006
6.9	0.98	0.960
5.1	–0.82	0.672
5.7	–0.22	0.048
8.3	2.38	5.664
5.2	–0.72	0.518
4.3	–1.62	2.624
4.9	–1.02	1.040
Average = $\frac{118.4}{20}$	Average = 0	Average = $\frac{60.644}{20}$
= 5.92		= 3.032
= Mean		= Variance

Figure 11 Calculating a variance. (Source: data from Table 1)

gauge of how discrepant individual values are from the mean, and hence how discrepant they are from each other. A rule of thumb for histograms is this: Nearly all measurements fall within ±2 standard deviations from the mean. In other words, one can expect the range of a typical set of data to be about four standard deviations. For the data of Table 1, we noted above that the range was 7.2°. This is close to 4 × 1.74° = 6.96°, in accord with the rule of thumb.

Thus far we have exclusively considered univariate data, that is, measurements pertaining to a single numerical quantity such as time, direction, salary, and so on, or to a single qualitative variable such as sex, occupation, marital status. Inventories of such measurements lend themselves to organization in the form of tables, bar graphs, histograms, which in appropriate cases allow for further reduction to a measure of location and one of variabilty.

Sometimes this is enough, especially if all that is required is an assertion of simple fact: "The life expectancy of a Saudi Arabian is presently 42 years"; "the proportion of 15-to-18-year-olds enrolled in education in the U.S. was 84% in 1976"; "the infant mortality rate is 15 per 1,000 births in the U.S.; on average in the U.S., someone is murdered every 23 seconds, and every 6 minutes a woman is raped."

There are many classes of statements that are rather more complex: "From 1963 to 1980, average verbal scores on the College Board's Scholastic Aptitude Test dropped over 50 points, and average mathematics scores dropped nearly 40 points"; "Warning: The Surgeon General has determined that cigarette smoking is dangerous to your health"; "Psychologists have shown a connection between viewing violence on TV and aggressive behavior"; "It's easier to recognize a face than it is to recall the right name"; and so on. When dissected, such statements are seen to involve two or more variables or two or more sets of measurements. For instance, the Surgeon General's warning means, in large part, that there is a difference in the incidence of various diseases (lung cancer, emphysema, heart ailments, etc.) for those who smoke cigarettes and those who do not and, moreover, that such differences cannot reasonably be attributed to other possible sources (alcohol, place of domicile—urban vs. rural—anxiety, etc.).

The ability to detect change, to recognize differences, to notice that one variable (say, height) is linked to another (say, weight) are all crucial for what is perhaps the major ambition of science: to provide a simple yet highly precise description of the world. No encyclopedia of bare facts is adequate to this task.

The question "Does juvenile delinquency increase with population density?" is one that typifies many research efforts in the social sciences. It is often dealt with by the use of *correlational* algorithms, two of which we deal with below. They are distinguished by the type of variables involved (whether the variables are quantitative or qualitative), but their purpose remains the same: to decide if two or more variables *covary* (vary together).

Suppose we grab forty high school seniors, twenty male, twenty female, and submit them to a battery of tests designed to assess "ability in mathematics." We compile the results of these forty individual ability scores and compute the median. Why median? This allows individuals of both sexes to be classified as "above the median" or "below the median." In short, we record the number of students falling into each of the four categories "male-above," "male-below," "female-above," "female-below." It is convenient to record these counts in a 2×2 table.

A glance at the table reveals that those who score above the median are typically male, while those who score below are typically female. In other words, the variables "gender" and "mathematics ability" are positively *associated*. We can go further and compute an index of *strength and direction* of association, designated by the Greek letter ϕ. The index ϕ is set up so as to vary between two extreme values, -1 (complete negative association), and $+1$

	Male	Female	Totals
Above	13	7	20
Below	7	13	20
Totals	20	20	

Table 5 A 2x2 cross classification of 20 male, 20 female students according to mathematics ability.

(complete positive association). Speed and accuracy are usually negatively associated, (quickness begets sloppiness), whereas motivation and effort are often positively correlated. Values of φ near zero indicate little or no association.

The algorithm for computing φ for any 2×2 table is given in the following table.

		B		
		B₁	B₂	Totals
A	A₁	a	b	a + b
	A₂	c	d	c + d
	Totals	a + c	b + d	

$$\phi = \frac{ad - bc}{\sqrt{(a+b)(c+d)(a+c)(b+d)}}$$

Table 6 Computation of coefficient of association φ for an arbitrary 2x2 frequency table.

Applying the algorithm to the data of Table 5, we compute φ = .3 confirming what our eye told us already, that there is a modest positive association between gender and mathematics ability.

Now, ladies, do you accept this conclusion without protest? Surely not. There is good reason to believe that the observed association may be a by-product of complex social circumstances that conspire to the detriment of women. (To what extent this more complex and subtle explanation is true is an area of current investigation.) As this example suggests, it is a mistake to confuse association with the notion of cause. While no one anymore doubts that cigarette smoking is a causal agent for a number of horrible diseases, it took about ten years of research to replace the phrase "may be" with the definitive "is" in the warning that appears on the side of every pack of cigarettes on sale in the U.S. Why? Because taking into account other relevant factors can change an observed association between two variables quite dramatically, turning a large value of φ into a small one, or even reversing its sign.

When covariation is suspected between a pair of quantitative variables, a simple *scatter plot* is useful.

County	Index of exposure	Cancer mortality per 100,000 person-years
Clatsop	8.34	210.3
Columbia	6.41	177.9
Gilliam	3.41	129.9
Hood River	3.83	162.3
Morrow	2.57	130.1
Portland	11.64	207.5
Sherman	1.25	113.5
Umatilla	2.49	147.1
Wasco	1.62	137.5

Table 7 Radioactive contamination and cancer mortality. (Source: Fadeley, 1965, as quoted by Anderson & Sclove, 1978)

The data recorded in Table 7 concern county-by-county *pairs* of measurements taken in the state of Oregon following leakage of radioactivity contaminated waste into the Columbia River. One measurement is an index of exposure, large values indicating more serious exposure than small values. The other is the mortality rate due to various forms of cancer. These pairs of measurements are readily plotted in the plane as in the scatter plot presented in Figure 12.

The relationship between death from cancer and radioactive exposure is obvious. An index called *coefficient of correlation*, denoted r, is often employed for the same purpose as the measure φ; r is set up,

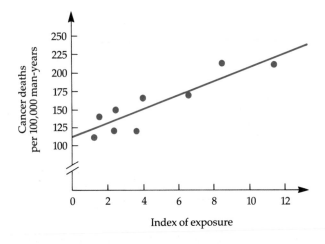

Figure 12 Scatter plot of data of Table 7. (Source: data after Fadeley, 1965, as quoted by Anderson & Sclove, 1978)

like φ, to range between −1 and +1 and has roughly the same interpretation. More precisely, r is a measure of how well the relationship between two quantitative variables conforms to a simple straight line (see Figure 12). The value of r for the present data turns out to be about .93, a value which again merely bolsters what we see by eye in the scatter plot of Figure 12.

Correlations can be terribly misleading if accepted uncritically. The scatter plot of Figure 13 shows a definite, very nearly linear relationship between human population size and stork population size in the German city of Oldenburg. The value of r for these data is .95. Do storks bring babies? The answer is surely "no"—in fact, it is closer to the truth to say that babies bring storks. For, as the Oldenburg population increases, more housing is built, a byproduct of which is chimneys, ideal nesting sites for storks. The very large correlation between the populations of inhabitants and storks would drop to zero if the number of chimneys was kept constant and not allowed to increase with new housing.

The problems associated with the interpretation of indices such as r and φ make the task of the social scientist quite difficult. It is not a problem so much for statistics as it is for scientific explanation. There *is* a large positive correlation between numbers of storks and numbers of babies; that is all that a statistical index is required to report. But the scientific explanation of covariation is not to be found in accepting such indices at face value. Other, nonmeasured or hidden variables (e.g. chimneys) may be responsible for superficial appearances.

Problems of interpretation of data are usually traced to lack of *control*. It is often difficult to control natural events, so science has invented the laboratory, a place where the individual scientist can, in principle, have the last word as to what will vary and what will remain fixed. A good deal of technology, common sense, intuition, and creative effort goes into a well-controlled scientific experiment. Each scientist brings to bear one or more techniques from a bag of tricks called *scientific method* so as to achieve as much control as he or she can. When successful, scientific explanation and statistical interpretation practically coincide. But in psychology, as in other social sciences, control may not always be possible without disturbing important features of the system being studied. And even in the context of a laboratory, control is often only partially achieved. While scientific method is a branch of metaphysics, statistics is a branch of applied mathematics. They should never be confused.

STATISTICAL INFERENCE

Descriptive techniques play a very useful role in the preliminary search for regularity in variable data. But there are a number of vexing questions that remain unanswered, indeed unanswerable, without further consideration. For instance, in the context of our introductory remarks it is natural to ask the simple question: Has the wind changed? We might mean any one of a number of things by this. We might mean, Has the breeze shifted its mean direction from 5.9° east of north, to a new value?; or we might mean, Has the breeze become more variable than before?; or we might have in mind both questions. The issue may more generally be put thus: if the data represented in the histogram of Figure 5 were collected at 10 A.M. and we take another set of measurements on the same flag at, say, 2 P.M. and construct a new histogram from those measurements, can we tell the difference between the two

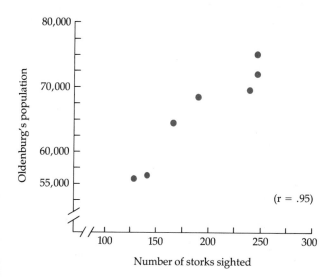

Figure 13 The population of Oldenburg, Germany, and the corresponding stork population for the years 1930–36. (Source: Glass & Hopkins, 1984)

histograms? Of course, large differences will show up quite clearly; one needs no elaborate statistical apparatus to distinguish two clearly different sets of measurements. But what would you say of the two histograms pictured in Figure 14? While they are literally different all right, would you be willing to attribute this difference to a genuine trend?

The problem of detecting change, especially "small," difficult-to-discern differences, is a very common one in scientific research. Its resolution calls for a new language, supplied by the theory of probability. We do not have the space here to enter into this mathematical theory in any serious way, and we shall content ourselves with the briefest indication of the role it plays.

Probability theory is used by statisticians as a framework for modeling *inherently* variable measurements. It is commonly observed, especially in the behavioral sciences, that do what one will to control matters, variability of measurement cannot be

eliminated. Sometimes this may be attributed to "individual differences" among people, but such inherent variation is also present in the behavior of each one of us. For instance do you chew your food or blink your eyes at precise, regular intervals? While the sun rises each morning, on time and in the right place, can you say the same about your own behavior or that of anyone else? Even for people who pride themselves on being punctual, the best we can say is something like "there is a 90 percent chance that Mr. Discipline will be under the shower between 7:00 and 7:05 A.M. on any given day."

To be sure, not all variability is due to chance, and it is the responsibility of each scientist to attempt the difficult job of partitioning it into a component that is controllable and a separate component due to uncontrollable, chance events. A characteristic signature of chance is that its effects disappear in *large* batches of independently repeated measurements. In the parlance of everyday language, this phenomenon is often termed the "law of averages." It is no empirical law or phenomenon, but a mathematical theorem, an inevitable consequence of "averaging out" the annoying obfuscations of chance. It is testimony to the appropriateness of probability theory for application to data that batches of empirical observations do behave in the manner dictated by that theory.

Not to be outdone by nature, science has exploited the theory of probability to good end in the process of *sampling*. The Nielsen ratings, which influence practically the whole of the television advertising industry, are based on measurements taken in 1,000 households. This is a tiny proportion of the 100 million or so dwellings in the U.S. Political polls, famous for a few outstanding blunders, also deserve to be credited with an otherwise flawless track record. (In fact they may be "too" good. These days it is not uncommon for the results of an election to be announced before voting has ended.)

While there are various forms of sampling, that is, of selecting a few from a larger *population* of possible measurements, the most useful forms are those called *probability sampling*, in which chance is injected *deliberately* by the scientist or pollster. This is done so that the results of a scientific endeavor, survey, or poll may be subject to the description afforded by probability theory, and to gain from the precision offered by that theory.

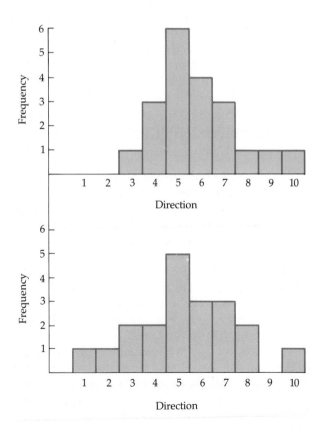

Figure 14 Are these histograms representative of the same breeze; or has the breeze changed its direction?

The simplest form of probability sampling is known as *random sampling*. Here, all samples of a given size (i.e., all samples containing a specified number of measurements), are conceptually laid out on a table, and just one of these is chosen "at random," without bias or emotion. It is usually the failure to carry out this conceptual random selection that causes problems in practice. For example, a convenient practical way to research people for survey purposes is to call them on the phone. This excludes people who do not own telephones, who have limited access to them, who have unlisted numbers, and the like. Such departures from the strict requirements of random sampling can and do lead to unwarranted conclusions in research or to incorrect predictions in a close political contest. For related reasons, psychology has sometimes been dubbed (not entirely without justification) as the "science of college sophomores."

Let us pick some simple notion to examine, such as the average height of American 10-year-old males. This measure is not entirely frivolous. For example, the government department of Health and Human Services might be interested in determining whether providing free milk in schools has a measurable effect on mean height. The cost of locating, measuring, and recording an individual height is say $1 per 10-year-old child. It is not worth the $1 million to measure every one, so a simple random sample of 1,000 10-year-old-males is selected. The average value of these 1,000 measurements is computed. Now the question arises: To what extent is this sample average indicative of the true, but unknown, population mean? The answer turns out to depend on the variance of the population, *an unknown quantity*, and on the size of the sample. In fact, the "error" of our sample mean is gauged as ± the quantity

$$2 \times \frac{\text{unknown population standard deviation}}{\sqrt{\text{sample size}}}$$

We can take a rough guess at the value one would expect of the unmeasured population standard deviation. Remember the rule of thumb mentioned earlier: Almost all measurements of a single numerical quantity fall between ±2 standard deviations of the mean. Common experience tells us that the range of heights of typical 10-year-old boys is surely no more than 2 feet, so a reasonable guess at the unknown

population standard deviation should be no more than 6 inches. The "error" incurred by quoting our sample mean as if it were the true population mean is thus (using the formula above)

$$\frac{2 \times 6''}{\sqrt{1000}} = 0.38''$$

Our sample mean (whatever its value) is seen to be an excellent *estimate* of the true population value. We could improve our accuracy further by increasing sample size to say 10,000; the error now drops to 0.12". Or, if we were not interested in such precision, a sample size of 100 incurring an error of 1.2" might be tolerable and would certainly be cheaper to obtain.

The use of sample means as estimates of population means is widespread in scientific and commercial enterprises alike. Similar sample quantities are available for estimating other *parameters* of populations; for instance, it is intuitively reasonable, and theory confirms, that a sample variance provides a pretty good estimate of population variance, at least for large samples.

Now that we know how to estimate mean height of U.S. 10-year-old males with an accuracy that improves with sample size, we are pretty close to being able to address more serious matters. For instance, we should have a go at the question that prompted the measurement of height in the first place: Does the school milk program have the effect of increasing height? To address this question requires two samples, one taken just before the program is instituted, one taken, say, five years later. Entirely different 10-year-olds characterize each sample. And each sample typifies different populations, one who received no free milk, one who did.

The question may thus be put: Do these populations differ in their means? This question is handled by *statistical inference*, the major application of which involves *hypothesis testing*. Briefly put, a skeptical attitude is adopted and the hypothesis of "no effect," that is, "no difference in height," is made. The hypothesis allows the observed difference in the (undoubtedly different) sample averages to be evaluated under the assumption that all one really has are two samples from the *same* population. Roughly, the procedure runs as follows. Imagine that the heights from each sample are listed side by side in long columns of 1,000 entries each. Suppose the initial sample is listed in the left-hand column, the final sample on the right. Proceeding line by line, subtract the left-hand number from the right, recording the 1,000 differences in yet a third column. What do you expect the average of those 1,000 differences to be? Well, according to the skeptical hypothesis of no difference, each sample average provides a good estimate of the same population mean; so their difference should be close to zero. Simple algebra tells us that an average of differences is the same as a difference of averages, and we have answered our question: the average of the 1,000 differences should be close to zero, if indeed the sample means are estimating a common population value.

What if the hypothesis is wrong; what if milk does in fact have an effect on height? Why, we should then expect many more of our 1,000 differences to be positive and consequently the average difference to be positive. The only question that remains unanswered is this: How discrepant from zero is a *significant* positive difference. This question can be put another way: How likely is it to observe a positive difference of any stated amount?

Such questions are answered by probability theory. Alas, we have no space here for details, so we shall again call into play our rule of thumb about the scatter of any distribution of numerical data. Differences are numerical data, so we apply our rule to them: We expect almost all differences to fall within ±2 standard deviations of their mean (which we are temporarily assuming is zero). We have to somehow come to terms with the standard deviation of differences, and once again it is probability theory that provides the answer: the "error" of our sample differences is $\sqrt{2}$ times the error incurred by either sample mean alone. For samples of size 1,000, we saw above that this latter error was at most 0.38". Multiplying by 2 we find that almost all average differences in height should lie in the interval −0.54" to +0.54", provided, of course, that milk has no effect. Thus, if we observe an average difference of say 0.25", we attribute it to chance and give up on the milk program (at least insofar as it affects height); but if we observe a mean difference of 1", we stay with the program and maybe hire some more high school basketball coaches.

While this example is fictitious, and anyway might strike you as a bit lame, it does illustrate a common design strategy. Another, more realistic example along similar lines is provided with the 1954 Salk vaccine trials, which constituted possibly the largest public health experiment ever conducted anywhere in the world.

The Salk vaccine was developed as a means of reducing the incidence of poliomyelitis, a crippling disease to which young children are especially prone. Two very large random samples of young children (grades 1, 2, 3) were chosen, roughly equal in number. One group, the "control" group, received a placebo—each child received injection(s) of a harmless substance. Each child in the "treatment" group received injection(s) of the vaccine. No child, parent, or administering medical staff had any knowledge as to the true nature of the substance being injected into any particular individual; that is, the study was run *double blind*. (This very useful device helps to offset any bias that might otherwise contaminate the interpretation of results.)

Partial data from this experiment are given in Table 8.

Notice the large sample size, about 200,000 for each group. Why so large? The answer is partially contained in the "placebo" column: the rate of the naturally occurring disease is estimated as 110/201,229; or about one case per two thousand children. A sample of 1,000 children would not be expected to reveal a single case of polio. To obtain an accurate estimate of the incidence of any rare event, such as contracting polio, calls for large sample sizes.

There is another reason for the large numbers of children studied. While it is important to be conservative in evaluating differences between treatment and control groups, so that "small" differences are

	Placebo	Vaccine	Totals
Children contracting polio	110	33	143
Children not contracting polio	201,119	200,712	401,831
Totals	201,229	200,745	

Table 8 Incidence of poliomyelitis. (Source: Francis et al., 1957; as quoted by Anderson & Sclove, 1978)

not inappropriately interpreted as an effect of treatment, it is also important to pick up genuine effects of treatment when they do in fact exist. The ability of a statistical test to satisfy the latter requirement involves the notion of *power*. To achieve a high likelihood of detecting genuine effects of vaccine in the polio trials calls for high power, which, in the present context, is also achieved by employing very large sample sizes.

We have a tool for evaluating the effect of the vaccine, namely the coefficient of association, ϕ introduced in Table 6. Calculation reveals $\phi = .01$, a shocking result that taken at face value would seem to implicate the vaccine as worthless. But this conclusion is unwarranted. Tiny as it is, the .01 value of ϕ is wildly significant, that is, could not have been produced by chance (except in about one of every 200 or so such experiments). This example points to the often dramatic difference between a purely descriptive use of statistical indices and a more refined statistical analysis of the same data. A value of ϕ close to zero may be highly significant; and, contrariwise, it is routine in smaller-scale experiments to observe nonsignificant values of ϕ in the neighborhood of .5 or so.

There are extensions of the above simple design. One common extension involves two or more *levels* of some treatment. For example, the vaccine may be available in two or more concentrations; all concentrations may be effective; but is one more effective than another?

A more important extension involves the simultaneous experimental manipulation of two or more *independent variables,* so as to study their *joint* effect on a single *dependent variable.* For example, age could have been incorporated into the vaccine trials so that the effectiveness of the vaccine on adults as well as children could be assessed simultaneously.

When two or more variables influence a third, it cannot usually be expected that their joint effect is predictable in any simple way from the effect of each of them taken alone. Consider the influence of fear and rage on the aggressiveness of an animal. We probably expect a frightened animal to be passive while, on the contrary, we would expect an enraged animal to be relatively dangerous. What then can we expect of a frightened, angry animal? It is quite possible that the situation depicted in Figure 15 obtains. Notice that a dog in a state of moderate fear and

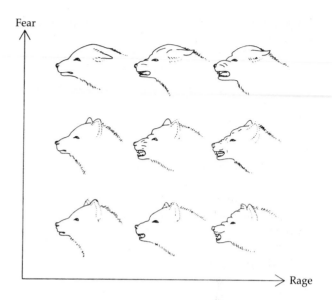

Figure 15 The joint effects of fear and rage on aggressiveness. (Source: Zeeman, 1976)

moderate rage appears more vicious than one in a state of no fear and moderate rage. This is contrary to what would have been anticipated from our earlier conjecture about the effect of increasing fear alone. In the jargon of *analysis of variance*—statistical machinery developed for analyzing the effects of two or more variables on a single dependent measure—we say that fear and rage *interact* in their influence on aggressiveness.

Let me add a few final remarks. Contrary to popular impression, statisticians do not normally spend much of their time scratching out arithmetic calculations on a piece of paper. Computers compute; statisticians, however, occupy themselves with "good" methods of organizing data, "good" methods for estimating population quantities, and "good" inferential procedures. The emphasis is always on the term "good" and what that term means in a given context.

The advantages of an informed data analysis, tailored to the requirements of some set of specific data and keeping in prominent view questions that arise naturally from the empirical context generating those data, are obvious and many. All too frequently the conservative ("no effect") null hypothesis of the working scientist is confirmed. More often than not this occurs not because an effect is absent, but as a by-product of an insensitive analysis chosen naively for reasons of convenience or tradition. A competent statistician can often turn an apparently uninteresting set of data into a highly revealing, thought-provoking one; and, if for no other reason, I leave you with the following advice: Support your local statistician.

Glossary

A

absolute threshold The least amount of physical energy necessary for us to register a stimulus. It is defined as the minimum strength for a stimulus to be noticed by an observer 50 percent of the time. See also **difference threshold.**

accommodation When a new event cannot be easily assimilated into one's knowledge structure, the knowledge structure must be disrupted and changed—accommodated to the new event. See also **assimilation.**

acetylcholine (ACh) One of the major transmitters in the nervous system, it is involved in the arousal of the organism and is most concentrated in the brain during sleep. See also **neurotransmission.**

achievement motivation The form of motivation, postulated by McClelland, that enables us to carry through and complete the goals we set for ourselves. Achievement motivation varies in different cultures and in different subgroups within a culture. In many experiments, it has been found that achievement motivation can be developed. See also **goals.**

action potential The electrical impulse of the neuron, which releases its stored energy. The action potential sweeps down the axon and releases the neurotransmitters, which completes the process.

activation The major physiological effect of emotion. See also **emergency reaction.**

activation synthesis An influential theory of dream interpretation proposed in 1977 by Hobson and McCarley. It assumes that the brain is activated in REM sleep and that dreams are a conscious *interpretation* or *synthesis* of the bizarre varieties of information available during dream states; this information may come from the internal state of the dreamer and from events of the day and long-term preoccupations.

adaptation The process wherein an organism changes in order to fit better in its environment. Varieties of adaptation include sensory adaptation, perceptual adaptation, and biological adaptation through the long processes of evolution.

adaptation level The adjustment an organism makes to respond to differences in its external environment. It is determined by three factors: focal stimuli, background stimuli, and residual stimuli. The general finding in adaptation level research is that we adjust our perceptions to match the average of our external surroundings. If we are watching a group of tall people, such as basketball players, those "only" 6'5" seem small.

adaptive value Any trait is said to have adaptive value if it enables an organism to function better in its environment. See also **adaptation.**

adipocites The body's fat cells. It seems that the number and size of fat cells a person has are genetically determined, and it is very difficult to change them. Fat cells are established in the first two years of life, and overfeeding in those years results in an increased number of fat cells.

affect A term used by psychologists to refer to the feeling dimension of life. Someone with a *flat affect* displays little or no emotion.

affective disorders A psychological disorder in which a disturbance of mood is the distinguishing feature; such disorders include depression, manic depression, mania.

afferent neurons Nerve cells in the spinal cord that convey information to the brain from the sensory system. Efferent neurons take messages from the brain and activate muscles and glands. Interneurons connect afferent and efferent neurons.

affordance Each object in the environment offers a rich source of information about its nature. This is its affordance.

aggression The intentional harming of another. According to Freud, it is an instinct. According to social learning theory, it is learned behavior. In social psychology, the *situation* is analyzed to determine how people can be coerced to become aggressive.

agoraphobia The fear of being alone in public places that might be difficult to escape. See also **phobia.**

algorithms A thought strategy for guaranteeing a solution if one keeps working at it long enough; if you follow the procedure exactly, you will reach a correct solution to the problem.

altruism Behavior characterized by kindness and concern for others, which in extreme situations may extend to sacrificing one's life for others. The question for evolutionary biologists, since natural selection is presumed to operate on individuals, is why would an individual give up his or her life for another. See also **sociobiology.**

amniocentesis The prenatal test in which a small amount of amniotic fluid (the liquid surrounding the fetus inside the womb) is withdrawn and subjected to chromosome analysis.

amygdala A small structure between the hypothalamus and the hippocampus. Its functions are not completely understood, but it seems to have to do with the maintenance and gratification of internal bodily needs and the storage of some memory processes.

analgesics Drugs, such as morphine, that reduce the experience of pain; also known as painkillers.

analytical psychology An offshoot of psychoanalysis, developed by Jung, that studied individuation, the development of the person through the process by which the unconscious and the conscious unite.

anchoring A common effect of comparisons, by which once a standard has been used to solve a problem it becomes less likely that the problem solver will change or adjust his or her approach, having become "anchored" in that strategy.

angiotensin II The "thirst substance," which acts upon receptors in the hypothalamus and other parts of the limbic system. These, in turn, activate the sensation of thirst.

anniversary effect The apparent postponing of death until after a special occasion—such as a birthday, election, or special holiday—by persons very near death who might otherwise not be expected to live that long.

antipsychotic drugs Substances, often called major tranquilizers, used in the treatment of severe mental disorders. See also **pharmacotherapy.**

antisocial personality A personality disorder that is characterized by an extremely calm mood, no sense of responsibility or shame, lack of genuine concern or caring for other people. Also called psychopathic or sociopathic.

anxiety A general emotional reaction that develops in response to the anticipation that something may occur in the future. This could be something physical or psychological, such as a threatened insult or a threatened embarrassment.

appraisal The understanding of the meaning of an event. Among the many dimensions along which people evaluate events is whether there is harm or loss, whether the situation is a threat, a challenge, or benign.

artificial categories Systems of classification that refer to attributes of constructed objects, like chairs or buildings.

assertiveness training A form of behavior therapy used when the problem entails difficulties in interpersonal relationships. Generally, assertiveness training teaches people that they have a right to their own feelings and opinions, which matter as much as anyone else's.

assimilation The incorporation of a new event into one's existing knowledge structure. See also **accommodation.**

association The postulated bond that forms in the mind when two events occur often enough together: the dinner bell and the taste of dinner, for instance.

attachment The special bond between the infant and the mother or other caregiver. It probably is an innate bond that develops due to the necessity for mother love, the gratification of needs, the infant's cognitive development, and the communication between the caregiver and the child.

attribution The process by which we explain the causes of our own or others' actions or behavior. We try to determine whether people's actions are attributed to a specific situation or whether their behavior reflects something enduring about their personal disposition.

Australopithecus A hominid, dating from 3 to 4 million years ago, that might be considered the earliest direct ancestor of humans.

automatization When a series of movements or actions are repeated many times, as in writing or walking, the behavior is accomplished automatically—"without thinking." Automatization is an important aspect of cognitive functioning; without it we would have to "pay attention" to the many actions we must take during the day.

autonomic nervous system (ANS) A division of the peripheral nervous system primarily responsible for running the internal organs, such as the heart, kidneys, liver, and gastrointestinal tract. It's processes are "autonomic"; that is, they seem to work without conscious control. See also **somatic nervous system.**

availability A thought judgment that refers to the ease with which relevant instances come to mind. We use availability to judge the frequency or the probability of events. See also **heuristics.**

awareness Keeping track or monitoring a set of activities, actions, or behaviors.

axon A part of the neuron that extends outward from the cell body. The axon is the "transmitter" end of the neuron. See also **dendrites; neurotransmission.**

B

basic level category That part of a categorization system that children learn first—such as table, apple, house—and that is the level at which we most naturally divide the world.

basilar membrane A structure in the ear at the base of the cochlea. It moves like a whip being cracked and creates a traveling wave that is transduced into sound.

behavioral repertoire A set of abilities that each organism is born with. This repertoire varies greatly between the species: some can fly, some cannot; some can swim, some cannot.

behaviorism Growing out of a desire, in the late nineteenth century, to make psychology objective, it is an approach that studies external, observable behavior of organisms and attempts to infer what caused that behavior.

behavior modification A form of therapy based on operant conditioning, which attempts to change behaviors by changing the stimuli and conditions. Behavior modification may employ reinforcement or extinction to teach people new learned responses and to alter problem situations.

behavior therapy A form of psychotherapy, based primarily on classical conditioning. It attempts to "decondition" anxiety-producing responses.

biases Factors in the decision-making process that prevent impartiality in certain kinds of judgments. Such biases include availability, representativeness, and vivid information.

binaural disparity The difference in sound information received by each ear, which provides us with cues to distance, since the sound slightly to the left will strike the left ear before the right and vice versa.

binocular disparity The difference in information received by the left and right eyes, which are in slightly different locations on the head. This difference is analyzed by the brain to provide cues to distance.

biofeedback A method of training people to control internal processes not normally controlled by consciousness, such as glandular and muscular activity, brain waves, blood pressure, and heart rate.

biological adaptation See **adaptation; evolution.**

biological approach The approach to psychology that emphasizes the relationship of the brain and nervous system to human experience.

bipedalism Walking on two legs instead of all four limbs. Humans are the only organisms that typically walk on the hind limbs. This enables them to carry, to share, to use their delicate forelimbs to manipulate objects, and to accomplish many other tasks that contribute to human uniqueness.

birth order An individual's rank in the family, which seems to influence personality and psychosocial development.

brain stem The oldest and deepest area of the brain, which evolved over 500 million years ago. It sets the general level of alertness and warns the organism of important incoming information.

C

cardinal traits In Allport's theory of personality, these are highly generalized dispositions that organize the whole personality, such as competitiveness and conscientiousness.

case history A psychologist's report of unique experiences for which little or no other evidence is available.

catharsis An ancient idea, first proposed by the Greeks, that strong emotional experience will "cleanse the mind" and release some form of stored energy. In more technical terms, catharsis is the reduction of emotional stress by releasing the emotion in controlled circumstances.

cathexis According to Freud, the investment of energy in an object, action, individual, image, or idea that will gratify an instinct.

central nervous system (CNS) This is comprised of the brain and the spinal cord. It forms the overall network wherein brain activity is relayed through nerve junctions in the spinal cord to the body. See also **peripheral nervous system.**

chromosome A substance like a string on which the genes are arranged. The chromosomes carry an individual's entire genetic program. Each human chromosome contains thousands of genes.

chronic life strains Certain conditions that persist in a life, such as an unhappy marriage or poor working conditions, that may be very stressful. Such chronic life strains can also be produced by the way a society is organized.

chunking A memory process that reorganizes individual bits of items into chunks by using a code. IBM and FBI are not mere sequences of letters—they are chunked into their code.

circadian From the Latin *circa dies*, or "about one day." A term used to denote phenomena that have a rhythm of approximately one day—the light-dark cycle of the earth.

classical conditioning See **respondent conditioning.**

client-centered therapy See **person-centered therapy.**

clinical approach The attempt to understand human behavior through an analysis of "where things go wrong." It may involve biological malfunctions, mental errors, or psychological paralysis.

clinical psychologist A Ph.D. in psychology who may specialize in a particular form of psychotherapy, such as behavior modification, sex therapy, and so on. Many clinical psychologists are involved in testing and research.

coaction effect A phenomenon in which the presence of other people intensifies and directs an individual's behavior.

cochlea The part of the inner ear that contains an ideal medium for the transmission of sound waves.

cognitive consistency A common theory in social psychology that postulates that we are motivated to make our attitudes more simple and more

consistent with one another. We do not, in this view, like to have discrepant cognitive attitudes.

cognitive dissonance A social cognition theory by Festinger that states that whenever an individual holds two cognitions (such as beliefs, attitudes, or consciousness of behaviors) that are inconsistent with one another, a disharmony results. There is then, it is hypothesized, a desire to reduce such disharmony either by changing cognitions or changing behaviors. This theory has been a most influential one in social psychology and has led to many imaginative experiments. See also **cognitive consistency.**

cognitive modifiability A concept of Feuerstein's in assessing intelligence. It refers to the ability to *change* one's mental structure and content.

cognitive psychology The study of the mind, which, unlike the brain, is not an observable entity. It involves many hidden activities, such as thinking, memory, language, and consciousness.

cognitive restructuring therapy A form of therapy developed by Beck. It assumes that disorders result from individuals' negative beliefs about events in the world and about themselves. The aim of cognitive restructuring therapy is to encourage the clients to engage in experiments that will help them confirm or disconfirm their beliefs and obtain a more realistic picture of themselves in their situation.

cohort effect In a sample of people of different age groups, a group that begins in the same period of time. People are grouped into cohorts so as to avoid the distorting effects of different environmental experiences. For example, people born in the 1960s are, on the average, taller than are people born in the 1920s.

collective unconscious Perhaps the most important of Jung's contributions to psychology, it is considered to be the inherited foundation of personality and contains the common reservoir of experience available to all human beings. It consists largely of archetypes, which are the inherited predispositions to have certain experiences or to react to the world in a certain way.

companionate love After passionate love fades, it is often replaced (especially in successful relationships) with this more sober, "everyday" kind of love, in which there is less arousal and excitement but more friendly affection and deep attachment.

competence One of the indicators (with planning and concern for standards) that a child has developed consciousness of himself or herself.

complexes In the usage developed by Jung, these are organized groups of constellations of memories, thoughts, feelings and perceptions that can influence or even control a person's personality.

concern with standards One of the indicators (with competence and planning) that a child has developed consciousness of himself or herself.

concrete operational stage The stage of cognitive development, according to Piaget, that lasts from ages seven to twelve years. In this stage, thinking is no longer dominated by sensory information; children begin to reason abstractly. They become more organized and more able to focus and direct attention for longer periods.

conditioned response (CR) A response that comes to be associated with a conditioned stimulus, such as salivating at the dinner bell. See also **respondent conditioning.**

conditioned stimulus (CS) Something that has no inherent meaning, such as a light, a sound, a puff of air, but comes to acquire meaning through a specific learning situation. For example, a puff of air may always signal a loud noise; thus the puff of air will become a conditioned stimulus to the noise. See also **respondent conditioning.**

conditioning The study of the *conditions* under which simple associations are formed. Extensive experiments in conditioning in psychology have been conducted by Ivan Pavlov and B. F. Skinner, among others. See also **operant conditioning; respondent conditioning.**

cones Photoreceptors in the retina that are responsible for color vision and are less sensitive than rods. They need bright light to be activated. Three kinds of cones exist, each of which responds primarily to a different range of wavelengths. One responds best to red/orange, one responds best to green, and one responds best to blue/violet. See also **photoreceptors.**

conservation The understanding that an object is the same, even if it looks different. For instance, a ball of clay is the same whether it is spread out into a disc or made into a cylinder. Piaget felt that children under three do not understand this principle.

conformity pressure See **social pressure.**

consistency The degree to which a person's behavior is the same from situation to situation.

constancy A goal of the perceptual process is to achieve a stable, constant world. So we experience surprisingly little change, even though the sensory information changes radically. A building may first appear like a small dot, then larger than anything on the horizon, but you see the building as the same constant building. There are three varieties of constancy: shape, size, and brightness.

constructivist approach Sensory information reaching the brain is chaotic and disorganized. Thus, in this view, perception must be a process of constructing a "representation" or model of the world, as a globe is fashioned to represent the earth. In this view, the information from the senses merely "sparks off" the creation of an image of what could have caused a sensation.

continuous reinforcement (CRF) A form of reinforcement in which each time the animal makes the correct response, it is reinforced. See also **operant conditioning; partial reinforcement.**

control group That part of the sample similar in every way to the experimental group except that it is observed in the absence of the independent variable. See also **experimental group; sample; variables.**

conventional morality In Kohlberg's theory of moral development, the level of moral reasoning that goes beyond individual considerations and takes the view of society as a whole. See also **postconventional morality; premoral level.**

conversational maxims According to Grice, the four maxims that speakers usually obey when they speak. These are quantity, quality, relation, and manner. The existence of these maxims makes it possible to understand the general rules people follow when they have a conversation. See also **cooperativeness principle.**

cooperativeness principle The principle that describes the relationship between two speakers: each speaker tries to understand *why* the other said what he or she did.

coping Thought or behavior that is directed at managing a problem or an emotional situation or stress.

cornea A transparent membrane that covers the front of the eye.

corpus callosum An enormous structure of 300 million neurons that connects the two separate cerebral hemispheres. Fibers in the corpus callosum run from one area in the left hemisphere to corresponding areas in the right, serving as an enormous network of communication.

correlation A statistic that measures the relationship between two sets of numbers. Usually used in psychology to measure the relationship between two factors, such as years of drinking and decline in intelligence.

cortex This is the "executive branch" of the brain. In humans the cerebral cortex constitutes about 85 percent of the brain's weight. It contains more unspecialized neurons than the rest of the brain. These neurons can be programmed and reprogrammed presumably in many different ways, thus accounting for human flexibility and creativity.

counterconditioning A method of therapy using extinction and generalization, often used to help people overcome their fears. In this method, an unwanted conditioned response is eliminated by conditioning the subject to another stimulus (a conditioned stimulus) that elicits a new conditioned response, less disruptive than the unwanted conditioned response.

covariation principle A method of understanding how we attribute other people's behaviors; it involves multiple observations rather than a single one. In this view, developed by Kelly, we assess the degree to which the other person's behavior occurs in the presence of every possible cause. If, for instance, we know a person always says positive things when paid large sums of money, we may infer that money is the dispositional cause of that individual's behavior. See also **discounting principle.**

Cro-Magnon The first modern humans, members of our own species, *Homo sapiens.* See also **Lascaux.**

crystallized abilities Mental abilities hypothesized by Cattel to derive from specific cultural experiences. See also **fluid abilities.**

cultural deprivation A concept of Feuerstein's, which notes that individuals who are culturally *deprived* are lacking something in their own culture.

cultural differences The culturally *different* have a different idea of the answer to a question than those who are culturally deprived. A wrong answer on a test to the culturally different might simply be due to not knowing the language or the usual usage of a word.

cultural evolution The sum of developments in science, arts, humanities, and technology. Physical, biological evolution may take millennia or even millions of years to produce changes. Cultural evolution can produce profound changes in weeks.

D

decentration According to Piaget, at each stage of development, children and adults become increasingly aware of the world outside of themselves and less focused on themselves. They become progressively less and less egocentric.

decision analysis Thinking about decisions in terms of alternatives, outcomes, preferences, and probabilities.

declarative sentence A sentence that conveys specific information, such as "Jamaica is a country in the Caribbean."

defense mechanisms Unconscious ways of distorting reality to ward off unpleasant facts that might produce anxiety. Among defense mechanisms are denial, repression, rationalization, displacement, projection, and reaction formation.

dendrites Part of the neurons named after the Greek word for tree, indicating the branches of one neuron connecting with another. They receive information from the axons of other neurons. See also **neurotransmission.**

dependent variable See **variables.**

depression A severe mental disorder consisting of an overwhelming sadness that immobilizes and arrests the entire course of a person's life. See also **affective disorders; mania.**

deviation IQ In the Stanford-Binet IQ Test, a precise statistical method for defining the relative position of an individual testee in comparison with others. Currently, tests are standardized with a norm of 100, meaning someone who scores 116 is one standard deviation above the norm.

dexterity The ability in humans to use the forelimbs (hands) in a delicate manner. Human dexterity, allowed by bipedalism, encouraged toolmaking and other factors important to human evolutionary development.

difference threshold More commonly called the just noticeable difference (j.n.d.). The minimum increase in a physical stimulus necessary for us to notice a difference. The j.n.d. is not constant; the experience of a stimulus is always relative to its surroundings. See also **absolute threshold.**

discounting principle A rule of attribution developed by Kelly to describe how people attribute the behavior of a single person in a single situation on a single occasion. In this view, you discount one factor in favor of another. If, for instance, you discover that a person was paid a large sum of money to do something, you will conclude that this was the reason for that individual's behavior. See also **covariation principle.**

discrimination The ability to notice differences between stimuli. See also **generalization.**

disengagement theory The proposal that it is normal for the elderly to withdraw or disengage from society. This is a controversial theory that inspired numerous studies showing that the elderly who keep active are the most satisfied with their lives.

dissociation A division of consciousness, described by Janet, in which certain experiences can only be recovered under specific conditions. Under hypnosis, for instance, people can be made either to forget or to remember certain experiences that are not accessible to the remainder of consciousness.

distress From the Latin, dis = bad. The form of stress that is usually thought to last a long time and to become physically harmful. Selye divided stress into distress and eustress—the bad and good forms of stress.

DNA Deoxyribonucleic acid. Each molecule is made of two chains twisted into a spiral. The chains consist of four chemical building blocks: adenine, thymine, guanine, and cytosine. Virtually every living thing is made up of these elements.

dominant/recessive genes Gene selection operates on a dominant/recessive basis. If a dominant gene is present, the trait it governs appears in the individual's physical makeup. A recessive trait would normally be expressed only if both parents contribute the recessive gene.

dopamine An important neurotransmitter whose pathway connects the limbic system to the cortex; it also participates in the brain's reward system and in the control of motor activity. The lack of dopamine causes Parkinson's disease.

dopamine hypothesis The theory that schizophrenia is caused by a surplus of dopamine, a neurotransmitter of the catecholoamine group. Alternatively, it is proposed that there may be a surplus of dopamine receptor sites.

double-bind theory An interesting and controversial theory of schizophrenia proposed by Bateson. The double bind is a situation in which a person is called on to respond to a message that contains two meanings, such as "I love you" and "I hate you." Such double messages are thought, in this view, to contribute to the development of schizophrenia.

double-blind procedure An experimental procedure in which the experimenter as well as the subjects is unaware, "blind," of which is the experimental group and which is the control group, and is thus unable to influence the results.

Down's syndrome A genetic condition caused by an extra chromosome in pair 21. The child so affected will be very short, have a malformed heart, and will be severely retarded. It is quite a common birth defect.

drives Physiologically based goads to behavior: they literally move us to action, as a hungry person is "driven" to find food. A drive is often experienced as a specific feeling, such as thirst, hunger, or sex. See also **goals; needs.**

E

ecological approach A theory of perception that emphasizes the richness of the information available to be "picked up" by the perceiver. In this view, perception is a direct function of stimulation.

efferent neurons The nerve cells in the spinal cord that take messages from the brain and activate muscles and glands. See also **afferent neurons; interneurons.**

ego An important part of the personality as described by Freud. It mediates between the demands of the id and the reality of the external world. See also **id; superego.**

egocentric bias A bias in judgment of other people and ourselves. We tend to overestimate our own contributions to situations, mainly because we "know" everything that *we* have done but do not know everything about the other person.

egocentrism An important principle in psychology emphasizing that individuals' experience tends to be centered upon themselves. With normal development a human being becomes progressively less egocentric from childhood to adulthood. See also **decentration.**

electroconvulsive therapy (ECT) A form of therapy for severe cases of schizophrenia and depression. It involves the passing of an electric shock through one or the other hemisphere of the brain. In many cases, it is extremely effective. In other cases, it is of marginal use.

electroencephalogram (EEG) The EEG is a record of voltage that the brain produces, usually recorded on the scalp. The voltages recorded are typically quite small—in the *millionths* of a volt. Changes in the EEG often relate to changes in arousal and alertness.

electromagnetic energy The band of energy that contains light among forms of waves, such as radio waves, X-rays, and others.

embryonic period The first period of pregnancy, lasting until about the ninth week. It is the critical stage of development for the nervous system.

emergency reaction The activation reaction of the body, preparing us to respond to the unexpected. Most of the emergency reaction involves stimulating the mechanisms of the sympathetic nervous system: increases in norepinephrine, heart rate, blood pressure, and blood volume. Skin resistance decreases; respiration, sweating, salivation, and gastric motility all increase; pupil size increases.

emotions Relatively specific involuntary and automatic patterns of short-lived physiological and mental responses.

emotion solid A theoretical analysis proposed by Plutchik, which describes that emotions are most distinct from one another at the highest levels of intensity and least distinguishable at the lowest level of intensity. See also **emotion wheel.**

emotion wheel A theoretical approach to how emotions are organized. In this framework, proposed by Plutchik, the eight primary emotions are arranged in a circle of opposites. See also **emotion solid; primary emotions.**

empty nest period The period for a woman in which the children leave home and become increasingly independent.

endorphins Stemming from the word

meaning "the morphines within," they are a class of neurochemicals (peptides) that serve as modulators of nervous system activity and seem to be involved in pain and healing and in relief from noxious stimulation.

episodic memory A record of our own individual and personal experiences, memories that are unique to ourselves, such as a movie, a relationship, or experiences in learning.

Eros According to Freud, the sexual instinct, the primary source of libido.

estrus The period in most animal's lives when the female is sexually receptive. During estrus, she communicates her sexual receptivity to others. See also **ovulation.**

eustress From the Greek, eu = good. The stress associated with the exhilaration of a change in one's life. Eustress is thought to be less harmful than distress. Perhaps this is because eustress lasts only a short time, while distress is a chronic condition.

evoked potential The sum of electrical activity in the brain associated with a specific event.

evolution The long series of physical changes through which species develop specific characteristics that allow them to adapt to their environment. See also **adaptation.**

experimental group That part of the sample with whom the researcher intervenes by manipulating the independent variable and observing this group's reactions. See also **control group; sample; variables.**

experimenter bias An experimenter's subtle and often unconscious influencing of the results of an experiment.

extinction The process whereby a conditioned response (CR) gradually decreases as a result of no longer being reinforced, because of the conditioned stimulus (CS) being presented without the unconditioned stimulus (UCS). See also **reinforcement.**

extrasensory perception (ESP) The ability to communicate and acquire information about the world by means other than those familiar to us.

F

factor analysis A technique devised by Spearman in 1927 to measure the relationship of different test scores. Spearman developed it because he assumed that a single factor would be found that would correspond to general intelligence.

false assumptions The characterization by Gould that major life stages in adulthood are characterized by misconceptions about one's identity and intimacy. At different ages, different false assumptions are to be challenged: for instance, in early adulthood a false assumption is "If I do things the way my parents did, I will get ahead;" in late adulthood, "There is no evil or death in the world."

false consensus An error in attribution, it is the tendency of individuals to overestimate the commonness of their own responses and to underestimate the commonness of the responses of others who acted differently.

fear An immediate and specific emotional reaction to a threatening stimulus. For example, young birds show fear if the shadow of a hawk passes over them.

feature analyzers Cells in the visual area of the cerebral cortex that respond best to certain features in the environment. See also **receptive field.**

feedback Information about the operation of a system, used within the system to attain its goal.

feedback loop The cyclic action by which information from one part of a system affects another, which in turn affects the part of the system that initiated the cycle of feedback. See also **feedback; negative feedback; positive feedback.**

feelings The subjective experience of emotions. Feelings can be more complex than simple emotions. Jealousy, for instance, is a feeling comprised of several emotions, including envy and anger.

fetal alcohol syndrome An ailment suffered by babies born of alcoholic mothers. These newborns have cone-shaped heads and may be mentally retarded.

"fight or flight" emergency reaction See **emergency reaction.**

fixation In Freud's view, many individuals' personalities become fixed at a given stage of mental development. Therefore, their adult personality will reflect this tendency. For example, a person who is overly dependent and derives a lot of satisfaction from oral activities, such as eating, is said to be fixated at the oral stage. See also **regression.**

fixed interval (FI) One of the four kinds of partial reinforcement schedules, in which reinforcement is presented at regular intervals after the correct response. See also **variable interval (VI); fixed ratio (FR); variable ratio (VR).**

fixed ratio (FR) In this schedule of reinforcement, the reward is given after a certain number of responses.

flooding A form of behavior therapy similar to systematic desensitization. In flooding, the therapist fills, literally "floods," the client's mind with a continuing narrative of situations that evoke fear and anxiety.

fluid abilities Mental abilities hypothesized by Cattel to be involved in the perception and registration of the world. These are thought to be genetically based. See also **crystallized abilities.**

formal operational stage A stage from age twelve to adulthood, in Piaget's framework for cognitive development. In this higher-order thinking, abstract thinking begins, complex scientific experiments can be followed, and hypotheses can be formulated and tested.

fovea At the center of the retina, it contains the greatest concentration of cones and has no rods.

fraternal twins Developed when the mother releases two eggs and each is fertilized by different sperms. The individuals are no more alike than would be any two siblings.

free association A technique developed by Freud. It is a fundamental feature of psychoanalytic therapy. The patient is asked to say anything that comes into his or her mind, without criticism or editing. Free association is designed to allow normally "forbidden" thoughts to arise to the surface of consciousness.

frontal lobes A part of the cortex intimately connected to the limbic system, so much so that many psychologists regard the frontal lobes as part of the limbic system. They are also involved in forward planning and seem to contain different emotions: the left side seems to be involved in positive or "happy" emotions; the right, negative or "sad" emotions.

frustration Results when a desired outcome is thwarted or delayed. It is a normal reaction to stress and to the hassles of everyday life.

functional autonomy The tendency for any action repeated often enough to become a motive in its own right. For instance, a person who initially strives to make money may continue to try to make money even after becoming very rich.

fundamental attribution error A mistake that people often make in judgment: What little information is available is overused. In judging other people, we tend to overgeneralize from this small sample we have and to underestimate situational forces and overestimate dispositional forces. So if we see someone acting brusquely, we may conclude that person is rude.

G

ganglion cells The third layer of nerve cells in the retina. Each ganglion cell has a long axon and all these axons exit the eye at the same point, where they are bundled together and form the optic nerve that carries visual information to the brain. See also **retina.**

gender identity When a child knows and identifies with what sex he or she is.

gene The basic unit of heredity in all living things. Genes are made of a substance called DNA (deoxyribonucleic acid). See also **chromosome.**

general adaptation syndrome The physiological reactions to extreme change, which occur in three stages: (1) alarm reaction, (2) resistance, and (3) exhaustion. It was first identified by Selye, who set out to study the "syndrome of just being sick"— those phenomena that occur in all illnesses. See also **emergency reaction.**

general enrichment Training programs devised to generally raise the stimulation in the environment or the amount of interaction that a caregiver or other person has with a child. Such programs include Head Start, the toy demonstrators program, and many others. Most have been shown to be successful in some way and increase the child's ability to function in school.

generalization Once a specific stimulus has become a conditioned stimulus, similar stimuli can elicit the conditioned response. For instance, someone who has an aversion to eating a hamburger may also avoid eating steak. See also **discrimination.**

generalized anxiety People suffering from generalized anxiety live in constant tension and worry. They are uneasy around people and are sensitive to comments and criticism. They are often so terrified of making a mistake that they cannot concentrate or make decisions. Generalized anxiety is a very common anxiety disorder.

general paresis A slow degenerative disease that eventually erodes mental faculties. A scourge in the late nineteenth century, it was discovered to be caused by syphilis. This understanding of the biological roots of a supposedly mental disorder gave psychiatrists the hope that other biological causes would be found for many mental disorders.

genetic code The sequence of instructions contained in the four chemical building blocks of the genes, which guides the construction of any particular organism. The essential differences between human beings and turtles, at the molecular level, is only the arrangement of the chemical substances along the DNA molecule. See also **DNA.**

genetic potential The specific genetic endowment that may predispose an individual to an ability or a trait. See also **range of reaction.**

genetics The study of how specific characteristics are passed physically from one generation to the next.

genotype The entire complement of an individual's genetic inheritance. See also **phenotype.**

Gestalt Gestalt means to "create a form." In psychology, it is an immediate organizing of the form of an object. One of the principles of Gestalt psychology is that the whole is greater than the sum of its parts.

goals Desired outcomes that have not yet occurred. See also **achievement motivation; needs.**

grammar The study of the rules for formation of a specific language. See also **syntax.**

H

hassles The common, daily annoyances—like traffic jams, waiting in long lines, foul-ups with the computer, dealing with editors—that add measurably to our emotional conflict and to stress.

Head Start A large-scale experimental program of preschool enrichment in underprivileged areas of the United States, which was initiated in 1965.

heuristics Simplifying strategies that we use to make judgments and solve problems—our usual mental "rules of thumb."

hidden observer An important demonstration of the hypothesis that many experiences below consciousness may enter consciousness through hypnosis. In this demonstration, a person was instructed that he would feel no pain during hypnosis. While his conscious report indicated that he felt no pain, through "automatic writing," his "hidden observer," operating below consciousness, could still report the experience of pain, indicating that this experience was simply dissociated from consciousness.

hippocampus A structure in the limbic system that seems to be involved in three related functions: learning, the recognition of novelty, and the storage of memory.

homeostasis Literally, a return to the same state. It describes the general principle whereby the body maintains a constant environment. Changes in one direction are neutralized, and body functions remain at a constant. For instance, changes in blood flow, heartbeat rate, blood temperature, and breathing rate are all regulated to maintain constant internal processes. The best-known of these is the "normal" body temperature of 98.6°F. See also **negative feedback.**

hominids All humans and their humanlike ancestors.

Homo erectus Probably one of the first true humans, this so-called "upright man" stood fully erect and walked much as we do, had a relatively large brain and a complex culture and technology that included mastery of fire.

Homo habilis Literally "handy man," this hominid was a maker and user of tools, and an efficient worker and hunter who was probably a direct ancestor of later humans.

Homo sapiens Literally "intelligent man," our own species. See also **Cro-Magnon.**

homunculus A representation of how various portions of the brain correspond to different parts of the body.

hormones Chemicals manufactured and secreted by special glands, such as the endocrine glands; they are carried through the blood to specific target cells in the body.

human adaptation The simultaneous development, in a positive feedback loop, of all those characteristics that set humans apart from other animals. See also **adaptation.**

humanistic approach An attempt to analyze human experience by understanding important, positive aspects of life, such as "growth and development."

humanistic psychology A field of psychology that argues that psychology should study primarily the healthy, growth-oriented side of human nature.

hunter-gatherers The typical human group through most of our evolutionary history. In this kind of society there are two main activities: the search for meat and the gathering of available fruits, vegetables, and grains.

hyperphagia Extreme overeating.

hypnogogic See **hypnopompic and hypnogogic states.**

Hypnopompic and hypnogogic states Borderline states that we enter just before complete awakening (hypnopompic) and just before we go to sleep (hypnogogic). Consciousness in both states is receptive. Images in the mind have the qualities of vividness, originality, independence of conscious control, and changeableness.

hypnosis A form of dissociation in which individuals relinquish the normal control of their consciousness to another person. People under hypnosis have been able to recall events otherwise inaccessible to their waking consciousness. They can also withstand pain and follow quite detailed suggestions.

hypochondriasis An individual's misinterpretation of bodily functions, leading usually to fear of disease or belief that one is already suffering from a disease.

hypothalamus A pea-sized organ that weighs about 4 grams. It is located in the limbic system and regulates many activities relating to survival: eating, drinking, sleeping, waking, body temperature, balance, heart rate, hormones, sex, and emotions.

hypothesis A specific statement about what will happen if certain events take place: "if A, then B." An important aspect of hypothesis is that in order to be scientific, it should be able to be confirmed or disconfirmed.

hypothesis testing The systematic consideration of a series of hypotheses until all are eliminated except the one that solves your problem.

I

id According to Freud, it is the initial, infant personality and is composed of the primary instincts (those largely concerned with survival) and other inherited psychological characteristics. See also **ego; superego.**

identical twins See **monozygotic (MZ) twins.**

immaturity Human beings are born "immature." This means that the infant is not fully developed at birth. The father and mother need to care for the human infant longer than is the case in other species. The many learning experiences during their long childhood make human beings much more distinct from one another than are other animals.

independent variable See **variables.**

innate Inborn, unlearned, fixed at birth. Usually applied to such characteristics as instincts. See also **instincts.**

insight A vision of how all the parts of a problem fit together or of how to represent the problem differently. The experience of insight can come at the end of a process of hypothesis testing or seemingly all at once.

instinctive drift A phenomenon identified by Breland and Breland that indicates various organisms have difficulty learning arbitrary responses because learned behavior "drifts" toward instinctive behavior.

instincts Innate, fixed patterns of behavior typical of every member of a given species, which are thought to be programmed to satisfy needs and which appear without learning as soon as they are needed. The salmon's inevitable return to the river of its birth is instinctual.

instrumental conditioning See **operant conditioning.**

instrumental enrichment (I.E.) A program devised by Feuerstein in Israel, which attempts to develop a special set of techniques to increase intelligence and to assess increases in intelligence.

intermediate layer One of the three main layers of nerve cells in the retina, comprising bipolar cells, horizontal cells, and amacrine cells. See also **ganglion cells; photoreceptors; retina.**

interneurons Nerve cells in the spinal cord that connect afferent and efferent neurons. See also **afferent neurons; efferent neurons.**

interposition A cue to depth, provided when one object stands in front of another and blocks part or all of the other object.

interpretation After organization, interpretation is the second step in discovering meaning. A question we answer when we interpret phenomena is: What is the simplest meaningful stimulus that gives rise to my experience?

introspection The primary research method used by late-nineteenth-century psychologists, it involved studying their own minds and examining the contents of their own experience.

invariance A constant pattern of stimulation. For instance, from every perspective we can see that a post has right angles and is always perpendicular to the horizon.

IQ An abbreviation of "Intelligence Quotient," used first by Binet when testing individuals for their suitability for either normal or remedial school. The IQ test is probably psychology's most visible contribution to society, and its most controversial. Many psychologists feel that it is a useful predictor of how well a person will do in society, while many more feel that it is only a measure of a kind of achievement and reflects more on an individual's background than his or her potential.

J

just noticeable difference (j.n.d.) See **difference threshold.**

K

kinethesis Kinesthetic feedback is the feedback from the joints of the body, which allows us to know and coordinate the movement of different body parts (where our limbs are, what their angle is, and what they are doing).

L

Lascaux The site in France where magnificent cave paintings attest to Cro-Magnon's powers of abstraction and use of symbolism in inventing art.

latent learning Learning that can occur without being manifested in an observable performance improvement.

lateral inhibition Retinal cells fire and affect one another. The brighter the light, the more they fire. Whenever a cell fires, it inhibits the firing of a cell next to it (laterally). This mechanism sharpens perception of sharp changes, like corners and edges. It sometimes makes edges appear when there are none.

learned helplessness The discovery that one has no control over events and that one's actions do not lead to one's goals. This can decrease motivation, decrease the ability to learn new responses, and increase emotional disturbance.

learning potential assessment device (LPAD) An intelligence testing and enrichment program aimed at remediation of retarded individuals.

levels of awareness Awareness may take several levels: from full consciousness, as in an action we are deliberately attending to; to preconscious, nonconscious, and unconscious processes.

levels of processing A theory of memory stating that all information presented to us is "processed" at different "depths" or "levels." According to this theory, the greater the "depth of processing," the more likely something is to be remembered. The "deepest" processing is that which relates information to oneself.

libido In Freud's theory, the "animal" instincts provide the "fuel" for actions and for the human mind. In human beings, this biological fuel is transformed into "psychic energy," which is called libido.

life change units (LCU) The major life changes a person has experienced in the recent past. Certain events are set on this scale at arbitrary values, such as marriage at 50 life change units. Different experiences, such as divorce, the birth of a child, changing a job, are also assigned values in relation to marriage. The number of life change units a person experiences during a year is strongly related to one's propensity for becoming ill.

limbic system A group of cellular structures between the brain stem and the cortex, which evolved about 150 million years ago. It is the area of the brain that helps maintain constant environment in the body. The limbic system's many critical activities include regulating the maintenance of body temperature, blood pressure, heartbeat rate, and levels of sugar in the blood. See also **homeostasis.**

lock and key The principle recently discovered about transmission in the nervous system. Each neuro-transmitter has a specific shape, and the shape of its molecule forms a "key" that "fits" a receptor whose shape matches it, as a key fits into a lock. This lock and key relationship describes how chemical messages of the body can connect with their target cells.

longitudinal study Research in which a group or panel of people are studied over a number of years or even decades. See also **cohort effect.**

long-term memory A kind of memory thought by many psychologists to store permanent records of our experiences, including both episodic and representational memory.

M

mania Excessive elation. An individual in a manic episode may be caught up in a frenzy of overexcitability and activity. Grandiose and impossible plans may be made during such manic episodes. Mania is a serious condition, but it is treatable, often by chemical means.

maturation The emergence of individual characteristics through normal growth processes. It is controlled by the information contained in the genes, is relatively unaffected by learning or experience and follows a universal pattern.

mean The arithmetic average of a set of numbers.

means-end analysis With this method of problem solving, one works backward from the goal through things one needs to achieve it. For example, if the goal is to cook spaghetti, one needs a kitchen to cook it in and all the ingredients for spaghetti.

measurements See **quantitative and qualitative distinctions.**

median From the Latin word for middle. It is the middle figure in a distribution of numbers.

mediated learning experience The information about the world, events, and experiences *interpreted* by others, usually a parent or sibling. Thus the *meaning* of events is given to us by other people. In Feuerstein's theory of instrumental enrichment, the hypothesis is made that the roots of intelligence will be found in the ade-quacy of the mediated learning experience.

meditation A system of mental training that often involves relaxation and an attempt at knowledge of oneself and one's place in the world. It is a different form of knowledge than the intellectual and academic knowledge taught in schools.

menarche The onset of first menstruation.

mental age Based on the concept that intellectual abilities increase with age, it attributes various levels of attainment (ages) to different IQ test scores.

mentor Someone who eases a youth into adulthood. A mentor ideally aids a person in developing his or her own autonomy and interests.

method of loci A memory method developed by the Greeks. With it, the person tries to ceate a new and different association to improve recall by visualizing the items to be recalled.

midlife crisis A hypothesized state in middle adulthood in which people review and assess their early adulthood. They may try to change the facets of life with which they are dissatisfied in an attempt to resolve the psychological issues introduced by entering the final half of life. A midlife crisis may be triggered by awareness of their own mortality and by discovery that they are not happy with life, and this may lead to radical changes, such as job and family disruptions.

mitosis The process of cell division that underlies normal organismic growth.

mnemonics A technique for aiding memory. It involves making up a context in which certain meaningless items can be remembered, such as "Spring forward, fall back" to remember which way to change your clocks for Daylight Savings Time.

monozygotic (MZ) twins Identical twins, developed from the same fertilized egg. See also **fraternal twins.**

moods Long-lasting states of feeling. See also **affective disorders.**

morality The knowledge of what is right and what is wrong. According to Kohlberg, morality develops in several stages, from the premoral stage through the conventional moral stage to the postconventional stage of morality. These stages, in most part, parallel developments in cognition and are based on them.

morphemes The smallest units of meaning in language. A morpheme can be a word, such as car, but, or teach. It can be fragments, such as common prefixes and suffixes of words.

motion parallax The differences in apparent speed and direction of movement by objects at varying distances from a moving observer.

mutation A spontaneous change in the structure of one or more genes.

myelin sheath A fatty substance coating the axons of many neurons. It serves to insulate, to accelerate neuronal transmission, and to isolate neurons from one another.

MZ twins See **monozygotic (MZ) twins.**

N

natural categories Systems of classification that reflect the structure of the physical world. An example would be categories of color.

natural selection Natural selection was described by Darwin in 1859 to elucidate how populations can change over time. It involved two insights: (1) those individuals who do survive must in some way be more fit, better able to live in and adapt to their environment; and (2) the offspring differ in important respects from the parents. Therefore, differences that are passed on to the offspring are differences that usually enable them to fit better in their environment. The "natural" selection is made by the environment. See also **adaptation.**

nature/nurture In psychology there is a controversy over whether we are completely determined either by our innate characteristics or by experiences in the environment. Both of these views are extreme. Neither is considered sufficient now to explain the full range of human behavior. Most human behavior is the product of both factors, as the area of a rect-

angle is determined by its length and width.

Neanderthal The cave man of popular folklore, but with mental abilities and a culture far more advanced than was once suspected. Very like modern humans in many ways.

needs In psychological terms, the specific deficits that any animal must satisfy, such as hunger and thirst. See also **goals.**

negative feedback A form of feedback in which information triggers changes in the opposite (negative) direction; for instance, low blood sugar signals us to increase blood sugar levels. Negative feedback is important to the maintenance of the body's internal state. See also **homeostasis; positive feedback.**

neuroendocrine system The system comprising the autonomic nervous system (ANS) and the endocrine glands, which is one of the means through which the brain controls the body.

neurons Nerve cells that are the building blocks of the brain and nervous systems. The nucleus of the neuron is called the cell body. There are approximately ten billion neurons in the human brain, each neuron having as many as thousands of different interconnections.

neuroses In the definition of Freud, these are unconscious conflicts between the desires of the id and the demands of the superego. He felt they often occurred as a result of traumatic experiences in early childhood.

neurotransmission The process by which nerve cells in the brain and other parts of the body communicate with one another. This process is largely chemical. When a neuron fires, it releases chemicals at its axon, which then migrate across the synoptic cleft to a second cell.

nonconscious A level of awareness that is primarily concerned with the autonomic functioning of the body, such as the pumping of the heart, blood circulation, breathing, digestion, and other biochemical and neurological activities.

nonsense syllables Such as "dof," "zam," and "fok," devised by Ebbinghaus to test memory in his con-

trolled research on recall and forgetting.

norepinephrine Formerly called adrenaline, this neurotransmitter is important in coding of memory and in the reward system of the brain.

norms. Standards of permissible thought and behavior shared by members of a group.

O

object permanence An important demonstration first pointed out by Piaget: that children, at about eight months, begin to be able to form a representation of an object not present. They will follow an object that they have previously seen and attempt to find it. Younger children will not look for such a vanished object. They are at the stage of "out of sight, out of mind."

observational learning Also called social learning, it involves learning through watching others and modeling or imitating their behavior.

obsessive-compulsive disorders In an obsession the mind is flooded with a specific thought. In a compulsive disorder the person feels compelled to repeat a certain action over and over again.

occipital lobes The area at the back of the brain that is devoted entirely to vision.

ocular accommodation In order to focus on objects close to oneself, the lens of a camera must bend the light so it falls on the film. The eye works in a similar way. When we look at objects at different distances, the width of the lens needs to change to focus light on the retina. This change is called ocular accommodation.

olfactory cilia The receptors for smell, located at the end of the nasal cavity.

olfactory epithelium This means "smell skin." The end of the nasal cavity containing the receptors for smell.

operant conditioning Also called instrumental conditioning, it was developed by B. F. Skinner beginning in the 1930s. In this form of conditioning, it is the organism's *opera-*

tions or actions that are conditioned. Operant conditioning is very useful for teaching organisms new responses and the contingencies of different situations. See also **conditioning; reinforcement; respondent conditioning.**

operant level In operant conditioning, the number of times a specific response is made before the conditioning trials begin.

operant strength In operant (instrumental) conditioning, the measure of the rate of response after conditioning, of the strength of association between a behavior and its reinforcement. See also **operant level.**

operations In Piaget's theory of cognitive development, operations are rules for transforming and manipulating information in the world. A simple arithmetic operation is: If you have two and add two, you will have four.

optical expansion The so-called looming effect, which creates the impression that, as you approach a scene, objects closer to you are moving toward you faster than those far away.

organization Perceptual organization is the connection and coordination of separate sensory stimuli into something meaningful. When something becomes organized as an illusion, it is difficult to disorganize it.

organizational stress The combination of tensions, pressures, and dangers that impinge upon people in their work environment and which may outstrip their capacity to adapt to it.

orgasm The most brief and intense phase of the sexual response cycle, during which arousal, muscle tension, heart rate, and respiration increase rapidly to a kind of peak, which for males also involves ejaculation.

orienting reflex (OR) The physiological changes that prepare the organism for action: muscles tense, neurotransmitters increase, sensory acuity sharpens. See also **emergency reaction.**

ossification The development and fusing of the bone structure.

ovulation The time when the female egg is developed and released from the ovary, and thus can be fertilized. In human females this takes place every month, rather than only during estrus, a more limited period of ovulation during which other female mammals are fertile and sexually receptive to males.

P

pair bonding The sexual bond that is the basis of the family, that encourages fathers to stay with, care for, and care about their mates and their offspring, permitting families to expand faster through the sharing of food and child rearing responsibilities.

parasympathetic nervous system A division of the autonomic nervous system, it acts to return the body to normal after emergencies. See also **sympathetic nervous system.**

parietal lobes The area between the frontal lobes and the occipital lobes, which are involved in the integration and analysis of sensory input, although its functions are not all that clearly understood.

partial reinforcement (PR) In this form of reinforcement, each time the animal makes a correct response, the reinforcement does not always occur. See also **continuous reinforcement; operant conditioning.**

passionate love This is the strong form of being in love; a state of intense absorption in another person. It includes arousal, longing, and activation of many different emotions.

perceptual adaptation See **adaptation.**

perceptual cycle A concept by Neisser that helps to explain that perception is an active process guided by schemata. When something is seen, it stimulates direct exploration; then the sensory information provided by these exploratory movements modifies the view of the world and the schemata change again. New movements are directed and exploration begins anew. This is why different people may carve out different perceptual experiences from the same scene for themselves. They "select" the world differently.

perceptual-motor memory This form of memory is sometimes called "skill memory." It contains the rules for operating certain routine actions, such as throwing a ball, getting dressed, or playing a game like football.

peripheral nervous system (PNS) Nerves from the spinal cord that conduct commands to the muscles and organs of the body and comprise the peripheral nervous system, gather information about body states, muscle position, limb position, and internal states of organs. See also **central nervous system.**

person-centered therapy An influential form of psychotherapy developed by Rogers. In this humanistic therapy, the most important element is the relationship between the therapist and client. Clients are encouraged by means of *nondirective* statements to explore and reveal their feelings about themselves and their life situations. Once these situations can come to consciousness, a clarification of beliefs and action are hoped to follow.

pharmacotherapy An attempt to treat psychological problems by administering drugs in four major categories: antipsychotics, antidepressants, antianxiety drugs, and lithium compounds.

phenotype The portion of the genotype (genetic inheritance) that is "expressed" in the organism.

pheromones Chemical substances used by members of various animal species to communicate with others of their kind.

phobia From the Greek word for fear. But in psychology the term refers to an extreme or unfounded fear of an object or place.

phonemes The specific sound elements of language. A particular sound is considered a phoneme only if it is used in language.

photoreceptors The rods and cones, nerve cells containing photochemicals that respond to light. They constitute the main layer of the retina. See also **retina.**

pituitary The control gland of the neuroendocrine system, it lies below the hypothalamus in the limbic system.

planning One of the indicators (with competence and concern for standards) that a child has developed consciousness of himself or herself.

pleasure principle In Freud's theory of personality, the principle that organisms seek to reduce tension created by the build-up of libido.

polarity In Plutchik's theory of emotions, the variation between emotions that makes them opposites, such as love being the opposite of hate, sadness the opposite of joy. See also **emotion solid; emotion wheel.**

pontine reticular formation A network of cells located in the pons of the brain, which activates eye movement neurons during REM sleep. During this period, the pontine reticular formation also inhibits another part of the brain, which in turn blocks muscle movements.

positive feedback A process by which things may change dramatically. Changes in one element of the system change the rest of the system in the same direction. For instance, increases in grumpiness, hostility, or happiness lead to further increases in the same direction. See also **negative feedback.**

positron emission tomography The so-called PET scan, a method for measuring glucose uptake within the brain, enabling investigators to "see" into the deeper workings of the brain.

postconventional morality In Kohlberg's theory of moral development, moral reasoning based on individual principles of conscience, which respect both the moral rights of individuals and the welfare of the community. See also **conventional morality; premoral level.**

potency A component of emotional appraisal proposed by Osgood. In this, a person judging an emotional experience asks, "Is it alive or dead, strong or weak, fast or slow?"

Power Law A principle of sensation described by Stephens, which shows that the different senses transform the information they select differently. Within each sensory system, equal ratios of stimulus intensity produce equal ratios of change in experience. See also **Weber's Law.**

preconscious A level of awareness that includes memories that enable us to operate in the world.

prehumans Creatures having both apelike and humanlike characteristics. See also **hominids.**

prejudice A negative judgmental attitude toward an identifiable group of people. This is usually based on a simplistic overgeneralization.

premoral level In Kohlberg's theory of moral development, moral reasoning in which individuals consider only their own interests. See also **conventional morality; post-conventional morality.**

preoperational stage In Piaget's view of cognitive development, the stage (from two to seven years) at which a child begins to be able to represent objects in drawings or words and in which schemata become more integrated and coordinated.

preparedness An influential concept developed by Seligman, which hypothesized that certain animals are more predisposed (prepared) to learn certain responses better than are other animals.

prepotence In Maslow's hierarchy of motivation, prepotence denotes the relative strength of different needs. In this view, the "stronger" needs are lower on the hierarchy. The need for water, for instance, is a stronger need than the need for friendship.

pressure receptors Specific receptors in the veins that detect even the smallest reduction in water content of the blood. This is an important mechanism in the transmission of thirst signals to the brain.

primacy An example is our enhanced recall of beginnings in learning: the first words in a list are easier to learn than the latter ones; the first lessons of a course are easier to learn and remember than the latter ones. See also **recency.**

primary emotions Many psychologists now hypothesize that there are several primary emotions, as there are primary colors. Plutchik further states that there are eight primary emotions: joy, acceptance, fear, surprise, sadness, disgust, anger, and anticipation.

proactive interference This occurs when previous knowledge interferes with present memory. See also **retroactive interference.**

problem representation The way a person thinks about or *represents* a problem may make it harder or easier to solve. Some problems need to be represented visually, some purely mathematically. The wrong representation to a problem may dramatically change how it works.

proprioception The sense that allows us to know where each part of the body is in relation to all other parts.

prosocial behavior Behaving in such a way as to enhance social integration and to enhance the actions of others.

protocol analysis A method of analysis of thought, used by Newell and Simon to study how people solve puzzles. This method involves recording verbatim the statements made by a person while he or she is solving a problem, and analyzing the protocol by means of a problem behavior graph.

prototype The sample that most typifies a category. A house evokes up the prototype of four walls, ceiling, paintings on the wall.

proxemics An analysis of personal space developed by Hall. Personal distance is classified in four different ways: intimate, personal, social, and public.

psychiatric drugs Subtances—such as antidepressants, antipsychotics, antianxiety drugs, and lithium—that help to "normalize" consciousness by correcting neurochemical imbalances.

psychiatric social worker The holder of an advanced degree, such as an M.S. or Ph.D. Usually concentrates on social and community-based problems.

psychiatrist A medical doctor whose specialty is the treatment of psychological problems and who is licensed to dispense drugs.

psychoactive drugs Substances—such as marijuana, mescaline, and LSD—that change the overall structure of consciousness.

psychoanalysis The most famous and one of the most influential theories in psychology. Proposed by Freud and developed from the late nineteenth century until 1940, it is a complete theory of personality and a method of treatment. It specifies what motivates people, how personality develops, and how it is built. Its primary aim is to show that the relationship between conscious and unconscious processes is often the root of much of our behavior, especially behavior that causes us difficulties.

psychoanalyst A psychotherapist trained in the psychoanalytic techniques formulated by Freud; almost all psychoanalysts are physicians.

psychokinesis The ability to affect the physical world by mental force alone. A demonstration of this would be transporting objects merely by willing, although such demonstrations have not been scientifically verified.

psychopath See **antisocial personality.**

psychosocial development The individual relationship with various groups—family, community, nation—and the socialization and development of the individual. Also, the recognition, by Erikson, that development processes occur in a psychosocial context. Erikson viewed the life course as a series of eight successive stages, each with its characteristic crisis to be resolved.

pyramid of motivation A theoretical description of motivation by Maslow, which places emotions in an ascending pyramid of relative strength. At the bottom are physiological needs, such as hunger and thirst. Following those are belonging and safety needs, for shelter and the need for friendship. Above those are the goals of competence and self-esteem, the desire for knowledge, for self-actualization, and for transcendence.

Q

quantitative and qualitative distinctions A quantitative distinction tells us the degree of difference between two measurements—how much taller someone is than another, how much stronger, etc. A qualitative distinction points to the qualities that are possessed by an individual—X is aggressive, Y is friendly, etc.

questionnaire A formal method for asking specific questions that will provide researchers dependable answers on which to base their judgments.

R

range of reaction The portion of an individual's genetic potential that predisposes him or her to a certain ability or trait. Whether the predisposition develops into a reality depends on experience, on environmental factors.

Rational-emotive therapy (RET) A form of therapy, developed by Ellis, in which the therapist determines what the underlying belief system of the individual is, confronts the client with that belief system and directly forces him or her to examine it against reality.

reality principle The principle, postulated by Freud, in which the ego operates. It specifies that actions are tested against reality, and the feedback from those actions modifies behavior. See also **ego.**

recall The ability to summon up stored information in the absence of the actual object or event.

recency There is enhanced recall of the latest thing that one has learned or experienced: the last word in a list is better remembered; the last lesson in a series of lessons is better remembered. See also **primacy.**

receptive field The area of stimulation that a retinal cell responds best to. Different cells have been found to have different shaped receptive fields.

recessive gene See **dominant/recessive genes.**

recognition The ability to correctly identify an object or an event.

reference group In social comparisons, we must learn to compare ourselves to other people on a number of dimensions, such as the speed with which we run, our writing ability, and the like. The group we choose to compare ourselves to is our reference group, often a group of peers or appropriate individuals.

reflexes Inborn, unlearned responses of newborns, many of which involve sophisticated motor skills. Reflexes include sucking and head turning in response to noise.

regression Under stress, according to Freud, a person may regress to earlier stages of personality. Thus, people will act more as they did when they were younger, when the foundations of their personality were formed. See also **fixation.**

reinforcement Any event that strengthens the possibility that a certain response will reoccur. When something is given to an animal after a desired response, this is called *positive reinforcement*. When something unpleasant is taken away from the animal after a desired response, this is called *negative reinforcement*.

reliability The necessity that test scores be reproducible and consistent. See also **validity.**

REM sleep Rapid eye movements (REM) during sleep were first discovered in the 1950s. Since then, they have been taken as an unequivocal sign that the sleeper is in a dream state, and hundreds of experiments since then show a consistent association between REM sleep and dreaming.

replication Psychological experiments need to be repeated, *replicated*, by others. If the findings of a second experiment confirm those of the first, then the findings of the first experiment are more likely to be accepted.

representational memory A record of general knowledge of the world, such as how to speak, how to ride a bicycle, where Chicago and Scotland are. Representational memory is generally assumed to be common to all members of a culture. See also **episodic memory.**

representational thought At about 18 months, children begin to be able to develop the capacity to represent objects in their minds. One important kind of symbol is language.

representativeness The judgment that an object is *typical* of its category. Because we tend to judge vivid examples of a category as representative, a single case, considered representative, can have a disproportionate influence on us.

resistance In psychoanalysis, a characteristic way that the patient unconsciously works *against* revealing his or her feelings or thoughts. For instance, every time a patient might start to talk about his or her mother, he or she might change the subject, tell a joke, or say the thought is too silly.

respondent conditioning The process whereby a previously neutral stimulus (NS) comes to have a significant effect on an organism's behavior is called "classical" or respondent conditioning. See also **conditioned response; conditioned stimulus; conditioning; operant conditioning; unconditioned response; unconditioned stimulus.**

retention A process in memory in which new information must be stored and kept. This is a hypothetical stage in the cycle of memory, used by many psychologists. See also **retrieval.**

reticular activating system (RAS) The RAS arouses the cortex to important incoming stimulation. It seems to serve a general alarm function—it tells the cortex that something visual, auditory, or olfactory is on its way. The RAS controls the existence and the intensity of consciousness.

retina The center of the process of vision, comprised of neural tissues and about the thickness of this page.

retrieval A process hypothesized by many psychologists in which stored information is brought forward into consciousness at the appropriate time. See also **retention.**

retroactive interference This occurs when new information interferes with memory of old. See also **proactive interference.**

risky shift The concept that people are more likely to take risks in an extreme position in groups than while alone. Also called the extremity shift.

rods Photoreceptors in the eye that respond most to light energy at low levels, particularly those of a wave length of 480 nm. There are about 120 million rods distributed over the

retina; the heaviest concentration is at the sides. See also **cones; photoreceptors.**

role playing A form of psychotherapy in which the therapist creates a hypothetical situation that is likely to cause the client anxiety and which they act out together. For instance, a person may think he or she deserves a raise but cannot come to ask his or her boss for one. The therapist asks the client to act out the scene in which he or she asks for more money.

S

sample The group of subjects, representative of an entire population, in an experiment or study.

schema (plural, **schemata**) The unit of mental life, the internal, mental organization of how actions relate to one another, how different internal stimuli relate to one another, and how outside stimuli relate to specific actions. Schemata are the cognitive generalizations about oneself that guide the processing of information and interpretation about oneself.

schizophrenia The group of psychological disorders that involve severe deterioration of mental abilities, fundamental disorganization that causes disturbances in every area of life: social functioning, feeling, behavior.

secondary traits In Allport's theory of personality, these are traits that only occur in a few specific situations. For example, a person may be generally calm but may become anxious on airplanes. See also **cardinal traits.**

sedatives Drugs, such as barbiturates, that induce relaxation and sleep.

self-actualization Maslow theorized that we all have within us certain "potentials" and that we strive to make those potentials "actual." Thus, self-actualization is the drive within individuals to actualize their potential.

self-awareness The typically human consciousness of our own existence, our own mortality—the knowledge of who we are and the sense of our own personal self.

self-monitoring The degree to which people are concerned about how they appear to others and how appropriately they behave. High self-monitors are concerned about how they appear to others; low self-monitors are not so concerned about others and look to their own standards as a guide.

self-schemata Cognitive generalizations that guide the processing of information and interpretation about the self.

semantic memory The knowledge of a specific language, of what words mean and how they are used within a specific culture. The average college student has a vocabulary of about 50,000 words in semantic memory.

sensorimotor stage In Piaget's view of cognitive development, the stage (up to two years of age) during which a child learns primarily through motor and sensory play, begins to develop a sense of self, and starts to be capable of representational or symbolic thought. See also **object permanence.**

sensory acuity Used by Galton in the late nineteenth century to judge a person's intelligence. Sensory acuity is measured by such tests as reaction time for sound, speed in naming colors, how tightly the hand can squeeze, and other measures of the efficiency of the senses.

sensory adaptation See **adaptation.**

sensory-motor areas This part of the cortex is located at the juncture of the frontal and parietal lobes. Sensory areas receive information about body position, muscles, touch and pressure from all over the body.

separation anxiety The extreme distress shown by infants, usually around eight months of age, when the mother leaves them in the care of someone else. See also **attachment.**

serotonin A neurotransmitter that connects the brain stem and reticular activating system to the cortex and to the limbic system. It is thought to be very much involved in sleep and sleep regulation.

set point The body tends to maintain a set point for weight, set as is the temperature on a thermostat. The hypothalamus can control eating and drinking and metabolic level to raise or lower caloric expenditure. The implications of this set point are that weight is much more difficult to either gain or lose than we would like and that people's normal weight is more likely to be higher than the current social norm. See also **homeostasis.**

sex roles Society's expectations of how a male or female should behave.

sexual response cycle The regular physiological changes involved in sexual intercourse and sexual activity, described by Masters and Johnson as comprising four phases: excitement, plateau, orgasm, resolution.

short-term memory The process by which information is thought to be stored for temporary retention of only a few seconds. Its capacity is about seven items, such as a seven-digit number.

sleep spindles The appearance of 12–14 Hz rhythms on the EEG during stage-two sleep.

social comparison An important theory in social psychology by Festinger. If there is no objective measure of comparison, we tend to seek out other people, whom we admire or believe are like us, and compare our attitudes and behavior to theirs. There is no generally accepted yardstick for determining such questions as: How smart am I? Am I well behaved? The only way to achieve such comparisons is to compare oneself to others.

social environmental perspective The study of how other people and our environment affect us.

social learning See **observational learning.**

social learning theory An outgrowth of the learning theory analyses of conditioning in the 1930s. It emphasizes that most behavior is learned rather than instinctually determined. It generally rejects the idea of an unconscious and favors an analysis of the situational and immediate determinants of behavior.

social pressure Pressure inherent in many group situations that forces us to be like everybody else.

social support The company and attention of others. In a large number of studies, it has been shown that the more social support a person has, the less likely he or she is to become ill when under stress.

sociobiology A new field of study that attempts to account for much social behavior in biological terms. Important questions dealt with by sociobiologists are altruism, male/female sex differences, and territoriality.

sociopath See **antisocial personality.**

somatic nervous system (SNS) A division of the peripheral nervous system that controls voluntary movements of the body.

somatoform disorders Disorders in which the individual complains of a physical ailment for which there is no organic or physiological explanation.

somesthetic system Part of the vestibular senses, it conveys to the brain information concerning sensations in the internal environment (body), such as deep pain or nausea.

species-specific behavior See **instincts.**

split brain In this surgical operation devised by Sperry and his colleagues, the corpus callosum is severed, producing a person or animal whose hemispheres can no longer communicate with one another. Many studies have been performed on split-brain people and have revealed the dramatic differences between the two hemispheres.

spontaneous remission The process by which people "spontaneously" recover from psychological disorders without the intervention of psychotherapy. Such spontaneous remission is now used as a control in studies evaluating the outcome of specific therapies.

SQ3R The method of remembering, which stands for "Survey, Question, Read, Recite, Review." It involves (1) surveying a chapter before you read it, (2) questioning the material before you read it, (3) reading the material only after a framework for remembering is in place, (4) reciting what you have learned, and (5) reviewing the material after retaining the important information.

statistics The formal, mathematical set of rules for the evaluation of evidence, which enables scientific judgments to be more precise and quantitative than ordinary judgments.

stereotype A generalized assumption attributing identical characteristics to all members of a group: for instance, blondes are dumb, Americans are materialistic, and the like.

stimulants Drugs, such as amphetamines and cocaine, that elevate mood and increase alertness.

storage space The amount of memory capacity taken up by given experiences, which helps us construct our sense of time, because we judge periods of time by how much is remembered about them, by how much storage space they take up.

stranger anxiety Infants' fear of strangers, which often develops around the last quarter of the first year and may cause them to scream and cry if a stranger approaches. See also **attachment.**

strange situation In this experiment, developed by Ainsworth, a stranger enters the room where a baby and mother are playing with toys. The mother leaves the room so that the child is alone with the stranger. The experimenter observes how the baby reacts to the mother's departure. See also **attachment; separation anxiety.**

stress The failure of adaptability, which occurs when environmental or internal demands exceed the adaptive resources of an organism. Also defined, by Selye, as the general reaction of the body to change. See also **emergency reaction; general adaptation syndrome.**

stress inoculation therapy A therapy proposing that by altering the way people talk to themselves, the way they approach stressful problems will be changed. The training takes place in three phases: (1) the therapist and client examine a stressful situation, (2) the client rehearses and learns a new set of statements to help avoid stress, and (3) the client puts these new statements into application and practice.

structure of intellect A model of the mind hypothesized by Guilford, which describes human intelligence as a set of abilities, each different and distinct from one another. In this model, the abilities are arranged in a cube. Each side of the cube represents a different function of the mind.

subgoals A method of thinking that is useful in problem solving. It involves breaking a large problem into shorter problems and setting intermediate or subgoals.

subjects The people (or sometimes animals) whose behavior is observed as part of an experiment. See also **control group; experimental group; sample.**

substance use disorders Psychological disorders in which there is a consistent pattern of excessive substance use resulting in impairment of social or occupational functioning and that may involve physical dependence on the substance.

superego In Freud's theory, this is the last part of the personality to develop. It is the internal representation of society's values and morals. The superego restrains aggression and sexual impulses of the id, pressures the ego to act in a more moralistic than realistic way, and encourages the individual to strive for perfection. See also **ego; id.**

symbolic thought See **representational thought.**

sympathetic nervous system A division of the autonomic nervous system, it prepares internal organs for emergencies. It operates "in sympathy" with the emotions, telling the body to "go." See also **parasympathetic nervous system.**

synapse The point at which two neurons meet—usually between the axon of one and the dendrite of the other—where the chemicals involved in neurotransmission pass from the transmitting neuron to the receiving.

syntax How words in a specific language are arranged to convey meaning. See also **grammar.**

system Any group of things that function together for a common purpose. A system can be as wide ranging and complex as the educational system or as specific as the visual system.

systematic desensitization A form of

behavior therapy based on the phenomenon of counterconditioning. In this therapy, the aim is to *eliminate* an unwanted conditioned response by conditioning the client to another stimulus that elicits a response (usually relaxation) that is incompatible with the original response.

T

tactile sensory replacement (TSR) A technique using a device that impresses "televised" images onto the skin so that blind persons can feel the pattern of stimulation and recognize objects in front of them.

taxonomy A system of classification, an orderly organization of things by similarities and differences.

teaching story A story form predominant in the Sufi tradition, which aims to entice the mind into operating in an unfamiliar manner. Examples of such tales include "The Elephant in the Dark" and "The Man with the Inexplicable Life" by Idries Shah. (See pp. 274–75.)

temperament The enduring emotional characteristics of a person's life.

temporal lobes The area on the side of the brain devoted in part to hearing as well as perception, memory, and dreaming. Damage to the temporal lobes may result in a condition known as aphasia, the disruption of the ability to use language.

terminal drop A marked decline in intelligence and other measures of cognitive and biological functioning, a few months to a year before death.

Terra Amata The site in southern France where archeologists uncovered a well-preserved *Homo erectus* settlement and unlocked many of the secrets of *Homo erectus* culture.

tests Formal measurements of such psychological abilities as intelligence, verbal and spatial skills, the ability to get along with others.

texture gradient As you look over a uniform surface, the density of the texture increases with distance. This texture gradient can be analyzed for information about distance and the angle of the surface.

thalamus The brain stem structure that relays information to the appropriate areas of the cortex. It appears that certain areas of the thalamus are specialized for specific kinds of sensory information—auditory, visual, and the like—and that these forms of sensory information are sent to the cortex.

Thanatos In Freud's theory, the death instinct: organisms seek a quiescent state, and death is, of course, the ultimate of this. "The aim of life" Freud wrote in a famous passage, "is death." See also **Eros.**

thermometer neurons Nerve cells that measure blood temperature and can alter their firing rate to trigger actions either to warm or cool the blood. See also **homeostasis.**

timetables Within each culture, there are generally agreed upon times for entering or completing certain roles, such as when one graduates from college, when one has a family, when one is financially secure.

tool use The characteristic of human adaptation made possible by the dexterity of hands freed for such use by bipedalism. Although largely confined to humans, tool use is attributed to prehumans and other species, notably chimpanzees.

transcendence The form of motivation that drives people to go beyond the ordinary understanding of life. Many people try to search for knowledge at the highest level and ask questions, such as "What is the meaning of life?" or "What is God?"

transduction A sensory process that transforms each particular kind of physical energy (light, sound, etc.) into neural firing. The eye transduces light, the ear transduces sound waves, the nose transduces gaseous molecules.

transference An important concept of psychoanalytic theory. During therapy, the patient tends to "transfer" his or her general feelings about life onto the therapist. A person who has difficulty getting along with people in authority may suddenly start to have that problem with the therapist; a person who is suspicious of other people may be suspicious of what the therapist is doing.

The clarification of the transference is held to reveal fundamental ways in which the patient acts in the world. Psychoanalysis then proceeds to a "working through" of that transference.

transformational grammar An influential theory that holds that there is a distinction in syntax between "surface" and "deep" structure. This theory presupposes that the human brain is designed to produce language and that the structure of language is in some way innate.

trephining A medieval method of treatment of mental disorder. In what must have been a heroic treatment, holes were drilled into a person's head to let out the demons who were thought to be causing the disorder. Trephining is not a current method of treatment.

Type A behavior The behavior of individuals who have specific reactions to the stresses of life: They tend to be aggressive, hostile, competitive, time-urgent, fast-paced, impatient, and irritable. They are deeply involved in their work and often deny failure, fatigue, and illness. They try to get more and more done in less and less time and are twice as likely to develop heart disease as Type B people, who may be as successful but tend to be calm.

typicality Having characteristics of a category that thereby make something an example of that category closest to the prototype.

U

unconditioned response (UCR) A response that is made without any specific sort of learning, such as salivation to food.

unconditioned stimulus (UCS) A stimulus, such as food or a loud noise, that elicits an unconditioned response, such as salivation or being startled.

unconscious A level of awareness, postulated by Sigmund Freud, in which memories and thoughts that are difficult to deal with are supposedly hidden.

unconscious inferences The nineteenth-century scientist Helmholz described a perceiver as one who must make inferences, fill in gaps in the information reaching him or her. These inferences transform a set of disconnected lines into the living world of objects: cube, train, car.

uplifts Positive life events that give a great deal of pleasure and may, in some instances and to varying degrees, balance the impact of negative events.

V

validity A required characteristic of tests, such as intelligence tests, assuring that they measure what they are intended to measure. See also **reliability.**

variable interval (VI) In this reinforcement schedule, the intervals between reinforcement vary randomly around an average.

variable ratio (VR) In this reinforcement schedule, the reward occurs after a randomly varying number of responses.

variables In experiments, only a few things are allowed to change—these are called variables. Variables are of two kinds: *independent* variables are those the experimenter may attempt to manipulate, such as how many hours an animal is deprived of food; *dependent* variables are those which the experimenter measures, those that change after the experimenter's manipulations, such as how much the animal might eat.

vasocongestion The increase of blood flow to the genitals, which is one of the physical changes during the excitement phase of the sexual response cycle.

vestibular system This consists of organs sensitive to motion, position, and balance.

visual cliff In order to test whether depth perception develops only when a baby can move around, Gibson developed a visual cliff, which is the effect created by two surfaces under glass, both of which have a checkerboard pattern. It gives the illusion of a visual drop, but there is of course no drop.

W

Weber's Law The first major principle of sensation, discovered by Ernest Weber (1834), noted the consistent proportional relationship between a physical stimulus and our psychological response to it.

References

ABRAMOWITZ, S. I. (1969). Locus of control and self-reported depression among college students. *Psychological Reports, 25,* 149–150.

ADAM, K., & OSWALD, I. (1977). Sleep is for tissue restoration. *Journal of the Royal College of Physicians, 11,* 376–388.

ADLER, A. (1929). *The practice and theory of individual psychology.* New York: Harcourt Brace Jovanovich.

ADORNO, T. W., FRENKEL-BRUNS-WICK, E., LEVINSON, D. S., & SANFORD, R. N. (1950). *The authoritarian personality.* New York: Harper & Row.

AIELLO, J. R., DE RISI, D. T., EPSTEIN, Y. M., YAKOV, M., & KARLIN, R. A. (1977). Crowding and the role of interpersonal distance preference. *Sociometry. 40,* 271–282.

AIELLO, J. R., & THOMPSON, D. E. (1980). When compensation fails: Mediating effects of sex and locus of control at extended interaction distances. *Basic and Applied Social Psychology, 1,* 65–82.

AINSWORTH, M. D. S. (1967). *Infancy in Uganda.* Baltimore: Johns Hopkins University Press.

AINSWORTH, M. D. S., & BELL, S. M. (1970). Attachment, exploration and separation: illustrated by the behavior of one-year-olds in a strange situation. *Child Development, 41.*

AINSWORTH, M. D. S., BLEHAR, M., WATERS, E., & WALL, S. (1978). *Patterns of attachment: A psychological study of the strange situation.* Hillsdale, NJ: Lawrence Erlbaum.

AINSWORTH, M. D. S., & WITTIG, B. A. (1965). Attachment and exploratory behavior of one year olds in a strange situation. In B. M. Foxx (Ed.), *Determinants of infant behaviour: Vol. 4.* London: Methuen.

ALBERT, M. A., & OBLER, L. K. (1978). *The bilingual brain.* New York: Academic Press.

ALBRECHT, S. (1980). Reactions and adjustments to divorce: Differences in the experiences of males and females. *Family Relations, 29,* 59–68.

ALEXANDER, R. D., HOOGLAND, J. L., HOWARD, R. D., NOONAN, K. M., & SHERMAN, P. W. (1979). In N. A. Chagnons & W. G. Irons (Eds.), *Evolutionary biology and human social behavior: An anthropological perspective.* North Scituate, MA: Duxbury Press.

ALLEN, I. M. (1951). Cerebral injury with shock treatment. *New Zealand Medical Journal, 50,* 356–364.

ALLISON, R. (1980). *Minds in many pieces.* New York: Rawson-Wade.

ALLPORT, G. W. (1937). *Personality: A psychological interpretation.* New York: Holt, Rinehart & Winston.

ALLPORT, G. W. (1950). *The individual and his religion: A psychological interpretation.* New York: Macmillan.

ALLPORT, G. W. (1954). *The nature of prejudice.* Cambridge, MA: Addison-Wesley.

ALLPORT, G. W. (1955). *Becoming.* New Haven: Yale University Press.

ALLPORT, G. W. (1961). *Pattern and growth in personality.* New York: Holt, Rinehart & Winston.

ALLPORT, G. W., & ODBERT, H. S. (1936). Trait-names: A psycholexical study. *Psychological Monographs, 47,* 1–171.

ALLPORT, G. W., & ROSS, J. M. (1967). Personal religious orientation and prejudice. *Journal of Personality and Social Psychology, 5,* 432–443.

ALPER, T. G. (1974). Achievement motivation in college women: A now-you-see-it-now-you-don't phenomenon. *American Psychologist, 29,* 194–203.

ALPERS, B. J., & HUGHES, J. (1942). Changes in the brain after electrically induced convulsions in cats. *Archives of Neurology and Psychiatry, 47,* 385–398.

ALTROCCHI, J. (1980). *Abnormal behavior.* New York: Harcourt Brace Jovanovich.

AMERICAN INSTITUTE OF PLANNERS NEWSLETTER, 1967.

AMERICAN PSYCHIATRIC ASSOCIATION. (1980). *Diagnostic and statistical manual of mental disorders* (3rd ed.). Washington, DC: Author.

ANAND, B. K., & BROBECK, J. R. (1951). Hypothalamic control of food intake in rats and cats. *Yale Journal of Biology and Medicine, 24,* 123–140.

ANDRES, R. (in press). *The ideal weight.*

ANONYMOUS. (1978). *Problems of pregnancy: A report.* Ontario: Commission on Mental Health, Toronto, Ontario.

ANTONOVSKY, A. (1979). *Health, stress, and coping.* San Francisco: Jossey-Bass.

ARENBERG, D., & ROBERTSON-TCHABO, E. (1977). Learning and aging. In J. E. Birren & K. W. Schaie (Eds.), *Handbook of the psychology of aging.* New York: Van Nostrand Reinhold.

ARGYLE, M. (1978). *The psychology of interpersonal behavior.* New York: Penguin Books.

ARON, A. (1977). Maslow's other child. *Journal of Humanistic Psychology, 17*(2), 9–24.

ARONSON, E. (1958). The need for achievement as measured by graphic expression. In J. W. Atkinson (Ed.), *Motives in fantasy, action and society* (pp. 249–265). Princeton, NJ: Van Nostrand Reinhold.

ARONSON, E. (1978). *The jigsaw classroom.* Beverly Hills: Sage Publications.

ARONSON, E. (1984). *The social animal.* San Francisco: W. H. Freeman.

ARONSON, E., & OSHEROW, N. (1980). Cooperation, prosocial behavior, and academic performance: Experiments in the desegregated classroom. In L. Bickman (Ed.), *Applied social psychology annual: Vol. 1.* Beverly Hills: Sage Publications.

ASCH, S. E. (1946). Forming impressions of personality. *Journal of Abnormal and Social Psychology, 41,* 258–290.

ASCH, S. E. (1951). Effects of group pressure upon the modification and distortion of judgments. In H. Guetzkow (Ed.), *Groups, leadership, and men* (pp. 177–190). Pittsburgh: Carnegie Press.

ASCH, S. E. (1956). Studies of independence and conformity, a minority of one against a unanimous majority. *Psychological Monographs,* *70*(9, Whole No. 416).

ASCHOFF, J. (1965), *Circadian clocks.* Amsterdam: North-Holland.

ASCHOFF, J. (1967), Human circadian rhythms in activity, body temperature, and other functions. In A. H. Brown & F. G. Favoite (Eds.), *Life Sciences and Space Research.* (pp. 159–173). Vol. 5. Amsterdam: North-Holland.

ASERINSKY, E., & KLEITMAN, N. (1953). Regularly occurring periods of eye motility and concomitant phenomena during sleep. *Science, 118,* 273–274.

AUSTIN, J. L. (1962). *How to do things with words.* Oxford: Oxford University Press.

AVERILL, J. R. (1978). The emotions. In E. Staub (Ed.), *Personality: Basic issues and current research.* Englewood Cliffs, NJ: Prentice-Hall.

AVERILL, J. R. (1980). A constructivist view of emotions. In R. Plutchik, (Ed.), *Theories of emotion,* New York: Academic Press.

AYLLON, T., & AZRIN, N. (1968). Intensive treatment of psychotic behavior by stimulus satiation and food reinforcement. *Behavior Research and Therapy 1,* 53–61.

AYLLON, T., & AZRIN, N. (1968a). *A motivating environment for therapy and rehabilitation.* New York: Appleton-Century-Crofts.

AYLLON, T., & AZRIN, N. (1968b). *The token economy: A motivational system for therapy and rehabilitation.* New York: Appleton-Century-Crofts.

AZJEN, I., & FISHBEIN, M. (1977). Attitude-behavior relations: A theoretical analysis and review of empirical research. *Psychological Bulletin, 84,* 888–918.

BAASTRUP, P. C. (1980). Lithium in the treatment of recurrent affective disorders. In F. N. Johnson (Ed.), *Handbook of lithium therapy.* Baltimore: University Park Press.

BAGCHI, B. K., & WENGER, M. A. (1957). Electrophysiological correlates of some yogi exercises. *Electroencephalography and Clinical Neurophysiology, 7,* 132–149.

BAHNSON, C. B., & BAHNSON, M. B. (1964). Cancer as an alternative to psychosis: A theoretical model of somatic and psychological regression. In D. M. Kissen & L. L. Leshan (Eds.), *Psychosomatic aspects of neoplastic disease.* London: Pitman.

BAHNSON, M. B., & BAHNSON, C. B. (1969). Ego defenses in cancer patients. *Annals, New York Academy of Science, 164,* 546–559.

BAHRICK, H. P., BAHRICK, P. O., & WITTLINGER, R. P. (1975). Fifty years of memory for names and faces: A cross-sectional approach. *Journal of Experimental Psychology: General, 104,* 54–75.

BAKAN, P. (1977). Left-handedness and birth order revisited. *Neuropsychology, 15.*

BANDURA, A. (1965). Vicarious processes: A case of no-trial learning. In L. Berkowitz (Ed.), *Advances in experimental social psychology: Vol. 2.* New York: Academic Press.

BANDURA, A. (1973). *Aggression: A social learning analysis.* Englewood Cliffs, NJ: Prentice-Hall.

BANDURA, A. (1977a). Self-efficacy: Toward a unifying theory of behavioral change. *Psychological Review, 84,* 191–215.

BANDURA, A. (1977b). *Social learning theory.* Englewood Cliffs, NJ: Prentice-Hall.

BANDURA, A. (1978). Social learning theory of aggression. *Journal of Communication, 28,* 12–29.

BANDURA, A. (1979). *Aggression: A social learning analysis* (2nd ed.). Englewood Cliffs, NJ: Prentice-Hall.

BANDURA, A., & ADAMS, N. E. (1977). Analysis of self-efficacy theory of behavioral change. *Cognitive Therapy and Research, 1*(4), 287–310.

BANDURA, A., & McDONALD, F. D. (1963). The influence of social reinforcement and the behavior of models in shaping children's moral judgments. *Journal of Abnormal and Social Psychology, 67,* 274–281.

BANDURA, A., ROSS, O., & ROSS, S. A. (1961). Transmission of aggression through imitation of aggressive models. *Journal of Abnormal and Social Psychology, 63,* 575–582.

BANE, M. S. (1976). *Here to stay: American families in the twentieth century.* New York: Basic Books.

BANKS, W. C., McQUARTER, G. V., & HUBBARD, J. L. (1977). Taskliking and intrinsic-extrinsic achievement orientations in black adolescents. *Journal of Black Psychology, 3*(2), 61–71.

BARON, R. A. (1977). *Human aggression.* New York: Plenum.

BARON, R. A., & KEPNER, C. R. (1970). Model's behavior and attraction toward the model as determinants of adult aggressive behavior. *Journal of Personality and Social Psychology, 14,* 335–344.

BARR, J., LANGS, R., HOLT, T., GOLDBERGER, L., & KLEIN, G. (1972). *LSD: Personality and experience.* New York: John Wiley.

BARSLEY, M. (1979). *Left handed people.* North Hollywood: Wilshire.

BART, P. (1971). Depression in middle-aged women. In V. Goinich & B. K. Moran (Eds.), *Women in sexist society.* New York: Basic Books.

BARTLETT, F. C. (1932). *Remembering: A study in experimental and social psychology.* Cambridge: Cambridge University Press.

BARTROP, R. W., LAZARUS, L., LUCKHURST, E., KILOH, L. G., & PENNY, R. (1977). *Lancet, 1,* 834–839.

BATESON, G. (1959). *The double bind.* Palo Alto: Science and Behavior Books.

BATESON, G., JACKSON, D. D., HALEY, J., & WEAKLAND, J. H. (1972). Toward a theory of schizophrenia. *Behavioral Science 1*(4).

BATSON, C. D., NAIFEL, S. V., & PATE, S. (1978). Social desirability, religious orientation and racial prejudice. *Journal for the Scientific Study of Religion, 17,* 31–41.

BECK, A. T. (1976). *Cognitive therapy and the emotional disorders.* New York: International Universities Press.

BECK, A., RUSH, A. J., SHAW, B., & EMERY, G. (1979). *Cognitive therapy of depression: A treatment manual.* New York: Guilford Press.

BEE, H. (1978). *The developing child,* (2nd ed.). New York: Harper & Row.

BEECHER, H. W. (1885). *Evolution and religion.* New York.

BEERS, R. F., JR. (1979). *Mechanisms of pain and analgesic compounds.* New York: Raven Press.

BEHAVIORAL AND BRAIN SCIENCES. Published quarterly. New York: Cambridge University press.

BELLAH, R. N. (1973). Evil and the American ethos. In N. Sanford & C. Comstock (Eds.), *Sanctions for evil* (pp. 187–188). San Francisco: Jossey-Bass.

BELLER, S., & PALMORE, E. (1974). Longevity in Turkey. *The Gerontologist, 14*(5), 373–376.

BELLOWS, R. T. (1939). Time factors in water drinking in dogs. *American Journal of Physiology, 125,* 87–97.

BELOFF, J. (1978). Why parapsychology is still on trial. *Human Nature, 1*(12), 68–76.

BEM, D. J. (1967). Self-perception: An alternative interpretation of cognitive dissonance phenomena. *Psychological Review, 74,* 183–200.

BEM, D. J. (1970). *Beliefs, attitudes and human affairs.* Belmont, CA: Brooks/Cole.

BEM, D. J. (1972). Self-perfection theory: In L. Berkowitz (Ed.), *Advances in experimental social psychology: Vol. 6.* New York: Academic Press.

BEM, D. J., & ALLEN, A. (1974). On predicting some of the people some of the time: The search for cross-situational consistencies in behavior. *Psychological Review, 81,* 506–520.

BENNETT, W. (1983). *Implications of setpoint theory for treatment and research strategies.* Lecture given at Nutrition and the Brain symposium, Los Altos, CA Institute for the Study of Human Knowledge.

BENNETT, W. (1984). *Set point regulation of body weight* [Tape]. ISHK.

BENNETT, W., & GURIN, J. (1982). *Dieter's dilemma: Eating less and weighing more.* New York: Basic Books.

BENSHOOF, L., & THORNHILL, R. (1979). The evolution of monogamy and concealed ovulation in humans. *Journal of Social and Biological Structures, 2*(2), 95–105.

BERDYSHEV, G. D. (1966). *Ecologic and genetic factors of aging and longevity.* Moscow: Nauka.

BERGER, K. (1980). *The Developing Person.* New York: Worth.

BERGER, P. A., WATSON, S. J.,

AKIL, H., BARCHAS, J. D., & LI, C. H. (1980). Clinical studies with Naloxone and Beta-endorphin in chronic schizophrenia. In E. Usdin, T. L. Sourkes, & M. B. H. Youdim (Eds.), *Enzymes and neurotransmitters in mental disease* (pp. 45–64). United Kingdom: John Wiley.

BERKOWITZ, L. (1970). Aggressive humor as a stimulus to aggressive responses. *Journal of Personality and Social Psychology, 16,* 710–717.

BERLIN, B., & KAY, P. (1969). *Basic color terms: Their universality and evolution.* Berkeley and Los Angeles: University of California Press.

BERLYNE, D. E. (1960). *Conflict, arousal, and curiosity.* New York: McGraw-Hill.

BERLYNE, D. E. (1966). Curiosity and exploration. *Science, 153,* 25–33.

BERLYNE, D. E. (1967). Arousal and reinforcement. *Nebraska Symposium of Motivation* (pp. 1–110). Lincoln: University of Nebraska Press.

BERLYNE, D. E. (1972). Humor and its kin. In J. H. Goldstein & P. E. McGhee (Eds.), *The psychology of humor* (pp. 43–60). London: Academic Press.

BERMAN, W., & TURK, D. (1981, February). Adaptation to divorce: Problems and coping strategies. *Journal of Marriage and the Family,* pp. 179–189.

BERNARD. (1972). *The future of marriage.* New York: Bantam Books.

BETCHER, R. (1981). Intimate play and marital adaptation. *Psychiatry, 44,* 13–33.

BETTELHEIM, B. (1960). *The informed heart: Autonomy in a message.* Glencoe, IL: Free Press.

BIBRING, G. (1959). Some consideration of the psychological processes in pregnancy. *Psychoanalytic Study of the Child, 14,* 113–121.

BINFORD, S. R., & BINFORD, L. R. (1969, April). Stone tools and human behavior. *Scientific American,* 96.

BIRREN, J. E. et al. 1981. *Developmental psychology: A life-span approach.* Boston: Houghton Mifflin.

BIRREN, J. E., BUTLER, R. N., GREENHOSE, S. W., SOKOLOFF, L., & HARROW, M. R. (Eds.). (1963). *Human aging: A biological and*

behavioral study. (Publication No. HSM 71–9051). Washington, DC: U.S. Government Printing Office.

BJORK, R. A., & LANDAUER, T. K. (1979). On keeping track of the present status of people and things. In M. M. Gruneberg, P. E. Morris, & R. N. Sykes (Eds.), *Practical aspects of memory.* New York: Academic Press.

BJÖRNTORP, P. (1972). Disturbances in the regulation of food intake. *Advances in Psychosomatic Medicine, 7,* 116–147.

BLANCHARD, F. A., ADELMAN, L., & COOK, S. W. (1975). Effect of group success and failure upon interpersonal attraction in cooperating interracial groups. *Journal of Personality and Social Psychology, 31,* 1020–1030.

BLANCHARD, F. A., WEIGEL, R. H., & COOK, S. W. (1975). The effect of relative competence of group members upon interpersonal attraction in cooperating interracial groups. *Journal of Personality and Social Psychology, 32*(3), 519–530.

BLASI, A. (1980). Bridging moral cognition and moral action: A critical review of the literature. *Psychological Bulletin, 88,* 1–45.

BLASS, E. M., & KETY, F. S. (1974). Medial forebrain bundle lesions: Specific loss of feeding to decreased glucose utilization in rats. *Journal of Comparative and Physiological Psychology, 86,* 679–692.

BLOCK, J. (1971). *Lives through time.* Berkeley: Bancroft Books.

BLOCK, J. (1981). Some enduring and consequential structures of personality. In A. I. Rabin, J. Aronoff, A. M. Barclay, & R. A. Zucker (Eds.), *Further explorations in personality.* New York: Wiley-Interscience.

BLOCK, J. H. (1978). Another look at sex differences in the socialization of mothers and fathers. In J. Sherman & F. Denmark (Eds.), *The Psychology of women: Future directions in research.* New York: Psychological Dimensions.

BLOCK, J. H. (1979). Socialization influences on personality development in males and females. In M. M. Parkes (Ed.), *APA master lecture series* on issues of sex and gender in psychology. Washington, DC: American Psychological Association.

BLOCK, J. H., & BLOCK, J. (1980). The role of ego-control and ego resiliency in the organization of behavior. In W. A. Collins (Ed.), *Minnesota Symposium on Child Psychology: Vol. 13*. Hillsdale, NJ: Lawrence Erlbaum.

BLOOM, B. L., ASHER, S. J., & WHITE, S. W. (1978). Marital disruption as a stressor: A review and analysis. *Psychological Bulletin, 85*, 867–894.

BLOOM, B. L., & WHITE, S. W. (1981). Factors related to the adjustment of divorcing men. *Family Relations, 30*, 349–360.

BLUMENTHAL, H., & BURNS, A. (1964). Autoimmunity in aging. In B. Strehler (Ed.), *Advances in gerontological research: Vol. 1*. New York: Academic Press.

BLYTH, R. (1979). *The view in winter: Reflections on old age*. New York: Harcourt Brace Jovanovich.

BOLLES, R. C. (1970). Species-specific defense reactions in avoidance learning. *Psychological Review, 71*, 32–48.

BOLLES, R. N. (1972). *What color is your parachute: A practical manual for job-hunters and career-changers*. Berkeley: Ten Speed Press.

BOLLES, T. C. (1974). Cognition and motivation: Some historical trends. In B. Weiner (Ed.), *Cognitive views on human motivation* (pp. 1–32). New York: Academic Press.

BORGES, J. L. (1966). Funes the memorius. In D. A. Yates & J. E. Irbt (Eds.), *Labyrinths*. New York: New Directions.

BORQUIST, A. (1906). Crying. *American Journal of Psychology, 17*, 149–205.

BOTWINICK, J. (1977). Intellectual abilities. In J. E. Birren, & K. W. Schaie (Eds.), *Handbook of the psychology of aging*. New York: Van Nostrand Reinhold.

BOTWINICK, J., WEST, R., & STARANDT, M. (1978). Predicting death from behavioral test performance. *Journal of Gerontology, 33*, 755–762.

BOUCHARD, T., & McGUE. (1981) Familial studies of intelligence: A review. *Science, 212*, 1055–1059.

BOWER, G. (1973). How to . . . uh . . . remember! *Psychology Today, 7*, 62–67.

BOWER, G. H. (1978). Improving memory. *Human Nature, 7*, 62–67.

BOWER, G. H. (1981). Mood and memory. *American Psychologist, 36*, 129–148.

BOWER, G. H., & GILLIGAN, S. G. (1980). Remembering information related to one's self. *Journal of Research in Personality, 13*, 420–432.

BOWER, G. H., GILLIGAN, S. G., & MONTEIRO, K. P. (1981). Selectivity of learning caused by affective states. *Journal of Experimental Psychology: General, 110*(4), 451–473.

BOWER, G. H., & HILGARD, E. R. (1981). *Theories of learning* (5th ed.). Englewood Cliffs, NJ: Prentice-Hall.

BOWER, S. A., & BOWER, G. H. (1976). *Asserting yourself*. Reading, MA: Addison-Wesley.

BOWER, T. G. R. (1974). *Development in infancy*. San Francisco: W. H. Freeman.

BOWER, T. G. R. (1977). *A primer of infant development*. San Francisco: W. H. Freeman.

BOWLBY, J. (1969). *Attachment: Vol. 1. Attachment and loss*. New York: Basic Books.

BRADY, J. V. (1958). Ulcers in "executive" monkeys. *Scientific American, 199*, 95–100.

BRAINERD, C. (1978). *Piaget's theory of intelligence*. Englewood Cliffs, NJ: Prentice-Hall.

BRANCH, A. Y., FINE, G. A., & JONES, J. M. (1973). Laughter, smiling, and rating scales: An analysis of responses to tape recorded humor. *Proceedings of the 81st Annual Convention of the American Psychological Association*.

BRAND, R. J., ROSENMAN, R. H., SHOLTZ, R. I., & FRIEDMAN, M. (1976). Multivariate prediction of coronary heart disease in the Western Collaborative Group Study compared to the findings of the Framingham Study. *Circulation, 43*(2), 348–355.

BRANDWEIN, R. A., BROWN, A., & FOX, S. M. (1974). Women and children last: The social situation of divorced mothers and their families. *Journal of Marriage and the Family, 36*, 495–514.

BRANSFORD, J. D., & JOHNSON, M. K. (1974). Contextual prerequisites for understanding: Some investigations of comprehension and recall. *Journal of Verbal Learning and Verbal Behavior, 11*, 717–726.

BRAY, G. A. (1974). Endocrine factors in the control of food intake. *Federal Proceedings, 33*, 1140–1145.

BRECHER, E. M., & CONSUMER REPORTS (Eds.). (1974). *Licit and illicit drugs*. Boston: Little, Brown.

BRELAND, H. (1977). Family configuration and intellectual development. *Journal of Individual Psychology, 31*, 86–96.

BRELAND, K., & BRELAND, M. (1961). The misbehavior of organisms. *American Psychologist, 16*, 661–664.

BRENNER, M. H. (1973). *Mental illness and the economy*. Cambridge: Harvard University Press.

BRENNER, M. H. (1976). *Estimating the social costs of economic policy: Implications for mental and physical health, and criminal aggression* (Paper No. 5, report to the Congressional Research Service of the Library of Congress and Joint Economic Committee of Congress). Washington, DC: U.S. Government Printing Office.

BREUER, J., & FREUD, S. (1955). Studies in hysteria. In J. Strachey (Ed.), *The standard edition of the complete psychological works of Sigmund Freud*. London: Hogarth Press (Original work published 1895).

BREWER, V., & HARTMANN, E. (1973). Variable sleepers: When is more or less sleep required. *Sleep Research, 2*, 128.

BRICKMAN, P. (1975). Adaptation level determinants of satisfaction with equal and unequal outcome distributions in skill and chance situations. *Journal of Personality and Social Psychology, 32*, 191–198.

BRIDGES, D. (1927). Occupational interests of three-year-old children. *Journal of Genetic Psychology, 34*, 415–423.

BRIDGES, K. M. B. (1932). Emotional development in early infancy. *Child Development, 3*, 324–341.

BRIM, O. G., JR. (1968). Adult socialization. In J. A. Clausen (Ed.), *Socialization and society*. Boston: Little, Brown.

BRIM, O. G., JR. (1976). Theories of the male mid-life crisis. *Counseling Psychologist, 6*(1), 2–9.

BRIM, O. G., JR. (1978–1979). In *Lifespan development and behavior* (P. Baltes Ed., Vols. 1–2). New York: Academic Press.

BROADBENT, D. E. (1961). *Behavior*. New York: Basic Books.

BROADHURST, P. L. (1957). Emotionality and the Yerkes-Dodson law. *Journal of Experimental Psychology, 84*, 345–352.

BROBECK, J. R. (1946). Mechanics of the development of obesity in animals with hypothalamic lesions. *Physiological Review, 26*, 541–559.

BROOKS, C. McC., & LAMBERT, E. F. (1946). A study of the effect of limitation of food intake and the method of feeding on the rate of weight gain during hypothalamic obesity in the albino rat. *American Journal of Physiology, 147*, 695–707.

BROOKS, G. W., & MUELLER, E. (1966). Serum urate concentrations among university professors: Relation to drive, achievement, and leadership. *Journal of the American Medical Association, 195*(6), 415–418.

BROWN, J. (1977). *Mind-brain and consciousness*. New York: Academic Press.

BROWN, L. B. (1964). Classifications of religious orientation. *Journal for the Scientific Study of Religion, 4*, 91–99.

BROWN, R. (1965). *Social psychology*. New York: Free Press.

BROWN, R., & HERRNSTEIN, R. J. (1975). *Psychology*. Boston: Little, Brown.

BROWN, R. W., & LENNEBERG, E. H. (1954). A study in language and cognition. *Journal of Verbal Learning and Verbal Behavior, 49*, 454–462.

BRUNER, J. S. (1978) Learning the mother tongue. *Human Nature 1*, 52–59.

BRUNER, J. S., & GOODMAN, C. C. (1946). Value and need as organizing factors in perception. *Journal of Abnormal and Social Psychology, 42*, 33–44.

BRUNER, J. S., & TAGIURI, R. (1954). Person perception. In G. Lindzey (Ed.), *Handbook of social psychology: Vol. 2*. Reading, MA: Addison-Wesley.

BRYAN, J. H., & TEST, M. (1967). Models and helping: Naturalistic studies in aiding behavior. *Journal of Personality and Social Psychology, 6*, 400–407.

BRYDEN, M. P. (1973). Auditory-visual and sequential-spatial matching in relation to reading ability. *Child Development, 43*(3), 824–832.

BUDZYNSKI, T. (1977). Biofeedback and the twilight states of awareness. In G. Schwartz & D. Shapiro (Eds.), *Consciousness and self-regulation*. New York: Plenum.

BUDZYNSKI, T. (1981). Lecture at "The Healing Brain," University of California.

BUFFREY, A., & GRAY, J. (1972). Sex differences in the development of spatial and linguistic skills. In C. Ounsted & D. Taylor (Eds.), *Gender differences, their ontogeny and significance*. New York: Churchill Livingstone.

BURNES, K., BROWN, W. A., & KEATING, G. W. (1971). Dimensions on control: Correlations between MMPI and I-E scores. *Journal of Consulting and Clinical Psychology, 36*, 301.

BUTLER, R. N. (1963). The life review: An interpretation of reminiscence in the aged. *Psychiatry, 26*, 65–76.

CABANAC, M. (1971). Physiological role of pleasure. *Science, 173*(4002), 1103–1107.

CADORET, R. J., WINOKUR, G., & CLAYTON, P. J. (1971). Family history studies: VI. Depressive disease types. *Comprehensive Psychiatry, 12*, 148–155.

CALHOUN, J. B. (1973). Population density and social pathology. *Scientific American, 206*, 139–148.

CAMPBELL, B. G. (1982). *Humankind emerging* (3rd ed.). Boston: Little, Brown.

CAMPBELL, D. T. (1960). Blind variation and selective retention in creating thought as in other knowledge processes. *Psychological Review, 67*, 380–400.

CAMPBELL, D. T. (1963). Social attitudes and other acquired behavioral dispositions. In S. Koch (Ed.), *Psychology: A study of a science: Vol. 6*. New York: McGraw-Hill.

CAMPBELL, R. (1978). Asymmetries in interpreting and expressing a posed facial expression. *Cortex, 14*, 327–342.

CANGEMI, J. J. (1976). Characteristics of self-actualizing individuals. *Revista de Psicologia General Aplicada, 31*, 88–90.

CANNON, W. (1929). *Bodily changes in pain, hunger, fear and rage: An account of recent researches into the function of emotional excitement* (2nd ed.). New York: Appleton-Century-Crofts.

CANNON, W. (1932). *Wisdom of the body*. New York: W. W. Norton.

CANNON, W. B. (1977). "Voodoo" death. In A. Monat & R. S. Lazarus (Eds.). *Stress and coping*. New York: Columbia University Press.

CANTOR, J., ZILLMAN, D., & BRYANT, J. (1974). Enhancement of humor appreciation by transferred excitation. *Journal of Personality and Social Psychology, 30*, 812–821.

CANTOR, N., & MISCHEL, W. (1977). Traits and prototypes: Effects on recognition memory. *Journal of Personality and Social Psychology, 35*, 38–48.

CANTOR, N., & MISCHEL, W. (1979). Prototypes in person perception. In L. Berkowitz (Ed.). *Advances in social experimental psychology: Vol. 12*. New York: Academic Press.

CARLSMITH, J. M., & ANDERSON, C. A. (1979). Ambient temperature and the occurrence of collective violence: A new analysis. *Journal of Personality and Social Psychology, 37*, 337–344.

CARMICHAEL, L., HOGAN, H. P., & WALTERS, A. (1932). An experimental study of the effects of language on the reproduction of visually perceived form. *Journal of Experimental Psychology, 16*, 73–86.

CARVER, C., & GLASS, D. (1977). *The coronary prone behavior pattern and interpersonal aggression*. Unpublished manuscript, University of Texas.

CATTELL, R. B. (1971). *Abilities: Their structure, growth and action*. Boston: Houghton Mifflin.

CHANCE, P. (1977). *Learning and be-*

havior. San Francisco: Wadsworth.

CHAPMAN, A. J. (1976). Social aspects of humorous laughter. In A. J. Chapman & H. C. Foot (Eds.), *Humour and laughter: Theory, research and applications*. London: John Wiley.

CHASE, W. G., & SIMON, N. A. (1973). The mind's eye in chess. In W. G. Chase (Ed.), *Visual information processing*. New York: Academic Press.

CHIRIBOGA, D. (1951). The developmental psychology of middle age. In J. Howells (Ed.), *Modern perspectives in the psychiatry of middle age*. New York: Brunner/Mazel.

CHIRIBOGA, D. (1977). Life event weighting systems: A comparative analysis. *Journal of Psychosomatic Research, 21*, 415–422.

CHIRIBOGA, D., & CUTLER, L. (1977). Stress responses among divorcing men and women. *Journal of Divorce, 1*(2), 95–106.

CHIRIBOGA, D., ROBERTS, J., & STEIN, O. (1978). Psychological well-being during marital separation. *Journal of Divorce, 2*(1), 21–35.

CHOMSKY, N. (1966). *Aspects of the theory of syntax*. Cambridge: MIT Press.

CHRISTIAN, J. J., FLYGER, V., & DAVIS, D. C. (1960). Factors in the mass mortality of a herd of Sika Deer, Cervus Nippon. *Chesapeake Science, 1*, 79–95.

CHUKOVSKY, K. (1963). *From two to five*. Berkeley: University of California Press.

CLARK, K., & CLARK, M. (1947). Racial identification and preference in Negro children. In T. M. Newcomb & E. L. Hartley (Eds.), *Readings in social psychology*. New York: Holt, Rinehart & Winston.

CLECKLEY, H. (1954). *The mark of sanity*. St. Louis: C. V. Mosby.

COBB, S., & KASL, S. V. (1977, June). *Termination: The consequences of job loss* (Report No. 76–1261). Cincinnati: National Institute for Occupational Safety and Health, Behavioral and Motivational Factors Research.

COBB, S., & ROSE, R. M. (1973). Hypertension, peptic ulcer, and diabetes in air traffic controllers. *Journal of the American Medical Association, 224*, 489–492.

COFER, C. N., & APPLEY, M. H. (1964). *Motivation: Theory and research*. New York: John Wiley.

COHEN, F., & LAZARUS, R. (1973). Active coping processes, coping dispositions, and recovery from surgery. *Psychosomatic Medicine, 35*, 375–389.

COHEN, M., BAKER, G., COHEN, R. A., FROMM-REICHMANN, F., & WEIGERT, E. V. (1954). An intensive study of twelve cases of manic-depressive psychosis. *Psychiatry, 17*, 103–137.

COHEN, S., GLASS, D. C., & SINGER, J. E. (1973). Apartment noise, auditory discrimination, and reading ability in children. *Journal of Experimental Social Psychology, 9*, 407–422.

COLEMAN, J. C., BUTCHER, J. N., & CARSON, R. C. (1980). *Abnormal psychology and modern life*. Glenview, IL: Scott, Foresman.

COLEMAN, P. O. (1974). Measuring reminiscence: Characteristics from conversation as an adaptive feature of old age. *International Journal of Aging and Human Development, 5*, 281–294.

COMFORT, A. (1974). *The joy of sex*. New York: Simon & Schuster.

CONDRY, J., & CONDRY, S. (1976). Sex differences: A study in the eye of the beholder. *Child Development, 47*, 812–819.

CONDRY, J. & DYER, S. (1976). Fear of success: Attribution of cause to the victim. *Journal of Social Issues, 32*(3), 63–83.

CONNORS, J. R., & DIAMOND, M. C. (1982). A comparison of dendritic spine number and type on pyramidal neuron of the visual cortex of old adult rats from social and isolated environments. *Journal of Comparative Neurology, 210*, 99–106.

COOPER, C., & MARSHALL, J. (1976). Occupational sources of stress: A review of the literature relating to coronary heart disease and mental ill health. *Occupational Psychology, 94*, 11–28.

COOPER, J. E., KENDELL, R. E., GURLAND, B. J., SHARPE, L., COPELAND, J. R. M., & SIMON, R. (1972). *Psychiatric diagnosis in New York and London*. London: Oxford University Press.

CORAH, N., & BOTTA, J. (1970). Perceived control, self-observation, and response to aversion stimulation. *Journal of Personality and Social Psychology, 16*(1), 1–4.

COREN, S., PORAC, C., & WARD, L. M. (1979). *Sensation and perception*. New York: Academic Press.

CORSO, J. (1977). Auditory perception and communication. In J. Birren & K. Schaie (Eds.), *Handbook of the psychology of aging*. New York: Van Nostrand Reinhold.

COSTA, P. T., McCRAE, R. J., & ARENBERG, D. (1980). Enduring dispositions in adult males. *Journal of Personality and Social Psychology, 38*, 793–800.

COTMAN, C., & McGAUGH, J. (1980). *Behavioral neuroscience*. New York: Academic Press.

COWAN, C., COWAN, P., COIE, L., & COIE, J. (1978). Becoming a family: The impact of a first child's birth on the couple's relationship. In W. Miller & L. Newman (Eds.), *The first child and family formation*. Chapel Hill: Carolina Population Center.

COYNE, J., ALDWIN, C., & LAZARUS, R. S. (1981). Depression and coping in stressful episodes. *Journal of Abnormal Psychology. 90*, 439–447.

CRAIK, F. (1977). Age differences in human memory. In J. Birren & K. Schaie (Eds.), *Handbook of the psychology of aging*. New York: Van Nostrand Reinhold.

CRAIK, F. I. M., & LOCKHART, R. S. (1972). Levels of processing: A framework for memory research. *Journal of Verbal Learning and Verbal Behavior, 12*, 599–607.

CRAIK, F. I. M., & TULVING, E. (1975). Depth of processing and the retention of words in episodic memory. *Journal of Experimental Psychology: General, 104*, 268–294.

CUMMING, E., & HENRY, W. (1961). *Growing old: The process of disengagement*. New York: Basic Books.

CUMMINGS, S. (1977). Family socialization and fatalism among black adolescents. *Journal of Negro Education, 46*(1), 62–75.

CURTIS, H. J. (1966). *Biological mechanisms of aging*. Springfield, IL: Charles C. Thomas.

CUSTANCE, J. (1951). *Wisdom, madness, and folly: The philosophy of a lunatic.* New York: Pellegrini Cudahy.

CZEISLER, C., WEITZMAN, E. D., MOORE-EDE, M. C., ZIMMERMAN, J. C., & KNAUER, R. S. (1980). Human sleep: Its duration and organization depend on its circadian phase. *Science, 210,* 1264–1267.

DARBY, W. J. (1978). The benefits of drink. *Human Nature, 1,* 30–37.

DARLEY, J. M. & BATSON, C. D. (1973). From Jerusalem to Jericho: A study of situational and dispositional variables in helping behavior. *Journal of Personality and Social Psychology, 27,* 100–108.

DARLEY, J. M. & LATANÉ, B. (1968). Bystander intervention in emergencies. *Journal of Personal and Social Psychology, 8,* 377–383.

DARWIN, C. (1872). *The expression of the emotions in man and animals.*

DARWIN, C. (1968). *The origin of species.* New York: Penguin Books. (Original work published 1859)

DAVIDSON, R. (1984). Hemispheric asymmetry and emotion. In K. Scherer & P. Ekman (Eds.), *Approaches to emotion.* Hillsdale, NJ: Lawrence Erlbaum.

DAVISON, G. (1976). Homosexuality: The ethical challenge. *Journal of Consulting and Clinical Psychology, 44,* 156–162.

DAVISON, G., & NEALE, J. (1982). *Abnormal psychology* (3rd ed.). New York: John Wiley.

DAWKINS, R. (1976). *The selfish gene.* New York: Oxford University Press.

DAWSON, J. (1975). Socio-economic differences in size judgments of discs and coins by Chinese primary VI children in Hong Kong. *Perceptual and Motor Skills, 41,* 107–110.

DECI, E. L. (1972). Intrinsic motivation, extrinsic reinforcement and inequity. *Journal of Personality and Social Psychology, 22,* 113–120.

DECI, E. L. (1975). *Intrinsic motivation.* New York: Plenum.

DEIKMAN, A. (1966). Deautomatization and the mystic experience. *Psychiatry, 29,* 329–343.

DELGADO, J. M. R. (1969). *Physical control of the mind.* New York: Harper & Row.

DeLONGIS, A., COYNE, J. C., DAKOF, G., FOLKMAN, S., & LAZARUS, R. S. (1982). Relationship of daily hassles, uplifts and major life events to health status. *Health Psychology, 1,* 119–136.

De LUMLEY, H. (1969). A Paleolithic camp at Nice. *Scientific American, 220*(5), 47–59.

DEMBER, W. N. (1974). Motivation and the cognitive revolution. *American Psychologist, 29,* 161–168.

DEMBER, W. N., EARL, R. W., & PARADISE, N. (1957). Response by rats to differential stimulus complexity. *Journal of Comparative and Physiological Psychology, 50,* 514–518.

DEMENT, W. C. (1974). *Some must watch while some must sleep.* San Francisco: W. H. Freeman.

DEMENT, W. C., & KLEITMAN, N. (1957). Cyclic variations in EEG and their relation to eye movements, bodily motility and dreaming. *Electroencephalography Clinical Neurophysiology, 9,* 673–690.

DEMENT, W. C., & WOLPERT, E. (1958). The relation of eye movements, bodily motility and external stimuli to dream content. *Journal of Experimental Psychology, 55,* 543–553.

DENES, P. B., & PINSON, E. N. (1963). *The speech chain.* Murray Hill, NJ: Bell Laboratories.

DENGERINK, H. A., O'LEARY, M. R., & KASNER, K. H. (1975). Individual differences in aggressive responses to attack: Internal-external locus of control and field dependence-independence. *Journal of Research in Personality. 9*(3), 191–199.

DENNIS, W. (1960). Causes of retardation among institutional children: Iran. *Journal of Genetic Psychology, 96,* 47–59.

DENNIS, W., & DENNIS, S. G. (1948). Development under controlled environmental conditions. In W. Dennis (Ed.), *Readings in child psychology.* New York: Prentice-Hall.

DENNIS, W., & NAJARIAN, P. (1957). Infant development under environmental handicap. *Psychological Monographs, 71*(7).

DENTON, D. A. (1967). Salt appetite. In C. F. Code (Ed.), *Handbook of physiology: Alimentary canal: Vol. 1* (pp. 433–459). Washington, DC: American Physiological Society.

DEREGOWSKI, J. B. (1973). Illusion and culture. In R. L. Gregory & G. H. Gombrich (Eds.), *Illusion in nature and art* (pp. 161–192). New York: Scribner's.

DEROGATIS, L. R., ABELOFF, M. D., & McBETH, C. D. (1976). Cancer patients and their physicians in the perception of psychological symptoms. *Psychosomatics, 17*(4), 197–201.

DEUTSCHER, I. (1964). The quality of post-parental life. *Journal of Marriage and the Family, 26*(1), 263–268.

DEYKIN, E. Y., KLERMAN, G. L., & ARMOR, D. J. (1966). The relatives of schizophrenic patients: Clinical judgment of potential emotional resourcefulness. *American Journal of Orthopsychiatry, 36*(3), 518–528.

DIAMOND, M. (1978, January/February). The aging brain: Some enlightening-optimistic results. *American Scientist.*

DIAMOND, M. C. (1980, June). Environment, air ions and brain chemistry. *Psychology Today.*

DIAMOND, M. C., & CONNORS, J. R. (1981). A search for the potential of the aging cortex. In M. Diamond (Ed.), *Brain neurotransmitters and receptors in aging and age related disorders.* New York: Raven Press.

DINARELLO, C., & WOLFE, S. (1979). Fever. *Human Nature, 2*(2), 66–74.

DOBRZECKA, C., & KONOROWSKI, J. (1968). Qualitative versus directional cues in differential conditioning. *Acta Biologiae Experimentale, 28,* 61–69.

DOBZHANSKY, T. (1962). *Mankind evolving.* New Haven: Yale University Press.

DODSON, J. D. (1917). Relative values of reward and punishment in habit formation. *Psychobiology, 1,* 231–276.

DOHRENWEND, B. S., & DOHRENWEND, B. P. (1974). A brief historical introduction to research on stressful life events. In B. S. Dohrenwend & B. P. Dohrenwend (Eds.), *Stressful life events: Their nature and effects.* New York: John Wiley.

DOLLARD, J., DOOB, L. W., MIL-
LER, N. E., MOWRER, O. H., &
SEARS, R. R. (1939). *Frustration and
aggression.* New Haven: Yale University Press.

DONALDSON, M. (1978a). *Children's
minds.* London: Croom Helm.

DONALDSON, M. (1978b). The mis-
match between schooling and children's minds. *Human Nature, 2,* 60.

DONER, J. F., & LAPPIN, J. S. (1980).
Commentary in S. Ullman, Against
direct perception. *The Behavioral and
Brain Sciences, 3*(3).

DOOLING, D. J., & LACHMAN, R.
(1971). Effects of comprehension on
retention of prose. *Journal of Experimental Psychology, 88,* 216–222.

DOUVAN, E. (1956). Social status and
success striving. *Journal of Abnormal
and Social Psychology, 52,* 219–223.

DUA, P. S. (1970). Comparison of the
effects of behaviorally oriented action and psychotherapy reeducation
on introversion-extroversion, emotionality, and internal-external control. *Journal of Counseling Psychology,
17,* 567–572.

DUBOS, R. (1968). *So human an animal.*
New York: Scribner.

DUBOS, R. (1978). Health and creative
adaptation. *Human Nature, 1*(1), 14–
21.

DUBOS, R. (1979, April). The price of
adapting to work. *Human Nature,*
29–35.

DUNN, J. P., BROOKS, G. W.,
MAUSNER, J., RODMAN, G. P., &
COBB, S. (1963). Social class gradi-
ent of serum uric acid levels in
males. *Journal of the American Medical
Association, 185*(6).

DUTTON, D., & ARON, A. (1974).
Some evidence for heightened sexual attraction under conditions of
high anxiety. *Journal of Personality
and Social Psychology, 30,* 510–517.

DWORKIN, E. S., & EFRAN, J. S.
(1967). The angered: Their susceptibility to varieties of humor. *Journal of
Personality and Social Psychology, 6,*
233–236.

DYER, W. G. (1962). Analyzing marital adjustment using role theory.
Marriage and Family Living, 24(4),
371–375.

EBBINGHAUS, H. (1885). *Über das
gedächtnis (Memory).* Leipzig: Dunch-
er Humbolt. (Translated by H. A.

Ruger and E. Bussenius, 1913, and
reissued by Dover Publications,
1969.)

ECKERMAN, J., WHATLEY, J., &
KUTZ, S. (1975). The growth of social play with peers during the second year of life. *Developmental Psychology, 11,* 42–49.

ECKHOLM, E. (1978). Vanishing fire-
wood. *Human Nature, 1*(5), 58–67.

EHRHARDT, S. A., & MEYER-BAHL-
BURG, H. (1981). Effects of prenatal
sex hormones on gender-related behavior. *Science, 211,* 1312–1318.

EHRLICH, P., & FELDMAN, S.
(1977). *The race bomb.* New York:
Quadrangle.

EHRLICH, P., HOLDREN, J., & EHR-
LICH, A. (1977). *Ecoscience.* San
Francisco: W. H. Freeman.

EIBL-EIBESFELDT, I. (1970.) *Ethology,
the biology of behavior.* New York:
Holt, Rinehart and Winston.

EIBL-EIBESFELDT, I. (1971). *Love and
hate: The natural history of behavior patterns* (G. Strachan, Trans.). New
York: Holt, Rinehart and Winston.

EIBL-EIBESFELDT, I. (1972). Similarities and differences between cultures in expressive movements. In
R. A. Hinde (Ed.), *Non-verbal communication.* Cambridge: Cambridge
University Press.

EIBL-EIBESFELDT, I. (1980). Strategies of social interaction. In R. Plutchik & H. Kelerman (Eds.), *Emotion:
Theory, research, and experience.* New
York: Academic Press.

EINHORN, H. J., & HOGARTH, R.
M. (1981). Behavioral decision theory: Processes of judgment and
choice. *Annual Review of Psychology,
32,* 53–88.

EINSTEIN, A. (1956). My life as a scientist. In J. Bronowski (Ed.) *The
structure of science.* New York: Dou-
bleday.

EKMAN, P. (Ed.). (1982). *Emotion in
the human face* (2nd ed.). Cambridge:
Cambridge University Press.

EKMAN, P. (1984). Expression and the
nature of emotion. In K. Scherer &
P. Ekman (Eds.), *Approaches to emotion.* Hillsdale, NJ: Lawrence Erlbaum.

EKMAN, P., & FRIESEN, W. (1983).
Unmasking the face. Palo Alto, CA:
Consulting Psychologists Press.

EKMAN, P., FRIESEN, W. V., &

ELLSWORTH, P. (1972). *Emotion in
the human face.* Elmsford, NY: Pergamon Press.

ELKIND, D. (1974). *Children and adolescents: Interpretive essays on Jean Piaget*
(2nd ed.). New York: Oxford University Press.

ELKIND, D. (1978). *A sympathetic understanding of the child: Birth to sixteen*
(2nd ed.). Boston: Allyn & Bacon.

ELLIOTT, J. (1977). The power and
pathology of prejudice. In P. G.
Zimbardo & F. L. Ruch (Eds.), *Psychology and life* (9th ed.). Glenview,
IL: Scott, Foresman.

ELLIS, A. (1970). *Reason and emotion in
psychotherapy.* New York: Lyle Stuart.

ENGEN, T. (1977). Taste and smell. In
J. E. Birren & J. W. Schaie (Eds.),
Handbook of the psychology of aging.
New York: Van Nostrand Rein-
hold.

ENGEN, T., & ROSS, B. M. (1973).
Long term memory of odors with
and without verbal descriptions.
*Journal of Experimental Psychology,
100,* 221–227.

EPSTEIN, S. M. (1967). Toward a unified theory of anxiety. In B. A.
Maher (Ed.), *Progress in experimental
personality research: Vol. 4.* New York:
Academic Press.

EPSTEIN, S. M. (1979). The stability of
behavior: I. On predicting most of
the people much of the time. *Journal
of Personality and Social Psychology,
37,* 1097–1126.

EPSTEIN, S., & SMITH, R. (1956). Repression and insight as related to reaction to cartoons. *Journal of Consulting Psychology, 20,* 391–395.

ERICSSON, K. A., & SIMON, H. A.
(1980). Verbal reports as data. *Psychological Review, 87,* 215–251.

ERIKSON, E. H. (1950, 1953). *Childhood and society.* New York: W. W.
Norton.

ESTES, W. K. (1980). Is human memory obsolete? *American Scientist, 68,*
62–69.

EYSENCK, H. J. (1952). The effects of
psychotherapy: an evaluation. *Journal of Consulting Psychology, 16,* 319–
324.

FADELEY, R. C. (1965). As quoted by
T. W. Anderson & S. L. Sclove
(1978). *An Introduction to the Statistical Analysis of Data.* New York:

Houghton Mifflin.

FANTZ, R. L. (1961). The origin of form perception. *Scientific American, 204,* 66–72.

FARB, P., & ARMELAGOS, G. (1980). *Consuming passions: The anthropology of eating.* Boston: Houghton Mifflin.

FARIS, R. E. L., & DUNHAM, H. W. (1965). *Mental disorders in urban areas.* Chicago: University of Chicago Press. (Original work published, 1939)

FARR, L. E. (1967). Medical consequences of environmental noises. *JAMA, 202,* 171–174.

FEIN, R. A. (1978). Consideration of men's experiences and the birth of a first child. In W. Miller & L. Newman (Eds.), *The first child and family formation.* Chapel Hill: Carolina Population Center.

FELDMAN-SUMMERS, S., & KIESLER, S. B. (1974). Those who are number two try harder: The effect of sex on attributions of causality. *Journal of Personality and Social Psychology, 30,* 846–855.

FERENCZI, S. (1954). *Thalassa: A theory of genitality.* New York: W. W. Norton.

FERNSTROM, J. D., & WURTMAN, R. J. (1975). Nutrition and the brain. *Scientific American, 230*(2), 84–91.

FESTINGER, L. (1954). A theory of social comparison processes. *Human Relations, 7,* 117–140.

FESTINGER, L. (1957). *A theory of cognitive dissonance.* Stanford: Stanford University Press.

FESTINGER, L., & CARLSMITH, J. M. (1959). Cognitive consequences of forced compliance. *Journal of Abnormal and Social Psychology, 58,* 203–211.

FESTINGER, L., SCHACHTER, S., & BACK, K. (1950). *Social pressures in informal groups: A study of human factors in housing.* New York: Harper & Row.

FEUERSTEIN, R. (1979). *The dynamic assessment of retarded performers.* Baltimore: University Park Press.

FEUERSTEIN, R. (1980). *Instrumental enrichment.* Baltimore: University Park Press.

FEUERSTEIN, R., & RAND, Y. (1977). *Studies in cognitive modifiability. Instrumental enrichment: Redevelopment of cognitive functions of retarded early*

adolescents. Jerusalem: Hadassah-Wizo-Canada Research Institute.

FISCHER, C. S. (1976). *The urban experience.* New York: Harcourt Brace Jovanovich.

FLAVELL, J. H. (1963). *The developmental psychology of Jean Piaget.* New York: Van Nostrand Reinhold.

FALVELL, J. H. (1977). *Cognitive development.* Englewood Cliffs, NJ: Prentice-Hall.

FLINN, M. W. (1966). *The origins of the industrial revolution.* London: Longmans, Green.

FOLKMAN, S., & LAZARUS, R. (1980). An analysis of coping in a middle-aged population. *Journal of Health and Social Behavior, 21,* 219–239.

FORT, J. (1970). *The pleasure seekers: The drug crisis, youth and society.* New York: Grove Press.

FOUCAULT, M. (1978). *The history of sexuality: Vol. 1: An introduction* (Robert Hurley, Trans.). New York: Random House.

FOZARD, J., WOLF, E., BELL, B., FARLAND, R., & PODOLSKY, S. (1977). Visual perception and communication. In J. Birren & K. Schaie (Eds.), *Handbook of the psychology of aging.* New York: Van Nostrand Reinhold.

FRAIBERG, S. (1971). Blind infants and their mothers: An examination of the sign system. In M. Lewis & L. A. Rosenblum (Eds.), *The effect of the infant on its care-giver* (pp. 215–232). New York: John Wiley.

FRANCIS, T. et al. (1957). As quoted by T. W. Anderson & S. L. Sclove (1978). *An Introduction to the Statistical Analysis of Data.* New York: Houghton Mifflin.

FRANQUEMONT, C. (1979). Watching, watching, counting, counting. *Human Nature, 2,* 82–84.

FREEDMAN, D. (1979). Ethnic differences in babies. *Human Nature, 2,* 36.

FREEDMAN, J. L. (1975). *Crowding and behavior.* New York: Viking Press.

FREEDMAN, J. L., LEVY, A. S., BUCHANAN, R. W., & PRICE, J. (1972). Crowding and human aggressiveness. *Journal of Experimental Social Psychology, 8,* 528–548.

FREEDMAN, J. L., SEARS, D. O., & CARLSMITH, J. M. (1978). *Social*

psychology. Englewood Cliffs, NJ: Prentice-Hall.

FRENCH, E., & LESSER, G. S. (1964). Some characteristics of the achievement motive in women. *Journal of Abnormal and Social Psychology, 68,* 119–128.

FRENCH, J., & CAPLAN, R. (1970). Psychosocial factors in coronary heart disease. *Industrial Medicine, 39,* 383–397.

FREUD, S. (1896). *Further remarks on the neuro-psychoses of defence. Standard edition: Vol. 3,* (p. 159). London: Hogarth Press.

FREUD, S. (1920). *Beyond the pleasure principle. Standard edition,* Vol. 18. London: Hogarth Press.

FREUD, S. (1955). *The interpretation of dreams.* London: Hogarth Press. (Original work published 1900).

FREUD, S. (1962). *New introductory lectures on psychoanalysis.* London: Hogarth Press.

FREY, A. (1982). Personal communication.

FREY, W. H., II, DeSOTA-JOHNSON, D., HOFFMAN, C., AND McCALL, J. T. (1981). Effect of stimulus on the chemical composition of human tears. *American Journal of Ophthalmology, 92*(4), 559–567.

FRIEDL, E. (1978). Society and sex roles. *Human nature, 1*(4), 68–75.

FRIEDMAN, M., & ROSENMAN, R. (1974). *Type A behavior and your heart.* New York: Alfred A. Knopf.

FRIEDMAN, M. I., & STRICKER, E. M. (1976). The physiological psychology of hunger: A physiological perspective. *Psychological Review, 83,* 409–431.

FRIEDMAN, M. I., THORESON, C. E., & GILL, J. J. (1982). Feasibility of altering Type A behavior pattern after myocardial infarction. *Circulation, 66,* 83–92.

FROHMAN, L. A., & BERNARDI, L. L. (1968). Growth hormone and insulin levels in weanling rats with ventromedial hypothalamic lesions. *Endocrinology, 82,* 1125–1132.

FROMM, E. (1941). *Escape from freedom.* New York: Holt, Rinehart & Winston.

GALANTER, E. (1962). Contemporary psychophysics. In R. Brown, E. Galanter, E. Hess, & G. Mandler (Eds.), *New directions in psychology,* (pp. 87–157). New York: Holt, Rinehart & Winston.

GALIN, D., & ORNSTEIN, R. (1972). Lateral specialization of cognitive mode: An EEG study. *Psychophysiology, 9,* 412–418.

GALIN, D., ORNSTEIN, R. E., & ADAMS, J. (1977). Midbrain stimulation of the amygdala. *Journal of States of Consciousness, 2,* 34–41.

GALIN, D., ORNSTEIN, R. E., HERRON, J., & JOHNSTONE, J. (1982). Sex and handedness differences in EEG measures of hemispheric specialization. *Brain and Language, 16(1),* 19–55.

GALLUP, G. G. (1977). Self-recognition in primates: A comparative approach to the bi-directional properties of consciousness. *American Psychologist, 32,* 329–338.

GALLUP, G. G. (1979). Self-awareness in primates. *American Scientist, 67,* 417–421.

GALTON, F. (1895). *British men of science.* London: Longmans.

GALTON, F. (1979). *Hereditary Genius.* New York: St. Martin's Press. (Original work published 1874).

GARCIA, J., & KOELLING, R. (1966). Relation of cue to consequence in avoidance learning. *Psychonomic Science, 4,* 123–124.

GARDNER, H. (1978). The loss of language. *Human Nature, 1(3),* 31–40.

GARDNER, H. (1984). *Frames of mind,* New York: Basic Books.

GARNER, W. R. (1974). *The processing of information and structure.* Potomac, MD: Lawrence Erlbaum.

GARRISON, W. (1971, March). Tears and laughter. *Today's Health,* 29–32.

GARVEY, C. (1977). *Play.* Cambridge: Harvard University Press.

GELMAN, R. (1978). Cognitive development. In L. W. Porter & M. R. Rosenzweig (Eds.), *Annual review of psychology, 29.* Palo Alto, CA: Annual Reviews.

GERBNER, G., & GROSS, L. (1976). The scary world of TV's heavy viewer. *Psychology Today, 89,* 41–45.

GESCHWIND, N. (1972). Language and the brain. *Scientific American, 226(4),* 76–83.

GESCHWIND, N., & LEVITSKY, W. (1976). Left-right asymmetries in temporal speech region. *Science, 161,* 186–187.

GIBSON, E., & WALK, R. (1960). The visual cliff. *Scientific American, 202,* 64–71.

GIBSON, J. J. (1960). *The perception of the visual world.* Boston: Houghton Mifflin.

GIBSON, J. J. (1966). *The senses considered as perceptual systems.* Boston: Houghton Mifflin.

GIBSON, J. J. (1970). On theories for visual space perception: A reply to Johansson. *Scandinavian Journal of Psychology, 11,* 73–79.

GIBSON, J. J. (1979). *The ecological approach to visual perception.* Boston: Houghton Mifflin.

GIBSON, J. J., OLUM, P., & ROSENBLATT, F. (1955). Parallax and perspective during aircraft landings. *American Journal of Psychology, 68,* 372–385.

GIEDION, S. (1948). *Mechanization takes command.* New York: W. W. Norton.

GLASER, R., & BOND, L. (Eds.). (1981). Testing: Concepts, policy, practice, and research [special issue]. *American Psychologist, 36(10).*

GLASS, A. L., HOLYOAK, K. J., & SANTA, J. L. (1980). *Cognition.* Reading, MA: Addison-Wesley.

GLASS, D. C., & SINGER, J. E. (1972). *Urban stress: Experiments on noise and social stressors.* New York: Academic Press.

GLASS, D. C., SINGER, J. E., & FRIEDMAN, L. N. (1969). Psychic cost of adaptation to an environmental stressor. *Journal of Personality and Social Psychology, 12,* 200–210.

GLASS, G. V. & HOPKINS, K. D. (1984). *Statistical Methods in Education and Psychology.* Englewood Cliffs, NJ: Prentice-Hall.

GLEESON, P. A., BROWN, J. S., WARING, J. J., & STOCK, M. J. (1979). Themogenic effects of diet and exercise. *Proceedings of the Nutrition Society, 38,* 82.

GLICK, F. O., WEISS, R. S., & PARKES, C. M. (1974). *The first year of bereavement.* New York: John Wiley.

GLICK, P. C., & NORTON, A. J. (1977). Marrying, divorcing and living together in the U.S. today. *Population Bulletin.*

GMELCH, G. (1978). Baseball magic. *Human Nature, 1,* 32–40.

GOLDBERG, P. (1968, April). Are women prejudiced against women? *Trans-Action,* 28–30.

GOLDBERG, S., & LEWIS, M. (1969). Play behavior in the year-old infant: Early sex differences, *Child Development, 40,* 21–31.

GOLDSTEIN, J. H., DAVIS, R. W., & HERMAN, D. (1975). Escalation of aggression: Experimental studies. *Journal of Personality and Social Psychology, 31(1),* 162–170.

GOLDSTEIN, K. (1947). *Human nature in the light of psychopathology.* Cambridge: Harvard University Press.

GOLDSTEIN, M. J. (1959). The relationship between coping and avoiding behavior and response to fear-arousing propaganda. *Journal of Abnormal and Social Psychology, 58,* 247–252.

GOMBRICH, E. H. (1961). *Art and illusion* (2nd ed.). Princeton, NJ: Princeton University Press.

GOODCHILDS, J. D. (1972). On being witty: Causes, correlates and consequences. In J. H. Goldstein & P. E. McGhee (Eds.), *The psychology of humor.* London: Academic press.

GOODE, W. (1956). *Women in divorce.* New York: Free Press.

GOODMAN, M. J., STEWART, G. J., & GILBERT, F., JR. (1977). A study of certain medical and physiological variables among Caucasian and Japanese women living in Hawaii. *Journal of Gerontology, 32(3),* 291–298.

GOODY, J. (1976). *Production and reproduction: A comparative study of the domestic domain.* Cambridge: Cambridge University press.

GORDON, B. (1979). *I'm dancing as fast as I can.* New York: Harper & Row.

GOSS, A., & MOROSKO, I. E. (1970). Relations between a dimension of internal-external control and the MMPI with an alcoholic population. *Journal of Consulting and Clinical Psychology, 34,* 189–192.

GOTTESMAN, I. I. (1974). Developmental genetics and ontogenetic psychology. *Minnesota Symposia on Child Psychology, 8.* Minneapolis: University of Minnesota Press.

GOTTESMAN, I. I., & SHIELDS, J.

(1972). *Schizophrenia: A twin study vantage point.* New York: Academic press.

GOTTMAN, J. M. (1979). *Marital interaction: experimental investigations.* New York: Academic Press.

GOULD R. L. (1972). The phases of adult life: A study in developmental psychology. *American Journal of Psychiatry, 129*(5), 521–531.

GOULD, R. L. (1978). *Transformations: Growth and change in adult life.* New York: Simon & Schuster.

GOULD, S. J. (1979). *Ever since Darwin.* New York: W. W. Norton.

GOVE, W. R. (1972). Sex roles, marital roles, mental illness. *Social Forces, 51,* 34–44.

GRAFF, H., & STELLAR, E. (1962). Hyperphagia obesity and finickiness. *Journal of Comparative and Physiological Psychology, 55,* 418–424.

GRANICH, S., & PATTERSON, R. (Eds.). (1971). *Human aging II: An eleven year follow-up biomedical and behavioral study* (Publication No. HSM 71–9037). Washington, DC: U.S. Government Printing Office.

GRASTYAN, E., KARMOS, G., VORECZKEY, L.; MARTIN, J., & KELLENYI, L. (1965). Hypothalamic motivational processes as reflected by their hippocampal electrical correlates. *Science, 149,* 91–93.

GRAUNT, J. "Natural and political observations made upon the bills of mortality." In *The world of mathematics,* J. R. Newman (Ed.) Vol. 3. New York: Simon & Schuster.

GRAVES, C. W. (1966). Deterioration of work standards. *Harvard Business Review, 44,* 117–128.

GRAY, J. A. (1972). *The psychology of fear.* New York: McGraw-Hill.

GRAY, J. A. (1973). *The psychology of fear and stress.* New York: McGraw-Hill.

GRAY, J. A. (1978a). Anxiety. *Human Nature, 1*(7), 38–46.

GRAY, J. A. (1978b). The neuropsychology of anxiety. *British Journal of Psychology, 69,* 417–34.

GRAY, R., & SMITH, T. (1960). Effect of employment on sex differences in attitudes toward the parental family. *Marriage and Family Living, 22,* 36–38.

GREELY, A., & SHEATSLEY, P.

(1971). The acceptance of desegregation continues to advance. *Scientific American, 225*(6), 13–19.

GREENBERG, R., & PEARLMAN, C. A. (1974). Cutting the REM nerve: An approach to the adaptive role of REM sleep. *Perspectives in Biology and Medicine, 19,* 513–521.

GREENOUGH, S. (1975). Experiential modification of the developing brain. *American Scientist, 63,* 37–46.

GREENOUGH, W. T. (1982). Lecture to the Developmental Psychology Research Group, Estes Park, CO.

GREENOUGH, W. T., & JURASKA, J. M. (1979). Synaptic Pruning. *Psychology Today, 13,* 120.

GREER, S. (1981, August). *Psychological response to breast cancer and eight-year outcome.* Paper presented at the Annual Meetings of the American Psychological Association, Los Angeles.

GREGORY, R. L. (1973, 1977). *Eye and brain,* (2nd & 3rd eds.). New York: McGraw-Hill.

GRICE, G. R. (1948). The relation of secondary reinforcement to delayed reward in visual discrimination learning. *Journal of Experimental Psychology, 38,* 1–16.

GRICE, H. P. (1967). Utterer's meaning, sentence-meaning and word-meaning. *Foundations of Language, 4,* 225–242.

GRIFFITH, R. M., MIYAGI, O., & TAGO, A. (1958). The universality of typical dreams: Japanese vs. American. *American Anthropologist, 60,* 1173–1179.

GRINKER, R. R. (1953). *Emotions and emotional disorders.* New York: Hoeber.

GRINKER, R. R., & SPIEGEL, J. P. (1945). *Men under stress.* Philadelphia: Blakiston.

GRINSPOON, L., & BAKALAR, J. B. (1979). *Psychedelic drugs reconsidered.* New York: Basic Books.

GRIVES, P. M., & THOMPSON, R. F. (1973). A dual process theory of habituation: Neural mechanisms. In H. M. S. Pecks & M. J. Herz (Eds.), *Habituation, physiological substrates II.* New York: Academic Press.

GROSS, C. G.., ROCHA-MIRANDA, C. E., & BENDER, D. B. (1972). Visual properties of neurons in infero-

temporal cortex of the macaque. *Journal of Neurophysiology, 35,* 96–111.

GROSSMAN, F. K., EICHLER, L. SL., & WINICKHOFF, S. A. (1980). *Pregnancy, birth, and parenthood.* San Francisco: Jossey-Bass.

GROSSMAN, S. (1979). The biology of motivation. *Annual Review of Psychology, 30,* 209–242.

GUILFORD, J. P. (1967). *The nature of human intelligence.* New York: McGraw-Hill.

GUILFORD, J. P., & HOEPFNER, R. (1971). *The analysis of intelligence.* New York: McGraw-Hill.

HAAN, N. (1977). *Coping and defending.* New York: Academic press.

HAAS, J. (1978). *Teenage sexuality.* New York: Simon & Schuster.

HABER, R., & STANDIG, L. G. (1966). Direct measures of short-term visual storage. *Quarterly Journal of Experimental Psychology, 21,* 43–54.

HAITH, M. M. (1980). *Rules that babies look by: The organization of newborn visual activity.* New York: Lawrence Erlbaum.

HALDANE, J. B. S. (1932). *The causes of evolution.* London: Longmans, Green.

HALER, R. N. (1958). Discrepancy from adaptation level as a source of affect. *Journal of Experimental Psychology, 56,* 370–375.

HALL, C. (1966). *The meaning of dreams.* New York: McGraw-Hill.

HALL, C. S., & LINDZEY, G. (1978). *Theories of personality,* (3rd ed.). New York: John Wiley.

HALL, E. (1978). *Why we do what we do: A look at psychology.* Boston: Houghton Mifflin.

HALL, E. et al. (1982). *Child psychology today.* New York: Random House.

HALL, E. T. (1969). *The hidden dimension.* New York: Anchor Press.

HALL, R. C., GARDNER, E. R., STICKNEY, S. K., LeCANN, A. F., & POPKIN, M. K. (1980). Physical illness manifesting as psychiatric disease. II. Analysis of a state hospital inpatient population. *Archives of General Psychiatry, 37*(9), 989–995.

HAMBREE, W. C., NABAS, G. G., & HUANG, H. F. S. (1979). Changes in human spermatozoa associated with high dose marihuana smoking. In G. G. Nahas, & W. D. M. Paton (Eds.), *Marihuana: Biological effects.* New York: Pergamon Press.

HAMILTON, C. L. (1963). Interactions of food intake and temperature regulation in the rat. *Journal of Comparative and Physiological Psychology, 56,* 476–488.

HAMILTON, W. D. (1964). The genetical evolution of social behavior. *Journal of Theoretical Biology, 7,* 1–52.

HANDAL, P. S. (1965). Immediate acceptance of sodium salts by sodium deficient rats. *Psychorem. Sci., 3,* 315–316.

HANEY, C., BANKS, C., & ZIMBARDO, P. G. (1973). Interpersonal dynamics in a simulated prison. *International Journal of Criminology and Penology, 1,* 69–97.

HARE, R. D., & CRAIGEN, D. (1974). Psychopathy and physiological activity in a mixed-motive game situation. *Psychophysiology, 11,* 197–206.

HARLOW, H., & HARLOW, M. H. (1966). Learning to love. *American Scientist, 54,* 244–272.

HARLOW, H. F. (1950). Learning and satiation of response in intrinsically motivated complex puzzle performance by monkeys. *Journal of Comparative and Physiological Psychology, 43,* 289–294.

HARRELL, R. F., WOODYARD, E. R., GATES, E. R., & GATES, I. A. (1956). The influence of vitamin supplementation in the diets of pregnant and lactating women on the intelligence of their offspring. *Metabolism, 5,* 555–62.

HARRINGTON, D. M., BLOCK, J. H., & BLOCK, B. (1978). Intolerance of ambiguity in preschool children: Psychometric considerations, behavioral manifestations and parental correlates. *Developmental Psychology, 14,* 242–256.

HARRIS, MARVIN. (1971). *Culture, people, nature.* New York: Thomas Y. Crowell.

HARTLINE, H. K., & RATLIFF, F. (1957). Inhibitory interaction of receptor units in the eye of Limulus. *Journal of General Physiology, 40,* 357–376.

HARTMANN, E. (1973). *The functions of sleep.* New Haven: Yale University Press.

HARTON, J. J. (1938). An investigation of the influence of success and failure on the estimation of time. *Journal of General Psychology, 21,* 51–62.

HARTSHORNE, H., & MAY, M. A. (1928). *Studies in the nature of character: Studies in deceit.* New York: Macmillan.

HARTSHORNE, H., & MAY, M. A. (1929). *Studies in the nature of character: Studies in self-control.* New York: Macmillan.

HASKELL, W. (1979). Physical activity in health maintenance. In D. Sobel (Ed.), *Ways of health.* New York: Harcourt Brace Jovanovich.

HASTORF, A. H. (1950). The influence of suggestion of the relationship between stimulus, size and perceived distance. *Journal of Psychology, 19,* 195–217.

HASTORF, A. H., & CANTRIL, H. (1954). They saw a game: A case study. *Journal of Abnormal and Social Psychology, 49,* 129–134.

HAVIGHURST, R. J., & GLASER, R. (1972). An exploratory study of reminiscence. *Journal of Gerontology, 27,* 245–253.

HAVIGHURST, R. J., NEUGARTEN, B. L., & TOBIN, S. S. (1968). Disengagement and patterns of aging. In B. L. Neugarten (Ed.), *Middle age and aging.* Chicago: University of Chicago Press.

HAYES-ROTH, F. (1980). Comment regarding "Against direct perception", *The behavioral and brain sciences 3(3),* 367–368.

HAYFLICK, L. (1980). The cell biology of human aging. *Scientific American, 242(1),* 58–65.

HEATH, R. G. (1963). Electrical self-stimulation of the brain in man. *American Journal of Psychiatry, 120,* 571–577.

HEATH, R. G., & MICKLE, W. A. (1960). Evaluation of seven years' experience with depth electrode studies in human patients. In E. R. Ramey, & D. S. O'Doherty (Eds.), *Electrical studies of the unanesthetized brain.* New York: Holber.

HEBB, D. O. (1949). *The organization of behavior.* New York: John Wiley.

HECKHAUSEN, H. (1967). *The anatomy of achievement motivation.* New York: Academic press.

HEIDER, F. (1946). Attitudes and cognitive organization. *Journal of Psychology, 21,* 107–112.

HEIDER, F. (1958). *The psychology of interpersonal relations.* New York: John Wiley.

HELD, R., & HEIN, A. (1963). Movement produced stimulation in the development of visually guided behavior. *Journal of Comparative and Physiological Psychology, 56,* 872–876.

HELSON, H. (1964). *Adaptation level theory: An experimental and systematic approach to behavior.* New York: Harper & Row.

HENRY, J. P., & STEPHENS, P. M. (1977). *Stress, health and social environment: A sociobiological approach to medicine.* New York: Springer-Verlag.

HENRY, W. (1956). *The analysis of fantasy.* New York: John Wiley.

HERBERT, M. J., & HARSH, C. M. (1944). Observational learning by cats. *Journal of Comparative and Physiological Psychology, 37,* 81–95.

HERMAN, J. H., & ROFFWARG, H. P. (1983). Modifying oculomotor activity in awake subjects increases the amplitude of eye movement during REM sleep. *Science, 220,* 1074–1076.

HERRMANN, D. J., & NEISSER, U. (1978). An inventory of everyday memory experiences. In M. M. Gruneberg, P. E. Morris, & R. N. Sykes (Eds.), *Practical aspects of memory.* New York: Academic Press.

HERRNSTEIN, R. J. (1973). *IQ in the meritocracy.* Boston: Little, Brown.

HERRON, J. (1980). *Neuropsychology of left-handers.* New York: Academic Press.

HERZBERG, F. (1966). *Work and the nature of man.* Cleveland: World Publishing.

HERZBERG, F. (1968, January/February). One more time: How do you motivate employees? *Harvard Business Review.*

HESS, E. H. (1975). *The tell-tale eye: How your eyes reveal hidden thoughts and emotions.* New York: Van Nostrand Reinhold.

HESTON, L. (1966). Psychiatric disorders in foster home reared children of schizophrenic mothers. *British Journal of Psychiatry, 112,* 819–825.

HETHERINGTON, A. W., & RANSON, S. W. (1940). Hypothalamic lesions and adiposity in the rat. *Anatomical Record, 78,* 149–172.

HETHERINGTON, A. W., & RANSON, S. W. (1942). The spontaneous activity and food intake of rats with hypothalamic lesions. *American Journal of Physiology, 136,* 609–617.

HETHERINGTON, E., COX, M., & COX, D. (1977). Divorced fathers. *Family Coordination, 25,* 417–428.

HETHERINGTON, E., COX, M., & COX, R. (1978). The aftermath of divorce. in J. Stevens, Jr. & M. Mathews (Eds.), *Mother/child, father/child relationships.* Washington, DC: NAEYC.

HILGARD, E. R. (1966). *The experience of hypnosis.* New York: Harcourt Brace Jovanovich.

HILGARD, E. R. (1977). *Divided consciousness: Multiple controls in human thought and action.* New York: Wiley-Interscience.

HILGARD, E. R. (Ed.). (1978a). *American psychology in historical perspective.* Washington, DC: American Psychological Association.

HILGARD, E. R. (1978b). Hypnosis and consciousness. *Human Nature, 1,* 42–51.

HILGARD, E. R., & MARQUIS, D. G. (1940). *Conditioning and learning.* New York: Appleton-Century.

HILGARD, E. R., & MARQUIS, L. (1961). *Conditioning and learning.* Boston: Appleton-Century-Crofts.

HILGARD, J. R. (1970). *Personality and hypnosis: A study of imaginative involvement.* Chicago: University of Chicago Press.

HILLYARD, S. A., & KUTAS, M. (1980). Reading senseless sentences: Brain potentials reflect semantic incongruity. *Science, 207,* 203–207.

HINTON, J. (1967). *Dying.* Baltimore: Penguin Books.

HIRST, W., NEISSER, U., & SPELKE, E. (1978). Divided attention. *Human Nature, 1,* 54–61.

HOBART, C. W. (1958). The incidence of romanticism during courtship. *Social Forces, 36,* 362–367.

HOBSON, J. A., & McCARLEY, R. W. (1977). The brain as a dream state generator: An activation-synthesis hypothesis of the dream process. *The American Journal of Psychiatry, 134*(12), 1335–1348.

HOCHBERG, J. E. (1978). *Perception.* (2nd ed.). Englewood Cliffs, NJ: Prentice-Hall.

HOCKETT, C. F., & ASHER, R. (1964). Human revolution. *Current Anthropology, 135,* 142.

HOEBEL, B., & TEITELBAUM, P. (1962). Hypothalamic control of feeding and self-stimulation. *Science, 135,* 375–376.

HOFFMAN, A. (1968). Psychotomimetic agents. In A. Burger (Ed.), *Drugs affecting the central nervous system: Vol. 2.* New York: Marcel Dekker.

HOFFMAN, L. W. (1974). Fear of success in males and females: 1965 and 1972. *Journal of Consulting and Clinical Psychology, 42,* 353–358.

HOFFMAN, L. W. (1978). Effects of the first child on the woman's role. In W. Miller & L. Newman (Eds.), *The first child and family formation.* Chapel Hill: Carolina Population Center.

HOFSTADTER, R. (1959). *Social Darwinism in American thought.* New York: George Braziller.

HOGARTY, G. E., & GOLDBERG, S. C. (1973). Drug and sociotherapy in the aftercare of schizophrenic patients. *Archives of General Psychiatry, 28,* 54–63.

HOLLAND, J. L. (1973). *Making vocational choices: A theory of careers.* Englewood Cliffs, NJ: Prentice-Hall.

HOLMES, L. (1978). How fathers can cause the Down Syndrome. *Human Nature, 1*(10), 70–73.

HOLMES, T. H., & RAHE, R. H. (1967). The social readjustment rating scale. *Journal of Psychosomatic Research , 11,* 213–218.

HONORTON, C. (1974). Psi-conducive states of awareness. In E. Mitchell & J. White (Eds.), *Psychic exploration: A challenge for science* (pp. 611–638). New York: Putnam.

HORN, J. L., & KNAPP, J. R. (1973). On the subjective character of the empirical base of Guilford's structure of intellect model. *Psychological Bulletin, 80,* 33–43.

HORN, J. M., LOEHLIN, J. C., & WILLERMAN, L. (1982). Personality resemblances between unwed mothers and their adopted-away offspring. *Journal of Personality and Social Psychology, 42*(6), 1089–1099.

HORNER, M. S. (1968). *Sex differences in achievement motivation and performance in competitive and non-competitive situations.* Unpublished doctoral dissertation, University of Michigan. (University Microfilms No. 69–12, 135).

HORNEY, K. (1950). *Neurosis and human growth.* New York: W. W. Norton.

HUBEL, D. H. (1979). The brain. *Scientific American, 241,* 44–53.

HUBEL, D. H., & WIESEL, T. N. (1962). Receptive fields, binocular interactions and functional architecture in the cat's visual cortex. *Journal of Physiology, 160,* 106–154.

HUBEL, D. H., & WIESEL, T. N. (1979). Brain mechanisms of vision. *Scientific American, 241,* 150–162.

HUDSON, W. (1960). Pictorial depth perception in sub-cultural groups in Africa. *Journal of Social Psychology, 52,* 183–208.

HULICKA, I. M., & GROSSMAN, J. L. (1967). Age group comparisons for the use of mediators in paired associate learning. *Journal of Gerontology, 22,* 46–51.

HULL, C. L. (1943). *Principles of behavior.* New York: Appleton-Century-Crofts.

HUMPHREY, N. K. (1978). The origins of human intelligence. *Human Nature, 1*(12), 42–49.

HUNT, J. McV. (1965). Intrinsic motivation and its role in psychological development. *Nebraska · Symposium on Motivation 1965,* (pp. 189–282). Lincoln: University of Nebraska Press.

HUNT, M. (1974). *Sexual behavior in the 1970's.* New York: Dell.

HURVICH, L. M., & JAMESON, D. (1957). An opponent-process theory of color. *Psychological Reviews, 64,* 384–404.

HURVICH, L. M., & JAMESON, D. (1974). Opponent processes as a model of neural organization. *American Psychologist, 29,* 88–102.

HUTCHINGS, B., & MEDNICK, S. A. (1974). Registered criminality in the adoptive and biological parents of registered male adoptees. In S. A. Mednick, F. Schulsinger, J. Higgins, & B. Bell (Eds.), *Genetics, environment and psychopathology*. New York: Elsevier.

HUXLEY, A. (1971). Fifth philosopher's song. In D. Watt (Ed.), *The collected poetry of Aldous Huxley*. New York: Harper & Row.

ITTLESON, H. (1952). The constancies in perceptual theory. In F. R. Kilpatrick (Ed.), *Human behavior from the transactional point of view*. Hanover, NH: Institute for Associated Research.

IZARD, C. E. (1977). *Human emotions*. New York: Plenum.

JACOBS, B., & MOSS, H. (1976). Birth order and sex of sibling as determinants of mother-infant interaction. *Child Development, 47*, 315–322.

JACOBS, J. (1959). *Death and life of great American cities*. New York: Vintage Books.

JACOBS, J. (1971). *Adolescent suicide*. New York: John Wiley.

JACOBSON, J. (1977). *The development of peer play and cautiousness toward peers in infancy*. Doctoral dissertation, Harvard University.

JACQUES, E. (1951). *The changing culture of a factory*. London: Tavistock.

JACQUES, E. (1965). Death and the midlife crisis. *International Journal of Psychoanalysis, 46*, 502–514.

JAHODA, M., & WEST, P. (1951). Race relations in public housing. *Journal of Social Issues, 7*, 132–139.

JAMES, W. (1970). *The principles of psychology: Vol. 1*. New York: Dover. (Original work published 1890).

JAMES, W. (1970). *The principles of psychology: Vol. 2*. New York: Dover. (Original work published 1890).

JAMES, W. (1980). *The varieties of religious experience*. New York: Longmans Green. (Original work published 1917)

JANIS, I. L. (Ed.). (1977). *Current trends in psychology: Readings from American scientists*. Los Altos, CA: William Kaufmann.

JANIS, I., & MANN, L. (1977). *Decision-making*. New York: Free Press.

JARVICK, L. F., & DECKARD, B. S.

(1977). The Odyssean personality: A survival advantage for carriers of genes predisposing to schizophrenia. *Neuropsychobiology, 3*(2–3), 179–191.

JENKINS, J. G., & DALLENBACH, K. M. (1924). Oblivescence during sleep and waking. *American Journal of Psychology, 35*, 605–612.

JENKINS, R. L. (1966). Psychiatric syndromes in children and their relation to family background. *American Journal of Orthopsychiatry, 36*, 450–457.

JENKINS, R. L. (1969). Classification of behavior problems of children. *American Journal of Psychiatry, 125*(8), 1032–1039.

JENSEN, A. R. (1969). How much can we boost IQ and scholastic achievement? *Harvard Educational Review, 39*, 1–123.

JENSEN, A. R. (1980). *Bias in mental testing*. New York: Free Press.

JESSOR, R., & JESSOR, S. L. (1977). *Problem behavior and psychosocial development: A longitudinal study of youth*. New York: Academic press.

JESSOR, S. L., & JESSOR, R. (1975). Transition from virginity to nonvirginity among youth: A social-psychological study over time. *Developmental Psychology, 11*, 473–484.

JOHANSEN, D., & EDEY, M. (1981). *Lucy: The beginnings of human kind*. New York: Simon & Schuster.

JOHNSON, A. (1978). In search of the affluent society. *Human Nature, 1*(9), 50–60.

JOHNSON, D. M. (1972). *Systematic introduction to the psychology of thinking*. New York: Harper & Row.

JOHNSON-LAIRD, T. N., & WASON, P. C. (Eds.). (1977). *Thinking: Readings in cognitive science*. New York: Cambridge University Press.

JOINER, B. L. (1975). Living histograms. *International Statistical Review, 43*, 339–340.

JONES, E. E., & HARRIS, V. A. (1967). The attribution of attitudes. *Journal of Experimental Social Psychology, 3*, 1–24.

JONES, E. E., & NISBETT, R. E. (1971). *The actor and the observer: Divergent perception of the causes of behavior*. Morristown, NJ: General Learning Press.

JONES, M. C. (1924). A laboratory

study of fear: The case of Peter. *Journal of Genetic Psychology, 31*, 308–315.

JOSEPH, S. A., & KNIGGE, J. M. (1968). Effects of VMH lesions in adult and newborn guinea pigs. *Neuroendocrinology, 3*, 309–331.

JULIEN, R. M. (1978). *A primer of drug action*. San Francisco: W. H. Freeman.

JUNG, C. G. (1921). Psychological types. In *Collected works: Vol. 6*. Princeton: Princeton University Press.

JUNG, C. (1953). *Collected works*. H. Read, M. Fordham & G. Adler (Eds.), New York: Bollingen Series/ Pantheon Books.

KAGAN, J. (1978). *The growth of the child: Reflections on human development*. New York: W. W. Norton.

KAGAN, J. (1981). *The second year: The emergence of self-awareness*. Cambridge: Harvard University Press.

KAGAN, J., KEARSLEY, R. B., & ZELAZO, P. R. (1978). *Infancy: Its place in human development*. Cambridge: Harvard University Press.

KAGAN, J., & KLEIN, R. E. (1973). Cross-cultural perspectives on early development. *American Psychologist, 28*, 947–961.

KAHN, M. (1970). Non-verbal communication and marital satisfaction. *Family Process, 9*, 449–456.

KAHN, R. L., HEIN, K., HOUSE, J., McLEAN, A., & KASL, S. (1980, July). *Stress in organizational settings*. Paper prepared for the National Academy of Sciences, Institute of Medicine, Committee on Stress in Health and Disease.

KAHNEMAN, D., SLOVIC, P., & TVERSKY, A. (Eds.). (1982). *Judgment under certainty*. New York: Cambridge University Press.

KAHNEMAN, D., & TVERSKY. (1973). On the psychology of prediction. *Psychological Review, 80*, 237–251.

KALISH, R. A. (1976). Death and dying in a social context. In R. H. Binstock, & E. Shanas (Eds.). *Handbook of aging and the social sciences*. New York: Van Nostrand Reinhold.

KAMIN, L. (1979). Psychology as social science: The Jensen affair, ten years after. Presidential address to Eastern Psychological Association,

Philadelphia, April 1979.

KAMIN, L. (with Eysenck, H. J.). (1981). *The intelligence controversy.* New York: John Wiley.

KANNER, A. D., COYNE, J. C., SCHAEFER, C., & LAZARUS, R. S. (1971). Comparison of two modes of stress measurement: Daily hassles and uplifts vs. major life events. *Journal of Behavioral Medicine, 4*, 1–39.

KAPLAN, E. A. (1960). Hypnosis and pain. *A.M.A. Archives of General Psychiatry, 2*, 567–568.

KAPLEAU, P. (1980). *The three pillars of Zen.* New York: Anchor Press.

KASAMATSU, A., & HIRAI, T. (1963). An electroencephalographic study on the Zen meditation (Zazen). *Folia Psychiatria et Neurologia, 20*, 315–336.

KASTENBAUM, R. (1965). Wine and fellowship in aging: An exploratory action program. *Journal of Human Relations, 13*, 266–275.

KASTENBAUM, R. (1977). Is death a crisis? In Daton N., and Ginsberg (Eds.) *Life-span developmental psychology.* New York: Academic Press.

KASTENBAUM, R., & AISENBERG, R. (1972). *Psychology of death.* New York: Springer.

KATCHADOURIAN, H. (1977). *The biology of adolescence.* San Francisco: W. H. Freeman.

KATZ, M. L. (1973). *Female motive to avoid success: A psychological barrier or a response to deviancy?* Princeton: Educational Testing Service.

KAUFMAN, L. (1974). *Sight and mind: An introduction to visual perception.* New York: Oxford University Press.

KEESEY, R., & POWLEY, T. (1975, September–October). Hypothalamic regulation of body weight. *American Scientist, 63*, 558–565.

KELLEY, H. H. (1967). Attribution theory in social psychology. In D. Levine (Ed.)., *Nebraska Symposium on Motivation, 15*, 192–238. Lincoln: University of Nebraska Press.

KENNEDY, J. M. (1974). *A psychology of picture perception.* San Francisco: Jossey-Bass.

KESSEN, W., HAITH, M., & SALAPATEK, P. H. (1970). Infancy. In P. H. Mussen, (Ed.), *Carmichael's manual of child psychology* (3rd ed.).

New York: John Wiley.

KESSLER, S. (1980). *Schizophrenic families.* New York: Raven Press.

KEYS, A., BROZEK, J., HENSCHEL, A., MICKELSON, O., & TAYLOR, H. (1950). *The biology of human starvation* (Vols. 1–2). Minneapolis: University of Minnesota Press.

KIDSON, M. A., & JONES, I. H. (1952). Psychiatric disorders among aborigines of the Australian western desert. *Archives of General Psychiatry,* American Psychiatric Association.

KIMBLE, G. A. (1961). *Hilgard and Marquis' conditioning and learning* (2nd. ed.). New York: Appleton-Century-Crofts.

KIMMEL, D. C. (1980). *Adulthood and aging: An interdisciplinary developmental view* (2nd ed.). New York: John Wiley.

KIMURA, D. (1963). Right temporal lobe damage. *Archives of Neurology, 8*, 264–271.

KING, B. M., & GASTON, M. G. (1977). Reappearance of dynamic hyperphagia during the static phase in medial hypothalamic lesioned rats. *Physiology and Behavior, 18*, 463–473.

KINSEY, A., POMEROY, W., & MARTIN, C. (1948). *Sexual behavior in the human male.* Philadelphia: W. B. Saunders.

KINSEY, A., POMEROY, W., & MARTIN, C. (1953). *Sexual behavior in the human female.* Philadelphia: W. B. Saunders.

KISSEN, D. M. (1962). Relationship between primary lung cancer and peptic ulcer in males. *Psychosomatic Medicine, 24*, 133–147.

KISSEN, D. M. (1963). Personality characteristics in males conducive to lung cancer. *British Journal of Medical Psychology, 36*, 27–36.

KISSEN, D. M. (1966a). Psychosocial factors, personality and prevention in lung cancer. *Medical Officer, 166*, 135–138.

KISSEN, D. M. (1966b). Psychosomatic histories in the relatives of male hospital chest unit patients with special reference to lung cancer. *International Journal of Social Psychiatry, 12*, 199–208.

KISSEN, D. M. (1966c). The significance of personality in lung cancer

in men. *Annals of the New York Academy of Science, 125*, 820–826.

KLEINKE, C. (1978). *Self-perception: The psychology of personal awareness.* San Francisco: W. H. Freeman.

KLONOFF, H. (1974). Effects of marijuana on driving in a restricted area and on city streets: Driving performance and physiological changes. In L. L. Miller (Ed.), *Marijuana: Effects on human behavior* (pp. 359–397). New York: Academic press.

KLONOFF, H., McDOUGALL, G., CLARK, C., KRAMER, P., & HORGAN, J. (1976). The neuropsychological, psychiatric, and physical effects of prolonged and severe stress: 30 years later. *Journal of Nervous and Mental Disease, 163*, 240–252.

KNITTLE, J. (1971). Childhood obesity. *Bulletin of the New York Academy of Medicine, 47*, 579–589.

KOBASA, S. (1979). Stressful life events, personality and health: An inquiry into hardiness. *Journal of Personality and Social Psychology, 87*(1).

KOBASA, S. (1984). *The stress resistant personality.* [Tape]. Institute for the Study of Human Knowledge.

KOESTLER, A. (1974). *The heel of Achilles: Essays 1968–1973.* London: Hutchinson.

KOGAN, N., & WALLACH, M. A. (1967). Risk taking as a function of the situation, the person, and the group. In G. Mandler (Ed.), *New directions in psychology: Vol. 3.* New York: Holt, Rinehart & Winston.

KOHLBERG, L. (1969). Stage and sequence: The cognitive developmental approach to socialization. In D. A. Goslin (Ed.), *Handbook of socialization theory and research.* Chicago: Rand McNally.

KOHLBERG, L. (1976). Moral stages and moralization. In T. Lickona (Ed.), *Moral development and behavior: Theory, research and social issues.* New York: Holt, Rinehart & Winston.

KÖHLER, I. (1962). Experiments with goggles. *Scientific American, 206*, 62–86.

KÖHLER, W. (1925). *The mentality of apes.* New York: Harcourt Brace Jovanovich.

KOHN, B., & DENNIS, M. (1974). Selective impairments of visual-spatial abilities in infantile hemiplegics after right hemidecortication. *Neuropsy-*

chologia, 12, 505–512.

KOHN, M. L. (1971). Bureaucratic man: A portrait and interpretation. *American Sociological Review 36,* 461–474.

KOHN, M. L. (1978) "The Benefits of Bureaucracy", *Human Nature* 1(8), 60–66.

KOLB, B., & MILNER, B. (1980). Observations on spontaneous facial expression in patients. In B. Kolb & I. Whishaw (Eds.), *Fundamentals of human neuropsychology.* San Francisco: W. H. Freeman.

KOLB, B., & WHISHAW, I. Q. (1984). *Fundamentals of human neuropsychology.* (2nd ed.). San Francisco: W. H. Freeman.

KORNER, A., HUTCHINSON, C., KORPERSKI, J., KRAEMER, H., & SCHNEIDER, P. A. (1981). Stability of individual differences of neonatal motor and crying patterns. *Child Development, 52,* 83–90.

KOZMA, A., & STORES, M. J. (1980). Bereavement in the elderly. In B. M. Schoenberg (Ed.), *Bereavement counseling: A multidisciplinary handbook.* Westport, CT: Glenwood Press.

KRECH, D., CRUTCHFIELD, R. S., & LIVSON, N. (1974). *Elements of psychology* (3rd ed.). New York: Alfred A. Knopf.

KRECH, D., ROSENZWEIG, M., & BENNETT, E. L. (1962). Relations between brain chemistry and problem-solving among rats raised in enriched and impoverished environments. *Journal of Comparative and Physiological Psychology, 55,* 801–807.

KRECHEVSKY, D. (1932). "Hypotheses" in rats. *Psychological Review, 39,* 516–532.

KRINGLEN, E. (1967). *Heredity and environment in the functional psychosis: An epidemiological-clinical twin study.* Oslo: Universitsforlaget.

KRUEGER, A. (1978). Ions in the air. *Human Nature, 1*(7), 46–53.

KÜBLER-ROSS, E. (1969). *On death and dying.* New York: Macmillan.

KÜBLER-ROSS, E. (1975). *Death: The final stage of growth.* Englewood Cliffs, NJ: Prentice-Hall.

KUHN, T. S. (1962). *The structure of scientific revolutions.* Chicago: University of Chicago Press.

KURTINES, W., & GREIF, E. B. (1974). The development of moral thought: Review and evaluation of Kohlberg's approach. *Psychological Bulletin, 81,* 453–470.

KUTAS, M., & HILLYARD, S. A. (1980). Reading senseless sentences: Brain potentials reflect semantic incongruity. *Science, 207,* 203–204.

KYUCHARYANTS, V. (1974). Will the human life-span reach one hundred? *The Gerontologist, 14*(5).

LABERGE, S. P., NAGEL, L. E., DEMENT, W. C., & ZARCONE, V. P. (1981). Lucid dreaming verified by volitional communication during REM sleep. *Perceptual and Motor Skills, 52,* 727–732.

LACEY, J. I. (1950). Individual differences in somatic response patterns. *Journal of Comparative and Physiological Psychology, 43,* 338–50.

LACEY, J. I., BATEMAN, D. E., & VAN LEHN, R. (1953). Autonomic response specificity and Rohrschach color responses. *Psychosomatic Medicine, 14,* 256–260.

LACEY, J. I., & LACEY, B. C. (1958). Verification and extension of the principle of autonomic response stereotypy. *American Journal of Psychology, 71,* 50–73.

LAING, R. D. (1959). *The divided self.* London: Tavistock.

LAMARK, J. B. P. A. DE. (1951). Evolution through environmentally produced modifications. In *A source book in animal biology,* trans. of original statement of hypothesis by Lamark.

LAMB, C. W. (1968). Personality correlates of humour enjoyment following motivational arousal. *Journal of Personality and Social Psychology, 9,* 237–241.

LANCASTER, J. L. (1978). Carrying and sharing in human evolution. *Human Nature, 1*(2), 82–89.

LANGER, E., & RODIN, J. (1976). The effects of choice and enhanced personal responsibility for the aged: A field experiment in an institutional setting. *Journal of Personality and Social Psychology, 32*(2), 191–198.

LANGER, E. J., & ABELSON, R. P. (1974). A patient by any other name . . . clinician group difference in labelling bias. *Journal of Consulting and Clinical Psychology, 42,* 4–9.

LANGLOIS, J. H., & DOWNS, A. C. (1980). Mothers, fathers and peers as socialization agents of sex-typed behaviors. *Child Development, 51,* 1237–1247.

LASSWELL, H. D. (1948). *Power and personality.* New York: W. W. Norton.

LATANÉ, B., & DORLEY, J. M. (1970). *The unresponsive bystander: Why doesn't he help?* New York: Appleton-Century-Crofts.

LATANÉ, B., & NIDA, S. (1980). Social impact theory and group influence: A social engineering perspective. In P. B. Paulus (Ed.), *Psychology of group influence.* Hillsdale, NJ: Lawrence Erlbaum.

LATANÉ, B., & RODIN, J. (1969). A lady in distress: Inhibiting effects of friends and strangers on bystander intervention. *Journal of Experimental Social Psychology, 5,* 189–202.

LAWICKA, W. (1964). The role of stimuli modality in successive discrimination and differentiation learning. *Bulletin of the Polish Academy of Sciences, 12,* 35–38.

LAZARUS, R. S. (1968). Emotions and adaptation: Conceptual and empirical relations. In W. J. Arnold (Ed.), *Nebraska Symposium on Motivation XVI.* Lincoln: University of Nebraska Press.

LAZARUS, R. S. (1976). *Patterns of adjustment* (3rd ed.). New York: McGraw-Hill.

LAZARUS, R. S., & LAUNIER, R. (1978). Stress-related transactions between the person and the environment. In L. A. Pervin & M. Lewis (Eds.), *Internal and external determinants of behavior.* New York: Plenum.

LEAKEY, R., & LEWIN, R. (1977). *Origins.* New York: E. P. Dutton.

LECONTE, P., HENNEVIN, E., & BLOCH, V. (1972). Increase in paradoxical sleep following learning in the rat: Correlation with level of conditioning. *Brain Research, 42,* 552–553.

LEE, M. L., NOVOTNY, M., & BARTLE, K. D. (1976). Gas chromatography/mass spectrometric and nuclear magnetic resonance spectrometric studies on carcinogenic polynuclear aromatic hydrocarbons in tobacco and marijuana smoke condensate. *Analytical Chemistry, 48,* 405–416.

LEFCOURT, H. (1976). *Locus of control: Current trends in theory and research.* New York: John Wiley.

LEFF, J. P., & WING, J. K. (1971). Trial of maintenance therapy in schizophrenia. *British Medical Journal,* 3(5775), 599–604.

LEHMAN, H. C. (1953). *Age and achievement.* Princeton: Princeton University Press.

LEHMAN, H. C. (1962). The creative production rates of present vs. past generations of scientists. *Journal of Gerontology,* 14(4), 409–417.

LEHMAN, H. C. (1966). The psychologist's most creative years. *American Psychologist,* 21(4), 363–369.

LEIBOWITZ, S. F. (1976). In D. Novin, W. Wyrwicka, & G. A. Bray, *Hunger: Basic mechanisms and clinical implications* (pp. 1–18). New York: Raven Press.

LE MAGUEN, J. (1969). Peripheral and systematic actions of food in the caloric regulation of intake. *Annals of the New York Academy of Sciences, 147,* 1126–1157.

LeMASTERS, E. E. (1957). Parenthood as crisis. *Marriage and Family Living, 19,* 352–355.

LENNEBERG, E. H. (1967). *The biological foundations of language.* New York: John Wiley.

LEONARD, C. V. (1971). Depression and suicidality. *Journal of Consulting and Clinical Psychology, 42,* 98–104.

LETTVIN, J. Y., MATURANA, H. R., McCULLOCH, S. W., & PITTS, W. H. (1959). What the frog's eye tells the frog's brain. *Proceedings of the Institute of Radio Engineers, 47,* 140–151.

LEUTENEGGER, W. (1977). Scaling of sexual dimorphism in body size and breeding system in primates. *Nature, 272,* 610–611.

LEVENSTEIN, P. (1970). Cognitive growth in pre-schooler through verbal interaction with mothers. *American Journal of Orthopsychology. 40,* 426–432.

LEVINE, J. D., & FIELDS, H. (1979). Role of pain in placebo analgesia. *Proceedings National Academy of Science, 3528*–3531.

LEVINE, S., & URSIN, H. (1980). *Coping and health.* New York: Plenum.

LEVINGER, G. A. (1976). A social psychological perspective on marital dissolution. *Journal of Social Issues, 32,* 21–47.

LEVINSON, D. J. (1977). The mid-life transition: A period in adult psychosocial development. *Psychiatry, 40.*

LEVINSON, D. J. (1978). (with C. Darrow, E. B. Klein, M. H. Levinson, & B. McKee). *The seasons of a man's life.* New York: Alfred A. Knopf.

LEWIN, J., & GOMBOSH, D. (1973). Increase in REM time as a function of the need for divergent thinking. In W. P. Koella & P. Lewin (Eds.), *Sleep: Physiology, biochemistry, psychology, pharmacology, clinical implications.* Basel, Switzerland: Karger.

LEWINSHOHN, P. M., MISCHEL, W., & BARTON, R. (1980). Social competence and depression: The role of illusory self-perceptions. *Journal of Abnormal Psychology, 89*(2), 203–212.

LEWIS, C. N. (1971). Reminiscing and self-concept in old age. *Journal of Gerontology, 26,* 240–243.

LEWIS, M. (1964). Behavior resulting from calcium deprivation in parathyroid-ectamized rats. *Journal of Comparative and Physiological Psychology, 57,* 348–352.

LEWIS, M., & FREEDLE, R. (1973). Mother-infant dyad: The cradle of meaning. In P. Pliner, L. Kramer, & T. Alloway (Eds.), *Communication and affect: Language and thought.* New York: Academic Press.

LIEBERMAN, M. A., & FALK, J. (1971). The remembered past as a source of data for research on the life cycle. *HD, 14,* 132–141.

LIEBERT, R. M., & BARON, R. A. (1972). Some immediate effects of televised violence on children's behavior. *Developmental Psychology, 6,* 469–478.

LIFTON, R. J. (1963). *Thought reform and the psychology of totalism: A study of "brainwashing" in China.* New York: W. W. Norton.

LINDEMANN, E. (1944). The symptomatology and management of acute grief. *American Journal of Psychiatry, 101,* 141.

LINDSAY, P. H., & NORMAN, D. A. (1977). *Human information processing* (2nd ed.). New York: Academic Press.

LIVINGSTON, R. B., CALLAWAY, D. F., MACGREGOR, J. S., FISCHER, G. J., & HASTINGS, A. B. (1975). U.S. poverty impact on brain development. In M. A. B. Brazier (Ed.), *Growth and development of the brain: Nutritional, genetic, and environmental factors.* New York: Raven Press.

LOCKE, H. J. (1951). *Predicting adjustment in marriage: A comparison of a divorced and a happily married group.* New York: Henry Holt.

LOCKE, J. (1964). *An essay concerning human understanding.* New York: Meridian. (Original work published 1670).

LOFTUS, E. F. (1978). Shifting human color memory. *Memory and Cognition, 5,* 696–699.

LOFTUS, E. F., MILLER, D. G., & BURNS, H. J. (1978). Semantic integration of verbal information into a visual memory. *Journal of Experimental Psychology, 4* 19–31.

LOFTUS, E. F., & PALMER, J. C. (1974). Reconstruction of automobile destruction: An example of the interaction between language and memory. *Journal of Verbal Learning and Verbal Behavior, 13,* 585–589.

LOFTUS, G. R., & LOFTUS, E. F. (1974). The influence of one memory retrieval on a subsequent memory retrieval. *Memory and Cognition, 3,* 467–471.

LOFTUS, G. R., & LOFTUS, E. F. (1975). *Human memory: The processing of information.* New York: Halsted Press.

LOPATA, H. Z. (1973). *Widowhood in an American city.* Cambridge, MA: Schenkman.

LOPATA, H. Z. (1979). *Women as widows: Support systems.* New York: Elsevier.

LORENZ, K. (1966). *On aggression* (M. K. Wilson, Trans.). New York: Harcourt Brace Jovanovich.

LOVEJOY, C. O. (1974). The gait of Australopithecines. *Yearbook of Physical Anthropology, 17,* 147–161.

LOVEJOY, C. O. (1981). The origin of man. *Science, 211,* 128–130.

LOWENSTEIN, W. R. (1960). Biological transducers. *Scientific American, 203,* 98–108.

LOWENTHAL, M. F. (1964). *Lives in distress.* New York: Basic Books.

LOWENTHAL, M. F., THURNER, M., & CHIRIBOGA, D. (1975). *The four stages of life.* San Francisco: Jossey-Bass.

LUBORSKY, L., SINGER, B., & LUBORSKY, L. (1975). Comparative studies of psychotherapies. *Archives of General Psychiatry, 32,* 995–1008.

LUCE, G. (1970). *Biological rhythms in psychiatry and medicine.* U.S. Public Health Service Publication No. 2088.

LUCE, G., & SEGAL, J. (1966). *Sleep.* New York: Lancet.

LUCERO, M. (1970). Lengthening of REM sleep duration consecutive to learning in the rat. *Brain Research, 20,* 319–322.

LUCHINS, A. (1942). Mechanization in problem solving. *Psychological Monographs, 54*(248).

LUCHINS, A. S., & LUCHINS, E. H. (1959). *Rigidity of behavior: A variational approach to the effect of Einstellung.* Eugene, OR: University of Oregon Books.

LUDEL, J. (1978). *Introduction to sensory processes.* San Francisco: W. H. Freeman.

LURIA, A. R. (1968). *The mind of a mnemonist.* New York: Basic Books.

LURIA, A. R. (1973). *The working brain.* New York: Penguin Books.

LUTSKY, N., PEAKE, P. K., & WRAY, L. (1978). *Inconsistencies in the search for cross-situational consistencies in behavior: A critique of the Bem and Allen study.* Paper presented to the Midwestern Psychological Association, Chicago.

LYKKEN, D. T. A. (1957). A study of anxiety in the sociopathic personality. *Journal of Abnormal and Social Psychology, 55,* 6–10.

LYNCH, J. (1977). *The broken heart: The medical consequences of loneliness.* New York: Basic Books.

MACCOBY, E. (1980). *Social development: Psychological growth and the parent-child relationship.* New York: Harcourt Brace Jovanovich.

MACCOBY, E. E., & JACKLIN, C. N. (1974). *The psychology of sex differences.* Stanford: Stanford University Press.

MACFARLANE, A. (1978). What a baby knows. *Human Nature, 1,* 74–81.

MACLEAN, P. (1978). The triune brain. *American Scientist, 66,* 101–113.

MAGOUN, H. (1969). Advances in brain research with implications for learning. In J. Kagan. (Ed.), *On the biology of learning.* New York: Harcourt Brace Jovanovich.

MAHER, B. (1964). *Progress in experimental personality research.* New York: Academic Press.

MAHONEY, M., & ARNKOFF, D. (1978). Cognitive and self-control therapies. In S. Garfield & A. Bergin (Eds.), *Handbook of psychotherapy and behavior change: An empirical analysis.* New York: John Wiley.

MAIN, M. (1973). *Exploration, play and level of cognitive functioning as related to child-mother attachment.* Unpublished doctoral dissertation, Johns Hopkins University.

MAKINODAN, T. (1977). Immunity and aging. In C. Finch & L. Hayflick (Eds.), *Handbook of the biology of aging.* New York: Van Nostrand Reinhold.

MALINKOWSKI, B. (1955). *Sex and repression in savage society.* New York: Meridian. (Original work published 1928)

MANDLER, G. (1980). *Mind and emotion.* New York: John Wiley.

MARGOLIS, B. L., KROES, W. H., & QUINN, R. P. (1974). Job stress: An unlisted occupational hazard. *Journal of Occupational Medicine, 16,* 654–661.

MARGULES, D. L., & OLDS, J. (1962). Identical "feeding" and "rewarding" systems in the lateral hypothalamus of rats. *Science, 135,* 374–375.

MARKUS, H. (1977). Self-schemata and processing information about the self. *Journal of Personality and Social Psychology, 35,* 63–78.

MARSDEN, H. M. (1972). Crowding and animal behavior. In J. F. Wohlwill & D. H. Carson (Eds.), *Environment and the social sciences: Perspectives and applications.* Washington, DC: American Psychological Association.

MARSHAK, A. (1978). The art and symbols of Ice Age man. *Human Nature, 1*(9), 32–41.

MARSHALL, G. D., & ZIMBARDO, P. G. (1979). Affective consequences of inadequately explained physiologically arousal. *Journal of Personality and Social Psychology, 37*(b), 970–988.

MARSHALL, J. F., TURNER, B. H., & TEITELBAUM, P. (1971). Sensory neglect produced by lateral hypothalamic damage. *Science, 174,* 523–525.

MASLOW, A. H. (1970). *Motivation and personality* (2nd ed.). New York: Harper & Row.

MASLOW, A. H. (1971). *The farther reaches of human nature* (2nd ed.). New York: Viking Press.

MASLOW, A. H. (1976). *Religions, values and peak experiences.* New York: Penguin Books.

MASTERS, W. H., & JOHNSON, V. E. (1966). *Human sexual response.* Boston: Little, Brown.

MATAS, L., AREND, R., & SROUFE, L. A. (1978). Continuity of adaptation in the second year: The relationship between quality of attachment and later competence. *Child Development, 49,* 547–556.

MAWHINNEY, V. T., BOSTON, D. E., LAWS, D. R., BLUMENFELD, G. J., & HOPKINS, B. L. (1971). A comparison of students studying: Behavior produced by daily, weekly, and three-week testing schedules. *Journal of Applied Behavior Analysis, 4,* 257–264.

MAYER, A. D., & ROSENBLATT, J. S. (1979). Hormonal influences during the ontogeny of maternal behavior in female rats. *Journal of Comparative and Physiological Psychology, 93,* 879–898.

MAYER, J. (1953a). Genetic, traumatic and environment factors in the etiology of obesity. *Physiological Review, 33,* 472–508.

MAYER, J. (1953b). Glucostatic mechanism of regulation of food intake. *New England Journal of Medicine, 249,* 13–16.

MAYNARD SMITH, J. (1978). The evolution of behavior. In Scientific American *Evolution.* San Francisco: W. H. Freeman.

McCLELLAND, D. C. (1961). *The achieving society.* New York: Van Nostrand Reinhold.

McCLELLAND, D. C. (1971). *Motiva-*

tional trends in society. Morristown, NJ: General Learning Press.

McCLELLAND, D. C. (1973). Testing for competence rather than for "intelligence." *American Psychologist, 28,* 1–14.

McCLELLAND, D. C. (1975). *Power: The inner experience.* New York: Irvington.

McCLELLAND, D. (1984). *Achievement motivation.* New York: Free Press.

McCLELLAND, D. C., ATKINSON, J. W., CLARK, R. A., & LOWELL, E. L. (1953). *The achievement motive.* New York: Appleton-Century-Crofts.

McCLELLAND, D. C., & WINTER, D. G. (1971). *Motivating economic achievement: Accelerating economic development through psychological training.* New York: Free Press.

McCLINTOCK, M. K. (1971). Menstrual synchrony and suppression. *Nature, 229,* 244–245.

McCONNELL, P. & BERRY, M. (1978). The effects of undernutrition on Purkinje cell dendritic growth in the rat. *Journal of Comparative Neurology, 177,* 159–171.

McGINTY, D. J. (1969). Effects of prolonged isolation and subsequent enrichment on sleep patterns in kittens. *Electroencephalography and Clinical Neurophysiology, 26,* 335.

McGLONE, J. (1980). Sex differences in human brain asymmetry: A critical survey. *The Behavioral and Brain Sciences, 3*(2), 215–263.

McGRATH, M. J., & COHEN, D. B. (1978). REM sleep facilitation of adaptive waking behavior: A review of the literature. *Psychological Bulletin, 85*(1), 24–57.

McGREGOR, D. (1960). *The human side of enterprise.* New York: McGraw-Hill.

McLEAN, A. (1979). *Work stress.* Reading, MA: Addison-Wesley.

McMAHON, A. W., & RHUDICK, P. J. (1967). Reminiscing in the aged: An adaptational response. In S. Levin & R. J. Kahana (Eds.), *Psychodynamic studies on aging: Creativity, reminiscing and dying.* New York: International Universities Press.

McMILLEN, M. M. (1979). Differential mortality by sex in fetal and neonatal deaths. *Science, 204,* 89–91.

McNEIL, E. B. (1967). *The quiet furies:*

Man and disorder. Englewood Cliffs, NJ: Prentice-Hall.

MECHANIC, D. (1978). *Students under stress: A study in the social psychology of adaptation.* Madison: The University of Wisconsin Press.

MEDNICK, S. A. (1977). A bio-social theory of the learning of law-abiding behavior. In S. A. Mednick & K. O. Christiansen (Eds.), *Biosocial bases of criminal behavior.* New York: Gardner Press.

MEDVEDEV, Z. A. (1974). Caucasus and Altay longevity: A biological or social problem. *The Gerontologist, 14*(5), 31–37.

MEDVEDEV, Z. A. (1975). Aging and longevity: New approaches and new perspectives. *Gerontologist, 15*(3), 196–201.

MEGARGEE, E. (1966). Undercontrolled and overcontrolled personality types in extreme antisocial aggression. *Psychology Monographs, 80.*

MEICHENBAUM, D. (1974). *Cognitive behavior modification.* Boston: General Learning Press.

MEICHENBAUM, D. (1977). *Cognitive behavior modification: An Integrative Approach.* New York: Plenum.

MELLEN, S. L. W. (1981). *The evolution of love.* San Francisco: W. H. Freeman.

MENNINGER, K. A. (1945). *The human mind* (3rd ed.). New York: Alfred A. Knopf.

METROPOLITAN LIFE INSURANCE CO. (1969). Changes of dependency. *Statistical Bulletin, 50,* 10–11.

MEYER, M. B. (1978). How does maternal smoking affect birth weight and maternal weight gain? Evidence from the Ontario Perinatal Mortality Study. *American Journal of Obstetrical Gynecology, 131*(8), 888–893.

MICHAEL, R. P., BONSALL, R. W., & WARNER, P. (1974). Human vaginal secretions: Volatile fatty acid content. *Science, 186,* 1217–1219.

MICHAELS, C. F., & CARELLO, C. (1981). *Direct perception.* Englewood Cliffs, NJ: Prentice-Hall.

MIDDLETON, R., & MOLAND, J. (1959). Humor in negro and white subcultures: A study of jokes among university students. *American Sociological Review, 24,* 61–69.

MILGRAM, S. (1970). The experience

of living in cities. *Science, 13,* 1461–1468.

MILGRAM, S. (1974). *Obedience to authority.* New York: Harper & Row.

MILLER, E. (1971). Handedness and the pattern of human ability. *British Journal of Psychology, 62,* 111–112.

MILLER, G. A. (1951). *Language and communication.* New York: McGraw-Hill.

MILLER, G. A. (1981). *Language and speech.* San Francisco: W. H. Freeman.

MILLER, G. A., & BUCKHOUT, R. (1973). *Psychology: The science of mental life* (2nd ed.). New York: Harper & Row.

MILLER, G. A., GALANTER, E., & PRIBRAM, K. H. (1960). *Plans and the structure of behavior.* New York: Holt, Rinehart & Winston.

MILLER, J. (1978). *General systems theory.* New York: McGraw-Hill.

MILLER, J. (1980). *The body in question.* New York: Holt, Rinehart & Winston.

MILLER, L. B., & DYER, J. L. (1975). Four preschool programs: Their dimensions and effects. *Monographs of the Society for Research in Child Development, 40*(5, 6).

MILLER, N. (1978). Biofeedback and visceral learning. *Annual Review of Psychology, 29,* 421–452.

MILLER, N. (1980). Lecture at "The Healing Brain," Albert Einstein College of Medicine.

MINEKA, S., & SUOMI, S. J. (1978). Social separation in monkeys. *Psychological Bulletin, 85,* 1376–1400.

MINKLER, M. (1981). Applications of social support theory to health education: Implications for work with the elderly. *Health Education Quarterly, 8*(2).

MINKLER, M. (1984). Social networks and health: People need people. Institute for the Study of Human Knowledge.

MISCHEL, W. (1968). *Personality and assessment.* New York: John Wiley.

MISCHEL, W. (1973). Toward a cognitive social learning reconceptualization of personality. *Psychological Review, 80,* 252–283.

MISCHEL, W. (1976). *Introduction to personality* (2nd ed.) New York: Holt, Rinehart and Winston.

MISCHEL, W. (1979). On the interface

of cognition and personality: Beyond the person-situation debate. *American Psychologist, 34,* 340–354.

MISCHEL, W. (1981a). *Introduction to personality* (3rd ed.). New York: Holt, Rinehart & Winston.

MISCHEL, W. (1981b). *Personality and assessment* (3rd ed.). New York: John Wiley.

MISCHEL, W., & PEAKE, P. K. (1982). Beyond deja vu in the search for cross-situational consistency. *Psychological Review, 89,* 730–755.

MONTGOMERY, K. C. (1954). The role of the exploratory drive in learning. *Journal of Comparative and Physiological Psychology, 47,* 60–64.

MONTGOMERY, K. C., & SEGALL, M. (1955). Discrimination learning based upon the exploratory drive. *Journal of Comparative and Physiological Psychology, 48,* 225–228.

MORGAN, W. P. (1978). *Introduction to sport psychology.* St. Louis: C. V. Mosby.

MORRIS, P. (1958). *Widows and their families.* London: Routledge.

MORRIS, P. (1974). *Loss and change.* New York: Pantheon Books.

MOSCOVITCH, A., & LORORDO, V. M. (1968). Role of safety in the Pavlovian backward fear conditioning procedure. *Journal of Comparative and Physiological Psychology, 66,* 673–678.

MOSCOVITCH, M., & OLDS, J. (1980). *Asymmetries in spontaneous facial expressions and their possible relation to hemispheric specialization.* Paper presented at the meeting of the International Neuropsychology Society, Holland.

MOSS, H. A. (1967). Sex, age and state as determinants of mother-infant interaction. *Merrill-Palmer Quarterly, 13,* 19–36.

MOUNTCASTLE, V. B. (1976). The world around us: Neural command functions for selective attention. *Neurosciences Research Program Bulletin, 14*(Suppl.) 1–47.

MUMFORD, L. (1970). *The pentagon of power.* New York: Harcourt Brace Jovanovich.

MURSTEIN, B. I., CERRETO, M., & MACDONALD, M. G. (1977). A theory and investigation of the effect of exchange-orientation on marriage and friendship. *Journal of Marriage and the Family, 39,* 543–548.

MYERS, A. K., & VILLER, N. E. (1957). Failure to find a learned drive based on hunger: Evidence for learning motivated by "exploration." *Journal of Comparative and Physiological Psychology, 47,* 428–436.

MYERS, D. G., & LAMM, H. (1975). The polarizing effect of group discussion. *American Scientist, 63,* 297–303.

MYERS, D. G., & LAMM, H. (1976). The group polarization phenomenon. *Psychological Bulletin, 83,* 602–627.

MYERS, R. D. (1969). Temperature regulation: Neurochemical systems in the hypothalamus. In W. Haymaker, E. Anderson, & W. J. Nauta (Eds.), *The hypothalamus.* Springfield, IL: Charles C. Thomas.

MYERS, R. D. (1971). Hypothalamic mechanisms of pyrogen action in the cat and monkey. In G. E. V. Wolstenholme & J. Birch (Eds.), *Ciba Foundation symposium on pyrogens and fever* (pp. 131–153). London: Churchill.

NAGLE, J. J. (1979). *Heredity and human affairs* (2nd ed.). St. Louis: C. V. Mosby.

NAVRAN, L. (1967). Communication and adjustment in marriage. *Family Process, 6,* 173–184.

NEBES, R. (1972). Dominance of the minor hemisphere in commissurotomized man in a test of figural unification. *Brain, 95,* 633–638.

NEISSER, U. C. (1976). *Cognition and reality.* San Francisco: W. H. Freeman.

NEISSER, U. C. (1982). *Memory observed: Remembering in natural context.* San Francisco: W. H. Freeman.

NEISSER, U. C. (1979). *Cognitive psychology.* New York: Appleton-Century-Crofts.

NERHARDT, G. (1970). Humor and inclination to laugh: Emotional reactions to stimuli of different divergence from range of expectancy. *Scandinavian Journal of Psychology, 11,* 185–195.

NEUGARTEN, B. L. (1964). Summary and implications. In Neugarten et al., *Personality in middle and late life.* New York: Atherton.

NEUGARTEN, B. L. (1974, September). Age groups in American society and the rise of the young-old. *The Annals of the American Academy of Political and Social Science,* 187–198.

NEUGARTEN, B. L. (1977). Personality and aging. In J. E. Birren & K. W. Schaie (Eds.), *Handbook of the psychology of aging.* New York: Van Nostrand Reinhold.

NEUGARTEN, B. L., & HAGESTAD, G. O. (1976). Age and the life course. In R. H. Binstock & E. Shanas (Eds.), *Handbook of aging and the social sciences.* New York: Van Nostrand Reinhold.

NEUGARTEN, B. L., HAVIGHURST, D. J., & TOBIN, S. S. (1968). Personality and patterns of aging. In B. L. Neugarten (Ed.), *Middle age and aging.* Chicago: University of Chicago Press.

NEUGARTEN, B. L., MOORE, J. W., & LOWE, J. C. (1965). Age norms, age constraints, and adult socialization. *American Journal of Sociology, 70*(6), 710–717.

NEUGARTEN, B. L., & PETERSON, W. (1957). A study of the American age-grade system. *Fourth Congress of the International Association of Gerontology, Vol. 3.* Firenzi, Italy: Tito Mattiolo.

NEUGARTEN, B. L., & WEINSTEIN, K. (1964). The changing American grandparent. *Journal of Marriage and Family, 24*(2), 199–204.

NEUGARTEN, B. L., WOOD, V., KRAINES, R. J., & LOOMIS, B. (1963). Women's arttitudes toward the menopause. *Vita Humana, 6*(3), 140–151.

NEVILLE, H. (1977). Electroencephalographic testing of cerebral specialization in normal and congenitally deaf children: A preliminary report. In S. J. Segalowitz & F. A. Gruber (Eds.), *Language development and neurological theory.* New York: Academic Press.

NEWCOMB, T. M. (1943). *Personality and social change.* New York: Dryden Press.

NEWCOMB, T. M., KOENIG, K. E., FLACKS, R., & WARWICK, D. P. (1967). *Persistence and change: Bennington College and its students after twenty-five years.* New York: John Wiley.

NEWELL, A., & SIMON, H. A. (1972). *Human problem solving.* Englewood Cliffs, NJ: Prentice-Hall.

NEWMAN, J., McCAULEY, C. (1977). Eye contact with strangers in city, suburb, and small town. *Environment and Behavior, 9*(4), 547–558.

NEWMAN, O. (1979). Community of interest. *Human Nature, 2*(1).

NEWTON, N., & MODAHL, C. (1978). Pregnancy: The closest human relationship. *Human Nature, 1*(3), 40–50.

NISBETT, R. E. (1968). Taste, deprivation, and weight determinants of eating behavior. *Journal of Personality and Social Psychology, 10,* 107–116.

NISBETT, R. E. (1972). Hunger, obesity, and the ventromedial hypothalamus. *Psychological Review, 79*(6), 433–453.

NISBETT, R. E., & BELLOWS, N. (1977). Verbal reports about causal influences as social judgments: Private access versus public theories. *Journal of Personality and Social Psychology, 35,* 613–624.

NISBETT, R. E., CAPUTO, C., LEGANT, P., & MARACEK, J. (1973). Behavior as seen by the actor and as seen by the observer. *Journal of Personality and Social Psychology, 27,* 154–164.

NISBETT, R. E., & ROSS, L. (1981). *Human inference: Strategies and shortcomings of social judgment.* Englewood Cliffs, NJ: Prentice-Hall.

NORMAN, D. A. (1982). *Learning and memory.* San Francisco: W. H. Freeman.

NORTON, D. (1976). *Personal destinies: A philosophy of ethical individualism.* Princeton: Princeton University Press.

NORTON, A., & GLICK, P. (1976). Marital instability: Past, present and future. *The Journal of Social Issues, 32,* 5–20.

OFLER, D. (1967). *The psychological world of the teenager.* New York: Basic Books.

OFLER, D., & OFLER, J. (1975). *From teenage to young manhood: A psychological study.* New York: Basic Books.

OLDHAM, G. R., HACKMAN, J. R., & PEARCE, J. L. (1975, September). *Conditions under which employees respond positively to enriched work* (Tech. Rep. No. 4). New Haven: Yale University Department of Administrative Sciences.

OLDS, J. (1958). Self-stimulation of the brain. *Science, 127,* 315–323.

OLDS, J., & MILNER, P. (1954). Positive reinforcement produced by electrical stimulation of septal area and other regions of rat brain. *Journal of Comparative Physiological Psychology, 47,* 419–427.

OLWEUS, D. (1969). Prediction of aggression on the basis of a projective test. *Skandinavista Test Forlaget.*

OMARK, D. R., & EDELMAN, M. (1973). *Peer group social interactions from an evolutionary perspective.* Paper presented at the meetings of the Society for Research in Child Development, Philadelphia.

ORNSTEIN, R. E. (1969). *On the experience of time.* London: Penguin Books.

ORNSTEIN, R. E., (Ed.). (1973). *Nature of human consciousness.* San Francisco: W. H. Freeman.

ORNSTEIN, R. E. (1977). *The psychology of consciousness* (2nd ed.). New York: Harcourt Brace Jovanovich.

ORNSTEIN, R. E., HERRON, J., JOHNSTONE, J., & SWENCIONIS, C. (1979). Differential right hemisphere involvement in two reading tasks. *Psychophysiology, 16*(4), 398–401.

ORNSTEIN, R. E., & SWENCIONIS, C. (in press). Analytic and synthetic problem-solving strategies in hemispheric asymmetry. *Neuropsychologia.*

ORNSTEIN, R. E., THOMPSON, R., & MACAULAY, D. (1984). *The amazing brain.* Boston: Houghton Mifflin.

OSBORN, D. K., & ENDSLEY, R. C. (1971). Emotional reactions of young children to TV violence. *Child Development, 42,* 321–331.

OSGOOD, C., SUCI, G. J., & TANNENBAUM, P. H. (1971). *The measurement of meaning.* Urbana: University of Illinois Press.

OSIS, K., & HANALOSEN, E. (1977). *At the hour of death.* New York: Avon Books.

OSWALD, I. (1962). *Sleeping and waking.* Amsterdam, NY: Elsevier.

PAPEZ, J. W. (1937). A proposed mechanism of emotion. *Archives of Neurology and Psychiatry, 38,* 725–743.

PARKER, D. General review of the sex situation (1954). *The portable Dorothy Parker* (Rev. & expanded ed.). (p. 115). New York: Viking Press.

PARKES, C. M. (1972). *Bereavement: Studies of grief in adult life.* New York: International Universities Press.

PARKES, C. M., BENJAMIN, B., & FITZGERALD, R. G. (1969). Broken heart: A statistical study of increased mortality among widows. *British Medical Journal, 1,* 740.

PATTISON, E. M. (1977). The will to live and the expectation of death. In E. M. Pattison (Ed.), *The experience of dying* (pp. 61–74). Englewood Cliffs: NJ: Prentice-Hall.

PAUL, G. L. (1965). Effects of insight, desensitization, and attention-placebo treatment of anxiety: An approach to outcome research in psychotherapy. *Dissertation Abstracts, 25*(9), 5388–5389.

PAVLOV, I. P. (1927). *Conditioned reflexes.* London: Oxford University Press.

PAVLOV, I. P. (1928). *Lectures on conditioned reflexes.* New York: International Publishers.

PAVLOV, I. P. (1941). *Conditional reflexes and psychiatry* (W. H. Gantt, Ed. and Trans.). New York: International Publishers.

PAXTON, A. L., & TURNER, E. J. (1978). Self-actualization and sexual permissiveness, satisfaction, prudishness, and drive among female undergraduates. *Journal of Sex Research, 14*(2), 65–80.

PEARCE, T. V. (1930). In Kendall, *Advanced Statistics.*

PEARLIN, L. (1980). Life strains and psychological distress among adults. In N. J. Smelser & E. H. Erikson (Eds.), *Themes of work and love in adulthood.* Cambridge: Harvard University Press.

PEARLIN, L., & JOHNSON, J. (1977). Marital stress, life strains and depression. *American Sociological Review, 42,* 704–715.

PEARLIN, L., & SCHOOLER, C. (1978). The structure of coping. *Jour-*

nal of Health and Social Behavior, 19, 2–21.

PECK, M. A., & SCHRUT, A. (1971). Suicidal behavior among college students. *HSMHA Health Reports, 86*(2), 149–156.

PECK, R., & BERKOWITZ, H. (1964). Personality and adjustment in middle age. In B. L. Neugarten et al., *Personality in middle and late life* (pp. 15–43). New York: Atherton.

PECK, R., & HAVIGHURST, R. (1960). *The psychology of character development*. New York: John WIley.

PEDERSEN, E., & FAUCHES, T. (1978). A new perspective on the effects of first-grade teachers on children's subsequent adult status. *Harvard Educational Review, 48*, 1–31.

PENFIELD, W. (1975). *The mystery of the mind*. Princeton: Princeton University Press.

PERRIS, C. (1971). Abnormality on paternal and maternal sides: Observations in bipolar (manic-depressive) and unipolar depressive psychoses. *British Journal of Psychiatry, 118*(543), 207–210.

PETERSEN, C., SCHWARTZ, S., & SELIGMAN, M. (1981). Self-blame and depressive symptoms. *Journal of Personality and Social Psychology, 41*, 253–259.

PETTIGREW, J. (1972). The neurophysiology of binocular vision. In R. Held & W. Richards (Eds.), *Recent progress in perception: Readings from Scientific American* (pp. 55–66). San Francisco: W. H. Freeman.

PETTIGREW, T. (1961). Social psychology and desegregation research. *American Psychologist, 15*, 61–71.

PHARES, E. J., WILSON, K. G., & KLYVER, N. W. (1971). Internal-external control and the attribution of blame under neutral and distractive conditions. *Journal of Personality and Social Psychology, 18*, 285–288.

PHILLIPS, D. P., & FELDMAN, K. A. (1973). A dip in deaths before ceremonial occasions: some new relationships between social integration and mortality. *American Sociological Review, 38*, 678–696.

PHILLIPS, J. L. (1981). *Piaget's theory: A primer*. San Francisco: W. H. Freeman.

PIAGET, J. (1960). *The moral judgment of the child*. Glencoe, IL: The Free Press. (Original work published 1932)

PIAGET, J. (1952). *The origins of intelligence in children*. New York: International Universities Press.

PILBEAM, O. (1972). *The ascent of man*. New York: Macmillan.

PLUTCHIK, R. (1980). *Emotion: A psychoevolutionary synthesis*. New York: Harper & Row.

PLUTCHIK, R. (1984). Emotions: A general psychoevolutionary theory. In K. Scherer & P. Ekman (Eds.), *Approaches to emotion*. Hillsdale, NJ: Lawrence Erlbaum.

POINCARÉ, H. (1921). The value of science. In G. B. Halstead (Trans.), *The foundations of science*. New York: Science Press.

POLIVY, J., & HERMAN, P. (1983). *Breaking the diet habit: A natural weight alternative*. Boston: Houghton Mifflin.

POLLIO, H. R., EDGERLY, J. W., & JORDAN, R. (1972). The comedian's world: Some tentative mappings. *Psychological Reports, 30*, 387–391.

POLYA, G. (1957). *How to solve it*. Garden City, NY: Doubleday/Anchor.

PREMACK, D. (1965). Reinforcement theory. *Nebraska Symposium on motivation, 1965* (pp. 123–188). Lincoln: University of Nebraska Press.

PREMTICE, N. M. (1972). The influence of live and symbolic modeling on promoting moral judgment of adolescent delinquents. *Journal of Abnormal Psychology, 80*(2), 157–161.

PRESIDENT'S COMMISSION ON MENTAL HEALTH. (1978). *Report*. Washington, DC: U.S. Government Printing Office.

PREVOST, F. (1975). An indication of sexual and aggressive similarities through humour appreciation. *Journal of Psychology, 91*, 283–288.

PRICE, J. S. (1968). The genetics of depressive disorder. In A. Coppen & A. Walk (Eds.), *Recent developments in affective disorders, British Journal of Psychiatry, Special Publication, 2*.

PROSSER, H. A. (1978). Social factors affecting the timing of the first child. In W. Miller & L. Neuman (Eds.), *The first child and family formation*. Chapel Hill: Carolina Population Center.

QUAY, H. C. (1965). Psychopathic personality as pathological stimulation-seeking. *American Journal of Psychiatry, 122*, 180–183.

RABKIN, S. W., MATHEWSON, F., & TATE, R. B. (1980). Chronobiological cardiac sudden death in men. *Journal of the American Medical Association, 244*, 1357–1358.

RACHMAN, S. (1978). *Fear and courage*. San Francisco: W. H. Freeman.

RADLOFF, L. (1975). Sex differences in depress: The effect of occupation and marital status. *Sex Roles, 1*, 249–265.

RAHE, R. H., & ARTHUR, R. J. (1978, March). Life change and illness studies: Past history and future directions. *Journal of Human Stress*.

RAHULA, W. (1969). *What the Buddha taught*. New York: Grove Press.

RANDI, J. (1975). *The magic of Uri Geller*. New York: Ballantine Books.

RAUDICH, A., & LOLORDO, V. M. (1979). Associative and nonassociative theories of the UCS preexposure phenomenon: Implications for Pavlovian conditioning. *Psychological Bulletin, 86*, 523–548.

RAZRAN, G. (1939). A quantitative study of meaning by conditioned salivary technique (semantic conditioning). *Science, 90*, 89–91.

REDMOND, D. E., HUANG, Y. H., BAULU, J., SNYDER, R. V., & MAAS, J. W. In R. A. Vigersky *Anorexia nervosa* (pp. 81–96). New York: Raven Press.

REES, W. D. (1971). The hallucinations of widowhood. *British Medical Journal, 4*, 37–41.

REES, W. D., & LUTKINS, S. G. (1967). Mentality of bereavement. *British Medical Journal, 4*, 13.

REICH, J., & ZAUTRA, A. (1981). Life events and personal causation: Some relationships with satisfaction and distress. *Journal of Personality and Social Psychology, 41*, 1002–1012.

REICHARD, S., LIVSON, F., & PETERSON, P. (1962). *Aging and personality: A study of eighty-seven older men*. New York: John Wiley.

REID, D. K. (1977). *Early identification of children with learning disabilities*. New York: Regional Access Project, Region 11, New York University.

RESCORLA, R. A., & LOLORDO, V. M. (1965). Inhibition of avoidance behavior. *Journal of Comparative and Physiological Psychology, 69,* 406–412.

REVUSKY, S., & GARCIA, J. (1970). Learned associations over long delays. In G. H. Bower (Ed.), *The psychology of learning and motivation: Advances in research in theory: Vol. 4.* New York: Academic Press.

RHEINGOLD, H. L., & COOK, K. U. (1975). The contents of boys' and girls' rooms as an index of parents' behavior. *Child Development, 46,* 459–463.

RIEGEL, K. F., & RIEGEL, R. M. (1972). Development, drop, and death. *Developmental Psychology, 9,* 306–319.

RIESMAN, D., GLAZER, N., & DENNEY, R. (1950). *The lonely crowd: A study of the changing American character.* New Haven: Yale University Press.

RING, K. (1980). *Life at death: A scientific investigation of the near-death experience.* New York: Coward-McCann.

RIOSEN, A. H. (1960). Effects of stimulus deprivation on the development and atrophy of the visual sensory system. *American Journal of Orthopsychiatry, 36,* 23–36.

RIZZO, R., & VINACKE, E. (1975). Self-actualization and the meaning of critical experience. *Journal of Humanistic Psychology, 15*(3), 19–30.

ROBERTS, D. C. S., PRICE, M. T. C., & FIBIGER, H. C. (1976). The dorsal tegmental noradrenergic projection: An analysis of its role in maze learning. *Journal of Comparative and Physiological Psychology, 90,* 363–372.

ROBINSON, B., & THURNER, M. (1979). Taking care of aged parents: A family cycle. *Transition Gerontologist, 19*(6).

ROCHE, R. (1971). *Roche Report: Drug Abuse in America.* Newark, NJ: R. Roche.

RODIN, J. (1978). On social psychology and obesity research: A final note. *Personality and Social Psychology Bulletin, 4*(1), 185–186.

RODIN, J., & LANGER, E. (1977). Long-term effects of a control-relevant intervention with the institutional aged. *Journal of Personality and Social Psychology. 35*(12), 897–902.

ROFFWARG, H., BOWE-ANDERS, C., TAUBER, E., & HERMAN, J. (1975). Dream imagery: The effect of long-term perceptual modification. *Sleep Research, 4,* 165.

ROGERS, C. R. (1951). *Client-centered therapy.* Boston: Houghton Mifflin.

ROGERS, C. R. (1959). A theory of therapy, personality and interpersonal relationships, as developed in the client-centered framework. In S. Koch (Ed.), *Psychology: A study of a science: Vol. 3* (pp. 184–256). New York: McGraw-Hill.

ROGERS, C. R. (1963). The actualizing tendency in relation to "motives" and to consciousness. *Nebraska symposium on motivation, 1963.* Lincoln: University of Nebraska Press.

ROGERS, C. (1970). *On becoming a person: A therapist's view of psychotherapy.* Boston: Houghton Mifflin.

ROGERS, C. R. (1972). Some social issues which concern me. *Journal of Humanistic Psychology,* Fall, 12(2), 45–60.

ROGERS, C. R. (1974). In retrospect: Forty-six years. *American Psychologist, 29,* 115–123.

ROGERS, T. B., KULPER, N. A., & KIRKER, W. S. (1977). Self-reference and the encoding of personal information. *Journal of Personality and Social Psychology, 35,* 677–688.

ROKEACH, M. (1960). *The open and closed mind.* New York: Basic Books.

ROKEACH, M. (1973). *The nature of human values.* New York: Free Press.

ROSCH, E. (1973). Natural categories. *Cognitive Psychology, 4,* 328–350.

ROSCH, E. (1975). Cognitive representation of semantic categories. *Journal of Experimental Psychology, 104,* 192–233.

ROSCH, E. (1978). Principles of categorization. In E. Rosch & B. L. Lloyd (Eds.), *Cognition and categorization.* Hillsdale, NJ: Lawrence Erlbaum.

ROSCH, E., & MERVIS, C. B. (1975). Family resemblances: Studies in the internal structure of categories. *Cognitive Psychology, 7,* 573–605.

ROSCH, E., MERVIS, C., GRAY, W., JOHNSON, D., & BOYES-BRAEM, P. (1976). Basic objects in natural categories. *Cognitive Psychology, 8,* 382–439.

ROSE, J. E., BRUGGE, J. F., ANDERSON, K. J., & HIND, J. E., Phase locked response to low frequency tunes in single auditory nerve fibers of the squirrel monkeys. *Journal of Neural Physiology 30,* 769.

ROSEKRANS, M. A., & HARTUP, W. W. (1967). Imitative influences of consistent and inconsistent response consequences to a model on aggressive behavior in children. *Journal of Personality and Social Psychology, 7,* 429–434.

ROSEN, B. C. (1956). The achievement syndrome: A psychocultural dimension of social stratification. *American Sociological Review, 21,* 203–211.

ROSEN, B. C. (1959). Race, ethnicity, and the achievement syndrome. *American Sociological Review, 24,* 47–60.

ROSEN, G. (1946). Mesmerism and surgery: A strange chapter in the history of anaesthesia. *Journal of the History of Medicine, 1,* 527–550.

ROSENHAN, D. L. (1973). On being sane in insane places. *Science, 179,* 250–258.

ROSENMAN, R. H. (1978). The role of the Type A behaviour pattern in ischaemic heart disease: Modification of its effects by Beta-blocking agents. *British Journal of Clinical Practice, 32*(Suppl. 1), 58–89.

ROSENMAN, R. H., & FRIEDMAN, M. (1980). The relationship of Type A behavior pattern to coronary heart disease. In H. Selye (Ed.), *Selye's guide to stress research: Vol. 1.* New York: Van Nostrand Reinhold.

ROSENTHAL, D. (Ed.). (1963). *The Genain quadruplets.* New York: Basic Books.

ROSENTHAL, D. (1970). *Genetic theory and abnormal behavior.* New York: McGraw-Hill.

ROSENTHAL, D., WENDER, P. H., KETY, S. S., WELNER, J., & SHULINGER, F. (1971). The adopted-away offspring of schizophrenics. *American Journal of Psychiatry, 128*(3), 307–311.

ROSENTHAL, R. (1966). *Experimenter effects in behavioral research.* New York: Appleton-Century-Crofts.

ROSOW, J. (1974). *Socialization to old age.* Berkeley: University of California Press.

ROSS, L. (1969). *Cue- and cognition-controlled eating among obese and nor-*

mal subjects. Unpublished doctoral dissertation, Columbia University.

ROSS, L. (1974). Effects of manipulating the salience of food upon consumption by obese and normal eaters. In S. Schachter & J. Rodin (Eds.), *Obese humans and rats.* Hillsdale, NJ: Erlbaum/Halsted.

ROSS, L. (1977). The intuitive psychologist and his shortcomings: Distortions in the attribution process. In L. Berkowitz (Ed.), *Advances in experimental social psychology: Vol. 10.* New York: Academic Press.

ROSS, L., AMABILE, T. M., & STEINMETZ, J. L. (1977). Social roles, social control, and biases in social-perception process. *Journal of Personality and Social Psychology, 35,* 485–494.

ROSS, L., GREENE, D., & HOUSE, P. (1977). The false consensus phenomenon: An attributional bias in self-perception and social perception processes. *Journal of Experimental Social Psychology, 13,* 279–301.

ROSSI, A. (1968). Transition to parenthood. *Journal of Marriage and the Family, 30,* 26–39.

ROSSMAN, I. (1977). Anatomic and body composition changes with aging. In C. Finch & L. Hayflick (Eds.), *Handbook of the biology of aging.* New York: Van Nostrand Reinhold.

ROTHWELL, N. J., & STOCK, M. J. (1979). Regulation of energy balance in two models of reversible obesity in the rat. *Journal of Comparative and Physiological Psychology, 93*(6), 1024–1034.

ROTTER, J. B. (1966). Generalized expectancies for internal versus external control of reinforcement. *Psychological Monographs, 81*(1 Whole No. 609).

ROUTENBERG, A. (1976). The reward system of the brain. *Scientific American, 239,* 154–164.

ROUTENBERG, A., & LINDY, J. (1965). Effects of the availability of rewarding septal and hypothalamic stimulation on bar pressing for food under conditions of deprivation. *Journal of Comparative and Physiological Psychology, 60,* 158–161.

RUBIN, D. C. (1977). Very long term memory for prose and verse. *Journal of Verbal Learning and Verbal Behavior, 16,* 611–621.

RUBIN, J. Z., PROVENZANO, F. J., & LURIA, Z. (1974). The eye of the beholder: Parents' view on sex of newborns. *American Journal of Orthopsychiatry, 44,* 512–519.

RUBIN, L. B. (1976). *Worlds of pain.* New York: Basic Books.

RUBIN, Z. (1980). *Children's friendships.* Cambridge: Harvard University Press.

RUSH, A. J., KHATAMI, M., & BECK, A. T. (1975). Cognitive and behavior therapy in chronic depression. *Behavior Therapy, 6,* 398–404.

RUSSEK, H. I., & ZOHMAN, B. L. (1958). Relative significance of heredity, diet and occupational stress in CHD of young adults. *American Journal of Medical Sciences, 235,* 266–275.

RUSSELL, B. (1929). *Marriage and morals.* New York: Liveright.

RUSSELL, B. (1979). In D. Tennov, *Love and limerance* (p. 56). New York: Stein & Day.

RUTTER, M. (1980). *Changing youth in a changing society: Patterns of adolescent development and disorder.* Cambridge: Harvard University Press.

SACKHEIM, H. A., GUR, R. C., & SAUCY, M. C. (1978). Emotions are expressed more intensely on the left side of the face. *Science, 202*(4366), 434–436.

SAFER, M. A., & LEVENTHAL, H. (1977). Ear differences in evaluating emotional tones of voice and verbal content. *Journal of Experimental Psychology, Human Perception and Performance, 3,* 75–82.

SAHLINS, M. (1972). *Stone Age economics.* Chicago: Aldine.

SALAPATEK, O., & KESSEN, W. (1966). Visual scanning of triangles by the human newborn. *Journal of Experimental Child Psychology, 3,* 111–122.

SALONTO, M. V., & HAMBURG, M. D. (1979). DDC-induced amnesia and norepinephrine: A correlated behavioral-biochemical analysis. *Psychopharmacology, 66,* 167–170.

SCANLON, J. V. (1975). *Self-reported health behavior and attitudes of youths 12–17 years, United States* (DHEW Publication No. HRA 75–1629). U.S. National Center for Health Statistics.

SCARR, S. (1981). *Race, social class, and*

individual differences in IQ. Hillsdale, NJ: Lawrence Erlbaum.

SCARR, S., & WEINBERG, R. A. (1978). Attitudes, interests, and IQ. *Human Nature, 1*(4), 29–37.

SCHACHTER, D. L. (1976). The hypnagogic state: A critical review of the literature. *Psychological Bulletin, 83,* 452–481.

SCHACHTER, S. (1959). *The psychology of affiliation: Experimental studies of the sources of gregariousness.* Stanford: Stanford University Press.

SCHACHTER, S. (1971). Some extraordinary facts about obese humans and rats. *American Psychologist, 26*(2), 129–144.

SCHACHTER, S., & RODIN, J. (1974). *Obese humans and rats.* Potomac, MD: Lawrence Erlbaum.

SCHACHTER, S., & SINGER, J. (1962). Cognitive, social, and physiological determinants of emotional state. *Psychological Review, 69,* 379–399.

SCHAFFER, H. R., & EMERSON, P. E. (1964). The development of social attachments in infancy. *Monographs of the Society for Research in Child Development, 29*(3, Serial No. 94).

SCHEFF, T. J. (1979). *Catharsis in healing, ritual, and drama.* Berkeley: University of California Press.

SCHILDKRAUT, J. J., SCHANBERG, S. M., BREESE, G. R., & KOPIN, I. J. (1967). Norepinephrine metabolism and drugs used in the affective disorders: A possible mechanism of action. *American Journal of Psychiatry, 124*(5), 600–608.

SCHMALLEGER, F. (1979). World of the career criminal. *Human Nature, 2*(3), 50–58.

SCHNEIDER, D. J., HASTORF, A. H., & ELLSWORTH, P. C. (1979). *Person perception* (2nd ed.). Reading, MA: Addison-Wesley.

SCHONFIELD, P., & ROBERTSON, B. A. (1966). Memory storage and aging. *Canadian Journal of Psychology, 20,* 228–236.

SCHREIBER, F. (1973). *Sybil.* New York: Warner Books.

SCHULSINGER, F. (1972). Psychopathy, heredity, and environment. *International Journal of Mental Health, 1,* 190–206.

SCHWARTZ, G. E., DAVIDSON,

R. J., & MAER, F. (1975). Right hemispheric lateralization for emotion in the human brain: Interactions with cognition. *Science, 190*(4211), 286–288.

SCIENTIFIC AMERICAN. (1979). *Evolution*. New York: Author.

SEARLE, L. V. (1949). The organization of heredity maze-brightness and maze-dullness. *Genetic Psychology Monographs, 39*, 279–325.

SEGAL, M. H., CAMPBELL, D. T., & HERSKOVITS, M. J. (1963). Cultural differences in the perception of geometric illusions. *Science, 139*, 769–771.

SELFE, L. (1977). Nadia, a case of extraordinary drawing ability in an autistic child. London: Academic Press.

SELIGMAN, M. E. P. (1970). On the generality of the law of learning. *Psychological Review, 77*, 406–418.

SELIGMAN, M. E. P. (1973). Fall into hopelessness. *Psychology Today, 7*(1), 43–48.

SELIGMAN, M. E. P. (1975). *Helplessness: On depression, development and death*. San Francisco: W. H. Freeman.

SELIGMAN, M. E. P., & HAGER, J. (1972). *Biological boundaries of learning*. New York: Appleton-Century-Crofts.

SELMAN, R. (1980). *The growth of interpersonal understanding*. New York: Academic Press.

SELMAN, R., & JAQUETTE, D. (1977). Stability and oscillation in interpersonal awareness: A clinical developmental approach. In H. Howe & C. Keasey (Eds.), *Nebraska Symposium on Motivation, 25*. Lincoln: University of Nebraska Press.

SELMANOWITZ, V. J., LORER, W., & ORENTREICH, N. (1970). Multiple noduli, cutanei and urinary tract abnormalities: A possible significant association. *Cancer, 26*, 1256–1260.

SELYE, H. (1956). *The stress of life*. New York: McGraw-Hill.

SELYE, H. (1978). They all looked sick to me. *Human Nature, 1*(2) 58–63.

SHAH, I. (1970). *Tales of the dervishes*. New York: E. P. Dutton.

SHAH, I. (1971). *The pleasantries of the incredible Mulla Nasrudin*. New York: E. P. Dutton.

SHAH, I. (1972). *The exploits of the in-*

comparable *Mulla Nasrudin*. New York: E. P. Dutton.

SHAH, I. (1982). *Seeker after truth*. New York: Harper & Row,

SHANAS, E. (1979). Social myth as hypothesis: The case of the family relations and old people. *The Gerontologist, 19*(1), 3–9.

SHANAS, E., TOWNSEND, D., WEDDERBURN, D., FRIIS, H., MILHOJ, P., & STENOUWER, J. (1968). *Older people in three industrial societies*. New York: Atherton Press.

SHANON, B. (1979). Yesterday, today and tomorrow. *Acta Psychologica, 43*, 469–476.

SHATAN, C. (1978). Stress disorders among Vietnam veterans: The emotional context of combat continues. In C. R. Figley (Ed.), *Stress disorders among Vietnam veterans*. New York: Brunner/Mazel.

SHEEHY, G. (1976). *Passages: Predictable crises of adult life*. New York: E. P. Dutton.

SHEFFIELD, F. D., & ROBY, T. B. (1950). Reward value of a nonnutritive sweet taste. *Journal of Comparative and Physiological Psychology, 43*, 471–481.

SHEFFIELD, F. D., WULFF, J. J., & BACKER, R. (1951). Reward value of copulation without sex drive reduction. *Journal of Comparative and Physiological Psychology, 44*, 3–8.

SHEPARD, R. N. (1967). Recognition memory for words, sentences, and pictures. *Journal of Verbal Learning and Verbal Behavior, 6*, 156–163.

SHEPARD, R. N., & SHEENAN, M. M. (1963). Immediate recall of numbers containing a familiar prefix or postfix. *Perceptual and Motor Skills, 21*, 263–273.

SHEPHER, J. (1978). Reflections on the origins of the human pair-bond. In *Journal of Social and Biological Structures, 1*(3), 253–263. New York: Academic Press.

SHERIF, M., HARVEY, O. J., WHITE, B. J., HOOD, W., & SHERIF, C. (1961). *Intergroup conflict and cooperation: The robbers cave experiment*. Norman: University of Oklahoma Institute of Intergroup Relations.

SHERMAN, P. W. (1979). *Evolutionary biology and human social behavior*. North Scituate, MA: Duxbury Press.

SHIRLEY, M. N. (1933). The first two

years. *Institute of Child Welfare Monograph, 7*. Minneapolis: University of Minnesota Press.

SHOCK, N. W. (1977). System integration. In C. Finch & L. Hayflick (Eds.), *Handbook of the biology of aging*. New York: Van Nostrand.

SHRAUGER, J. S., & SILVERMAN, R. E. (1971). The relationship of religious background and participation to locus of control. *Journal for the Scientific Study of Religion, 10*, 11–16.

SHULINGER, F. (1977). Psychopathy and environment. In S. Mednick & K. O. Christiansen (Eds.), *Biosocial bases of criminal behavior*. New York: Gardner Press.

SIEGEL, R. (1981). Accounting for "afterlife experiences." *Psychology Today, 15*, 64–75.

SIEGEL, R. K. (1980). The psychology of life after death. *American Psychologist, 35*, 911–931.

SIEGEL, S. (1976). Morphine analgesic tolerance: Its situational specificity supports a pavlovian conditioning model. *Science, 193*, 323–325.

SIMON, W., BERGER, A. S., & GAGNON, J. S. (1972). Beyond anxiety and fantasy: The coital experiences of college youth. *Journal of Youth and Adolescence, 1*, 203–222.

SINGER, B., & LUBORSKY, L. (1975). Comparative studies of psychotherapies: Is it true that "everyone has won and all must have prizes?" *Archives of General Psychiatry, 32*(8), 995–1008.

SINGER, D. G. (1968). Aggression, arousal, hostile humor, catharsis. [Monograph Suppl.]. *Journal of Personality and Social Psychology, 8*, 1–14.

SINGER, J. L. (1966). *Daydreaming: An introduction to the experimental study of inner experience*. New York: Random House.

SINGER, J. L. (1976). *The inner world of daydreaming*. New York: Harper & Row.

SINGER, J. L. (1984). *The human personality*. New York: Harcourt Brace Jovanovich.

SINGER, J. L., & SINGER, D. G. (1981). *Television, imagination and aggression*. Hillsdale, NJ: Erlbaum.

SINGER, S., & HILGARD, H. (1978). *The biology of people*. San Francisco: W. H. Freeman.

SINGH, S. (1978). Motive to avoid success. *Asian Journal of Psychology and Education, 3*(1), 39–45.

SKEELS, H. M. (1966). Adult status of children with contrasting early life experience. *Monographs of the Society for Research in Child Development, 31*(3), 1–65.

SKEELS, H. M., & DYE, H. B. (1939). A study of the effects of differential stimulation of mentally retarded children. *Proceedings of the American Association on Mental Deficiency, 44,* 114–136.

SKEELS, H. M., & HAMS, I. (1948). Children with inferior social histories; their mental development in adoptive homes. *Journal of Genetic Psychology. 72,* 283–294.

SKINNER, B. F. (1938). *The behavior of organisms.* New York: Appleton-Century-Crofts.

SKINNER, B. F. (1972). *Cumulative record: A collection of papers* (3rd ed.). New York: Appleton-Century-Crofts.

SKINNER, B. F. (1981). Selection by consequences. *Science, 213,* 501–504.

SKINNER, B. F. (1982). *Notebooks.* R. Epstein (Ed.). Englewood Cliffs, NJ: Prentice-Hall.

SLATER, E., & COWIE, V. (1971). *The genetics of mental disorders.* London: Oxford University Press.

SLOBIN, D. I. (1970). Universals of grammatical development in children. In G. B. Flores d'Arcais & W. J. M. Levelt (Eds.), *Advances in psycholinguistics.* Amsterdam: North-Holland Publishing.

SMILANSKY, B. (1974). Paper presented at the meeting of the American Educational Research Association, Chicago.

SMITH, E. E., & MEDIN, D. L. (1981). *Categories and concepts.* Cambridge: Harvard University Press.

SMITH, M., COLLIGAN, M., HORNING, R. W., & HURREL, J. (1978). *Occupational comparison of stress-related disease incidence.* Cincinnati: National Institute for Occupational Safety and Health.

SMITH, M. L., GLASS, G. V., & MILLER, T. I. (1980). *Benefits of psychotherapy.* Baltimore: Johns Hopkins University Press.

SMITH, R. E. (1970). Changes in locus of control as a function of life crisis regulation. *Journal of Abnormal Psychology, 75,* 329–332.

SMITH, R. L. (1973). The ascending fiber projection from the principal sensory trigeminal nucleus in the rat. *Journal of Comparative Neurology, 148,* 423–446.

SMITH, W. A. (1970). *Gout and the gouty.* San Antonio, TX: Naylor.

SMITH, W. F. (1976). *The effects of social and monetary rewards on intrinsic motivation.* Unpublished doctoral dissertation, Cornell University, Ithaca, NY.

SNYDER, M. (1979). Self-monitoring processes. In L. Berkowitz (Ed.), *Advances in experimental social psychology: Vol. 12.* New York: Academic Press.

SNYDER, S. H. (1980). *Biological aspects of mental disorder.* New York: Oxford University Press.

SNYDER, S. H. (1980a). The interaction of psychoplasmacology and psychomalysis in the borderline patient. *Psychiatric Quarterly, 52*(4), 240–250.

SNYDER, S. H. (1980b). Brain peptides and neurotransmitters. *Science, 209,* 976–983.

SOLOMON, G. F., & AMKRAUT, A. A. (1981). Psychoneuroendocrinological effects on the immune response. *Annual Review of Microbiology, 35,* 155–184.

SOLOMON, R. L. (1980). The opponent-process theory of acquired motivation: The costs of pleasure and the benefits of pain. *American Psychologist, 35,* 691–712.

SOLOMON, R. L., & CORBIT, J. D. (1973). An opponent-process theory of motivation: I. Cigarette addiction. *Journal of Abnormal Psychology, 81,* 158–171.

SOLOMON, R. L., & CORBIT, J. D. (1974). An opponent-process theory of motivation: II. Temporal dynamics of affect. *Psychological Review, 81,* 119–145.

SPANIER, G. B., & GLICK, P. C. (1981). Martial instability in the U.S.: Some correlates and recent changes. *Family Relations, 31,* 329–338.

SPEARMAN, C. (1927). *The abilities of man.* New York: Macmillan.

SPEISMAN, J. C., LAZARUS, R. S., DAVIDSON, L., & MORDKOFF, A. M. (1964). Experimental analysis of a film used as a threatening stimulus. *Journal of Consulting Psychology, 28*(1), 23–33.

SPENCER, H. (1860). The physiology of laughter. *Macmillan's Magazine,* 395–402.

SPERRY, R. (1982). Some effects of disconnecting the cerebral hemispheres. *Science, 217,* 1223–1226, 1250.

SPERRY, R. W. (1952). Neurology and the mind-brain problem. *American Scientist, 40,* 291–312.

SPITZER, R. L., SKODOL, A. E., GIBBON, M., & WILLIAMS, J. B. (1980). *Diagnostic and statistical manual of mental disorders* (3rd ed.) (DSM-III). Washington, DC: American Psychiatric Association.

SPITZER, R. C., SKODOL, A. E., GIBBON, M., & WILLIAMS, J. B. W. (1981). *DSM-III Casebook.* (3rd ed.). Washington, DC: American Psychiatric Association.

SPRINGER, S., & DEUTSCH, G. (1984). *Left brain, right brain.* (2nd ed.). San Francisco: W. H. Freeman.

SQUIRE, L. R. (1977). ECH and memory loss. *American Journal of Psychiatry, 134,* 997–1001.

SQUIRE, L. R., & SLATER, P. C. (1978). Bilateral and unilateral ECH: Effects on verbal and nonverbal memory. *American Journal of Psychiatry, 135,* 1316–1320.

STANDING, L., CONEZIO, J., & HABER, R. N. (1970). Perception and memory for pictures: Single-trial learning of 2560 visual stimuli. *Psychonomic Science, 19,* 73–74.

STEFFENS, A. B. (1970). Plasma insulin content in relation to blood glucose level and meal pattern in the normal and hypothalamic hyperphagic rat. *Physiology and Behavior, 5,* 147–151.

STEFFENS, A. B., MOGENSON, G. J., & STEVENSON, J. A. F. (1972). Blood glucose, insulin, and free fatty acids after stimulation and lesions of the hypothalamus. *American Journal of Physiology, 222,* 1446–1452.

STEIGLEDER, M. K., WEISS, R. F.,

BALLING, S. S., WENNINGER, V. L., & LOMBARDO, J. P. (1980). Drivelike motivational properties of competitive behavior. *Journal of Personality and Social Psychology, 38,* 93–104.

STEIGLEDER, M. K., WEISS, R. F., CRAMER, R. E., & FEINBERG, R. A. (1978). The motivating and reinforcing functions of competitive behavior. *Journal of Personality and Social Psychology, 36,* 1291–1301.

STEIN, Z., SUSSER, M., SAENGER, G., & MAROLLA, F. (1972). Nutrition and mental performance. *Science, 178,* 703–713.

STERLING-SMITH, R. S. (1976, April). *A special study of drivers most responsible in fatal accidents* [Summary for management report]. (Contract No. DOT–HS–310–3–595).

STERMAN, M. B. (1978). Effects of sensorimotor EEG feedback training on sleep and clinical manifestations of epilepsy. In J. Beatty & H. Legewie (Eds.), *Biofeedback and behavior.* New York: Plenum.

STEVENS, S. S. (1956). The direct estimation of sensory magnitudes-loudness. *American Journal of Psychology, 69,* 1–25.

STEVENS, S. S. (1957). On the psychophysical law. *Psychological Review, 64,* 153–181.

STEVENS, S. S. (1961). The psychophysics of sensory functions. In W. A. Rosenblith (Ed.), *Sensory communication.* (pp. 1–33). Cambridge, MA: MIT Press.

STEVENS, S. S., WARSHOFSKY, F., & STAFF (1965). *Sound and hearing.* New York: Time-Life Books. (Original work published 1906).

STEVENSON, H. W., FRIEDRICHS, A. G., & SIMPSON, W. E. (1970). Interrelations and correlates over time in children's learning. *Child Development, 41,* 625–637.

STOKOLS, D. (1972). On the distinction between density and crowding: Some implications for future research. *Psychological Review, 79,* 275–277.

STRATTON, G. M. (1896). Some preliminary experiments on vision without inversion of the retinal image. *Psychological Review, 3,* 611–617.

STREHLER, B. L. (1977). *Time, cells and aging* (2nd ed.). New York: Academic Press.

STREIB, G. F., & SCHNEIDER, C. S. (1971). *Retirement in American society: Impact and process.* Ithaca, NY: Cornell University Press.

STREISSGUTH, A. P. (1978). Fetal alcohol syndrome: An epidemiological perspective. *American Journal of Epidemiology, 107*(6), 467–478.

STRICKLAND, J. F. (1959). The effect of motivational arousal on humor preferences. *Journal of Abnormal and Social Psychology, 59,* 278–281.

STRUBLE, J. H., & STEFFENS, A. B. (1975). Rapid insulin release after ingestion of a meal in the unanesthetized rat. *American Journal of Physiology, 229,* 1019–1022.

SULLOWAY, F. (1979). *Freud, biologist of the mind: Beyond the psychoanalytic method.* New York: Basic Books.

SUNDSTRUM, E. (1975). An experimental study of crowding: Effects of room size, intrusion, and goal blocking on nonverbal behavior, self-disclosure, and self-reported stress. *Journal of Personality and Social Psychology, 32,* 645–654.

SWARBRICK, L., & WHITFIELD, I. C. (1972). Auditory cortical units selectively responsive to stimulus "shape." *Journal of Physiology* (London), *224,* 68–69.

SYME, S. L. (1984). *Friends can be good medicine* [Tape]. ISHK.

SYMONS, D. (1978). *The evolution of human sexuality.* New York: Oxford University Press.

SYMONS, D. (1980). Precis of the evolution of human sexuality. *Behavioral and Brain Sciences, 3,* 171–214.

SZASZ, T. (1961). *The myth of mental illness.* New York: Harper & Row.

TAGNEY, J. (1972). Rearing in an enriched or isolated environment: Sleep patterns in the rat. *Sleep Research, 1,* 121.

TALBERT, G. B. (1977). The aging of the reproductive system. in C. Finch & L. Hayflick (Eds.), *Handbook of the biology of aging.* New York: Van Nostrand Reinhold.

TANNER, J. M. (1962). *Growth at adolescence* (2nd ed.). Oxford: Blackwell Scientific Publications.

TANNER, J. M. (1970). Physical growth. In P. H. Mussen (Ed.), *Carmichael's manual of child psychology: Vol. 1.* New York: John Wiley.

TARG, F., & PUTHOFF, H. (1977). *Mind reach: Scientists look at psychic ability.* New York: Delacorte Press.

TART, C. (1977). *PSI: Scientific studies of the psychic realm.* New York: E. P. Dutton.

TART, C. T. (1971). *On being stoned.* Palo Alto: Science & Behavior Books.

TART, C., PUTHOFF, H. E., & TARG, R., (Eds.). (1979). Mind at large. *Institute of Electrical and Electronics Engineers Symposia on the Nature of Extra-sensory Perception.* New York: Praeger.

TASKIN, D. P., CALVARESE, B. M., SIMMONS, M. S., & SHAPIRO, B. J. (1978). *Respiratory status of 74 habitual marijuana smokers.* Presented at the annual meeting of the American Thoracic Society, Boston.

TAVRIS, C. (1982). Anger defused. *Psychology Today, 16,* 25–35.

TAYLOR, F. W. (1967). *Principles of scientific management.* New York: W. W. Norton. (Original work published 1911)

TAYLOR, S. (1970). Aggressive behavior as a function of approval motivation and physical attack. *Psychonomic Science, 18,* 195–196.

TAYLOR, S. P., GAMMON, C. B., & CAPASSO, D. R. (1976). Aggression as a function of the interaction of alcohol and threat. *Journal of Personality and Social Psychology, 34*(5), 938–941.

TAYLOR, S. P., VARDARIS, R. M., RAWITCH, A. B., GAMMON, C. B., CRANSTON, J. W., & LUBETKIN, A. I. (1976). The effects of alcohol and delta-9-tetra hydrocannabinal on human physical aggression. *Aggressive Behavior, 2,* 153–161.

TEITELBAUM, P. (1955). Sensory control of hypothalamic hyperphagia. *Journal of Comparative and Physiological Psychology, 48,* 156–163.

TEITELBAUM, P. (1957). Random and food-directed activity in hyperphagic and normal rats. *Journal of Comparative and Physiological Psychology, 50,* 486–490.

TEITELBAUM, P., & EPSTEIN, A. N.

(1962). The lateral hypothalamic syndrome. *Psychological Review, 69,* 74–90.

TENNOV, D. (1979). *Love and limerence.* New York: Stein & Day.

TERKEL, J., & ROSENBLATT, J. S. (1972). Humoral factors underlying maternal behavior of parturition: Cross transfusion between freely moving rats. *Journal of Comparative and Physiological Psychology, 80,* 365–371, 309.

TERKEL, S. (1975). *Working.* New York: Avon Books.

TERMAN, L. (1916). *The measurement of intelligence.* Boston: Houghton Mifflin.

TERMAN, L. M., & MERRILL, M. (1937). *Measuring intelligence.* Cambridge, MA: Riverside.

TEYLER, T. (1978). *A primer of psychobiology.* San Francisco: W. H. Freeman.

THIGPEN, C. H., & CLECKLEY, H. M. (1957). *The three faces of Eve.* New York: McGraw-Hill.

THOMAS, L. (1982). *The youngest science.* New York: Viking Press.

THOMPSON, R. F. (1967). *Foundations of physiological psychology.* New York: Harper & Row.

THOMPSON, R. F. (1975). *Introduction to physiological psychology.* New York: Harper & Row.

THORNDIKE, E. L. (1911). *Animal intelligence.* New York: Macmillan.

THORNDIKE, R. L. (1954). The psychological value systems of psychologists. *American Psychologist, 9,* 787–789.

THURSTONE, L. L. (1938). Primary mental abilities. *Psychometrika Monographs, 1.*

TILLICH, P. (1957). *Dynamics of faith.* New York: Harper & Row.

TIMIRAS, P. S. (1972). *Development physiology and aging.* New York: Macmillan.

TINBERGEN, N. (1968, June). On war and peace in animals and man. *Science, 28.*

TINKELBERG, J. R., & DARLEY, C. F. (1975). Psychological and cognitive effects of cannabis. In P. H. Cornell & N. Dorn (Eds.), *Cannabis and man.* New York: Churchill Livingstone.

TOCH, H. (1969). *Violent men.* Chi-

cago: Aldine.

TOLMAN, E. C. & HONZIK, C. H. (1930). "Insight" in rats. *University of California Publications in Psychology, 4,* 215–232.

TOMKINS, S. (1984). Affect theory. In K. Scherer & P. Ekman (Eds.), *Approaches to emotion.* Hillsdale, NJ: Lawrence Erlbaum.

TOMKINS, S. S. (1962). *Affect, imagery, consciousness: Vol. 1. The Positive Affects.* New York: Springer-Verlag.

TOMKINS, S. S. (1963). *Affect, imagery, consciousness: Vol. 2. The Negative Affects.* New York: Springer-Verlag.

TOMKINS, S. S. (1975). The phantasy behind the face. *Journal of Personality Assessment, 39,* 551–562.

TOMKINS, S. S. (1979). Script theory: Differential magnification of affects. In H. E. Howe & R. A. Dienstbier (Eds.), *Nebraska Symposium on Motivation, 1978, 26.* Lincoln: University of Nebraska Press.

TOWNSEND, P. (1968). Emergence of the four-generation family in industrial society. In B. L. Neugarten (Ed.), *Middle age and aging.* Chicago: Chicago University Press.

TREPATHI, R. R., & AGRAVAL, A. (1978). The achievement motive in leaders and nonleaders: A role analysis. *Psychologies: An International Journal of Psychology in the Orient, 21(27),* 97–103.

TRESEMER, D. (1974, March). Fear of success: Popular but unproven. *Psychology Today,* 82–84.

TREVARTHEN, W. R. (1981). Maternal touch at first contact with the newborn infant. *Development Psychobiology, 14(6),* 549–558.

TRIPLETT, N. (1897). The dynamogenic factors in pace making and competition. *American Journal of Psychology, 9,* 507–533.

TRIVERS, R. L. (1971). The evolution of reciprocal altruism. *Quarterly Review of Biology, 46,* 35–57.

TRYON, R. C. (1940). Genetic differences in maze learning in rats. *Yearbook of the National Society for Studies in Education, 39,* 111–119.

TULVING, E. (1972). Episodic and semantic memory. In E. Tulving & W. Donaldson (Eds.), *Organization and memory.* New York: Academic Press.

TURNBULL, C. (1961). Some observations regarding the experiences and behavior of the Bambuti pygmies. *American Journal of Psychology, 74,* 304–308.

TURVEY, M. T., & SHAW, R. (1979). The primacy of perceiving: An ecological reformulation for understanding memory. In G. Nillson (Ed.), *Perspectives on memory research essays in honor of Uppsala University's 500th anniversary.* Hillsdale, NJ: Lawrence Erlbaum.

TVERSKY, A. (1977). Features of similarity. *Psychological Review, 84,* 327–352.

TVERSKY, A., & GATI, I. (1978). Studies of similarity. In E. Rosch & B. B. Lloyd (Eds.), *Cognition and categorization.* Hillsdale, NJ: Lawrence Erlbaum.

TVERSKY, A., & KAHNEMAN, D. (1973). Availability: A heuristic for judging frequency and possibility. *Cognitive Psychology, 5,* 207–232.

TVERSKY, A., & KAHNEMAN, D. (1981). The framing of decisions and the psychology of choice. *Science, 211,* 453–458.

ULLMAN, M., KRIPPNER, S., & VAUGHN, A. (1973). *Dream telepathy.* New York: Macmillan.

ULLMAN, S. (1980). Against direct perception. *The Behavioral and Brain Sciences, 3,* 373–381.

ULVUND, S. E. (1980). Cognition and motivation in early infancy: An interactionistic approach. *Human Development, 23,* 17–32.

U.S., BUREAU OF THE CENSUS. (1975, March). *Current population reports. Marital status and living arrangements* (Series P-20, No. 287). Washington, DC: U.S. Government Printing Office.

U.S. DEPARTMENT OF HEALTH, EDUCATION, AND WELFARE. (1971). *National Health Survey: Roche Report, 1(9),* 2.

U.S. PUBLIC HEALTH SERVICE. (1974). Vital statistics of the United States.

VAILLANT, G. (1977). *Adaptation to life.* Boston: Little, Brown.

VAILLANT, G., & MILOFSKY, E. (1978). Natural history of male psychological health: IX. Empirical evidence for Erikson's model of the life cycle. *American Journal of Psychiatry*, 137(11).

VALINS, S. (1966). Cognitive effects of false heart-rate feedback. *Journal of Personality and Social Psychology, 4*, 400–408.

VANDELL, D., WILSON, K., & BUCHANAN, N. (1980). Peer interaction in the first year of life: An examination of its structure, content, and sensitivity to toys. *Child Development, 41*, 481–488.

VIERLING, J. S., & ROCK, J. (1967). Variations in olfactory sensitivity to Exaltolide during the menstrual cycle. *Journal of Applied Physiology, 22*, 311–315.

VOGEL, G. W. (1978). An alternative view of the biology of dreaming. *American Journal of Psychiatry, 135*(12), 1531–1535.

VON BÉKÉSY, G. (1949). *Experiments in hearing.* New York: McGraw-Hill.

WALDROP, M. J., & HALVERSON, C. F., JR. (1975). Intensive and extensive peer behavior: Longitudinal and cross-sectional analysis. *Child Development, 46*, 19–26.

WALLERSTEIN, J. S., & KELLY, J. B. (1980). *Surviving the breakup: How children and parents cope with divorce.* New York: Basic Books.

WADDINGTON, C. H. (1957). *The strategy of the genes.* New York: Macmillan.

WALSTER, E., ARONSON, V., ABRAHAMS, D., & ROTTMANN, L. (1966). The importance of physical attractiveness in dating behavior. *Journal of Personality and Social Psychology, 4*, 508–516.

WALSTER, E., WALSTER, G. W., & TRAUPMANN, J. (1978). Equity and premarital sex. *Journal of Personality and Social Psychology, 37*, 82–92.

WARDEN, C. J. (1931). *Animal motivation: Experimental studies on the albino rat.* New York: Columbia University Press.

WARREN, R. M., & WARREN, R. P. (1970). Auditory illusions and confusions. *Scientific American, 223*, 30–36.

WASHBURN, S. (1960). Tools and human evolution. *Scientific American, 203*(3), 67–73.

WASHBURN, S. (1961). *Social life of early man.* Chicago: Aldine.

WASHBURN, S. L. (1978). The evolution of man. In *Evolution.* San Francisco: Scientific American.

WASON, P. C., & JOHNSON-LAIRD, P. N. (1972). *Psychology of reasoning: Structure and content.* Cambridge, MA: Harvard University Press.

WATERS, E., WIPPMAN, J., & SROUFE, L. A. (1979). Attachment, positive affect and competence in the peer group: Two studies in construct validation. *Child Development, 50*(3), 821–830.

WATSON, J. B. (1914). *Behavior, an introduction to comparative psychology.* New York: Henry Holt.

WATSON, J. B. (1925). *Behaviorism.* New York: W. W. Norton.

WATSON, J. B., & RAYNOR, R. (1920). Conditioned emotional reactions. *Journal of Experimental Psychology, 3*, 1–14.

WEBER, E. H. (1834). *De pulsu, resorptione, auditu et tactu: Annotationes anatomical et physiological.* Leipzig: Koehler.

WEBER, M. (1930). *The Protestant ethic and the spirit of capitalism* (T. Parsons, Trans.). New York: Charles Scribner's Sons. (Original work published 1904)

WEIL, A. (1979). *The natural mind.* Boston: Houghton Mifflin.

WEINER, A., GERBER, I., BATTIN, J., & ARLON, A. (1975). The process and phenomenology of bereavement. In B. Schoenberg et al., (Eds.), *Bereavement: Its psycho-social aspects.* New York: Columbia University Press.

WEINER, H. (1977). *Psychobiology and human disease.* New York: Elsevier.

WEINRAUB, M., & LEWIS, M. (1979). *Infant attachment, play behavior and sex of child and sex of parent differences.* Unpublished manuscript.

WEISMAN, A. D., & KASTENBAUM, R. (1968). The psychological autopsy: A study of the terminal phase of life [Monograph]. *Community Mental Health Journal.* New York: Behavioral Publications.

WEISS, A. D. (1959). Sensory functions. In J. E. Birren (Ed.), *Handbook of aging and the individual* (pp. 503–542). Chicago: University of Chicago Press.

WEISS, J. M. (1968). Effects of coping response on stress. *Journal of Comparative and Physiological Psychology, 65*, 251–260.

WEISS, R. S. (1976). The emotional impact of marital separation. *Journal of Social Issues, 32*, 135–145.

WEISZ, P. B. (1971). *The science of biology.* New York: McGraw-Hill.

WEIZENHOFFER, A. M., & HILGARD, E. R. (1959). *Stanford hypnotic susceptibility scale, forms A and B.* Palo Alto, CA: Consulting Psychologists Press.

WESTON, P. J., & MEDNICK, M. T. (1970). Race, social class and the motive to avoid success in women. *Journal of Cross-Cultural Psychology, 1*, 284–291.

WHITE, R. W. (1952). *Lives in Progress.* New York: Dryden Press.

WHITE, R. W. (1959). Motivation reconsidered: The concept of competence. *Psychological Review, 66*, 297–333.

WHITE, R. W. (1960). Competence and the psychosexual stages of development. *Nebraska Symposium on Motivation, 1960* (pp. 97–141). Lincoln: University of Nebraska Press.

WHITE, R. W. (1961). *Lives in progress.* New York: Holt, Rinehart & Winston.

WHITE, S. H. (1965). Evidence for a hierarchical arrangement of learning processes. In L. P. Lipsitt & C. C. Spiker (Eds.), *Advances in child development and behavior: Vol. 2.* New York: Academic Press.

WHITE, S. H. (1966). Age differences in reaction to stimulus variation. In O. J. Harvey (Ed.), *Experience structure and adaptability.* New York: Springer-Verlag.

WHITE, S. H., & WHITE, B. N. (1980). *Childhood pathways of discovery.* New York: Harper & Row.

WHITE, W. (1980). Street life. *Natural History, 89*, 63–69.

WHITFIELD, I. C. (1976). *The auditory pathway.* London: Arnold.

WHITING, J. W. M., WHITING, B. B., AND LONGABAUGH, R. (1974). *Children of six cultures: A psycho-cultural analysis.* Cambridge: Harvard University Press.

WHORF, B. (1942). *Language, thought, and reality: Selected writings of Benja-*

min Lee Whorf (J. B. Caroll Ed.). New York: John Wiley.

WHYTE, W. H. (1956). *The organization man.* New York: Simon & Shuster.

WICKELGREN, W. A. (1977a). *Learning and memory.* Englewood Cliffs, NJ: Prentice-Hall.

WICKELGREN, W. A. (1977b). Speed-accuracy tradeoff and information processing dynamics. *Acta Psychologica, 41,* 67–85.

WICKELGREN, W. (1979). *Cognitive psychology.* Englewood Cliffs, NJ: Prentice-Hall.

WICKER, A. W. (1969). Attitudes versus actions: The relationship of verbal and overt behavioral responses to attitude objects. *Journal of Social Issues, 25,* 41–78.

WILDER, D. A., & ALLEN, V. L. (1973). Veridical dissent, erroneous dissent, and conformity. Unpublished master's thesis.

WILLEMSEN, E. (1979). *Understanding infancy.* San Francisco: W. H. Freeman.

WILLERMAN, L. (1979). *The psychology of individual and group differences.* San Francisco: W. H. Freeman.

WILSON, C. P. (1979). *Jokes: Form, content, use and function.* London: Academic Press.

WILSON, E. O. (1975). *Sociobiology.* Cambridge: Harvard University Press.

WINNICK, M. (1979). Starvation studies. *Human Nature Manuscript Series, 4.*

WINNICK, M., MEYER, K. K., & HARRIS, R. C. (1975). Malnutrition and environmental enrichment by early adoption. *Science, 190,* 1173–1175.

WINOGRAD, T. (1980, February). Face savings memory. *Psychology Today* p. 81.

WINOKUR, G. (1981). *Depression: The facts.* New York: Oxford University Press.

WINOKUR, G., & CLAYTON, P. J. (1967). Family history studies: I. Two types of affective disorders separated according to genetic and clinical factors. In J. Wordin (Ed.), *Recent advances in biological psychiatry; Vol. 9.* New York: Plenum.

WINOKUR, G., CLAYTON, P. J., & REICH, T. (1969). *Manic-depressive illness.* St. Louis: C. V. Mosby.

WISDOM, C. S. (1977). A methodology for studying noninstitutionalized psychopaths. *Journal of Consulting and Clinical Psychology, 45,* 674–683.

WISHNER, J. (1960). Reanalysis of "Impressions of personality." *Psychological Review, 67,* 96–112.

WITELSON, S. F. (1976). Sex and the single hemisphere: Specialization of the right hemisphere for spatial processing. *Science, 193,* 425–427.

WOLFE, J. B. (1936). Effectiveness of token-rewards for chimpanzees. *Comparative Psychology Monograph, 12,* 5.

WOLMAN, B. (Ed.). (1982). *Handbook of developmental psychology.* Englewood Cliffs, NJ: Prentice-Hall.

WOLPE, J. (1958). *Psychotherapy by reciprocal inhibition.* Stanford: Stanford University Press.

WOLPE, J. (1981). The experimental model and treatment of neurotic depression. *Behavior Research and Therapy, 17*(6), 555–565.

WORKS, E. (1961). The prejudice-interaction hypothesis from the point of view of the Negro minority group. *American Journal of Sociology, 67,* 47–52.

WRIGHT, J. C., & VLIETSTRA, A. G. (1975). The development of selective attention: From perceptual exploration to logical search. In H. W. Reese (Ed.), *Advances in child development and behavior: Vol. 10.* New York: Academic Press.

WYNNE, L. C., CROMWELL, R. L., & MATTYSSE, S. (Eds.). (1978). *The nature of schizophrenia: New approaches to research and treatment.* New York: John Wiley.

YAMAMOTO, J., OKONOGI, K., IWASAKI, T., & YOSHIMURA, S. (1969). Mourning in Japan. *American Journal of Psychiatry, 125*(12), 1660–1665.

YARROW, L. J., RUBINSTEIN, J. L., PEDERSEN, F. A., & JANKOWSKI, J. J. (1972). Dimensions of early stimulation and their differential effects on infant development. *Merrill-Palmer Quarterly, 18,* 205–218.

YERKES, R. M., & DODSON, J. P. (1908). The relation of strength of stimulus to rapidity of habit-formation. *Journal of Comparative*

Neurological Psychology, 18, 459–482.

YOUNG, M., BENJAMIN, B., & WALLIS, C. (1963). Mentality of widows. *Lancet, 2,* 454.

ZAJONC, R. B. (1980). Feeling and thinking: Preferences need no inferences. *American Psychologist, 35*(2), 151–175.

ZAJONC, R. B., & MARKUS, G. B. (1975). Birth order and intellectual development. *Psychological Review, 82,* 74–88.

ZAJONC, R. B., MARKUS, H., & MARKUS, G. P. (1979). The birth order puzzle. *Journal of Personality and Social Psychology, 37,* 1325–1341.

ZEEMAN, E. C. (1976, April). Catastrophe theory, *Scientific American,* p. 67.

ZEIGLER, H. P., & KARTEN, H. J. (1973). Brain mechanisms and feeding behavior in the pigeon (Columbia Livia). II. Analysis of feeding behavior deficits after lesions of quinto-frontal structures. *Journal of Comparative Neurology, 152,* 83–101.

ZEIGLER, H. P., & KARTEN, H. J. (1974). Central trigeminal structures and the lateral hypothalamic syndrome in the rat. *Science, 186,* 636–638.

ZERBING, R, & RUDIN, E. (1968). Endogene Psychosen. In P. Becker (Ed.), *Humangenetik: Ein Kurzes Handbuch in Funt Banden: Vol. 2.* Stuttgart: Verlag.

ZILLMAN, D., JOHNSON, R. C., & DAY, K. D. (1974). Attribution of apparent arousal and proficiency of recovery from sympathetic activation affecting activation transfer to aggressive behavior. *Journal of Experimental Social Psychology, 10,* 503–515.

ZILLMAN, D., KATCHER, A. H., & MILOVSKY, B. (1972). Excitation transfer from physical exercise to subsequent aggressive behavior. *Journal of Experimental Social Psychology, 8,* 247–259.

ZIMBARDO, P. G. (1972). The tactics and ethics of persuasion. In B. T. King & E. McGinniss (Eds.), *Attitudes, conflict and social change.* New York: Academic Press.

ZIMBARDO, P. G. (1973). A field experiment in auto-shaping. In C.

Ward (Ed.), *Vandalism*. London: Architectural Press.

ZIMBARDO, P. G. (1973). The psychological power and pathology of imprisonment. *Catalog of Selected Documents in Psychology, 30*, 45.

ZIMBARDO, P. G. (1977). *Shyness: What it is, what to do about it.* Reading, MA: Addison-Wesley.

ZIMBARDO, P. G. (1978). *Shyness.* New York: Harcourt Brace Jovanovich.

ZIMBARDO, P. G., ANDERSEN, S. M., & KABAT, L. G. (1981). Induced hearing deficit generates experimental paranoia. *Science, 212*(4502), 1529–1531.

ZIMMERMAN, B. J., & DIALESSI, F. (1973). Modeling influences on children's creative behavior. *Journal of Educational Psychology, 65*, 127–135.

ZIMMERMAN, J., STOYVA, J., & METCALF, D. (1970). Distorted visual feedback and augmented REM sleep. *Psychophysiology, 7*, 298.

ZUCKERMAN, M. (1979). *Sensation seeking: Beyond the optimal level of arousal.* Hillsdale, NJ: Lawrence Erlbaum.

Copyrights and Acknowledgments

Illustration Credits/Figures

Chapter 1

Page 3 Donna Salmon from Ornstein, R. E., *The psychology of consciousness*, 2nd ed. New York: Harcourt Brace Jovanovich, 1977. **1–1** Penfield, W., *The mystery of the mind*. Princeton University Press, 1975. **1–8** Selfe, L., *Nadia, a case of extraordinary drawing ability in an autistic child*. London: Academic Press, Inc., 1977. **1–9** Grives, P. M., & Thompson, R. F., A dual process theory of habituation: neural mechanisms, in Pecke, H. M. S., & Herz, M. J. (eds.), *Habituation, physiological substrates II*. New York: Academic Press, Inc., 1973. **1–10** Metzger, Wolfgang, *Gesetze des sehens*. Frankfurt: Verlag Waldemar Kramer, 1953.

Chapter 2

Pages 40–41 & 2–8 Leakey, R. E., & Lewin, R., *Origins*. New York: E. P. Dutton, 1977. **2–10** Johnson, A., The original affluent society, *Human Nature*, September 1978. **2–15** Campbell, B. G. (ed.), *Humankind emerging*, 2nd ed. Boston: Little, Brown and Co., 1979. **2–22** Gottesman, I. I., Developmental genetics and ontogenetic psychology, from Pick, A. D. (ed.) *Minnesota symposia on child psychology*, Vol. 8. Minneapolis: University of Minnesota Press, 1974.

Chapter 3

3–2 Waddington, C. H., *The strategy of the genes*. New York: Macmillan Publishing Co., 1957. **3–6** Franz, R. L., The origin of form perception, *Scientific American 204*, May 1961. **3–7** Salapatek, P., & Kessen, W., Visual scanning of triangles by the human newborn, *Journal of Experimental Child Psychology 3*: 111–22, 1966. **3–9** Shirley, Mary N., The first 2 years, *Institute of Child Welfare Monograph # 7*. Minneapolis: University of Minnesota Press, 1933. **3–11** Hall, Elizabeth, et al., *Child psychology today*. New York: Random House, 1982. Reprinted by permission of Random House, Inc. **3–12** Goren, Carolyn, *Form perception, 1970: Innate form preferences, and visually mediated head-turning in human neonates*. Unpublished doctoral dissertation, Committee on Human Development, University of Chicago. **3–13** Braun, J., & Lindner, D., *Psychology today: an introduction*, 4th ed. New York: CRM Books, a Division of Random House, Inc., 1979. **3–20** Ainsworth, M. D. S., & Bell, S. M., Attachment, exploration and separation: Illustrated by the behavior of one-year-olds in a strange situation, *Child Development 41*, 1970. By permission of The Society for Research in Child Development, Inc. **3–22** Tanner, J. M., *Growth at adolescence*, 2nd ed. Oxford: Blackwell Scientific Publications, 1962.

Chapter 4

4–2 Hillyard, Steven A., & Kutas, Marta, Reading senseless sentences: brain potentials reflect semantic incongruity, *Science, 207*: 203–207, January 1980. **4–4** Thompson, R. F., *Foundations of physiological psychology*. New York: Harper and Row, 1967. Copyright © 1967 by Richard F. Thompson. Reprinted by permission of Harper & Row, Inc. **4–8** Vannini, V., & Pogliani, G., *The color atlas of human anatomy*. New York: Harmony Books, 1979. **4–12** Truex, R. C., & Carpenter, M. B., *Human neuroanatomy*. Baltimore: Williams and Wilkins, 1964. **4–13** Penfield, W., & Rasmussen, T., *The cerebral cortex of man*. New York: Macmillan Publishing Company, 1950. Copyright renewed 1978 by Theodore Rasmussen. Adapted

with permission of Macmillan Publishing Company. **4–19** Sperry, R. W., The great cerebral commissure, *Scientific American, Inc.*, 1964. **4–20** Levy, J., Trevarthen, C., & Sperry, R. W., Perception of bilateral chimeric figures following hemispheric disconnection, *Brain 95*: 68, 1972. **4–21** Bogen, J., The other side of the brain, I, *Bulletin of the Los Angeles Neurological Societies 34*, July 1969. **4–32** McConnell, P., & Berry, M., The effects of undernutrition on Purkinje cell dendritic growth in the rat, *Journal of Comparative Neurology 177*: 159–171, 1978.

Chapter 5

5–2, 5–13, 5–14 Hubel, D. H., & Wiesel, T. N., *Journal of Physiology 160*: 106–154, 1962. **5–3** Stevens, S. S., The psychophysics of sensory function, in Rosenblith, W. A. (ed.), *Sensory communication*. Cambridge: MIT Press, 1961. **5–5, 5–16, 5–17** Cornsweet, T. N., *Visual perception*. New York: Academic Press, 1970. **5–9** Hurvich, L. M., & Jameson, D., Opponent processes as a model of neural organization, *American Psychologist 29*: 88–102, 1974. **5–12** Gross, C. G., Inferotemporal cortex and vision, *Progress in physiological psychology* New York: Academic Press, 77–123, 1973. **5–22** Lindsay, P. H., & Norman, D. A., *Human information processing*, 2nd ed. New York: Academic Press, 140, 1977. **5–24, 5–25, 5–26** Ludel, J., *Introduction to sensory processes*. New York: W. H. Freeman and Co., 1978. **5–27** Snyder, S. H., Opiate receptors and internal opiates, *Scientific American 51*, March 1977.

Chapter 6

6–1, 6–4 Thurston, J., & Carraher, R. G., *Optical illusions and the visual arts*. New York: Litton Educational Publishing Co., 1966. **6–2** Hochberg & McAllister, *Perception*, 2nd ed. Englewood Cliffs, NJ: Prentice-Hall, 1953. **6–3** Gibson, J. J., *The perception of the visual world*. Boston: Houghton Mifflin Co., 1977. **6–11** Coren, S., Subjective contours and apparent depth, *Psychological Review 79*: 359–367, 1972. **6–14** Neisser, U., *Cognition and reality: principles and implications of cognitive psychology*. New York: W. H. Freeman and Co., 1976. **6–25** Kennedy, J. M., *A psychology of picture perception*. San Francisco: Jossey-Bass Inc., 1974. **6–27** Hudson, W., Pictorial perception and education in Africa, *Psychologia Africana 9*: 226–239, 1962.

Chapter 7

7–7 Hirst, W., Neisser, U., & Spelke, E., Divided attention, *Human Nature 57*, June 1978. Copyright © 1978 by Human Nature, Inc. Reprinted by permission of the publisher. **7–11** Van de Castle, R., *The psychology of dreaming*. Morristown, NJ: General Learning Corporation, 1971. **7–12** Hartmann, E., *The biology of dreaming*. Springfield, IL: Charles Thomas, 1967. **7–14** Hilgard, E. R., Hypnosis and consciousness, *Human Nature 48*, January 1978. Copyright © 1977 by Human Nature, Inc. Reprinted by permission of the publisher.

Chapter 8

8–13 Garcia, J., & Koelling, R. A., Relation of cue to consequence in avoidance learning, *Psychometric Science 4*: 123–214, 1966.

Chapter 9

9–1 Nickerson, R. S., & Adams, M. J., Long-term

memory for a common object, *Cognitive Psychology 11*: 297, 1979. **9–3** Shanon, B., Yesterday, today and tomorrow, *Acta Psychologica 43*: 469–476, 1979. Reprinted by permission of North-Holland Publishing Company. **9–6** Neisser, U., *Memory observed*. San Francisco: W. H. Freeman, 1982. **9–7** Bahrick, H. P., Bahrick, P. O., & Wittlinger, R. P., Fifty years of memory for names and faces, *Journal of Experimental Psychology 74*: 81–99. **9–8** Rubin, D. C., Very long term memory for prose and verse, *Journal of Verbal Learning and Verbal Behavior 16*: 611–12. **9–9** Shepard, R. N., Recognition memory for words, sentences, and pictures, *Journal of Verbal Learning and Verbal Behavior 6*: 156–163. **9–13** Loftus & Loftus, Reconstruction of automobile destruction: An example of the interaction between language and memory, *Journal of Verbal Learning and Verbal Behavior 13*: 585–589, 1974. **9–14** Rogers, T. B., Kulper, N. A., & Kirker, W. S., Self-reference and the encoding of personal information, *Journal of Personality and Social Psychology 35*: 677–88, 1977.

Chapter 10

10–8 Chomsky, *Aspects of the theory of syntax*. Cambridge: MIT Press, 1966.

Chapter 11

11–1–A Bayley, N., Development of mental abilities, in Mussen, P. (ed.), *Carmichael's manual of child psychology*, Vol. 1. New York: John Wiley & Sons, 1970. **11–1–B** Schaie, K. W., & Strother, C. R., A cross-sequential study of age changes in cognitive behavior, *Psychological Bulletin 70*: 677, 1968. **11–4** Adapted from Terman & Merrill, *Manual for the third revision of the Stanford-Binet intelligence scale*. Boston: Houghton Mifflin Co., 1973. Reprinted by permission of The Riverside Publishing Company, Chicago. **11–7** Guilford, J. P., *The nature of human intelligence*. New York: McGraw-Hill, 1967. **11–10** Scarr, S., & Weinberg, R. A., Attitudes, interests, and IQ, *Human Nature 32*, April 1978. Copyright © 1978 by Human Nature, Inc. Reprinted by permission of the publisher. **11–11** Gottesman, I. I., Genetic aspects of intelligent behavior, in Ellis, N. (ed.), *Handbook of mental deficiency: psychological theory and research*. New York: McGraw-Hill, 1963. **11–12, & Page 423** Feuerstein, R., *The dynamic assessment of retarded performers*. Baltimore: University Park Press, 1979. Reprinted by permission of the publisher.

Chapter 12

12–1 Ekman, Paul (ed.), *Darwin and facial expression*. New York: Academic Press, 1973. **12–2** Plutchik, R., *Emotion: A psychoevolutionary synthesis*. New York: Harper & Row, 1980. Copyright © 1980 by Robert Plutchik. Reprinted by permission of Harper & Row, Inc. **12–13** Sackheim, H. A., Gur, R. C., & Saucy, M. C., Emotions are expressed more intensely on the left side of the face, *Science 202*: 434–36, 1978. **12–14** Speisman, J. C., Lazarus, R. S., Davison, L., & Mordkoff, A. M., Experimental reduction of stress based on ego-defense theory, *Journal of Abnormal and Social Psychology 68*: 367–80, 1964. **12–16** Masters, W. H., & Johnson, V. E., *Human sexual response*. Boston: Little, Brown & Co., 1966. **12–17** Kinsey, Pomoroy, Martin, & Gebhard, *Sexual behavior in the human female*. Philadelphia: W. B. Saunders, 1953.

Chapter 13

13–2 Maslow, A. H., *Motivation and personality*, 2nd ed. Data based on Hierarchy of Needs in "A Theory of Human Motivation." Copyright © 1970 by Abraham Maslow. Reprinted by permission of Harper & Row, Inc. **13–5–A** Powley, T. L., & Keesey, R. E., Relationship of body weight to the lateral hypothalamic feeding syndrome, *Journal of Comparative and Physiological Psychology 70*, 25–36, 1970. **13–5–B** Hoebel, B. G., & Teitelbaum, P., Effects of force-feeding and starvation on food intake and body weight of a rat with ventromedial hypothalamic lesions, *Journal of Comparative and Physiological Psychology 61*: 189–93, 1966. **13–13** Hebb, D. O., Emotion arousal and performance, *Textbook of psychology*, 3rd ed. Philadelphia: W. B. Saunders, 1972.

Chapter 15

15–2 Rahe, R. H., The pathway between subjects' recent life changes and their near-future illness reports: Representative results and methodological issues, in Dohrenwend, B. S., & Dohrenwend, B. P. (eds.), *Stressful life events: Their nature and effects*. New York: John Wiley & Sons, 1974. **15–3** Vinokur, A., & Selzer, M. L., Desirable versus undesirable life events: their relationship to stress and mental distress, *Journal of Personality and Social Psychology 32*(2): 329–337, 1975.

Chapter 17

17–2 Gray, J. A., Anxiety, *Human Nature 43*, July 1978. Copyright © 1978 by Human Nature, Inc. Reprinted by permission of the publisher.

Chapter 18

18–1 Milgram, S., Behavioral study of obedience, *Journal of Abnormal and Social Psychology 67*: 371–78, 1963. **18–2** Asch, S. E., Effects of group pressure upon modification and distortion of judgments, in Maccoby, E. E., Newcomb, T. M., & Hartley, E. L. (eds.), *Readings in social psychology*, 3rd ed. New York: Holt, Rinehart and Winston, 1958. **18–3** Festinger, L., & Carlsmith, J. M., Cognitive compliance, *Journal of Abnormal and Social Psychology 58*: 203–10, 1959. **Page 641** Schenkel, R., Submission, its features and function in the wolf and dog, *American Zoology 7*: 319–329. **18–6** Darley, J. M., & Latané, B., Bystander intervention in emergencies: Diffusion of responsibility, *Journal of Personality and Social Psychology 8*: 377–83, 1968. **18–7** Newman, O., Community of interest, *Human Nature 58–9*, January 1979.

Appendix

8 Rose, J. E., Brugge, J. F., Anderson, K. J., & Hind, J. E., Phase-locked response to low frequency tones in single auditory nerve fibers of the squirrel monkeys, *Journal of Neural Physiology 30*: 769, 1967. **9** Pearce, T. V., in Kendall, *Advanced statistics*, 1930. Reproduced in Moroney, M. J., *On the average and scatter*, Chapter 5, Vol. 3. New York: Simon & Schuster. **10** Joiner, B. L., Living histograms, *International statistical review 43*: 339–340, 1975. **12** Fadeley, R. C., Oregon malignancy pattern physiographically related to Hanford, Washington radioisotope storage, *Journal of Environmental Health 27*: 883–897, 1965. As quoted by Anderson, T. W., & Sclove, S. L., *An introduction to the statistical analysis of data*. Boston: Houghton Mifflin, 1978, p. 592. **13** Glass, G. V., and Hopkins, K. D., *Statistical methods in education and psychology*, 2nd ed. Englewood Cliffs, NJ: Prentice Hall, 1984, p. 105. Reprinted by permission of the publisher. **15** Zeeman, E. L., Catastrophe theory, *Scientific American* April 1976, p. 67.

Ilustration Credits: Pictures

Page 4 (top left) © Jill Cannefax/EKM Nepenthe; (bottom left) © Joel Gordon 1983; (right) © 1977 Imogen Cunningham Trust. **5** (top left) Monte S. Buchsbaum, M. D., University of California Irvine; (bottom left) Frank Siteman/© The Picture Cube; (top right) © James H. Karales/Peter Arnold, Inc.; (bottom right) © Joel Gordon 1979. **9** (top) Dr. Nicholas Pastore, New York City; (bottom) Sea World Photo. **10** (top & bottom) Courtesy Dr. Albert Bandura. **11** © Arthur Tress/Photo Researchers, Inc. **13** (left) © Francis Miller, Life Magazine © Time, Inc.; (top right) Bettmann Archive; (bottom right) Culver Pictures. **15** Dr. Peter Hauri, Dartmouth Sleep Clinic. **17** Courtesy of New York Port of Authority. **25** © Bob Krueger/Photo Researchers, Inc. **37** C. Edelman, © Black Star 1980. **39** Peter Jones, © National Geographic Society. **53** Colorphoto Hans Hinz, Basle. **63** © Zoological Society of San Diego 1974. **70** Photos Brookhaven National Laboratory. **72** Cytogenics Laboratory, University of California, San Francisco. **73** Richard A. Boolotian, Science Software. **75** Culver Pictures. **83** © David Scharf/Peter Arnold, Inc. **86** © H. Hammid/Photo Researchers, Inc. **87** © Jason Laure/Woodfin Camp & Associates **89** © Doris Pinney **94, 95** Gerry Cranham/Photo Researchers, Inc. **99** © Zimbel/© Monkmeyer **101** (top left) Colin Graham Young; (top right) Eric McNaul; (bottom) from Gaitskell, Hurwitz, & Day, *Children and their art*, 4th ed. Harcourt Brace Jovanovich, Inc. © 1982 **102** Mimi Forsyth/Monkmeyer **105** David S. Strickler/The Picture Cube **109** World Health Organization **110** © Erika Stone **111** © Sponholz, University of Wisconsin Primate Laboratory **114** © Joel Gordon 1983 **115** (left) © Joel Gordon 1979; (right) Steve Herzog/Black Star. **117** (left) © Suzanne Szasz/Photo Researchers, Inc.; (right) © Landau Mayer/Monkmeyer **121** © 1982 Hildegard Adler. **125** © Erika Stone/Peter Arnold, Inc. **141** (top) Neal Miller. **147** Woolsey & van der Loos, *Brain research*, Elsevier Science Publishing Co., Inc., © 1970. **154** © Eric Arnesen from Ornstein, R. E., *The psychology of consciousness* 2nd ed. New York: Harcourt Brace Jovanovich, Inc., © 1977. **157** (top) © Manfred Kage/Peter Arnold, Inc.; (bottom) Carolina Biological Supply Co., Inc. **167** McConnell & Berry, *Journal of Comparative Neurology*. Alan R. Liss, Publisher. **168** (both) © Robin Risque. **183** © Mahon/Monkmeyer. **197** Yorbus, O. L., *Eye movements and vision*. Plenum Publishing Corp. © 1967. **203** Judy Porter 1974/Photo Researchers. **208, 209** © Hazel Hankin. **223** (all) Norman Snyder. **229, 230, 231** © Robin Risque. **233** William Vandivert. **234** Gregory, R. L., *Eye and brain*. McGraw-Hill, Inc., © 1977. **235** British Information Service. **236** Kennedy, J. M., *A psychology of picture perception*. San Francisco: Jossey-Bass, © 1974. **237** Ralph Crane, Life Magazine © Time, Inc. **240** (left) Vincent van Gogh, Hospital Corridor at Saint Remy, 1889, gouache and watercolor, $24\frac{1}{8} \times 18\frac{5}{8}''$. Collection, The Museum of Modern Art, New York. Abby Aldrich Rockefeller Bequest; (right) © M. C. Escher Heirs, c/o, J. W. Vermeulen. Prilly, CH. **241** Chase Manhattan Bank. **242** (top) U.S. Dept. of Agriculture; (bottom) © Grant Heilman. **256** (left) S. Hurok; (right) © Mimi Forsyth/Monkmeyer. **257** © Robin Risque. **263** Philadelphia Museum of Art: Given by Mr. & Mrs. Rodolphe M. de Schaueusee. **272** © Judy Porter/Photo Researchers. **278** © Mimi Forsyth/Monkmeyer. **280** American Cancer Society. **283** (top) © Rhoda Sidney/Monkmeyer; (bottom) © Polly Brown/ The Picture Cube. **284** © Melanie Kaestner/Zephyr. **286** © B. Griffith/The Picture Cube. **287** *Triangle*, No. 3, 1955. The Sandoz Journal of Medical Science, © Sandoz, Ltd., Basle, Switzerland. **289** © Mary Evans Picture Library/Photo Researchers. **291** © Ken Robert Buck/The Picture Cube. **300** Culver

Pictures. **308** Harvard University. **311** Yerkes Regional Primate Research Center. **313** © Frank Siteman 1983/The Picture Cube. **315** (both) AP/Wide World. **316** Yerkes Regional Primate Research Center. **320** © Janet Robertson 1984. **322** (left) © George W. Gardner 1979; (right) © Ken Karp. **323** © Tom Ballard/EKM Nepenthe. **330** © Imogen Cunningham Trust, 1977. **333** © Hazel Hankin. **335** © Ken Karp. **345** 1963 Yearbook, *The Tartan*, Helix, H. S., La Mesa, CA, courtesy Candy Young. **358** © Mimi Forsyth/Monkmeyer. **373** Courtesy Needham Harper & Steers and the American Honda Motor Company. **381** © Lilo Hess/Three Lions. **384** HBJ Collection. **390** N. R. Farbman. © 1946, Time-Life, Inc. **402, 403** © Judith Sedwick/The Picture Cube. **409** © Harvey Stein. **417** (top) © Paul Conklin; (bottom) © Jill Cannefax/EKM Nepenthe. **419** © David S. Strickler/Monkmeyer. **420** © Jean-Claude Lejeune. **431** © Jeffrey Jay Foxx. **435** © Melanie Kaestner/Zephyr. **439** (center) © Earl Dotter/Archive; (lower left) © Paul Ekman; (lower center) © Spencer Carter 1983/Woodfin Camp; (bottom right) Robert V. Eckert Jr./EKM Nepenthe. **440** (left) Standard Oil (N.J.); (right) © George Zimbel/Monkmeyer. **442, 443** (all) © Paul Ekman except (bottom right) UPI/Bettmann Archive. **444** (top both) © Paul Ekman; (bottom) HBJ Collection. **446, 448** Art Resource. **447** From Sackheim, H. A., Gur, R. C., & Saucy, M. C., *Science*, 1978, *202*, 434–36 with the permission of the American Association for the Advancement of Science. **450** © James H. Karales/Peter Arnold, Inc. **455** (top) © Robert V. Eckert, Jr./EKM-Nepenthe; (bottom left) © Marjorie Pickens 1983; (bottom right) © Joel Gordon 1974. **465** © David E. Kennedy/TeraStock. **475** © Catherine Ursillo/Photo Researchers. **478** National Gallery of London. **479** (left) © David Burnett 1981/Woodfin Camp; (right) AP/Wide World. **484** (center) © Paul Conklin; (bottom) © Abigail Heyman/Archive. **487** (top) Nik Kleinberg/Picture Group; (bottom) The National Foundation. **488** © Fred Sponholtz. **490** © Ron Cooper/EKM–Nepenthe. **497** © Joel Gordon 1982. **498, 499** © Erika Stone 1984/Peter Arnold, Inc. **513** (top) © Barbara Rios/Photo Researchers; (bottom) HBJ Collection. **516** (center) National Safety Council; (bottom) © Gerhard Gscheidle/Peter Arnold, Inc. **517** (center) Erika Stone 1984; (bottom) © Paula Allen/Archive. **526** UPI/Bettmann. **527** © Michael Yada/Zephyr. **530** © P. Damien, Click/Chicago. **531** © Earl Dotter/Archive; (right) AP/Wide World. **539** National Archives. **541** Dorothea Lange, FSA. **543** © Paul Conklin. **546** © Joel Gordon 1978. **547** © Sylvia Johnson 1980/Woodfin Camp. **554** © Paul Conklin. **558** © Jean-Claude Lejeune. **560** © Harvey Stein. **561** © Pamela Price/Picture Cube. **572** Jack Manning/NYT Pictures. **576** © Nancy Hayes/Monkmeyer. **578** (center) Victoria and Albert Museum, London; (bottom) Guttmann-Maclay Collection, The Bethlem Royal Hospital and the Maudsley Hospital, Beckenham, Kent. **581** © Grunnitas/Monkmeyer. **592** Museo del Prado. **593** (left) Culver Pictures; (right) Bettmann Archive. **596** © Edmund Engleman. **607** Michael Rougier, Life Magazine © 1966 Time, Inc. **609** (center) © Jerry Cooke/Photo Researchers; (bottom) Vista Hill Foundation. **610** © Bernard Pierre Wolff 1982/Photo Researchers. **612** © Joel Gordon 1980. **615** © Sybil Shelton/Peter Arnold, Inc. **621** © Peter Read Miller 1983/Focus West. **624** (left) © Audrey Topping 1976/Photo Researchers; (right) © Werner H. Muller/Peter Arnold, Inc. **626** Copyright 1965 by Stanley Milgram from the film *Obedience*, distributed by the Pennsylvania State University, PCR. **628** © Klaus D. Francke/Peter Arnold, Inc. **634** © Jack Prelutsky 1977/Stock Boston. **640** © Melanie Kaestner/Zephyr. **641** From *Love and hate*. I. Eibl-Eibesfeldt, Holt Rinehart and Winston © 1971, 1972. **643, 644** Philip G. Zimbardo. **645** © Jeff Albertson/Stock Boston. **652, 653** UPI/Bettmann Archive. **654** © Human Nature Magazine, 1979. **672** AP/Wide World. **673** © Robin Ris-

Index